# *RxFiles* - Drug Comparison Charts - 8th Edition

## Critical Appraisal of Drug Studies [6,7]

### A) Is the study valid?

1. Were patients **randomized** to treatment (tx) groups & was allocation **concealed** (AC). {Without concealment, 37% bias in favor of tx. Sealed, opaque envelopes or central registry used to attain AC} [8,9]
2. Was everyone (patients, physicians, investigators, assessors) **blinded** to tx? {Especially important for assessors of subjective outcomes.}
3. Was the study **controlled**? (e.g. inclusion of placebo or active control group/arm; in an "N of 1" trial, patient is own control.)
4. Were treatment & control **groups similar** in prognostic factors for outcome of interest at beginning of study? If not, were adjustments made?
5. Were all patients accounted for at end? {Missing patients addressed?}
6. Was data analyzed based on groups patients were initially randomized to? {Intent to treat or ITT; protects integrity of prognostic randomization; per protocol (**PP**) analysis may also be of interest (e.g. non-inferiority trials}
7. Were patient groups treated similarly except for study intervention?
8. How was the study funded (role of funder)? Was study stopped early?
9. Was active comparator drug & dose a good choice?

### B) What are the study results?

1. What was the primary (1°) endpoint? What were the secondary (2°) endpoints? Were endpoints & subgroups pre-specified? [10] Avoid data mining!
2. What was the difference between treatments? (Harm vs Benefits)
3. Were the differences statistically significant? Clinically significant? {What were the 95% confidence intervals (CIs) or p values? Does the CI cross line of no effect?}
4. What are the absolute and relative risk reductions or increases?
5. What is the number needed to treat (NNT) or harm (NNH)?

### C) Does this study matter to my patients?

1. How clinically relevant/important are the outcomes?
2. Were the patients similar to those in my practice? {Consider inclusion & **exclusion** criteria; very sick, old, young, drug interactions & complicated/comorbidity patients often excluded.}
3. Do treatment benefits outweigh the risks, costs & impact on life?

## Types of Studies (from low to **high level** of evidence) [11]

- **Case-control study**: a retrospective observational study which selects patients with the outcome of interest (cases) & patients without that outcome (controls); attempts to find features linked to the outcome.
- **Cohort study**: an observational study in which two groups (cohorts) are observed over time for an outcome of interest. One cohort has exposure to a condition or treatment that the other does not. {Observational studies: Association does not prove causation! Strength of association: RR: 1.01-1.5 *weak*; 1.51-3 *moderate*; >3 *strong*.[12]}
- **Crossover study**: a design in which each patient receives both treatments in two phases separated by a washout period. Each patient serves as own control, thus less variability in outcomes, & smaller sample size required; period effects may limit findings.
- **Randomized controlled trial** (**RCT**): a prospective study in which patients are randomized to treatment or control groups (equal chance at being assigned to any group). Groups are followed for outcome of interest.
- **Systematic Review** (**SR**): a systematic collection, review & presentation of available studies addressing a clinical question. Uses specific criteria & methods; may include meta-analysis. e.g. *Cochrane Reviews*[13] {**Meta-analysis**: the combining of studies meeting prespecified criteria & addressing a clinical question. Results are calculated for data from each study. Data is then pooled. ↑ sample size & statistical power useful if individual trials underpowered or subgroup analysis.}

[**Level of evidence**: SR > RCT > observational study > expert opinion.[14] **Caution**: lots of low quality RCTs may not be better than 1 good quality RCT!]

## Terms: Related To Validity

- **Bias**: design flaws leading to over/underestimation of treatment effect e.g. recall bias, selection bias, publication bias; confounding factors esp observational studies
- **Blinding**: if investigators & patient unaware of who receives tx vs control, they are less likely to inappropriately report better results with tx.

## Study Results: Size Of The Treatment Effect [15,16,17,18]

- **Event rate** (**ER**): the number of people experiencing the event as a proportion of total number of people in the population or group
  - -Experimental ER (**EER**): {# events in experimental group / total in exp. group}
  - -Control group ER (**CER**): {# events in control group / total in control group}
- **Relative risk** (**RR**) or risk ratio: {EER/CER}
- **Relative risk reduction** (**RRR**): the RR subtracted from 1 {RRR=1–RR} [Whereas ARR varies with type of population treated, RRR is often more constant.]
- **Absolute risk reduction** (**ARR**): the arithmetic difference between the 2 event rates {CER – EER} [If ↑ risk: **ARI**= absolute risk increase]
- **Number needed to treat** (**NNT**): the number of patients who would have to be treated with the studied intervention for the studied time period for 1 of them to benefit. {NNT= 100 / ARR%}
- **Number needed to harm** (**NNH**): number of patients who would have to be treated with the studied intervention for the studied time period for 1 of them to experience an adverse event. {NNH = 100 / ARI%}
- **Odds ratio** (**OR**): = experimental event odds / control event odds; especially used in case-control studies where baseline risk is not known; also used in metaanalysis. When events are rare, the OR is similar to the RR; however, OR rate exaggerated relative to RR when events more common. {Link www.cebm.net: tool for converting OR to NNT[19]}
- **Point estimate**: the trial result used as best estimate of the true effect
- **Hazard ratio** (**HR**): like RR but more accurate; accounts for the time each participant was in the study before having event or withdrawing.

## Study Results: Precision of Treatment Effect [20]

- **Confidence Interval** (**CI**): a 95% CI provides the range of values we are 95% certain that overlaps the true value. CI's indicates the precision of the estimate; where CIs are wide, they indicate less precise estimates of effect (just an estimate of the worst & best case scenario of the outcome) {For ratios, a CI that includes 1 means possibility of no difference. For ARR, ARI, NNT, NNH, a CI that includes zero means possibility of no difference between treatments. Non-significant trends may provide clues for future research.}
- **Type 1 (or α) error**: *the false positive*; to find a difference when there is none. **p-value**: reflects type 1 error. A p <0.05 suggests a <1 in 20 probability that any difference is due to chance (statistically significant by convention). The smaller the p-value, the less likely that the result is due to chance.
- **Type 2 (or β) error**: *the false negative*; to conclude there is no difference when there really is a difference (e.g. if not enough patients enrolled)
- **Heterogeneity**: when study results within a meta-analysis have more variation than expected; may indicate inappropriate to combine studies.[21]

## Do the study results matter to me & my patients?

- **Clinical significance vs statistical significance**: some studies may detect extremely small statistically significant differences between groups; however magnitude of effect (e.g. NNT) may be too small to change practice. Evaluate both 1) the endpoint, & 2) the NNT or NNH. {e.g. small cognitive score improvement not noticeable to patient.[22,23]}
- **Composite endpoints**: combining endpoints can increase a study's power allowing for smaller or shorter trials. Outcomes should have **similar value**. Examination of individual outcomes can be important in interpretation as one endpoint may be the primary *driver*. {e.g. In DREAM, outcome of diabetes diagnosis the driver **or** death example of unequal endpoints.[24]}
- **Surrogate endpoints**: an endpoint meant to reflect / be correlated with another endpoint (e.g. BP/LDL/A1c for CV events; CD4 cell count for HIV mortality). Clinical outcomes are more important since surrogate endpoints assume correlation with an outcome which may or may not always be true. {e.g. lower A1C target ≤6% in ACCORD led to ↑ death.}
- **Other considerations**: What uncertainties remain? Has drug been studied in enough patients to detect serious rare adverse events? What duration of intervention is studied & what are the potential benefits & risks over a longer term of exposure? Does real-world experience appear to be consistent with clinical trial data? Cost? How benefits & risks are described will also affect decisions.[25]
- **What patient specific and societal values need to be considered?**

## Heads Up! Know what the numbers are telling you.

⇨ *You double your chance of winning a lottery if you buy a 2nd ticket; however your chance of winning is more related to whether 2 tickets or 2 million tickets are sold!*

- ***Beware of the Relatives*** ☺
  - Benefits are often given as **relative** numbers, whereas harms are often given as **absolute** numbers. This tends to exaggerate benefits & minimize the harms. ⇨ Look for NNTs & NNHs. {e.g. Vioxx monograph 2004 CPS: reported ~ 50% ↓ in GI complications with Vioxx 50mg/day vs naproxen 500mg BID & a thrombotic event rate of 1.8% (Vioxx) vs 0.6% (naproxen). Actual GI complications reductions 0.59% vs 1.37% (ARR=0.78; NNT=**129**); whereas thrombotic risk was worse (NNH=**83**).} {e.g. Oral contraceptives: risk of DVT in a younger, non-smoking ♀ may be ↑300% but absolute risk is <1.5/10,000 /yr & lower than risk in pregnancy}
- ***Non-Equivalent Durations & Risk/Benefit Perception***
  - Benefits are often given for total duration of trial which may be several years, whereas harms are often given per year. {e.g. UKPDS-33: aggressive glucose control benefit on microvascular endpoints given per **10 years**; risks of hypoglycaemia were given **per year**.[26]}
- ***Analysis: Pooling Together or Dividing Out***
  - Discussing the multiple benefits of a composite endpoint while individually sorting out risks may minimize risk perception. {e.g. In WHI, risk of just breast ca with HRT was **8/10,000 pt-years**; yet risk of any harm (DVT, CHD, stroke, PE & breast cancer) was **1/66** over 5.2yrs. [27]}

| Calculations Example: 1 yr trial | RRR | ARR | NNT | NNH: if 60% of patients in Tx group experienced *headaches* compared with 27% in control group (ARI=33%) |
|---|---|---|---|---|
| •200 patients in Control grp<br>•200 patients in Treatment (Tx) group<br>•Deaths: Control grp: 40. **CER**=40/200=0.2<br>Tx grp: 30. **EER**=30/200=0.15 | = (0.20 - 0.15)/0.20 X 100<br>= 25% {risk of event is reduced by 25%} | 20% - 15% = 5%<br>{absolute risk of event is reduced by 5%} | = 100 / 5%<br>= 20 | NNH= 100 / 33% = 3 |
| | For every 20 patients treated for 1yr, there is 1 less *death*; & for every 3 patients treated there will be 1 extra *headache*. | | | |

| A few NNTs / NNHs of interest | NNT |
|---|---|
| ↓ mortality with simvastatin 20-40mg/day over 5.4yrs vs placebo in patients with CHD 4S | 30 / 5.4yrs |
| ↓ mortality with metformin 2550mg/day over 10 years vs non-intensive in obese T2DM patients UKPDS-34 | 14 / 10 yrs |
| ↓ CV death/MI/stroke; clopidogrel 75mg/day + ASA vs ASA alone in ACS pts (↑ bleeding: NNH=99) CURE | 48 / 9mo |
| ↓ pain by ≥50% with TCAs (e.g. amiltriptyline 100mg/day) vs placebo in neuropathic pain (short term trials) | 2 |

**What makes for a good NNT?** *It all depends!!!* NNTs will vary greatly with variations in baseline population risk, duration of tx, & type & number of endpoints included in composite. The value of the endpoint also varies from patient to patient.

# Alternate CVD 5yr Risk Assessment Tables

Includes heart & stroke risk. (Adapted from New Zealand Guideline 2009 Group with permission) - http://www.nzgg.org.nz/guidelines/0154/090311_CVD_poster_Final.pdf [1]; also BMJ [2] & CMAJ [3] {Based on Framingham}

- Canadian 10yr Framingham CVD Risk Tables are at RxFiles.ca on page 2 of this chart (alternate risk calculation approaches: web, PDA etc.)

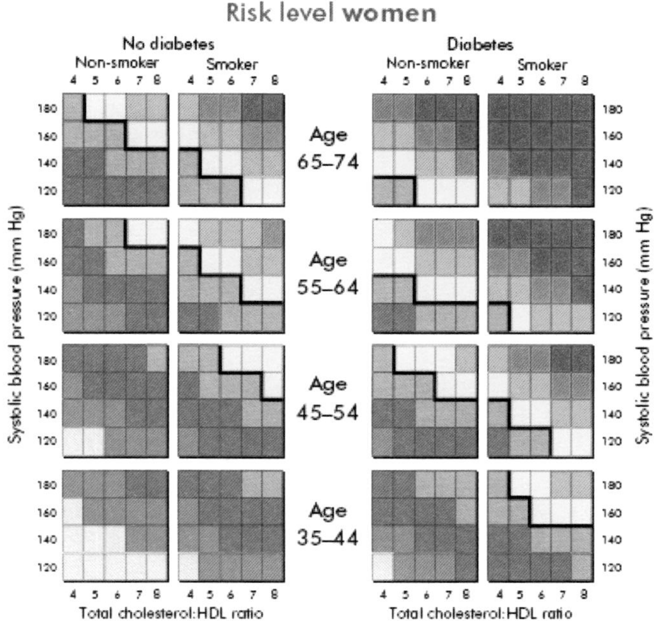


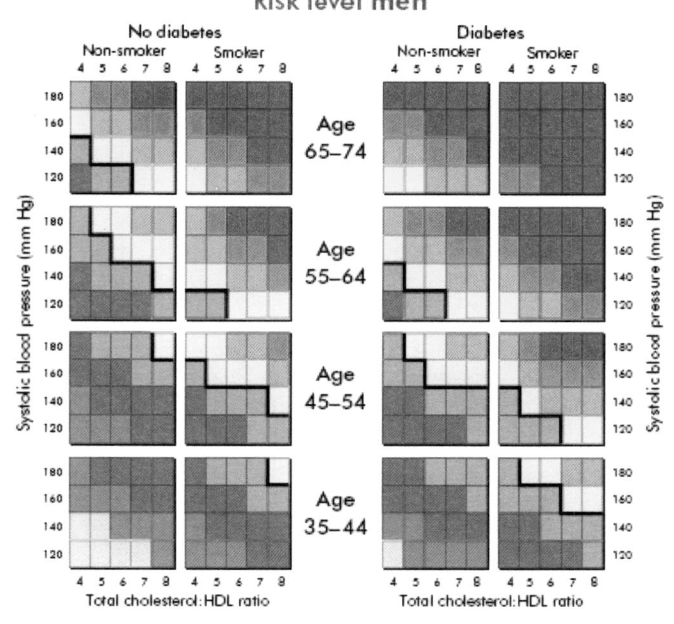


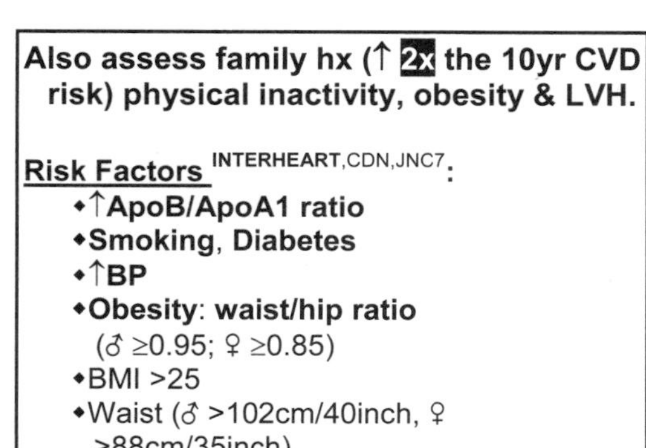

**Also assess family hx (↑ 2x the 10yr CVD risk) physical inactivity, obesity & LVH.**

**Risk Factors** INTERHEART,CDN,JNC7:

- **↑ApoB/ApoA1 ratio**
- **Smoking, Diabetes**
- **↑BP**
- **Obesity**: waist/hip ratio (♂ ≥0.95; ♀ ≥0.85)
- BMI >25
- Waist (♂ >102cm/40inch, ♀ >88cm/35inch)
- **stress & depression;**
- **lack of: vegetables, fruits, exercise & alcohol;**
- Low HDL ≤1
- Family hx of premature heart dx (Age: ♂ <55, ♀ <65)
- Age (♂ >55, ♀ >65)
- Microalbuminuria

### Key

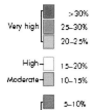

5-year cardiovascular disease (CVD) risk (fatal and non-fatal)

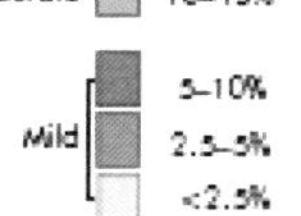

- Very high: >30%, 25–30%, 20–25%
- High: 15–20%
- Moderate: 10–15%
- Mild: 5–10%, 2.5–5%, <2.5%

### Using the Charts

- Identify the chart relating to the person's sex, diabetic status, smoking history and age.
- Within the chart choose the cell nearest to the person's age, systolic blood pressure (SBP) and total cholesterol (TC) TC:HDL ratio. People who fall exactly on a threshold between cells are placed in the cell indicating higher risk.

Note: The risk charts now include values for SBP alone, as this is the most informative of conventionally measured blood pressure parameters for cardiovascular risk. Diastolic pressures may add some predictive power, especially at younger ages (eg. a diastolic pressure consistently >100 mm Hg in a patient with SBP values between 140 and 170 mm Hg).

Certain groups may have CVD risk underestimated using these charts. See Cardiovascular Guidelines Handbook (2009 Edition) for details.

| Risk level: 5-year CVD risk (fatal and non-fatal) | Benefits: NNT for 5 years to prevent one event (CVD events prevented per 100 people treated for 5 years) | | |
|---|---|---|---|
| | 1 Intervention (25% risk reduction) | 2 Interventions (45% risk reduction) | 3 Interventions (55% risk reduction) |
| 30% | 13 (7.5 per 100) | 7 (14 per 100) | 6 (16 per 100) |
| 20% | 20 (5 per 100) | 11 (9 per 100) | 9 (11 per 100) |
| 15% | 27 (4 per 100) | 15 (7 per 100) | 12 (8 per 100) |
| 10% | 40 (2.5 per 100) | 22 (4.5 per 100) | 18 (5.5 per 100) |
| 5% | 80 (1.25 per 100) | 44 (2.25 per 100) | 36 (3 per 100) |

NNT = Number needed to treat
Based on the conservative estimate that each intervention:
**aspirin**, **BP treatment** (lowering SBP by 10 mm Hg) or **lipid** modification (↓ LDL-C by 20%) reduces cardiovascular risk by about 25% over 5 years.
Note: Cardiovascular events are defined as MI, new angina, ischemic stroke, TIA, PVD, HF & CV death.

**NZ-CVD-5yr Risk Tool:** quick/easy way to estimate risk of **CHD and stroke**; the Framingham **10yr** risk assessment may also be used to estimate CHD risk. Antihypertensive benefit greater in those at highest risk!

## TARGETS: Canadian (Adult)

### BLOOD PRESSURE 2010, 4

↓ salt intake & Importance of accurate measurement e.g. 5 min resting

{BP: Optimal <120/<80; Normal <130/<85; High Normal: <140/<90 (~ ½ of these will develop HTN within 2yrs!)}

| | Consider Treatment | Target |
|---|---|---|
| NO RISK FACTORS; no target organ damage | ≥160/100 | <140/90 |
| ISOLATED SYSTOLIC HTN (ISH) | SBP >160 | SBP <140 |
| MODERATE-HIGH RISK Patient | ≥140/90 | <140/90 |
| ◆If HOME BP Measurement | ≥135/85 | <135/85 |
| DIABETES or RENAL Disease | ≥130/80 | <130/80 |

### LIPID 2009, 5

+Target **<2** or ↓LDL≥50%. If **LDL is <3.5**, then for ♂>50yr or ♀>60yr check **hsCRP** check twice 2 weeks apart, not during acute illness, **if hsCRP>2 mg/l**→then consider treatment. Jupiter trial

Caution: High statin dose in low risk pts..

| Risk (CDN based on Framingham 10yr CVD risk) | | | LDL | Apo B | T.Chol/HDL |
|---|---|---|---|---|---|
| **HIGH** * | (10yr CVD ≥20%) | Target→ | <2 or ↓LDL≥50% | <0.8 | <4 |
| **MODERATE** | (10yr CVD 10-19%) | Treat if→ | >3.5 + | >0.8 | >5 |
| **LOW** | (10yr CVD <10%) | Treat if→ | ≥5 → Target ↓LDL ≥50% | | >6 |
| | | | Primary target | -alternate to LDL | |

***High Risk:** ALL with CAD, CVD & PAD. Most DIABETES older with risk factors & chronic renal dx. Cl<30ml/min
HIGH Risk: Treat with medication & lifestyle changes concomitantly.
LOWER Risk: May try lifestyle changes for 3-6 months before drug therapy if targets not met.
If **Low/Mod risk**: guidelines suggest **↓LDL by ≥50% but** remember simvastatin 40mg, atorvastatin 10mg & pravastatin 40mg, has strong outcome evidence eg. ↓MI, stroke & death from landmark trials but only ↓LDL by 18-35%.

### BLOOD GLUCOSE 2008, 6

| | Target for most | Normal range | →consider achieving |
|---|---|---|---|
| **A1C** q3-6 mon (calibrate meter q-yr) | ≤ **7** (≤6.5 for some) | ≤ **6** | **if** can be done |
| **FPG** (mmol/L) | **4-7** | **4-6** | **safely** without |
| **PPBG** (mmol/L) 2hr post | **5-10** (5-8 if A1C not met) | **5-8** | hypoglycemia etc. |

**Individualized Target Treatment Goals:** consider age[7], life expectancy, co-morbidity and risk of hypoglycemic side effects. **Monitor**: A1C q3-6 months; calibrate meter yearly.

**A1C**=glycosolated hemoglobin $A_{1C}$ **BP**=blood pressure **CAD**=coronary artery disease **CVD**= cardiovascular disease **Dx**=disease **FPG**=fasting plasma glucose **HDL**=high density lipoprotein **HF**=heart failure **Hx**=history **LDL**=low density lipoprotein **MI**=myocardial infarction **PAD**=peripheral arterial disease **PPBG**=postprandial (2hr) blood glucose **TG**=triglycerides **TIA**=transient ischemic attack ♂=male ♀=female

# ACE INHIBITOR (ACEI) / ANGIOTENSIN II RECEPTOR BLOCKER (ARB): Comparison Chart [1,2,3,4,5,6,7,8,9,10,11,12,13,14,15,16,17,18,19,20,21,22,23,24] L. Regier, B. Jensen © www.RxFiles.ca May 10

| Generic=g / TRADE (Dosage strength & forms) — Pregnancy rating: C/D All ACEI & ARBs | FOOD EFFECT | Class / Prodrug | ONSET & (PEAK) | Duration (hrs) [21] | INDICATIONS: ✓HPB (CDN); *Other Indications-US FDA* | DOSE: INITIAL (Maximum) | USUAL DOSE # RANGE | $ COST / 30 Day |
|---|---|---|---|---|---|---|---|---|
| **ANGIOTENSIN CONVERTING ENZYME INHIBITORS ACEI: ROLE: 1ST LINE: HF, Diabetes, Post MI, Uncomplicated HTN, LVH, Prior CVA/TIA, renal disease & ALL Coronary Artery Disease pts.** | | | | | | | | |
| **Benazepril** LOTENSIN,generic<br>(5ς, 10ς, 20ς mg tab) | ↓ rate not extent | carboxy / PD-YES | 60min (2-4hr) | 24 | ✓BP<br>{ACCOMPLISH 2008: amlodipine 5-10mg + benazepril 20-40mg/day (e.g. LOTREL combination product in USA)} | 5mg OD (40mg OD) | 10mg po OD<br>20mg OD CKD pts: 10mg bid | 29<br>32 |
| **Captopril** CAPOTEN,generic<br>(6.25, 12.5, 25ς, 50ς, 100ς mg tab) | ↓ absorption | sulfhydryl/ **PD-NO** | 15-30min (1-2hr) | 6-12 | ✓BP ✓HF ✓Post MI<br>✓Diabetic Nephropathy; HTN Urgency | 6.25mg BID (150mg TID) | 25mg po BID<br>50mg po TID HFTD | 28<br>62 |
| **Cilazapril** (1ς, 2.5ς, 5ς mg tab) INHIBACE,generic<br>**Cilazapril/HCT•** (5mg/12.5ς mg tab) INHIBACE PLUS ,generic | ↓ absorption | carboxy / PD –YES | 60min (3-7hr) | 12-24 | ✓BP<br>✓HF | 1mg OD (10mg OD) | 2.5-5mg po OD<br>10mg po OD<br>5mg/12.5mg po OD | 23<br>40<br>37/28 g |
| **Enalapril** maleate 5mg=4mg enal sodium VASOTEC approved 1987,generic<br>(2.5ς, 5ς,10ς, 20ς mg tab) (**Enalaprilat Vial 1.25mg/ml**)<br>**Enalapril/HCT•** VASERETIC<br>(5mg/12.5mg, 10mg/25ς mg tab) | **NONE** | carboxy / PD-YES | 60min (4-6hr) | 12-24 | ✓BP (including Age >6yr)<br>✓HF (10-20mg bid) HFTD<br>*Post MI, Pheochromocytoma, Scleroderma Renal Crisis* | 2.5mg OD (20mg BID) | 10mg po OD<br>20mg po OD<br>10mg po BID<br>10mg/25mg po OD | 45/25 g<br>53/28 g<br>83/42 g<br>46/32 g |
| **Fosinopril** MONOPRIL,generic<br>(10ς, 20mg tab) | ↓ rate not extent | phosphoryl / PD-YES | 60min (2-6hr) | **24** | ✓BP<br>*HF* | 10mg OD (40mg OD) | 20mg po OD<br>40mg po OD | 27<br>47 |
| **Lisinopril** (5ς, 10, 20mg tab) ZESTRIL,PRINIVIL<br>**Lisinopril/HCT•** ZESTORETIC, PRINZIDE<br>(10mg/12.5mg; 20mg/12.5mg; 20mg/25mg tab) ,generic | **NONE** | carboxy / **PD-NO** | 60min (4-6hr) | **24** | ✓BP (10-40mg od ALLHAT) ✓**Post MI**<br>✓HF (10 – **35**mg od) HFTD ATLAS<br>*Uremic hypertrophic cardiomyopathy* | 2.5-5mg OD (40mg OD) | 10-20mg po OD<br>10mg/12.5mg po OD<br>20mg/12.5mg po OD | **28**-33 g<br>37/26 g<br>43/30 g |
| **Perindopril** COVERSYL (2, 4ς ,8 mg was new generic tab)<br>**Perin./Indapamide** COVERSYL PLUS (4/1.25mg tab) (8/2.5mg tab ⊗) | may ↓ effect | carboxy / PD-YES | 60min (2-4hr) | **24** | ✓BP,HF [CAD pts→EUROPA 8mg od] PROGRESS<br>↓stroke when indapamide added to perindopril | 2mg OD Hyvet -very elderly (16mg OD) | 4-8mg po OD<br>4/1.25mg OD 25 Advance | **35-46**<br>42 |
| **Quinapril** 5ς,10,20,40mg tab) ACCUPRIL<br>**Quinapril/HCT•** ACCURETIC<br>(10mg/12.5ς mg; 20mg/12.5ς mg; 20/25mg ) | ↓ rate not extent | carboxy / PD-YES | 60min (2-4hr) | **24** | ✓BP<br>✓HF<br>(not help scleroderma) Gliddon 2007 | 5mg OD<br>20 mg OD Quiet NS<br>(40mg OD) | 10mg po OD<br>40mg po OD Imagine NS<br>20mg/12.5mg po OD | **38**<br>38<br>38 |
| **Ramipril** ALTACE,generic new<br>(1.25,2.5,5,10,15✗⊗mg caps)(ALTACE HCT 2.5&5&10/12.5mg; 5&10/25mg <$25) | **NONE** | carboxy / PD-YES | 60min (4-6hr) | **24** | ✓**BP, Post MI,** HF (5-10mg bid) HFTD<br>✓**High CV** risk HOPE (vs placebo),(15mg od Dream NS) | 1.25-2.5 OD (20mg OD) | 5mg po OD (or bid)<br>10mg **HS** Hope 26, Ontarget | **35**/26 g<br>43/29 g |
| **Trandolapril** MAVIK<br>(0.5, 1, 2, 4mg capsule) | ↓ rate not extent | carboxy / PD-YES | 30min (2-4hr) | **24** | ✓BP<br>✓**Post MI** (with or without HF) | 0.5-2mg OD (4mg OD) | 2mg po OD BENEDICT<br>4mg po OD TRACE, PEACE | **35**<br>42 |
| **ANGIOTENSIN II RECEPTOR BLOCKERS ARBs: ROLE: 1ST LINE: Diabetes, uncomplicated HTN, ISH, LVH** & alternative for patients **who do not tolerate ACE** inhibitor-induced cough/side effects. | | | | | | | | |
| **Candesartan** cilexetil (4⊗,8ς,16ς, 32ς mg tab) ATACAND<br>16/12.5ς mg, (**32**/12.5, 32/25mg) ς⊗ HCT• ATACAND PLUS | **NONE** | PD-**YES** | ? (3-5 hr) | 24 | ✓BP [✓heart failure Class II-III EF≤40% → (CHARM 32mg od $48)] | 4mg OD (32mg OD) DIRECT NS | 8mg po OD<br>16mg po OD TROPHY | **48**<br>48 |
| **Eprosartan** (400, 600 mg tab) TEVETEN<br>600/12.5mg HCT• tab TEVETEN PLUS | ↓ rate | PD-NO | ?(4hr) | 12-24 | ✓BP | 400mg OD (800mg OD) | 600mg po OD MOSES<br>600/12.5mg po OD | **44**<br>44 |
| **Irbesartan** (75,150,300mg tab) AVAPRO<br>**Irbesartan/HCT•** AVALIDE<br>(150mg /12.5mg, 300mg/12.5mg & 300mg/25mg tabs) | **NONE** | PD-NO | 60min (2-4 hr) | 24 | ✓BP<br>✓**Delay diabetic/early nephropathy** IRMA II, IDNT | 75mg OD (300mg OD) | 150mg po OD<br>300mg po OD I-PRESERVE NS<br>150mg/12.5mg po OD | **50**<br>50<br>50 |
| **Losartan** (25,50,100mg tab) COZAAR approved in 1995<br>**Losartan/HCT•** HYZAAR<br>(50mg / 12.5mg tab; **DS** =100mg/12.5mg tab; 100mg/25mg) | **NONE** | Active Metabolite: *E-3174* | 60min (3-6hr) | 12-24 | ✓**BP,Delay diabetic nephropathy** RENAAL<br>**Peds** 6-16yr<br>[LVH pts→losartan 100mg od $52 ↓stroke vs atenolol 5vs6.7%; NNT=59 LIFE] | 25mg OD (100mg OD) 150mg HEALL | 25mg po OD<br>50mg po OD<br>50mg/12.5mg po OD | 52<br>**52**<br>52 |
| **Telmisartan** (40ς,80ς mg tab) MICARDIS<br>80// 12.5/ 25mg HCT• tab MICARDIS PLUS | **NONE** | PD-NO | 60min (3hr) | 24 | ✓**BP & High CV** risk if ACE intolerant<br>Arbs: ?concern of ↑cancer Meta-Sipahi'10, NNH=143/4yr | 40mg OD (80mg OD ProFESS NS & TRANSCEND NS ) | 80mg OD DETAIL, Ontarget<br>80mg/12.5mg po OD | **47**<br>47 |
| **Valsartan** (40ς, 80, 160, 320 mg tab) DIOVAN<br>**Valsartan/HCT** •80/12.5 & 160&**320**mg//12.5/25 tab DIOVANHCT | ↓ rate not extent | PD-NO | 2 hr (4-6 hr) | 12-24 | ✓BP<br>**Peds** 6-16yr USA<br>[✓heart failure→**Val-HeFT** 160mg bid $92<br>✓post MI → **Valiant** 160mg bid $92<br>Diabetes prevention Navigator NS for CV events] | 80mg OD (320mg OD $49 2° Gissi-AF NS) | 80-160mg po OD VALUE<br>160mg/12.5mg po OD | **49**<br>49 |

• Accuretic, Altace HCT, Coversyl PLUS, Inhibace PLUS, Prinzide, Vaseretic, Zestoretic; Atacand PLUS, Avalide, Diovan HCT, Hyzaar, Micardis PLUS, Olmetec PLUS & Teveten PLUS →**synergistic low-dose** combos→ ↓BP more **than doubling the ACEI/ARB dose.**

**# IF Renal Dysfx** →use low dose; MONITOR[27]: SCr, BUN, fluid balance & lytes upon & after 1-2week of starting. If ↑ **K >5.6** or ↑ **SCr rise >30%** over baseline this may warrant stopping the ACEI or ARB (if not related to ↓ volume).

ς=scored tab ✗ =non formulary SK. **ACE**=angiotensin converting enzyme **BP**=blood pressure **CKD**=chronic kidney dx **COST**=markup & fee **HCT**=hydrochlorothiazide **HF**=heart failure **HFTD**=heart failure target dose **ISH**=isolated systolic htn **LVH**=left ventricular hypertrophy **MI**=myocardial infarction **PD**=prodrug

**Renal Risk factors** for acute renal failure: **bilateral renal artery stenosis**, stenosis of a solitary kidney, **HF** with aggressive **diuretic therapy** or excessive **vasodilation**, or **volume depletion** from any cause. ⊗ not covered by NIHB

**HF**: Relatively high TARGET DOSES often used in HF studies with **reduced mortality** as outcome (NOT all patients able to tolerate target dose). May use lower initial dose & titrate as tolerated (monitor BP & renal function)

**DIs ACEI:** diuretic K sparing→↑K+, gold inj nitritoid rx, lithium ↑ Li level, NSAID ↓ BP effect & K/Bactrim/Spironolactone ↑K+ **ARB:** ↑**lithium & K+**; **losartan→**fluconazole & rifampin ↓ losartan effect, ↓uric acid level; **telmisartan→** ↑digoxin level; **irbesartan→** fluconazole ↑ irbesartan effect.

**SE**: cough 10% with ACEI (↑in East Asians), dry/nonproductive, loss of taste, rash esp. captopril (sulfa), headache, dizziness, ↓BP, fatigue, ↑K+, acute renal failure, angioedema ~0.5%(esp. in blacks), ↑↑LFT, dysguesia, pancreatitis & blood dyscrasias (**ARB** may ↓cough, headache & dizziness than ACEI; ? ↑cancer NNH=143/4yr).

**Contraindications: ACEI & ARBs**: bilateral artery stenosis (or solitary kidney stenosis if only 1 kidney), history of angioedema & pregnancy (↑malformations 1st trimester ACEI ,↑ fetal mortality 2nd/3rd trimester).

**ACE/ARBs** not as effective in blacks but still use for compelling indications eg. MI,HF,CKD. **Combo**: ACEI+ARB: **no better** CV benefit & ↑**SE** ↓BP, ↑K+, & worse renal outcomes Ontarget; small benefit in proteinuria Calm,Cooperate & persistent HF Charm; but ↑SE & no greater efficacy MI trial; VALIANT.

New: **Aliskiren ✗** ⊗**RASILEZ** HCT, TEKTURNA 150,300mg OD tab ↓ by fat $45; Direct renin inhibitor DRI SE: diarrhea, headache, ↑K+, rash, allergy & pharyngitis. Rare: cough ~1%, angioedema, gout 0.2%. (rats:colonic mucosal hyperplasia). CI:Pregnancy. DI:cyclosporine,furosemide,irbesartan,ketoconazole.

**Olmesartan** OLMETEC 20 & 40mg tabs, **OLMETEC PLUS** 20/12.5mg HCT , & 40/12.5 & 40/25mg HCT tabs. 20-40mg OD $42, a prodrug. **Peds** 6-16yr USA

# BETA-BLOCKER (BB): Comparison Chart [1,2,3,4,5,6,7,8,9,10,11,12,13,14,15,16,17,18,19,20,21,22,23]

Prepared by: L. Regier, B. Jensen BSP © www.RxFiles.ca — May 10

| Generic name / TRADE g=generic avail. / (Dosage strength & form) — Pregnancy rating | ○Lipid *,** / ♦WATER SOLUBILITY | ISA + | EFFECT on LIPIDS | ↓Dose: [kidney] [liver] | Half-Life & Active Metab. | COMMENTS | APPROVED INDICATIONS ✓CDN; *italics USA* | INITIAL & MAX DOSE | USUAL DOSAGE RANGE | COST/ MONTH |
|---|---|---|---|---|---|---|---|---|---|---|
| **CARDIO-SELECTIVE: Alternate agent⇨ for DIABETICS.** Cardioselectivity **may be lost at higher dosages. Also esmolol** BREVIBLOC **IV (2500mg/250ml** infusion; **100mg/10ml vials** direct IV**) for aortic dissection, A. fib or post-op hypertension.** | | | | | | | | | | |
| **Acebutolol** B/D<br>MONITAN D/c by Co, SECTRAL g<br>(100ς, 200ς, 400ς mg tablet) | ○○ / ♦♦ | YES + | **neutral** | [kidney] | 3-8hrs **YES** | • less coldness of extremities?<br>• ?preferred in hypercholesterolemia pts<br>• ?less bradycardia but reports in breastfed infants<br>• positive antinuclear antibody test & lupus reported | ✓BP (od or bid)<br>✓ANGINA (bid)<br>*VENTRICULAR ARRHYTHMIA* | 100mg OD<br><br>400mg BID | 100mg po BID<br>200mg po BID<br>400mg po OD | 17<br>**22**<br>22 |
| **Atenolol** D<br>TENORMIN g (25, 50ς, 100ς mg tablet)<br>TENORETIC/Apo-Atenidone g<br>(50ς, 100ς mg with 25mg **chlorthalidone**) | ♦♦♦ | NO | slight | [kidney] | 6-14 hrs NO | • commonly used, but **lacks** compelling outcome evidence in BP trials [24]<br>• ↑breast milk levels: infant ↓HR & ↓glucose<br>Ⓜ 50-150mg per day<br>• ?cause reduced fetal growth & weight [25] | ✓BP<br>✓ANGINA<br>*POST MI*<br>(Used in high risk long QT syndrome pts) | 12.5-25mg OD<br><br>200mg OD | 50mg po OD<br>100mg po OD<br>100mg po BID<br>50/25mg po OD | **18**<br>24<br>40<br>22 |
| **Bisoprolol** C/D<br>MONOCOR g (5ς, 10mg tablet) | ○○ / ♦♦ | NO | **neutral** | [kidney] [liver] | 10-12hrs NO | • ↓ morbidity/mortality in HF<br>Ⓜ 5mg per day | ✓BP<br>HF | 2.5mg OD<br>(20mg OD) | 5mg po OD<br>10mg po OD **HFTD** | 15<br>**21** |
| **Metoprolol** Tartrate C/D<br>LOPRESOR, BETALOC g (Vial 1mg/ml;<br>25ς, 50ς, 100ς mg; **SR** g:100mg, 200mg tab)<br>10mg/ml susp manufactured at some pharmacies | ○○ / ♦♦♦ | NO | slight | [liver] | 3-7 hrs NO | ✓ **SR form combines β1 selectivity, 24hr BP control & efficacy in angina, post-MI & HF. DIs:**↑ levels by 2D6 inhibitors<br>• 100mg 2-4hr pre-op ↓CV events but ↑death/stroke Poise | ✓BP<br>✓ANGINA<br>✓POST MI [26Commit]<br>✓*HF* | 12.5-25mg BID<br><br>200mg BID | 50mg po BID<br>100mg po BID **HFTD**<br>100-200mg **SR** po OD | 14<br>18<br>**15-21** |
| **NON-SELECTIVE** | | | | | | | | | | |
| **Nadolol** C/D<br>CORGARD g (40ς, 80ς, 160ς mg tablet) | ♦♦ | NO | moderate | [kidney] | 10-24hr NO | • only BB to ↑ renal blood flow<br>Ⓜ 20-160 mg/d;?Tx:esophageal **varices** [27] | ✓BP<br>✓ANGINA | 40mg OD<br>160mg BID | 40mg po OD<br>80mg po OD | 16<br>**20** |
| **Oxprenolol** TRASICOR C/D<br>(40ς, 80ς mg tablet) | ○○ / ♦ | **YES ++** | **neutral ?** | [liver] | 1-2 hr YES | • avoid post-MI | ✓BP | 20 mg TID<br>160mg TID | 80mg po BID<br>"D/C by company 2008" | 37 |
| **Pindolol** B/D<br>VISKEN g (5ς, 10ς, 15ς mg tablet)<br>VISKAZIDE (10mg with 25ς,50ς mg **HCT**) | ○○ | **YES +++** | **neutral** | [liver] | 3-4hr NO | • avoid post-MI<br>• ?preferred in symptomatic bradycardia pts | ✓BP (bid; ?od)<br>✓ANGINA (tid-qid) | 5mg OD-BID<br><br>20mg BID | 10mg po BID<br>15mg po BID<br>10/25mg po OD | **29**<br>45<br>37 |
| **Propranolol** C/D<br>INDERAL g (10ς,20ς,40ς,80ς & 120ς mg tab;<br>**LA** 60, 80, 120, 160mg cap; Vial 1mg/ml) | ○○○○ / ♦ | NO | moderate | [liver] | 3-4hr **YES** | Ⓜ >80mg per day<br>• Uses: GI tract bleeds due to esophageal **varices** [28], thyrotoxicosis & anxiety<br>• for lithium tremor ~10-20mg tid | ✓BP ✓ANGINA<br>✓POST MI<br>✓ARRHYTHMIA<br>✓ATRIAL FIB<br>✓**TREMOR**<br>✓HEADACHE | 10-40mg BID<br><br>320mg LA OD | 40mg po BID<br>80mg po BID<br>120mg LA po OD<br>160mg LA po OD | 10<br>**12**<br>**41**<br>49 |
| **Sotalol** B/D<br>SOTACOR g (80ς, 160ς mg tablet) | ○ / ♦♦ | NO | moderate | [kidney] | 10-13hr NO | • Class 2 & 3 antiarrhythmic may be preferred for SVT's<br>• not suitable post-MI due to pro-arrhythmic effect | ✓VENTRICULAR ARRHYTHMIA<br>✓*ATRIAL ARRHYTHMIA* [29] | 40mg BID<br><br>160mg TID | 40mg po BID<br>80mg po BID<br>160mg po OD | 23<br>**38**<br>25 |
| **Timolol** C/D<br>BLOCADREN g (5ς, 10ς, 20ς mg tablet) | ○○ / ♦♦ | NO | moderate | [liver] | 4-5hr NO | Ⓜ ~10mg bid; **not** prevent varices [30]<br>• ophthalmic suspension for Tx of glaucoma (0.25,0.5%) | ✓BP (bid; ?od)<br>✓POST MI<br>✓ANGINA (bid)<br>✓HEADACHE | 5mg OD-BID<br><br>20mg TID | 10mg po BID<br>20mg po OD | **26**<br>26 |
| **NON-SELECTIVE BETA & ALPHA -1 BLOCKADE** | | | | | | | | | | |
| **Carvedilol** ☎▼ C/D<br>COREG g<br>(3.125, 6.25, 12.5 & 25mg tablet) | ○○○ | NO | **neutral** | [liver] | 6-8hr **YES** | • for stable **HF**; reports of ↑LFTs (start with 3.125mg po bid & ↑ q2-wks)<br>• ? Prevent: esophageal varices | ✓HEART FAILURE<br>COMET-Lancet Jul03 (effective but expensive) | 3.125mg - 6.25mg BID<br><br>50mg BID | 6.25mg po BID with food<br>12.5mg po BID<br>25mg po BID **HFTD** | ☎▼ **53**<br>53<br>53 |
| **Labetalol** Vial 5mg/ml C/D<br>TRANDATE g (100ς, 200ς mg tablet) | ○○○ / ♦ | +? | **neutral** | [liver] | 6-8hr NO | β:∝ blockade ratio = 3:1<br>• postural hypotension; reports of ↑LFTs<br>• IV HTN emergencies; PO HTN urgency | ✓BP<br>✓ANGINA<br>*ECLAMPSIA*<br>Used in pregnancy | 100mg OD<br><br>600mg BID | 100mg po BID<br>200mg po BID<br>200mg po TID | **27**<br>42<br>59 |

ς=scored tab ☎ **EDS**=Exception Drug Status ✆=prior NIHB approval ▼=covered NIHB Ⓜ =migraine prophylaxis **ALT**=alternate **COST**=to pt **HF**=heart failure **HR**=heart rate **HFTD**=heart failure target dose **LA**=Long-acting **LVH**=left ventricular hypertrophy **SR**=sustained release

* **Water-soluble:** tend toward longer t 1/2's; renal elimination ( [kidney] =↓ dose in renal failure); ** **Lipid-soluble:** tend toward shorter t 1/2's; hepatic elimination ( [liver] =↓ dose in ↓ hepatic fx); drug interactions due to altered metabolism.

**DIs**: amiodarone, antidiabetics, calcium channel blockers synergistic & ↓ heart rate, cimetidine ↑β blocker effect, clonidine hypertension crisis, digoxin ↓ heart rate, fluconazole, insulins, NSAIDS ↑ blood pressure & ↓ renal function & phenobarbital ↓β blocker effect.

**Side Effect**: fatigue, insomnia, dream vivid, ↓HR, impotence, ↓exercise tolerance, dizzy, cold extremitiy, bronchospasm Tx: ipratropium, headache, mask & delay Sx hypoglycemia, ↑TG, ↓HDL, hallucinate, depression & ?↑psoriasis, ?↓seizure c ECT. **Taper** over 2-4week if D/C.

**t 1/2** does not necessarily correlate with duration of action. **+ ISA** (intrinsic sympathetic activity): may have less negative effects on heart rate useful if bradycardic on other BBs, glucose, lipids, respiratory system; **AVOID** agents with ISA in patients **post MI or CHF.** [7]

Overdose: consider specific therapy for acute poisoning eg. glucagon IV, calcium gluconate IV, epinephrine, insulin euglycemia therapy, & sodium bicarbonate when indicated.

**Angina**: May require high dose. **HF:** Use initial **low** dose & titrate up. **USEFUL**: to **prevent migraine**, tremor, **atrial arrhythmia**, perioperative HTN/CV risk, thyrotoxicosis & ?peritonitis SBP. **Beneficial**→limit infarct size & ↓arrhythmia. (?↓benefit in blacks)

**ROLE**: 1st line⇨ **ANGINA** Stable**, Post MI, LVH <60yr, uncomplicated HTN ≤60yr; +ACEI in SYSTOLIC Dysfx; Alt ⇨DIABETICS** (**cardioselective** agents). Not 1st line in elderly unless post-MI, HF or angina. Blacks less effective!

**Contraindication**: asthma, 2nd or 3rd degree heart block or PR>0.24sec, uncompensated HF & severe PAD peripheral arterial dx, pheochromocytoma if no alpha -blockade 1st. May **WORSEN**→ PAD, HF & Raynauds. **SUDDEN WITHDRAWAL** can ↑angina/MI.

**Perioperative** [31,32,33 AHA'09]: Continue→**if on BB for cardiac indication**, vascular surgery if **myocardial ischemia** & probably if CAD or high cardiac risk ie. multiple risk factors such as: MI hx, angina, HF, severe valve dx, ventricular arrhymias with heart dx, SV arrhythmia with uncontrolled ventricular rate, diabetes, stroke or ↓renal fx. Start days to weeks **before** surgery. Target resting HR 60-80 & SBP>100. Post-op HR<80. Metoprolol 25-50mg bid or bisoprolol 2.5mg Decrease-IV -10mg od or atenolol 50-100mg od used. Taper if DC ?d/c in 2-4wk. Risk of perioperative CV event 1-5% in general, but 11-34% in high risk pts. SE:↓BP & ↓HR. Poise ↓CV events but ↑death/stroke

# CALCIUM CHANNEL BLOCKER (CCB): Comparison Chart [1,2,3,4,5,6,7,8,9,10,11,12,13,14,15,16,17,18]

Prepared by Loren Regier, Brent Jensen BSP  May 10

| Generic Pregnancy Rating<br>TRADE (Dosage & form) ⇓ | ONSET; & DURATION of effect | SA NODE AUTO-MATICITY | AV NODE CON-DUCTION | Periph. Vascular Resistance | HEART RATE | CONTRAC-TILITY | CARDIAC OUTPUT | APPROVED INDICATIONS | COMMENTS | INITIAL & (MAX Dose) | USUAL DOSE RANGE | $COST / MONTH 🍁 |
|---|---|---|---|---|---|---|---|---|---|---|---|---|
| **DIHYDROPYRIDINE (DHP)** | | | | | | | | | | | | |
| **Amlodipine** C<br>NORVASC/new generics<br>5ς & 10mg tab | ~6 hr;<br>24 hr | ↔ | ↔ | ↓↓↓ | ↔ | ↔/↑ | ↑ | ✓HTN (2.5-10mg od ALLHAT)<br>{+ ACEI ACCOMPLISH}<br>✓Stable Angina<br>(ALT systolic Dysfx CND 2007) | DI: grapefruit juice, PI<br>•↓dose in hepatic dysfx<br>•CCB option in HF, but ↑risk in ALLHAT; ?preferred CCB in non-ischemic HF Praise | 2.5-5mg OD<br>(ACCOMPLISH 2008 amlodipine 5-10mg + benazepril 20-40mg/day)<br>(10mg OD) | 2.5mg po OD<br>5mg po OD<br>10mg OD ASCOT,VALUE<br>(Bedtime dosing may decrease edema) | $17_g$/30<br>$26_g$/53<br>**$35_g$**/75 |
| **Amlodipine//atorvastatin** CADUET 5 & 10mg// 10 & 20 & 40 & 80mg tabs $90-120 | | | | | | | | | | | | |
| **Felodipine** C<br>RENEDIL,PLENDIL$_g$<br>2.5, 5 & 10mg tab ext. release | 2-6 hr;<br>24 hr | ↔ | ↔ | ↓↓↓ | ↔/↑ | ↔/↑ | ↑ | ✓HTN<br>(ALT systolic Dysfx CND 2007)<br>(ESRD[19]-adding felodipine to ramipril: no added benefit REIN-2) | DI: **grapefruit juice** CYP3A4 (↑ absorption >2X)<br>•do not chew or crush<br>•CCB option in HF | 2.5-5mg OD<br>(20mg OD) | 5mg po OD<br>10mg po OD HOT<br>15mg po OD | $25_g$/31<br>$32_g$/**43**<br>$46_g$/80 |
| **Nifedipine** C<br>ADALAT/generic<br>**REG**$_g$ 5, 10mg cap<br>PA$_g$ 10, 20mg tab : D/C<br>**XL** 20, 30, 60mg tab<br>-shell may appear in stool | <20 min; 6 hr<br><60 min; 12 hr<br>2 hr; 24 hr | ↔ | ↔ | ↓↓↓ | ↔/↑ | ↔/↓ | ↑↑ | ✓HTN (PA & XL forms)<br>✓Stable Angina (Reg. & XL)<br>✓Coronary Artery Spasm Reg cap<br>• may help achalasia<br>• (Reg. caps **NOT** recommended for acute BP reduction due to assoc. of ↑ MI & stroke) | DI: grapefruit juice<br>SE: reflex tachycardia with short acting forms; more headache & edema<br>•caution in CHD & HF (potential negative inotrope)<br>•used in pregnancy | 5mg TID<br>10mg PA BID<br>30mg XL OD<br>(120mg/d) | 10mg po TID<br>10mg PA po BID<br>20mg PA po BID<br>30mg XL po OD<br>60mg XL po OD<br>90mg XL po OD | 55<br>36<br>53<br>50<br>**38**<br>82 |
| **NON-DIHYDROPYRIDINE** | | | | | | | | | | | | |
| **Diltiazem** C<br>CARDIZEM/generic<br>**REG.**$_g$ 30, 60ς mg tab<br>SR$_g$ 60,90,120mg cap: D/C<br>**CD**$_g$ 120, 180, 240, 300mg cap<br>**TIAZAC**$_g$ **reg** cap & **XC** tab 120,180,240, 300 & 360mg<br>Vial- 50mg/10ml * | <30min; 4-8 hr<br><60min; 12 hr<br><60min; 24 hr<br><60min; 24hr<br>3-7min; 1-3hr | ↓ | ↓ | ↓ | ↓ | ↓ | ↔/↑ | ✓HTN (SR & CD & Tiazac reg/**XC** form)<br>✓Stable Angina (All dosage forms; initial titration with reg. tabs recommended)<br>✓Coronary Artery Spasm (Reg. tabs) | DI 3A4: ↑**cyclosporine** & carbamazepine level; PI, pimozide; simvastatin (↑myopathy) & ranolazine.<br>SE: heart failure, AV block & headache<br>• Tiazac: macrocap bead technology with similar cost as CD<br>• AVOID in CHD & HF (negative inotrope) | 30mg TID<br>60mg SR BID<br>120mg CD/TiazacOD<br>(420-540mg/d)<br>generic Tiazac ↓$ | 30-60mg po TID<br>120mg SR po BID<br>120mg CD po OD<br>240mg CD po OD<br>300mg CD po OD<br>120mg Tiazac OD<br>240mg Tiazac OD<br>300-360mg Tiazac OD<br>240-360mg **XC** HS | 25-38<br>81<br>33<br>**54**<br>65<br>g=generic<br>$25_g$/38<br>$37_g$/**61**<br>44-52g/75-90<br>**57** |
| •CD or Tiazac caps: can sprinkle contents but do not chew/crush -not interchangeable. | | | | | | | | | | | | |
| **Verapamil** C<br>ISOPTIN/generic REG<br>ISOPTIN SR tab<br>**REG**$_g$ 80, 120mg tab<br>**SR**$_g$ 120,180ς,240ς mg tab<br>COVERA-HS –D/C by Co (CV) (Controlled Onset Extended Release) 180, 240mg tablet -shell may appear in stool<br>Vial 5mg/2ml * | <30min; ~8 hr<br><30min; 24 hr<br>4-5hr post ingestion;11 hr post ingestion<br>1-5min; 30min | ↓↓ | ↓↓ | ↓↓ | ↓ | ↓↓ | ↓/↑ | ✓HTN (Reg. CV & SR)<br>✓Stable Angina & Coronary Artery Spasm (Reg & CV Tabs)<br>✓Atrial Fib<br>✓SV arrhythmias<br>✓Cardiomyopathy: obstructive hypertrophic<br>Useful for migraine prophylaxis | DI amiodarone;↑ alcohol effect; ↑carbamazepine,**cyclosporin**, **digoxin**~70% & dofetilide level; erythromycin, grapefruit juice; lithium, pimozide, ranolazine, rifampin; simvastatin ↑ myopathy & terazosin<br>(Verapamil is a Cyp 3A4 inhibitor)<br>SE: heart failure, AV block, **constipation**<br>•SR tabs may be halved<br>•AVOID in CHD & HF (negative inotrope) | 40-80mg TID<br>120mg SR OD<br>(480mg/d) | 80mg po TID cc<br>120mg po BID cc<br>120mg SR po OD cc<br>180mg SR po OD cc<br>240mg SR po OD cc<br>CV: 180mg po HS<br>CV: 240mg po HS | 31<br>35<br>30<br>**30**<br>31<br>36<br>39 |
| •CHRONOVERA dosed at **HS** for peak effect in am & early pm. **NOT** uniquely beneficial (CONVINCE trial [15])<br>• verapamil 180-240mg SR less effective than trandolapril 2mg od at ↓ microalbuminuria in ↑BP & type 2 diabetic pts (BENEDICT trial [16]) | | | | | | | | | | | | |

ς =scored tablet ☎=**EDS** status in Sask. **ALT**=alternate **cc**=with food **CD**=controlled delivery **CHD**=coronary heart dx **COST**=markup & dispensing fee **DI**=drug interaction **HF**=heart failure **HTN**=hypertension **PI**=protease inhibitor **SE**=side effect **SR**=sustained release

* IV diltiazem & IV verapamil indicated for atrial fibrillation/flutter & paroxysmal supraventricular tachycardia. $_g$=generic avail. **Pregnancy** C rating =possible fetal risk

**Drug Class**: **Dihydropyridine (DHP)**: - amlodipine, felodipine, nicardipine, nifedipine, nimodipine {relatively: **more peripheral vasodilation (edema)**, **less effect on heart**};Cyp3A4 substrates.
**NON-Dihydropyridine**: **Benzothiazepine** - diltiazem; **Phenylalkylamine** - verapamil (relatively: **more negative chronotrophic** effect on heart, less on peripheral vasodilation).

**Dosage adjustments:** every 2-4 weeks in HTN (HTN dose often higher than anti-anginal dose.) **Combination** with ACE inhibitors & diuretics reasonable; Dihydropyridines (e.g. nifedipine) may be given with a beta blocker to prevent reflex tachycardia; however use PRECAUTION as possible negative inotropic effects. Generally neutral effect on lipids & glucose tolerance.

**SE: (General)**: dizziness, headache, **edema** esp. with dihydropyridines (?↓if dosed at hs) & in women, flushing, rash, gingival hyperplasia esp. nifedipine + cyclosporine; constipation esp. with verapamil; dyspnea & pulmonary edema in pts. with LV dysfx, may worsen HF.
Overdose: consider specific therapy for acute poisoning eg. glucagon IV, calcium gluconate IV, epinephrine, insulin euglycemia therapy, & sodium bicarbonate when indicated.

**Grapefruit juice** can inhibit metabolism via the cytochrome-P-450 system (CYP 3A4) resulting in significant increases in drug levels, especially with **felodipine**.

**ROLE**: 1ST LINE: Long acting CCB→**Uncomplicated HTN**, **Left Ventricular Hypertrophy** & Angina Stable; 1ST LINE: Long-acting **DHP**→ **Isolated Systolic HTN** & **Diabetic** without nephropathy
Long acting Calcium Channel Blocker: Preferred in vasospastic angina; Alternate in diabetics, CAD with ACEI & angina. Non-dihydropyridines (diltiazem & verapamil) useful for atrial fibrillation & SVT's.
CAD pts: When combination tx needed for high risk pts, an ACE inhibitor with a dihydropyridine CCB is preferred if tolerated (Long-acting CCBs).

**Other Uses**: **blacks**, esophageal disorders, ↓migraines (flunarizine SIBELIUM), ↓panic attacks, **Raynaud's phenomenon** (dihydropyridines), thyrotoxicosis, tardive dyskinesia , aid stone passage & Tourette's Sx.

**Contraindications**: severe hypotension (SBP<90), recent MI with pulmonary edema, sick sinus syndrome or 2nd or 3rd degree AV block ; & if Systolic dysfx or CHF **avoid** diltiazem & verapamil.

| NAME: Generic Pregnancy Rating TRADE (Dosage strength & form) g=generic avail. | Comments (response usually seen within 4 weeks, esp. in low-renin or salt-sensitive hypertensive pts eg. elderly, blacks, obese) | Usual Low Dose (for hypertension) | $ Cost 30 Days |
|---|---|---|---|
| **Hydrochlorothiazide** HYDRODIURIL g (HCT) 12.5,25ˢ,50ˢ,100ˢ ✗▼mg tab -works primarily on distal tubule **B/D** | •low-dose (≤**12.5mg**-25mg) effective; minimal side (rash, photosensitivity) & metabolic effects: ↑ (calcium, uric acid, glucose, cholesterol,TG); ↓ (Na, K+ esp. with salbutamol, magnesium, zinc); Rare: pancreatitis & sexual dysfunction. • **DI**: digoxin↑ toxicy if K+ low ↑ lithium level, NSAID, steroids. •6.25mg enough to augment other agents •scored •low-dose 12.5mg combos with ACEI & ARBs (Altace HCT, Accuretic, Inhibace Plus, Vaseretic, Prinzide, Zestoretic; Atacand Plus, Avalide, Diovan HCT, Hyzaar, Micardis Plus, Olmetec Plus & Teveten Plus) & 25mg with some ACEI/ARB/β-blockers | 12.5-25mg OD up to 50mg (Less diuresis if **CrCl less than 30ml/min**) HF may require bid dosing | 4 **Diuretics**:3 months dispensed in Sask. |
| **Chlorthalidone** HYGROTON g 50ˢ,100ˢ D/C 2005 mg tab **B/D** | •Advantage: best outcome evidence SHEP, ALLHAT & more **potent** 1.5-2x & **longer** acting than **HCT** (Allhat: K+↓0.3, glucose↑0.28, chol↑0.044)mmol/l @ 2-4yr •Disadvantage: low dosage requires quartering or halving of tablets or every other day dosing •scored tablet; • 25ˢ mg avail. combo with atenolol (**Tenoretic** 50/25 or 100/25) but higher cost | 12.5-25mg OD SHEP, ALLHAT (or 25mg EOD) | 4 |
| **Indapamide** LOZIDE g 1.25, 2.5mg tab **B/D** | •less effect than higher-dose HCT on lipids & glucose metabolism. •may be preferred in patients with hyperlipidemia or diabetes • combination with perindopril ↓ stroke PROGRESS •high cost for a diuretic but low cost for an antihypertensive •?more effect if ↓CrCl | 1.25 Hyvet -very elderly -2.5mg OD | 8-11 |
| **Combination Diuretics** | •for *Low Dose* consider using ½ tablet or every other day dosing; K+ sparing combo often not necessary with low-dose HCT, but consider if baseline $K^+ \leq$ 3.8mmol/l | | |
| **Aldactazide-25**ˢ g (also–50ˢ) **C/D** | •HCT(25mg) & spironolactone(25mg) •aldosterone antagonist; K+ sparing | 1 tab EOD-OD | 5 |
| **Nu-Triazide/Dyazide**ˢ g tablet **C/D** | •HCT(25mg) & triamterene(50mg) •triamterene: K+ & Mg sparing; Rare: nephritis, urolithiasis (Use **only if** K+ sparing needed) | ½ - 1 tab OD | 4 |
| **Moduret**ˢ g tablet **B/D** | •HCT(50mg) & amiloride(5mg) •K+ & Mg sparing •use ½ tab for low dose | ½ tab EOD-OD | 5 |

**ROLE**: 1st line: **Uncomplicated**, **Diabetes with normal albuminuria**, **LVH** & **Isolated Systolic HTN**.; *Thiazide Diuretics for Most* JNC 7, Wright-Cochrane 2009, initial or as add-on tx
Alternate 1st line: **RENAL disease**. 2nd line: **SYSTOLIC dysfunction**. Effective in **blacks**.

**Contraindications**: anuria, severe sulpha allergy, gout (symptomatic hyperuricemia) & hyponatremia.

- **Ethacrynic acid** EDECRIN ☎▼ - used esp. for treatment of pts. who can't tolerate furosemide, No sulfur group; Dose 25-200mg/d. Typical: 25mg po od ($30) 50ˢmg po od ($35), ototoxic **B/D**
- **Furosemide** LASIX g, loop diuretic – esp. for diuresis if ↓ **renal function** or nephrotic syndrome; HF may need bid. Dose 20-240mg/d. Typical: 20mg po od-bid $4, 40ˢmg po od-bid $5, 10mg/ml oral soln 40mg od=$39 **C/D**
- **Metolazone** ZAROXOLYN - used **with furosemide** for diuresis in patients with ↓ **renal function** or nephrotic syndrome; Dose 1.25-5mg/day; Typical: 2.5mg po od ($8) 5mg po od ($14) **B/D** (Max 10-20mg/d)
- **Spironolactone** ALDACTONE g - for hyperaldosteronism, diuresis in cirrhosis, **resistant** HTN & **SYSTOLIC** Dysfx HF Class III-IV; Dose 12.5-200mg/d; Typical: 25ˢ-50mg po od ($5-8)•NOT a sulpha SE: ↑K+ **C/D**

## Miscellaneous Antihypertensives

| NAME: Generic /Pregnancy Rating TRADE (Dosage strength & form) g=generic avail. | Comments | Usual Dosage (Max/day) | $ Cost x 30 days | |
|---|---|---|---|---|
| **Central Alpha Agonists** • 2nd or 3rd line agents; an option for pheochromocytoma tx; may worsen depression; impotence | | | | |
| **Clonidine** **C** CATAPRES g 0.1ˢ, 0.2ˢ mg tab DIXARIT g 0.025 mg tab☎▼ | •AVOID in HF/heart block/autonomic neuropathy •rebound HTN on withdrawal taper when D/C over days • **SE**: sedation, dry mouth • **DI**: cyclosporine, mirtazapine, TCA •may tx **acute** ↑BP eg. Initial 0.2mg, then 0.1mg q1h •overdose Tx naloxone •Onset: 30-60min; Peak: 2-4hr; can repeat q1-2hr; **Max**: 0.6-0.8mg • ? abused | 0.1mg BID (0.2mg TID) | 0.1-0.2mg po BID | 20-28 |
| **Methyldopa** ALDOMET g 125, 250, 500mg tab **B** APO-METHAZIDE g **15, 25** 250mg + 15,25 mg HCT Co D/C | •1st line for hypertension in **PREGNANCY** **SE**: sedation, dry mouth, depression, **hepatotoxic**, lupus like Sx & ↓ platelets/RBC •avail. in with HCT(15, 25mg) **DI**: levodopa ↓BP, TCAs ↑BP | 125mg BID (500mg QID) | 250mg po BID<br>Aldoril-15 po BID Co D/C | 17<br>20 |
| **Alpha Blockers**[26] •3rd line agent; option for pheochromocytoma/prostatism[27]; **SE**=sedation, **orthostatic hypotension**, nasal congestion & priapism; **Doxazosin pulled from ALLHAT#** | | | | |
| **Doxazosin** CARDURA g 1,2ˢ,4ˢ mg tab **C** | •once daily; postural hypotension so start with **1 mg** | 2-8mg HS (16 mg HS) | 2mg po HS | 21 |
| **Prazosin** MINIPRESS g 1ˢ,2ˢ,5ˢ mg tab **C** | •multiple daily dosing; esp. first dose syncope, may ↑ # of stillbirths | 0.5mg BID (5mg TID) | 2mg po BID | 25 |
| **Terazosin** HYTRIN g 1,2,5,10mg tab **C** | •once daily; postural hypotension so start with **1 mg** | 1mg HS (10mg BID) | 5mg po HS | 25 |
| **Other Agents** • 2nd or 3rd line agents - vasodilators (often **add a Beta-blocker/centrally acting** drug to minimize reflex tachycardia & a **diuretic** to avoid sodium & water retention) | | | | |
| **Hydralazine** APRESOLINE g 10ˢ,25,50mg tab (20mg **amp**) | **C** **SE**: Lupus syndrome, reflex tachycardia, headache & edema •AVOID in left ventricular hypertrophy | 10mg QID (50mg QID) 37.5-75mg tid with isosorbide A-HeFT 28 | 25mg po QID | 37 |
| **Minoxidil** LONITEN 2.5ˢ, 10ˢ mg tab | **C** **SE**: ↑heart rate, edema, pericardial effusion, lupus, rash, ↑hair face | 2.5mg BID (50mg BID) | 10mg po BID | 59 |

ˢ=scored tablet **COST**=markup & dispensing fee **DI**=drug interaction **HCT**=hydrochlorothiazide **HF**=heart failure **HTN**=hypertension **ISH**=isolated systolic hypertension (ISH) **SE**=side effect (kidney symbol) = ↓ dose for **renal dysfx**
#: doxazosin (α blocker) arm of **ALLHAT** study was stopped early due to ↑ **HF** & stroke compared to chlorthalidone (even though BP lowering effect similar) ☎ **EDS**=Exception **D**rug **S**tatus ▼ covered by NIHB

New: **Aliskiren** RASILEZ HCT, TEKTURNA ✗ ⊗ 150,300mg OD tab ↓ by fat $45; Direct renin inhibitor DRI SE: diarrhea, headache, ↑$K^+$, rash, allergy & pharyngitis. Rare: cough ~1%, angioedema, gout 0.2%. (rat:colonic mucosal hyperplasia). CI:Pregnancy. DI:cyclosporine, furosemide, irbesartan, ketoconazole.

| | Generic/ TRADE / Strength | Comments/ Drug Interactions [11] DI | Side Effects [8,10] | 2010 CND Guidelines by CLASS Indications ✓ ContraIndication CI | Initial Dose (MAX dose) | Usual Dose $/30days |
|---|---|---|---|---|---|---|
| DIURETIC | **Hydrochlorothiazide HCT** HYDRODIURIL 12.5,25ς,50ς mg tab | **12.5**-25mg effective & less SEs •evidence for ↓ morbidity/mortality; •Ineffective→**CrCl<30ml/min** (Avoid if Cl<10ml/min). If Scr>150umol/l → **LASIX** for volume control. **DI**: digoxin↑ toxicy if K+ low ↑ lithium level, NSAID, steroid. Low dose 12.5mg combos→ Accuretic, Altace HCT, Inhibace Plus, Prinzide, Vaseretic, Zestoretic; Atacand Plus, Avalide, Diovan HCT, Hyzaar, Micardis Plus, Olmetec Plus & Teveten Plus | **Low doses well tolerated** but rash, allergic sulfa rx, photosensitivity rx esp UVA, ↑ (calcium, uric acid, glucose, cholesterol,TG) ↓ (Na, K+ esp. with salbutamol, magnesium, zinc), pancreatitis & sexual dysfunction. (Allhat: K+↓0.3, glucose↑0.28, chol ↑0.044) mmol/l@2-4yr | ***Diuretic: First among equals*** [12] initial or add-on. **1st line⇨uncomplicated HTN,ISH,LVH & DIABETES** normal albuminuria (HCT ≤25mg) Add-on 1st line⇨Renal disease & proteinuria **2nd line⇨SYSTOLIC** Dysfunction Class III-IV. | 6.25-12.5mg OD (25-50mg OD HTN; 50-100mg other) | 12.5-25mg OD $4. **Diuretics:3 months** dispensed in Sask. |
| | **Chlorthalidone** HYGROTON 50ς,100ς mg tab | similar to HCT; best trial evidence @ 12.5-25mg od SHEP, ALLHAT (minimal lipid & lyte changes, more potent & longer acting than **HCT**) | | **Useful**: ↓bone loss; effective in **blacks** | 12.5-25mg OD | 12.5-25mg OD $4 |
| | **Indapamide** LOZIDE 1.25,2.5mg tab | less effect on lipid/glucose; still THIAZIDE type; ?more effect if ↓CrCl | **Indapamide**→ headache, dizziness | **CI:** gout (symptomatic hyperuricemia), sulfa allergy, anuria, hyponatremia | 1.25mg OD (5mg OD) | 1.25-2.5mgOD $12 |
| | **Spironolactone** 25ς,100ς mg tab ALDACTONE | If renal dysfunction→↑Scr,↑BUN,↑K & hyperchloremic acidosis. | ↑**K+** esp. if CrCl<30ml/min, diabetic, on ACE/ARB/NSAID, ↓Na, rash, gynecomastia, menstruation abnormal & ?↑GI ulcers | ✓CHF Class III-IV, **BP, hyperaldosteronism, edema, cirrhosis** **Alt 1st line⇨SYSTOLIC Dysfx** | 12.5mg OD (100mg BID) | 25-50mg OD $5-8 |
| | **DYAZIDE** tabς→HCT 25mg/triamterene 50mg; MODURET→HCT 50ς mg/amiloride 5mg | | | | | |
| β BLOCKER | **Metoprolol** LOPRESOR, BETALOC 25ς,50ς,100ς mg tab; **SR**:100,200mg tab | •**β1 cardioselective**→, acebutolol, atenolol, bisoprolol & metoprolol •Evidence in **CHF** → bisoprolol, carvedilol & metoprolol •<u>ISA</u> Intrinsic Sympathetic Activity →<u>acebutolol, oxprenolol & pindolol</u> (less bradycardia, lipid changes & cold extremities but **NOT** recommended in angina/Hx MI[8]) •Non-selective β blockers nadolol, oxprenolol, pindolol, propranolol, sotalol & timolol | fatigue, insomnia, dreams vivid, ↓ HR, impotence, ↓ exercise tolerance, dizzy; worsens→ PAD, CHF, Raynauds; cold extremities, bronchospasm, headache, mask & delay Sx hypoglycemia, ↑TG, ↓HDL, hallucinations, depression; & sudden withdraw→exacerbate angina/MI **acebutolol** also→positive antinuclear antibody test & lupus | **1st line⇨ ANGINA** stable, **MI, LVH** <60yr, **uncomplicated HTN for age ≤60yr; +ACEI for SYSTOLIC Dysfunction; Alt⇨DIABETICS** (cardioselective agents) | 12.5-25mg BID (200mg BID) | 50mg BID $14; 100mg <u>SR</u> OD $15 |
| | **Bisoprolol** MONOCOR 5ς,10mg tab | | | | 2.5mg OD (20mg OD) | 5mg OD $15; 10mg OD $21 |
| | **Atenolol** TENORMIN 25,50ς,100ς mg; TENORETIC/chlorthalidone 50/25ς,100/25ς tab | **DI**: amiodarone, antidiabetics, CCB synergistic, cimetidine ↑β blocker, clonidine HTN crisis, digoxin ↓HR, insulins, NSAIDS ↑BP & phenobarbital ↓β blocker | | **Useful**: migraine, tremors, atrial arrhythmias, perioperative hypertension & thyrotoxicosis | 25mg OD (200mg OD) | 50-100mg OD $18-24 |
| | **Propranolol** INDERAL Reg:10ς,20ς,40ς,80ς,120ς mg tab LA:60,80,120,160mg cap | •? ↑ CNS SE; ↑lipids; **Use**: GI bleed, thyrotoxicosis, migraine & anxiety | | **CI:** asthma/COPD; 2nd/3rd degree heart block, uncompensated HF & severe PAD | 10-40mg BID (320mg LA OD) | 80mg BID $12; 160mg LA OD $47 |
| | **Acebutolol** SECTRAL 100ς,200ς,400ςmg tab; **Carvedilol** ☎▼ COREG 3.125,6.25,12.5&25mg tab 3.125-25mg bid=$53 with food; **Nadolol** CORGARD 40ς,80ς,160ς mg tab; **Pindolol** VISKEN 5ς,10ς,15ς mg tab, VISKAZIDE 10/25ς mg,10/50ς mg(/**HCT**) tab; **Sotalol** SOTACOR 80ς,160ς mg tab; **Timolol** BLOCADREN 5ς,10ς,20ς mg tab | | | | | |
| ACEI | **Lisinopril** ZESTRIL, PRINIVIL 5ς,10,20mg tab; **ZESTORETIC** 10/12.5mg; 20/12.5mg; 20/25(/**HCT**) tab | If ↑ **K** >5.6 or ↑ **SCr** rise >30% over baseline may warrant discontinuation.[1] Less effective in African Americans unless add a THIAZIDE,[2,8] but still use for compelling indications eg. MI, HF, renal disease. | cough 10% (↑in East Asians), dry/nonproductive, loss of taste, rash esp. captopril (sulfa), headache, dizziness, ↓BP diuretics/volume depletion, fatigue, ↑K+ K supplements/K sparing diuretics/↓renal fx; acute renal failure with bilateral renal artery stenosis, angioedema 0.5% (esp. in blacks), hepatotoxicity, dysguesia, pancreatitis & blood dyscrasias. | **1st line ⇨uncomplicated HTN, LVH & DIABETICS & SYSTOLIC Dysfx & MI, RENAL Dx., Past CVA/TIA** combo c HCT **& ALL Coronary Artery Disease pts.** | 2.5mg OD (40mg OD) | 5-10mg OD $25-28; 10/12.5mg OD $26; 10→35mgOD CHF ATLAS |
| | **Ramipril** (new generics: ↓ cost) ALTACE 1.25,2.5,5,10mg cap; Altace HCT | **DI**: diuretics K sparing→↑K, lithium ↑levels, NSAIDS ↓effect & potassium ↑K | | **CI:** artery stenosis (solitary kidney or bilateral), Hx angioedema, pregnancy ↑fetal mortality 2nd/3rd trimester ↑malformations 1st trimester | 1.25mg OD (20mg OD) | 5mg OD $26 g/ 35; 10mg HS HOPE $29g/ 43 |
| | **Captopril** CAPOTEN 6.25,12.5,25ς,50ς,100ς mg tab | •short acting; option for initiation of Tx / hypertensive urgency | | | 6.25mg BID (150mg TID) | 25mg BID $28; 50mg BID $44 |
| | **Benazepril** LOTENSIN 5ς,10 od=$29ς,20ς mg tab; **Cilazapril** INHIBACE 1ς,2.5 od=$23ς,5ς mg tab, INHIBACE PLUS 5/12.5ς mg(/**HCT**) tab; **Enalapril** VASOTEC 2.5ς,5ς,10ς od=$25,20ςmg tab, VASERETIC 5/12.5mg,10/25ςmg(/**HCT**) tab, **inj**; **Fosinopril** MONOPRIL 10 od=$25ς, 20mg tab; **Perindopril** COVERSYL 2,4 od=$35ς, 8mg tab, COVERSYL PLUS 4/1.25 indapamide;8/2.5⊗ mg; **Quinapril** ACCUPRIL 5ς,10 od=$38,20,40mg tab, ACCURETIC 10+20/12.5ςmg; 20/25 mg(/**HCT**) tab; **Trandolapril** MAVIK 0.5,1,2 od=$35, 4mg cap | | | | | |
| ARB | **Irbesartan** AVAPRO 75,150,300mg tab; **AVALIDE** 150/12.5mg; 300/12.5 & 25mg (/**HCT**)tab | If ↑ **K** >5.6 or ↑ **SCr** rise >30% over baseline may warrant discontinuation.[1] Less effective in African Americans unless add a THIAZIDE,[8] but still used for compelling indications esp if ACEI intolerance eg. MI, HF, renal dx. | Well **tolerated** in general but fatigue, headache, rash, ↓BP diuretics/volume depletion, ↑ K+ K supplements/K sparing diuretics/↓ renal fx & acute renal failure with bilateral renal artery stenosis, angioedema less than ACEI, dysguesia, pancreatitis & blood dyscrasias. <u>Less</u> cough, headache, dizziness than ACE. ?concern of ↑cancer Meta-Sipahi'10, NNH=143/4yr | Delay diabetic nephropathy PRIME→irbesartan; RENAAL→losartan. Heart failure Val-HeFT→valsartan, CHARM→candesartan; HTN LIFE→losartan | 75mg OD (300mg OD) | 150-300mg OD $50 |
| | **Losartan** COZAAR 25,50,100mg tab; **HYZAAR** 50/12.5mg (/**HCT**) tab; **HYZAAR DS** 100//12.5/25mg (//**HCT**) tab | **DI**: ↑ lithium; losartan→fluconazole&rifampin ↓losartan, &↓uric acid level; telmisartan→ ↑ digoxin level; irbesartan→ fluconazole ↑'s irb effect. | | **1st line ⇨uncomplicated HTN,ISH,LVH & DIABETICS. Alt⇨ SYSTOLIC Dysfunction/MI,CAD** | 12.5-25mg OD (100mg OD) | 50-100mg OD $52 |
| | **Valsartan** DIOVAN 40ς,80,160,320mg tab; **DIOVAN HCT** 80/12.5 & 160&320mg//12.5/25 tab /**HCT** tab | **COMBO**: ACE & ARB CALM→signif. ↓ BP but not sig. ↓ microalbuminuria vs lisinopril. ARB's are priced ~$1.15 per tab/cap→use **scored tablets** ς to ↓ cost. | | **CI:** artery stenosis (solitary kidney or bilateral), Hx angioedema, pregnancy ↑fetal mortality 2nd/3rd trimester | 80mg OD (320mg OD) | 80-320mg OD $49 |
| | **Candesartan** ATACAND 4⊗,8ς,16ς,32ς CALM mg tab, ATACAND PLUS 16/12.5ς od=$48; 32//12.5/25ς⊗ mg (/**HCT**) tab; **Eprosartan** TEVETEN 400,600mg, PLUS 600/12.5mg od=$44 tab; **Olmesartan** OLMETEC 20,40 od $42 mg tab, OLMETEC PLUS 20/12.5mg & 40/12.5 & 40/25 od $42 mg HCT tabs; **Telmisartan** MICARDIS 40ς,80ς mg tab, PLUS 80//12.5/25mg (/**HCT**) tab od=$47 | | | | | |
| CCB | **Felodipine** RENEDIL (new generic) PLENDIL 2.5,5,10mg ext. release tab | •less negative inotropic effects than nifedipine •Don't crush/chew •safe HF **DI**: carbamazepine, ?cyclosporin, fluconazole, **grapefruit** juice↑↑effect | dizzy, headache nifedipine 12%, rash, flushing dose related, constipation verapamil 7%, peripheral edema esp. with dihydropyridines & ♀, ↑HR dihydropyridines, ↓HR diltiazem, verapamil, gingival hyperplasia >20%, gynecomastia; dyspnea & pulmonary edema in pts. with LV dysfunction, as some may worsen CHF. **Diltiazem** also→ **lupus like rash**. **LA-Dihydropyridine**→amlodipine, felodipine, nicardipine, nifedipine & nimodipine (Relatively: more peripheral vasodilation & <u>less heart</u> effect) | ✓**Felodipine** HTN, ALT systolic Dysfx ✓**Amlodipine** HTN, Stable Angina, ALT systolic Dysfx ✓**Nifedipine** HTN: PA&XL form; Stable Angina: Reg& XL; Coronary Artery Spasm: Reg caps ✓**Diltiazem** HTN: SR, CD & Tiazac; Coronary Artery Spasm: Reg; Stable Angina: All dosage forms→ titrate Reg. ✓**Verapamil** HTN: Reg&SR; Stable Angina & Coronary Artery Spasm: Reg; A.Fib, SV arrhythmia, Cardiomyopathy- obstructive hypertrophic | 2.5-5mg OD (20mg OD) | 5-10mgOD HOT $25-32 |
| | **Amlodipine** (new generic) NORVASC 5ς,10mg tab | •long acting→long t½ **DI**: ?cyclosporin, fluconazole, **grapefruit** juice↑effect •may be beneficial in diastolic dysfunction | | | 2.5-5mg OD (10mg OD) | 5-10mg OD $26-35 |
| | **Nifedipine** ADALAT Reg 5,10mg cap (PA 10,20mg tab **D/C**) XL 20,30,60mg tab | •negative inotropic potential •reflex ↑HR **DI**: cimetidine, digoxin, grapefruit juice •Reg. caps **NOT** for <u>acute</u> ↓ BP due to assoc. of ↑ MI/stroke •used in pregnancy | | | 30mg XL OD (120mg XL OD) | 30mg XL OD $50; 20mg PA BID $53; 60mg XL OD $38 |
| | **Diltiazem** CARDIZEM CARDIZEM CD, TIAZAC reg/XC Reg: 30,60ςmg tab (SR:60,90,120mg D/C) CD/ER: 120,180,240,300,360mg Tiazac/XC cap | •negative inotropic **DI**: carbamazepine ↑carb level, cimetidine & PI ↑diltiazem, **cyclosporin** ↑cyclo level, digoxin ↑dig level; lovastatin & simvastatin ↑myopathy | | **1st line uncomplicated, LVH, ISH** LA-DHP **& Diabetic** non-nephro LA-DHP; **ANGINA. CAD: combo of ACEI with DHP.** | 120mg CD OD $33 (420mg CD OD) generic Tiazac ↓$ | 60mg TID $38; 240mg CD OD $54; 240mg Tiazac OD $37 {XC ↓$ at ≥240mg/d} |
| | **Verapamil** ISOPTIN Regular/ SR tab **Reg**: 80,120mg tab **SR**: 120,180ς,240ςmg tab (COVERA-HS: 180, 240mg tablet **D/C**) | •Chronovera not uniquely beneficial (CONVINCE trial 2003) •<u>most negative inotropic & chronotropic</u> •**DI**: amiodarone, dofetilide, carbamazepine, **cyclosporine, digoxin**, grapefruit juice, rifampin, simvastatin & terazosin. | | **Useful:** A.Fib, SVT, Raynaud's & **blacks**. **CI:** SBP <90, recent MI or pulm. edema, sick sinus Sx or 2nd/3rd degree AV block; Systolic dysfx/CHF→ diltiazem, verapamil | 120mg SR OD (480mg SR OD) | 80mg TID $31; 180mg SR OD $30; 240mg CV OD $39 |

ς=scored tablet ☎ Exception Drug Status Sk **Cost**=markup & fee **ACE**=angiotensin converting enzyme **ARB**=angiotensin receptor blocker **Alt**=alternative **CD**=controlled delivery **CNS**=central nervous system **DI**=drug interaction **Dx**=disease **HCT**=hydrochlorothiazide **HF**=heart failure **HR**=heart rate **HTN**=hypertension **Hx**=history **ISH**=isolated systolic htn **K**=potassium **LA**=Long-acting **LVH**=left ventricular hypertrophy **MI**=myocardial infarction **Na**=sodium **PAD**=peripheral arterial dx **PI**=protease inhibitor **Rx**=reaction **SE**=side effect **SR**=sustained release **Sx**=symptom **TG**=triglycerides (kidney symbol) =↓dose for **renal dysfx**

**NEW: Aliskiren** RASILEZ HCT, TEKTURNA ✗ ⊗ 150,300mg OD tab ↓by fat $45; Direct renin inhibitor (DRI) SE: diarrhea, headache, ↑K+, rash, allergy & pharyngitis. Rare: cough ~1%, angioedema, gout 0.2%. (rats: colonic mucosal hyperplasia). CI: Pregnancy. DI: cyclosporine, furosemide, irbesartan, ketoconazole.

**OTHER**

| Generic/ TRADE / Strength | Comments/ Drug Interactions [11] DI | Side Effects [8,10] SE | 2010 CND (Guidelines by CLASS) Indications ✓ ContraIndication CI | Initial Dose (MAX) | Usual Dose $/30days |
|---|---|---|---|---|---|
| **Clonidine** CATAPRES 0.1[s],0.2[s] mg tab | • used for acute ↓BP **DI**: cyclosporine,mirtazapine,TCA's **CENTRAL ALPHA AGONIST** (2nd/3rd line) →if others CI/ refractory HTN | **sedation,dry mouth**,↓HR,depression & **rebound HTN** on withdrawal,impotence | **CI**:CHF/heart block,diabetes autonomic neuropathy | 0.1mg BID (0.2mg TID) | 0.1-0.2mg BID $19-28 |
| **Methyldopa** ALDOMET 125,250,500mg tab | **DI**: levodopa ↓BP,TCAs ↑BP [Methyldopa/HCT APO-METHAZIDE 250/15,250/25; 1 tab po OD=$14] Co D/C | sedation, dry mouth, impotence, depression, **hepatotoxic**, lupus like Sx & ↓ platelets/RBC | 1st line HTN in pregnancy; an option for pheochromocytoma | 125mg BID (500mg QID) | 250mg BID $17 |
| **Prazosin** MINIPRESS 1[s],2[s],5[s] mg tab | **ALPHA BLOCKERS** (2nd/3rd line) →if others CI/ refractory HTN | sedation, dizziness, vertigo,headache, palpitations, ↑HR, fluid retention, weakness, nasal congestion & priapism. **First dose syncope** → minimize by gradual dose titration & give @HS | **Useful→ for prostatism;** [8,19] an option for pheochromocytoma | 0.5mg BID (5mg TID) | 2mg BID $25 |
| **Terazosin** HYTRIN 1,2,5,10mg tab | Doxazosin CARDURA 1,2[s],4[s] mg tab ALLHAT removed → due to ↑CHF/stroke | | | 1mg HS (10mg BID) | 5mg HS $25 |
| **Hydralazine** APRESOLINE 10[s],25,50mg tab | **VASODILATOR** reflex ↑HR,edema & renin Sx activation often add β-blocker/diuretic | ↑↑HR,aggravate angina,headache,dizzy, fluid retention,lupus like >200mg/d & hepatitis | Alt Systolic Dysfx hydralazine with isosorbide A-HeFT **CI:** in left ventricular hypertrophy | 10mg QID (50mg QID) | 25mg QID $37 |
| **Labetalol** TRANDATE 100[s],200[s] mg tab | **ALPHA & BETA BLOCKADE** ↓ BP more than other β-blockers | postural hypotension & **hepatotoxicity** more than other β-Blockers 7 | Used in pregnancy **CI:** as per β-Blockers above | 100mg BID (400mg TID) | 200mg BID $42 |

**2010 CND Recommendations: Disease & Risk Factors (consideration for Trials)** [2,3,4,5,6,7,8,9,10,11,12,13,14,15,16,17,18,19,20,21] **Lifestyle change** for DIET ↓Na Ideal <1.5g,Max 2.3g/d,<100mmol/d,DASH, **EXERCISE, ↓alcohol** use **& stop SMOKING!**

| DISEASE or RISK FACTOR | 1ST LINE INITIAL THERAPY Wright-Cochrane'09 | SECOND STEP THERAPY | NOTES & CAUTIONS |
|---|---|---|---|
| **Uncomplicated Hypertension {Hypertension without other compelling indications}** | **Thiazide** like diuretic (eg.HCT or chlorthalidone 12.5-25mg od) β blocker (for age ≤60 years ); ACE inhibitor,ARB not rec. in blacks unless compelling indication 2,8 CCB→Long Acting {Consider: ASA esp. if >50yr & BP not ↑ & statins ↑risk pts} | **COMBOS** of 1st line drugs. (Not ACE+ARB) Wald'09 **If SBP≥20 or DBP≥10**mm Hg above target consider combo: **TWO** 1st line drugs INITIALLY,but cautious in elderly due to falls; dose titration & adverse reaction management more difficult. | α blockers not recommended as initial therapy (If used may consider additional antihypertensive agent). **Monitor** for hypokalemia: seldom if on low dose thiazide (consider K+ sparing diuretics if baseline K+ ≤ 3.8mmol/l) |
| **Isolated Systolic Hypertension (ISH)** | **Thiazide** like diuretic (eg.HCT or chlorthalidone 12.5-25mg od) Calcium channel blockers→LA-DHP , ARBs | **COMBINATIONS** of 1st line drugs (ACE+CCB more effective than ACE +HCT) Accomplish | Hypokalemia→seldom if using low dose thiazide (K+ sparing diuretics rarely needed) |
| **Diabetes mellitus with nephropathy*** *albumin:creatinine ratio (ACR): ≥ 2mg/mmol in men; ≥2.8 mg/mmol in women or chronic kidney disease | ACE inhibitor or ARBs (Monitor K+ & SCr carefully) (Evidence from IDNT irbesartan/RENAAL losartan ) {Note: 3-4 drugs may be needed} | Addition of one or more: Thiazide (HCT ≤ 25mg od), Long acting calcium channel blockers (amlodipine had less kidney protection than ramipril or metoprolol AASK) {If β blocker , cardioselective acebutolol, atenolol,bisoprolol & metoprolol} | If Scr 150 umol/l, use a loop diuretic rather than thiazide if needed to reduce edema. (If CrCl <30ml/min→thiazide diuretic less effective) May consider **ACEI + ARB** combination CALM,COOPERATE |
| **Diabetes mellitus without nephropathy** (ACR): <2mg/mmol in men; <2.8 mg/mmol in women | ACE inhibitor or ARB, or Thiazide ALLHAT or LA-DHP CCB {Note: more than 3 drugs may be needed} | Combination of 1st line drugs or addition of cardioselective β blocker, or LA Non-DHP-CCB. ACE+ARB→renal benefits but may ↑Scr&K+& hypotension. | Low dose **thiazides** have evidence for CV outcome benefits in diabetes & minimal effect on glucose. **ALLHAT** included **>15,000** patients [2,13] **with diabetes**, the largest antihypertensive trial ever in this population. |
| **Diabetes mellitus without nephropathy & with systolic hypertension** | ACE inhibitor or ARB, or Thiazide diuretic ALLHAT or Calcium channel blockers →LA-DHP | | |
| **CAD- Coronary Artery Disease** | ACE inhibitor or ARB (except in low risk pts) | Long-acting CCBs. When combo used for high risk pts, an ACE inhibitor/dihydropyridine CCB is preferred | Avoid short-acting nifedipine. Combo of an ACE with an ARB is specifically not recommended. |
| **Angina, stable** | **β blocker** (strongly consider adding ACE inhibitors) Or Long acting calcium channel blocker | | Vasospastic angina→long acting CCB (avoid β-blocker). AVOID short-acting nifedipine. |
| **Prior MI** | **β blocker and ACE inhibitor** (ARBs if ACE intolerant) | If β blocker contraindicated/ineffective, consider CCB | If using CCB, only LA-DHP if also HF not diltiazem or verapamil. |
| **Systolic Dysfunction (Heart Failure)** -titrate to HF trial doses ACEI+BB if possible | **ACE inhibitor** (ARB if ACE contraindicated or not tolerated) & β blocker (bisoprolol, carvedilol COMET, metoprolol), +/- diuretic; (spironolactone if Class III-IV HF) | ARBs or (Hydralazine + isosorbide dinitrate A-HeFT 22), Amlodipine or felodipine (helpful in diastolic dysfx; but ↑ HF ALLHAT ); thiazide/loop diuretic as additive Tx. | AVOID non-dihydropyridine CCB (diltiazem & verapamil). Use ICD devices & CRT in select pts. Watch for ↑K+ with spironolactone. [23] If ACE+ARB→may↑Scr&K+& ↓BP. |
| **Past Cerebrovascular Accident or TIA** | **ACE inhibitor & diuretic combo** (Not an ACE + ARB) ↓ BP after acute phase of non-disabling stroke (↓ recurrent CV events) | Antihypertensives may ↑ death in **acute** TIA/stroke but ↓ long term risk. Evidence supports {chlorthalidone or amlodipine ALLHAT}, {perindopril + indapamide PROGRESS}, {losartan +/- HCT LIFE}, {ramipril HOPE} & {diltiazem NORDIL}. | |
| **Renal disease & proteinuria *** *albumin:creatinine ratio >30mg/mmol or urinary protein >500mg/24hr | ACE inhibitor (diuretics as additive therapy) {monitor K+ and SCr carefully if ACEI or ARB} | Combinations of agents (incl. ACEI + ARB watch K & Crcl) (If ACE intolerance→Angiotensin receptor blocker) | AVOID ACE if renal artery stenosis, (bilateral or solitary) Loop diuretics if volume overload, advanced disease. |
| **Left Ventricular Hypertrophy (LVH) Dyslipidemia Peripheral Arterial Disease (PAD)** | LVH: ACE inhibitor,ARB,CCB→LA,diuretics; β blocker if <60yr Dyslipidemia & PAD -Does Not affect initial treatment In LVH patients→ losartan ↓ stroke (NOT CV death or MI) vs atenolol (5%vs6.7%; NNT=59) LIFE Lancet 2002 | Does not affect initial treatment recommendation | LVH→AVOID hydralazine & minoxidil. PAD→AVOID β blocker in pts with **severe** disease. PAD → CCB useful option (eg. Raynaud's Syndrome Sev). |

ACE=angiotensin converting enzyme **ARB**=angiotensin receptor blocker **CCB**=calcium channel blocker **HCT**=hydrochlorothiazide **HF**=heart failure **TIA**=transient ischemic attack **LA-DHP**: Long-Acting Dihydropyridines: amlodipine, felodipine, nifedipine, nimodipine.

**Drugs which ↑BP**: appetite suppressants,caffeine,cocaine & other illicit drugs,cyclosporin,ephedra,erythropoietin,fludrocortisone,licorice in chewing tobacco,nasal decongestant,midodrine,nicotine,NSAID's & COX-2,oral contraceptive,steroids adrenal,sympathomimetics,tacrolimus, VEGF inhibitors bevacizumab,pazopanib,sorafenib,sunitinib & venlafaxine.

**CONTRAINDICATIONS**: **DIURETICS**: symptomatic gout, sulpha allergy, anuria, hyponatremia. **β-BLOCKERS**: asthma, 2nd or 3rd degree heart block,severe bradycardia, uncompensated heart failure, severe PAD.
**ACEI / ARB**: bilateral artery stenosis (or solitary kidney stenosis if only 1 kidney), history of angioedema, pregnancy- 2nd & 3rd trimesters (but new info now on ACE harm in 1st trimester).
**CCB**: systolic BP <90, recent MI with pulmonary edema Non-LA-DHP, sick sinus syndrome or 2nd/3rd degree AV block, systolic dysfunction/HF (especially diltiazem & verapamil).

**MONITOR**: urinalysis, CBC, lytes, calcium, BUN/Scr, ECG, fasting glucose & lipids. {Baseline: rule out secondary causes ie. Mineralocorticoid esp. if K+ is low; assess end-organ damage & identify CV risk factors}

**PROBLEM COMBO'S**:
- ♦**hydralazine and diuretic** ⇨stimulate renin & sympathetic activity unless used with β-blocker
- ♦**verapamil or diltiazem** with a **β-blocker** ⇨negative effects on heart (e.g. ↓ heart rate & ↓ cardiac output)
- ♦**β-blocker and clonidine** ⇨ concern about rebound hypertension if clonidine withdrawn abruptly
- ♦**CCBS and α-blockers** ⇨ potential for excessive hypotension; increased risk of falls, etc.
- ♦**ACEI+ARB**: no better CV benefit & ↑**SE** ↓BP, ↑K+, & worse renal outcomes in hypertension trial: Ontarget; small benefit in reducing proteinuria Calm,Cooperate & persistent HF Charm; but ↑SE & no greater efficacy MI trial; VALIANT.

**SYNERGISTIC COMBO'S: AB ⇔ CD:** **A:** **ACEI or ARB**→with diuretic or CCB **B:** **β-BLOCKER**→with diuretics or CCB (+ACEI if post MI/HF) **C:** **CCB**→ with β-Blocker or ACEI **D:** **DIURETICS**→with β-Blocker, ACEI or ARB

**RISK Factors** [13,24]: ↑**Cholesterol**: ↑LDL (↑ApoB/ApoA1 ratio studied in INTERHEART), **Smoking, Diabetes,** ↑**BP** esp. systolic, **Abdominal obesity**: **waist/hip** ratio (♂ >0.9; ♀ >0.85), BMI >25, Waist size 15 (♂≥94-102cm,~40inch S.Asian 90cm; ♀ ≥80-88cm,~35inch S.Asian 80cm), **stress & depression; lack of vegetables, fruits, exercise** (30-60mins 5-7x/week) & **alcohol** (0-2drinks/d ♂=14/week ♀=9/week); Low HDL ≤1, Family history of premature heart disease [15] (Age: ♂ <55, ♀ <65), Age (♂ >55, ♀ >65) & Microalbuminuria [15].

**BP TARGETS** **Uncomplicated HTN**⇨140/90 **ISH**⇨SBP <140 **Home/Self BP** best⇨135/85 **RENAL Dysfx/DIABETES**⇨130/80 **Ambulatory 24hr avg**⇨130/80; {**Normal BP** <120/80; **Optimal BP**<130/85; **High Normal BP** 130-139/85-89}

**Resistant Hypertension**: careful technique taking BP; rule out white-coat by ambulatory monitoring if prn; look for 2° causes eg. Obstructive sleep apnea, renal artery stenosis, 1o aldosteronism, NSAIDs; ↓wt, drinking moderate, ↓salt; maximize diuretic & consider spironolactone; use combos.

# Antihypertensives: Landmark & Recent Trials pre 2006–Summary (for more detailed trial summary chart, see *Antihypertensives: Landmark & Recent Trials* at © www.rxfiles.ca)

| TRIAL | PRIMARY AGENTS | POPULATION STUDIED | CONTRIBUTION TO CURRENT KNOWLEDGE |
|---|---|---|---|
| **AASK** [1] 3-6.4yr, n=1,094 | Ramipril ALTACE 2.5-10mg od, Metoprolol 50-200mg od, Amlodipine NORVASC 5-10mg od | **African Americans with hypertensive nephrosclerosis** | **Ramipril provided best renal protection**, followed by metoprolol (amlodipine arm halted early - safety concerns) Group with lower target BP goal no better than group with higher target (achieved goal: 128/78 vs **141/85**). |
| **ALLHAT** [1,3,2] 4.9yr n=42,418→33,357 | Doxazosin CARDURA 2-8mg/day; study arm **stopped early**; Amlodipine NORVASC 2.5-10mg od, Lisinopril ZESTRIL 10-40mg od, Chlorthalidone 12.5-25mg od | **↑BP & 1 other risk factor** (prev MI, stroke, LVH, diabetes, smoke, ↓HDL, hx CVD) ♀47%, black35%, hispanic16%, diabetes36% | **Chlorthalidone (thiazide): well tolerated, as effective & least expensive in lowering CV events.** Chlorthalidone had: much less HF than amlodipine; less stroke and HF than lisinopril; much less HF & stroke than doxazosin. Study design limits lisinopril interpretation: blacks respond less to ACEI; ACEI + β-blocker less synergistic than ACEI + diuretic. (See also Q&A How ALLHAT compares to the **ANBP2** trial at http://www.rxfiles.ca/acrobat/HTN-Q&A-ANBP2.pdf) |
| **ASCOT-BPLA** [3,4] 5.5yr, n=19,257 See also Q&A Ascot | amlodipine NORVASC 5-10mg od +/- perindopril 4-8mg od vs atenolol 50-100mg od +/- bendroflumethiazide 1.25-2.5mg od | **↑BP & ≥3 other risk factor** moderate risk without prev heart dx (eg. ♂ 77%, age mean 63, smoking 33%, albuminuria 62%, diabetes 27% & family hx CHD 26%) | Amlodipine 5-10mg od + perindopril 4-8mg od was superior to atenolol 50-100mg od + bendroflumethiazide 1.25-2.5mg od on many secondary but not the primary outcome. (Trial did not compare more common ACE + diuretic combinations. Beta blockers known to be less effective in **elderly** (Ascot mean age 63) & recent meta analysis showed disappointing results with atenolol. A BP difference of 2.7/1.9 mmHg favoring amlodipine could account for these results.) |
| **CALM** [5] 24 wk, n=199 | Candesartan ATACAND 16mg od, Lisinopril ZESTRIL 20mg od, Combination | **Type 2 diabetes, ↑BP & microalbuminuria** | Lisinopril esp. & candesartan ↓BP & microalbuminuria in Type 2 diabetes. **Combo ACEI & ARB** may be more effective to ↓BP & albuminuria. {**COOPERATE** [6] **retracted**: trandolapril 3mg od + losartan 100mg od: ??? renal benefit, but trial **irregularities**} |
| **CAPPP** [7] 6.1yr, n=10,985 | Captopril CAPOTEN 50-100mg po od/bid, Conventional tx (eg. atenolol/metoprolol 50-100mg od/HCT 25mg od) | **DBP>100** (BP 162/100 captopril, BP 160/98 conventional) | Captopril & conventional arms were equal in preventing CV morbidity & mortality; however less strokes in the conventional arm. In patients with diabetes, captopril had less cardiac & fatal events. This trial had baseline flaws. |
| **ELITE II** [8] 1.5yr, n=3,152 | Losartan COZAAR 50mg od, Captopril CAPOTEN 50mg tid | **Heart Failure II-IV** EF <40% (Mean 31%), Mean 71yr | **Losartan 50mg od not superior to captopril in HF**, but less losartan discontinued due to side effects (9.7 vs 14.7%) (Previous smaller ELITE findings suggested losartan may be superior to captopril in reducing mortality in HF). |
| **FACET** [9] 2.5yr, n=380 | Fosinopril MONOPRIL 20mg od, Amlodipine NORVASC 10mg hs | **↑BP & Type 2 diabetes** | Fosinopril significantly decreased major vascular events vs amlodipine, despite amlodipine decreasing BP by 4/2 mmHg more than fosinopril. Note: Trial was non blinded & 1/3 of patients were receiving both drugs. |
| **HOPE** [10, 11, 12] 4.5yr, n=9,297 | Ramipril ALTACE 10mg po **hs**, {**Initial BP** mean **139/79**} **Placebo** | **High CV risk**(Hx: CAD80%, PVD44%, stroke/TIA11%) or (diabetes 38% & 1 other risk factor); LVH 8%; **≥55yr** | **Ramipril** significantly **reduces MI, stroke, CV death & all-cause death** vs **placebo** in **high-risk patients** (especially the 47% with hypertension [13]) not known to have a low ejection fraction or HF. Benefits greater in **diabetes**. BP reduction may be greater than the "modest" reported (due to HS dosing & differences in nighttime vs morning BP readings [14]). |
| **HOT** [15] 3.8yr, n=18,790 | BP→ **3 DBP target groups: ≤90, ≤85, ≤80** mmHg (**Felodipine** RENEDIL 5→10mg od, +/-**ACE**, +/- **Beta-blocker**, +/-**diuretic**) | ↑BP 170/105→to **3 DBP gps**: ≤ 90 gp =144/85, ≤ 85 gp=141/83, ≤80 gp=140/81 | **Most benefits** achieved at a BP of **~140/90** mmHg, small additional benefit obtained by further lowering BP. Lowest major CV events at 139/83 mmHg; Lowest CV mortality at 139/87 mmHg. **Patients with diabetes did better with DBP ≤80, supporting aggressive BP lowering in these patients**. {ASA 75mg od: ↓ CV events, but ↑ non fatal major bleeds}. |
| **IDNT** [16] 2.6yr, n=1,715 | Irbesartan AVAPRO 75→**300mg** od, Amlodipine NORVASC 2.5→ **10mg** od, **Placebo** {other agents} | **Type 2 diabetes & Nephropathy**, BP~159/87 | **Irbesartan** is effective in **delaying** the **progression of nephropathy** due to type 2 diabetes (amlodipine no better than placebo despite a BP that was similar to irbesartan group). (Unfortunately, not compared to ACEI). |
| **INSIGHT** [17] ~3.5yr, n=6,321 | Nifedipine ADALAT 30-60mg GITS od, HCT 25mg/amiloride 2.5mg (=½ MODURET) 1-2 tabs od | **↑BP & 1 other risk factor** | Nifedipine & co-amilozide equal in preventing CV death, stroke & all MI. Less fatal MI & heart failure in the diuretic arm. (Nifedipine: ↑peripheral edema stopped early in 8% pts; severe adverse events in mid-high dose co-amilozide 28 vs 25%). |
| **IRMA II** [18] 2yr, n=590 | Irbesartan AVAPRO 150mg od or 300mg od, **Placebo** {CCB 27%, diuretic 25%, β-blocker 19%, other 15%} | **↑BP, Type 2 diabetes, normal GFR & microalbuminuria** | **Irbesartan delays progression to nephropathy** in **Type 2 diabetes patients with microalbuminuria**. The effect was **dose related** with 300mg od having the greatest effect. (Unfortunately, not compared to ACEI). |
| **LIFE** [19, 20, 21] 4.8yr, n=9,193 | Losartan COZAAR 50-100mg od +/-HCT 12.5-25mg od, Atenolol TENORMIN 50-100mg od +/-HCT 12.5-25mg od {HCT used in 44% of losartan & 38% of atenolol pts, but not directly compared to diuretics in the trial} | ↑ BP 174/98 →144/81 losar; 145/81aten. & **left ventricular hypertrophy (LVH);** (diabetes 13%) (black 5.8%) age mean 67; range 55-80 | **Losartan** was more effective than atenolol in preventing **stroke** in hypertensive patients with **LVH** (**no** difference in **CV mortality** or **MI** or **stroke in blacks**). Unfair since Beta blockers known to be less effective in **elderly** (Life mean age 67). In **LVH patients with diabetes,** losartan **decreased CV death & total mortality**, but not MI or stroke (Atenolol group was at higher baseline risk. Fewer than 40% of all patients attained a SBP <140; Mean BP ~147/79). In **ISH** patients, losartan reduced stroke, CV & total mortality but not CV events. |
| **NORDIL** [22] 4.5yr, n=10,881 | Diltiazem CARDIZEM 180-360mg od +/- ACEI, diuretic, α blocker, Diuretic +/- Beta-blocker +/- ACEI, α blocker | **DBP >100** | **Diltiazem** as effective as diuretic & β-blocker in reducing CV events (fatal/non-fatal stroke, MI & CV death). Diltiazem reduced fatal & non-fatal **stroke**. Treated **BP's were high** (diltiazem 155/89; diuretic/β-blocker 152/89). |
| **OPTIMAAL** [23] 2.7yr, n=5,477 | Losartan COZAAR 12.5→50mg od, Captopril CAPOTEN 6.25x1→12.5→50mg tid | **High risk, post MI,** ~BP 123/71 | **Captopril** ≤50mg TID ↓ **CV death** more **than losartan** 50mg od in **post MI patients**. Medication discontinued due to adverse reactions: 7% for losartan vs 14% with captopril. |
| **PROGRESS** [24] 3.9yr, n=6,105 | Perindopril COVERSYL 4mg od +/- indapamide LOZIDE 2.5mg od, **Placebo** | Previous stroke/TIA within 5yr, Normal BP 136/79 or hypertensive 159/94 | **Perindopril + indapamide** ↓BP 12/5 & significantly ↓ **rate of stroke** in normal & hypertensive patients with previous stroke/TIA. Perindopril **alone did not** ↓ stroke (↓BP only 5/3). The **hypertensive group benefited most**. |
| **QUIET** [25] 2.3yr, n=1,750 | Quinapril ACCUPRIL 10→20mg od, {BP 123/74} Placebo | **Post-angioplasty/atherectomy** with **preserved LV fx** EF 59% | **Quinapril** was well tolerated in patients after angioplasty with normal LV function, but **no effect** on the overall frequency of clinical outcomes or the angiographic progression of coronary atherosclerosis. |
| **RENAAL** [26] 3.4yr, n=1,513 | Losartan COZAAR 50-100 71% mg od {+ other agents}, **Placebo** {diuretic 84%, CCB 81%, α-blocker 46%, β-blocker 37%, other 22%} | **Type 2 diabetes with Nephropathy**, BP~153/82 | **Losartan** is more effective than placebo in **protecting** against the **progression of nephropathy** due to type 2 diabetes despite a BP that was similar in both groups. (Unfortunately, not compared to ACEI). |
| **SHEP** [27, 28] 4.5yr, n=4,736 | Chlorthalidone 12.5→25mg od +/-Atenolol 25-50mg od/ Reserpine 0.05-0.1mg/d; Vs **Placebo** | **ISH**,↑BP 170/77; **elderly** Mean 72yr, (diabetes 12%) | **Diuretic chlorthalidone** ↓ **stroke & CV events** in **elderly ISH** patients & had greater absolute **benefit in patients with diabetes**. **DBP<65** mm Hg was associated with an ↑ **risk of stroke & CV disease (CVD)**. [29] |
| **STOP-Hypertension 2** [30] ~5yr, n=6,614 | 1.Conventional Metoprolol/Atenolol/ Pindolol; +/- HCT/amiloride 2.Felodipine/Isradipine 2.5mg od +/- β-blocker 3.Enalapril/Lisinopril 10mg od +/- HCT≤25mg od | **Elderly** Mean 76yr ↑**BP** 194/98(→ ~159/81 in all 3 gps) | **Conventional & newer drugs** were **similar in CV mortality** & overall major events in this open trial of elderly hypertensives. 1/2 of all patients received more than one BP med. **Of the newer antihypertensives: ACE inhibitors had less MI & HF** than the calcium channel blockers. |
| **SYST-EUR** [31,32] 2yr, n=4,695 | Nitrendipine (dihydropyridine) 10-20mg bid +/- enalapril 5-20mg hs & HCT 12.5-25mg od Vs **Placebo** (2/3 rec'd BP meds) | **ISH**, ↑BP 174/86; **elderly** Mean 70yr,(diabetes 10.5%) | In **elderly with ISH**, antihypertensive drug treatment **starting with nitrendipine** ↓ rate of CV complications, stroke & possibly dementia [33]. The **benefit was significantly greater** in the **diabetes** arm. ↓ CV mortality & all CV events |
| **UKPDS-38** [34] **UKPDS-39** [35] 8.4yr, n=1,148 | **-38**: Tight vs Conventional BP control **-39**: Captopril 25-50mg BID vs Atenolol 50-100mg OD {Other: Furosemide, Nifedipine SR, Methyldopa, Prazosin} | **Type 2 diabetes,↑BP** ~160/94, Mean 56yr, **8.4yr study** | **Tight blood pressure** (**~BP 144/82**) control in hypertensive patients with **type 2 diabetes** reduces diabetes related morbidity & mortality. Captopril and atenolol were similarly effective (BP reduction, preserve renal function & proteinuria & CV complications). |
| **Val-HeFT** [36, 37] 1.9yr, n=5,010 | Valsartan DIOVAN 40→160mg bid, **Placebo** | **Heart Failure Class II-IV** EF < 40% (Mean 27%), Mean 63yr | Valsartan appears to benefit **ACE inhibitor-intolerant HF patients** (benefits predominantly seen in the 7% of patients **not** treated with an ACEI). {Concerns: **increased mortality** in subgroup already receiving **both** ACEI & β-blocker}. |

**ACEI**=angiotensin converting enzyme inhibitor **ARB**=angiotensin receptor blocker **BP**=blood pressure **CAD**=coronary artery disease **CV**=cardiovascular **DBP**=diastolic blood pressure **Dx**=disease **EF**=ejection fraction **ESRD**=end stage renal disease **GFR**=glomerular filtration rate **HCT**=hydrochlorothiazide **HF**=heart failure **ISH**=isolated systolic hypertension **LVH**=left ventricular hypertrophy **MI**=myocardial infarction **pts**= patients **PVD**=peripheral vascular disease

**See next page for trials 2007- present.**

## Antihypertensives: Landmark & Recent Trials Since 2007– Summary

| TRIAL | PRIMARY AGENTS | POPULATION STUDIED | CONTRIBUTION TO CURRENT KNOWLEDGE |
|---|---|---|---|
| **Accomplish** [38]<br>39 months, n=11,290 | Benazepril $^{20\to40\text{mg od}}$ + Hydrochlorothiazide $^{12.5\text{-}25\text{mg od}}$<br>**vs Benazepril** $^{20\to40\text{mg od}}$ **+ Amlodipine** $^{5\text{-}10\text{mg od}}$<br>(Both combos given as a single daily pill: Lotensin HCT vs Lotrel) | SBP≥ 160; Age >55yr $^{\text{Mean} \sim 68\text{yr}}$, high risk with CV/renal disease (diabetes ~60%) | **Either combo lowers BP into normal in >70% of pts within 6months. Trial stopped early because benazepril plus amlodipine — was more effective on major CV outcomes** $_{\text{non-fatal MI/stroke, CV death NNT=77 over 3yrs}}$ **than benazepril plus hydrochlorothiazide. Benazepril plus amlodipine was also more effective in diabetics & progression of renal dx. Limitations exist: lower BP in amlodipine arm** $^{0.9/1.1\text{mm Hg}}$**, chlorthalidone not used & heart failure pts excluded. Amlodipine had more edema & hydrochlorothiazide had more dizziness & hypokalemia.** |
| **Accord-BP** [39]<br>4.7 years, n=4733 | **Non-blinded**,<br>intensive therapy {**target SBP<120mmHg**} $^{\text{Actual } 119.3}$<br>**vs**<br>standard therapy {**target SBP<140mmHg**} $^{\text{Actual } 133.5}$ | T2DM, $^{47.7\%}$ ♀, A1c $^{\text{Mean } 8.3\%}$, age $^{\text{mean}\sim 62\text{yr}}$, high risk of CVD (dyslipidemia $^{\text{LDL}=2.85}$, hypertension $^{\text{baseline}139/76}$, smoking $^{13.2\% \text{ current}}$, or obesity $^{\text{BMI}=32.1}$) | **After 4.7 years, there was no significant difference between target SBP < 120mmHg vs target SBP < 140mmHg in the primary outcome of nonfatal MI, nonfatal stroke, or death from CV causes** $^{1.87 \text{ vs } 2.09\% \text{ NS}}$ **with significantly more adverse events** $^{\text{intensive vs. standard } 3.3 \text{ vs } 1.3\%}$ **(hypotension** $^{0.7 \text{ vs } 0.04\%}$**, bradycardia/arrhythmia** $^{0.5 \text{ vs } 0.13\%}$**, hyperkalemia** $^{0.4 \text{ vs } 0.04\%}$**, hypokalemia** $^{2.1 \text{ vs } 1.1\%}$**, ↑Scr** $^{\sim 11 \text{ vs } \sim 8\%}$**) and lower incidence of macroalbuminuria** $^{6.6 \text{ vs } 8.7\%}$**. There was significant difference of any or nonfatal stroke** $^{1.5 \text{ vs } 2.6\%}$ **in favour of the intensive group (NNT=89 in 5 yrs).**<br>**Targeting SBP < 120 mmHg in patients with T2DM may be beneficial in reducing stroke and macroalbuminuria, with potentially more adverse effects, but did not reduce the primary composite of major cardiovascular events.**<br>{**Tight control** of systolic BP among pts with diabetes & CAD was **not** associated with improved CV outcomes compared with usual control. $^{\text{Invest}}$} |
| **Advance** [40]<br>4.3yr, n=11,140 | Perindopril $^{2\to4\text{mg od}}$ + Indapamide $^{0.625\to1.25\text{mg od}}$ **vs placebo** | BP145/81→~135/75 $^{\text{combo}}$ vs ~140/77 $^{\text{placebo}}$<br>Age >55yr $^{\text{Mean} \sim 66\text{yr}}$,<br>Diabetes $^{\sim 8\text{yr}}$ (CV hx or risk factor) | **Routine use of perindopril & indapamide versus placebo to patients with type 2 diabetes reduced combined macro & microvascular** $^{\text{renal}}$ **complications (but macrovascular not individually significant). All cause mortality was reduced to 7.3 vs 8.5% NNT=84 over 4.3yr.**<br>**Treating type 2 diabetics to a lower blood pressure (BP 135/75) is beneficial.** |
| **Hyvet** [41]<br>1.8yr, n=3,845 | **Indapamide** $^{1.5\text{mg od}}$ **+/- Perindopril** $^{2\text{-}4\text{mg od } (75\% \text{ of pts})}$<br>vs Placebo | SBP≥ 160; **BP 173/91**, Scr ~89 (BP ↓ by 15/6mm Hg in tx gp) **Elderly Mean 84yr**, diabetes $^{7\%}$, **12%** hx of heart dx & 60% ♀ | **The results provide evidence that antihypertensive treatment to a target of BP 150/80mm Hg with indapamide (sustained release), with or without perindopril, in persons 80 years of age or older is beneficial to reduce heart failure, death from stroke & death from any cause** $^{\text{NNT}=47/1.8\text{yr}}$**. This benefit begins to be apparent within the first year. Almost 60% of all the strokes were fatal. Caution since risk for drug-induced orthostatic hypotension and its potentially serious consequences (e.g., falls, hip fractures) is likely to be much higher in actual practice.** |
| **Moses** [42]<br>2.5yrs, n=1,405 | **Eprosartan** $^{600\text{mg od}}$ vs Nitrendipine $^{10\text{mg od}}$<br>Plus mainly diuretics & beta-blockers to target BP <140/90.<br>(Patients had therapy with ASA ~80% and statins ~30%) | BP 150.7/87→137.5/80.8 $^{\text{Epro}}$<br>BP 152/87.2→136/80.2 $^{\text{Nitr.}}$<br>**↑BP; previous stroke** $^{\text{within 2yrs}}$<br>BMI ~28, **Age ~ 68yr,** (diabetes $^{\sim 37\%}$) | **MOSES was the first to compare an ARB with a calcium antagonist in secondary stroke prevention. In these high-risk hypertensive stroke patients, an early normotensive and comparable blood pressure was achieved. The combined primary end point (**total mortality and all cardiovascular and cerebrovascular events, including all recurrent events**) was significantly lower in the eprosartan group** $^{30 \text{ vs } 38\%}$**. However a larger trial, telmisartan** $^{80\text{mg od}}$ **initiated soon after an ischemic stroke and continued for 2.5 years did not significantly lower the rate of recurrent stroke, major cardiovascular events, or diabetes. PROFESS** $^{2008 \text{ n}=20,332 \text{ NEJM Aug/08}}$ |
| **Ontarget** [43]<br>56 months, n=25,620 | **Ramipril** $^{5\text{mg od x 2wk} \to 10\text{mg od}}$ vs Telmisartan $^{80\text{mg od}}$<br>vs Combo of each | **↑BP 142/82; high risk** with vascular disease or (diabetes with end organ damage), but **without** heart failure; BMI ~28 **Age ~ 66yr, (diabetes ~38%)** | **Telmisartan was equivalent to ramipril in patients with vascular disease or high-risk diabetes & assoc. with less angioedema** $^{\text{NNT}=500, 0.1 \text{ vs } 0.3\%}$ **& cough** $^{\text{NNT}=33, 1.1 \text{ vs } 4.2\%}$**, but more hypotension** $^{\text{NNH}=112, 2.6 \text{ vs } 1.7\%}$ **symptoms. The combination of the two drugs was assoc, with more adverse events leading to discontinuation** $^{\text{NNH}=24}$ **vs ramipril (hypotension** $^{\text{NNH}=33}$**, diarrhea, syncope, renal dysfunction** $^{\text{NNH}=31, 13.5 \text{ vs } 10.2\%. \text{ Renal study: } \uparrow \text{ doubling of creatinine \& need for dialysis}}$**, & ↑ potassium** $^{\text{NNH}=45}$**) without an ↑ in benefit. Ramipril lowered BP less than comparators, but had equal clinical benefit.** A substudy suggests ↑ CV death in diabetics with SBP<130. (However, telmisartan fared no better than placebo on the primary outcome, in **TRANSCEND** $^{\text{trial n}=5926 \text{ 56months}}$ patients at high risk of CV disease unable to tolerate ACEIs) |

Treating healthy persons (60 years or older) with moderate to severe systolic and/or diastolic hypertension **reduces all cause mortality and cardiovascular morbidity and mortality**. The decrease in all cause mortality was limited to persons **60 to 80 years of age**. (Musini VM, Tejani AM, Bassett K, Wright JM. Pharmacotherapy for hypertension in the **elderly**. Cochrane Database Syst Rev. 2009 Oct 7;(4):CD000028)

### Hypertension Guidelines:

American JNC VII 2003 http://www.nhlbi.nih.gov/guidelines/hypertension/index.htm

British Hypertension Society http://www.bhsoc.org/default.stm

Canadian Hypertension Society (**Canadian** recommendations **2010 & slides**) http://www.hypertension.ca

New Zealand http://www.nzgg.org.nz/index.cfm?screensize=800&ScreenResSet=yes

NICE: National Institute for Health and Clinical Excellence 2006 http://www.nice.org.uk/CG034

### Books:

Hypertension Guidelines for Family Practice 2008 MUMS Guideline Clearinghouse, Suite 901-790 Bay Street, Toronto. ON M5G 1N8, Ph: 416-597-6867. www.mumshealth.com

### Other associations/agencies:

American Heart Association http://www.americanheart.org/presenter.jhtml?identifier=1200000

American Society of Hypertension (ASH) http://www.ash-us.org/

Bandolier Preventing Hypertension http://www.jr2.ox.ac.uk/bandolier/band107/b107-6.html

Best Practice of Medicine -Hypertension (Merck Medicus) http://www.merckmedicus.com/pp/us/hcp/hcp_home.jsp

Canadian Cardiovascular Society http://www.ccs.ca/

Canadian Heart & Stroke Foundation http://ww2.heartandstroke.ca/Page.asp?PageID=24

Dash Diet http://www.nhlbi.nih.gov/health/public/heart/hbp/dash/

Hypertension Online http://www.hypertensiononline.org/

National Institutes of Health: Cardiovascular Information: http://www.nhlbi.nih.gov/health/public/heart/

National Institutes of Health: Cholesterol (ATP III) Guidelines http://www.nhlbi.nih.gov/guidelines/cholesterol/index.htm

Palm: Stat Cholesterol Cardiac Risk Calculator (Free) http://www.statcoder.com/

| Generic/ TRADE (Strength & forms) g=generic avail. | INDICATIONS | | ADVERSE EFFECTS | COMMENTS/ CONTRAINDICATIONS (CI) / MONITOR (M) | DOSE $ /30 Day |
|---|---|---|---|---|---|
| **Acetylsalicylic acid (ASA) –irreversibly inhibit COX-1 to ↓thromboxane** inhibit platelet for 5-7day; **antiplatelet resistance occurs in 5-10% of pts with stable heart dx** NEJM May 02; **administer @hs to↓BP** | | | | | |
| **Aspirin/ASA**[101] **C/D** OTC<br>**ENTROPHEN**/Generics<br>150ˣ▼ & 650ˣ▼mg supp OTC;<br>80ˣ▼,325ˣ▼mg regular tab OTC;<br>80ˣ▼mg chew tab OTC;<br>81ˣ▼,162ˣ▼,325▼,500ˣ⊗,650▼, 975ˣ⊗mg EC tab OTC.<br>(Note: only **325 & 650mg EC** tabs **covered** on Sask. formulary)<br>325ˣ⊗,650ˣ⊗mg EC caplet OTC<br>**ASA Preop** continue if ↓ bleeding risk dental, cataract or if ↑ thrombosis risk recent stent or CV history. If ↑bleed or ↓CV risk, hold ASA for 7-10days prior. | **Primary MI Prevention**[7,331] **only if:**<br>(**consider** ASA if 10yr CAD risk ≥10% AHA 2010[19])<br>-USPSTF[09]: ♂↓MI 45-79yr, ♀↓stroke 55-79yr if low GI risk<br>◆**diabetes** if high risk ♂≥45yr, ♀≥50 CDA08;405 ADA'10: consider if high risk, ♂≥50yr or ♀≥60yr; & 1 additional risk<br>◆**>50 yrs AND…≥ 1 risk factor**: smoking, ↑BP, ↑lipids, hx of young parental MI, albuminuria<br>◆**no ASA contraindication** & not ↑BP<br>(**NNT=175** 3.8yr to prevent 1 major CV event in treated hypertensive pts HOT)<br>{In ♀≥45: ↓ stroke NNT=500/10yr but for ♀≥65: ↓CV event NNT=50/10yr, Maj. Bleed NNH=125} WHS | **Secondary Prevention**<br>to ↓ MI, stroke or death in:<br>**ACS** Acute Coronary Syndrome, **CAD**, **CVD**, Angioplasty & Coronary Artery Bypass Surgery<br>(**NNT=22** 2.6yr to prevent 1 stroke or death in post TIA/stroke pts SALT; Meta-analysis[2]: 16%→12.9% NNT=33)<br>ASA not help Alzheimer's pts.[298]<br>If ASA GI bleed & ↑CVD risk pt, may restart ASA in ≥7day.[414, 422] | **GI upset ~ 5%**<br>Fatigue, rash 4.6% CAPRIE<br>Muscle weakness<br>{ **Any GI bleed 2.7%** CAPRIE<br>{ **Severe GI bleed 0.7%** RR↑1.4<br>Leuko/thrombocytopenia rarely <1%<br>Renal: can ↓ renal fx esp. if CrCl < 30ml/min<br>Gout at low ASA doses rare | ◆**Drug of choice in many pts** (~25% ↓ in relative risk)<br>◆80/81mg tabs ↑ expense; can use ¼ x 325mg<br>◆>81mg not more efficacious but ↑ SE bleeding<br>◆**chew** EC tab: ↑onset of action eg. ≥ 160mg x1 acute stroke/MI<br>◆**Options to ASA in STROKE prevention**<br>**(no options clearly offer more benefit vs risk):**<br>•do nothing if options are CI (but stop smoking)<br>•AGGRENOX (Chest'08→ maybe drug of choice)<br>•PLAVIX or (TICLID not recommended)<br>•ASA + PLAVIX but ↑bleeding MATCH NNH=77 1.5yr; ? use 1-3 months<br>•↑dose of ASA (?≤325mg/d if on ~80mg/d)<br>◆in select pts mortality benefit seen with other therapies (eg. thiazides, ACEIs & statins). Warfarin: ↑↑SE & not more effective vs ASA 650mg bid for intracranial arterial stenosis WASID<br>**CI**: Bleeding disorders, allergy, bleed/ulcer active & ? asthma<br>**M**: CBC if indicated [**Not** useful for DVT prophylaxis] | **80mg od $5**<br>**81mg EC od $5**<br>-option in high risk preeclampsia<br>(75mg od) HOT, SALT<br>**325mg od** CAPRIE, SPAF I **$2**<br>**325mg every other day** PHS **$1**<br>**100mg every other day** WHS ♀<br>**325mg EC $8**<br>≤100mg od Popadad/JPAD NS; AAA NS<br>(Primary prevention: Diabetes/PAD) |
| | **✱ ASA Combination Treatment Options:** but combo ASA&clopidogrel ↑bleeding MATCH DAC (5.8 months v 4.3 months) 376.<br>1) **ASA + Dipyridamole** for recurrent stroke, ? hemodialysis graft patency<br>2) **ASA + Clopidogrel** x ≥52 wks post coronary stent if DES; CABG ASA 75-100mg for NSTE ACS indefinitely<br>3) **ASA ~81mg + Warfarin** INR 2-3 for recurrent systemic embolism in mitral valve stenosis/regurgitation; mitral mechanical valve; aortic mechanical valve & atrial fibrillation; (not for peripheral arterial dx Wave)<br>4) **ASA ~81mg + Warfarin** INR 2-3 post MI x 3months in high risk pts[45] (if on ASA 81mg + Clopidogrel + Warf ⇒ INR 2-2.5)<br>5) **ASA ~81mg + Warfarin** INR 2.5-3.5 mechanical valve + (recurrent systemic embolism or other cardiac risks) | | | **ASA 75-162mg od** AHA Secondary Prevention 2006, CABG/PCI+stent ASA≤325mg, ASA 50-325mg od Chest 08 & Primary Prevention 75-100mg od; ASA 75-150mg od Antithrombotic Trialists' BMJ'02 & '09; ♀ stroke ♂↓MI | |
| **Dipyridamole (with ASA) – antiplatelet and vasodilatory effects via inhibition of cAMP and blockade of adenosine uptake** | | | | | |
| **Dipyridamole + ASA**<br>**AGGRENOX**<br>200mg extended release + ASA 25mg capsule **C/D** | **Secondary Prevention:** ◆dipyridamole + ASA **NNT=37** over 2yr to prevent 1 stroke/death in pts with hx of stroke/TIA **vs** ASA 25mg bid ESPS2 n=6602 2yr<br>◆dipyridamole + ASA **NNT=34** over 3.5yr to prevent 1 stroke/MI, ↑bleed or death 13 vs 16% in pts with hx ischaemic stroke/TIA **vs** ASA 30-325mg od, ~75mg ESPRIT n=2739 3.5yr<br>◆dipyridamole+ASA **vs** clopidogrel PRoFESS Stroke 9vs8.8%, Death 7.3vs7.4%; n=20332; 2.5yr<br>**EDS criteria**: pts with recurrent stroke or TIA while on ASA | | **More SE vs ASA alone:**<br>**Headache ~ 30%**, diarrhea<br>GI upset ~15%, Dizziness ~10%<br>Any GI bleed 1.2% ESPS2<br>-Discontinued tx: 34 vs 13% ESPRIT<br>-Vs Plavix: ↑ intracranial bleed PRoFESS | **Good choice** CHEST'08 maybe drug of choice for embolic stroke or TIA (but **poor tolerability**) ESPS2<br>**More effective**: than aspirin 25mg bid alone & than aspirin 30-325mg od (~75mg) alone ESPRIT 160<br>**CI**: Bleeding disorders, allergy, bleed/ulcer active & ? asthma<br>**M**: CBC if indicated | **200/25mg bid** ESPS2, ESPRIT<br>**$66**<br>May be cost effective for ≥70yr 416 |
| **Thienopyridine– irreversibly via P2Y12** (major ADP platelet receptor) **prevents platelet aggregation. Both are prodrugs with delayed onset, metabolism** via Cyp 2C19/3A4 ? **before being active.** 2-14% pts ↓↓ 2C19 | | | | | |
| **Clopidogrel**<br>**PLAVIX**<br>75mg tablet (300mg tabˣ⊗)<br>(1st approved 1998) **B**<br>**Prasugrel Effient** FDA'09, CDN'10 ˣ⊗ Load 60mg po x1then 5-10mg po daily<br>↓MI risk during & after angio PCI. Caution: ↑bleed (esp. if ↓wt, old, CABG, or prev stroke/TIA), ??cancer<br>**Ticagrelor**: not in CDN/USA; Plato ACS trial 180mg po x1, 90mg bid reversible ADP θ; SE: dyspnea, ↓HR, ↑uric acid & Scr | **Secondary Prevention:**<br>**CAPRIE**: PLAVIX (**NNT= 200** / yr to prevent 1 vascular death, MI, or stroke **vs** ASA 325mg/d; although **most benefit** in pts with **peripheral arterial disease** (& more benefit in diabetics): **1⁰ : no better than ASA in pts groups with recent MI or recent stroke)**<br>(**Substudy**: For pts with Prior Stroke or MI History the NNT was **71**/yr)[40,51]<br>**CURE**: PLAVIX {**NNT= 48** for 9months to prevent 1 CV death, MI, or stroke when combined **with ASA vs** ASA 75-325mg/d alone in pts with **ACS** (but ↑major **bleeding** 3.7 vs 2.7%, **NNH=99; ↓bleeding with ≤100mg ASA** without loss of efficacy[25]; most benefit in first 3 months Dalhousie'06)}<br>**CLASSICS**: no difference between PLAVIX or TICLID in 1st 28days **post-stenting**<br>**MATCH**:[48] with TIA hx 21% or ischemic stroke 79% →PLAVIX +/-ASA 75mg od {ischemic events 15.7 combo vs 16.7% NS; major **bleeding** 2.6 combo vs 1.3%; n=7599 ~18mon}<br>**CHARISMA**:[131] PLAVIX + ASA **no** better than ASA 75-162mg/d CV death, MI, or stroke 6.8 vs 7.3% in atherosclerosis/high CV risk pts (but ↑bleeding Moderate 2.1 vs 1.3% NNH=125; Severe 1.7 vs 1.3%) n=15,603 ~28mon **Subgroups**: Asymptomatic pts: ↑ harm (bleed, ↑CV events, ↑CV death); Documented atherosclerosis pts: some benefit NNT=100 but ↑bleed.<br>Reductions in stroke incidence for PLAVIX (CAPRIE 5.7→5.3% & CURE 1.4→1.2%) were NOT statistically significant {Expert Reviewer comment} | | GI upset ~10% (⇨**diarrhea**)<br>Headache, dizziness >5%<br>**Rash** 6%→severe 0.26% Caprie<br>**Any GI bleed** 2.0% Caprie<br>**Severe GI bleed** 0.5% Caprie<br>Blood dyscrasias rarely <1%<br>-aplastic anemia, neutropenia 0.1%, **thrombotic thrombocytopenic purpura (TTP) 20 cases** -often in 1st 2 weeks of starting & can relapse; (? occurs in >20 per 3 million pts NEJM Bennett '00) | **PLAVIX**: Good choice CHEST'08 for embolic stroke/TIA<br>Stop 5-10day prior to scheduled **CABG** & ?transbronchial biopsy.<br>**Acute MI**: COMMIT/CCS-2 56 (N=45,852) Plavix 75mg + ASA 162mg vs ASA 162mg od x~15day; Death/MI/stroke 9.2 vs 10.1%; Major Bleed both equal ~0.6%). Tx ≥ 2-4 weeks<br>**Post-stent**: 300-600mg x1[94] →75mg od x 4-52 if DES wks ACC'09: if BMS or DES stent use clopidogel for ≥ 12 months.<br>(Stenting→If on ASA+warfarin INR 2-3 for anticoagulation then D/C Plavix after: ≥1month-bare metal; ≥12month drug eluting stents; If only on ASA+Plavix→D/C after ~1yr)[45]<br>Initially ↑ASA 162-325mg if PCI+stent: minimum 1month→bare metal, 3month→sirolimus & 6month→paclitaxel AHA 06 (only in special circumstatnaces consider just 2 weeks tx for BMS)<br>Initially if PCI+DES stent ↑ASA 325mg x 3month then ≤100mg; + Plavix 75mg ≥12month Chest 08<br>↑stent thrombosis risk: diabetes, ACS/MI, ↓EF, ↓renal fx; lesion: bifurcation, longer stent, residual dissection, small stent diameter. DES=Drug eluting stent<br>**Acute Coronary Syndrome** (ACS): 75mg od x3-12mo<br>**Previous ulcer pts**[52]: ASA 80mg od + Esomeprazole 20mg bid ↓ recurrent bleed more than clopidogrel 75mg od 0.7 vs 8.6%; n=320 ~1yr<br>**CI**: Bleeding disorders & allergy<br>**M**: CBC q-week x 4 weeks **if** indicated → catch TTP | **75mg od** CAPRIE, CLASSICS, CURE, CHARISMA, MATCH CLARITY 55, COMMIT/CCS-2 56<br>▼ **$99**<br>No loading dose for 2° prevention. Load for ACS & stenting STEMI 75mg if >75yr.<br>If using ASA ↑RR 3.9+ **Plavix, ASA dose ≤100mg helps to** minimize risk of bleeding[25,289] & limit NSAID use ↑RR 2.9<br>Perioperative issues[291]<br>Consider PPI if on dual antiplatelet tx; but pantoprazole may avoid 2C19 DI. Less 2C19: Caucasian 30%, Asian 50% |
| **Ticlopidine** ▼<br>**TICLID/Generics**<br>250mg tablet **B** | **AAASPS**: **black pts** n=1809; ≤2yr; recurrent MI, stroke or vascular death 14.7% (Ticlid 250mg bid) vs 12.3% (**ASA** 325mg po bid). P=0.12<br>**EDS**: Plavix & Ticlid: Pts with **recurrent** vascular episodes TIA/stroke or MI<br>◆ while on ASA or intolerant ie GI bleed or allergic ie nasal polyps, asthma<br>Plavix: Acute coronary syndrome & post stenting for ≤1yr; or in PAD pts intolerant/allergic to ASA | | GI upset ~10%, ↑ LFT ~1%<br>**Diarrhea** 20%→severe 6% TASS<br>**Rash** 12%→severe 3% TASS<br>**Neutropenia 2.4%** WBC< 1.2<br>Blood dyscrasias <1%<br>-aplastic anemia, **TTP** (>**1/ 5000** -peak incidence at **3-4weeks, seldom relapses**) | **Clopidogrel PLAVIX preferred vs TICLID:**<br>◆similar efficacy but ↓ **toxicity** (less rash, GI upset, blood dyscrasias)<br>◆no comparative trial of clopidogrel vs ticlopidine in 2° prevention<br>**TICLID** not recommended CHEST'08 esp. because of side effects<br>**M**: CBC q2wk x 3months→catch neutropenia/TTP;LFT | **250mg bid** CATS, TASS, AAASPS<br>▼<br>**$47**<br>No loading dose for 2° prevention |

✱ Most likely scenarios where combo therapy indicated; other situations possible. References at www.RxFiles.ca

Evidence Interstroke 465: **Lifestyle changes for DIET (↑ fruits & vegetables, ↓ fat), EXERCISE (30-60mins 4-7x/week), moderate alcohol use & stop SMOKING!** Consider **Thiazides** (HCT 12.5-25mg od $4) Multiple Trials, **ACEIs: (ramipril** 10mg od $29) HOPE; **(perindopril** 4mg od $35 + **indapamide** 2.5mg od $12) PROGRESS-perindopril alone did NOT ↓ stroke<br>**Statins: Atorvastatin** 80mg od $87 Sparcl; **Pravastatin** 40mg od $42; **Simvastatin** 20-40mg od $41. **Vitamins** NO benefit→Norvit 132, Hope2 133; await Vitatops 42; WAFACS 191; ($B_{12}$ 400ug, $B_6$ 25mg, **Folate** 2.5mg: **no benefit** VISP 41)

| Name/ TRADE (strength & forms) | INDICATIONS { Oral Antiplatelet & Antithrombotic Agents, Pg 10 - © www.RxFiles.ca} | ADVERSE EFFECTS | COMMENTS / CONTRAINDICATIONS (CI) / MONITOR (M) | $/30 Days |
|---|---|---|---|---|
| **Warfarin**<br>(**S** & R enantiomer)<br>-for VTE & prevent cardioembolic events in atrial fibrillation pts.<br>Consider LMWH or heparin if pregnant:<br>**D or X**<br>-Malformation ~ 10%: CNS,bone,nose,eye esp. 1st trimester<br>-breastfeeding compatible<br>**WARFARIN/ COUMADIN/ g**<br>1mg ς *pink*<br>2mg ς *lavender*<br>2.5mg ς *green*<br>3mg ς *tan*<br>4mg ς *blue*<br>5mg ς *peach*<br>6mg ς ✗ ▼ *teal*<br>7.5mg ς ✗ ▼ *yellow*<br>10mg ς *white*<br>ς=scored tab<br>**Generics in SK** are **interchangeable**<br>**New in Canada:**<br>**Dabigatran** ✗ ⊗<br>**Pradax** 75&110mg cap<br>-a direct thrombin inhibitor -a prodrug<br>-prevent VTE post hip & knee surgery;<br>(A. fib 110-**150**mg bid RE-LY vs warf 1o NNT=173,NNH MI=477/yr)<br>(VTE 150mg bid Re-Cover vs warf 1o 2.4 vs 2.1% NS, Bleed 1.6 vs 1.9%; Dab:↑ dyspepsia & D/C due to SE)<br>DI: amiodarone, rifampin, quinidine, verapamil<br>≤ 220mg po od $260<br>**Rivaroxaban Xarelto**<br>-factor Xa inhibitor<br>**10mg po od** $320 ☎▼<br>**6-10**hr after **surgery** x2-5wk<br>DI: azoles,CBZ,phenytoin | **– inhibit vitamin K dependent clotting factors (II, VII, IX, X)** t ½ 6-72hrs<br>**Primary and Secondary Prevention of thrombus:**<br>**Indication** — **Duration** — longer if higher-risk<br>**Venous**<br>◆post-op prophylaxis total hip or total knee replacement (up to **35days** for total hip/knee or hip fracture surgery)[411] — ≥10d<br>◆treat VTE [264] or PE [307] (Dx: eg. Wells rule, D-dimer, ultrasound, imaging) (Start Heparin/LMWH with warfarin & continue ≥**5day** until INR≥2 x2d)<br>calf vein thrombosis (symptomatic, isolated)……….. — ≥3mon<br>proximal thrombosis (known, reversible risk factor)… — ≥3mon<br>1st episode idiopathic VTE ♀ ≤ 6months if 0-1 risk factors; ♂ may need continued tx — ≥6-12mon<br>recurrent idiopathic VTE or continued risk factor (ie **cancer** consider LMWH first 3-6 months, clotting factor problems). — indefinite<br>[2.0 to 3.0]<br>◆1st DVT/PE + antiphospholipid antibody[130] or ≥2thrombophilic conditions — 12 mon ? indefinite<br>◆1st episode DVT/PE + thrombophilic condition (testing considerations see 412) — 6-12 mon ? indefinite<br>{After ≥3mon, warfarin (INR **1.5-2** vs placebo) is effective to prevent recurrent VTE [17], but warfarin (**INR 2-3** vs 1.5-1.9;NNT=100) was more effective without increased bleeding. [21])<br>**Arterial {atrial flutter** same as **AF}**[93; **Warf** better than ASA+Plavix Active W; then **ASA** 75-100mg **+ Plavix** better than **ASA** NNT=125 **Active A** 373, but ↑major bleed NNH=143, intracranial NNH=500/yr] — indefinite<br>◆atrial fibrillation † [169, BAFTA 285] (persistent or paroxysmal AF, & any HIGH risk or more than 1 MODERATE risk factors)<br>◆atrial fibrillation ≥48hr or for unknown duration (elective pharmacological or electrical cardioversion) — 3 week before & ≥4week after successful cardioversion (continue longer if >1 episode of AF or if risk factors warrant)<br>◆atrial fibrillation ≥48hr , post cardiac surgery — for 4 weeks following reversion to NSR<br>[2.0 to 3.0]<br>**Intracardiac**<br>◆native valve dx with embolism history or atrial fib... — indefinite<br>◆mitral valve strands or prolapse + Hx TIA/stroke — not warfarin<br>◆rheumatic mitral valve dx + AF or Hx systemic embolism — longterm+?+ASA<br>◆rheumatic mitral valve dx + NSR + left atrial diameter >5.5cm — long term<br>◆MVP + systemic embolism or recurrent TIA despite ASA — long term<br>◆bioprosthetic/tissue valve♥…………………………… — varies<br>Mitral 3 mon; Aortic 3mon (or ASA 81mg/d); Hx of systemic embolism 3-12mon; AF long term<br>◆mechanical valve♥ (St. Jude bileaflet aortic; Carbomedics bileaflet or Medtronic-Hall tilting disk + aortic + normal left atrial size + NSR) — indefinite<br>◆mechanical valves♥ in aortic position + atrial fibrillation — indefinite<br>◆mechanical valves♥ in mitral position (tilting disk & bileaflet) — indefinite<br>◆mechanical valves♥ + risk factors (AF, MI, left atrial enlargement, endocardial damage or low EF) or caged ball/disk valves or prosthetic valve + systemic embolism despite therapeutic INR — indefinite +ASA 81mg<br>[2.5-3.5]<br>◆**post-MI esp. if high risk** pts (eg. ↑anterior MI, sig. heart failure, A. fib, intracardiac thrombus on echo, Hx VTE/PE) (WARIS-II n=3,630 over 4yr) [20] warfarin INR 2.8-4.2 or warfarin INR 2-2.5 + ASA 75mg od or ASA 160mg od<br>Warfarin +/- ASA most effective but ↑non-fatal major bleed NNH= 250/yr — 3mon-indefinite- (ACC/AHA 2007) — 2-3[45] with ASA ~81mg/d | **Common**: nausea, diarrhea, abdominal cramping, fever<br>**Rare**: alopecia, urticaria, hematoma, skin necrosis ~1/10,000 in 1st 10 days, purple toe syndrome in 1st few weeks, dermatitis, renal tubular necrosis ≤ 1%, hepatitis & vasculitis<br>**Bleeding** ≤10%; major bleed 1.3% RR ↑ 1.9 if INR 2-3 but ↑ to 7% in **high risk** pts Chest 01. {**13.7%** in **1st yr** if **age ≥80** AF}[275]<br>Intracranial bleed <0.5%/yr.<br>(May need fresh frozen plasma ~3units or Vitamin K)<br>**Vit K** 1-10mg **PO**/IV [27-33] Not IM.<br>↑Vit K dose⇒**warfarin resistance** ~1 week<br>If HIT: Vit K 10mg po or 5-10mg IV<br>↓'s INR if required.<br>Not all ↑INR's need Vit K.<br>(Avail. as tab or an ampule, but given PO if only mild/moderate ↑INR without major bleeding)<br>**INR <5 & no significant bleeding**: Lower 10-20% or omit warfarin dose; monitor<br>**INR ≥5 but <9 & no sig. bleeding**: Omit 1-2 warfarin doses or omit 1 warfarin dose & give Vit K **1 - 2.5mg** po. INR may be lowered in 24hrs.<br>**INR≥9 & no significant bleeding**: Hold warfarin & give Vit K **2.5 - 5mg** po. INR will reduce substantially in 24-48hrs.<br>**Serious bleeding** at any elevated INR: Hold warfarin & give Vit K **10mg** IV & fresh plasma or prothrombin complex concentrate; recombinant factor VIIa an option; may need to **repeat** Vit K q12h<br>**Life threatening bleeding**: Hold warfarin & give Vit K **10mg** IV, & prothrombin complex concentrate eg. Octaplex or recombinant factor VIIa an option; may need to **repeat** based on INR<br>**INR 3-4.5** had ↑↑ **major bleeding** in pts with TIA/minor stroke SPIRIT. | ◆Dosing per therapeutic INR Range (INR =2.5 usually 2-3)<br>◆Hold ~5days before surgery (heparin/LMWH maybe needed)<br>◆Bridge with LMWH/heparin esp if $CHADS_2$ is ≥5 consider if 2-4; or any mechanical mitral valve, older aortic valve or a recent (< 3-6 month) stroke/TIA/VTE hx.<br>◆Holding generally not needed for tooth extractions [343], skin biopsies, cataract or injections or aspirations of soft tissues/joints.<br>◆Overlap heparin/LMWH x **5-7days** until INR≥2 for ≥2 day<br>◆Loading dose often not good: ↓ risk of high INR & hypercoaguable state via ↓protein C&S<br>◆**Initially** give ≤5mg OD x2 (10mg x1 an option for low risk outpts [16]), [**↓dose** if: ↑bleed risk, DI's, elderly >70yr [59], nutrition poor, liver dx or HF], Start same day as heparin/LMWH. Small dose changes 15% of a weekly regimen. Consider pharmacy coagulation clinic or self-management. [71,92]<br>◆After proximal DVT, using compression stockings within 1month & continuing for ≥2yr will ↓ post thrombotic syndrome.<br>**Monitior M: CBC & INR as indicated** Initial: platelet, LFT, albumin & Scr.<br>Initial tx: INR in **3 & 5** days, then 2 INR's in 1st wk; then INR weekly until stable x 2wks. Then INR q2 wks untl stable x 1 month, then consider INR ≤q monthly. Check INR in days 4-6d of new meds. After a change in dose, check INR at least weekly until stable. Coagulation factors half-life vary from 6-72h & the half-life of warfarin is 2.5 days-thus **changes** made in the warfarin dose are **not completely reflected** in the INR **until day 3 or 4.**<br>**Algorithm** Target INR 2-3: **INR<1.5** ↑dose 10-20%; **INR 1.5-1.9** ↑dose 5-10%; **INR 2-3** No change; **INR 3.1-3.9** ↓weekly dose 5-10%, **INR 4-4.9** Hold 0-2 doses, ↓dose 10-20%<br>If **INR variable** consider Vit K 100-200ug po daily to stabilize INR GNC Vit K 100ug tab, Vita-Vim 50+ & ♀)<br>**Drug Interactions** (if new med added, generally recheck INR within 4-6days)<br>**↑ Warfarin Response/↑Bleed**: Also by diarrhea, fever, ↑thyroid, liver dx, ↓Vit K intake<br>**Major** Significance: acetaminophen, **alcohol**, **Allopurinol**, Amiodarone, Anabolic steroids, Azole antifungals (eg. fluconazole), Bactrim, **Cimetidine**, Ciprofloxacin, Clopidogrel, Erythromycin, **Fibrates**, fluoxetine, fluvoxamine, Metronidazole, **NSAIDs** & Salicylates (warfarin & **ASA** may be combined with close supervision), Omeprazole, Paroxetine, Phenylbutazone, Quinidine, Quinine, Sitaxsentan, Sorafenib, Statins some, Steroids, Sulfinpyrazone, Sulfonamide, Sunitinib, Thyroid hormone, Ticlopidine, & Vit E > 800iu.<br>◆**herbal preps** can ↑warfarin response / bleeding (e.g. chamomile, Dong quai, fenugreek, ginkgo, garlic, ginseng…; see Herbal RxFiles Chart)<br>**↓ Warfarin Response**: Also by edema, ↑ Vit K intake, ↓thyroid, nephrotic Sx, cancer.<br>**Major** Significance: Antithyroid drugs (e.g.PTU), **barbiturates** (e.g. phenobarbital) , carbamazepine, griseofulvin, Kaletra, nevirapine, phenytoin, rifampin, St .John's wort. Vit. K rich supps/**foods** eg. avocados, broccoli, brussel sprouts, cabbage, canola oil, green tea, mayonnaise, parsley, soybean oil, spinach & swiss chard<br>**SE**: bleeding, skin necrosis ~1/10,000 in 1st 10 days, purple toe syndrome, N/V/D, flatulence<br>**CI**: Pregnancy, Active bleed, Hemorrhagic disorder/tendencies, Previous warfarin-induced skin necrosis, Recent/contemplated surgery of: CNS, eye, or surgery resulting in large open spaces.<br>**Caution**: Noncompliant or unreliable patients & Fall history.<br>**Hemorrhagic Risks** **Pt factors**: Age >80, Hx of GI bleeding, Hx of cerebral vascular dx, Serious co-morbid condition (e.g. kidney/liver dx), **Interacting** meds, **INR above** therapeutic range & **length** of therapy. **More bleeding** when warfarin combined with **ASA** RR ↑6.5, **NSAIDs** RR ↑4.6 or **clopidogrel**. [289,418] | 13-18 for ≤5mg od<br>Dosing calculator: (Clinical & Geneetic variables VKORC1, CYP2C9*1 *2 or *3) www.warfarindosing.org |

**Cost**: drug & markup. **ACE**=angiotensin converting enzyme **AF**=atrial fibrillation **BP**=blood pressure **Dx**=disease **EC**=enteric coated **EF**=ejection fraction **Fx**=function **GI**=stomach **Hx**=history **LFT**=liver function test **MI**=myocardial infarction **MVP**=mitral valve prolapse **NNH(T)** number needed to harm (treat) **NSR**=normal sinus rhythm **OTC**=over the counter **PE**=pulmonary embolism **Pts**=patients **SE**=side effects **TIA**=transient ischaemic attack **VTE**=venous thromboembolism **WBC**=white blood cell ☎EDS in Sask. ✗ Non formulary in Sk. prior approval for NIHB ⊗ not covered by NIHB ▼ covered by NIHB

**† Atrial Fibrillation Risk** 54,169 ACC'06 (SPAF & CHADS2 rule,CHEST'08)→ **High** 8-12%/yr, CHADS2=≥3 **prior stroke/TIA, embolus** systemic, **stenosis** mitral, **prosthetic** valve. Tx:**warfarin** ↓RR 60% **Moderate** ~4%/yr,CHADS2=1-2 hypertension, HF, ↓EF≤35%, >75yr, diabetes. If only 1 risk factor Tx:**warfarin** ?ASA+clopidogrel **or ASA 81-325mg/d** **Low** <2%/yr, CHADS2=0-1 60-74yr & no other risk factor, Tx:**ASA 81-325mg/d.** ↓RR 25%, <60yr ?no Tx. Overall AF stroke risk **~4.5%/yr**. {Warf **vs** ASA: Primary 2x more effective; 3x in Secondary [37]}

♥ Onset of anticoagulant effect ranges from 2-7days; if rapid anticoagulation required (eg VTE, post valve insertion) then heparin or LMWH and warfarin should be initiated the same time with overlap of at least 4 days. Heparin or LMWH is continued for ≥5days and then stopped when INR therapeutic for 2 consecutive days. Certain situations (eg chronic stable atrial fib) are not urgent & warfarin can be initiated without heparin or LMWH.

**VTE Risk Factors**: Surgery, Trauma major or lower extremity, **Immobility** paresis, **Malignancy**/Cancer tx (hormonal, chemo or radiation), **Previous VTE**, Older **age** >60yr, Pregnancy & postpartum, Birth control pills? hold 4week before elective surgery, erythropoiesis-stimulating meds, Hormone replacement tx, Raloxifene, thalidomide, **acute medical illness/infection**, **heart** or **respiratory failure**, Inflammatory bowel dx, Nephrotic sx, Myeloproliferative dx, Paroxysmal nocturnal hemoglobinuria, Obesity BMI≥30, Smoking, Varicose veins, Central venous catheterization, Inherited/ acquired thrombophilia. & ↑ D-dimer.

**Stroke Risk Factors** Modifiable: atrial fibrillation, **hypertension**, diabetes, high cholesterol, left ventricular hypertrophy, high fat & salt diet, obesity, **smoking** & high alcohol intake. Non modifiable: older age, hx of TIA & family hx, race & ♂'s.

Early TIA/stroke risk scores (ABCD) may be useful (Score of 6→30% risk of stroke in next 7 days Rothwell 80) 81,82. CT imaging also useful. The $ABCD^2$ →stroke risk within 7 & 90day of TIA. High stroke risk if score ≥4. (**RRE-90** score) 415 Consider rehabilitation after stroke 58,74,194

**Bleeding Risk**: GI ulcer previous, on NSAIDs, antiplatelets, anticoagulants, female, elderly >75yr, ↑Scr, ↓weight, ↑heart rate, ↑↓systolic BP, ↓hematocrit, heart failure/MI, liver dx, diabetes, previous stroke noncardioembolic www.crusadebleedingscore.org

## What are the clinical presentations of HF?

⇨**Cardinal triad=FED: Fatigue, Edema, Dyspnea**

⇨**Common:** dyspnea, orthopnea, paroxysmal nocturnal dyspnea, fatigue, weakness, exercise intolerance, wt gain, dependent edema, cough, abdominal distension, nocturia, cool extremities

## What is the NYHA functional classification?

{NYHA =New York Heart Association; common HF classification}

**Class I** –No symptoms (Sx); **Class II** –Sx with ordinary activity

**Class III** – Sx with less than ordinary activity

**Class IV** – Sx at rest or minimal activity

{AHA Stages of HF: A:at risk, B:structural but non-symptomatic, C:structural & symptomatic HF, D:refractory HF}

## Trivia: *Take it with a grain of salt* (NaCl) [4,5,6,7]

- **1 teaspoonful = ~ 6g of NaCl; ~ 2.4g Na**
- Normal diet: 2-3g Na (e.g. >5g salt) per day {↑ Na: effervescent antacids etc.}
- Normal Saline (NS) **IV solution** = 9g NaCl or 3.6g Na in 1L {e.g. NS 0.9% @125ml/hr ⇨10.8g Na (or 27g salt) /3L in 24hr}
- **Food/Drink**: {Often very high Na+: bacon, canned soups, condiments, cheese, frozen dinners, lunch meats, pickles, sauces, salted nuts, snacks}
  - 12 oz 360ml Coke/Sprite = 50/70mg Na
  - 1 oz salted pretzels = 150-300mg Na
  - 12 Baked Lays Crisps = 210mg Na
  - 1 cup Cottage cheese = 400-500mg Na
  - 1 Big Mac + 1 Lg Fries (McD) = 1000mg + 450mg Na
  - ⇨ Look for low sodium/serving size e.g. < 170mg Na.

Caution if Na is listed in the first 5 label ingredients!

## If hyperkalemia, caution with high $K^+$ foods

- E.g. apricots, bananas, beans, bran, cantaloupe, carrots, chocolate, figs, nuts, juices carrot, grapefruit, orange, prune & vegetable, milk, raisins, potatoes, pumpkins, salt substitutes, spinach, tomatoe & yogurt. Avoid liquid from canned fruit/vegetable & cooked meat. (Herbs: alfalfa, dandelion, horsetail, milkweed & nettle)

## Non-pharmacological Management of HF?

### Exercise (after Stress Test assessment):

- Regular physical activity is recommended for all patients with stable HF Sx & impaired LV systolic function
- Exercise training 3-5x per wk for 30-45 min/session (include warm-up & cool-down) for NYHA class II - III with LVEF < 40%

### Salt, fluid restriction & weight management:

- All HF pts: no-added salt diet (2-3g salt/day).
- Advanced HF & fluid retention: ≤2g salt per day (approx. ¼ tsp/d)
- **Daily morning weight** nude & after voiding should be monitored in HF, especially with fluid retention, congestion or renal dysfx. **Furosemide *sliding scale*** may be useful in management of select patients able to adjust dose depending on weight; E.g. If rapid 1kg wt ↑, double furosemide dose; if wt ↓1kg hold furosemide. {See "Warning Signs & Symptoms" box at bottom of this page.}
- Fluid intake: **1.5-2 L/day** for all patients with fluid retention or congestion that is not easily controlled with diuretics, or in patients with significant renal dysfunction or hyponatremia. {Fluid intake includes more than just water e.g. soups, puddings, etc.}
- Not more than 1 alcoholic drink per day[3]

### *For all symptomatic pts with systolic HF:*

- *Education* {e.g. self-monitoring weight; action plan when to seek help}
- *Aggressive risk reduction (BP, AF, statins, glucose, wt & ASA)*
- *Vaccinations: Influenza annual & pneumococcal one-time*
- *Salt/fluid vigilance; smoking cessation* • *Tailored diuretic Rx*
- Possibly add fish oils (1g/day n-3 PUFA) GISSI-HF trial: ↓ all-cause death NNT=56 / 3.9yr; {n-3-PUFA = n-3 polyunsaturated fatty acids; Sources: salmon, herring, mackerel & flax.}

## What is the treatment management of HF?[1]

- If Sx severe, refer to specialist: acute⇨ER, chronic⇨HF clinic
- If HF Sx & LVEF>40%, treat cause (eg, HTN, ischemia)
- If LVEF ≤ 35%, consider ICD referral; if QRS ≥ 120ms, CRT referral eg. biventricular pacing; If refractory, consider transplant.

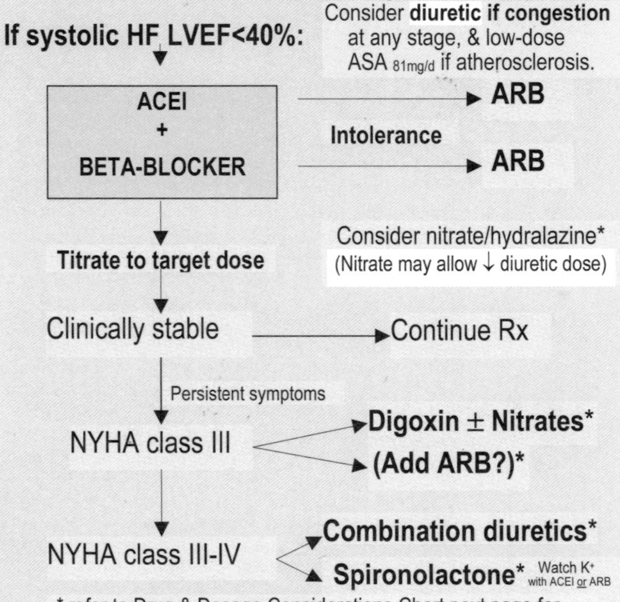

**If systolic HF LVEF<40%:** Consider **diuretic if congestion** at any stage, & low-dose ASA 81mg/d if atherosclerosis.

- **ACEI + BETA-BLOCKER** → **ARB**; Intolerance → **ARB**
- ↓ **Titrate to target dose** — Consider nitrate/hydralazine* (Nitrate may allow ↓ diuretic dose)
- ↓ Clinically stable → Continue Rx
- ↓ Persistent symptoms
- NYHA class III → **Digoxin ± Nitrates***; → **(Add ARB?)***
- ↓ NYHA class III-IV → **Combination diuretics***; → **Spironolactone*** Watch $K^+$ with ACEI or ARB

* refer to Drug & Dosage Considerations Chart next page for further considerations on when to use in specific cases.

**ACEI**=Angiotensin Converting Enzyme Inhibitor **AF**=Atrial fibrillation **ARB**=Angiotensin II Receptor Blocker **BB**=Beta-blocker **BNP**=Brain natriuretic peptide **CRT**=Cardiac Resynchronization Therapy **EF**=Ejection fraction **ER**=Emergency Room **HF**=Heart Failure **HTN**=Hypertension **ICD**=Implantable Cardioverter Defibrillator **LV**=Left ventricle **LVEF**=Left Ventricle Ejection Fraction **Na**=Sodium **NaCl**=Sodium chloride **NYHA**=New York Heart Assoc. **Rx**=Prescription **Sx**=Symptoms **tsp**=teaspoonsful **Tx**=treatment **wt**=weight

---

**Incidence/Prevalence: 1%** self-reported HF 1; 400,000 people in Canada live with HF[1]

- Annual Mortality: 5-50% per year[1]. Up to 40-50% of people with HF die within 5 years of diagnosis[1]
- In 2000, 1.38 million HF associated hospital days; 15.8% died in hospital; ave. hospital stay ~ 13 days[1]

**Precipitating Cause:** other cardiac (e.g. **HTN**, CAD, AF, acute MI, valve dx, cardiomyopathy, pericarditis) & non-cardiac (e.g. pulmonary edema or emboli, COPD, ARDS, lung infection); non-adherence (lifestyle, drug tx)

- Acute exacerbations very often avoidable therefore investigate precipitating causes (e.g. *Diet* & *Drugs*)!

**Initial Assessment:** (When able or appropriate include twelve-lead ECG, chest radiograph & echo)

**HISTORY**: weakness, fatigue (low-output HF), lightheaded, exercise tolerance change, wheezing, nocturia, orthopnea, paroxysmal nocturnal dyspnea, dyspnea on exertion; drug exacerbating causes eg. NSAIDs, CCBs, antiarrhythmics

LV involvement: dry cough, ↑weight, cognitive change, pink frothy sputum if severe;

RV involvement: edema, nausea, jaundice {Note: gut edema can dramatically reduce drug absorption.}

**PHYSICAL**: hepatojugular reflux, edema, ↑**JVP**, S3 gallop, rales, hepatosplenomegaly; anxiety, sweating, cyanosis

**LAB**: lytes Ca&Mg, SCr, BUN, LFT, TSH, lipid. (? **BNP**: may be useful if diagnosis unclear/unexplained dyspnea/risk stratification)

**Special Considerations:**

- To achieve target doses, systolic BP <100mmHg OK if no hypotension symptoms
- Optimize the role of diuretics in systolic HF. [Note; in diastolic HF, overdiuresis may make HF worse.]
- "Wet beriberi consider if HR > SBP ": ↑↑↑HR & low SBP & 3rd space tendency ⇨high output HF; consider if post-op, or eating poorly x ≥3 mo & getting sicker quite common; may be due to low thiamine, alcohol; Tx Thiamine 100mg od
- If $K^+$ is low & does not respond to K+ supplement, check $Mg^{++}$ **level** & supplement if low (250-500mg elemental/day) {e.g. $Mg^{++}$ oxide 420mg/tab▼ (=252mg elemental $Mg^{++}$) 1-2 tab po daily; $Mg^{++}$ glucoheptonate Soln 3g/30ml▼ (=150mg elemental $Mg^{++}$)}

**Acute Heart Failure Management:**[3]

- Clinical assessment of perfusion (cold/warm) and volume status (wet/dry)
- Initial investigations (CBC, lytes, BUN, SCr, eGFR, troponin, BNP, ECG, chest x-ray, echocardiogram)
- Tx precipitating causes: tachyarrhythmia, ischemia, infection pneumonia, HIV, Hep C, anemia, thyroid dysfx, adherence issues.
- Death risk↑: if ↑SCr, ↓BP systolic, older age, ↑HR, new onset AF, ↓serum Na, anemia, ↓EF, ↑QRS, ↑NYHA class.
- Monitor heart rate, blood pressure, oxygen saturation, response to therapy
- Warm (well perfused, stable BP) & Wet (volume overloaded):
  - **IV diuretic** congestion (furosemide→double usual PO dose & give it IV, reassess response after 60-90 min & titrate prn), vasodilators (nitroglycerin SL, IV, PO; nitroprusside IV), morphine
- Cold (poor perfusion, hypotensive) and Wet (cardiogenic shock)
  - Positive inotrope [dobutamine 2-5ug/kg/min (preferred) or dopamine or milrinone (0.25ug/kg/min)]
- Once stabilized: consider combined IV diuretics & inotropes, initiate vasodilators (**ACEI**, hydralazine, nitrates)

**PEARLS for ↓ Morbidity & Mortality in HF**

(1) Patient education is key (consider referral to interprofessional HF clinic where available).
(2) Make sure ALL patients with reduced EF are on the maximally tolerated dose of a BB & ACEI (or ARB).
(3) After HF controlled, titrate BB dose ↑ gradually (q2-4wks); patient will feel worse before feeling better.
(4) To optimize ACEI & BB doses, consider: ↓ dose of diuretic, nitrates &/or doses of other antihypertensives.
(5) Consider adding a 3rd drug (e.g. spironloactone, digoxin, nitrate) if patient still symptomatic on ACEI + BB.

**Warning Signs & Symptoms**: ↑shortness of breath esp. with mild exercise, waking up at night with sudden breathlessness, chest pain or discomfort, ↑ fatigue or weakness, swelling in feet/ankles, or rapid ↑ weight {1 kg (2 lbs) in 2days, or 2.5kg (5 lbs) in 7days}

# Heart Failure - Drug & Dosage Considerations[1,2]

Prepared by M. Jin, B. Jensen, L. Regier © www.RxFiles.ca May 2010

| form/strength g=generic | Start / ⇨Target Dose in Trials | $/30d |
|---|---|---|

**PLACE IN THERAPY / COMMENTS / Outcome Evidence / Side effect SE / Contraindication CI**

## ANGIOTENSIN CONVERTING ENZYME INHIBITORS (ACEI)

| Drug | Start / ⇨Target Dose | $/30d |
|---|---|---|
| **Ramipril** ALTACE, g<br>1.25, 2.5, 5, 10, (15*®mg) caps<br>2.5 & 5 & 10/12.5mg; 5 & 10/25mg HCT Altace HCT | 1.25-2.5mg BID po / ⇨**5mg BID** - 10mg OD<br>Max 10mg bid | 43-29 |
| **Lisinopril** ZESTRIL/PRINIVIL, g<br>5ᵍ, 10, 20mg tab<br>10 & 20/12.5mg; 20/25mg tab HCT Zestoretic | 2.5-5mg OD po ⇨**20-40mg OD** ATLAS ave 35mg<br>Max 20mg bid | 28-58 |
| **Perindopril** COVERSYL, g<br>2, 4ᵍ, 8 mg tab; 4/1.25mg tab HCT Coversyl Plus | 2mg OD po / ⇨**4mg OD** PEP-CHF 9<br>Max 4-8mg bid | 35 |
| **Enalapril** VASOTEC, g<br>2.5ᵍ, 5ᵍ, 10ᵍ, 20ᵍ mg tab; 1.25mg/ml vial<br>5mg/12.5mg, 10mg/25 mg tab HCT Vaseretic | 1.25-2.5mg BID po / ⇨**10mg BID**<br>Max 20mg bid | 42 |
| **Captopril** CAPOTEN, g | 6.25-12.5mg TID po /⇨**25-50mg TID** | 62 |
| **Trandolapril** MAVIK | 0.5-1mg OD po /⇨**4mg OD** TRACE | |

✓ ACEI should be used in all pts as soon as safely possible after AMI & continued indefinitely if LVEF < 40 or if AHF complicated the MI [1]
✓ ACEI should be used in all asymptomatic pts with a LVEF < 35% & in all pts with Sx of HF & LVEF < 40% [1]
(ACEI's improve ventricular fx, patient well being, reduces hospital admission for HF & increases survival; appears to be class effect but ACEIs with HF evidence listed)

**CI**: bilateral renal artery stenosis or unilateral stenosis if only 1 kidney, angioedema, pregnancy & SBP<85mmHg. {HF clinic may exceed usual max dose.}

**M**: SCr & K⁺ upon initiation & after 3-7days of starting or adjusting dose (a 30%↑ in **SCr** & a **K⁺** of 5.6mmol/L may be reasonable)

**SE**: cough<10%, esp. Asians, hypotension/dizzy, ↑K⁺, renal insufficiency. {If ↑SCr >30% in euvolemic pts, consider hydralazine/nitrate combo.}

**DI**: diuretics K sparing→↑K, lithium↑ levels, NSAIDS↓ effect & potassium↑K; generally avoid combination of ACE+ARB+spironolactone.

◆Good evidence for ↓mortality in HF; may use in combo with diuretic (if ↓wt or ↓BP occurs, hold or ↓diuretic dose & maintain ACEI dose)

◆ACEI vs. Pl.: All-cause **mortality**: 15.8% 611/3870 vs. 21.9% 709/3235, NNT=16 [8]; All-cause mortality or Hospitalization for HF: 22.4 vs. 32.6%, NNT=10 [8 META-ANALYSIS]
{Inclusion: patients with symptomatic CHF. Most patients were classified as class II-III at entry. LVEF at entry <0.35 to <0.50}

Start low dose; titrate up as tolerated eg. Ramipril 2.5mg OD x1wk, 5mg od x 3wk then 5mg BID or 10mg daily Hope. May ↑dose more quickly eg. q2day. Aim for max tolerated **target** dosages!

## BETA BLOCKERS (BB) {bisoprolol, metoprolol β1-selective; carvedilol β1,β2 & α1}

| Drug | Start / ⇨Target Dose | $/30d |
|---|---|---|
| **Bisoprolol** MONOCOR, g<br>5ᵍ, 10mg tablet [USA: ZEBETA] | 1.25mg OD po / ⇨**10mg OD** Max 20mg/d | 21 |
| **Carvedilol** COREG, g ▼<br>3.125, 6.25, 12.5 & 25mg tab | 3.125mg BID po / ⇨**25mg BID** Max 50mg BID<br>with food | 53 |
| ------------------ | ------- | --- |
| ✦ **Metoprolol SR** LOPRESOR, g<br>SR: 100mg, 200mg tab (SR form preferred chronically)<br>{Regular 25ᵍ, 50ᵍ, 100ᵍ mg tabs;<br>10mg/ml susp manufactured at some pharmacies} | 12.5-25mg OD po / ⇨**200mg SR OD**<br>(start with lowest dose if Class III HF) Max 200mg BID | 21 |

{✦Tartrate salt in Canada; but the most studied succinate salt TOPROL XL→only available in the USA; some consider Canadian formulation unproven in HF.}

Start low dose; titrate up as tolerated (~double dose q2-4wks); HF symptoms may get worse before they get better! Aim for maximally tolerated target dose. ↓HR assoc⇨↑benefit. If DM/hypoglycemia, bisoprolol or metoprolol may be preferred. {64% of Merit-HF pts reached metoprolol 200mg/d}

✓ All HF pts with LVEF ≤40% should receive a BB[1]; If NYHA class IV symptoms, **stabilize** patient/congestion before initiation of a BB [1]
(BB's improve ventricular fx, pt well being, ↓ hospitalizations, tx AF & ↑ survival). Avoid abrupt withdrawal! Down-titrate in acute CHF. Caution with IV inotropes & right sided HF.

**CI**: severe/poorly controlled asthma, 2nd or 3rd degree heart block without a permanent pacemaker, or a PR>0.24sec, symptomatic bradycardia (or HR<50), SBP<85mmHg, decompensated HF,[10] or on cocaine. BB not normally started in pts with symptomatic hypotension despite adjustment of other meds [1]. {Note: Stable COPD is not a CI [1].} Useful for exercise induced ↑HR **M**: HR; SCr, BUN, lytes after 3-7day.

**SE**: ↓BP, ↓HR, dizziness, fatigue<10%, insomnia, dream vivid & sexual dysfx ~4%; PAD, cold extremity; hypoglycemia may mask, **fluid** retention,? ↑ psoriasis

**DI**: amiodarone, antidiabetics, CCB synergistic, cimetidine ↑β blocker, clonidine hypertensive crisis, digoxin↓HR, insulins, NSAIDS ↑BP & phenobarbital↓β blocker

Metoprolol IV CCS-2 trial 11: ↑ cardiogenic **shock** esp. in those with HF or hypotension. {In severe HF, add low dose inotropes or stop BB.}

◆Carvedilol vs. Pl: All-cause **mortality**: 11.2% 130/1156 vs. 16.8% 190/1133, NNT = 18 in 10.4 months [12 COPERNICUS]
◆Bisoprolol vs. Pl: All-cause **mortality**: 11.8% 156/1327 vs. 17.3% 228/1320, NNT=19 in 1.3 years [13 CIBIS II]
◆Carvedilol 25mg BID vs. Metoprolol 50mg BID (suboptimal: formulation & dose): All-cause **mortality**: 33.9% 512/1511 vs. 39.5% 600/1518, NNT=18 after 58 months [14 COMET]
◆Metoprolol CR/XL 200mg CR/XL OD vs. Pl; All cause **mortality**: 7.2% 217/1990 vs. 11% 237/2001, NNT=28 after 1 year [15 MERIT-HF] {This succinate formulation not in Canada}

## Angiotensin Receptor Blockers (ARB)

| Drug | Start / ⇨Target Dose | $/30d |
|---|---|---|
| **Valsartan** DIOVAN<br>40ᵍ, 80, 160, **320** mg tab;<br>80/12.5 & 160&320mg//12.5/25mg tab HCT Diovan HCT | 40mg BID po / ⇨160mg BID | 49/92 |
| **Candesartan** ATACAND<br>4ᵍ, 8ᵍ, 16ᵍ, 32ᵍ mg tab; 16/12.5ᵍ, 32/12.5/25ᵍ®mg HCT Atacand Plus | 4mg OD po / ⇨32mg OD CHARM 22 | 48/48 |
| **Losartan** COZAAR<br>25, 50, 100mg tab; 50mg/12.5mg HCT tab;<br>100mg/12.5mg HCT tab; DS =100mg/25mg HCT Hyzaar | →not officially indicated; 25-150mg HEALL OD | 52-74 |

Start low dose; titrate up. Aim for max tolerated dose.

✓ ARBs should be used in pts who **cannot tolerate ACEI** (especially cough), although renal dysfunction & hyperkalemia may occur [1]
✓ ARB+ACEI if persistent HF Sx & ↑'d risk of hospitalization despite optimal tx; or when BB contraindicated/not tolerated after careful attempts [1]
◆Valsartan vs. Pl: All-cause mortality: 19.7% 495 / 2511 vs. 19.4% 484 / 2499, NS; Hospitalization for HF: 13.8% vs. 18.2% Pl, NNT=23 @23 months [17 Val-HeFT]
◆Candesartan vs. Pl: CV death: 21.6% 219/1013 vs 24.8% 252/1015, NNT=31; Hospitalization for HF: 20.4% vs 28.2% Pl, NNT=13 @34months [18 CHARM-Alternative]
◆Candesartan+ACEI vs. Pl: CV death: 23.7% 302 / 1276 vs 27.3% 347 / 1272, NNT=28; Hospitalization for HF: 24.2% vs 28.0%, NNT=26 @41months [19 CHARM-Added]
◆Losartan 50mg od vs. captopril 50mg tid – **NS** after 1.5 years [20 ELITE II] ◆Irbesartan 300mg od vs. placebo – **NS** after 49.5mon [21 I-PRESERVE, HF & EF ≥45%, n=4128]

## Aldosterone Antagonist (for neurohormonal benefit, not just diuretic effect)

| Drug | Start / ⇨Target Dose | $/30d |
|---|---|---|
| **Spironolactone** ALDACTONE, g | 12.5mg OD po / ⇨25mg OD see dose note | 9 |
| **Eplerenone** INSPRA✗® 25,50mg tab NEW Jun09<br>{?? may have ↓gynecomastia & impotence than spiron.} | 25mg od; ↑ to 50mg od @ 4 wks EPHESUS (Post-MI HF)<br>**DI** with strong CYP3A4 inhibitors e.g. azoles, clarith, PIs; K+ salts | 95 |

✓ Option for pts with LVEF <30% & severe HF sx's despite tx optimization, or AHF with an LVEF <30%. (Also useful in right sided HF.) following **AMI**, if SCr <200umol/L & K⁺ < 5.2 mmol/L [1]. Consider ↓ or discontinue K+ supplements when starting! Counsel re K⁺; Hold if diarrhea.

**DI**: ↑ K⁺ with ACEI +/or ARB +/or NSAID ∴ **M**: **K⁺** avoid if K+ ≥5mmol/L & **renal fx** **SE**: gynecomastia, ↑K⁺, ↓Na, rash, erectile dysfx, menstruation abnormal & ?↑GI ulcers.

All-Cause **mortality**: 34.5% 284/822 vs. 45.9% 386/841 placebo, NNT=9 after 2 years for severe HF Class III-IV [23 RALES] [Note: 50mg/day target dose, but 25mg/day average achieved.]

## Vasodilators (Nitrate + Hydralazine used concurrently conventionally)

| Drug | Start / ⇨Target Dose | $/30d |
|---|---|---|
| **Isosorbide dinitrate** ISORDIL, g<br>5mg SL; 10ᵍ, 30ᵍ mg tabs; 60ᵍ mg ER tab IMDUR®, g | 20mg TID po ac / ⇨40mg TID ac | 15/23 |
| **Hydralazine** APRESOLINE, g<br>10ᵍ, 25, 50mg tabs; 20mg amp | 37.5mg TID po / ⇨75mg TID | 41/48 |

Nitroglycerin patch (0.2, 0.4, 0.6, 0.8mg/hr x12hr) may be ISDN alternative; nocturnal dyspnea.

✓ **Combination** isosorbide dinitrate (**ISDN**) & **hydralazine** should be considered in addition to standard therapy for **African-Americans** with systolic dysfx; also for HF pts unable to tolerate other standard tx[1] & chronic renal failure. {~12hr nitrate free interval prevents tolerance.}

**CI**: Isosorbide: hypersensitivity; PDE5 inhibitor eg. sildenafil, severe anemia, & shock. Hydralazine: Dissecting aortic aneurysm & rheumatic heart dx mitral valve.

**SE**: Isosorbide: hypotension, HA, ↑HR, dizzy, flushing & methemoglobinemia; GI upset. Hydralazine: Lupus Sx, ↑HR, HA, edema & peripheral neuropathy.

◆All-cause **mortality**: 6.2% 32/518 vs. 10.2% 54/532 placebo, NNT=25 after 18 months [24 Class III-IV A-HeFT]

## Diuretics – use IV in acute HF (if gut edema, ↓absorption will make PO route less effective)

| Drug | Start / ⇨Target Dose | $/30d |
|---|---|---|
| **Furosemide** LASIX, g<br>20, 40ᵍ mg tabs; 10mg/ml soln; 40 & 250mg vials | 20-40mg po OD-BID (Max: 600mg/d) | 5-5 |
| **Hydrochlorothiazide** HYDRODIURIL, g<br>12.5, 25ᵍ, 50ᵍ, (100ᵍ✗▼) mg tab - ↓effect if CrCl<30 | 12.5-25mg po OD-BID (Max: 200mg/d) | 5-5 |
| **Metolazone** ZAROXOLYN 2.5mg tab | 2.5-5mg po OD (Max: 10-20mg/d) | 10-17 |

✓ Loops, like **furosemide**, for most HF pts & **congestive Sx**. Once ↓acute congestion, use **lowest** effective dose ? sliding scale for stable S&S[1].
✓ For pts with persistent **volume overload** despite optimal medical therapy & ↑'s in loop diuretics, cautious addition of a 2nd diuretic (eg. a thiazide or low dose metolazone ≥30min pre-loop) may be considered if possible to closely monitor **M**: AM daily weight, Cr, BUN, eGFR, K⁺; Mg⁺⁺

◆↓/hold diuretic if SCr ↑ >30% from baseline. **DI**: digoxin↑ toxicity if K+ low, ↑ lithium levels, NSAIDs, steroids. **CI**: gout symptomatic hyperuricemia, sulfa allergy?, anuria, ↓ Na+

**SE**: rash, allergic sulfa rx, photosensitivity rx, ↑ (calcium, uric acid, glucose, cholesterol, TG), ↓ (Na, K⁺ esp. with salbutamol, magnesium, zinc), pancreatitis & sexual dysfx.

## Other

| Drug | Start / ⇨Target Dose | $/30d |
|---|---|---|
| **Digoxin** TOLOXIN, LANOXIN g<br>0.0625, 0.125ᵍ, 0.25ᵍ mg tab; 0.05mg/ml elixir;<br>Injectable: 0.25mg/ml amp; 0.05mg/ml amp | MD: 0.0625 - 0.125mg po OD<br>Usual Max in HF: 0.25mg po OD<br>Optional LD: 10ug/kg LBW 0.75-1.25mg PO<br>(eg. 0.5mg IV/po x1, then 0.25mg q6h IV/po x2 doses) | 15-15 |

{Routine levels not recommended in HF[1]; target in HF is ≤**1.3**nmol/l; (usual range in A.fib 1.3-2.6 nmol/L) In HF, ≥ 1.5 nmol/L associated with harm.[26,27]} {Trough level or at least >8hr post-dose.}

✓ Sinus rhythm pts with moderate-sev persistent Sx despite optimized HF tx, digoxin recommended to ↓Sx esp if EF<30% & hospitalizations[1]
✓ Chronic **AF** pts & poor control of ventricular rate despite BB tx, or when BB cannot be used, consider digoxin [1] Also ↑exercise tolerance.

**CI**: hypersensitivity, ventricular fibrillation. Caution: acute MI, AV block, chronic constrictive pericarditis, ↓↓ HR, thyroid dx. (DIGIBIND if overdose.)

**SE / Toxicity**: anorexia, nausea/vomiting, weakness, dizzy, visual change (Digoxin less effective if ↓Ca⁺⁺ or ↓K⁺; but ↑toxic if ↓or↑K⁺, ↑Ca⁺⁺, ↑TSH or ↓Mg⁺⁺)

◆**No** digoxin role in HF pt & preserved LVEF with normal sinus rhythm [2] **DI**: amiodarone, azoles, CCB, clarithromycin, cyclosporine, eryc & quinidine ↑dig level, BB.

◆Digoxin vs Pl: All cause mortality 34.8% vs 35.1%, NS; **Hospitalization** for HF: 26.8% vs. 34.7%, NNT=13 [25 DIG]

**Other Meds**: **Amlodipine** (2.5-10mg po daily $30-75) appears to be safe, & may benefit diastolic dysfx & non-ischemic dilated cardiomyopathy. **Felodipine** (2.5-10mg od $24-32) is an option for systolic HF. **Amiodarone** 200mg od $50: option in atrial fib & HF. ↑↑SE

= Exception Drug Status in SK ✗ = Non-formulary in SK = prior approval by NIHB ⊗=not covered NIHB ▼ covered NIHB $=retail cost ᵍ=scored tab ACEI=angiotensin converting enzyme inhibitor AHF=Acute heart failure AMI=acute myocardial infarction ARB=angiotensin receptor blocker BB=beta blocker BUN=blood urea nitrogen CCB=calcium channel blocker CI=contraindication Cr=serum creatinine CV=cardiovascular eGFR=estimated glomerular filtration rate HA=headache HCT=hydrochlorothiazide HF=heart failure HR=heart rate K⁺=potassium JVP=jugular venous pressure LBW=lean body weight LD=loading dose LVEF=Left Ventricle Ejection Fraction M=monitor MD=maintenance dose NNT=number needed to treat NS=not significant PAD=peripheral arterial disease PI=Placebo S&S=signs & symptoms SCr= serum creatinine SE=side effects Sx=symptom TG=triglycerides

**For all asymptomatic pts with systolic HF:** Education, aggressive risk reduction, lifestyle, salt/fluid vigilance, tailored diuretic Rx. **NOT recommended:** Coenzyme Q10, vitamins, herbal supplements & chelation therapy.

**Drugs that ↑HF:** Alcohol, antiarrhythmic amio & drone-darone, disopyramide, dofetilide, ibutilide, flecainide, propafenone, CCB esp. verapamil > diltiazem > nifedipine, dutaseride, glitazones pioglitazone, rosiglitazone, itraconazole, mitoxantrone, nitric oxide, **NSAIDs** incl. celecoxib, steroid cortico & anabolic, stimulants cocaine, ephedra, amphetamine & TNF blockers. **Chemotherapy:** anthracyclines (doxorubicin→dexrazoxane a cardioprotectant; daunorubicin), bleomycin, cetuximab, cyclophosphamide high dose, cytostatic agents, dasa-, ima-, lapa-, nilo-, suti-**tinib**, interferons, interleukin-2 & **trastuzumab**.

# Figure 3. ALL-CAUSE MORTALITY OUTCOMES from MAJOR LIPID TRIALS

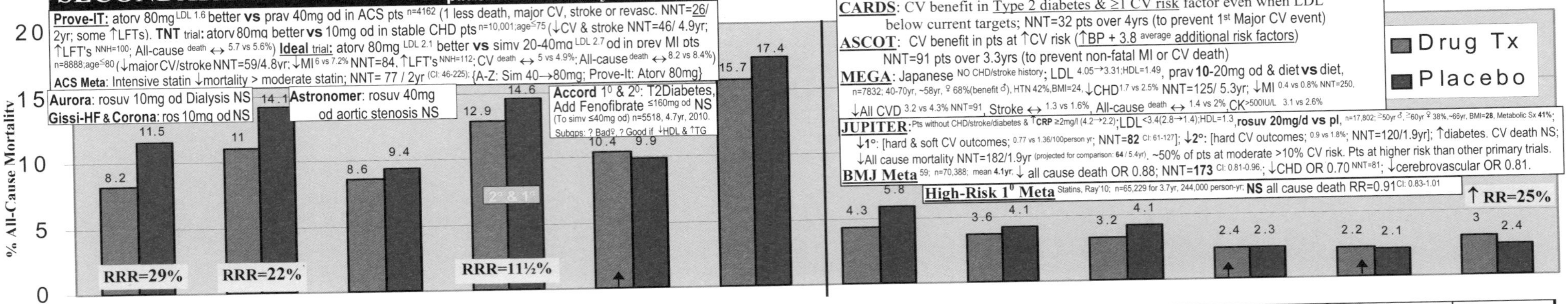

## SECONDARY PREVENTION patients with history of CHD

**Prove-IT:** atorv 80mg LDL 1.6 better **vs** prav 40mg od in ACS pts n=4162 (1 less death, major CV, stroke or revasc. NNT=26/2yr; some ↑LFTs). **TNT** trial: atorv 80mg better **vs** 10mg od in stable CHD pts n=10,001;age≤75 (↓CV & stroke NNT=46/ 4.9yr; ↑LFT's NNH=100; All-cause death ↔ 5.7 vs 5.6%) **Ideal** trial: atorv 80mg LDL 2.1 better **vs** simv 20-40mg LDL 2.7 od in prev MI pts n=8888;age≤80 (↓major CV/stroke NNT=59/4.8yr; ↓MI 6 vs 7.2% NNT=84, ↑LFT's NNH=112; CV death ↔ 5 vs 4.9%; All-cause death ↔ 8.2 vs 8.4%)
**ACS Meta**: Intensive statin ↓mortality > moderate statin; NNT= 77 / 2yr (CI: 46-225); {A-Z: Sim 40→80mg; Prove-It: Atorv 80mg}

**Aurora**: rosuv 10mg od Dialysis NS
**Gissi-HF & Corona**: ros 10mg od NS

**Astronomer**: rosuv 40mg od aortic stenosis NS

**Accord** 1° & 2°: T2Diabetes, Add Fenofibrate ≤160mg od NS (To simv ≤40mg od) n=5518, 4.7yr, 2010. Subgps: ? Bad♀, ? Good if ↓HDL & ↑TG

## PRIMARY PREVENTION pts without CHD trials

**CARDS**: CV benefit in Type 2 diabetes & ≥1 CV risk factor even when LDL below current targets; NNT=32 pts over 4yrs (to prevent 1st Major CV event)
**ASCOT**: CV benefit in pts at ↑CV risk (↑BP + 3.8 average additional risk factors) NNT=91 pts over 3.3yrs (to prevent non-fatal MI or CV death)
**MEGA**: Japanese NO CHD/stroke history; LDL 4.05→3.31;HDL=1.49, prav **10**-20mg od & diet **vs** diet, n=7832; 40-70yr, ~58yr, ♀ 68%(benefit ♂), HTN 42%,BMI=24, ↓CHD 1.7 vs 2.5% NNT=125/ 5.3yr; ↓MI 0.4 vs 0.8% NNT=250, ↓All CVD 3.2 vs 4.3% NNT=91, Stroke ↔ 1.3 vs 1.6%, All-cause death ↔ 1.4 vs 2%, CK>500IU/L 3.1 vs 2.6%
**JUPITER**: Pts without CHD/stroke/diabetes & ↑**CRP** ≥2mg/l (4.2→2.2); LDL <3.4(2.8→1.4);HDL=1.3, **rosuv 20mg/d vs pl**, n=17,802; ≥50yr ♂, ≥60yr ♀ 38%,~66yr, BMI=**28**, Metabolic Sx **41%**; ↓**1°**: [hard & soft CV outcomes; 0.77 vs 1.36/100person yr; NNT=**82** CI: 61-127]; ↓**2°**: [hard CV outcomes; 0.9 vs 1.8%; NNT=120/1.9yr]; ↑diabetes. CV death NS; ↓All cause mortality NNT=182/1.9yr (projected for comparison: **64** / 5.4yr). ~50% of pts at moderate >10% CV risk. Pts at higher risk than other primary trials.
**BMJ Meta** 59; n=70,388; mean **4.1yr**; ↓ all cause death OR 0.88; NNT=**173** CI: 0.81-0.96; ↓CHD OR 0.70 NNT=81; ↓cerebrovascular OR 0.81.
**High-Risk 1° Meta** Statins, Ray'10; n=65,229 for 3.7yr, 244,000 person-yr; **NS** all cause death RR=0.91 CI: 0.83-1.01

% All-Cause Mortality (0, 5, 10, 15, 20) — ■ Drug Tx ■ Placebo

4S: 8.2 / 11.5 (RRR=29%); LIPID: 11 / 14.1 (RRR=22%); CARE: 8.6 / 9.4; HPS: 12.9 / 14.6 (RRR=11½%) (2° & 1°); BIP: 10.4 / 9.9; VA-HIT: 15.7 / 17.4; CARDS: 4.3 / 5.8; ASCOT: 3.6 / 4.1; WOSCOPS: 3.2 / 4.1; AFCAPS: 2.4 / 2.3; HHS: 2.2 / 2.1; WHO-CLOF: 3 / 2.4 (↑ RR=25%)

| | 4S | LIPID | CARE | HPS | BIP | VA-HIT | CARDS | ASCOT | WOSCOPS | AFCAPS | HHS | WHO-CLOF |
|---|---|---|---|---|---|---|---|---|---|---|---|---|
| **Drug & dose used** | **Simvastatin** 20-40mg/day[1,2] | **Pravastatin** 40mg/day[3,4] | **Pravastatin** 40mg/day[5] | **Simvastatin** 40mg/d[6,7,8,9,10] | **Bezafibrate** 400mg/day[11] | **Gemfibrozil** 600mg BID[12] | **Atorvastatin** 10mg/day[13] | **Atorvastatin** 10mg/day[14] | **Pravastatin** 40mg/day[15] | **Lovastatin** 20-40mg/day[16] | **Gemfibrozil** 600mg BID[17] | **Clofibrate** 1.6g/day[18] |
| **ARR** all death | 3.3% p=0.0003 | 3.1% p<0.001 | NS | 1.7% p<0.001 | NS | NS | NS | NS | 0.9% p=0.051 | NS | NS | (-0.6%) p<0.05 |
| **NNT** mortality | 30 | 32 | NS | 57 | NS | NS | NS | NS | 111 (p=0.051) | NS | NS | NNH=167 |
| **Duration** | 5.4 yrs | 6.1 yrs | 5 yrs | 5 yrs | 6.2 yrs | 5.1 yrs | 4 yrs | 3.3 yrs | 4.9 yrs | 5.2 yrs | 5 yrs | 5.3 yrs |
| **All-cause mortality in *English*** Based on NNT | **Treat 30 patients for 5.4 yrs to prevent 1 death** | **Treat 32 patients for 6.1 yrs to prevent 1 death** | No statistical difference in all-cause mortality | **Treat 57 patients for 5 yrs to prevent 1 death** | No statistical difference in all-cause mortality (? better with ↑HDL) | No statistical difference in all-cause mortality | No statistical difference in all-cause mortality; trial halted early | No statistical difference in all-cause mortality; trial halted early | **Trend: 1 death prevented per 111 patients over 4.9yrs** | No statistical difference in all-cause mortality | No statistical difference in all-cause mortality | Treating 167 patients for 5.3yrs caused 1 extra death |
| **n= (♂+♀)** *publication yr* | 3617+827 *1994* | 7498+1516 *1998* | 3583+576 *1996* | 15454♂+5082♀ *2002* | 2825♂ + 265♀ *2000* | 2531♂ *1998* | 1929 ♂ + 909 ♀ *Aug 2004* | 8363♂+1942♀ *2003* | 6595♂ *1995* | 5608+997 *1998* | 4081♂ *1987* | 15745♂ *1978* |
| **Patients Studied** | pts with angina or previous MI & TC >5.5 age 35-70 | recent hx of acute MI or unstable angina; age 31-75 | recent hx of acute MI & average LDL; age 21-75 | High risk patients: MI, CHD, PVD, CVA, DM, HTN; TC ≥3.5; age 40-80 | recent hx of MI or stable angina; age 45-74 | ♂ with CHD, low HDL & normal LDL; age <74 | Type 2 **Diabetes** & ≥1 risk factor; no CHD/CVD, LDL ≤4.14;age 40-75 avg~62 | **≥3** risk factors CHD **TC ≤6.5 & HTN** (24% diabetes) age 40-79 ~63 | ♂ with cholesterol ≥7; (44% smokers) age 45-64 ~55 | **↓HDL** but normal LDL & TC; ♂ 45-73yr & ♀ 55-73yrs ~58 | ♂ with high levels of non-HDL cholesterol age 40-55 | ♂ with normal or high TC; age 30-59 |
| **LDL (ave) initial⇨end** | **4.9⇨3.2** ↓35% ↓MI / death CHD 19.4 vs 28% NNT=12 | 3.9⇨2.9 ↓26% | 3.6⇨2.5 ↓31% ✝ | 3.3⇨2.3 ↓30% (Adjusted ~ 3.9)[19] | 3.9⇨3.6 | 2.9;↔LDL | 3.0⇨2.1 ↓30% | 3.4⇨2.3 ↓32% | 5⇨4.1 ↓18% | 3.9⇨3.0 ↓23% | 4.9⇨4.5 | not available |
| **1° Endpoint** Placebo/Drug | ↓ **total mortality** 11.5%/8.2% NNT=31 | ↓ **death** CHD 8.3%/6.4% NNT=53 | ↓ **MI / death** CHD 13.2/10.2% NNT=34 | ↓**Vascular** fatal & non 25.2/19.8% NNT=19 | **MI** or **death** sudden NS 15% / 13.6% | ↓ **MI / death** CHD 21.7/17.3% NNT=23 | ↓**1st CHD Event** 9.0%/5.8% NNT=32 | ↓**MI /death** CHD 3%/1.9% NNT=91 | ↓**MI /death** CHD 7.9%/5.5% NNT=42 | ↓ **1st CV event** 10.9/6.8% NNT=25 | ↓ **MI / death** CHD 41.4/27.3% NNT=8 | ↓ **heart disease** |
| **Comment** | impact after~1 yr 10yr data NNT=42 | | benefit most in ♀ & high LDL baseline | benefits similar in low & high LDL | benefit only in pts with *TG* >2.3 | some benefit in ↑HDL & ↓TGs | benefit even in LDL ⇨ <2 | benefit only in ♂; especially >60yrs | higher risk ♂ pts | Serious adverse outcome events 34% in **both** groups | ↑ in non-CHD mortality? | ↑ death; ↑ liver/GI risk |
| | **STATINS** | | | | **FIBRATES** | | **STATINS** | | | | **FIBRATES** | |

**ACS**=acute coronary syndrome **ARR**=% absolute risk reduction **CHD**=coronary heart disease **CV**=cardiovascular **CVD**=cardiovascular death **DM**=diabetes **GI**=stomach **hx**=history **HF**=heart failure **LFT**=liver function tests **MI**=myocardial infarction **MI NF**=nonfatal MI **NNH**= # needed to harm one **NNT**= # needed to treat to benefit one (e.g. in 4S trial, treating 30patients for 5.4yr would prevent 1 death) **NS**= not statistically significant **pts**=patients **RRR**= relative risk reduction (**HDL**= high density lipoprotein **LDL**= low density lipoprotein **TC**= total cholesterol **TG**= triglycerides **Tx**= treatment)
✝ in the CARE trial pts with initial LDL < 3.2 did not receive CV benefit from pravastatin; **Lipid values in mmol/L**
**NOTE**: This collection of data is from different studies of varying patient groups and with varying methodology; it presents data and demonstrates overall trends but can not be used for direct quantitative comparison.

### Summary of All-Cause Mortality Evidence

{ many studies not powered to evaluate this endpoint ; of published trials, only the **4S & HPS** "overall" had this as the primary (1°) endpoint }

Trials support *statins* for **high risk** rather than just *high TC or LDL*; few *treat to target* trials

- **Statins**[20,21]: strong evidence for 2° prevention (incl. high-dose atorvastatin 80mg in post MI, stable CHD & ACS[22]); some evidence for 1° prevention in diabetes & males at ↑'d risk of CHD and in subset of patients with low HDL, TG's >2.3 &/or pts with diabetes
- **Fibrates**: **no** evidence yet for reductions in 1° or 2° all-cause mortality[23]; possible benefit in subset of patients with low HDL, TG's >2.3 &/or pts with diabetes
- **Lack data** to assess **risk vs benefit** in: 1) age >82 2) combination therapy 3) 1° prevention in low risk pts esp. females 4) aggressive pursuit of targets in low-moderate risk patients.
- **High-dose statin**: mortality benefit in very high risk ACS, but also ↑ SE liver, muscle. • **Niacin**: some evidence for long term ↓ mortality (no difference at 6yrs; difference at 15yr NNT=25, ♂) CDP

**TNT/IDEAL**: CV benefit in 2° prevention with achieved LDL 3.9→2.0 ↓LDL 49% TNT mmol/L & 3.1→2.1 ↓LDL 33% IDEAL mmol/L in the **80mg atorv** arms; but a non significant ↑non-CV death 3.2 vs 2.5% in **TNT** (not in **IDEAL**) & ↑LFTs NNH=~100

# LIPID LOWERING THERAPY: DYSLIPIDEMIA Comparison Chart [1,2,3,4,5,6,7,8]

Prepared by: Brent Jensen BSP, L Regier BSP © www.RxFiles.ca May 2010

| Generic/TRADE/ g=generic avail. Pregnancy | LDL[2,7] (dose effect) | HDL[2] | TG[2] | SIDE EFFECTS /CONTRAINDICATIONS (CI) /COMMENTS/MONITOR (M) | DRUG INTERACTIONS | THERAPEUTIC BENEFITS/USES | USUAL Dose Range (Max dose/day) Studied doses in 1° or 2° prevention | $ / Month |
|---|---|---|---|---|---|---|---|---|
| **STATINS / HMG** | | | | | | | | |
| **Atorvastatin** X LIPITOR g ATO 1997 approved (10,20,40,80 eliptical mg tablet) | ↓ 35 - 60%; Amlodipine//atorvastatin CADUET 5 & 10mg//10 & 20 & 40 & 80mg tabs $95-120 | ↑ 5 - 15%; ROS & SIM may ↑ HDLs most [8,12] | ↓ 7 - 30%; ATO, ROS & SIM may ↓ TGs most [3,12,15] | **SE≤10%**; Generally better tolerated than other agents. Common: upper **GI**, **headache**, rash, sleep problems, muscle pain (not ↓ by coenzyme Q10 Young'07 (but ?? helps) ??Vit D helps). Rare: peripheral neuropathy, lupus like Sx, impotence[9] ?↑hemorrhagic stroke, pancreatitis, diabetes NNH=255/4yr. ↑ **LFT** (AST & ALT >3X Normal in < 2%)[4,7]; **dose** dependent (high vs low dose NNH=96); reversible if stop statin. **Myopathy**[10]: <1%; concern esp. if muscle pain & (SLCO1B1 variants) weakness present; check CK (concern if CK>3-5x). **Rhabdomyolysis** <0.2%[6] (CK>10x, darkened urine, renal failure) -risk ↑10 fold [11-39] with combo/DI's; perioperative (cautious use). ↓ CNS SE: **ATO,FLU,PRA** due to ↓ CNS penetration. **CI**: Active Liver Dx, ↑ alcohol intake & Pregnancy. **M**: Routine LFT's & CK not indicated for all pts [23,30] (LFT: 0,3,6,12 months & annually if high dose/combo or at risk). ROS: potent; ↑levels in Asians; Jupiter outcome data[12,13]; postmarketing safety concerns relative to other statins[14] | ↑ **effect of**: digoxin ATO ↑20%, warfarin FLU,LOV,ROS,SIM. FOR: LOV, SIM, ATO less effect. ↑ **toxicity with HMG &**: amiodarone; **clarithromycin**, conivaptan, colchicine, cyclosporine, danazol, daptomycin, diltiazem, ethinyl estradiol, **erythromycin**, fenofibrate, fluoxetine, fusidic acid, **gemfibrozil**, **grapefruit juice**, imatinib, isoniazid; keto & itra & posa & vori-**conazole**, **niacin**, **nefazodone**, **PI's**[HIV], raltegravir, telithromycin & **verapamil**. ↓ **effect of HMG by**: Bosentan; cholestyramine/colestipol (space ≥2hr); carbam & oxcab-azepine, efavirenz, nevirapine, phenytoin, pectin, phenobarb, St. Johns Wort & rifampin. PRA & ROS: few DIs, but some transplant & HIV meds | ↓ Cholesterol (esp ↓ LDL) ATO,FLU,LOV,PRA,SIM,ROS. ↓ Atherosclerosis ATO,FLU,LOV,PRA,SIM,ROS. ↓ Coronary Heart Disease ATO,FLU,LOV,PRA, ROS, SIM. Diabetes ↓heart & stroke ATO CARDS, SIM (American Diabetes 2008 consider statin if age >10yr & LDL >4). ↓ Stroke ATO,PRA,SIM. Pediatric AHA≥10yr FDA approval ATO,FLU,LOV,PRA,ROS,SIM. Effective in secondary causes such as diabetes & in nephrotic syndrome. In general **doubling** the statin **dose ↓LDL** by a further **6%**. High vs low dose: ACS NNT=80/2yr death | 10mg po hs 1° ASCOT, CARDS, TNT, ASPEN NS; 20mg po hs 4D NS 80mg/d $87 AVERT, MIRACL, PROVE IT, TNT, IDEAL, SPARCL, LEADe NS; 40mg po od/hs | 67; 81; 87 |
| **Fluvastatin** X LESCOL FLU (20 & 40mg cap)(80mg XL ✗▼) | ↓ 20 - 35% | | | | | | 20mg po hs; 40mg po hs; 40mg po bid cc LIPS (80mg/d) | 37; 49; 92 |
| **Lovastatin** LOV 1987 approved MEVACOR g X (20 scored, 40mg tab) ? in red yeast | ↓ 25 - 40% | | | | | | 20-40mg po hs 1° AFCAPS; 40mg po bid cc → 40-80mg/d POST CABG (cc=with meal ↑absorption)(80mg/d) | 34 - 73; 140 |
| **Pravastatin** PRA PRAVACHOL g X (10,20 & 40mg tablet) | ↓ 20 - 35% | | | | | | 20mg po hs (80mg/d); 40mg po hs 1° WOSCOPS; 2° → CARE, LIPID, PROSPER {Adjust for severe renal impairment[7]} | 36; 42 |
| **Rosuvastatin** ROS CRESTOR X (5,10,20,40mg tablet) | ↓ 40 - 65% | | | | | | 5-10mg od CORONA -Heart Failure & Gissi-HF & Aurora NS; 20mg po od 1° JUPITER; 40mg po od/hs Astronomer NS (40mg/d) | 53-56; 68; 78 |
| **Simvastatin** SIM ZOCOR g X (5,10,20,40, 80 rectangle mg tab) | ↓ 35 - 50% | | | | | | 20-40mg po hs 2° 4S, IDEAL, Accord; 40mg po hs 2° MRC/BHP: HPS; 80mg po hs A to Z, Search. Max ≤80mg/d esp. with DI, but ↑muscle SE at 40mg/d. | 41; 41; 41 |

**Pravastatin & Rosuvastatin few DIs**-some transplant meds like cyclosporin & GEM. **Fluvastatin** less DIs→ still with glyburide, phenytoin, rifampin & warfarin. **Atorvastatin similar** DIs but less dramatic. {**Primary Mechanisms**[3,11] **of DI**: PRA⇨sulfation; ATO/LOV/SIM⇨CYP-3A4; FLU⇨CYP-2C9}

| Generic/TRADE/ g=generic avail. Pregnancy | LDL | HDL | TG | SIDE EFFECTS /CI /COMMENTS/MONITOR | DRUG INTERACTIONS | THERAPEUTIC BENEFITS/USES | USUAL Dose Range | $ / Month |
|---|---|---|---|---|---|---|---|---|
| **FIBRATES** | | | | | | | | |
| **Bezafibrate** U BEZALIP g BEZ ☎▼ (200mg tab; 400mg SR tab) | LDL shifts to larger more buoyant forms[3]; ↓ 5-20% (LDL may ↑ if TG very high initially) | ↑ 10-20% | ↓ 20-50% | Common: GI upset, rash & **abdominal pain**. Less common: headache, pruritis, ↓ libido, dizzy, drowsy, arthralgia, ↑glucose, sleep/vision changes. Rare: ↓ renal fx, anemia, ↑ LFT's, **myopathy**, pancreatitis, impotence (reversible) & ↑**gallstones** by 1-2%[3]. **CI**: severe hepatic & renal Dx & ?**smoking** (↑ in cardiac events in smokers + gemfibrozil[VA-HIT]). **M**: CBC, Scr (↓ dose if ↑ Scr), Glucose, **LFT's** (?CK's). ☎ **Criteria**: if gemfibrozil/fenofibrate intolerance or ineffective ➜ bezafibrate | ↑ **toxicity/levels with**: cyclosporin, furosemide, MAOI's, probenecid, & **statins**. ↓ **effect by**: cholestyramine & colestipol (space by ≥ **2hrs**); rifampin. ↑ **effect of**: chlorpropamide, furosemide, homocysteine, **pioglitazone**, **repaglinide**, **rosiglitazone**, **sulfonylureas** & **warfarin**. | ✓↓Cholesterol & ↓TG; ↑HDL. ✓Combo with HMG/Niacin (to ↑ HDL & ↓ TG). ↓ Atherosclerosis. ✓**Type III** dyslipidemia. May be useful if: BIP, HHS ♦**TG >2.3**mmol/l -virtually **all** clinical benefits in patients with **diabetes & ↑ insulinemia**[7]. - lack all-cause mortality ↓ | 200mg po bid cc; 200mg po tid cc (600mg/d); 400mg SR po od 2° BIP | ☎▼ 65; 94; 69 |
| **Fenofibrate** LIPIDIL MICRO g 67 ✗▼ & 200mg cap; LIPIDIL SUPRA g (✗▼→ 100 & 160mg tab) | -fenofibrate may ↓LDL & TG & uric acid more than GEM[37] -& with statin combo may have ↓rhabdo than GEM | | | | | | FIELD NS; 200mg MICRO po od cc DAIS (200mg/d); 160mg SUPRA od cc Accord NS (160mg/d); Lipidil EZ 48 & 145mg tab | 43; ✗▼35; $20-45 |
| **Gemfibrozil** LOPID g GEM (300mg cap, 600mg tablet) | -current outcome evidence best with gemfibrozil -clofibrate was associated with ↑ mortality WHO | | | | | | 300mg po bid ac (ac=before meals); 600mg bid ac 1° HHS, 2° VA-HIT (1500mg/d) | 27; 57 |
| **RESINS** | | | | | | | | |
| **Cholestyramine** QUESTRAN g CME B (4gram regular, 4gram **light**) | Option: mix with metamucil & orange juice/lemonade the night before; refrigerate & give next day, ½ before breakfast & ½ before supper (shake well) | | | Common(<30%): **constipation**, nausea & bloating. Rare: hyperchloremic acidosis[CME] in peds/↓renal fx[3]. **CI**: biliary obstruction, dysbetalipoproteinemia, **TG >4.6** mmol/l (Caution TG >2.3 mmol/l); phenylketonurics ("light" & "orange granules"). ↑ fluid & bulk in diet→ **metamucil** may be required. **Mix** →**juice**/milk/water/applesauce **M**: LFT's, TGs | **Space other meds** (by ≥ **2hrs**) with resins since ↓ absorption of: amiodarone, cyclosporin, digoxin, diuretics, fat soluble vitamins (A,D,E,K), **folate**, **HMG's**, l-thyroxine, methotrexate, NSAIDS, propranolol, raloxifene, steroids, sulfonylureas, valproate, **warfarin**, mycophenolate | ✓↓ Cholesterol & ↓ LDL (Questran: **pregnancy** & age >2yr). ✓Combo with HMG (to ↓ LDL). ✓Pruritus esp. with certain biliary/liver dx. ✓Bile acid induced diarrhea | 4g po bid ac → +/- 8g/day POST CABG; 8g po bid ac (16-24g/d); **Start** 4g od-bid to ↑ tolerability | 97; 188 |
| **Colestipol** COLESTID B (5g granules; 7.5g **orange** granules; 1gm tab) | ↓ 15-30% | ↑ 3-5% | NO Change or **Possible INCREASE** | | | | 2g po bid ac; 4g po bid ac (20-30g/d); **Start** 2-5g od-bid to ↑ tolerability | 42; 77 |
| **OTHER** | | | | | | | | |
| **Ezetimibe**[16] 2003 approved C EZETROL 10mg tab rectangle ✓ | ↓18% 5mg ↓16% | ↑ 1.3% | ↓ 6% | ↓'s intestinal cholesterol absorption; synergistic ↓ in LDL **when added to statin** **CI**: hepatic **M**: LFT's | •levels ↑'d by cyclosporine, fibrates •resins interfere with absorbtion | ✓↓Cholesterol(+/-Statin or fenofibrate) -lacks outcome data Sands CIMT + | 10mg od with or without meal ENHANCE & SEAS NS {when added to statin, may allow ↓ statin dose} | ✓ 69 |
| **Nicotinic acid**[17,18] NIACIN (100ᶜ, 500mg tab): ✗⊗; NIASPAN (500 & 750mg, 1g ER tab); Advicor (500 & 1g/20mg LOV tab) ✗⊗; SR / No-flush niacin: non-Rx in Canada, less effective; better tolerated?; ↑ hepatic SE? C/A/X | ↓5-25%-shifts to larger buoyant forms[3]; ~2g niacin/day helps HDL & TG, but only higher doses affect LDL[3,7]; NICOTINAMIDE-NOT EFFECTIVE !! | ↑ 15-35% | ↓ 20-50% | **Flushing** (↓ by ASA/Advil 1/2hr pre), dry eyes, pruritus, headache, GI upset, ↑ LFT's, ↑uric acid & ↑ **glucose**, macular edema (rare). **CI**: severe peptic ulcer Dx, chronic liver Dx, overt diabetes & severe gout. **M**: LFT's, glucose, uric acid | •Low dose or 325mg/d **ASA**: useful on initiating/↑ niacin dose to ↓ flushing; some pretreat X3d. ASA may also ↑ niacin levels. **HMG's**: ?↑ myopathy if with lovastatin[19] | ✓↓Cholesterol & ↓TG; ↑HDL. ✓Combo with HMG/Fibrate (to ↑ HDL & ↓ TG). ✓Niacin deficiency (Pellagra) | **Start 50-100mg bid-tid** (↑ tolerability) **(increase weekly by ~100mg/week)**; 500mg po tid (**all with meals/snack**); 1500mg po bid 1° ADMIT; 1g po tid cc 2° CDP (3-6g/d); Niaspan ER 500-750mg-2g Arbiter 6-Halts hs; Advicor 500mgER/20mg (2gER/40mg hs) | 9; 12; 16; 16; ✗⊗86; ✗⊗48(70) |

**Major RISK Factors**[1,2,22]: **Diabetes** (most), Smoking, Hypertension (≥140/90/BP meds), Low HDL≤ 1, Family hx (~2x 10yr CVD Risk) 1st degree relative (Age<60) CAD, Age(♂≥45, ♀≥55). **MODIFIABLE** ↑BP, ↑Lipid/**LDL**, Obesity: BMI>25 (>23 Asian), Waist(♂>102cm, 40"; ♀>88cm, 35"), Diet, Smoking, Alcohol & sedentary lifestyle. **Screen**: q1-3yr ♂≥40, ♀≥50 or postmenopausal; pts with CAD/PVD/atherosclerosis/stroke/HIV, diabetes, xanthomata or other dyslipidemia stigmata; HTN; obesity; dyspnea; family hx dyslipidemia/CAD even for kids; smoker; erectile dysfx; Lupus/RA/Psoriasis or if CKD renal.

**DRUG INDUCED HYPERLIPIDEMIA**[20,21]: alcohol, amiodarone, beta-blockers (non ISA), carbamazepine, clozapine, cyclosporin, danazol, contraceptives esp. levonorgestrel, efavirenz, phenytoin, phenobarb., protease inhibitors, progestins, retinoids, steroids, temsirolimus & thiazides≥50mg/d.

**CHOICE of AGENT**: ↑↑LDL⇨HMG +/- resin +/-ezetimibe; ↑↑LDL & ↑TG⇨HMG; ↑↑LDL & ↓HDL⇨HMG +/- fibrate/niacin; **Normal LDL & ↑↑TG**⇨fibrate/niacin/omega 3 (fatty acid 22) or combo; **Normal LDL & ↓HDL**⇨fibrate/niacin or combo

**TARGETS 2009**[23]: **HIGH Risk** (10yr CVD risk **≥20%**) **Target LDL<2** or ↓LDL≥50% **+Apo B** <0.8 (or Total Chol/HDL<4) {**High risk→ ALL pts with CAD,CVD,PAD; most with DIABETES** (♂>45yr, ♀>50yr, younger with risk factors) **& chronic renal dx** (eGFR<30ml/min)}

for patients at: (Primary target: LDL) **MODERATE Risk***(10yr CVD risk **10-19%** **Treat if LDL>3.5 ⇒Target LDL <2** or ↓LDL ≥50% or Total Chol/HDL>5 **+**Apo B <0.8). **LOW Risk** (10yr CVD risk **<10%** **Treat if LDL≥5** or Total Chol/HDL >6⇒Target LDL ↓LDL ≥50% {Ensure **2x** CVD risk if family hx}

*If LDL is <3.5, then for ♂>50yr or ♀>60yr check **hsCRP** (check twice 2 weeks apart, not during acute illness), **if hsCRP>2 mg/l→then consider treatment**. (Jupiter trial)

**High risk pts: treat meds & lifestyle changes concomitantly. Lower risk pts: use meds after 3-6months of lifestyle changes.** Low/Mod risk: suggest ↓**LDL≥50%** (but simv 40mg, ator 10mg & prav 40mg has strong outcome data).

♦ ***Lifestyle***: **DIET** (↓sodium, fat & calories), **EXERCISE**, ↑fiber, **alcohol** (moderate use) **& stop SMOKING!** (will also ↑HDL). Consider **ASA** ~81mg/d. ***Highest*** risk benefit most!

**Metabolic Sx**: Abd obesity (ethnic dependent) ♂≥94cm, ♀≥80cm; & (2 or more of) **TG** ≥1.7; **HDL** ♂<1, ♀<1.3; **BP**>130/85; **Glucose** (fasting)>5.6mmol/l. ☎ EDS Sask. ✗ Non-formulary SK ✓prior NIHB ⊗not covered NIHB ▼covered NIHB ✓Indication/Use **DI**=Drug Interaction **Dx**=disease **dysfx**=dysfunction

**GI**=stomach **HDL**=high density lipoprotein **HMG** CoA reductase inhib→STATIN **LDL**=low density lipoprotein **NS**=non significant **SE**=side effect **TG**=triglyceride ⇒↓dose for renal dysfx. **Baseline Monitoring**: Fasting lipid, glucose, TSH, liver function, creatinine, creatine kinase, apoB & apoAI per clinical judgment.

Caution: High statin dose in **lower** risk pt. Unclear if benefit solely from achievement of target eg. ↓LDL alone [24 & page14] **+Apo B**: Alternate to LDL, non fasting useful, esp. if ↑TG/metabolic Sx/on statin. **Optimal TG**<1.5mmol/l (if >10mmol/l ↑pancreatitis; Tx: ↓refined carbohydrate, ↓alcohol, ↓weight, ↑exercise & ↑omega-3 fatty acids).

**Rhabdomyolysis** Statin Risk Factors (NNH=22,700/yr but ↑ if): ↓renal fx, drug interaction (eg. fibrate NNH=1670/yr, amiodarone, azole antifungal, cyclosporine, macrolide, niacin & protease inhibitor), high statin dose, pts with diabetes, Asians, elderly & hypothyroidism. Mortality ~10%.

# Post-MI – Drug & Dosage Considerations [1]

| Class | POST-MI TARGET DOSES (CONTROLLED TRIALS) | $/30d | BENEFITS | RISKS | COMMENTS |
|---|---|---|---|---|---|
| ACEI | Ramipril ALTACE (new generic) 10mg HS HOPE 2.5mg BID AIRE 3<br>Trandolapril MAVIK 4mg OD TRACE 4<br>Lisinopril ZESTRIL/PRINIVIL 10mg OD GISSI-3 5<br>(high dose) ~35mg OD ATLAS 6 (HF)<br>Perindopril COVERSYL 8mg OD EUROPA 7<br>Enalapril VASOTEC 20mg OD CONSENSUS-II 8<br>Captopril CAPOTEN 50mg TID SAVE 9, BID in ISIS4 10 | 29<br>42<br>28<br>60<br>46<br>28<br>62 | • all-cause mortality: 17-29% RRR when started 2-16 days after event & continued for 4-5 yrs in pts with LV dysfx AIRE, TRACE, SAVE; {TRACE: NNT=13 over 4yrs 42.3 vs 34.7%, n=1749}<br>• prevents ventricular remodeling; ↓proteinuria<br>• 16% RRR in all cause mortality when started in high risk pts with remote history of MI and continued for 5 years HOPE; NNT HOPE = 56 | • Adverse effects include cough <10%, hypotension/dizzy ~2%, hyperkalemia ~2-11%, renal insufficiency (in pts with renal artery stenosis) & angioedema 0.4%, Blacks 0.7% 11; taste changes, rash; Rare: pancreatitis & blood dyscrasias. | • AHA STEMI Guidelines 2007 suggest to use ACE inhibitors in **all pts indefinitely** if **EF≤0.4** & for those with hypertension, diabetes & CKD. Most benefit if anterior infarction, pulmonary congestion or ↑HR, in the absence of hypotension SBP <100mm Hg or < 30mm Hg below baseline<br>• Contraindicated in pts with bilateral renal artery stenosis (or unilateral stenosis if only 1 kidney), history of angioedema to ACEI & pregnancy<br>• Combo ACEI+ARB: benefit in persistent HF CHARM (but caution of ↑SE & no greater efficacy MI trial; VALIANT) |
| | **Generally start low-dose & titrate up to target dose if tolerated. eg. ramipril 2.5mg OD x1wk, 5mg od x3wk then 10mg od** HOPE >50% POST MI | | | | |
| ARB | Valsartan DIOVAN 160mg BID VALIANT 12<br>Candesartan ATACAND 32mg OD CHARM (HF trial) 13,14 | 92<br>48 | • all-cause mortality: valsartan, captopril 50mg TID, or combo equally effective VALIANT, n=14703, ~2yr<br>• ↓ proteinuria 15 even in pts with SCr<265 16, 17 | Angioedema (17 of 26 pts safely put on ARB after ACEI) 18;<br>More: ↓BP & ↑SCr 4.9 vs 3% VALIANT<br>Less: cough 1.7 vs 5% VALIANT, rash & taste changes than ACEI. VALIANT | • **Alternative if ACEI not tolerated & HF/LVEF<0.4** [1] (ARB: less cough & somewhat less angioedma)<br>• captopril 50mg TID reduced CV-death in post-MI pts more than losartan 50mg OD OPTIMAAL 19 |
| | **Generally start low-dose & titrate up to target dose if tolerated. eg. candesartan 4-8mg od, doubling ~q2wk →32mg od** (>50% Ischemic Heart Disease in the CHARM Heart Failure trial) | | | | |
| β-BLOCKER | Metoprolol♥ LOPRESSOR 100mg BID HJALMARSON 20<br>≤200mg SR OD MERIT-HF 21,22,23,24<br>Atenolol♥ TENORMIN 100mg OD ISIS-1 25<br>Carvedilol COREG ☎ ▼ 25mg BID with food CAPRICORN 26<br>Propranolol INDERAL 60-80mg TID BHAT 27<br>Timolol BLOCADREN 10mg BID NMCG 28<br>Acebutolol♥ & ISA MONITAN 200mg BID APSI 29 | 18<br>21<br>24<br>53<br>14<br>27<br>22 | • all-cause mortality: 23% RRR when started in any pt within 5-28 days of MI & continued for up to 4yr; Meta-analysis: NNT=42 over 2yr (best long-term evidence with propranolol, metoprolol & timolol) FREEMANTLE n=24,974 30<br>• ↓ sudden death, reinfarction & arrhythmias<br>• Less benefit: ISA agents (pindolol; acebutolol?) 1,31<br>• Cardioselective agents (♥) preferred for mild asthma & diabetes | SE: 32 ↓BP, ↓HR, dizziness, fatigue <10%, insomnia, vivid dreams & sexual dysfx ~4%; PAD, ?↑ psoriasis, cold extremities; may mask hypoglycemia. Metoprolol IV CCS-2 trial 33: ↑ cardiogenic **shock** esp. in those with HF or hypotension. | • AHA STEMI Guideline 2007 suggest to use ß-blockers in **all pts indefinitely** MI, ACS, LV dysfunction {benefit less in low-risk pts eg. ~normal left ventricular fx, successful reperfusion, absence of significant ventricular arrhythmias}<br>• Contraindicated in pts with severe/poorly controlled asthma, $2^{nd}$ or $3^{rd}$ degree heart block or a PR>0.24sec, HR<50, SBP <90, decompensated HF, 34 or on cocaine.<br>• some data suggests carvedilol better than metoprolol but equivalent doses may not have been used HF trial; COMET 35<br>• CNS adverse effects (depression, impotence, fatigue) overestimated; common in placebo groups & may not be solely related to beta-blockers 30 |
| | **Start low-dose & titrate up to target dose if tolerated, eg. metoprolol 12.5mg BID; double dose ↑ q2wk.** (atenolol 25mg OD; carvedilol 3.125mg BID).<br>**Tolerability**: Gradual dose titration & pt education regarding initial side effects improves tolerability. (e.g. 64% of MERIT-HF reached metoprolol 200mg/d) 22<br>**If withdrawing** beta-blocker therapy, do so gradually if possible over a few weeks to minimize risk of precipitating angina/MI. | | | | |
| STATINS | Simvastatin ZOCOR 20-40mg OD 4S 36, HPS 37<br>Atorvastatin LIPITOR 10mg OD ASCOT (not post-MI) 38<br>(high-dose in ACS) 80mg OD PROVE IT 39,40<br>Pravastatin PRAVACHOL 40mg OD LIPID 41, CARE 42<br>Rosuvastatin CRESTOR -outcome trial Jupiter 20mg od; 43,44 10mg OD<br>Higher levels in Asians; rhabdomyolysis cases at doses ≥10mg/d) | 41<br>67<br>87<br>42<br>56 | • all-cause mortality: 22-29% RRR in post MI pts with ↑ cholesterol (LDL 3.9-4.9mmol/L) 4S, LIPID; 4S NNT=30 11.5 vs 8.2%, n=4444 simvastain 20-40mg/d, 5.4yr<br>• ↓ in major CV events NNT=18 & stroke NNT=62 in pts at high CV risk (over 5 years) HPS 34<br>• most trials enrolled pts >3months post-MI HPS, LIPID, CARE<br>• No major statin trial enrolled pts age >82yrs 45 | • Adverse effects include GI upset, muscle aches, elevated LFTs <2%, myopathy <1%, rhabdomyolysis <0.2%, impotence; Rare: lupus-like symptoms, periph neuropathy. | • AHA STEMI Guidelines 2007 suggest to use statins **in all patients** (even when baseline LDL < 2.5mmol/L)<br>• ATP-3 LDL target option: 1.8 mmol/L if very high risk 46<br>• If TG >5.6mmol/L, consider niacin or fibrate<br>• Options for low HDL: lifestyle (exercise, ↓wt, smoking), fibrate (gemfibrozil 600mg BID VA-HIT $61) 47 or niacin<br>• Contraindicated in pts with active liver disease, high alcohol consumption & pregnancy |
| | **May start at target dose unless high risk for side effects** (ie. elderly, renal/hepatic dysfx, niacin or fibrate combos, drug interactions, high dose or hx of intolerance) | | | | |
| ANTI-PLATELET | ASA (160-325mg po x1 acute STEMI) **80-162mg OD** ISIS-2 48<br>Generally start at ~ 81mg enteric coated OD; {ASA 75-100mg as effective/less bleeding than 325mg, especially with Plavix CURE} 49<br>{see also RxFiles Antiplatelet & Antithrombotic Chart 50}<br>Clopidogrel PLAVIX ☎♥ 75mg OD CURE 51, CAPRIE 52, CLARITY 53 COMMIT/CCS-2 54, CHARISMA<br>Warfarin COUMADIN 1-10mg OD WARIS II 55 | 5<br><br><br>99<br><br>15 | • all-cause mortality: 10% RRR, NNT=91 over 2yr ATC<br>• 25% RRR in vascular events in previous MI pts treated with antiplatelets x 27months ATC 56<br>• STEMI: add clopidogrel 75mg od ≥2-4wk +ASA<br>• Stenting→ If on ASA+**warfarin** INR 2-3 for anticoagulation then D/C Plavix after: ≥1month-bare metal; ≥3month-sirolimus; ≥6month-paclitaxel. If only on ASA + Plavix →then D/C Plavix after ~1 yr. [1]<br>ACC'09: if BMS or DES stent use clopidogel for ≥ 12 months.<br>Initially ↑ASA 162-325mg if PCI+stent: Min 1mo→bare metal, 3mo→sirolimus & 6mo→paclitaxel AHA 07<br>Initially if PCI+DES stent ↑ASA 325mg x 3month then ≤100mg; + Plavix 75mg ≥12month Chest 08<br>• If on all 3 recommend: warfarin INR2-2.5, clopidogrel & ASA 81mg | • Adverse effects: GI upset, hypersensitivity, GI bleed; major bleed.<br>• Maj bleed/ hemorrhagic stroke ~ 0.5% / 5 years (NNH=200) ATC, USPSTF 57<br>{high risk pts, i.e. CAPRIE ASA 325mg/d 1.9 yrs; Bleeding: GI= 2.7%; All severe = 1.6%} 48 | • AHA STEMI Guidelines 2007 suggest **ASA indefinitely** 75 to 162 mg/d if not contraindicated. (ASA 75-165mg Chest'08)<br>• Contraindicated in pts with recent/active bleeding, major GI intolerance or history of ASA allergy<br>• For true ASA allergy pts consider clopidogrel 75mg OD or warfarin (INR target **2-3**) as useful alternatives. [1]<br>• Acute STEMI: clopidogrel 300mg load if ≤75yr; 75mg od ≥2-4wks<br>• Combo: ASA+PLAVIX: ↑efficacy in ACS/stents but ↑bleeds {CURE NNT=48, NNH 99, over 9 months; MATCH 58 post stroke NNH=77; CHARISMA in high CV risk pts, no benefit, but ↑ moderate bleeding NNH=125}<br>• If triple tx: ASA 81mg + Clopidogrel + Warf ⇒aim for INR of 2-2.5 |

**OTHER**: **Spironolactone** ALDACTONE 12.5-25mg OD $9 severe HF Class III-IV RALES 59; DI: ↑ K+ with ACEI +/or ARB +/or NSAID, ∴ monitor K+ avoid if K+≥5mmol/L & **renal fx**. {Eplerenone new Canada: 25& 50mg tab $95: in select post-MI pt with LV dysfx EPHESUS 60}

$=retail cost ☎=Exceptional Drug Status ♂=male ♀=female **A1C**=glycosylated hemoglobin **ACEI**=angiotensin converting enzyme inhibitor **ARB**=angiotensin receptor blocker **ATC**=Antithrombotic Trialists' Collaboration **ARR**=absolute risk reduction **BMI**=body mass index **BP**=blood pressure **CK**=creatine kinase **CV**=cardiovascular **DI**=drug interaction **EF**=Ejection Fraction **Fx**=function **FPG**=fasting plasma glucose **GI**=stomach **HF**=heart failure **HQC**=Health Quality Council **HR**=heart rate **Hx**=history **K+**=potassium **LV**=left ventricular **MI**=myocardial infarction **NNT(H)**=number needed to treat (harm) **PAD**=peripheral arterial disease **PPBG**=postprandial blood glucose **Pts**=patients **RRR**=relative risk reduction **SCr**=Serum creatinine **TG**=triglycerides **wk**=week **wt**=weight

**RISK Factors**: 61,63 **Cholesterol: ↑LDL** (ApoB/ApoA1 ratio used in INTERHEART), **Smoking**, **Diabetes**, ↑**BP** esp. systolic, **Abdominal obesity**: **waist/hip ratio** (♂ ≥0.9; ♀ ≥0.85), BMI >25, Waist size 62 (♂ >102cm, 40inch; ♀ >89cm, 35inch), **stress** & **depression**; ?migraine ♀with aura **lack of vegetables, fruits, exercise** (30-60mins ≥5-7x/week) & **alcohol** (0-2drinks/d ♂=14/week ♀=9/week); Low HDL ≤1, Family Hx of premature heart dx (Age: ♂ <55, ♀ <65) 61, Microalbuminuria 61, renal dysfx 63 & Age (♂ >55, ♀ >65). not moderate coffee intake 63; cocaine abuse.

**Targets**: **BP** Canadian 2010 (64): General <**140/90**; Diabetes < **130/80** **LIPID** Canadian 2009 (65) Post MI/High Risk→ LDL<**2** or ↓ by ≥50%; Total Cholesterol/HDL Ratio<**4** (If serum sodium <136 mEq/L then poorer prognosis)

**GLUCOSE**: Canadian 2008 (66) Target for most: **A1C ≤7%**; **FPG 4-7** mmol/L; **PPBG** 2hr post **5-10** mmol/L **if** can be done **safely** without hypoglycemia.

*Post-MI*: **Do Not** recommend: NSAID/Cox 2's, vitamin C or E & HRT [1]
**Do...: Lifestyle changes for DIET, EXERCISE & stop SMOKING!**

About 30% of MI patients die before receiving medical attention (mainly from ventricular fibrillation). In-hospital mortality rates went from 11.2% in 1990 to 4.6% in 2005 Grace. REFERENCES AVAIL. at www.RxFiles.ca

# QT PROLONGATION and TORSADES DE POINTES: DRUGS and SUDDEN DEATH

## What is Torsades de Pointes (TdP)?

- TdP or "twisting of the points" refers to a polymorphic ventricular tachycardia
- It is associated with a prolonged $QT_c$ interval and bradycardia; patients may also report shortness of breath or syncope
- TdP is thought to be caused by early after-depolarizations during prolonged repolarization[1]
- It is often self-limiting but may be **potentially fatal**, sometimes leading to syncope and/or sudden death
- TdP can be either 1° (congenital) or 2° (acquired) due to metabolic disturbances, medical conditions, or **most commonly**, drugs [1,10]
- Recent USA black box **FDA WARNINGS** due to QT prolongation: amiodarone, cisapride, droperidol, itraconazole & thioridazine [13]
- Recent drug **FDA REMOVALS** due to QT prolongation: astemizole (Hismanal), grepafloxacin (Raxar) & terfenadine (Seldane). [13]

## Who is at risk?[1-6,14]

- The "**multiple hit**" theory suggests that a culmination of several factors is required to induce TdP [2]
- Generally, these factors promote early after-depolarizations or prolongation of the action potential [1]

**Table 1: Risk Factors for QT interval Prolongation and TdP [1-6]** * greatest significance

| Cardiac (underlying conditions) | Metabolic | Other |
|---|---|---|
| Bradycardia < 50 bpm | Altered nutritional status: | ***Age** - ↑ risk with ↑ age |
| ***Cardiomyopathy**: | Alcoholism | Cerebrovascular disease |
| Heart failure | **Anorexia**, starvation | ***Female sex** –sex hormones regulate channel expression |
| Left ventricular hypertrophy | Diabetes | |
| *Myocardial infarction | Electrolyte disturbances: | **Hypothyroidism** |
| ***Congenital long QT interval** | **Hypokalemia** | Obesity |
| (incidence ~ 1 / 2,500)[8, AHA-Hospital'10] | **Hypomagnesemia** | Pituitary insufficiency |
| Hypertension | Hypocalcemia | Poisoning –arsenic, organophosphates, nerve gas |
| Ischemic heart disease | Hypoglycemia | **Renal** & liver disease |
| | Hypothermia | ***DRUGS (see Table 2), esp. at high-dose & if IV** |

## Which drugs are implicated?

- Many **drugs** from a variety of therapeutic classes have been associated with **QT interval prolongation** and/or TdP **(see table)**
- All of these drugs have in common their ability to block the *I* kr potassium channel; this results in increased repolarization time and a prolonged QT interval (beginning of QRS complex to end of T wave) on ECG.[1] Inward Na+ and Ca+ influx channels may also be affected [8]
- Prolongation of the QT interval is thought to be **dose-related** and can occur within therapeutic range for some agents (eg amiodarone) but only at supra-therapeutic concentrations for others (eg. clarithromycin)
- Effects of different drugs can be **additive** {Besides effect on QT & DI's, a metabolic effect may be important eg. ↓ $K^+$ ⇒ **diuretics, laxatives**}.
- Since many of these drugs are also metabolized by the **cytochrome P450 system**, serious and sometimes lethal drug interactions can occur when combined with drugs which **inhibit** or compete for binding to these isoenzymes (see Table 2 column 5)

## How to avoid trouble:[2,6]

- **Identify those at risk** (Table 1); be aware however, that individuals' vulnerability can vary greatly due to a complexity of genetic and environmental factors which are not completely understood. Check family hx for syncope!
- **For patients with major or multiple risk factors, obtain a baseline ECG** and determine the QTc interval (corrected for heart rate – equation described elsewhere[7]). Long QTc interval is >470ms postpubertal males & >480ms for postpubertal females.
  - **Short [2] QTc ≤ 0.41 sec ..........................VERY LOW RISK**
    -may not require ECG monitoring after initiating a QT-prolonging agent but should have if additional risk factors develop or if a drug interaction is likely
  - **Intermediate QTc 0.42-0.44 sec .........LOW - MODERATE RISK**
    - repeat ECG after initiating any QT prolonging agent, again at steady state, weekly for 1st month, then q6months and when any other QT prolonging agent is added or if a drug interaction is likely
    - if QTc >0.45 sec, reduce dosages or avoid these agents and use alternatives
  - **Prolonged QTc ≥0.45 sec ...................MODERATE - HIGH RISK**
    - repeat ECG after initiating any QT prolonging agent, again at steady state, weekly for 1st month, then q6months and when any other QT prolonging agent is added or if a drug interaction is likely
    - if **QTc >0.50 sec or > 60ms over baseline avoid** these agents and use alternatives
    - regular **monitoring of serum K+ and Mg+** also advised

**Rule of thumb**[8]**: A QTc change of < 10msec is acceptable as long as there are no other significant risk factors; If the QTc change is >10msec, reduce dosage or eliminate the drug(s), monitor more closely.**





## How to treat TdP:

**Emergency:** [9]

- *Do not use standard antiarrhythmic agents*
- Give **magnesium** sulphate 2 grams IV over 2 minutes. If ineffective, consider isoproterenol , dobutamine, or atropine IV
- Consider giving potassium if serum K+ is low; bicarbonate for TCP (phencyclidine) or quinidine poisoning
- Lidocaine & phenytoin have also been used, alternatives are cardiac pacing & isoproterenol.

**Later:**

- Stop the offending agent
- Maintain normal K+ , Mg++ and $HCO_3^-$
- Keep out of trouble as above

**Table 2: Drugs which can prolong QT Interval [1,3,6,9,12,13,14]** -see www.torsades.org

| Cardiovascular Agents | CNS Agents / Psychotropics | Anti-Infective Agents | Miscellaneous Agents | Cytochrome P450 Inhibitors (DIs: Column 5) |
|---|---|---|---|---|
| **Anti-arrhythmics**<br>**Amiodarone** (low risk of TdP compared to other class III agents such as sotalol; however potential for DIs)<br>**Bepridil**<br>Bretylium<br>**Disopyramide**<br>**Dofetilide**<br>**Dronedarone**<br>**Flecainide**<br>**Ibutilide**<br>**Mexiletine**<br>**Procainamide**<br>**Propafenone**<br>**Quinidine** less at ↑ dose<br>**Sotalol**<br><br>Dobutamine<br>Dopamine<br>Isradipine<br>Moexipril/HCTZ<br>Nicardipine<br>Norepinephrine<br>Ranolazine<br>-------------------------<br>**ADHD agents**<br>Amphetamine<br>Atomoxetine<br>Dextroamphetamine<br>Lisdexamfetamine<br>Methylphenidate &Dex-<br>**Antiemetics**<br>**Dolasetron**<br>**Domperidone**<br>Droperidol<br>Granisetron<br>Metoclopramide<br>Ondansetron<br>Promethazine | **Anticonvulsants**<br>Felbamate, Fosphenytoin, Lithium<br>**Antipsychotics**<br>Asenapine<br>Aripiprazole<br>Butyrophenones<br>**Haloperidol** esp. with ↑ dose or IV<br>Clozapine<br>**Phenothiazines (PZs)**<br>**Chlorpromazine**<br>**Mesoridazine**<br>Perphenazine<br>**Thioridazine**<br>Iloperidone<br>Paliperidone<br>**Pimozide**<br>*Quetiapine*<br>*Risperidone*<br>Thioxanthines<br>**Ziprasidone**<br>Chloral Hydrate<br>Mirtazapine<br>**SSRIs**<br>Citalopram (in overdose)<br>Escitalopram (in overdose)<br>Fluoxetine<br>Paroxetine (esp. ↑ pimozide)<br>Sertraline<br>**SNRI**<br>Des & -venlafaxine<br>**TCAs**<br>**Amitriptyline**<br>**Amoxapine**<br>**Clomipramine**<br>**Desipramine**<br>**Doxepin**<br>**Imipramine**<br>**Maprotiline**<br>**Nortriptyline**<br>**Protripyline**<br>**Trimipramine** | **Antibiotics**<br>Cotrimoxazole<br>Fluoroquinolones<br>Gatifloxacin<br>Gemifloxacin<br>Levofloxacin<br>Moxifloxacin<br>Norfloxacin<br>Ofloxacin<br>**Sparfloxacin**<br>Macrolides<br>Azithromycin<br>**Clarithromycin**<br>**Erythromycin** [11]<br>Roxithromycin<br>Telavancin<br>Telithromycin<br><br>**Azole Antifungals**<br>*Fluconazole*<br>Itraconazole<br>Ketoconazole<br>Posaconazole<br>Voriconazole<br><br>**Antimalarials**<br>Artemether-lumefantrine<br>**Chloroquine**<br>**Halofantrine**<br>Mefloquine<br>Quinine<br><br>**Pentamidine** | Alfuzosin, Amantidine,<br>**Arsenic** trioxide,<br>Atazanavir,<br>**Cisapride**(Special Access)<br>Cocaine, Cyclosporin,<br>dasatinib, Degarelix,<br>donepezil, Foscarnet,<br>gallantamine, Ginseng,<br>Hydroxyzine, Indapamide,<br>Kaletra, Lapatinib,<br>Levomethadyl, Lopinavir,<br>**Methadone,** Midodrine,<br>nilotinib, Octreotide,<br>Orphenadrine, Oxytocin,<br>Pazopanib,<br>Phenylephrine<br>**Probucol**<br>Pseudoephedrine<br>Ritodrine, Ritonavir<br>Romidepsin<br>Saquinavir, Sibutramine<br>Solifenacin, Sunitinib<br>Tacrolimus, Tamoxifen<br>Tizanidine, Tolterodine,<br>Triptans (Recently off QT list)<br>Vardenafil<br>**Antihistamines**<br>*Diphenhydramine*<br>*Clemastine*<br>*Loratidine*(but no reports)<br>Withdrawn:<br>Astemizole & terfenadine<br>**Appetite suppressant**<br>Ephedrine, Fenfluramine<br>Phentermine, Sibutramine<br>**Bronchodilators**<br>Epinephrine<br>Isoproterenol<br>Levalbuterol<br>Metaproterenol<br>Salbutamol/albuterol<br>Salmeterol<br>Terbutaline | **CYP3A4**<br>**amiodarone**<br>**Azole antifungals:**<br>*Fluconazole*<br>Itraconazole<br>Ketoconazole<br>**Calcium channel blocker**:<br>Diltiazem<br>Verapamil<br>Cimetidine<br>**Ciprofloxacin**<br>Grapefruit juice<br>**HIV: protease inhibitors**<br>**Macrolides:**<br>**Erythromycin**<br>Clarithromycin<br>Troleandomycin<br>(not with Azithromycin)<br>Methadone<br>Telithromycin<br>**SSRI's:**<br>Fluvoxamine<br>Norfluoxetine<br>Nefazodone<br>**Paroxetine**<br>Trazodone<br>**CYP2D6**<br>Beta Blockers (BBs)<br>Haloperidol<br>Phenothiazines<br>Quinidine<br>SSRIs (not interact with citalopram)<br>Terbinafine<br>TCAs<br>-------------------------<br>*less significant*<br>**CYP1A2**<br>Fluoroquinolones<br>Fluvoxamine<br>Grapefruit juice |

**AVOID COMBINATIONS of PHENOTHIAZINES with TCAs, BETA BLOCKERS, and ANTICONVULSANTS**

**Some drugs** (eg. erythromycin & amiodarone) **prolong the QT Interval AND act as inhibitors to potentially increase levels or QT effects of concomitant medications.**

**BOLD=major significance (well-documented)** REGULAR=low-moderate significance (fewer case reports) *ITALIC=minor significance (theoretical, few if any case reports)*

{**Long QT syndrome**: a familial condition associated with recurrent syncope & sudden cardiac death resulting from ventricular arrhythmias; may be misdiagnosed as epilepsy. Triggers for arrhythmias: meds that prolong the QT interval or subtype specific factors such as swimming & other exercise (long QT1), auditory stimuli & emotional stress (long QT2), & rest or sleep (long QT3). **β blockers** are usually effective; **implantable cardioverter defibrillators** reserved for people deemed at high risk or refractory to medical treatment. Thoracoscopic left cardiac sympathectomy an option -highly effective & useful if β blockers not tolerated or an implantable cardioverter defibrillator is contraindicated.} [Abrams 2010]

**References:**


1. Wolbrette D. Drugs that cause TdP & increase the risk of sudden cardiac death. Curr Card Reports 2004; 6: 379-84.
2. Wojciech Z & Lin D. Antipsychotic drugs and QT interval prolongation. Psychiatr Q 2003; 74(3): 291-306.
3. Taylor D. Antipsychotics and QT prolongation. Acta Psychiatr Scand 2003;107:85-95.
4. Vieweg W. New generation antipsychotic drugs abd QTc interval prolongation. Prim Care Companion J Clin Psychiatry 2003;5 (5):205-15.
5. Roden D. Drug-induced prolongation of the QT interval. N Engl J Med 2004; 350: 1013-22.
6. Crouch M et al. Clinical relevance & management of drug-related QT interval prolongation. Pharmacotherapy 2003; 23(7):881-908.
7. Witchel H et al. Psychotropic drugs, cardiac arrhythmia, & sudden death. J Clin Psychopharmacol 2003; 23(1):58-77.
8. Brown et al. Cardiovascular effects of anti-psychotics. Clin Pharmacokinet 2004; 43(1): 38-56 (see Roden NEJM'08)
9. Gowda RM, et al. Torsade de pointes: the clinical considerations. Int J Cardiol. 2004;96:1
10. Sudden Arrhythmia Death Syndromes Foundation The long QT syndrome. SADS Foundation http://www.sads.org/LQTflyer.pdf (Cardiac Arrhythmia Reasearch & Education Foundation www.longqt.org)
11. Ray WA, et al. Oral erythromycin & the risk of sudden death from cardiac causes. N Engl J Med. 2004 Sep 9;351(11):1089-96.
12. Liu BA, Juurlink DN. Drugs and the QT interval - caveat doctor. N Engl J Med. 2004 Sep 9;351(11):1053-6.
13. Woeffel JA. Drug-Induced Long QT Interval & Sudden Cardiac Death. Pharmacist's Letter Nov 2004;20:201111
14. Al-Khatib SM, LaPointe NM, Kramer JM, Califf RM. What clinicians should know about the QT interval. JAMA. 2003 Apr 23-30;289(16):2120-7. Review. Erratum in: JAMA. 2003 Sep 10;290(10):1318.

**Basic Care**
- D/C acnegenic moisturizers/substances; • Use oil free makeup
- D/C manual lesions manipulation • Avoid stress, astringents, scrubs
- **Shaving:** shave area lightly, only once & follow grain of hair growth
- **Wash face:** preferably **once daily** & no more than BID with… mild soap (e.g., Glycerin Bar, Petrophyllic, Pears, Aveeno, Dove & Olay) and water or soapless cleanser (e.g., Cetaphil, Spectro Jel)
- **Avoid Soaps:** such as Dial, Irish Spring, Ivory, & Zest that are more irritating, & associated with erythema, dryness, & itching [1]
- Moisturizers – in dry seasons (e.g. Complex-15 Moisturizing Lotion)
- **Sunlight:** evidence lacking [2]; may be helpful for some; however, long-term exposure ↑ risk of skin cancer.
- **Diet:** chocolate=MYTH; individualize diet recommendations

**Suggested Step-wise Approach for Initial Therapy**[3,4,5,6,7,8,9] **{Step-down in treatment intensity for maintenance following remission}**

Severity of Acne: Mild → Severe

- **Isotretinoin** Accutane, Clarus {Avoid topicals as ↑ drying effect & not tolerated}
- Systemic antibiotics ± Topicals {Resistance concerns: systemic ABX "pulse therapy" for more severe/inflammatory acne}
- **Women**: Oral Contraceptives (COCs) or Diane 35 {Spironolactone may be an alternative}; ± Topicals
- **If papulopustular (inflammatory) +/- comedonal: Add topical ABX to BP** [10](may need lower BP strength to ↓ dryness); ± retinoid e.g. combo topical products (Benzamycin, Clindoxyl / BenzaClin) ± retinoid' OR Stievamycin. To maintain, may step down to retinoid. **If comedonal (white-blackheads):** Start **topical retinoid** {tretinoin 0.025-0.05% has cost advantage; adapalene less irritating}; may add BP.
- 1) General measures (discontinue drying agents); 2) Initiation of **Benzoyl Peroxide (BP) 2.5% or 5% $H_2O$-based** gel e.g. Panoxyl Aquagel or 4% Solugel; or lotion {if starting at 2.5%, consider increase to 5% $H_2O$-based BP; acetone- or alcohol-based gel option if oily skin.} Patient education important!!!

| Severity | MILD | MODERATE | SEVERE |
|---|---|---|---|
| Description[11] | < 20 comedones (whitehead/blackhead), or <15 inflammatory papules, or a lesion count <30 | 15-50 papules & pustules with comedone; cysts are rare; Total lesion count may range from 30-125 | Primarily nodules & cysts; also present are comedones, papules & pustules or total lesion count of > 125. Scarring. |

**GENERAL APPROACH for topical therapies: Oily skin → Use solution or gel; Dry skin → Use cream or lotions. Potency of a given drug in various vehicles: Solution > gel > cream / lotion. Apply to affected areas, not just lesions!!!**

**Context**: affects 85% of those age 12-24; duration varies ~4+ yrs. **Concerns include**: scarring, pain, self esteem, social life, suicide. **Contributing factors**: hormonal, mechanical, contact, environmental, emotions, drugs. **Family hx** predictive of acne severity/duration.

## Acne - TOPICALS [12,13,14]

www.RxFiles.ca

| | Generic/TRADE g=generic avail.<br>-Strength/forms, **Pregnancy Category**[15] | Side effects (SE)/ Contraindications CI | Response Time<br>Allow at least 8 wks! | √ = therapeutic use / ☒= Disadvantage / Comments / Drug Interactions DI / Monitor M | USUAL DOSE | $ per pkg |
|---|---|---|---|---|---|---|
| **Antibacterial, Keratolytic** | **Benzoyl Peroxide** = BP (≤ 5% OTC)<br>H2O-based: **Solugel**▼x 4%, 8% gel; **Benzac^ AC**▼ or **W**▼ 5%x, 10% gel; **Desquam X** 10%▼x gel; **Panoxyl Aquagel**▼x 2.5%, 5% gel<br>**Proactiv** soln 2.5%x⊗ (System: cleanser, toner, lotion, $$$)<br>Alcohol-based: **Benzagel** 5%▼x, 10% gel; **Panoxyl** 5%▼x, 10%▼, 15%▼, 20%▼ gel **C**<br>Acetone-based: **Acetoxyl**▼x 2.5, 5, 10% gel<br>Lotion: **Oxy 5**▼x 2.5%; **Benoxyl** 5%▼x, 10%▼; **Benzagel 5**▼. Select list above - see references for a more complete list<br>Less Useful: **Soap**: Panoxyl 5%▼x, 10%▼; **Wash**: Benzac W 5%▼x, 10%; Benzagel 5%▼x; Desquam X 5%▼x, 10%▼x; Panoxyl | **Common**: contact dermatitis[50%], dryness[8%] & peeling[20%] appear after a few days; erythema[14%]; burning[1%]; & pruritus[2%]; may **bleach** hair/clothes; odor on clothing & bed sheets.<br>{Temporary reduction in application may help.}<br>Irritation: ↑ conc. = ↑ irritation<br>$H_2O$-based < alcohol=acetone-based<br>**Serious**: Allergic reactions & contact sensitization dermatitis[1-2%] | 8-12 weeks for noted improvement;<br>2-4 weeks: clinical worsening may occur before improvement | √**1st line medication** for mild-moderate acne vulgaris as monotherapy; **low cost**<br>√In combination with other agents for mod-severe acne; helps prevent ABX resistance!<br>√Benzac AC gel for sensitive/dry skin & Benzac W $36 (Water) for oily/normal skin.<br>☒ BP >5% no more efficacious than 2.5-5% & more irritation (but covered on some drug plans)<br>☒ Washes & Soaps least effective → little residual contact time<br>**DI**: ↑ **skin irritation or drying effect** – concomitant topical medication, medicated abrasive soaps & cleansers, soaps & cosmetics with strong drying effect; products with high concentrations of alcohol, astringents, spices or lime; isotretinoin<br>**BP's oxidizing action degrades antibiotics or retinoids:** space admin times!<br>{Or use premixed combination products such as Clindoxyl, BenzaClin, Benzamycin}<br>To **reduce irritation** initially apply **q2-3days** then ↑ frequency as tolerated or apply for 2 hrs for 4 nights, 4hrs for 4 nights, & then leave on all night if tolerated. | Apply to entire affected area QHS or BID<br>2.5% or 5%; H20 based generally better tolerated<br>{if 2.5% ineffective, then ↑to 5%.}<br>**OTC**: 2.5, 4, & 5%<br>**Rx**: 8, 10, 15, 20% | **OTC**: 10-15<br>**Rx**: 15-25<br>18 bar |
| **Retinoid** | **TRETINOIN** = TRE **C**<br>**Retin-A** 0.01% crm, 0.025% crm, 0.05% crm, 0.1%▼ crm, 0.01% gel, 0.025% gel; **Stieva-A** 0.01% crm, 0.025% crm, 0.05% crm, 0.1%▼ forte crm, 0.01% gel, 0.025% gel, 0.05% gel, 0.025% soln; **Vitamin A Acid** 0.01% gel, 0.025% gel, 0.05% gel **{0.025-0.05% useful/tolerated}**<br>{**Pregnancy**: Motherisk deems fairly safe}<br>**ADAPALENE** = ADA **C**<br>**Differin** 0.1% crm & gel (XP 0.3% gel ⊗x)<br>**TAZAROTENE** = TAZ **X**<br>**Tazorac** 0.05 & 0.1% crm, gel | **Common**: erythema, dryness, burning, photosensitization (less with adapalene)<br>**Irritation**: TAZ > TRE* >ADA *(except Retin-A Micro)<br>{TAZ often reserved for tough skin areas, or a desire for strong therapy despite irritation}<br>**Serious**: rare true contact allergy<br>**CI** eczema; pregnancy; sunburn may be less with adapalene -may wish to stop for 1 week before a sunny vacation | ~12 weeks for max response; {continue till no new lesions}<br>2-4 weeks: clinical worsening may occur | √**1st line medication for mild-moderate comedonal** (blackheads/whiteheads) acne<br>√**Tretinoin** 0.025-0.05% has cost advantage; **Adapalene** 0.1% has less irritation advantage<br>After successful course, consider step-down to less frequent (q2-3 night) maintenance tx<br>☒Use sunscreen SPF 15-30 esp. for TRE & TAZ {Retisol A: SPF-15 + tretinoin 0.01%, 0.025%, 0.05%, 0.1% $40/45g cr⊗x}<br>**DI**: ↑ **skin irritation or drying effect**– concomitant topical medication, medicated abrasive soaps & cleansers, soaps & cosmetics with strong drying effect; products with high concentrations of alcohol, astringents, spices or lime; isotretinoin<br>√ ↓ noninflammatory & inflammatory lesions counts by 38-71%[16]<br>Retin-A Micro▼x 0.04% gel, 0.1% gel $35 emollient, less penetrating/irritation (may be useful near eyes?; anti-aging?)<br>Renova⊗x 0.05% crm indicated for fine wrinkles, mottled hyperpigmentation & roughness of skin (not acne) | QHS<br>Apply 30-45 min after wash; start low conc. TRE 0.025%; apply **q2-3 nights** initially to ↓SE.<br>•May give **ADA** in **AM** less photosensitivity<br>•TAZ may be effective with <5 min contact, thus reducing irritation | TRE: **16** 25g, **21** 20g Micro<br>ADA: **58** 45g<br>TAZ: **54** 30g |
| **Antibiotic** | **Clindamycin** = CLI; Topical Soln<br>**Dalacin T**, g 10mg/ml; **Clindets** 1%⊗x;<br>CLI 1% Cream & SPF-15 **Clindasol** ⊗x<br>**Erythromycin** = ERY **B**<br>**Erysol**⊗x 2% gel contains SPF-15 sunscreen | **Common**: less irritating than BP & TRE, erythema, peeling, itching, dryness & burning[17]<br>**Serious**: PMC rare<br>**CI** CLI – previous colitis, regional enteritis, ulcerative colitis, PMC | 8-12 weeks for noted improvement | √Most effective for inflammatory lesions. Stop when/if no further inflammation.<br>**Use in combination with BP to prevent bacterial resistance** !!![18,19,20]<br>√Most effective when used in combination with BP or topical retinoids[21,22,23,24]<br>{CLI may be preferred over ERY for prolonged effect &/or less resistance} Expert Opinion | Dalacin T: BID<br>Clindets: BID<br>ERY: OD-BID | **24** 60ml<br>**50** 60s Clindets<br>**26** 25g |
| **Combination** | **Benzamycin**⊗ = BP 5%/ERY 3% gel *<br>**BenzaClin**⊗, **Clindoxyl**⊗ = BP 5%/CLI 1% gel * -50g Pump<br>**Stievamycin**x▼ gel = TRE+ERY **C**<br>**Mild** TRE 0.01%/ERY 4%,<br>**Regular** TRE 0.025%/ERY 4%,<br>**Forte** TRE 0.05%/ERY 4% | As for individual ingredients above.<br>{for Neomedrol corticosteroid: burning sensation, itching, irritation, dryness, folliculitis, acneiform eruptions, hypopigmentation; rare true contact allergy}<br>[BP/CLI combination no better than BP alone for non-inflammatory acne McKeage] | 2-4 weeks for noted improvement;<br>8-10 weeks for optimal results | √BP combined with ERY or CLI has not shown resistance[17] Similar or ↑ efficacy.[18,25]<br>•Refrigerate Benzamycin (3 month expiry); Clindoxyl at room temp (4 mo. expiry)<br>☒ Combinations that are not generally recommended for long-term acne treatment:<br>Neo-Medrol Acne Lotion⊗x NEOSPORIN 0.25%/ METHYLPREDNISOLONE 0.25%; OD-BID; may exacerbate acne $24 75ml<br>Sulfacet-R Lotion⊗ = SS 10%/Sul 5%; BID-TID; acne:less efficacious; useful: acne rosacea $33 25g (tinted preparation may be useful as camouflage) | **Benzamycin**: qHS-BID*<br>**BenzaClin**: qHS-BID*<br>**Clindoxyl**: qHS-BID*<br>**Stievamycin**: QHS | **63** 46.6g<br>**58** 50g<br>**53** 45g<br>**22** 25g |
| | **Salicylic Acid** = **SA**▼x 0.5, 1, 2 & 3.5% Oxy, Clearasil, Neutrogena, others →☒Not commonly recommended (less potent than equal strength BP); option if retinoid intolerance e.g. skin irritation | | | | OD or BID | 10-15 |

χ=Non-form Sk ☎=Exception Drug Status Sk ⊗=not covered by NIHB ▼=covered by NIHB Δ=change **ABX**=antibiotic **crm**=cream **DI**=drug interaction $H_2O$=water **MET**=methylprednisolone **NEO**=neomycin **OTC**= over-the-counter **PMC**= Pseudomembranous colitis
**SS**=sodium sulfacetamide **Sul**=sulfur **Rx**=prescription ◊ Adjunctive BP ± Retinoids ± topical Antibiotics is beneficial ^Benzac AC: **AC**rylates Polymer =microscopic beads that absorb excess oil while releasing a small amount of glycerine to moisturize the skin.

***Practical Tips for Combo Tx:** Give BP/ABX at night (avoid BP staining of clothing during day); may follow with adapalene in AM (minimal sun concern). **Tea tree oil 5%**: 1 small trial showed efficacy but relatively slow onset.[26]

| Class | Generic/TRADE g=generic avail.<br>Strength/forms, pregnancy category[15] | Side effects (SE)/ Contraindications CI | Response time | √ = therapeutic use / ☒= Disadvantage / Comments / Drug Interactions DI / Monitor M | INITIAL; USUAL DOSE | $ 90 days |
|---|---|---|---|---|---|---|
| Antibiotics | **Oral Antibiotics** | **√ Indicated for moderate-severe acne; acne on the chest, back, or shoulders; in pts with inflammatory disease in whom topical combinations have failed or are not tolerated; in moderate acne with tendency for scarring or substantial post-inflammatory hyperpigmentation. Lack of Response**: may relate to resistance, especially with ERY; less with TET, DOX, MIN | | | | |
| | **Tetracycline** = TET, g<br>250mg cap **D** | **Common**: GI upset, vaginal candidiasis, photosensitivity (DOX>TET>MIN) dose-dependent, esp UVA<br>MIN: hyperpigmentation of skin (rare bluish skin) & mucous membranes, lightheadedness, dizziness, **vertigo**, ataxia, drowsiness & fatigue<br>**GI upset: TET > DOX = MIN**<br>**Serious**: rare azotemia, pseudotumor cerebri (benign intracranial hypertension)<br>MIN: rare lupus-like reaction, autoimmune hepatitis & hypersensitivity syndrome (some suggest **avoid**[27])<br>CI Children < 9, severe renal or hepatic dysfunction;<br>DOX: myasthenia gravis possible association with muscle weakness | Allow 8-12 weeks for optimal response.<br><br>"Pulse tx": Use po ABX **2-4 months** & follow-up with topical ABX + BP. Shorter courses ↓ development of resistance | √TET has a 50-60% rate of improvement in inflammatory lesions[28] after 8 wks<br>√DOX, MIN & TET: equally effective lesion count.[53,29,30,31]. (MIN >antimicrobial effect)[32]<br>√DOX: advantage of daily dosing without the severe SEs or cost of MIN.<br>☒Absorption of TET is ↓ by food & dairy– take on **empty** stomach<br>☒Use Sunscreen SPF 15-30 {photosensitivity less of a problem with doxycycline at 100mg/day}<br>☒NO TCN before sleep b/c pills may lodge in the esophagus & cause ulceration<br>☒DOX has cross resistance with TET, not MIN<br>DI: ↓GI absorption: $Fe^{++}$, BIS, $Al^{++}$, $Ca^{++}$, Mg (separate dose by 2 hr); ↑INR:warfarin; **ABX**: may ↓ birth control pills effectiveness; isotretinoin (intracranial HTN/hemorrhage)<br>M: MIN: consider LFTs & antinuclear factor baseline & q3-4 months | 500mg bid initial; 250-500mg od **ac if** maintenance | **32** 500bid<br>**21** 500/d<br>**15** 250/d |
| | **Doxycycline** = DOX, g<br>**Doxycin** 100 mg cap, tab **D** | | | | 100mg od<br>(ac best, but may take cc) | **57** |
| | **Minocycline** ☎ ✆ = MIN, g<br>**Minocin** 50 & 100mg cap **D** | | | | 100mg od initial, 50mg od if maintenance<br>May give with food | **109** 100/d<br>**60** 50/d |
| | **Erythromycin** = ERY, g<br>**Eryc, Erybid**, others<br>250, 333 & 500mg, others **B** | **Common**: GI: N, V, D, vaginal candidiasis<br>**Serious**: rare estolate-induced cholestatic jaundice<br>**CI:** ERY estolate – pre-existing liver disease | | √67% ↓ of inflammatory lesion & 22% ↓ of noninflammatory lesions [33] in 8 weeks<br>☒Not first line ABX because of ↑ Resistance & GI effects<br>DI: inhibits CYP1A2 & 3A4: ↑ levels of: carbamazepine, cyclosporine, theophylline & warfarin | 500mg bid initial, 250-500mg od maintenance | **84** 500bid<br>**43** 500/d<br>**26** 250/d |
| | **Trimethoprim**, g = TRI<br>**Proloprim** 100 & 200mg tab **C** | **Common**: GI upset; rash 3% usually self limiting<br>**Rare**: hepatic/renal toxicity, agranulocytosis & TEN | | √3rd line agent; may be effective and useful when other antibiotics can not be used<br>May worsen megaloblastic anemia due to **folate** deficiency | 200 bid to 300mg bid | **111**<br>**159** |
| Anti-androgenic | **Combination Oral Contraceptives (COCs)**<br>**Tri-Cyclen** EE 35ug+ Norgestimate 0.18-0.215-0.25mg<br>**Alesse** EE 20ug+Levo 0.1mg<br>**Diane 35/Cystra-35** ▼ χ { EE 35ug + cyproterone (CPA) 2mg }<br>**Yasmin** EE30ug+drospirenone 3mg | **Refer to Oral Contraceptive RxFiles chart** (e.g. CI: smoking, migraine with aura…)<br>**Common**: Breakthrough bleeding, headache<br>**Serious**: hepatotoxicity cyproterone: rare; venous thromboembolism (3.4 / 10,000 woman-yrs in 1st yr); {March 2010: some controversy regarding potentially ↑ VTE risk with Yas and Yasmin.}<br>Diane 35 lacks indication in Canada for contraception although has this indication in other countries e.g. Australia. | 3-6 months for optimal response.<br>Acne may worsen early in cycle. | √For females with moderate to severe acne + seborrhoea ± hirsutism ± androgenic alopecia ± late onset acne ± requiring contraception (overall >50% improvement)<br>√All COCs beneficial likely due to estrogen's effect on SHBG sex hormone binding globulin, resulting in an anti-androgen effect.[34] Evidence for superiority of one progestin over another is conflicting.[35] **Yasmin** as efficacious as Tri-cyclen[36] & Diane 35 [37] {Yaz EE 20ug+drospirenone 3mg ⊗: new in Canada & also has official acne indication}<br>☒ Relapses are common after discontinuation of treatment[38]<br>DI: Oral antibiotics may ↓ contraceptive efficacy {significance controversial} | OD x21 day, x7 days off / cycle<br>Tri-cyclen or Alesse, Aviane<br>Yasmin/Yaz<br>Cyestra 35 / Diane 35 | <br><br>**69**<br>**62, 43 g**<br>**52 / 63**<br>**88 g / 107** ▼χ |
| | **Spironolactone**, g<br>**Aldactone** 25 & 100mg tabs **C/D** | **Common**: Menstrual irregularity, mild GI upset, headache, ↑ K+, gynecomastia, breast tenderness<br>CI Anuria, acute renal insufficiency, significant impairment of renal function, or hyperkalemia. | 2-3 months for optimal response | √Used to treat late onset acne in **adult women** when other treatments have been ineffective, not tolerated or contraindicated<br>M: Potassium (lytes): baseline & q1month | 25-200mg daily<br>Usual: 50mg od or 100mg po od | **21 - 28** |
| Retinoid | **Isotretinoin** = ISO, g<br>**Accutane** 1-888-762-4388<br>**Clarus** 1-877-776-7711 (CNS, ears, eyes, heart) **X**<br>10 & 40mg caps, ⊗ soybean/peanut oil<br>♀:****Test for pregnancy twice before** (once at initial assessment & the other within **11 days prior** to initiating), **during** (monthly) **& 1 month after d/c**<br>◆**2 reliable contraception forms are recommended,** unless abstinence is chosen method; Initiate after 2-3 days of next normal menstrual period<br>◆**Not a major issue for males/sperm**<br>**Web:** www.claruscleargprogram.com | **Common**: dryness of the mucous membranes [lips 93%, mouth 33%, eyes 35%, nose 80%; nose bleeds 20%], peeling of fingertips 20%, dry skin 80%, itching 41%; hair loss, thirst 30%, rash/red face 34%, headache 13%, myalgia, back pain 5%; ↑chol ~20% ↑ over baseline, ↑LDL >15% ↑ from baseline, ↑TG >5.7 mmol/L in 25% pts, ↑pancreatitis, ↓HDL ~15% from baseline.<br>**Dryness** worse in 1st 8 weeks;⇨ treat with **lip balm**, temporary removal of contact lens; **eye lubricants**, Vaseline or **nasal** moisturizers e.g. Rhinaris/Secaris helpful<br>**Sun Sensitivity**: caution ⇨use sunscreen SPF ≥15, esp UVA<br>**Minor aches**⇨treat with acetaminophen or NSAIDs (SE dose related; consider lower dose, slow titration)[39,13]<br>**Serious**: abrupt ↓ night vision (D/C ISO); depression & suicide controversial: no direct evidence but monitor)[40]; ?IBD, ?SJS/TENS<br>CI Hepatic/renal dysfx, hypervitaminosis A, ↑↑ lipids; peanut allergy DI: COCs, methotrexate, TCNs, Vitamin A | 2-3 months for optimal response. Usually 3-4 months for complete suppression. Improvement persists after 1-2 months of stopping!<br>{T1/2=10-20h} | √**Role**: severe nodulocystic acne, acne associated with scarring, failure to respond to or inability to tolerate systemic antibiotics &/or hormonal therapy, significant psychological distress because of acne, acne fulminans, gram-negative folliculitis, or pyoderma faciale [41]<br>**{If severely inflamed acne, initial ↓dose** can ↓initial flare!**} Recommend** in **≥12yrs**<br>√Remission rates as high as 70-89%[42,43,44]; 55-80% long-term remission after 1 course<br>√Most effective therapy for mod-severe inflammatory acne[45] ↓sebum, comedone formation, P. acnes, inflam<br>√Lesions localized on the face, upper arms & legs tend to clear more rapidly than trunk[46]<br>☒ **Initial acne flare up** may occur during the 1st 2 months of tx (in ~6% of patients) [47] (If acne flare up is severe, D/C ISO & restart at 0.1mg/kg/d & slowly ↑ to 0.5mg/kg/d; or give prednisone 0.5-1mg/kg/d x 2-3 wks with a gradual taper)<br>☒ **Relapse**: wait ≥ 8wks after completion (usual 4-5 months before considering retreatment)<br>◆Delay follow-up topical retinoid for **~4months** after stopping ISO; dry-sensitive skin persists!<br>M: CBC, LFTs (transient↑), LDL, Triglyceride: O,1 & q3mon, Pregnancy tests**, mood {Link: **FORM**} | **0.5mg/kg/d** divided OD-BID **CC** x4wks then **1mg/kg/d x3-7** months[48] (Max: 2mg/kg/d) -e.g.<br>**60kg (40mg caps)** 40mg od x 1 mon, then alternating 40mg on day 1 & 80mg on day 2 x4-5mon<br>**60kg (10mg caps)** 20mg bid x 1 mo, then 30mg bid x 4-5 months<br>Lower-dose options?[49,43,50,51] Not generally recommended. | Pk size: 30 tabs; Suggest limit to 1 month supply<br>**510** / 5months 40mg caps<br>**970** / 5months 10mg caps |
| | | | | Total optimal cumulative dose = **120-150 mg/kg/course**: >150mg/kg/course no further benefit; <120mg/kg/course ↑ rates of postreatment relapse (eg. 60kg = 7,200mg - 9,000mg per course, ~ 5 month therapy course). **Avoid:** other acne topicals due to dryness & Vitamin A supplements due to ↑ toxicity. | | |

χ=Non-formulary Sk ☎=Exception Drug Status SK ⊗=not covered by NIHB ▼=covered by NIHB ✆ prior approval by NIHB ⊗=soybean **ABX**=antibiotic **ac**=before meals **Al**=aluminum **BIS**=bismuth **Ca**=calcium **cc**=with food **chol**=cholesterol **D**=diarrhea **EE**=ethinyl estradiol **Fe**=iron **GI**=stomach **IBD**=Inflammatory bowel dx **K+**=potassium **Levo**=levonorgestrel **Mg**=magnesum **mon**=month **N**=nausea **temp**=temporary **SE**=side effect **TEN**=toxic epidermal necrolysis **TG**=triglyceride **TCNs**=tetracyclines **V**=vomiting **wt**=weight {Chemical peels glycolic & SA useful to correct scarring}

**Other Meds**: **Clindamycin (oral)** & **Bactrim** not commonly used → pseudomembranous colitis & TEN, respectively[47]; **Azithromycin** 250mg 3x/wk is being used in acne, but studies are preliminary [32]; **Prednisone** 2.5-7.5mg or **dexamethasone** 0.125-0.5mg qhs for congenital adrenal hyperplasia or temporary benefit in severe inflammatory acne; **Flutamide** 250-375mg/d for hirsute females x 1-6 months but potential hepatic toxicity & **Triamcinolone** 0.25-0.5mg injected into inflammatory cysts for acute cosmetic purposes.

**Other Topicals**: Dapsone gel marginally effective. **Sulfur & Resorcinol** less efficacy than above meds; **Azelaic Acid** not avail. in Canada, ↓irritate & ↓effect, √post-inflammatory pigmentation. **Drug induced**: Anabolic steroids, androgens in women, COCs high in progestin, corticosteroids, corticotrophin ACTH, bromides, cetuximab, chlorides, coal tar topical, crystal meth, cyanocobalamin, cyclosporine, dantrolene, erlotinib, gabapentin, gefitinib, gold salts, halothane, iodides, lithium salts, panitumumab, Provera/Norplant[52], phenobarbital, phenytoin, psoralens, quinidine, quinine.

| DRUG/STRENGTH (grouped by formulation & potency) | BRAND NAME | 1 | 2 | 3 | 4 | 5 | 6 | 7 | SIZE / COMMENTS | |
|---|---|---|---|---|---|---|---|---|---|---|
| **CREAMS** → cause less occlusion, are suitable for non-acute, wet lesions & tend to be cosmetically more acceptable | | | | | | | | | | |
| **Clobetasol propionate 0.05%** | *Dermovate, Others* | $22 | | | | | | | 15,50g | PG |
| Halobetasol propionate 0.05% | *Ultravate* (D/c by the company) | ■ | | | | | | | 15,50g | |
| Desoximetasone 0.25% | *Topicort* PB, WA | | $29 | | | | | | 20,60g | • |
| Fluocinonide 0.05% | *Lyderm (Emollient Base•)* | | $24 $27 | | | | | | 15,60g | PG • |
| Halcinonide 0.1% | *Halog* | | $26 | | | | | | 15,30,60g | PG |
| Betamethasone dipropionate glycol 0.05% | *Diprolene Glycol, Topilene Glycol* PB | | $26 | | | | | | 15,50g | PG, • |
| **Betamethasone dipropionate 0.05%** | Diprosone, Taro-Sone PG; *Lotriderm*1% clotrimazole OH PG | | | $15 | | | | | 15,50,450g | • |
| Amcinonide 0.1% Ratio, *Taro* $17 | *Cyclocort* (lanolin,paraben,PG,tartrazine,urea free•) | | | $25 | | | | | 15,30,60g | OH, • |
| Beclomethasone dipropionate 0.025% | *Propaderm* ▼ | | | | $23 | | | | 15,45g | OH |
| Clobetasone butyrate 0.05% (OTC) | *Spectro Eczema Care* | | | | $21 | | | | 30g | |
| Desoximetasone 0.05% | *Topicort Mild* PB, WA, *Desoxi* | | | | $23 | | | | 20,60g | • |
| Diflucortolone valerate 0.1% | *Nerisone Cr* PB, *Nerisone Oily Cr* (NP),(Nerisalic oily 3%SA x▼) | | | | $21 | | | | 30g,60g | • |
| Mometasone furoate 0.1% | *Elocom* (Once daily recommended) | | | | $33 | | | | 15,50,100g | PG |
| Fluticasone propionate 0.05% | *Cutivate* (D/c by the company) | | | | ■ | | | | | PG |
| Triamcinolone acetonide 0.1% | *Triaderm, Aristocort-R* R=reg | | | | $10 | | | | 15,30,500g | PG |
| **Betamethasone valerate 0.1%** / 0.05% | *Betaderm* PG, *Ratio-Ectosone* PB / *Betaderm* PG, *Ratio-Ectosone Mild* PB | | | | | $10 | | | 15,-450g | • low cost |
| Fluocinolone acetonide *Fluoderm* - (D/c by the company) 2005 | | | | | | ■ | | | | |
| Hydrocortisone valerate 0.2% | *Hydroval* PB | | | | | $14 | | | 15,45,60g | PG, • |
| Triamcinolone acetonide 0.025% *Triaderm* | (D/c by the company) 2005 | | | | | | ■ | | | |
| Desonide 0.05% | *Desocort, PMS-Desonide* | | | | | | $17 | | 15,60g | PG |
| Hydrocortisone/Urea 1%/10% | *Uremol-HC* | | | | | | $14 | | 50,225g | PG ;8-15°C |
| **Hydrocortisone** 2.5% / 1% / 0.5% (OTC) | *Emo-Cort* / *Hyderm, Emo-Cort* / *Hyderm, Cortate* others | | | | | | | $15 / $9 / $13 | 45,225g / 15,-450g | OD-QID / low cost |
| **OINTMENTS** → Ointments are more occlusive, greasy; more effective in dry, scaly, or hyperkeratinized skin areas | | | | | | | | | | |
| Betamethasone dipropionate glycol 0.05% | *Diprolene glycol, Topilene glycol* | $26 | | | | | | | 15,50g | PG |
| Betamethasone dipropionate 0.05%+SA 3% | *Diprosalic* (SA=Salicylic Acid-karatolytic) | $38 | | | | | | | 15,50g | •psoriasis |
| **Clobetasol propionate 0.05%** | *Dermovate* PG, Others PG | $22 | | | | | | | 15,50g | PB & lanolin free |
| Halobetasol propionate 0.05% | *Ultravate* (D/c by the company) | ■ | | | | | | | 15,50g | PG |
| Amcinonide 0.1% | *Cyclocort* $25 (tartrazine free); *Ratio* | | $17 | | | | | | 15,30,60g | OH |
| **Betamethasone dipropionate 0.05%** | **Diprosone, Topisone** | | $14 | | | | | | 15,50,450g | |
| Desoximetasone 0.25% | *Topicort* | | $27 | | | | | | 20,60g | PG |
| Fluocinonide 0.05% | *Lyderm* | | $20 | | | | | | 15,60g | PG |
| Halcinonide 0.1% | *Halog* x ▼ | | $25 | | | | | | 30g | |
| **Betamethasone valerate 0.1%** | **Betaderm** | | | $11 | | | | | 454g | low cost |
| Mometasone furoate 0.1% | *Elocom,PMS,Ratio,Taro* (Once daily recommended) | | | $20 | | | | | 15,50,100g | PG |
| Triamcinolone acetonide 0.1% / 0.1% oral top | *Aristocort R* (NP) / *Oracort Dental* •7.5g | | | | $13 / $16 | | | | 15,30,454g | • / • |
| Clobetasone butyrate 0.05% | *Eumovate* (D/c by the company) | | | | $21 | | | | 15,30g | |
| Diflucortolone valerate 0.1% | *Nerisone* (NP) | | | | $21 | | | | 30 g | |
| Fluocinolone acetonide 0.025% | *Synalar Reg* (D/c by the company) (NP) 60g | | | | $23 | | | | 15,454g | • |
| Hydrocortisone valerate 0.2% | *Hydroval* PB | | | | $12 | | | | 15,60g | PG, • |
| **Betamethasone valerate 0.05%** | **Betaderm** | | | | | $9 | | | 454g | low cost |
| Desonide 0.05% | *Desocort, PMS Desonide* | | | | | | $17 | | 15,60g | |
| **Hydrocortisone 1%; 0.5% (OTC)** | Cortoderm PB (1% *Cortate* D/C'd 2004) | | | | | | | $8-13 | 15,-450g | OD-QID |

Comments (creams): **High Potency agents:** reserve for resistant conditions/ thick skin areas due to potential for local & systemic side effects. **Ultra Potent agents:** • max ~50g/week; • limit duration (e.g. ≤3 weeks) • apply OD-BID. **Low Potency:** preferred when necessary on thin skin areas, in elderly, young children or infants or if used long-term. Caution if on face or thin skin areas!

Comments (ointments): **High Potency agents:** -see comments above in the cream section. **Ultra Potent agents:** -see comments above in the cream section. Ointments MORE potent than creams! **Low Potency:** -see comments above in the cream section.

**Other steroidal**: prednicarbate 0.1% crm,oint; *Dermatop*; Potency Group 5 ; $15/20g ; $40/60g X ⊘ {possibly less skin atrophy than other mid-potency agents} 5,6

**Non-steroidal**: **Topical calcineurin inhibitors**: tacrolimus 0.03%, 0.1% oint adults only; *PROTOPIC* $89/30g ☎⊘. Pimecrolimus 1% crm; *ELIDEL* $86/30g ☎⊘→.Use BID; ↓**atrophy**; burning, not adrenal suppression, not ocular side effects, may ↑ skin infections vs corticosteroids. **Tacrolimus** seems to be more **potent**. Both approved in kids ≥ 2yrs. FDA 2005 **cancer warning**: a few human reports causal relationship has not been established & in 3 different animal species as amount of drug ↑ so did cancer risk.[7] Greatest concern in kids.

**Indications for topical steroids**: Clinical data supports efficacy in psoriasis, vitiligo, eczema, atopic dermatitis, phimosis, acute radiation dermatitis, & lichen sclerosus. Limited evidence: melasma, chronic idiopathic urticaria, and alopecia areata. **Topical Azole Antifungals** – anti-inflammatory potency: itraconazole > ketoconazole > fluconazole



| DRUG/STRENGTH (by formulation & potency) | BRAND NAME | 1 | 2 | 3 | 4 | 5 | 6 | 7 | SIZE / COMMENTS | |
|---|---|---|---|---|---|---|---|---|---|---|
| **GELS** → Gels are non-occlusive, non-greasy, quick drying, & do not leave residue; useful on hairy areas, face; irritating | | | | | | | | | | |
| Desoximetasone 0.05% | *Topicort Gel* | | $24 | | | | | | 20,60g | OH |
| Fluocinonide 0.05% | *Lyderm* | | $20 | | | | | | 15,60g | PG, • |
| **LOTIONS / SOLUTIONS** → Least occlusive; preferred for acute weeping lesions, axilla, foot, groin & hairy areas. {FOAM x ⊗: new formulation for hairy areas; alcohol base causes burning, etc.} | | | | | | | | | | |
| Betamethasone dipropionate glycol 0.05% lot. | *Diprolene Glycol, Topilene Glycol* | $26 | | | | | | | 30,60ml | PG, OH |
| Betamethasone dipropionate 0.05%+SA 2% lot. | *Diprosalic,Topisalic* (SA=Salicylic Acid) | $37 | | | | | | | 30,60ml | OH, • |
| **Clobetasol propionate 0.05% scalp lot.** / 0.05% topical solution / 0.05% topical spray | *Dermovate, Others* / *Taro-clobetasol* x ▼ / *Clobex spray* x⊗ | $31 / $31 / $75 | | | | | | | 20,60ml | OH |
| Amcinonide 0.1% lotion Ratio $24 | *Cyclocort* (lanolin,PG,tartrazine,urea free•) | | | | $38 | | | | 20,60ml | OH, • |
| Beclomethasone dipropionate 0.025% lotion | *Propaderm* (D/c by the company) | | | | ■ | | | | 20,60ml | PG |
| Mometasone furoate 0.1% lotion | *Elocom* | | | | $41 | | | | 30,75ml | PG, OH |
| **Betamethasone dipropionate 0.05% lot.** | ***Diprosone, Topisone, Taro-sone*** | | | $22 | | | | | 30,75ml | OH |
| **Betamethasone valerate 0.1% scalp lot.** / 0.1% lotion / 0.05% lotion | ***Valisone, Ectosone, Betaderm*** / ***Ratio-Ectosone*** / ***Ratio-Ectosone Mild*** | | | | | $14 / $25 / $21 | | | 30,75ml / 60ml / 60ml | OH / OH, PB / OH, PB |
| Fluocinolone acetonide shampoo / topical oil | *Capex* (12mg capsule+shampoo base) / *Derma-Smoothe/FS* OH, peanut oil | | | | | $49 / $25 | | | 60ml / 180ml / 118ml | PG; NP / PG, PB |
| Desonide 0.05% lotion | *Desocort* | | | | | | $19 | | 60,120ml | PB, PG |
| Hydrocortisone / Urea 1%/10% | ***Uremol-HC*** keratin softening/hydrating | | | | | | $15 | | 150ml | |
| **Hydrocortisone 2.5% scalp solution** / 2.5% lotion / 1% lotion / 0.5% lotion | *Emo-cort* OH / ⊠*Sarna-HC (camphor & menthol)* / *Emo-Cort* / ⊠*Sarna-HC (camphor & menthol)* / *Emo-Cort* / *Cortate* (D/C by company 2004) | | | | | | | $21 / $20 / $22 / $15 / $18 / $15 | Emo-Cort=60ml; Sarna-HC 2.5%=75ml, 1%=150ml; Cortate=30ml | |

Comments (lotions, ultra potent): Max ~50ml/wk with Ultra potent agents

**Cost** =total cost for **30g/60ml** in Sask. Lowest price alternative used where avail. ⊠ =not interchangeable in Sask. X non-formulary in SK ▼=covered by NIHB ⊗=not NIHB • = brand specific info in brand section; **OH** = benzyl or isopropyl alcohol (drying!); **NP** = no preservatives; **PB** = parabens (preservative; may rarely cause irritation); **PG** = propylene glycol (may rarely cause irritation if sensitive); WA = wool alcohol (avoid if wool allergies)

**Table 4: Potency* Classification[1,2,3] - Ultra high potency steroids are up to 1000 times more potent than hydrocortisone**

| | |
|---|---|
| **Group 1=Ultra High Potency** | •reserve for **resistant conditions**; high potential for serious side effects (local & systemic) •suitable for **short term** intermittent use in severe eczematous dermatoses & psoriasis •often required for palms, soles, & scalp where thickened skin may require prolonged Tx •{alopecia areata, resistant atopic dermatitis, discoid lupis, hyperkeratotic eczema, lichen planus/sclerosus/simplex chronicus, severe poison ivy, psoriasis, severe hand eczema} |
| **Group 2,3 = High Potency** | •generally limit to OD-BID, & length of Tx. to **≤2-4 weeks** followed by less potent agent •**avoid** use on large areas, thin skin areas, skin folds, face; **caution** in young children/infants |
| **Group 4,5 = Mid Potency** | •suitable for intermittent long term use, chronic use in thick skin areas (hand eczema) {anal inflammation (severe), asteatotic eczema, atopic dermatitis, lichen sclerosus (vulva), nummular eczema, scabies (after scabicide), seborrheic dermatitis, severe intertrigo (short-term), stasis dermatitis.} •**avoid** on thin skin areas; **extreme CAUTION** if used on **face**, intertriginous areas (severe adverse effects) |
| **Group 6,7 = Low Potency** | •safest in children, infants & elderly or for covering large or higher risk areas (**face, eyelids, skin flexures, scrotum, perianal**); **CAUTION** still required! •suitable for **maintenance** of most chronic conditions after initial control obtained •often applied BID-QID; less frequent (OD-BID) if ongoing |

*Actual potency may vary considerably depending on: site of application, skin condition, use of occlusion, and individual patient variation.
**SE**: striae, skin atrophy*; if on eyelids rarely: glaucoma & cataracts; rare adrenal suppression esp. with high potency +/- occlusive dressing, ↑ dose & in young kids.

**Table 5: Quantities of Cream Required in an Adult[8]**

| Single Application | Area {1 fingertip unit = approximately 0.5g} | Amount Needed to Apply BID X7 Days |
|---|---|---|
| 1g | 1 hand | 15g |
| 2g | 2 hands; head; face; genital | 30g |
| 3g | 1 arm; front or back of trunk | 45g |
| 4g | 1 leg | 60g |
| 30-60g | Whole body | 500-1000g |

1g of cream should cover ~100cm² of area. Ointments spread easier than creams ∴ 5-10% less ointment may be required than cream. {*Concurrent topical tretinoin 0.1% may ↓incidence of atrophy from chronic use.}

**Table 6: Non-steroid Emollients**

**Alpha-Keri**® (bath oil / soap) • mineral oil, lanolin / glycerin
**Aveeno**® (bath oil, lotion, oilated powder & bar) •colloidal oatmeal
**Eucerin**® (cream, lotion) •petrolatum & petrolatum liquid
**Hydrous Emulsifying Ointment** (HEO). **Glaxal Base**
**Keri**® (lotion) • mineral oil, lanolin
**Lubriderm AHA**® (cream, lotion) •lactic acid; **Lubriderm**® lotion
**Nicotinamide 2%** in HEO or Glaxal base (compounded) restore skin barrier / UV protect
**Neutragena** (cream, lotion glycerin, etc.)
**Nutraderm**® (lotion) •light mineral oil
**Sarna**® Lotion •contains camphor-menthol-phenol
**Uremol**® **10%**, (cream, lotion); **20%** (cream) • urea {more potent}
**Vaseline**® (ointment); **Vaseline Intensive Care**® (lotions,creams)

# GLAUCOMA: TOPICAL OPHTHALMICS FOR POAG: Comparison Chart [1,2,3,4,5,6,7]

Originally prepared by C.Anderson. B. Jensen BSP © www.RxFiles.ca May 10

| Generic=g TRADE Name (Dosage forms) | Dose / Frequency | Cost / 30day 🇨🇦 | Comments: Remove contact lenses prior to instilling any eyedrops. Occlude the lacrimal punctae after instillation or shut eyes tightly for at least 1-5min. Shake suspensions prior to use. Use 1 drop & wait 5 minutes between consecutive drops. Allergies to preservatives (benzalkonium often present) possible. |
|---|---|---|---|
| **Prostaglandin F2α Analogue** [PAs]: active metabolite (latanoprost acid) ↑'s outflow via uveo-scleral route *(~25-30% ↓IOP)* -PGAs | | | **Monotherapy or can be used as an adjunctive agent**; reasonable 1st line option (additive ↓ IOP with β-blockers, dipivefrin, and CAInh (po or topical)<br>Latan: Refrigerate prior to opening; once opened may store at room temp. for a max of 6 weeks[8]; Trav & Bimat: room temp is ok •no advantage of >1 gtt/d<br>Well-tolerated, fewer systemic SE & better night-time IOP control vs. timolol but more ocular reactions. (**Bimatoprost**: may ↓ IOP 1mmHg more than latanoprost) [9]<br>**Systemic side effects: (up to 10% incidence)**, skin reaction (toxic epidermal necrolysis possible), upper respiratory tract infection/cold/flu (4%), chest pain, muscle & joint pain (1-2%)<br>**Topical SE: (up to 15% incidence)** altered iris pigmentation (7-22% ) (esp. in patients with mixed pigmentation), foreign body sensation, blurred vision, & burning on instillation (>10%), mild conjuctival hyperemia (improves after 2-4weeks), dry eye, tearing, pain, photophobia, edema; darkening, thickening, & lengthening of the eyelashes PGAs found in as adulterant: Age Intervention Eyelash, darkening of the eyelid (esp. NB if tx is in one eye only) or discolor contacts. Rare anterior uveitis.<br>**Drug Interactions**: thimerosol preservative→immediate precipitate forms (thus give >5mins apart). Don't use 2 PG F2α concurrently.[10] ?Topical NSAIDs. |
| **Latanoprost**<br>XALATAN 0.005% soln | 1 gtt q hs<br>1 study showed hs better than am dosing | $39 (2.5ml) | |
| **Travoprost**<br>TRAVATAN reg & Z 0.004% sol | 1 gtt qhs<br>(Z :no benzalkonium) | $72 (2.5, **5** ml) | |
| **Bimatoprost**<br>LUMIGAN 0.03% sol (0.01% RC soln ⊗)<br>-also work by trabecular pathway | 1 gtt qhs | $46 (3ml) | |
| **β-Blockers:** ↓ aqueous production/secretion via sympathetic receptor blockade in the ciliary body *(~20-25% ↓ in IOP)* | | | β-blockers are a reasonable **1st line** option for POAG **if no CI exists** (asthma, COPD, bradycardia, heart block, overt CHF, cardiogenic shock)<br>Dose once or twice a day. Dosing at night seems to be less effective in reducing IOP.<br>**Systemic side effects (up to 10% incidence)**: ↓HR, ↓BP, CHF, cold extremities, bronchospasm, ↓ symptoms of hypoglycemia, ↓ libido, itchy red skin, alopecia, CNS SE's (H/A, depression, fatigue, weakness etc.), tolerance to IOP ↓'ing effect may occur with prolonged therapy<br>-systemic side effects are more likely to occur with timolol & levobunolol (non-selective β1β2 antagonism) vs betaxolol (β1-selective) but may be less effective at ↓ eye pressure<br>**Topical SE: (up to 10% incidence)** stinging, dry eyes, foreign body sensation, itching, photophobia, blurred vision, ↓ visual acuity, eyelash crusting<br>-allergic reaction has been reported (no cross-reactivity between agents, therefore may switch within the class)<br>**Drug interactions**: caution with other drugs that ↓ HR/BP (eg. digoxin, other systemic beta-blockers, diltiazem & verapamil) |
| **Betaxolol**<br>BETOPTIC S 0.25% susp | 1 gtt q12-24h | $34 (10ml) | |
| **Levobunolol**<br>BETAGAN 0.25, **0.5**% soln | 1 gtt q12-**24**h | $26 (5,**10**ml) | |
| **Timolol**<br>TIMOPTIC **0.25**,0.5% soln | 1 gtt q**12**-24h | $25 (10ml) | |
| TIMOPTIC XE **0.25**,0.5%gelsoln | 1 gtt q24h | $28 (5ml),$21 g | |
| **α2 Agonists:** ↓ aqueous production via local α2 agonist action, but may also ↑ uveo-scleral outflow *(~18-27% ↓IOP)* | | | Note: Brimonidine may also ↑ uveoscleral outflow & useful addition to prostaglandin tx Bournias'09<br>Dipivefrin Propine : Discontinued in 2005, was a prodrug of epinephrine therefore ↑ potency & ↑ tolerability (but still not great) vs. epinephrine ophthalmic drops.<br>Apraclonidine for perioperative control of IOP (1%) and as short-term adjunctive therapy in POAG (0.5%) (2nd-3rd line tx)<br>-may not provide ↑ benefit when given with β-blockers or carbonic anhydrase inhibitors because they have common MOA's<br>-usually only short-term therapy b/c tachyphylaxis develops (apraclonidine>brimonidine) and topical side effects<br>**Systemic side effects: (up to 10% incidence)** dry mouth/nose, arrhythmias, H/A, ↓ HR, anxiety, sleep disturbances,↓ BP, lethargy, fatigue, drowsiness<br>-CNS SE's more common with brimonidine (>10%) (vs. apraclonidine) due to ↑ lipophilicity. Toxic in kids with inadvertent oral overdose. brimonidine; eg. respiratory arrest<br>**Topical SE: (up to 10% incidence)** burning/stinging, photophobia, blurred vision, mydriasis (dipivefrin), blanching , eyelid elevation.<br>Allergic reaction with apraclonidine (incidence as high as 50%): hyperemia, pruritis, discomfort, edema & ++tearing. May be better tolerated with Alphagan P.<br>**Drug interactions:** ↑ effect of CNS depressants (eg. alcohol, benzodiazepines, etc.), MAOI's contraindicated with apraclonidine, other drugs that ↓BP |
| **Apraclonidine**<br>IOPIDINE **0.5**%; 1% soln⊗ | 1 gtt q**8**-12h | $32 (5ml) | |
| **Brimonidine**<br>ALPHAGAN/PMS/Apo0.2% soln | 1 gtt q8-12h | $30 (5&**10**ml) | |
| ALPHAGAN P ✆ 0.15%soln;generic | 1 gtt q8-12h | $35 (5&**10**ml),$26 g | |
| **Carbonic Anhydrase Inhibitors (CAIs):** ↓ production of aqueous humour by 40-60% *(Topicals: ~15-20% ↓IOP)* | | | Well tolerated and can be used as both monotherapy (q8h) or as adjunct treatment (q12h). **Caution**: in diseases that may induce acidosis (COPD, diabetes, hepatic/renal insufficiency), if Creatinine Cl <30mL/min (eliminated renally) & possible cross-sensitivity with **sulfonamides.** {Note: **Oral CAIs** may ↓ IOP by 30-50%, but many SEs.}<br>**Systemic side effects: (up to 10% incidence)** bitter taste (25%), H/A, nausea, fatigue<br>-possible blood dyscrasias (as seen with PO acetazolamide: rare, non-dose-dependent effect)<br>**Topical SE: (up to 10% incidence)** immediate ocular discomfort (33% with dorzolamide, **improved with brinzolamide**), superficial punctate keratitis (10-15% with dorzolamide), blurred vision, allergy.<br>**Drug interactions:** salicylates have caused accumulation of oral acetazolamide (=CNS toxicity, metabolic acidosis); never been shown with eyedrops but it is possible, as ophthalmic CAInh's are absorbed systemically. {**Corneal transplantation**: CAIs long term may lead to graft decompensation.} |
| **Brinzolamide**<br>AZOPT 1% susp | 1 gtt q8-12h | $26 (5ml) | |
| **Dorzolamide**<br>TRUSOPT **2**% soln | 1 gtt q8-12h | $28 (5ml) | |
| **Parasympathetic agents: (Direct and Indirect)** ↑ aqueous outflow via trabecular meshwork *(~20-30% ↓IOP)* | | | Pilocarpine has similar efficacy to β-blockers in terms of IOP reduction but not as well tolerated (2nd line tx)<br>-2% soln 1 gtt q6-12h produces desired response in most patients (patients with darkly pigmented eyes may require higher doses of pilocarpine)<br>Cholinesterase inhibitor reserved for those who don't respond to other agents (3rd or 4th line tx) due to their high incidence of ocular and systemic side effects<br>-miosis occurs within 10-30 min of echothiophate administration and can last up to 4 weeks<br>-Refrigerate echothiophate until reconstituted, then stable for 1 month at room temp or 3 months if kept in the refrigerator<br>**Systemic side effects: (up to 10% incidence)** headache/**browache** (tends to reduce with longer term use), nervousness, polyuria, hypersensitivity reactions<br>-H/A, sweating, tremor, salivation, N/V, diarrhea, cramps, ↓ BP/HR (more likely with AchE inhibitors) (<1%). {Atropine can reduce systemic toxicity symptoms}<br>**Topical SE: (up to 10% incidence)** local burning and stinging, photophobia, myopia leading to decreased vision at night, fixed small pupils. Cataracts can occur especially with echothiophate, and its prolonged use may cause formation of rounded nodules (cysts) of the pigmentary epithelium which may interfere with vision (usually reversible if discontinue drug). **Drug interactions:** Stop echothiophate prior to surgery because prolonged apnea with general anaesthetic |
| **Direct Acting Cholinergic Agonists:** | | | |
| **Pilocarpine** mimics acetylcholine effect<br>1,2,4,6⊗ % soln; | 1 gtt q4-**12**h | $10 (10ml) | |
| 4% gel PILOPINE-HS | ½ " at HS | $23 (5g) | |
| **Indirect Acting Agonist (AchE inhibitor):** | | | |
| **Echothiophate** soln ✗<br>PHOSPHOLINE IODIDE | **Summer 2001 - D/C by Co** | | |

| **Combination Therapies:** multiple mechanisms of action (synergy) | Sig | Cost# | |
|---|---|---|---|
| **Timolol/Dorzolamide:** COSOPT (0.5%/2%) soln -bottle/Ocumeter Plus 0.2ml unit dose ✗⊗ | 1 gtt q12h | $41 (5,10ml) | Timolol and pilocarpine have additive effects on IOP (i.e. ~↓ 40-70%) |
| **Timolol/ Brimonidine:** COMBIGAN (0.5%/0.2% ) susp | 1 gtt q12h | $55 (**10**ml) | Dorzolamide and timolol have additive effects on IOP (i.e. ~↓ 35-65%) |
| **Timolol/ Latanoprost:** XALACOM (0.5%/0.005% ) susp ⊗ | 1 gtt hs | $44 (2.5ml) | XALACOM was better tolerated & more effective than COMBIGAN in one 6 month trial[11] |
| **Timolol/ Travoprost:** DUOTRAV (0.5%/0.004% ) susp | 1 gtt od am | $44 (2.5ml) | Combinations may offer both **cost & convenience advantages** over same agents given separately |
| **Timolol/ Brinzolamide:** AZARGA (0.5%/1% ) susp ⊗ (Formulary recommendation: CDR'10) | 1 gtt q12h | $32 (5ml) | {TIMPILO 2 & 4 & Levobunolol/Dipivefrin PROBETA **-Discontinued by Co**} |

**Notes**: **POAG**= primary open angle glaucoma; **IOP**= intraocular pressure **Cost** =month of therapy in Sask.. incl. mark-up & dispensing fee (when multiple strengths/intervals exist, **bolded strength/interval** used to calculate cost) ▼=covered by NIHB ✆=prior approval NIHB ✗=non-form ☎=EDS **AchE**=acetylcholinesterase **BP**=blood pressure **CAInh**=carbonic anhydrase inhibitors **CI**=contraindication **CNS**=central nervous system **H/A**=headache **MOA**=mechanism of action **PNS**=Parasympathetic nervous system **SE**=side effect ⊗=not NIHB

**Drug Induced IOP**: eg. antidepressants TCA's, antihistamines 1st generation, atropine, benzodiazepines, caffeine, corticosteroids, decongestants, ketamine, muscle relaxants, naphazoline, oxybutynin, phenylephrine, phenothiazines, salbutamol, scopolamine, succinylcholine & tolterodine.

**Target IOP**: Consider setting individualized target IOP for treatment based on **staging of severity** (suspect, early, moderate, advanced). see tables on web page Re-evaluate at each visit based on disease progression; patient's quality of life & ability to tolerate treatment. Canadian Guidelines 2009

**Pregnancy**: Treat topically with caution. **Consider**: α2 agonists (but toxic brimonidine overdoses in kids reported), β-Blockers (monitor fetal heart rate, arrhythmia), cholinergics. **Avoid**: PGA's (may cause uterine contraction & influence fetal circulation theoretical), CAI's (? teratogenic po). [12]

# INTRANASAL CORTICOSTEROIDS (INCS) [1,2,3,4,5,6,7,8,9,10,11,12,13,14,15,16,17,18]

Prepared by: B. Jensen, L. Regier © www.RxFiles.ca May 10

| Generic/ TRADE g=generic — Pregnancy Category [19] | Side Effects (Common & Rare) | Contraindications CI Precautions | Systemic Bioavailability [2] | Dose: For Perennial & seasonal allergic rhinitis **USUAL & MAX** | $ per bottle (~30-50cents/day) **Scented** vs Non | Comments 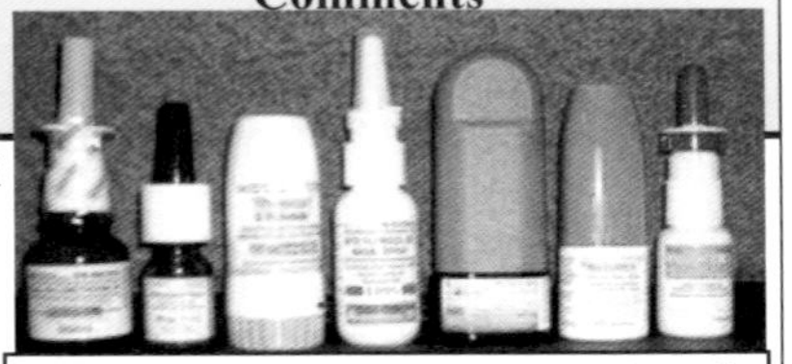 |
|---|---|---|---|---|---|---|
| **Beclomethasone dipropionate** C<br>generic only<br>50ug aqueous spray [i]<br>(previously available as BECONASE AQ) | **Common:**<br>Transient nasal irritation (burning/stinging[<10%]), epistaxis[<10%], pharyngitis[<5%], sneezing[<3%] in hyperactive nose, rhinitis[<3%], headache[<3%], & taste/smell/voice changes. | **Contraindications**<br>Hypersensitivity reaction to any component of the medication; in pts. With untreated fungal, bacterial, tuberculosis & viral infections<br>**Precautions:**<br>Excess Nasal | High: 44%<br>400ug/day did not affect HPA; however 800ug/day did ↓ urinary cortisol<br>Growth retardation: small but sig. effect in 6-9yr olds over 1yr [20] | 1-2 spray in EACH nostril BID Max 3 spray EN BID<br>(Kids <6yr not rec.)<br>Also indicated for: ↓ nasal polyps if >5yr | **$22** / 200 doses<br>(metered pump & nasal applicator in amber glass bottle)<br>◆ **Scented** | i<br>◆ **Storage**: protect from light, discard after 3 months use; shake well<br>◆ effectiveness / safety established with >20yrs of experience |
| **Budesonide**<br>RHINOCORT AQUA generic<br>64ug [ii], 100ug aqueous suspension nasal spray B<br>RHINOCORT Turbuhaler (100ug dry powder [iii]) | **Rare:**<br>Ulceration of mucous membranes, Pharyngeal candidiasis, | Secretions: may ↓ effectiveness (blowing first +/- decongestants important)<br>Steroid Withdrawal: can occur if pt. **stops systemic steroid** | Moderate: 31%<br>(Turbuhaler 22% [29])<br>HPA:none [21,22,23,24]; ? some effect [25]<br>Growth retardation: none at 2yr [26], some in asthma [27,28] | 1-2 spray in EACH nostril OD Max 1 spray EN BID<br>(Kids <6yr not rec.)<br>Also indicated for: ↓ nasal polyps if >5yr | **$20** / 10ml / ~120 doses 64ug<br>**$24** / 10ml / ~165 doses 100ug<br>{1 spray EN OD→ lowest price @ ~30¢/day}<br>(metered dose, nasal adapter in amber glass bottle)<br>**$34** Turbuhaler / 200 doses | **ii** (Rhinocort Aqua), **iii** (Turbuhaler)<br>◆ **Turbuhaler** has no additives, & less bioavailability vs spray [29]; may be favored if post nasal drip is bothersome<br>◆ effectiveness / safety established with >20yrs of experience<br>◆ **DI**: itraconazole ↑ Cushing's risk [30] |
| **Flunisolide** C<br>RHINALAR, generic<br>~25ug (0.025%) nasal spray [iv] | ↓ wound healing esp. in nasal area, & skin rash. | therapy too quickly, after starting INCS (pain, depression & adrenal suppression can occur; also can | High: 40-50%<br>Growth retardation: none at 1yr [31] in asthma | 1-2 spray in EACH nostril BID Max 3 spray EN BID<br>Kids 6-14yr 1spray EN TID<br>(Kids <6yr not rec.) | **$24** / 25ml / ~225 doses<br>(metered pump & nasal applicator in a plastic bottle) | **iv** (Rhinalar)<br>◆ Contains polyethylene glycol which may keep nose moist |
| **Fluticasone** propionate<br>FLONASE, generic<br>50ug aqueous nasal spray [v]<br>**Fluticasone furoate** ≥2yr<br>AVAMYS nasal spray ✗ ⊗ C | **Very rare:**<br>Nasal septal perforation, ? atrophic rhinitis, | **unmask** existing asthma or eczema)<br>↓ Thyroid & Cirrhosis: ↑ corticosteroid effects | **Very Low:** ~0.5%<br>HPA: none [2], some effect [32]<br>Growth retardation: none at 1yr [33, 34] (in asthma) | 1-2 spray in EACH nostril OD Max 2 spray EN BID<br>(Kids <4yr not rec.)<br>Also: sinusitis acute if ≥12yr | **$31** g [$43] / ~120 doses<br>(metered pump & nasal applicator in amber glass bottle)<br>◆ **Scented** | **v** (Flonase) -also new generic avail.<br>◆ **Storage**: shake gently before use<br>◆ **DI:** ketoconazole, rito- & ataza-navir ↑ risk of Cushing's [35] |
| **Mometasone** furoate monohydrate<br>NASONEX C<br>~50ug (0.05%) aqueous nasal spray [vi] | face/tongue edema, ↑ intraocular pressure & hypertrichosis.<br>Systemic effects may be more of a | Nasal Structure: so far, biopsies normal[30]<br>**Growth retardation**: Minimal effect, but a beclomethasone trial[1yr] found a small effect.[20] | **Very Low:** ~0.5%<br>HPA: no effect<br>Growth retardation: none at 1yr [36] | 1-2 spray in EACH nostril OD Max 4 spray EN BID<br>(Kids <3yr not rec.)<br>Also: sinusitis acute if ≥12yr<br>polyposis if ≥18yr; 200ugBID | **$40** / ~140 sprays<br>(metered pump & nasal applicator in a plastic bottle)<br>◆ **New: Scent free Oct/06**<br>**Also as Scented** | **vi** (Nasonex)<br>◆ **Storage**: protect from light, shake before use |
| **Triamcinolone** acetonide<br>NASACORT AQ C<br>~55ug aqueous nasal spray [vii] | concern if on other corticosteroids (e.g. for asthma) † | Not seen in products that have **low** systemic bioavailability. | High: 46%<br>HPA: no effect<br>Growth retardation: none at 2yr [37] | 1-2 spray in EACH nostril OD<br>(Kids <4yr not rec.) | **$35** ~120 sprays<br>(metered pump & nasal applicator in a plastic bottle) | **vii** (Nasacort Aq)<br>◆ **Storage**: shake before use |
| **Non Steroidal Nasal Anti-inflammatory:** B<br>Cromoglycate sodium **Rhinaris** Cromolyn 2% nasal pump soln OTC ▼, Covered Sask | Adults & ≥2yr : 1 spray TID-QID [14,15] -effective prophylaxis if before isolated allergy exposure[18] (eg. cats/cutting lawn); low potency but very safe (even for **pregnancy & kids ≥2 yrs**), but benefits for seasonal allergic rhinitis in ~1-2weeks. {Expert Opinion: **Opthalmic formulation** often useful for eye symptoms whereas **Intranasal formulation** often not very helpful.} | | | | | |

☎=Exception Drug Status ✗ =non-form Sask. **BP**=blood pressure **EN**=each nostril **HPA**=hypothalamic pituitary adrenal axis **OTC**=Over the Counter **Pts**=patients **rec**=recommended C=Pregnancy: possible fetal risk (evident in animals) ▼=covered NIHB

**Efficacy**: potent & effective for nasal symptoms (blockage, rhinorrhoea, sneezing, itching) in mod-severe allergic rhinitis. Also for **nasal polyps** & **chronic sinusitis** not acute. No evidence one INCS more efficacious than another.[13]

**Therapeutic Tips**: ◆**Ensure adequate dose & duration!** ◆Optimal effects of INCS seen within **~3-14days** (whereas decongestants work quickly) ◆**Best given regularly & ~1week before allergen exposure** ◆ Seasons of heavy allergen challenge may necessitate additional therapy especially for eye symptoms ◆Topical route: requires lower doses than with oral steroids & lowers side effect potential ◆BID dosing of agents may ↑ efficacy (even if same daily dose is used). ◆With chronic dosing a dose reduction is often possible & desirable ◆**Initial Priming**: a few actuations to create uniform spray (re-prime if spray used infrequently). ◆**Concern** if unilateral Sx.

**Administration**: Blow nose, then insert nozzle into the nostril; avoid placing nozzle tip in too far; compress the opposite nostril & actuate the spray while inspiring through the nose, with closed mouth. Avoid blowing nose for ~15mins. **Medication is aimed away from the septum** towards the turbinates (outer part of the nose) to lessen nasal bleeding. Vaseline may be used to lubricate the anterior nasal septal area. {The **Contralateral Hand Nostril technique** has been recommended. It uses the alternate hand method – the **right hand to spray in the left nostril**; and vice versa.[38]}

† **Systemic Steroid Cautions**: **(unlikely with low→normal dose INCS)**: ↑ BP, diabetes, infections, thin skin, ↑ weight, cause cataracts & osteoporosis (treat: Calcium 1500mg/d, Vit. D 800iu/d, +/- bisphosphonates).

**Drug Induced Rhinitis**: α & β blockers (eg. prazosin), **ASA/NSAIDs** in susceptible individuals, chlorpromazine, cocaine abuse, eye drops, methyldopa, oral contraceptives & **topical decongestants** (rebound congestion with overuse).

**Other Therapy**: **Antihistamine**:[39] for itching, sneezing & rhinorrhoea; combo with INCS may lack ↑efficacy vs INCS alone.[6,40] **Decongestant**: for congestion. **Ophthalmics**: for eye symptoms. **Atrovent nasal**: for rhinorrhoea. Neti Pot

Not avail. in Canada: Azelastine ASTELIN nasal & ocular antihistamine: 2 sprays each nostril BID (5-11yr: 1 spray each nostril BID [15]) -has rapid onset, but sometimes leaves a bitter taste & rarely sedation; useful for patients with mucosal irritation/nose bleeds.
New to Canada: Ciclesonide OMNARIS ⊗ nasal pro-drug corticosteroid spray, 2 x 50ug hypotonic aqueous sprays in each nostril daily, Max 200ug/day [$35 / 120 doses], approved for ≥12yr for seasonal allergic rhinitis [eg. hayfever] & perennial allergic rhinitis [eg. dust mites, animal dander, mould].

| Route of Administration | Drug | Trade Name (g=generic avail.) | Formulation | Usual Dosage Range (adult men androgen deficiency) | $ /30 days | Comments |
|---|---|---|---|---|---|---|
| **ORAL** | **Testosterone undecanoate** | **ANDRIOL** ✗ ⊗ (new: **generic**) **Males**: 120-160mg/d x2-3weeks as loading dose; 40-120mg/d maintenance dose | 40mg cap | **80mg AM + 40mg PM**<br>80mg BID **after meals** swallow without chewing<br>40mg every other day ♀? | **$108** [77g]<br>$142 [99g]<br>$ 25 [19g] | ◆ taking **after meals** greatly enhances absorption [1,2]<br>◆ no effect on liver function over 10yrs (observation)[3]<br>◆ new castor oil & propylene glycol formulation thus up to **2yr** shelf-life when stored at room temp. |
| **TRANSDERMAL -GEL -pump** ✗ ⊗ | **Testosterone 1% Gel** (5g **packet** delivers 50mg testosterone & approx. 10% absorbed) | **ANDROGEL** (1 **actuation** delivers 12.5mg testosterone, 1st use→ prime 5times) | -2.5g, 5g **packet**<br>-metered 60 dose **pump** | **-5g daily in AM** *initial dose* ♂<br>7.5-10g daily in AM<br>-5g (4 actuations) daily<br>10g(8 actuations) daily | **$131**<br>$131-253<br>$150 [2pump]<br>✗ ⊗ | ◆ apply to shoulder/abdomen/upper arms then wash hands<br>◆ patient should wait >6hrs before showering, etc.<br>◆ can **transfer** to partner/kids ∴T-shirt before hugging<br>◆ **gel** generally better tolerated than patch but flammable when wet |
| ✗ ⊗ | **Testosterone 1% Gel** -?↑ absorption vs Androgel | **TESTIM** | 5g | **-5g daily in AM** *initial dose* ♂<br>7.5-10g daily in AM | **$125**<br>✗ ⊗ | ◆ apply to shoulder/arm upper; avoid **transfer** to others wash hands<br>◆ patient should wait >2hrs before showering, etc. |
| **TRANSDERMAL PATCH** ✗ ⊗ | **Testosterone** (in alcohol based gel) | **ANDRODERM**<br>12.2g patch delivers 2.5mg/24hr;<br>24.3g patch delivers 5mg/24hr. | 2.5mg, 5mg patch<br>reservoir<br>-contains aluminum thus remove prior to MRI scan | 2.5mg patch daily at HS<br>**5mg patch daily at HS**<br>7.5mg patch(s) daily at HS<br>(Apply between 8 & 12 PM) | $71<br>**$135**<br>$198<br>✗ ⊗ | ◆ produces stable – normal testosterone levels (8-12hrs after nightly application)<br>◆ **skin irritation** at site; burn-like blister >10%; if mild may use low potency topical corticosteroid<br>◆ apply to back, abdomen, thigh or upper arms; avoid bony areas; ROTATE site weekly<br>◆ contact with water does not affect patch |
| **INJECTABLE**<br>**Cost:** also consider cost of additional visits to receive injections. | **Testosterone cypionate** | **DEPO-TESTOSTERONE**g | 100mg/ml (10ml Vial) | 100mg IM q2wks<br>150mg IM q2-3wks Alternating buttocks | $ 14<br>$ 19 | ◆ supratherapeutic levels during first few days; subtherapeutic levels thereafter; ∴**more** prone to side effects (eg. mood disturbance, ?↑polycythemia, inj pain)<br>◆ testosterone levels: 7th day injection (mid range)<br>◆ range: 50mg q2wk – 200mg q2wk - 400mg q4wks |
| | **Testosterone enanthate** | **DELATESTRYL**g [smaller injection volume advantage] | **200mg/ml** (5ml Vial) | 100mg IM q2wks<br>150mg IM q2-3wks<br>100mg IM q4wks ♀? | $ 25<br>$ 30<br>$ 19 | |

☎ =Exception Drug Status ✗ =non-formulary Sask ⊗=not covered NIHB ♂ =male; ♀ =**dose in women; {caution -data lacking!** [4] Dose must be individualized}. **Conversion Factor:** Testosterone ng/dL x **0.0347**=nmol/L

**Major Contraindications:** polycythemia, cancer prostate/testicular/breast, paternity, criminal sexual behavior, prostate hypertrophy IPSS>19 with severe urinary retention & heart failure Class 3/4 **Precautions:** mild prostate hypertrophy, sleep apnea

**Goal of Androgen Therapy:** primarily to improve symptoms of hypogonadism and to bring testosterone levels into the normal range **Therapeutic Trial Duration:** ≥ 3-6 months

**↓ Testosterone Effect:** [5,6] **DRUGS**: alcohol, ?atorvastatin, cimetidine, flutamide, glucocorticoids, ketoconazole, opioids, phenytoin, ?ramelteon, spironolactone; **LIFESTYLE**: smoking, stress, obesity [7]; chronic medical conditions **MEDICAL CONDITIONS**: HIV AIDS, hypothyroidism, hyperprolactinemia (drug induced or prolactinoma), Klinefelter's syndrome, pituitary adenomas or tumors affecting pituitary e.g. meningiomas, chromaphobe adenomas

**Related Conditions & Therapies:** **DEPRESSION** ⇨ antidepressants, mood stabilizers; **ERECTILE DYSFUNCTION** ⇨ **VIAGRA, MUSE**, other; **OSTEOPOROSIS** ⇨ bisphosphonates, $Ca^{++}$ & Vitamin D; **HYPOTHYROIDISM** ⇨ levothyroxine; **LIBIDO** ⇨ multifactorial; **LIFESTYLE** ⇨ exercise, diet, sleep, avoid excess alcohol & caffeine, positive social support/relationships

**CAUTION**: Treatment safe & effective in true hypogonadism but not well established in Partial Androgen Deficiency in the Aging Male (**PADAM**). Trials too small & too short term for heart & prostate outcomes.

### Potential BENEFITS of Androgen Therapy [5,8,9]

- ↓↓ body fat; ↑ lean body mass (LBM) [17]
- ↑ bone density*; lack data on fracture outcomes
- ↑ hand-grip **strength*** (less effect on lower body)
- improvement in **mood***; mixed effects on cognition[5]
- antidepressant effect in depressed refractory ≥4 weeks men with low testosterone levels (preliminary data) [18]
- ↑ libido; possible improvement in sexual function but **often not useful in erectile dysfunction** [15] *; {impotence multifactorial and testosterone often not beneficial; one study found placebo (8 wks) as effective as testosterone undecanoate in treating impotence [19]}
- HIV-AIDS patients: improved quality of life, ↑LBM [20,21]

* **(improvements specifically seen in men with the very low/lowest of testosterone levels)**

### Potential RISKS of Androgen Therapy [10,11,12,13,22]

- **Cardiovascular- ↓HDL**; unknown long-term, ↑CV risk Basaria'10
- **Fluid retention**; exacerbation of heart failure
- **Polycythemia (↑Hgb; ↑Hct) -** ↑stroke risk; less with oral/ transdermal forms which provide stable levels
- **Gynecomastia** (especially if **hepatic/renal** disease)
- **Testicular:** atrophy or infertility[22]
- **Prostate:** ↑ prostate size; ↑ PSA but usually within normal range; possible acceleration of prostate cancer; **Difficulty with urination** - 2° to benign prostatic hypertrophy (one study found retardation in BPH [23])
- **Sleep apnea? -** may exacerbate caution in obese, smokers, COPD
- **Pregnancy**–may cause ♀ sexual changes pseudohemaphroditism
- **Other**: acne; exacerbation of aggression, hostility, alopecia, inappropriate sexual behavior or psychotic illness [24]

{Hepatotoxicity only with anabolic 17-α-alkylated forms e.g. stanozolol}

### MONITORING of Androgen Patients [14,15,16,22]

- **Clinical evaluation** of symptom response & SE (from pt &/or spouse or family member). Sx's may be: ↓ frequency of morning erection & sexual thoughts, & erectile dysfx.
- **Prostate assessment**: baseline & annually; some references suggest more frequent in first year [14,16,22]
  - questionnaire regarding urinary/prostate symptoms
  - digital rectal exam (DRE) & **PSA** (range: 0-4 ug/L)
- **Lab Tests**: Hct concern if >54%, Hgb, Liver Function Tests
- **CV assessment**: lipid/TG profile, edema, weight gain
- **Testosterone** in AM total level (normal = **6-29**nmol/L SK Prov Lab) **Free Androgen Index** ⇨**provides better measure of bioavailable testosterone** (normal ♂ = **14.8-94.8**); (accounts for effect of sex hormone binding globulin SHBG)
- **Sleep** disturbance: excessive snoring; sleep apnea
- **Mood** changes

Monitor: at baseline; for efficacy at 1-2 months; q3-6months in 1st yr; & annually thereafter. [22]

**See also:** **Sexual Dysfunction Chart:** http://www.rxfiles.ca/rxfiles/uploads/documents/members/CHT-Sexual-Dysfx-Drugs-Overview.pdf ; **Erectile Dysfunction Chart:** http://www.rxfiles.ca/rxfiles/uploads/documents/members/Cht-erectile-dysfx.pdf

# ⇨ APPROACH TO MANAGEMENT OF TYPE 2 DIABETES (T2DM) in Adults

## Nonpharmacologic Therapy: {nutrition & activity ⇨ weight loss of ≥5% or ≥4kg can ↓ hyperglycemia}

☆ •**Lifestyle Modifications** [1] portion plate,pedometer & **Patient Education** are important at all levels! [2,3,4]

*If individualized goals for glucose are not achieved in 2-3 months, ⇨reassess; advance to next level of therapy*

See Health Canada's Food & Fitness Guides &/or CDA Guidelines.{Consider low-glycemic,Mediterranean diet.Shai 08}

## Oral Hypoglycemic Monotherapy {Note: if A1C ≥ 9%, consider MF + 2nd agent concurrently.}

☆ •**For most, especially if obese or overweight**

FYI: MF target dose in UKPDS-34 (obese, age ≤65): 1700mg am + 850mg @ supper (↓ mortality NNT=14/10yr)

⇨ start **metformin (MF) 250-500mg po OD**
(Titrate dose up slowly to improve GI tolerance!; **over 3-4 weeks or longer if GI side effects**;
usual dose ≤ 2,000mg/day; lower doses in elderly &/or ↓renal fx (see Table 6)

⇨ alternative agents used if metformin contraindicated/not tolerated
eg. secretagogues (e.g. sulfonylureas, repaglinide), TZDs not rosiglitazone-ADA'08, insulin, acarbose; see chart
{In rare "young, thin T2DM", sulfonylurea (SU) low-moderate dose or metformin suitable for initial tx}

⇨ If TZDs considered, these agents can take a long time before full effect seen (6+ weeks). There are theoretical advantages to early use but also concerns about ↑ weight, HF, fractures (♀) & possibly cardiovascular (CV) risk. {CV & MI risk concerns mostly with rosiglitazone.}

*Repeat A1C ; Reassess lifestyle modifications in 2-4 months* {Attain target A1C in 6-12 months.}

⇨*If targets for glucose control not achieved, consider advancing to combination therapy*

## Oral Combination Therapy (2 agents often needed: after 3yrs 50%; after 9yrs 75%)

•a variety of 2-drug combinations e.g. (MF + SU lower half of dose range) may be considered (see Table 7); repaglinide +sulfonylurea not usually recommended; consider risks & benefits of other combos.
{2rd line/agent options: basal insulin NPH, detemir or glargine; a TZD e.g. pioglitazone; new agents? (Consider early insulin!)

*Repeat A1C ; Reassess lifestyle modifications in 2-4 months,*

⇨*If targets for glucose control not achieved, consider next level of therapy* (Note lack good evidence for combos)

## Add Insulin Therapy +/- Oral Agents (MF will limit wt gain & insulin dose required)

•**Option 1: Bedtime basal insulin** (e.g. NPH or N) **+ daytime oral hypoglycemics** e.g. metformin 4-T trial

⇨**if** on SU + other oral agent, consider discontinuing or reducing the dose of the SU (or could use a metiglinide)

**-add intermediate or long-acting insulin, 5-10 units at HS** (or initial dose: ~ 0.1 - 0.2 units/kg; very obese ~ 15 units)

-↑ **insulin: Option 1)** by 2 units every 3-4 days until FPG of 4 -7 (or by 1 unit/day till target is reached.)

{or **Option 2**) Titration is patient specific; however an **example of a q-weekly titration regimen** could be: if FPG in previous few days: [7.1-8 mmol/L, 2 units]; [8.1-10 mmol/L, 4 units]; [10.1-12 mmol/L, 6 units]; No ↑ or may need ↓ if ≥ 2 episodes of BG <4 mmol/L at any time in preceding week, if severe hypoglycemia (i.e. requiring assistance), FPG < 3.1 in preceding week or any nocturnal hypoglycemia.}

-if target BG not achieved at 30units/day, or ↑ in daytime BG, may switch to split-mixed or more intensive regimen (usual range: 0.25-1unit/kg/d). To add bolus insulin to basal insulin, take [current basal insulin dose ÷ 10] = bolus dose at largest meal; reduce basal insulin dose by the same amount; titrate. 2nd & 3rd mealtime injections can be added similarly in succession.

•**Option 2: Switch to insulin therapy 1-4x/day**

⇨if starting mealtime insulin, discontinue SUs &/or glitinides (see Table 7)

-adjust insulin dose & frequency to achieve targets without hypoglycemia

Some patients may eventually require very high doses of insulin due to insulin resistance (max 400units/day used in UKPDS)

e.g. Split-mixed regimen: total starting daily dose (depends on patient, other drugs, etc.; 0.1-0.5 units/kg; safer to start lower!)
Basal/bolusTID or QID: ≥40% of total dose as basal; other 60% as bolus/prandial divided TID at mealtimes adjust per diet/exercise
BID: divide daily dose: 2/3 pre-breakfast; 1/3 in evening pre-supper; divide each dose: 2/3 basal & 1/3 bolus (or 30/70 mix)

(**Note:** insulin temporarily indicated in any pt with metabolic decompensation, severe fasting hyperglycemia, or severe illness.)

| GLUCOSE TARGETS CDN '08 Adult | Target for most | Normal | Frail elderly AGS'03 |
|---|---|---|---|
| **A1C** q3-6mon (calibrate meter q-yr) | ≤ 7 (≤6.5% in some) | ≤ 6 | ≤ 8 |
| **FPG** (mmol/L) | 4-7 | 4-6 | |
| **PPG** (mmol/L) 2hr post | 5-10 | 5-8 (consider if A1C not met) | |

Note: pursue targets **if** can be done **safely** without hypoglycemia etc. ADA'08 30

**Individualize targets:** More aggressive in young adult with recent diagnosis STENO-2; less aggressive in **frail elderly** [32]. **ACCORD** A1C arm halted due to ↑death NNH= 95 / 3.5yr in aggressive target group (A1C <6 Achieved=6.4) vs standard target group (A1C: 7-7.9 Achieved=7.5); in patients with established T2DM at high CV risk ~ 10 yr hx.

**Screen**: if BP >135/80 USPSTF'08; FPG: screen q3yrs if risk factors or ≥40yrs old. Estimate **average glucose** eAG: 8.5mmol/l = an A1C 7%

**Diagnosis**: A1C since fast, easy, non-fasting (Prediabetes: 5.7-6.4%; Diabetes: ≥6.5%) ADA 2010; FPG≥7 mmol/l; OGTT 2hr plasma glucose ≥ 11.1 mmol/l

**BP** 2010 Diabetes→**130/80** **LIPID** 2009 Diabetes most→LDL<**2** or ↓ by ≥50% Total Chol/HDL<**4** (Lower risk: younger without risk factors)

| RENAL | Normal | Microalbuminuria Start ACEI or ARB | Macroalbuminuria |
|---|---|---|---|
| Albuminuria | <30mg/day (<20ug/min) | 30-300mg/day (20-200ug/min) | >300mg/day( >200ug/min) |
| Albumin mg/Creatinine mmol Ratio | Male <2; Female <2.8 | Male 2-20; Female 2.8-28 | Male >20; Female >28 |

| BMI (kg/m²) | | 45kg | 50 | 55 | 60 | 65 | 70 | 75 | 80 | 85 | 90 | 95 | 100 | 105 | 110 | 115 | 120 | 125 | 130 |
|---|---|---|---|---|---|---|---|---|---|---|---|---|---|---|---|---|---|---|---|
| HEIGHT (Cm; inches) cm. | in. | 99lbs | 110 | 121 | 132 | 143 | 154 | 165 | 176 | 187 | 198 | 209 | 220 | 231 | 242 | 253 | 264 | 275 | 286 |
| 155cm | 61 | 18½ | 21 | 23 | 25 | 27 | 29 | 31 | 33 | 35½ | 37½ | 39½ | 41½ | 43½ | 46 | 48 | 50 | 52 | 54 |
| 160 | 63 | 17½ | 19½ | 21½ | 23½ | 25½ | 27 | 29 | 31 | 33 | 35 | 37 | 39 | 41 | 43 | 45 | 47 | 49 | 51 |
| 165 | 65 | 16½ | 18½ | 20 | 22 | 24 | 26 | 27½ | 29½ | 31 | 33 | 35 | 36½ | 38½ | 40½ | 42 | 44 | 46 | 48 |
| 170 | 67 | 15½ | 17 | 19 | 21 | 22½ | 24 | 26 | 27½ | 29½ | 31 | 33 | 34½ | 36 | 38 | 40 | 41½ | 43 | 45 |
| 175 | 69 | 14½ | 16 | 18 | 19½ | 21 | 23 | 24½ | 26 | 28 | 29½ | 31 | 32½ | 34½ | 36 | 37½ | 39 | 41 | 42½ |
| 180 | 71 | 14 | 15½ | 17 | 18½ | 20 | 21½ | 23 | 24½ | 26 | 28 | 29 | 31 | 32½ | 34 | 35½ | 37 | 38½ | 40 |
| 185 | 73 | 13 | 14½ | 16 | 17½ | 19 | 20½ | 22 | 23½ | 25 | 26 | 28 | 29 | 30½ | 32 | 33½ | 35 | 36½ | 38 |

Underweight = <18.5kg/m²; **Normal** = 18.5-24.9kg/m²; Overweight = 25-29.9kg/m²; **Obese = ≥30kg/m²**

**Waist Circumference:** ♂ **<94**cm ideal, >102cm high risk; ♀ **<80**cm ideal, >88cm high risk {better risk predictor than BMI} ethnic variable

## Table 6: Individualization of Drug Therapy: Special Considerations

| Patient Factor | Consider ⇨ possibly preferred drugs |
|---|---|
| **Renal failure** * | TZDs Caution: edema, repaglinide; insulin; (also tolbutamide or gliclazide [5]) |
| **Hepatic disease** | **Insulin, repaglinide;** acarbose; (Caution:glyburide,metformin & TZDs) |
| **Hypoglycemia** {consider risk of combos below} | **Metformin**, metformin+sitagliptin, TZDs; also: repaglinide; gliclazide or glimepiride less than long-acting SUs; acarbose; {basal insulin: glargine or detemir somewhat less than intermediate e.g. NPH/ N} |
| **Obese / Overweight** | **Metformin** drug of choice if no CI's; ↓mortality (UKPDS-34); {acarbose; I-Det; new agents?} |
| **Irregular mealtimes** | **Repaglinide** (may be preferred over SU) |
| **PPG >10mmol/L & FPG minimally ↑'d** | **Repaglinide** (or **Acarbose**); Metformin + sitagliptin; Diet ↑fiber **Rapid Acting Insulin** (if PPG very high >10mmol/L) e.g. Lispro, Aspart |
| **IGT/IFG** "Prediabetes" | **Lifestyle** (↓wt, diet/exercise) DPP, FDP; **MF** 850mg BID DPP; orlistat Xendos, acarbose Stop-NIDDM |

* **Metformin dosing**: lactic acidosis assoc. with metformin is rare (<1:10,000 treated pts) [6,7,8]

**MAX Metformin Dose** [9] for CrCl: 60 ml/min ≤1700mg/d; >30 ml/min ≤850mg/d; ≤30 ml/min→contraindicated

## Table 7: Combination Therapy/Insulin Therapy in Type 2 Diabetes [10,11]

| Drug combination | ↓ in A1C | hypo-glyc. | Wt | Comments re Combinations (long-term clinical outcomes not studied!) |
|---|---|---|---|---|
| MF + SU | ↓↓↓ | ↑↑ | ↑/↓ | •if MF initially, may add SU e.g. **gliclazide** or repaglinide •if SU initially, may add MF or TZD; SU+MF may further ↓A1C by 1.7%; 1 study ↑ mortality[12], but ADVANCE neutral* •**MF combos generally result in less weight gain than SU combinations**; •MF+Pioglitazone: positive lipid effects but ↑ edema; MF+rosiglitazone: lower A1C but ↑edema •MF+acarbose: ↓wt & PPG but ↑GI SEs |
| SU + TZD [13] | ↓↓ | ↑↑ | ↑↑ | |
| MF+ repaglinide [14] | ↓↓ | ↑ | ↑ | |
| MF+ sitagliptin | ↓↓ | - | ↓ | |
| MF+ TZD [15,16,17] | ↓↓↓ | -/↑ | ↑ | |
| MF+ acarbose [18] | ↓ | - | ↓ | |
| Exenatide+MF+SU [70] | ↓↓↓ | ↑↑ | ↓ | |
| Insulin monotherapy | ↓↓↓ | ↑↑↑ | ↑↑↑ | •tight BG control but **hypoglycemia/weight gain** |
| Insulin + SU (UKPDS 57 ultralente @ evening) | ↓↓↓ | ↑↑ | ↑↑ | •evening basal insulin; lower A1C & less hypoglycemia than insulin alone; caution in elderly (hypoglycemia) |
| **Insulin + MF** (FINFAT STUDY [19]) | ↓↓↓ | ↑ | ↑ | •**overcomes insulin resistance**; MF has positive effect on wt & lipids; preferred in obese patient; superior to insulin+SU; insulin sparing ~20-25% |
| Insulin+ pioglitazone or rosiglitazone | ↓↓[20] | ↑↑↑ | ↑↑↑ | •overcomes insulin resistance; but potential harms (e.g. ↑ **wt, edema & risk of HF**[21]); risk/benefit?. |
| Insulin+ repaglinide | ↓↓ | ↑↑ | ↑↑ | •option to ↓ PPG, ↑wt more than metformin non-obese Lund'09 |
| Insulin + acarbose | ↓↓ | ↑↑↑ | ↑↑↑ | •↓ PPG diet high in CHOs; also ↓ wt & triglycerides |
| Insulin + 3 orals* | ↓↓↓ | ↑↑↑↑ | ↑↑↑ | •**ACCORD**: >50% of pts on 3 orals+insulin; ↑ **death** * |

***ACCORD**: baseline A1C=8.3%, wt=93kg & very aggressive intervention (>50% on 3 orals + insulin); ↓A1C to 6.4% but ↑ death NNH=95 /3.5yr (& ↑wt. & hypoglycemia). In **ADVANCE**: baseline A1C=7.5%, wt=78kg; most on SU **gliclazide + MF**; ↓A1C to 6.5% & ↓ microvascular NNT=67 /5yr (esp. nephropathy) but also ↑ severe hypoglycemia NNT=83 /5yr & ↑ hospitalizations NNT=42 /5yr.

**A1C** = glycosylated hemoglobin **BG**= blood glucose **CHO**= carbohydrate **FPG**= fasting plasma glucose **HF**= heart failure **MF**= metformin **PPG** = postprandial blood glucose **SE**= side effects www.RxFiles.ca **SU**= sulfonylurea **TZD**= pioglitazone & rosiglitazone **Wt**= weight

**Self monitoring** of BG in **T2DM** has limited effect on A1C ↓~0.25%, yet ↑cost $160 - $2400 / yr & ↑depression. Consider if: using insulin or secretagogue, in select new/motivated diabetics, to aid motivation or if at ↑hypoglycemic risk acute illness, dose Δ's. DiGEM,ESMON,Farmer

# Oral Anti-Hyperglycemic Agents (OAHA) - Comparison Chart [22,23,24,25,26,27,28,29,30 ADA, 31,32,33 CDA, 34,35]

Prepared by: Loren Regier, Brent Jensen, © www.RxFiles.ca May 10

| Generic/TRADE/ (Strength) Pregnancy | KINETICS | EFFECTS ON: FPG | PPG | A1C ↓% | LDL | HDL | TGs | Wt | DRUG INTERACTION | COMMENTS | INITIAL & (Max.) DOSE | USUAL DOSE RANGE | $ (Canada) /100 day |
|---|---|---|---|---|---|---|---|---|---|---|---|---|---|
| **BIGUANIDES – reduces hepatic glucose production; increase insulin sensitivity & cellular glucose uptake & utilization; ↓ morbidity & mortality [NNT=14/10yr] in obese patients (UKPDS-34)** | | | | | | | | | | | | | |
| **Metformin** [36] **(MF)** B<br>GLUCOPHAGE, GLYCON<br>generic (500ς, 850mg tab) | P = 3h<br>D = 8-12h | ↓ | ↓ | ↓<br>1-1.5 | ↓ | ↑ | ↓ | -/↓<br>↓2.9kg Adopt 4yr | • **EtOH** and cimetidine ↑ effect<br>• contrast media (long-term ↓ $B_{12}$ & folate absorption)<br>{**Caution/**↓ dose **CrCl ≤60**ml/min} | Does **not** by itself cause **hypoglycemia.** Possible **wt loss**; ⇨ **DOC for OBESE !** **First line agent** (Used in PCOS[37])<br>**SE: To avoid GI SEs, start low & titrate up q2-4wk**<br>**Avoid**: ↓ renal fx (<**30** ml/min), acute/decompensated HF, liver dx[severe]; 48hr post [iodinated contrast]. {(Lactic acidosis <1:10,000)[7], watch Na bicarb}. Long-term ↓B12 absorption [7%]; anemia [may occur]. **Elderly:** ↓ dose.[38] **Prevents** NIDDM [39 DPP]. ↓ breast [milk levels] | **250-500mg od**<br>(Max: 850mg tid; but usual max 1g bid) | 500mg po bid<br>850mg bid [DPP]<br>1g po bid [Adopt]<br>1700mg po am, 850mg po pm: **UKPDS** | (↓ dose for renal dysfx) 22<br>**43**<br>**35**<br>61 |
| | | **+'ve effect on lipids & wt!** | | | | | | | | | TID dosing option for larger doses to ↓ GI intolerance (dyspepsia, nausea & diarrhea). Consider oral B12 supplement. | | |
| **Metformin** GLUMETZA ✗ ⊗ 0.5&1g ER tab, Max 2g/day[$240] (OD with evening meal).<br>**Metformin/Rosiglitazone** AVANDAMET ☎ ⊗ tabs: (500mg/1,2,4mg BID =$155, $270, $360 /100day tab; 1gm/2,4mg =$290, $390). {**Not in Canada: Metformin/Pioglitazone** ACTOplus met ✗ ⊗ tabs 500/15mg, 850/15mg BID}. MF/Rosi ↓A1c by ~2%; ↑edema & hypoglycemia vs MF alone.<br>**Metformin//Sitagliptin JANUMET** ✗ ⊗ -new in Canada (500/850/1000mg//50mg BID) | | | | | | | | | | | | | |
| **SULFONYLUREAS (SU) Insulin Secretagogue – stimulates β cell insulin release; ↑peripheral glucose [utilization] (↑ #/sensitivity of insulin receptors?); ↓hepatic [gluconeogenesis]; may stop if on insulin** | | | | | | | | | | | | | |
| **Chlorpropamide** ⊗ C<br>DIABINESE,g;(100ς, 250ςmg tabs) | P = 6-8h<br>D =24-**72h** | chlorpropamide **not recommended** due to ↑BP & ↑ retinopathy (UKPDS-33) | | | | | | ↑↑ | **Yes:** ↑ by 2C9 inhibitors eg. amiodarone, Bactrim, fluvastatin…<br>• ↑ Hypoglycemia with: cimetidine, **EtOH**, fluconazole, fluoxetine, MAOIs, NSAIDs, quinolones, salicylates & sulfonamides.<br>• β-Blockers may mask hypoglycemia<br>• Disulfiram rx. with EtOH & chlorpropamide<br>• rifampin ↓ effect | Many (~75%) require 2nd agent for BG control [eg. + MF or TZD]<br>**Hypoglycemia**: most with chlorpropamide & glyburide (see note below); **least**: tolbutamide, glimepiride[40,41] & gliclazide [42]<br>Caution in elderly (hypoglycemia risk) & obese (wt gain).<br>**Require consistent food intake** to avoid problems with hypoglycemia (↑risk: elderly, debilitated, malnourished)<br>**SE: Wt gain,** headache, dizziness, **sulfa** skin rx (rash/ photosensitivity [~1%]),GI SE [1-3%]; tooth discolor [kids-glyburide];<br>Concern: cardiac [toxicity], hyperinsulinemia, hyponatremia & G6PD.<br>Reduce dose if hypoglycemia or renal/hepatic dysfx<br>**Dose titration q1-2 weeks**. Failure rates ~5-10%/year.<br>In general, SUs achieve ~75% of effect at **1/2 their max dose**.<br>Breast milk level minimal likely with glyburide & glipizide.[Glatstein09] | 100mg od<br>(500mg od) | 100mg po od<br>250mg po od | (↓ dose for renal dysfx) 16<br>**13** |
| **Gliclazide**,generic<br>DIAMICRON 80ςmg tab ✗;<br>DIAMICRON MR,g 30 mg tab C | P = 4-6h<br>D=10-**24h** | ↓ | ↓ | ↓<br>1-1.5 | - | - | - | ↑1.6kg Adopt4yr | | Total Wt gain with glyburide >4kg vs **>6kg insulin** (UKPDS-33)[10yr] | 40mg (160mg bid)<br>30mg MR<br>(120mg daily [Advance]) | 80mg po bid<br>60mg MR po od<br>120mg MR po od | **68**<br>41<br>74 |
| **Glyburide** B/C<br>DIABETA,generic<br>(2.5, 5mg scored tabs) | O=<60min<br>P= 2-4h<br>D=12-**24h**<br>↓placenta[transfer] | | | | | | | | | | 1.25-2.5mg od<br>(10mg bid $31) | 5mg po od-bid<br>7.5mg bid [Adopt]<br>Peds: 0.05-0.45mg/kg/d | (↓ dose for renal dysfx) 14-19<br>26<br>←Kir6.2[mutation] |
| **Tolbutamide**,generic C<br>ORINASE (500mg scored tab) | P= 3h<br>D=6-**12h** | | | | | | | | | | 250mg od<br>(1000mg tid) | 500mg po bid<br>500mg po tid | 31<br>**43** |
| | | **Glimepiride** AMARYLg ✗ ⊗(1,2,4mg ς tabs) 1mg od ($61); 2mg od ($61); 4mg od ($61) /100days (↓ dose for renal dysfx)<br>**Glimepiride/rosiglitazone** AVANDARYL ✗ ⊗ (1,2,4/4mg tabs) od with a meal ($325) (↓ dose for renal dysfx)<br>**Glimepiride/pioglitazone DUETACT** ✗ ⊗ in USA C | | | | | | | | | | | |
| **THIAZOLIDINEDIONES (TZDs) or GLITAZONES –Insulin Sensitizers: ↓ hepatic output of glucose & ↑ peripheral insulin uptake; ~ 4-6+ weeks before effect (adjust dose at ~2 months)** | | | | | | | | | | | | | |
| **Pioglitazone** ☎ ✆<br>ACTOS,generic<br>(15, 30, 45 mg tab) C | **Delayed action**…<br>Onset ~3wks | ↓ | ↓ | ↓<br><1<br>or<br>1-1.5 | - | ↑ | ↓ | -/↑<br>↑3.6kg Proactive3yr | • Cholestyramine ↓ absorption ~70%<br>• Hepatic CYP 2C8<br>• rosigl. not CYP 3A4<br>• ?? may ↓ oral contraceptives [pioglitazone]<br>• ↑ by gemfibrozil & ↓ by rifampin | More effective in obese or hyperinsulinemia pts. **Doesn't by itself cause hypoglycemia**; ovulation resumption in anovulatory ♀ [premenopausal PCOS]. **CI**: any HF; triple tx [?MF+SU+ TZDs.]<br>**SE: Edema 4.8% (HF 2x** [43,44];HTN);**↑Wt**; anemia [~1% mild] (due to hemodilution?);↑fractures [esp ♀,2X];monitor **liver fx (ALT)** when indicated; pioglitazone may have more +ve lipid effect[45,46]<br>**ROLE**: +MF, or SU [if MF CI]; (↑↑ HF with insulin); Rosi: ↑MI risk?[60] | 15mg od<br>(45mg/day) | 15mg po od<br>30mg od [Periscope]<br>45mg od [Proactive] | 122g,380<br>162g,**380**<br>228g,550 |
| **Rosiglitazone** ☎ ✆<br>AVANDIA ; 1st approved 2000<br>(2, 4, 8mg tab) =Rosi C | **Max effect in 8-16 wks** | ↓ | ↓ | | 47,48<br>-/↑ | 49,50<br>↑ | -/↓ | -/↑<br>↑4.8kg Adopt 4yr | | | 4mg od<br>{4mg max if with SU}<br>(4mg bid)<br>bid dose ~more effective (51) | 4mg po od<br>4mg po bid [Adopt]<br>8mg od [Dream,Record] | 260<br>495<br>**360** |
| ?? May ↑MI, CV risk [Nissen, DREAM?, FDA];?↑ Macular edema; advise against using rosi ADA'08 | | | | | | | | | | | | | |
| **MEGLITINIDES (GTN) – short-acting insulin secretagogue; bind to β cell to stimulate insulin release at different site than SUs; (adjust dose at ~7days); discontinue if on insulin recommended** | | | | | | | | | | | | | |
| **Nateglinide** ☎ ▼<br>STARLIX<br>(60, 120 mg tab) C | O = **<20min**<br>P=60-120min<br>D = ~**4h** | ↓ | ↓↓ | ↓<br>**0.5** | - | - | - | -/↑ | • CYP [3A4] inhib [↑ effect]: Amiodarone, azole-[antifungal], cipro, clari-/ery-thromycin, cyclosporine, diltiazem, gemfibrozil & PI [HIV meds.]<br>• CYP [3A4] inducers ↓ effect: barbs, carbamaz & rifampin | Restores 1st phase insulin release - (↓ PPG)<br>Rapid, short duration ⇒ May ↓ risk of hypoglycemia vs SUs ∴option in elderly; **{Flexibility with food intake: skip dose if skip meal; take extra dose if add meal}**<br>If stop other hypoglycemics begin next day & watch for hypoglycemia. **ROLE**: alone or + MF, TZD, or insulin<br>Agents lack outcome data on morbidity &mortality. | 60mg tid ac [Navigator NS]<br>(180mg po tid) | 60mg po tid<br>120mg po tid | 199<br>199 |
| **Repaglinide** ☎ ▼<br>GLUCONORM<br>(0.5, 1, 2mg tab) C | O=15-60min<br>P=60-90min<br>D = ~**4-6h** | | | ↓<br>1-1.5 | | | | | | | 0.5mg tid ac {if no prev tx or A1C <8%}<br>(4mg qid) | 0.5mg po tid<br>1-2mg po tid<br>4mg po tid | } **118**<br>235 |
| **α GLUCOSIDASE Inhibitors –inhibit α-glucosidases in brush border of small intestine; prevent hydrolysis & delay carbohydrate digestion** {Tx hypoglycemia with glucose tablets [Dex4], honey or milk; (sucrose not absorbed)} | | | | | | | | | | | | | |
| **Acarbose**<br>GLUCOBAY(prev Prandase)<br>(50,100mg scored tabs) B | **Meal-time dosing**;<br>~8 wks for max. effect | acarbose minimally absorbed; monitor 2hr PPG<br>↓ | ↓↓ | ↓<br>.5-.8 | - | - | -/↓ | -/↓ | • ↓ digoxin effect<br>• Cholestyramine & cathartics ↑ effect<br>• Enzymes[amylase/pancreatic] ↓ effect; • ↓ Fe++? | **SE: GI intolerance**: **flatulence** >41%, **diarrhea** >28%; little hypoglycemia. Acarbose: ↑ LFTs [3%] & hepatic failure. Accumulation in renal failure. Avoid in chronic GI disease.<br>↑ **dose q4-8wks**. **ROLE** minimal: if ↑**PPG**; + SU, MF; (+Insulin?) | **25mg od**<br>(100mg tid) [STOP-NIDDM 52] | 50mg po tid<br>100mg po tid | 100<br>**135** |
| **Miglitol** ✗ ⊗ (not in Can.) | | miglitol GLYSET (25,50,100mg tab) well absorbed | | | | | | | | | 25mg od (100mg tid) | 25-50mg po tid | n/a |
| **Sitagliptin** New 2008 U<br>JANUVIA ✗ ⊗<br>100mg tab (free base) | Onset ≤4wks;<br>~18 wks for max effect | **Dipeptidyl peptidase-4 inhibitor** [DPP-4]<br>↓ | ↓↓ | ↓0.7<br>(0.5-1) | - | - | - | - | • minimal experience<br>• digoxin: small ↑ in dig levels (AUC 11%; Cmax 18%) | ↑insulin secretion [via ↑incretin; ↓glucagon]. **ROLE**: combo MF/SU, mono tx<br>**SE**:throat [sore] (↑infection [URTI, UTI])[Cochrane08], HA,nausea,diarrhea; arthralgia; ↑LFT/SJS/pancreatitis [rare (FDA caution)],less hypoglycemia [but ↑ with SU];edema? | 100mg po OD<br>[25mg & 50mg avail. in USA]<br>100mg/day | 100mg po OD<br>**New**: **no** outcome data & unknown safety! (Not a tier 1 or 2 choice by ADA'08) [72] | (↓ dose for renal dysfx) $305 |

(kidney symbol) = ↓ dose for renal dysfx ς =scored tab **$** Cost =total cost & markup in Sask; ☎ = Exception Drug Status in SK ✗ = Non-formulary in SK ✆ =prior approval for NIHB ⊗=not covered by NIHB ▼ covered by NIHB; '+' denotes combination options

**A1C** = glycosolated Hemoglobin (reflects glycemic control over prior 8-10 weeks) **BP**= blood pressure **DOC**= drug of choice **dysfx**= dysfunction **EtOH**= alcohol **FPG**= fasting plasma glucose **GI**= gastrointestinal **HA**= headache **HDL**= high density lipoprotein **HF**= heart failure **Ins.**= Insulin **KINETICS**: **O**= onset **P**= peak **D**= duration; **LDL**= low density lipoprotein **PPG**= postprandial blood glucose **SE**= side effects **Wt**= weight ς = scored tablet

**Drug induced ↑glucose**: antipsychotic [clozapine, olanzapine…], corticosteroid, cyclosporine, diuretic [thiazide e.g. >25mg HCT], estrogens, GnRH [agonists], interferon [alpha], nicotinic [acid ↑ dose], phenytoin, sympathomimetic [decongestant], siro-, tacro-, temsiro-limus, statin & thyroid [med].
Beta-blockers minimal risk of altering glucose control but may alter/mask hypoglycemic response. **Pregnancy:** Encourage diet, moderate exercise; **Insulin** preferred; generally avoid oral hypoglycemics[53] (See Insulin Management Chart)

**Hypoglycemia risk -UKPDS**: risk of ≥1 **MAJOR** hypoglycemic events/yr (ITT): chlorpropamide=1%, glyburide=1.4%, **insulin 1.8%**; risk of **ANY** hypoglycemic event/yr chlorprop.= 16%, glyburide=21%, insulin 28%.

**Oral agents +/- insulin**: with T2DM progression, combo tx with oral &/or addition of insulin will eventually be required.

**PPG** may reflect risk of CV dx & all-cause mortality [observational,54]; FBG & A1C are predictors of microvascular complications.

• **Consider:** [55] **lipids/statin**, orlistat [56],↓ **hypertension** [ACE Inhibitor/ARB/thiazide] **& DC smoking! ASA** ~81mg/d. **Lifestyle:** ↓5-10% wt {↑fiber, ↓fat, low glycemic index CHO food, whole grains; exercise: aerobic150min/wk, resistance 3x/wk; but start with 5-10 minutes}

**New**:not in (Canada): **Exenatide BYETTA** ✗ ⊗ an incretin mimetic; 5-10ug SC bid ac (↓ dose for renal dysfx);↓PPG,↑insulin [secretion],↓A1C 1%; may ↓wt, GI ↓[gastric emptying] & ↑N&V; rare: pancreatitis [acute]. **Pramlintide SYMLIN** ✗ ⊗ an amylinomimetic,15-60-120ug SC tid ac; ↓wt & ↑N&V.
**Saxagliptin ONGLYZA** ✗ ⊗ new in Canada, dipeptidyl peptidase-4 inhibitor with MF or SU; 5mg tab, 5mg po od=$300, (↓ dose for renal dysfx) DI: 3A4/5 (eg clarithromycin), SE: anemia, ↓ lymphocytes, edema?,hypersensitivity reactions, ↑infection [URTI, UTI], less hypoglycemia [but ↑ with SU], & weight neutral.
**Liraglutide VICTOZA** ✗ ⊗ new in Canada, a glucagon-like peptide-1 [GLP-1] receptor agonist [incretin-mimetic]; 0.6-1.2mg [$550; 1.8mg] SC daily [+/- MF,SU]; A1C↓ 0.8-1.4%. SE: headache, nausea, diarrhea, hives, may ↓wt, low hypoglycemica, pancreatitis [n=7] & thyroid cancer [in mice].

## *To test or not to test…*

- SMBG is widely used to support diabetes management.
- The value of routine SMBG, especially in patients not on insulin, has come into question, due to uncertain or marginal benefits & significant costs.[1,2,3,4,5,6,7,8,9,10] A possible association with depression[11] & lower quality of life[12] has also been noted. {See also: 1) Weighing the Benefits & Risks of Intensive Therapy in the Extras section online & 2) Landmark Trials chart.}
- Some still favour SMBG in all individuals with T2DM, but acknowledge that it is an ineffective use of time & money if it does not result in positive behaviour change.[13]

## *Highlight Recommendations from the CADTH Review**

1. **For most adults with T2DM who are <u>using insulin</u>:**
   a. SMBG should be tailored to best guide them in fine-tuning their insulin therapy to achieve optimal BG control.
   b. This should require no more than 14 tests, on average, each week for most patients on basal insulin (≤2x per day).
   {Some individuals on MDI, may benefit from more frequent testing. See Consider testing …section}
2. **For most adults with T2DM who are taking <u>medication by mouth</u> to control their diabetes:**
   a. Routine SMBG is <u>not</u> required.
   b. Periodic testing may be required in some situations, but only if it helps determine a specific course of action. See Consider testing more …section
3. **For most adults with T2DM who control their diabetes through <u>diet alone</u>:** Routine SMBG is <u>not</u> required.

*Note: In **gestational & pre-gestational DM**, SMBG ≥4x a day (pre & post-prandially) recommended.[14]

## *Cost Considerations**

<u>The cost of SMBG</u> is a significant consideration, especially for patients not using insulin, where testing may not change therapy or offer much benefit.[15,16]

- ○ Cost to drug plans public & private = $330 million 2006 Canadian data
- ○ Cost per QALY (quality adjusted life year) is estimated at $113,643 for routine use of SMBG (at least 1 strip each day on average).
- ○ Annual cost per patient: $165 - $2,400 (see Table below).

## *CADTH Clinical Analysis* [17] (From the Report Summary)

### Methods

- A systematic review of randomized controlled trials (RCTs) and observational studies comparing SMBG with no SMBG, or comparing different SMBG frequencies, was performed. Studies were identified through electronic databases, grey literature, reference lists, and stakeholder consultation. Meta-analyses were conducted to pool trial results, when appropriate.

### Patients with diabetes using insulin:

- In general, the COMPUS systematic review identified few studies that explored the optimal frequency of SMBG in patients with either type 1 diabetes, or insulin-treated type 2 diabetes. Moreover, the studies that were identified reported mixed results, and were of low quality. In patients <u>with insulin-treated type 2</u> diabetes, low-quality evidence suggests that use of SMBG is associated with improvements in glycemic control.

### Patients with type 2 diabetes (T2DM) <u>not</u> using insulin:

- The COMPUS systematic review elicited more robust studies for patients with non–insulin-treated T2DM, including several RCTs.
- Pooled results from 7 RCTs showed that SMBG is associated with a statistically significant improvement in glycemic control (**WMD* in A1C** [95% CI]* = **-0.25%** [-0.36, -0.15]). [However, a change of <0.5% is of questionable clinical significance.]
- In 1 RCT, performing SMBG was beneficial to ↓ the number of symptomatic hypoglycemic events in patients using sulfonylureas.
- For patients with T2DM not using diabetes pharmacotherapy, improvements in glycemic control were less pronounced & statistically non-significant.
  (**WMD* in A1C** [95% CI]* = **- 0.05** [-0.33, 0.23]).
- Overall, the quality of the available evidence regarding SMBG varied, depending on the patient population.

*{**CI**= confidence interval, **WMD**=weighted mean difference}

## *Other Considerations:*

- <u>SMBG is often used</u> to provide feedback to newly diagnosed patients regarding the effects of lifestyle and dietary choices on BG levels. Over time, the value of such SMBG may decrease, and less frequent testing may suffice.
- <u>Consider factors</u> such as motivation, comprehension level, age, hypoglycemia risk (e.g. especially when on insulin or secretagogues), exercise, illness, drug dose adjustments.
- <u>Choice of meter</u> should accommodate individual needs.
  - ○ Vision impairment: consider display size or voice option
  - ○ Size/feel: assess portability, speed, dexterity & other needs (e.g. arthritis)
  - ○ Alternate site testing: may be useful if significant pain from finger pokes
  - ○ Simple vs many features, remote reading/transmission etc.
  - ○ Test strip cost: meters often complimentary; strips are major cost over time

## *If testing, when?*

⇨<u>Diet Only</u>: occasional testing, especially of 2 hr post-prandial may be useful to reinforce diet/lifestyle changes

⇨<u>OAHA only</u>: at staggered times; eg. pre- & 2hr post-prandial, 1 or 2x weekly

⇨<u>OAHA & bedtime insulin</u>: 1-2x/day at variable times (≤14 tests/wk); eg. fasting, pre- & 2hr post-prandial

⇨<u>Insulin: multiple daily injections +/-OAHA</u>: individualize CADTH; ≥TID CDA; pre- & 2hr post-prandial; **

**{Some patients with very intensive regimens may require paired meal testing; up to 7 tests/day.}

◆**<u>Paired meal testing</u> (AC before & 2hr PC after)**: to match regimen to BG patterns; stagger times and days:

⇨ <u>Day 1</u>: AC & PC breakfast; <u>Day 2</u>: AC & PC lunch; <u>Day 3</u>: AC & PC supper; & HS somewhere. (This gives a good cross sectional representation of pattern of hypo- & hyperglycemia, with <u>less testing</u>.)

◆**<u>Consider testing more often</u>:** in pregnancy; illness; prior to driving in patients on insulin to detect & treat hypoglycemia; when diet &/or activity changes; after adjusting insulin/pills over 1-2 weeks; if hypoglycemic unawareness; exercise.

## Blood Glucose Meter Considerations [18,19,20,21] {Note: list of meters is not exhaustive}

| Consideration | Accu-Chek | | | | Bayer | | | Freestyle | | Guardian | iTest | NovaMax | One-Touch | | | | Oracle | Precision | TRUE |
|---|---|---|---|---|---|---|---|---|---|---|---|---|---|---|---|---|---|---|---|
| | Aviva | Aviva-Nano | Compact Plus Meter/Strips/Lancer | Voicemate Plus | Breeze 2 | Contour (New: **USB**) | Contour Link | Freedom Lite | Lite previously Freestyle Mini | Real-Time [22] Continuous Monitoring | BGMS | Monitor | Ping | Ultra2 | UltraMini | Ultra-Smart | (French or English) | Xtra BG & Ketone | track |
| Reagent A,B,C or D (see notes**); Picture | A | A | A | A | B | C | C | A | A | | B | B | | B | B | B | B | D | B |
| Automatic Coding | X | X | ✓ | ✓ | ✓ | ✓ | ✓ | ✓ | ✓ | | ✓ | ✓ | ✓ | X | X | X | ✓ | ✓ | X |
| Impaired Vision | - | backlight | backlight | ✓✓ voice | ✓ large | ✓ large | - | ✓ large | ✓ lighting | {Transmitter, sensor & monitor. Can upload data for provider. ↑cost; interstitial BG.} | ✓ large /backlit | - | - | ✓ large /backlit | - | ✓ large | ✓✓ voice | ✓ large | ✓ large |
| Drop size: mcL | 0.6 | 0.6 | 1.5 | 1.5 | 1 | 0.6 | 0.6 | 0.3 | 0.3 | | 0.5 | 0.3 | 1 | 1 | 1 | 1 | 0.7 | 0.6 BG | 1 |
| Test Time: seconds | 5 | 5 | 5 | 5 | 5 | 5 | 5 | 5 | 5 | | 4 | 5 | 5 | 5 | 5 | 5 | 6 | 5 | 10 |
| Range: mmol/L | 0.6-33.3 | 0.6-33.3 | 0.6-33.3 | 0.6-33.3 | 0.6-33.3 | 0.6-33.3 | 0.6-33.3 | 1.1-27.8 | 1.1-27.8 | | 1.1-33.3 | 1.1-33.3 | 1.1-33.3 | 1.1-33.3 | 1.1-33.3 | 1.1-33.3 | 1.1-33.3 | 1.1-27.8 | 1.1-33.3 |
| Memory / Battery | 500 Li3V | 500 2x Li3V | 500 2x AAA | 5,000 4x AAA | 420 Li3V | 480 2x Li3V | 480 2x Li3V | 400 Li3V | 400 2x Li3V | 3x AAA | 300 2x Li3V | 400 1x Li3V | 20,000 2x AAA | 500 2x Li3V | 500 1x Li3V | 3,000 2x AAA | 450 2x AAA | 450 1x Li3V | 365 1x Li3V |
| Expiration (test strips) | As labelled (checks strip condition) | As labelled | 3 month prompt to change drum & check strip accuracy. No strip handling. | | As labelled | 6 months after opening | 6 months after opening | As labelled | As labelled | N/A | As labelled | 3 months after opening | | As labelled; 6 months after opening | | | 3 months after opening | As labelled. Ketone: limited | 4 months after opening |
| Other {Note most strip pkg sizes in 50s & 100s} ♬ = reminder function | Download.IFR ≤30day ave. Ergonomic; easy to hold. ♬ x4 /day | As per Aviva. Smaller. Pre/post ave up to 90 days. | Downloadable.IFR; ≤30day ave. ♬ x3/day; pre/post Preloaded drum with 17 strips. | Downloadable via USB cable. Meter+voice unit. Preloaded drum with 17 strips. | Downloadable "Arthritis friendly" Alternate site:No Disc of 10 strips | Downloadable; ≤30 day ave. Record pre/post. Easy to use.[20] | As per Contour + Wireless remote to Guardian & Paradigm monitoring systems ♬ | Downloadable; ≤30day ave. Up to 1 min to apply blood. Simple to use | As per Freedom, but ♬ x4 programmable, Backlight & strip light. | Can be used with an insulin pump. Under skin; 288 transmissions/day. Customized alerts. | Downloadable; ≤90day ave. ≤6 daily ♬; Compact, non-slip. | Downloadable. ≤30 day ave. {Link version if pump} | Downloadable Remote; for use with insulin pump. Waterproof 12ft | Downloadable. 30 day ave. Flags pre/post readings. | As per Ultra2 but no ave. Small: for pocket/purse. | Download. As per Ultra2 + graphs… | Downloadable Shows 7-90 day averages If BG>13.3, warns to check ketones. | Downloadable. Blood ketone optional (↑ size 1.5mcL drop & ↑ price/test) | Downloadable. 30day,AM ave May not be easy to use.[20] Low cost strips. |
| Strip cost | **Annual cost:** range from **$165** (1 test/day) to **$1100 - $2400** (7 tests/day). **Cost per 100 strips**: *most brands:* $75-100; ***lower cost brands*** e.g. TRUEtrack, SideKick, Life = $60+. Cost varies with brand, frequency of testing & pharmacy variables. | | | | | | | | | | | | | | | | | | |

**A1c**=hemoglobin A1c **ac**=before meals **ave**=averaging **BG**=blood glucose **CADTH**=Canadian Agency for Drugs & Technologies in Health **CI**=confidence interval **COMPUS**=Canadian Optimal Medication Prescribing and Utilization Service **CV**=cardiovascular **IFR**=infrared data transfer **OAHA**=oral anti-hyperglycemic agent **RCT**=randomized controlled trial **SMBG**=self monitor blood glucose pc=after meals **T2DM**=Type 2 diabetes **WMD**=weighted mean difference {ReliOn Micro & ReliOn Ultima are low strip cost options but only available at Walmart in the USA (Not in Canada).} **Alternate Site:** Most newer meters allow for testing from forearm, upper arm, palm, thigh or abdomen as well as usual fingertip.

**<u>**Reagent Interactions**</u>: **A**: Strips with GDH glucose dehydrogenase PQQ pyrroloquinolinequinone: cross react with maltose, glactose or xylose (but not $O_2$) e.g. some immunoglobulins, icodextrin peritoneal dialysis soln, Orencia, Bexxar; **B**: glucose oxidase (+/- ferricyanide): affect by $O_2$; **C**: GDH glucose dehydrogenase FAD Flavin adenine dinucleotide: affected by xylose; **D**: no interaction

**Sidekick**: <u>Good choice</u> for a simple, **low cost**, small, easy to use, no frills, disposable combination of strips & meter (in lid of vial). Specs: 1 mcL sample required; 5 sec; glucose oxidase "B".

| Device | Picture (actual size will differ) | For use with… | Comments/ Considerations |
|---|---|---|---|
| **Device for use with cartridge (Reusable)** -ensure right cartridge for the specific pen device but only last a few years (New HumaPen Memoir is a reusable pen for Lily 's insulins that confirms the date, time & amount of last 16 insulin injections) | | | |
| **HumaPen Luxura** (3ml penfill) 1-60 units in 1 unit increments {Champagne or Burgundy shown with hard case.} | | HUMULIN (R, N, 30/70) HUMALOG (lispro) HUMALOG Mix25 (lispro+lispro protamine) HUMALOG Mix50 (lispro+lispro protamine) | • 1st pen free [1 for each type of insulin] at diabetes education centers, pharmacies; additional pens avail. for ~$90 • has dial back capability, decreases wastage • audible click on dialing doses • dark numbers on a white background • if insufficient insulin in cartridge, number remaining on dial will show remaining dose to be given HD half dose: small increment dose adjustment possible - useful: children & insulin sensitive patients |
| **HumaPen Luxura HD** half dose (3ml penfill) {Green} 1-30 units in ½ unit increments | | | |
| **NovoPen 4** Novolin-Pen 4 (3ml penfill) 1-60 units in 1 unit increments {Silver or Blue; with soft zipper case that can accommodate 2 pens} | | NOVOLIN GE (Toronto, NPH, 30/70, 40/60, 50/50), LEVEMIR (detemir) NOVORAPID (aspart) NOVOMIX 30 (aspart + aspart protamine) | • free from diabetes education centers, pharmacies • has dial back capability, decreases wastage • has locking mechanism, does not allow for an injection higher than insulin remaining in cartridge if <60 units • audible click on dialing doses • dark numbers on white background |
| **Novolin-Pen Junior** (3ml penfill) 1-35 units in ½ unit increments {Blue with green or yellow with green} | | | • free from diabetes education centers, pharmacies • small increments useful: children & insulin sensitive pts • does **NOT** have dial back capability; barrel and cartridge holder should be pulled apart & button reset to correct dose • small white numbers on a black background • if insufficient insulin in cartridge, number remaining on dial will show remaining dose to be given |
| **ClikSTAR** (3ml penfill) 1-80 units in 1 unit increments | | LANTUS (glargine) APIDRA (glulisine) | • dark numbers on a white background; does not have number window (e.g. number not magnified.) • dial back capabilities • if insufficient insulin in cartridge, cannot turn dosage selector past the number of units left in the cartridge • up to 4 years use, after initial use • audible click when adjusting dose |
| **OptiClik pen** * available in USA | *Not available yet in Canada* | Insulin glulisine (APIDRA), LANTUS | • has a digital display; left handed grip may read incorrectly |
| **Pre-loaded device (Disposable)** -does not require loading of cartridges, benefit for patients with decreased dexterity; less eco-friendly | | | |
| **Humalog Pen** 1-60 units in 1 unit increments | | HUMALOG (lispro) | • window magnification **NOT** as clear as other pens • may use a symbol instead of 0 to indicate dose complete • has dial back capability, decreases wastage • audible click on dialing doses • dark numbers on a white background |
| **Humalog Mix 25 Pen** 1-60 units in 1 unit increments | | HUMALOG MIX 25 (lispro + lispro protamine) | |
| **Humulin N Pen** 1-60 units in 1 unit increments | | HUMULIN N | |
| **SoloStar** (3ml penfill) 1-80 units in 1 unit increments | | LANTUS (glargine) APIDRA (glulisine) | • has dial back capabilities, decreases wastage • dark numbers on a white background • dials only up to the max amount of insulin in the cartridge |
| **Humalog KwikPen** 1-60 units in 1 unit increments (3ml penfill) | | HUMALOG, MIX 25, MIX 50 (lispro) | • has dial back capabilities, decreases wastage • even numbers printed on the dial • dials only up to the max amount of insulin in the cartridge |

**General Comments regarding Pens vs Vial/syringe**: Advantages: convenient; potentially less painful- needle not dulled entering insulin vial stopper.
Disadvantages: potentially more wastage of insulin, may require more injections (as insulins not mixed), little higher cost, upper limit to single dose.

**Mixing**: Mix insulin suspensions prior to admin. by inverting pen & rolling pen between palms up to 10 times until insulin looks uniformly white and cloudy. Ensure enough insulin is present to properly mix.

**Needle compatibility**: NovoFine, BD Ultra-fine, & Unifine Pentips: compatible with all pens. Various sizes & lengths: {28,29,30,**31**,**32G** (gauge); **4**,**5**,**6**,8,12,12.7mm length}. Use shorter needle in thin pts. New: click into place.

**Prime pen with new cartridge & before each dose to remove air** and ensure proper dose delivery. Small amount of insulin must be wasted with priming, amount varies with pen and reason for priming.

**Stability**: All cartridges, when in use stable, at room temp (<30 degrees) x 28days (except detemir x 42 days). Do not freeze or overheat.

**Storage**: Do not store pen with needle attached, insulin may leak out (may change concentration of suspension), air bubbles may form, & may increase risk of needle clog. **Never share** pens or cartridges with others!

**Supplies**: Diabetic supplies (needles, strips) possibly eligible for 3rd party & NIHB coverage if written prescription given. **Link to RxFiles SMBG & Glucose Meters chart**: http://www.rxfiles.ca/rxfiles/uploads/documents/CHT-Diabetes-SMBG.pdf

# INSULIN Comparison Chart

1,2,3,4,5,6,7,8,9,10,11,12,13,14,15,16,17,18,19; CDN Guidelines Sept 2008; ADA Oct 2009

Prepared by L Regier, B Jensen, S Downey - © www.RxFiles.ca

May 10

**Indications:** Type 1, gestational (not controlled with diet & activity); lactation; Type 2 not controlled with meals, activity & oral agents; if severe hyperglycemia/infection; major surgery; CI to oral agents; ketoacidosis; hyperosmolar nonketotic Sx.

| Type of Insulin [generally 100 unit/mL] avail. OTC ("clear" = solution appears clear) | Form 100u/ml | Source, Given | Onset (variable) | Peak (variable) | Duration (hrs) | ~$/ 15ml |
|---|---|---|---|---|---|---|
| **Bolus / Prandial** | | | | | | |
| **Rapid acting** (give just before or within 20min of starting meal) | {clear} | Recombinant DNA tech analog -SC,IV,IM | 10-15 min | 60-90 min | 3.5 – 6h | |
| Insulin lispro Humalog ▼ [B] | v, c, p✗▼ | | | | | 53V 69c 81P |
| Insulin aspart NovoRapid ▼ [B] | v, c | | | | | 54V 70c |
| (Rapid analogs:) • ↓ variability between sites, flexible, less need for snacks • less early night hypoglycemia than regular (R) • better control of postprandial glucose (PPG) • 1 unit is equal to ~ 10-15g of carbohydrate but VARIABLE! | | | | | | |
| Insulin glulisine Apidra ▼ *New* • prefilled disposable SoloStar pen | v,p,c | (Aspart & glulisine SC only) | 10-30 min | 60min | ≤5h | 48V 62P |
| **Short-acting / Regular Insulin** | {clear} | Recombinant DNA tech. Human -SC,IV,IM | | | ~ 6.5hr | 43V |
| Humulin R [B] | v, c | | 0.5 – 1h | 2 – 3h | 5 – 10h | 54c 44V |
| Novolin ge Toronto [B] | v, c | | Note: For **very large doses, a special 500 U/ml** Humulin R is avail. via Special Access Program | | | 55c |
| Hypurin II R (**rarely** used!) | V ⊗ | Pork-SC,IV,IM | | | | 160V |
| **Basal** | | | | | | |
| **Intermediate-acting or NPH** [B] | | Recombinnt DNA tech. Human -SC | 2 – 4h | 4 – 10h | 12 – 18h (range 12-24) | |
| Humulin N | v, c, p✗▼ | | | | | 43V 54c |
| Novolin ge NPH | v, c | | | | | 44V 52c |
| Hypurin NPH (**rarely** used!) | v⊗ | Pork -SC | | | | 160V |
| **Premixed** *Humulin* 20/80 - Not available | c✗▼ | | | | | |
| *(regular/intermediate)* 30/70 | v, c | | | | | 43V 54c |
| Novolin GE (10/90; 20/80) Plan D/C July 2007 | c | | | | | |
| 30/70 | v, c | | | | | 44V |
| 40/60; 50/50 | c | | | | | 55c |
| Humalog Mix25 ✗; Mix50 ✗⊗ lispro & lispro protamine | c,p | Recombinant DNA tech. Human -SC | 0.5 – 1h | 2-12h Dual Peak | 14 – 18h (range 12-24) | 52c 64c |
| NovoMix30 aspart 30%, aspart protamine 70% ✗⊗ | c | | | | | 61c |
| Discontinued (DC'd) 2003: *Novolin ge Ultralente, Novolin ge Lente*; DC'd 2004: *Iletin II Lente* Pork; DC'd 2006: *Humulin L, Humulin U* | | | | | | |
| **Long-acting (LAIA)** 4-T trial [C] Insulin detemir neutral PH Levemir ⊗ • give daily or twice daily~20% of pts; (room temp: good **42days** after open) | {clear} c | Analog -SC | 1h initial ~3.5 50% effect | 6 - 8h | 16 - 24h if dose ≥0.4U/kg, duration longer with ↑ dose | 115P |
| Insulin glargine Lantus ? Type 1 [C] • acidic PH→ some inj site pain; a bit more absorption variability than detemir • forms microprecipitates in sc tissue⇒slow release • given once daily (HS or morning); may split dose if > 50-100 units • prefilled disposable SoloStar pen max 80u/inj/Autopen max 42u/inj | {clear} v, c, p✗⊗ vial: stable 28days | Analog -SC | >2 - 4h | No Peak | 20 - 24h | 105V 105c |

• **Human analog insulins** generally shorter acting than Beef/Pork insulins.
• **Beef** insulin no longer in Canada; available from the UK through Health Canada-Special Access Program at 613-941-2108.

**Premix**: May give 1, 2 or 3 times a day, but avoid giving at bedtime! May be useful if non-intensive regimen for T2DM patient with consistent lifestyle (bedridden/institutional/elderly).
**Premixed analogues**: Similar control to premixed human insulin, & tighter BG control but ↑ hypoglycaemia than LAIA. Lack clinical outcome data. Ann Int Med 2008 #78
**Administer**: Humalog/NovMix just before meal; other premixes ~30min before meals.

If switching from **daily** NPH, use ≤ same total daily dose;
If switching from **BID** NPH to daily LAIA, use ~**80%** of total NPH daily dose;
Start ≤10units if not previously on NPH

## Comments
See also *Insulin Management: Evidence, Tips & Pearls*

**DOSING**: (see Insulin Management chart)
Note re bolus admin: **regular** given 20-30min ac; **rapid acting**: give just before or within 20 min starting meal

**Cost**: Vial $; Cartridge $$↑30%; Humalog $$$; NovoRapid $$$; Hypurin/Detemir/Glargine **$$$$** {vials good for ~**28 days** at room temp after opening}

**MIXING**:
• **Compatabilities**: Regular with all insulins; NPH with Regular; Lispro & Aspart with NPH if used immediately after mixing; {Glulisine, Glargine or detemir-do **NOT** mix per CPS}
• **always draw up short-acting/R first** to prevent contamination with longer acting
• **inject mixtures immediately** as alterations in formulation's pharmacodynamics occur dependent on concentration & elapsed time {If delayed, be consistent with mix to inj. Time}
{**Novolin-Pen 4**: for all Novolin products & Levemir; **HumaPen Luxura** for Humulin & Humalog}

**HYPOGLYCEMIA**: see also Insulin Management Chart 4-T trial -less hypoglycemia with basal
• **Symptoms**:
**Mild/moderate** = sweating, tremor, tachycardia, hunger, lethargy, weakness
**Severe** = confusion, disorientation, altered behavior/speech, seizures, coma
• **Incidence**: higher with intensive vs conventional; (in UKPDS risk of ANY hypoglycemic event/year: glyburide=21%; **insulin=**28% {1.8% severe}
• **Treat Mild:** 15g glucose tabs; orange juice ¾ cup, 3 sugar cubes, honey/syrup/sugar 1 tablespoonful, 9 jelly beans, 6 LifeSavers® (glucose/dextrose absorbed directly, don't require prior digestion)
**If Severe** (e.g. unconscious) = 1mg glucagon IM/SC > $100/dose; or D50W 20-50mL IV
• **Prevention**: regular monitoring/exercise/↓↓ alcohol, balanced meals; adjust regimen

**OTHER SIDE EFFECTS**: 4-T trial -less weight gain when basal insulin added vs biphasic or prandial at 3yrs.
• **Weight ↑**: more with intensive vs conventional (4.6kg/5yrs DCCT 11,12); diet & exercise encouraged; less with detemir & ?glargine • **Lipodystrophy** – rotate sites within anatomical area {limited long-term / safety data with newer analogues; (FDA: evaluating ?? ↑ association with cancer for glargine)[102]}

**SC VARIABILITY**:
• onset/peak/duration for SC insulins is **highly variable** between pts & even at different times for same pt; the longer acting the insulin, the greater the variability seen (e.g. +/- 15% with Reg; +/- 30% **with NPH**) not the case with detemir & glargine

**SUPPLEMENT DOSING**: rapid or short acting insulin used to correct hyperglycemia; conservative dose. Individual requirements will vary, somewhat according to total daily dose & response. Insulin to carbohydrate ratios used to guide bolus CSII & MDI. {Caution if <3 hrs since previous insulin, or planning exercise}.

**Pregnancy**: Category **B**. *Regular or Rapid* preferred. **C** (Caution): detemir, glargine & glulisine.
Tight glucose control critical in the first 42 days of pregnancy organogenesis. Minimize hypoglycemia.
Hyperglycemia: ↑ of macrosomia & pre-eclampsia. Neonatal hypoglycemia if maternal BG high before/during delivery.
If antenatal steroids used in preterm labour ↑ insulin dose. Postnatal care: insulin dose ↓ after the birth.

| INSULIN REGIMEN | SCHEDULE | COMMENT –treat to effect, no maximum dose for insulin |
|---|---|---|
| **Conventional Regimens** | OD insulin: N, D or G at HS (or rarely before breakfast) | Useful with daytime oral hypoglycemics in T2DM. Simple but poor control; <24hr coverage |
| **RAIA= Lispro** (ILis), **Aspart** (IAsp), **Glulisine** (IGlu) | BID insulin: N or D before breakfast & supper | Improved morning control & overnight coverage; no provision for meal coverage |
| **R= Human Regular or Toronto** **N= NPH or N** | BID insulin: {also **premixed** options} {R or RAIA ac breakfast & supper **and** N (or D) ac breakfast & supper} | More common; better meal control (Or *breakfast & bedtime*; less hypoglycemia) |
| **D= Detemir** (IDet); **G= Glargine** (IGla) | TID insulin: {R or RAIA ac breakfast & supper **and** N ac breakfast & bedtime} | Most likely to last till next morning; (may substitute D or G for N) |
| | | • Shorter acting insulins given before meals help prevent meal related hyperglycemia! • BID regimens require regular lifestyle (e.g. institutional) • 50-75% as long acting & 25-50% as short acting |
| **Multidose Intensive Regimens (MDI)** | R or RAIA TID ac; N or D ac supper or hs (or G in am or hs) | Good control, flexible regarding meals; demands frequent & consistent testing at start! |
| (≥40% of total insulin dosed as basal insulin; | **Eg.** 1) Lispro/Aspart/Glulisine/R 4-8 units tid ac & Glargine/Detemir/NPH 8-16 units hs. 2) Breakfast 25% R & 45% N; Dinner 15% R; Bedtime 15% N. Based on total daily dose. | |
| bolus/prandial dosing adjusted with meal/CHO) | R or RAIA TID ac; **&** N or D BID (ac breakfast & supper or bedtime) | Better suited for people with varying schedules; flexibility with regards to meals |
| **Intensive Continuous SC Infusion (CSII)** | R or RAIA; basal & boluses prn; rapid analogues preferred most flexible | More flexible, better control; ↑$ >$5000+$250/mo; ↑ risk of rapid ketoacidosis, etc. if discontinued. |
| **Insulin + Oral Hypoglycemics** esp. if A1c>9% (in **Type 2** Diabetes) | Common: N, G (or D) **at bedtime**, with **1-2 oral agents during day** See Approach to ...Diabetes & Insulin Management charts for dosing information, etc. | Less insulin required ~0.1u/kg eg. 5-10u & ↓weight gain than insulin alone (esp. with Metformin!) **Tip:** If ↑ PM blood sugar may need bid insulin regimen. If ↑ PPG may need short acting insulin with meals, (or premix). |

**Form:** v=vial c=cartridge (for reloadable pen) p=pen (disposable pre-loaded pen) ; **ac**=before meals **CSII**=continuous subcutaneous insulin infusion **d/c**=discontinuation **pt**=patient ☎=Exception Drug Status (EDS) in SK. ✗ =Nonformulary Sk. ▼ covered by NIHB

**Tips**: Fix the **lows first** & highs later, **correct morning blood glucose, assess Somogyi effect** if unexplained highs in the am **& only adjust one insulin** at a time. ✆=prior approval NIHB ⊗=not NIHB =↓dose for renal dysfx

EXUBERA : **Discontinued!** Inhaled (✗ ⊗)adults type 1&2;dry powder given 10min ac, rapid acting, no difference in A1c from regular/NPH regimens; pts may prefer over sc; SE: cough, hypoglycemia,↓pulmonary fx tests short term, anti-insulin antibodies; CI: COPD, smoking if within prev 6 months; long term lung safety ?cancer; $$$$.

**Diabetes** if it was diagnosed within the first 6months of age consider genetic testing, since **Kir6.2 mutations** successfully **switched from insulin to sulfonylureas** (eg. glyburide 0.05-**0.45**-1.5mg/kg/d) Pearson NEJM Aug/06

## Indications for the Use of Insulin[1]

- Type 1 Diabetes Mellitus (**T1DM**); gestational diabetes not controlled with diet & activity; Type 2 Diabetes Mellitus (**T2DM**) not controlled with meal choices, activity & use of oral agents; T2DM with severe infection, major surgery, oral hypoglycemics contraindications, lactating, or requiring corticosteroid; ketoacidosis or hyperosmolar nonketotic syndrome; severe hyper-glycemia where rapid glucose reduction/control is desired. {Also: Low rate of drug interactions.}

{Note: Recent Chinese trial: early intensive insulin till normal glycemia achieved x2 weeks induced remission in new T2DM.[2]; n=382; evaluated at 1year; remission in 50% CSII vs 27% oral hypoglycemics. Preliminary!}

## Administering Insulin - Subcutaneous (SC) Injection

- Abdomen (**not** within a 5cm radius of the umbilicus), upper arms, anterior/lateral thigh, buttocks.
- Alcohol is no longer recommended for topical preparation of the skin; soap & $H_2O$ adequate.
- Give insulin injections at a 90° angle subcutaneously to ensure adequate absorption.
- DO NOT pinch skin {Pinching of the skin prior to inj. is only necessary when using a 12 mm pen/syringe needles, if individual is thin &/or in children. (Most needles 4-8mm; e.g. ≤**8**mm for most; 6mm for young T1DM)}
- People with a BMI >27 kg/m² may use the 12mm length needle if thin 4-5mm may be used (Becton Dickson)
- If leaking is occurring at the injection site, check that the client is:
  - Injecting at a 90° angle & using the appropriate needle length
  - Leaving the needle under the skin for 5 seconds after injecting

**[Insulins generally given SC, but rapid & short acting formulations can be given IV]**

## Variables That Can Affect Insulin Action

1. **Mixing insulin together**
   a. Regular (short acting) insulin can be mixed with NPH with no effect on insulin action (draw up short acting first to avoid contamination with NPH e.g draw *clear before cloudy*)
   b. Lispro *Humalog* binds rapidly with NPH & must be injected immediately after mixing
   c. Aspart *NovoRapid* may be mixed with NPH & must be injected immediately e-CPS
   {Best not to mix rapid acting IAs, & not necessary with most devices. (b., c.)}
   d. Glargine *Lantus*: mixing with any other insulin not recommended {but some studies report that mixing with bolus insulin for BID administration in T1DM Pediatric suitable[3,4]}.
   e. Detemir *Levemir*: not to be mixed with any other insulin (potential for crystallization)
2. **Insulin dosage and absorption variance factors**
   a. Larger doses of insulin may have slightly longer duration of action. For lispro & aspart an increase in dose has no effect on the duration of action.
   b. Daily absorption can vary up to 30% using same site at the same time
   c. Speed/consistency of absorption: Fast to slow: abdomen → arm → thigh → buttock
   d. Absorption ↑ by exercise, heat, massage, injection into muscle
   e. Absorption ↓ by cold, lipohypertrophy, decreased blood flow (avoid areas of scar tissue)
   f. Avoid injecting into SC tissue adjacent to the main muscles being used in exercise
3. **Injection site**: Systematically rotate injection site by at least 1-2 inches to prevent lipodystrophy. The abdomen is often the preferred site; most consistent & fast rate of absorption
4. **Other**: improper storage (too hot or too cold); proper re-suspension of suspension insulins important! (Store insulin in a cold place 2 to 8°C, preferably a fridge, but not a freezer. Avoid direct sunlight.)

## Canadian Guidelines - Notes Regarding Insulins [5]

- CDA Guidelines 2008 & some specialist reviewers advocate for a more prominent role for the newer insulin analogues, if economic and drug plan coverage issues are not major considerations. Primary advantage valued is less hypoglycemia in some patients. (A1C & weight endpoints lack meaningful differences.) [5,6,7,8]
- Trend in current clinical thinking is to pursue tighter BG control, both basal & postprandial. Newer insulin analogues theoretically may allow for more precise tailoring of regimen if patients willing to be highly aggressive in carbohydrate counting, BG testing & titrating of insulin. Limited evidence, hypoglycemia risk together with varying appreciation of economic analysis result in conflicting viewpoints in this area.

*References available online at www.RxFiles.ca*

## Insulin Analogues (IA): Systematic Reviews (Tables 1 & 2)

**Insulin Analogue Systematic Reviews (SR)**: 1) Cochrane SAIA[6]; 2) Cochrane LAIA[7]; 3) COMPUS – IA[8,34]. {Many studies; however none assess long-term complications or mortality & most of low-quality.} Related LINKs[9].

### Table 1: IAs: Guide to Advantages/Disadvantages of Insulins [6,7,8,10]

| | Insulins | Advantages | Disadvantages |
|---|---|---|---|
| Bolus | **HI** Short Acting<br>Human Regular<br>Humulin R; Novolin ge Toronto | ◆more long-term & safety experience<br>◆low cost (10ml/mo x1yr: \$430 vs \$550 ILis-\$590 IAsp)<br>◆pregnancy-extensive safety experience | ◆injecting 20-30min pre-meal impractical (short acting but not rapid acting) |
| Bolus | **RAIAs** Rapid Acting<br>**Lispro (ILis)** Humalog<br>**Aspart (IAsp)** NovoRapid<br>-rapid onset may ⇨ better PPG control if pre-meal (significance uncertain)<br>{Glulisine (IGlu) Apidra} | ◆inject & eat convenience (may give just before or within 20min of starting meals); valuable when dietary/activity patterns unpredictable, e.g. adolescents<br>◆may have less hypoglycemia<br>◆↑ patient satisfaction in T1DM<br>◆safe in pregnancy (less extensive experience) | ◆moderately high cost utility in T2DM (but reasonable cost utility in T1DM)[8]<br>◆lack evidence for any clinical outcome or A1C advantage over HI {T1DM studies: A1C difference was < -0.2%}<br>◆limited long-term & safety evidence |
| Basal | **NPH** Intermediate Acting<br>Human NPH<br>Humulin N, Novolin ge NPH | ◆long-term safety & outcome evidence<br>◆low cost (10ml/mo x1yr: \$430 vs \$830 IGar-\$1040 IDet)<br>◆may avoid need for lunchtime bolus injection (↑convenience) e.g. in children | ◆NPH vial must be mixed before withdrawing dose affects absorption<br>◆intermediate action & peak at 4-12hrs predispose to hypoglycemia |
| Basal | **LAIAs** Long Acting<br>**Detemir (IDet)** (daily or BID) Levemir<br>**Glargine (IGlar)** (daily) Lantus | ◆↓ hypoglycemia, nocturnal subjective, not blinded ( T2DM: Estimated NNT= ≥6 / 6-12 mo[7,8])<br>◆slight ↓ in weight (<1kg) vs NPH (in T2DM, only detemir had ↓ weight*)<br>◆OD dosing; IDet: some will require BID | ◆ relative to NPH: very high cost utility; no difference in **severe** hypoglycemia<br>◆ limited safety data; (?:↑ca with glargine) FDA Jul09<br>◆↑# of injections if not mixed with bolus<br>◆↑caution in pregnancy (IDet may be an option)[5] |
| - | **Premixed** | ◆convenience;↓A1C more than HS only T2DM | ◆limited fixed dose flexibility; cost ? |

## Insulins: Selection Considerations (Evidence & Economic)* Systematic Reviews 8,6,7;34,35

**◆A1C differences of Insulin Analogues (IAs) compared to Regular & NPH:**
-Rapid Acting IA: range from -0.03% to -0.18% vs R; Long Acting IA: range from -0.12% to 0.28% vs NPH. adult
-There are no clinically significant differences in A1C control likely to impact clinical outcomes.[6,7,8]

**◆T1DM – Bolus (rapid or short acting):**
- **Adults**: Regular HI, Lispro or Aspart may be used. {ILis vs Reg: ↓ severe hypoglycemia (est. NNT=54/yr CI: 32-260)}
  -Consider a Rapid Acting IA especially if meal flexibility and/or hypoglycemia concerns.
- **Adolescents**: Lispro & Aspart offer convenience, flexibility & ↓hypoglycemia & preferred over regular HI.

**◆T1DM – Basal (intermediate or long-acting):**
- NPH preferred in COMPUS SR[8]; Detemir or Glargine are suitable if major hypoglycemia history or concern. {less hypoglycemia with IDet BID vs IGla OD[11]; but ↑ FG (7.7 vs 7.0) & ↑ serious adverse events (8.7% vs 6.9%) not Tx related?}
- Preadolescent: a twice daily NPH regimen not requiring a lunch time injection may be useful in some.

**◆T2DM – Bolus:** ◆Regular HI preferred in COMPUS SR[8]; Lispro or Aspart suitable if hypoglycemia history or concern.

**◆T2DM – Basal:** ◆NPH preferred in COMPUS SR[8]; Detemir or Glargine suitable if hypoglycemia history or concern.
{IDet vs IGla[12]: similar A1C; but 55% of IDet required BID where wt gain advantage lost & 2x daily dose required; ↑ site rx's with IDet}

**◆Pregnancy, Pre-existing T1DM / T2DM or Gestational:**
- Most safety experience with HI; RAIAs also safe & allow for tight PPG control, but no evidence of superiority.
- Detemir & Glargine do not have sufficient safety data to recommend in pregnancy or preconception state.

*Evidence for insulin analogues is often limited (small, short-term trials) and benefits modest; anecdotal experience is favorable. The COMPUS systematic & economic reviews rigorously assessed benefits, risks and incremental cost.[8]

**Weight** change with LAIA vs NPH: (T1DM: -0.73 to - 0.4kg); (T2DM: IDet: -1.27 to -0.8 kg less than NPH; IGlar: no difference) [8]
{There is question as to the clinical significance of the minor weight changes of <1.3kg here, (or <5% in general).}

**Hypoglycemia**: Most pronounced ↓ risk for LAIA is on nocturnal hypoglycemia. {LAIA vs NPH: NNT ≥6 (CI range 4-33)}[7]

**Cost** Approx: Bolus: Regular \$2–3/ml; Aspart \$3-4/ml; Lispro \$3-5/ml. Basal: NPH \$2-3/ml; Glargine \$6/ml; Detemir \$8/ml.
{Cost estimate for converting 50% of patients to new insulin analogues ranges from \$50-100million/yr Canada[13] The COMPUS economic analysis modeled the overall impact of these costs & the potential benefits of lower A1C & hypoglycemia over the lifetime of the patient. Compared to regular insulin T2DM, the cost per Quality Adjusted Life Year (QALY) for RAIAs ranged from \$22,448 - \$130,865. The analysis comparing LAIAs with NPH insulin in T2DM was less favourable; for IGla the cost per QALY was \$642,994 & for IDet the value was not calculated as it was less effective than NPH in terms of A1C.[14]}

## MONITORING (BG, A1C, Ketones)

### Blood Glucose (BG) Targets

- Preprandial: Optimal BG 4-7 mmol/L before meals
- Postprandial (PPG): BG 5-10 mmol/L 2hrs after meals (5-8 mmol/L if A1C target not being met) {Limited observational data suggests PPG as a potential risk factor for mortality [15]}
- Prevent extreme lows (<3.5 mmol/L) and high BG levels (>14mmol/L)
- Individualize with each person [16]: e.g. ambitious targets may be counterproductive in elderly (risk of hypoglycemia, etc.); for patient who has coronary artery disease (CAD), low BG can trigger atrial fibrillation therefore ambitious targets may not always be achievable/beneficial.[17]

### Self Monitoring Blood Glucose (SMBG)[1,5] ( >$300 million spent in 2006 for SMBG strips in Canada)

- No gold standard of testing frequency established. {Systematic/Economic Review Draft: COMPUS [32]}
  - Diet Only: may check occasional postprandial ($/QALY: non-insulin T2DM, ≥1strip/day = $113,643; 1-4 strip/wk=$6,322-46,445)
  - **OHA only**: routine self monitoring not necessary in T2DM pts not on insulin & without hypoglycemia [18,19,20] {If done, twice a day at staggered times, eg. pre- & post-prandial, 1 or 2 times weekly}
  - OHA & bedtime insulin: test once daily at variable times recommended.[5] Up to 14 times/wk COMPUS
  - OHA & insulin MDI: individualize
  - Insulin monotherapy: individualize eg. ≥Tid, pre & post prandial

    ♦AC/PC meals, up to 7x/day in patients with intensive regimens
  - **Strips: yearly cost** (1 test/day= >$165; 3 tests/day= >$500; 7 tests/day=$1100-2400) generics: Life, Sidekick, Truetrack
- Paired meal testing (AC & 2hr PC) helpful to match regimen to BG patterns; may stagger times:
  - Day 1: AC & PC breakfast; Day 2: AC &PC lunch; Day 3: AC & PC supper; Check HS somewhere.
  - This gives a good cross sectional representation of pattern of hyperglycemia, with less testing.
- Test more often: in pregnancy; illness; before driving to detect & treat hypoglycemia; when diet & activity changes; after adjusting insulin/pills over 1-2 wks; if hypoglycemic unawareness; exercise?; driving?
- Rapid-acting insulin analogues, oral glitinides: e.g. repaglinide (Gluconorm®) – may be particularly important to check 2 hours postprandial to determine if the dose is accurate
- Testing at ~3:00am or overnight expected insulin peak time may be required to rule out nocturnal hypoglycemia

### Variables Affecting Accuracy Of Self-Monitoring Blood Glucose (SMBG)

- Sample Size: ↓blood on strip problem for some meters • if GDH-PQQ strip may falsely ↑BG if on dialysis soln or immunoglobulins
- Test strips: if expired or exposed to extreme temperature or humidity.
- Clean finger needed (especially sensitive to sugar containing foods or drinks).
- Meter inaccuracy: if old, dirty, or exposed to extreme temperatures. Lab/meter comparison recommended (annually). A fasting lab/meter comparison should be done annually to check meter accuracy; acceptable reading could be within 15-20% higher or lower than the lab value.
- Hematocrit: most test strips make allowance for this (results vary from 4-30% for every 10% change in hematocrit)
  - Anemia can falsely ↑ & polycythemia can falsely ↓ the BG values obtained by meters
- Alternate site testing or misrepresentations of BG results (clients falsify the test results)

### Glycated Hemoglobin (A1C): an indicator of overall glycemic control in the preceding 3 months

- [For **diagnosis** since fast, easy, non-fasting (Prediabetes: 5.7-6.4%; Diabetes: ≥6.5%)] ADA 2010
- A1c may be measured every 3 months in all clients taking insulin & every 6 months in people on nutrition therapy, oral antihyperglycemic agents (OHA) or during tx & lifestyle stability
- **Accuracy** affected by: anemia falsely ↑ if slow RBC turnover eg iron deficiency; falsely ↓ if fast RBC turnover e.g. hemolysis; PRBC transfusion; Hemoglobinopathies eg. sickle cell, haemoglobin C; ESRD assay dependent; meds HIV, Epo; age, race
- **Target A1c for most:** ≤ 7%. A1c targets should consider patient factors & intervention intensity. (Overly intensive regimens may cause harm in T2DM populations ACCORD; see Diabetes Trials chart)
- **Blood Glucose & A1c relationship** (derived from DCCT in T1DM) [21]
  - Mean BG (mmol/L) = [1.98 x A1C(%)] – 4.29. (E.g., A1c = 10, Mean BG= 19.8-4.29 = 15.5mmol/L)

⇨**Estimated Average Glucose (eAG)** is another new way to reflect A1c; reported as mmol/L [22]

- eAG (mmol/L) = 1.59 x A1C(%) – 2.59

| A1c: 6% = eAG 7mmol/L<br>7% = eAG 8.5mmol/L<br>10% = eAG 13.3mmol/L | Or commonly:<br>(2x A1C) – 4 = eAG<br>**But** inflates a high A1C. |
|---|---|

### Urine Ketone Testing (Primarily in T1DM)

- Required during significant hyperglycemia periods to assess risk of life-threatening ketoacidosis e.g., when pre-prandial BG >14mmol/L (or commonly >16 – 20), nausea, vomiting, abdominal pain, illness &/or if dehydration
- May test urine ketones during pregnancy to ensure mother & baby's nutritional needs are met

**Blood ketone testing** with suitable meter often preferred over urine testing, since assoc. with earlier detection of ketosis & response to tx.

## HYPOGLYCEMIA:



- Clinically hypoglycemia is defined as a state that results in:
  - Biochemical low – e.g BG <3.5 or < 4 mmol/L (common definition in DM trials)
  - Autonomic (adrenergic) OR neuroglycopenic symptoms {better recognition if infrequent occurrence}

  {Symptoms may occur at euglycemic BG levels in chronic hyperglycemia; typically resolves with time.}
- Mild: autonomic symptoms: tremors, palpitations, sweating, excessive hunger; able to self-treat
- Moderate: autonomic & neuroglycopenic symptoms – headache, mood △, irritability, ↓ attentiveness, paresthesias, visual disturbances; may be able to self-treat
- Severe hypoglycemia = distinguished by unresponsiveness, unconsciousness, seizures or coma; unable to self-treat, requires assistance. (Some studies also use thresholds e.g. ≤2.8mmol/L)
- Nocturnal: night sweats, nightmares; patient may not be aware. (Subjectively defined in studies.)
- Causes - Iatrogenic: dose of insulin or sulfonylureas is too high; diabetes therapy too intensive; decreased renal function can result in increased frequency of hypoglycemia in those on insulin or sulfonylureas; increase in the level of activity; insufficient carbohydrates in diet; Drug Causes [23]: insulin, sulfonylureas (chlorpropamide & glyburide); alcohol delayed, beta-blockers, salicylate, chromium, marijuana {Tight glucose control in critically ill hospitalized pts may ↑mortality & ↑↑risk of hypoglycemia. JAMA'08; 24 Nice-Sugar NNH=38/90day}
- Other: develop meal & activity plan; a bedtime snack may be helpful in those at risk (if BG <7mmol/L)
- If severe hypoglycemia or unawareness; raise glycemic targets for **several weeks**, to avoid hypos ADA'10
- **4-T trial** -less hypoglycemia when basal insulin added vs biphasic or prandial insulin at 3yrs.

### Treatment For Mild To Moderate Hypoglycemia

- **15g of carbohydrate (glucose or sucrose tablets)** should ↑BG about 2.1 mmol/L in 20min {15g examples: ¾ cup juice or regular soft drink, 3 teaspoonfuls table sugar or honey, 6 LifeSavers®, 3 sugar cubes, 9 jelly beans, 4 x 4g glucose tabs Dex4. (glucose/dextrose absorbed directly)}
- Children – 0.3g/kg (10g carbohydrate in child <5yrs or <20kg)
- Wait 15 minutes, retest BG and retreat with another 15g glucose/sucrose if BG < 4.0mmol/L
- After initial glucose treatment, another carbohydrate containing snack should be taken within 1 hour. If meal more than 1 hour away, a snack with 15g carbohydrate & protein source is also recommended.
- If on Acarbose - use glucose tablets, milk or honey; (sucrose will not be absorbed!!!)

### Treatment For Severe Hypoglycemia Occurring Outside Hospital Setting*

- If **conscious** and able to take oral treatment:
  - Treat with 20g glucose in tablet form, then wait 15 minutes (if possible).
  - Retest BG & retreat with another 15g glucose if BG <4.0mmol/L. (Repeat till sustained >4mmol/L)
- If **unconscious / unable to swallow**: (BG <2.8mmol/L associated with unconscious)
  - Administer **glucagon** (details below). {**Kits available** > $100; portable for emergencies}
  - Once the individual is conscious & able to take oral food, hospitalization is probably not necessary; however, cause should be determined so that recurrence can be avoided.
  - Glucose gel should NOT be used buccally since minimal absorption through mucosa. Glucose gel is slow to react (< 1mmol/L rise in 20 min) & must be swallowed.

### Table 2: Glucagon Treatment Of Acute Hypoglycemia

⇨Converts stored glycogen in the liver to glucose. Glucagon is only helpful if liver glycogen is available. {Less effective if from starvation, chronic hypoglycemia, adrenal insufficiency &/or >2 std drinks of alcohol.}

- Adult: glucagon dose SC/IM **1mg** (if IM, administer in the deltoid or anterior thigh)
  - BG may rise from 3 -12 mmol/L within 60 min
- Child: glucagon SC/IM 15-30mcg/kg [MAX 1mg/dose] {<5yrs: 0.25-0.5mg; 5-10yrs: 0.5-1mg; >10 yrs: 1mg}
  - {Also: mini-dosing for impeding hypoglycemia due to refusal to eat (20mcg/yr of age; Max 150mcg)}
- BG response is greater in T2DM than in T1DM. Glucagon side effects: may cause nausea & vomiting
- Following glucagon administration: turn patient on side to avoid aspiration; never leave alone.
- When individual becomes alert, usually 10-15 min after receiving glucagon IM/SC, he/she should be given a fast acting carbohydrate (e.g., glass of juice, or glucose/sucrose tablets) followed by a carb. snack such as crackers & cheese or a sandwich (to prevent recurrent hypoglycemia). Ongoing monitoring is essential!

* If access to hospital/medical care, IV dextrose will act rapidly (Dextrose 10 to 25 g (20 to 50 cc of D50W) should be given over 1 to 3 minutes. Repeat BG in 15-30minutes. (The pediatric dose of glucose for IV treatment is 0.5 to 1 g/kg). Follow with D5W IV.

## INITIATING INSULIN {Discuss insulin early, long before initiating, to deal with –'ve perceptions.}

### Type 2 DM (adult) on oral medications (see also RxFiles - Approach to Management of T2DM)

- Start low dose for safety, then titrate upward!!! {Tips: suggest 1 month trial; use easier/newer device; access a CDE.}
- 5-10 units of intermediate insulin e.g. NPH or 0.1-0.2 units/kg of total body weight (TBW) at hs; titrate by 2 units every 2-3days. {More cautious with initiation & titration in elderly & non-obese (e.g. start with 5 units)}
- Adding insulin to already established **metformin** may be very useful to ↓ insulin dose required; also may result in less weight gain & less hypoglycemia
- Secretagogues e.g. sulfonylureas useful with hs basal insulin; should be stopped if mealtime insulin given
- **Caution/Avoid**: TZD glitazone & insulin combinations; ↑ heart failure, weight gain & edema[25].

### Type 1 DM

Starting insulin in T2DM: http://www.cadth.ca/media/pdf/c1109-guide-to-starting-insulin-final-e.pdf

- Adult: 0.1-0.5 units/kg of body weight. (Typical requirement 0.5 units/kg.) If newly diagnosed, but not acutely ill or ketotic – start with lower dose (e.g. 0.3 units/kg or 4 units ac meals and hs).
- Adolescent: start similar to adult; but expect eventual higher requirement e.g. ≤1 unit/kg (tight follow-up required)

## SWITCHING INSULINS* {temporary ↑BG monitoring required; ↓ dose to 80% for more conservative approach}

Short-acting human insulin → Rapid Acting IA: may be transferred on a unit for unit basis
NPH OD → glargine OD: may use same total number of units/day
NPH BID → glargine or detemir OD: ↓ total daily dose to 80% of the NPH daily dose
NPH OD → detemir OD: may use up to the same total # of units/day (↑ in dose is likely after switch; some may require BID)
Basal only hs → premixed given BID: use same or less total number of units/day (as ↑'d effect)[16]
***If hypoglycemia** history or reason for switching, may be more conservative in initial dose chosen.

## TIPS FOR INSULIN DOSE ADJUSTMENT

1. Fix the lows first & the highs later. Once the lows gone, rebound hyperglycemia often eliminated.
2. Adjust insulin by 5-10% per week, or 1 or 2 units at a time to prevent hypoglycemia.
3. Adjust one insulin at a time. Begin with the insulin that will correct the 1st problem BG of the day.
4. Overnight control is difficult & requires the right basal dose. {Goal: keep BG between 4-8mmol/L from bedtime to morning without causing a low & usually without requiring a bedtime snack.}
5. To assess for Somogyi (nocturnal hypoglycemia <4mmol/L with rebound hyperglycemia in the AM) or overnight control, check BG at 0300 or 0400 not just once but a for a few nights, especially if experiencing unexplained morning highs. {Dawn phenomena also causes early AM rise but due to hormonal surge.}
6. Nightmares, restless sleep, headache on waking, wet pillow or sheets may be signs of sleeping through a low BG reaction. {One specialist uses BG from both 2AM & 5AM to assess.}
7. Postprandial targets are helpful when assessing the meal insulin. Assessing PPG control provides information to determine which insulin needs adjusting (the meal insulin or the basal insulin). The goal is to achieve PPG levels of 5-10mmol/L without lows between meals.
8. Sliding Scale Insulin: practice discouraged Nau'10. Consider basal/bolus & supplemental regimen. {Supplemental insulin useful in addition to daily regimen (**e.g.** 1 unit bolus insulin for every 3mmol/L greater than 7 mmol/L; **but will vary!**)}

### Activity/Exercise Principles:

Patient education important for success!!!

1. In general, insulin therapy does not require adjustment for periods of activity < 30 minutes.
2. If activity > 30 minutes, & the activity is spontaneous & not preplanned, supplemental CHO before and during the activity can be used to balance the effects of ambient (previously injected) insulin.
3. Self Monitoring of Blood Glucose (SMBG) is recommended post event period q1-2h to assess response to activity and food consumption and to avoid post activity hypoglycemia.
4. On days of planned activity, reduction of pre-activity dose of insulin will help prevent hypoglycemia induced by exercise. If exercise will be after breakfast, lower the dose of regular insulin that would be taken before breakfast. If rapid acting insulin is used (aspart or lispro), decrease insulin dose only if exercise takes places within 2-3 hours after injection. (See Table 3.)
5. BG readings before, after, and possibly during exercise should be used to determine the appropriate change in insulin dose or food intake the next time the activity is done.
6. Prolonged activity can have a delayed BG lowering effect; ∴ may require ↓ basal insulin & hs BG test. {If T1DM & BG acutely high >14-16mmol/L, exercise will speed up ketosis process & should be delayed till BG lowered.}

BG=blood glucose CDE: certified diabetes educator CHO= carbohydrate IA=insulin analogue SMBG=self monitoring of blood glucose

**Table 3: Exercise Intensity & % Of Insulin Dose Reduction**[26] VO2 max = max rate of $O_2$ consumption

| **Intensity** (% VO2 max) | **30 min of exercise** | | **60 min of exercise** | Commonly, a snack or ↑ calories prior, is easiest way to manage exercise! |
|---|---|---|---|---|
| **Mild** exercise (25%) | 25 | (patient variable) | 50 | |
| **Moderate** exercise (50%) | 50 | | 75 | |
| **Strenuous** activity (75% ) | 75 | | No insulin | |

## TRAVEL THROUGH TIME ZONES

| | |
|---|---|
| General comment: goal is to switch to new time zone as soon as possible after arrival at new destination. {North-South travel may involve little if any time change so no insulin adjustment required.} | |
| In North America (3 hours max) → no adjustment | |
| Travel EAST (lose hours, shorter day): usually need less intermediate or long-acting insulin & less sleep | |
| Canada →Europe<br>*Lose 5-7 hrs; shorter day* | • Decrease bedtime dose of intermediate-acting insulin (NPH) by 1/3 or ½ on the travel day (usually on the plane crossing the Atlantic) |
| Europe →Canada<br>*Gain 5-7 hrs; longer day* | • When arrive home, have an extra meal & extra dose of bolus insulin<br>• The dose will need to last 5-6 hours, until return to usual routine |

## SICK DAY GUIDELINES for Patients on Insulin

- Check BG before meals &/or q4h around the clock (more often if necessary); drink extra sugar-free fluids
- Acute illness has variable effect on insulin requirement; management patient & regimen dependent
- T1DM: additional doses of bolus insulin for elevated BG or urine ketones (if BG not low); may ↓ insulin dose to avoid low BG if unable to ingest required amounts of carbohydrate & BG is not high.
- T2DM: ↓ or hold mealtime insulin if not eating; ↑ or additional doses of bolus insulin if high BG
- If on oral hypoglycemics, may need to temporarily decrease dose
- If the individual cannot eat as usual, they should replace solid food with glucose containing fluids. They should try to take ≥10 grams of carbohydrate every hour (see *clear fluids* below).

## PRE-PROCEDURE CONSIDERATIONS e.g. outpatient with diet restrictions pre-gastroscopy [27]

- Management depends on: T1DM vs T2DM; duration of fasting; time/duration of procedure; insulin regimen
- E.g. Days Before Test: no change or ↓ basal insulin dose(s) by ~20%; ↓ bolus insulin dose(s) by ~50%. BG in range of 5-12mmol/L are OK for 1-2 days. On Day of Test: ↓ morning basal insulin by ~30% (up to 50% if very long procedure) & do not take bolus until test is done & ready to eat. Test BG before giving next insulin.
- Clear fluids containing sugar: (e.g. fruit/sports drink, pop, popsicle, regular Jell-O®); test BG more frequently (e.g. q4h); if BG <4mmol/L or symptoms, take 15-20g carbohydrate & retest in 15min

## PREGNANCY & PRE-EXISTING DIABETES – Targets & Comments [5]

| | |
|---|---|
| **Pre-pregnancy:** A1c (%) | ≤7.0 |
| **Once pregnant:** | |
| FBG & preprandial (mmol/L) | 3.8-5.2 |
| 1-hour PPG (mmol/L) | 5.5-7.7 |
| 2-hour PPG (mmol/L) | 5.0-6.6 |
| A1c (%) of somewhat limited value in pregnancy | ≤6.0 if possible |
| In some ♀, especially T1DM or obese, higher targets may be necessary to avoid excessive hypoglycaemia! | |

1. **Stop** OHAs, ACEI/ARB & statin prior to conception*,**
2. Use intensive insulin therapy - MDI or CSII
3. SMBG: pre & postprandial at least 4 x per day

{Hyperglycemia Effects: T1: developmental defects; T3: macrosomia, delivery & neonatal complications}

Postpartum: ◆ Insulin may not be required on the day of delivery & up to 24-48 hours postpartum
- 5-7 days post-delivery, insulin requirements have usually returned to pre-pregnancy levels. Encourage breastfeeding!
- screen for diabetes 6-12wks postpartum ADA 2010

**Pregnancy Category B**-*Likely safe*: Human regular, NPH; Aspart, Lispro. **Category C**-*Caution*: Detemir, Glargine theoretical early risk
*There is evidence that glyburide & metformin e.g. in PCOS may be safe & not contraindicated in all cases. **Give 5mg/d folic acid![28]

## GESTATIONAL DIABETES (GDM)[5] –screen using risk factor analysis

- **Targets**: same as "Pre-existing" in table above. Avoid FBG < 3.3 mmol/L & 1 hr PPG < 5.0 mmol/L.
- **Intervention**: Diet & light exercise (small plate; walk after meals). If targets not achieved within 2 wks with nutrition alone, insulin should be initiated. {Glyburide or metformin MiG are 2nd line "off-label" options.} Regimen & dose depends on the pattern of hyperglycemia. Follow up: screen OGT for DM @ 6weeks-6months post-partum.
- **Example of MDI regimen in GDM (dosing will depend on patient!)**
  - High FBG: NPH qhs 0.1 unit/kg body weight (or start 5-8 units NPH qhs); Avoid LAIAs (Glargine, Detemir)
  - High PPG: Regular or RAIA of 1.5 units/10g CHO at breakfast due to insulin resistance, & 1 unit/10g CHO at lunch & dinner (or start 5 units bolus insulin for each meal with high PPG)

# Diabetes - Glucose Control: Landmark Outcome Trials – Summary

Loren Regier, Brent Jensen – www.RxFiles.ca – May 10

| | Trials Mean follow-up | Population Risk, hx, age | Intervention | A1C: baseline⇨final | Results |
|---|---|---|---|---|---|
| Type 1 (T1DM) | **DCCT** [1]<br>~6.5yrs; n=1,441<br>{Conducted between 1983-1993.}<br>{note 1° & 2° endpoints, as well as 1° & 2° cohorts.} | T1DM; mean age 27 (13-39)yr; BMI=27<br>Excluded: if CV disease, ↑ BP,HC, complications.<br>1° & 2° cohorts (2° if 1-15yr hx, existing mild-mod retinopathy & microalbuminuria; 1°: 1-5yr hx) | Intensive insulin (3+ inj/day or pump) with target A1C of <6.05% (44% achieved once, but only 5% maintained), preprandial BG 3.9-6.7mmol/L, PPBG <10mmol/L, weekly 3A.M. BG >3.6mmol/L vs Standard insulin (1-2 inj/day) | Int. vs Std.:<br>8.8%⇨7.4%<br>vs 9.1%<br>{Pre-prandial mean BG Int. vs Std. 8.6 vs 12.8mmol/L}<br>{↑ Wt 4.6kg/5yr} | Endpoint 1° or 2° / △ Rate/100 pt yr NNT/H=100per pt yr / RRR<br>1 Retinopathy: 1° ↓3.5 NNT=29; 2° ↓4.1 NNT=24; 63%<br>2 Microalb.: 1° ↓1.2 NNT=83; 2° ↓2.1 NNT=48; 39%<br>2 Macroalb.: 1° ↓0.1 NS; 2° ↓0.8 NNT=125; 54%<br>2 Neuropathy @5yr: ↓6.7 NNT=15; ↓9.1 NNT=11; 60%<br>Hypogly SEVERE: ↑43 NNH=2.3; ↑Hosp 7.6% vs 4.9% |
| | **DCCT / EDIC** [2]<br>~17yrs; n=1,394 | 93% of DCCT in follow-up till Feb05. age 45; BMI=28; 24yr hx | As above, but 94% of standard group changed to intensive insulin. | 7.4%⇨7.9%<br>9.1%⇨7.8% | •↓ CV events (nonfatal MI, CV death, stroke, angina, revascularization) 5.8% vs 10.3% NNT=23/17yr CI=12-352. (RRR=42% ↓) |
| Type 2 (T2DM) | **UKPDS-33** [3] ✦<br>~10yrs; n=3,867 | New T2DM; age 54yrs; with FPG 6.1-15 on diet alone | Intensive SU or insulin vs diet. Target FBG <6mmol/L vs <15mmol/L | 7%⇨ 7%<br>vs 7.9% | •↓microvascular endpoints NNT=42/10yr; mostly retinal<br>•no effect on CV events✦ •↑ hypoglycemia esp insulin |
| | **UKPDS-34** [4] ✦<br>~10.7yrs; n=1,704 | Obese T2DM; age 53yrs Wt=87kg; BMI=31 | Metformin 1700mg am, 850mg pm vs conventional (diet mostly) | 7%⇨7.4%<br>vs 8% | •↓diabetes endpoint NNT=10/10yr (RRR=32%) ✦<br>•↓ all-cause death NNT=14/10yr; ↓stroke NNT=48/10yr |
| | **Kumamoto** [5]<br>6yrs; n=110 | Japanese with 2° & without 1° retinopathy; UAE<300mg/24hr | Multiple insulin injection tx (MIT) vs conventional insulin tx (CIT) | 9.2-9.4⇨7.1<br>vs 8.9⇨9.4 | •↓ early microvascular complications (retinopathy [2+ steps on 19 step scale]; nephropathy & neuropathy) |
| | **PROACTIVE** [6]<br>~2.9yrs; n=5,238 | High CV risk; Age 61; BMI=30; A1C≥6.5 | Pioglitazone 45mg po daily vs Placebo (>10% higher rate of insulin use) | 7.8%⇨7%<br>vs 7.5% | •1° composite-no effect; 2°↓CV events NNT=50/2.9yr<br>•↑wt 3.6kg/yr; ↑HF NNH=30/2.9yr & edema. |
| | **ACCORD** [7]<br>~3.5yrs; n=10,251 | High CV risk; ~10yr hx T2DM; age 62; 93kg; North American | Intensive A1C target <6% {most on 3 oral hypoglycemics + insulin} vs standard A1C target 7-7.9% | 8.1%⇨6.4%<br>vs 7.5% | •↑ all-cause death ↑22% in intensive group at 3.5yr resulted in halting trial (NNH=95/3.5yr); also severe hypoglycemia (NNH=9/3.5yr) & ↑ weight 3.5 vs 0.4kg |
| | **ADVANCE** [8]<br>~5yrs; n=11,140 | Hx of CV disease; 8yr hx T2DM; age 66; 78kg; Austral-Asian/European | Intensive A1C target 6.5% {most on SU (gliclazide) + metformin} vs standard A1C target ~ 7% | 7.5%⇨6.5%<br>vs 7.3% | •↓ microvascular events over 5yrs (NNT=67/5yr), mostly nephropathy indicators; also ↑ severe hypoglycemia (NNH=83/5yr) & minimal wt change |

**RECORD** [31]: n=4447, ~ 5.5yr; T2DM (A1C mean ~ 7.9%⇨7.4-7.9%); open label; metformin or SU + rosiglitazone vs metformin + SU. No difference in CV death, MI; ↑HF & fracture.

**STENO-2** [9]: n=160, T2DM & microalbuminuria; multifactorial intensive (A1C <6.5% <20% achieved @13yrs, 8.4→7.7%; BP, lipid, ACEI, ASA) vs conventional tx for 7.8yr+ 5.5yr follow-up; ⇨ ↓ death, NNT=5 / 13.3yrs p=0.02, ↓ macro & microvascular events. (Only 1 pt achieved all 5 targets at 13yrs)

**UGDP** [10]: (1971) n=1027; ~8yrs; T2DM. Tolbutamide ↑ CV mortality 2.9x; Phenformin ↑ CV 4x & all cause mortality. Insulin, even with adjustable dosing was no better than diet alone, but no harm. Results criticised e.g. ↑ death in more poorly controlled, etc. 13 yr follow-up.

**VADT** (Dec08) [11]: n=1791, ~5.6yr, Age ~60yr, ♂ mostly, T2DM x 11.5yrs; 40% CAD Hx (Veterans Affairs). Intensive vs standard A1C Achieved: 6.9% vs 8.4%. No significant effect on CV events, deaths 102 vs 95 or microvascular complications; but ↑ serious adverse events 17.6 vs 24.1% mostly hypoglycemia.

✦ **UKPDS 80**: 10 year observational follow-up to UKPDS 33 & 34 (Sep08): glycemic difference lost in follow-up, however risk reduction emerged/sustained for endpoints (MI & Death), especially with MF. {SU/Insulin vs control: ↓Death 30.3⇨26.8 per 1000 patient-yrs; MF vs control: ↓ Death 33.1⇨25.9 per 1000 patient-yrs.} 12

## Summary of RCT Outcome Evidence

**Type 1 Diabetes** {ENDIT nicotinamide & DPT-1 low-dose insulin not effective in T1DM prevention}

- ✦↓ in microvascular complications in initial 6.5yrs (1° endpoint: retinal surrogates) (mostly ↓ retinal △ on fundus photo 3 steps / 25 stage scale, microalbuminuria & neuropathy)
- a 10% relative reduction in A1C (regardless of what the initial A1c value was) resulted in a 43% relative risk ↓ in progression of retinopathy & a 25% relative risk ↓ in microalbuminuria. (Substantially less at lower A1C levels.)
- ↑severe hypoglycemia including coma/ seizures NNH=9 /100pt-yr & hospitalizations 54 vs 36
- possible ↓ in macrovascular complications in long-term follow up(~17yrs); however, limitations such as unmasking could bias results.

**Type 2 Diabetes**

- intensive glucose control **may ↑ or ↓ risk depending on type of patient & treatment** {e.g. in ACCORD type patients, overly intensive pursuit of A1C target associated with ↑death; no benefit in VADT; whereas in ADVANCE type patients, not quite as intensive tx had some benefit; UKPDS 33,34 reveal variability between extent of BG control & outcomes.}
- glucose control offers predominantly microvascular benefit
- **metformin** in newly diagnosed obese T2DM: reduces macrovascular events & all-cause death without ↑ weight or hypoglycemia UKPDS-34, 80
- pioglitazone may ↓CV events (2° outcome & statistical concerns)[6], but ↑ HF & wt {rosiglitazone: ↑HF, wt, fractures; uncertain CV outcomes (neutral in RECORD, but limitations) 31
- **macrovascular benefits** seen with **multifactorial approach** to Tx
  - -lifestyle, ↓smoking, diet, exercise, BP, ACEI, statin, ASA, A1C<6.5% STENO-2
  - -statin therapy { simvastatin 40mg/d HPS; atorvastatin 10mg/d CARDS }
  - -ACEI, BP reduction {e.g. ramipril 10mg/d MICROHOPE}

## T2DM "Prevention" Trials *Pre-diabetes*

| | Trials | Population | Intervention | Results |
|---|---|---|---|---|
| Effective Options | **FDPS** [13]<br>4yr, n=522<br>(Finnish Diabetes Prevention Study) | Age 40-65 (ave 55yrs); BMI ≥25 (mean 31); IGT (a FBG < 7.8mmol/L; 2hBG >7.8 but <11 mmol/L) | Intensive lifestyle vs control<br>{Lifestyle: detailed, individualized counseling with nutritionist; individualized exercise circuit. Goals: ↓ weight >5%, fat <30% of all energy, fibre >15g/1000kcal, & moderate exercise > 30 minutes/day.} | 1°: incident diabetes (4yrs): 11% vs 23%<br>**RRR= 58%** HR = 0.4 (0.3-0.7) **NNT/4yrs = 8**<br>△Body wt: -4.2kg (-4.8 to -3.6) vs -0.8kg (-1.3 to -0.3) control<br>**7 yr follow-up: effect persists** 4.3 vs 7.4cases/100 person-yrs<br>**10yr** follow-up: no effect on CV or total mortality |
| | **DPP** [19]<br>2.8yr, n=3,234<br>(Diabetes Prevention Project)<br>[Troglitazone arm stopped early due to liver toxicity[20]] | Age >25 (mean 51yrs); BMI≥24 (mean=34); IGT (FBG of 5.3-6.9 mmol/L, 2hBG of 7.8-11 mmol/L.)<br>68% ♀; ~45% ethnic | Intensive lifestyle* n=1079<br>Lifestyle+ metformin 850mg po BID n=1073<br>Lifestyle + placebo n=1082, or<br>*{Lifestyle: ↓ weight by 7% (healthy diet & exercise ≥ 150 minutes/week), & 16 individualized lessons, covering diet, exercise & behaviour modification. [Low-cal diet: ↓450kcal/day ave; e.g. 1500kcal/d for 80-95kg ☺]} | 1°: incident diabetes (2.8yrs):<br>4.8 cases/100 person yrs for intensive lifestyle<br>7.8 case/100 person yr metformin; 11 case/100 person yr placebo,<br>•**NNT= 7 / 2.8yrs** for lifestyle (RRR: 58%; 71% age 60+)<br>•**NNT= 14 / 2.8yrs** for metformin (MF) (RRR: 31%)<br>Weight ↓: 5.6kg Lifestyle, 2.1kg MF, 0.1kg (p<0.001)<br>**10yr** follow-up: delays diabetes ⇒ lifestyle by 4yr, MF by 2yr |
| | **IDPP** [21] (India)<br>2.5yr, n=531 | Mean age 46yrs; BMI 26 IGT – in Asian Indians | Lifestyle vs metformin 250mg po BID vs control | 1°: incident diabetes (2.5yrs): lifestyle 39.3%, **NNT=6**; metformin 40.5%, **NNT=7**; 55% control |
| | **Stop-NIDDM** [22]<br>3.3yr, n=1,429 | Age 40-70 (mean 54yrs); IGT (2hBG ≥ 7.8 & <11.1mmol/L, FBG of 5.6-7.7 mmol/L). | Acarbose 100mg TID vs placebo {also encouraged exercise; met with dietitian} | 1°: incident diabetes (3.3yrs): 32.4% vs 41.5%; **NNT=11** / 3.3 yrs {↓CV events 2.5%; NNT=40}[23]<br>{GI SE's 83% vs 60%; Stop Tx: 31% vs 19%} |
| | **XENDOS** [24]<br>4yr, n=3,305 | Age 30-60;(mean 43yrs); BMI≥30; no CV disease; 21% had IGT | Orlistat 120mg TID vs placebo (weight loss study) {also ↓calorie diet & physical activity encouraged.} {High drop-out rate.} | 2°: incident diabetes: 6.2% vs 9% **NNT=36/4yrs**; ↓ diabetes in IGT subgroup only 18.8% vs 28.8%; NNT=10<br>{1°: ↓weight 5.8kg vs 3kg; ↑ GI SE's: 91% vs 65%/1yr} |
| | **DREAM-Rosi** [25]<br>3yr, n=5,269<br>{Canoe Rosi 2mg+MF500mg bid n=207 3.9yr, NNT=4} | Age ≥30yrs (~55yrs); IGT +/- IFG or IFG<br>Mean FBG=5.8mmol/l | Rosiglitazone 8mg po daily vs placebo {Trial stopped 5months early due to ↓diabetes; but ↑CV event rate approaching statistical significance.} | 1°: incident diabetes or death: 11.6% vs 26%; **NNT=7/3yrs** (driven by diabetes; no difference in death); CV events: 2.9% vs 2.1% HR=1.37; CI 0.97-1.94 |
| | **DREAM-Rami** [26]<br>3yr, n=5,269 | No DM or CV disease (eligibility expanded during trial) | Ramipril 15mg po daily (start 5mg/d x2 months, then ↑10mg/d till 1 yr) vs placebo | 1°: incident diabetes or death: 18.1% vs 19.5% NS {Also, no difference in CV event rate 2.6% vs 2.4%} |
| | **NAVIGATOR** [27] 5yr | IGT & ↑CV risk/disease | Nateglinide: no ↓ in progression to diabetes or ↓CV event. Valsartan ↓diabetes RR 14% but no CV benefit. | |

## Summary {Note: "prevention of DM" a non-clinical outcome.}

1) **Intensive Lifestyle Interventions ✓**
   a. Most effective intervention for patients with IGT
   b. How intensive was *intensive lifestyle*?
      i. Individualized counseling/education important
      ii. Weight loss: goal of at least 5-7% (& up to 10%)
      iii. Exercise: moderate activity of 30 minutes/day or 150 minutes/week
      iv. Diet: healthy, low calorie, low fat (<30% of total kcal & <10% saturated fat), ↑ fibre (>15g/1000kcal).
2) **Pharmacological Options** (+ some lifestyle measures)
   a. Effective but less so than intensive lifestyle*
      i. Metformin 250-850mg po BID (Meta-analysis[14])
         - 6 trials, n=3119, abd. obesity, IGT, family hx: ↓ time to diabetes onset ≤ 3yrs; NNT=12.5 CI: 9.1-20 (better if age <60yr)
      ii. Orlistat 120mg po TID
         - Effective if able to tolerate GI side effects; high cost >$150/mo
      iii. Acarbose 100mg po TID (CV benefit did not persist)
         - Effective if able to tolerate GI side effects; high cost >$120/mo
   b. Not Effective or Harm/Outcome Concerns*
      i. Ramipril: not effective; valsartan ↓diabetes RR 14%, not CV
      ii. Glitazones (Rosiglitazone & Pioglitazone): effective but concerns {↑wt, ↑ HF, ↑ fracture, (& ?CV Rosi)}[15,16]
      iii. Nateglinide: ↑ risk of hypoglycemia without any benefits

*Prevention strategies that utilize drugs risk harming otherwise healthy people; knowledge of long term efficacy, safety & impact on healthcare resources need to be established.[17]

**Of note**: early intensive insulin Tx (x2 wks) may induce remission in some **new T2DM**.[18]

2hBG=2hr blood glucose BMI=body mass index CV=cardiovascular FBG=fasting blood glucose HC=hypercholesterolemia HF=heart failure hx=history IGT=impaired glucose tolerance MF=metformin PPBG=post-prandial blood glucose SU=sulfonylurea Tx=treatment wt=weight yr=year

Links: CDA Professional: http://www.diabetes.ca/for-professionals/resources/2008-cpg/ ADA Prevention/delay of type 2 diabetes. http://care.diabetesjournals.org/cgi/content/full/30/suppl_1/S4#SEC14. AACE Prediabetes link[28] NICE T2DM: http://www.nice.org.uk/guidance/index.jsp?action=byID&o=11983 COMPUS: link[29] Ann Int Med: link[30]

# WEIGHT LOSS AGENTS COMPARISON CHART[1,2,3,4,5]

Brent Jensen , Loren Regier, Lynette Kolodziejak © www.RxFiles.ca May 10

| Generic/TRADE g=generic avail. (Strength & forms) Pregnancy | Class | Side effects / Contraindications CI: | √ = Therapeutic use / Comments / Drug Interactions DI / Monitor M / Safety | DOSE *Starting* / Usual | month |
|---|---|---|---|---|---|
| **Agents WITH An Official Indication for Weight Loss (For BMI≥30 or BMI≥27 with other risk factors** hypertension, diabetes, dyslipidemia & excess visceral fat **)** | | | | | |
| **Sibutramine**[6] **MERIDIA** (REDUCTIL UK)<br>10, 15mg cap ✗⊗ C<br>• may help by ↑ fullness sensation or ↓ snacking<br>**Several non-Rx products found to contain sibutramine**[1]**:** ARMA - Sin Gang San, Chao Nongsu Qingzhi Jiaonang Slim Hong Kong, Dai Dai Hua Jiao Nang, Dan Bai Shou Shen Su, Detox Peptide, Energy II, Fat Rapid Loss (Xin Yan Zi Pai Mei Zi Jiao Nang, Lexscl), Hanguo shoushen Yihao, Karntien Easy to Slim, Lasmi, LiDa Daidaihua Slimming Caps, Miaozi Slimming Caps, More Slim, Qianweisu Slimming Herb, Qing Zhi, Reduce Weight, Slim 3in1, Soloslim, Super Fat Burning, Xin Yi Dai & Xian Zhi Wei II etc. **FDA**: http://www.fda.gov/bbs/topics/NEWS/2009/NEW01977.html<br>**Health Canada List**: http://www.hc-sc.gc.ca/ahc-asc/media/advisories-avis/_fpa-ape_2009/index-eng.php | **Anorexiant** – inhibits reuptake of NE, 5-HT >dopamine | **Common**: dry mouth, headache, constipation, dizziness (to ↓SE: med with plenty of water may help); insomnia, menstrual changes, dyspepsia, rash, nervousness; ↓HDL<br>**Serious**: ↑HR (4-5 beats/min), ↑BP (1-3mmHg) (in some pts); seizure, cholelithiasis, ↑LFT (?↑ CV events Scout 11.4 vs 10%)<br>**Rare**: depression, abnormal bleeding, pulmonary hypertension, serotonin syndrome, ↑ QT interval<br>**CI**: anorexia nervosa, bulimia, **heart**/CVD/↑BP/liver dx; use of central acting appetite suppressants or MAOIs | **Wt loss** **~4.2kg / 1 yr** (95% CI -4.7 to -3.6kg) dose-related; peak weight loss at 6 months and maintained with continued treatment. ◆ Continuous vs intermittent therapy: no difference in efficacy, similar safety.<br>**DI**: ergots, lithium, MAOI (2wk wash-out period), meperidine, SSRI's, tramadol & triptans (↑risk of serotonin syndrome); stimulants (↑BP & HR)<br>**M**: blood pressure & heart rate (q2wks for first 12 wks; then q1-3months)<br>**Safety**: 2yr data. Not studied in <12 yrs old. Limited data in 12-16yrs.[7,8,9,10,11]<br>No additional benefit when agents (sibutramine & orlistat) combined. | *10mg od*; *Reassess dose after 1-2mo*<br>10mg po od<br>15mg po od STORM<br>{Europe- D/C 2010}<br>Max 15mg/d<br>(note some trials used up to 20mg/d) | **$120**<br>**$145** |
| **Orlistat**[12,13] **XENICAL** B<br>120mg cap ✗⊗<br>◆Roche offers the Xenical **BodyWellness Support Program** with free counselling by a dietitian (1-888-320-3131)<br>◆60mg FDA USA approved for OTC sale (**ALLI**). internet conterfeit version: may contain sibutramine | **GI Lipase inhibitor** - decreases fat breakdown & absorption ~↓30%<br>Minimally absorbed | **Common**: diarrhea , oily/fatty stools esp if ≥60g fat/d; oily spotting, ↑ bowel movements, flatulence, abd pain, bloating, nausea, vomiting, dry skin, pedal edema<br>* GI side effects ↓ with continued use.<br>**Negative reinforcement** (worse with high fat meal)!<br>* Discontinuation rates double vs placebo (8% vs 4%)[13]<br>**Serious, Rare**: anaphylaxis, angioedema, gallstones, urticaria<br>**CI**: chronic malabsorption syndrome, cholestasis (N=6 liver failure FDA Aug/09) | **Wt loss** **~2.9kg/1yr** (95% CI -3.2 to -2.5kg) **dose-related**; ↓wt regain up to 3yrs<br>{Diabetes: ↓$A_{1C}$ 0.38% 1yr[14]; ↓ need for hypoglycemics. ↓progression to diabetes in IGT: NNT=17}<br>**DI**: warfarin ↑INR, cyclosporine ↓levels, space 2 hrs; amiodarone monitor , levothyroxine<br>**Safety**: 4yr data. Not studied in <12 yrs old. Appears safe in 12-16yrs.[15] Recommend a **multivitamin** to prevent fat soluble vitamin deficiency. Take Vitamin 2hr before or after orlistat. With metamucil may ↓GI SE.<br>**Initiation**: weekend start, once daily, slowly ↑ up to TID to ↓SE (Note: some report better compliance with noon & evening meal dosing only) | *120mg po od*<br>120mg po bid cc<br>120mg po tid cc XENDOS<br>Give during or <1hr of a meal. Omit dose if no meal or no fat. | **$110**<br>**$160** |

| Generic/TRADE/Strength | Class / Use | Comments Regarding Weight Loss (See psychotropic charts for additional information www.RxFiles.ca) | Dose weight loss | $/mo |
|---|---|---|---|---|
| **Agents WITHOUT An Official Indication for Weight Loss** | | | | |
| **Bupropion SR** WELLBUTRIN g C<br>100,150mg SR tab (150,300mg **XL**tab)⊗ | Antidepressant | **Weight loss**: ~2.8kg (95% CI, -4.5 to -1kg); not enough evidence to recommend for weight loss. Consider for use when bupropion may be otherwise indicated. (↑seizure risk at >300mg/day in at-risk patients) | 150-200mg po bid<br>300mg XL od | $40-55<br>$45 |
| **Fluoxetine** PROZAC g C<br>10,20,40✗▼mg **cap** & 4mg/ml **soln** | Antidepressant | **Weight loss**: Too much variability in results to pool data (range from -14.5 to +0.4kg). Dose-dependant. May lose effectiveness over time. Consider if depression ± anxiety. Modest ↓ in wt & $A_{1C}$ in Type 2 diabetes.[16] | 60mg po od | $75 |
| **Topiramate** TOPAMAX g C<br>25,50⊗,100,200mg tab; 15, 25mg sprinkle cap | Mood stabilizer, anti-seizure, migraine | **Weight loss**: ~6.5% of total body weight; dose related; may minimize wt gain by other psychotropics;<br>◆with metformin & exercise in obese type 2 diabetes: ↓ wt ~5% vs 1.7% Pl; ↓A1C by ~0.5% vs 0.1% Pl n=646; 24wks[17]; SE's limit use | 50-100mg po bid | Generic/Trade<br>$75-90 |

=↓dose for renal dysfunction χ=Non-formulary Sk =Exception Drug Status Sk =prior approval NIHB ⊗=not covered by NIHB ▼=covered by NIHB 5HT=serotonin **BP**=blood pressure **CB1**-cannabinoid-1 receptor blocker **cc**=with meal **CI**=contraindication g=generic **DI**=drug interaction

**Drugs not recommended for wt loss:** amphetamines & thyroid replacement. **Dx**=disease **HR**=heart rate **LBM**= lean body mass **NE**= norepinephrin **OTC**=over the counter **Pl**=placebo **Pt**=patient **SE**=side effect **Tx**= treatment **wt**=weight

**Other Meds**: Potentially useful: **metformin** diabetes[18]. [Not in Canada: exenatide BYETTA[19] & pramlintide SYMLIN (for diabetics); phendimetrazine BONTRIL, **rimonabant** ACOMPLIA (CB1 blocker; 20mg/d; ↓4.7kg; SE: mood/depression 12%, drop out >45% & nausea)[20,21,22], zonisamide ZONEGRAN.]

**Discontinued Drugs:** fenfluramine+phenteramine PHEN-FEN & dexfenfluramine ⇨ heart valve abnormalities & primary pulmonary hypertension; phenylpropanolamine ⇨ strokes in ♀; phentermine IONAMIN, diethylpropion TENUATE & mazindol SANOREX.

**Drug Induced Weight Gain**: From Most → Least (**Bolded** drugs may be **preferred**)

- **Antidepressants**: mirtazapine, amitriptyline, phenelzine > desipramine, nortriptyline; weight neutral/loss: **bupropion, SSRIs** (esp. **fluoxetine,** but with paroxetine ↑weight possible), **moclobemide, venlafaxine**
- **Antipsychotics**: clozapine > olanzapine > quetiapine > **risperidone > haloperidol/loxapine, aripiprazole, ziprasidone**
- **Diabetes meds**: insulin > glitazones > sulfonylureas, repaglinide > acarbose {↓PPBG & $A_{1c}$}[23,24]; metformin; {less wt gain with **metformin** monotherapy or metformin combinations such as metformin + insulin[25]}
- **Anticonvulsants**: valproic acid > lithium, pregabalin > gabapentin, **carbamazepine**, vigabatrin; {weight loss/neutral: **topiramate**, zonisamide not in Canada, **lamotrigine, levetiracetam & phenytoin**}
- **Other**: cetirizine, corticosteroids, cyclosporine,flunarizine, medroxyprogesterone, megesterol, propranolol; raloxifene > tamoxifen. Smoking cessation: (Pl gain @12 weeks=3kg > varenicline gain 2.6kg > bupropion gain 2kg[26]).

**Diets**[27,28,29] Health Canada: http://www.hc-sc.gc.ca/fn-an/index_e.html; DASH Hypertension: http://www.nhlbi.nih.gov/health/public/heart/hbp/dash/; USA NCEP Cholesterol: http://www.nhlbi.nih.gov/guidelines/cholesterol/index.htm; USA Dietary Ref Intakes: www.iom.edu; USA Food Pyramid: http://mypyramid.gov

**Common Diet Types**: **Balanced**: Weight Watchers. **Low Fat**: Pritikin Diet. **Low Carbohydrate**: Atkins Diet {initial limit of 20g carbohydrate/day; can lead to ketosis and rapid short term wt loss}. **CND Guidelines** Lau 2006 www.cmaj.ca [Short term results encouraging, but often poor long term efficacy. Dietary ↓ of 500 kcal/day leads to loss of 0.5kg/week. **PHYSICAL ACTIVITY**: Moderate exercise such as 30-**60mins** walking x5-7 days/week supports wt loss[30] & prevents diabetes[31].]

**Wt Risk Assessment (Adult)**: Waist Circumference: ♂ <94cm ideal; >102cm high risk; ♀ <80cm ideal; >88cm high risk; {measure midway between lower rib margin & iliac crest}. Waist/Hip Ratio: ♂>0.9; ♀>0.85. BMI: >25=overweight, >30=obese.

## Natural / Herbal Weight Loss – Product Components & Side Effects

**Suitable Goal for Wt Loss:** ~ 5-10%, individualize, make realistic, consider long-term, sustainability (eat slowly,quit before full).

| Product | Comments |
|---|---|
| Bitter Orange | ◆stimulant with synephrine; similar to ephedra⇨ ↑BP, ↑HR |
| Caffeine, guarana, yerba mate, kola | ◆caffeine 40-1200mg ZANTREX-3 >150mg/cap; max 6/d ⇨ headache, anxiety, ringing, arrhythmias |
| Chitosan[32] | ◆some evidence, but quality trials suggest any benefit modest |
| Chromium[33] (especially picolinate) | ◆ineffective; Cr III from foods/dairy; Cr VI from industrial source, toxic/carcinogenic |
| Ephedra (Ma Huang) for wt loss | ◆banned 2004 due to MI & death; ↓ of ~0.6kg/mo; ↑psych, GI, autonomic, CV risk[34] |
| Green Tea (Camellia); relatively safe | ◆conflicting evidence[35,36;37] ↓mortality?; caffeine 10-80mg/cup; stimulant, diuretic; high doses hepatotoxic |
| Hydroxycitric Acid, garcinia | ◆"↓ fat storage & appetite" but mixed results; possible lead contamination! |
| 7-Keto-DHEA | ◆"3-acetyl-7-oxo-dehydroepiandrosterone"; not converted to androgens or estrogens like DHE; 200mg may ↑ basal metabolism & cause weight loss |
| Pyruvate | ◆from glucose metabolism; used to ↑exercise capacity and LBM; evidence weak |
| Conjugated Linoleic Acid | ◆isomer of linoleic acid found in dairy/beef sources; may ↓fat mass but not wt |
| Hoodia gordonii | ◆non-stimulating appetite suppressant; evidence weak |

**General Comments:**

- **Overall evidence is weak** for alternative dietary weight reduction products.[38] Products often expensive!
- Some of these products have potential for serious complications ◆{**Iodine** sometimes included to stimulate thyroid}
- **Fiber** products may assist in promoting satiety; however, guar gum & psyllium are ineffective for wt loss.
- Health Canada Warnings: e.g. *Herbal Diet Natural, Slimming Coffee, Lose Weight Coffee, Revolution DS Weight Loss, Anti-Aging Acai Berry, Guarana Blast, Brazillian Pure,* Weight Loss VitalAcai, Dietary Supplement, *Acai Power Blast* and *Muscle Mass M2 Formula & Energy 2000* (toxic ingredients – heart & kidney); *Emagrece Sim* Brazilian Diet Pill & *Herbathin* (may contain fluoxetine, chlordiazepoxide); *HydroLean, 4Ever Fit, Kaizen* (ephedrine ± caffeine).

**Drink**: Coke 591ml=240Kcal, Frappuccino Venti =323Kcal, Slurpee 1.18L=570Kcal, Big Gulp Double 1.9l=800Kcal. **Snack**: Donut=300Kcal 15g fat, Mars Bar=294Kcal 11g fat, Fries Supersize=570Kcal 28g fat, Milkshake Triple Thick=1160Kcal 28g fat. **Activity:** 60min: Walk >300 Kcal or Run >800 Kcal. **Surgery** 40 SOS

**Lifestyle**: Daily activity: Walk 10,000+ steps pedometer; Take stairs. 6x10min activity bursts. Self-weighing. Consider membership at suitable gym e.g. Curves & Limit computer & TV "**screen-time**" for kids. (Regular meal times include breakfast , ↑fiber, ↓fat & ↓portion sizes.)

**Obesity Complications**: tired, depression, stroke, clot, cataract; lung, **heart** ↑BP, liver, skin & gall bladder dx; pancreatitis, **diabetes**, ↑lipids, gyne abnormalities, **cancers** esophagus, colorectum, pancreas, breast, endometrium, & kidney, osteoarthritis, GI reflux, phlebitis, **sleep apnea** & gout.

| Product | Ingredients | Cautions {NOTE: effects may be dose dependent & rare at lower doses} | Cost |
|---|---|---|---|
| **Herbal Magic** http://www.herbalmagic.ca/index.asp<br>CBC-Marketplace suggests costs often more than initially appear. 05 Feb, 2010 http://www.cbc.ca/marketplace/2010/magic_in_a_bottle/main.html | • Involves diet changes with use of herbal supplements, vitamins & special food products. Many products. List of product contraindications, but not all-inclusive<br>• Intensive one-on-one counseling & review of food diary (i.e. 3 times/week) | • Most people will take 2-3 herbal products in addition to vitamins & food (therefore expensive)<br>• Herbal products range from single elements (chromium) to multi-ingredient (WM-2000: hydroxycitric acid, ginseng, d&elion, ginger, gymnema, kelp; WM-4000: garcinia, chromium, kola, ginseng, centaury, betony, ho shu wu, beet powder; Platoria: iodine, minerals, glucomannan, tyrosine, guarana, ginseng, yerba mate, green tea, kola, caleus forskonlii, ashwag&ha; PB-5: juniper, uva ursi, agrimony, gravel root, hydrangea, butcher's broom, couchgrass, cornsilk, marshmallow) | program costs $500-$600, plus food, & supplements {may end up costing thousands} |
| **Hydroxycut**<br>-Caffeine-Free Hydroxycut does not have anhydrous caffeine & the tea sources are decaffeinated<br>-Hydroxycut 24 uses regular product in AM & caffeine-free in PM | Calcium hydroxycitrate, chromium polynicotinate, potassium hydroxycitrate, garcinia cambogia, gymnema sylvestre, soy phospholipids, rhodiola rosea, withania somnifera, green tea, anhydrous caffeine, white tea, oolong tea | • Green tea, anhydrous caffeine, white tea & oolong tea are caffeine sources. (~ 600mg caffeine/day)<br>• Phosphotidylserine in soy phospholipids can cause GI upset & insomnia & may originate from bovine cortex (theoretical concern: possible rare risk of bovine spongiform encephalopathy or "BSE")<br>• Garcinia may contain lead & cause GI upset & headaches; Withania somnifera can cause sedation<br>• Hydroxycut associated with seizures with use of an older version that contained both caffeine & ephedrine. Hepatotoxicity has been reported with the ephedra-free formulation[1]<br>• **Health Canada**: nausea, tremor, dizziness, palpitations, chest pain, SOB, vomiting, sleep difficulties, syncope; one report of fatal MI in Canada (**FDA** May/09: **liver toxicity** 23 cases from Iovate and MuscleTech brands) | $45 for 72 caps (Days 1-3: 1 cap TID; Days 4 & beyond 2 caps TID); $113 for 30 days |
| **Relacore** | Vitamins [supratherapeutic amounts of C, B1 (thiamine), B2 (riboflavin), B6]; B12, calcium, biotin, panthenic acid, magnesium, magnolia, passion flower, scutellaria, niacinamide, panax ginseng, pinellia, poria, jujuba, perilla, phosphotidylserine | • Magnolia is a CNS depressant; Pinellia contains ephedrine alkaloids; Passion flower has been associated with sedation, dizziness, confusion, ataxia, vasculitis & possible liver & pancreas toxicity<br>• Scutellaria associated with sedation; high doses associated with hepatotoxicity, seizures<br>• Phosphotidylserine can cause GI upset & insomnia & may be sourced from bovine cortex (?BSE risk)<br>• Panax ginseng associated with insomnia, drowsiness, tachycardia, labile blood pressure & ↑ bleeding. May have estrogen-like effects. DIs: May inhibit CYP1A2, 2C9, 2D6 & 3A4 isoenzymes | $40 for 90caps (2 caps TID); $80 for 30 days |
| **Trimspa X32**<br>-Trimspa Energy also contains guarana, l-tyrosine & ATP<br>-Trimspa Ultra: adds grapefruit extract | Chromium dinicotinate glycinate, glucomannan, cocoa, green tea, hoodia gordonii, sodium carboxymethylcellulose, glucosamne, citrus naringin, vanadium | • Glucomannan can cause esophageal & GI obstruction, esp. if taken with ↓ fluid; may ↓ BG<br>• Cocoa is a caffeine source & contains tyramine. DIs: Citrus naringen may inhibit CYP3A4<br>• Vanadium has been associated with GI upset & nephrotoxiciy; Glucosamine may theoretically ↑BG | $50 for 90 tabs (4 tabs daily); $65 for 30 day |
| **Meta-Slim Weight Reduction Formula**<br>Carb Neutralizer & Fat Blocker: has phaseolamine, cassia nomane & gymnema sylvestre | Bitter orange, yerba mate, green tea, cayenne pepper, ginger | • Yerba mate & green tea are caffeine sources; Bitter orange is similar to ephedrine; Cayenne pepper(see chart next page); Ginger is used to ↓ GI upset; however can also cause GI upset & a pepper-like irritant effect on mouth/throat | $15 for 60 tabs (1-2 tabs daily); 30 days |
| **Zantrex-3** | Niacin, yerba mate, caffeine, guarana, damiana, schizopeta, green tea, piper nigrum, tibetan ginseng, panax ginseng, maca root, cola nut, thea sinensis complex | • Yerba mate, guarana, green tea, cola nut & thea sinensis are caffeine sources (600-900 mg/day)<br>• Piper Nigum is a CYP3A4 inhibitor & may inhibit p-glycoprotein; Panax ginseng has been assoc. with insomnia, drowsiness, tachycardia, labile blood pressure, & ↑ bleeding. It may inhibit CYP1A2, 2C9, 2D6 & 3A4<br>• **Health Canada reports**: headache, nervousness, tachycardia, nausea, diarrhea, palpitations, tremor, sweating; abnormal crying & feeding in 1 year old child (breastfeeding) | $95 for 28 day supply; take 2 caplets before "main meals" |
| **Xenadrine EFX**<br>Xenadrine NRG: has a methylxanthine complex<br>Xenadrine 40: has Uncaria tomentosa (Cat's Claw)<br>Xenadrine Hard-Core: blue-green algae potentially hepatotoxic, yohimbine & brown algae contains iodine | Vitamins C, B6, pantothenic acid, magnesium, l-tyrosine, green tea, cocoa, yerba mate, guarana, calcium tribasic, di-methinione, quercetin, fisetin, ginger, bitter orange, long pepper, red cayenne pepper, DMAE (dimethyl aminoethanol) | • Cocoa, yerba mate, guarana are caffeine sources; provides 400 mg/day caffeine<br>• Cocoa contains tyramine; Bitter orange similar to ephedrine; L-tyrosine assoc. with GI upset & arthralgia<br>• Quercetin is assoc. with GI upset, dizziness, drowsiness, irritability & aggravation of liver damage (↑ NE)<br>• DMAE is associated with urticaria, HA, drowsiness, insomnia, vivid dreams, confusion, hypertension & tardive dyskinesia; is a precursor for choline; Cayenne pepper(see chart next page)<br>• Ginger can cause GI upset & a pepper-like irritant effect on mouth/throat<br>• **Health Canada reports**: tachycardia, palpitations, abdominal cramps, "tingling skin", nausea, vertigo, xerostomia, tremor, chest pain, SOB, anxiety, & ↑ amylase | $40 for 90 caps (2 caps BID); $53 for 30 days |
| **Ezee Slimming Patch** | Ocean kelp (bladderwrack) | • Ingredients not listed on package. Product website indicates contains "minimal iodine", but no amount of iodine listed. Iodine can lead to hyper/hypothyroidism; May contain iodine, arsenic & cadmium<br>• **Health Canada reports**: leukopenia, thrombocytopenia, neutropenia, ↓ hemoglobin, menstrual irregularities, agitation. **One report** of jaundice, hepatitis & coagulation disorders that was **fatal**. | $30 for 15 patches (apply 1 patch every 2 days) =30 days |
| **Natural Factors SlimStyles, Appetite Control Fibre Blend**, or **WellBetX** | Polyglycoplex (PGX)-contains fibre from konjac mannan (glucomannan), sodium alginate & xanthan gum. Mulberry extract. Program with numerous products http://www.naturalfactors.com/index.asp | • PGX absorbs 600 times its weight in water to produce satiety; reports of GI obstruction exist but likely risk only with excessive intake; may cause gas, diarrhea, abdominal distention. No ARs in 8wk trial.[2]<br>• SlimStyles menu plan suggests lower amount of fruits/vegetables, dairy or meat products than recommended by Canada's Food Guide<br>• May ↓ absorption of oral meds. Take meds at least 1 hour prior or 3 hours after PGX | $30-$60 for single product |

**BG**=blood glucose **DI**=drug interaction **GI**=stomach **HA**=headache **MI**=heart attack **NE**=norepinephrine **SOB**=shortness of breath {Commercial programs beneficial but require motivation; group support programs may be most effective long-term.[3]}

## Caffeine: Recommended Maximums and Average Content

| Population | Max Recommended Caffeine Intake/day |
|---|---|
| Children (based on average weight & limits of 2.5 mg/kg/day of caffeine) | 45 mg 4-6 yrs; 62.5 mg 7-9 yrs; 85 mg 10-12 yrs |
| Women planning to become pregnant, or who are pregnant or breast feeding | 300 mg |
| Other adults | 400-450 mg |

## Average Caffeine Content:

| Product | Caffeine Content (mg) | Product | Caffeine Content (mg) |
|---|---|---|---|
| Coffee | 118 percolated to 179 drip /237 ml | Tea | 30 green to 50 leaf or bag /237 ml |
| Red Bull | 80 /250 ml | Chocolate milk | 8 /237 ml |
| Cola | 36-46 regular to <50 diet /355 ml | Chocolate bar or candy | 7 milk chocolate, 19 sweet chocolate, 28-58 unsweetened baking chocolate /28 g |
| Akavar 20/50 | 100mg / capsule | | |

**Caffeine** by law, does not have to be listed on ingredient lists unless it is added as a pure substance. Caffeine in many sources eg. **guarana, kola & yerba mate**. **Pregnancy** concern esp. if ≥ 150mg/day.



| Ingredient | Notes: {Potential adverse effects, usually dose dependent} |
|---|---|
| 7-Keto-DHEA | "3-acetyl-7-oxo-dehydroepi&rosterone"; not converted to &rogens or estrogens like DHE; 200 mg may ↑ basal metabolism & cause weight loss |
| Agrimony | Photosensitivity; affects BP & BG; astringent |
| Bitter Orange | Stimulant with synephrine; similar to ephedra ⇒ ↑BP, ↑HR.[4] Case report of associated MI.[5] |
| Caffeine | Headache, anxiety, ringing, arrythmias. ↑HR & BP. Diuretic effect. Some evidence for weight loss when combined with other stimulants (e.g. ephedra). |
| Cassia nomame | Inhibits lipase; may cause diarrhea & limits absorption of fat soluble vitamins; no evidence of efficacy |
| Cat's claw (uncaria tomentosa) | Not studied for weight loss; usually used for arthritis; has immune-stimulating properties |
| Cayenne pepper | Common spice; large amounts may cause liver & renal damage; flushing, sweating, lacrimation, rhinorrea, headache |
| Chitosan | Some evidence, but quality trials suggest any modest benefit. Claims to bind fat and block fat absorption. May ↓ valproate levels or ↑ effect of warfarin. |
| Chromium | Ineffective; CIII from foods/dairy, CrVI from industrial source, toxic/carcinogenic |
| Citrus naringen | CYP3A4 inhibitor; source of insoluble fibre |
| Cocoa | Contains tyramine & caffeine; limited evidence of efficacy |
| Conjugated Linoleic Acid | Isomer of linoleic acid found in dairy/beef sources; may ↓ fat mass but not wt |
| Ephedra (Ma Huang) | Banned 2004 due to MI & death, ↓ 0f 0.6kg/mo; ↑psych, GI, autonomic, CV risk |
| Gravel root (Joe Pye) | Hepatotoxic if contains pyrrolizidine alkaloid & its metabolite which is carcinogenic/mutagenic; hypersensitivity if ragweed allergy; assoc. with veno-occlusive disease |
| Green Tea {also consider that this has been used for 1,000+ yrs} | Conflicting evidence; contains caffeine (stimulant, diuretic); very high doses hepatotoxic; contains ECGC (epigallocatechin gallate), a flavenol which may suppress appetite & ↑ fat metabolism, but may also inhibit dihydrofolate reductase leading to folic acid deficiency. Oral absorption of ECGC is questionable. |
| Guarana | **Caffeine** source; insufficient evidence (only studied with damiana & mate) |
| Hoodia gordonii | Non-stimulating appetite suppressant; evidence weak |
| Hydroxycitric acid (garcinia) | "↓ fat storage & appetite" but mixed results (3 month RCT found no effect)[6]; possible lead contamination |
| Iodine/kelp | Can lead to hyper/hypothyroidism; evidence suggests no benefit |
| Juniper | Prolonged high doses neprotoxic; convulsions; ↑ uterine tone; diuretic |
| Kola (cola nut) | **Caffeine** source; only studied in combination with ephedra |
| Konjac mannan (glucomannan) | Tablet form associated with esophageal & GI obstruction; evidence of benefit for weight loss conflicting; may ↓ absorption oral meds |
| Panax ginseng | Has caused insomnia, drowsiness, tachycardia, labile BP; estrogen-like effects; may inhibit CYP 1A2, 2C9, 2D6, 3A4; limited evidence of efficacy in reducing BG in diabetics |
| PGX (polyglycoplex) | Contains konjac mannan, xanthan gum & sodium alginate; insufficient evidence of efficacy; fibre souce; reports of GI obstructions. {contains glucomannan: unabsorbable polysaccharide (glucose + mannose).} |
| Phaseolamine | Derived form white kidney bean; probably not effective. Claims to prevent starch from breaking down to glucose. |
| Pinellia | Contains ephedra alkaloids |
| Piper nigrum | CYP3A4 inhibitor; may inhibit p-glycoprotein; insufficient evidence of efficacy |
| Pyruvate | From glucose metabolism; used to ↑ exercise capacity & LBM; evidence weak |
| Schizonepeta | May cause photosensitivity, dizziness, teeth discolouration, diuresis & hepatotoxicity |
| Scuttellaria | Associated with sedation; high doses associated with hepatotoxicity & seizures; not usually used for weight loss |
| Sodium alginate (algin) | Isolated from brown algae; may ↓ cholesterol absorption from gut |
| Thea sinesis | Caffeine source; scientific name for tea (also known as camellia sinensis) |
| Uva ursi | Not recommended for prolonged use because of mutagenic/cardinogenic hydroquinone; use not recommended for >1 wk; used as adjunct for people with urinary problems |
| Vanadium | Trace mineral; GI upset, nephrotoxicity; insufficient evidence of effects on BG |
| Withania somnifera (ashwag& ha) | Sedating; insufficient evidence of efficacy |
| Xanthan gum | Bulk-forming laxative; may ↓ absorption oral meds; not studied individually for weight loss |
| Yerba mate (mate) | **Caffeine** source; contains theophylline & theobromine; insufficient evidence for weight loss |

- **Other**: Some use "bowel cleansers" to ↓ weight. Often contain laxatives (cascara sagrada, rhubarb), bulk-forming agents (psyllium, flax); or goldenseal, fennel, ginger, marshmallow, slippery elm & probiotics.
- **Links**: -See www.dietitians.ca for information on eating well, finding a registered dietitian, & track your eating & activity patterns
  -The Government of Canada also provides information on eating right & exercising at www.eatwellbeactive.gc.ca

- General References [7,8,9,10,11,12]

## Classification of Thyroid Disorders [1, 2, 3, 4, 5, 6, 7, 8, 9] (American Thyroid Association-ATA, American Association of Clinical Endocrinologists-AACE, British Thyroid Association-BTS)

| | Normal values will vary; check standard for lab | HYPOthyroid | Subclinical HYPOthyroidism | HYPERthyroid | Subclinical HYPERthyroidism | Comments |
|---|---|---|---|---|---|---|
| TSH ultra-sensitive | 0.3–5.5 mIU/L* Euthyroid: TSH <4 -not treat | ↑↑ (>10) | ↑ (4-10) (guidelines vary) | ↓↓ (<0.1) | ↓ (<0.3) | •Best screening test for hyper/hypothyroidism (draw blood in am) •**If abnormal measure FT4 & FT3** •Will not identify pts with pituitary or hypothalamic disease •**Clinical assessment & Tx based on SYMPTOMS** |
| FT4 -free T4 | 9-19 pmol/L | ↓↓ | Normal | ↑↑ | Normal | •In unstable thyroid state (e.g. recently hyperthyroidism tx, on excess T4 replacement) FT4 more accurate than TSH •↑/↓ in a clinically hyper-/hypothyroid pt, with non-suppressed/non-elevated TSH = 2° causes |
| FT3 -free T3 | 2.6-5.7 pmol/L | ↓ not useful for hypo or tx | Normal | ↑ pure T3 toxicosis common | Normal | •May be useful early in tx to assess level of **active** hormone |

**Other test:** •**Hyperthyroidism:** U/S volume, echo texture, nodules; RAIU & scan differential once hyperthyroidism established (e.g. thyroiditis has ↓ RAIU, Graves' has diffuse RAIU), TRAbs not routine (? clinical utility, expensive, long turn around time from lab), helpful in pregnancy to determine fetal risk, EKG not routine, (cardiac disease, irregular rhythm)
•**Hypothyroidism:** U/S volume, echo texture, nodules; anti-TPO not routine monitoring; may do once for diagnosis **Extra**: Bone Density not routine, unless clinically indicated. **Seriously ill Pt**→ TFTs not assessed unless strong suspicion of thyroid dysfunction. LT4 tx of little benefit & may be harmful.

**Screening:** ↑screening reasonable in ↑risk pts ♀>45, pregnancy/postpartum, T1DM, strong family history, goiter, signs/symptoms, autoimmune dx, vitiligo, neck radiation, pernicious anemia, ↑lipids, hypoadrenalism, Down's/Sjogren Sx [1, 4, 7, 10] (Routine adult screening controversial →? Clinically important benefits, ? cost effectiveness)[6, 7, 10]
* Possible change to upper TSH limit→ ? ↓upper limit to 2.5 mIU/L →No evidence of adverse consequence for TSH 2.5-5 mIU/L; level has a number of limiting factors assay problem, circulating abnormal TSH, etc.; this may ↑↑ pts dx with subclinical disease.

## HYPOTHYROIDISM

{Prevalence: ~2% of women, 0.1% of men; ↑'s with age}

Symptoms: ↓HR, fatigue, ↑weight, **cold** intolerance, dry skin/hair, constipation, hair loss, menorrhagia, emotional lability, poor concentration & ↑cholesterol

**1° Hashimoto's Thyroiditis** most common; iatrogenic, congenital; ↓I rare in developed countries

**2°** ~1% of cases pituitary >Sx of pituitary insufficiency: abnormal menses, ↓libido, galactorrhea, acromegaloid; hypothalamus rare eg. tumor, inflammatory conditions, infiltrative diseases, infection, pituitary surgery or radiation, & head trauma⇒ do MRI / CT scan.

**1° Hypothyroidism: Permanent condition in most pts. Tx: LT4**

**Myxedema coma**: rare decompensated hypothyroidism: ↓mental status, hypothermia, ↓BP, HR, hypoventilation, esp. in elderly
Tx: hydrocortisone 100 mg IV q8h untill adrenal suppression ruled out; LT4 100-400μg IV Day 1, 50-100μg IV/d until stable→LT4 po

**Congenital:** asymptomatic at birth maternal hormone crosses placenta; S&S appear after ≥6-12wk: poor feeding, growth failure, lethargy, slow movement, hoarse cry;
Tx: LT4; Goal= FT4 ≥ upper half of the normal range adjusted for age

**Monitoring**: •Re-evaluate TSH/FT4/FT3 too variable q6-8wks until stable TSH can remain abnormal for months→FT4 more reliable indicator initially •Clinical improvement in 2 wks, complete recovery in several months •**Goal**=maintain TSH & FT4 in normal range (? Goal TSH ≤2.5 mIU/L >2.5 often have S&S & Tx Sx's ) •Once euthyroid, maintenance LT4 dose does not fluctuate greatly→monitor **TSH** q6-12 months •Re-evaluate TSH q4-6 wk following any Δ **in LT4 brand/dose** or Δ **in weight ≥10lb** •**LT4: life long therapy**

**Subclinical**: [6, 7, 13, 14, 15] TSH above reference limit & **FT4/T3** within **range** 4-10% of the population
•Clinical Significance: ?↑atherosclerosis, CHD, MI, depression, ↓BMD, metabolic sx
•Tx: TSH >10 mIU/L→**LT4** (Good to **recheck TSH** in 6-8wks before initiating tx)
TSH 4-10 mIU/L→**consider Tx** esp if hypothyroid S&S, DM, ↑lipid, HTN, pregnant/planning, depression, ↑↑ goiter, ↑antibody⊕
•If no Tx, monitor q 6-12 months for Δ in clinical status & TSH.
•Cochrane review suggests: treatment does not improve survival or ↓CV morbidity [16].

**Hypothyroidism in Pregnancy**: Hashimoto's autoimmune thyroiditis most common
•Clinical Significance: Serious **maternal** miscarriage, C-section, pre-eclampsia→↑↑ hypothyroid risk later, etc. & **fetal** complications cognitive impairment, lower IQ score, stillbirth, low birth weight, delays in mental/motor development, etc.
•Tx: LT4 dose Δ's(often ↑ dose **25-50%**)→check FT4/TSH when pregnant & q4 wk.
•**Subclinical hypothyroidism** evidence of benefit is limited, but benefits > risks
•Dose increase often greater with previous thyroidectomy than with Hashimoto's

•**Very elderly >85** with TSH 4.5-10, esp. with CVD Tx usually not recommended. Tx if Sx's: cognitive etc but go slow with LT4
• **Elderly** presentation of hypo-/hyperthyroidism can be atypical. (eg. apathy or ↑weight in hyperthyroidism)
• **Athletes:** use of LT4 not on prohibited substance list
• **Smoking** → ? worsen ophthalmopathy, ↓remission & response to MMI/PTU, larger goiter at presentation, ↓TSH/↑FT3 during pregnancy.

## HYPERTHYROIDISM

Symptoms: ↑HR, tremor, ophthalmopathy, **heat** intolerance, ↓weight ↑rarely, ↑BMR, menstrual Δ's, ↑$Ca^{2+}$, diarrhea, weakness, apathy elderly

**Graves' Disease** most common esp. in young: autoimmune disorder due to TRAbs⇒stimulate thyroid growth, hormone synthesis & release May have proptosis, pretibial myxedema
Tx: Thionamide **MMI** or PTU; 1st line Europe, esp ♀ young fertile, RAI destroys gland; 1st line USA; CI if active eye dx: steroids may help, Surgery, Symptom control β-Blocker

**Solitary toxic nodules & toxic MultiNodular Goiter** Multi Nodular Goiter: esp older pts, RAIU is ↑: autonomous thyroid nodules that secrete excess thyroid hormone
Tx: Thionamides to attain euthyroid before Tx with RAI or surgery; esp. for elderly/CVD with mod-severe Sx; or RAI 1st line US; may need ↑dose, often weeks wait time, SE: edema; Surgery; ?ethanol inj (If pretreat with thionamides the required dose of I131 will be larger, & the cure rate after first treatment will be lower.)

**Thyroiditis** painless/subacute: ↑ESR/postpartum: Inflammatory damage to the gland→↑release of T4 & T3; ↓RAIU; initially hyperthyroid likely followed by transient hypothyroid
Tx: Self-limiting; β-Blockers; NSAIDs pain control; Glucocorticoids reserved for severe cases; Thionamides not indicated does not ↓ preformed hormone release

**Thyroid Storm**: life threatening decompensated thyrotoxicosis fever, tachycardia, dehydration, delirium, coma, N/V, diarrhea; causative factors: trauma, surgery, RAI
Tx: β-Blocker propranolol po→40-80mg q6h (not long acting form); PTU preferred; Iodide ↑dose, SSKI 5 drop po q6h (Potassium iodide)/Lugol's **after PTU**; Hydrocortisone ≥100mgIV q8h; Supportive Tx

**Thyroid cancer (ca):** papillary, follicular cancers differentiated; anaplastic undifferentiated → arise from differentiated
Tx: Surgery →RAI adjuvant ablation **where appropriate**→ LT4/TSH suppression ↓TSH induced tumor growth; If high/immediate ca risk (eg.stage 3-4) →TSH≤ 0.1mIU/L; If ca stage 1-2 →TSH=0.1-0.5 mIU/L (11,12)

**Monitoring**: •Re-evaluate TSH/FT4/FT3 q4-6 weeks until stable **frequency will depend on severity of illness** •TSH can remain suppressed for months→FT4 more reliable indicator initially •In 3-4 wks will see Sx improvement •In 4-12 wks most pts are euthyroid or improved considerably must ↓ dose of MMI/PTU
•**Goal**=maintain TSH & FT4 in normal range •Stable dose identified →monitor **TSH** q2-6month depends on illness severity •MMI often 1st ,if SE consider PTU.
•**>18 months of Tx not associated with improved relapse rates in Graves' disease; often treat until euthyroid for ~1year**
•Relapse ~50% in Graves' occurs within 1st 3 months alternate tx with RAI if hyperthyroidism persists >6months, preferred to 2nd MMI/PTU course •↑ monitoring required if d/c MMI/PTU after remission.

**Nodules:** Do TSH & ultrasound. If TSH low then do I-131 or technetium scan. If nodule is <1cm or unchanged & no family risk→likely not cancer.
**FNAB if:** nodule growing; >1cm & history unknown; if ultrasound suggests cancer; family/pt history of thyroid cancer; if neck radiation, or vocal/swallowing problems.

**Subclinical**: [6, 7, 17] TSH below lower reference limit & FT4/FT3 within range (**Lab error common** = Repeat before you treat!)
•Clinical Significance: •2% of the population •link with **osteoporosis** esp. in postmenopausal ♀, cardiac abnormalities especially **AF in elderly**, mortality ↑41%
•Tx: **↑ risk for complications** eg. elderly, postmenopausal (1) **TSH <0.1 mIU/L**→tx for hyperthyroidism.
(2) **TSH 0.1-0.3 mIU/L** → consider tx esp. if thyroid scan shows high uptake or ↓BMD, otherwise observe if medical conditions repeat TSH in 2 wks, or 3 months otherwise
**↓ risk for complications** e.g younger, healthier (1) **TSH <0.1 mIU/L** → tx for hyperthyroidism esp. if thyroid scan shows high uptake or ↓BMD
(2) **TSH 0.1-0.3 mIU/L** → follow up TSH in 3 months. •Clinical implications may suggest to tx very mild thyroid hyperfunction even in asymptomatic older pts

**Hyperthyroidism in Pregnancy**: 1) Gestational assoc. with hyperemesis gravidarum -if low TSH, check T3 & if ↑, may need tx. 2) True Grave's thyrotoxicosis-tx. 2/1000 pregnancies; Worse during 1st trimester→improve later→worse after delivery. Assess newborn for hypothyroidism if MMI/PTU given. If initial maternal thyroid stimulating **antibodies levels are high**, consult pediatrician early.
•Clinical Significance: Serious maternal miscarriage, preterm labour, HTN, heart failure, etc. & **fetal** complications stillbirth, low birth weight, goiter, etc.; **NO RAIU or Scans**
•Tx: Mild hyperthyroidism →monitor without Tx as long as mother/fetus are not symptomatic; expect altered lab values (TSH=low normal; FT4=high normal)
PTU is DOC for **overt** dx→maintain FT4 in upper ½ of normal by 2nd/3rd trimester most can ↓dose or d/c & stay euthyroid. Do **FT4/FT3**/TSH q 4-6 wk. MMI an alternative;
If need surgery→optimal during 2nd trimester •**Subclinical hyperthyroidism** adverse pregnancy outcomes not reported →Tx not currently recommended.

•**β-Blocker**: ↓Sx palpitation, anxiety, tremor, heat intolerance; no effect on thyrotoxicosis; Use short acting non-selective βB easy to titrate & withdraw: **propranolol** 20 mg BID, ↓ to d/c, ?metoprolol, ?atenolol
•**RAI**: defer pregnancy ≥6 months; Cardiac/Elderly may need thionamide before RAI to ↓stored hormone→ ?↑RAI failure→ **d/c MMI/PTU >1wk if feasible**
**CI:** pregnancy/lactation/eye dx active Graves; **SE**: hypothyroid: most in 1st yr→3%/yr, thyroiditis esp. if volume 45-50 ml,? ↑ca risk; follow-up q4-6wk until euthyroid; TSH slow to recover→FT4 more accurate early on
•**Surgery**: Option for Graves' •Consider if severe ophthalmopathy, large thyroid, drug failure or toxic nodules. [**Caution: RAI** mush **& amiodarone** bubble gum; effects thyroid consistency!]
•**Iodides**: (SSKI 38mg I /drop: 1-2 drop bid pre-op, Lugol's 6.3 mg I /drop); Wolff-Chaikoff effect & ↓size/vascularity of gland; rapid effect ↓Sx in 2-7 day; short-term effect 1-2 wks usually
**Tx role** very limited: thyroid storm; rapid hormone release inhibition. **SE**: hypersensitivity, salivary gland swelling; iodism metallic taste, burning mouth, GI upset/diarrhea; gynecomastia; **Caution=OTC meds** containing iodine supplements, kelp, herbals for ↓weight can induce hyper-/hypothyroidism

## DRUG-INDUCED THYROID DISORDER:

**Hypothyroidism→** •**↓TSH secretion**= amiodarone, bexarotene, dopamine, glucocorticoids, hormones endogenous, metformin, somatostatin •**↓T4 absorption**= See LT4 DIs •**↓T4→T3 conversion**= amiodarone, β-Blockers, glucocorticoids, x-ray contrast iodinated.
•**↓ Hormone synthesis/release**= aminoglutethamide, **amiodarone**, expectorant iodinated glycerol, iodide including x-ray contrast, **lithium**, thalidomide, thionamides & topical antiseptics povidone iodide •**↑T4/T3 metabolism**= carbamazepine, phenobarbital, phenytoin & rifampin no effect on normal thyroid fx, but ↑LT4 doses may be needed •**Induction of autoimmune dx**= amiodarone, **interferon-α**, interferon- β, interleukin-2 & lithium •**Unknown mechanism**= sertraline, sorafenib & sunitinib.

**Hyperthyroidism→** •**↑TSH secretion**=antipsychotics, metoclopramide, theophylline •**↑thyroid hormone synthesis/release**=amiodarone, iodine, lithium •**Immune reconstitiution**=alemtuzumab, after highly active HIV tx

**Amiodarone**: •causes hypo 5-25% & hyperthyroidism <5%, ↑ risk if: thyroid dx or family hx, goiter, thyroid antibodies ⊕ •if ↑risk monitor TFTs TSH/FT4/FT3 q1mon x3, q3 mon x4-8, then q6-12 mon •Hypo thyroidism Tx=LT4 & continue amiodarone •Hyper thyroidism difficult to distinguish Type 1 or 2; & amiodarone blocks ↑HR & tremor; pt can deteriorate rapidly & if toxic thyroidectomy may be best. •RAIU & scan rarely helpful; gland saturated with iodine via amiodarone ≥40x daily amount; Tx=d/c amiodarone if possible, propranolol ↑dose if able, Prednisone 40-80mg od, MMI •**Dronedarone** 400mg po bid with food; related but ↓effective than amiodarone; less thyroid SE; but ↑ HF risk.

**Lithium**: •can appear to cause hypo-/hyperthyroidism ?non-clinical •goiter in ≤5% & hypothyroidism ≤20% •↑risk elderly, ♀, prior disease • TSH @3 months , then q6-12 months •Hypothyroid Tx=↓lithium dose ideal or LT4 •Hyperthyroidism rare Tx= d/c lithium

☆ **Pearls**: 1) Wait **6-8 weeks** after LT4 change before rechecking **TSH**. 2) Correlate what has happened in **last 8 weeks** to the pt when interpreting TFT's. 3) If **nodule >1cm & history unknown** then do a fine needle aspiration biopsy (FNAB) 4) If LT4 tx response poor, consider **compliance, malabsorption** celiac dx, **drug interactions** Ca, iron, antacids etc. **& other diagnosis** adrenal. 5) Thyrotoxicosis: 1st do FT4/FT3, I-131 uptake & scan, β-blocker, then **MMI/PTU** after discuss all options with the pt. 6) Hyperthyroid Diagnosis missed.

ς=scored tab χ=Non-formulary Sask ☎=Exception Drug Status Sask. ⊗=not covered by NIHB ▼=covered by NIHB Δ=changes **AAP**=American Academy of Pediatrics **AF**=atrial fibrillation **anti-TPO**= antithyroid peroxidase antibody **ATA**=American Thyroid Assoc. **BMD**=bone mineral density **BMR**=basal metabolic rate **BP**=blood pressure **CHD**=coronary heart dx **CI**=contraindication **CVD**=cardiovascular dx **CV**=cardiovascular **d/c**=discontinue **DI**=drug interaction **DM**=diabetes mellitus **DOC**=drug of choice **dx**=diagnosis/disease **FNAB**=fine needle aspiration biopsy **FT4**=free thyroxine **fx**=function **HF**=Heart Failure **HR**=heart rate **HTN**=hypertension **I**=iodine **LT4**=levothyroxine **MI**=myocardial infarction **MMI**=methimazole **N/V**=nausea & vomiting **Pt**=patient **PTU**=propylthiouracil **RAI**=radioactive iodine iodine-131 **RAIU**=radioactive iodine uptake **rhTSH**=recombinant TSH **S&S**=signs & symptoms **SE**=side effects **ss**=steady state **Sx**=symptom **T1DM**=Type 1 diabetes mellitus $T_{1/2}$=half life **T3**=triiodothyronine **TFT**=Thyroid Function Tests (TSH/FT4/FT3) **TRAbs**=thyroid receptor antibodies **TSH**=thyroid stimulating hormone **Tx**=treatment **U/S**=ultrasound **wks**=weeks **wt**=weight.

# Thyroid Treatment Chart [18, 19, 20, 21, 22, 23, 24, 25]

Prepared by Jason Kielly, Brent Jensen © www.RxFiles.ca May 2010

| Generic/TRADE (Strength & forms) | Class / Pregnancy category | Side effects / Contraindications CI | √ = therapeutic use / Comments / Drug Interactions DI / Monitor M | Dosing | $/mo |
|---|---|---|---|---|---|
| **Levothyroxine (LT4)**<br>50,100,150,200,300ug tabs<br>**(all scored) ELTROXIN**<br>25,50,75,88,100,112,125,137 x▼,<br>150,175,200,300ug tabs<br>**(all scored) SYNTHROID**<br>**No evidence either brand superior**<br>{Liquid Drops available in Europe}<br>Option to give **SL if malabsorption** a problem.<br>If **allergies: white pills** do not contain dye.<br>**Considered interchangeable, but less TFT variation if same brand used.**<br>LT4 500µg/10ml for **inject**<br>•IV/IM when rapid repletion is required or po admin precluded<br>•initial 50-80% of established **po** dose | **Thyroid Supplement**<br>synthetic form of T4<br><br>Pregnancy: Category **A**<br>Dose adjustments may be necessary as pregnancy progresses.<br>Dose of LT4 likely will be **25**-50% higher during pregnancy-follow TSH.<br>(Some ↑ 2 tabs/week if pregnant)<br><br>Breastfeeding:<br>Compatible | **Common:**<br>- usually due to **over** treatment (palpitations, ↑HR, tremors, anxiety, diarrhea, etc.)<br>- may aggravate existing CVD (arrhythmias-A fib, angina, MI), ?↓BMD<br>**Serious (rare):**<br>CI: Acute MI, adrenal insufficiency if untreated; **tx of obesity/weight loss**: may produce serious/life threatening SE, esp if given with certain weight reduction aids;<br>does not ↑ thyroid cancer.<br>**Precautions:**<br>•Careful dose titration to minimize SE<br>•CVD, ↓BMD, DM, Elderly ↑CV effects<br>•Psyc history of anxiety or depression start slowly with LT4 replacement | √ 1st line for treatment of hypothyroidism<br>**Peak** effect: **2-4**hr; $T_{1/2}$: 6-7day; **Absorption**: 40-80% ↓ by age / food / med<br>Little or no effect on multinodular **goiter** size. **Protein** bound: 99%<br>DI: **↓ Levels** (Space > **2-4**hrs apart): **aluminum hydroxide, calcium supplements, iron salts, magnesium salts**, orlistat cholestyramine, chromium, ciprofloxacin, colestipol, sevelamer, simethicone, sodium polystyrene<br>**↓ Level**: Coffee/tea 1hr spacing, H2 blockers & PPI's due to ↑gastric pH, estrogens, raloxifene 12hrs spacing, sucralfate 8hrs spacing, meals 30 min spacing<br>**↓ Level**: by inducers concern if intermittent dosing eg. carbamazepine, phenobarb, phenytoin, **rifampin**<br>M: TSH during maintenance tx q6-**12**months (draw blood in **am**) | •Euthyroid quicker with **weight based dosing** vs slow titration, but Sx's & QofL improve at same rate<br>•Few pts require > 200 µg/day<br>•6-8 weeks before ↑dosage (as LT4 has long T1/2)<br>•No effect on infant during pregnancy or lactation & will ensure adequate milk supply<br>•Individualize dose based on patients symptoms 50, 75, 100, 112ug po daily<br>(60kg x 1.6ug/kg/d=100ug/d; 70kg x 1.6ug/kg/d=112ug/d)<br>•**Take dose same time each day!** AM, before breakfast | 9-11 |
| | | | ***Young-healthy***: •1.6 µg/kg/day Ideal Body Wt (full replacement dose) •TFTs 6-8 wk **2-3 wk if severe** •↑by 12.5-25 µg increments until normal TSH & ↓S&S<br>***> 50 or <50 with CVD***: •25-50 µg/day •↑q6-8 wks prn {more cautious titration to minimize CV risk}<br>***Elderly w/ CVD***: •12.5-25 µg/day & ↑q4-8wk •if ↑CVD S&S: ↓dose. ***Severe dx***: •12.5-25 µg/day & ↑25µg/d q2-4wk until TSH norm<br>***Congenital Hypothyroidism***: •initial 8-15µg/kg/day **(~25-50 µg/day)**; AAP recommends 50 µg/day initially for term and full-size infants<br>***Pregnancy***: •Hypothyroid **prior** to pregnancy: Adjust LT4 to **TSH<2.5mIU/L**; Expect ↑ LT4 dose by 4-6wk gestation ↑25-50% possible<br>•Hypothyroidism **during** pregnancy: Titrate LT4 dose rapidly to **TSH<2.5mIU/L in 1st trimester** or **3 mIU/L in 2nd & 3rd trimester** | | |
| **Liothyronine (LT3)** x ⊗<br>5, 25 µg tab (not scored)<br>**CYTOMEL**<br>**(LT3 25 µg = LT4 100 µg)** | **Thyroid Supplement**<br>synthetic form of T3<br>Pregnancy: Category A<br>LT4 is better than LT3 in pregnancy.<br>Breastfeeding:<br>Compatible | •Sx of hyperthyroidism if overtreated<br>•↑ incidence of **cardiac events** compared to LT4<br>•Rapid absorption & short $T_{1/2}$ vs LT4 leads to marked **fluctuations** in T3 levels & S&S.<br>**Trials of LT4 vs. LT4/LT3 combo have shown no benefit for combination therapy** | **Not 1st line alone or in combo with LT4 for hypothyroidism**<br>√ simple (nontoxic) goiter may be tried to ↓ size of goiter<br>√$T_3$ suppression test differentiate hyperthyroidism from euthyroidism<br>√Thyroid Carcinoma radioimaging ⇨may replace T4 due to rapid clearance which allows for sooner radioimaging without hypothyroid symptoms<br>Possible augmentation in refractory depression Very limited evidence<br>**Peak effect**: 1-2 hours; $T_{1/2}$: 1.5 days; **Absorption**: 95-100% | *Mild Hypothyroidism*<br>•Initially 25 µg daily.<br>•↑ by 12.5-25 µg q1-2 weeks.<br>•Maintenance dosage = 25-75 µg daily<br>•Titration of dose harder than LT4; but if intolerant to LT4, patient may tolerate LT3 | 45-125 |
| **Desiccated Thyroid**<br>30,60,125mg tab **THYROID** | **Thyroid Supplement**<br>T3 & T4 from **porcine** thyroid glands | •Sx of hyperthyroidism if over treated<br>•Animal protein derived antigenic in allergic or sensitive pts<br>•Unpredicatable stability & batch variation | •**Guidelines suggest should be avoided**<br>•Never compared with LT4 or LT4/LT3 in a randomized study | Initial dose: 60 to 300 mg daily.<br>Maintenance dose: 30-125 mg daily<br>****60 mg = LT4 100 µg or LT3 25 µg** | 12-16 |
| **Methimazole (MMI)**<br>5mg (10mg x ⊗) tab<br>**TAPAZOLE**<br>**MMI ~10x more potent than PTU**<br>*Can be given rectally if necessary* | **Thionamides**<br>Inhibits T4 to T3<br>Pregnancy: Category D<br>•craniofacial malformation, esp. 1st trimester<br>•alternative if PTU SE<br>•similar fetal concentration for PTU or MMI<br>Dose often less in 2nd & 3rd trimester.<br>Breastfeeding:<br>Compatible Caution if >10mg/d | **Serious (rare)**: Lupus like, vasculitis<br>**Agranulocytosis** 0.1-0.5% of pts; possibly more with PTU<br>• Baseline WBC regular CBC not cost effective<br>• Consult Dr if Sxs fever, sore throat, mouth ulcers<br>•Neutropenia→same maybe with PTU► **Refer**<br>**Reversible cholestatic** jaundice: if D/C→slow complete recovery<br>•Occurs usually in first 3 months incidence 1.3%<br>**Minor***: skin rash if persistent use antihistamine or topical steroid, arthralgias, abnormal taste/smell<br>* may subside with continued use > 4 wks<br>CI: thionamide allergy<br>**Precautions**: bleeding disorders or easy bruising, liver dx, S&S of infection fever, headache, malaise, skin eruptions, sore throat, surgery | **√ MMI 1st choice for Tx of hyperthyroidism** adults & kids<br>**Clinical Response→days; Lab Response 4-6wk**.<br>**Peak** effect: **0.5-1**hr; $T_{1/2}$: 4-6hr; **Absorption**: 93% ? effect of food<br>Not protein bound; CYP450 metabolism no active metabolites<br>Renal excretion<br>DI: **Warfarin** may ↓INR; **Digoxin** ↑dig level; **2D6** inhibitor→ DI with TCA, codeine, paroxetine **RAI** impair uptake & ↓ efficacy<br>Liver dx: No dosage adjustment ? ↓Clearance<br>Renal dx: No dosage adjustment<br>M: TSH; CBC & LFT: Baseline & at 1wk. (see monitoring above)<br>**Block-replace regimen** High dose thionamide + T4 **not indicated** ↑SEs. | *Mild hyperthyroidism*<br>10-15 mg daily initially; 5-15 mg daily maintenance<br>*Mod-severe hyperthyroidism*<br>20-30 mg daily initially; 5-15 mg daily maintenance<br>*Severe hyperthyroidism-large goitres*<br>30-40 mg daily initially; 5-15 mg daily maintenance<br>•Initially divided doses to ↓ GI upset<br>•Max blocking dose = 60-120 mg/day<br>•↑dose if no improvement in TSH & T4 levels in 4–6 weeks.<br>•No dosage adjustment in elderly<br>*Pediatric hyperthyroidism*<br>Initial= 0.4-0.7 mg/kg/day ÷ q 8-12 hours<br>Maintenance= 0.2 mg/kg/day ÷ q 8-12 hours | 15-35<br><br>Formulary: not covered by some. |
| **Propylthiouracil**<br>**PROPYL- THYRACIL**<br>**50,100mg tab scored (PTU)**<br>*Can be given rectally* *as an enema or suppository*<br>↑liver failure:<br>? restricting PTU to pt with toxic reaction to MMI where RAI/surgery not an option | **Thionamides**<br>•Inhibits T4 to T3<br>•PTU only:<br>↓peripheral conversion of T4→T3 prefer for thyroid storm<br>Pregnancy:<br>Category D - Compatible *<br>**PTU is DOC**; MMI is an alternative if not tolerated<br>* Maternal Benefit outweighs Fetal Risk esp. in 1st trimester.<br>Dose often less in 2nd & 3rd trimester.<br>Breastfeeding:<br>Compatible Caution if >200mg/d | **Serious (rare)**: Lupus like, vasculitis<br>**Agranulocytosis** 0.1-0.5% of patients<br>• Baseline WBC **regular CBC not cost effective**<br>• Consult Dr if Sx fever, sore throat, mouth ulcers<br>•Neutropenia→same maybe with MMI► **Refer**<br>**Severe liver** 0.1%: **hepatitis with hepatocellular injury**<br>• liver transplants 3rd most common drug cause<br>• d/c PTU immediately if S&S<br>**Minor***: skin rash if persistent Tx: antihistamine or topical steroid, arthralgias, GI upset divide dose<br>*may subside with continued use > 4 wks<br>CI: liver dx (S&S fatigue, weakness, abdominal pain, itching, easy bruising, yellowing of the eyes/skin), allergy<br>**Precautions**:<br>hematologic abnormalities may occur agranulocytosis, leukopenia, thrombocytopenia, aplastic anemia | √ Thyroid storm (inhibits T4 to T3), Pregnancy esp 1st trimester<br>Use PTU only in pts who have an allergy/intolerance to MMI, have thyroid storm or are pregnant.<br>**Clinical** Response→**days; Lab** Response **4-6wk.**<br>**Peak** effect: **0.5-1.5** hr; $T_{1/2}$: 1-2hr; **Absorption**: 75% food no effect<br>Protein bound ~**75%**; Liver metabolism; Renal excretion<br>DI: **Warfarin** may ↓INR; **Digoxin** ↑dig level ; **RAI** impair uptake & ↓ efficacy<br>No dose adjustment = elderly, renal or liver disease.<br>M: TSH; CBC & LFT: Baseline & at 1wk signs of liver dx esp. during 1st 6months (see monitoring above)<br>**Block-replace regimen** High dose thionamide + T4 **not indicated** ↑SEs | *Graves' Disease*<br>*Initial*= 300mg/day divided q8h max. 900-1200 mg/day<br>*Maintenance*=100–150mg/day divided q8–12h<br>•For doses >300 mg = divide dose<br>•If no improvement after 4–6 wks ↑ dose.<br>•Once euthyroid, ↓dose gradually q4–6 wks to the lowest effective dose<br>*Thyroid Storm*<br>600–1200 mg/day divided every 4–6 hours<br>•As Sx resolve, slowly ↓dose to maintenance dose<br>*Pregnancy*<br>•Initial= full PTU dose, monitor TFTs monthly<br>•Stable= Use lowest effective dose, monitor<br>•Dose often less in 2nd & 3rd trimester. | 20-35 |

*LIOTRIX* (LT4 & LT3 in 4:1 ratio) available in the USA. OTC preparations (Thyroid American Biologics; Thyroid Complex The Vitamin Shoppe) have not been evaluated by Health Canada (some concern ⇨ may contain unregulated animal products).

## Patient Education & Information:

American Academy of Family Physicians http://familydoctor.org/

The College of Family Physicians of Canada

http://www.cfpc.ca/English/cfpc/programs/patient%20education/default.asp?s=1

US FDA Consumer Drug Information Web Site http://www.fda.gov/cder/drug/DrugSafety/DrugIndex.htm

Public Health Agency of Canada http://www.phac-aspc.gc.ca/chn-rcs/index-eng.php

## Health Web Sites:

ACP Journal Club http://hiru.mcmaster.ca/acpjc/default.htm

American Family Physician http://www.aafp.org

Bandolier http://www.jr2.ox.ac.uk/bandolier/

Cochrane Collaboration http://www.cochrane.org/

Doc Guide http://www.docguide.com

Health Canada Advisories, Warnings & Recalls

http://www.hc-sc.gc.ca/dhp-mps/medeff/advisories-avis/index_e.html

Health Knowledge Central http://www.healthknowledgecentral.org/

HealthOntario.com http://www.healthyontario.com/

Medical Letter http://www.medletter.com/

Medscape http://www.medscape.com

MotherRisk http://www.motherisk.org/index.jsp

NHS **Clinical Knowledge Summaries** (formerly PRODIGY) http://cks.library.nhs.uk/home

NICE (National Institute for Health and Clinical Excellence) http://www.nice.org.uk

RxFiles (Comparative Objective Comparative Drug Charts) http://www.rxfiles.ca/

Therapeutics Initiative (University of British Columbia) http://www.ti.ubc.ca/

Travel Health Canada http://www.phac-aspc.gc.ca/tmp-pmv/index.html

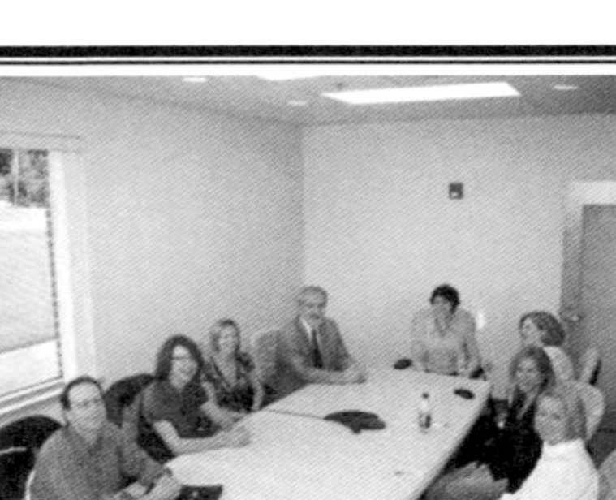

***Academic detailing Training Workshops***

RxFiles has been privileged to both host and help facilitate academic detailing workshops in Saskatoon, Hamilton, Halifax and Boston. In 2009, RxFiles hosted the 2nd of such workshops benefiting again from the leadership of Frank May (Australia), staff from other programs, and the goodwill of several Saskatoon physicians who stole some hours away from the office to assist. *Loren Regier* RxFiles

Originally prepared by Adrienne Lindblad PharmD, Loren Regier, Brent Jensen © www.RxFiles.ca


## ULCERATIVE COLITIS (UC)

{Symptoms: abd. pain/cramping, diarrhea, blood in stool, ↓weight, fever, eye problems, arthritis, fatty liver...}

**UC Disease Severity**[1,2]: {*Primarily mucosal involvement; starts at anus/rectum & may extend up colon*}

- Mild: <4 stools/day (blood can be present); no systemic manifestations & normal ESR
- Moderate: >4 stools/day (blood can be present) with minimal systemic effects
- Severe: >6 stools/day with blood & systemic toxicity (fever, anemia, tachycardia, ESR>30)
- Fulminant: >10 stools/day, continuous bleeding, systemic toxicity, need for blood transfusions, dilated colon, abdominal tenderness/distention

**UC Treatment Pearls:**

- **Consider** disease location, severity, #pills/day, size of dose & cost.[3] **Surgery** is curative.
- **Topical therapies** achieve higher concentrations in mucosa than oral formulations; may have higher efficacy & lower risk of systemic adverse effects. Topicals have faster response times & are dosed less frequently. Some patients may prefer oral treatment. Topicals can stain clothing & cause pain/irritation with insertion (lubricating gel may help)
  - ◆**Suppositories** reach 10cm. **Foam** reaches 15-20cm & **Enemas** may reach splenic flexure[9].
  - ◆5-ASA & steroid enemas effective in inducing remission; oral steroids not effective for maintaining remission[1,4]
  - ◆Left colon *Rectosigmoid* disease: particularly suitable for topical 5-ASA products[4]
  - ◆Distal disease: topical treatment more effective than oral, combination PO/PR good
- **Oral**: Sulfasalazine (**SSZ**) preferred due to cost efficacy but 5-ASA may be better tolerated
  - ◆SSZ/5-ASA products effective in 40-80% patients {equally effective in maintenance}.
- If requiring chronic steroid pred >20mg/d, check adherence & consider alternatives (AZA/6-MP or surgery)
- **Antidiarrheals** eg. codeine, diphenoxylate, loperamide: use ≤ twice/day; try alternative tx if requiring more opinion
- **Monitor**: Hbg, iron indices, nutritional status consider multi-vitamins, folic acid, growth peds, BMD if ↑ OP risk
- **Cancer**: UC with onset, duration (decades), extensive disease, primary sclerosing cholangitis & family history of ca associated with ↑colon ca risk→regular colonoscopy within 8yrs of IBD onset; after 2 negative exams, screen 1-3yr; if extensive dx or left sided colitis screen 1-2yr after initial endoscopy; colectomy: if non-adenoma-like dysplasia; polypectomy & surveillance: if adenoma-like dysplasia & not flat dysplasia. 125
- **Complications**: intestinal: bleeding, perforation, toxic megacolon; extra-intestinal: arthritis, osteoporosis, mood, fatty liver.

## CROHN'S DISEASE (CD)

{Symptoms: abdominal pain, diarrhea, blood in stool, ↓ weight, fever, perianal fissures, arthritis,...}

Presents at any age but often 16-30yrs. **Investigations**: CBC, CRP, Urea, Lytes, LFT, Stool Culture & Micro.

**CD Severity**[5]: {*May occur in all layers of bowel at any point from mouth to anus (including perianal);* also non-GI}

- Mild-moderate: ambulatory pts able to tolerate oral intake; absence of dehydration, abdominal pain/tenderness, painful mass, obstruction, systemic toxicity (high fevers, rigors) or >10% weight loss
- Moderate-severe: patients unresponsive to treatment for mild-moderate disease or with symptoms, fever, weight loss, nausea or vomiting, anemia, abdominal pain or tenderness
- Severe-fulminant: symptoms persist despite PO steroids; high fevers, intestinal obstruction, rebound tenderness, persistent vomiting, cachexia or abscess
- Remission: patients without symptoms or inflammatory sequelae; "steroid-dependent" patients require steroids to maintain wellbeing & are not considered to be in remission

**CD Treatment Pearls:** (Patient info page JAMA April 9,2008 http://jama.ama-assn.org/cgi/reprint/299/14/1738 )

- Location of disease important in selecting drug. **Monitor** as per suggested UC monitoring.
- **Surgery** not curative; 5-ASA often used to prevent post-op recurrence (minimal supportive evidence)
- 5-aminosalicylic acid does not contain acetylsalicylic acid; thus no significant antiplatelet effects
- **Smoking** can ↑ risk of and worsen disease (in contrast to UC where improvement reported)
- 2/3-3/4 patients with mild-moderate disease remain in remission for up to 2 years without drug tx
- Budesonide CIR less effective than conventional steroids in acute treatment & more costly, but less SE's; may delay time to relapse (although corticosteroids not effective for maintaining remission long-term).
- Efficacy of 5-ASA products questionable in CD (Hanauer meta-analysis found Pentasa not clinically superior to placebo)[6]; SSZ effective for active disease.
- Use of probiotics for maintenance promising, but requires further study. (More promising in UC.)
- Antibiotics role uncertain. There are concerns with long-term use neuropathy, tolerability, antimicrobial resistance & concerns if also on an immunomodulator. May be beneficial if infection suspected or fistulas.
- **Cancer**: Crohn's with onset, duration (decades), extensive disease, primary sclerosing cholangitis & family history of ca associated with ↑colon ca risk→regular colonoscopy within 8yrs of IBD onset; after 2 negative exams, screen 1-3yr; if extensive dx or left sided colitis screen 1-2yr after initial endoscopy; colectomy: if non-adenoma-like dysplasia; polypectomy & surveillance: if adenoma-like dysplasia & not flat dysplasia. AGA'10 125

| | UC: Acute Therapy | UC: Maintenance Therapy |
|---|---|---|
| Mild - Mod | **Distal disease**[1,2]: ◆ combination (5-ASA PO 2.4g/day + enema 4g/day) or 5-ASA PO 2-4.8g/day or 5-ASA supp 500mg BID or 5-ASA enema 1-4g/day or steroid enema {1g 5-ASA enema may be as effective as 4g in left-sided colitis} | ◆Oral 5-ASA +/- 5-ASA enema (i.e. 2-3 g/day PO +/- 4g PR twice weekly), or ◆Mesalamine enema 2-4g q1-3days; 5-ASA supp 500mg daily-BID ◆ Effect: dose dependant |
| Mild - Mod | **Extensive**: SSZ 4-6g/d or PO 5-ASA 2-4.8g/d | ◆SSZ 2-4g/day or 5-ASA up to 4 g/day |
| Mod-Sev | See above for distal or extensive disease OR Prednisone 40-60 mg/day PLUS either SSZ 4-6g/day OR PO 5-ASA 3-6g/day (60 mg pred more effective, but ↑'d SE) -infliximab if inadequate response | Taper prednisone, then after 1-2 months decrease SSZ or 5-ASA to doses listed under mild/moderate disease; continue SSZ 2-4 g/day (2g preferred as better tolerated, but 4g more effective) or 5-ASA or 6-MP or AZA[8] -infliximab if used for induction |
| Sev-Fulminant | Hydrocortisone 100 mg IV Q6-8H or 60mg methylprednisolone/day if received steroids within prior month -if no response after 7-10 days, consider infliximab NNT=5 for refractory disease at 8wks (12) or colectomy; (cyclosporine an option e.g. for bridging while waiting for effect, though now rarely used given availability of anti-TNF agents) | Change to PO prednisone and taper over ~ 2-8wks; add SSZ or 5-ASA & attempt to withdraw steroids after 1-2 months. Use SSZ maintenance dose if remission achieved. -6MP or AZA can be used -infliximab (if successfully used for induction) |

**5-ASA**=mesalamine **AZA**= azathioprine **CIR**=controlled ileal release **NNT**=number need to treat to benefit one **OP**= osteoporosis **SSZ**= sulfasalazine

**Note**: Consider OP prevention in IBD, especially if on frequent steroids {Vit D, Ca++, exercise; bisphosphonates} 13,14

**Nutrition**: important in IBD patients; prevent malnutrition; enteral feeds may be effective 1° therapy esp peds

**Depression/anxiety**: common; consider non-drug interventions psychotherapy; TCAs useful if also diarrhea?; may avoid SSRIs?

| | CD: Acute Therapy | CD:Maintenance Therapy |
|---|---|---|
| Mild - Mod | Prednisone 40-60 mg/day, taper after 2-4 weeks **Small Bowel Disease:** Prednisone as above; 5-ASA 3.2-4g/day controversial; **Ileocolonic/colonic**: SSZ 3-6 g/day for ≤16wks; Budesonide 9mg/day x 8-16 weeks & taper {for ileo & right colonic only}[7] **Perianal:** SSZ &/or (metronidazole ± cipro) esp. if fistula&abscess | Tx not always required in mild disease! Some use 5-ASA for in mild disease but may be no better than placebo. Consider use of AZA or 6MP if >1 recurrence/yr; MTX injectable (SC) if fail AZA or 6MP; SSZ may prevent recurrence after ileocolonic resections |
| Mod-Sev | Prednisone 40-60 mg/day; consider addition of AZA or 6MP due to long onset of effect[9] -If ineffective, consider MTX injectable (SC) -Infliximab if continuing symptoms despite steroids & immunomodulator or if rapid onset required[10] or if fistulating disease ± AZA or 6-MP | -AZA or 6MP (delayed effect; useful for long term maintenance NNT=7; NNH=19; Steroid Sparing NNT=3)[11] -AZA especially useful in peds -MTX injectable (SC) if fail AZA or 6MP or if can't wait for AZA or 6MP -Anti-TNF e.g. Infliximab (if induction successful); also 3 doses useful for fistula. **{Current debate whether *step-up* or *top-down* better.}** |
| Sev-Fulminant | Hydrocortisone 100 mg IV Q6-8H; Infliximab or anti-TNF | |

| Potential 5-ASA Sites of Action | Duodenum | Jejunum | Ileum | Terminal ileum may also be affected by UC. | Proximal colon | Distal colon | Rectum |
|---|---|---|---|---|---|---|---|
| | *Crohn's only* affected areas | | | | *UC & Crohn's* affected areas | | |
| Pentasa | ✓ | ✓ | ✓ | | ✓ | ✓ | ✓ |
| Salofalk or Mesasal | | ? | ✓ | | ✓ | ✓ | ✓ |
| Budesonide CIR | | | ✓ | | ✓ | ✓ | ✓ |
| Asacol / Mezavant Lialda / Apriso | | | ✓ | | ✓ | ✓ | ✓ |
| Sulfasalazine or Olsalazine | | | | | ✓ | ✓ | ✓ |
| 5-ASA Enema or Steroid Enema "TOPICAL" | | | | | | ✓ | ✓ |
| 5-ASA Suppository "TOPICAL" | | | | | | | ✓ |

| Name & Dosage Form g = generic | Side Effects (SE)/ Contraindications (CI) | Therapeutic Use/Comments Drug Interactions (DI) /Monitor (M) | Dose: Active disease & Maintenance (Maint); Peds shaded blue [15,16,17,18] | $/mo |
|---|---|---|---|---|
| **SULFASALAZINE (SSZ)** | | **Time to effect: 2-4 weeks** | | |
| **Sulfasalazine (SSZ)**<br>**SALAZOPYRIN** g<br>500 ☺ mg tab;<br>500 mg EC tab (EN-tabs).<br><br>-can make suspension (HSC)<br>B | CI: hypersensitivity to sulfonamides or salicylates, porphyria, <2 yrs of age, intestinal/urinary obstruction; G6PD caution<br>SE: more common on initiation & ↓ as tx continues. If SE troublesome, may stop drug & restart at lower dose; use EN-tabs or change to 5-ASA<br>Dose-related: GI 33%, HA 33%, arthralgia, anorexia<br>Non-dose related: rash, fever, hepatotoxicity, bone marrow suppression, pancreatitis, nephrotoxicity, photosensitivity, oligospermia 33%, revresible after d/c, alveolitis; can discolour skin, tears, urine | -used in acute & maintenance therapy for UC; for acute therapy in CD; & may prevent post-op recurrence in CD. Lower cost than 5-ASA.<br>-cleaved into 5-ASA & sulfapyridine by colonic bacteria<br>-consider folic acid supplements as absorption impaired (1-5mg/day)<br>-preferred option for patients with rheumatoid arthritis or IBD-related arthropathies [4] (monitor as below)<br>M: CBC, Hct, renal+ hepatic function, urinalysis q1-2 weeks→q1-3 months<br>DI: ↑phenytoin level, ↑myelosuppression with AZA /6MP due to TMPT inhibition, ↑toxicity methotrexate, ↑thrombocytopenia with thiazide diuretics, ↓digoxin & ↓cyclosporine level; ↓effect with: $Fe^{++}$, digoxin, PABA/PABA metab. procaine, tetracaine | Start with low dose & ↑q2-3d to ↓ SEs; 500mg EC po daily cc<br>Active UC: 4-6g/day divided TID-QID; 1g EC po QID (after meals)<br>Maint UC: 2-4g/day divided BID-TID; 1g EC po BID (after meals)<br>(4g/day most effective, but less SE with 2g/day); ↑ if deterioration<br>Active CD: 3-6g/day divided TID-QID; 1-2g EC po TID (after meals)<br>Maint CD: not recommended; except to prevent post-op recurrence<br>Peds Active: **25-35 kg**: 1 tab TID; **35-50kg**: 2 tabs BID-TID 40-70mg/kg/d PO divided TID-QID PC max 6g/d HSC<br>Peds Maint: 25-35kg: 1 tab BID; 35-50kg: 1 tab BID-TID 20-50mg/kg/day PO divided BID-QID (max 2g/day) HSC | 18<br>99<br>50<br><br>71-135 |
| **5-ASA (MESALAMINE)** | **If pH dependent 5-ASA release: caution co-administering with antacids,PPI's & H2RAs.** | **Time to effect: 2-4 weeks {See previous page for sites of action!}** | | |
| **ASACOL**<br>400mg EC tab, (800mg EC tab ®)<br>"Eudragit S" coated; (Novo-5-ASA g 400mg tab)<br>B | CI: hypersensitivity to salicylates, existing gastric or duodenal ulcer, urinary tract obstruction, <2 years of age;<br>enemas: hypersensitivity→metabisulfite | -pH-dependent release (terminal ileum→rectum); -do not break or chew<br>-many people ~80% tolerate 5-ASA if they do not tolerate SSZ [1]<br>M: CBC, renal function, allergy symptoms, liver function<br>DI: ↑myelosuppression from AZA/6MP; ↓ digoxin bioavailability; varicella virus vaccine (Reye's syndrome); heparin possible ↑ bleeding | 800mg po BID<br>800mg po TID<br>800mg po QID<br>1.6g po TID<br>(NIHB: 800mg tab ⊗) | 79/59 g<br>115/85 g<br>152<br>224 |
| **PENTASA**<br>500 ☺ mg ER tab;<br>1g & 4g rectal enema;<br>1g suppository<br>"Ethylcellulose coated"<br>B | SE: GI nausea, vomit, abdominal pain 18%, headache 14%, rash 6%, flu-like 3%, edema 3%, dizziness 3%, acne 2%, yellow-brown urine<br>Rare: blood dyscrasias, hepatotoxicity, alopecia, lupus like, nephrotoxicity, pericarditis & pancreatitis | -5-ASA microgranules; time-dependent release (duodenum→ rectum)<br>-can break along score line (avoid knife/pill cutter protect release mechanism)<br>-all 5-ASA used in acute/maintenance therapy for UC<br>-role in CD controversial | 500mg po QID<br>1g po TID-QID<br>4g Enema PR HS<br>1g Rect Supp PR HS<br>1g Rect Supp PR 3x/wk [21] | 87<br>127-167<br>167<br>65<br>32 |
| **MESASAL**<br>500mg EC tab<br>B | -enema contents darken with time (do not use if dark brown); retain >30min | -pH-dependent release (terminal ileum→ rectum) | 500mg po TID<br>1g po TID | 73<br>139 |
| **SALOFALK**<br>500mg EC tab;<br>500 & 1000mg supp;<br>2 & 4g rectal susp<br>B | -enemas SE: difficulty in retention, abdominal bloating, discomfort on administration, stain [19] | -pH-dependent release (terminal ileum → rectum)<br>-swallow whole before meals with lots fluid<br><br>Some evidence that every 2nd or 3rd night dosing of enemas + suppositories may be effective Cohen 2000, Bergman 2006; Marteau 1998,; little evidence compares to daily administration [4,10,11] | 500mg po TID<br>1g po QID<br>2-4g Enema PR HS<br>2-4g Enema PR HS q3days<br>1g Rect Supp PR 3x/wk | 60<br>148<br>133-220<br>49-78<br>32 |
| | **New**: MEZAVANT, LIALDA, **once daily** mesalamine 1.2g tab for UC; (2-4 tab/day $100-200) ⊗; compliance advantage (MMX-pH dependent release: terminal ileum→ rectum<br>**In USA:** APRISO, **once daily** mesalamine granule; mild-mod maint. UC (1.5g= 4 cap od); pH dependent coat around polymer matrix core; released distal ileum & colon; has aspartame | | Active UC:<br>Combo PO 2.4g/day divided & enema 4g/day;<br>PO 2.4-8 g/day divided TID; supp 500mg BID; or enema 1-4g/day (x3-6wks; then ↓ to lowest effective dose) [20]<br>• 4.8 g/day improves response over 2.4 g/day, but remission rates similar<br>• remission rate higher when enema used for 4 wks compared to 2 wks [4]<br>Maint UC:<br>COMBO: PO 1.6g/day + enema 4g twice wkly,<br>5-ASA enema 2-4g/d or every other day or q3d;<br>5-ASA supp 500mg daily-BID; or<br>5-ASA PO up to 4g/day divided BID-QID<br>Active CD: 3.2-4g/day<br>Maint CD: not recommended<br>Peds Active (UC or CD): 30-50mg/kg/day divided BID-QID<br>Peds Maint: lowest effective dose | |
| **OLSALAZINE** | | **Time to effect: 2-4 weeks** | | |
| **DIPENTUM**<br>250mg cap<br>{1g delivers 0.9g 5-ASA}<br>C | CI: hypersensitivity to salicylates<br>SE: as for 5-ASA above, plus diarrhea 20%<br>{efficacy uncertain; confounded by dose-related diarrhea} | -used in acute & maintenance therapy for UC; but prefer SSZ or 5-ASA<br>-inactive till cleaved into 2 molecules of 5-ASA by colonic bacteria<br>M: CBC, renal + hepatic function, allergy, diarrhea; DI: As above | Start 500 mg/day & ↑over 1 wk; max 3g/day; no single dose >1g<br>Active UC: 1.5-3g/day divided TID-QID; 500mg po TID-QID cc<br>Maint UC: 500mg po BID cc | 114-150<br>78 |
| **CORTICOSTEROIDS -** | | **Time to effect: 7-10 days (tech review); experience: may see benefit within a few days! AVOID abrupt withdrawal to prevent relapse!** | | |
| **Prednisone** g<br>1, 5 ☺ & 50 ☺ mg tabs<br>**Prednisolone** g<br>1mg/ml susp (120ml)<br>**Methylprednisone**<br>4 ☺ & 16 ☺ mg tabs **Medrol**<br>C | SE: cushingoid features, ↑ blood glucose, infections, skin thinning, psychiatric SE, impaired wound healing, GI bleeds, cataracts, osteoporosis/osteopenia, fluid & electrolyte imbalances may ↑BP, fat redistribution<br>{Consider $Ca^{++}$, Vitamin D & bisphosphonates if long term.} | M: annual eye exam, HPA axis suppression, blood glucose, s/sx infection, CBC, electrolytes; BMD if indicated Rx: OP prevention strategies.<br>Begin **taper** once significant clinical improvement seen, by 5-10 mg weekly until 20mg/day then ↓ by 2.5 mg/week ( tapering to ↓ symptom relapse)<br>DI: aspirin (GI effects), fluoroquinolone (↑ tendon rupture), carbamazepine & phenytoin (↓steroid efficacy), vaccines (↓ efficacy) | Active UC & CD: 40-60 mg PO daily (60mg more effective, but ↑ SE)<br>Pred 40-**50**-60mg po daily x 2wks; taper.<br>Peds: prednisolone 1-2 mg/kg/day (max 60mg) for 2-4 weeks, then ↓ 5 mg/day each week upon remission [22]<br>{Not effective for maintenance; taper more gradually for worse disease}<br>Medrol 32-48mg po daily x 2wks; taper. | ~10<br><br><br><br>20-40 |
| **Betamethasone 5mg enema** BETNESOL | ◆ caution if abdominal abscess | | Enema: 5mg PR HS | 320 |
| **Budesonide**<br>**ENTOCORT**<br>3mg CIR caps ☎✆;<br>2mg retention enema<br>C | **Budesonide SE**: as above, but ↓ incidence due to low bioavailability (first pass effect) | **Use**: ileal + right-sided colonic acute CD (Tech & Sandborn 2003)<br>{CIR=controlled ileal release}<br>DI: a 3A4 substrate (eg. rifampin ↓ levels; grapefruit juice/kietoconazole ↓ levels)<br>{Not as effective as prednisone but ↓ SE & more expensive.[23]} | 9mg PO OD ac; taper after 8-16 wks, ↑ by 3mg over 2-4 wks [24] {3-9mg od<br>Enema: 2mg PR QHS<br>{Not effective for long-term maint., but may prolong time to relapse} | 60-170 ✓}<br>290 |
| **Hydrocortisone**<br>**CORTIFOAM** 10% 15g,<br>**HYCORT & CORTENEMA**<br>100mg/enema, boxes of 7<br>C | **Foam**: easily retained; pts often prefer over enema; more cost; coats last ~20cm of colon | -lie on left side for administration of rectal forms<br>-retain enema for as long as possible (>60 min or all night if possible) | Active UC & CD: Solu-Cortef 100mg IV Q6-8H<br>{Not effective for maintenance} Enema: 80-100mg PR QHS<br>Enema: 80-100mg PR 2x/ wk<br>Foam 80mg: 1 applicator PR 2x/ wk | >450<br>190<br>59<br>75 |
| | **Hydrocortisone Solu-Cortef** (100 & 250 mg vials) 100mg IV q6-8h. **Methylprednisolone Solu-Medrol** (40 & 125mg vials) 60 mg **IV** daily for severe disease can be used in place of hydrocortisone (esp if heart or renal failure). {**Equivalencies** Glucocorticoid: Prednisone 5mg = Methylprednisolone 4mg = Hydrocortisone 20mg most mineralcorticoid effect} | | | |

| Drug | Side Effects / Contraindications | Comments / Drug Interactions / Monitoring | Dose | $ |
|---|---|---|---|---|
| **PURINE ANTIMETABOLITES -** | ⇨**Time to effect: 3-6 months. May tolerate mercaptopurine if intolerance (eg. hepatotoxicity or arthralgia/myalgia) to azathioprine.** | | | |
| **Azathioprine**=AZA **IMURAN** g 50 ς mg tab dumbbell shape (Can make susp) 50mg/17 ml vial; -prodrug of 6-MP **D** | **SE**: flu-like fever (2-3 weeks into treatment), bone marrow suppression 2-5%, dose dependent, unpredictable (esp. leukopenia), infections, hepatotoxic 2%, allergy <5%, pancreatitis (as hypersensitivity rxn 2%-occurs within 1st 3-4 wks), ?lymphoma 111 {controversial} | -Used in mod-severe UC ? & CD for pts not responding to PO steroids & pts unable to wean from steroids; useful in fistulating CD. -May ↓ post-op recurrence in CD 115; use if high-risk for recurrence -Educate pts on sx pancreatitis; pancreatitis reappears on re-challenge **DI**: **allopurinol/febuxostat** (↑ ↑levels/toxicity), ↑infections with steroids; ACEI/Bactrim may ↑ leukopenia/anemia; live vaccine; anti-TNF's may ↓ antibodies {5-ASA, sulfasalazine & olsalazine may inhibit TPMT enzyme} | Start at 50mg once/day & ↑ by 25mg q1-2wks until target UC: 1.5-2.5mg/kg/day 50-100mg po daily CD: 2-3mg/kg/day 26 (Sonic 2.5mg/kg) 150mg po daily CD Peds: 2.5 mg/kg/day (Cinn); {in RA: 0.1mg/kg/day, ↑by 0.5mg/kg/day up to 2.5mg/kg/day} AZA & 6MP: Maintenance dose same as induction dose | 25-43 61 renal dysfx, hepatic |
| **6MP** (Mercaptopurine) **PURINETHOL** 50 ς mg tab round **D** | -GI SE dose-related & improve with time[25] | **M**: CBC every other week while doses adjusted, then q1-3month; LFTs; (If ↑plasma level &/or ↓**TPMT genotype** 6 per 1000, esp. African-Caribbean pts have ↑↑ level & SEs, but routine monitoring of limited value; vs routine pt/other blood work follow up) | Start at 50mg once/day & ↑ by 25 mg every 1-2 wks until target UC & CD: 1-1.5 mg/kg/day; 50-75-100mg po daily CD Peds: 1.5 mg/kg/day (Cinn) | 138-260 ▼;☎: Crohn's |
| **BIOLOGIC RESPONSE MODIFIER -** | ⇨**Time to Effect: 2 weeks (ACT). Anecdotal: may start to see benefit within few days. Endoscopic remission "mucosal healing" observed!** | | | |
| **Infliximab REMICADE** 100mg vial inj Mouse-human **Anti TNF-α** Monoclonal Antibody **B** Etanercept **Enbrel** - not effective | **CI**: infection (active TB, serious/opportunistic fungal); optic neuritis; demyelinating disorders e.g. MS, heart failure NYHA class 3-4; recent malignancy **SE**: infections, infusion reactions (headache, dizziness, flushing, fever, chills, chest pain, cough, dyspnea & pruritis), nausea, abdominal pain, fatigue, rash; delayed reactions (3-14 days post-infusion; serum-sickness like); infection risk -Severe SE more frequent in peds: ↑ LFTs, anemia, infection, flushing, blood dyscrasias, fractures, acute reaction -Rare lymphoma*, drug-induced lupus *rates unknown; one estimate of **lymphoma 2/1000** & **mortality 4/1000** in CD **at 1 year** 27 | -used in mod-sev UC ACT-1,2 & CD ACCENT-I,II, Sonic not responsive to standard tx -taper steroids if achieve remission -concomitant use AZA/6MP, MTX can ↓ formation of antibodies ? benefit -**Health Canada warnings**: hepatitis B reactivation, hepatosplenic T-cell lymphoma in pediatrics/young adults, malignancies, including lymphomas and Hodgkin's disease {FDA warning: malignancy, hepatic rx's, HF} -↓ response in smokers 2; May ↓ extra-intestinal manifestations **M**: baseline tuberculin test, symptoms of infection e.g. shingles/PHN, candidiasis **Use**: hospitalized patients with moderately-severe or fistulating disease where rapid onset required; as bridge to immunomodulator, other manifestations Crohn's (erythema nodosum; pyoderma gangrenosum) **DI**: abatacept, anakinra, live vaccines (may ↑ infections) | Active CD & UC: 5mg/kg/dose over 2 hrs at weeks 0, 2, 6 (FDA: age ≥6yr for CD) -if no response after 3 doses, stop drug Maint CD & UC: 5mg/kg/dose q8weeks; some evidence for "as needed" dosing, rather than regularly scheduled dosing If respond initially & then lose response: ↑ frequency to q4weeks OR ↑dose to 10mg/kg q8weeks {CDN guide: ↑dose first; trough may be important} 300mg IV x 3 doses (~5mg/kg x 60kg) Week 0, 2, & 6; 300mg IV q8wks (~5mg/kg x 60kg); 600mg IV q8wks (~10mg/kg x 60kg) **Pretreat** infusion (acetaminophen 650mg & diphenhydramine 50mg po x1); ↓'s reactions. Give over ≥ **2-4hr** in 250ml normal saline. infuse ≥1hr if tolerated long term | 8,800 (3 doses) 17,800 (1 year) 35,400 (1 year) ✆,☎: Crohn's & UC |
| **Adalimumab HUMIRA** -TNF ∝ inhibitor antibody;RA,JRA,PA, Psoriasis plaque, ankylosing spondylitis; **CD** Induction 160mg week 0, 80mg week 2 → 40mg SC every other Week ☎ ✆ $19,250/yr (MTX may ↑adalimumab level) **B** | | | | |
| **Certolizumab pegol CIMZIA** -TNF ∝ inhibitor antibody approved in USA April/08; CDN: moderate or severe adult **CD**, moderate-severe RA; Dose 400mg sc q2week x3 then 400mg sc q4week ✗ ⊗ $17,600 | | | | |
| **OTHER** | | | | |
| **Methotrexate** g 2.5 ς & 10mg tabs; (20 & 50mg/2ml inj ✗▼) Dihydrofolate reductase inhibitor D/C 90days before → **X** | **CI**: pregnancy, breast-feeding, liver disease **SE**: leukopenia, GI, HA, dizziness, fatigue, thrombocytopenia, photosensitivity, alopecia, stomatitis, rash, cough & reversible sterility in men Rare: hepato & nephro-toxicity, Stevens Johnson Sx, hypersensitivity pneumonitis 3 cases/100 pt yrs 28 | **Time to Response:** 4 wks {evidence for parenteral form; PO not as effective}[29] **Use**: CD when not responding to AZA/6MP; insufficient evidence for UC **M**: CBC, liver indices, SCr, albumin at baseline & within 4 weeks of starting therapy, then monthly 28; ?annual CXR 30 **DI**: Bactrim ↑ myelosuppression, alcohol, live vaccine, cyclosporine, anti-TNF's may ↓ antibody NSAIDs may ↑ MTX level Consider **folic acid** supplementation (1mg/day or 5mg/week) | CD: 25mg SC/IM weekly (or PO? 70% bioavailable) 15-25 mg IM weekly; can use 25 mg IM weekly for 16 weeks followed by 15 mg SC/IM weekly 28 Peds CD: 15 mg/m² SC/IM weekly (up to 25 mg); {Wk 1: 50% of dose; Wk 2: 75% dose; Wk 3: 100% of dose 31}; once steroid stopped & pt stable, ↓ dose by 20%, further ↓ by 20% in another 3-6 months if stable 30 | 70 IM / 230 PO 70 renal dysfx, hepatic |
| **Metronidazole** Tab 250mg; cap 500mg ✗▼; IV 500mg FLAGYL g **X/B** | **CI**: 1st trimester pregnancy **SE**: nausea, metallic taste, HA, dry mouth, furry tongue; peripheral neuropathy with long-term use (often not reversible) | -role not well defined; added to 5-ASA or steroids when monotherapy not effective; helpful in ruling out GI infection; may be helpful in those with abscesses or fistula & disease limited to perianal disease **DI**: alcohol (disulfiram reaction), warfarin (↑ bleeding) | 10-20mg/kg/d in divided doses 500mg po/IV BID -no benefit when added to IV **steroids** ?; but, still used if sx persist with UC {Often used in combo with cipro for 2 wks followed by metronidazole monotherapy for 2 wks Opinion} | 15 / 120 |
| **Ciprofloxacin** g Tab 250,500 & 750mg; 500mg & 1g XL⊗; IV 200+400mg; Susp 100mg/ml **C** → Use after 1st trimester | **SE**: somnolence, dizziness, rash, GI nausea/vomit/diarrhea, arthralgias, photosensitive, rare tendon rupture | **Use**: occasional; may be used in conjunction with or in place of metronidazole **DI**: divalent cations, glyburide, mirtazapine, QTc prolonging drugs, tizanidine & warfarin | 500 mg PO BID >90% oral bioavailability 400 mg IV Q12H | 111 1350 renal dysfx |
| **Cyclosporine** g **NEORAL/ SANDIMMUNE** **C** 10, 25, 50 & 100mg caps; 100mg/ml oral susp; 50mg/ml (1 & 5 ml vials) Calcineurin inhibitor=CsA | **SE**: ↑BP, paresthesias, HA, abnomal LFTs, hyperkalemia, gingival hyperplasia, hypertrichosis, tremor; nephrotoxicity Rare: infection, seizure; ?lymphoma 30, anaphylaxis **Time to Response:** 2-3 weeks 30 **DI**: many **[Generally avoided given newer agents!]** | **Use**: **rare!**; main role may be in severe UC to bridge to thiopurine 28 (eg. surgery-sparing agent in the acute tx of severe, steroid-refractory UC) -not adequately studied in CD; rarely use beyond 3-6 months **-watch for DIs!** -add if no response to IV hydrocortisone after 7-10 days; -concomitant IV steroids recommended Tech; withdrawal may lead to Sx recurrence; consider PJP prophylaxis **Target trough concentration**: unknown; 200-800 ng/ml (via monoclonal radioimmunoassay) or 200-400 ng/ml (via HPLC) 2; 150-250 ng/ml 32 **M**: CBC, lytes, SCr, LFTs?, CsA levels, BP; baseline Mg++ & ?cholesterol | UC: 2mg/kg/day IV infusion for 7-10 days. {150mg iv/d x 10day= Start AZA/6-MP prior to change to PO & ? temporarily stop AZA if starting CsA 30 UC: Change to PO, taper steroids and use AZA/6-MP -continue AZA/6-MP for maintenance 33 {Tapering: change to PO 5-8 mg/kg/day given BID for 1–3 months 30} Neoral > Sandimmune for bioavailability 150mg PO q12h= | 150 (10 days) ☎ ✆ (not IBD in SK) renal dysfx 570 |

ς =scored **5-ASA**=5-aminosalicylic acid **6MP**=mercaptopurine **AZA**=azathioprine **BMD**=bone mineral density **CBC**=complete blood count **CD**=Crohn's **CsA**=cyclosporine **EC**=enteric coated **ESR**=erythrocyte sedimentation rate **GI**=stomach **HA**=headache **Hbg**=hemoglobin **Hct**=hematocrit **MS**=multiple sclerosis **MTX**=methotrexate **SE**=side effects **SSZ**=sulfasalazine **supp**=suppository **sx**=symptoms **tx**=treatment **UC**=ulcerative colitis ☎=Exception Status SK ✗ =Non-formulary SK ✆ =prior NIHB ⊗ =not NIHB (kidney)=↓ dose for renal dysfx

**New / Other Drugs**: **Balsalazide COLAZOL** -N/A in Canada; FDA: UC ≥5yrs. **Etanercept** not effective [34]. **FK506** (**tacrolimus**)-low bioavailability, 0.05 mg/kg BID (target serum concentration: 10-15 ng/ml); mainly open-label, small trials; SE: HA, ↑SCr, ↑BUN, insomnia, leg cramps, tremors, parasthesias. **MMF**-inadequate efficacy evidence, safety concern. **Natalizumab TYSABRI** -300mg IV Q4wk, ↑caution after 42 cases fatal progressive multifocal leukoencephalopathy in MS & ↑LFT (restricted USA for Crohn's & MS; MS in Canada 2006). **SPD476**-once daily formulation of 5-ASA-effective at inducing remission in preliminary studies. **Transdermal nicotine** ≥21mg/day (UC): benefits mainly ex-smokers, not as effective as 5-ASA; long-term SE unknown.

**Probiotics**: **VSL#3**: lactobacilli, bifidobacteria, Strep. Slivarins; 1 small, controlled, open-label trial suggests benefit in treating **mild-mod UC**; small, placebo-controlled trials suggest benefit in preventing **pouchitis** and preventing relapse of pouchitis; various dosing regimens used in trials. Further data on efficacy & safety needed before routine use [35]; caution if on immunomodulators. Other probiotics: further evidence on efficacy and safety needed, but results look promising. Concerns with lack of live bacteria in some products.

**Omega 3's**: insufficient evidence to support/refute; benefit mainly with enteric coated capsules for maintenance of remission in CD [36, 37, 38]

**Other**: Avoid food triggers (varies for different patients) i.e. lactose deficiency **Complications**: obstruction, bleeding, perianal disease, fistulae, prolapse, malnutrition, renal stones, malignancy & toxic megacolon.

**Differential Diagnosis**: appendicitis, colitis C. diff, ischemic, radiation,TB, enterocolitis campylobacter or yersinia, small bowel lymphoma, IBS, pancreatitis, Overuse NSAIDS, laxatives. **CD**: delayed diagnosis (~2yrs) is common; consider early in differential diagnosis.

## Five Key Decision Points in the Approach to Patients with Uninvestigated Dyspepsia (pain or discomfort in upper abdomen)[3]

1. Are there other possible causes for the symptoms? Consider cardiac, hepatobiliary, medication-induced, lifestyle or dietary indiscretion
2. Is the patient **>50yrs**, or does the patient have alarm symptoms? Alarm features and increased age identify patients at higher risk of organic causes, including cancer and ulcers. Alarm symptoms - ***VBAD*⇨** (**V**omiting, **B**leeding/anemia, **A**bdominal mass/uninvestigated wt loss, **D**ysphagia) ⇨ warrant prompt investigation
3. Is the patient regularly using conventional NSAIDs (including ASA)? Stop therapy if possible
4. Is the dominant symptom heartburn or acid regurgitation, or both? If yes, these are reliable indicators of GERD (gastroesophageal reflux disease)
5. Is the patient infected with *Helicobacter pylori*? Considering this question last will assist in legitimate indications for *H.pylori* testing

## GERD

- symptomatic response to antisecretory therapy with proton pump inhibitor (**PPI**) or H2 antagonist (**H2RA**) is generally considered to support the presumptive diagnosis of GERD.
- mild symptomatic GERD <3x/week,↓ duration& intensity can often be managed with lifestyle & dietary changes along with OTC antacid or H2RA

### PHARMACOLOGICAL CONSIDERATIONS

**Initial therapy**

- Standard dose PPI is more efficacious than H2RA[1]; double dose PPI is generally no more efficacious than standard dose for initial therapy in erosive esophagitis[1]

**Reassess therapy at 4-8 wks**

- if symptoms respond to 4-8weeks of therapy STOP therapy, if symptoms recur repeat original therapy
- if symptoms not resolved,
  →if not on a PPI, switch to a PPI x 4-8 weeks
  →if on a PPI give bid x 4-8 weeks or consider investigation;
  {Ensure PPI taken ~30 minutes before am meal, or pm meal if primarily nocturnal symptoms}

**Long-term therapy**

- REASSESS NEED FOR THERAPY following initial therapy & periodically thereafter.
- Tailor the dose and frequency to control symptoms. Patients should be maintained on the lowest dose of therapy that was adequate to provide symptom relief.

**On-Demand PPI after response to initial PPI**

- patients who respond to initial PPI therapy, subsequent "on-demand" PPI is more efficacious than continuous H2RA, but less efficacious than standard dose PPI {in uninvestigated GERD}[1]

### STANDARD DOSES OF PPIs

**There are no clinically important differences among standard doses of PPIs in treatment of symptomatic GERD, ENRD and esophagitis[1] Patient variation in response may be seen.**
{Standard dose: Omeprazole, rabeprazole & esomeprazole 20mg od; lansoprazole 30mg od; pantoprazole 40mg od}.

PPIs are **not efficacious** in **asthma** associated with GERD, in improving **laryngeal** symptoms associated with reflux or improving **chronic cough** with or without GERD[1, Mastronarde]

## PUD & *H.pylori* (Non-NSAID PUD)

- ≈90% of DU & 70% of GU may be *H.pylori* positive
- the standard of care for all patients with GU/DU is *H. pylori* testing & treating if positive (~**30%** of Canadians are infected ↑ with age)
- smoking cessation improves ulcer healing rates and reduces ulcers not related to *H.pylori* infection

### *H.pylori* TESTING – Noninvasive

- diagnostic testing for *H. pylori* should only be performed in pts suspected of having *H pylori*-related conditions such as PUD and if treatment is intended. (test and treat strategy)

**Urea Breath Test (UBT)**

- should be used for routine diagnosis, unless endoscopy is indicated for another reason
- excellent sensitivity, specificity and ease of use
- to prevent false –'ve results Helikit, patients should **stop** for: antibiotics 4 weeks, bismuth 2 weeks, PPIs 3 days & H2RA 1 day (prn use of antacids can be used for Sx while awaiting tests)

**Serology:**

- appropriate if no access to UBT or endoscopy, higher rate of false positives results (≈20%)

**Repeat H.pylori testing after *H.pylori* eradication**

- confirmation of *H.pylori* eradication is not required unless symptoms persist, pt with bleeding or perforated ulcers, MALT lymphoma or gastric cancer do 4weeks after tx
- serology cannot be used to determine cure from infections (IgG antibodies still detectable 6-12 months after eradication)

***H. pylori* Regimens** (see *H.pylori* Chart; all PPIs equally effective)

- *H. pylori* regimens 1-2-3 =**1** week, **2** times a day, **3** drugs commonly used, but quadruple regimens also an option
- single and two drug regimens not recommended
- 7 & 10 regimens equally effective, but 14 day regimens more efficacious than 7 day regimens[1,(American ACG recommends 10-14days) 9]
- consider the following when selecting regimen: allergy history, recent antibiotic metronidazole/clarithromycin or EtOH use (avoid metronidazole), potential compliance issues (1-2-3 regimens, Hp-PAC®), DIs
[See RxFiles H. Pylori Eradication chart http://www.rxfiles.ca/rxfiles/uploads/documents/members/CHT-Hpylori.pdf ]

**PPI treatment after *H. pylori* eradication**

- for uncomplicated duodenal ulcer, once HP has been eradicated, continued PPI use does not produce higher ulcer healing rates and is generally not indicated[1]
{Note: PPI may be indicated for acute healing of gastric ulcer}

## PUD & NSAIDs - Prevention

- NSAIDS are responsible for the majority of HP negative PUD
- routine concomitant antiulcer prophylaxis is not warranted for all pts taking NSAIDs; assess patient risk

**Preventing NSAID Induced Ulcer in High Risk Patients**

High Risk: especially if hx of ulcers/UGIB. See note at bottom.* Those with several risk factors are at highest risk for NSAID-induced GI toxicity (up to 9% at 6 months)

- avoid NSAID if possible (use alternatives e.g. acetaminophen)
- if NSAID must be used, use lowest dose & shortest duration
- **GI Ulcer Prophylaxis** (often a gastric ulcer with NSAIDs)
  →standard dose PPI (all PPIs, similar efficacy)[1]
  →misoprostol 200ug tid-qid $50-64 (SE: GI upset & diarrhea)
  {H2RAs are **not** recommended for GI prophylaxis in NSAID pts}

**HP Eradication and NSAID Use**

- *H.pylori* & NSAID additive on the risk of PUD/UGIB
- Testing for H. pylori in patients starting long-term ASA or NSAID therapy has been proposed, but is not routinely recommended.[9] Those at greatest risk (hx of peptic ulcers, dyspepsia, steroids, and/or warfarin) most likely to benefit.

**COXIBs:**

- The GI sparing effect of COXIBs is compromised when used concurrently with low dose ASA, therefore the GI advantage of a COXIB especially at high-dose is lost. When a COXIB is used with warfarin concurrently, the risk is similar to NSAIDS.
- COXIB risks {e.g. cardiac, renal, gastric} are dose dependent
- COXIB vs {NSAID + PPI} appear to have similar efficacy in prevention and recurrence of ulcer/bleeding in patients with previous NSAID associated UGIB[1]

**TREATMENT OF NSAID INDUCED ULCER**

- Discontinue NSAID, *H.pylori* test & treat if positive, treat like a non-NSAID ulcer {e.g. PPI or H2RA (x4wk in DU); (x8wk in GU)}
- Healing rates: standard dose PPI x4-8weeks is more efficacious than H2RA or misoprostol[1]

**If NSAID MUST BE CONTINUED**

- PPI more effective than H2RA, but similar efficacy to misoprostol 400-800ug/day endoscopic evidence 1
- *H. pylori* –'ve pts (ulcer bleeding history) on **low dose ASA+PPI** have lower risk of ulcer complications vs **clopidogrel** alone[1] (Chan'05 & Lai'06)

**COXIB**=Selective cyclooxygenase 2 inhibitor **DI**=drug interaction **DU**=duodenal ulcer **ENRD**=endoscopic negative reflux disease **EtOH**=alcohol **GERD**=gastroesophageal reflux disease **GI**=gastrointestinal **GU**=gastric ulcer ***H.pylori***=*helicobacter pylori* **H2RA**=H2-receptor antagonist **NSAID**=nonsteroidal anti-inflammatory drug **OTC**=over the counter **PPI**=proton pump inhibitor **PUD**=peptic ulcer disease **UBT**=urea breath test **UGIB**=upper GI bleed. [See also http://www.rxfiles.ca/rxfiles/uploads/documents/members/CHT-AcidSuppression.pdf ]


**References**

1. CADTH. Scientific Report: Evidence for PPIs use in Gastroesophageal Reflux Disease, Dyspepsia and Peptic Ulcer Disease (Mar 2007) www.cadth.ca
2. 2006 UpToDate® • www.uptodate.com [See also RxFiles NSAID/COXIB chart: http://www.rxfiles.ca/rxfiles/uploads/documents/members/CHT-NSAID-Cox2.pdf ]
3. Veldhuyzen van Zanten SJ, Flook N, Chiba N, Armstrong D, Barkun A, Bradette M, et al. An evidence-based approach to the management of uninvestigated dyspepsia in the era of Helicobacter pylori. Canadian Dyspepsia Working Group. CMAJ 2000;162(12 Suppl):S3-S23.
4. e-therapeutics www.e-therapeutics.ca
5. Preventing NSAID-Induced Ulcers.. Pharmacist's Letter/Prescriber's Letter 2002; 18(3):180306.
6. Armstrong A, et al. Canadian Consensus Conference on the management of GERD in adults – update 2004. Can J Gastroenterol 2005;19(1):15-35.
7. Hunt RH, et al. Canadian Helicobacter Study Group. Consensus Conference Update: Infections in Adults. Can J Gastroenterol 1999;13(3): 213-217.
8. Hunt R, Thomson ABR. Canadian Helicobacter pylori Consensus Conference. Can J. Gasteroenterol 1998;12(1):31-41.
9. Chey et al; Practice Parameters Committee of the American College of Gastroenterology. American College of Gastroenterology guideline on the management of Helicobacter pylori infection. Am J Gastroenterol. 2007 Aug;102(8):1808-25. Epub 2007 Jun 29.




***NSAID Ulcer Complication Risk Factors** (x=↑ **odds ratio**): •hx complicated ulcer x13.5 •multiple NSAID x9 •high dose NSAID x7 •concomitant anticoagulant use x6.4 •age≥70 x5.6 •SSRI use 3.6 •age ≥60 x3.1 •concomitant steroids x2.2 •heart disease x1.8

# ORAL ACID SUPPRESSION - Comparison Chart [1,2,3,4]

Prepared by: Loren Regier, Brenda Schuster, Brent Jensen © www.RxFiles.ca May 10

| g=Generic/TRADE/Pregnancy Category | Comments / Drug Interactions (DI) / Side Effects (SE) | Dose (Adult) [5,6], Use, ~Duration | $ / 30d |
|---|---|---|---|
| **H2-Receptor Antagonists (H2RA's)**: **nocturnal** acid suppression (may dose at HS with a daytime PPI, but tachyphalaxis may develop ≥ 7d; limited efficacy in GERD) [22] Good initial agent for new onset dyspepsia (e.g. step-up tx: similar efficacy, ↓cost than PPI)[23] Uninvestigated GERD: PPI somewhat more effective than H2RA (pantoprazole 20mg od vs ranitidine 150mg bid: complete Sx control: 77 vs 59% at 12 month NNT=6) Talley 2002 n=307, 12month (early 4wk results favored PPI) | | | |
| **Cimetidine** USA approved 1977 **TAGAMET**,g<br>200✗▼,300,400,600,800✗▼mg tab; 60mg/ml soln D/C **B** | •useful: dyspepsia esp maintenance, GERD esp mild, prn for dietary indiscretion; Not NSAID prophylaxis<br>•few significant differences between H2RA's: **ranitidine** may be preferred H2RA's due to comparable safety, efficacy & lower cost<br>- **may avoid cimetidine** in patients who are **elderly** or at ↑**risk of DIs**<br>•**DI**: **Cimetidine** ☞ inhibit $CYP_{450}$ 1A2,2C19,2D6 eg. warfarin, phenytoin, theophylline... ($CYP_{450}$: ranitidine minor effect; midazolam; nizatidine/famotidine little or no effect on).<br>- space **antacid** administration 30-60 minutes apart from H2RA's<br>•**SE**: Uncommon: diarrhea, constipation, headache, fatigue, confusion (risk ↑in elderly and in patients with ↓renal function). Rare: thrombocytopenia<br>**SE: Cimetidine** ☞ slightly higher side effect risk seen with higher doses for a prolonged time; reversible gynecomastia (< 1%); weak antiandrogenic effect; may cause transient ↑ in SCr & LFTs<br>•↓ **dosage** in patients with ↓ **renal function**, ↓ **hepatic function, or elderly**<br>•higher dosages may be suitable for some patients/conditions | **800mg po HS** – GU acute x 8wk, DU acute x 4-8wk<br>600mg po BID – GERD | 15<br>17 |
| **Famotidine** **PEPCID**,g<br>20, 40mg tab {20mg, 40mg Vial} **B** | | **40mg po HS** – GU acute x 8wk, DU acute x 4-8wk<br>20mg po HS – PUD maint.<br>20mg po BID–GERD Famous ↓PUD on ASA 75-325mg/d; Ped ≥3month USA<br>20mg **IV** q12h | 34<br>24<br>38<br>200 |
| **Nizatidine** **AXID**,g<br>150, 300mg cap **B** | | **300mg po HS** – GU acute x 8wk, DU acute x 4-8wk<br>150mg po HS – PUD maint.<br>150mg po BID – GERD; Peds ≥12yr in USA | 39<br>24<br>42 |
| **Ranitidine** USA approved 1983 **ZANTAC**,g<br>150, 300mg tab; 15mg/ml oral solution **B**<br>{50mg Vial} | | **150mg po bid or 300mg HS** – GU acute x 8wk, DU acute x 4-8wk<br>150mg po HS – PUD maint.<br>150mg po BID – GERD; Peds ≥1month in USA<br>50mg **IV** q12h *or* 150mg **oral** solution BID | 20<br>14<br>20<br>125 |
| **Proton Pump Inhibitors-PPI**: **Superior efficacy vs H2RAs** incl. double dose **esp for daytime/meal related acid secretion** give 30min before meals. [22] GERD: BID dose if severe persistent sx. (Reassess dose q2-3months)[6,22]. **Peptic ulcer bleed**: PPI ↓rebleed risk NNT=12, need for surgery NNT=20, but NO mortality benefit.[21] IV≈po Liver failure: ↓dose. **DI**: **levels ↓** for **meds** dependent on **low pH** for **absorption** →[ $Ca^{++}$ carb, dasa & erlo-tinib, keto & itra -conazole, $Fe^{++}$, PI's HIV & thyroxine]; **can give with antacids**; some CYP450 metab eg. clopidogrel. **Long term**: ↓ B12 serum level esp. elderly, ?↓$Mg^{++}$ level; may ↑pneumonia, *C. difficile* & hip fracture [7,8]. Rare: interstitial nephritis, rash & allergy. PPI's have equivalent clinical efficacy at standard doses.[9] Pt variation in response to one PPI vs another may be seen. **Reassess** double dose & need for ongoing tx regularly, esp. after being **inpatient**. Consider PPI if on dual antiplatelet tx. **Erosive esophagitis**: standard PPI's doses recommended; relapse rates ↑ with step down therapy. [9] **Rebound hypersecretion**: common when H2RA or PPIs stopped after a few months of continuous use. Effective for NSAID GI prophylaxis | | | |
| **Esomeprazole** **NEXIUM** **B**<br>20, 40mg long football shaped tab Delayed Release; 10mg✗⊗ sachet | •**S-isomer** of **omeprazole**: ↑bioavailability; 20mg/day=standard dose but 40mg/day common; Similar DI's/SE's[10]; Clarithromycin ↑s levels. ZES 40-80mg BID. **NG tube** with water | 40mg po OD ac – GERD acute x 2-8wk Peds≥1yr Reflux/NERD<br>**20mg po OD** ac – GERD maint.[22] | ☎⊗ 82<br>82 |
| **Lansoprazole** **PREVACID**,g<br>15,30mg Delay Release cap (15, 30mg FasTab & IV✗) ⊗ **B**<br>Can **mix** in applesauce for swallowing difficulties.<br>Dex-lansoprazole **Dexilant**, Kapidex previous: R isomer avail USA | •**DI**: ↓theophylline levels 10%; some CYP 2D6 & 2C19 inhibition; tacrolimus ↑?, mycophenolate ↓?<br>•**SE**: diarrhea 4.1%, HA 2.9%, nausea 2.6%, rash<br>•effective in hypersecretory conditions e.g. ZES: dose range 30-90mg po BID<br>•may give contents via **NG tube** in apple juice or water; or use FasTab $79 | 30mg po OD ac – GU acute x 4-8wk Peds ≥1yr GERD<br>30mg po OD ac – DU acute x 2-4wk<br>**30mg po OD** ac – PUD refract x 8-12wk, GERD acute x 2-8wk<br>≥15mg po OD ac – GERD maint. | 57, g, 79<br>57 g, 79<br>☎ 57g,79<br>57g,79 |
| **Omeprazole** **LOSEC**, g interchangeable in Sask<br>10,20mg Delayed Release tab; OTC in USA; USA approved 1989 **C**<br>Losec **MUPS** (micropellets): available "hospital only" | •**DI**: inhibit CYP2C19: ↑level of diazepam, dig, mycophenolate?, phenytoin?, Tegretol, triazolam & warf.<br>•**SE**: HA 2.4%; diarrhea 1.9%; nausea 0.9%, rash, sweating •long-term safety good; approved 1988<br>•effective in hypersecretory conditions eg. ZES: dose range: 60mg OD–120mg TID<br>•**NG tube**: use **MUPS** or Susp compounded or mix tab with sodium bicarbonate •On NIHB | 20mg po OD ac – GU acute x 4-8wk Peds ≥1yr in USA<br>**20mg po OD** ac – DU acute x 2-4wk, GERD acute x 2-8 wk<br>40mg po OD ac – PUD refractory x 8-12 wk<br>≥10mg po OD ac – GERD maint. ☎▼ Losec, ▼ 10 & 20mg generic | 46 Losec cap<br>43 g, 86<br>80 g, 165<br>34 g, 70 |
| **Pantoprazole** **PANTOLOC**, **TECTA**, g<br>40mg Enteric tab, 20mg⊗ tab; 40mg Vial,g **B**<br>(suspension manufactured by some pharmacies) | •rapid onset / similar outcomes vs omeprazole **SE**: HA; diarrhea; nausea; pruritus<br>•**less DI's** less CYP450 effect 2C19; ↑dig? •**IV** 40mg **IV od** or GI bleed 80mg bolus; 8mg/hr x72hr<br>•✓ hypersecretory conditions e.g. ZES: Dose range 40-120mg po BID; 80mg IV BID-TID | **40mg po OD** ac –GU acute x 4-8wk, DU acute x2-4wk, GERD acute x 2-8 wk<br>≥20mg po OD ac – GERD maint. 40mg **IV** OD $350 | 52 g,80<br>☎<br>50 |
| **Rabeprazole** **PARIET**,g **B**<br>10, 20mg Enteric coated tab (USA name=Aciphex) | •**SE**: HA 2.4%, rash, diarrhea. ZES: 30-60mg po BID •On NIHB formulary<br>•**less DI's** as less CYP450 effect & non-enzymatic metabolism; ↑dig. | **20mg po OD** ac – GU & DU acute, GERD x 4-8 wk<br>≥10mg po OD ac – GERD maint. Peds ≥12yr in USA:GERD | ☎▼ 37 g,55<br>23 g,30 |

= ↓dose for renal dysfx **Cost** =total cost in Sask.; Considerations of cost should be given to the potential for shorter duration of therapy & ↑ efficacy of PPIs vs H2RAs. ▼ =covered by NIHB ⊗ =not covered by NIHB ▮=Max. allowable cost ☎ =Exception Drug Status SK. ✗ =non-formulary SK. ✆=prior approval required for NIHB **ac**=before meals **CYP** =cytochrome P450 enzymes **DI** =drug interaction **dig**=digoxin **DU**=duodenal ulcer **GERD**= gastroesophageal reflux disease **GI**=gastrointestinal **GU**=gastric ulcer **HA**=headache **Hx**=history **LFTs**=liver function tests **PUD**=peptic ulcer disease **SCr**= creatinine serum **SE**=side effect **SX**=symptoms **ZES**=Zollinger-Ellison Syndrome ▮ =*H. pylori* eradication preferable to long-term acid suppression in PUD; **PREVENT NSAID induced ulcers** in high-GI risk: **standard dose PPI** [18] or misoprostol **X** 200ug TID $50 (range BID-QID)

## OTC H2-Receptor Antagonists

| | | | |
|---|---|---|---|
| Famotidine* | **PEPCID AC** coated /chewtab | 10-**20**mg Tab | x30/ ≥ $12 |
| Ranitidine | **ZANTAC-75-150** | 75-**150**mg Tab | x30/ ≥ $12 |

**Generic versions** of famotidine/ranitidine available; cost of 30 tablets/ <$10
* Pepcid Complete = (famotidine/calcium carb./magnesium hydroxide; 10 tabs ≅ $9)

## Special Considerations [11,10]

☑=may use if benefit outweighs risk ☒=avoid if possible

- **Pregnancy**: H2RAs ☑-all **B**; **ranitidine** preferred.[12] PPIs ☒: lansoprazole & pantoprazole **B**; omeprazole most experience **C**
- **Lactation**: H2RAs ☑-famotidine may be preferred. PPIs ☒- avoid due to lack of data & potential adverse effects
- **Pediatrics**: H2RAs –limited trials in kids <12 yrs; PPIs -caution, not well established; omep, esomep & lansop-razole ☑ [13]

**NSAID Ulcer Complication Risk Factors**[4]: (x= ↑ in O.R.) Hx of ulcer complications x13.5, Multiple NSAIDS x9, High dose NSAIDS x7, Concomitant anticoagulant use x6.4, Age≥70 x5.6, Age ≥60 x3.1, Concomitant steroids x2.2, Hx of CVD x1.8
**Red Flags**: age>50, or **VBAD**: **V**-persistent vomiting>7day, **B**-bleeding (anemia, melena), **A**-abdominal mass/weight loss (eg. 3kg/10% body weight), **D**-dysphagia; jaundice, family hx of gastric cancer or prior ulcer dx; then immediate **endoscopy**.
• **Lifestyle** changes for **DIET** (minimize foods that worsen Sx, eat lighter meals & chew well), **AVOID** (lying down for >2hr after eating & tight clothing), **ELEVATE** head of bed, **EXERCISE, moderate alcohol** use **& stop SMOKING!**
**Meds** ↑**GERD**: anticholinergic, B-blocker, barbiturate, benzos, caffeine, digoxin, CCB dihydropyridine, erythromycin, estrogen, ethanol, narcotic, nicotine, NTG, orlistat, progesterone & theophylline. ↑**irritation**: ASA, bisphosphonate, erlotinib, iron, KCL, **NSAIDs** & quinidine.
**Dyspepsia**: chronic peptic ulcer dx<15% (H. pylori causes up to 90% of duodenal & up to 70% of the gastric ulcers, or caused by the use of NSAIDs), GERD +\- esophagitis~25%, malignancy<2% & functional or nonulcer dyspepsia~60%. **PUD** complications: Perforation <10%, Obstruction~2%, Bleed~15%.

# **H. pylori Eradication** (eg. Tx: 1[week], 2[x/day], 3[meds]) {**Indicated** esp. for **1.** ***peptic ulcer disease*** **2.** ***gastric MALT lymphoma***}[? also ↓ gastric cancer post resection Fukase'08] 



⇨Consider pts previous antibiotic exposure to maximize efficacy. If fails one triple regimen; repeat therapy with a different antibiotic combo, or treat for 2week rather than one, or use quadruple tx.

| | Selected Regimens | Days | Cost | ITT ≥80% | Comments[1] (PPIs are best given ~30min before meals) |
|---|---|---|---|---|---|
| *First-Line* **Triple Therapy** **(PPI + amoxicillin + clarithromycin)** C | *Hp-PAC* ☎ ▼: lansoprazole 30mg po BID ☎▼; amoxicillin 1000mg po BID; clarithromycin **500**mg po BID ☎▼ | **X7d** | **$ 105** | ✓ | • **Hp-PAC**: all 3 meds in a **single** 7day blister pack only 1 dispensing fee<br>• lower dose of clarithromycin (250mg) was effective in some studies but is not currently recommended; using two of the **500mg XL** od **with food** is ~$5more than the regular formulation<br>• **SE**: diarrhea (~28%), taste disturbance (~15%)<br>• **CI**: avoid if penicillin allergy<br>•**esomeprazole** NEXIUM 1-2-3-A ☎ ⊗ **20mg po BID** $100 regimen as effective as omeprazole 20mg BID and an option to listed PPIs[2]<br>•**rabeprazole** PARIET ☎▼ **20mg BID** -approved; similar efficacy[3]; 7day rabeprazole/amoxicillin/clarithromycin =$79 generic |
| | *LOSEC 1-2-3-A*: omeprazole 20mg po BID ☎; amoxicillin 1000mg po BID; clarithromycin **500**mg po BID ☎▼ (Agents used in peds trial 4) | **X7d** | $82 generic▼<br>$101 Losec tab▼ | ✓ | |
| | **Pantoprazole** PANTOLOC 40mg po BID ☎✆; **amoxicillin** 1000mg po BID; **clarithromycin** BIAXIN **500**mg po BID ☎▼ | **X7d** | $86 generic<br>**$98** | ✓ | |
| *First-Line* **Triple Therapy** **(PPI + metronidazole + clarithromycin)** C | **lansoprazole** PREVACID 30mg po BID ☎✆; **metronidazole** FLAGYL 500mg po BID; **clarithromycin** BIAXIN **250**mg po BID ☎▼ | **X7d** | **$64** generic<br>**$74** | ✓ | **Drug-Lab Interaction:** PPIs & H2RA should be stopped ≥1**week** & antibiotics **4 weeks** prior to culture & histology for *H. pylori*. {For the $^{13/14}$C-**urea breath** test **stop** for: antibiotics 4 weeks, bismuth 2 weeks, PPIs 3 days & H2RAs 1 day to prevent false negative results Helikit. Concurrent antacids will **not** affect the urea breath test}<br>• **250mg dose of clarithromycin** preferred as better tolerated, equal or better efficacy (MACH I study [5]), and less costly than using the 500mg dose as in the PPI + amoxicillin regimens<br>• pantoprazole & rabeprazole regimens less potential DI's than omeprazole, but the **generic forms of omeprazole, pantoprazole** & **rabeprazole** regimens are the least expensive<br>• avoid alcohol! (DI: metronidazole→disulfiram rx; ↓clarithromycin by rifampin)<br>• **SE**: taste disturb. (~14%), diarrhea (~13%), headache (~6%); Also (less common): neuropathy, coated tongue<br>•**esomeprazole** NEXIUM ☎ ⊗ 20mg BID $77 regimen an option to listed PPIs<br>•**rabeprazole** PARIET ☎▼ **20mg BID $56** generic regimen an option to listed PPIs |
| | *LOSEC 1-2-3-M*: omeprazole 20mg po BID ☎; metronidazole 500mg po BID; clarithromycin **250**mg po BID ☎▼ | **X7d** | $59 generic▼<br>$78 Losec tab▼ | ✓ | |
| | **pantoprazole** PANTOLOC 40mg po BID ☎✆; **metronidazole** FLAGYL 500mg po BID; **clarithromycin** BIAXIN **250**mg po BID ☎▼ | **X7d** | $62 generic<br>**$75** | ✓ | |
| *Alternate First-Line* **Quadruple Tx Regimens (PPI + bismuth + 2 antibiotics)** | Omeprazole ☎ or rabeprazole ☎▼ or other PPI 20mg po BID; + bismuth subsalicylate-PEPTO BISMOL 30mls po QID✗▼; metronidazole 250mg po QID; tetracycline 500mg po QID ac D | **X7d**<br>**X14d** | $60 generic▼<br>$75 Losec tab▼<br>$90 generic▼ | ✓ | • **14 day quadruple tx most effective but less well tolerated & more $$. 10-14 day option for 1st line [6] or treatment failure.**<br>• PEPTO BISMOL **suspension preferred** to tablets to avoid drug interaction with tetracycline (*PEPTO BISMOL* tablets contain calcium carbonate which can interfere with tetracycline)<br>• **SE**: temporary **darkening of stool and tongue**, diarrhea<br>• **CI**: porphyria, renal dysfx (CrCl <25ml/min), pregnancy, children; **avoid alcohol** |

☎ =**EDS** Exceptional Drug Status Sask. ✆=prior approval NIHB coverage ▼ =covered NIHB ⊗ =not covered by NIHB **DI**=Drug interactions **ER**=eradication rate **MCI**=major contraindications **PPI**=Proton pump inhibitors **SE**=Side Effects

**Length of Tx:** 7day regimens ↓cost & ↑compliance; but ↑ER's with 14 day regimens American ACG→ 10-14day; suggest 14d for kids[7] **Compliance** & resistance determines eradication success; warn pts for SE.

**Resistance:** **Cdn** 2004 [14]: **metronidazole** ~20% relative, clarithromycin ↑from 2% to 8% absolute & amoxicillin ~1% (may affect ERs) [8] Bismuth/metronidazole combos appear effective even if ↑ metronidazole resistance.

**Follow-up acid suppression** (with PPI or H2RA) not generally indicated esp duodenal ulcers once *H. pylori* eradicated [9] except for acute ulcer healing esp gastric ulcers, if symptomatic or if complicated/high risk pts.

**Other regimens:** **1.** Quadruple 14 day therapy (ranitidine 300mg po BID + bismuth 30ml po QID +metronidazole 250mg po QID + tetracycline 500mg po QID; ER >80% ITT).
**2.** Classic triple therapy (bismuth 30ml po QID + metronidazole 250mg po QID + tetracycline 500mg QID x14days; ER~78% ITT). **3.** Maclor 5day regimen:[10] PPI or high dose H2RA + metro + amox + clarithromycin
**4.** Quadruple 1 day regimen[11]: PPI double dose + Pepto Bismol 2 tab qid + metronidazole 500mg qid + amoxicillin 2gm qid Needs more validation: **5.** Levofloxacin regimens [13] **6.** Sequential treatment Jafri'08 Gatta'09

Intention to treat analysis **(ITT):** Canadian Consensus Conference 1998 classified treatments as "recommended" when controlled trials had at least 80% eradication efficacy by ITT analysis. [11]

**Search & treat beneficial if: symptomatic with high risk ethnic background (Aboriginals, Asians, Hispanics), family hx** of **gastric cancer, ?long-term NSAID/ASA tx.**[12] Overall ~ **30%** of Canadians are infected ↑'s with age.

H. pylori **causes** ~90% of duodenal & ~70% of gastric ulcers. If GERD, H. pylori testing often not required. • **Lifestyle changes for DIET** moderation, **EXERCISE, moderate alcohol use & stop SMOKING!**

Risk of Reinfection: Low at 3.4% per pt year in developed countries; & 8.7% in developing countries. Fuccio BMJ'08

Confirmation of Eradication: Confirm H. pylori eradication usually in pts who have had an H. pylori–assoc. ulcer or gastric MALT lymphoma or have undergone resection for early gastric cancer.

| Generic/TRADE (Strength & forms) g=generic avail. | Class | Side effects / Contraindications CI: | Comments / Drug Interactions DI: / Safety | Adult Dose Starting / Max | $/ month |
|---|---|---|---|---|---|
| **⇨ CONSTIPATION Related IBS Symptoms (IBS-C) –more common in females (New in USA: Lubiprostone Amitiza 8-24ug po bid for IBS-C in women ≥18yr; SE: anorexia, nausea, dyspnea)** | | | | | |
| **Psyllium** **METAMUCIL**,g {powder (original, smooth, sugar-free, flavoured, unflavoured)} χ▼, (wafers, capsules) χ⊗ {dose varies between formulations} -psyllium/ ispaghula is a **soluble** fiber (but an insoluble fibre like bran not very beneficial [42]) B | Bulking agent (fiber) | **SE:** abdominal pain/bloating, flatulence, borborygmi; cramps<br>*Palatability poor. Try different formulation or mix in beverage to mask taste.<br>CI: intestinal obstruction, fecal impaction, hypersensitivity<br>* Phenylketonurics – smooth texture, orange flavoured and sugar free preparations contain phenylalanine from aspartame.<br>**Caution:** Dextrose-containing formulations ↑ glucose in diabetics | **3.4g** are in each of the following preps:<br>• 1 tsp smooth, unflavoured, sugar-free<br>• 1 tsp/pk smooth, orange flavoured, sugar-free<br>• 1 tbsp smooth, orange flavoured<br>• 1 tsp original, unflavoured; 2 wafers or 5 caps<br>**DI:** lithium, carbamazepine, acarbose. Suggested that doses be separated from other meds by 2-3 hrs.<br>**Safety:** ↑'ing fluid intake is helpful. Rare impaction. | 1 tsp/packet/tbsp; 2 wafers; 5caps = 3.4g (see comments)<br>⇨*3.4g BID with meals* ↑gradually, up to 12-20g/day[4,21] as tolerated.<br>Mix: in 8oz H2O/ beverage. | **OTC**<br>Pwd: 8-17<br>Waf: 50-95<br>Cap: 40-80 |
| **Calcium Polycarbophil** 625mg caplet χ⊗ **PRODIEM** U {other formulations also available} | Bulking agent (fiber) | **SE:** abdominal pain/bloating, epigastric fullness, flatulence<br>If flatulence occurs, try smaller & more frequent doses.<br>CI: intestinal obstruction, fecal impaction, difficulty swallowing | **Comments:** does not degrade via fermentation, ∴ less chance of causing gas or bloating[5].<br>**DI:** tetracyclines (space by 2 hours) | *2 caps po OD-QID with 8oz of water*<br>8 caplets/day | OTC<br>$13-52 |
| 1) **MOM** ▼ (milk of magnesia)<br>2) **Lactulose** ▼ 3) **Sorbitol 70%** C/B<br>4) **PEG Soln** (polyethylene glycol) Lax-A-Day 250ml od▼ | Osmotic laxatives | **SE:** abdominal pain/bloating; ↑Mg for MOM; ↑glucose possible for sorbitol<br>CI: GI obstruction, ↓ renal fx (Mg++ containing)<br>Fiber preferred; however when other laxatives necessary, osmotics can be used carefully long-term; GI stimulant (bisacodyl) may be necessary for some. | **DI:** for Mg++: quinolones & tetracyclines (space 2 hrs)<br>♦ lack of long-term trials in IBS patients | 1)15-30ml OD-BID<br>2)15-30ml OD-BID<br>3)30ml OD-QID | 5-10<br>30<br>? |
| **⇨ ABDOMINAL PAIN RELATED IBS SYMPTOMS** | | | | | |
| **Antispasmodics** Use scheduled before meals in patients with postprandial abdominal pain or prn for acute attacks. Caution in patients with constipation. Evidence for efficacy limited & conflicting! | | | | | |
| **Dicyclomine** **BENTYLOL**,g (10χ, 20ς mg **tab** & 2mg/ml **sol**)⊗ B<br>Peppermint oil is helpful for some. | Anti-cholinergic {↓ contractions in colon & small bowel} | **SE, Common:** sweating, constipation, nausea, dry mouth, dizziness, somnolence, blurred vision, urinary retention<br>**SE, Serious:** tachyarrhythmia, psychosis, apnea, dyspnea<br>CI: GI obstruction/severe colitis/toxic megacolon, glaucoma, GERD, myasthenia gravis, obstructive uropathy, unstable CV status in acute hemorrhage | **Comments:** if inadequate response during the first week, increase dose to 160mg/day as tolerated. Discontinue if inadequate response after 2 weeks.<br>**DI:** belladonna, cisapride, betel nut<br>**Safety:** lack data for >80mg/day for >2 weeks | *10-20mg po qid*<br>40mg po qid<br>{generally given as needed; before meals} | $22-36<br>$65 |
| **Pinaverium** **DICETEL** (50, 100mg **tab**) χ⊗ U | GI calcium antagonist | **Side effects:** epigastric pain, constipation, distention, diarrhea, N&V, heartburn, ↓BP, rash, drowsiness, vertigo, dry mouth<br>**Caution:** duodenal, esophageal or gastric ulcers | **DI:** indinavir, Ma Huang, peppermint oil, SJW, Yohimbine<br>**Safety:** lack data for >150mg/day >4wks.<br>Esophageal irritation⇨ Avoid prior to bedtime or lying down & take with water or food! | *50mg po tid*<br>100mg po tid | $41<br>$68 |
| **Trimebutine** **MODULON**, g (100ς, 200ς mg **tab**) χ⊗ U | Peripheral opiate antagonist | **Side effects:** epigastric pain, dyspepsia, diarrhea, constipation, foul taste, hot/cold sensations, N&V, fatigue, dry mouth | **Comments:** most patients will require 200mg po tid.<br>**DI:** cisapride **Safety:** lack data >600mg/day for >6months | *100mg po tid*<br>200mg po tid | $33<br>$59g-71 |
| **⇨ DIARRHEA RELATED IBS SYMPTOMS (IBS-D) –more common in males** | | | | | |
| **Loperamide** **IMODIUM**, g 2ς mg caplet▼ & quick dissolve tabς χ⊗; 2mg/10ml soln▼ B<br>**Diphenoxylate LOMOTIL** 2.5mg tab ⊗{2.5-5mg po QID PRN}; Not studied/recommended in IBS; crosses BBB→ causing CNS SE.<br>**Cholestyramine**: **QUESTRAN**: useful post-cholecystectomy 4g BID | Opioid receptor agonist | **SE:** N&V, dry mouth, abdominal cramps, anorexia, flatulence, constipation, rash, urticaria {no CNS penetration with loperamide}<br>CI: abdominal pain without diarrhea, bacterial enterocolitis, dysentery, antibiotic-induced pseudomembranous colitis. Avoid in IBS patients with constipation or if painful diarrhea. | **Comments:** can use for '**anticipatory**' diarrhea<br>**DI:** gemfibrozil, itraconazole, saquinavir, SJW, valerian<br>**Safety:** Caution in alternating IBS, & in abdominal pain. Longest trial 4mg/day x 5 weeks.[6] Highest scheduled dose 12mg/day x 2 weeks.[7] | *2-4mg po od-bid prn* (1/2hr **before** meals)<br>12mg/day (6 caplets/tablets) | OTC<br>25-150 |

| Class | Comments (see psychotropic charts for additional information on antidepressants www.RxFiles.ca) | Sample Agents | | Dose | $ /30day |
|---|---|---|---|---|---|
| **⇨ DIARRHEA & PAIN** | | | | | |
| **Tricyclic Antidepressants** (TCAs) {2° amines (desipramine, nortriptyline) often better tolerated} | • May be used for abdominal pain if also psychiatric comorbidity e.g. anxiety / depression.<br>• May relieve abdominal pain exacerbated by meals **SE:** anticholinergic dry mouth, drowsiness<br>• Avoid in pts with constipation, or alternating constipation & diarrhea. (may ↓ diarrhea)<br>• Quality of life improved at 10mg/day.[29,30] May require 25-100 mg/day.[8-10] (similar to that for pain) | Amitriptyline<br>Imipramine<br>Doxepin<br>Desipramine<br>Nortriptyline | **ELAVIL**<br>**TOFRANIL**<br>**SINEQUAN**<br>**NORPRAMIN**<br>**AVENTYL** | ***10-25mg po HS***<br>↑slowly by 10-25mg increments q5-7 days till effect (see comments) | $10-55 |
| **⇨ CONSTIPATION & ABDOMINAL PAIN RELATED IBS SYMPTOMS** | | | | | |
| **Selective Serotonin Reuptake Inhibitors** (SSRIs) | • May be used for abdominal pain if also psychiatric comorbidity e.g. anxiety / depression.<br>• Only 3 agents have been investigated (paroxetine[11], fluoxetine[12], citalopram[13])<br>• May be trialed if suffering from diarrhea; monitor for worse GI sx. (may ↓ constipation) | Paroxetine<br>Fluoxetine<br>Citalopram | **PAXIL**<br>**PROZAC**<br>**CELEXA** | 10-20-40mg po OD<br>20mg po OD<br>20-40mg po OD | $41-32-57<br>$30<br>$27-27 |

ς =scored tablet ✗ =Non-formulary SK ⊘=prior approval NIHB ⊗=not NIHB ▼covered NIHB **BP**=blood pressure **CV**=heart **GERD/GI**=stomach **Hx**=history **Mon**=month **SE**=side effect **SJW**=St. Johns Wort **sx**=symptom **tbsp**=tablespoon **tsp**=teaspoon

**Lifestyle**: Encourage exercise & frequent smaller meals; ↓alcohol, caffeine, & dietary fat. Avoid dietary triggers. Stress management & cognitive behavioral therapy. Dietary/soluble fibre (eg. ispaghula, oats): start with 1 tbsp cc po od & gradually ↑ to 1-2 tbsp po bid-tid, up to 12-20g/day. Trial 4-6 weeks, if intolerable/ineffective/symptoms worsen switch to a bulking agent.[14,15] CI: gluten sensitivity. May worsen IBS symptoms. Patient Handout: http://www.healthknowledgecentral.org/pdf/ibshandout.pdf.

**Opioids**: Most suggest avoiding opioid analgesics, due to concerns involving adverse events, the abuse potential, & the lack of evidence in this population.[13] Option in select pain patients. {If diarrhea, may not absorb SR formulations.}

**Probiotic**: {VSL#3 po BID; Probiotic mix po OD; Encapsulated *Bifidobacterium infantis* 35624 Align po OD}; limited evidence for modest ↓in IBS symptoms low quality trials ≤ 6 mo; ensure ≥1month indiv. trial; lack standardization; safety concern if critically ill & immunosuppressed.

**Red Flags**: fever; wt loss>10lbs; bleeding rectal/stools, anemia; family IBD hx; GI cancer or celiac dx; new symptoms in pts age>50; nocturnal symptoms; persistent diarrhea; severe constipation; abdominal mass [8,15-17] (ACG 2009) → **colonoscopy**

**Discontinued Drugs**: **Alosetron** LOTRONEX (2000 -severe constipation & ischemic colitis) avail. in USA ♀ special access 5HT3 antagonist. Not avail. in Canada. **Benzodiazepines**: not recommended (tolerance, dependence, worsening depression)

**Tegaserod** **ZELNORM**: Mar07- suspended due to CV ischemic events; but Apr08-FDA for Emergency IND situations only use in IBS-constipation & chronic idiopathic constipation in ♀<55yr with no hx of heart problems. 6 mg po bid $160 (NNT=14) 5HT4 agonist Not avail in Canada.

**Drugs that cause constipation**: $Al^{+2}$ containing antacids, anticholinergics (esp. TCAs), anticonvulsants, calcium channel blockers (esp. verapamil), calcium & iron supplements, diuretics high dose & narcotics.

**Drugs that cause diarrhea**: antibiotics, antiarrhythmics, chemotherapy, laxatives, magnesium containing antacids/supplements & NSAIDs. **Drugs that cause abdominal pain**: antibiotics, corticosteroids, iron supplements & NSAIDs.

**Differential Diagnosis**: Inflammatory bowel dx Ulcerative/Microscopic colitis, Crohn's, colorectal polyp/cancer, malabsorption lactose intolerance or celiac dx or pancreatic insufficiency, infectious diarrhea giardia, bacterial overgrowth, thyroid & gyne dx or psychological depression, anxiety. (To help exclude other diagnoses, in those who meet the IBS diagnostic criteria consider: CBC, ESR, CRP & antibody testing for **celiac** disease) NICE guidelines 2008 Other optional tests: TSH; Stool occult blood/ova/parasites Mayer'08

**Rome III Criteria** [25]: **IBS** if at ≥3mon, with onset ≥ 6mon previously of recurrent abdominal **pain or discomfort** not described as pain assoc. with ≥2 of: Improve with **defecation**; &/or onset assoc. with a change in **frequency** of stool; &/or change in **form** appearance of stool (present ≥3day/mon)

# NAUSEA & VOMITING (n&v) - Symptom Management [1]



## MANAGEMENT

### A) Non-drug Interventions

- Stimulus Reduction
  - Avoid unpleasant odours (e.g. foods); fresh air
  - Present small, attractive meals *{eat less more often}*; (after oral intake of clear fluids); loose clothing
  - If symptoms are related to medication: ↓ dosage, change drug, select a different form/route
- Cognitive Therapy; relaxation, distraction, guided imagery, systematic desensitisation
- Rest, avoid rapid head movements (if motion-induced)
- TENS can enhance antiemetic drug effect
- Acupuncture/acupressure + antiemetics in CINV
- Reassurance, explanation, information (for patient/family/caregivers)
- Gastric pacing: option for gastroparesis
- Post op –give IV Dextrose 5% solution

### B) Selection of an Antiemetic Strategy

- Identify likely cause(s) of n&v
- Identify pathway for each cause
- Identify neurotransmitters in suspected pathway(s)
- Choose most potent antagonist for target receptor
- Consider previous n&v history & be pre-emptive
- Choose a route that allows the drug to be absorbed & reach the site of action
- Why give IM when you can give **SC**! e.g. Gravol, Haldol… {Insert **SC butterfly catheter** for repeat SC doses}
- Suppository *PR* - sometimes a handy route option!
- **Administer regularly**; **titrate dose (repeat if pt vomits within 30 minutes of an oral dose)**
- Reassess frequently, at least every 2 to 3 days
- ***Add-on* tx** rather than *substitute* till n&v controlled

## EVIDENCE CONSIDERATIONS for Nausea & Vomiting (n&v) [1]

**Pregnancy n&v (NVP)** - Cochrane Reviews: {2003: 28 studies}[2]; Motherisk [3] www.motherisk.org ; Briggs[4]; Micromedex[5]

- Diclectin (doxylamine 10mg/pyridoxine B6 10mg): best studied; effective & "**A**" safety rating Briggs; Motherisk
- Dimenhydrinate: effective RR=0.34; Category "**B**" FDA or "**A**" Australia; likely no or ↓ teratogenicity {case control study}[6], {however 5 CV defects & 8 inguinal hernias; association not confirmed in CPP study n= 319 1st trimester & 697 anytime exposure}[7]. Caution late in pregnancy (oxytocic effect: ↑ uterine activity which may cause premature labour).
- Other options, effective but less safety data: metoclopramide 32b; phenothiazines; ondansetron[8]
- Pyridoxine (B6): safe, effective (↓ severity); 10-25mg TID Bnatal. P6 acupressure[9] (wristband e.g. *Sea-Band*) probably safe landmark with 3 fingers; efficacy unproven trials equivocal. Psychotherapy, hypnosis: unproven, likely safe.
- Ginger root: safety not proven; efficacy proven {Dose: 250mg-1g QID in pregnancy & post-op n&v} (SE uncommon, but may include GI upset, mouth irritation, & ↑ risk of fibrinolysis); tabs, caps, fresh, biscuits…

**Post-operative n&v (PONV)**: **Cochrane 2006**: 1) 737 studies, 103,237 patients; Four endpoints: n, v, n&v, rescue [10]; 2) P6 Acupoint 26 studies; 3,347 patients [11,12]

- Eight drugs similarly effective: cyclizine, dexamethasone, dolasetron, droperidol, granisetron, metoclopramide, ondansetron & tropisetron; RR=0.5-0.8 vs Pl; NNT ≤3; NNH ≥20 e.g. sedation, headache {PONV: **Ondansetron vs Pl. NNTs**: Early: 1mg NNT=3.8; 4mg NNT=3.2; 8mg NNT=3.1; 24hr: 1mg NNT=4.8; 4mg NNT=3.9; 8mg NNT=4.1}[8]
- Dimenhydrinate: effective for v, n&v[2]; metaanalyisis $_{n=3,000}$: effective/similar to metoclopramide.[13]
- Haloperidol 2mg IV = ondansetron 4mg IV for efficacy & SEs (given 30min prior to end of surgery)[14]
- Wrist acustimulation P6 acupoint: effective vs sham tx; as effective for "N" but not "V" as drug tx

**Chemotherapy Induced n&v (CINV)**: {Emetogenicity of chemo agents; see Hesketh list[15]} www.cancercare.on.ca

- 5-HT$_3$A agents have similar clinical efficacy; PO appears equal to IV (if tolerated & dose adjusted)[16,17]

## DRUG CLASSES – Overview - {combine for severe/refractory cases}

**1) Dopamine (D$_2$) Antagonists (eg. haloperidol, metoclopramide, domperidone)**

- Act at chemoreceptor trigger zone (**CTZ**): haloperidol has high **central** potency on the CTZ e.g. useful for opioid n&v
- Metoclopramide & domperidone have some central antidopaminergic activity **and** also antagonize dopamine (D$_2$) in gut; useful as prokinetics ➔ reverse gastroparesis via serotonin (5-HT$_4$) antagonism
- Metoclopramide readily crosses the blood-brain barrier causing AEs 10-20% (EPS, tardive dyskinesia) FDA: Use ≤3months
- Since CTZ is on "blood" side, domperidone maintains activity but does not cross the barrier to cause SEs

**2) Phenothiazines (eg. prochlorperazine, promethazine, chlorpromazine)**

- Weaker central D$_2$ antagonists with variable effects at other receptors in CTZ, gut & Vomiting Center (VC)
- Significant anticholinergic effects especially sedation & dry mouth; EPS symptoms are common {Haloperidol useful alternative for less sedation, anticholinergic & hypotensive effects}; hypotension via α-adrenergic stimulation (especially chlorpromazine), & rarely NMS, blood dyscrasias & cholestatic jaundice.}

**3) Serotonin (5-HT3) Antagonists (eg. ondansetron, granisetron, dolasetron)**

- Act both centrally (CTZ) and peripherally (gut); used primarily for post-chemo or radiation-induced n&v
- Do not reverse nausea mediated by dopamine pathways (eg. opioid-induced)
- Well tolerated; low rates of side effects (SE: headache, constipation); rare ↑QT interval with dolasetron.

**4) Antihistamines (H1 antagonists) (eg. dimenhydrinate, diphenhydramine, cyclizine)**

- Antagonize both histamine (H$_1$) and muscarinic cholinergic (Ach) receptors
- Exert central antiemetic effects at vestibular apparatus and vomiting center
- Can be effective for various causes (especially motion)
- Drowsiness & dry mouth are common side effects

**5) Anticholinergics (M1 antagonists) (eg. scopolamine patch)**

- Little central antiemetic effect but especially useful in the prevention & treatment of motion sickness
- Primarily reduce GI peristalsis & decrease exocrine secretions
- Limited by frequent SE's esp. dry mouth (consider saliva substitute eg. Oral Balance Gel), sedation & blurred vision

**6) Benzodiazepines (eg. lorazepam, clonazepam, diazepam)**

- Have no direct antiemetic effect; may be useful as adjunctive therapy of post-chemo n&v
- Used to reduce **anxiety** when symptoms are related to psychological factors

**7) Corticosteroids (eg. dexamethasone;** others likely effective but less studied)

- A preferred agent for severe or refractory n&v; & in combo with 5-HT3-A, for CINV prevention & treatment
- High doses used as primary intervention for nausea due to ↑'d intracranial pressure, bowel obstruction
- Often employed to manage refractory n&v of unknown origin and delayed n&v; mechanism unknown

**8) Somatostatin Analogues (eg. octreotide)**

- ↓ peristalsis & gastric secretions (via inhibition of growth, thyroid-stimulating & adrenocorticotropic hormone)

**9) Neurokinin-1 (NK-1; e.g. substance P) Receptor Antagonist (eg. aprepitant PO; fosaprepitant IV; prodrug)**

- Active centrally & peripherally; used with steroids & 5-HT$_3$ drugs for highly emetogenic regimens {see chart} {DI: aprepitant may ↑ levels of drugs metabolized by CYP3A4 eg. chemo agents, pimozide; and ↓ levels of drugs metabolized by CYP2C9 eg. birth control pills, warfarin}

**Differential Diagnosis:** **CNS**: closed head injury, ↑ intracranial pressure (e.g CVA, meningitis/encephalitis/abscess, mass lesion), migraine, seizure, vestibular; **GASTROINTESTINAL**: functional (e.g. gastroparesis, IBS), obstruction, organic (e.g. appendicitis, cholangitis, hepatitis, IBD, PUD); **INFECTIOUS** : bacterial, viral, toxins; **METABOLIC**: adrenal, diabetic ketoacidosis, pregnancy, thyroid, uremia; **MISCELLANEOUS**: acute glaucoma, AMI, renal, pain, psych & eating disorders.

**Drug Causes** (abridged list): antiarrhythmics, antibiotics, anticonvulsants, chemo, digoxin, ethanol overdose, hormonal preps, illicit substances (e.g. cannabis & CVS), NSAIDs, opiates, overdoses/withdrawal, SSRIs.

**History Clues:** Abrupt onset {⇨cholecystitis, food poisoning, gastroenteritis, pancreatitis, drug related}; Insidious onset {⇨GERD, gastroparesis, medication, metabolic, pregnancy}; Pain {⇨obstructive, organic, functional}; Timing of symptoms: {*before breakfast*⇨EtOH, ↑intracranial pressure, pregnancy, uremia; *with eating*⇨psych related, or PUD; *1-4hrs post-meal*⇨obstruction, gastroparesis}; Diarrhea, myalgia, malaise {⇨viral}; Also assess: nature of vomit; ↓ wt.

**PONV**[18]: Prediction Models: e.g. Koivuranta[19], Apfe[20]; treat mod-high risk; ↑ **Risk** if ♀, previous hx PONV or motion sickness, non-smoking, post-op opioids. [**# of risk factors: PONV risk**: (0-1:≤ 20%), (2: 40%), (3: 60%), (4: 80%)]. Other: surgery duration >60min, etc. Prevention Options: haloperidol 0.5-1mg, dimenhydrinate 25-100mg, ondansetron 2-4mg, dexamethasone 4-5mg; scopolamine patch (pre-4hr), pain control. Consider using 3 agents for high-risk. Acute tx: use agent from other class[12]; as for prevention; also metoclopramide.

**Pediatric Considerations:** 1) Viral gastroenteritis: self limiting typically; 1° tx is hydration; ondansetron may ↓vomiting NNT=5 but ↑diarrhea & no difference in admission/readmission; option if prolonged; however insufficient evidence Level B & not recommended [21,22,23]
2) **CINV** [24]: determine emetogenicity of chemo/radiotherapy regimen: High - Very High: ondansetron 5mg/m² (max 8mg) IV or po (see po dose below-note 3) pre-chemo and q8h PLUS dexamethasone 4.5 - 8mg/m² (max 8 - 20mg/dose) pre-chemo po/IV over ≤10min & q12-24h thereafter. Moderate: ondansetron 5mg/m² (max 8mg) IV or po (see dose note 3) pre-chemo & q12h thereafter. Low: ondansetron 3mg/m² (max 8mg) IV or po x1 pre-chemo. Minimal: none. Breakthrough n&v management: consider lorazepam, ondansetron & dexamethasone. (granisetron 20ug/kg/dose IV pre & q12h; metoclopramide & nabilone used in refractory cases). 3) **Ondansetron PO dose per BSA (m²)** CINV: <0.3m² ⇨1mg; 0.3-0.6m² ⇨2mg; 0.61-1.5 m² ⇨4mg; >1.5m² ⇨8mg

# NAUSEA & VOMITING: Drug Treatment Options [1]

Adapted/expanded from Timmins Palliative Centre (P. Critchley, T. Dolanjski); L. Regier, B. Jensen © www.RxFiles.ca **May 10**

| Indication/ Problem | Cause/ Site | Clinical Feature(s) | Receptor(s)/ Pathway | Drug (highlight / bold for emphasis) & Pregnancy category ↓ | Dosage, Typical for N&V ($ Cost /month po; $ other cost / dose) | Adverse Effects (most common) & Comments |
|---|---|---|---|---|---|---|
| **Chemically-Induced N&V**<br>1) Opioids, etc., & 2) Chemo induced N&V (**CINV**)<br>Need for & degree of prophylaxis depends on chemo emesis potential.<br>**Hesketh Level**: [15]<br>1) **Min** <10% e.g. Vincristine; No routine prophyl.<br>2) **Low** 10-30% eg Paclitaxel; Routine pre-chemo, but prn post-chemo<br>**Routine pre & post chemo:**<br>3) **Moderate** 31-90% eg: cytarabine, Dauno-Doxo-Epi-Idar-rubicin, Carbo-Oxali-platin, Irinotecan<br>4) **High** >90% e.g. Carmustine, Cisplatin, Cyclophosphamide >1.5g/m2, Dacarbazine, Mechlorethamine, Streptozocin | **Drugs** (**opioids**, NSAIDs, antibiotics, cytotoxics) or **Toxins** (food poisoning, tumour products) | → Tolerance to N&V from drugs develops quickly; antiemetic treatment can then be discontinued | D$_2$ in CTZ<br>See also RxFiles Antipsychotic chart<br>{Metoclopramide & domperidone also CTZ} | **Haloperidol** HALDOL **C**<br>0.5ς, 1ς, 2ς, 5ς, 10ς mg tab; 2mg/ml soln; 5mg/ml amp | **0.5** to 2mg Q6-**12**H *for n&v* $10-15 po; $4/amp<br>po/SC/IM (may start 0.5mg HS); PONV: 1mg | Sedation, EPS, agitation/restlessness. CINV: PRN option<br>{low rate of sedation & EPS with low doses for n&v}; ↑QT? |
| | | | | **Prochlorperazine** STEMETIL, (COMPRO$_{USA}$) **C**<br>5ς, 10 mg tab; 10mg supp; 10mg/2ml inj | 5 to 10mg Q6-8h $20 po $1/supp; $1.80/amp<br>po/IV/IM/pr/(SC?)** (Max 40mg/day) | Sedation, EPS, hypotension, dry mouth, blurred vision<br>[best tolerated phenothiazine]. CINV: PRN option; PONV: 5-10mg |
| | | | | Droperidol INAPSINE 5mg/2ml amp | 0.625-2.5mg IM/IV$^{slow}$; ?ECG$_{prior}$ $5/amp χ ⊗ | As above (esp. akathisia); ↑QT ? interval & sudden death (controversial) [25] |
| | Metabolic ( hypercalcemia) e.g. 2° to cancer/bone mets | → Lethargy, anorexia, thirst, polydipsia, dehydration | Bisphosphonates ↓ bone resorption | Clodronate BONEFOS 400mg cap | **1.6**-2.4g Daily po $245; 300mg/5ml iv/x1 $?? χ ⊗ ♣ | GI ≤10%: Gastric pain/GERD, diarrhea, n+v; |
| | | | | Pamidronate AREDIA **D** | 30-**60**-90mg IVx1 over ≥2hr $200 /x1 ☎ ▼ | Also zoledronic Aclasta 5mg IV/yr ☎ $700 {See RxFiles Post-menopausal chart} |
| | Post Chemo (**CINV**)<br>{Acute <24hrs; Delayed 1-5days}<br>Delayed: cisplatinin, cyclophosphamide, carboplatin, anthracyclines<br>Post Radiation (**RINV** Radiation induced n&v)<br>◆Dexamethasone added to a 5-HT$_3$ for ↑effect acute & **delayed**.<br>◆Aprepitant (**EMEND**) new NK-1; see note at page bottom. | → Varies with Chemo regimen<br>◆5-HT$_3$A's useful pre-chemo or pre-procedure +/- first 24hrs post<br>◆low efficacy for delayed CINV (beyond 24hrs, there is only a small, 4.6–8.2% ↓ in late onset n&v). [26,27]<br>◆Not effective after n&v occurs.<br>◆Other antiemetics may be needed for up to 4 days.} | 5-HT$_3$ in gut → vagus → vomiting centre<br>{in PONV, 5-HT$_3$ more effective for vomiting than nausea; ondansetron lower rescue rate than KYTRIL in one analysis, but ?due to dose.} | **Ondansetron** χ ▼ ♣ generic **B**<br>ZOFRAN 4, 8mg tab;<br>ZOFRAN **ODT** 4, 8mg tab<br>ODT=oral disintegrating tablet ↑$<br>4mg/5ml soln;<br>(2mg/ml inj: 2,4,20ml vials) χ ⊗ | 4-8mg Q12H x3 IV/po $8 / 4mg tab; $16 / 4mg vial<br>PONV: 2-4mg iv (Max 16mg); 4 mg po 1hr pre-op;<br>CINV: 8-16mg 1hr pre (Max 32mg)<br>Peds CINV: 0.15mg/kg/dose pre-chemo 30 min; 4, 8hr post & Q8H x24-48hrs; or 0.45mg/kg/day x1<br>PONV: ≤40kg: 0.1mg/kg IV x1; >40kg: 4mg IV x1 | Headache 9-27%, malaise 9-13%, constipation 6-11%; transient ↑LFTs?<br>Serious (rare): anaphylaxis, bronchospasm, dysrhythmia<br>{5-HT$_3$ agents have similar efficacy; PO equal to IV} [16]<br>{**ODT**: easier swallowed; not faster; contains phenylalanine}<br>[8- ≤15kg: 2mg po x1; 15- ≤30kg: 4mg po x1; >30kg: 8mg po x1] [24] |
| | | | | **Granisetron** KYTRIL **B** | 10ug/kg x1 IV $12 / 1mg vial; 1-2mg po x1 $18 /1mg tab χ ▼ ♣ | [Other 5-HT$_3$A: Dolasetron ANZEMET 100-200mg/day χ ▼ tab, inj: CINV only; ↑QTc] |
| | | | | **PLUS Dexamethasone** **C/D** | 8-20mg x1; 4-8mg po/IV/SC q12h | Mood change, ↑appetite/energy, ↑glucose. PONV: 4-8mg iv |
| | Refractory Post Chemo CINV<br>Combine agents with different mechanisms first! | → Severe | CB$_1$ & CB$_2$<br>See also RxFiles Cannabinoids chart | Dronabinol MARINOL **C** | 2.5-5mg po TID-QID χ ⊗ $200 -500 | Sedation 4-89%; ataxia, dizziness 12-65%, euphoria 27%, |
| | | | | Nabilone CESAMET **C** | 0.5-1-2mg po Daily-BID ☎ ▼ $130 - 830 | ↓or↑ BP, dry mouth 6-62% {start at lowest-dose} |
| **GI / Dysmotility**<br>May be caused by drugs or disease e.g. overall tumour load. | Drug (opioid, anticholinergic) or Irritation ( iron, potassium, NSAIDs, some antibiotics) or Mechanical / Gastroparesis | → Gastric stasis can feature fullness, acid reflux or projectile vomiting<br>→ n&v usually develop over time & become chronic if not resolved promptly | 5-HT$_3$ in gut → vagus → vomiting centre CTZ peripheral D$_2$;<br>{may also consider antacid/H2RA/PPI if GERD} | **Domperidone** (MOTILIUM) 10mg tab **C** | 5-**10**-20mg TID-QID po ac ~$20<br>[CINV: 20mg po QID ac & HS (NOT available IV) | Galactorrhea, gynecomastia (Overall SE's: 5-10%);<br>SE: diarrhea ≤45%, abdominal cramps; |
| | | | | **Metoclopramide** **B**<br>MAXERAN 10mg vial χ ⊗<br>REGLAN 5, 10mg tab; 1mg/ml soln<br>{may + diphenhydramine to ↓EPS, n&v} | 5-**10**-20mg TID-QID po/IV/SC ac ~$15<br>*Or* 3 to 6mg/hr continuous SC; $2 / vial<br>[CINV: 10-20mg or 1–2 mg/kg IV 30min pre +/-2hr post]<br>PONV: 10mg iv. Peds: 0.1-0.2mg/kg/dose po/IV q6h | May ↑ pain if GI obstruction present. CINV: PRN option<br>EPS-akathesia 3% initial 48hrs, sedation mild, ↑prolactin<br>Serious rare: dysrhythmia, NMS; EPS oculogyric crisis;<br>Overall SE's: 10-20%; most common in peds & elderly |
| | Bowel obstruction | → Abdominal distention | | **Dexamethasone** **C/D** | 4-8mg BID-QID po/IM/SC – see 2 rows below for $ | Mood changes, ↑appetite/energy, hyperglycemia, ↑GI SE |
| | | | | Octreotide Sandostatin ☎ ▼ **B** | 50-150ug BID-TID SC 50,100,500ug amp $8 / 100ug | Pain at injection site, diarrhea, nausea 1000ug / 5ml vial = $80 |
| **↑ Intracranial Pressure** | Tumour, infarction or hemorrhage | →Symptoms often diurnal (morning headache, nausea) & may exclude nausea | H$_1$ in cortex + H$_1$, Ach, 5-HT$_3$ in vomiting centre | **Dexamethasone** ♣ **C/D**<br>0.5ς, 0.75ς, 2ς, 4ς mg tab; 20mg/5ml vial (0.5mg/5ml elixir, 100mg/10ml vial) χ ▼ | 4-8 mg BID-QID po/IV/SC $60-200 po<br>$10 / 5ml vial | Mood changes, ↑appetite, hyperglycemia, ↑energy; ↑BP<br>{Corticosteroids in **Pregnancy**: avoid in 1st 10 weeks if possible; ↑oral clefting} |
| **Sensory/ Psych; Anticipatory** | Anxiety, fear, annoyance, anticipation. {Also non-drug treatment options, e.g distraction} | → "Waves" of nausea<br>→ Anticipatory n+v occurs in ≤50% by 4th chemo course CINV | See also RxFiles Benzodiazepine chart<br>**D** | **Lorazepam** 0.5, 1ς, 2ς mg po tab; (0.5, 1, 2mg sl tab ▼; 4mg/ml vial ⊗) χ | 0.5 to 1mg Q6H PRN po/sl/SC $12 po<br>0.5 to 1mg po/sl pre chemo CINV $2/ amp | Lorazepam - Peds: 0.025-0.05mg/kg/dose IV/po/SL; max 4mg/dose; 8mg/12hr or 0.1mg/kg/12hrs whichever is less. |
| | | | | **Clonazepam** 0.25 χ ▼; 0.5ς, 1, 2ς mg tab | 0.25 to 0.5mg BID-TID po ~$16 | Sedation ≤80%, confusion; falls in elderly |
| | | | | Diazepam 2ς, 5ς, 10ς mg tab | 5 or 10mg HS po/pr 5mg rectal gel $75⊗ $11 po | {Lorazepam advantages: SL option, short acting} |
| **Motion Related;**<br>Meniere's disease | Vestibular disorder, labyrinthitis, movement<br>{note P6 wristbands eg. Sea-Band may also be effective} | → Often accompanied by autonomic symptoms (pallor, diaphoresis, salivation) | H$_1$, Ach → vomiting centre<br>Ach; some H$_1$ | **Dimenhydrinate** GRAVOL **B**<br>15 χ ▼, 50mg tab; 3mg/ml soln; (25,50) χ ▼, 100mg supp | 25-50-100mg Q4-6H PRN OTC ~$10 po<br>po/SC/pr $1/supp /(IM) $4/ 50mg amp | Sedation >10%, dry mouth. OTC Over the Counter; PONV: 25-100mg<br>Peds: **2-5yr**: 12.5-25mg q6-8hrs, max 75mg/day; **6-12yr**: 25-50mg q6-8h, max 150mg/day |
| | Betahistine SERC 16ς-24ς mg BID PRN CC $30-40 SE: Skin rash, GI, & headache | | | **Meclizine** BONAMINE **B** | 12.5-25mg 1hr pre-travel; & Q12H PRN $40 | Sedation, dry mouth. {Vertigo: up to 50mg BID} .OTC 25ς mg chew tab |
| | For **dry mouth**, may consider saliva substitutes e.g. Oral Balance Gel, or pilocarpine 1% eye drops: 1-2 drops into mouth q6h prn. | | | **Scopolamine:** 1) **SC** HBr **C**<br>2) **Patch** TRANSDERM V 1.5 | 0.3 to 0.6mg Q3-6H PRN SC $2 / amp<br>1 patch q72h (1mg over 3day) $4/patch-aluminum OTC ⊗ | Dry mouth+++; sedation, blurred vision {PONV: Patch **4hr** till onset}<br>{more effective vs Pl; appear equal to antihistamines} Cochrane,[28] |

**Pregnancy** [29,30,31]
- Peaks at 9wks; often resolves by 14 wks
- **Motherisk helpline**: 1-800-436-8477

**Step 1:** **Doxylamine / Pyridoxine** DICLECTIN; 10/10mg; **A**; Dose: {2 tabs HS, 1 in AM, 1 mid-afternoon} Max 8 tab/d $180; H$_1$ blocker; SE: drowsiness, anticholinergic (dry mouth etc.), DI: CNS depressant/herbs e.g. valerian. {?may add Folic Acid 5mg supplement.}
**Step 2:** options/add-on tx: **Dimenhydrinate** GRAVOL 50-100mg q4-6h po/pr; **Promethazine** PHENERGAN 12.5-25mg q4-6h po/pr not sc/iv. **If dehydration**: hydration tx (IV fluid; IV vitamins; dimenhydrinate 50mg/50ml over 20min q4-6h IV)
**Step 3:** in order of declining fetal safety: chlorpromazine 10-25mg q4-6h po/im or 50-100mg q6-8hpr; prochlorperazine 5-10mg q6h im/po/pr; promethazine im/po; **metoclopramide** 5-10mg q8h sc/im/po; ondansetron 4-8mg q12h po. **Step 4:** IV med options; NG tube [32]
**Links**: **SOGC**: http://www.sogc.org/health/pregnancy-nausea_e.asp, **Guideline** SOGC: http://www.sogc.org/guidelines/public/120E-CPG-October2002.pdf; **Pt Info** SOGC: http://www.sogc.org/health/pdf/OBS-Nausea_e.pdf; **CFP-Algorithm** Motherisk: http://www.cfp.ca/cgi/reprint/53/12/2109.pdf. **Lifestyle**: ↓meal/drink size, frequent nibble, biscuit before rising; GERD tx?; P6 acupressure

**Unknown Causes**: {H$_1$, Ach, 5-HT$_3$}; consider dexamethasone, dimenhydrinate. **Cyclic Vomiting Syndrome** CVS: supportive tx, H2RA or PPI; TCA 50mg/day or migraine prevention drugs. [33,34] **N&V Links**: AFP PONV Prediction: http://www.aafp.org/afp/20070515/poc.html; AFP Evaluation n&v: http://www.aafp.org/afp/20070701/76.html; Australia FP: http://www.racgp.org.au/afp/200709

**Legend:** (SC)** Prochlorperazine has been given subcutaneously, but many references discourage this, due to local irritation & burning. H$_1$=Histamine 5-HT$_3$=serotonin Ach=Acetylcholine χ=Non-formulary Sask ☎=Exception Drug Status SK ς=scored ▼covered NIHB ♣Sk. Cancer Agency free med coverage ⊗not NIHB ac=before meal AE=adverse event CINV=chemo induced n&v CTZ=chemoreceptor trigger zone D$_2$=dopamine EPS=extrapyramidal symptom GI=stomach NMS=neuroleptic malignant syndrome NNT/NNH=number needed to treat / harm PL=placebo PONV=post-op n&v QTc=cardiac QT interval SE=side effect tx=treatment

## THERAPEUTIC TIPS:

1) **Typical favorites** in Palliative Care: Metoclopramide (or domperidone), haloperidol (or prochlorperazine), dexamethasone; sometimes dimenhydrinate. (po,pr or SC routes).
2) Prokinetic agents may induce colic if there is GI obstruction; anticholinergic drugs may exacerbate n&v secondary to colonic obstruction or constipation.
3) Anticholinergics can reduce the effectiveness of prokinetic agents (caution when combining other antiemetics e.g. dimenhydrinate with domperidone)
4) Symptoms from metabolic causes respond to higher doses of a central D2 antagonist (eg. haloperidol). Suggest writing "…***for nausea***" to haloperidol Rx.
5) Single evening doses of a long half-life benzodiazepines e.g. clonazepam are preferred to PRN use for ongoing symptoms due to psychological factors

Ensure patients take antiemetics regularly & on time!

**OTHER**: **Aprepitant** EMEND χ : PO (IV new); antagonist NK-1-receptor (substance P), SE: h/a, fatigue, dizzy, ?↑LFTs CINV: {125mg ORAL 115mg IV 1 hr pre-chemo day 1, THEN 80mg po daily in morning on day 2 & 3 (**Emend Tri-Pack** $116)}; in combo with ondansetron 32mg IV 30mins prior to chemo on day 1 only & dexamethasone 12mg ORALLY 30min prior to chemo on Day 1 & 8 mg ORALLY daily in AM on Days 2, 3, & 4}; **DI**: ↑dexamethasone level via Cyt-P450; {PONV: 40mg po 1-3hr prior to anesthesia; no change in renal dysfx}. **Palonosetron** ALOXI (**NOT in Canada**) CINV: 0.25mg IV x1 or 0.5mg po; & PONV; most potent & long-acting 5HT$_3$A (2-5days; t ½=40hr).
**Compounded combination suppositories**: e.g. "Triple Suppository", sometimes made to include multiple antinauseants for PR administration (various; e.g. metoclopramide 10mg, dimenhydrinate 50mg, haloperidol 0.5mg). http://www.paddocklabs.com/images/PadSec_v9n2.pdf

| Generic/TRADE (Strength & forms) | Class / Pregnancy category [9] | Side effects / Contraindications CI | √ = therapeutic use / Comments / Drug Interactions DI / Monitor M | INITIAL;MAX; USUAL DOSE | $ 8 doses |
|---|---|---|---|---|---|
| **Sildenafil** VIAGRA =S 25, 50, 100mg tab χ⊗ [10,11,12,13,14]; approved 1999 (**Revatio** 20-80mg tab tid ⊗≥$1050 per month, new: USA IV form→**PAH**) **Tadalafil** CIALIS =T 2.5,5,10,20mg tab [15,16] χ⊗ (**Adcirca** 20-40mg tab od χ⊗ FDA'09; USA is IV form→**PAH**) **Vardenafil** LEVITRA =V 5,10, 20mg tab χ⊗ [17,18,19,20,21,22,23,24,25,26] | **Oral selective phosphodiesterase-5 PDE5 inhibitor**: -reduce catabolism of cGMP resulting in smooth muscle relaxation of the corpus cavernosum and ↑ blood flow into penis (need sexual stimulation to produce actual erection) **-considered FIRST LINE** unless CI, but ~30% of men may still **not** respond to PDE5's monotherapy. **B** | **Common**: **flushing**[10%], diarrhea [4%], dizziness[2%], **headache** [>10%], **dyspepsia** [<8%], blurry vision (visual disturbance > with S,V), myalgia (T=6%[35]), **nasal congestion** & rash [2% esp S]; GI upset [dose-related] & visual disturbance [(>10% at dose high)], ?(↓smell, amnesia, hearing loss). [hot flashes if used in ♀] **Serious**: rare MI & *priapism; **QT** prolongation –V, very rare cases of **NAION**[23], ?seizures, ?sickle [cell crisis] CI: **nitrates:** ↑↑ hypotensive effect & ↑↑ heart rate (AVOID within 24h of S,V; 48h of T [31]); α-1 blockers (if new pt or if given ≤ 4hrs) S >25mg, T,V **Precautions**: anatomical penis deformation; CV dx (eg. arrhythmia, recent MI/stroke, uncontrolled HTN, coronary ischemia, HF); ↑ risk of **priapism*** (eg, sickle cell anemia, multiple myeloma, or leukemia); liver dx; multi BP meds; ↓ renal fx; NAION [27]; | √idiopathic, postencephalitic, symptomatic (Option: SSRI induced ED) (**Onset similar**: generally 30-60min [V,S,T]; as early as 10-15min [V,S]); S&T: pulmonary arterial HTN. **Peak** effect: S &V ~1hr; T ~2hr; **Duration**: S&V~4-12hr T ≤ **36hr** DI: **↑ hypotension**: α-1 blockers (especially in new pt; avoid or space by **>**4hrs); nitrates (CI or caution); antihypertensives (esp. vasodilators) & alcohol **Nitrate washout period**: S & V~24hr; T ~48hr. V:QT [see QT chart p.17] **↑ levels of PDE5 by**: CYP **3A4** [inhibitors] (azole [antifungals], cimetidine, cipro, erythromycin/ macrolides, tacrolimus), doxycycline, grapefruit [juice], isoniazid, protease [inhibitors], quinidine, verapamil. (PDE5: use lowest dose; S,V: [Max interval q24h] T: [Max interval q72h]) **↓ effect:** enzyme inducers [carbamazepine, phenytoin, phenobarb, rifampin]; ↓S&T by bosentan. **high fat meals** may delay and reduce efficacy of S & V. M: S,T= liver & renal fx, V=liver fx tests (Initial workup usually: glucose, lipid, TSH, testosterone) **Dose Adjustments**: **>65years** old: initial; S=25 mg T= by CrCl V=5mg **Liver dx**: Initial S=25 mg, T=10mg V=5mg **Renal dx** [CrCl <30mL/min]: Initial S=25 mg T=5mg V= no adjustment **Daily or 3x/week** dosing may be more efficacious for **poor responders** [36] < 5% of Non-responders will respond to a different PDE-5 inhibitor [36] | S 25-50mg→ 100mg x1/24h **50**-100mg, 30-60min pre-sex T 5-10mg→ 20mg x1/24h 10-**20**mg 1-2hr pre-sex 2.5-**5**mg daily option V 5-10mg→ 20mg x1 /24h **10**-20mg, 30-60min pre-sex | $99-102 $109 $125 $122 $132 30days $102-111 $119 |
| **Frequently as adulterants in herbs**: Acai Berry [products], Actra-Sx, Adam Free, Armstong Natural, Aspire36 & Aspire Lite, Aspire Lite, Axcil, 4Everon, Actra-Rx, Blue Steel, China Vigour, Chong Cao Ju Wang, Chongcaoliubian Jiaonang, Darling Caps, Dali Caps, Deguozhanjiang, Deguozonghengtianxia, Desirin, Dr. Life, Ehanix New Extra Men's Formula, Encore tabs for Men, Energy Max, Erextra, Excite, Firm Dose, Granite Rooster, Herb Vigour, Hero, HS Joy of Love, Jia Yi Jian, Jolex, Jiu Bian Wang, Kang Da, King Power Oral Soln, Lady Shangai, Libidfit, Libidus, Libimax, Libipower [Plus], Liviro3, Max [V8 Rhino], Lover Liquid Nutriment, Lu Quan, Meng Rong, Nangen Zengzhangsu, Nasutra, Naturalë Super Plus, NaturalUp, Natural Vigour, Neophase, Once More, Onyo, Oyster Plus, Platinum [Power 58 Extra], Power 58, Power 1 Walnut, Powertabs, Power Up, Santi Scalper [Penis Erection], Rize 2 The Occasion Caps, Rockhard Weekend, Rose 4 Her Capsules, Sanbianwan, Satis 60hr [Ever Lasting], Shangai Regular & Ultra & X, Spanish Fly, Stamina Rx, Steam, Stiff Nights, Stretch Up, Strong Testis, Super Shangai, Super X, Sweet Energizer Vitality, Tian Li, Tian Huang Gu Shen Dan, Top Gun [for Men Herbal Extracts], True Man, Ultimates, Urat Madu, Valentino, Vigoureux, VG, Vigor-25, Vigorect, Viril-ity Power vpxl No1, Yilishen, Yixinjiaonang, Xiadafil VIP, XOX [for men], XP Tongkat Ali Supreme, Viapro, Viril-Ity-Power, Wodibo, Zencore & Plus, Zhong Guo Shen Fang, Zhong Hua Niu Bian, Zhuang Yao Gu Shen, Zhuang Tjar Gere, Zui Xian Dan Gong Shi Z, Zimaxx **etc.** | | | | | |
| **Alprostadil** χ⊗ CAVERJECT, 20 ug vial (powder) **intracavernosal inj.** MUSE [28] 250, 500, 1000 ug **urethral supp** (refrigerate; otherwise 14days at RT) [29,30,31] Prostaglandin χ⊗ E1[32] **(PGE1) = E1** **inj** corpora cavernosa; transurethral **gel** | **Prostaglandin E** -activates cAMP which relaxes smooth muscle and produces vasodilation (also inhibition of platelet aggregation and gastric secretion, stimulation of intestinal smooth muscle, uterine smooth muscle) -most efficacious of injectable agents **X** | **Common**: ↓ HR[7%], dizziness, fever[14%], headache, hypotension[4%], penile pain[37%], penile fibrosis[3%], tachycardia[3%], urethral burning, vaginal itch (in partner with transurethral systems) **Serious**: seizures[4%], priapism* [<4%], HF, second degree heart block, supraventricular tachycardia, ventricular fibrillation[<1%], disseminated intravascular coagulation[1%] & cortical proliferation of long bones CI: anatomical penis deformation, penile implant, predisposition to priapism* (sickle cell anemia or trait, leukemia, myeloma), Peyronie's disease **Precautions:** concurrent anticoagulant, vasoactive agents or bleeding abnormalities | √ vasculogenic, psychogenic, neurogenic & mixed Onset = rapid Duration= <1hr Initial dosage/titration should occur under medical supervision (due to risk of syncope). Pts receiving intracavernosal inj should be assessed by Dr. q12months **Vascular ED requires larger doses (>20ug) vs neurogenic ED (2-5ug)**[33] Injection: no more than 3 doses/week (with 24 hours between doses) Suppositories: no more than 2 within 24 hours ↓ dose if erection lasts greater than one hour with either system Seek medical assistance if tx results in erection that lasts >4 hr. DI: heparin (↑ partial thromboplastin time & thrombin time); ↑ risk of symptomatic hypotension, syncope with vasodilators, antihypertensives, alcohol M: *priapism (erection lasting >4hr) tx=needle aspiration of penile blood; intracavernosal inj phenylephrine 200ug q5min up to 500ug if needed) [34] | **Neurogenic ED**: Titrate from 1 ug Usual: 2-5ug **Vascular ED**: Titrate from 4ug Usual: 5-20ug Severe: 40-60ug Inject 10-30mins pre-sex 125-250ug; 1000ug x1/24h 250-500ug 10-30mins pre-sex (dose depends on venous anatomy not ED etiology) | $248 10 doses CAVERJECT $200 8 doses MUSE $55-85 5ml vial 0.5-1ml/dose compounded |
| **Papaverine** = **Pv** 30mg/ml inj. soln (2ml vials) χ⊗ | **Vasodilator** (non-selective PDE [2,3,4] inhibitor) -produces generalized arteriolar dilation & smooth muscle relaxation -can be combined with prostaglandin &/or phentolamine **C** | **Common:** abdominal discomfort, anorexia, constipation, diarrhea, nausea, vomiting, drowsiness, headache, vertigo, hypertension, tachycardia, pruritis, rash & blurred vision? **Serious:** acidosis, ↑intercranial pressure, hepatotoxicity & priapism* CI: complete atrioventricular block **Precautions:** glaucoma, liver dx, recent MI, stroke, Parkinsonism & sickle cell anemia | √ idiopathic, postencephalitic & symptomatic (not FDA indication) Papaverine in any ischemic type condition is not recommended. Do not use more than 3 times weekly or 2 days in succession. Combos: -0.5-1 mg phentolamine intracavernosal; phentolamine & alprostadil by intracavernosal inj Consult Dr. if erection lasts more than 4 hours after self inj T½= 0.5-2hr DI: levodopa (↓ levodopa affect), ginkgo (↑ SE of papaverine) M: intraocular pressure in glaucoma patients, liver fx | 30 mg 60mg 30mg-60mg intracavernosal over 1-2 min | $40 10x2ml vials |
| **Phentolamine** χ⊗ = **Pt** **Rogitine**, generic 5mg lypholized powder for injection **As adulterants in**: Desire | **Alpha-Adrenergic Blocker** -antagonizes anti-erectile sympathetic tone, ↑perfusion - poor efficacy alone so usually combined with prostaglandin &/or papaverine **C** | **Common:** chest pain, diarrhea, dizziness[3%], headache[3%], hypotension[2%], nasal congestion[10%], nausea, palpitations[1%], ↑HR[1-7%] & vomiting **Serious:** arrhythmia CI: myocardial infarction, CAD, angina pectoris, hypersensitivity to phentolamine or mannitol, renal impairment, coronary or cerebral arteriosclerosis **Precautions:** arrhythmia, cerebral vascular spasm or occlusion, hypertension, ↑HR | √ idiopathic, postencephalitic & symptomatic (not FDA indication) Take one hour prior to sexual activity Peak activity: 30-60min Onset of action: 30-40min Duration: 5-7hr Compounded mixes may ↑ efficacy and ↓ pain associated with prostaglandin DI: **↑ hypotension**: beta blockers, tadalafil & vardenafil; disulfiram like rx with alcohol; ↓ effect with ephedrine (OTC cough/cold products, diet & "wake-up" pills) M: blood pressure changes, heart rate | **Compounded Products** **Bi-mix inj = Pt + Pv** 6ml vial = $60 0.5-1ml/dose **Tri-Mix inj =Pt + Pv + E1 in 3 strengths** $60-80 per 5ml vial 0.2-1ml per dose **TriMix also available in Transurethral gel** $40-120 / 5x1ml syr 0.5-1ml per dose | |

= ↓dose for renal dysfx ς=scored tab χ=Non-formulary Sk ☎=Exception Drug Status Sk ⊗=not covered by NIHB ▼=covered by NIHB **ac**=before meal **BP**=blood pressure **cc**=with meal CI=contraindication **CrCl**=creatinine clearance **DI**=drug interaction **Dx**=disease **ED**=Erectile dysfx **fx**=function **HF**=heart failure **HR**=heart rate **MI**=myocardial infarction **NAION**=nonarteric ischemic optic neuropathy **n/v**=nausea/vomiting **pc**=after meal **Pt**=patient **RT**=room temp. **Sx**=symptom **SE**=side effect **T½**=half life **Tx**=treatment

**Remedy for penile inj pain**: Sodium bicarbonate to restore isotonicity. **Other Meds**: apomorphine[42], testosterone [33], yohimbine [34 ? Prelox], surgical (eg. revascularization/penile prosthesis implantation)[35] & **vacuum** devices[~$350]. * priapism=any erection lasting >4hr

**Diagnosis**: ED is a couple's entity. Involve partner; may be reasons not to tx **Rule out**: low sex drive, relationship & psychological problems **Non Drug**: Quit smoking, regular exercise [avoid prolonged cycling >3hr/wk 36], ↓excess wt, & ↓alcohol consumption.

**Drug induced**: acetazolamide, alcohol, barbiturate, beta-blocker, carbamazepine, cimetidine, clonidine, cocaine, cyproterone, digoxin, finasteride, flutamide, ketoconazole, labetalol, lithium, MAOI, methadone, methyldopa, marijuana, methotrexate, opioid, phenytoin, phenothiazine, spironolactone, SSRI, TCA & thiazide.

# Sexual Dysfunction: Drug Causes / Considerations[1,2,3,4,5]

L. Regier, B. Jensen 

## Initiating Discussions About Sexual Function (Acronyms)

| | | BETTER[6] |
|---|---|---|
| **ALLOW** | ○ *Ask* about sexual function and activity<br>○ *Legitimize* problems; acknowledge as a clinical issue<br>○ Identify *Limitations* to the evaluation of sexual fx<br>○ *Open* up the discussion; *option* for referrals<br>○ *Work* with patient to develop goals & management plan | ○ **B**ring up topic<br>○ **E**xplain sexuality part of quality of life<br>○ **T**ell about available resources |
| **PLISSIT** 7,8 | ○ Obtain *permission* (e.g. I routinely discuss sexual issues with my patients; is that OK with you?)<br>○ Give *limited information* (don't inform about "normal" fx)<br>○ Give *specific suggestions* that the patient may try<br>○ Consider *intensive therapy* with specialist(s) | ○ **T**ime discussion to a time of patient's preference<br>○ **E**ducate on impact of treatment on sex & sexuality<br>○ **R**ecord that topic discussed |

## Female Sexual Dysfunction

**Epidemiology**: 40% of ♀ have sexual concerns; 12% distressing. Often associated with depression/anxiety.

**Types:** 1) Hypoactive sexual desire disorder 2) Female sexual arousal disorder 3) Female orgasmic disorder (inability to achieve orgasm) 4) Sexual pain disorder: Dyspareunia (pain with intercourse); Vaginismus (difficulty with intercourse)

## Drug Treatments for Female Sexual Dysfunction[1,2,9,10]

| Drug | Used for | Comment |
|---|---|---|
| **Estrogens**,<br>◆systemic (tablets, patches, gel)<br>◆vaginal (tablets, creams, ring) | ◆vaginal atrophy<br>◆dryness<br>◆dyspareunia | ◆systemic estrogen for vasomotor symptoms<br>◆vaginal estrogen for local symptoms & atrophy<br>{testosterone 2% sparingly to posterior fourchette x3 months has been tried.}[4]<br>{see Postmenopausal Chart (RxFiles 8th Ed – pg 90) [11]} |
| **Testosterone (Androgens)**<br>◆oral ANDRIOL; gel. 150-300ug/day *INTRINSA* **patch** in **Europe** | ◆↓ sexual desire | ◆limited efficacy/study; lack official indication in ♀ Canada;<br>{Masculinization with doses used for males! see Androgens Chart [12].} |
| **Bupropion** WELLBUTRIN | ◆↓ sexual desire (magnitude of role uncertain) | ◆may be useful in SSRI-induced sexual dysfunction (switch to or add on) [13]; limited study.[14] {Avoid if seizure risk.} |
| **Phosphodiesterase Inhibitors (PDE-5 inhibitors)**<br>e.g. Sildenafil VIAGRA<br>(also tadalafil CIALIS, vardenafil LEVITRA) | ◆↓ sexual desire &/or arousal | ◆limited data; may be effective in ♀ with autonomic nerve damage such as in multiple sclerosis patients<br>◆official indication only in ♂; conflicting results in studies<br>{see Erectile Dysfunction chart (RxFiles 8th Ed – pg 46 )[15]} |
| **Vaginal Moisturizers, etc.**<br>◆ Replens OTC (Moisturizer)<br>◆ KY Jelly OTC (Lubricant) | ◆vaginal dryness / dyspareunia<br>◆↓arousal | ◆Replens requires regular use daily or 3x/wk; minimal SEs<br>◆KY generally used intermittently before intercourse<br>◆Can help resolve issues 2° to drugs causing dryness! |
| Other: | ◆Alprostadil CAVERJECT: local application of compounded cream has been tried to ↑ arousal<br>◆Apomorphine APOKYN: investigational orally for ↑ arousal; causes emesis | |

- ◆Psychological & relational issues are key factors in sexual function/dysfunction.
- ◆"Don't forget to set the mood"; good long-term relationships require ongoing investment of time, effort, energy, ideas…
- ◆Age/menopause: apart from dryness/trouble lubricating, sexual problems do not necessarily ↑ with age.
- ◆Surgical menopause may have greater impact than natural menopause (perhaps due to ↓ androgen production).
- ◆Pelvic floor or bladder dysfunction, endometriosis, uterine fibroids: may be associated with dyspareunia.
- ◆Other: ↑ prolactin, renal failure, stoma [16], cancer [7] (active or history of) may ⇨pain, ↓desire, anxiety/fear/guilt, body image issues

## Male Sexual Dysfunction (See also Erectile Dysfunction pg 46 [15] & Androgen pg 23 [12] charts) [17]

- ◆**Always assess potential interpersonal issues, conflict, etc**. Tx ⇨ counselling, etc. "Merely restoring erections is usually not sufficient to restore a poor sexual relationship"[18].
- ◆**Pornography**: frequent access can contribute to loss of libido, impotence/ED, critical of partner, relationship issues, etc. [19]
- ◆**↓ Libido:** age, androgen deficiency, psychological/depression, recreational drugs including alcohol, nicotine & marijuana.
- ◆**Erectile dysfunction** (ED): may reflect ↓ blood flow to corpora cavernosae. Tx: PDE5, alprostadil inj or urethral suppository, vacuum device, prosthesis penile {if rapid onset (& not post-surgery): often performance anxiety, disaffection with partner or emotional issue; Tx ⇨ counselling.}
- ◆**Ejaculation disorders**: e.g. delayed ejaculation (DE): caused by tissue damage in prostate surgery or failure of α-adrenergic clamping of bladder neck sphincter resulting in retrograde ejaculation. Also may be caused by medication.
- ◆**Gradual/complete loss of nocturnal erections**: suggests neurologic or vascular disease.
- ◆**Non-sustained erections** after penetration: due to 1) anxiety or 2) vascular steal syndrome (↑ oxygen demand during sex)
- ◆**Premature ejaculation:** common ~30% of ♂. "persistent or recurrent …with minimum stimulation before or shortly after penetration"; in trials, normal latency is 2+ minutes; PE is <1 minute. **Tx** [18,20]: 1) reassurance; 2) pause & squeeze technique; 3) start-stop technique; 4) SSRI (regularly x1-2 wks with citalopram, paroxetine, sertraline or fluoxetine); 5) clomipramine 25-50mg x1; 6) anesthetic creams (e.g. Emla; remove excess pre-intercourse, or condom)
- ◆**Uremia/renal failure**[21]: common (causes: neuropathy, PVD, hypogonadism, drug induced, psychological); Tx: maximize dialysis, correct anemia; <u>Options</u>: PDE5 inhibitor, psychotherapy, testosterone, vacuum device, alprostadil, zinc supplement, penile prosthesis.

## Potential Drug Causes of Sexual Dysfunction

⇨NOTE: Sexual desire, arousal & function is psychologically complex; investigate non-drug causes (e.g. take a good sexual/relationship history) before assigning causation to a drug. {**Other disease causes:** diabetes, atherosclerosis, cardiac, central nervous system diseases, depression, obesity.[22] Note: sexual health & sexually active life will benefit from good health[23]; some drug treatments can help maintain health.

| Drug Class | Examples | Male (♂) | Female (♀) |
|---|---|---|---|
| **Analgesics** | Opiates (potential to ↓ testicular function with chronic use)<br>Indomethacin; possibly other NSAIDs | ED, AnO, ↓Lib<br>ED, ↓Lib | AnO, ↓Lib<br>↓Lib |
| **Anticholinergics** [24] | 3° TCAs (e.g. amitriptyline, imipramine); 2° TCAs,<br>Oxybutynin, tolterodine | ED; Pain desipramine | SD, Dryness vag<br>Dryness vag |
| **Anticonvulsants**[25]<br>[Lamotrigine may improve fx[26]] | Phenytoin, phenobarbital, carbamazepine,<br>Gabapentin, topiramate. [Valproate:↑5HT] | ED, ↓Lib,<br>ED, AnO | AnO, ↓Lib<br>AnO |
| **Antidepressants**<br>[**Tx**: PDE-5 inhibitors useful; bupropion in lieu of, or added to SSRIs[27]; buspirone[28]; resolution of depression helps.] [See Antidepressants: Table 1] [29] | MAOIs (e.g. phenelzine, tranylcypromine)<br>Mirtazapine, venlafaxine esp ↑doses, duloxetine [30]<br>SSRIs (e.g. citalopram, escitalopram, fluoxetine, fluvoxamine, paroxetine, sertraline)<br>TCAs (e.g. amitriptyline, imipramine, other)<br>Trazodone | ED, DE<br>DE, AnO<br>DE50%, ED, AnO<br>DE, ED, Pain<br>Pria | SD<br>AnO, ↓arousal<br>↓Lib, AnO<br>↓Lib; Dryness<br>SD |
| **Anticonvulsants/Mood Stabilizers** | Carbamazepine, phenytoin [not lamotrigine][31]<br>Lithium (less of a problem then many psychotropics) | ED<br>(ED, ↓Lib) | SD |
| **Antihistamines** | Dimenhydrinate, diphenhydramine, hydroxyzine, meclizine, promethazine | ED | Dryness vag |
| **Antihypertensives**<br>(see also *Diuretics* below)<br>[Less likely to cause: ACEI, ARBs & most CCBs] | Alpha-blockers (e.g. doxazosin, prazosin, terazosin)<br>Beta-blockers ( e.g. atenolol, bisoprolol, carvedilol, metoprolol, propranolol)<br>Methyldopa<br>Other: clonidine, reserpine, verapamil | ED, Pria<br>ED, ↓Lib?<br>DE, ED, ↓Lib<br>ED | <br>↓Lib?<br>AnO, ↓Lib<br>SD? |
| **Antiparkinson agents** | Bromocriptine<br>Levodopa, trihexyphenidyl | ED<br>ED | Pain |
| **Antipsychotics**<br>Tx: switch drugs; sildenafil ED [32]; ↓dose. See Antipsychotic Tables.[33] | Antipsychotics (e.g. haloperidol, phenothiazines)<br>[inhibit DA & ∴ ↑prolactin ⇨gonadal suppression]<br>Less likely to cause: olanzapine, quetiapine, risperidone & clozapine | DE, ED, Pain, ↓Lib, Pria | ↓Lib ; SD; Dryness vag |
| **Antispasmotics** | Baclofen | DE | |
| **Cardiovascular, other** | Digoxin, disopyramide<br>Fibrates (e.g. gemfibrozil)<br>Amiodarone | ED<br>ED, ↓Lib<br>↓Lib | |
| **Cytotoxic agents** | Methotrexate, other (cyclophosphamide); see also "hormone" | ED | Dryness vag |
| **Diuretics**<br>(uncommon with low doses) | Spironolactone<br>Thiazides | ED, ↓Lib<br>ED | ↓Lib |
| **GI** | Cimetidine, metoclopramide, rarely ranitidine<br>Sulfasalazine | ED, ↓Lib<br>ED | |
| **Hormone, hormone antagonists, etc.** | 5-α-reductase inhibitors; corticosteroids; estrogen; progesterone?; contraceptives?; aromatase inhibitors [34] | ED | ?? ↑ or ↓Lib; Dryness vag |
| **Immunomodulators** | Interferon-alfa | ED | |
| **Opiates** (↓ testosterone) | Codeine, hydromorphone, morphine, fentanyl, etc. | ED, ↓Lib | ↓Lib |
| **Sedatives/Anxiolytics**<br>(Can also cause disinhibition issues.) | Benzodiazepines (e.g. diazepam) esp. at higher doses<br>Buspirone (but 60mg/day may improve sexual fx in some)[28] | DE, ED, ↓Lib<br>Pria | ↓Lib, AnO |
| **Substances of abuse**[35,36]<br>**Alcohol** - esp chronic use (↓ hormones, ↓ orgasm),<br>**Nicotine/smoking** (ED)[37] | Amphetamines<br>Barbiturates<br>Cocaine regular use<br>Marijuana; smoking (♂: 1.5x risk of ED)<br>*It provoketh desire & taketh away the capacity.* Shakespeare's Macbeth on **alcohol** | DE, ED<br>ED<br>ED, Pria<br>ED, ↓Lib | AnO<br><br>AnO<br>↓Lib |

**AnO**=anorgasmia (or delayed/↓ orgasm) **DA**=dopamine **DE**=delayed or no ejaculation **ED**=erectile dysfunction **↓Lib**=↓ libido **Pain**=pain with intercourse or on ejaculation **PE**=premature ejaculation **Pria**=priapism **Tx**=treatment **SD**=sexual dysfunction (general)

<u>**Herbal/Natural Products**</u>[38]: ◆Yohimbe: possibly effective for SSRI induced sexual dysfx. ◆DHEA 300mg x1 probably ineffective in premenopausal ♀ for arousal. ◆Ginkgo: probably ineffective for sexual dysfx caused by antidepressants

## Types & Treatment Considerations- Rule out: UTI, cancer, stones, & inflammatory causes (by urinalysis & MSU for C&S). **Bladder diary** [47] for 3+ days (working & leisure), physical exam +/- PVR to determine type of UI [1].

3 Questions: In the last 3 months, have you leaked urine? What activity (coughing / sneezing / lifting / exercise, or a feeling / urge, or no feeling / urgency) were you doing when you leaked urine? What activity made you leak urine most often? 122

**1) Overactive bladder (OAB) / Urge Incontinence:** syndrome with urinary urgency +/- urgency UI, usually with frequency & nocturia; includes detrusor muscle overactivity (DO); more in ♀ than ♂ up to 44yr, but evens by age 75 [2]. **OAB is most responsive type of UI to drug tx!**

**Treatment:** (goal to ↓ urinary urgency, frequency &/or nocturia if present)

1. Anticholinergics/antimuscarinics (**AC**): **most useful** (act at detrusor smooth muscle; mainly $M_2$ & $M_3$ receptors [44])
2. Bladder training: gradual time lengthening between voids/urge suppression [1]: Useful, especially in addition to AC.
3. Estrogens topical or oral in estrogen deficient ♀: controversial, conflicting data; may worsen UI in some.
4. Tricyclic antidepressants (TCAs) – less commonly used; *dual mechanism* (AC detrusor & adrenergic urethral effects)
5. Other drugs: via intravesicular instillations compounded 10ml (oxybutynin for kids rarely, capsaicin irritating) or detrusor injections; (Also botulinum toxin A inject 20-30 sites with ~10units/site; may last 6months or longer if non-neurogenic, ↑dose if neurogenic) [2,34-36]
6. Neuromodulation/surgery augmentation, urinary diversion, detrusor myectomy

**2) Stress Urinary Incontinence (SUI):** due to underlying anatomical factors. Occurs with **exercise, coughing & sneezing**; more common in ♀ (hx of pregnancy). Perform a stress/cough test→ cough & strain to detect leakage.

**Treatment:** {Vaginal cones: biofeedback PFMT therapy,~15mins twice a day, LadySystem/Aquaflex}

1) Pelvic floor muscle training (**PFMT**, **Kegels** prophylactic & therapeutic.): 1st line in SUI [1]; Other lifestyle, pessaries, etc.
2) Surgery (>80% success) [1,54] retropubic suspension , suburethral slings, trans vaginal tape or artificial sphincter for ♂; peri urethral injectables (bulking)
3) Pharmacologic [1,5]: weak/conflicting data for estrogen. Some use of TCAs & pseudoephedrine if surgery not an option

**3) Mixed UI:** has characteristics of both OAB & SUI. Tx: as per the dominant category, OAB or SUI [1]; or TCAs.

**4) Overflow UI:** treat constipation, stop/↓ meds, double voiding, α- blocker trial in ♂, catheter decompression, IC preferred

**Other Related**

- **Neurogenic bladder** – multiple factors may be involved and management of each case individualized!
  - -e.g. from damage to peripheral pelvic surgery, lumbar disc prolapse or spinal nerves or cerebral lesion (e.g. Parkinson's, MS, Alzheimer's, stroke);
  - -drugs only as per OAB if detrusor overactivity (DO) is present otherwise, timed voiding, absorbent pads & catheterization intermittent, clean (IC). Assess PVR. Detrusor sphincter dyssynergia e.g. brainstem has been treated with catheterization IC, AC, α-blockers & baclofen [3].
  - -Autonomic dysreflexia: e.g. spinal cord injury above T5; ↑BP, ↓HR & headaches may actually resolve with bladder emptying; IC cath.; α-blocker?
  - -Spinal Cord patients: lying down (afternoon & evening) effective to ↓ peripheral fluid load & ↓ nocturia! (May be safer than DDAVP)
  - -Lower motor neuron lesion sacral, pelvic, cauda equine (↓'d detrusor & sphincter stimulation): Tx: Cath. IC, pads; ?pseudoephedrine; not AC!
- **Male UI** - **bladder outlet obstruction** (**BOO**) or underactive detrusor muscles & often associated with BPH. Treatment: α-blockers, dutasteride, finasteride, catheterization, surgery & non-drug (e.g. urethral milking). {If α-blocker ineffective, a switch to, or addition of an AC may be considered (caution: rare urinary retention)} [63,76-79,82,87].

## Non-Drug Urinary Incontinence (UI) Treatment: Great resource→ Nurse Continence Advisor [33; 96]

- ↓**Fluid** intake to ~1.5L/day depending on UI cause [1]. Restrict intake **after 6pm**. (To prevent dehydration/constipation, sometimes ↑ fluid)
- ↓**Weight** helps if BMI>30 [1] • ↓**Caffeine & alcohol/smoking** elimination can assist with OAB & possibly SUI [1,2].
- **Pelvic floor muscle training** (PFMT) strength & relaxation: self-taught or physiotherapy referral [33] Useful in ♂ post TURP/prostatectomy.
  - Tx of choice in SUI & useful in Mixed UI: 3 months minimally. More effective if younger (age ≤50). {14x more likely to report cure vs no tx) (95% CI 2-140)} [4]
  - Less effect in OAB but RR of improvement/cure of 2.2 [4]. PFMT trial ≥ 6 weeks b/c lower relapse rates than with AC.[1]

  PFMTs (Kegels): Test by interrupting stream or prevent gas passing; Biofeedback: uses probe device to measure PFM tone; ensures PFMT done correctly.
- **Bladder training** – useful in OAB, especially in addition to AC [4,93] {avoid last minute rush, map out bathrooms, urge suppression quick Kegels}

  Timed voiding: void regularly q1hr; ↑ by 15min each wk or until 2 days without incontinence episodes / satisfied with voiding; goal of 3-4hrs with no leaks [1,80]

  Distraction techniques eg. friends, crossword puzzles: can be helpful to relax & distract when urge comes
- **Absorbent products & toileting aids** are not treatment, but should be in treatment plan. {coping strategy while awaiting definitive tx or adjunct to ongoing therapy. Used long-term only after exhausting other treatment options [1].}
- **Intravaginal Pessaries**: ↓leakage in ♀ Cost <$100 Milex, no discomfort (physical exercise,prolapse,SUI) ↓SUI score by 47%; 50% ♀ used for full year of study, 76% if successful fit @2wks [1,92]
- Catheterization [1] {e.g. intermittent, clean (**IC**) catheterization may be option for some with overflow incontinence}
- Neuromodulation: Stoller stimulation above ankle; or implantable InterStim device for sacral nerve • Acupuncture: ↓ in frequency ARR = 10 ? but not UI episodes [1]

## Medications / Foods Contributing to UI [5]:

- Caffeine (contained in coffee, tea, chocolate, pop, etc... ); Alcohol
- Diuretics (especially if late in the day, high dose or before going out)
- Anticholinergics (AC) (⇨urinary/fecal retention⇨overflow incontinence). Total **AC load** of all meds [43] patient is on is important ↑ delirium / SEs

  AC list: http://formulary.drugplan.health.gov.sk.ca/FormularyBulletins/Bulletin86Apr2001.pdf
- Acetylcholinesterase inhibitors (donepezil, rivastigmine, galantamine) [83,84]: direct ↑ on OAB symptoms
- Psychotropics (antidepressants, antipsychotics, sedatives) ↑AC SEs & ↓ bladder awareness
- Narcotic analgesics (⇨urinary retention)
- α-blockers (e.g. tamsulosin, doxazosin, terazosin)
- α-adrenergic agonists ephedrine, pseudoephedrine ⇨ urinary retention
- β-agonists / -antagonists (variable effects)
- CCBs (calcium channel blockers): nocturnal enuresis, reports of retention, ↑ frequency <1%)
- ACEI/ARBS (angiotensin converting enzyme inhibitors): cough

## Considerations for UI in the Frail Elderly [6,80]

- History & clinical assessment crucial:

  ⇒**D**elirium **I**nfection **A**trophic vaginitis **P**harmaceuticals **P**sychological **E**xcess urine output **R**educed mobility **S**tool impaction...
  - **Environmental** (toilet access, physical barriers)
  - **Functional** – physical, mobility & cognitive impairments (arthritis, stroke, fracture); assess clothing, footwear, lighting & home layout
  - **Iatrogenic** (drug induced urinary & fecal retention, surgical complications)
  - **Other** (↑fluid intake, fluid shift from periphery, delirium, **UTI**, atrophic vaginitis, **constipation**, psychological, cancer, BPH)
- Address factors & reassess to determine if treatment still warranted
- **SUI** tx in elderly would ideally not include TCAs (→ fall risk)
- **OAB** may be treated with cautious trial of AC (start very low dose). Timed/assisted/prompted toileting q2-4h based on diary if cognitive impairment.

## The Cognitive Impairment/Urinary Incontinence Balance

- **Older patients**, > 60y/o (even w/o dementia) are at high risk for cognitive impairment 2° to ACs. Caution warranted [7,42,43,64,65,80]. Use lowest effective AC dose (*start low & go slow*).
- **Alzheimer's & Parkinson's patients** may have acute agitation, anxiety, panic attack, confusion & delusions when placed on ACs for UI. Rapidly reversible upon discontinuation [8,9,10].
- **Are any ACs preferred in this population?** OXY & tolterodine can both cause cognitive impairment [8,9,10]; however tolterodine is favored by some especially if low-dose OXY is problematic. There are a lack of adequate trials in this population setting. Theoretically ↓ *lipophilicity* (↓ BBB penetration) with tolterodine & trospium and *M3 specificity* (1° receptor for bladder response to AC) of trospium, solifenacin & darifenacin have **not** yet translated into clear clinical advantages in terms of CNS adverse effects compared to oxybutynin [11]. One RCT [12] showed lack of detrimental effect of darifenacin vs. OXY ER 15-20mg/day or placebo on memory name-face association, however design issues (E.g. high OXY dose & no difference vs OXY for 15 other endpoints.)

**Epidemiology** Canada: 17.3% of ♀ & 3.4% of ♂ have urinary incontinence [5,46]. (Europe: OAB prevalence of 42% in ♂ >74yr & 31% in ♀ >74yr [2]). **AC**=anticholinergic **BBB**=blood brain barrier **MSU**=midstream urine **PVR**=post void residual 50-100ml acceptable

**Contributing factors**: obstruction (tumors, calculi, prostate enlargement), impaired urinary sphincter contractility/weakness, bladder abnormalities, or estrogen deficiency (in ♀), **RR**=relative risk **UI**=urinary incontinence peripheral edema (fluid shifting), neurologic diseases (Alzheimer's, Parkinson's, stroke, multiple sclerosis, diabetic neuropathy) [2], hyperglycemia/hypercalcemia & congestive heart failure.

**Risk factors** [1,97]: pregnancy, parity, obstetric factors, menopause, hysterectomy, obesity, lower urinary tract symptoms, functional impairment, cognitive impairment, smoking, family history, genetics, & diet alcohol, caffeine, ↑ fluids.

**Red Flags** for referral: recurrent incontinence, incontinence assoc. with: pain, urinary tract anomalies, hematuria, recurrent infection, fistulas, prostate irradiation, previous radical pelvic surgery, pelvic mass, or lack of response to treatment.

**Concerns**: social isolation, deleterious sexual effects, depression, sleep disruption, falling & fracture (known issue in post-menopausal women) [2], & skin integrity breakdown.

**Patient info**: PFMT (Kegels) hold & relax ≤10 seconds each, do 10 times QID; breathe; http://www.continence-fdn.ca/pdf/pelvicmuscleexercises.pdf; UI info: www.continence-fdn.ca, www.simonfoundation.org, www.womensbladderhealth.com; www.continence-foundation.org.uk; Dermatitis: www.nursingcenter.com/pdf.asp

# Urinary Incontinence: Drug Treatment Comparison Chart

Initial workup by K. Mulherin, BSP, PharmD Candidate; L. Regier, B. Jensen - © www.RxFiles.ca - May 10

| Generic/TRADE g=generic avail. Strength/forms[13]; pregnancy category[14] | INITIAL; USUAL range & (maximal dose) | $ / 30days | Side effects (SE); Contraindications CI; Drug Interactions DI[2,18]; Monitor M √ = Therapeutic use / Comments |
|---|---|---|---|
| **Anticholinergics=AC** | Renal dysfunction ; Liver | | AC/antimuscarinics: competitively block bladder $M_{2\&3}$ receptors: ↓ detrusor muscle contractions & relax bladder / ↓ urge.[19] Most useful in **OAB** |
| **Oxybutynin (OXY)** -over 30yrs use<br>DITROPAN, g -has active metabolite N-DEO<br>IR 2.5✗▼, 5mg$^{s}$ tab; 5mg/5ml soln<br>DITROPAN XL ✗ ⊗ 5,10mg tab B<br>OXYTROL ✗ ⊗36mg Patch -3.9mg/d delivered<br>UROMAX ☎ ⊗ 10,15mg FC tab ER | IR: 2.5mg bid or hs<br>5mg bid-tid; Max qid<br>Peds: >5y/o 5mg bid<br>Ditropan XL 5-10mg od<br>15-20mg daily (Max 30mg/day)<br>Apply twice/wk alternate sites<br>Uromax 10-15mg daily 20mg/d | 14<br>19-25 $30<br><br>80<br>150<br>70<br>54-58 $99 | |
| **Tolterodine (Tolt)**-approval USA 1998<br>DETROL IR ✗ ✆ 1, 2mg tab<br>DETROL LA ☎ ✆ 2, 4mg cap C<br>-M1-5 nonspecific, but less lipid soluble<br>-has an active metabolite | IR 1-2 mg bid<br>LA 2-4mg daily Max 4mg/day<br>Renal / Liver: Max 2mg/day<br>Peds: limited trials[37,38,39] | 72<br>73 | |
| Fesoterodine TOVIAZ ✗ ⊗ 4,8mg ER tabs –new USA, prodrug, active Tolt metabolite, DI 3A4 | | | |
| **Trospium** -approval USA 2004<br>TROSEC 20mg tab USA: Sanctura XR ☎ ✆ C<br>-low BBB penetration? quaternary amine, hydrophilic<br>-M2 & 3 receptors, ↑active drug in urine | Adult: 20mg bid<br>(1hr before or 2-3hr after meals)<br>Geriatric / Renal <30ml/min:<br>20mg daily at bedtime | 61<br><br><br>34 | |
| **Darifenacin** ENABLEX ☎ ✆ C<br>7.5, 15mg XR tab -approval USA 2005<br>-M3 specific +++, low BBB penetration? ↑molecular wt | Adult: 7.5mg daily;<br>may ↑at 2wks to 15mg od<br>If Liver/Cyp3A4 inhibitors: 7.5mg od | 59<br>59<br>59 | |
| **Solifenacin** VESICARE ☎ ✆ C<br>5, 10mg FC tab -approval USA 2005<br>-M3 specific +, long half life (T½=45-68hrs) | Adult: 5-10mg daily; Max 10mg<br>Liver / Renal / & with CYP 3A4 inhibitors: 5mg daily | 61-61<br><br>61 | |

**Anticholinergics – comments:**

**An Approach**: Oxybutynin gold standard experience/trials/safety & limited advantages with other agents. Start oxybutynin 2.5-5mg hs/bid & slowly ↑ dose if necessary. **PRN dosing** may be useful for pts only requiring continence for daily outings. Tolterodine, trospium, oxybutynin ER & patch, (darifenacin & solifenacin) less experience/evidence are alternatives if lack of efficacy, SE or convenience or QOL issues. Cost is a factor. (Individualize treatment based on the patient's age, concurrent medications, cognitive function & social/financial situation.)

**Efficacy**: Defined for some as complete cessation of incontinence; for others as being able to complete ADLs outside the home. Patient perception of cure/improvement directs care. **Improvement seen after 1 week to 1 month after starting AC.**

- ACH vs Placebo: a) Pts perceive cure or improvement: 56% vs 41%; NNT=7; b) about 4 less leakage episodes & 5 less voids per week.[20]

OXY ER vs Tolterodine ER: more OXY patients achieve continence & ↓ incontinence episodes, but ↑dry mouth; poor study designs[11]

Comparisons between OXY & other AC's: have shown a lack of meaningful efficacy differences.[15,16,17,19,21] (study dose & design limitations)

**Side Effects (SE) / Safety**:

General comments: common, especially in elderly. Long-acting forms often less SE. Change of drug &/or dose may help.

Common: **dry mouth, blurred vision, constipation** trospium > oxybutynin IR 5mg bid & darifenacin=solifenacin > tolterodine[11], GI discomfort, GERD, dizziness, headache drowsiness, heat intolerance & pruritis. **Patch specific**: pruritis[17%], erythema[50%][2]; less dry mouth. Avoids 1st pass effect; ↓ N-DEO metabolite.[91]

Serious: traffic accidents, ↓ **cognition, confusion**[90], convulsions, **falls**, bradycardia, **tachycardia**, flushing anxiety, urinary retention rare, allergy, angioedema tolterodine,?darifenacin,?solifenacin, QTc prolongation[62] (in at-risk pts: tolterodine, solifenacin) & sweating (solifenacin); asthenia, SJS ? tolterodine

Overdose Toxidrome: Blind as a bat, mad as a hatter, red as a beet, hot as a hare & dry as a bone.

**Dry mouth:** common reason to stop tx. Range 13-41%. Severe 8%[11]. {OXY IR > OXY XL> darifenacin = solifenacin > tolt IR > tolt ER > trospium = OXY patch}[18,21,23]

- To prevent 1 case of dry mouth over 8wks[11]: tolt 2mg bid vs oxy 5mg bid: NNT=4; tolt LA 4mg daily vs tolt IR 2mg bid: NNT=14; oxy ER 10mg daily vs oxy IR 5mg bid: NNT=17
- **MANAGEMENT:** sugarless candy; OTC saliva substitutes e.g. ORAL BALANCE GEL, MOUTH KOTE; (useful esp. @ HS); Rx Pilocarpine 1% Eye Drops: 1-2 drops qid prn into mouth

**DI**: KCl (↑ risk of GI lesions); **Tolterodine** –↑ levels by CYP 3A4 inhibitors such as ketoconazole; **Solifenacin** - azole antifungals; **Trospium** – food, digoxin, metformin, morphine, pancuronium, procainamide, tenofovir & vancomycin (no CYP 450 DIs). **Darifenacin** - desipramine, flecainide, ketoconazole & other azoles, imipramine probable, nelfinavir, ritonovir; theoretical: clarithromycin & thioridazine.

**CI**: gastric & urinary retention, uncontrolled narrow angle glaucoma, hypersensitivity, myasthenia gravis; worsens delirium/dementia

{CDR Recommendations: Trospium[15] & Darifenacin:[16] - option if failing/SE to oxybutynin; Solifenacin: yes was no initially. if failing/SE to oxybutynin for formulary[17]}

| Generic/TRADE | INITIAL; USUAL range & (maximal dose) | $ / 30days |
|---|---|---|
| **Estrogens** - in estrogen deficient ♀ | See also postmenopausal chart. | |
| **Vaginal**: X | | |
| PREMARIN 0.625mg/g cream | 0.5-2g per vag twice/week | ~6-15 |
| VAGIFEM 25ug vaginal tab | 1 tab per vag twice/week | 28 |
| ESTRING 2mg vaginal ring | Ring per vag every 90 days | 25 |
| **Patch**: 25, 37.5, 50, 75, 100ug/day | Twice/wk e.g Estradot, or weekly Climara | ≥20 |
| **Gel**: ESTROGEL 2.5g/day | Apply daily as directed | 25 |
| **Oral**: PREMARIN, CES 0.3, 0.625, 0.9, 1.25mg tab | PO 0.3-1.25mg/day | ~10 |

**Efficacy**: Conflicting data with WHI showing HRT (progesterone + estrogen) & unopposed estrogen worsening UI regardless of type (SUI or OAB)[24] & Cochrane[25] review indicating estrogen treatment without progesterone having a statistically significant subjective improvement but not objective for either SUI or OAB. {Note: may offer benefit for other bladder symptoms e.g. ↓ urge even if not curative for UI.}

- SOGC[26] and British guidelines[1] specifically **exclude** the use of estrogens for UI
- There is insufficient efficacy data to recommend one formulation (po/vaginal) over another[25]; **vaginal** may have more local effect, & may be given less frequently with less systemic risk (although there can be significant systemic absorption via vaginal route).

**Safety**: WHI study cautions on the use of oral HRT/estrogen tx for indications other than relief of vasomotor symptoms (use at lowest dose & for **shortest** duration necessary) due to ↑ in breast cancer, cardiac events, stroke & pulmonary emboli (NNH=66 / 5yrs; ave age 63yrs)[24;WHI].

| Generic/TRADE | INITIAL; USUAL range & (maximal dose) | $ / 30days |
|---|---|---|
| **Antidepressants - TCAs**<br>Imipramine TOFRANIL g C<br>10, 25, 50; 75✗▼mg tab<br>Others: Amitriptyline, nortriptyline, desipramine… | Imip.: 10-25mg hs (or tid)<br>Usual 50-100mg/day.<br>Dose bid - tid optimal in some.<br>Ped: 6-12 yr 10-50mg hs | 15<br>18-30 |

**Efficacy**: OAB: Limited efficacy evidence[27,28]. Nocturia: TCAs have anectodal evidence to support hs use in this population (pediatric & adult). SUI: Used in practice however efficacy data lacking[29]. {**Duloxetine** CYMBALTA 40-60mg po BID $138 ☎⊗; antidepressant; limited SUI evidence}[70-75] Mixed: as per SUI[30]. Anecdotal reports suggests more effective for mixed than in SUI or OAB. (Dual action: have AC & adrenergic effects)

**Safety**: For SE see RxFiles antidepressant chart. (**Other TCA options**: **nortriptyline** 10-50mg HS esp. if elderly or patient with concomitant chronic pain)

| Generic/TRADE | INITIAL; USUAL range & (maximal dose) | $ / 30days |
|---|---|---|
| **Alpha (α) blockers** | | |
| **Alfuzosin** XATRAL g 10mg XR tab B | Alfuzosin 10mg daily after meal | 43 (32 g) |
| **Doxazosin** CARDURA g 1,2$^{s}$,4$^{s}$ mg tab C | Doxazosin: 1-4mg hs Max 8mg | 19-25[43] |
| **Prazosin** MINIPRESS g 1$^{s}$,2$^{s}$,5$^{s}$ mg tab C | Prazosin: 1-5mg bid Max 15mg/d | 21-32[45] |
| **Tamsulosin** FLOMAX g C<br>0.4mg SR cap after meals, 0.4mg CR tab B | Tamsulosin: 0.4-0.8mg daily<br>{Take SR caps 30min after meal; CR tabs may be taken anytime} | 27-50 |
| **Terazosin** HYTRIN g 1,2,5,10mg tab C | Terazosin: 1-5mg hs Max 20mg | 17-25[65] |

**Efficacy**: ↓BPH in ♂ improves UI Sx in most. No definite efficacy advantage of 1 drug over another[98]. Option if **bladder outlet obstruction** is present. {Finasteride PROSCAR g 5mg daily $38-70 ✆ / Dutasteride AVODART 0.5mg daily $64 ✆ options if large prostate}[88]. Tamsulosin? help eliminate ureteral stone 96a

**Combos**: AC + α-blocker for **OAB & BPH** in select ♂ patients has been recently studied; ↑ efficacy but possible ↑ in urinary retention.[63,76-79,82,87] BPH: Finasteride+doxazosin: benefit if ↑prostate eg. >40ml & >1yr tx, but ↑cost & sexual SE.[94,95] {Combo of tamsulosin+ tolterodine not effective in♀}[68]

- Some agents have advantages in ease of use, dose titration & SEs (e.g. tamsulosin CR tabs are taken daily, without regards to both food or 1st dose syncope)

**Safety**: SE: Dizziness <8%, asthenia ~5% & **postural hypotension** ~5% & often dose-related; ↑dose gradually. Rare: floppy iris Sx tamsulosin 114; DI: Cyp3A4 HIV. Some **more selective** for prostatic tissue α1A {ie. alfuzosin & tamsulosin} & may have less potential SE e.g. less hypotension. Sulfa allergy tamsulosin. Doxazosin arm of ALLHAT hypertension study stopped early due to ↑**heart failure & stroke** compared to thiazide (chlorthalidone)

| Generic/TRADE | INITIAL; USUAL range & (maximal dose) | $ / 30days |
|---|---|---|
| **Desmopressin** ☎,▼ DDAVP g B<br>0.1, 0.2mg tablets; -Metabolic agent<br>10ug intranasal spray pump & soln<br>Intranasal: NOT for primary nocturnal enuresis FDA & CND[69]<br>4ug/ml inj; DDAVP **Melt** 60,120,240ug tab ↑bioavail<br>(150ug intranasal soln hemophilia A/von Willebrand's) ☎⊗ | PNE: 0.1-0.2mg po 1-2hr pre hs; Max 0.6mg<br>20ug intranasally qhs initially,<br>titrate to 10-40ug qhs x 4-8 wk<br>Pediatric: >6 yr/o: 0.1-0.2mg qhs<br>{Intranasal: Not for 1° nocturnal enuresis; start 20ug; titrate 10-40ug qhs x4-8 wks} | 40-72<br><br>85<br><br>M: ISMP link |

- Antidiuretic: ↓H2O elimination. Used for: 1) **nocturnal enuresis/diuresis** where over 30% of urine occurs at night. 2) Central diabetes insipidus

**Efficacy**: Pediatric trial poorly designed: 30ug/night vs. imipramine 0.9mg/kg found 20 vs 37% wet nights[18]. Extreme caution in elderly! hyponatremia, trials lacking 18

**EDS SK**☎: for nocturia with recognized neurologic dx which causes DO confirmed by cystogram in absence of obstruction who have not responded/SE to at least 2 AC drugs; diabetes insipidus; enuresis in kids >5yr refractory to bed-wetting alarms or alternative formulary txs tabs (1.3 fewer wet nights/week vs placebo)121

**Serious SE**: water intoxication (fluid restriction 2hr before - 8hrs after tabs!!!): **hyponatremia** rapid; monitor lytes baseline, @72hr & periodically, **seizure**; ↑or↓BP, ↑HR; thrombotic dx

**CI**: hypersensitivity, CrCl<50 ml/min, acute illness-risk of electrolyte imbalance, CHF. **DI**: TCA, SSRI, alcohol: ↑hyponatremia risk; Li++, NSAID

ς=scored ✗=Non-formulary Sk ☎=Exception Drug Status SK ⊗=not covered NIHB ▼=covered NIHB ✆ prior approval NIHB **AC**=anticholinergic **GI**=stomach **NNH/NNT**=number needed to harm / treat **PNE**=Primary nocturnal enuresis **PVR**=post void residual **SE**=side effect **Sx**=syndrome

**Other Meds**: ephedrine & pseudoephedrine cardiac SE; propantheline, dicyclomine & flavoxate ↑SE; phenazopyridine urinary analgesic;?D/C: 200mg tid after meal, Belladonna & Opium supp ↓urethal spasm pain post-op & propiverine AC in Britian.[53], botox☎

Kavita Parihar SPEP Student, Brent Jensen BSP, Loren Regier BSP, BA www.RxFiles.ca May 10

## General Statements

- **Physicians are strongly advised** to check with **local public health** departments for current guidelines, advice & patient's immunization **record** (if available)!!! This document intended to highlight vaccine awareness. **Provincial policy & cost/coverage issues will impact use!!!**

**Links:** **Canadian**: Public Health Agency of Canada Immunizations & Vaccine Info: http://www.phac-aspc.gc.ca/im/index-eng.php
**Provincial-Links:** http://www.phac-aspc.gc.ca/im/ptimprog-progimpt/table-1-eng.php; **BC**: http://www.bccdc.org
{**American**: Adult Immunization Schedule 2010 Recommendations: http://www.cdc.gov/mmwr/preview/mmwrhtml/mm5901a5.htm?s_cid=mm5901a5_x}
**SK**: http://www.health.gov.sk.ca/immunization-**schedule**; http://www.health.gov.sk.ca/immunization-**manual**
**NACI:CIG Online** Canadian Guidelines: www.naci.gc.ca (BOOK); **Other**: http://immunize.cpha.ca/en/default.aspx; http://www.cdc.gov/vaccines/

## Common Myths / Misunderstandings

**Reactions**: http://www.phac-aspc.gc.ca/im/aefi-form_e.html

- Vaccines & autism. Best available evidence suggests that vaccines, including MMR & those containing thimerosal are not linked to the development of autism.[4,5,6] (Impossible to rule out risk completely. Thimerosal present in very few Canadian vaccinations.)
- Hepatitis B & Multiple Sclerosis: Current evidence suggests no link between HB vaccination & MS.[7]

## Precautions & Contraindications (Consult specific product monographs & guidelines!)

- Immunodeficiency: **Avoid** live vaccines (yellow fever, oral typhoid, rotavirus, varicella, MMR, FluMist, BCG, zoster).
- Pregnancy: **Avoid** use of live vaccines. Assess benefit/risk. (Those contraindicated in pregnancy may be given post.)
- Hypersensitivity: inquire regarding any previous reactions: thimerosal, egg, latex, preservatives

**Storage & the "Cold Chain"**: **Cold storage** & **transport** of vaccines is critical!!! (Direct, door-to-door from pharmacy to physician office for **same day appointment; transport in cool container** 2-8° C). See Q&A pg 2.

## Practice Pearls & Common Q&As {for more detail, see next *Extras* page (available online)}

**Considerations for Immigrants**[8]: Useful Links: http://www.immunize.org/izpractices/p5120.pdf ; http://www.immunize.org/izpractices/p5121.pdf

- Immigration medical examinations (IME's) do not routinely cover immunization status, tuberculosis or HB testing.
- Compare: age of immunization, number of doses & intervals between doses; may need additional vaccinations
- Other country vaccination schedule information: http://www.who.int/vaccines/GlobalSummary/Immunization/ScheduleSelect.cfm {Note: Developing countries: measles vaccine often given alone, without mumps & rubella. Vaccines in limited use include Haemophilus influenzae type b conjugate, hepatitis B, varicella, pneumococcal conjugate, meningococcal C conjugate.}
- When immune status uncertain, usually safe to give routine vaccinations (even if repeat) if no adverse reaction history & HIV **-ve**
- In temperate climates a higher proportion of varicella infections occur in adults. As such adolescents and adults from such countries may be susceptible to varicella, and require vaccination.
- Foreign born individuals from endemic areas may be more likely to be carriers of hepatitis B.
- HA immunity may be more prevalent in individuals from endemic countries. May test prior to vaccination.

**Considerations for Travel**: Links: http://www.travelhealth.gc.ca (Travel Medicine Program PHAC; travel clinic list); www.cdc.gov/travel ; www.who.int/ith

- Clients should consult/obtain current info from travel health clinics or public health agencies. (2-3months prior!)
- Ensure routine immunizations are up to date (poliomyelitis, HB, measles, rubella, Td, pertussis).
- May require: Meningococcal (MCV4), Yellow Fever, HA, Influenza, Japanese encephalitis, Typhoid, Cholera, TBE
- Accelerated **Hepatitis** Vaccine Schedule age >18: **Twinrix** (**HA+HB**): Reg Schedule: 0,1 & 6 months. Rapid schedule at 0,7,21 days, with 4th dose at 1yr. **Engerix-B** (**HB**): Reg Schedule: 0, 1, 6months or 0, 1, 2, 12months. Rapid schedule 0, 7, 21days, with 4th dose at 1 yr.
- Accelerated schedules: immunity starts to build after 1st dose, so useful even if completion is after return.

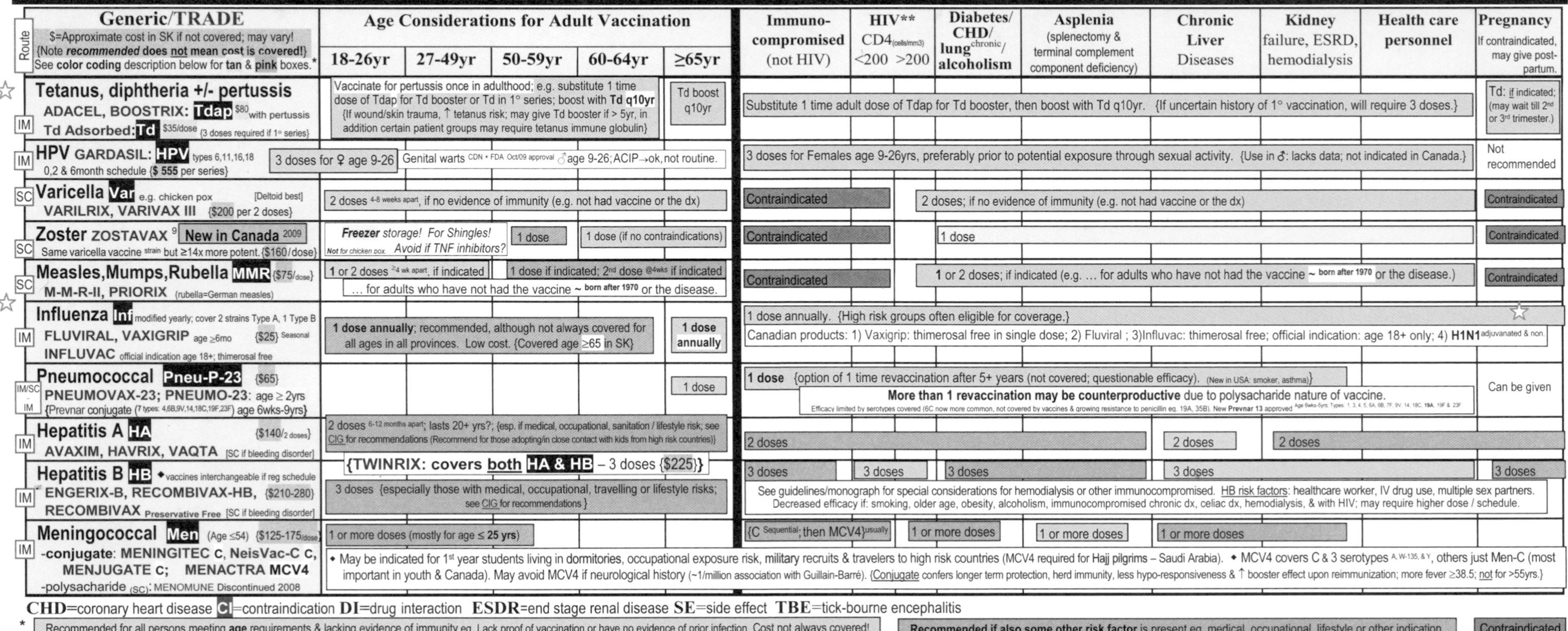

| Route | Generic/TRADE — $=Approximate cost in SK if not covered; may vary! {Note *recommended* does not mean cost is covered!} See color coding description below for tan & pink boxes.* | 18-26yr | 27-49yr | 50-59yr | 60-64yr | ≥65yr |
|---|---|---|---|---|---|---|
| IM | ☆ **Tetanus, diphtheria +/- pertussis** ADACEL, BOOSTRIX: **Tdap** $80 with pertussis; Td Adsorbed: **Td** $35/dose (3 doses required if 1° series) | Vaccinate for pertussis once in adulthood; e.g. substitute 1 time dose of Tdap for Td booster or Td in 1° series; boost with **Td q10yr** {If wound/skin trauma, ↑ tetanus risk; may give Td booster if > 5yr, in addition certain patient groups may require tetanus immune globulin} | | | | Td boost q10yr |
| IM | **HPV** GARDASIL: **HPV** types 6,11,16,18; 0,2 & 6month schedule {$ 555 per series} | 3 doses for ♀ age 9-26 | Genital warts CDN + FDA Oct/09 approval ♂ age 9-26; ACIP→ok, not routine. | | | |
| SC | **Varicella Var** e.g. chicken pox [Deltoid best]; VARILRIX, VARIVAX III {$200 per 2 doses} | 2 doses 4-8 weeks apart, if no evidence of immunity (e.g. not had vaccine or the dx) | | | | |
| SC | **Zoster** ZOSTAVAX [9] New in Canada 2009; Same varicella vaccine strain but ≥14x more potent. {$160/dose} | ***Freezer** storage! For Shingles!* Not for chicken pox. *Avoid if TNF inhibitors?* | | 1 dose | 1 dose (if no contraindications) | |
| SC | **Measles, Mumps, Rubella MMR** {$75/dose}; M-M-R-II, PRIORIX (rubella=German measles) | 1 or 2 doses ≥4 wk apart, if indicated … for adults who have not had the vaccine ~ born after 1970 or the disease. | | 1 dose if indicated; 2nd dose @4wks if indicated | | |
| IM | ☆ **Influenza Inf** modified yearly; cover 2 strains Type A, 1 Type B; FLUVIRAL, VAXIGRIP age ≥6mo {$25} Seasonal; INFLUVAC official indication age 18+; thimerosal free | **1 dose annually**; recommended, although not always covered for all ages in all provinces. Low cost. {Covered age ≥65 in SK} | | | | **1 dose annually** |
| IM/SC - IM | **Pneumococcal Pneu-P-23** {$65}; PNEUMOVAX-23; PNEUMO-23: age ≥ 2yrs; {Prevnar conjugate (7 types: 4,6B,9V,14,18C,19F,23F) age 6wks-9yrs} | | | | | 1 dose |
| IM | **Hepatitis A HA** {$140/2 doses}; AVAXIM, HAVRIX, VAQTA [SC if bleeding disorder] | 2 doses 6-12 months apart; lasts 20+ yrs?; {esp. if medical, occupational, sanitation / lifestyle risk; see CIG for recommendations (Recommend for those adopting/in close contact with kids from high risk countries)} | | | | |
| | {TWINRIX: covers both **HA & HB** – 3 doses {$225}} | | | | | |
| IM | **Hepatitis B HB** ◆vaccines interchangeable if reg schedule; ENGERIX-B, RECOMBIVAX-HB, {$210-280}; RECOMBIVAX Preservative Free [SC if bleeding disorder] | 3 doses {especially those with medical, occupational, travelling or lifestyle risks; see CIG for recommendations} | | | | |
| IM | **Meningococcal Men** (Age ≤54) {$125-175/dose}; -conjugate: MENINGITEC C, NeisVac-C C, MENJUGATE C; MENACTRA MCV4; -polysacharide (SC): MENOMUNE Discontinued 2008 | 1 or more doses (mostly for age ≤ 25 yrs) | | | | |

| Vaccine | Immuno-compromised (not HIV) | HIV** CD4 (cells/mm3) <200 | HIV** CD4 >200 | Diabetes/ CHD/ lung chronic/ alcoholism | Asplenia (splenectomy & terminal complement component deficiency) | Chronic Liver Diseases | Kidney failure, ESRD, hemodialysis | Health care personnel | Pregnancy (If contraindicated, may give post-partum.) |
|---|---|---|---|---|---|---|---|---|---|
| Tetanus, diphtheria +/- pertussis | Substitute 1 time adult dose of Tdap for Td booster, then boost with Td q10yr. {If uncertain history of 1° vaccination, will require 3 doses.} | | | | | | | | Td: if indicated; (may wait till 2nd or 3rd trimester.) |
| HPV | 3 doses for Females age 9-26yrs, preferably prior to potential exposure through sexual activity. {Use in ♂: lacks data; not indicated in Canada.} | | | | | | | | Not recommended |
| Varicella | Contraindicated | Contraindicated | 2 doses; if no evidence of immunity (e.g. not had vaccine or the dx) | | | | | | Contraindicated |
| Zoster | Contraindicated | Contraindicated | | 1 dose | | | | | Contraindicated |
| Measles, Mumps, Rubella | Contraindicated | Contraindicated | 1 or 2 doses; if indicated (e.g. … for adults who have not had the vaccine ~ born after 1970 or the disease.) | | | | | | Contraindicated |
| Influenza | 1 dose annually. {High risk groups often eligible for coverage.} Canadian products: 1) Vaxigrip: thimerosal free in single dose; 2) Fluviral ; 3)Influvac: thimerosal free; official indication: age 18+ only; 4) **H1N1** adjuvanated & non. | | | | | | | | |
| Pneumococcal | **1 dose** {option of 1 time revaccination after 5+ years (not covered; questionable efficacy). (New in USA: smoker, asthma)} **More than 1 revaccination may be counterproductive** due to polysacharide nature of vaccine. Efficacy limited by serotypes covered (6C now more common, not covered by vaccines & growing resistance to penicillin eg. 19A, 35B). New **Prevnar 13** approved Age 6wks-5yrs: Types: 1, 3, 4, 5, 6A, 6B, 7F, 9V, 14, 18C, **19A**, 19F & 23F | | | | | | | | Can be given |
| Hepatitis A | 2 doses | | | | | 2 doses | 2 doses | | |
| Hepatitis B | 3 doses | 3 doses | | 3 doses | | 3 doses | | | 3 doses |
| | See guidelines/monograph for special considerations for hemodialysis or other immunocompromised. HB risk factors: healthcare worker, IV drug use, multiple sex partners. Decreased efficacy if: smoking, older age, obesity, alcoholism, immunocompromised chronic dx, celiac dx, hemodialysis, & with HIV; may require higher dose / schedule. | | | | | | | | |
| Meningococcal | {C Sequential; then MCV4} usually | | 1 or more doses | | 1 or more doses | 1 or more doses | | | |

◆ May be indicated for 1st year students living in dormitories, occupational exposure risk, military recruits & travelers to high risk countries (MCV4 required for Hajj pilgrims – Saudi Arabia). ◆ MCV4 covers C & 3 serotypes A, W-135, & Y, others just Men-C (most important in youth & Canada). May avoid MCV4 if neurological history (~1/million association with Guillain-Barré). {Conjugate confers longer term protection, herd immunity, less hypo-responsiveness & ↑ booster effect upon reimmunization; more fever ≥38.5; not for >55yrs.}

**CHD**=coronary heart disease **CI**=contraindication **DI**=drug interaction **ESDR**=end stage renal disease **SE**=side effect **TBE**=tick-bourne encephalitis

* Recommended for all persons meeting **age requirements** & lacking evidence of immunity eg. Lack proof of vaccination or have no evidence of prior infection. Cost not always covered! | **Recommended if also some other risk factor** is present eg. medical, occupational, lifestyle or other indication. | Contraindicated

** HIV Considerations: 1) Before immunizing an HIV positive person, consult an ID specialist or Medical Health Officer. 2) HB may not be necessary in all HIV patients, although may be given routinely due to rapid progression if exposed.

**OTHER:** YF-VAX: Yellow Fever $140; IMOVAX-Rabies, RabAvert: Rabies $700/3 doses; Rabies Immune Globulin (acute exposure; give within 24hrs or up to 7 days after 1st dose of rabies vaccine); TYPHIM-VI, TYPHERIX: Typhoid IM $70; VIVOTIF: Typhoid oral; VIVAXIM: HA & Typhoid HA-Typh-I; JE-VAX/Ixiaro: Japanese Encephalitis $615/series; DUKORAL: oral for select cholera strains $130-195/series; Polio $80; Haemophilus influenzae type b **Hib**: not generally for age ≥5yr, may consider in sickle cell dx, leukemia, HIV, splenectomy pt. [Canada Feb/10, FDA Oct/09: **CERVARIX** ASO4: HPV types 16, 18; ♀ age 10-25.]

**Passive Agents:** Antitoxin: botulism & diphtheria; Immuglobulin: human, HB, rabies, RSV, tetanus & varicella; Antivenom: snake & spider. **Some Peds Products:** INFANRIX HEXA: 6wk – 2yrs diphtheria, tetanus, pertusis, HB, polio, Hib; RotaTeq: for infants rotavirus 5 types

**VACCINES ROUTINELY GIVEN to MOST KIDS in Canada:** between age 0month – 18year: tetanus, diphtheria, pertussis, polio, measles, mumps, rubella, HPV, varicella, pneumococcal PCV7, influenza, hepatitis B, meningococcal, & Hib.

## Onychomycosis [8,9]

**Key signs**: nail thickening, discoloration, & separation from nail bed.[10,11,12,13] **Culture to confirm** prior to tx. (**Clip, scrape & deep nail sample** to avoid false negatives.) **Cause**: toenail→commonly dermatophytes; fingernail→may be yeast[14] [**yeast** i.e. candida; **dermatophyte**=filamentous fungi]
Pearls: uncommon to have finger without toenail involvement; file & mark margin of fungus on nail at completion of tx to monitor success!

**Risk factors:** ↑ prevalence with ↑ age (15-20% in pts ≥ 40 yrs); swimming, barefoot, tinea pedis, diabetes, immunodeficiency, living with an infected family member [15,16]

**Tx**: ◆**Oral terbinafine** or itraconazole: **x12-16wks** toe; success:50-80%; relapse: ~25-30%[17]; topical terbinafine weekly to prevent relapse?
{Effectiveness: terbinafine > itraconazole >> fluconazole if unable to tolerate other tx; consider cost, success rate, SE risk}[18]
- Itraconazole pulse tx less $$ & SE, but requires scheduling; however terbinafine pulse treatment lower cure rate than daily dose[19]
- Topical: Nail lacquer in mild, distal dx, minimal penetration; combo with po no added benefit

**Prevention**: tx tinea pedis; wear sandals/slippers in communal areas bathing places, locker rooms, gyms, mosque
- Home remedies eg. Vicks VapoRub, vinegar no proven tx benefit. Tea tree oil: little evidence for benefit[20]; allergy.

## Common Fungal Skin Infections [36,37,38]

**Causes**: Candida, epidermophyton, trichophyton, microsporum **Risk factors:** animal exposure (eg. vets, vet techs), skin trauma (eg. wrestlers), diabetes, immunodeficiency, ↓ circulation, poor hygiene, warm/humid climate.

**General tx info:** Apply antifungal to **affected & surrounding area** (**1-2 inches beyond rash**).
- Continue x **1wk after** sx's gone & skin looks healed to ensure eradication (often ~10-14 days).
- Keep area clean & dry (use non-scented talc or powder baby powder, Goldbond, tolnaftate as prophylaxis).
- Nystatin not useful for dermatophyte infections; effective for candidal infections.
- Oral tx: nail, scalp Kerion: inflammed purulent mass, from livestock,? add prednisone, beard, severe/widespread or if recurrent.
- Combination with **steroids not usually recommended** due to ↑ SE, cost & ↓ cure rates.

**Prevention:** Avoid sharing personal items & towels. Avoid wearing tight or occlusive clothing. Wash linens & clothing in hot water & hot dryer or line dry & expose to UV rays; disinfect shoes.

i) **Seborrheic dermatitis**[30] Commensal overgrowth of yeast. Topical/shampoo azoles & ciclopirox olamine useful. Intermittent shampoo use once weekly or every other week after tx may ↑remission. {limited comparison data}

ii) **Tinea capitis (Scalp)**: **Common in kids** cats, cows; oral terbinafine DOC x 4-**8**wks +/- selenium sulfide shampoo 2-3x per wk (x5mins) to ↓ spread. Other options: oral fluconazole, itraconazole, (griseofulvin).

iii) **Tinea corporis (Body)**: Tx options: topical azoles (clotrimazole, miconazole) & terbinafine. Consider topical azoles first, terbinafine slightly more effective/rapid but ↑ cost. Tx: x2-**4** wks.

iv) **Tinea Cruris (Groin)**: Common in adolescent & young adult ♂; if wear tight jean/pantyhose. Overdiagnosed? **Tx**: Topical azole clotrimazole, miconazole x 2-4wk or terbinafine cream/ spray daily x 2-**4**wk. Assess for tinea pedis.

v) **Tinea pedis (Foot)**: **Tx** Effective: terbinafine > azole (clotrimazole, miconazole) > tolnaftate; consider cost & dosing schedule[31]. **Treat topically x 4wks.** {Common: elderly⇨dry cracked skin; adolescent⇨between toes.}

vi) **Tinea Pityriasis versicolor**:[32,33] Commensal overgrowth of Malassezia yeast. Use topical antifungals 1st mild dx. Apply azole to whole affected area (ie. chest) every day x 1wk, then q. weekly for prophylaxis). If severe/recurrent consider **short-term** 1-5 days po (keto-, flu-, itra-conazole (↑ SE). Oral terbinafine ineffective[34]. Suggest selenium sulfide 2.5% or **ketoconazole** 2% **shampoo** ↓ recurrence weekly or 1-2x /month x 40+ yrs (ie. long-term)

**Candidal Intertrigo**[35]: Common in moist skin folds (especially in obese, ostomy, etc.); results in tender, burning, pruritic areas with satellite lesions; **Tx:** consider nystatin **powder**, topical antifungals

## Oral Candidiasis [21,22]

**Key Signs:** Pseudomembranous form: white plaques on oral mucosa; atrophic form: erythema without plaque (common in elderly with dentures denture stomatitis). Angular cheilitis may be present.

**Causes:** commonly *Candida albicans* **Risk factors:** smoking, poor dental hygiene, inhaled or systemic **steroid use**, antibiotics, diabetes, immunodeficiency (HIV?), ↓ saliva

**Tx:** ◆***Mild dx***: Topical nystatin or oral fluconazole effective x **7days** minimum (or 2+days after improved.)
- ***Dentures***: disinfect chlorhexidine rinse ~20-30min & tx with topical antifungal to mucosa & denture base[23].
- ***Refractory, recurrent or esophageal*** infections need systemic azoles fluconazole; topical tx ineffective. May indicate compromised immune system; consider referral to ID (? HIV).

**Prevention:** If on inhaled steroid, use aerochamber, rinse mouth & spit after each use. Dentures: daily cleaning recommended (chlorhexidine useful, rinse well)[24]; +/- nystatin but not at same time

**Infant**: ◆ Nystatin safe, ↓cost but ↓effective → poor oral adherence & QID. comparison data limited [25,26]
- Fluconazole more effective, once daily dosing but ↑ cost; not officially approved in newborns.
- Gentian violet 0.5-1% aqueous soln BID effective, but longer tx period, messy, & associated with ulceration.[27,28]
- Breastfeeding infant: consider topical tx of nipple[29] (eg. clotrimazole, miconazole, nystatin) lack safety data

## Vulvovaginal Candidiasis [39]

**Key signs**: pruritus, soreness, dyspareunia, external dysuria; possibly thick & curdy discharge

**Causes:** *Candida albicans*, occasionally non-albicans; associated with antibiotic use; rule out UTI/STI

**Tx:** Topical azoles (see table) or oral fluconazole. Oral route often preferred by pts; consider cost.[40] {Cochrane: no difference in effectiveness of fluconazole oral vs intra-vaginal OTC routes}
- 1-3days topical as effective as 6-7days with better compliance. **Allow ~3 days** for sx resolution.
- **Recurrent** cases (≥4/yr) may benefit by addressing risk factors uncontrolled diabetes, high dose estrogen OC (?HIV); try: 1) longer initial course of topical (7-14days) then clotrimazole 200mg pv 2x weekly or 500mg Supp pv wkly x 6mon; or 2) fluconazole 150mg q72h x 3doses[41] then 150mg po wkly x 6 mon. Treat male partner?: controversial, but may benefit if *Candida balanitis* present.; tx-topical azole BID x 1 week[42,43,44]
- **Complicated** vaginitis~10% : ≥7days topical tx or fluconazole 150mg q72hr for 3 doses-IDSA guidelines
- **Pregnancy**: require longer tx interval (**7 days azoles** topical; 14 days nystatin; 1 day fluconazole po) topical azole (clotrimazole, miconazole) more effective & convenient than nystatin; tx topical 1st line systemic absorption low; ↓ risk of birth defects[45]; oral fluconazole 2nd line Avoid 1st trimester & ≥ 400mg daily as teratogenic.
- Topical boric acid 600mg cap PV hs x2wks an option if *C. glabrata* (rare); compounded not commercially available[46]
- Dietary yogurt with live culture or Lactobacilli oral cap: NOT prevent post-antibiotic vulvovaginitis, but may help restore normal flora[47] {Vaginal yogurt, homeopathy Yeast Gard, Azo Yeast: controversial}
- topical vaginal tx containing mineral or vegetable oil {e.g. miconazole vaginal ovules problem} may ↓ effectiveness of **condoms**, or other vaginal contraceptive devices (eg. **diaphragms**) during treatment & up to 3 days post-tx[48] {Okay: clotrimazole products & miconazole cream.}

## Diaper Rash [49]

- Apply antifungal underneath barrier cream until rash is resolved.
  ⇨Topical nystatin, clotrimazole, miconazole, or ketoconazole if rash candidal or >3 days.
- Combo topical corticosteroid/antifungal products not routinely recommended as may result in dilution,↑ SE & mask Sx of infection. eg. Viaderm-KC, Kenacomb If necessary: use only **low**-potency, short-term corticosteroid!!! Best to apply creams separately allowing a few minutes between applications. {Alternately, add hydrocortisone powder 1% to azole cream. See also OTC dermatology section.}

| Antifungals: Topicals & Vaginal: therapeutic use ⇨ ⇨ ⇨ ⇨ ⇨ | Tinea pedis/cruris/corporis |
|---|---|
| **Ciclopirox** olamine LOPROX Pr 1% top crm ⊗ (45gm); 1% top lotion ⊗ (60ml)<br>PENLAC Pr 8% Nail lacquer x ⊗; STIEPROX Pr 1.5% Shampoo x ⊗ (100ml) | Apply bid x 2-**4** weeks |
| **Clotrimazole** CANESTEN OTC 1% top crm ▼ (15,30 & 500gm); 200,500mg **vag tab**; 1, 2 & 10% **vag crm**<br>Generic OTC 1% top crm ▼ (20,30,50 & 500gm); 1, 2% **vag cream** [higher % for shorter term tx] | Apply bid x 2-**4** weeks |
| **Ketoconazole** Generic(Pr) 2% top crm ▼ (30gm) NIZORAL OTC 2% Shampoo x ▼ (60,120ml) | Apply once daily x 2-**4** wk (x 6wks tinea pedis) |
| **Miconazole** MONISTAT-DERM OTC 2% top crm ▼ (15,30gm)<br>MONISTAT, Generic OTC 100, 400,1200mg **vag ovules**; 2, 4% **vag cream**; | Apply bid x 2-**4** weeks |
| **Nystatin** MYCOSTATIN, Generic 100,000 U/G top crm & oint ▼ {bulk powder available for compounding topical powder}<br>OTC (15,30 & 450gm); 25,000 & 100,000 U/G **vag cream** Pr ▼ | **Nystatin NOT effective for dermatophytes!** |
| **Terbinafine** LAMISIL Pr 1% crm ▼ (15,30gm); 1% top **spray** soln ⊗ (30ml) | Apply daily x 2-**4**wk (x 1-2wk mild tinea pedis) |
| **Tolnaftate** TINACTIN x,▼ OTC 1% top crm; powder; soln; top **spray**<br>Others(Undecylenic acid-Desenex / Fungicure, Tolnaftate-Dr. Scholl's OTC products): less data, less effective | Apply bid x 2-4wks |

**Comments:**
- **Cost Considerations:**
  - terbinafine more expensive but more rapid effect ∴azoles generally used first; consider amount of product required, dosing schedule & length of tx
  - Cost/30gm tube:
    - clotrimazole $12-15;
    - miconazole $12-15;
    - terbinafine $20-25
- Consider **oral tx** if widespread, recurrent or failure with topical tx
- **Creams or spray soln preferred** over powders, except in skin folds.

| Vaginal candidiasis All OTC | Cost |
|---|---|
| CANESTEN 1 Combi Pak 500mg pv / 1%crm ▼ or Cream 10% ⊗ x 1 day,<br>CANESTEN 3 Combi Pak 200mg pv / 1%crm ▼ or Cream 2% ▼ x 3 days,<br>CANESTEN 6 Cream 1% ▼ x 6 days. | $14-18 |
| MONISTAT 1 Vag Ovule 1200mg ⊗ x1 day or Combi Pak 1200mg/2%crm ⊗ x1day,<br>MONISTAT 3 Dual Pak 400mg pv / 2%crm ▼ or Vag Ovule 400mg ▼ or Vag Cream 4% x, ⊗ x3 day,<br>MONISTAT 7 Dual Pak 100mg pv / 2%crm ▼ or Vag crm 2% ▼ x 7day. | $16-20 |
| TERAZOL 3 Supp 80mg x, ▼ or Dual Pak 80mg pv / 0.8% crm ▼ or Vag crm 0.8% x3day<br>TERAZOL 7 0.4% crm ▼ x 7 day. | $20-30 |
| CanesOral fluconazole 150mg po; & CombiPAK | $25-33 |

**AZOLE antifungals**: Topical: butocon-, clotrim-, ketocon-, micon-, tercon-azole. Oral: fluconazole, itraconazole, ketoconazole, posaconazole, voriconazole. IV: fluconazole, voriconazole. **Fungal infection: *ask yourself why*** - ? risk factors, ? immune suppression, ? HIV.

| Generic/TRADE<br>(Strength & forms) g=generic | P<br>50 | Side effects / Contraindications CI<br>Cautions | √ = therapeutic use / Comments /<br>Drug Interactions DI (not exhaustive)[51]/ Monitor M | INITIAL; MAX /USUAL DOSE<br>{Drug of Choice highlighted in brown.} | $<br>/course |
|---|---|---|---|---|---|
| **Terbinafine** HCL ▼g<br>**Lamisil**<br>250mg tab ς<br>**(Susp 25mg/ml compounded by some pharmacies)** | B | **Common**: PO: headache, GI diarrhea, dyspepsia, abdominal pain, taste disturbance may persist after tx stopped, rash mild<br>**Serious**: (≥0.01% to 0.1%) ↑AST & ALT or hepatotoxicity, (≤0.01%) SJS, toxic epidermal necrosis, erythema multiforme, pancytopenia, neutropenia<br>**Precaution: liver**/kidney disease, lupus erythematosus | √ Onychomycosis & skin infections due to dermatophytes<br>Tx severe tinea corporis, cruris, pedis unresponsive to topicals<br>DI: **CYP2D6** inhibitor: ↑effect of: TCA ↑TCA level, Possible: Beta blockers & Antipsychotics<br>↓level of terbinafine: rifampin.<br>M: LFT's at baseline & at 4-6 wks of tx [52] | **Onychomycosis**: 250mg po daily<br>(**Fingernail**: x 6wks; **Toenail**: x12-16 wks)<br>**Tinea capitis**: 250mg po once daily x 4-**8**wk<br>Pediatric dosing: (e.g. Tinea capitis x4wk)<br><20kg: 62.5mg/day po, 20-40kg: 125mg/day po, >40kg: 250mg/day po [53] | 108/6wks<br>225/12wk<br>41-75/<br>2-4wks |
| **Fluconazole** g<br>**Diflucan**<br>(50, 100mg tab) ▼ ☎ ;<br>150mg cap▼, regular benefit SK formulary<br>[CanesOral: new OTC formulation of fluconazole 150mg tab +/- clotrimazole 1% vag cream]<br>10mg/ml powder for oral suspension (P.O.S.) **Diflucan**<br>IV soln 200mg/100ml vial, 400mg/200ml vial | C | **Common**: well tolerated; headaches, GI upset, rash<br>**Serious**: Stevens-Johnson syndrome(SJS), hepatotoxicity, QT prolongation<br>CI: cisapride: ↑↑ drug level cause ↑QT & torsades des pointes; ergot alkaloids : ↑↑ ergot levels<br>**Cautions**:<br>-High dose≥ 400mg/d in pregnancy & 1st trimester.<br>-Pts on rifampin, phenytoin, valproic acid, isoniazid & po sulfonylureas may be at ↑ hepatic risk.<br>Thrush in Newborns: NOT officially indicated but is an off-label, more effective alternative to nystatin.<br>- Full-term (37-44 wk GA) & 0-14 days: 3mg/kg q48h<br>- Full-term (37-44wk GA) & >14 days: 3mg/kg q24h[54]<br>Dose varies on site &/or severity of infection | √ Active against most *Candida* species except *C.krusei* & some *C. glabrata*, *Coccidioides*, *Histoplasma*, *Cryptococcus* sp. in high doses<br>Consider for oropharyngeal, esophageal or vaginal candidiasis<br>DI: ↓ fluconazole level: rifampin. [Less DI's than azoles in general.]<br>Moderate CYP3A4 inhibitor: ↑level of alfentanil, carbamazepine, cyclosporine, midazolam, quinidine, rifabutin, statins, tacrolimus,& triazolam.<br>Strong **CYP 2C9,2C19** inhibitor: ↑level of ergot alkaloid, glimepiride, nevirapine, phenytoin, warfarin, zidovudine.<br>Prolong QT interval: amiodarone, cisapride, clarithromycin, TCA's<br>Renal dx: **no** adjustment needed for single-dose vaginal candidiasis<br>M: liver enzymes, renal function; baseline & periodically if risk factors/long-term tx<br>Comments: • Bioavailability of PO similar to IV; use PO if possible<br>• ↓ DI due to ↑ renal excretion~80% & ↓ hepatic metabolism effect<br>• Compatible with breastfeeding<br>• May require dose ↑ if obese with severe/systemic infection | Dose range:100-800mg /day.<br>Pediatric: 3mg/kg/day-12mg/kg/day. (≤ adult dose.)<br>**Onychomycosis**: 150mg po once weekly<br>(**Fingernail**: x 3mos; **Toenail**: x 6-12mos) [55]<br>(3rd line adults; useful if ++DI's, peds pts)<br>**Oropharyngeal** candidiasis: Load: 200mg po x1 →100mg po daily x 7 day<br>(Peds: Load 6mg/kg→ 3mg/kg/day x 14day)<br>**Esophageal** candidiasis: 200-400mg od x 2-3wk<br>**Tinea versicolor**: 400mg po x 1 dose<br>**Vulvovaginitis** candidal:150mg po once OTC<br>**Candidemia** neutropenic & non-neutropenic:<br>Load day 1:800mg→400mg daily until 14day post-signs/sx & after last +ve blood culture ; obese patients: consider 6-12mg/kg IDSA (56) | (renal)<br>141/3mos<br>282/6mos<br>64 /wk<br>178-349 /2 wks<br>32<br>17<br>178/wk |
| **Itraconazole** ▼ ☎<br>**Sporanox**<br>100mg cap<br>[Give cap with food acidic PH ↑ absorption; In past, was often given with cola.]<br>10mg/ml solution<br>-soln more bioavailable than cap[57]; solution prefered for oral/esophageal candidiasis. [Take on empty stomach]<br>**Dosage forms NOT interchangeable** | C | **Common**: dose-related nausea, diarrhea, abdominal discomfort, rash, edema, hypokalemia , ↑ transaminases, & dizziness<br>**Serious**: SJS, hepatotoxicity failure, HF dose related negative inotropic effect at 400mg/d<br>CI: pts with ventricular dysfunction or HF; pts on negative inotropics or erythromycin; pts using drugs metabolized by CYP 3A4 (ie. cisapride, dofetilide, eletriptan, ergot alkaloids, lovastatin, midazolam, nisoldipine, pimozide, quinidine, simvastatin, triazolam);<br>: pregnant women<br>**Caution**: hepatic dysfunction, pts at risk for arrhythmias<br>[See note at bottom for "Hepatic Risk" comment.] | √ Broader spectrum of activity than fluconazole: including *Candida* spp., *Cryptococcus neoformans*, *Aspergillus* spp., *Blastomyces dermatitidis*, *Coccidioides immitis*, *Histoplasma capsulatum*, & dermatophytes.<br>Consider for fluconazole resistant mucosal candidiasis<br>DI: Strong **CYP3A4** inhibitor: ↑ level of: amio-/drone-darone, astemizole, atorvastatin some, buspirone, CCB nifedipine, nisoldipine, felodipine, cisapride, cyclosporine, digoxin, dofetilide, eletriptan, ergot alkaloids, fentanyl, indinavir, lovastatin, midazolam, pimozide, quinidine, ritonavir, saquinavir, simvastatin, sirolimus, steroids ↑ level: budesonide, dexamethasone, fluticasone, methylprednisolone , tacrolimus, triazolam & vincristine.<br>↑ itraconazole level: indinavir, ritonavir<br>↓ itraconazole level: antacids, H2 receptor blockers, PPI due to ↓ acidity; carbamazepine, efavirenz, grapefruit juice, nevirapine, phenytoin, rifampin, rifabutin<br>↓ levels of oral contraceptives. ↑ level of: warfarin<br>M: liver enzymes (every month if on long-term tx ie >1month)<br>Comments: • most DI's, ↑ toxicity compared to other azoles | Dose range:100-400mg/day<br>**Onychomycosis** (if terbinafine contraindicated)<br>Toenail: 200mg po daily x12wks or "pulse" tx: 200mg po BID x 1wk (3wks off & rpt 1wk x 2 cycles)<br>Fingernail: 200mg po daily x 6wks or "pulse" tx: 200mg BID x 1 wk (3wks off & rpt x 1wk)<br>**Oropharyngeal** candidiasis: if fluconazole resistant 200mg po once daily of soln x 14 days<br>**Esophageal** candidiasis: if fluconazole-resistant 200mg po daily of soln x 14-21 days<br>**Tinea versicolor**: 200mg po daily x 5-7 days (pityriasis versicolor) or 400mg x 1 dose [58,59]<br>*Caps less expensive (~half the cost) but less bioavailable; solution used for pricing of oral/esophageal candidiasis only.* | 822 /12wks<br>408/6wks<br>(daily dose)<br>423/3mos<br>282/2mos<br>(pulse tx)<br>283/<br>14days<br>55/5days-<br>74/7days<br>26/single dose |
| **Nystatin** ▼g<br>500,000 unit tab po<br>100,000 units/ml susp | A<br>C | **Common**: well-tolerated; nausea, vomiting, diarrhea at high doses<br>**Caution**: contains sucrose; may ↑ risk for dental caries | √ Fungi-static & cidal; may be used for candidal skin infections, Oropharyngeal & vulvovaginal candidiasis; for topical skin & vaginal candidal infections during **pregnancy**<br>• slightly less effective for most conditions but safe, inexpensive | Children & adults: {liquid; swish & swallow!}<br>**Thrush** (mild): 500,000units (5ml) qid **x 7days or 2days after** improvement.<br>Pediatric: [may use 0.5ml & swab for infants]<br>Infants⇨thrush: 100,000-200,000 units qid | 15<br>/ 7days |

(renal symbol) =↓ dose for renal dysfunction ς=scored tab χ=Non-formulary SK ☎=Exception Drug Status SK ⊗=not covered by NIHB ▼=covered by NIHB ⊘=prior NIHB approval **CCB**=calcium channel blocker CI=contraindication **crm**=cream **DI**=drug interaction **DOC**=drug of choice **Dx**=disease **fx**=function **g**=generic avail. **GA**=gestational age **GI**=gastrointestinal **HF**=heart failure **LFT**=liver function tests **n/v**=nausea/vomiting **OC**=oral contraceptive **OTC**=over the counter **pc**=after meals **po**=oral **PPI**=proton pump inhibitor **Pr**=prescription **Pt**=patient **pv**=per vagina **SAP**=special access program **SE**=side effect **SJS**=Stevens-Johnson syndrome **STI**=sexually transmitted infection **Sx**=symptoms **TCA**=tricyclic antidepressant **Tx**=treatment **UTI**=urinary tract infection **vag**=vaginal **wt**=weight

When choosing drug keep in mind: frequency of dosing, dosing with regards to food, & organism coverage.

**Comments**: When not to use fluconazole: positive fungal urine cultures without symptoms, systemic candidiasis, or an impending genitourinary tract procedure; positive sputum cultures.

**Special Considerations**: **Hepatic Risk**: Overall incidence <2% for all; for oral tx of onychomycosis treatment: ketoconazole>itraconazole>terbinafine. Pulse treatment may reduce risk, but less effective for terbinafine.

**Useful links**: www.dermnet.com www.RxFiles.ca **See page 53** (book or online) **for**: voriconazole VFEND, posaconazole SPRIAFIL, POSANOL, ketoconazole , echinocandins CANCIDAS, MYCAMINE, ERAXIS, amphotericin B.FUNGIZONE, ABELCET, AMBISOME

**Other drugs**: flucytosine SAP – add-on po tx of Candida endocarditis/meningitis with Amphotericin B. •griseofulvin FULVICIN: not available in Canada but bulk supply available for compounding; is available in some areas of the world; especially useful in T. capitis; newer options available for tinea infection. •butoconazole – 2% vag crm available, more expensive, no advantages over other indicated treatment for vaginal candidiasis; contains mineral oil: caution with condoms, diaphragms.

**Investigational Drugs**: Ravuconazole, Isavuconazole invasive aspergillosis & candidiasis, Pramiconazole & Albaconazole onychomycosis.

**Acknowledgements**: Contributors & Reviewers: Dr. P. Hull (MD, Dermatology, Saskatoon) Dr. D. Lichtenwald (MD, Dermatology, Saskatoon); Y. Shevchuk (PharmD, C of Pharmacy, U of S, Saskatoon); S. Sanche (MD, Infectious Diseases - Internal Med, Saskatoon), S. Skinner (MD, Infectious Diseases - Internal Med, Saskatoon), B.Tan (MD, SHR-Ped ID), M Jin (Pharm D, Hamilton), A Bhalla (Pharm D, Ontario) & the RxFiles Advisory Committee. Prepared by: *Shannon Stone* BSP; *Brent Jensen* BSP, *Loren Regier* BSP BA

| Drug | Preg. | Adverse Effects | Spectrum / Drug Interactions / Monitoring / Comments | Dosing | $ |
|---|---|---|---|---|---|
| **Ketoconazole** ▼ ☎<br>**Nizoral**<br>200mg tab<br><br>(see topicals section above for topical, shampoo) | C | **Common**: poorly tolerated; anorexia, nausea, vomiting high doses; pruritus, rash dizziness, ↓ testosterone level: gynecomastia, ↓ libido & loss of potency in ♂, menstrual irregularities in ♀<br>**Serious**: ↓steroidogenesis adrenal & ↓cortisol; hepatotoxic<br>**CI**: astemizole, cisapride, triazolam | √ Rarely used orally<br>**DI**: similar to itraconazole (see above)<br>Strong **CYP3A4** inhibitor: ↑ level of amio-/drone-darone, cyclosporine, digoxin potential, ergot alkaloid, lovastatin, pimozide, quinidine, rifabutin, simvastatin, tacrolimus, (similar to itraconazole)<br>**M**: liver transaminases<br>Comment: ◆With food & at bedtime to ↓SE ◆ breastfeeding compatible | 200; 400mg<br>200-400mg once daily at bedtime<br>Pediatrics ≥ 2 yrs:<br>3.3-6.6mg/kg/day po once daily<br>**Tinea versicolor** [60,61] (pityriasis versicolor): 400mg x 1 dose or 200mg daily x 5-7 days | 10 /400mg dose<br><br>15-17/ 5days |
| **Voriconazole** ✆ ☎<br>**Vfend**<br><br>50, 200mg tab;<br>(Good oral absorption)[62]<br>(Take on empty stomach)<br><br>IV 200mg/vial {if ↓ renal fx, give po}<br><br>Relatively new drug; often requiring Infectious Disease Service consult! | D | **Common**: rash ~7%, photosensitivity, confusion, hallucinations, ↑ transaminases, transient visual disturbances ~20+ % including blurred vision, photophobia, & altered perception of color/image {may resolve early; avoid night-time driving}<br>**Serious**: SJS rare, hepatotoxicity<br>**CI**: astemizole, barbiturates, carbamazepine, cisapride, efavirenz, ergot alkaloids, pimozide, quinidine, rifabutin, rifampin, high dose ritonavir >400mg BID, sirolimus, St. John's wort & terfenadine.<br>D: pregnant women<br>**Caution:** hepatic dysfunction, pts at risk for arrythmias | √ Similar spectrum to itraconazole;<br>More active: *Aspergillus* spp & *Candida* *glabrata & krusei*, *Fusarium*<br>**DI**: ↓ levels of voriconazole: barbiturates, carbamazepine, efavirenz, phenobarbital, phenytoin, rifampin, rifabutin, ritonavir, & St John's wort.<br>Moderate **CYP3A4** inhibitor ↑ levels of: alfentanil, amio-/drone-darone , cisapride, cyclosporine, efavirenz, methadone, midazolam po (& higher iv dose), omeprazole, sirolimus, tacrolimus, triazolam & vincistine<br>Strong **CYP 2C9**, weak **2C19** inhibitor ↑ levels of: methadone, warfarin<br>Liver dx: Initial loading dose, but half maintenance dose if liver cirrhotic<br>Renal dx: if CrCl<50 ml/min-use only po formulation solubilizing agent can accumulate<br>**M**: liver enzymes; serum level monitoring for serious infections only<br>Comments: ◆ DOC-invasive aspergillosis [63] ◆ serum levels may vary [64]<br>◆ poor CYP2C19 metabolizers (ie Asian ~20-30%) [65] -↑drug level | Dose range: 200-600mg/day<br><br>**Aspergillosis**:<br>6mg/kg q12h x 1day → then 4mg/kg<br>or: if >40kg ⇨ 200-300mg po q12h<br>If <40kg ⇨ 100-150mg po q12h<br>Adjust dose based on levels if not responding.<br>{Above dosing higher then previously recommended (200mg po q12h >40kg)}<br>**Oropharyngeal**: if fluconazole resisitant<br>200mg po bid x 14-21day<br>**Esophageal** candidiasis: if fluconazole-resistant<br>200mg po bid x 14-21day | 148 /200mg vial<br><br>1,515-2,270 /14-21 days |
| **Posaconazole** [66] χ ⊗<br>**Posanol** Spirafil<br><br>40mg/ml suspension (cherry flavored)<br>(Take with **high-fat** meal or meal replacement to ↑ absorption)<br><br>Relatively new drug; often requiring Infectious Disease Service consult! | C | **Common**: fairly well-tolerated; diarrhea, nausea ~6%, vomiting, headache ~6%, hypokalemia ↑transaminases similar to fluconazole<br>**Serious**: hepatic necrosis, QT prolongation & arrhythmias<br>**CI**: ↑level of astemizole, cisapride, ergot alkaloid, pimozide, quinidine, sirolimus, terfenadine<br>: pregnant women<br>**Caution:** hepatic dysfunction, pts at risk for arrythmias | √ Similar spectrum to itraconazole with activity against Zygomycetes (alternative to amphotericin B), *Cryptococcus*, *Aspergillus*; refractory oropharyngeal/esophageal candidiasis; prophylaxis of Aspergillus & Candida infection in neutropenics & stem cell transplant recipients; option for prophylaxis & tx of invasive fungal dx (broad spectrum; potentially less resistance)<br>**DI**: Moderate-strong **CYP3A4** inhibitor [67]: ↑level of amio-/drone-darone theoretical, atazanavir, cyclosporine, digoxin potential, midazolam[68], rifabutin, sirolimus, tacrolimus, terfenadine, triazolam & vincristine<br>↓ levels of posaconazole: cimetidine, efavirenz, phenytoin, rifabutin.<br>**M**: liver enzymes; electrolytes ($K^+$, $Mg^{++}$, $Ca^{++}$)<br>Comments: ◆ **Less DI's**; metabolized by glucuronidation | **Consult with Infectious Disease Specialist/Service for Posaconazole use!**<br>Dose range:100-800mg/day {Pts > 13yrs}<br>**Oropharyngeal** candidiasis:<br>Load: Day 1: 100mg bid→100mg od x 13day<br>Fluconazole-refractory oropharyngeal dx:<br>400mg po BID x3d → 400mg daily x 4wk IDSA [69]<br>**Esophageal, fluconazole refractory**:<br>400mg po BID x 14-21 day;<br>**Prophylaxis** of invasive infection:200mg tid - duration based on neutropenia/ immunosuppression recovery<br>**Tx invasive** aspergillosis: 200mg po qid then 400mg bid if stable {If no food 200mg qid} | 410 /14 d<br>3,659 /4wks<br>3,015-4,519/ 400mg BIDx14-21days |
| Echinocandins - **IV**:<br>**Caspofungin acetate** C<br>**Cancidas** 50, 70mg vial<br><br>**Micafungin sodium** M<br>**Mycamine** 50mg vial<br><br>**Anidulafungin** A<br>**Eraxis** 100mg vial<br><br>Broad spectrum; often requiring Infectious Disease Service consult! | C | **Common**: well tolerated!<br>C: fever, phlebitis infusion site, ↑ALT & AST, histamine-like effects: rash , pruritus, facial swelling<br>M: nausea, vomiting, ↑ALT, AST & ALP<br>A: diarrhea & hypokalemia, ↑ALT<br>**Serious:**<br>C: hepatotoxicity<br>M: anaphylaxis rare, febrile neutropenia, hepatic abnormalities, renal insufficiency, hemolytic anemia<br>A: anaphylaxis, hepatic abnormalities, DVT, low BP & flushing (minimize with infusion rate<1.1mg/min) | √ Active: most *Candida* spp(incl. azole-resistant), *Aspergillus* spp;<br>C: invasive & esophageal candidiasis; invasive Aspergillosis refractory/intolerant<br>M: esophageal candidiasis & prevent stem cell transplant invasive candidiasis;<br>A: esophageal candidiasis & candidemia<br>**DI**: ↓ levels of caspofungin: enzyme inducers ie. carbamazepine & rifampin; dexamethasone, efavirenz, nevirapine, phenytoin → consider ↑dose 70mg OD<br>↑caspofungin levels: cyclosporine ↑ hepatic enzymes<br>M: ↑ level of: itraconazole, nifedipine, sirolimus<br>Do not adjust in renal failure; **C** requires adjustment in liver failure.<br>**M**: A: LFT's; C: $K^+$, LFT's;<br>M: Lytes ($K^+$, $Mg^{++}$), Scr, BUN, LFT's, CBC<br>Comment: Preferred for *C. Glabrata* candidemia IDSA guidelines | **C**: Candidemia neutropenic & non-neutropenic:<br>Load: 70mg iv x 1 →50mg iv once daily<br>Esophageal candidiasis: 50mg iv once daily<br>Liver impairment (Child-Pugh score 7-9):<br>70mg load → 35mg iv once daily<br>**M**: Candidemia neutropenic & non-neutropenic:<br>100mg iv daily;<br>Esophageal candidiasis: 150mg iv daily;<br>Prophylaxis stem cell transplant : 50mg iv daily<br>**A**: Candidemia neutropenic & non-neutropenic:<br>Load:200mg iv x1→100mg iv od x 14day minimum;<br>Esophageal candidiasis:<br>Load 100mg iv x 1→50mg iv od x 14day minimum | 446 /70mg vial<br>271 /50mg vial<br><br>98 /50mg vial<br><br>214 /100mg vial |
| **Amphotericin B - IV**<br>**Amphotericin** B deocycholate (AmBd): **Fungizone** 50mg vial<br>**Lipid formulations**:<br>i)Amphotericin B lipid complex (ABLC): **Abelcet** 100mg vial<br>ii)Liposomal Amphotericin B (L-Am B): **Ambisome** 50mg vial<br>iii)Amphotericin B colloidal dispersion (ABCD) in US<br>Infectious Disease consult! | B | **Common**: infusion reactions: fever, chills, shakes, headache, nausea, vomiting, hypotension & tachypnea (worse with early infusions; may pretreat with acetaminophen/NSAID, diphenhydramine & meperidine) [70,71], malaise, weight loss, mild leukopenia, thrombocytopenia<br>**Serious**: nephrotoxicity (may reduce with $Na^+$ loading /lipid formulations), cardiac toxicity, $K^+$ & $Mg^{++}$ wasting (may tx with po spironolactone), myopathy ◆liver toxicity lipid formulations<br>**Precautions**: nephrotoxic drugs; liposomal amphoB (L-Am-B) has 900mg sucrose/vial –caution diabetes | √Active against most fungi & protozoa including Zygomycetes; reserved for serious infections; low therapeutic index, ↑↑toxicity; traditional ampho $B_{AmBd}$ preferred tx for severe fungal infections during **pregnancy.**<br>**DI**: ↑ nephrotoxicity: aminoglycosides, cyclosporine, tacrolimus, & other nephrotoxins including chemotherapy<br>↑ toxicity: digitalis low $K^+$<br>**M**: CBC, electrolytes $K^+$, $Mg^{++}$, liver transaminases if lipid, renal fx BUN, Scr<br>Comments: good CNS penetration; lipid formulations: better tolerated, less nephrotoxicity & less infusion reaction problems, but expensive | Dose varies based upon formulation used & indication/organism treated; duration dependent on response; poorly dialyzed.<br>{usual dose range: AmBd: 0.25-1mg/kg/day; Other formulations: 3-5mg/kg/day}<br>◆no longer need for traditional test dose or gradual titration<br>Broad spectrum; often requiring Infectious Disease Service consult! | Fungizone 68 /50mg vial<br><br>Abelcet 198 /100mg vial<br><br>Ambisome 121 50mg vial |

**Extras: Tinea alba**: sometimes confused with tinea versicolor; non-fungal in origin and does not require treatment beyond usual care for eczema; **Tinea barbae** : fungal infections of the beard area; oral antifungal required.

# Anti-infectives for Common Infections – Overview [1,2,3,4,5,6]

Originally prepared by: Kevin Hamilton; L. Regier, B. Jensen - www.RxFiles.ca **Jun 2010**

| Infection | Subclass | Pathogen(s) | Treatment / DOC | Typical Dose Adult/Peds | Duration | $ | Comments / Alternative (Alt) Treatments |
|---|---|---|---|---|---|---|---|
| **SKIN** | | | | | | | |
| **Impetigo** | | *S. aureus** (bullous), GAS (honey crusted) | mild: topical Mupirocin 2% or | tid topically Apply sparingly | 7-10 days | 20-25 | Systemic ABX if multiple/extensive/recurrent lesions, outbreaks, fever/constitutional symptoms/lymphadenopathy, immunocompromised, valvular heart dx |
| | | | Fusidic acid 2% | tid-qid topically Apply sparingly | | 28 | |
| Epidemics: ⇨ report to public health. Highly contagious! | - Crusts do not need to be removed for topical tx - If recurrence, consider eradication of carrier state. e.g. mupirocin 2% or fusidic acid 2% topically bid-tid to anterior nares &/or perineum x3-5 day. (Patients often their own carriers) | | mod-sev.: Cloxacillin or (Systemic ABX) | 250-500mg PO qid; 45-50mg/kg/d div PO qid | Some suggest 5-7 days | 25/10d | Alt/βLA: adults: erythromycin 250mg qid x7 days or clindamycin 150-300mg qid x7 days. |
| | | | Cephalexin Keflex | 250-500mg PO qid; 50-100mg/kg/d PO div qid | | 25/10d; 19/10d | Kids: erythromycin estolate 30-40mg/kg/day divided q6h or clindamycin 20mg/kg/day divided q6h (range 10-30mg/kg/day) |
| **Folliculitis & Furuncles** (boils) | | *S. aureus** {if MRSA: TMP/SMX} | Hot compress + antiseptic cleanser/drying agent. Topical mupirocin Bactroban 2% or fucidic acid Fucidin 2% topically tid | | 7 days | ~25 | Usually self limiting; non-drug tx. Drainage occasionally required. Oral ABX if on scalp. Tx recurrence by eradication of carrier state e.g. mupirocin 2% topically bid to nares x3-5 days.[7]; or Alt: PO [rifampin + TMP/SMX] |
| | Hot-tub related folliculitis may be due to *P. aeruginosa*; usually self limiting! If severe, may treat with ciprofloxacin 500mg PO bid. | | | | | | |
| **Carbuncles** | Mod-severe | *S. aureus** | Cloxacillin or | 250-500mg PO qid | 7-10 days | 25/10d | Systemic tx if: surrounding cellulitis, fever/constitutional sx's/ located in central area of face. Alt: clindamycin or TMP/SMX |
| | Incision & drainage often all that is required! Obtain C&S if tx necessary. | | Cephalexin | 250-500mg PO qid | | 25/10d | |
| **Cellulitis** ⇨if severe, may add gentamicin IV for synergy! | Mild (&/or when switching IV to PO) | *S. aureus**, GAS; *Strep. agalactiae* Group B | Cephalexin (1st choice) or | 500mg PO qid | 7-10 days | 25/10d | Alt/βLA: clindamycin 150-300mg PO qid x 7-10d for mild or 450-600mg IV/PO q8h x 10d for mod-severe; or ceftriaxone? |
| | | | Cloxacillin | 500mg PO qid | | 25/10d | |
| | Severe, Non-facial | Group a,b,c or g strep, *S. aureus** | Cefazolin Ancef | 1-2 g IV q8h | 10 days | ≥200 | If once daily cefazolin desired: give probenecid 1g PO 30min, pre |
| | | | or Clindamycin | 300 PO qid (or 600mg IV q8h) | 10 days | 50/10d | Prophylaxis of close household contacts may be considered if GAS (eg. cephalexin, erythromycin, or clindamycin x 7-10d) |
| {Also r/o other cause: e.g. bites, dermatitis, foreign body, tinea, vascular} | Severe, Facial, Adult | GAS, *S. aureus**; (*H. influenzae* if <5yrs) | Cefazolin or | 1-2 g IV q8h | 10 days | ≥200 | **Necrotizing fasciitis** (rapid progression): medical emergency!!! |
| | | | Ceftriaxone Rocephin | 1g IV/IM q24h | | ≥250 | **Diabetic foot** infection prevention is key- proper foot care! |
| | Will often get worse in 1st 48hrs before it gets better. | | [? Cloxacillin only if *S. aureus*] | [1-2g IV q6h] | 10 days | 250 | Tx choice & duration dependant on culture & clinical picture. |
| **Cellulitis, Diabetic Foot** (Tx only if inflammatory) | Mild- non-limb threatening | As above; +/- mixed aerobic & anaerobic, *enterococci*. | TMP/SMX Bactrim + | 1-2 tabs DS PO bid | 14-21 days | 10 | Alt: amox/clav ▼ 875mg PO bid x 10-14+ d or |
| | | | Metronidazole Flagyl (or Pen V) | 500mg PO bid | | 10 | cephalexin 500mg PO qid + metronidazole 500mg bid x14+ d |
| | **For severe/limb-threatening, culture; see other references**: options include: {3rd Gen Ceph IV e.g. ceftriaxone + (metronidazole or clindamycin IV or PO)}; or {ciprofloxacin ▼ Cipro IV or PO + clindamycin IV or PO.} | | | | | | |
| **Bites, non-severe** -ensure tetanus status up to date (give booster if >5yrs) | Cat 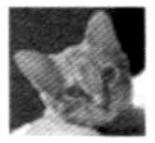 | Pasteurella spp, *Streptococcus* spp, *Staphylococcus* spp, oral anaerobes, CDC-group EF-4 | Amox/clav Clavulin ▼ [for Tx of mod-sev bites, ceftriaxone IM/IV +/- metronidazole x2-4days, then po amox] | 875mg PO bid; Kids: 40mg/kg/day divq8h | Prophylax: 3-5 days; Tx:7-10 days; longer if bone. | 35/10d; 24/10d | Irrigation & debridement !! Culture if established infection. Cat: prophylaxis within 12 hrs of bite for all significant **cat** bites b/c of high rate of infection (up to 80%). {Human bites ~50%.} Alt/βLA: Prophylaxis: doxycycline 100mg bid x1d, daily x7-10d. -Tx: clindamycin + ciprofloxacin ▼ (or 2nd gen. Ceph) |
| -clean/irrigate/debride -assess rabies risk | Dog  | Same + *Capnocytophaga* spp, *Eikenella* spp & *Weeksella* spp | If treating, Amox/clav ▼ as for cat (see comment ⇨ | Dog bites: infection rate ~ 5% [4] ∴ **only prophylax if**: mod-sev., crush injury/edema, age >50, puncture wounds, bone/joint involvement, immunocompromised, injuries to hand/foot/face/genitalia, spleenectomised. | | | |
| **Cold Sores** {Recurrent: at least >3 episodes/year} | Severe or recurrent, normal immunity | *Herpes Simplex Virus* (HSV) type 1 or 2; *fever blisters* | Topical docosanol 10% Abreva, apply 5x/day OTC antiviral cream; may ↓ symptoms by 1 day. | | | | Self limiting! Topical acyclovir not very effective! Start tx with prodrome tingling/burning. No benefit if start after lesions present. Tx results in ↓ symptoms only by ½ - 2 days. |
| | | | Valacyclovir Valtrex or (↓ by 1d) | 2g PO bid x1 | 1 day | 29 | |
| | | | Famciclovir Famvir or (↓ by 2d) | 500mg PO bid | 7 days | 70 | Chronic daily suppression: if ≥6 episodes/yr or immunosuppressed/HIV. |
| | 1st, mild, or occasional episodes do not require tx | | Acyclovir Zovirax (↓ by ½ d) | 400mg PO 5 times daily | 5 days | 75 | (e.g. famcyclovir 500mg bid; valacyclovir 500mg bid; acyclovir 400-800mg bid)[4] |
| **Shingles** | Normal Immunity | *Varicella zoster* (VZV) | Famciclovir or | 500mg PO tid | 7 days | 100 | Best if initiate ≤72hr of onset. If immunocompromized, longer Tx required (e.g. till crusting complete). Alt: acyclovir 800mg 5x daily for 7 days. |
| | | | Valacyclovir | 1g PO tid | 7 days | 125 | |
| **Chicken Pox** ⇨report to public health | Children >12yrs or ↑ risk, & Adults | *Varicella zoster* (VZV) | Acyclovir (see comments & Alt) - best if ≤ 24hrs of rash onset - pregnancy: likely safe (Category B) | 20mg/kg (max 800mg) PO qid; symptomatic tx often preferred, esp in kids. {or 800mg 5x/day Adult [4]} | 5 days; 10 days if lung / visceral or immuno-compromized | 45 | Tx only if: >12yrs old, chronic skin or lung disorder, recent corticosteroid use. {IV acyclovir if severe & immunocompromized} Alt: famciclovir 500mg PO tid or valacyclovir 1g PO tid x5days |
| | Vaccination: to prevent rare but very severe complications! | | | | | | |
| **EYE/EAR** | | | | | | | |
| **Otitis Externa** ⇨associated with pain when touching outer ear; also pruritis. Consider general tx measures / flushing of canal. | Acute | *P. aeruginosa, S. aureus**, *Enterobacteriaceae*, ?fungal in humid areas (prevent: ketoconazole *Nizoral* shampoo) | Buro-Sol OTC (Al++acetate/benzethonium) | 2-3+ drops to ear tid-qid | Max 7-10+ days | 13 | Corticosteroid part useful when there is underlying dermatitis. |
| | | | Garasone betamethasone/gent or | 3-4+ drops in affected ear tid | 5-7 days | 20 | Gent: Ototoxicity risk if perforated ear drum, ear tubes or >7d tx. |
| | | | Ciprofloxacin/dexameth Ciprodex | 4+ drops in each ear bid | 5-7 days | 40 | Pain: ibuprofen or acetaminophen; +/- hot packs/heating pads. |
| | | | Sofracort framacetin/gramicidin/dexameth | 2-3+ drops tid-qid | 5-7 days | | Fungal: clotrimazole crm 1% bid; Locacorten Vioform drops; fluconazole 200mg x1, 100mg x3d[4] |

**Eye: Conjunctivitis-Pink eye** Most viral & self-limiting! Bacterial likely if <6yr, pus/glue eyed. **Tx-Adult** (non-Chlamydia) {Drop: 1 drop to eye qid; or Oint}: Gramicidin-Polymyxin B Polysporin OTC, Gentamicin 0.3% $10, Polymyxin B/Trimethoprim Polytrim $15 or Sulfacetamine 10% $10. Fluoroquinolones if severe eye disease eg. Besi- 0.6% soln ✗ ⊗, Cipro- 0.3% oint & soln ☎ ▼, Gati- 0.3% soln ☎ ⊗, Moxi- 0.5% soln ☎ ⊗, O-floxacin 0.3% soln ☎ ▼. **Tx-child** (not newborn): Bacitracin-polymyxin B or Erythromycin oint 0.5% qid. **Steroid**: eg. Garasone may cause epithelial toxicity, cataracts, ↑intraocular pressure & mask/worsen other conditions (eg. herpetic keratitis). Contagious bacterial for 1-2 day post tx. [Conjunctivitis: more on extras page online]. (For severe bacterial inf., drops given q2h while awake x2 day then q4-8h x5+ days.)

☎ = Exception Drug Status in SK ✗ = Non-formulary in SK ✓ =prior approval for NIHB ⊗=not covered by NIHB ▼ covered by NIHB **ABX**=antibiotic **alt**=alternative **βLA**=β-lactam allergy **d**=day **CAD**=coronary artery disease **DS**=double strength **dx**=disease **DOC**=drug of choice **DRSP**=drug resistant *Streptococcus pneumonia* **FQ**=fluoroquinolone **GAS**=Group A. Streptococci **new macrolide**=clarithromycin or azithromycin **pt**=patient **RSV**=respiratory syncytial virus **Sx**=symptoms **TMP/SMX**=cotrimoxazole. Sanford's Guide[4]: www.sanfordguide.com

**See also**: RxFiles UTI Chart; Community Acquired Pneumonia Chart; Influenza Chart; Oral Antibiotic (ABX) Chart. **Guideline & Links**: CBSN: http://microbiology.mtsinai.on.ca/research/cbsn/default.asp ; MUMS[2] http://www.mumshealth.com/ Anti-infective Guidelines 2010; Bugs & Drugs[1]: http://www.bugsanddrugs.ca/

**CDAD** *Clostridium difficile* Associated Diarrhea: • >3 loose stool/day x1-2days •Tx: metronidazole 500mg po q8h x10d or 250mg po QID x10d; vancomycin ≥ 125mg po qid $345 (only if severe or >2 tx failures); •Anti-motility drugs discouraged. ?Prevention: probiotics (S. boulardii) 1g/d. Other [8]

**Endocarditis Prophylaxis** [9]: **Dental** Procedures: **only in high risk** e.g. previous endocarditis, valve replacement, 6mo after congenital heart repair, cardiac transplant pts with valve regurgitation due to a structurally abnormal valve. Tx Adult: Amoxicillin 2g (or Clinda 600mg) PO x1, 30-60min prior. Alt: Ampicillin IV.

**Skin Trauma**: **Nail puncture**: Ensure irrigation / cleaning of the wound; tetanus booster if >5yrs since last one. ABX prophylaxis if <24hrs; ciprofloxacin 750mg po q12h x5d. **Wound**: Apply suitable dressing cover & keep moist. Topical antibiotics e.g. Polysporin, of limited value.

* **MRSA** methacillin resistant *S. aureus*: consult infection control; eradication of MRSA colonization controversial (↑ mupirocin resistance in Canada). *Community acquired MRSA tx (afebrile, outpatient)*: TMP-SMX DS (may require higher dose; I tab po BID-QID) or doxycycline; *If febrile*: consult ID service.

RTI

| Infection | Subclass | Pathogen(s) | Treatment / DOC | Typical Dose Adult/Peds | Duration | $ | Comments / Alternative (Alt) Treatments |
|---|---|---|---|---|---|---|---|
| **Pharyngitis: When to treat? Centor score** useful in predicting likelihood of bacterial/GAS cause, & when ABX tx may be more useful.[10] <u>One Point for each of following</u>: 1) Temp >38° C, 2) absence of cough, 3) swollen/tender anterior nodes, 4) tonsillar swelling/exudates, 5) age 3-14; Subtract 1 point if ≥45yrs. <u>Total score:</u> **0-1** <1 – 10%: no culture or ABX required; **2-3** 11–35% may test culture or rapid antigen, Tx if positive; **4+** >50%: start ABX empirically. | | | | | | | Conjunctivitis, cough, hoarseness, rhinorrhea & diarrhea are suggestive of a **viral** etiology. ABX tx can be delayed while waiting for swab C&S. <u>Goal</u>: prevent acute rheumatic fever (rare), shorten course ~1 day, & ↓ transmission. |
| **Pharyngitis / Tonsillitis** -self limiting (8-10 days) | Adult | Viral (80-90%), GAS, other rare | No tx if likely viral; GAS: **Pen V** | 600mg PO bid | 10 days | 10 | Alt: erythromycin; {cephalexin, clindamycin options but too broad for routine use} |
| | *F. necrophorum* a concern in age 15-24. Tx: pen or ceph. | | | | | | |
| | Child | GAS ↑likely if age 3-14yrs. | Penicillin V <u>or</u> Amoxicillin ☺ better tasting if susp | 25-50mg/kg/d div bid 40mg/kg/d div bid-tid | 10 days | ≤ 20 | (Kids: erythromycin estolate 20-40mg/kg div bid-tid x10 days) {Eradication of asymptomatic carrier if high-risk e.g. for rheumatic fever. [Clindamycin or amox/clav▼ <u>or</u> pen V] x10 days + rifampin x4 days} |
| **Laryngitis** | | Viruses | Antibiotics <u>not</u> needed! | n/a | | | |
| **Rhinitis, Acute** | Eg. common cold | Viruses (*rhinovirus*), Allergies | Antibiotics <u>not</u> needed | {Symptomatic Tx e.g. decongestant} | n/a | | Yellow/green discharge NOT indicative of bacterial infection. |
| **Sinusitis** ⇨bacterial etiology ↑ if sx >10days, or worsening >5 days | Acute | Viruses (>98% initially) *S. pneumoniae*, *H. influenzae*, *M. catarrhalis* | Symptomatic tx | {Tx with decongestants, analgesics} | n/a | | ~70% resolve spontaneously. Sxs can last up to 14 d. Refer to specialist if ≥4 episodes/year. No role for nasal corticosteroids in <u>acute</u>. |
| | | | Amoxicillin | 500mg PO tid (up to 1g PO TID)[4] | 10 days Possibly shorter | 17 | **Reserve antibiotics** for severe symptoms/ moderate Sx that don't improve in **7 to 10 days** or get worse. |
| | | | Alt/βLA:TMP/SMX; <u>or</u> Doxycycline | 1 DS tab bid; 100mg PO daily | | | |
| ABX often <u>not</u> effective in chronic sinusitis.[4] | Chronic sx ≥12 wks | As above + *S. aureus*, GAS, *Enterobacteriaceae, anaerobes* | Amox/clav ▼ (also Alt for acute) | 875mg PO bid | 21 days | 65 | Alt: cefuroxime▼, cefprozil▼, macrolide, fluoroquinolone e.g. moxifloxacin |
| | | | **Saline irrigation** e.g. Neti Pot may be useful if used properly (e.g. cleaning, etc.) | | | | |
| **Acute Otitis Media** (AOM)[11] Consider **watchful waiting**[i] x48-72hrs if suitable patient (e.g. deferred Rx); **see note below!!** | Child, mild – mod,; if willing to watchful wait | Viral *S. pneumonia* *H. influenzae* *M. catarrhalis* | 1) Symptomatic tx; Decongestants <u>not</u> approved for <6yrs; <u>not</u> effective for effusion. acetaminophen, ibuprofen <u>or</u> naproxen OTC age ≥12 in Canada | 10-15mg/kg q4-6h Max 65mg/kg/d 5-10mg/kg q6-8h 2.5-5mg/kg bid | Especially in 1st 48hrs | | See RxFiles Pediatric Pain chart pg 73 for analgesic dosing, etc. Topical corticosteroids / antibiotic preps are not recommended. Alt/βLA: clarithromycin Biaxin ▼ 15 mg/kg/day div BID x 5-10 day. or azithromycin▼, or cefixime▼, or cefprozil▼ (see ABX chart) |
| | Child – mod-sev; when treating | As above | 2) **Amoxicillin** (See comments for alternatives) | 75-90mg/kg PO div q12h {~ up to 2-3g/day Max 4g/day} | 5 days ≥2yrs (10 days) → | 20 30 | Alt: [amox/clav (7:1) ▼ 45mg/kg/d PLUS amox 45mg/kg/d divided BID] if no improvement after 2 days or recent ABX tx (Amox/clav + Amox allows for high-dose amox, without excessive clavulinic acid ∴ less diarrhea) |
| | Child: perforation / tubes | *S. aureus, P. aeruginosa*, Viridans Streptococcus sp. | Ciprofloxacin/ dexamethasone Ciprodex | 4 drops in affected ear bid | 7 days | 40 | Tx for 10 days if ≤2 yrs, perforation or frequent recurrent AOM. Effusion middle ear: persists up to 1 & 3 months in 50% & 10% of pts. |
| **Bronchitis** {Higher risk patients have poor lung fx, co-morbidity, frequent AECB, etc.; they may require broader ABX (see comments)} | Acute | Viral >90% (Adults: *M. pneumoniae, C. pneumoniae*. Kids: *Adenovirus, RSV*) | Antibiotics not indicated! Symptomatic tx. {Cough often lasts 2-3+ weeks!} {If productive cough continues >10days, may consider ABX (doxycycline or macrolide)} | | | | <u>**AECB:**</u> Smoking cessation important! ABX Tx if ≥2 of: ↑sputum **volume**, **purulence** or ↑ **dyspnea**. |
| | AECB if severe {Acute Exacerbation of Chronic Bronchitis} ⇨role of antibiotics debated.[4] | *H. influenzae*, *S. pneumoniae*, *M. catarrhalis*, H. species [*K. pneumoniae*] if higher risk | Amoxicillin, Doxycycline, Erythromycin (<u>or</u> new macrolide) TMP/SMX [12] Cefuroxime axetil Ceftin Cefprozil Cefzil | 500mg PO tid 200mg PO x1→100mg bid 333mg PO tid 1 DS tab PO bid 500mg PO bid 500mg bid | 5-10 days | 17/10d 15/10d 26/10d 10/10d 51/10d 56/10d | Alt: clarithromycin▼ 500mg bid; or azithromycin▼ 500mg x1, then 250mg daily x4 <u>Consider broader spectrum ABX if</u>: >65yrs, CAD, FEV1 <50%, 3+ exacerbations/yr, ABX in last 3 months. E.g a **fluoroquinolone** (**moxifloxacin** 400mg daily x5-10d <u>or</u> **Amox/clav**▼ 875mg bid x7-10d). -FQ may provide ↑ eradication, accelerated recovery & ↑ disease free intervals GLOBE, MOSAIC Adjunct tx with prednisone 25-50mg/day x 7-14 d in mod-sev; |
| **Whooping Cough** (Pertussis) | {Symptoms: coughing⇨vomiting; *whoop* on inhalation.} | *B. pertussis* {remain infectious for 21 days post cough or 5 days post start of tx} | Erythromycin Erythromycin estolate | 333mg PO tid range 1-2g/day 30-40mg/kg/day divided q6-8h | 7 days | 22 | Notify public health & offer all household contacts prophylaxis. Alt: clarithromycin Biaxin ▼ or azithromycin Zithromax ▼ |
| | | | <u>Alt.</u> Azithromycin adult: 500mg po x1, then 250mg daily x4d. Kids >6mo: 10mg/kg po x1, then 5mg/kg daily x4days. Infants <6mo not officially indicated; literature dosing varies (5 or 10mg/kg daily x5days). | | | | |

STD / STI[13]; (at risk age groups expanding[14]; ii)

| Infection | Subclass | Pathogen(s) | Treatment / DOC | Typical Dose Adult/Peds | | Duration | $ | Comments / Alternative (Alt) Treatments |
|---|---|---|---|---|---|---|---|---|
| **Epididymitis** (Epididymoorchitis) | - eitiology may differ for age <35 vs >35yrs - r/o testicular torsion | *Chlamydia trachomatis*, *N. gonorrhoeae*; {<u>if age >35</u>: also coliforms, *P. aeruginosa*} | Ceftriaxone + doxycycline {FQ <u>or</u> TMP/SMX if >35yrs} | 250mg IM 100mg PO bid | | 1 dose 10 days {x10d} | 15 15 | Pt & contact(s) remain infectious until tx is complete or in the case of single-dose therapy for 7 days. Alt: Ciprofloxacin▼ 500mg PO bid (option for **age >35**; but ↑ resistance) |
| **Syphilis** | Early: 1°, 2°, & latent <1yr | *Treponema pallidum* | Benzathine Pen G Bicillin LA | 2.4 million units IM x1 | | 1 dose | 90 | <u>Alt/βLA</u>: doxycycline 100mg bid x 14 day. (Alt: ceftriaxone 1g IV/IM x8-10d [4]) Test & tx sexual contacts of early syphilis. |
| | Benz Pen G available through provincial/territorial STD clinics; safe in pregnancy. Painful; may give ½ dose to each gluteal side. | | | | | | | |
| **Gonorrhea** Eg. cervicitis, urethritis | [Tx also for Chlamydia] | *N. gonorrheoeae* | Cefixime Suprax ▼ (or Ciprofloxacin ▼ <u>if</u> sensitive locally) | 400mg PO x1 500mg PO | STI drugs often free if through sex health programs. -- Also tx partner? Eg. EPT | 1 dose 1 dose | 10 10 | All pts should also be treated for chlamydial infection unless nucleic acid test negative. Cefixime safe in pregnancy. |
| | [Alt. tx: **Ceftriaxone** 125mg IM x1 (250mg IM x1 in USA)] | | | | | | | |
| **Chlamydia** Eg. cervicitis, urethritis [usually tx also for *N. gonorrhea*] | Adults | *C. trachomatis* | Azithromycin ▼or doxycycline | 1g PO x1 100mg PO bid | | 1 dose 7 days | 20 15 | Disease under-diagnosed; majority of infected individuals are asymptomatic. Test & treat recent (≤ 60days) sex contacts. Prevented by use of consistent safe sex practices. |
| | Pregnant or lactating ♀ | - watch for co-infection with *N. gonorrhea* | Amoxicillin or erythromycin base | 500mg PO tid 500mg PO qid | | 7 days 7 days | 15 19 | Alt to Azithro.: Erythromycin base 500mg PO qid x7 days |
| **Nongonococcal Urethritis/cervicitis** | | *C. trachomatis, U. urealyticum, M. genitalium* | Doxycycline or Azithromycin ▼ | 100mg PO bid 1g PO x1 | | 7 days 1 dose | 15 20 | Similar cure rate for ABX listed; azithromycin resistance in USA. GI side effects more common with erythromycin. |

*<u>VULVOVAGINITIS</u>*: **Candidiasis** (see antifungal chart)[15]. **Trichomoniasis**: Tx with metronidazole 2g po x1; if failure/recurrence 500mg PO bid x7 days or 2g daily x3-5days. **Bacterial vaginosis**: asymptomatic & tx not required unless high-risk pregnancy, pre-IUD/gyne surgery; Tx metronidazole 500mg PO bid x7 days or metronidazole 0.75% gel, 5g intravaginally HS x 5days <u>or</u> clindamycin 2% crm 5g intravaginally HS x7days (topicals not recommended in pregnancy). **Genital Herpes: 1° episode** (HSV-1, HSV-2): Tx x5-<u>7</u> days PO with: acyclovir 400mg tid, famciclovir 250mg tid, or valacyclovir 500-1000mg bid, within 72hrs onset. (Recommendations differ for recurrence & pregnancy); **Genital Herpes: Episodic Recurrences** (HSV-1, HSV-2): <u>Non-HIV Tx</u>: acyclovir 800mg PO tid x2days or 400mg tid x5days; or famciclovir 1g PO bid x1day or 125mg PO bid x5days; or valacyclovir 500mg bid x3days, or 1g PO daily x5days; (<u>HIV</u> patients: acyclovir 400mg PO tid x5-10d, or famciclovir 500mg bid x5-10d; valacyclovir 1g bid x5-10d.)

**i) Watchful Wait or ABX**: ABX <u>should</u> be prescribed if age <6mons, oral temp >39°C, immunodeficient, heart or lung disease, craniofacial abnormalities, a history of otitis media complications & Down's syndrome. (Aboriginals may also be at higher risk.). Must be able to ensure observation & follow-up over 24-72 hours. Risk factors PRSP include children <2 yrs of age, who attend daycare (defined as greater than 4hr per wk with at least two unrelated children), who have frequent AOM and/or recent antimicrobial use (within the past 3 mos).

**ii) STI/STD**: those with STI are at ↑ risk of HIV transmission & acquisition; ∴ counsel & screen routinely!!!

**Antibiotic Resistance**:
- Growing bacterial resistance has led to efforts to reduce unnecessary ABX use, & encourage use of narrow spectrum agents, adequate doses & shortest effective durations whenever possible! **Don't tx viruses**!
- Resistance trends will vary by geographic location, local ABX usage, & population demographics (e.g. vaccinations, risk factors)
- **Penicillin resistant** strep pneumo (**PRSP**) Canada 2008: 6% high-level & 10% intermediate resistance; **20% macrolide resistance**.
- **Fluoroquinolone resistant** strep pneumonia: levofloxacin 1.5%; moxifloxacin 0.5% {growing resistance, especially in age >64.}
- *N. gonorrhea* Ontario [16]: 28% resistant to fluoroquinones. <u>Other concerns</u>: **MRSA, VRE, *Clostridium difficile*, DRSP & *N. meningitidis*.**

| Antibiotic /Pregnancy code Generic / TRADE g=generic | Strength / Formulation (in mg or mg/5ml) | | Flavour | Ped. Dose mg/kg/day | Dosing Interval | Usual Max/d | Dose: 1 {10kg child ~1yr} 2 Adult | COST $ /10d | Comments (see page 57 - EDS criteria abbreviation key) |
|---|---|---|---|---|---|---|---|---|---|
| **PENICILLINS** B ←Pregnancy category | Rare- aminopenicillins such as amoxicillin & ampicillin have an ↑risk of Stevens-Johnson syndrome. | | | | | | | | |
| **Amoxicillin** | 125 & 250mg | ChewT | cherry | 40-50 | Q8H | 1.5g | {125-250mg Q8H} | 25 | •great middle ear level & drug of choice for initial Tx of acute otitis media. CPS'09,170 [Watch & wait option if kid >6month. |
| AMOXIL,g | 125mg/5ml | Susp | strawberry | 75-90mg/kg/d given bid in kids at ↑risk | | | (may give q12h Sanford's) | 13 | Antibiotic more useful in kid<2yr with bilateral AOM or |
| | 250mg/5ml | Susp | ☺banana/other | of resistant S. pneumo up to 1.5-3-4g/day eg. recent previous antibiotic use, daycare, not given Prevnar | | | | 15 | if AOM & otorrhoea.] •sinusitis <10day & acute bronchitis is often viral |
| | 250 & 500mg | Cap | | | | | *500mg-1g Q8H* | 17-27 | •Novamoxin has sugar reduced susp,(Amoxil Susp. is bubble-gum flavoured but NOT usually stocked) |
| **Amox/Clavulanate** | 125F & 250F /5ml (4:1) | Susp | rasp-orange | 45 | Q8-12H | 1.5g amox | {125mg Q8H cc} | 19 | ☎▼EDS -a,c,d,e,g,i,m,p bites,q •↑absorb. with food(cc) |
| CLAVULIN,g | 200 & 400 /5ml 70ml (7:1) | Susp | | (range 20-90) | Q12H | | {200mg Q12H cc} | 24 | •↑activity vs resistant *H. flu but not PRSP*; ↑LFT's rare •diarrhea ~25% with q8h regimen; **less** frequent |
| (amox/clavulanate 6.4mg/kg/day ratio varies) -dose listed=amoxicillin component | 250(2:1), 500(4:1), 875mg (7:1) | Tab | Caution preterm: neonatal enterocolitis | | Q8-12H | | *875mg Q12H cc* | 35 | (~10%) with **higher ratio** formulation given q12h |
| **Combination of {Amoxicillin 40mg/kg/d + Amox/Clavulanate 40mg/kg/d}** sometimes recommended to provide high-dose of amoxicillin for pen-resistant *S. pneumoniae* and regular dose amox/clavulanate for excellent *H. influenzae* & *M. catarrhalis* coverage without excessive clavulanate, which may cause excessive diarrhea & increased cost (i.e. option in resistant/recurrent OM). | | | | | | | | | |
| **Ampicillin,g** | 250 & 500mg | Cap | | 50-100 | Q6H | 2g | {250mg Q6H ac} | 22 | •recommend amox (better absorption; q8h; less |
| | | | | | | | *500mg Q6H cc* | 33 | rash/diarrhea)unless shigella/citrobacter/enterobacter |
| **Cloxacillin,g** | 125 mg/5ml | Susp | cherry | 50-100 | Q6H | 4g | {125-250mg Q6H ac} | 27 | •primarily for *Staph. aureus*; also *strep* coverage |
| | 250 & 500mg | Cap | | | | | *500mg Q6H ac* | 25 | • liquid poor tasting; consider cephalexin as alternative |
| Penicillin V (Benzathine) PEN-VEE | 300mg/5ml | Susp | fruity | 25-50 | Q6-12H | 3g | {150mg Q8h ac} | 13 D/C | D/C by company 06 |
| **Penicillin V (Potassium)** | 125 & 300mg✗▼/5ml | Soln | fruity | 25-50 | Q6-12H | 3g | {125mg Q6H ac} | 20 | •Drug of choice for adult pharyngitis (esp. when Strep. confirmed by C&S); **q12h** dosing appears effective. |
| PEN-VK,g | 300mg (=500,000 I.U.s) | Tab | | | | | *300mg Q8H ac/600mg bid* | 10 | |
| **CEPHALOSPORINS** (generation) B | Cephs lacks atypical & Enterococcus activity. About 1-10% of adult pts with penicillin allergy will develop ceph allergy. If penicillin "rash only", cephs often ok. Med Let Sep/03; side chain esp. important 41 | | | | | | | | |
| **Cefaclor** (2nd) | 125,250 & 375mg/5ml | Susp | ☺strawberry | 20-40 | Q6-8H | 2g | {125mg Q8H} | 25 | •serum sickness <1% |
| CECLOR,g ✗ | 250 & 500mg | Cap | | | Q8H | | *500mg Q8H* | 70 | ✗▼ **Delisted** from Sask. formulary **2003** |
| **Cefixime** (~3rd) | 100mg/5ml | Susp | ☺strawberry | 8mg | Q24H | 400mg | {80mg Q24H} | 26 | ☎▼ EDS -b,c,v & uncomplicated gonorrhea |
| SUPRAX | 400mg | Tab | | | | | *400mg Q24H* | 49 | •diarrhea ~15% •not recommended if Staph infection |
| **Cefprozil**-new generic (2nd) | 125&250mg/5ml | Susp | ☺bubblegum | 15-30mg | Q12H | 1g | {150mg Q12H} | 22 | ☎▼EDS -a,b,c,d,e,i •diarrhea only ~3% •room temp 24hrs |
| CEFZIL,g | 250 & 500mg | Tab | | | | | *500mg Q12H* | 56g 88 | •500mg od = $43 –adequate for some indications |
| **Cefuroxime axetil** (2nd) | 125mg/5ml;sachet 250mg✗⊗ | Susp | tutti-fruiti | 20-30mg | Q12H | 1g | {125mg Q12H cc} | 27 | ☎▼ EDS -a,b,c,d,e,i • Susp-bitter tasting; |
| CEFTIN,g | 250 & 500mg | Tab | | | | | *500mg Q12H cc* | 51 | absorption concerns: may ↑absorption with food |
| **Cephalexin** (1st) | 125 & 250mg | Susp | bubblegum, cherry, orange, banana ☺ | 25-100mg | Q6H | 4g | {125mg Q6H} | 26 | •poor mid-ear penetration; no coverage of *H. flu or* |
| KEFLEX,g | 250 & 500mg | Tab/cap | | | | | *500mg Q6H* | 25 | *atypical* ∴not for empiric Tx of OM/CAP |
| Ceftriaxone -ROCEPHIN 50mg/kg IM X1 (Max2g) effective for acute OM incl. areas with high PRSP rates (X3 if recurrent OM)††; Cost 500mg < $30✗; inj. painful ∴often mixed with lidocaine; rare SE: biliary sludge DI: calcium | | | | | | | | | |
| **FLUOROQUINOLONES** C | •**Generally reserve** use for 1st line, in patient with true allergies to 1st line tx; as ↑gram –ve resistant organisms & MRSA outbreaks. **Not for MRSA, & ↑ resistance to N. *gonorrhoeae* in USA >10%** CDC MMWR April 2007 •concern for articular damage in kids; rare: photosensitivity, tendon rupture esp. elderly on steroids, transplants, seizure, allergy •**safety in <18yr not established** • **DI:chelation with cations (eg. Al++, Ca++, Fe++)** •FQ's likely absorbed in the duodenum, ∴less drug may be absorbed when administering via a jejunostomy tube •Clostridium difficile: ↑ incidence & severity possible with FQs. •FQ's removed from market: trovafloxacin (hepatic SE), grepafloxacin (cardiac SE), gatifloxacin TEQUIN 2006 (↑diabetes). | | | | | | | | |
| **Ciprofloxacin** CIPRO,g | 500mg/5ml ✆ | Susp | strawberry | (20-30mg) | Q12H | 1.5g | *250mg Q12H* (for UTI) | 38 | ☎▼EDS-b ≥2 ABX,c C & S resistance,h,j,l,m prolonged,o,r & gonorrhea |
| 500mg & 1g XL® tabs, | 250,500 & 750mg | Tab | •coverage incl. PRSP, atypicals, & gm –ves, (some pseudomonas) | | | | *500mg Q12H;1g XL od* | 43;43 | •**antipseudomonal** (rarely in peds-cystic fibrosis) •DIs •Travelers' diarrhea: FQ good choice unless in Asia Campylobacter. |
| **Levofloxacin** LEVAQUIN,g | 250, 500 & 750mg | Tab | •rare QT prolongation <3/million; | na | Q24H | 500mg | *500-750mg Q24H* | 46-80 | ☎⊗EDS-c resistant,d,e,j, PID.Generic was avail., rare ↑LFTs |
| **Moxifloxacin** AVELOX | 400mg | Tab | •↑/↓ glucose changes <300/million but more common in elderly diabetics (Gatifloxacin the worst offender) | na | Q24H | 400mg | *400mg po Q24H* | 74 | ☎✆EDS-c resistant,d,e,j •covers **anaerobes**, rare ↑LFT •not for UTIs (low concentrations/low renal elimination) |
| **Norfloxacin** NOROXIN,g | 400mg | Tab | | na | Q12H | 800mg | *400mg po Q12H before meals* | 37 | ☎▼ **EDS-b,c,l for genitourinary tract inf's only** & gonococcal urethritis/cervicitis |
| Gemifloxacin FACTIVE | 320mg | Tab | | na | Q24H | 320mg | *320mg po Q24H* | 85 | ✗⊗; Few DI's; approved for CAP,AECB; rash 2.8% |
| **Telithromycin** KETEK C | 400mg (a KETOLIDE) | Tab | Not 1st line due to potential of ADRs (liver toxicity & death in relatively young healthy pts! | na | Q24H | 800mg | *800mg po Q24H* (only for pneumonia FDA/CND) | 80 | ☎⊗↑DI 5: disopyramide,ergots, pimozide...; Rare:↑↑LFT's, TEN & myasthenia gravis. SE: GI, vision blurry. Cover resistant strep |

☺ tastes good ☎ =Exception Drug Status in Sask ✆=prior approval required for NIHB coverage ▼ covered by NIHB ⊗ not covered by NIHB **ABX**=antibiotic(s) **CAP**=community acquired pneumonia **ChewT**=chewable tab **COST $**=total cost to consumer for 10 day therapy **GI** = gastrointestinal **inf**=infection **na**=not applicable **OM**=otitis media **Ped**=pediatric **PMC**=pseudomembraneous colitis **PRSP**=penicillin resistant Strep. pneumoniae **pts**=patients **Susp**=suspension TEN=toxic epidermal necrolysis **Tx**=treatment. **Ped. Dose**: dosages in the higher end of the range should generally be used for treatment of OM †† References: (Ped Inf Dis 1999;18-5:403-9. Sanford's 2002:p7)

**Probiotics** i,ii Probiotics (*Saccharomyces boulardii, Lactobacillus rhamnosus GG*, & probiotic mixes) ↓ antibiotic-associated diarrhea (AAD) but separate 2hrs from abx. Only *S. boulardii* 1g od effective for *C. difficile* diarrhea caution if immunocompromised, pancreatitis.

| Antibiotic /Pregnancy code<br>Generic / TRADE | Strength/Formulation<br>(in mg or mg/5ml) | | Flavour | Ped. Dose † mg/kg/day | Dosing Interval | Usual Max/d | Dose: 1 {10kg child~1yr †}<br>2 *Adult* | COST $ /10d | Comments |
|---|---|---|---|---|---|---|---|---|---|
| **MACROLIDES**: Erythro- & clarithro- can ↑QT interval[iii] & more DI's CYP 3A4,↑ level of other meds eg. digoxin than azithro-mycin. Rare ototoxicity. May ↑resistance with azithro. ◆cover atypical organisms; not for MRSA | | | | | | | | | |
| **Azithromycin** [B]<br>ZITHROMAX, ,generic<br>Z-PAK= 6x 250mg tabs | 100 & 200mg/5ml 15ml | Susp | ☺ cherry; but generic PMS poor taste | Day 1: 10mg<br>Day 2-5: 5mg | Q24H | 500mg | {**D1**: 100mg; **D2-5**: 50mg} | 21 | ☎▼ **EDS -a.b.f.k,s,t,u** & *chlamydia trachomatis*<br>◆**5days** ≅10days therapy; also 1&3day regimens<br>◆Travelers' diarrhea: option in Asia, kids or in pregnancy. |
| | 250mg | Tab | | | | | **D1**: 500mg; **D2-5**: 250mg | 28 | |
| | 600mg | Tab | | | | | ***See other sources*** | - | ☎▼ for disseminated MAC in pts with HIV |
| **Clarithromycin** [C]<br>BIAXIN,generic 10day tx ~↓$10 than XL | 125& 250mg/5ml 105ml | Susp | fruity | 15mg | Q12H | 1g | {75mg Q12H} | 27 | ☎▼ **EDS -a,b,f,k,s,u,w, MAC** prophylaxis in HIV pts, & 1wk for *H. pylori tx;* susp @room temp;DI colchicine |
| | 250&500mg; 500mg XL | Tab | | | Q12-24H | | ***500-1000mg XL OD cc*** | 37-67 | |
| **Erythromycin** [B] Non estolate<br>i)Base Tab ii) ERYC<br>iii) PCE D/C'd by Company | i) 250mg, 500mg✗▼<br>ii) 250 & 333mg | Base<br>EC Cap | | | Q6-8H | 2g | ***250mg Q6H*** Erythro, ERYC<br>***333mg Q8H*** ERYC | 15[i],30[ii]<br>26 | ◆↑absorption on empty stomach, but with food ↓GI upset. Kids:ERYC→sprinkled on food useful<br>◆**Estolate form** preferred in **kids** as most acid stable; not recommended in adults/pregnancy<br>◆Coverage for *H. influenzae* poor with erythro (better with new macrolides); there is some PRSP cross-resistance<br>◆ Option in acute gastroparesis ◆ DI colchicine ◆ þ concern |
| | iii) 333mg | EC Tab | | | Q8H | 2g | *333mg Q8H* PCE | 25 D/C | |
| **Eryth. Estolate** ILOSONE | 125 & 250mg/5ml | Susp ☺ | orange/cher | 30-40mg | Q6-8H | 2g | {125mg Q8H cc} | 17 | |
| **Eryth. Ethylsuc.** EES | 200 & 400mg/5ml | Susp | strawb/bana | 30-40mg | Q6-8H | 2g | {100mg Q6H} after meals | 18 | |
| **Eryth.Stearate** ERYTHROCIN | 250mg | Tab | | | Q6-8H | 2g | ***250mg Q6H*** | 17 | |
| **SULFA COMBINATIONS** 43 [C],but near term [D] -Trimethoprim has antifolate effect. ↑ $K^+$ with ACEI/ARBs. **Rare** SE: Stevens Johnson Sx & Toxic epidermal necrolysis ◆**CI: infant <2months old, G6PD, þ concern.** | | | | | | | | | |
| **Cotrimoxazole (SMX/TMP)**<br>BACTRIM/SEPTRA,g<br>(Sulfamethoxazole/Trimethoprim)<br>DS="double strength" | 200/40 /5ml (10ml=1 tab) | Susp | cherry | 6-12mg TMP | Q12H | 320mg of TMP | {(200/40) **5ml** Q12H} | 17 | ◆UTI prophylaxis Adult: 40-80mg as TMP daily or 3X/wk<br>◆PJP prophylaxis: SMX/TMP (1 reg daily or 1 DS M,W,F) or TMP (20mg/kg/d) ◆?use for MRSA esp CA<br>◆store suspension at room temp.; rare: thrombocytopenia |
| | 100/20 Pediatric | Tab | | | | | {**ii** tab Q12h} | 12 | |
| | 400/80 & 800/160 (DS) | Tab | | | | | ***(800/160) i tab Q12H*** | 10 | |
| Eryth/Sulfisoxazole D/C by Company PEDIAZOLE | 200mg/600mg /5ml | Susp | strawberry-banana | 40-50mg Eryth | Q6-8H | 2g Eryt, 6g Sulf | {(160/480) 4ml Q8H} | 24 D/C | ◆disadvantage: ↑'d resistance & ↑SE e.g. GI allergy rash; b/c of 2 drugs ◆refrigerate& best after meals |
| **TETRACYCLINES** [D] ◆TCN & doxycycline **not recommended in kids <8yr** (minocycline <13yr) ◆ **1hr before or 2hr after any $Ca^{++}$** (dairy products) **& $Fe^{++}$ ◆ Concern: phototoxicity, GI irritating** | | | | | | | | | |
| **Doxycycline** VIBRAMYCIN,g | 100mg | Tab/Cap | √ atypical RTIs | 2-5mg | Q12-24H | 200mg | ***100mg Q12H x1d, Q24H*** | 15 | ◆better tolerated than TCN; useful Lyme dx/?CA-MRSA |
| **Minocycline** MINOCIN,g | 50 & 100mg | Cap | | 4mg/kg X1, 2mg/kg | Q12H | 200mg | ***200mg X1, 100mg Q12H*** | 31 | ☎ ✆Tx: acne unresponsive to TCN. SE: lupus, vertigo |
| **Tetracycline**,g | 250mg | Cap | | 25mg | Q6H | 2g | ***250mg Q6H ac*** | 11 | ◆take on empty stomach with water ◆avoid if ↓renal fx |
| **OTHER** | | | | | | | | | |
| **Clindamycin** [B]<br>DALACIN C,g | 75mg/5ml | Soln | cherry | 10-30mg | Q6-8H | 1.8g | {100mg Q8H} | 34 | ◆Gram +ve, anaerobes, vaginosis & CA-MRSA<br>◆store suspension at room temp (b/c ↑ thickness) |
| | 150 & 300mg | Cap | | | Q6-12H | | ***300mg Q6H*** | 50 | |
| **Linezolid** ZYVOXAM [C]<br>-bacteriostatic agent | 600mg (600mg IV ✗✆) | tab | | 30mg | BID | 1.2g | ***600mg BID*** | 1475 | ☎ ✆**EDS**-Gram +ve resistant/intolerant to vanco.<br>◆weak MAOI & serotonin action; thrombocytopenia if >3wk |
| **Methenamine mandelate** [C]<br>MANDELAMINE | 500mg | EC Tab | | 50-75mg | Q6H | 2g | ***1g Q12H*** | 23 | ✆ ◆requires acidified urine (pH <5.5)∴often given with ascorbic acid |
| **Metronidazole** [B]<br>FLAGYL,g | 250mg, (500mg cap▼$) | Tab/<br>Cap | | 30mg<br>(range 15-50) | Q6-12H | 4g | {75mg Q6H}<br>***250-500mg Q8H*** | 11 | ◆Susp. compounded-poor taste; Disulfiram Rx; **DI**: phenytoin, warfarin<br>◆Tx: anaerobic, antiprotozoal, vaginosis & PMC inf's |
| **Fosfomycin** MONUROL [B] | 3g oral powder | sachet | | >1 yr 2g x1 | x 1 | 3g | ***3g x1 empty stomach*** | 34 | ☎ ✆ **EDS-b,c,x for UTIs only!** |
| **Nitrofurantoin** [B/D]<br>ii) MACRODANTIN,g<br>iii) MACROBID<br>{Avoid if CrCl <40-60ml/min ↓ effect} | 50 & 100mg | Tab | | 5-7mg | Q6H | 200-400mg | ***50mg Q6H cc*** | 14 | ◆**UTI only**; pregnancy: avoid at term (36wks),or G6PD<br>◆UTI prophylaxis: Kid >1mo 1-2mg/kg/d (max 100mg/d); Adult 50-100mg po HS. Long term ↑SE & rarely causes pneumonitis, neuropathy & ↑LFTs |
| | ii)50mg macrocrystals | Cap | ped. formulation not avail. but recipe in CJHP Feb'06 or round to the nearest ¼ tab =12.5mg | | Q6H | | ***50mg Q6H cc*** | 23 | |
| | iii)100mg macrocrystal | Cap | | | Q12H | | ***100mg Q12H cc*** | 23 | |
| **Probenecid** BENURYL [C] | 500mg | Tab | | 40mg | Q6H | 2-3g | ***1g OD or 500mg QID*** 30-45min prior to IV antibiotics | 15 | ◆Action: ↑ levels of penicillin/cephalosporins. CI <2yrs. |
| **Trimethoprim** PROLOPRIM [C] | 100 & 200mg | Tab | | {na} | Q12-24H | 200mg | ***200mg Q24H*** | 14 | ◆Option: sulfa allergy ◆QID dose in PCP ◆May ↑Scr |
| **Vancomycin** VANCOCIN [B] | 125 & 250mg | Cap | vial sometimes used to make up oral solution | 40mg | Q6-8H | 2g | ***125mg Q6H*** | 345 | ☎ ✆ Not absorbed ∴only po use for PMC *C. diff* |

(kidney symbol) = ↓ dose for renal dysfunction  PJP= pneumocystis jiroveci pneumonia (previously PCP)

**Abbreviation Key to EDS (Exception Drug Status) criteria in SK:**

**a)** Upper & lower RTI's in pts NOT responding to 1st line ABX **b)** Pts ALLERGIC to alternative ABX **c)** Inf's known to be resistant or not responding to alternate ABX(s) **d)** RTIs in nursing home pts
**e)** Pneumonia in pts in the community with comorbidity (ie. COPD, diabetes, renal insufficiency, heart failure, stroke) **f)** Pneumonia **g)** Pneumonia caused by aspiration **h)** Pts with bronchiectasis or cystic fibrosis
**i)** Completion of Tx initiated in hospital **j)** Completion of ABX Tx initiated in hospital when alternatives are not appropriate **k)** Completion of ABX Tx initiated in hospital with macrolides or quinolones
**l)** *Pseudomonas aeruginosa* inf's **m)** Inf's in pts with neutropenia **n)** Inf's & prophylaxis in neutropenic pts **o)** UTI in pts allergic or not responding to alternate ABX **p)** For human, cat & dog BITES
**q)** Diabetic foot inf's **r)** Severe diabetic foot inf's in combo with other ABX **s)** Non-tuberculous *Mycobacterium* inf's & prophylaxis **t)** *Chlamydia trachomatis* inf's **u)** Pts intolerant to erythromycin &/or other ABX
**v)** Uncomplicated gonorrhea **w)** *H. pylori* -1 week when used in combo regimens for eradication **x)** Tx of UTI in pregnancy when first line agents inappropriate PMC =pseudomembraneous colitis (*C. difficile*)

## Table 1: Approach to Treatment (Tx)

- **The complexities of HIV require that patients be treated by physicians/clinics with expertise in HIV.**
- Goals: 1) to achieve & maintain an undetectable viral load (HIV RNA < 40copies/ml) within 6mths of tx; 2) prevent opportunistic infections (OI)
- Resistance testing key to drug selection; >95% adherence required
- Individualize tx with respect to comorbidities (CV, liver & renal dx; chemical dependency, psych hx, TB), pt compliance, convenience (pill burden, dosing frequency, & food/fluid requirement), SEs & DI's
- Initial tx - a 3 drug regimen: e.g. 2 NRTI's + (1 NNRTI or boosted PIs or ?integrase inhibitor) (Choice complexity too complicated for scope of this chart!)
- Drug interactions (DI): critical; review with new or change in Rx see links

## Table 2: Antiretrovirals (ARV's): Common Side Effects (SEs) & Their Management

**Diarrhea, ARV-induced:**
- rule out infectious or medical causes before chronic treatment;
- loperamide 2mg PRN (Max 16mg/day), diphenoxylate, & codeine useful (see OTC chart)
- other tx agents: elemental calcium 500mg bid; oat bran 1500mg bid, psyllium 1 tbsp or 2 bars daily, pancrelipase (Viokase, Ultrase MT 20) 1 cap tid-qid, l-glutamine 10g tid x1 wk (if response inadequate continue 10g bid x 1wk, then 10g od)

**Nausea**: (See N&V chart)
- Various causes (e.g. stimulation of the CTZ, ↓ GI motility, taste, etc.)
- May resolve in few wks. Tx: dimenhydrinate, metoclopramide, etc.

**Rash :** [7] (Common with ARV tx; may resolve over weeks)
- Abacavir: hypersensitivity common ~2-9% [8] & occurs < 6 wks after start Sx includes: fever, rash, GI sx (n&v, diarrhea, stomach pain), lack of energy, muscle or bone pain, & respiratory sx (cough, SOB, sore throat). Stop abacavir; DO NOT restart.[9,10] ⇨ HLA screen all pts
- Nevirapine: to ↓ rash risk, start with 200mg daily even if reinitiating
- If very severe (e.g. fever, systemic, mucosal involvement) stop drug tx, arrange to reassess drug options & tx rash (below)
- Drug Tx: consider antihistamines to relieve itch & discomfort (1st generation: diphenhydramine 25-50mg q4-6h; max 150mg/day, hydroxyzine; 2nd generation- cetirizine, loratadine, and fexofenadine) see OTC chart. {Corticosteroids & low dose doxepin may be options if severe}[11]

**Pregnancy**: ARVs started after 14 weeks(& by 28weeks) significantly ↓ mother to child transmission (mtct); intrapartum ARV + infant ARV prophylaxis (6wk) essential to ↓ mtct transmission ~30%⇨<2%

## Table 3: HIV – Drug Treatment Comparison Chart

| Generic/TRADE (Strength & forms) g=generic avail. | Adult Dose Starting / Max | $/mo | Side effects (SE) / Drug Specific Comments Drug Interactions (DI) {key select, not exhaustive!} | P [12,13] ← Pregnancy Category | General Comments & Considerations |
|---|---|---|---|---|---|
| **⇨ Nucleoside Reverse Transcriptase Inhibitors NRTIs** | | | | | |
| **Abacavir ABC** ZIAGEN (300mg tab, 20mg/ml soln) ☎▼ | 300mg po bid<br>600mg po daily | 470<br>470 | **SE:** hypersensitivity reaction(**HSR**); ?↑MI risk DAD study [14,15]<br>**Caution:** Test for **HLA-B*5701** prior to tx to ↓risk of hypersensitivity. Do **not** rechallenge if hypersensitivity occurs. See Table 2 - Rash above. | C | ♀ on NRTI's during PREGNANCY should continue all ARV's, but should have AZT intrapartum to prevent transmission to child.<br>few DI's[16] (DI: ddI+ribavirin→lactic acidosis, hepatic injury) |
| **Didanosine ddI** VIDEX EC (4g solution) χ ▼ (125, 200, 250 & 400mg EC cap) ☎▼ | 400mg po od wt>60kg<br>250mg po od wt<60kg<br>(↓ dose with tenofovir-see comments) | 380<br>250 | **SE:** peripheral neuropathy dose-related, pancreatitis, GI upset, portal hypertension<br>retinal Δ's, optic neuritis, ?↑MI DAD study **DI:** allopurinol,ribavirin,methadone ddI soln | B | can be taken without regards to food (except ddI on empty stomach)<br>**SE** long-term: lactic acidosis (d4T,AZT,ddI); hepatic steatosis; lipodystrophy syndrome with central fat accumulation worst d4T, ↑ lipids & insulin resistance/diabetes (common with d4T,AZT,ddI)[17]; anemia; myopathy; osteopenia[18] |
| **Lamivudine 3TC** 3TC, HEPTOVIR (100,150,300mg tab;10mg/ml soln) ☎▼ | 150mg po bid<br>300mg po daily | 340<br>340 | **SE:** pancreatitis<br>**Comment:** well tolerated NRTI, common in pregnancy | C | **SE short-term**: GI disturbances, headache |
| **Stavudine d4T** ZERIT 15,20,30 & 40mg cap ☎ ▼; 1mg/ml soln SAP | 40mg po bid wt>60kg<br>30mg po bid wt<60kg | 330<br>320 | **SE: hyperlipidemia, lactic acidosis, lipoatrophy**, peripheral neuropathy 15-20%, pancreatitis | C | ddI soln must be mixed as a buffered solution with antacid<br>ddI +TDF not 1st line tx; ↓ dose ddI: 250mg if wt>60kg od; 200mg if wt<60kg od |
| **Zidovudine AZT,ZDV** RETROVIR (100mg cap;10mg/ml soln & IV⊗) ☎▼ | 300mg po bid | 260 | **SE: anemia** may occur after long-term tx, neutropenia, muscle wasting & pain, leukocytoclastic vasculitis case reports, lipoatrophy. Common in pregnancy | C | 3TC, FTC, TDF used for Hep B. Hepatitis flare with abrupt discontinuation.<br>{Controversial: shorter time to SE presentation, & early virologic failure with |
| **Emtricitabine FTC** EMTRIVA 200mg cap χ ⊗; (10mg/ml soln in USA) | 200mg po daily (cap)<br>(240mg po daily (liquid)USA) | 290<br>NA | **SE:** discoloration of skin(palms & soles) more common on dark skin<br>Used as the combo product TRUVADA with tenofovir in Canada | B | ABC/3TC vs TDF/FTC in pts with HIV RNA >100,000 copies/ml ACTG5202}[19] |
| **⇨ Nucleotide Reverse Transcriptase Inhibitors NRTIs** | | | | | |
| **Tenofovir DF, TDF** VIREAD ☎✆ 300mg tab (▼ for chronic hepatitis B) | 300mg po daily | 570 | **SE:** renal impairment, Fanconi-like Sx, GI upset, osteopenia.<br>**DI:** ddI ↑ddI level; ATV ↓ATV level; use RTV 100mg to boost level | B | **Comments:** less lipoatrophy than ddI & d4T [20,21]; lipid friendly.<br>**M:** renal fx, urinalysis, lytes (phosphate). Hepatitis flare if Hep B & D/C tx abruptly |
| **⇨ Non-Nucleoside Reverse Transcriptase Inhibitors NNRTIs –resistance common (less with etravirine)** | | | | | |
| **Efavirenz EFV** SUSTIVA ☎▼ 50,100χ & 200mg cap; 600mg tab | 600mg po daily<br>(hs dosing for ↓CNS SE) | 485 | **SE: rash** 26%(mild-moderate), **CNS SE** ↓ with hs dosing,time: vivid dreams, dizziness, insomnia, headache, ↓concentration, psychiatric Sx; ↑LFT, ↑chol, ?↓Vit D | D | **General:** NNRTI's more likely to have **resistance;** less # of pills/day<br>**EFV & NVP**: stop ~ 2 wks in advance of other ARVs due to long half life |
| **Nevirapine NVP** VIRAMUNE 200mg tab ☎ ▼ 10mg/ml soln SAP-EDS | Start 200mg daily x14day<br>then 200mg BID or 400mg daily | 340<br>180 | **SE: rash** mild-severe, rare SJS; **hepatic failure** esp. ♀ with pre-tx CD4+ >250, & ♂ with pre-tx CD4+ >400; hepatitis, nausea, diarrhea, lipid friendly | B/C | **EFV**: 1) **Teratogenic**: avoid in ♀ of child bearing age; 2) **DI**: methadone ↓ meth level 45% [22], ↓ PI level, ↓ voriconazole level [23]; ↑ midazolam & triazolam levels; caution if psych hx |
| **Etravirine ETR** INTELENCE ☎⊗ 100mg tab | 200mg po bid | 730 | **SE:** rash occurs early in tx, ↑ in ♀, diarrhea, nausea, headache; ↑TG & cholesterol<br>**M:** TG, cholesterol FDA Aug/09: rare severe skin rx & liver failure | B | **NVP**: Caution Hep B/C coinfection [24]. Pregnancy option: use if CD4+<250;may ↓ perinatal transmission; **M**: LFT; **DI**: methadone ↓ level (AUC ↓ 40-65%), ↓ PI level<br>**ETR** less resistance?; not for tx naïve. **DI**: Avoid TPV/RTV, FPV/RTV, ATV/RTV [25,26] |
| **Delavirdine DLV** RESCRIPTOR (100mg tab) ☎ ⊗; rarely used, more frequent dosing (400mg TID $300), & potentially less antiviral activity | | | | | |
| **⇨ Fixed dose NRTI Combinations** {SE: see above} | | | | | |
| **Abacavir/Lamivudine** KIVEXA | 1 tablet once daily | 750 | 600/300mg tab ☎ ▼ | C | more convenient, lower pill burden |
| **Abacavir/Lamuvudine/Zidovudine** | 1 tablet bid | 1100 | TRIZIVIR 300/150/300 tab ☎ ▼ low virological response | C | less flexible for dosage adjustments |
| **Lamivudine/Zidovudine** COMBIVIR | 1 tablet bid | 690 | 150/300mg tab ☎ ▼ well tolerated | C | combine with a PI or NNRTI |
| **Emtricitabine/Tenofovir** TRUVADA | 1 tablet once daily | 810 | 200/300mg tab ☎ ✆ well tolerated, convenient **M**: renal function | B | Trizivir not recommended, use only if other options unsuitable; less effective |
| **⇨ Fixed dose NNRTI/NRTI Combinations** {SE: see individual drugs for SE's} | | | | | |
| Efavirenz/Emtricitabine/Tenofovir ☎ | 1 tablet once daily | 1240 | ATRIPLA 600/200/300mg tab ☎ ✆; "one tab, once daily" | D | Convenient; Avoid: in pregnancy and ♀ of child bearing age, renal dysfunction |

ς =scored tablet **#**=fracture χ=Non-formulary Sask ☎=Exception Drug Status SK ✆ =prior approval for NIHB ⊗=not covered by NIHB ▼covered by NIHB **ART**=antiretroviral therapy **ARV**=antiretroviral **BG**=blood glucose **BP**=blood pressure **CTZ**=chemoreceptor trigger zone **CV**=heart **DX**=disease **GERD/GI**=stomach **LFT**=liver function tests **P**=pregnancy category **SAP**=special access **SX**=symptoms **TB**=Tuberculosis **TG**=Triglycerides **VL**=Viral load **Red Flags**-for more urgent investigation: fever, night sweats, thrush **Lifestyle**: Encourage exercise, no smoking; prevent transmission

**Regimens for Tx Naïve Pts: A) NNRTI Based** (1 NNRTI + 2 NRTIs). **B) PI-Based** (1 or 2 PIs + 2 NRTIs): (ritonavir boost usually preferred). **Regimens for Tx Experienced Pts**: guided by resistance testing etc.; at least 2-3 active ARVs

☆**HIV Links**: **Guidelines**: http://aidsinfo.nih.gov/contentfiles/AdultandAdolescentGL.pdf; **Pregnancy:** http://aidsinfo.nih.gov/contentfiles/PerinatalGL.pdf **Metabolic diseases**: http://www.eacs.eu/guide/2_Prevention_and_Management_of_Metabolic_diseases_in_HIV.pdf **DIs**: University of Liverpool http://www.hiv-druginteractions.org/; HIVInsite http://www.hivinsite.com/insite?page=ar-00-02 [27] Toronto General Hospital HIV clinic http://www.hivclinic.ca/

## ⇨ Protease Inhibitors (PI) –consider using PI if tx started before drug resistance tests available

| Drug | Dose | Cost | Side effects / Notes | Preg. |
|---|---|---|---|---|
| **Atazanavir ATV REYATAZ** (150,200,300mg cap) ☎ ▼ | 300mg/100mg RTV OD 1st (400/100mg RTV if with EFV) 400mg once daily | 750 770 700 | **SE:** ↑ unconjugated bilirubin no Tx required, nephrolithiasis; ↓ lipid[28] & BG effects ◆ECG: ↑PR interval~5%. Boost ATV if used with TDF or EFV tx naive | B |
| Darunavir DRV **PREZISTA** 300,400,600mg tab ☎ ▼, (75mg)X⊗ | 600mg/100mg RTV po bid 800/100mg RTV once daily | 1040 740 | **SE:** hepatotoxicity, ↑ lipids & TG ≤21%, headache, rash, ?sulfa allergy ◆Boost with ritonavir {800/100mg once **daily** -CDN/FDA tx naive} ◆Age ≥ 6yr | C |
| **Fosamprenavir FPV TELZIR,** LEXIVA (700mg tab; 50mg/ml susp) ☎ ▼ | 1400mg/100-200mg RTV po daily 1st (tx naïve) 1400mg bid (tx naïve) 700mg/100mg RTV bid | 660 1050 660 | **SE:** rash[19%, SJS]; (?↑MI risk Heath Canada July/09) Dose varies based on dosing frequency & other meds; sulfa allergy ◆Bid dosing in tx experienced pts. ↑↑DIs ◆rare: nephrolithiasis | C |
| Indinavir IDV **CRIXIVAN** (200,400mg cap) ☎ ▼ | 800mg po q8h 800mg/100-200mg RTV po bid | 550 500 | **SE:** renal toxicity, renal calculi, ↑ bilirubin without ↑ LFT's, alopecia & dry skin, nail changes, gallstones & hypertension, ↑MI DAD study (36) Note: take with ≥ 2 glasses H2O/dose. **Used infrequently** due to ↑ SE. | C |
| **Lopinavir/Ritonavir LPV/r KALETRA** (133.3/33mg cap D/C; 200/50mg tab; 80/20mg/ml soln; 100/25mg pediatric tab) ☎ ▼ {Pill burden less with tab} | 400/100mgRTV bid 1st 800mg/200mg RTV po once daily tx experience/ naive (except pregnancy[37]) | 720 720 | **SE: GI (diarrhea++** , nausea), ↑ **lipid** esp ↑ TG, ↑MI DAD study, insulin resistance, pancreatitis, ↑ LFT, ↑ bilirubin[38] ↑↑DIs: ↑ benzodiazepine level, bosentan… ◆OD dosing may not be sufficient for VL>100,000 copies/ml & has ↑ diarrhea ◆**PI of choice in pregnancy** ◆caps, solution store in fridge, room temp<42days | C but DOC |
| **Nelfinavir NFV VIRACEPT** 250,625mg tab☎▼; (50mg/g powder for susp)X ▼ | 1250mg po q12h 750mg po q8h | 610 550 | **SE: diarrhea** ~35% ◆**Do not boost** with RTV; not effective ◆Previously avoided in pregnancy, but is now an option (level of EMS corrected) | B |
| **Ritonavir RTV NORVIR** (100mg cap; 80mg/ml soln) ☎ ▼ | ***With other PI's**** at 100-200mg od-bid | 75-215 | ◆Used low-dose as *booster;* **SE:** nausea, diarrhea; not tolerated well, ↑QT with saquinavir ◆Cap: store in fridge; room temp<30day, Soln at room temp {100mg tab FDA; store room temp} | B |
| Saquinavir SQV **Invirase,** Fortovase discontinued (200mg cap; 500mg tab) ☎ ▼ | 1000mg/100mg RTV po bid | 690 | **SE:** rash, ↑LFT, ↑QT or PR interval ◆Boost with ritonavir ◆Alternate choice in pregnancy | B |
| Tipranavir TPV **APTIVUS** 250mg cap ☎ ✆ (soln avail. USA, contains ↑ Vit E) | 500mg/200mg RTV po bid | 1265 | **SE:** intracranial hemorrhage 8 reports, hepatotoxicity, rash, sulfa allergy Boost with ritonavir; **CI:** hepatic insufficiency Caution: hemophilia **M:** liver fx; store in fridge, room temp for<60days | C |
| Amprenavir APV **AGENERASE** (50,150mg cap; 15mg/ml soln) ☎ ✆, often replaced by fosamprenavir since amprenavir no longer avail. in the USA | | | | |

1st: in dosing column denotes a 1st line dosing option (many dosing variations)

***Boosting**: low dose RTV given with other PI's to ↓ metabolism & ↑ levels {where common, the combination RTV dose used is shaded orangy-tan.}

◆**Class SE:** rash, GI disturbances-nausea, diarrhea (less for ATV)[29], headache, paresthesias(RTV), hyperglycemia, insulin resistance/diabetes, ↑ lipids, ↑ bleeding in hemophiliacs, peripheral lipoatrophy & central fat accumulation, hepatotoxicity

**Important drug interactions:**

- PI's are inhibitors of or are metabolized by CYP3A4: ↑↑ **DI's** eg. ↑ benzos
- **RTV many DI's:** Inhaled/intranasal fluticasone + RTV and RTV boosted PI's: cause Cushing's syndrome; alternatives: budesonide, beclomethasone, triamcinolone, flunisolide[30]. ◆Statins (see Table 4) ◆Garlic
- GI meds[31,32,33]: ATV & TPV DI with antacids give 2hrs before or 1hr after antacids; ATV + (H2RA or PPI) DI complicated= ↓↓ ATV level (Discourage use of PPI, but if PPI needed use ≤20mg omeprazole equivalent 12hours prior to ATV/RTV dose.)
- LPV/r: methadone ↓ levels, **M** for withdrawal. LPV/r: gemfiibrozil ↓AUC 41%
- TPV/r + estrogen ↑ rash risk ◆TPV/r + raltegravir ↑ LFT's[34].
- ATV + (EFV or TDF) ↓ ATV level, avoid in tx experienced

**Comments:**

- **DRV** and **TPV** may be used in treatment experienced pts
- **TPV** option for resistant cases & good responses when given with enfuvirtide [35]
- **FPV** use boosted dose with efavirenz (700mg/100mg RTV bid or 1400mg/300mg RTV od)
- **LPV/r** + efavirenz/nevirapine: use higher dose in tx-experienced 600mg/150mg bid
- **Pregnancy**: LPV/RTV drug of choice (DOC); ATV/RTV, NFV, SQV/RTV also ok. (based on ARV in Pregnancy guidelines; considers tolerability as well as overall safety rating & experience.)

## ENTRY INHIBITOR ⇨ Fusion Inhibitor

| Drug | Dose | Cost | Side effects | Preg. | Comments |
|---|---|---|---|---|---|
| Enfuvirtide **T20 FUZEON** vial 108mg=90mg ☎⊗ | 90mg SC bid | 2450 | **SE:** local inj site rx, ↑ bacterial infections, hypersensitivity rx <1%, eosinophilia | C | **Comments:** SC, expensive; use in treatment experienced pts |

## ENTRY INHIBITOR ⇨ Chemokine Coreceptor 5 (CCR5) Antagonist

| Drug | Dose | Cost | Side effects | Preg. | Comments |
|---|---|---|---|---|---|
| Maraviroc **CELSENTRI, Selzentry USA** (150,300mg film coated tab) ☎ ⊗ | 300mg po bid 150-600mg po bid (Dose adjust if with 3A4 inhibitors/inducers) | 1050 1050-2080 | **SE:** cough, fever, colds URTI's, rash, muscle & joint pain, abdominal pain, dizziness (postural hypotension)[39], ?hepatotoxicity **M:** liver function Tropism assay: performed on samples with >1000 copies/ml HIV-1 RNA Caution: prior liver dysfunction, coinfection with Hepatitis B or C virus | B | **Comments:** specific for CCR5-tropic HIV-1 virus (not for use in dual /mixed or CXCR4-tropic virus); use in tx experienced pts(with resistance) & naïve pts; Tx failure often due to tropism changes [40] **DI:** many potential DI's (CYP3A4 substrate); St. John's Wort (↓maraviroc levels) |

## Integrase Strand Transfer Inhibitor (INSTI)

| Drug | Dose | Cost | Side effects | Preg. | Comments |
|---|---|---|---|---|---|
| Raltegravir **ISENTRESS** 400mg film coated tab ☎ ✆ | 400mg po bid | 875 | **SE:** diarrhea, nausea, headache, thrombocytopenia rare **M:** CK **DI:** ↑rhabdomyolysis, myopathy with simvastatin, rosuvastatin[41] | C | **Comments:** for naïve & **tx experienced** TRIO (42) pts; low genetic barrier for resistance **DI:** rifampin may ↓ levels of raltegravir |

## Table 4 : HIV – Common Concomitant Diseases/Conditions

**Contraception considerations** [43] {counsel HIV positive ♀ to use **2 methods of contraception**: barrier & hormonal}

- ARV's that ↓ hormone levels: ritonavir, lopinavir/ritonavir, tipranavir/ritonavir, darunavir, nelfinavir, nevirapine, saquinavir
- Options with Few DIs: 1) NRTIs can be used safely with most hormonal contraceptives; 2) maraviroc, raltegravir, or etravirine
- Combinations of hormonal contraceptives + ARV's that maintain potency of hormones are:
  - Depo medroxyprogesterone acetate Depo-Provera + nevirapine or nelfinavir (or efavirenz however pregnancy category D)
- some OC's ↓ARV levels & should not be used together: fosamprenavir

**CV disease**[44] {pts have ↑risk of cardiovascular disease due to HIV disease related ↑in pro-inflammatory effects}

- Framingham equation can be used but may underestimate risk; new tool to be developed. ◆ Treat modifiable risk factors

**Cholesterol**[45,46,47,48,49,50] {ART causes ↑ in cholesterol; lipid lowering medications often necessary [51]}

- DI's with ART may ↑ or ↓ statin levels – consult DI charts for appropriate dosing (see links)
- Statins: consider pravastatin & fluvastatin as few DI's with HIV meds; rosuvastatin & atorvastatin may be used with caution if started at low doses. AVOID: lovastatin/ simvastatin + PI's and some NNRTI's; pravastatin + DRV/RTV
- Fibrates (fenofibrate, gemfibrozil) are tx options for ↑ triglycerides. DI with RTV & NFV – fibrate dose may need increase (lpv/rtv+gemfibrozil- ↓ gemfibrozil AUC 41%)[52] ◆ other tx options include niacin, ezetimibe (minimal PI interactions) & fish oil ↓ TG

**Lipodystrophy:** {syndrome including: fat redistribution with ↓ fat in arms, neck & face; ↑central fat in neck (buffalo hump) & abdomen; associated with ↑chol, ↑TG, ↑LDL;↓HDL; impaired glucose tolerance & insulin resistance}

- common (up to 40-50% of people on ARV tx); seen with NRTI's (d4T,AZT), PI's ◆ treatment somewhat controversial

**GERD/PUD**[53]: Certain PI's (ATV, FPV, IDV,TPV) have the most significant DI's with antacids, H2RA's & PPI's

- other ARV classes have minimal DI's with antacids, H2RA's & PPI's

**Immunizations :** ◆give pneumococcal vaccine soon after initial diagnosis or when CD4+count >200cells/mm³. Additional booster if CD4+ count <200 cells/mm³ on initial administration & count ↑ > 200cells/mm³. Repeat in 5-6 years.[54] ◆influenza vaccine yearly. ◆vaccinate for hepatitis B (Hepatitis A if at risk)see vaccine chart. Additional injections may be required if Hep B antibody indicates no immunity[55]. ◆Caution: live attenuated vaccines (except perhaps varicella); dependent on CD4+ counts; check with specialist.

**Osteoporosis**[56,57,58,59,60,61] {Osteoporosis/penia is a metabolic complication of HIV disease}

- periodically assess pts for low BMD & risk factors (↑ age & steroid exposure; ↓ body wt, low BMI, smoking/alcohol, duration of HIV)
- Calcium 1-1.5g / day & Vit D 400-1000IU / day. Targeted tx of high fracture risk if # hx or ↑↑↑risk: bisphosphonates (alendronate 70mg once weekly most studied)

**TB: disease or latent** {Mycobacterium tuberculosis: complexities of tx are beyond the scope of this document (referral required)}

- delay initiation of ART for 8week in ART naïve pts starting TB tx. All rifamycins have major DI's with NNRTI's & PI's.

**Pneumonia** [62,63,64]**:** {NOTE: if >2 episodes of pneumonia per year, indicator of potential AIDS illness}

- if CD4+ cell count > 200 cells/mm³ : *Strep pneumoniae, H . influenzae, Staph aureus* IV drug user,&/or aerobic Gm- bacilli see CAP chart.
- if CD4+ cell count < 200 cells/mm³ consider PJP(pneumocystis jirovecii pneumonia); if pneumocystis moderate-sev, treat with high dose prednisone (40mg po BID x 5 day, then 40mg po od x 5day, then 20mg po x 11days) **at start of tx** with TMP/SMX 15-20mg TMP/75-100mg SMX po q8h x21days
- if using macrolide in ART patient, consider azithromycin instead of clarithromycin due to ↑ DI's (HIV DI resource: see link below)
- consider **PJP** primary prophylaxis if CD4+ count <200 cell/mm³ or hx of oropharyngeal candidiasis: TMP-SMX: 400/80mg tab daily or one DS tab 3x/wk. Other tx options: dapsone, dapsone + pyrimethamine + leucovorin, aerosolized pentamidine via Respirgard II nebuliser, atovaquone[65]
- Stop 1° & 2° prophylaxis in pts on ART with CD4+ cell count >200 cells/mm³ for > 3 months; restart prophylaxis if CD4+ <200; consider lifetime 2° prophylaxis if PJP occurred with CD4+ >200 or PJP recurs
- Delay ART tx until end of PJP tx or ≥2 wks after starting tx for PJP {to prevent immune reconstitution inflammatory syndrome (IRIS)}

**Erectile dysfunction:** ↑↑ levels of sildenafil/tadalafil/vardenafil when combined with PI's; use lowest doses

**Acute HIV infection / Retroviral Syndrome**: Symptoms: flu-like (fever, myalgias/arthralgias), skin rash, lymphadenopathy, pharyngitis, etc. Consider screen for HIV if suspect due to symptoms &/or risk factors. Data unclear if initiating tx during acute infection beneficial. More studies required to determine benefits vs risks. Genotypic resistance testing recommended. **Treatment Interruptions**:[66] AVOID if possible. {may result in ↑ viral load, ↑ infections, & clinical progression; does not ↓ SEs.} **Infection**[67]: Initiating ART during tx of opportunistic infections (OI) can result in immune reconstitution inflammatory syndrome (IRIS). Symptoms: unexpected worsening of underlying infection. Common associated infections include: mycobacterium (e.g. TB, MAC), PJP, & herpes viruses. Delaying initiation of ART in the early phases of tx of the OI may ↓ risk of IRIS.

# ANTIVIRALS (Drugs for Influenza): AMANTADINE -*SYMMETREL* Dosage by Age & Renal Function [1,2]

| No recognized renal dysfunction | TREATMENT DOSAGE | |
|---|---|---|
| Children 1-9 yrs old [a] | 5mg/kg OD or divided BID (total daily dose not to exceed 150mg) | |
| Children >10 yrs old | 200mg OD or divided BID [b] (if less than 40 kg, give 5mg/kg per day) | |
| Adults ≤ 64 yrs old | 200mg OD (or 100mg BID) [b] (Note: **100mg OD** adequate/better tolerated for **prophylaxis**) | |
| Adults ≥ 65 yrs old | 100mg OD | |
| **Renal dysfunction: CrCl * in ml/second** (ml/min in brackets) | | **Alternate dosing adjustment schedule**[2] |
| >1.33ml/s (80-99 ml/min) | 100mg po OD | 100mg Day 1, 100mg/day starting Day 2 |
| 1.00-1.32 ml/s (60-79 ml/min) | Alternating daily doses of 100mg & 50mg | 100mg Day 1, 75mg/day starting Day 2 |
| 0.67-0.99 ml/s (40-59 ml/min) | 100mg every 2 days | 100mg Day 1, 50mg/day starting Day 2 |
| 0.50-0.66 ml/s (30-39 ml/min) | 100mg twice weekly | 100mg Day 1, 25mg/day starting Day 2 |
| 0.33-0.49 ml/s (20-29 ml/min) | 50mg three times per week | 100mg Day 1, 25mg/day starting Day 2 |
| <0.32 ml/s (10-19 ml/min) | Alternating weekly doses of 100mg & 50mg | If outbreak continues, repeat 100mg dose every seven days during the outbreak. |
| **Hemodialysis** | 200mg every 7 days | |

**Emphasize importance of vaccination!**
(In Canada ~20% get the flu & leads to >4000 deaths/yr)
**{Especially for Healthy kids 6-23months** (give 2 doses of vaccine 4 weeks apart for kids <9yrs who were previously unvaccinated); **People providing regular care to young kids** [<2yr]**, if heart, renal, cancer, diabetes or lung disease; & in elderly ≥65; & in pregnant women; & encourage in those capable of transmitting to high risk people such as health care workers or in anyone if adequate vaccine supplies exist}. Efficacy to prevent is ~70%.**
**Protection begins ~2 weeks post vaccination & persists ~6months** [~4months in elderly] **or longer.**
**Vaccine contraindicated in severe egg allergy, previous severe reaction or if currently has a serious acute febrile illness.** Watch ~15mins post-vaccination for a reaction.
**CDN**: Vaxigrip [thimerosal free in single dose only]; Fluviral; & Influvac [thimerosal free]
(FluMist: live attenuated intranasal vaccine in USA only).
Usually give 0.5mL ≥ 3yrs [0.25mL 6-35months] **IM** [in deltoid] in **Oct or Nov** but offer thru March.

* **Calculation of creatinine clearance (CrCl):** ♦CrCl ml/second = {(140-age) x weight (kg)} / {serum creatinine (umol/L) x 50} ♦ Female: CrCl = 0.85 x CrCl (male) | Watch units for ml/second !!!

[a] **Use in children** < 1yr old has not been evaluated  [b] **Patients with history of seizures**: consider reduction in amantadine dose (<100mg OD) or use alternate neuraminidase inhibitor

## ANTIVIRAL AGENTS for Influenza [3,4,5] -treatment within ~48hr of symptom onset shortens course by ~1 day & relieves symptoms to some extent [8, conflicting data]

-treat patients with **severe illness** or those likely to **suffer complications or death** due to influenza (also encourage fluids, rest & analgesics)
-persons **not** at higher risk for complications or do **not** have severe influenza requiring hospitalization generally do not require antiviral meds for treatment or prophylaxis.

| | M2 INHIBITORS | NEURAMINIDASE INHIBITORS (NI) | |
|---|---|---|---|
| | **Amantadine** C *SYMMETREL* | **Oseltamivir** C *TAMIFLU* ✗ ⊗ | Zanamivir C *RELENZA* ✗ ✆ |
| Influenza coverage | Influenza **A only** {H3N2, H1N1, H1N2} except resistance now high (↑ H3N2 Resistance 0.4% (1994)→12.3%(2004); >70% China & Hong Kong) | Influenza **A** including **H1N1** & Influenza **B** | Influenza **A** including **H1N1** & Influenza **B** |
| Route of administration | Oral | Oral | Oral Inhalation (<2 % oral bioavailability) |
| Dosage forms available | 100mg **capsules;** 10mg/ml **syrup** | 30,45,75 mg **caps;** or **powder for susp.** 12mg/mL (**susp** has 26g **sorbitol** thus not use if fructose intolerance) | 5mg per inhalation via **Diskhaler** Show & give info to use **device** properly. Contains **lactose**. |
| Approved for **prophylaxis** [c] (A 10 day tx of postexposure prophylaxis with zan- or oselt-amivir results in **8% less** incidence of symptomatic influenza.) [8] | Currently **not** for prophylaxis because of resistance {Previously: "approved for - ≥ 1yr old"} | Yes ≥ 13yrs old →75mg po od x 7-14day ⚙ CrCl 10-30ml/min 75mg every other day or 30mg OD suspension Kids 1-12yr ≤ 15-40kg of age 30-60mg od x 10day | Yes ≥ 7yrs old [d] (FDA: Adult & Kids ≥5yr: 10mg od x 10-28d) ♦NOT for nebulizer/ventilator mechanical; not for reconstitution |
| Approved age for treatment | ≥ 1yrs old | ≥ 1yr old But CNS SE in young kids {<1yr for pandemic tx 3-3.5mg/kg bid} | ≥ 7 yrs old Concern: Diskhaler difficult to use in young kids |
| Dosage for **treatment** (usually 5 days) | **Currently not for prophylaxis or treatment** (because resistance has risen to > 99 %) ⇨ **except** if severe H5N1 or resistant/multiple A subtypes may **combo** Tx with NI. | Adult or Kids>40kg: 75mg po BID x 5 days; Kids: ≤15kg: 30mg bid x5days; 15-23kg: 45mg bid x5days; 24-40kg: 60mg bid x5day | 2 inhalations's (10mg) q12h x 5days [e] |
| Adjustment for renal failure | YES - see above Table ⚙ | YES treatment-if CrCl < 30ml/min 75 mg OD ⚙ | NO dose adjustment necessary. |
| Side Effects | **CNS** - lightheadedness, insomnia, irritability (less when ↓dose for age & renal fx); GI upset, edema Use in Pregnancy **not** recommended. WHO | **Nausea, vomiting**, insomnia, vertigo & bronchitis, headache, rash & ↑ liver enzymes Rare: behavior changes self-injury & delirium esp. in kids | Nasal/throat irritation, Headache, GI upset, Bronchitis & Cough Rare ?: behavior changes self-injury & delirium esp. in kids |
| Cost in Sask. for **5days** | **~$10 (cap); $13 (syrup)** | **~ $50** | **~ $46** |
| Comments/ Precautions ⇨Check with local Medical Health Officer for current local area recommendations before prescribing!!! | ♦Adverse CNS effects related to & progressive with high serum concentrations ♦↓dosage for age, renal function & **seizure** history ♦institutional outbreaks: Tx 6-8wk→80% preventive ♦avian 2004 virus isolates are resistant to amantadine ♦↑**resistance** H3N2 esp. in Asia, **CDN** & USA CDC'06 | ♦ prodrug requiring hepatic activation ♦ ~10% incidence of **nausea** +/- vomiting 6%; taking with food may help ♦ concern of resistance in kids & **H1N1** strains [6] ♦ stockpiling: for avian H5N1 & swine H1N1 flu (In **pregnant** women recommend to give for H1N1) ♦ DI: probenecid ↑ oseltamivir levels, clopidogrel ↓ effect; | ♦may cause **bronchospasm**, in people with asthma or COPD avoid or use cautiously with access to a SABA eg. salbutamol Ventolin ♦? an option in pregnancy due to ↓**bioavailability** ♦ resistance not a great concern yet ♦ stockpiling: for avian H5N1 & swine H1N1 flu (In **pregnant** women recommend to give for H1N1) |

⚙ =↓ dose for renal dysfunction ✗ =non formulary Sask ⊗=not covered NIHB ✆=prior NIHB **COPD**=chronic obstructive pulmonary disease **fx**=function **SABA**=short acting beta agonist **Sx**=symptoms **Tx**=treat **Wks**=weeks

[c] **Prophylaxis**: Institutional exposure Tx at least 2wks & continued for **1 wk after** the end of the outbreak; Household post-exposure 60-90% effective Tx 7-14days may be effective. **Infection**: Tx usually 5days. (Med Letter Nov/2005)
[d] Zanamivir trials show 80-85% effective at 1/2 of the usual dose. [e] **Zanamivir -Recommended on first day**: 2 inhalations stat; repeat after 2 hrs then begin 2 inhalations q12h the next day for 4 days. **WHO**: http://www.who.int/csr/disease/influenza/en/
**Amantadine for prophylaxis &/or therapy** within a family, facility or institution is **NO longer** advised because of ↑ viral resistance.[7 (NACI), 8] **Canada** http://www.phac-aspc.gc.ca/fluwatch/ **CDC** http://www.cdc.gov/flu/about/season/index.htm

# MALARIA PROPHYLAXIS

## General Statements [1,2,3,4,5,6,7,8,9]

- **Physicians are strongly advised** to recommend that all travelers to malaria endemic areas, developing or tropical countries, extreme environments and those travelers with significant underlying medical conditions consult with a **certified travel medicine provider** or public health international **travel clinic** well in advance.
- **Malaria recommendations change frequently** and unpredictably in response to changing drug resistance patterns and the occurrence of malaria outbreaks in low risk destinations including popular tourist destinations. Review of current travel recommendations is essential!!
  - **Canadian**: http://www.phac-aspc.gc.ca/tmp-pmv/index.html
    - -Travel Clinics: www.travelhealth.gc.ca
    - -Advisories: http://www.phac-aspc.gc.ca/tmp-pmv/pub_e.html
  - **CDC**: http://www.cdc.gov/malaria/ **(Ph. 770-488-7788)**
  - **WHO**: http://www.who.int/topics/malaria/en/
- **Travel to a malaria risk zone (MRZ) within the past year** is a risk for malaria even if prophylaxis was used, especially if a **fever** develops **within 3 months** of return.
- Individuals originally from a MRZ who return back to **visit relatives** are at high risk for malaria and high risk to not seek prophylaxis. {**Immunity wanes** over 3+ months.}
- **Symptoms**: fever & rigors with other **flu-like** symptoms (myalgias, headache, vomiting, back/abdominal pain). May progress to breathlessness, impaired consciousness, seizures, shock, haemoglobinuria, bruising. {Residual neurological deficits can occur; most resolve by 6 months.}
- **Refer malaria patients to a specialist early!**
- Malaria can lead to seizures, coma, organ failure & death. {**The time from onset of symptoms to death** can be **<48hrs**; therefore **a suspected case is a medical emergency**. Blood slides require processing within hours. Prompt treatment / referral should not be delayed even if lab results not available.}
- **Epidemiology**: Worldwide: >300 million cases/year and >2 million deaths/year (mostly infants & children). {Canada[2]: ~400 malaria cases imported & ~1 death/yr[2004]}
- **Malaria is caused by** Plasmodium protozoa transmitted from female ***Anopheles*** mosquito[quiet, active dusk to dawn] bites.
  ****Plasmodium falciparum*** is the most common cause of serious morbidity & mortality. *P. vivax, P. ovale, P. malariae* (& *P. knowlesi*) generally present as less severe, but have a dormant stage. *P. vivax, P. ovale* may cause relapsing malaria.
- **ABCD**: A[awareness of risk] B[bite avoidance] C[compliance of meds] D[diagnosis]

## Who's at risk? Awareness of risk

- **Travelers** who enter a malaria risk zone (**MRZ**) in tropical latitudes & some temperate regions. **CDC Map**
- **Those with ↑ risk factors of acquiring malaria:**
  - a destination that includes rural exposure
  - camping versus air-conditioned accommodations
  - duration of stay especially high risk season
  - low altitude at destination (< 2000m or 6500ft)[2]; NOTE: low risk at altitudes >1500m, virtually nonexistent >2500m.

**We would like to acknowledge the following contributors and reviewers:** Dr. J. Opondo (SHR-Pub Health), Dr. T. Diener (RQHR-Pub Health), Dr. K. McClean (SHR-Infectious Disease), Dr. J. Kriegler (Saskatoon-FP) & the RxFiles Advisory Committee. *Prepared by Joseph Dagenais, Loren Regier* BSP, BA, *Brent Jensen* BSP



## What can be done to prevent malaria? Bite avoidance

- **Reduce physical exposure to mosquito bites** from dusk to dawn. Wear light coloured, tucked-in, tight weaved, long sleeved shirts, pants & socks.
- **Use DEET (30%) insect repellent** for all ages >2 months while in the MRZ. Reapply q4-6 hrs or sooner PRN. {Microencapsulated slow release forms ↑ duration ≤ 8hrs with ↓ concentration USA:Ultrathon. >30% DEET: not avail. in Canada & little added protection.} {Alternatives: **Picaridin** Bayrepel, lemon eucalyptus oil & soybean oil 2%. This is not available in Canada; may be obtained outside Canada e.g. in airports/online}
- **Postpone travel until low risk season,** especially for elderly, children & pregnant women who must travel
- **Impregnated clothing with insecticide** {Instructions at: www.phac-aspc.gc.ca/publicat/ccdr-rmtc/04pdf/ccdr_malaria_0604_e.pdf}
- **Impregnated bed netting:** {Instructions for replacement e.g. after 6 months & washing at: http://www.healthbridge.ca/malaria_control_e.cfm
- **Ask travelers about potential "misconceptions";** (not a trivial disease, herbals e.g. citronella oils not proven, repellent safety).

## Malaria Prophylaxis - Chemotherapy Compliance

- No chemoprophylaxis is 100% effective in prevention.
- If patient is concerned with the side effects & tolerability of their malaria meds, may start 3-4 wks prior to travel.
- Weekly malaria prophylaxis (**MP**) has been associated with ↑compliance & maintains sufficient drug blood levels longer than the daily regimen if a dose is missed.
- Purchase MP in Canada before leaving. Agents purchased or couriered from overseas may not be effective due to insufficient amounts of active drug, contamination, or the wrong drug. **Counterfeit** drugs are common.[10] {Some agents used overseas are associated with severe toxicities e.g. Halofantrine (HALFAN) – cardiotoxicity.}
- Choice of prophylaxis will depend on resistance trends. Types: chloroquine-sensitive, chloroquine-resistant *P. falciparum*; mefloquine-resistant *P. falciparum*; Chloroquine-resistant *P. vivax*; & case reports of chloroquine-resistant *P. malariae*.
- Chloroquine is the drug of choice (**DOC**) for malaria prevention only in regions with solely chloroquine-sensitive P. *falciparum/ vivax/ ovale & malariae*
- Terminal Prophylaxis "post-exposure" with primaquine may be considered **if travel for >8wks** in a MRZ with exposure to P. vivax or P. ovale

## PREGNANCY & LACTATION:

- Due to the ↑ risk of both malaria and pregnancy complications it is recommended that women who are or who may become pregnant should not travel to a MRZ
- For those who must travel, consult with travel specialist.
- Risks of malaria considered to outweigh risks of drugs!
- All antimalarial drugs listed in chart enter breast milk. Safety of the mother's anti-malarial medication with the infant must be considered. Insufficient levels of drug are obtained in breast milk which may necessitate infant MP.
- **DEET 20% is considered safe in pregnancy and lactation**
- {Falciparum malaria in preganancy often complicated by recurrent hypoglycemia, pulmonary oedema, premature delivery, & stillbirth.}

**Table 2: Malaria Prophylaxis** [11,12,13,14,15,16,17,18,19,20,21,22,23,24,25,26,27,28,29,30,31,32,33] © www.RxFiles.ca May 2010

| Drug (g=generic avail.) Role, etc. Pregnancy | Dose (po) for Prevention | $ Tx course | Comments {Major Contraindications, Side Effects, Drug Interactions, etc.} |
|---|---|---|---|
| **If Chloroquine Sensitive Area** {Resistance changes; check current recommendations. {Choroquine sensitive areas: travel to Caribbean incl. Haiti & rural areas of Dominican Republic; travel to most of Central America (EXCEPT Panama); travelers visiting resort areas not generally at risk.} Resistance: esp. sub Saharan Africa, much of S. America & SE Asia. | | | |
| **Chloroquine** phosphate (ARALEN),g 250mg tab (500mg = 300mg chloroquine base)<br>First-line: DOC chloroquine sensitive malaria [2]<br>**Consult travel clinics if available!!!**<br>See current listings for malaria risk zones MRZ[34]. {Area risk changes over time as do resistance patterns.}<br>• **DOC**: All Plasmodium except CR(PF& P. vivax); in areas without CRPF<br>• **DOC**: in Pregnancy if chloroquine sensitive (but SE concern for nursing infants) **C**<br>May use long term if tolerating well[2]. 60 year safety record {Opthalmological exam periodically if used weekly low dose long term; risk very low in first 5yrs; if >5yrs (BMJ,CDC), or high risk (ACP)}. | Pediatric: 8.3 mg/kg (5 mg base/kg) oral weekly<br>• Loading dose: 16.7 mg/kg (10 mg/kg base) if not started 2 wks prior to exposure)<br>Adult: 500 mg **weekly** (=300 mg base)<br>Loading dose: 1g in two divided doses 6 hr apart if not initiated 2 wks prior to exposure<br>• Begin **1-2wk prior** to entering MRZ, continue during stay & **4 wks after** leaving MRZ (to cover delayed mechanism of action) | Assuming 4 week trip<br>15 | • **CI**: **visual** field changes (if continuous for 5 yrs & further prophylaxis required), myasthenia gravis. **Precaution**: generalized psoriasis, epilepsy<br>• **Caution**: pts with hepatic failure, **G6PD deficiency**, pre-existing auditory damage. OK in pt with CrCl >10 ml/min.<br>• **SE**: N/V/D, pruritus in blacks, headache & dizziness. {Uncommon: alopecia, hair de-pigmentation, fatigue, skin eruptions, tinnitus, blurred vision, ↓platelets, retinopathy, psychosis & seizures.}<br>• **DI**: Inhibits CYP 2D6, cimetidine, cyclosporine, antacids; quinine, quinidine, mefloquine; high-dose acetaminophen, agalsidase α & β; amp[2hr], amiodarone, chlorpromazine, digoxin, methotrexate; bupropion ↑ seizure risk?.<br>• Vaccine Interaction[17]: Typhoid, Cholera, Rabies[ID]<br>• **Missed dose**: Take ASAP then wait 7 days for next dose.<br>**Take with food;** may crush tablets in jam, fruit juice or chocolate syrup, bananas or formula to mask bitter taste. Caps compounding option. Chocolate syrup recipe: http://www.sickkids.ca/pharmacy/custom/chocolate_cherry_syrup.asp |
| **Hydroxychloroquine** PLAQUENIL,g | • Seldom used; alternative to chloroquine if pt already on, or if chloroquine not available (400mg/weekly). More info on ref page [35]. | | |
| **If Chloroquine Resistant Area** (DOC: Mefloquine; if mefloquine resistant DOC: Doxycycline, Atovaquone/Proguanil) | | | |
| **Mefloquine** HCL 250mg tab LARIAM,g ✗ ⊗<br>• ≥ 95% effective against CRPF<br>First-line: DOC chloroquine resistant **C**<br>**DOC**: 2nd & 3rd trimester of pregnancy if CRPF [2]. {1st trimester: safety not established; however may consider as benefit may outweigh potential risk of early pregnancy loss}<br>• Wait 3 months after DC before trying to conceive.<br>• Neuropsychiatric SEs not common (but noted in media) Serious (seizure/psychosis) 1 in ≥ 6,500. Less severe (anxiety, depression, irritability) 1 in ≥ 200. ?pneumonitis<br>• Increased risk of neuropsychiatric SE in women, first-time users, and BMI ≤20; well tolerated in males without past history of psychiatric disorders [20].<br>• Long-term prophylaxis well tolerated. Good evidence up to 1 yr. CDN Guidelines recommend not to arbitrarily restrict use if well tolerated & pts at risk[2] {Monitor: Periodic LFT & Ophthalmic exams}<br>40% of **neuropychiatric** adverse events occur after 1st dose & 75% by 3rd dose; 1-4% DC due to SE | • Pediatric: 5mg/kg weekly. <5 kg no data; assess risk vs benefit<br>5 - 9 kg: 5mg/kg weekly<br>10 -19 kg: ¼ tab weekly<br>20-29 kg: ½ tab weekly<br>30-45 kg: ¾ tab weekly<br>>45 kg: 1 tab weekly<br>Tablets taste bitter; pharmacist may compound syrup with sugar or chocolate.<br>• Adult: 250 mg weekly<br>• Begin **1-2 wk* prior** to entering MRZ; use during stay & **4 wks after** leaving MRZ<br>*Begin 3 wk prior if worried about SE or loading dose 250mg od x3→weekly | 56 | • **CI**: Epilepsy, history of depression, psychosis, anxiety, schizophrenia & heart conduction problems. Do not use with halofantrine, quinine & quinidine (due to ↑QT effect).<br>• Caution: activities involving coordination or in situations where vertigo is life threatening; hepatic dysfx., myasthenia gravis.<br>• **SE** (> in ♀): (1-10%) N/V/D, dizziness, headache, sleep disorders (vivid dreams[≥15%]/insomnia), vomiting (can persist after DC); (<1%) anxiety, confusion, paranoia, psychosis depression, hallucinations, seizures, abnormal heart beat<br>• 1-6% discontinue due to SE; similar to other antimalarials<br>• **Take with food (after main meal) and 8 oz of water**<br>• **Missed dose** - Take ASAP, however; if almost time for next dose, skip the missed dose & resume normal dosing regimen.<br>• **DI**: anticonvulsants, bupropion, cardiac conduction meds, β-blockers concern if arrhythmia hx, ketoconazole, rifampin; acetaminophen high-dose, anti-psychotics, warf?, cimetidine, metoclopramide. Vaccine DI[17]: Typhoid, Rabies?.<br>• Resistance to mefloquine: esp. select areas around Thailand |
| **Atovaquone/Proguanil** ✗ ⊗<br>250mg/100mg tab MALARONE<br>62.5mg/25mg tab MALARONE PEDIATRIC<br>• Wait 3 weeks after DC before trying to conceive. **U**<br>• First-line: CRPF {although emerging resistance}<br>• 2nd-line: chloroquine sensitive & multi-drug resistant malaria (e.g Thailand border region, west Cambodia, east Myanmar). Not 1st-line; lack of evidence[2]<br>• Good safety data up to 12 wks. Supportive evidence up to 26 wks. Use with caution longer than 26 wks[8]. | • Pediatric (FDA ≥11kg; CDC off-label <11kg):<br>5-8kg: ½ Ped tab OD<br>9-10 kg: ¾ Ped tab OD<br>11-20 kg: 1 Ped tab OD<br>21-30 kg: 2 Ped tab OD<br>31-40 kg: 3 Ped tab OD<br>> 40 kg: 1 Adult tab OD<br>*Malarone Adult (250mg/100mg): 1 tab OD<br>• Begin **1-2day prior** to entering MRZ, continue during stay, & **1 wk after** leaving MRZ | 65 Based on 1 tab OD<br>185 | • **CI**: children <5 kg & CrCl ≤30 ml/min; pregnancy lack data<br>• **SE**: Well-tolerated. N/V/D [7-15%], rash, headache; mouth ulcers, seizures rare<br>• **Take with food or milk. Missed dose:** Take ASAP, skip dose if <3 hrs of next dose & continue normal regimen.<br>• **If switching from mefloquine or doxycycline:** there are special considerations for duration of prophylaxis required [9]. Since confusing contact local travel clinic or CDC-Malaria Line @ 770-488-7788.<br>• **DI**: indinavir, metoclopramide, tetracycline, rifabutin, rifampin, warfarin; resins: separate admin times.<br>• Vaccine Interaction[17]: Oral Typhoid |
| **Doxycycline** 100mg tab/cap VIBRA-TABS,g<br>• ≥ 95% effective against CRPF<br>• First-line: chloroquine & multi-drug resistant malaria[2]<br>**DOC**:Thailand border region Cambodia, Mynamar, & for scuba divers {less SE's/seizure issues}<br>• 2nd-line: chloroquine sensitive<br>• Persons on long-term minocycline & tetracycline for acne should cease 1-2 days prior to travel & commence doxycycline until full course of doxycycline is completed; then restart previous tx. **D**<br>• Duration: considered safe <3 months; use documented in troops up to 1 year; UK Guidelines suggest safe up to 2 yrs[8]. Monitor CBC, CrCl, LFTs with >3mon use. | • Pediatric ≥8yrs: 2 mg base/kg OD (max 100 mg/day)<br>25-35 kg or 8-10 yrs: 50 mg OD<br>36-50 kg or 11-13 yrs: 75 mg OD<br>≥ 50 kg or ≥ 14 yrs: 100 mg OD<br>• Adult: 100 mg OD<br>• Begin **1-2day prior** to entering MRZ, continue during stay, & **4 wks after** leaving MRZ<br>{also prevents leptospirosis} | 39 | • **CI**: <25kg or < 8yrs, breastfeeding, pregnancy, myasthenia gravis<br>• **SE**: Common: nausea, ↑**sun sensitivity** (may be less common with 100mg/day dose expert opinion), ↑vag. **Candidiasis** (♀ may wish to take along med for self treatment of Candidiasis)<br>• **Take with plenty of water** to ↓GI irritation. (Food may ↓ absorption by 20%); remain upright for 30min<br>• **Missed dose:** Take ASAP, skip dose if within 3 hrs of next dose and resume normal dosing regime.<br>• **DI**: Inhibits 3A4; anticonvulsants phenytoin, digoxin, warf; ↓ absorption with antacids/ multivitamins/ iron; resins separate admin times, acetaminophen high dose, Pepto-Bismo, retinoids, rifampin, sucralfate, MTX.<br>• Vaccine Interaction[17]: Typhoid, Oral Cholera; BCG bladder ca |
| **Terminal Prophylaxis / Prevent Relapse due to P. vivax and P. ovale** (*presumptive antirelapse therapy*) | | | |
| **Primaquine:** Terminal Prophylaxis: Effective against *P. vivax* & *P. ovale* only. Used for pts that have had long exposure to malaria endemic areas (>8wks) [2]. **C/D**<br>• Only therapy to prevent relapse from P. vivax & P.ovale due to dormant hypnozoites in liver (relapse may occur within 5 years of exposure). Also 2nd line for CRFP.<br>• More info on reference page online at www.rxfiles.ca . {Primaquin 15mg/kg/day + Chloroquine x14days more effective for preventing P. vivax relapses than shorter courses or Chloroquine alone.Cochrane 07} | | | |

**ASAP**=as soon as possible **CBC**=complete blood count **CI**=contraindication **CrCl**=creatinine clearance **CRPF**=Chloroquine Resistance *P. falciparum* **d**=day **DEET**=Meta-N,N-diethyl toluamide insect repellant **DC**=discontinue **DI**=drug interactions **DOC**=drug of choice **ID**=intradermal **LFT**=liver function tests **mon**=months **MP**=malarial prophylaxis **MRZ**=malaria risk zone **MTX**=methotrexate **NVD**=nausea, vomiting & diarrhea **Pts**=patients **rh**=rheumatoid **SE**=side effects **wk**=weeks **[B]** =pregnancy category χ=Non-formulary SK ☎=Exception Drug Status SK ⊗=not covered NIHB ▼=covered NIHB

**Long term use of prophylaxis**: There is no absolute limit for long term use of any agent. **CDC Map**: http://www.cdc.gov/travel/destinat.htm

| Patient Characteristics | Likely Pathogens | Recommended Empiric Antibiotics {Canadian-adapted from 1) 2010 Anti-infective Guideline CDN 2) IDSA 2007 Update Mandell & 3) 2000 CIDS/CTS guidelines} | | Specific Agents & Sample Adult Dosages | $ per 10 d | Comments |
|---|---|---|---|---|---|---|
| **OUTPATIENTS** | | **Canadian** 2,9 (2010) | **USA** 5 (2007), 6 (2003 Med Let) | **Resistance** DRSP possible if: elderly, antibiotics last 3months, alcoholic, steroid use, comorbidity or child day care. | | |
| No modifying factors<br>Some Reserving FQs for: •more severe cases with co-morbidity •those intolerant or failed on alternates •PRSP -penicillin resistant Strep. pneumoniae (MIC ≥4mg/L) | •Mycoplasma pneum. (not as prevalent in elderly)<br>•Chlamydophila pneumoniae<br>•Strep. pneumoniae | 1st -Amoxicillin or Macrolide<br>2nd -Doxycycline 1st Bugs&Drugs'06 (Ketolide: may be option if Tx failures or DRSP) | •Macrolide or<br>•Doxycycline<br>If recent antibiotic Tx:<br>•Respiratory FQ alone<br>•Macrolide new &<br>amox↑dose or amox-clav↑dose<br>If recent Abx use: Add Amox↑dose B&D'06 | Doxycycline 100mg po bid; or<br>100mg bid x1d, then 100mg od<br>Erythromycin base 250-500mg po qid<br>Erythromycin ERYC 333mg po tid<br>☎▼Azithromycin 500mg po Day1; then 250mg po Days 2 thru 5<br>* long t½; 5day tx ≈ 10d or 500mg od x3 | 19<br>15<br>15-24<br>26<br>*28 5d | •compared to erythromycin, new macrolides ↑$ but ↓GI SE, od dose & better H. flu coverage (**but** S. pneumo **resistance** ~20% & recent macrolide use may ↑multi-drug resistant strep)<br>•5 day tx with azithromycin & 7-10 day tx with clarithromycin or **FQs** is adequate [6,7,8] |
| **Comorbidity – no recent antibiotics or oral steroids** within past **3** months | Above plus:<br>•H. influenzae<br>•M. catarrhalis | 1st -New Macrolide, Amoxil or Doxycycline Bugs&Drugs'06 (Ketolide: if Tx failures/DRSP) | Macrolide new or FQ Resp.<br>Aspiration: Amox-clav or clindamycin | ☎▼Clarithromycin 500mg po bid<br>1g XL po od cc | 55<br>67 | •Doxycycline preferred over TCN due to ↓GI SE, ↑bioavailabilty, BID (or OD) dosing; covers atypicals & ↓Strep resistance than macrolides.<br>•Ciprofloxacin **not** recommended –poor Strep. coverage/treatment failures |
| **Comorbidity – recent antibiotics or oral steroids** within past **3** months<br>**Comorbidity** may include: **COPD**, diabetes, malignancy, renal failure, heart failure, alcoholism, malnutrition, etc. | Above plus:<br>•H.influ, βlactamase +<br>•M. catarrhalis<br>•Legionella pneumophilia<br>(rare in SK) •Gram -ve rods | -(Amox↑dose or Amox/clav or 2ndG Ceph)+(Macrolide new or doxycycline) {Ketolide: alternative to macrolide if Tx failure or DRSP}<br>or<br>-Respiratory FQ | •Respiratory FQ alone<br>•Macrolide new & βlactam (amoxicillin↑dose, amox-clav↑dose, cefprozil or cefuroxime) | Amoxicillin 500-**1000**mg po tid<br>☎⊗Telithromycin 800mg po od<br>☎✆Levofloxacin 500-750mg po od<br>☎✆ Moxifloxacin 400mg po od<br>✗ ⊗Gemifloxacin 320mg po od | 17-27<br>80<br>46-80<br>74<br>85 | •Cephalosporins **lack** atypical coverage & show increasing pneumococcal resistance<br>•Penicillin for S. pneumoniae if MIC≤2mg/L; amoxicillin preferred: better absorption, dose TID & good MICs (S. pneumonia high level resistance~6%, intermediate resistance~10%) |
| **Nursing home resident,** outpatient management (if hospitalized, treat as below)<br>FQ **resistance** as high as 4%. | •Strep. & C. pneumoniae<br>•H. influenzae, S. aureus<br>•Gram –ve rods<br>•aspiration pneumonia | (Amox↑dose or Amox/clav or 2ndG Ceph) +(Macrolide new or doxycycline) {Ketolide: if Tx failure / DRSP}<br>or<br>-Respiratory FQ | •Respiratory FQ alone<br>or<br>•Macrolide new & amox-clavulanate | ☎▼Amox/clav **875**-2000mg po bid<br>☎▼Cefuroxime axetil 500mg po bid<br>☎▼ Cefprozil 500mg po bid | 35-89<br>51<br>56 | •Telithromycin: option if Tx failure or DRSP but has DI's, vision + **LFT** SE & ↑$. |
| **HOSPITALIZED Inpatients** (antibiotic within 4hr likely assoc. with **lower mortality**) [10] (FINE risk class I-III or CURB-65 score 0-1 may treat as outpt) [12] IV to oral antibiotic step down when stable. | | | | | | |
| **General Ward admission**<br>{Gram – **rod** more likely if: nursing home, CV/lung dx, recent antibiotics use or steroid use} | •**Strep.** & M. pneumoniae<br>•Chlamydophila pneumoniae<br>•H. influenzae •gram **-ve**<br>•Legionella pneumophilia | - (2nd or 3rd or 4thG Ceph or Amoxil or Amox/clav) + (Macrolide new or doxycycline) {Ketolide: if Tx failures/DRSP}<br>Or -Respiratory FQ alone | •Respiratory FQ alone<br>•(Macrolide new or doxy Med Let) & βlactam {cefotaxime, ceftriaxone, ertapenem; mero or imipenem Med Let if resistance} | Levofloxacin 500-750mg IV q24h<br>Moxifloxacin 400mg IV q24h<br>(or **po** fluoroquinolones as above)<br>Cefuroxime 750mg IV q8h<br>Cefotaxime 1-2 g IV q8h | 450<br>380<br>(49-72)<br>100<br>250 | •Cdn CAP group favor monotherapy with FQs; US IDSA is concerned that misuse & overuse of FQs may ↑↑ resistance rates (S. pneumonia FQs resistance <2%) CBSN'05<br>•choice of 2nd, 3rd, or 4th gen cephalosporin dependent on local resistance |
| **ICU**<br>If antibiotic usage history in past 3 months, consider selecting antibiotic from different **class**. If pneumonia onset >5days after admission to hospital, more resistant organisms usually present.<br>**CA-MRSA**: If suspicion/at risk athlete, military, inmate, young, aboriginal, IV drug user, prior viral infx ? add or use Bactrim, clindamycin, **vancomycin** +/- rifampin or linezolid. [40] | Above plus:<br>•Enteric gram – **rods** (eg. Klebsiella, Enterobacter, Serratia, Acinetobacter)<br>•S. aureus (eg. CA-MRSA, MRSA) | -3rdG Ceph IV + Macrolide new<br>Or<br>- 3rdG Ceph IV + Respiratory FQ<br>{Using βlactam/lactam Inh or the 3rdG Ceph in CND2000 guidelines}<br>If beta-lactam allergy: Respiratory FQ + clindamycin | •βlactam {cefotaxime, ceftriaxone, ertapenem; (pip/taz, mero or imipenem -in Med Let if resistance issues)} & Macrolide new or FQ Resp.<br>{if severely ill +AMG Med Let}<br>•If βlactam allergy: Respiratory FQ +/- Clindamycin | Ceftriaxone 1-2 g IV q24h DI: calcium<br>Cefepime 1g IV q12h covers peudomonas<br>Erythromycin 500mg IV q6h<br>Azithromycin 500mg IV q24h **x5d** or **po** as above<br>Tazocin 4.5g IV q8h covers peudomonas<br>(**dose/cost of oral agents above**)<br>Tigecycline 100mg x1, 50mg IV q12h | 240<br>250g 320<br>600<br>110<br>610<br><br>**1700** | (S. pneumonia ceftriaxone resistance<2%) CBSN'05<br>•adjust doses for severity/renal function<br>•penicillin 3MU IV q6h or ampicillin 1-2g IV q6h still OK for *Strep. pneum* if MIC≤2 mg/L, but if MIC >2mg/L a FQ Resp. or vancomycin 1gm IV q12h watch for ↓ platelets or linezolid 600mg IV/PO q12h may be needed [6] |
| **ICU, risk of Pseudomonas** (Cystic Fibrosis, HIV, **structural lung disease**, bronchiectasis, recent stay in hospital esp. in the ICU) | Above plus:<br>•**Pseudomonas** species | 1st - antiP FQ + antiP βlactam (+/- AMG)<br>2nd - triple IV therapy:<br>•antiP βlactam+Macrolide (or FQ) + AMG {or as guided by C&S} | •antiP βlactam + ciprofl.<br>•antiP βlactam + AMG + (FQ Resp. or Macrolide)<br>•If βlactam allergy Med Let: ciprofloxacin & AMG & (clindamycin or vancomycin)<br>(dose/cost of other agents as above) | Ciprofloxacin 400mg IV q12h<br>Ceftazidime 2g IV q12h (or 1-2g q8h)<br>Imipenem 500mg IV q6h<br>**Dori**-500mg IV Q8h/**Mero**-penem 500mg/1g IV q8h<br>Gentamicin 3-7mg/kg IV q24h<br>Tobramycin 3-7mg/kg IV q24h | 450<br>880<br>1000<br>≥1000<br>200<br>230 | •Aminoglycoside cost based on **5mg/kg/d** x70kg adult, normal renal fx; {lengthen dosing interval if elderly, ↓ renal fx, etc.}<br>5-7mg/kg if younger, normal CrCl<br>7mg/kg for more severe infection<br>•Tobra better than gent for Pseudomonas |
| **Aspiration Pneumonia** (assess teeth & mouth area) | •Oral anaerobes esp if loss of consciousness & alcohol/ drug overdose or seizure<br>(dose/cost of other agents as above) | 1st -Amox/clav or cefuroxime (+/-Macrolide or metronidazole)<br>2nd -Clindamycin or {Metronidazole + (FQ or ceftriaxone)} | •Amox-clavulanate or clindamycin or (metronidazole Med Let)<br>(consider Tazocin if severe/ICU & gram -ve suspected) Sanford | Clindamycin 300mg po qid<br>600mg IV q8h<br>Metronidazole 250mg po tid<br>500mg IV q12h | 50<br>300<br>10<br>30 | •Moxifloxacin has anaerobic coverage (~ option for monotherapy 2nd line)<br>•po bioavailability: metronidazole~100%; clindamycin~90% |

☎ = EDS in Sask ✗ = non-formulary in Sask ✆=prior approval for NIHB coverage ▼=covered by NIHB ⊗=not NIHB **Cost= approximate $ drug cost per 10 days** unless noted otherwise noted = ↓ dose for renal dysfunction

**Amox/clav**= amoxicillin+clavulanate CLAVULIN **AMG**= aminoglycoside (tobramycin>gentamicin against Pseudomonas) **βlactam/lactam Inh (inhibitor)** = Amox/clavulanate (oral), piperacillin/tazobactam TAZOCIN

**2ndG Ceph** (cephalosporin)= cefuroxime CEFTIN, cefprozil CEFZIL; **3rdG Ceph**= cefotaxime CLAFORAN, ceftriaxone ROCEPHIN, cefixime SUPRAX (oral); **4thG Ceph**= cefepime MAXIPIME **B&D'06**=Bugs & Drugs 2006

**Macrolide**= erythromycin, clarithromycin BIAXIN, azithromycin ZITHROMAX **New macrolide**= clarithromycin, azithromycin **Ketolide**=Telithromycin KETEK **PRSP** = penicillin resistant S. pneumoniae (ie MIC ≥4mg/L).

**Respiratory fluoroquinolones (FQ Resp.)** = gatifloxacin TEQUIN D/C by Co, levofloxacin LEVAQUIN, moxifloxacin AVELOX (NOT ciprofloxacin unless pseudomonas suspected); **TCN** = tetracycline **DRSP**=drug resistant S. pneumo

**Antipseudomonal: antiP βlactam** = imipenem PRIMAXIN, meropenem MERREM, ceftazidime FORTAZ, cefepime MAXIPIME, piperacillin/tazobactam TAZOCIN; **antiP FQ** = ciprofloxacin CIPRO, levofloxacin 750mg LEVAQUIN

**Dose** -may need adjustment for severity of illness, renal function, etc. **Treatment duration** variable (typically 7-14day or 4-5day post-improvement; longer if complicated; 2-3 weeks suggested for Legionella, S. aureus, Gram -, also for C. pneumoniae & M. pneumoniae due to risk of relapse). **Pregnancy: 'B'** no evidence of risk (in animal studies or uncontrolled human studies) cephalosporins, penicillins, erythromycin , azithromycin, clindamycin & metronidazole.

**Pathogens for select conditions**: Airway obstruction & poor dental hygiene anaerobes; Bats/bird droppings Histoplasma capsulatum; Birds Chlamydia psittaci; Farm animals/cats Coxiella burnetti; IV drug use S. aureus, anaerobes, M. tuberculosis & Rabbits Francisella tularensis.

**Prevention**: stop smoking, vaccinate for pneumococcal all persons ≥65yr & select high-risk eg. comorbidity; revaccination after 5yrs in some & influenza most people if adequate vaccine supplies, annual revaccination, treat comorbidities, & have pandemic preparations in place.

**Pneumonia Risk Score Option #1:**

## Prediction Model for Identification of Patient Risk for Person with COMMUNITY-ACQUIRED PNEUMONIA (CAP) Pneumonia Severity Index (PSI) Algorithm

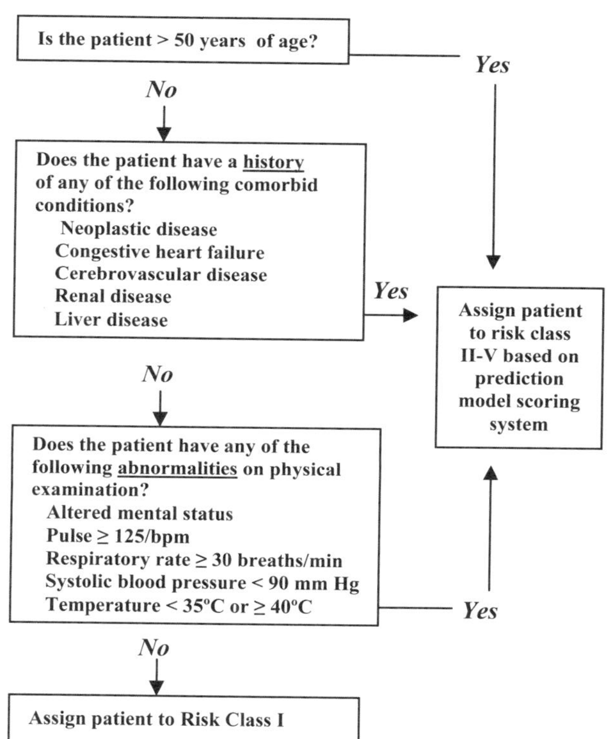
Is the patient > 50 years of age?
Yes
No
Does the patient have a history of any of the following comorbid conditions?
Neoplastic disease
Congestive heart failure
Cerebrovascular disease
Renal disease
Liver disease
Yes
Assign patient to risk class II-V based on prediction model scoring system
No
Does the patient have any of the following abnormalities on physical examination?
Altered mental status
Pulse ≥ 125/bpm
Respiratory rate ≥ 30 breaths/min
Systolic blood pressure < 90 mm Hg
Temperature < 35°C or ≥ 40°C
Yes
No
Assign patient to Risk Class I

**This model may be used as a guide in conjunction with clinical judgement in the decision on the most appropriate site of care for patients with CAP.**

Adapted from: 1. **Fine** MJ et al. A prediction rule to identify low risk patients with CAP. N Engl J Med 1997;336:243-50. 2. Mandell LA et al. Canadian guidelines for initial management of community acquired pneumonia. Clin Infec Dis 2000;31:383-421. 3. Bartlett JG et al. Practice guidelines for the management of community acquired pneumonia in adults. Clin Infec Dis 2000; 31: 347-82. 4. Lim WS, et al. Defining community acquired pneumonia severity on presentation to hospital: an international derivation and validation study. Thorax. 2003 May;58(5):377-82. (Kollef KE, Reichley RM, Micek ST, Kollef MH. The modified APACHE II Score outperforms CURB65 Pneumonia Severity Score as a predictor of 30day mortality in MRSA pneumonia. Chest. 2007 Oct 20).

### Pneumonia-Specific Severity of Illness Scoring System

| Patient's Characteristics | Points Assigned | Your Pt |
|---|---|---|
| **DEMOGRAPHIC FACTOR** | | |
| Age, yr | | |
| Male | (age) | |
| Female | (age-10) | |
| Nursing home resident | +10 | |
| **COMORBID ILLNESS** | | |
| Neoplastic disease | +30 | |
| Liver disease | +20 | |
| Congestive heart failure | +10 | |
| Cerebrovascular disease | +10 | |
| Renal disease | +10 | |
| **PHYSICAL EXAMINATION FINDING** | | |
| Altered mental status | +20 | |
| Respiratory rate>30/min | +20 | |
| Systolic BP<90 mm Hg | +20 | |
| Temperature<35°C or>40°C | +15 | |
| Pulse>125/min | +10 | |
| **LABORATORY FINDING** | | |
| pH<7.35 | +30 | |
| BUN>10.7 mmol/L | +20 | |
| Sodium<130 mmol/L | +20 | |
| Glucose>13.9 mmol/L | +10 | |
| Hematocrit<30% | +10 | |
| $PO_2$<60mm $Hg^2$ or $O_2$ sat <90% | +10 | |
| Pleural effusion | +10 | |
| **Total Score** | | |

### Stratification of Risk Score

**Score ≤90: send home; score ≥91: admit to hospital**
(possible short-course admission of those with 71-90 points)

| Risk | Risk Class | Based on Algorithm | Mortality |
|---|---|---|---|
| Low | I | 0 total points | ~0.1% |
| | II | ≤70 total points | ~0.6% |
| | III | 71-90 total points | ~0.9-2.8% |
| Moderate | IV | 91-130 total points | ~9% |
| High | V | >130 total points | ~28% |

**Above may underestimate risk in young otherwise healthy pts. May overestimate dx severity in elderly. Does not consider for example COPD, HIV or social factors.**

### SMART-COP

-an ICU intensive respiratory or vasopressor support (IRVS) **prediction score when CAP is confirmed on X-ray.**

| | Point |
|---|---|
| -low **S**ystolic BP <90 mmHg | 2 |
| -**M**ultilobar chest Xray involvement | 1 |
| -low **A**lbumin level <3.5g/dl * | 1 |
| -high **R**espiratory rate (age adjusted)<br>-If age ≤ 50yr then ≥ 25 breaths/min<br>-If age > 50yr then ≥ 30 breaths/min | 1 |
| -**T**achycardia ≥ 125 beats/min | 1 |
| -**C**onfusion (new onset) | 1 |
| -poor **O**xygenation (age adjusted) | 2 |

| Age | ≤ 50yr | > 50yr |
|---|---|---|
| $PaO_2$ * | < 70 mmHg | <60 mmHg |
| Or $O_2$ saturation | ≤ 93% | ≤ 90 % |
| Or (if on $O_2$) $PaO_2$ / $FiO_2$ * | < 333 | <250 |

-low arterial **p**H < 7.35 * 2

**Total Score=**

Interpretation: (This is not a predictor of mortality)

| | |
|---|---|
| 0-2 Points | Low risk of needing IRVS |
| 3-4 Points | Moderate risk (1 in 8) of needing IRVS |
| 5-6 Points | High risk (1 in 3) of needing IRVS |
| ≥7 Points | Very high risk (2 in 3) of needing IRVS |

* For primary care doctors, results for albumin, arterial pH, & $PaO_2$ can be overlooked & the following interpretation can be used:

| | |
|---|---|
| 0 Points | Very low risk of needing IRVS |
| 1 Point | Low risk (1 in 20) of needing IRVS |
| 2 Points | Moderate risk (1 in 10) of needing IRVS |
| 3 Points | High risk (1 in 6) of needing IRVS |
| ≥4 Points | High risk (1 in 3) of needing IRVS |

(Adapted from Charles et al. Used with permission.)

**Option #2:**

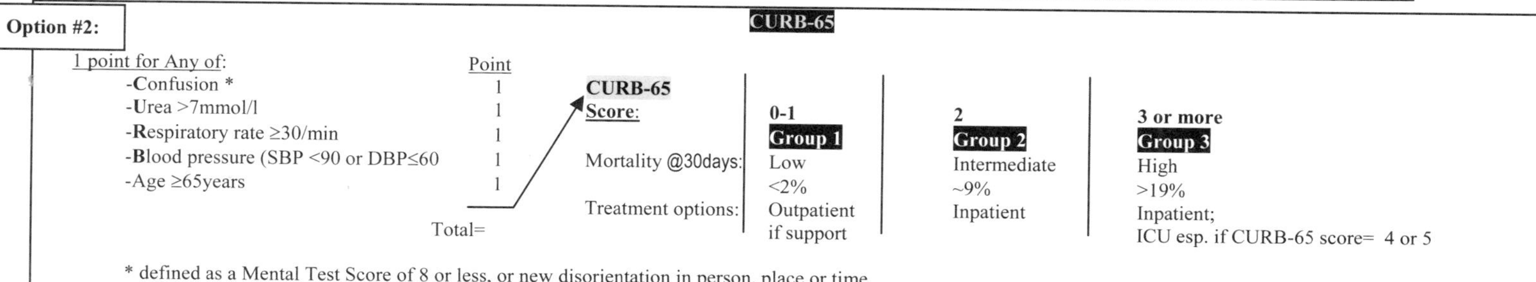

### CURB-65

| 1 point for Any of: | Point |
|---|---|
| -**C**onfusion * | 1 |
| -**U**rea >7mmol/l | 1 |
| -**R**espiratory rate ≥30/min | 1 |
| -**B**lood pressure (SBP <90 or DBP≤60 | 1 |
| -Age ≥65years | 1 |
| Total= | |

| **CURB-65 Score:** | 0-1 **Group 1** | 2 **Group 2** | 3 or more **Group 3** |
|---|---|---|---|
| Mortality @30days: | Low <2% | Intermediate ~9% | High >19% |
| Treatment options: | Outpatient if support | Inpatient | Inpatient; ICU esp. if CURB-65 score= 4 or 5 |

* defined as a Mental Test Score of 8 or less, or new disorientation in person, place or time.
This scoring does **not** take into account comorbidities or extent of the pneumonia. (The CRB-65 is another version which does not incorporate the Urea into the score).

# URINARY TRACT INFECTIONS (UTI), ADULT – TREATMENT OPTIONS

Prepared by: Loren Regier © www.RxFiles.ca


| CLASS | Drug (Strength) | TRADE name | Comments (related to use for genitourinary infections) | Acute ♀ Cystitis >12yrs | Recurrent (<1mo) | Prophylact. see note re. dose | Pregnancy, Asymptomatic | Complicated Tx: x10-14+ d | Pyeloneph. Out-patient | Pyeloneph In-patient | Prostatitis >35yrs Acute; Tx x2-4wks | Typical Dose for Genitourinary Infections (↓ dose in ↓Renal Fx; consult additional references/ pharmacy if CrCl <10ml/min) | $ (per 10 days) |
|---|---|---|---|---|---|---|---|---|---|---|---|---|---|
| | Shaded Rows = IV Formulations | | Cochrane Review 2008: PO = to parenteral in treating severe UTI. **Follow-up cultures in pregnancy.** | | | | | | | | | | |
| MISC. PO ABX | **SMX/TMP (Cotrimoxazole)** (100/20ς,400/80ςmg,800/160mgς DS tab; susp) | BACTRIM/SEPTRA (DS=double strength) | = sulfamethoxazole+trimethoprim; maintain hydration. *E. coli* resistance ≤15% in SK; enterococci resistant | ✓1 x3d | ✓1 x10-14d | ✓1* | ✓2 ✝ x3-7d | ✓1 C&S? | ✓2? C&S? | | ✓1 C&S? | 2 tabs (or 1 DS tab) PO BID; ↓*dose if CrCl<30ml/min* | 10 |
| MISC. PO ABX | **Trimethoprim** (100ς,200ς mg tab) | PROLOPRIM | Alternative to SMX/TMP in sulpha allergy. Max 200mg BID. | ✝ ⌛ | **Except for acute cystitis, antimicrobial treatment guided by urine C&S; ↑ bacterial resistance in more complicated patient** | | | | | | | 200mg OD; 200mg PO BID | 12, 22 |
| MISC. PO ABX | **Nitrofurantoin** (50ς,100ς mg tab) | NITROFURANTOIN | MACROBID well tolerated & convenient (BID) | | | | | | | | | 50mg PO QID cc Plain | 14 |
| MISC. PO ABX | **Nitrofurantoin** (50mg cap) | MACRODANTIN | Effective 1st line option in acute lower UTI. Note 7day tx recommended for acute cystitis. Avoid CrCl <40-60ml/min | ✓1 X5-7d ✝ | ✓1 x10-14d | ✓1* | ✓1 ✝ x3-7d | Not for upper UTI or systemic infection | | | | *Avoid if CrCl<40-60ml/min* Macro | 23 |
| MISC. PO ABX | **Nitrofurantoin** (100mg cap) | MACROBID | Good activity vs E. coli! (SE: rash, GI upset, ↑LFTs) | | | | | | | | | MACROBID 100mg PO BID cc | 23 |
| MISC. PO ABX | **Fosfomycin** (3g oral powder sachet) | MONUROL | Single dose tx; diarrhea 9% | ✓2 | | | | | | | | 3g PO x1; dissolve in ½ cup $H_2O$ | ☎ ✆34 |
| PEN | **Amoxicillin** (125,250mg chew tab; 250,500mg cap; susp) | AMOXIL | High rate >35% of *E. coli* resistance in SK! Option if C&S Ampicillin sensitive | ✓2 x7d | | | ✓1? x3-7d | | | | | 500mg PO TID; *BID if CrCl<50ml/min* | 17 |
| PEN | **Amox/Clavulanate** (susp) (250,500,875mg tab) –dose by amoxicillin component | CLAVULIN | Less *E. coli* resistance ~20% & broader coverage than amoxicillin; *875mg BID* convenient & less diarrhea | | ✓2 | | | ✓2 | ✓2 | | | 875mg PO BID; *500mg if CrCl<50ml/min* | ☎ ▼ 35 |
| PEN | **Ampicillin** (+AMG gent/tobra) IV | AMPICILLIN | Amp adds coverage for streptococcus & enterococcus | | | | | ✓1 | | ✓1 | ✓ | 500mg-1g IV Q6H | 80-140 |
| PEN | **Piperacillin/Tazobactam** IV | TAZOCIN | Broad spectrum; covers pseudomonas; poor evidence | | | | | ✓3? | | | | 3g/0.375g IV Q6H; ↓*dose if CrCl<50ml/min* | 600 |
| ? | **Imipenem** IV {Or: ertapenem **Invanz** 1g IV q24h $**500** not for Pseudomonas} | PRIMAXIN | Broad spectrum; covers pseudomonas; good evidence {Or: meropenem **MERREM** 500mg-1g IV q8h $720-1,430} {Or: doripenem **DORIBAX** 500mg IV q8h $1000} | | | | | ✓3 | | ✓3 | | 500mg IV Q6-8H | 999-790 |
| CEPH | **Cephalexin** (250,500mg tab/cap; susp) | KEFLEX | Safe in **pregnancy**; option if C&S suggests sensitivity. *E. coli* resistance in SK ~10% | ✓2 x7d | | ✓2* | ✓2 x3-7d | | | | | 250-500mg PO QID | 16-25 |
| CEPH | **Ceftriaxone** IV | ROCEPHIN | 3rd Gen IV Ceph's: | | | | | ✓2 | ✓ | ✓2 | ✓ | 1g IV Q24H | 240 |
| CEPH | **Cefotaxime** IV | CLAFORAN | -no coverage of enterococcus (Ceftriaxone: concern re calcium concurrently→precipitates) | | | | | ✓2 | ✓ | ✓2 | | 1g IV Q8-12H; ↓*dose if CrCl<50ml/min* | 250-180 |
| CEPH | **Ceftazidime** IV | FORTAZ | Reserve ceftazidime→**pseudomonal coverage** | | | | | ✓3 | | ✓3 | | 1g IV Q8H | 660 |
| FQ | **Norfloxacin** (400mg tab) | NOROXIN | **Fluoroquinolones (FQs)** useful if allergy or intolerance to other agents. **Reserve (preserve) for more severe, complicated or resistant infections.** | | | | | ✓3 | | | ✓1 | 400mg PO BID ac | ☎ ▼37 |
| FQ | **Ciprofloxacin** (250,500,750mg tab; 500mg & 1g XL⊗ tab, susp✆) | CIPRO | Concern regarding ↑ing resistance by both Gm-ve & Strep pneumo; **CIPRO covers pseudomonas.** | ✓2 x3d ⌛ | ✓2 x10-14d | ✓2* | AVOID | ✓2 | ✓1? | ✓2 | ✓1 | 250-500mg PO BID; 500mg-1g XL PO daily; ↓*dose if CrCl<50ml/min* | 38-42; 43⊗; ☎ ▼ |
| FQ | **Ciprofloxacin** IV | CIPRO | Other FQs: moxifloxacin AVELOX 400mg po OD has lower renal concentrations therefore not indicated for UTI | | | | AVOID | ✓2 | | ✓3 | ✓3 | 200-400mg IV Q12H | 240-450 |
| FQ | **Levofloxacin** (250, 500 & 750mg tab); 250,500,750mg inj PO/IV. Less pseudomonal coverage than Cipro! | LEVAQUIN/generic | **PO ≈ IV**; consider early switch (**IV→ PO**) e.g. 3-4days. **(Cipro 1g XL⊗ po od: 3 days=$17, 10days=$40)** Use higher doses for pyelonephritis; lower for cystitis. | ✓3 x3d ⌛ | ✓3 x10-14d | ✓3 | AVOID | ✓2 | ✓3 | ✓3 | ✓3 | {*250-500mg IV q24h* $130-250}; 250-500mg PO OD | ☎✆; 41-46 |
| AMG | **Gentamicin** (+/- Ampicillin) IV | GARAMYCIN | Excellent Gm –ve coverage. Q24H dosing safe & effective; levels not necessary for <7day therapy. **Treat ≤ 7days to ↓ toxicity; lower doses required in elderly/↓ renal fx.** | | | | | ✓1 | ✓ | ✓1 | ✓1 | 4-7mg/kg IV Q24H; e.g. 300-350mg IV Q24H | ~120 |
| AMG | **Tobramycin** IV | NEBCIN | Reserve tobramycin for **pseudomonal coverage** | | | | | ✓2 | | | ✓2 | *adjust dose for ↓renal fx* | ~90 |

**Suggested role in therapy**: ✓1 = 1st line option; ✓2 = 2nd line option; ✓3 = 3rd line option. (References: 2010 Anti-infective Guidelines, Anti-infective Review Panel, Ontario; Sanford Guide-Antimicrobial Therapy 2010) ς=scored tab
⚙ =↓ dose for renal dysfunction; $=10day cost (incl. markup & dispensing fee); ☎ = Exception Drug Status Sask. ✗ =non-formulary in SK ▼=covered by NIHB ✆=prior NIHB; avail. of IV formulations may vary. Consider **STDs** e.g. *C. trachomatis*: ⇨Doxy 100mg BID x7d or Azithro 1g x1
**AMG**= aminoglycoside **C&S**= culture & sensitivity **CEPH**= cephalosporins **FQ**= fluoroquinolones **GI**= gastrointestinal **LFT**= liver function tests **PEN**= penicillins **SK**= Sask **Tx**= Treat

- **Acute Cystitis (uncomplicated)** ⌛: **3day** tx option for SMX/TMP, TMP, FQs; **7day** tx for nitrofurantoin, amoxicillin & cephalexin; longer course in: diabetes, symptomatic >7days (& older women?).
- **Recurrent Cystitis**: reassess, culture & tx **10-14day**; * **Consider Prophylaxis**: if **3+ episodes per year**: eg. SMX/TMP or TMP 100mg 1 tab qHS or post-coital; Nitrofurantoin 50mg qhs or post-coital; Cephalexin 250mg qhs or post-coital; Low-dose FQs {(Cipro 250mg po or Norf 200mg) OD or every other day}. Short-course patient-initiated tx option for some; Vaginal estrogens option for post-menopausal ♀. ?Cranberry juice.
- **Antibiotics in Pregnancy**: ✝=**avoid nitrofurantoin at term** 36+ wks, or G6PD ⇨risk of hemolytic anemia; **avoid SMX/TMP in last 6wks** ⇨displacement of bilirubin or G6PD. **Avoid TMP** products **in 1st trimester; if use, give folic acid!**
- **Complicated UTI**: includes men, obstruction, chronic catheter (symptomatic), structural abnormalities & spinal cord injury. Tend toward mixed bacteriology/more resistant organisms. C&S important!
- **Pyelonephritis**: Culture. Treat **10-14days** (or ≥7 days for FQs). IV route if severe (convert from IV⇨PO after afebrile/improving x 1-2days); in diabetes & pregnancy, add ampicillin for Group B Strep.
- **Prostatitis**: if unable to void⇨hospitalization/catheterization. Chronic Prostatitis: may require longer duration of tx but often non-bacterial; if no response to ABX 4-6wks, may refer; Other options: α-blockers[1]
- **Asymptomatic Bacteriuria**[13] **- elderly, chronic cath., spinal cord injury**: **no indications for screening & no benefit in treating** (**except** pre-genitourinary procedures, pre-op prosthetic, immunosuppression, pregnancy)

**Common organisms**: **E. coli, Staphylococcus saprophyticus, Proteus species, plus other gram-negative rods (P. aeruginosa, Klebsiella) & enterococci.**

## LOW BACK PAIN - NON-PHARMACOLOGICAL TREATMENT OPTIONS*

Prepared by Loren Regier BSP, P. Taillon MD © www.RxFiles.ca May 10

| | |
|---|---|
| **Activity as tolerated** ✓<br>{suggest a structured exercise program} | ◆for acute or recurrent low back pain (**LBP**) of less than 3 weeks, **resuming ACTIVITY AS TOLERATED is encouraged!** For uncomplicated back pain, **bed-rest generally unnecessary & actually associated with longer recovery**[1] Specific exercises helpful in chronic LBP.[2,3] **Home exercise program (HEP)** useful!!! |
| **Physiotherapy** [4,5] | ◆useful in acute (<30 days), subacute (30-90 days), persistent (3-6 months) and chronic (>6 months) LBP; active exercise better than passive tx |
| **Spinal Manipulation** [6] | ◆conflicting results; some short-term improvement in pain & activity levels[7]; most useful in subacute illness; **Massage** – somewhat effective in persistent LBP[8] |
| **Psychosocial intervention** | ◆**important** for interrupting progression to **chronic pain behavior pattern**; factors should always be explored when progress is slower than expected |
| **Multidisciplinary intervention** | ◆intensive coordinated multidisciplinary programs are effective for recurrent/persistent low back pain of 3 months or more duration[9,10] |

**Patient education:** re. pain, posture, etc.; **Heat therapy** -useful acute relief; **TENS** -some efficacy?; **Lumbar support** -not particularly effective[11]; **Acupuncture** -unclear[12,13]; **Radiofrequency neurotomy**...; **Glucosamine**-not effective

## LOW BACK PAIN – PHARMACOLOGICAL TREATMENT OPTIONS*

| Class | Role | Comments | Sample Agents | Trade Name | Sample Dose | /30day |
|---|---|---|---|---|---|---|
| **Acetaminophen** | ✓✓ option in **mild-mod** pain; **≤4g/day** | ◆if chronic, **M** hepatic/renal fx; ≤3200mg/day | Acetaminophen 325,500mg | Tylenol | 650mg-1g QID | $20 OTC ✗▼ |
| **Acetaminophen with Codeine** | ✓ useful in **acute**, uncomplicated back pain (but little additional effect).<br>☒ not generally recommended in subacute/chronic pain | ◆Caution: may be **habit forming** in some patients; hepatotoxicity when used with muscle relaxants; adverse **GI effects** common with codeine | Acet.300mg + Caffeine +Codeine 8mg<br>Acet.300mg + Caffeine +Codeine 30mg | Tylenol #1 OTC (little additional effect)<br>Tylenol #3 | 2 tabs q4-6h (max 12tabs/d)<br>1-2 tabs q4-6h (max 12tabs/d) | $40 OTC* ✗ ⊗ *max 50tab/month in SK<br>$40 |
| **NSAIDs**<br>◆see also NSAIDs chart | ✓ **effective for acute**, uncomplicated low back pain; **equal efficacy** but pts may respond to one & not another [14]<br>◆less effective if sciatica or nerve root complications; lack evidence in chronic | ◆Caution: risk of **ulcers**; worsening **renal** fx, HF, HTN, MI?; CNS effects<br>◆If significant GI risk factors, consider prophylaxis with PPI std dose or misoprostol; coxib may also ↓ GI risk | Ibuprofen 200,300,400,600mg; **susp**<br>Ketorolac 10mg tab;30mg **inj**<br>Naproxen 125,250,375,500mg<br>Celecoxib 100,200mg | Motrin/Advil<br>Toradol {7d max}<br>Naprosyn; Aleve<br>Celebrex | 600-800mg TID<br>10mg po QID<br>220 - 375mg BID<br>200mg OD-BID | $15 OTC ≤400mg tab<br>$70 ✗ ✆<br>$16; OTC 220mg<br>$54-99 ☎ ✆ |
| **Opioids**<br>*Treatment Agreement* regarding usage is important to avoid overuse/abuse!<br>{Also morphine pump options} | ◆useful for **short-term use in severe/ acute pain**, if NSAIDs ineffective, not tolerated or contraindicated; short-acting forms for short-term/titration<br>◆**in sub-acute & chronic pain, long-acting** (SR) opioids may be indicated in conjunction with non-drug therapies **if** pain a significant barrier to **function!** | ◆Caution!!: **sedation, constipation**; sporadic use/overuse may adversely affect **cognitive/overall function**<br>◆**careful patient selection** and use of a *treatment agreement* important to limit dependence, abuse or diversion.<br>◆**Duragesic**® **cautions**: 12hr delay in onset; potent (not for opioid naïve); delayed resp. depression, sedation, etc. | Codeine regular; Codeine CR<br>Hydromorphone SR 3,6,12,24,30mg cap<br>Morphine SR[12hr] 15,30,60,100,200mg<br>Morphine SR[24hr] 20,50,100mg<br>Fentanyl **Patch** 12,25,50,75,100ug/hr | regular g; Codeine-Contin<br>Hydromorph-Contin<br>MOS-SR 30,60mg<br>MS-Contin/Ratio<br>Kadian<br>Duragesic | ≤60mg q4h; 50-200mg q12h<br>3-6mg q12h<br>30mg q12h<br>15-30mg q12h<br>20-50mg **q24h**<br>25ug/hr ≅ 90mg/d morphine | $40-70 ☎ ✆<br>$53-76 ✆<br>$40<br>$32-44<br>$35-58<br>$+++ ☎ ✆ new |
| | | | Tramacet (tramadol + acetaminophen; short acting) or tramadol SR also options. See opioid chart. | | | |
| **Muscle Relaxants**<br>◆misnomer?:- some suggest mostly sedation & little/no actual relaxant effect.<br>◆most centrally acting (except dantrolene & Botox) | ✓ possible **short-term role** of non-benzodiazepines for symptom relief in first **week**[15,16]; ≤ 2wks, but little evidence. **Effect linked to sedation!**. Studies do not support chronic use in LBP. {e.g. cyclo-benzaprine meta-analysis: 14 RCTs, efficacy modest & ↓ after 4 days use; adverse effects >50%} {Tizanidine 18mg/day also has some evidence for ↓ tension headache.} | ◆Caution: CNS SEs: **drowsiness, impaired cognitive/overall fx; falls, dependence**; hepatic toxicity with chronic use &/or acetaminophen. **(risk may often exceed benefit)**<br>DI:↑ tizanidine levels by CYP450 1A2 inhibitors like cipro & fluvoxamine→↑SE/hallucinations | Baclofen 10,20mg tab; intrathecal<br>**Cyclobenzaprine** 10mg<br>Dantrolene 25, 100mg cap (many SEs)<br>Tizanidine 4mg tab (2mg tab ✗)<br>Diazepam / Clonazepam<br>Methocarbamol +Acetam.<br>Methocarbamol +ASA<br>Methocarbamol +Ibuprofen | Lioresal<br>Flexeril **(TCA like)**<br>Dantrium<br>Zanaflex, generic<br>Valium / Rivotril<br>Robaxacet /ES<br>Robaxisal /ES<br>Robax Platinum | 5-10mg TID<br>5-10mg TID<br>25-100mg TID<br>2-4mg TID<br>various<br>2 tabs QID<br>2 tabs QID<br>1-2 caps q4-6h Max 6/24hrs | $18-28<br>$27-47 ☎ ✆<br>$45-87<br>$34-62 ☎ ✆<br>$15-25<br>$75 OTC ✗ ✆<br>$75 OTC ✗ ✆<br>$75 OTC ✗ ✆ |
| | Antispastic drugs (baclofen SE: weakness, dantrolene, tizanidine SE: hypotension, benzodiazepines, botox, & clonidine) sometimes used longer term for specific disease states (e.g. spinal cord/brain injury, multiple sclerosis). | | | | | |
| **Tricyclic Antidepressants** (TCAs)<br>(antidepressants with both serotonegic/ norepinephrine activity appear to have better efficacy in tx of pain; some non-TCAs may also be effective)[17] | ◆**may be indicated if comorbidities: depression, poor sleep, neuropathic** (burning) pain or persistent **headache**<br>◆some non-TCA antidepressants (e.g. venlafaxine) also alternatives<br>◆literature equivocal re. efficacy in LBP[18], but useful in **chronic pain**[19] (**amitriptyline** most studied in chronic pain) | ◆Caution: **dose-dependant SE's** - hypotension, dry mouth, drowsiness, confusion, constipation, urinary retention, wt gain; arrhythmia potential<br>◆**start low-dose HS,↑ slowly &/or consider 2° amine TCAs** (e.g. **nortriptyline**[20] & desipramine) often **better tolerated** than amitriptyline | 2° TCAs<br>Desipramine 10,25,50,75,100mg (10-150mg HS)<br>**Nortriptyline** 10,25mg cap (**10-100mg** HS) | Norpramin<br>Aventyl | 25-100mg HS<br>10-50mg HS | $17-35<br>$11-25 |
| | | | 1° TCAs — If sleep disturbance & chronic pain, consider amitriptyline 10-100mg hs, trazodone 25-100mg hs, mirtazapine 15-45mg hs. | | | |
| | | | **Amitriptyline** 10,25,50mg (10-150mg HS) | Elavil | 25-100mg HS | $12-23 |
| **Anticonvulsants**<br>Gabapentin, pregabalin; Others: carbamazepine... | ◆useful if neuropathic pain (e.g. burning/stabbing)<br>◆radiculopathy: small short-term benefit | ◆Caution: somnolence, dizzy, euphoria, etc.; many DI's with carbamazepine | Gabapentin 100,300,400mg<br>Pregabalin 25,50,75,150,300mg | Neurontin<br>Lyrica ☎ ⊗ | 300mg BID-TID<br>75-300mg BID | $40-56<br>$110-160 |

**Other: Topical Rubs**OTC ◆Often contain menthol or capsaicin; may provide some temporary local relief but not particularly useful in LBP ◆**Epidural steroids** - cautiously useful in spinal stenosis ◆**Herbal?**: devil's claw, willow bark, capsicum ◆**Botox injection** ☎✆ costly; effectiveness dependent on expertise ◆**Miacalcin** ☎✆ if vertebral fractures ◆**Bisphosphonates** ☎✆ in Paget's, OP etc. ◆**Methotrimeprazine** – additive analgesic/sedation ◆**Orphenadrine** Norflex ◆**Topical NSAIDs?**

=↓ dose for renal dysfx **DI's**=drug interaction **fx**=function **GI**=stomach **HF**=heart failure **HTN**=hypertentsion **OTC**=over the counter **SE**=side effect **SR**=sustained release **tx**=treatment ✗ =non-formulary in SK ☎= exception drug status SK ✆=prior NIHB ⊗not NIHB

***Overall approach to low back pain is to MOVE FROM PASSIVE modalities** (drugs, chiropractic therapy, massage therapy and passive physical therapy) **TO ACTIVE rehabilitation consisting of EXERCISES!** ▼=covered by NIHB

◆ **acute** (<30 days), **subacute** (30-90 days), **persistent** (3-6 months), **chronic** (>6 months) ➡ **Red Flags** (possible fracture, tumor or infection, or cauda equina syndrome) are potentially serious conditions. See http://www.rxfiles.ca/rxfiles/uploads/documents/members/CHT-BackPain-2pg.pdf

# PAIN – CHRONIC NON-MALIGNANT (CNMP): General Pharmacological Considerations [1]

## Medication / Analgesic History:

- Ask about use of over-the-counter (OTC) products including acetaminophen, Tylenol #1 with codeine, ibuprofen, relaxants, herbals, laxatives, etc. Trends in when various medications are used is helpful. Evaluate total acetaminophen dose & risk of toxicity from overuse.
- **Common Statements**:
  - "I've tried that and it didn't work!" Assess whether dose & duration of trial was adequate: what exactly was taken, at what dose, and for how long?
  - "It had too many side effects!" Evaluation of side effect history should consider whether initial dose was too high, and whether patient knew that many side effects go away over time. Dry mouth is common, and can often be relieved with an **artificial saliva agent** (e.g. Oral Balance Gel).
- Ask about drugs of abuse: street drugs, alcohol, etc. These can affect how drugs may work or are tolerated.

## Non-pharmacologic Therapy:

- Behavioral, psychosocial & physical therapies are essential in the successful long-term management.
- Interdisciplinary intervention may ↓drug requirements
- Pain reduction and improved function, not pain elimination, is the goal of drug therapy. Those with CNMP must be helped to refocus on positive, incremental gains. Dedicated therapists and/or CNMP programs are helpful. {Consider role of: exercise, pacing, heat, ice, TENS, cognitive-behavioral, relaxation, spiritual, acupuncture, etc.}

## Medication Induced Headache (MIH):

- *Analgesic rebound* or *medication overuse - headache*
- Generally resolves on discontinuation of drug up to 8wks {acetaminophen, NSAIDs, opioids, caffeine, ergots, triptans rare etc.}
- Outpatient: gradual taper; switch to longer-acting agents 1st; headache prevention agent {e.g. amitriptyline; DHE intranasal} x 3-6mo}
- Inpatient: dihydroergotamine (DHE) IV in NS Protocol given with metoclopramide 10mg may be effective.[2,3]

## Approach to analgesics:

- "One at a time" drug therapy changes allow for more accurate assessment of any beneficial or adverse effect.
- Specific pain syndromes or types of pain may have preferred drug options based on varying levels of evidence and practicality (see Table 1: Pain Conditions). {Evidence limited; trials small, short duration, & moderate quality.}
- Adequate trial of suitable non-opioid analgesics and/or adjunct agents is recommended before considering opioids.
- Try alternate drugs within a therapeutic class before determining that the class is ineffective.
- Continuous pain: use regularly administered agent(s); this will serve to prevent pain, and allows tolerance to develop to most of the bothersome side effects.
- Intermittent pain: consider whether an agent can be used just prior to activity or in conditions that trigger pain.
- Pain, Geriatric: http://www.americangeriatrics.org/education/final_recommendations.pdf

## Table 1: Pain Conditions – Specific Drug Therapy Options

L Regier May 10

| Pain Related Conditions | Specific Drug Therapy Options – {Daily target doses based on trials to date} [1] |
|---|---|
| **Neuropathic Pain** Cochrane07; CADTH09 TI (gabapentin) 2010: http://ti.ubc.ca/letter75 | TCAs: NNT=3.6, NNH AMI - major=28, minor=6, (not effective for HIV-related neuropathies); Venlafaxine: NNT=3.1, NNH major=16.2, minor=9; Gabapentin, Pregabalin, Carbamazepine: NNT≥3-8, NNH=8; Opioids; Tramadol NNT>3, NNH=8 major. **Drug causes**: alcohol, chemotherapy (platinum or taxane based), isoniazid, antiretrovirals. Freynhagen 2009 {Tips - TCA or anticonvulsant: start low but titrate up (e.g. weekly reassessment); SE: nortriptyline < amitriptyline; Cost: TCA < venla. & gaba} |
| **Trigeminal Neuralgia (TN)** (Facial pain) | **Anticonvulsant**: carbamazepine DOC,FDA 200mg qid; NNT=1.8 [4], may ↓effect at 3yrs, (+/-baclofen 60mg/d synergistic?); gabapentin 900-2400mg/d; lamotrigine 150-400mg/d; phenytoin; oxcarb.; **Topical anaesthetics**: 4% tetracaine & 0.5% bupivicaine option if not tolerating carbamazepine; BOTOX [5]. Little evidence for non-anticonvulsants.[6] Fluoxetine? {Drug Causes (rare): digoxin, nitrofurantoin} |
| **Painful Diabetic Neuropathy (DN)** 7,8, Wong, 89 | **TCAs** NNT 1.3-3; NNH=16: (amitriptyline, desipramine or imipramine) ~100mg/d; nortriptyline 20-50mg/d; **TCA +/- fluphenazine** 2-3mg/d; venlafaxine 150-225mg/d NNT=4.5@6wks [9]; **Anticonvulsants**: gabapentin ~1800mg/d; Cochrane:NNT=3, pregabalin 300-600mg/d; NNT>3, sodium valproate 1000mg/d [10], lamotrigine 200-400mg/d [11]; **SSRI's:** less effective than TCAs. **Topical Anaesthetics**: lidocaine patch 5%, **capsaicin crm** 0.025% or 0.075% qid; **glucose control** intensive -prevent progression; **Vitamins**: thiamine 25mg/d & pyridoxine 50mg/d; B12. **Duloxetine** CYMBALTA an SNRI 60-120mg/d $130-250, NNT≥5; no comparative trial [12; 13]. **Opioids** (oxycodone CR 10-40mg q12h NNT=2.6)[14]. **Tramadol** po; mexiletine 300-900mg/d ineffective in RCTs; ??topical isosorbide dinitrate, α-lipoic acid or TENs. |
| **Post-Herpetic Neuralgia (PHN)** 15,16,17,18 {Acute Herpes Zoster (shingles) if high PHN risk→ | **TCAs**: (nortriptyline, amitriptyline 75mg/d, desipramine) NNT<3; **Anticonvulsants**: gabapentin 1800mg/d, NNT=2.2; NNH=11.2, pregabalin 600mg/d, NNT=3.3; NNH=3.7 (16 for 300mg/d dose), divalproex sodium 1000mg/d; **Opioids** morphine, (oxycodone NNT=2.5; NNH=38); **Topical**: lidocaine 5% gel or patch; [negligible/marginal benefit: capsaicin 0.075% cream 8% patch FDA & ASA cream/oint] Acute Tx: antiviral within 72hrs (IMMUNOCOMPETENT: acyclovir 800mg po 5x/day x7-10d; famciclovir 500mg po tid x7d; valacyclovir 1g po tid x7d; IMMUNOCOMPROMIZED: acyclovir 10mg/kg IV q8h x7-10d); +/- prednisone x21days; +/- TCA 25mg hs} |
| **Post-Stroke Pain** | **TCAs**: amitriptyline 75mg/d, NNT=1.7 more effective than carbamazepine [19] (consider nortriptyline if elderly); **Anticonvulsants**: lamotrigine 200-400mg/d [20]; BOTOX for spasticity |
| **Spinal Cord Injury (SCI) Pain** | Gabapentin ≤3600mg/d-conflicting results (dose related?)[21,22]; most effective if duration <6months. Lamotrigine ≤400mg/d benefit only if incomplete SCI; allodynia a predictor of benefit[23]. Ketamine infusion [24]; Baclofen intrathecal infusion for refractory spasm/spasticity [25] Amitriptyline & valproate –not useful [26,27]. Pregabalin ?benefit [28] |
| **Post Mastectomy Pain** | Topical capsaicin 0.025% (open label trials only) [29,30]; TCA (amitriptyline 100mg/d NNT=2.5; NNH=5; Pre-emptive studies: amitriptyline & venlafaxine effective in 3 studies); NSAIDS |
| **Complex Regional Pain Syn.** Type I: Reflex Sympathetic Dystrophy (RSD) {Type II: previously "Causalgia"} 31,32,33,34 | DMSO 50% Crm 5x/day x2 months; Bisphosphonates IV short course in early phase; Prednisone short-term tapering regimen; Calcitonin: conflicting data; Nifedipine ≤60mg/d; Baclofen intrathecal for leg/foot pain in MS; TCAs & Anticonvulsants - options but lack data. [Gabapentin 1800mg/d NO long-term benefit [35].] Opioids?; Lidocaine 5% topical, 10% SC infusion ≤5 days; Regional Sympathetic Block–conflicting data; NSAIDs lack benefit but role in early inflammatory phase?; Vitamin C 500mg?; NMDA antagonists: amantadine, ketamine? **Clonidine** 0.05mg BID, ↑'d to 0.1mg BID may be useful if sweating or changes in skin temp/color. Max~ 0.4mg/BID. |
| **Musculoskeletal - Non-OA** | **NSAIDs**-useful in acute; less useful in chronic? **Opioids** (long-acting). **Injection therapies** sometimes option but evidence of benefit poor or inconsistent. |
| **Osteoarthritis (OA)** {Mild-moderate Exercise: hydrotherapy somewhat more effective than land based} | **Acetaminophen**[36]- effective for some; some consider DOC if effective; **NSAIDs** more effective than acetaminophen for pain but not function (consider SE, cost) some consider DOC; Exercise ✓ ![37] **Glucosamine**[38]–safe, effective short-term, but long-term?; **Intra-articular Corticosteroid** Knee[39]- short-term benefit; **Viscosupplementation** Knee-short-term ↓ pain & improved fx [40,41,42]; **Opioids** (incl. tramadol NNT=6; NNH=8) -option if more severe or if CI to other meds. Herbal: Avocado/soybean unsaponifiables + NSAID [43,44,45] -possible benefit NNT=4; ?duloxetine |
| **Psychological Factors - (Concomitant): Consider using…** | Depression/Anxiety[46]: nortriptyline, venlafaxine, mirtazapine, SSRIs. Insomnia: amitriptyline, nortriptyline, fluvoxamine, trazodone 50-100mg HS, methotrimeprazine NOZINAN. Bipolar/Mood: carbamazepine, divalproex, lamotrigine. Weight Gain: topiramate; gabapentin over pregabalin; nortriptyline over amitriptyline |
| **Headache, Chronic Daily** 47,48 | **Amitriptyline** 25-100mg HS; **SSRIs**; **Divalproex** 500mg-1.5g/d (retrospective study); Topiramate 50-200mg/d, Gabapentin ≥900mg/d; BOTOX q3mo. See also RxFiles Migraine chart. |
| **Phantom Limb Pain (PLP)** | Carbamazepine 200mg QID effective in case report; Gabapentin: somewhat effective in RCT [49] ≤2400mg/d; n=19 & case series n=7 (some patients able to taper off); Ketamine effective in case reports; Propranolol 80mg/d effective in 3 case reports; Opioids; Amitriptyline – not effective ≤125mg/d, RCT 6wk, n=39 [50]; Memantine – not effective. |
| **Fibromyalgia** 51,52,53,54 {may try trigger point injections if myofacial} | Amitriptyline 10-50mg hs, NNT=4 [55], cyclobenzaprine 10-30mg hs, NNT=5 [56]; SSRIs: fluoxetine conflicting data; {combination fluoxetine 20mg AM + amitriptyline 25mg HS}[57]; venlafaxine ≥150mg, duloxetine 30-60mg od $70-130 NNT=6; {antiepileptics-marginal benefit; gabapentin 1200-2400mg/d, pregabalin≤450mg/d [58] FDA& CDN approved}; zopiclone for sleep short-term; tramadol ≤400mg/d?; Non-drug Tx Exercise!. Other?: sodium oxybate (Xyrem) 4.5g (NNT=5); naltrexone 3-4.5mg hs (compounded; low quality trial, anecdote) |

**DOC**=drug of choice **fx**=function **NNT**=number needed to treat to benefit one **NNH**=number needed to treat for one extra harm resulting in discontinuation of treatment **RCT**=randomized controlled trial **SE**=side effect = ↓dose for renal dysfunction

## Table 2: Overview of Drugs Used in Treatment of Chronic Non-Malignant Pain (CNMP) [1,59]

Loren Regier - © www.RxFiles.ca May 10

| Therapeutic Class | Drug | TRADE NAME | Initial Dose | Usual Dose (Usual Max) | $/mo | General Comments for Use in CNMP |
|---|---|---|---|---|---|---|
| **Analgesic** | Acetaminophen | TYLENOL | 650-1,000mg q6-8h (**Max 4g/d**) ✗ ▼ OTC | | 20 | ◆Consider LFTs q6-12mo if hepatic risk (hx, long-term, EtOH, DI's-e.g. muscle relaxants) [60] |
| | Acetaminophen ER | ER = Extended Release → | TYLENOL ARTHRITIS 1,300mg q8h | | 25 | ◆Limit to ≤3200mg/d in elderly & chronic use; & ≤2600mg/d & high risk use (EtOH, cirrhosis) |
| **NSAID / Analgesic**<br>(various: see also RxFiles NSAIDs/COXIBs chart: http://www.rxfiles.ca/rxfiles/uploads/documents/members/CHT-NSAID-Cox2.pdf | Celecoxib | CELEBREX | 200mg OD Max 400mg/d ☎ ✆ | | 54 | ◆Effective in osteoarthritis; ≥ efficacy for acute pain than acetaminophen +/- weak opioid |
| | Diclofenac | VOLTAREN | 75mg SR BID Max 200mg/d | | 39 | ◆Dose listed is lowest anti-inflammatory dose; allow 1-2wks for anti-inflamatory effect |
| | Diclofenac+Misoprostol | ARTHROTEC 75 | 75mg+200mcg BID {or 50mg+200mcg BID-TID} | | 63 | ◆<u>Avoid</u> in **renal** dysfx, GI ulcer; <u>Caution</u> if CV disease (heart failure, HTN). {see NSAID chart} |
| | Ibuprofen | MOTRIN, ADVIL | 600mg po TID Max 2400mg/d OTC | | 13 | ◆Coxibs celecoxib: equal efficacy, similar renal toxicity to other NSAIDs; less GI ulcer Non-ASA pts; |
| | Meloxicam | MOBICOX | 7.5mg OD Max 15mg/d ☎ ▼ | | 25 | minimal platelet effects; ↑cardiac/serious[61,62,63] events: celecoxib ≥400mg/d, rofecoxib & valdecoxib. |
| | Naproxen | NAPROSYN, ALEVE | 375mg BID Max 1000mg/d ; 220mg q8-12h OTC | | 16 | |
| **Opioid**<br>See also Opioids-CNMP newsletter: www.RxFiles.ca<br>Note:<br>◆Recent concerns of abuse with <u>oxycodone</u>; some consultants note report of psychological symptoms (anxiety, apprehension) prior to end of dosing interval<br>◆<u>Dextromethorphan</u> (DM) in doses of 360-960mg/day effective in DN; but 1) high-dose=high cost & 2) potential abuse. Also used pre-op} | Codeine+Acetamin | TYLENOL #3 | <u>Lowest available:</u> *325/37.5mg* | 2 tablets q6h Max 12tabs/d | 35 | ◆Role in carefully selected CNMP patients, although long-term trials lacking! [65] |
| | Tramadol +Acetam. | TRAMACET ✗ ⊗ New g | | 2 tablets q6h Max 8 tabs/d | 190 170g | ◆Advantages: potent analgesics, lack of major organ toxicity with opioids |
| | Tramadol XL | ZYTRAM XL ✗ ⊗ New | *150mg* | 200mg q24h Max 400mg/d | 75 | ◆Disadvantages: concerns regarding abuse, diversion, tolerance, dependence |
| | Codeine | CODEINE CONTIN | *50mg* | 150mg q12h | 70 | ◆Keys to Success: 1) careful patient selection 2) documentation 3) use as part of |
| | Morphine q12h | MS-CONTIN, M-ESLON | *15mg* | 60mg q12h | 75 | comprehensive treatment plan non-drug components 4) use a treatment agreement 5) use long- |
| | Morphine q24h | KADIAN | *10 ✗▼ - 20mg* | 100mg q24h Dose dump c ethanol | 96 | acting formulations & minimize reliance/use of short-acting/PRN formulations 6) |
| | Hydromorphone | HYDROMORPH CONTIN | *3mg* | 12mg q12h ✆ | 125 | prevent/manage SE's constipation 7) Early follow-up for dose titration, etc. |
| | Oxycodone | OXYCONTIN | *10mg* | 10-20mg q12h ✆ | 97 | ◆**<u>Codeine</u>**: requires metabolism CYP2D6, ≤10% ↓ analgesia but ↑ SEs ◆**<u>DURAGESIC</u>**: potent; |
| | Fentanyl (new generic) | DURAGESIC PATCH | *25ug/hr* | 25ug/hr q48-<u>72</u>h ☎ ✆ | 72 | delayed but prolonged effect requires caution; not for opioid naïve or <18yrs; adjust dose q3-<u>6</u>days |
| | Methadone [64] powder ↓$ ▼ | METADOL scored tablets | *1-2.5mg* | {5-25mg q8h; $61-$168?} ✗ ⊗ | | ◆**<u>ZYTRAM XL</u>** Tridural/Ralivia; long acting; **<u>TRAMACET</u>** 325/37.5mg tab short acting $$$: requires metab by CYP2D6; |
| | Methadone requires <u>special license</u> to prescribe in SK; useful in rotation strategies or pts with chronic pain + addiction; used OD to prevent craving, but Q8H for pain. <u>Caution:</u> long half-life (~22hrs)& QT; dose ↑ after 5+ days. | | | | | neuropathic effect NNT>3 [66]; SE:dose related ↑seizure risk; ↑serotonin (5HT); caution with other 5HT. |
| **Antidepressant-TCA**<br>◆inhibit reuptake of 5HT & NE; block α-adrenergic, H1, ACH & NMDA receptors; block Na+ & Ca++ channels<br>◆higher doses if neuropathic pain; dose limited by side effects, CV disease<br>See Chart: http://www.rxfiles.ca/rxfiles/uploads/documents/members/cht-Psyc-Antidepressant.pdf | Amitriptyline 5HT & NE | ELAVIL | 10-25mg HS | 10-30mg HS pain/sleep | 12 | ◆Trial requires 2 weeks at adequate target dose; ↑dose gradually q1-2wks to minimize SEs & assess response; requires regular admin. Effective in neuropathic pain; improves sleep. |
| | Desipramine NE > 5HT | NORPRAMIN | (suggest taking | 75 - ≥ 100mg HS if | 30 | [NNT=2-3 [67,68, CADTH09]; NNH≥13 for ADR causing withdrawal. {Vulvodynia Ami 40-60mg hs}; <u>Not</u> for HIV neuropathic.] |
| | Imipramine 5HT & NE<br>--------------- | TOFRANIL | @ 8 or 9 PM) | neuropathic Max 300mg/d<br>------------- | | ◆Nortriptyline or desipramine: less SEs (esp anticholinergic); preferred in elderly |
| | Nortriptyline NE > 5HT | AVENTYL | 10mg HS | 20-25-<u>50</u>mg HS Max 150mg/d | 25 | ◆Avoid/Caution if arrhythmias or prolonged QT interval; hypotension less with nortriptyline |
| **Antidepressant-Other** [69] | Venlafaxine 5HT & NE | EFFEXOR XR | 37.5mg | 75-150mg OD Max 225mg/d | 50 | ◆Also effective in neuropathic pain NNT≥3; more effective than SSRIs SSRI NNT=7 |
| | **Duloxetine** CYMBALTA 30 - 60mg OD $72-138 Max 120mg/d. ☎ ⊗. Recently approved for DN ✆ & depression | | | | | ◆doses of 150mg-225mg/d often required [70] |
| **Anticonvulsant** [71]<br>◆often require relatively high doses; more expensive than TCAs without added benefit; SE's: amitript > nortrip, gaba, pregab<br>◆if SE's, ↑dose more slowly<br>◆may be useful for *sharp, stabbing, zinging*<br>◆all: pharmacodynamic DI's (e.g. ↑somnolence)<br>See: http://www.rxfiles.ca/rxfiles/uploads/documents/members/Cht-psyc-seizure.pdf | Gabapentin [72]<br>-few metabolic DI's | NEURONTIN<br>Useful in: PHN, DN, TN?, migraine prophylaxis & anxiety. | 300mg HS<br>↑by 100-300mg per day or weekly | 300mg am+600mg HS<br>600mg <u>TID</u>-QID<br><u>2.4</u>-3.6g/d common in trials | 56<br>115<br>125 | ◆Cochrane[73]: evidence in diabetic neuropathy NNT=3 & PHN NNT=4; doses <900mg not effective; harm major NNH=ns; or =18; harm minor NNH=3.7. Critical review2010: NNT=8; NNH=8; publication bias, etc.[89]<br>◆SE: dizzy 24%, somnolence 20%, headache 10%, diarrhoea 10%, confusion 10%, nausea 8%; weight ↑or↓, euphoria |
| | Carbamazepine<br>-many metabolic DI's | TEGRETOL | 100mg BID | 200mg BID<br>400mg BID | 14<br>19 | ◆Cochrane[74] : effective for trigeminal neuralgia NNT=2; no major harm NNH=ns; minor harm NNH=3.7 ◆SE: drowsiness, dizziness, constipation, nausea,ataxia,↑LFT |
| | Divalproex (DVA) | EPIVAL | 250mg OD ↑1wk | 500mg BID cc | 33 | ◆Option in chronic daily headache, migraine prophylaxis. CI: liver disease |
| | Topiramate | TOPAMAX | 25mg HS ↑weekly | 100mg BID or 50mg am;100mg HS | 90 | ◆limited role in CNMP; useful in preventing migraine & weight gain; DN lacks efficacy? |
| | Pregabalin<br>-few metabolic DI's | LYRICA (New 2005) | 50mg BID ↑1wk<br>**(or 25-50mg TID)** | 150mg BID ☎⊗<br>300mg BID Max 600mg/d | 165<br>165 | ◆Effective: PHN & DN NNT ≥3; NNH=13;FDA→Fibromyalgia; unknown if advantage over other meds[75,76,77]<br>◆SE RD: dizziness 20%, somnolence 14%, periph edema 5.3%, ≥7% ↑weight 5%, dry mouth 4.8%, blurred vision 4.5%; abnormal thinking/euphoria 3.4% ◆SE's causing withdrawal: overall NNH=13 [78]; 600mg/d NNH=4 [79] ◆glitazones: ↑edema |
| | No comparative trials yet; side effects common; high cost; new thus lack long-term data; vying for market now that gabapentin generic. | | | | | |
| **Herbal** | Glucosamine Sulfate | Various | 500mg OD | 500mg TID or 1500mg OD ✗ ⊗ OTC | 10 | ◆OA knee;benefit NNT=5 conflicting data 80,81,82; allow 4-8wks; well tolerated trials ≤3yrs |
| **Viscosupplementation** {Hyaluronic acid}[88] | Hylan G-F-20<br>Hyaluronic acid Na+<br>Na+ Hyaluronate | SYNVISC reg, One-$400<br>HYALGAN<br>NEOVISC New:Euflexxa | 16mg/2ml intra-articularly-knee / hip ?↑SE ✗ ⊗<br>20mg/2ml intra-articularly–shoulder / knee / hip $330/3<br>2ml intra-articularly to joint - avian protein free $200/3 | | 200-350 per 3 | ◆Cartilaginous Defect Repair Agent – OA (benefit up to 52wks knee); pseudosepsis SE rare<br>◆Dosing varies with product/indication (Knee–initial: weekly x3 Synvisc or x3-5 others); may repeat e.g. after 6 mo |
| **Other** | Calcitonin Salmon Nasal | MIACALCIN | 200 I.U. | OD alternating nostrils ☎ ✆ | 65 | ◆for pain from vertebral fractures ◆Adequate trial 1 wk ◆well tolerated |
| **Topical Anesthetic** | Lidocaine top 5% | USA: LIDODERM 5% Patch<br>CDN: MAXILENE 4% Cream | Also **Compounded Gel** 5% ✗ ⊗ | | 15 | ◆Effective in PHN[83]; apply on 12hrs, off 12hrs (systemic absorption is negligible) |
| **Topical Capsaicin** {from hot peppers} | Capsaicin **0.025%** | ZOSTRIX also A535 with Capsaicin 45g/$15 | | Apply TID {OA, RA} ✗ ▼ OTC | | ◆Adequate trial 4-8wks ◆neuropathic pain NNT=6 0.075% 8wks;musculoskeletal NNT=8 4wks |
| | Capsaicin **0.075%** | ZOSTRIX HP 60g | TID | Apply TID {for PHN, DN} | 25 | ◆SE causing withdrawal NNH=10 [84]; local burning, stinging, erythema. New generics |
| **Topical NSAID** [85,86]<br>{various base options for varying levels of penetration} | Diclofenac 1.5% | PENNSAID Soln | Apply 40drops to affected knee QID ✗ ⊗ | | 90 | ◆OA; allow 1wk; CI:GI ulcer; 40drops=16mg/dose; may be ineffective if using less |
| | Ketoprofen 5-15% | Compounded | Apply to affected area/joint TID ✗ ⊗ | | ? | ◆Limited evidence in CNMP musculoskeletal NNT=4.4 (at 2 weeks). ◆high concentrations in |
| | **Topical Salicylates** -limited data suggests little NNT=5.3 or no effect in chronic conditions. Overdose reported Bengay. | | | | | meniscus/cartilage & tendon sheath; [serum] 5% of oral. ◆ketoprofen may be preferred |
| **Topical-Compounded** | Small clinical trials suggest <u>possible</u> effect: amitriptyline 1% + ketamine 0.5% in chronic neuropathic pain n=20;7d [87]; clonidine 0.2% crm in oral neuralgia-like, but not neuropathic pain n=17[88]; **morphine**-painful open ulcers.[79] Single or multiple ingredient preps from pharmacies specializing in compounding: amitriptyline 1-4%, baclofen 2-5%, capsaicin 0.025-0.1%, carbamazepine 2%, clonidine 0.1-0.3%, doxepin 3%, gabapentin 6-10%, ketamine 0.5-1.5%, lidocaine 1-10%. | | | | | |

**CI**=contraindications **CV**=cardiovascular **DI**=drug interaction **EtOH**=alcohol **GI**=gastrointestinal **HA**=headache **LFTs**=liver function tests **ns**=not statistically significant **RD**=risk difference vs placebo **SE**=side effect **$**=retail cost/month SK ✗ =non formulary SK

**Muscle Relaxants**-CNMP– <u>not</u> generally recommended for use >2 wks; effect more from sedation than relaxation; PRN use - habit forming; ↑hepatic toxicity with chronic use & DI's e.g. with chronic acetaminophen; **RA**=rheumatoid arthritis baclofen LIORESAL 5-10mg TID-QID, tizanidine ZANAFLEX 2-4mg TID ☎ ✆, dantrolene DANTRIUM 25-50mg TID: effective for MS spasticity, spinal cord injury, cerebral palsy or stroke (<u>not</u> musculoskeletal injury). Gradual taper to discontinue. Also-BOTOX inj.

**Benzodiazepines**-CNMP: **<u>not</u>** generally recommended except for short term use; even then, the chronic nature of pain, and resultant pain behavior can easily result in long-term abuse (multiple adverse effects long-term e.g. falls)

**See also** - RxFiles Drug Comparison Charts at www.RxFiles.ca (NSAID/COXIB, Opioid, Antidepressant & Antiepileptic). ☎ =**EDS** Exception Drug Status in SK ✆=prior approval for NIHB coverage ▼=covered by NIHB ⊗=not covered by NIHB

# The Gout – Q&A & Treatment Options

"One of the most painful conditions experienced by humans" – Choi HK et al.[1]

Prepared by: Z Dumont; B Jensen, L Regier © www.RxFiles.ca May 10

## Gout: Overview of Causes, Risk Factors & Incidence[2]

- **Uric acid crystals** may deposit in joints, nephrons & tissues needle like, negative birefringent[3]. {↑serum uric acid (SUA) may contribute (>405µmol/L; theoretical saturation concentration)}
- **Pathophysiology**: ↑SUA: from ↓uric acid excretion 85% or ↑ purine breakdown; most commonly secondary 70% to drugs (chemotx, diuretics, ASA) disease (malignancies, renal dysfx, psoriasis), & dietary causes (beer, fish, red meat).
- **Risk factors**: ♂, CKD, HTN, obesity; hyperglycemia, hyperlipidemia, lead {Gout should prompt screen for conditions associated with CV risk!}[4,5,6] **Precipitating factors**: trauma, surgery, alcohol, starvation, ↑ purine foods & certain medications see Drug Induced.
- **Incidence**: <1%; mostly elderly, ♂ & postmenopausal ♀[7,8]. **Prevalence**: ≤7% in ♂ >65; ≤3% in ♀ >85[3].

## What are the stages and diagnostic criteria for gout?[3]

1) **Asymptomatic hyperuricemia**: ♂:>360-420µmol/L; ♀:>357µmol/L? estrogen effect
   - <25% go on to develop acute gout[7,9]. ↑ if SUA ≥500 µmol/L, >600µmol/L incidence ~6%[10].
   - ***Usually* does not require drug treatment!** [9,10,25,30]
2) **Acute gouty arthritis**: quick onset 6-12hrs, ***intense pain***, redness, heat & swelling, usually of one joint 90% of 1st attacks (commonly the big toe "podagra" 50%, ankle/foot, knee, finger, but also the olecranon, helix of the ear, &/or nephrons – uric acid tends to crystallize in the cooler parts of the body), pain peaks at 8-12hrs; often skin **desquamation** over affected joint. (May self-resolve in 3-7-14d [9,10]). SUA ↑or normal![7] **Elderly**: less pain; ↑ polyarticular, fever & delirium.
3) **Intercritical gout**: disease may progress despite symptom free period(s). {symptom free periods may decrease over time; initially may be years symptom free [10].}
4) **Chronic tophaceous gout**: tophi progression to, bony erosions, deformations, nephropathy, stones

## What is the concern of diuretics with gout?

- Loop e.g. furosemide & thiazide diuretics ↓excretion & ↑concentration of uric acid.
- Hydrochlorothiazide induced gout: ~1% [11]; risk ↑ when dose ≥25mg/d [12] Low dose thiazide (e.g. HCT12.5mg) often tolerated in patients with gout hx

## What non-pharmacological therapies are recommended?

- **Acute attack**: rest, elevate limb, ice [13], avoid contact
- **Maintenance**: useful & may ↓ the need for preventative medications
  **Diet**: compliance with low purine diets is poor[14], recommend one less portion of meat or fish each day; drink **wine** instead of beer; drink a glass of ***skimmed*** milk each day.[15] Low fat dairy, fiber, Vit C & whole grains assoc. with ↓ gout
  ***Low calorie diet*** *more beneficial/acceptable than low purine diet!*
  Avoid: liver, kidney, shellfish, gravy, sardine, sweetbread, sugary drinks[16] & yeast extract.
  **Lifestyle: Weight loss!!!** Smoking cessation! ↓ alcohol binging (especially **beer**)! ⇨ drink 2L water/day (unless CI'd), mild-moderate intensity exercise.

## Are there any special treatment considerations?

- Lifelong treatment may be required; however re-assess need for treatment if attack free for many years; SUA levels may be useful[17].
- **Renal dysfx & very elderly**: adjust dose for allopurinol & colchicine; consider using colchicine or corticosteroids[18] as alternatives to NSAIDs.
- With NSAIDs, GI prophylaxis should be considered if history of PUD/GI bleed or ↑GI risk age>70 {**PPI** omeprazole 20mg daily $46; or misoprostol 200mcg tid-qid $38-49}
- Review CV risk due to association of gout with CVD; CV protection with ASA 81mg po daily if 2° prevention; benefit supersedes the ↑risk of gout attacks.

## What are the primary drug treatment options for gout?

- **Acute attack**: *Rapid treatment initiation is key: <24-48hr.*
  **{Agent choice dependent on patient (severity, CI, DI, hx, SE, etc.)** [e.g. consider HF, renal fx, GI ulcer hx, diabetes, transplant hx, previous tx, age, DIs.]}
  - **Colchicine** (eg. 0.6mg BID x1-3 days, then daily); stop after ≥1-2wk {**FDA July/09**: 1.2mg po immediately, then 0.6mg once in 1hr}
  - **NSAIDs** - High doses to achieve pain relief until 48hrs after symptom resolution (or ~ 3 days); then stop or taper over 1-2 weeks
  - **Corticosteroid** IM methylprednisolone, PO prednisone (or Intra-Articular Betaject, Aristospan)[18,19,20] {May add acetaminophen to corticosteroid if NSAIDs & colchicine CI'd[21]}

  **NOTE**: Do not start, stop or adjust **allopurinol** during an acute attack!
- **Maintenance/Prophylaxis**[22]:
  - **1st attack**: lifestyle changes & remove drug causes if possible
    *Treat if*: 1) recurrent attacks (**≥3/yr**); 2) ↑SUA levels >800µmol/L; 3) pt undergoing chemotherapy; or 4) advanced disease
  - **1st Line: allopurinol**[23] (Start low, go slow, & prophylax as below!)
    - **Wait 1-2wks after inflammation settles before initiating allopurinol** (fluctuating SUA levels prolongs attacks, may destabilize crystals)
    - **Prophylax with colchicine** low dose **or an NSAID** not ASA[24] **while titrating allopurinol** (usually ~ 3 – 6+ months[17]) **unless CI'd**
    - **Target SUA** levels: <300 to **360µmol/L** [1,7,17]. Lifelong treatment.
  - **2nd Line: colchicine** (low dose ≤ 0.6mg daily); may not prevent complications {Alternative: **probenecid** may rarely be an option, but pts require good renal function}

## Table 1: Overview of Drugs Commonly Used in the Management of Gout

| | Generic/TRADE (Strength & forms) g=generic | Class / Pregnancy category[25] | Side effects / CI: Contraindications | √ = therapeutic use / Comments / Drug Interactions DI / Monitor M | Dosing: {for acute tx with NSAID & colchicine, Initial x 1-3 days ⇨ Follow-up x1-2+ wks} | $/30d |
|---|---|---|---|---|---|---|
| | **Naproxen** NAPROSYN,g ALEVE 125,250,375ς,500ς,750mg SR tab 500mg supp, 25mg/ml susp. | **NSAIDS (non-ASA)**/ -↓pain & inflammation B / D | **Common**: N/V (Indomethacin: GI upset, headache, ↑SE especially CNS, & in elderly) CI: ↓ Renal (Stage ≥IV CKD), GI ulcer, HF, transplant **Precautions**: CVD, (Avoid Indocid ≥65yrs) | √ Gout – for acute attack or when initiating allopurinol | 500-750mg x1; 500mg BID; ⇨ 375-500mg BID Max ≤ 1500mg/d x1day/short term. ⇨ Usual Max 1000mg/d | 16-20 |
| | **Ibuprofen** MOTRIN, ADVIL,g 300,600mg tab,(200χ▼,400mg)OTC | For more info on NSAIDs, Acet, & Coxibs, see **RxFiles PAIN charts** at www.rxfiles.ca | {Indomethacin used historically; however **others** effective & less CNS SE's!} | GI prophylaxis (if indicated) with a **PPI** or misoprostol[17] DI:Li⁺⁺; ACEI/ARBs (minor DI, except ↑K⁺ if on NSAID, spironolactone & ACEI or ARB) M:follow-up 4-6wks after acute attack to assess need of further tx; if at renal risk Na+ @ 24hr, SCr @72hr | 600-800mg po TID; ⇨ 400-600mg TID Max 2400-3200mg | 18-13 |
| | **Indomethacin** INDOCID,g 25,50mg cap; 50,100mg supp | | | {Can use in **CKD** stage 1-2 & dialysis; avoid in stage 3 if CrCl ≤40ml/min & CKD stage 4.} **Acute**: High doses for 1st 24-72hrs of attack. Then stop, or use lowest effective dose over 1-2wks. | 25-50mg po TID; ⇨ 25mg BID-TID Max 200mg/d {Historically used but other NSAIDs now preferred.} | 14-17 |
| | **Celecoxib** CELEBREX 100,200mg cap | **COX-2 specific inhibitor**/ C -↓ pain & inflammation | **Common**: GI maybe less than some other NSAIDS CI: **CVD**, Renal dysfx **Precautions**: GI ulcer | √Gout–acute attack or when initiating allopurinol DI:Lithium,ACEI/ARBs M: follow-up 4-6weeks after acute attack to assess need of further tx | 200mg po daily; ⇨ 100-200mg daily Max 400mg/d | 54 |
| | **Acetaminophen** TYLENOL,g 325,500,650mg tab ▼OTCχ | **Analgesic**/ B -↓ pain (minimally effective) | **Common**: rash **Serious**: hepatotoxicity **Precautions**: Liver dysfx &/or alcoholism | √ Mild gout associated pain &/or in combination with corticosteroids. DI:Warfarin if ↑ dose acetaminophen M: Liver function tests if long term & ↑EtOH intake | 650-1000mg po q6h (prn; adjunct to CS) Max 4000mg/d | 15-25 |
| | **Colchicine** COLCHICINE-ODAN,g 0.6ς,1ς mg tab [Colcrys USA] IV Colchicine not recommended →toxicity[10] | Anti-gout:↓ pain, inflammation: ↓'s urate crystal deposition by: (↓leukocyte motility, phagocytosis, etc.) B Familial Mediterranean Fever 1.2-2.4mg/d | **Common**: NVD 80% @ high dose; 4-25% @ low dose ⇨ ↓dose/stop; rash,alopecia. **Serious**: neutropenia, myopathy, rhabdomyolysis, liver. **Precautions**: CVD; ↓ renal fx ↓dose CI: blood dyscrasias, solid organ transplant; dialysis if possible | √ Gout –acute attack or if initiating allopurinol[24]; {SE with high doses however limiting to ≤3 tabs on 1st day then 1-2 tabs/day will ↓↓↓ diarrhea/GI side effects!!!} DI: cyclosporine ↑myopathy, P-gp & 3A4 inhibitors: clarithro & erythro-mycin, ketoconazole, verapamil, diltiazem M:CBC neutropenia, Creatine Kinase rhabdomyolysis: may ↑ with statin/fibrate & renal fx q6mon | Initial: 0.6mg po BID - TID x 1-3 days ⇨ then daily x 7-10+ days. **0.6mg OD** or BID **for ~ 3 - 6+ months if starting allopurinol** {If ↓**renal fx**, ↓dose to every other day if prolonged tx 10+ days} | 12-17 16 - 26 |
| | **Methylprednisolone** acetate DEPO-MEDROL,g 20χ▼,40,80mg vial **Triamcinolone** acetonide KENALOG 10 & 40,g 10mg/ml 5ml, 40mg/ml 1ml, 40mg/ml χ▼5ml vial | **Corticosteroids**/ C -↓ inflammatory response Hydrocortisone SOLU-CORTEF 100,200mg vial | **Common**: injection site reactions **Serious**: edema/HF; others rare in short term **Precautions**: systemic & viral infections, immunosuppression, local skin atrophy {Glucocorticoid: Prednisone 5mg = Methylprednisolone 4mg} | **Useful if CI/SE's to NSAIDs & colchicine** e.g. for renal, transplant, warfarin patients, etc. √IM or IA inj x1: **mono**articular attack √IM or oral: **poly**articular attack DI: aprepitant ↑CS levels, vaccines **DI**: rare with intra-articular minimal systemic absorption M:osteoporosis risk if prolonged / frequent use; diabetes: ?? ↑BG testing (IA: suggest minimum 3 months between treatments) {**Betamethasone** {sodium phosphate & acetate: Fast acting & Long acting} BETAJECT 3mg/1ml vial ⊗ IM,IA $9 / vial} {**Triamcinolone hexacetonide** ARISTOSPAN 20mg/1ml vial ☎ peds; ▼; $7/vial} | **IM**: Methylprednisolone: 40-80mg **IM** x1 Pending age / degree of inflam **IA: Small joints** Phalanges: Methylpred 4-10mg IA; 80mg Triamcin 2.5-5mg IA; 10mg Betameth 0.5-1ml IA; 1ml **IA: Large joints** Knees/ankles: Methylpred 20-80mg IA; 200mg? Triamcin 5-15mg IA; 40mg Betameth 0.5-1ml IA; 2ml | 5-9/vial 9/1ml vial 5/1ml vial |
| | **Prednisone** WINPRED,g 1,5ς,50ς mg tab (Prednisolone 1mg/ml susp) | **Methylprednisolone** C MEDROL 4ς,16ς mg tab | **Common**: insomnia, ↑BP, ↑BG, GI upset, mood △ **Serious**: most rare in short term; edema/HF | | 25-50mg po daily x 3-5 days & stop[20]; no taper! {If catch early e.g. 1st sign, 10mg x1-2 may be adequate} | 15 |
| | **URICOSURICS (rarely used!): Probenecid** BENURYL,g 500ς mg tab; 1g BID $34 (0.5-2g/d); SE: rash, GI upset; **CI**: nephrolithiasis Hx; renal: ineffective if CrCl<50mL/min; Drink 2L $H_2O$/d. DI:ASA, azathioprine, MTX. {Also **Sulfinpyrazone** ANTURAN g, 200mg tab; 100-200mg BID $17-27; no longer used.} | | | | | |
| **Prophylaxis** | **Allopurinol** ZYLOPRIM,g 100ς,200ς,300ς mg tab | **Xanthine oxidase (Xanthase) inhibitor**/ C -↓uric acid production -↓BP in young hypertensive pts -Adjunctive to K+ citrate for uric acid stones | **Common**: rash, diarrhea **Serious**: Allopurinol Hypersensitivity Syndrome <1% {20-30% mortality! ↑risk if ↓ renal fx (e.g. ACEI, NSAID), elderly, diuretic use}: start low! Stevens-Johnson syndrome 26, ↑with HLA-B*5801 CI: Acute gout **Precautions**: renal ↓dose or liver dysfx | √ **Maintenance; adjust dose** for SUA, renal fx, tolerability & response DI:rash maculopapular when used with ampicillin incidence 20% or amoxicillin; antacids; ↑ toxicity of 6-MP, azathioprine & cyclophosphamide[7]; warfarin ↑INR M:SUA & renal fx q3mon 1st year then q6mon[10] {See CPS for dosing info in ↓renal fx} **Note**: Allopurinol desensitization[27] possible (susp ↑'s from ≤50ug to 100mg over ≥28day). | Start at 100mg; ↑100mg q2-4wks ↓ risk of rash, etc. Usual dose: 300mg daily, preferably after food Usual range: 100-800mg (divide doses ≥300mg to ↓GI SE) If GFR<50ml/min, start 50mg/day; ↑ 50mg increments. MAX 300mg/d | 15 10-26 |

= ↓ dose for renal dysfunction ς=scored tab χ=Non-formulary Sask ☎=Exception Drug Status Sask. ⊗=not covered by NIHB ▼=covered by NIHB ∅=NIHB EDS **BG**=blood glucose **BP**=blood pressure **CS**=corticosteroids **CI**=contraindication **CKD**=chronic kidney disease **CVD**=cerebral vascular disease **DI**=drug interaction **dx**=diagnosis **fx**=function **GI**=stomach **HF**=heart failure **HR**=heart rate **HTN**=hypertension **hx**=history **IA**=intra-articular **Li**=lithium **M**=monitor **MI**=myocardial infarction **n/v**=nausea/vomiting **OTC**=over the counter **pt**=patient **SE**=side effect **SUA**=serum uric acid **sx**=symptoms **tx**=treatment **wt**=weight

**Other Meds for Tx**: **Oxypurinol**[28] oral allopurinol metabolite in clinical trial; **losartan** & fenofibrate[29]: modest uricosuric effect (potential losartan use if gout + hypertension); **Opioids** possible adjunct analgesic[30]; **ACTH**[10]; **Febuxostat**[31,32,33,34]: xanthine oxidase antagonist like allopurinol but unique structure, ↑LFT, UK/ USA 40-120mg po od, not CND; **Pegloticase**: urate oxidase Phase III; given IV q2-4weeks; **Benzbromarone** ↑urate excretion; orally special access Canada[35,36,37], & Ketorolac IA inj; **Rasburicase** IV in USA for tumor lysis syndrome in cancer pts. **HERBAL**: no documented efficacy; ?caffeine, devil's claw & garlic have been used. Anecdotal support: berry juice/ berries.

**Rule out**: **Pseudogout** (calcium pyrophosphate crystals in synovial fluid, commonly the knee), "Appears like OA, but in all the wrong places" possibly treat with colchicine 0.6mg/d or CS; **Septic arthritis** aspirate the joint, WBC, temperature & vitals, do gram stain & culture; & **Rheumatoid arthritis**.

**Drug induced**: acetazolamide, ASA low dose, chemo, cyclosporine, diuretic, ethambutol, lead, levodopa, niacin, tacrolimus, teriparatide **Food induced**: purine rich eg. red meat, fish, beer, spirits **Diagnosis**: Diagnostic certainty→ analyze synovial fluid for uric acid crystal or id'ing a tophus containing uric acid crystal under polarized light microscopy. May see "mouse bite" erosions. **Optional 24hr urine collection**: to see if ↓excretor or ↑producer[3,10] but does not alter tx; (if uric acid excretion ≥1g with reg. diet→over-producer, if $CL_{uric\ acid}$<6mL/min→under-excretor) since allopurinol effective for both[1].

# NSAIDS, COXIBs & OTHER ANALGESICS: Comparison Chart [1,2,3,4,5,6,7,8,9,10,11,12,13,14,15,16]

Prepared by: Loren Regier, Brent Jensen - © www.RxFiles.ca May 10

| Generic Name | TRADE | Products/Comments * | Usual Dosage | Max/d | ≅ Dose | $/30d | Class / Comments 🍁 |
|---|---|---|---|---|---|---|---|
| ASA-Plain (IR=immediate release)<br>**ASA-Enteric Coated** | **ASPIRIN**, generic OTC✗<br>**ENTROPHEN** | (150 & 650mg supp; 80,325mg tab)✗▼;<br>81✗▼,**325**,**650**,975✗⊗ mg EC tab | 325-650mg q4-6h<br>325-975mg QID | 4g | 650mg EC po QID | **$19** | ***Salicylates*** (ASA -CV protection). Caution: Reye's<br>• ASA: **irreversible** platelet inhibition ~7-10days<br>(↑GI-risk if used with other NSAIDs/COXIBs CLASS) |
| Diflunisal | **DOLOBID**, generic | 250,500mg tab | 250-500mg BID | 1.5g | 250mg po BID | $44 | |
| Indomethacin | **INDOCID**, generic | 25,50mg cap; 50,100mg supp | 25-50mg TID | 200mg | 25mg po TID | $17 | ***Indole Acetic Acids*** (Indomethacin: ↑SE CNS, elderly)<br>INDOCID SR: Special Access ankylosing spondylitis 613-941-2108<br>Sulindac: ↑**LFT**s reported |
| Sulindac | **CLINORIL**, generic | 150ς,200ς mg tab; PD | 150-200mg BID | 400mg | 150mg po BID | $32 | |
| Diclofenac | **VOLTAREN**, generic | 25,50mg EC tab; 50,100mg supp;<br>75,100mg SR tab | 25-50mg BID-TID | 150-200mg | 50mg po TID<br>**75mg SR po BID** | $40<br>$45 | ***Phenylacetic Acids***; recent <u>cardiac risk</u> concern<br>(♣ VOLTAREN RAPIDE 50mg tab ✗ ⊗ $75;<br>generic diclofenac K 50mg ✗ ⊗ $44 )<br>• diclofenac 75mg BID ↑**LFT**s AST >4% in **CLASS**; **MEDAL**, & gel |
| **Diclofenac + Misoprostol** ✚ | **ARTHROTEC-50**<br>**ARTHROTEC-75** ✗ | (50mg + 200µg) tab<br>(75mg + 200µg) tab | 1 tab BID-TID<br>1 tab OD-BID | 200mg/800µg | One tab po BID<br>One tab po BID | **$48**<br>$63 | |
| Ketorolac **PO** **IM** | **TORADOL**, generic ✗✆ | #; 10mg tab; 10 & 30mg amp injectable **IM** formulation avail. | 10mg po q6h <u>x7d max</u><br>10-30mg **IM** q4-6h | 40mg<br>120mg | 10mg po QID | $70# | ***Pyrolizine Carboxylic Acids***<br>• inj can be given **IM** (or IV) |
| Etodolac | **ULTRADOL**, gen. ☎✆ | ~COX-2 selective; 200,300mg cap | 200-600mg BID | 1.2g | 300mg po BID | $57 | ***Pyranocarboxylic Acids*** |
| Flurbiprofen | **ANSAID**, generic | 50, 100mg tab; 200✗▼mg SR cap | 50-100mg TID-QID | 300mg | 100mg po BID | $30 | ***Propionic Acids***<br>• ibuprofen 800mg tid Class & naproxen 500mg bid Vigor: similar overall withdrawal rates as celecoxib 400mg bid CLASS & rofecoxib 50mg od VIGOR respectively<br>• naproxen less HTN causing withdrawal (0. 1 vs 0.7%) vs rofecoxib VIGOR<br>• naproxen possibly a safer cardiac option |
| **Ibuprofen** (? DI with ASA: give 30min after ASA IR or 8hr before ASA IR) | **MOTRIN** OTC✗▼<br>generic 100,200,400mg | (100mg/5ml,200mg/5ml **susp** OTC, ✗,▼)<br>300,400,600mg tab (IV Caldolor 400-800mg q6h in USA 2010 | 200-800mg TID-QID<br>**Peds** RA: ≤50mg/kg/day | 2.4-3.2g | 400mg po TID<br>600mg po TID | **$18**<br>$13 | |
| Ketoprofen | **ORUDIS**, generic | 50,100mg EC; 200mg SR tab<br>50mg cap; 50,100mg supp | 25-100mg TID-QID | 300mg | 50mg po TID | $40 | |
| **Naproxen** (also naproxen sodium)<br>{Naprelan: 375 & 500mg CR tab ✗ ⊗} | **NAPROSYN**, generic {ALEVE 220mg OTC; limit to ≤440mg/day OTC} | 125,250,375ς,500ς mg; 750mg SR $33;<br>125mg/5ml **susp**; 500mg supp | 125-500mg BID<br>**>2yr: 10**mg/kg/day Max 20mg/kg/day | 1-1.5g | 375mg po BID<br>500mg po BID Vigor | **$16**<br>$20 | **Peds: ibuprofen** for **pain**/<u>**fever**</u>: **5-10mg/kg per dose** (≤40mg/kg/day).{?? help $FEV_1$ in cystic fibrosis} |
| Oxaprozin | **DAYPRO**, generic ✗✆ | 600ς mg caplet; long t1/2 (50h) | 600-1800mg OD | 1.8g | 600mg po OD | $30 | naproxen: ?help ↓cough for acute common cold Tx 5day<br>naproxen 250,375,500mg EC tab ✗▼: 375mg BID $41;<br>♣ANAPROX ✗▼275-550ς mg BID $50-85 (naproxen Na+) |
| Tiaprofenic Acid | **SURGAM**, generic | 200,300ς mg tab | 200-300mg BID | 600mg | 200mg po BID | $30 | |
| Piroxicam see comments | **FELDENE**, generic | 10,20mg cap & 10,20mg supp | 10-20mg OD | 20mg | 20mg po OD | $31 | ***Oxicams***- long t½ (>50h) –rare Stevens-Johnson Sx<br>Piroxicam: not for short-term pain/inflammation; ↑skin & GI reactions<br>• **meloxicam**-<u>**lacks**</u> **outcome data** for significant reductions in GI ulcer/complications SELECT, MELISSA but fairly well tolerated at low 7.5mg OD dose |
| Meloxicam | **MOBICOX**, gen. ☎▼ | ~COX-2 selective; 7.5,15ς mg tab | 7.5-15mg OD | 15mg | 7.5mg po OD | $25 | |
| Tenoxicam | **MOBIFLEX**, gen. ✗✆ | 20mg tab (only generic in Canada) | 20-40mg OD | 40mg | 20mg po OD | $45 | |
| Nabumetone | **RELAFEN** ☎✆ | ~COX-2 selective; PD; 500,750mg tab | 1-2g OD | 2g | 1g po OD | $40 | ***Naphthylalkanones***- long t½ (>24h) |
| Floctafenine | **IDARAC**, generic | 200,400mg tab | 200-400mg TID-QID | 1.2g | 200mg po QID | $62 | ***Anthranilic Acids***<br>• mefenamic acid - used for dysmenorrhea; other NSAIDs also effective |
| Mefenamic Acid | **PONSTAN**, generic | 250mg cap; (<u>initially</u> 500mg x1) | 250mg QID <u>x7d max</u> | 1.25g | 250mg po QID | $73# | |
| **Celecoxib** [32] | **CELEBREX** ☎✆<br>-approved 1999 | 100,200mg cap; Rare SULFA-type rx<br>**FAP**:400mg BID (not official indication) | 100mg BID (OA/AS) **$54**<br>200mg BID (RA) | 800mg | 200mg **OD**-BID<br>(**≥2yr** FDA approved)<br>10-25kg: 50mg BID | **$54-99** | **COXIBs -highly COX-2 selective:**<br><u>equal efficacy</u> & <u>similar renal/CV</u> toxicity to other NSAIDs; <u>**less GI**</u> ulcer/bleed <u>Non-ASA pts</u>; <u>minimal platelet</u> effects; concern re: <u>↑**cardiac**/serious</u> [17,18,19] events (VIOXX ≥25mg/d & CELEBREX ≥400mg/d); lumiracoxib TARGET [20,21]; warfarin DI's; **Valdecoxib** BEXTRA: Rare severe skin reactions (exfoliative dermatitis & Stevens-Johnson Sx.) |
| Lumiracoxib | **PREXIGE** D/C Oct/07 ✗⊗ | 100mg tab | **100**mg OD (≤ 400mg/day used) | 100mg | **100**mg od | **NA** | |

♦ **D/C** Oct/07: Cox-2 selective for OA, non sulfur moiety; less ↑BP (only 0.4 mmHg); ↔ ↑? cardiac events (0.65 vs 0.55% non-significant); but less GI ulcers **NNT=119** with lumiracoxib 400mg/d VS naproxen 500mg bid or ibuprofen 800mg tid; but <u>no</u> difference in ulcers when concurrently on aspirin therapy **TARGET (52 week n=18,325)** [20,21]; Rare-**severe hepatic toxicity** doses ≥200mg/d

**Discontinued**: Rofecoxib VIOXX 12.5 OA-25mg OA/RA OD (Discontinued, Sep04 Vigor: CV event NNH=83, GI NNT=129/8mos); Valdecoxib BEXTRA 10-20mg OD OA,RA (suspend CDN,USA,EU Apr05 Skin reaction)

| Generic Name | TRADE | Products/Comments | Usual Dosage | Max/d | ≅ Dose | $/30d | Class / Comments |
|---|---|---|---|---|---|---|---|
| **Acetaminophen** (= paracetamol) Pregnancy category **B** | **TYLENOL**, generic OTC✗<br>TYLENOL ARTHRITIS=ER Tab<br>**Caution: ingredient of many products!** | 80,160,325,500mg **tab**✗▼;<br>650mg **ER tab**✗⊗; various **susp's**✗▼<br>120,325,650mg **supp**✗▼ | 325-1000mg TID-QID<br>**(Peds: ≤75mg/kg/day)** | ≤4g | 650mg po QID<br>1,300mg ER Q8H | **$20**<br>$25 | **Non-Anti-inflammatory Analgesic**<br>lowest risk cardiac/GI ulcer/bleed; option in OA; ?↑INR; Watch **LFTs**: with chronic use & if ↑alcohol use Larson'05 |

Consider limit dose to ≤ 3250mg/day, esp long term & lower if hepatic/renal dx or chronic alcohol use! Acute Overdose-Hepatotoxic #1 transplant drug cause >140mg/kg or >7.5g; Level within 24hr predictive Rumack-Matthew Nomogram [36]

☎ **EDS**=**E**xception **D**rug **S**tatus Sask. ✆=prior approval NIHB ✗ Non-formulary Sask. ⊗=not covered NIHB ▼=covered NIHB **CV**=cardiovascular **DI**=drug interaction **EC**=enteric coated **ER**=extended release **FAP**=Familial Adenomatous Polyposis **GI**=stomach **HTN**= hypertension **LFT**=liver function tests **OA**=osteoarthritis **OTC**=over the counter (& non-formulary in SK) **PD**=Pro-drug **RA**=rheumatoid arthritis **SK**=Sask. **SR**=sustained release **supp**=suppository **susp**=suspension ς =scored tablet **COST**=generic if avail. with dispensing fee & based on **lowest usual anti-inflammatory dose**. Lower doses often effective for analgesia. Aspirin induced **asthma**: common [22], cross-react with other NSAIDS, rarely with acetaminophen. # cost/30days, but max. **7 days** recommended ketorolac & mefenamic.

**Discontinued Products**: Choline Mg Trisalicylate TRILISATE, Fenoprofen NALFON, Lumiracoxib PREXIGE, Piroxicam BREXIDOL, Rofecoxib VIOXX, Salsalate DISALCID, Tolmentin TOLECTIN.

♣ **Fast-acting forms**, but <u>non</u>-formulary Sask. (ANAPROX, VOLTAREN RAPIDE, NOVO-DIFENAC-K); <u>slightly</u> faster onset, but ↑$. **PREGNANCY**: weigh risk vs benefit (1st / 2nd trimester likely OK, but D/C ~6-8wks prior to delivery).[23] closes ductus arteriosus

**Topical NSAID**:[24] <u>May</u> be effective in localized pain esp. ≤2wk [25]; eg. diclofenac $Na^+$ PENNSAID 1.5% topical soln ✗⊗ -Apply 40drop (16mg) [26,27] QID or 50drop **TID** x3month to affected **knee**, allow to dry ($90/30d). Allow at least 1wk for effect. Diclofenac diethylamine 1.16% Voltaren Emulgel OTC topical gel 2-4g(4-8cm) tid-qid x 7day 50g=$10; 100g=$15; ✗ ⊗ ~6% absorbed, has propylene glycol: pain relief assoc. with recent acute, localized muscle/joint injury eg. sprains, strains or sports injury (eg. sprain of ankle, strain of shoulder or back muscles).

**GI ULCER Risk**[16]: ~annual risk 1-4% (x= ↑ odds ratio) Hx of ulcer complication x13.5, Multiple NSAID x9, High dose NSAID x7, Concomitant anticoagulant x6.4, Age≥70 x5.6, Age ≥60 x3.1, Concomitant steroid x2.2, Hx heart dx x1.8 {**Consider adding PPI**} ? use Cox-2

<u>**Suppository**</u> form **NOT** safer to GI tract. * Possible gastric bleeding; antiplatelet effects of NSAIDs may ↑ risk during **anticoagulant therapy**. ✚ Misoprostol **Cytotec** ✗ 200mcg po bid $35, tid $50, qid $64 is cytoprotective.

**RENAL RISK**: **Risk Factors** = underlying volume depletion (pts on ACEI/ARB & diuretics esp. high-dose loop), pre-existing renal insufficiency, heart failure, cirrhosis, age ≥70yrs, previous long-term daily use of ↑ NSAIDs/ASA. {Can use in **CKD** stage 1-2 & dialysis; <u>avoid</u> in stage 3 if CrCl ≤40ml/min & CKD stage 4.}

**MONITOR**: CBC, LFTs, SCr CrCL, lytes yearly (within 1-2wks if **cardio/renal** risk), BP, signs of **HF** (eg. edema, ↑wt), photosensitivity **DI**: ↓BP effect (diuretics, β-blockers, ACEI, ARBs); ↑toxicity (**lithium**, methotrexate, tenofovir, **warfarin**).

**Side Effect**: dyspepsia <20%, N/V, edema, GI bleed ~annual risk 1-4% (Indomethacin: ↑SE esp CNS in elderly: confusion). <u>**Precaution**</u>: asthma, CVD, HTN. **CI**: ↓ Renal Stage ≥IV CKD, (OK in **CKD** stage 1-2 & dialysis); GI ulcer, HF, transplant, cirrhosis, thrombocytopenia.

**CARDIAC**: Concern with all NSAID/Cox-2. Most trials done in ↓CV risk pts. Select pts carefully; use lowest effective dose. Naproxen, celecoxib ≤200mg/d & Ibuprofen ↓ dose appear neutral; ↑CV risk: diclofenac, indomethacin, rofecoxib, valdecoxib & ?meloxicam.

# OPIOID ANALGESIC: COMPARISON CHART [1,2,3,4,5,6]

Prepared by: Loren Regier - © www.RxFiles.ca

May 10

| Opioid Generic name (receptor target) | Route | TRADE Name(s) | Dosage Forms | Equivalent Dose approx. | Interval ~ duration | Comparative Dose & Cost | $ /30d | Comments Reassess regimens frequently when starting! |
|---|---|---|---|---|---|---|---|---|
| Morphine (mu) | PO | M.O.S; MS-IR; STATEX | Oral Soln: 1,5,10,20,50✗▼mg/ml<br>Tab: 5, 10, 20, 25, 30, 50mg | Oral 20-30mg in chronic dosing (po bioavailability ~35%) | 4 h | 20mg po q4h | $76 | ♦morphine: gold standard for opioids; {M-6-G metabolite-↑SEs if renal dysfx<br>♦may sprinkle M-Eslon or Kadian |
| Morphine SR (12h) | PO | MS CONTIN/PMS, RATIO SR, Novo<br>MOS-SR<br>M-ESLON | Tab:(15,30,60) 1st 3 brands, 100,200ς mg<br>Tab: 30,60mg<br>Cap: 10,15,30,60,100,200mg | | 12 h (q8-12h) | 60mg po q12h | $131/73<br>$64<br>$71 | ♦MS Contin may also be given pr<br>♦↑SE if renal failure ♦ 2D6 DI's but less 3A4<br>♦MS Contin, PMS & RATIO Morphine SR are ONLY interchangeable SR products. |
| Morphine SR (24h) | PO | KADIAN | Cap: 10mg✗▼,20,50,100mg | * (≤60mg in acute dosing studies) | 24 h | 100mg po q24h | $96 | |
| Morphine Supp | PR | STATEX supp | Supp: 5, 10, 20, 30mg | | 4 h | 20mg pr q4h | $459 | ♦addiction to opioids rare when no drug abuse hx & when used for pain management; consider *guidelines* for chronic pain & *treatment agreements*. |
| Morphine Inj. | SC/IM/IV | MORPHINE | Amp: 5,10,15,25,50 mg/ml<br>Syringe: 50ml X 50mg/ml | 10mg Inj. | 4 h | 10mg sc q4h | $195 | |
| Fentanyl (mu) {50ug/hr=5mg total patch} Transdermal {If skin irritation: steroid spray, or allow 1min for EtOH to evaporate} | | DURAGESIC, generic ☎✆<br>Patch; heat ↑absorption rate | Patches: 12; 25,50,75,100 ug/hr<br>Onset delayed~12-24hr. Matrix Duragesic Mat, PMS, Ran, Ratio, SDZ; Reservoir Ran, Duragesic | see comments / link 2010 | 72 h (q48-72h) | 25ug/hr q72h<br>50ug/hr q72h † | 72g-130<br>130g-240 | ♦25ug/hr ≅ 90mg oral morphine/day ♦DI 3A4<br>♦not suitable for opioid naïve, acute pain, <18yrs |
| Fentanyl / Sufentanil - SL | ✗⊗ | ♦inj. form given SL for breakthrough/incidental pain (5min prior to transfers/position change); {USA: FENTORA bucal, ACTIQ lozenge} | | | | | | ♦quick acting & very short duration |
| HYDROmorphone (mu) | PO | DILAUDID | Tab: 1,2,4,8ς mg<br>Oral Liquid: 1mg/ml | 4-6mg (as high as 7.5mg; wide variation in po bioavailability e.g. <30 - >90%) | 4 h | 4mg po q4h | $51<br>$60 | ♦may ↓SE's than morphine sedation, nausea, constip.<br>♦SC Pain Pump option ♦DI's but less 3A4<br>♦Jurnista ✗⊗ new once/day OROS; 4,8,16,32mg tabs, take whole. |
| HYDROmorphone SR (12h) | PO | HYDROMORPH- CONTIN ✆ | Cap: 3,6,12,18,24,30 mg (may sprinkle contents) | | 12 h (q8-12h) | 12mg po q12h | $128 | ♦EtOH may dramatically ↑↑ levels [7] of Palladone XL not avail., Kadian? & Avinza in USA |
| HYDROmorphone Supp | PR | DILAUDID, generic | Supp: 3mg | | 4 h | 3mg pr q4h † | $440 | ♦use laxatives (e.g. senna, lactulose) to prevent constipation; consider short-term/prn antinauseant in patients at risk. |
| HYDROmorphone Inj. | SC/IM/IV | DILAUDID | Inj: 2mg/ml; 10mg/ml; 20mg/ml; 50mg/ml; Sterile Powder: 250mg | 2-3mg (as low as 1.5mg) | 4 h | 1.5-2mg sc q4h | $230 | |
| IV may be slightly more potent than SC | | | | | | | | |
| Oxycodone SR (12h) | PO | OXYCONTIN ✆ | Tab: 5,10,15,20,30,40,60,80mg | 10-15mg; up to 30mg | 8-12 h | 30mg po q12h † | $132 | ♦biphasic; ↑abuse concern; ↑SE if ultra-rapid 2D6 met.; elderly |
| Oxycodone regular (mu & κ) | PO<br>PO / PR | OXY-IR<br>SUPEUDOL | Tab: 5ς,10ς,20ς mg<br>Tab: 5ς,10ς,20ς mg; Supp✗▼: 10,20mg | Misuse/abuse? FDA Potential Risk List-Mar08 | 4-6h | 15mg po q6h (cost based on 1½ x 10mg) | $62 | [Percocet ς ✗▼=oxycodone 5mg + acetamin. 325mg]<br>[Percodan ς ✗▼=oxycodone 5mg + ASA 325mg]<br>[Targin ✗⊗=oxycodone + naloxone]. DI's 3A4,2D6. |
| Methadone 1ς,5ς,10ς,25ς mg tab; 1&10mg/ml susp | PO | ♦tx opioid dependence; useful for opioid rotation & pain+addiction; require **special license**; long-acting, complicated dosing; Resp depression, ↑QT, DI 3A4. {SK: Pall Care only ☎} mu, δ, NMDA; ↑serotonin & noradrenalin | | | | | | |
| Meperidine (mu & NMDA) | PO | DEMEROL▼ 60 tabs/month; 2 weeks | Tab: 50ς mg (**poorly absorbed!**) | 300mg | 2-3 h | 100mg po q3h † | $89 | ♦**not for chronic pain**: short acting, requires frequent dosing. Metabolites accumulate esp. in ↓renal fx; ⇒ **CNS toxicity**: tremor, seizures |
| Meperidine Inj. (or Pethidine) | IM/SC/IV | DEMEROL▼ *See Comments* | Amp: 50,100mg/ml; (25,75 mg/ml)✗ | 75mg | 2-3 h | 50mg im q3h † | $260 | |
| Propoxyphene | PO | 642 ✗⊗ | Tab: 65mg | 100mg? | 2-4 h | 65mg po q4h † | $30 | ♦Max 390mg prop. plain/day; **abuse risk** |
| Propoxyphene napsylate | PO | DARVON-N ✗⊗ | Cap: 100mg (=65mg propox.) | 150mg? | 2-4 h | 100mg po q4h † | $79 | ♦DIs!!: alcohol & CNS depressants. |
| Codeine (mu) | PO | CODEINE | Tab: 15,30ς mg; Syrup: 5mg/ml | 200mg | 4 h | 60mg po q4h † | $40 | ♦Codeine: weak opioid; avoid daily doses ≥600mg po; practical analgesic ceiling |
| Codeine SR (12h) | PO | CODEINE CONTIN ☎✆ | Tab: 50,100ς,150ς,200ς mg | | 12 h | 150mg po q12h † | $70 | ≅200mg po or 120mg im /d, where low |
| Codeine Inj. | IM | CODEINE ✗▼ | Amp: 30,60mg | 120mg | 4 h | 30mg sc q4h † | $210 | doses of stronger opioids may be more |
| Acetaminophen (A.) +Codeine (C.) +/- Caffeine (Cf) | PO | TYLENOL + C. Elixir<br>TYLENOL # 1 Non-Rx ✗⊗<br>TYLENOL #2 /Ratio#2<br>ATASOL 15 & 30<br>TYLENOL # 3/Ratio #3<br>TYLENOL # 4/Ratio #4 | Elix: A. 320mg+C. 16mg/10ml<br>Tab: A. 300mg+C. 8mg +Cf. 15mg<br>Tab: A. 300mg+C. 15mg +Cf. 15mg<br>Tab: A. 325mg+C. 15ς & 30ς mg<br>Tab: A. 300mg+C. 30mg +Cf. 15mg<br>Tab: A. 300mg+C. 60mg | ≤200mg C. | 4+ h | 20ml po q6h †<br>ii tab po q4-6h †<br>"<br>i-ii tab po q4-6h<br>i tab po q4-6h | $300<br>$25<br>$35<br>$46<br>$45<br>$39 | effective & ↓SE ♦2D6 DI's but less 3A4<br>♦antitussive at dose of ≥15mg q4-6h<br>♦may cause ↑ constipation & GI upset;<br>♦caution with combination agents: -risk of: hepatotoxicity with >4g/d of acetaminophen; GI bleed with ASA |
| ASA/Codeine/Caffeine | PO | 292 ς ; 282 ς Tabs ✗▼ | 375mg/30mg/30 mg; 375mg/15mg/30 mg | ≤200mg C. | 4+ h | ii tab po q4-6h † | $80 | ♦concern with **breastfeeding** in rapid p450 metabolizers |

Codeine: morphine prodrug; requires CYP2D6 metabolism; ~10% genetically deficient; CYP inhibitors can ↓ analgesic effect (ie fluoxetine, paroxetine, Haldol). Ultra-rapid metabolizers (ie Ethiopians 39%, Saudi Arabians 20%, Spaniards 10%) have ↑ SE's

**Tramadol** -long acting tablet: ZYTRAM XL: 150, 200, 300 & 400mg tab od $60-140; TRIDURAL/RALIVIA: 100, 200, 300mg tab od $45-110, ✗⊗, Once daily dosing. (Not recommended: kids <18yr or pts with seizure/suicide hx. {100mg ≈ 10-20mg po morphine?} Low affinity for **mu**; also ↑serotonin & noradrenaline, Metabolized to active metabolite by CYP2D6. [**Acetaminophen** 325mg + **Tramadol** 37.5mg]=*TRAMACET*,g ✗⊗: New 2005. 2 tabs po q4-6h ~ $190 170g/mo (Max 8 tab/day).

**Pentazocine** *TALWIN* - Tab: 50ς✗▼mg (50mg po q4h $90 Max: 600mg/d; Amp: 30mg✗▼(30mg im q4h $280 Max: 360mg/d) ♦less effective than NSAIDs & other opioids; agonist-antagonist (**mu & κ**): can cause withdrawal in pts on opioids. **C/B₁**

New **Buprenorphine** partial mu agonist/κ antagonist + **Naloxone** mu, κ antagonist SUBOXONE ☎⊗2 /0.5mg, 8 /2mg SL tab: Tx opioid dependence; require **special license**; start 4 mg/day SL 24hr after last opiate; ↑or↓ by 2 - 4 mg to maintain patient & ↓withdrawal; range 4 to 24 mg/day. SE: sweat, GI, HA, ↓BP; hepatic. DI: 3A4 inhibitors; BZDs, opiates, CNS depressants

**Buprenorphine** partial mu agonist/κ antagonist *BuTrans* 5,10,20ug/hr patch ✗⊗, applied q7days for persistent moderate pain, steady state levels ~3days; SE: sweat, GI, HA, ↓BP; hepatic. DI: ↑ by 3A4 inhibitors; ↓ by 3A4 inducers carbamazepine, phenobarbital, phenytoin, rifampin; BZDs, opiates, CNS depressants.

Pregnancy Category: Strong Opioids ⇑ ⇑ C/D; Weak Opioids C/D ⇓

* with **chronic** admin., equivalent po morphine dose is ~**2-3X the inj. dose** but in acute pain, it may be ≤ 6X; † =dose listed not equivalent ☎ =EDS Sask ✗ =Non Formulary Sk **Cost**=to SK consumer ς=scored tab **d**=day ✆=prior NIHB ▼covered NIHB **CTZ**=chemoreceptor trigger zone **OTC**=over the counter. **Adverse Rx's**: nausea, constipation Tx: senna; methylnaltrexone 12mg sc EOD prn RELISTOR ✗⊗ $40/dose, sedation, confusion/CNS effect, sweating, miosis, resp depression, myoclonus, urine retention, dry mouth, hormonal (e.g. ↓testosterone & cortisol, ↑prolactin) & pruritus. Use short acting formulations ***PRN for breakthrough pain*** eg. 10-15% of total daily dose. Chronic opioid therapy in pts with **renal dysfx** ⇒ may lead to accumulation of toxic metabolites (esp. **meperidine**); switching opioids or opioid rotation strategies may be useful. **Drug Interactions**: CNS depressants (e.g. alcohol, sedatives, neuroleptics). **Patients intolerant to the side effects** of one opioid may be changed to a ≤ dose of another; True morphine **allergy** is very rare. **Switching** opioids, often 25-50% less than equivalent is given to account for variation & incomplete cross-tolerance. **SC Pain Pumps** available. **Adjuncts** NSAIDs, antidepressants TCA, anticonvulsants; dexamethasone 10mg sc/po bid.

**Antinauseants**: **metoclopramide** 10mg po/sc q4h prn, **domperidone** 5-10mg po tid ac (affect CTZ & GI motility); **haloperidol** 0.5-1mg po/sc bid prn (CTZ); **prochlorperazine** 5-10mg im/iv/po/pr q6h prn (effects CTZ but sedating); dimenhydrinate 25-50mg po/im/iv/sc/pr q6h prn

**Opioid Immunoassay (Urine):** Synthetic (meperidine, fentanyl series, propoxyphene, methadone) will be opiate negative & must be ordered independently. Semi-synthetic (hydrocodone, oxycodone, hydromorphone, oxymorphone, buprenorphine) may be opiate positive or negative, depending on the threshold. Interpret false negatives with caution. Drug specific confirmatory testing may be needed. Opiates may be detectable for a couple of days. May false positive⇒Poppy seeds

# Pediatric Pain: Treatment Considerations, Q&As



## Common Challenges in Pediatric Pain

- Myth: *children do not feel pain as their nervous system is not developed* [1]
- Myth: *Let's get it over with quickly; he won't remember, he's scared.*
- Failure to anticipate pain. (e.g. urethral caths, NG tube, labwork)
- Failure to assess[2] or difficulty in assessing pain in very young
- Fear of masking signs of a more serious etiology → No adverse outcome or delays in diagnosis attributed to admin of narcotic analgesia in acute abdominal pain[3,4,5]
- Fear of adverse events & overdose (sedation, respiratory depression)[6]
- Tendency to underdose (lack of parent/caregiver understanding of toxicity; dosing without dose calculation)[7]
- Transitioning: maintaining pain control from *Recovery* to *Ward* to *Home*

## Pain Assessment in Pediatrics

- ↑documenting of pain score assoc. with ↑analgesic use & ↓pain [8]
  Self-report scales[9]: 0-10 Numerical age 8+; Faces Pain Scale-Revised FPS-R[10], age 4+
- Observational scales Observe changes from usual in these cues:

| | |
|---|---|
| Vocal | ◆crying, screaming, yelling, moaning, whimpering |
| Social | ◆quietness, irritability, difficult to console |
| Facial | ◆furrowed brow, grimace, clenched teeth, tightly closed eyes |
| Activity | ◆less movement, agitated, guarding of a body part |
| Physical | ◆pallor, sweat, gasping/breathing change, tense/stiff |
| Other | ◆changes in sleeping & eating patterns |

See also FLACC scale: Face/Legs/Activity/Cry/Consolability[11]; Reviews[12,13]:

## Non-pharmacological Tips {↑ coping & pain threshold}

- Neonate/infant: bundle, kangaroo care, breast-feed, sucrose + sucking
  Toddler: distraction; Older child: preparation, explanation, distraction; assist parent on how to be calm; *non-procedural* talk most helpful.
- Sucrose Cochrane[17]: best for single painful procedure (infant <6 months[5,11,18]); + distraction. {Administer <2 minutes prior: 2ml of 25% sucrose solution e.g. TOOT SWEET 24% by oral syringe/dropper into mouth; or allow infant to suck from pacifier/breast. OK if NPO}
- Distraction/psychological techniques: Cochrane[19] very useful if age appropriate
  - toys, books, bubbles, music, humour, TV, imagery, breathing, blowing pinwheel
  - parent's presence; breastfeeding[20,21]; position for comfort!; *Cough Trick*[65]
- Pressure on injured or injection sites (e.g. immunizations 10 seconds prior)
- Cold/hot compresses (e.g. cold for sprains, warmth for earache)
- Splinting, elevation, bandaging or dressing (immobilize area & ↓ pain)
- Information giving: brief description, what to expect feels cold/warm, little pinch, will help you!
- *NEVER, NEVER use the word needle*[22]*; don't let them see the needle*

## Specific Therapeutic Considerations

| | |
|---|---|
| Abdominal acute<br>-consider pain, age, ... | **Opioid** does not delay surgical decision appendicitis[23];<br>*Relaxed patient ⇨ better exam & better diagnosis!* |
| Burns, Minor[24]<br><5% TBSA in children | Cold compress x20-30min before applying a dressing.<br>Give oral analgesic (ibuprofen or acetaminophen) |
| Chronic Daily Headache[25,26] | e.g. tension-type or transformed migraine; see migraine chart. TCAs, gabapentin, riboflavin, etc. Assess stressors & family hx!<br>- consider analgesic rebound/overuse (if use >4x/week) |
| Ear Ache<br>-acute otitis media (AOM): always treat pain whether "watchful waiting" or using antibiotics. | Acetaminophen or ibuprofen. Ensure adequate dose, initiate quickly (**1st dose in emerg** department/clinic!) Give round the clock x24-48hr.<br>Warm heat-pad or cloth often helps.<br>Ear drops: AURALGAN antipyrine & benzocaine: sensitizing; if perforated ear drum, avoid! Minimally effective but option |
| Emergency trauma (ex. Musculoskeletal) | **Ibuprofen** in musculoskeletal trauma (extremities, back & neck) better than acetaminophen or codeine for pain relief and length of relief[27]<br>**Opioids** suitable if moderate to severe pain |
| Heel poke | Breastfeeding, sucrose, sucking. Topical anaesthetic no effect! |
| Immunization*<br>{pressure at site helps}<br>Reviews:[28,29] Antipyretics may ↓ immune response. | 25% oral **sucrose** & pacifier 2 minutes pre; effective[30]<br>{RCT n=83: infants ↓ pain 3.8 vs 4.8 @7min; return to baseline @ 9min}<br>Topical anaesthetics: offer option to parents; OTC purchase; apply prior to appointment. Useful: ↓ pain 40%; (Table 2) |
| Lumbar puncture * | Topical anaesthetic; po acetaminophen or ibuprofen; may mix-in po midazolam 1yr +; sucrose if infant |
| NG Tube insertion | Lidocaine jelly; or endotracheal spray if >2yrs (burns & dose caution!) |
| Open wound<br>(**Not near eye!**)[32]<br>Explore to rule out retained foreign body! | **Anaesthetics:** administer topically e.g. LET, direct local infiltration or regional nerve block. Tetanus status?<br>**Tissue adhesive:** ↓pain in simple laceration <3cm[33] |
| IV insertion*:<br>*Use non-pharmacologic techniques.*<br>*Explain steps if appropriate* | **Topical anaesthetics** (Table 2): useful but pain relief not complete; takes time to absorb. Place in ≥ 2 sites over suitable vein. Use routinely!<br>{↑ in cannulation rate NNT=5; less procedure time[34]}<br>Avoid mucous membrane contact or ingestion<br>◆AMETOP superior to EMLA for needles[35]; Lipisomal lidocaine MAXILENE effective, fast , less vasoactive<br>**Vapocoolant Spray**: PAIN EASE; effect ≤60seconds[64] |
| Post-op analgesia:<br>{Concurrent opioids via IV & epidural: resp.depr <1%}[36] | Start analgesia **before child awakens** (e.g. supp).<br>Multimodal approach: pr naproxen or acetaminophen; if appropriate regional block (e.g. chest tube), epidural. |

***Preventing pain** may decrease analgesic requirement for future procedures!

## Q&As

### *Is alternating* acetaminophen with ibuprofen appropriate?*

- Not recommended by the Canadian Paediatric Society
- Increased risk of adverse effects e.g. renal & potential for errors
- Monotherapy sufficient & preferred for vast majority[38]. If not effective, may switch to or add the other. Mechanisms differ for pain; may give one round the clock, with other PRN for breakthrough.
- Reassess if pain unresolved; combining both is an option for pain

### *Alternatives in topical/local anaesthetic allergy?*

- True allergy to local anesthetic is rare[39]; often due to preservative
- Repeated use also ↑'s potential for hypersensitivity reactions
- Consider formulation without preservative if available/suitable[40]
- If allergy to amide (e.g. lidocaine, bupivicaine, mepivicaine, prilocaine): try an ester (procaine, tetracaine, benzocaine, cocaine) & vice versa.[41]
  {Allergy to both amide & ester: diphenhydramine 1% or benzyl alcohol; efficacy = to 1% lidocaine}

## Extras: Drugs for Procedural Sedation (sedative/hypnotic adjuncts)

– Monitor for Procedural Sedation [check institution or department **protocols** & be aware of guidelines / **liability implications**. Should not be providing sedation & doing procedure.]

◆**Midazolam**: as adjunct prior to minor procedures; PO onset 20-40min, duration 1hr; PO: <20kg: 0.5-0.75 mg/kg x1; ≥20kg: 0.3-0.5mg/kg/dose; Max 10-20mg PO;
Note IV midazolam dose is MUCH lower than PO dose!!! (1/10th the dose)
{IV: 0.05mg/kg/dose IV x1; repeat x1 prn; onset 10min}; SE: disinhibition, paradoxical agitation, apnea; Caution: ↓ hepatic or renal fx; DIs: CNS depressants ↓ dose of both.
{Nasal limited study: faster onset but ↓sedation & duration than po; less effective than intranasal ketamine.[51]}

◆**Ketamine**: see protocol(s)[52]; 0.5-2mg/kg IV; onset 1-5 min; duration 15-60min; SE: nystagmus, disassociative (looks awake but is asleep; inform parents); vivid dreams x48hrs {add low dose midazolam if ≥10 yrs to prevent nightmares}; ↑BP, HR, salivation (co-administer atropine with 1st dose)[53]; rash common but transient.
Rare-Severe SE: laryngospasm, apnea, resp depression; recovery agitation, Preserves pharyngeal & resp fx. CI: airway instability, URTI, ↑ICP, ↑BP, acute globe injury, glaucoma, thyrotoxicosis, psych disorder. Age >1yr preferred

◆$N_2O$:(50/50mix O2, demand valve) ∴ age >6yrs: quick 3 min, short acting good for IV starts; CI: pneumothorax, bowel obstruction

◆Fentanyl 1-4ug/kg IV x1 slow over 2min.; may repeat after 30-60min; rigidity possible with midazolam

◆Propofol: CAUTION - SIGNIFICANT TOXICITY! ⇨metabolic acidosis; ↑BP, ↑death in ICU! Reserve for anaesthesia. {Procedural sedation: 1mg/kg IVx1 then 0.5mg/kg q3-5min. Age >3yr}

⇨**Route of administration**: generally use IV, PO; but PR rarely
- Avoid the IM route (add to pain; erratic absorption)[56]
- PCA pump option in cancer pain for older children anaesthesia referral
- Epidural: option if AEs systemic meds; psychological prep important

⇨**Dosing**: by weight mg/kg or /BSA and by the hour!!!

⇨Be prepared to treat drug side effects as soon as they happen, or before {e.g. nausea, constipation & itch with opioids; dry mouth mouth care}

### Table 1: Pain Medication in Pediatrics - Overview (See also RxFiles pain related charts at www.RxFiles.ca)

| Drug | | Dose in Peds [PO unless otherwise indicated] | Comments {Acetaminophen po: Max 90mg/kg/day some refs.} |
|---|---|---|---|
| Acetaminophen TYLENOL ▼<br>{Liquids, chew-tab 80, 160mg, Tab 325mg; Supp 120mg, 325mg}<br>CAUTION! Calculate dose⇨ | | 10-15mg/kg q4-6h; Max **75**mg/kg/day >40wks<br>{Drops Infant: 80mg/ml; Liquid: 160mg/5ml<br>Supp PR: 15-20mg/kg/dose Max 5 dose/24hr}OTC<br>⇨overdose common - mix-ups e.g. formulation ! | ◆Caution if malnourished or dehydrated; ↑ hepatotoxicity?<br>◆{Loading dose x1: Emerg or post-op option; ≤30mg/kg po; ≤40mg/kg rectal[57]; (Toxic single dose <6yrs: ≥200mg/kg)}<br>[Newborn 4-40wks: Max 60mg/kg/day; may give drops PR for doses ≤80mg] |
| NSAID: Ibuprofen >6mo<br>Susp 20 & 40mg/ml; Tab 100 & 200mg | | 5-10mg/kg q6-8h; Max 40mg/kg/day<br>(Ibuprofen MOTRIN, ADVIL OTC. Naproxen ALEVE OTC ≥12yrs) | ◆may give acetaminophen & NSAID together for pain, not fever<br>◆some concern: long-term use may restrict healing fractures |
| (PO) Naproxen >2yrs<br>Susp 25mg/ml; Tab 125mg | | 2.5-5mg/kg BID; Max 20mg/kg/day;<br>[**PR**: 25-49kg: 250mg/dose; ≥50kg: 500mg dose] | ◆caution in ↓ renal fx, dehydration & ? bleeding disorder<br>◆celecoxib FDA approval: Juvenile RA >2yrs 10-25kg: 50mg po BID |
| Opioid | Codeine | 0.5-1mg/kg PO q4h (requires metab; ↑SEs) | ◆codeine ineffective in ≤ 1/3 of kids who can't metabolize |
| | Morphine<br>Soln: 1, 5 mg/mL; Supp: 5, 10mg<br>Tab: 5, 10mg; (also SR & ER tabs) | 0.2-0.4mg/kg PO q4h High alert drugs!<br>[IV: 0.05-0.1mg/kg IV/SC q2-4h] Check drug & dose! | ◆addiction not an issue when used appropriately for pain<br>◆monitor respirations ◆avoid meperidine (dysphoric, seizures) |
| | Hydromorphone | 0.04-0.08 mg/kg PO q3-4h | {reassess/titrate dose; forms: syrup & tab; codeine not PR} |
| | Fentanyl CAUTION! | Patch officially CI: <18yrs & opioid naive; | {potent; chest wall rigidity in neonates; alternative routes used for incidental pain} |
| Adjuncts for Neuropathic | | Antidepressants (e.g. TCAs), anticonvulsants (e.g. gabapentin), tramadol: limited evidence, off-label use. | |

◆Opioid Reversal: naloxone *Narcan* ◆Benzo Reversal: Flumazenil (short acting, rarely needed) RA= rheumatoid arthritis SHR= Saskatoon Health Region AEs= adverse events Crm=cream CI=contraindications PACU= post anesthesia care unit PCA=patient controlled analgesia SE=side effect

### Table 2: Topical Anaesthetics** OTC $6; Rx $15

| Table 2: Topical Anaesthetics** | Comments: use only on intact skin; avoid middle ear ototoxic |
|---|---|
| **AMETOP** tetracaine (amethocaine) 4% Gel ✗⊗ 1.5g/ $6 - 15<br>[ester] {write time on patch & remove per instructions blistering} | ◆Apply 30min prior; lasts 4hrs after removal; ?occlusion not required (if old enough to leave on);<br>Age: >1mo term infant; Vasodilation✓ (erythema; edema); Refrigerate✓; 1month @room temp |
| **EMLA** lidocaine 2.5%* + prilocaine 2.5% ✗▼: Crm 30g/$43, Patch 2/ $6<br>[amide] | ◆60+ min prior; occlusion required! Age: term infant; vasoconstriction {Rare: risk of methemoglobinemia: ↑ if <3mo; & in <1yr if DI's that ↑ Met-Hgb risk e.g. sulfonamides} |
| Lidocaine* Crm: 4% ✗⊗ **LMX-4, ELA-Max.** (also 5% ?) | ◆60+ min prior; occlusion required! {vasoconstriction: venous access more difficult.} |
| **MAXILENE** Liposomal* Lidocaine 4% ✗⊗ 30g/$50; 5g/ $6-15 | ◆30+ min prior; occlusion not required; minimally vasoactive. (Available: 4% or 5%) |

### Table 3: Other Local Anaesthetics**

| Table 3: Other Local Anaesthetics** | Comments: 45 minutes for good effect; Avoid mucous membranes[58] |
|---|---|
| **LET** lidocaine 4% */ epinephrine 0.1% / tetracaine 0.5%<br>Epinephrine (**E**): ↑ hemostasis, ↑ anaesthetic duration; **AVOID**: digits, nosetip, ear, penis (2° necrosis end artery). | ◆topical anaesthetic for **open wounds** esp facial/scalp if <5cm in length; max 3mL<br>1) mix with cellulose form gel, apply to wound, cover - occlusive dressing<br>2) place LET soaked cotton ball into wound; apply pressure x20min |
| Methylcellulose / epinephrine 0.05% / cocaine 11.8% (SHR) | ◆mixed solution with methylcellulose forms gel, preventing running; **LET preferred!** |

◆**Local Infiltration**: 1) warm anaesthetic 37° C, 2) use smaller gauge needle (e.g. 27 or 30-gauge), 3) inject at slow rate, proximal borders 1st, from inside wound edge, 4) pre-treat with topical anaesthetic, 5) consider buffering (sodium bicarb 9ml mix with 1ml 1mEq/ml bicarb), 6) pressure

| | | |
|---|---|---|
| **Lidocaine (L)**: onset rapid; duration ½ hr local - {duration 1-2hr if regional block}; Age 3yrs+ ✓<br>[L: 0.5%, 1%, 2%; L+E: 1%, 2%; (L+E no preservative: 1.5%)] | **Mepivacaine**: onset 6-10min; duration 1-3hrs;<br>- if Age <3yrs or weight <13.6kg, use [0.5-1.5%];<br>- little vasodilation & epinephine seldom needed | **Bupivacaine (B)**: onset 8-12min; duration 4-6hr;<br>Age 12yrs+ ✓; CI: sulfite allergy<br>[B: 0.25%, 0.5%; B+E: 1%, 2%] |

*avoid if amide allergy (rare); ** systemic toxicity (cardiac & CNS) possible but rare with appropriate use: (careful with dose & site).

Rx coverage: ☎=Exception Drug Status in SK ✗ =Non-formulary in SK ⌀=prior approval for NIHB ⊗=not covered by NIHB ▼=covered by NIHB (Indian Affairs)

Treat **High Absolute 10yr Fracture Risk, & Spine or Hip** # pts, NOT low or moderate # risk pt unless exceptional circumstances. Take age, sex, steroid use, family history, smoking & fragility # after age 40; not just BMD, into account.

| | Generic/TRADE<br>Strength & forms, g=generic avail. | Side Effects (SE) / Contraindications C | Hip # | Vertebral # | √ = therapeutic use / ×= Disadvantage / Comments /<br>NNT's may mislead; most OP trials had mix of low, moderate & high # risk pts. Drug Interactions DI / Monitor M | USUAL DOSE | $/year<br>g=generic |
|---|---|---|---|---|---|---|---|
| BISPHOSPHONATES anti-resorptive | **Alendronate, risedronate or zoledronic** acid ↓ vertebral ↓RR~50%, nonvertebral & hip # ↓RR~30% in **HIGH** risk OP pts; & FDA approved for OP in **MEN** & **GIO**. Glucocorticoid Induced Osteoporosis 2 (may ↓skeletal complications/pain in multiple myeloma, breast, lung & prostate cancer pts)<br>**Mechanism**: Anti-resorptive which binds to hydroxyapatite, inhibits the osteoclast, which decreases the resorption & turnover of bone, which increases BMD often a 2-6% increase in BMD over 1-3yr. Poor oral bioavailability <1% makes brand products hard to copy.<br>**M**: # risk, height, iliocostal distance, & BMD in 1-2yr. 6,7,8 Reassess existing pts Consider Indefinite **Drug Holiday** (?1-3-5yrs) after 5yr 9 FLEX,10, 11 of continuous tx only if not now or perhaps never were at high # risk. (effects **persist** since meds in bones for years).<br>**Caution**: bisphosphonate in **Stage 4-5 CKD** (1st rule out adynamic bone dx usually by lab +/- biopsy findings) or in **transplant** pts if only high OP risk but not #'s. **Ensure Bone Care/Hygiene**: lifestyle exercise-wt bearing, Vit D, Ca++, ↓falls/alcohol/smoking<br>**Possible long term Tx concerns**: 1) osteonecrosis of jaw (**ONJ**) avascular necrosis: rarely occurs; if cancer, extensive dental procedures & **high dose/long term IV** bisphosphonate used very rarely on oral tx, >1 in 100,000 pt yr; may benefit postponing tx until **invasive** dental work done. Dental exam with X-ray in high risk pts. Use good oral hygiene & report dental concerns. (Consider holding bisphos for invasive dental procedure: if on bisphos tx for >3yr, esp. if on steroids. If hold tx: stop 3month before; & until ~3months after dental procedure. Lacks evidence AAOMS'09)12,13,14<br>2) **Atypical sub-trochanteric #** very rare long term15 mid-shaft # eg. femur spike or beak configuration & cortical thickening at # site; ?↑ microcracks may present as **thigh pain** or hypersensitivity reaction. 3) **Atrial fibrillation** rare: reports with IV zoledronic acid 16 4) **esophageal cancer?** 17<br>**Others** not official OP indication: **Pamidronate** Aredia 30,60,90mg IV; 30mg IV 2hr D5W q3mon $450/yr, approved: Paget's dx & Hypercalcemia of Malignancy. **Clodronate** Bonefos 400mg cap; 300mg/5ml amp IV, approved: Hypercalcemia & osteolysis. | | | | | | |
| | **Alendronate**, **Fosamax**, g<br>(5 ×), 10, 40 Paget's & 70mg tabs<br>70mg/75mL oral soln (raspberry flavour) ⊗<br>(each pack = 4 bottles of 75mL)<br>---<br>**Alendronate/cholecalciferol** tabs **Fosavance**<br>70mg/70ug (2800IU Vit $D_3$), X<br>70mg/140ug (5600IU Vit $D_3$) OP<br>(Nitrogen containing⇒potent) | **Common: GI SE**: (abd pain ~7%, acid regurgitation ~2%, constipation ~3%, diarrhea 3%, dyspepsia ~4%, flatulence ~3%, nausea ~4%), headache ~2%, taste distortion ~1%<br>**Serious**: Esophagitis, esophageal ulcers 1.5%, erosions, stricture, perforation; gastric ulcer 1%; bone, joint ± muscle pain ~4%, muscle cramp ~1%, ocular disorders, ONJ rare<br>**C**: **esophagus** abnormalities which delay esophageal emptying stricture, achalasia; inability to stand/ sit up ≥30min; hypocalcemia; pregnancy & nursing moms; & renal dysfx: CrCl <35 mL/min weigh risk vs benefit if stable CrCl & definite OP | NNT = 91 for 3 yrs 1.1 vs 2.2% in ♀ with previous vertebral# 18 FIT<br>NS: **Primary** prevention<br>Cochrane 19 | NNT = 37 for 3 yrs 2.3 vs 5% in ♀ with previous vertebral# 20 FIT<br>Cochrane: 19 ~3yr<br>1° prev: NNT=50<br>2° prev: NNT=17 | **DI**: ↓ absorption alendronate: Calcium, antacids, iron, food/beverages water ok<br>Impair cholecalciferol absorption: bile acid sequestrants (eg. cholestyramine, colestipol), mineral oils, olestra & orlistat.<br>↑cholecalciferol catabolism: anticonvulsants, cimetidine, thiazide but ↑ ca++<br>**Men**: data only from secondary trial analysis. **Elderly**: studied up to age 91<br>Take at least **30 min before** first food/drink/medication of the day with a full glass of water (**240mL**); do not lie down for 30 minutes after.<br>Low cost, very good fracture outcome evidence & 10yrs of data. Approved 1995 | 10mg OD in am<br>70mg once **weekly**<br>70mg soln once **wkly**<br>---<br>70mg/2800IU once **wkly**<br>70mg/5600IU once **wkly** | 520 g<br>400 g<br>(710 Trade)<br>710<br>---<br>340 X<br>**360** |
| | **Risedronate** **Actonel**, g<br>5, 30, 35, (75 D/C, 150mg ⊗) tabs<br>**Actonel Plus Calcium X** ⊗ -D/C soon<br>4 Risedronate 35mg tabs & 24 calcium 1250mg tabs {500mg elemental calcium} – 28d supply<br>(Nitrogen containing⇒potent) | **Common: GI SE**: (abd pain ~4%, diarrhea ~3%, dyspepsia ~5%, flatulence 2%, gastritis 1%, vomiting ~1%), asthenia 1%, headache ~3%, pruritus 1%, rash 1.4%.<br>**Serious**: arthralgia ~2%, myalgia ~1%, gastritis erosive ~1%, iritis rare, uveitis rare, ONJ rare<br>**C**: Hypocalcemia, pregnancy & nursing moms, **esophagus** abnormalities which delay emptying (e.g., stricture, achalasia), renal dysfx: CrCl <30 mL/min weigh risk vs benefit if stable CrCl & definite OP | NNT=91 for 3 yr in ♀ with or without prev vertebral# 21 HIP<br>NS: **Primary** prevention<br>Cochrane 22 | NNT=15 or 20/ 3yr in ♀ without prev vert. # 23 or with # 24 VERT<br>NS: **Primary** prevention<br>Cochrane 22 | **DI**: ↓ absorption risedronate: Food, antacids/supplements which contain polyvalent cations (e.g., calcium, magnesium, aluminum & iron).<br>**Men**: data only from open label trials.<br>Take at least **30 min before** first food, beverage, or medication of the day with water (**≥120mL**); do not lie down for 30 minutes after.<br>**Elderly**: a few trials studied people over 100yrs.<br>Convenient monthly dosing with possibly less GI SE & 8yrs of data. | 5mg OD in am<br>35mg once weekly<br>150mg tab q **month**<br>150mg 75mg x2 q **mon**<br>(75mg soon D/C) | 870, 445 g ⊗<br>710, 360 g ⊗<br>840 ⊗<br>**690** |
| | **Zoledronic** acid **Aclasta**<br>5mg/**100mL IV** infusion, (Paget's),<br>(Nitrogen containing⇒potent)<br>**Zometa X** ⊗<br>(Osteolytic lesions of multiple myeloma, Hypercalcemia of Malignancy)<br>4mg vial (give as 100mL **IV** infusion)<br>For My Bones: 1-877-580-5338<br>Novartis program: gives IV clinic locations & helps to arrange monthly payment plan options. | **Common**: **Post-dose Sx**: fever 18%, myalgia 9%, headache 6%, flu-like 8%, arthralgia 7%, {mild-mod. in nature & resolve ~3day; some ≤7-14day ↓ in 2nd injection: acetaminophen/ibuprofen may help}<br>**Hypocalcemia** (usually asymptomatic, but Sx: numbness or tingling sensation, esp. near mouth, muscle cramp/spasm); redness, swelling &/or infusion site pain; eyes pain, redness, itching.<br>**Serious**: ?↑Atrial fib serious: 1.3 vs. 0.5% placebo, ONJ rare, acute **renal** failure may ↑with quick infusion rate; rare, musculoskeletal pain rare, bronchoconstriction in **Aspirin**-sensitive pts.<br>**C**: Pregnancy, nursing moms, non-corrected hypocalcemia, renal dysfx: CrCl <30 mL/min weigh risk vs benefit if stable CrCl & definite OP | NNT = 91 for 3 yrs in ♀ with or without a vertebral # 25<br>HORIZON | NNT = 13 for 3 yrs in ♀ with and without a previous vertebral # 26<br>HORIZON | Zoledronic acid is a potent antiresorptive, has ↓GI SE, & given IV q1-2yr<br>**DI**: Aminoglycosides (↓ serum calcium level), loop diuretics (↑ risk of hypocalcemia), nephrotoxic drugs such as NSAIDS<br>**Hydrate** prior to admin: drink ≥2 glasses of fluids/water before & after.<br>Post recurrent hip # trial Horizon: ↓ **mortality** 13.3 vs 9.6%, NNT=27 over 1.9yr 26<br>**Men**: 24% of pts in RCT 12 were men, but analysis not done by men only<br>**M**: Serum calcium, vitamin D, renal function (Scr, eGFR) before every tx.<br>Acetaminophen or ibuprofen may ↓ incidence of post-dose Sx's.<br>Criteria–symptomatic tx of **Paget's** disease of the bone (one tx/yr)<br>Least GI SE, infrequent q1-2yr IV infusion, but limited drug plan coverage. | Treat:<br>5mg IV infused over NO LESS than 15 minutes once/**yr**;<br>Prevent:<br>5mg IV infused over NO LESS than 15 min every 2yrs;<br>RCT trials out to 3yr. | **740**<br><br>365<br><br>X ⊗ for OP |
| | **Etidronate** (Eti) **Didronel**, g<br>200mg tab<br>**Didrocal kit**, g<br>14 x Etidronate 400mg white PLUS 76 Calcium Carbonate blue 1250mg (500mg elemental $Ca^{2+}$) | **Common** vs pl: **GI SE**: (diarrhea 37 vs 31%, dyspepsia 12 vs 11%, flatulence 17 vs 15%, nausea 18 vs 14%), dizzy 16 vs 11%, headache 2%<br>**Serious (rare)**: arthropathy (arthralgia, arthritis), ocular disorders, esophagitis, glossitis, angioedema, skin rashes, pruritus, Stevens-Johnson syndrome, urticaria, osteomalacia, leukopenia 1/100,000, agranulocytosis, pancytopenia<br>**C**: Overt osteomalacia, **esophagus** abnormalities stricture, achalasia, hypocalcemia, pregnancy & nursing moms. | NS compared to calcium ± vitamin D placebo 27<br>Cochrane | NNT = 20 for 3 yrs in ♀ who had a previous vertebral # 27<br>Cochrane | Etidronate is a **weak antiresorptive** agent & may be effective in ↓risk of vertebral # in those at high risk.2 ( not ↓ hip or non-vertebral #'s)<br>**DI**: Food/$Ca^{2+}$/Iron/$Mg^{2+}$ may ↓ absorption of etidronate; warfarin ↑INR reports, $Ca^{2+}$ may ↓ absorption of: cipro, HIV PI, iron, tetracycline, levothyroxine.<br>Etidronate on an **empty stomach**, with a full glass of water at **bedtime**, at least **2 hrs before or after** eating. Take calcium with food.<br>Lowest cost, but less fracture outcome evidence. | Eti 400mg hs x 14 d, then calcium 500mg daily x 76days ⇒ cycle therapy.<br>{**Continuous** eti can impair mineralization of the bone} | **160** g,<br>(230 Trade)<br>{Full formulary} SPDP&NIHB |
| SERM | **Raloxifene** **Evista**, g<br>60mg tab<br>-antiresorptive | **Common** vs pl: Vasodilatation **flushing** 10 vs 6%, flu like 14 vs 11%, leg **cramps** 7 vs 4%, ?↑diabetes mellitus 1.2 vs 0.5%<br>**Serious**: **VTE** 3.32/1000 ♀ yrs vs. 1.44 placebo (**OR**: 1.9 for PE, 1.5 for DVT)<br>**C**: ♀ of childbearing potential risk fo congenital defects in fetus, ♀ with active/past venous thromboembolic events (DVT, PE, retinal vein thrombosis) ↑ fatal **stroke** 0.22 vs 0.15% RUTH 28 | NS compared to placebo arm | NNT = 29 for 3yr in ♀ with & without a previous vertebral#29 MORE | Raloxifene ↓'s the risk of **vertebral** # 2, MORE, but not non-vertebral or hip #<br>Benefit pts with **breast cancer** risk. 30 STAR (Lipid: may ↑HDL-C, ↓ total cholesterol & LDL)<br>If **pt >65yr** & on raloxifene, consider switch to alternate agent. b/c stroke & VTE risk<br>**DI**: Cholestyramine ↓ raloxifene effect, warfarin ↓INR **M**: VTE<br>Limited role: weigh stroke/VTE risk against modest breast ca & OP outcomes. | 60mg PO OD | **630** g,<br>(870 Trade) |
| | **Calcitonin** Salmon<br>-antiresorptive **Miacalcin**, g<br>200IU/**nasal spray**,<br>14 doses/bottle {1 pack=2 bottles}<br>Unopened, store in fridge (2-8°C); after priming store at room temp (15-30 C) & use within 4 wks<br>{SC inj 100iu/ml Caltine, 400iu/4ml Calcimar} | **Common** vs pl: Rhinitis 8 vs 5%, nasal dryness 4 vs 3.6%, epistaxis 2.4 vs 2%, nasal discomfort 1.6 vs 1%, sinusitis 1.6 vs 0.5%, abd pain 3 vs 1.5%, nausea 1.7 vs 1%, dyspepsia 1.6 vs 0.3%, fatigue 1 vs 0.3%, hypertension 1.7 vs 0.8%, dizziness 1.6 vs 0.8%.<br>**Serious** vs pl: back pain 3 vs 0.8%, rhinitis ulcerative 3.4 vs 1.6%, cataract 3 vs 1.3% | NS compared to placebo arm | NNT = 12 for 5 yrs in ♀ who had a previous vertebral # 31<br>PROOF<br>**Trial Limitations** | Calcitonin considered to ↓ the risk of vertebral #s. but not non-vertebral or hip # 2<br>**Weak antiresorptive** agent (consider use in ♀ >5yrs PM, unless for pain)<br>√**Useful for pain from acute vertebral compression #s** esp. first ~3 months<br>**DI**: Lithium ↓lithium concentration. | 1 spray = 200IU/d, intranasally, alternating nostrils daily<br>Upon first use only, must prime pump. | **720** g |

| | Generic/TRADE Strength & forms, g=generic avail. | Side Effects (SE) / Contraindications CI | Hip # | Vertebral # | √ = therapeutic use / x= Disadvantage / Comments / NNT's may mislead; most OP trials had mix of low, moderate & high # risk pts. Drug Interactions DI / Monitor M | USUAL DOSE | $/year g=generic |
|---|---|---|---|---|---|---|---|
| PTH | **Teriparatide** *X*, ⊗ Forteo (1-34 PTH) 750ug/3mL prefilled pen syringe - **anabolic:** ↑ osteoblast activity {PTH I-84 PreOs} avail in Europe. Forteo Customer Care Program: 1-877-436-7836. Possible financial assistance by Eli Lilly. | **Common** vs pl: Nausea 9vs7%, dizzy 8vs5%, cramp leg 3vs1%, syncope 3vs1%. **Serious** vs placebo: Osteosarcoma rats, **hypercalcemia** symptomatic (eg. nausea, vomiting, constipation, lethargy, muscle weakness), hyperuricemia 3 vs 0.7%, angina pectoris 3vs2%, arthralgia 10vs8%, tooth disorder 2vs1%. **CI**: Pre-existing hypercalcemia, severe renal impairment, metabolic bone dx other than primary OP (incl. Paget's dx, hyperparathyroidism), unexplained ↑ alkaline phosphatase, prior skeleton external beam or implant radiation tx, bone metastases or skeletal malignancies hx, pregnancy, nursing moms, kids or young adults with open epiphysis. | NS compared to placebo arm [32] | NNT = 11 for 1.5 yrs in ♀ who had a previous vertebral # [32] | Teriparatide considered to ↓risk of vertebral & non-vertebral #s, not hip #'s in postmenopausal ♀ with very **severe** OP. [2] √Recommend if ⇒ prior fragility # + {very low BMD (below -3 to -3.5), pts who continue to #, or lose BMD despite taking antiresorptive tx's}. Osteoporosis in **MEN**: approved for tx some evidence for benefit, no # data available. Glucocorticoid Induced Osteoporosis **GIO**: approved for tx. If start PTH, D/C bisphosphonate usually; then when D/C PTH, restart bisphosphonate. **DI**: Digoxin ↑Dig level? | 20ug SC qd, up to 18 months 2yr FDA. Refrigerate, discard pen after 28 days | **9000** |
| Calcium & Vit D | **Calcium**, g *X*▼ Oral, chew, dissolvable tablet; liquid. NIHB covers ▼: Calcium 500mg, Calcium 500 + Vit D 125IU, & Calcium 500 + Vit D 400IU. Pt with chronic renal failure, NIHB ▼: Sandoz, Gramcal, Calsan, Os-cal 250mg, Calcium. $Ca^{++}$ content: carbonate 40%, citrate 21% | **Common**: Constipation, bloating. **Serious:** Renal stone {HR = 1.17, 95% CI, 1.02 to 1.34} [33 WHI] but uncertainty because no correlation with total daily calcium intake & kidney stone formation. The adverse effect of calcium supplement in excess of 2,500 mg/d may include high blood calcium levels, renal function complications, & renal calculi formation {There are no recorded cases of calcium intoxication from food.} | Ca+Vit D: RR=0.84, 95% CI 0.73-0.96 [34 Cochrane]. NNT=45 for 2-5 yrs in ♀ with or without a previous vertebral # [35] Meta-analysis. High 500,000 IU/yr⇒↑#'s Sanders'10 | NS [34] | Calcium & Vit D supplementation alone insufficient to prevent # in those with OP; but critical **adjunct** with antiresorptive & anabolic OP meds [2]. Consuming ≤500mg calcium elemental at one time maximizes absorption. [5] Include diet & supplemental calcium in daily intake needs. {Dietary calcium content: ~300mg in each⇒ a normal diet; 1 cup milk; 1 cup orange juice calcium fortified; ¾ cup yogurt; & cheese ~½ pack of cards sized serving}. Take calcium with a **meal**: ↑bioavailability calcium carbonate & adherence. **DI**: PPI's can ↓ calcium absorption calcium citrate may be better absorbed in this setting. ↓ absorption of: ciprofloxacin, iron, PI HIV, tetracycline, thyroid meds. | Ages 4-8 yrs: 800 mg/d; Ages 9-18yrs: 1300 mg/d; ♀ > 18 pregnant or lactating: 1000mg/d; Pre-menopausal ♀: 1000mg/d; Menopausal ♀ & ♂ > 50 yr: **1500mg**/day; ♂ 19-50yr: 1000mg/d | ~$50 |
| | **Vit D3** = cholecalciferol, g *X*▼ 400 & 1000IU combo with Calcium. Vit $D_2$ = Ergocalciferol *X* (10,000IU cap; 75,000 cap from powder made) {calcitriol: hypercalcemia risk, ↑cost} | Well tolerated. SE: GI nausea, vomiting, constipation, hypercalcemia. **Vit D3** is preferred over Vit D2 [36] May ↑ muscle strength, ↑ balance & ↓ falls. Risk ↓Vit D: skin dark, sunscreen SPF≥8, garment concealing, season, elderly institutionalized, obese, malabsorption, renal or liver dx, non-fish eating, meds anticonvulsants, cholestyramine, HIV, rifampin, steroids, latitude. | | | Vit D alone/low dose likely does not prevent hip, vertebral, or any new # [37]. **Serum** 25-OHD level desired: **>75 nmol/L** 30ng/mL, ~3months of tx to ↑ level, check level cool season. Some recommend **2,000 IU/d** in winter months & 1,000 IU/d in summer. [38] Consider single Vit D loading dose if severely deficient (eg. 75-150,000 IU). Vit D sources: dairy products, salmon, sardines & tuna. Sunscreens ↓↓ Vit D. Sun exposure 5-15min on arm/legs between 10am-3pm 3x/wk often adequate if Caucasian. | Vitamin D3: OP CDN 2010. If < 50 yrs: 400-1000 IU (10-25ug)/day. If > 50 yrs: **800**-2000 **IU** (20-50ug)/day | ~$30 |
| HT | **Hormone Therapy** (HT) ♀ -antiresorptive. {Males: ♂ with hypogonadism see RxFiles Andropause Testosterone Agents Chart} | **See also RxFiles Postmenopausal Chart page 90**. Combo with medroxyprogesterone WHI: ↑CHD/stroke, ↑breast cancer, ↑VTE. [40] Estrogen alone: ↑stroke & DVT (but not CHD or breast cancer). [40] Cognitive impairment & urinary incontinence may worsen. [39] After adjusted analysis hip # data was **not** significant ⇒ | NNT = 385 for 5 yrs in ♀ with or without a previous vertebral # [40 WHI] | NS compared to placebo arm | HT for symptomatic postmenopausal ♀ as the most effective tx for menopausal Sx relief vasomotor, vaginal atrophy & the prevention of bone loss / #. [2] Consider low conjugated estrogen 0.3mg or micronized estradiol 0.5mg & ultralow ½ of low dose, if both prevent OP & tx menopausal symptoms desired. Inform that it works for OP prevention, but limited data on ↓ of # risk. [2] | CES 0.3mg daily; Estrace 0.5mg daily; Climara 25ug weekly; Estradot 25ug 2x/wk | 84; 96; 325; 333 |

**Not** in Canada: **Denosumab Prolia** -target RANK ligand inhibits osteoclast, 60mg SC q6month FREEDOM, vertebral # NNT=20, non-vertebral # NNT=67, n=7,868 3yr; HALT; rash, limb pain, may ↑infection; & ? jaw necrosis & cancer. **Strontium ranelate Protelos**-2g at hs, nausea, diarrhea, seizure, rash DRESS Sx & VTE. Investigational SERMS: **Bazedoxifene**: 20-40mg/day approved in Europe, SE: ↑vasomotor sx, ↑VTE, leg cramps; **Lasofoxifene**: 0.25-0.5mg PEARL daily SE: ↑VTE but may ↓breast cancer. **Ibandronate Boniva** -2.5mg tab daily, 150mg tab po monthly; 3mg IV q3months.

X=non-formulary Sask. ⊗=not on NIHB ☎=EDS-Exception Drug Status Sask 1-800-667-2549 ∅=NIHB prior approval ▼=on NIHB ♀=women ♂=men **#**=fracture **BMD**=bone mineral density **$Ca^{2+}$**=calcium **CKD**=chronic kidney dx **DVT**=deep vein thrombosis **Dx**=disease **DXA**=dual energy x-ray absorptiometry **FDA**=Food Drug Admin **g**=generic **GIO**=glucocorticoid induced OP **HIV**=Human immunodeficiency virus **Ht**=height ≥2cm/yr loss **Hx**=history **$Mg^{2+}$**=magnesium **NNT**=number needed to treat **NS**=no significant difference **ONJ**=osteonecrosis jaw **OP**=osteoporosis **OR**=odds ratio **PE**=pulmonary emboli **pl**=placebo **PI**=protease inhibitor **PM**=postmenopausal **PTH**=parathyroid hormone **RR**=relative risk **Scr**=serum creatinine **Sx**=symptom **TSH**=thyroid stimulating hormone **Tx**=treatment **VTE**=venous thromboembolism event **WHO**=World Health Organization **Wt**=weight

**Drug Induced OP**: ↑ alcohol, antacids aluminum, anticonvulsants carbamazepine, phenobarbital, phenytoin, primidone, aromatase inhibitors anastrozole, letrozole, exemestane, **glucocorticoids** >3 months, drugs causing hypogonadism parenteral progesterone, gonadotropin-releasing hormone agonists (LHRH, GnRH), heparin if Tx > 30day, **immunosuppressants** cyclosporine, tacrolimus, lithium, medroxyprogesterone >2yr tx, methotrexate, proton pump inhibitors, smoking, SSRIs, tenofovir, ↓testosterone in ♂, thiazolidinediones pioglitazone, rosiglitazone, thyroid hormone excess & Vit A ↑dose.

**Metabolic Non-Osteoporosis Bone Diseases**: Osteogenesis imperfecta, Osteomalacia, Osteitis fibrosa cystica, **Renal osteodystrophy** check bone specific alkaline phosphatase & PTH eg. adynamic bone dx, Osteopetrosis & Paget's disease.

**General OP Information**: (Screen, BMD, Lab workup...)

**Osteoporosis** WHO 2002 Defined as T-score ≤ -2.5. Now by # risk.

**Prevalence**: 2 million OP # in USA in 2005; OP affect 1.4m CDN

**Screen**: all pts ≥50yr for OP risk factors,

**BMD** if ♀**≥65yr** ♂≥70yr ACPM'09, or younger PM ♀ or ♂ (50-69yr) if 1major or 2 minor OP risk factor; & BMD (DXA preferred) follow up q2-5yr if moderate risk, or q5-10yr if low risk.

**Initial Workup**: CBC, alk phos, Scr, Ca, Alb, 25-OH Vit D; elderly (protein electrophoresis, ?myeloma), ♂ testosterone, PTH, xray (thoracic & lumbar), phosphorus, & TSH.

**Exam**: Hx, X-ray, Ht, Wt, Iliocostal distance, kyphosis; BMD, # 's.

**Patient Goal**: Tx⇒ stronger bone & ↓ # risk. Prevent fractures!

**Education**: ↑compliance to meds & bone hygiene treatment.

**BMD Tx Follow-up**: Do once in 1yr after tx started. to catch no responder. If BMD same or ↑, then uncertain when or if repeat BMD. Use same DXA device if test is repeated.

❷ **Risk Graph according to bone mineral density reporting in Canada** [1]

10-year risk: lowest T-score of Lumbar 1-4 (minimum 2 valid vertebrae), total hip, trochanter and femoral neck

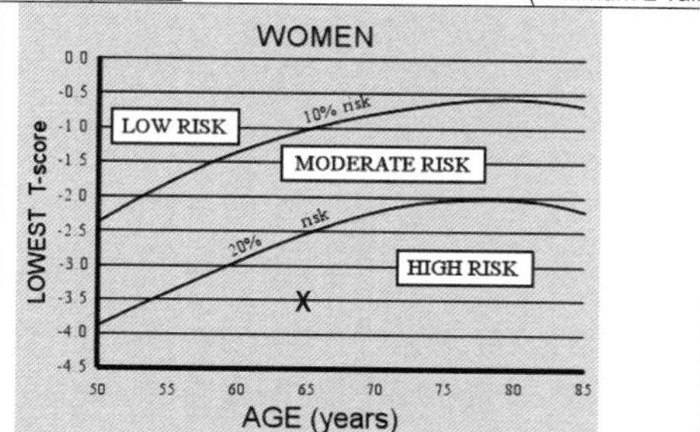


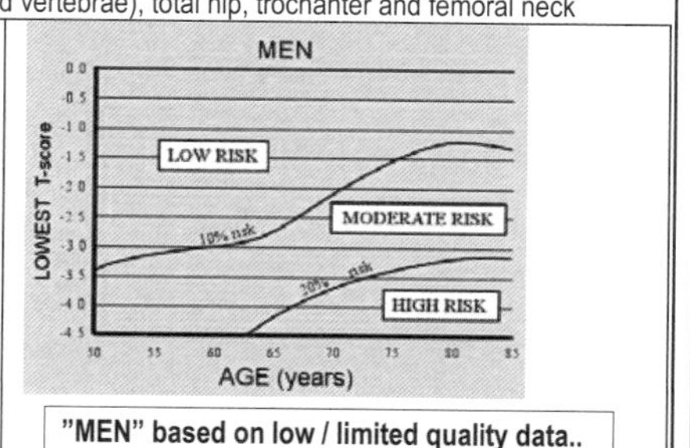


"MEN" based on low / limited quality data..

Example: Female, age 65, with T-score = -3.5, no hx of fragility fracture, no glucocorticoid use →**HIGH** Risk X marks the spot
Male, age 70, T-score= -3, no hx of fragility # & on **prednisone** 10mg/d >3month → Mod but→**HIGH** Risk b/c of prednisone
Most pts <50yr do **not need** osteoporosis tx unless exceptional circumstance. Both bone quality & density is important.

❸ **FRAX**=fracture risk assessment tool http://www.shef.ac.uk/FRAX/

For untreated pts (white, black, Hispanic & Asian) 40-90yr with osteopenia WHO. BMD is optional for calculating the FRAX risk score. **Canadian** & American FRAX dataset is now available.

Input⇒femoral neck BMD, age, sex, ht, wt, previous #, if parent hip #, smoker, steroid use, rheumatoid arthritis, 2° OP, alcohol ≥3unit/day, ↓BMI

Output⇒Calculates an **ABSOLUTE 10yr hip # & major # probability.**

**Consider Treating if**: NOT based on BMD or osteopenia only
1) hip or spine **FRACTURE**, or
2) **HIGH RISK** of Fracture: ↓ BMD (♀ PM, ♂ ≥50yr) & ↑ risk eg.**10yr Risk→hip fracture ≥ 3% or major # ≥ 20%** (spine, forearm, shoulder, hip).

**Major Risk Factors**: Age ≥ 65yr, Vertebral Compression #, Fragility # after age 40yr, Family hx osteoporotic # esp. hip # in mother, Propensity to fall, Osteopenia on radiograph, **Steroid** tx >3months of ≥ prednisone 2.5mg/day, Malabsorption Sx, hyperparathyroidism Primary, Hypogonadism, Early menopause before age 45yr.

**Minor Risk Factors**: Weight loss of >10% at age 25, weight <57kg, **Smoking**, Excess alcohol ≥3units/day, Excess caffeine >4cups/day, Low calcium intake, Rheumatoid arthritis, Hyperthyroidism, Anticonvulsant or heparin therapy long term.

☆ **Assess Risk**: Identify **HIGH risk pts to tx** by ❶) **age, sex, steroid** tx, **# fragility >40yr & BMD or 10yr Risk Score like** ❷) **Risk Graph** above **or** ❸) **FRAX.** **Low & Moderate Risk** pts usually do **NOT require tx**, except in exceptional circumstances.

**10yr ♀ Absolute # Risk**: ❶ **HIGH >20%** #→Age T Score=Age 50 T-3.9, Age 55 T-3.4, Age 60 T-3, Age 65 T-2.6, Age 70 T-2.2, Age 75 T-2.1, Age 80 T-2, Age 85 T-2.2. **Low <10%** # or **Moderate 10-20%** # **Risk**: ↑ to **next risk level** if on prednisone ≥2.5mg for >3mon or if fragility # after age 40.

**Treat OP with Calcium & Vit D PLUS First Line Agents**: alendronate, risedronate, zoledronic acid or **Second/Third Line Agents**: raloxifene, calcitonin, etidronate or teriparatide. **Good Bone Care/Hygiene**: Lifestyle (exercise, weight bearing), Vit D, Calcium, & ↓falls / alcohol / smoking.

| Generic/ TRADE — Pregnancy Category | √ USES / Comments / Onset — Contraindications CI | Side Effects (Common & Rare) — Monitor (ACR 2008 Guidelines) M | Drug INTERACTIONS 11,12 | Rheumatoid Dose: USUAL & MAX | $/Year |
|---|---|---|---|---|---|
| **Anakinra** KINERET (100mg/0.67ml syr ☎⊗) -Human IL-1 antagonist **B** | √Adult Mono Tx +/- DMARDs non TNF; **Onset**: 2-3month {Useful for new dx:DIRA}; **CI**: active infections, neutropenia | **Common**: **inj site reaction** ~75% esp. during 1st 4 wks, severe infection 2%, (headache, nausea) <10%, ↓glucose; **Rare**:**neutropenia** **M**: CBC(q1mon x3→q3mon[22]),ANA | **Enbrel, Humira… (& ? Remicade)**: ↓ WBC 3%, ↑ infections 7% | 100mg SC od (↓**dose** if ↓**renal** fx) -less effective than other biologics {store in Fridge} | ☎ 18,600 ⊗ |
| **Etanercept** ENBREL (25mg vial & 50mg syr ☎✆) -recombinant soluble p75 TNF fusion receptor protein & targets TNF-β, fairly short t ½ **B** | √**Mono Tx & with MTX** FDA; √Psoriasis plaque,arthritis, ankylosing spondylitis; **Onset**: 1-2 **weeks** (Up to 3 months); ↓joint erosions, May ↓steroid & MTX doses; **CI**: MS, sepsis, HF. Dx flare if drug D/C | **Common**(headache, nausea, rhinitis, cough)<10%, burning @**inj site**~50% 1st dose → ↓ after 5 doses, antibody to drug; **Rare**:pancytopenia, Lupus like, demyelination 9 cases, skin rx SJS, tuberculosis reactive, optic neuritis, severe infection 4.3/100 pt. yr incl. fungal, HBV reactivate; ?↑lymphoma risk **M**: CBC, tuberculin, ANA | Anakinra & live vaccines: ↑ infections; cyclophosphamide: ?↑ risk of solid cancers WGET NEJM05 | **25mg SC twice/wk**; **50mg SC weekly**; **Peds** FDA & Canada (Age 4-17): 0.4 mg/kg (Max 25mg) SC twice/wk or {0.8 mg/kg (Max 50mg) SC weekly FDA} | ☎ **20,875** ✆ **20,350**; 10yr data now avail.- well tolerated |
| **Adalimumab** HUMIRA-TNF ∝ inhibitor antibody; RA, JIR≥4yr 24mg/M2, PA, Psoriasis plaque, Crohn's, ankylosing spondylitis; 40mg SC every other Week ☎✆ | | | $19,250 (MTX may ↑adalim. level) **B** | | |
| **Hydroxychloroquine** PLAQUENIL **(HCQ)** (200mg tab) /generic **C** | √**Dx** short duration & low degree of Dx activity, without poor prognosis feature; √**mild/in combo** RA, Lupus; Well tolerated; Not ↓radiologic damage; **Onset**: 2-6month (trial 4mons); **CI**: G6PDH hemolysis, vision changes | **Uncommon**: GI (cramps & diarrhea), rash, headache; **Rare**:**ocular** toxicity, myopathy, skin pigment changes; **M**: CBC; **eye** exam (funduscopic & central field/q1-5yr) | digoxin: ↑ digoxin levels; methotrexate: ?↑ methotrexate levels; Beta blockers: ↑ β-blocker effect | 200mg po od (with food/milk); **200mg po bid, 400mg po hs**; (Max ≤ 6.5mg/kg/day) | 216; **330** |
| **Infliximab** REMICADE (100mg VIAL ☎ ✆) -**mouse**-human anti TNF α monoclonal antibody **B** | √**With MTX** official indication [23]; ↓ joint erosions & ↑ physical functioning; √Crohn's/UC, P&PA, ankylosing spondylitis-no NICE'08; **CI**: MS, sepsis, acute HF, watch for Dx flare if drug stopped; **Onset**: 1-2 **weeks** (Up to 4 months) | **Common**: (headache, nausea, lung infections)~10%, **infusion reaction** fever, urticaria, dyspnea, ↓BP for 1st few inj. Tx→↓rate, antibody reaction (10%→ antinuclear & DNA antibodies). Rare: SJS skin reaction; **Rare**:histoplasmosis, **TB** extrapulmonary, HBV reactivate, Lupus, HF, ↑LFT, Infection severe, demyelinating Dx 70cases, anemia aplastic, ?↑lymphoma; **M**:CBC, tuberculin test, ANA | Abatacept, anakinra & live vaccine: ↑ infections; ?↑Cancer NNH=154 over 6-12mo tx↑ with dose; ↑Infections Serious NNH=59 over 3-12 mo Bongartz 06 eg. shingles, Hep B+C, TB, fungal & other infections | 200mg 3mg/kg x ~70kg IV q 8 wks; **300mg** 5mg/kg x ~60kg **IV q 8 wks**; (Start Week 0, 2, 6, then every 8 wks); Range: 3-10mg/kg IV q8 wk or 3-5mg/kg IV q4wk. Peds: Crohn's ≥6yr | ☎ 11,920 ✆ **17,800**; 7yr data now avail. |
| | **Pretreatment** for infusion: (acetaminophen 650mg & diphenhydramine 50mg po x1) ↓'s reaction. Give over ≥ **2-4**hr in 250ml normal saline. over ≥ 1hr if tolerated | | | | |
| **Leflunomide** ARAVA (10, 20mg tab ☎ ✆) **(LEF)** /generic -pyrimidine synthesis inhibitor (prodrug) **X** | √**Mono Tx for Dx** any duration & degree of activity; **Active/severe RA** & slows progression; ↑ physical fx; **Onset**: 1-3 months; Drug in body up to 2yr after D/C→ **Questran** 8g TID x 11d if toxic/pregnant; **CI**: obstructive biliary & hepatic Dx, viral hepatitis, impaired immune Dx | **Common**:GI (**diarrhea**, nausea, ↓weight), rash, ↑BP, alopecia 8%, reversible & dose related, ↑ LFT 5%, lung infection; **Rare**: aplastic **anemia**, TENS, Stevens-Johnson 12 cases, hepatotoxic(130pts BMJ 2002 esp if **with MTX**) & pancytopenia, neuropathy peripheral, lung dx interstitial, TB; **M**: BP, CBC, Plt, LFT, Scr q2-4wk x≥3mon →q3mon | **↑ leflunomide level/toxicity by**: **methotrexate**( 2-3x ↑ of LFTs), **rifampin**; **leflunomide ↑ effects of**: NSAIDS, tolbutamide, warfarin; **↓ leflunomide level by**: activated charcoal, **cholestyramine**; live vaccines: ↑ risk of infection | 10mg po od; **20mg po od**; (?**Loading dose**= 100mg/day x 3 days or 100mg every other day x 3 doses may ↓GI side effects) | ☎ 2,500 ✆ **2,500** |
| **Methotrexate (MTX)** AMETHOPTERIN/ generics 2.5mg, 10mg tab (20 & 50mg/2ml inj x▼) D/C 90day before ♀&♂ **X** | √**Mono Tx for Dx** any duration & degree of activity; √**Active/severe RA** ↓radiologic progression; If AST or ALT ↑2-3x N→D/C & biopsy; **Onset**: **1-2 months** (often in 6 weeks); Adding Folic acid 5mg/wk: ↓ mouth ulcers; **CI**: liver, renal & lung Dx; ↑alcohol; breastfeeding | **Uncommon**:GI-nausea & diarrhea, stomatitis, rash, alopecia, pulmonary infiltrates→**cough**, men sterility; **Rare**: **pneumonitis** hypersensitivity <2%, nephrotoxic, hepatotoxic, **myelosuppression**, pulmonary & hepatic, **fibrosis**, phototoxicity & skin necrotizing vasculitis (?lymphoma); **M**: CBC, LFT, Scr, Plt, Alb q2-4wk x ≥3mon→q3mon | **↑ MTX level/toxicity by**: Bactrim, **cyclosporine**, doxycycline, ethanol, HCQ, **leflunomide**, live vaccines, **NSAIDs**, omeprazole, probenecid; **↑ myelosuppression with**: Bactrim, sulfasalazine, trimethoprim; **↓ MTX levels by**: cholestyramine, neomycin | **15-20mg po wkly**(Up to 25-30mg/wk split dose); 7.5-10mg po weekly (↓**dose** if ↓**renal** fx); 7.5mg IM/**SC** weekly (Max 25mg/wk); Peds: 5-10-15mg/m² per week; (JRA: MTX?> effect than leflunomide Silverman NEJM) | **295-375**; 190-230; 840 |
| **Sulfasalazine (SSZ)** SALAZOPYRIN/generic (500mg tab; 500mg EC tab) **B/D** | √**Dx** any duration & degree of activity, without poor prognosis features; √**Mild RA** -slows radiologic progression; **Onset**: ~2-3 months (?give folic acid); **CI**:G6PDH, sulfa allergy, GI obstruction | **Common**:**GI** nausea/abd pain, **rash**, photosensitivity, ↓sperm; **Rare**: leukopenia, **myelosuppression**, hepatitis, lupus, ↑Scr; **M**: CBC, Plt, LFT q2-4wk x≥3mon →q3mon | digoxin ↓dig level, warfarin ↓INR, azathioprine ↑toxic; **↓ sulfasalazine levels by**: cholestyramine, iron, phenobarb, rifampin | 500mg EC po bid -start low to ↓ side effects; **1000mg EC po bid (after meals)**; 1000mg EC po tid Peds: 30-50 mg/kg/day | 340; **630**; 850 |
| **Azathioprine** IMURAN/generic (50mg tab) -purine analog immunosuppressant **D** | √**Option:Refractory RA or vasculitis**; **Onset**: 2-3 months; **CI**: alkylating agents hx of tx, lymphoma | **Common**: GI, flu-like illness, ↑ LFT; **Rare**: **myelosuppression**, hepatotoxic, infection, pancreatitis; **M**: CBC, Plt, LFT, Scr q 1-2 wk →q1-3 mon | **azathioprine ↓effect of**: flu vaccine, warfarin; **↑ aza level by: allopurinol** (?↓dose by~70%); **↑ myelosuppression with**: captopril | 50mg po od; 100mg po od (Max 150mg po od); Range: 1-2.5mg/kg/day (? TPMT level if low then ↑ toxicity) | 315; 545 |
| **Cyclosporine** NEORAL (10, 25, 50, 100mg cap; 100mg/ml liquid generic) ☎✆ **C** | √ RA, Psoriasis (recalcitrant plaque); **Onset**:2->4month. Seldom used alone.; **CI**: ↓ renal fx, uncontrolled ↑BP | **Common**: GI, headache, paresthesia, **↑BP** dose related, ↑Wt; **Rare**:**nephrotoxic** dose related, **anemia**, cancer, papilledema, hypertrichosis, gingival hyperplasia ?TX azithro, tremor, ↑LFT, ↑K+; **M**: Scr q2wk→q1mon if stable, CBC, LFT, K+, uric acid, BP, Cp, TG, Mg | **↑ cyclo level by**: allopurinol, amiodarone, danazol, diltiazem, erythromycin, flu & keto & posa-conazole, grapefruit juice, verapamil. **↓cyclo level by**: aluminum, carbamaz., orlistat, phenobarbital, phenytoin, rifampin, St. Johns Wort, sulfasalazine. **↑ nephrotoxicity with**: aminoglycoside, amphotericin, melphalan, MTX, NSAIDs | 100mg po q12h (↓**dose** if ↓**renal** fx); 150mg po q12h (Max 4-5mg/kg/d); 2.5mg/kg/d bid, (↑ 0.5 mg/kg/d q 2-4 wk) | 4,700 ☎ 6,900 ✆ |
| **Tacrolimus** ☎✆PROGRAF g(0.5,1,5mg cap; 5mg/ml amp) 3mg po od $3270 | | | | | |
| **GOLD**:**Sodium aurothiomalate** MYOCHRYSINE (10,25,50 mg/ml inj); **Auranofin** RIDAURA (3mg cap) **C** | **Onset**:3-6 months(trial ~ 5months); **Oral**: ↓ efficacy & longer to effect than **IM gold** (~25% absorbed); **CI**: blood & skin Dx, lung fibrosis | **Common**:stomatitis, **rash**, **diarrhea**, edema, **proteinuria**; **Rare**: **myelosuppression**, ↓platelets, alopecia, colitis; **M**: CBC, Plt, Scr, urine protein q1-2 wk x 20wk then when inj or every other inj. {Oral: q1-3 mon} | Aspirin: may ↑ hepatotoxicity; Penicillamine: ↑ rash & suppress bone marrow | 3mg po bid ⇒ Clinically often IM used; 25mg **IM** q2-4 wks (↓ **dose** if ↓ **renal** fx); 50mg **IM** q2-4 wks (Peds: 1 mg/kg) | 1,810; 246; 324 |
| | | | Test dose: 10mg IM→Load 50mg/**wk** x ~20wk. Nitritoid rx flush, weak, nausea, dizzy may occur after injection. | | |
| **Minocycline** MINOCIN, generic (50 & 100mg cap ☎ ✆) **D** | √**Dx** short duration & low degree of Dx activity, without poor prognosis feature; **Onset**: 1-3month **CI**: kid ≤8yr, pregnancy last ½ | **Common**: GI upset, headache, dizziness, ↑**pigmentation**, yeast infection; **Rare**: vestibular dysfx, lupus, ↑ LFT, photosensitivity **M**: CBC, LFT | antacids, calcium, food, iron: ↓minocycline levels; warfarin ↑bleeding, isotretinoin ↑BP | 50mg po bid; 100mg po bid | ☎✆ 500; 900 |
| **Penicillamine** Infrequent use ( 250mg cap) CUPRIMINE **D** | **Onset**: 3-6 mon (Note:↓**iron** esp peds & menstruating ♀); **CI**: renal impairment, possible penicillin cross sensitivity | **Common**: GI (N/V, diarrhea), taste disorders, **rash**, gynecomastia; **Rare**: **myelosuppression**, **proteinuria**, Goodpasture's, myasthenia gravis, neuropathy **M**: CBC, Scr, urinary protein q2wk→ dose stable→ q1-3mon | antacids, calcium, food, iron: ↓penicillamine levels; digoxin ↓digoxin levels, gold ↑rash & ↓ bone marrow | 250mg po od, 250mg bid -start low & ↑ slowly; 250mg po tid **before meals** (Max 1-1.5g/day) | 1500, 2900; 4300 |

↓ dose for renal dysfx ☎=exception drug status Sask. ✆ prior NIHB x=NonForm. Sk. ⊗=not NIHB ▼covered NIHB ♀=females √Useful for/in **Alb**=albumin **ALT/AST**=liver test **BP**=blood pressure **CBC**=complete blood count **CI**=contraindication **Cp**=plasma level **d**=day **Dx**=disease **Dysfx**=dysfunction **EC**=enteric coated **FDA**=USA approved **fx**=function **GI**=stomach **HF**=heart failure **inj**=injection **K**=potassium **LFT**=liver fx test **Mon**=month **MS**=multiple sclerosis **N**=normal **P**=psoriasis **PA**=psoriatic arthritis **Peds**=pediatric **Plt**=platelet **RA**=Rheumatoid arthritis **Scr**=serum creatinine **TB**=tuberculosis **TENS**=toxic epidermal necrosis syndrome **TNF**=tissue necrosis factor **Tx**=treatment **WK**=week **yr**=year ς =scored tab

**Pregnancy**[2,14]: **B**=likely safe **C**=possible fetal risk **D**=fetal human risk **X**=teratogenic. Contraception required for most DMARDs. If possible: D/C med, ↓ dose, avoid in 1st trimester. **NSAIDS**: may use until last 6-8 wks of pregnancy. **DMARDs**: relatively safe→ HCQ, prednisone, SSZ.[7]

**GOAL**: Delay or prevent disability/joint damage, prevent loss of function & ↓ pain. Treat early, aggressive & often with combinations. Give patient info. Trial DMARDs for several months to ensure efficacy. Watch clinical symptoms, ↓ ESR & ↓ CRP.

**TREAT**: **DMARDs main tx** within 3 months; NSAIDS 1st few weeks, analgesics, local steroid inj ≥q3mon, prednisone ~ <10mg/day (↑BP, diabetes, infection, thin skin, ↑ weight, cataract, osteoporosis calcium 1500mg/d, Vit. D 800iu/d & bisphosphonates). Physio, recreation & occupational **THERAPY** when indicated.

**APPROACH**: **Mild Dx: HCQ** or **SSZ**; **Active Dx: MTX** or **Leflunomide** or **Combos** {(Common: MTX+HCQ; **Triple**=MTX,SSZ,HCQ); or Etanercept/Infliximab/Adalimumab +/- MTX/Leflunomide; …} **REFER**: for tx advice (diagnosis or complications).

**Diagnostic Criteria**[22]: morning stiffness >30mins; arthritis: of ≥3 joint areas, hand joints & symmetric -lasting at least 6wks; rheumatoid nodules, ↑ serum rheumatoid factor & radiographic changes. **Stop Smoking** is beneficial.

**C** **Abatacept** ORENCIA ☎✆ (250mg vial): RA, JIR≥6yr; CTLA4 fusion protein ~10mg/kg IV over 30min; $20,400/yr at Week 0,2,4 then monthly. Not with TNF meds MTX ok. SE: headache, nausea, hypersensitivity, ↑infection 3%, TB, & ?↑cancer 1.3 vs 1.1%. Caution COPD.

**Rituximab** RITUXAN ☎✆ (500mg vial): targets B-cells CD20+; 1g IV @50-400mg/hr Day 1 & 15; rpt in 6-12mon if response 4doses=$19,000 (with MTX) SE: itch, fever, chill & rash. Rare bowel obstruction, viral reactivation eg. PML, hep B (Pretreat: Tylenol, Benadryl & IV methylprednisone 40-100mg)

**Golimumab** SIMPONI x⊗-TNF ∝ inhibitor antibody; RA, PA, ankylosing spondylitis; 50mg SC Monthly $17,675 **Certolizumab pegol CIMZIA** x⊗ -TNF ∝ inhibitor antibody in USA 2008; mod-severe adult CD, RA mod-severe; Dose 400mg sc q2wk x3 then 400mg sc q4wk $17,600

**Tocilizumab** Actemra x⊗; inhibit IL-6 receptor; 4-8mg/kg over 1hr IV q4wk; Max: 800mg/dose 20mg/ml; 4,10 & 20ml vials; use alone or with MTX or other non-biologic DMARDs; SE: infection TB, fungal etc, HTN, GI ulcer, anaphylaxis, ?cancer; CI: vaccine live, infection active, liver dx; Pregnancy=C.

# Management of Behavioral & Psychological Symptoms of DEMENTIA (BPSD) [124] May/10

-very common (up to 90% during course of dementia), a major cause of distress to patients, families & caregivers; risk to self plus others, & huge cost in terms of institutionalization.

-not just agitation but non-agitated Sx (apathy, withdrawal, daytime somnolence {circadian rhythm disturbances}, depression, disinhibition etc.)

**Diagnosis**: (Evaluate behavior→**ABC's A**ntecedents (causes:Physical Intellectual Emotional Cultural Environmental Social), **B**ehaviors & **C**onsequences)

◆History Down's Sx, physical exam, cognitive tests Feldman CMAJ'08 & nurse observations; collateral family info essential! ◆Lab Tests-Recommended: CBC, electrolytes, calcium, B12, serum glucose & TSH; Optional: BUN & SCr, magnesium, LFTs, arterial blood gases, ECG, CT/MRI if suggestion of structural lesion eg. renal failure, brain tumor, normal pressure hydrocephalus, subdural hemorrhage ◆Eliminate delirium source Young BMJ'07 – eg. **meds** eg. opiates, benzos, anticholinergics **/withdrawal reactions /DI's**, dehydration & infections (if indicated: urinalysis/C&S, chest x-ray, lumbar puncture if suspicion of meningitis)

**Tx**: (attempt **taper/withdraw** of meds after a **3 month behavioral stability period**) {Tx comorbidity eg. infection, pain, constipation, depression, psychosis}

◆Appropriate **environmental, exercise & behavioral** measures should be explored! Reserve **drug therapy for situations** where non-pharmacological interventions have been fully explored & implemented or in cases of **significant dangerous risk**. Specify problem behavior (eg. "agitation" is less useful than "screaming", "hitting when bathed"). Identify what brings it on & what makes it go away. Identify whom the behavior is bothering (pt, caregiver/staff or other pts). Human interactions eg. activiy, adequate staff eg. nursing home & proper environment most critical.

◆If drug treatment (ie. Sx have no physical cause, are unrelated to other medications or unresponsive to non-pharmacological interventions), generally start with **1/3 to 1/2 of usual adult** dose & titrate up slowly individualizing dosages for each pt

***Start Low, Go Slow!***

◆If receiving treatment, **reevaluate** drug regimen & non-pharmacologic strategies at regular intervals (ie. **3**-6 months)

## DEPRESSION:

(anxiety often coexists thus use antidepressants with anxiolytic properties)

- ↓ mood, apathy may worsen & amotivation

*Mild*→ non pharmacologic

*Moderate* to *severe*→ **ANTIDEPRESSANT Tx**

**SSRI/venlafaxine →1st line**

In general →may be good for depression, depression assoc. agitation, emotionality & irritability

Allow >6 week for adequate trial at an adequate dose

⇩

**SSRIs: SE**: nausea, vomiting, restlessness, falls, insomnia, ↓weight, agitation initially & hyponatremia
**Citalopram** 10-30mg/d, **sertraline** 25-100mg/d, **fluvoxamine** 25-150mg/d, **paroxetine** 10-30mg/d etc.

**Venlafaxine:** 37.5-225mg XR od {Similar SE as SSRI, but has high GI SE & may ↑ blood pressure)

**Bupropion** ☎ ✆100-150mg bid or 150-300mg XL ☎ ✆ to activate pt with withdrawal or psychomotor retardation

**TCA's:** Avoid anticholinergics →less with **nortriptyline** 10-75mg hs & desipramine 25-150mg/d;
**SE**: hypotension, blurred vision, urinary hesitancy, cardiac conduction changes

**Mirtazapine:** consider if anorexia/anxiety/sleep problem; RD form if difficulty swallowing; ≤7.5-45mg/d

**Moclobemide**: role in anxiety & mood dx but may ↑ stimulation; 100mg od-300mg bid

**Trazodone**: low doses used for sedation & some anxiolytic effect;
monitor for hypotension, serotonin syndrome & rare priapism in ♂

Consider **ECT** in management of treatment resistant or severe depression

***Start Low, Go Slow, But go!***

## PSYCHOSIS/AGITATION:

Psychosis:
1) Positive Sx -delusions & hallucinations or paranoia
2) Negative Sx -poverty of thought, apathy & social withdrawal

***Start Low, Go Slow!***

BPSD:
Agitation -pacing, chanting, psychomotor, agitation etc.
Aggression

**ANTIPSYCHOTIC Tx**

-first designate target Sx (**not wandering or mild Sx**)
-try to minimize **sedation**,↑confusion,hypotension & **EPS**
-target Sx (hallucinations,delusions,hostility,**aggression**, agitation, & violent/high risk behavior)

**haloperidol** 0.25-2mg/day
**risperidone** 0.25-2mg/day
**quetiapine** 12.5-150mg/day
**olanzapine** ☎ ▼1.25-10mg/day
} monitor for SE & may attempt med tapering q6month

◆Newer agents as effective but generally better tolerated. Monitor for **SE**:sedation, hypotension, falls[125], EPS (drooling, rigidity & akinesia), anticholinergic SE dry mouth, delirium, constipation, ↑weight/lipids/diabetes , ? ↑stroke/death & tardive dyskinesia.

◆Pts with **Lewy bodies** (15% of dementias) have ↑sensitivity to neuroleptic meds (quetiapine an option)

## ANXIETY:

-use non-pharmacological intervention
-minimize provocation

-consider **antidepressant** therapy if anxiety is secondary to depression or very chronic in nature

-consider
**ANTIANXIETY Medication**

**lorazepam** 0.5-2mg/day
**oxazepam** 5-30mg/day
**buspirone** 10-30mg/day
**trazodone** 25-100mg/day
**alprazolam** 0.125-2mg/day
**clonazepam** 0.125-3mg/day
(caution long-acting)

**Benzodiazepines**-caution!
**SE**: sedation, ataxia, altered sleep architecture, motor & **cognitive** impairment & propensity to cause withdrawal Sx when D/C. Paradoxical excitation, **disinhibition** & **falls** may occur. An intermediate acting such as temazepam/oxazepam/lorazepam can be best used for short term, if possible sleep/anxiety states or before planned anxiety provoking situations

**Buspirone**: ✆
low sedation, ↓DI's, ↓ withdrawal & ↓ impairment of motor fx; option→ chronic anxiety but onset ~3wk delay

## APATHY

Tx with external activity & environmental measures. Possible options with concerns: methylphenidate & dopamine agonists.

**MOOD STABILIZERS:** some use in agitation, aggression, hostility, sleep-wake disturbance cycle & mania
◆ **divalproex** 125-750mg/day -fewer **SE**: sedation, diarrhea, tremor, nausea, weight gain, hair loss & ↑ liver tests & fewer DI's, but less evidence for use.
◆ **carbamazepine** 100-600mg/day -more **SE**: sedation, ataxia, falls, skin rash, headache, leukopenia & ↑ liver tests & multiple DI's

**BETA BLOCKER**-propranolol 10-80mg/d; possible ↓ aggression; SE:↓ heart rate & hypotension CI: asthma, PVD & possibly depression Hx

**CHOLINESTERASE INHIBITORS** -modest cognitive, functional & **behavioral** benefits; may help **apathy**, hallucinations & delusions (not better than placebo for agitation Howard NEJM/07), may help **Lewy Body dementia** to ↓ visual sx's .
Consider **cholinesterase inhibitors** in Alzheimer's (**donepezil**, **galantamine**, **rivastigmine**) ☎ ✆; SE: n/v, fatigue, anorexia, ↓ heart rate

Memantine ✗⊗ is a recently approved NMDA receptor antagonist which may have a role similar to cholinesterase inhibitors.

**CI** contraindication **DI** drug interaction **Dx** disorder **fx** function **HR** heart rate **Hx** history **n/v** nausea/vomiting **Pt** patient **PVD** peripheral vascular disease **SE** side effect **Sx** symptom **Tx** treatment ☎ Exception Drug Status Sask. ✗ non-formulary in Sask. ⊗not covered by NIHB ▼covered by NIHB ✆prior approval NIHB

| Generic/TRADE (Strength & forms) g =generic | Class / Symptoms / Tips | Side effects | Comments / Drug Interactions (DI [3,23,24]) (√ = therapeutic use) | INITIAL & MAX DOSE | USUAL DOSE RANGE geriatric | $ /Month |
|---|---|---|---|---|---|---|
| **Donepezil** ☎ ✆ **ARICEPT** [25-42]<br>5 ς, 10 ς mg tab; approved 1997 (5, 10mg RDT rapid dissolve tab) χ ⊗<br>acetylcholinesterase activity<br>t ½ ~75hr | **May**[43] temp. stabilize dementia & behavior (& **may** help apathy, hallucinations & delusions), may help ↓ visual sx's of Lewy Body dementia<br>May slow rate of functional loss<br>Not delay institutionalisation[36] AD2000 | (Nausea, vomiting, diarrhea) ~10%; ↑with ↑dose, anorexia, muscle cramps, insomnia, fatigue, wt loss ~3%, other cholinergic effects (**incontinence**, stomach, ↓**HR** esp with high dose, syncope, falls, nightmares) & agitation initially | √Mild to moderate (MMSE 10-26) & severe Alzheimer's; ? for moderate-**severe** FDA approved Oct/06 Alzheimer's [44,45];<br>**Not** better than placebo for **agitation** Howard NEJM/07<br>↑ dose **q 1month** if needed<br>(not effective for mild cognitive impairment) [46]<br>DI: ↑ level by erythromycin, grapefruit juice, ketoconazole, paroxetine & quinidine ; (2D6+3A4)↓ level by carbamazepine, dexamethasone, phenytoin, phenobarbital & rifampin | 2.5-5mg<br>10mg | 5mg po **od** in **am**<br>10mg po **od** in am<br>(with food may ↓SE) | 172<br>172<br>☎ ✆ |
| **Galantamine** ☎ ✆ **REMINYL** [47,48,49,50,51,52,53,54,55,56,57,58]<br>8,16,24 ER cap;<br>(4,8,12 ς mg tab-**D/C** June 2006);<br>acetylcholinesterase & nicotinic activity. t ½ ~6hr | NNT **12** minimal improvement [12]<br>NNT **42** marked improvement [12]<br>NNH **16** adverse event-dropout [12]<br>↑ADAS-Cog ~2-3pts vs placebo [8]<br>(~20% ↑ 4pts; ~10% ↑ 7pts vs placebo)<br>↑ MMSE ~1pt vs placebo [8,36] | (Nausea, vomiting, diarrhea) ~>10%; ↑with ↑dose, anorexia, wt loss ~3%, insomnia, abdominal pain other cholinergic effects (incontinence, stomach, ↓**HR**, syncope, falls, nightmares), agitation initially | √ Mild to mod Alzheimer's & to reverse neuromuscular blockers (not effective for mild cognitive impairment; ↑mortality 1.3vs0.1%) [59]<br>↑ dose **q 1month** if needed; ↓ dose in hepatic/renal dysfx<br>DI:↑level by antidepressants (amitriptyline, fluoxetine, fluvoxamine, paroxetine ~30%), (2D6+3A4) cimetidine 16%, erythromycin 10%, ketoconazole 30% & quinidine 30% | 4-8mg<br>24-32mg | 8,16,24mg ER cap OD cc in am | 186<br>☎ ✆ |
| **Rivastigmine EXELON**, g [60,61,62,63,64,65,66,67] ☎ ✆<br>1.5, 3, 4.5, 6 mg cap; 2mg/ml soln<br>acetyl & butyrylcholinesterase activity (**Patch** new 4.6+9.5mg od) χ ⊗<br>t ½ ~2hr | Takes **~3-6months** Tx→?modest benefit<br>Taper dose to ↓withdrawal SE eg fecal impaction.<br>If ChEIs therapy stopped temporarily then restarted later some pts may not return to baseline functioning level.<br>Acetylcholinesterase Inhibitor (**ChEIs**) | (Nausea, vomiting, diarrhea) ~>10%; ↑with ↑dose, ?↓ with patch, anorexia, muscle cramps, insomnia, fatigue, wt loss ~3%, asthenia, headache, confusion, other cholinergic effects (incontinence, stomach, ↓**HR**, syncope, falls, nightmares), agitation initially<br>{Patch: administration errors >1patch, cut ⇒death reported} | √Mild to mod Alzheimer's(MMSE 10-26),?Lewy body [68,69]<br>√Parkinson's dementia (tradeoff between benefit & SE) Almaraz'09<br>If Tx interrupted for several days→**restart** 1.5mg bid<br>Oral soln: stable for **4hrs** when mixed with juice/soda<br>↑ dose **q 1month** if needed. ↓↓ DI's but smoking ↓levels.<br>DI: **low** risk of DIs | 1.5mg<br>12mg | 1.5-3mg po bid cc<br>4.5-6mg po bid cc<br>4.5mg(2.25ml) bid<br>Patch χ ⊗ new option: with less n/v, avoid heat | 194/93 g<br>194/93 g<br>228/93 g<br>☎ ✆<br>150 |

**Relative Contraindications**: bradycardia, sick sinus syndrome, active peptic ulcer, severe asthma/COPD, anesthesia ↑ succinylcholine effect, **anticholinergic meds** antagonistic effects eg. oxybutynin, TCAs, Parkinson's ↑ EPS, Epilepsy ?↓Sz threshold & Beta-blockers ?↑bradycardia

☎ = **EDS** New pts: a) Dx of probable Alzheimer's b) MMSE 10-26 within 60 day before coverage c) Functional Activities Questionnaire (FAQ) within 60 days before coverage d) Stop all anticholinergic meds 14 days before MMSE & FAQ e) if intolerant: may switch to another ChEIs. **To continue coverage** must **not** have **both** >2pt ↓MMSE & 1pt ↑ FAQ in a 6month period.

**MMSE must always be ≥10**. Patients who do not meet criteria to continue can be re-evaluated within 3 months to confirm deterioration before coverage is discontinued. **Re-evaluate q 6 months.**

Memantine, g **EBIXA**/NAMENDA USA χ ⊗ 10mg scored tab: NMDA antagonist for mod-severe Alzheimer's; 5mg od (↑q1-2week)→5-10mg bid $85-160 20mg daily possible [70,71] Caution: with seizures & heart dx.
SE: dizzy, drowsy, confusion, insomnia, headache, restlessness inner & motor, akathisia, nausea,?cornea changes, seizures, ↑BP, ?↑LFTs, & over excitation. DI's: amantadine, DM & ketamine since also NMDA antagonists; sodium bicarbonate & acetazolamide.

| Generic/TRADE | Class / Symptoms / Tips | Side effects | Comments / Drug Interactions | INITIAL & MAX DOSE | USUAL DOSE RANGE | $ /Month |
|---|---|---|---|---|---|---|
| **Haloperidol** [72] **HALDOL** g<br>0.5 ς, 1 ς, 2 ς, 5 ς, 10 ς mg tab;<br>2mg/ml soln;<br>**DEPOT** 250 & 500mg/5ml Vials, 100mg/1ml Amp χ ⊗; 5mg/ml amp | Helps delusions, hallucinations, hostility & aggression.<br>↑EPS, ↑ALT ≤16%, **Weight gain ≤ 1 kg**<br>**Antipsychotics** (both old & new): (FDA: warning atypical antipsychotics may in BPSD pts ↑ **mortality** 4.5 vs 2.6% placebo, mainly by cardiovascular or pneumonia or DVT causes) [73] | Delirium, confusion, anticholinergic, **sedation**, constipation,↓BP,↑weight, EPS (extrapyramidal) esp. **parkinsonian**, akathisia, falls [74], neuroleptic malignant syndrome (NMS) & tardive dyskinesia.<br>(**ECG** useful to assess cardiac abnormalities) | Start low dose, go slow<br>Haloperidol: for acute tx delirium 0.5mg q30min prn day 1→ 0.5mg tid x 3-4days<br>Aim for **improvement** not resolution of hallucinations/delusions<br>Least EPS/Parkinson effect with **quetiapine** & clozapine.<br>**Minimal improvements** with olanzapine, risperidone & quetiapine in general, **offset with adverse effects** Catie-AD [75] | **0.25**-5mg po<br>25-100mg IM q4w | 0.25-0.5mg po bid<br>1mg po bid<br>25-50mgIMq2-4w | 10<br>12<br>20 |
| **Olanzapine** ☎ ▼ **ZYPREXA** g [76-77-78,79,80,81,82,83,84,85] new generic<br>2.5, 5, 7.5, 10, 15mg tab;<br>**ZYDIS** 5, 10, 15mg tab;<br>10mg IM χ ⊗ vial<br>(For IM use sterile water for injection; do not mix in same syringe with diazepam, haloperidol or lorazepam) | SE:somnolence, dry mouth, dizzy, headache, asthenia, **falls**, constipation, blurred vision, urinary incontinence, dyspepsia, ↑ ALT ≤ 6%, **diabetes**, **weight** ↑↑, **akathisia** >10%, postural hypotension, seizures 0.9%, **anticholinergic**, ?↑ stroke/death, ↑ triglycerides, ↑ cholesterol, ↔↑ **prolactin effect**<br>Health Canada as of Nov'08 received 69 total reports of agranulocytosis / **neutropenia** for olanzapine, quetiapine & risperidone. | | Antipsychotics in Lewy body dementia cause significant ↑ in EPS SE (if tx required & Parkinson's or Lewy body dementia, quetiapine or clozapine {12.5-50mg/d & watch WBC} is an option)<br>↑ weight gain/diabetes esp. with **clozapine** & olanzapine [86] | **1.25**-5mg<br>10-20mg | 2.5mg po od<br>5-7.5mg po od | 37 g, 70<br>66-96 g, [135-196]<br>☎ ▼ |
| **Quetiapine SEROQUEL** g<br>25, 100, 200, 300mg tab [87+88]<br>(**XR**: 50,150,200,300,400mg tab) ⊗ | SE: **somnolence**, dizzy, drowsy, constipation, dry mouth, **falls**, **lens changes** in beagles-annual slit lamp exam, ↓ BP, **weight** ↑, seizures ≤0.8%, dyspepsia, headache, urinary incontinence, diabetes, ↑ALT ≤ 9%, akathisia **>2%**, ↑ triglyceride 17%, ↑ cholesterol 11%, hypothyroidism 0.4%, ?↑stroke/death, **low EPS** effect (option in **Lewy Body Dementia & Parkinson's**) ↔ **prolactin effect** | | | **12.5**mg<br>150-750mg | 25mg po hs<br>50mg po hs<br>100mg po hs<br>50-100mg **XR** hs | 19 g, 25<br>30 g, 42<br>37 g, 54<br>42-77 |
| **Risperidone RISPERDAL** g [89,90,91,92,93]<br>0.25, 0.5 ς, 1, 2 ς, 3 ς, 4 ς mg tab;<br>**M-TAB** 0.5,1,2,3,4mg tab ;<br>1mg/ml soln. **DEPOT** Consta 12.5,25,37.5,50mg vial. | SE: sedation, headache, dry mouth, constipation, blurred vision, urinary incontinence, insomnia, asthenia, ↓**BP**, akathisia >10%, ↓ appetite, TTP, seizures ≤0.3%, photosensitive, ?↑ stroke/death, **weight** ↑. Oral liquid **not** mix with cola or tea. **DI:** ?furosemide ↑ associated mortality<br>Official BPSD indication (others are used off-label) **↑ EPS at doses > 2-4mg/day & ↑ prolactin effect** | | | **0.25**-1mg<br>2-6mg | 0.5mg po hs<br>1-2mg po hs<br>1-2mg **M-Tab** po hs | 23<br>27-47<br>44-80 |

Continued on page 77

| Generic/TRADE (Strength & forms) g=generic | Class / Symptoms / Tips | Side effects | Comments / Drug Interactions (DI [3,94,95]) (√ = therapeutic use) | INITIAL & MAX DOSE | USUAL DOSE RANGE geriatric | $ /Month |
|---|---|---|---|---|---|---|
| **Citalopram** [96,97,98] =CC CELEXA g<br>10✗▼, 20, 40mg **scored** tabs | escitalopram CIPRALEX✗ ⊗<br>S(+)citalopram 10ς-20ς mg od ~$60 | **SSRIs SE in General (GI & CNS)**<br>**nausea** {21%(F) - 36% (X)}, anxiety, insomnia {~14%}, agitation, anorexia, tremor, somnolence {11-26%}, sweating, dry mouth, headache, dizziness, falls, diarrhea {12% (F,P)-17% (S)}, constipation {13-18%}, sexual dysfx.[105,106], **D/C Syndrome** esp with P | CC & S -**few drug** interactions | CC 10-20mg am<br>60mg/d | 20mg po od<br>40mg po od | **27**<br>27 |
| **Fluoxetine** [99] =F PROZAC g<br>10,20,40✗▼ mg cap &<br>4mg/ml soln | Helps depression (mood, appetite, sleep or energy) & apathy may worsen which often occurs early in dementia | | F–most **anorexic** & stimulating; long half-life 5week washout | F 10-20mg od<br>80mg/d | 20mg po od am<br>40mg po od am | **30**<br>53 |
| **Fluvoxamine** [100] =X LUVOX g<br>50ς, 100ς mg scored tabs | **SSRI'S**<br>(not too useful for specific phobias) | | X-most **nausea**, constipating & sedating SSRI, ↑ DI's | X 25-50mg hs<br>300mg/d | 100mg po hs<br>150mg po hs | **36**<br>51 |
| **Paroxetine** [101,102] =P PAXIL g<br>10ς, 20ς, 30mg tab [renal] | | | P -most anticholinergic of SSRI's •↑weight & D/C reaction possible [107] | P 10-20mg am<br>60mg/d | 20mg po od am<br>40mg po od am | **32**<br>57 |
| **Sertraline** [103,104] =S ZOLOFT g<br>25, 50, 100mg cap | | **Serotonergic syndrome** with MAOI's -↓BP, tremor, agitation, hypomania | S -most diarrhea & male sexual dysfx of SSRIs DIADS-2 NS<br>**Trazodone** 25-50mg hs (helps sleep, sun downing & depression) -**flat dose response curve for depression**; however titration to ↑ doses sometimes required for anxiety.<br>**Start low, slow but go**. Elderly may need **>8week trial**. | S 25-50mg am<br>200mg/d | 100mg po od cc<br>100mg po bid cc | **34**<br>61 |
| **Venlafaxine** EFFEXOR g<br>(**Reg** 37.5,75mg tab-Co **D/C** Jul04) [renal]<br>(**XR** 37.5, 75, 150mg caps) g<br>(contents of XR may be sprinkled)<br>Desvenlafaxine ER Pristiq✗ ⊗ **50**-100mg po od [renal] new-avail; DI: Cyp 3A4 (?clarithromycin) $95 | **SNRI**<br>**5HT & NE**<br>(also some dopamine) | **As dose↑: ↑BP**, agitation, tremor, sweating, nausea {~37%}, sleep disturbances, headache, "clean TCA", SE similar to SSRIs | **Less weight** gain; **few drug** interactions<br>Caution: **D/C Syndrome**<br>(e.g. agitation, nausea, fatigue, dizziness, headache, etc.) | 18.75-37.5mg bid<br>375mg/d | 75mg **XR** po od<br>150mg **XR** po od<br>225mg **XR** po od (if 2-3 cap) | **46**<br>48<br>94-123 [renal] |
| **Desipramine** =D<br>NORPRAMIN g<br>10, 25, 50, 75, 100mg tab | **TCA's** | **CNS**: agitation initially, confusion, drowsiness, headache, tremors, seizures, **anticholinergic**: dry mouth, blurred vision, constipation etc.; nausea, sweating, rash, **cardiovascular**: ↑ heart rate, arrhythmias, ↓ BP; anorgasmia | May ↑ effect of anticholinergic & CNS meds.<br>~2-3 months for max effect. Trough plasma levels avail.<br>Fatal (≥2gm) **overdose** → to heart & CNS | 10-25mg<br>150-300mg | D 50mg po hs<br>D 75mg po hs | 21<br>**30** |
| **Nortriptyline** =N<br>AVENTYL g<br>10, 25mg cap [108] | | | •desipramine (the least anticholinergic, helps **apathy**) & nortriptyline are generally **better tolerated** than other TCA's | | N 25mg po hs<br>N 50mg po hs | 17<br>**25** |
| **Mirtazapine** REMERON g $T_{1/2}$=20-40hr 15ς, 30ς, 45mg tabs (**RD** g 15,30,45mg tab); **NaSSA** **5HT & NE**; **SE**: Dry mouth, sedation, edema, arthralgias, dizzy, rare neutropenia. DI-clonidine. May ↑appetite & weight with ↓ sexual dysfx; RD form useful if difficulty swallowing; **Useful** if Anxiety, anorexia, Somatization, or difficulty sleeping. Generic RD Novo-mirtaz OD is ↓$; Dose range: ≤7.5-45mg/day; Star*D Max <60mg/d; 15-30mg po hs (RD & reg) $20-33. | | | | | | |
| **Duloxetine** CYMBALTA (30,60mg cap) ☎ ⊗ SNRI [renal] **SE**: nausea, insomnia, somnolence, headache, diarrhea, ↓appetite, fatigue, ↑sweat, ↑BP, ↑**LFTs**, ↑DI 1A2,2D6, dry mouth; urinary retention FDA?. √depression adult & maintenance, GAD, diabetic neuropathic pain ✆, fibromyalgia & ?stress incontinence. 30-**60**mg/d $72-138 Max 120mg. | | | | | | |
| **Buspirone** BUSPAR g<br>5,10ς mg tab ✆ | **Azapirone** 5 $HT_{1a}$ agonist | Nausea, headache, dizzy;<br>Onset 1wk; Max effect 6 wks | √ Anxiety in Bz naive pt & for alcohol withdrawal; Non-addicting, DI's | 5mg; 60-90mg | 5-10mg po tid-qid | 55-71 |
| **Clonazepam**<br>RIVOTRIL g<br>0.25✗▼, 0.5ς, 1, 2ς mg tab<br>-long acting benzodiazepine | May help severe anxiety (use **cautiously/short term if at all**)<br>**Benzodiazepines** | **Drowsiness** (tolerance develops), **dizziness**, ↓ concentration, anterograde amnesia, falls, ↑ traffic **accidents**, physical **dependence** & paradoxical anger/hostility (disinhibition). Taper off slowly to ↓ rebound anxiety. | √ Anticonvulsant, Panic attack; Other uses: **sedative**, social phobia & akathisia, acute mania & neuralgic pain | 0.25mg<br>10-20mg | 0.5mg po tid<br>1mg po bid | **16**<br>21 |
| **Lorazepam** ATIVAN g<br>0.5, 1ς, 2ς mg tab;<br>(0.5,1,2mg sl▼ tab; 4mg/ml **amp**⊗)✗<br>-short acting benzodiazepine | | | √ Anxiety, Preanesthetic, Status epilepticus; ↓ **DI's**;<br>Other uses: **sedative**; muscle relaxant; or in delirium (due to alcohol withdrawal, those with Parkinson's or NMS) | 0.5mg<br>10mg | 0.5mg po tid<br>1mg po tid | 11<br>**12** |

[renal] =↓ dose for renal dysfunction ς=scored tab χ=Non-formulary Sask ☎=Exceptional Drug Status Sask. ⊗=not covered by NIHB ▼=covered by NIHB ✆=prior by NIHB **ADAS-cog**=cognitive section of the 70 point Alzheimer's Disease Assessment Scale **Bz**=benzodiazepine **BP**=blood pressure **cc**=with meal **DI**=drug interaction **Dx**=diagnosis **FAQ**=Functional Activities Questionnaire **HR**=heart rate **MMSE**=Mini-mental state examination (Scale 0-30) **NNH**=number needed to harm **NNT**=number needed to treat **Pt**=patient **Sx**=syndrome **Sz**=seizure **SE**=side effect **T½**=half life **Tx**=treatment **wt**=weight

**Other Meds**: See **RxFiles** Charts: Mood Stabilizers (Carbamazepine, Divalproex, Lithium,…); Antidepressants (Bupropion, …).

Option: NOT ASA 75mg od x 2yr [111] or estrogen[109,110], or NSAID[111,112,113] (ADAPT NS), no ginkgo[114,115,116] (GEM), ?statin[117,118,119] (Leade NS), ??Vit E[120;121] (not for mild cognitive impairment, concern: ↑mortality if >400iu/day), ?$B_{12}$[122] & vegetables.

**Prevent Dementia**: ↓cardiovascular risk if present by (↓BP[123], ↓cholesterol, stop smoking, ↑exercise & use ASA in high risk pts). If mild cognitive impairment, annual conversion rate of 5-10% to dementia.

**Epidemiologic**: 1.5% @65yrs; doubles q4yr; 30% @80yrs; average survival 8yr from Dx[6] **Non Drug**: involve family/caregivers in environmental & behavioral therapy; advance health care directive & discourage driving.

**Dementia**: **Type**: Alzheimer's most common >50% (short term **memory**, word & way finding), vascular ~25% (often stepwise evolution, apathy, dysexecutive Sx), mixture of these, Lewy body ~15% (fluctuations in cognition, hallucinations visual & spontaneous motor features of Parkinsonism), Frontotemporal ~5% (disinhibition, behavioral & social tactlessness, language changes, often younger onset) & hydrocephalus Normal pressure (rapid progressing, early gait abnormalities & incontinence). Progessive deterioration requires interventions to ↓ disease progression, ↓ symptoms (cognitive, behavioral & psychological) & ↓ caregiver burden. Comorbidity with diabetes & hypertension ↑ mortality.

**Drug induced delirium**: antiemetics (eg. dimenhydrinate, meclizine), antihistamines sedating (eg. chlorpheniramine & diphenhydramine), anticholinergics (antipsychotics like chlorpromazine, clozapine & olanzapine; benztropine, oxybutynin, procyclidine, scopolamine, TCAs like amitriptyline & imipramine; tolterodine), antiparkinsonian meds, benzodiazepines, digoxin, disopyramide, muscle relaxants, narcotics (eg. meperidine, pentazocine, propoxyphene) & NSAIDs (rarely eg. aspirin, indomethacin, sulindac).

# Essential Tremor (ET) - Treatment Options

## What are some general characteristics of "Essential Tremor"? [1,2,3,4,5]

- **Most common** adult tremor (in elderly [~5%]); autosomal dominant inheritance; offspring may have 50% chance of getting
- Affecting about 500,000 Canadians; starting at **any age** (Mean age 45yr; bimodal: 20s & 60s); equally men & women
- **Slowly progressive**; tremors esp. amplitude worsens over time; no bradykinesia, rigidity or postural instability. However, in cases with longstanding or severe ET, resting tremor may be seen (but without the other parkinsonian features).
- Often benign but can cause **functional** (occupation, activities, writing, drinking & eating) **& social impairment**
- **Tremor: postural & kinetic**, usually bilateral, symmetric & rhythmic; in forehands & **hands** [~95%] (dominant often first; eventually both hands); **head** [~34%] tremor & **voice** [~12%] shakiness may occur; occasionally trunk, legs, jaw & lip tremor

## What causes essential tremor?

- **Primary – Idiopathic/Essential**: most common (>60% will have a **positive family history**); ??environmental toxins
- **Rule out**: metabolic disturbances, drug eg. benzo or alcohol withdrawal, drugs, hypoglycemia, hyperthyroidism & panic disorder
- **Differential diagnosis**: Enhanced physiological tremor, Dystonic, Task-specific, Parkinsonian, Holmes (rubral tremor rare), & Wilson's disease (consider if <40yr without family history of tremor, esp. if dystonia, dysarthria & psychiatric features; liver abnormalities & Kayser-Fleischer corneal rings).
- **Drugs** which exacerbate physiologic tremor: amiodarone, amphetamines, antipsychotics, beta agonists eg. salbutamol, caffeine, calcitonin, cocaine, cyclosporin, dopamine, ephedrine, lead, $Li^{++}$, nicotine, procainamide, SSRIs, steroids, theophylline, thyroid hormones, TCAs & valproate.

## What non-pharmacological therapies can be recommended?

- Tremor is often the sole symptom but may be worsened by stress, fatigue, cold & social interaction. **Alcohol**, which may relieve the tremor, must be used appropriately. Adequate **REST** is important. Adding **wrist weights** to a limb may reduce amplitude of the tremor. **Relaxation** techniques such as meditation, yoga, hypnosis and biofeedback may help.

## When should drug treatment be considered for ET?

- Consider "**no drug treatment**" or "**treatment only for specific events**" (e.g. party, special events) if not severe.
- If disabling only during periods of stress & anxiety consider "**PRN**" use of propranolol or benzodiazepines
- Consider **regular** drug therapy if ET **significantly** impacts **daily activity or psychologic distress**. Meds don't cure or slow progression

## What are the primary drug treatments options for treating ET?

- Beta-blockers & anticonvulsants **alone or in combination** are the mainstays of therapy (>50% of the pts have symptomatic benefit). Dosages may have to be increased with time. Clonazepam, topiramate, gabapentin & botulinum toxin injections may be useful in select cases. Surgical intervention, if tremors are refractory to medical management, may be indicated. {Deep brain stimulation (DBS) to Vim nucleus of the thalamus has similar efficacy to thalamotomy of the Vim to improve contralateral limb tremor, but DBS has fewer serious SE.}

### Table 1: Drug Regimen Options in ET [1,6,7,8]

| Class | Drug (g=generic avail.) | Dose (po) in ET | $/month | Comments |
|---|---|---|---|---|
| **Beta-blockers** ⇨**1st line** in moderate to severe limb ET; may be helpful for head tremor; but review CI) | **Propranolol** INDERAL,g — FDA approved (best studied); ~ 50% respond to tx; Both regular & LA effective; Some OK on 10-40mg prn prior to stressful situations; More data/effective long term than other β-blockers; Non-selective β-blocker (vs metoprolol - β1-selective) | 10-20mg po bid initially<br>40-80mg po bid-tid<br>120-160mg **LA** po od<br>Range: 120-240-320mg/d | ~$10<br>$10-15<br>~$40-49 | CI: asthma, uncompensated heart failure, ↓ heart rate (<50), ↓BP (<90mmHg)<br>SE: wheezing, headache, dizziness, drowsiness & insomnia; ↓HR/BP<br>↓ **amplitude** not frequency of tremors {Also sotalol 80-160mg/d; non-selective & antiarrhythmic} |
| | Metoprolol LOPRESSOR,g | 50-100mg bid;100mg SR od | ~$15 | |
| **Anticonvulsants** [9] ⇨Primidone is **1st line** in moderate to severe limb ET; especially those intolerant to β- blockers (Primidone more effective than phenobarbital) | **Primidone** MYSOLINE,g — ~ 50% respond to tx; ~ similar efficacy to propranolol in trials; ~ one study found 250mg/d = 750mg/d (efficacy)[10]; ~ potential of 1st dose SE reaction, ∴ start low dose! | **62.5mg** hs (↑62.5mg q7d)<br>125-250mg po bid - tid<br>Range: ≤250-1000mg/d | $10<br>$15 | SE: dizziness/vertigo, ataxia/unstable gait, drowsiness, headache, polyuria & rash<br>**Combination** propranolol & primidone occasionally useful. |
| ⇨Others 2nd line (2nd Line Options) | Topiramate [11,Ondo 06] TOPAMAX,g — Effective in trials but high (40%) drop-out rates / poor tolerance | 100-200mg bid (Start: 25mg daily; ↑ by 25-50mg/wk to ↓ SE) | $90-140 | SE: dizziness, unstable gait, drowsiness, ↓weight, paresthesia, confusion & difficulty word finding |
| | Gabapentin NEURONTIN,g — Trial efficacy inconsistent | 400-600mg tid (Start: 100-200mg to ↓SE) | $66-115 | SE: sedation, dizziness, fatigue, euphoria, drowsiness & ↓ libido; abuse potential |
| | {Pregabalin ☎ ⊗ LYRICA | 75-300mg bid more studies needed} | $330-490 | SE: dizziness, flu symptoms, malaise, euphoria |
| **Benzodiazepines** [12] ⇨Intermittent use for stressful situations making tremor worse | Clonazepam RIVOTRIL,g | 0.25-0.5mg tid (Limited trial data; up to 6 mg/day but ↑ sedation) | ~$16 | Limited benefit on tremor, but has hypnotic effect & may help ↓ **anxiety.** |
| | Alprazolam XANAX,g | 0.25-0.5mg tid (Limited trial data) | ~$16 | SE: tolerance, falls, dependence, daytime **sedation** & **abuse / addiction** potential |
| **Botulinum Toxin A** [13] **(BTX)** | Botulinum BOTOX | Head: 50-100units Max 400<br>Voice: 0.6-15units<br>Repeated every ~3months | ~$4 per UNIT | SE: Hand tremor: muscle weakness & paresthesia. SE: Voice tremor: breathiness, hoarseness & swallowing difficulties.<br>Option: disabling head or voice tremor |

**BP**=blood pressure **CI**=contraindication **ET**=Essential Tremor **Li**=lithium **Pts**=patients **SE**=side effects

**Other Possible Options:** **amantadine** 100mg bid $30; **atenolol** 50-100mg od ~$20; **clonidine** 0.1mg tid $25; **clozapine** 12.5-75mg/d ~$100 (but sedation, agranulocytosis, etc.); **flunarizine** 5-10mg hs $26-45; **levetiracetam** [14] 500-1000mg bid $100-200; **methazolamide** 12.5-25-50mg tid ~$25-60; **phenobarbital** 30-60mg bid~$15; & **sotalol** 40-80mg po bid~$25-40. **Deep Brain Stimulation (DBS)** surgical option.

**NOT recommended**: acetazolamide, isoniazid, pindolol & trazodone.

**Drug treatment by ET type:** Limb/Hand: propranolol, primidone, anticonvulsants, benzodiazepines; Head: propranolol, BTX; Voice: BTX

See next page for: *Restless Legs Syndrome (RLS) Treatment Options*

**ET Websites**: www.essentialtremor.org
Specific drug charts at www.RxFiles.ca
RxFiles "Essential Tremor" in **CFP**, Mar 2010: http://www.cfp.ca/cgi/content/full/56/3/250



# Restless Legs Syndrome (RLS) - Treatment Options

## What are the diagnostic criteria for "restless legs"? [15,16,17] {Also known as: Ekbom's syndrome}

- Distressing desire to move legs or other body parts; often accompanied by uncomfortable sensations (e.g. creeping)
- Symptoms brought on by, or worsen with rest (sitting or lying down). Overall prevalence is ~10% in general population.
- Urge and sensation is relieved with movement or reduced temporarily (e.g. walking, stretching)
- Symptoms worsen in evening or at night (often worst between midnight-4am; thus causing major disruption of sleep)
- Optional: involuntary limb movements while awake; periodic limb movements while sleep (as per patient or partner)

## What causes restless legs?

- **Primary – Idiopathic**: most common (~ 50% will have a positive family history)
- **Secondary, non-drug**: uremia dialysis, diabetes, peripheral neuropathy, **iron** deficiency~5% serum ferritin, pregnancy; ↓Mg, $K^+$, $Ca^{++}$
- **Drug causes**: antihistamines, antinauseants, antipsychotics, dopamine antagonists, $Li^{++}$, metoclopamide, SSRIs & TCAs, CCBs.
  Other: Discontinuation of opioids may precipitate RLS. Caffeine containing products.

## What non-pharmacological therapies can be recommended? [18,19] (Note: non-drug therapies not well studied)

- *Avoiding* caffeine/chocolate, alcohol, smoking cessation; *keeping* a regular sleep routine, rubbing limbs, walking / exercise (combination resistance and aerobic), stretching; *doing* mentally alerting activities, warm or cool baths.
- Pneumatic compression devices effective: worn for 1hr upon symptom onset. inflated to 40cm H2O air pressure for 5 seconds during every minute

## When should drug treatment be considered for restless legs?

- Consider "**no drug treatment**" or "**treatment only for specific events**" (e.g. air travel, theatre) if not severe.
- Treat "**intermittently**" for intermittent symptoms. Levodopa's fast onset makes it suitable for intermittent use.
- Consider **regular** drug treatment if RLS significantly impacts daily activities or disturbs sleep.

## What are the primary drug treatments options for treating RLS?

- Dopaminergic therapy is often the current drug treatment of choice. "Rebound" and "Augmentation" can arise with dopaminergic agents, especially levodopa (**LD**). Rare: ↑gambling behavior {Other drugs have also been studied; see Table 1.}
  - **Rebound**: worsening of symptoms when LD levels fall, usually during **night** or early day
    Management Options: 1) Repeat dose; 2) Add Levodopa CR to IR
  - **Augmentation**: appearance of more severe RLS symptoms **earlier** in day, before dose.
    Management Options: 1) If on LD, switch to dopamine agonist

### Table 1: Drug Regimen Options in RLS [20,21,22,23,24,25,26]

| Class | Drug (g=generic avail.) | Dose (po) in RLS* | $/month | Comments |
|---|---|---|---|---|
| **Dopamine Agonists** (**1st line** in moderate to severe RLS; Gradually ↑dose q2-3days) NNT=~6; NNH=77 to D/C tx; SE: nausea, dizziness, fatigue, somnolence … | Pramipexole MIRAPEX,g (generic avail., but not officially indicated for RLS) | 0.125-1.5mg hs 1-3hrs pre hs | $50 0.5mg/d | Canadian & FDA approved, Effective; t½ =8-12hrs; Typical dose ≤**0.5mg/day**; scored tabs |
| | Ropinirole REQUIP,g | 0.25-4mg hs 1-3hrs pre hs | **$30** 2mg/d | FDA approved; RCT evidence, Level A; 12wks; Typical dose =**2mg/day**; t½ =6hrs |
| | Non-ergot dopamine agonists more effective than placebo at ↑QOL & sleep; however strong placebo effect & ↑ SEs (nausea, dizzy, somnolence, fatigue. Efficacy maintained for 1yr; minimal augmentation. **Pergolide** PERMAX, no longer available USA Mar'07 & CDN Aug'07 | | | |
| **Levodopa (LD)** [26], **Dopamine Precursor** (**1st line** for prn dosing in mild to moderate RLS) | LD/Benserazide PROLOPA<br>LD/Carbidopa SINEMET,g<br>SINEMET CR,g | 50/12.5mg hs<br>½-1, 100/25 mg tab hs<br>(may give regular & CR tabs together for rapid & sustained effect) | $17<br>$15<br>$45 (IR+CR) | (≤400/100 mg); **fast** onset ~20min if ac; useful for **intermittent** prn treatment<br>Rebound & Augmentation common if ≥200mg & requires discontinuation |
| **Benzodiazepines** [10] (2nd Line) | Clonazepam RIVOTRIL,g | 0.25-1mg hs | $15 | Hypnotic effect; limited benefit on sleep. Problems with tolerance, falls, dependence & daytime sedation. |
| | Temazepam RESTORIL,g | 15-30mg hs | $12 | |
| **Antiepileptics** [12] (2nd Line) | Carbamazepine TEGRETOL,g | 200mg hs; (200 am & 400mg hs) | $10-16 | Limited data, maybe effective; consider if pain; CNS effects (daytime sedation, etc.) Valproic acid may also be effective. |
| | Gabapentin NEURONTIN,g | 600-2400mg; trials:**1,800mg/d** | $115 | |
| **Opioids** [27] (2nd Line) | Oxycodone IR or OXYCONTIN | 5-10mg IR; 10-20mg SR hs or q12h | $60 20mg/d | Maybe effective; consider if pain, or failure or SEs on dopamine agents; CNS effects; ↑sleep apnea; dependency concern. |
| | Other opioid options; codiene 30-180mg/day, propoxyphene DARVON 100-600mg/day, etc. | | | |

**Ac**=before meals **CR**=controlled release **HS**=bedtime **IR**=immediate release **LD**=Levodopa **Mg**=magnesium **RLS**=Restless Legs Syndrome **SE**= side effects **t1/2**=half life

**Other options:** bromocriptine 5-15mg/d; clonidine 0.1-1mg/d; baclofen motor neuron disease; amantadine; sedatives; topiramate; cabergoline 0.5-2mg hs 24hr duration, but expensive; quinine 300mg hs for leg cramps SE: headache, ↓ platelets

***Dosing: HS effective for most, some may require daytime (e.g. afternoon) dose. If Depression may consider bupropion.** [13]

## RLS Differential Diagnosis:

- **Periodic limb movements of sleep (PLMS):** often occurs in addition to RLS. Involves involuntary movements during sleep; brief awakenings or arousal from sleep (unaware).
- **Nocturnal leg cramps:** always involve a specific muscle; they usually require stretching of the muscle more than non-specific movement to relieve symptoms; usually unilateral
- **Peripheral neuropathy:** not usually associated with restlessness or helped by movement; does not worsen in evening or hs; sensations (numbness, tingling, or pain). May coexist
- **Vascular disease (varicose veins, deep vein thrombosis):** usually accompanied by swollen legs & a change in skin color
- **Akathisia (often drug-induced):** usually involves spontaneous movement of the whole body without sensory complaints; lacks a circadian pattern.
- **Intermittent claudication:** usually worsens with exercise & improves with rest.
- **Rapid eye movement (REM) sleep behavior disorder:** complex, often violent, motor behaviors associated with dreams (dream may not be recalled). Typically after age 60+
- **Painful legs and moving toes:** rare disorder not involving an urge to move limb

**RLS Websites**: www.rls.org; www.aasmnet.org;
Specific drug comparison charts at www.RxFiles.ca; Clinical Knowledge Summary (**CKS**) http://www.cks.nhs.uk/
Evidence based reviews: http://www.jr2.ox.ac.uk/bandolier/booth/booths/RLS.html

| Generic/TRADE (Strength & forms) | Class / Pregnancy Rating [5] | Side effects SE / Contraindications CI | √ = Therapeutic use / Comments / Drug Interactions DI / Monitor M | INITIAL; MAX DOSE | USUAL DOSE RANGE | $ / year |
|---|---|---|---|---|---|---|
| **Interferon Beta-1A** (↓ dose for hepatic dysfx)<br>**REBIF** [6,7,8,9,10,11,12,13] =R<br>8.8ug, 6 (22ug), 12 (44ug) million IU Pre-filled syringe (66ug,132ug) ☎ ⊗<br>(new formulation ↓SE but still ↑flu sx)<br>**Interferon Beta-1A** (↓ dose for hepatic dysfx)<br>**AVONEX** [14,15,16,17,18,19] =A<br>30ug (6.6million IU) powder & Pre-filled syr for IM inj. ☎ ⊗<br>**Interferon Beta-1B** =B<br>**BETASERON** (Extavia) [20,21,22,23]<br>8MIU (0.25mg) (0.3mg (9.6miu) powder) ☎ ⊗<br>**STEP ONE agents in CIS, RRMS** | **Interferons (IFNB)**<br>Systematic review (Lancet'03 24)<br>(see comment re: bias in endnote [25]- "There was a biased selection of trials…and the many differences (in design and reporting) was not adequately addressed")<br>**Not a cure** but slows relapse rate ~30%. Long term efficacy unproven. No tx is option in select individuals. MRI data quite strong.<br>**C – all** | **Common**: **flu-like Sx**: fever, myalgia, chills (60%) → tx: acetaminophen/ibuprofen [26]; **inj site reactions SC>IM** (esp. necrosis with 1B), rash, asthenia, **depression, fatigue,** HA, sweating, Nabs (5-25%)<br>**Serious**: ↑LFT, ↓platelet, pancytopenia, ↑BP&↑HR<br>**Caution:** seizures, alcohol abuse, bone marrow suppression, depression/suicidal, liver/renal dysfx.<br>CI: concurrent illness likely to alter compliance or greatly ↓ life expectancy; pregnancy if planned/occurs; nursing women; active, severe depression; hypersensitivity to albumin | √efficacy (↓ relapse rate ~30%, 0.84 vs 1.3 at 2yr) in **RRMS** & CIS; less in SPMS<br>• Importance of staging at initiation, dosage, frequency & route with regard to efficacy as yet undetermined<br>• Agent selection often based on clinical experience & pt preference/compliance. {Avonex for less severe disease.}<br>• **Rebif** vs Avonex [27] (EVIDENCE): Rebif may be more effective but also more SE (↑'d injection site rxn, liver enzymes, & NAb)<br>• **Betaseron** vs Avonex [28] (INCOMIN): Betaseron may be more effective but ↑SE (↑'d injection site rxn, liver enzymes & NAb)<br>• IFN Beta 1A may be less likely than 1B to produce NAbs [4] but may also be related to route/frequency [28] (IM vs SC; 1x vs 3x/wk)<br>DI: live vaccines -↓ immune response; ↓ zidovudine clearance<br>M: CBC, LFT 0→q1mon x3→at 6month q6month; TSH @0&6mon | **R** 8.8ug 3x/wk x2, 22ug 3x/wk x2, 44ug 3x/wk<br>Initiation pack avail.<br>**A** 30ug weekly<br>(60ug =no ↑ in efficacy vs 30ug [29] but may be related to frequency of admin ie smaller dose more often better?)<br>Positive correlation between short term outcomes, dose, frequency & ?route (ETOMS, EVIDENCE, INCOMIN)<br>**B** 0.0625→0.1→0.2mg x 2 wk SC EOD | 22ug **SC**; 3x /wk (to ↓ SE)<br>44ug **SC** 3x/wk<br>{RebiSmart autoinjector avail.} ⇒<br>30ug **IM** weekly<br>30ug PS **IM** weekly<br>8MIU(0.25mg) **SC** every other day | 19,800<br>24,000-<br>**22,630**<br>20,170<br>20,170<br>20,830 |
| **Glatiramer** [30,31,32,33,34]<br>**COPAXONE**<br>20mg inj Pre-filled syringe ☎ ⊗<br>**Alternate STEP ONE (esp if intolerant to IFNB)** | **Immunomodulator**<br>Glatiramer – no beneficial effect on the main outcome measures in MS, i.e. disease progression [35] (Cochrane'04), but ↓ MS attacks & ↓brain lesions (on MRI testing) in **trials**. Long term efficacy unproven. **No tx** is an option in select individuals.<br>**B** -but caution | **Common**: **inj. site rx/pain** (frequent) **post-inj rx: chestpain** (26%), **palpitations** (17%), **nausea** (22%), **dizzy/flushing** (27%), anxiety (23%), hypertonia (22%), arthralgia (24%), asthenia (41%) & tremor (7%)<br>**Serious**: transient eosinophilia & ↑BP (frequent), transient dyspnea (19%), lymphadenopathy (12%)<br>**Caution**: anaphylaxis (potential), immune response (interference)<br>CI: mannitol hypersensitivity; concurrent illness likely to alter compliance or greatly ↓ life expectancy; pregnancy (if planned/occurs); nursing women | √efficacy (↓ relapse rate ~30%, 1.2 vs 1.7 at 2yr) in **RRMS, & CIS** (Precise); used esp. if SE to IFNBs since not assoc. with flu-like sx or depression<br>May have more effect on QOL measures than disease progression [36]; unknown affect of NAbs ? [36]<br>DI: not formally studied, no sig. interactions observed in studies between glatiramer & common MS therapy<br>M: no blood monitoring required<br>Glatiramer vs Rebif (REGARD) & Glatiramer vs Betaseron (BEYOND): -Essentially **no** clinical outcome difference, yet seen between interferons & glatiramer. | **Most treatment benefit** in presence of clinical & / or radiological markers of continuing active inflammation.<br>**Less benefit**: if more **benign** course eg. low EDSS score at 5yrs; **low chance of benefit** eg. progressive disease without signs of ongoing inflammation; **indeterminate prognosis** eg. CIS or early RRMS with infrequent mild attacks & favourable prognostic profile.<br>**Relapse rate**: most evident ↓ in the first year & then declines<br>**Disability**: prevent long term disability is the most important goal of therapy, but treatment effects are generally unknown.<br>20mg OD | 20mg **SC** daily | 16,580 |
| **Mitoxantrone** [37,38,39,40,41,42,43,44,45,46,47,48]<br>**NOVANTRONE**<br>20mg inj χ ⊗<br>**STEP TWO agent for pts failing on Step ONE or with SPMS** | **Immunosuppressant**<br>**D/X** May also cause permanent amenorrhea esp. in peri-menopausal women | **Common**: nausea, anxiety, fatigue, menstrual disturbances, alopecia, infection; blue-green discoloration of urine/sclera x24hr after admin<br>**Serious**: heart damage (~2%, ↑ with cumulative dose > 140mg/m2) (Systolic dysfunction ~12%, HF~ 0.4%) AAN'10<br>myleosuppression (neutropenia, leukopenia) (frequent)<br>**Caution**: pre-existing myleosuppression, CVD, liver dysfx, avoid GCSF (may trigger relapse)<br>CI: pregnancy, infection, liver (dysfx), **leukemia** (0.8%) / blood dx, heart dx (LVEF <50%), leukopenia | √ PRMS, **SPMS** (Aggressive relapsing forms with ↑dx & ↑MRI burden), esp. in younger pts<br>DI: live vaccines- ↓ immune response, valspodar - ↑ mitoxantrone toxicity<br>M: Baseline & prior to each infusion→ CBC, LFT, echocardiography, CXR, pregnancy test; MUGA scan prior to infusions once cumulative dose ≥ 60mg/m²<br>*(FDA: MUGA prior to each infusion & yearly for delayed toxicity)*<br>Assess left ventricular **ejection fraction** before each dose | 5-12mg/m²<br>q 3months | 12mg/m² **IV** q3mon<br>(in ≥50ml NS or D5W over 15mins)<br>(Investigational: induction regimen q month x6 )<br>**(Max lifetime limit** 100-140mg/m² or 2-3 yrs tx ) | 800<br>(based on 1.7m² BSA) |
| **Natalizumab** [49,50,51,52,53,54]<br>**TYSABRI** 300mg vial ☎ ⊗<br>Drug program 1-888-827-2827 | Alpha$_4$-integrin antagonist antibody<br>**C** (adhesion-molecule Inhibitor) | **Common**: headache, fatigue, arthralgias<br>**Serious**: infections (2%), depression (0.8 %), ↑LFT, **hypersensitivity** (1.3% within 2hr; rare delayed), cholelithiasis (0.8%)<br>**Caution**: use with immunosuppressives (within 3months) or if ↓ immune fx (eg. cancer, RA), ?melanoma | √RRMS (rapidly evolving severe; ↓relapse rate by > 60%, 0.26 vs 0.81 at 1yr. approved Canada Oct/06) (2nd line: if Nabs to IFNB or intolerant or continued disease progression while on IFNB/glatiramer)<br>→42 PML cases (progressive multifocal leukoencephalopathy 55: 1 in 1000 (USA: Crohn's dx indication)) (Clinically PML pts may present with unilateral acute onset hemiparesis)<br>May produce antibodies (~6%) that ↓serum drug level/clinical response<br>M: CBC, LFT 0→q1mon x3→at 6month q6month; TSH @0&6mon | 300mg q4wk<br>Controversy: ?**drug holiday**, since PML may ↑ with tx >18month, but potential of MS sx exacerbation after natalizumab stopped.<br>DI: Avonex (30% increase in natalizumab levels) | 300mg **IV** q4wk<br>(in 100ml NS over 1hr) | 30,280 |
| **Methylprednisolone** [56,57,58,59,60,61,62,63,64,65]<br>**SOLU-MEDROL** 1g vial χ⊗; -but in SK-covered by Health Region;<br>**MEDROL** 4,16mg tab [66,67,68,69]<br>**Prednisone**<br>1, 5 (scored), 50 (scored) mg tabs<br>**ADJUNCT for EXACERBATIONS** | **Immunosuppressant**<br>**U** | **Common**: ↑BP, $Na^+$ & $H_2O$ retention, ↑ LFT (mild), ↓ wound healing, ↑ infections, euphoria, depression, peptic ulcer, GI upset, hypokalemia, myopathy, skin atrophy<br>**Serious**: Cushing's syndrome, seizures, **osteoporosis**, cataracts, glaucoma, myopathy hyperglycemia, ↑ intracranial pressure, adrenocortical insufficiency, CHF<br>CI: vaccine (live/attenuated), systemic fungal infection, premature infants | √ Acute relapse, not enough info to support use in prevention or long term benefit [70]<br>• May speed up recovery following a relapse; but **DOES NOT** alter the course of the disease<br>• Some clinicians still may taper steroid dose, after pulse therapy eg. Prednisone 60mg po od x1 then ↓ 5mg each day until finished<br>DI: ASA, anticoagulants, CYP3A4 inhibitors/inducers, fluoroquinolones, hydrochlorothiazides, live vaccines (immunosuppressive doses ↓ immune response), neuromuscular blockers (antagonizes blocker effects), tacrolimus (↑ tacrolimus conc) | 1g IV OD (in AM) x3-5d; -esp. for severe disease<br>Option: Medrol po (Normims)<br>(Methylprednisone 4mg= Prednisone 5mg)<br>**Oral taper usually not required after short term tx due to fast recovery of HTPA axis** [71] | 1g **IV**/po OD in AM x 3-**5** days<br>Recommend to use ≥500mg dose (in 100ml NS or D5W over 1hr)<br>Monthly (pulses ineffective Mecombin)<br>**Prednisone**<br>1g-1250mg (25x50mg tabs) [72] **po** daily or every other day x 3-**5** doses | 250<br>(based on 1 relapse/ yr) [35]<br>25 |

(↓ dose for hepatic dysfx symbol) =↓ dose for hepatic dysfx χ=Non-formulary Sask ☎=Exception Drug Status Sask. ⊗=not covered by NIHB ▼=covered by NIHB ♀= women **BP**=blood pressure **CI**=contraindication **CIS**=clinically isolated syndrome **DI**=drug interaction **Dx**=diagnosis **fx**=function **HA**=headache **HR**=heart rate **IFNB**=interferon Beta **MS**=multiple sclerosis **NAb**=neutralizing antibody **ns**=non sig. **n/v**=nausea/vomit **Pt**=patient **RRMS**=relapsing remitting MS **Sx**=symptoms **SE**=side effect **SPMS**=secondary progressive MS **Tx**=treatment **wt**=weight

**Other TX** Options: [73] cyclophosphamide [74,75,76,77], azathioprine [78] {Cochrane 2007: ↓ disease progression & relapse (3yr); maintenance option if frequent relapse requiring steroids; limit to 10yr or 600g to minimize ca risk}, amantadine & modafinil ?for **fatigue** [79,80], **antispastics** -anxiety/stress worsens; stretching, positioning & bracing helps, –Meds: taper if stopping; ? difference: baclofen 10-60mg/d but weakness (for spinal cord), rarely intrathecal pump if pt non-ambulatory; dantrolene but peripherally acting; tizanidine but hypotension; botulinum toxin: 25-300IU IM/muscle, work in 1-2wk, lasts 3-6month, not if contracture developed, $4/IU, SE: focal weakness, [81]; ?Gabapentin for pain, SE-ataxia, balance, often 100-400mg tid.; ? dalfampridine 10mg po bid ↑walking; **Bowel**: fluid ≥8cup/d, fiber ~20g/d, activity, bowel regular schedule, defecation may take ≥1hr. Not oxygen hyperbaric [82], ?methotrexate [83], ?immunoglobulin [84,85], plasma exchange [86], ?donepezil [87], ?**Vit D** 1000- ≥2000iu/d [88], ?(alemtuzumab immune thrombocytopenic purpura: 3 vs 1%, rituximab [89], **fingolimod** [90], laquinimod, clardibine [91])

**Diagnosis**: MRI [92], visual/brainstem/sensory evoked potential testing, cerebrospinal fluid analysis eg. oligoclonal bands & serologic testing [2] **Rule out**: Vascular disease, spinal cord compression, Vit $B_{12}$ deficiency, CNS infection & inflammatory conditions [2]

**Red Flags for MS**: presence of steadily progressive disease; absence of clinical remission; absence of oculomotor, optic nerve, sensory or bladder involvement; normal CSF may signal further investigations

**Symptoms**: [93] monocular visual impairment with pain-optic neuritis, fatigue, weakness, impaired coordination, urinary bladder dysfx, sensory sx pain, numbness, vibration & position, Lhermittes sign, memory/cognitive problems, sexual dysfx [2]

**MS types**: **Relapsing-Remitting (RRMS)**: common 85% at onset, acute attacks over day/wks, then after wk/months often a complete recovery. **Secondary Progressive(SPMS)**: RRMS convert to SPMS 50% at 10yr, then acute attacks lessen, then steady ↓ of fx. ?? benefit from IFNB/glatiramer **Primary Progressive (PPMS)**: ~10% at onset steady decline in fx without acute attacks not benefit from IFNB/glatiramer. **Progressive-relapsing (PRMS)**: 5% at onset begins with a progressive decline, but also has occasional acute attacks.

**Non Drug**: involve patient & family for education, support, exercise, physiotherapy for lower extremity eg legs, speech therapy, occupational therapy for upper extremity eg. arms & driving [94] & nutrition counselling. www.mssociety.ca www.msfacts.org

**Criteria for coverage SK**: have clinical definite **relapsing & remitting MS**; have had **at least 2 attacks** of MS during the previous 2yrs (an attack is defined as the appearance of new Sx or worsening of old Sx lasting **at least 24hrs** in the absence of fever, preceded by stability for **at least 1 month**); are fully ambulatory 100 meters without aids (canes, walkers or wheelchairs) -Extended Disability Status Scale (**EDSS**) 5.5 or less; are age≥18 (used age <18yr in select cases).

**MIGRAINE: AGENTS FOR ACUTE TREATMENT**

Prepared by: L Regier BSP, B Jensen BSP, S Downey BSP © www.RxFiles.ca June 10

| Class | Generic/ TRADE (PREGNANCY CATEGORY) | INDICATIONS and CONTRAINDICATIONS (CI) | SIDE EFFECTS (SEs) | DRUG (DI) INTERACTIONS | COMMENTS | DOSING usual; MAX/24hr | $ per 6 doses |
|---|---|---|---|---|---|---|---|
| TRIPTANS (5HT1B/D Agonists) | **Naratriptan** C<br>AMERGE,g<br>(1,2.5mg D shaped tab);OTC in UK) | **1st line for mod & severe attacks**<br>• ≤40% of all attacks & 25% of all patients do not respond [1]; high recurrence rate (~40% @24hr IMITREX)<br>**CI** •cardiac or cerebrovascular disease (or high risk for the same); risk of MI ~1/5,000,000 migraine attacks treated [2,49]<br>•hypertension uncontrolled; PVD; ?diabetes<br>•hemiplegic or basilar migraine<br>**Caution: decrease dose/avoid**<br>•↑CV risk: e.g. ♂>40yrs; ♀ >50yrs; **smoker**<br>•Renal dysfunction with nara/suma<br>•Hepatic dysfn with all triptans<br>•Sulfa allergy?: Almo/Elet/Nara/Suma<br>•Aspartame ZOMIG Rapimelt, MAXALT wafer ⇨caution in PKU pts<br>EDS Criteria: Treat migraine headache (Age >18yr) | **For all:** (13 trials suggest no differences)[65]<br>Chest discomfort or tightness <7% (or tightness of neck/throat); {Actual CV events extremely rare if low CV risk}.<br>nausea, facial flushing, tingling & paresthesia; CNS: dizziness<10%, fatigue, somnolence;<br>poor taste Suma; Suma SC burning @ site<br>**Differences generally not clinically significant; trends:**<br>•Almo/Nara/Frova⇨less SEs slow onset<br>•Riza⇨more recurrence?<br>•Zolmi⇨more adverse effects?<br>**•Suma = 50mg dose often as effective as 100mg & as well tolerated as 25mg**[3]<br>• baseline cardiac evaluation/ECG recommended for ♂ >40yr & ♀ >50yr | **•Serotonin syndrome** (e.g. agitation, excitement, hypomania, myoclonus, **tremor**, hyperreflexia, ataxia, motor weakness, fever/chills, diarrhea) **with concurrent MAOIs, SSRIs, TCAs or lithium.**<br>MAOIs = stop at least 2 weeks prior to triptans (except Nara, Almo & Frova); caution with others<br>**•Do NOT use within 24hr of DHE**, other **ergot** preps or other **triptans** (risk of additive vasoconstriction/ coronary vasospasm)<br>•↑level of **Zolmi** use ≤ 5mg/24h with **cimetidine, propranolol, ciprofloxacin & fluvoxamine** | •Selective 5HT-1 receptor agonists 2hr response: NNT= 2 - 4<br>•Take at the earliest onset of migraine pain best, but taking during aura phase may be too early.<br>**•If failure** with one, can try another fast vs slow; route<br>**•Triptan + NSAID:** benefit some?↓recurrence• use≤2x/wk<br>**•Frequent use of triptans can cause rebound & chronic daily headache** (Some clinicians suggest 10-18 doses per month ok; lack of data[2])<br>•Less nausea vs DHE but ↑ recurrence rate | 1mg or **2.5mg**;<br>may repeat in 4h<br>**MAX=5mg/24h** | **61** generic **/112** |
| | **Rizatriptan** C<br>MAXALT<br>(5,10mg capsule shaped tab;<br>5,10mg wafer) | | | | | 5mg or 10mg;<br>may repeat in 2h<br>**MAX 20mg/24h**<br>If With Propranolol: 5mg; 15mg/24hr | **112** |
| | **Sumatriptan** C -most used<br>IMITREX<br>(25,50,100mg **DF tab**;<br>-generic 25,50 & 100mg tabs<br>5,20mg **Nasal spray**;<br>6mg/0.5ml **SC inj**);<br>50mg OTC in the UK<br>(Treximet in USA, Suma 85mg + naproxen 500mg) | | | | **SC IMITREX**[4] {most effective triptan form @2hr: NNT=2; OK if nausea; but less convenient & ↑cost; useful for cluster type HA or alternate rapid triptan e.g. Zolmig nasal}<br>•SC best bioavailability/**fastest** onset ~10-15min versus orals onset 30 - 120min; (nasal also fast! 15min)<br>**Nasal IMITREX**& DF (age >12yr[5]),**MAXALT Wafer, &/OR ZOMIG** RAPIMELT or nasal [4] may be preferred if<br>• **fast relief required** nasal ~15min; melt tab 30min, &<br>• **nausea &/or vomiting present** {wafer/melt: can take without water & inconspicuous} | **50-100mg PO**; 25-50mg<br>may repeat in 2h<br>(**MAX 200mg/24h**)<br>5mg or **20mg** in one nostril; may rpt in 2h<br>(**MAX 40mg/24h**)<br>6mg SC; may rpt x1in 1h; (**MAX 12mg/24h**) | **67** generic **/113**<br><br>**111**<br><br>**260** |
| | **Zolmitriptan** C<br>ZOMIG<br>(2.5mg tab; 2.5mg ZOMIG Rapimelt tab);<br>(5mg **Nasal** spray) | •**Eletriptan RELPAX** ✗ ⊗:20-40mg tab, ?sulfa allergy but ↑DI 3A4 with other meds; low recurrence $92/6 doses<br>•**Almotriptan AXERT**: 6.25-12.5mg tab may repeat x1 in 2hr; similar to po sumatriptan: $100/6dose. age ≥12yr FDA<br>•**Frovatriptan FROVA** ✗ ⊗: 2.5mg; may repeat after 2hr, MAX 5mg/24hrs; long t½= 25hr; slower onset 90-320min; ?less effective but less recurrence $94/6 doses. {?Menstrual migraine: has been used q12h short-term starting 2days prior to onset of period.}<br>(Review:Med Letter Feb05, Treatment Guidelines Mar08: Tepper 2009) | | | **AMERGE** [4] **- slower onset** 60-120min **but**<br>**•better tolerability, less drug interactions**<br>**•longest duration, lowest recurrence rate**<br>{2.5mg less effective?: at 2hr vs riza 10mg & at 4hr vs suma 100mg}[65] | 1.25mg or **2.5mg**;<br>may repeat after 2hr<br>**MAX 10mg/24h**<br>With Propranolol ↓ zolmi dose.<br>5mg nasal switch to oral | **103**<br><br><br>**198** |
| ERGOTS (5HT1B/D, 1A,1F,2A,2C, 3; α & β; DA1&2 Agonists) | **Dihydroergotamine** X<br>**DHE**<br>**MIGRANAL**/generic<br>(1mg/ml **injectable**)<br>(4mg/ml **nasal** spray = 0.5mg / spray)<br>NOTE: pump 4Xs into the air to prime nasal spray for 1st use. | **1st line agent for severe & ultra-severe attacks** (for status ⇨ migrainosus, pre-dose antiemetic, e.g. **metoclopramide**, x2-3 days)<br>**CI** •**cardiac** or cerebrovascular disease(or risk factors);uncontrolled hypertension, ?diabetes, pregnancy<br>•hemiplegic or basilar migraine<br>**Caution**: renal/hepatic dysfunction | Metoclopramide MAXERAN, REGLAN alone sometimes effective<br>Chest discomfort, tingling & paresthesia, nausea, drowsiness, dizziness, diarrhea, muscle cramp<br>Nasal spray = rhinitis, taste disturbance but ↓ nausea<br>• baseline cardiac evaluation/ECG recommended for ♂ >40yr & ♀ >50yr | **•Do NOT use within 12hr of triptans or 24hrs for naratriptan**[6] (risk of additive vasoconstriction/ coronary vasospasm)<br>•↑ toxicity (eg. severe ischemia) of ergot preps: with **clarithromycin, erythromycin, itraconazole, propranolol, protease inhibitors & itra-, posa- & vori-conazole.**<br>**•Sibutramine:**↑ risk of serotonin syndrome.<br>• þ -porphyria concern | •Non-selective 5HT agonist: (also α, ß & DA)<br>**•More nausea than triptans but less chest pain**<br>•May precede with 10mg **metoclopramide**, or **prochlorperazine** 5-10mg esp. if severe attack requiring repeat doses or if nausea present<br>**•IV** = rapid onset but more adverse effects so reserve for severe attack[6]<br>**•SC** = slower response rate vs IMITREX but longer acting & lower recurrence rate at 24hr [7]<br>**•Nasal spray** =response rate similar to oral triptans, or nasal IMITREX[5]; low recurrence rate | 0.5-**1mg** q1h **SC**, IM or IV; repeat q1h to **Max 3mg/24h** 6mg/wk<br>{IV 1mg/50ml over ≥15min<br>1 spray into each **nostril** stat;repeat in 15 minutes prn<br>**MAX 4 spray/attack; 8 sprays/24h** | **31**<br><br>**$ 44** per 1 pkg (3 bottles X4 doses per bottle) |
| | **Ergotamine/** ✗ X<br>**caffeine** (1/100tab[5])<br>CAFERGOT<br>Ergodryl avail.; Ergomar SL & Cafergot-PB Supp – DC'd by the company. | **2nd line** due to ↓ efficacy & ↑ toxicity<br>**CI** •**cardiac** or cerebrovascular dx or risk factors, uncontrolled BP, ?diabetes, **pregnancy**/?breastfeeding<br>•hemiplegic or basilar migraine<br>**Caution**: renal/hepatic dysfunction | Chest discomfort/ pain, tingling & paresthesia, nausea, vomiting, dizziness, drowsiness, diarrhea, muscle cramps<br>**Chronic daily headache** (with overuse; limit to 1-2 days/week) | | •Non-selective 5HT agonist<br>**•Most nausea of all abortive preps;** recent meta-analysis ?'s efficacy as mainly appeared to ↑ N&V[8]<br>• **Ergotism with overuse:** vasoconstriction⇨ numbness, tingling, paresthesia, blue hands/feet, (gangrene of extremities), HA, seizures, abdominal/chest pain, lack of pulse | 2 tab SL stat, then 1 tab Q30-60min,<br>**MAX** 6tab/24h;10/wk | **13** |
| NONSPECIFIC ANALGESICS | **NSAIDs** C/D<br>ASA, high dose, B/D<br>**Ibuprofen,**<br>**Naproxen** Na⁺ANAPROX ✗<br>or **Naproxen** (500mg Tab or Supp*) | **Treatment of mild-moderate attack**<br>**CI** •hypersensitivity to ASA/NSAID (ie bronchospasm, nasal polyps)<br>**Caution**: if cardiovascular or renal disease; GI ulcer risk.<br>{Useful for tension-type headache} | •GI irritation/upset/bleed, dizziness, fatigue, rash<br>•Renal impairment esp. if CrCl <30ml/min<br>See also NSAIDs chart for other drugs/formulations. | •↑ bleeding with **warfarin & antiplatelet agents**<br>•Displaces **DVA** & older **sulfonylureas** so↑ toxicity<br>•May blunt effect of some antihypertensives •others | •**Overuse** (ie >10-15x/wk) **can lead to rebound headache or medication-induced headache**<br>•for short-term, intermittent use; will increase effectiveness if used together with triptan<br>•Enteric ASA too slow. Buffered ASA OK OTC<br>•Fast acting useful (eg. ANAPROX, VOLTAREN RAPIDE ✗⊗, ibuprofen)<br>•Ibuprofen effective & acetaminophen useful:kids[5] | **ASA** 650-1300mg po q4h X2<br>**Ibuprofen** 400-800mg po q4-6h X2 (**MAX 3.2g/24h**)<br>**ANAPROX** 275-550mg po q4-6h X2 (**MAX 1.65g/24h**)<br>**Naproxen** 500-1000mg po<br>*Consider suppository if vomiting | (MAX 4g/24h) **$1**<br>**$1** OTC 400mg<br>**$ 15**<br>(MAX 1.5g/24h) **$2** OTC 220mg |
| | **292s, TYLENOL #3,** C/D<br>**FIORINAL** ✗ ⊗,others) | **Treatment of mild-moderate attack if**:<br>•not relieved with simple analgesics<br>•vasoconstrictors are contraindicated | Drowsiness, dysphoria, nausea, constipation (esp. with codeine);<br>{Opioids may ↑ risk of chronic HA} | •Products with ASA similar to above<br>•Additive effects with other **CNS depressants** | **•Overuse associated with rebound &** medication induced headache (esp. caffeine combos); for short-term & intermittent use<br>**•Dependency potential** •may mask pain without affecting underlying pathophysiology | 1-2 tabs/caps stat: may repeat 3-4h prn<br>**MAX 6-8 tabs/caps per 24h** | T3=$ 8<br>292= $ 8<br>Fc½= $ 20 |
| | **Acetaminophen** TYLENOL ▼ B: doses of ~1gram sometimes effective if taken early! [111] | | | | | | |
| | **Butorphanol** ✗ ⊗ C/D<br>10mg/ml **nasal** spray<br>(previous **STADOL**) 1mg/spray | **Reserve for rescue treatment or when DHE/triptans ineffective or contraindicated** | Drowsiness, dysphoria, nausea & vomiting, nasal irritation<br>(Dose ~ 1mg/spray) | •↑ CNS depression: **CNS depressants, MAOIs, alcohol** | **•Dependency potential**<br>•Mixed **agonist-antagonist** so can precipitate withdrawal in persons addicted to opiates | 1 spray in 1 nostril;<br>may repeat in 3-5hr<br>**MAX 16 sprays/24h** | **$53** (15 doses) |

**CORONARY VASOSPASM Potential:** still greatest concern; metaanalysis showed no clinically important differences between agents, thus one unlikely to be "safer" than others[9]; ⇨**patient selection & counseling** important! (♀ with aura ↑risk)

**ADJUNCT AGENTS:** •**metoclopramide** 10-20mg SC/IV {IV: 10-20mg /50ml over ≥15min}; 5-10mg PO •**chlorpromazine** 5-25mg IV (10-25mg PO) q4-6h {IV: pretreat with ≥ 500ml NS} •**domperidone** 20-30mg PO (or 60mg PR) tid-qid •**prochlorperazine** STEMETIL 5-10mg IV (25mg PR) q8h •**trimebutine** MODULON 200mg cap po x1 (may ↑ Tryptan efficacy with less nausea & photophobia[48]) •**haloperidol** HALDOL 5mg IV in 500ml normal saline or 5mg IV over 3mins •**diphenhydramine** BENADRYL 25mg IV combined with prochlorperazine or metoclopramide IV x1 to ↓ akathisia. Investigational: **Telcagepant**: cGRP antagonist; non-vasoconstrictive; ?↑LFTs]

**Migraine headache:** consider if recurrent severe disabling headache assoc. with nausea & sensitivity to light & a normal neurological exam. Characteristically is unilateral>60%, ?asymmetrical, pulsating, builds up over minutes to hours, & aggravated by routine physical activity.

Prepared by Loren Regier BSP, Brent Jensen BSP, S Downey BSP © www.RxFiles.ca June 10

| | Generic/ TRADE (PREGNANCY CATEGORY) | INDICATIONS AND CONTRAINDICATIONS CI | SIDE EFFECTS | DRUG (DI) INTERACTIONS | COMMENTS | DOSING *range* / typical | $ /month |
|---|---|---|---|---|---|---|---|
| TCAs | **Amitriptyline** C<br>ELAVIL/generic<br>(10, 25, 50,75χ▼ mg tab)<br>**Nortriptyline** C<br>AVENTYL/generic<br>(10,25mg cap) | **1st line** especially if associated depression, **chronic pain**, or **tension-type headache**<br>{fluoxetine possibly effective in some.}<br>**CI** •severe cardiac, kidney, liver, prostate or thyroid disease; glaucoma, hypotension •seizures •MAOI use | Anticholinergic effects: dry mouth, constipation, etc.; dizziness, **drowsiness**, postural hypotension, weight gain<br>**Nortriptyline** ⇨**less** drowsiness, dry mouth & weight gain than amitriptyline; but less evidence | Avoid with MAOI, cisapride, clonidine<br>↑ effects with MAOI, anticholinergics, other CNS depressants<br>↑ effect with CCBs, SSRIs cimetidine,phenothiazines, cipro (↓ TCA metabolism) | •Central neuromodulator of noradrenaline & serotonin (5HT) system<br>•**Start low & titrate up** to help ↓ side effects; may give **single dose at bedtime**<br>{nortriptyline ~1.5-2x more potent than amitriptyline}<br>•Caution in elderly ⇨ anticholinergic effects | *25-150mg/d*<br>50mg po hs<br>100mg po hs<br>*10-150mg hs*<br>50mg po hs<br>100mg po hs | *11-25*<br>**15**<br>**23**<br>*12-55*<br>**25**<br>**41** |
| β-BLOCKERS | **Metoprolol** C/D<br>LOPRESOR/generic<br>(25ς,50ς,100ς mg tab;SR 100,200mg)<br>**Atenolol** (25,50ς,100ς mg tab)<br>**Propranolol** C/D<br>INDERAL/generic<br>(10ς,20ς,40ς,80ς& 120ς mg tab; LA 60,80,120,160mg) | **1st line**<br>Can reduce frequency and some effect on intensity and duration<br>**CI** •asthma, heart block or uncompensated heart failure, peripheral vascular disease | Fatigue, bradycardia, hypotension, coldness of extremities, depression, impotence, sleep disturbance, bronchospasm | ↑ levels of rizatriptan (↓ dose of riza to 5mg)<br>↑ risk of peripheral ischemia with ergots<br>↑ cardiovascular effects with CCBs,clonidine<br>↑ levels of β-blocker with cimetidine,fluoxetine<br>Altered hypo-glycemic effect with sulfonylureas | •Modulation of central catecholaminergic system & brain serotonin<br>•May be class effect however β-blockers with intrinsic sympathomimetic activity may not be effective (data from small/poorly designed trials)[10]<br>•**Timolol** 20-30mg/day & **nadolol** (↓dose for renal dysfx) also used<br>•**Start low & titrate up**<br>•If failure with one→ may try another β-blocker<br>•Taper slowly before stopping to prevent rebound | ***Metopr*** *50-200mg/d*<br>50mg po bid<br>100mg SR po od<br>***Atenolol*** *50-150mg/d*<br>100mg po od (↓dose for renal dysfx)<br>***Propran*** *80-320mg/d*<br>80mg po bid<br>120mg LA po od | *10-20*<br>**14**<br>**15**<br>*18-32*<br>**24**<br>*10-15 /87LA*<br>**12**<br>**39** |
| CCBs | **Flunarizine** ☎▼ X<br>SIBELIUM /g (5mg cap)<br>**Verapamil** C<br>ISOPTIN, others<br>(120,180ς,240ς SR tab/cap) | Reduce frequency but little effect on intensity or duration<br>**CI** •CHF, arrythmias,hypotension (pregnancy with flunarizine)<br>**Caution: β-blockers, Parkinsons**<br>**Verapamil ~1st line option** expert opinion | **Flunarizine:** fatigue, weight gain, **depression**, parkinson like side effects (**EPS**)<br>**Verapamil:** bradycardia, hypotension, **constipation**, nausea, edema, headache | ↑ effect of CNS depressants<br>**Verapamil = many DIs**<br>ASA, barbs, β-blockers, carbamazepine, cimetidine, digoxin, erythromycin, ketoconazole, lithium, statins & theophylline | •? modulate transmitters rather than vasodilation<br>•**Maximum effect** may take several **months**<br>•**Overall benefit similar** to **β-blockers**<br>•Flunarizine seldom used (probably effective in kids[5]); Verapamil often used but less studied<br>•Verapamil **good** prophylaxis→**cluster** headache | *5-10mg/d*<br>5mg po hs (>6yrs old)<br>10mg po hs starting dose<br>*240-320mg/d*<br>240mg SR po od<br>(higher doses in cluster HA?) | <br>**31**<br>**55**<br><br>**30** |
| ANTICONVULSANT | **Divalproex** (DVA)<br>EPIVAL/generic D 93 Harm<br>(125,250,500mg EC tab;1000mg/10ml vialχ ⊗)<br>**Gabapentin** NEURONTIN<br>(100, 300, 400mg cap) C<br>**Topiramate** TOPAMAX<br>(25,50⊗,100,200mg tab; C<br>15, 25mg sprinkle cap) | **1st line for severe migraine**<br>(↓ severity and duration) but little effect on mild-moderate attacks;<br>•useful for **SSRI induced** migraine, prolonged atypical migraine aura & migraine with vertigo topiramate 50mg/day<br>**CI** •liver disease<br>**Caution: children → hepatotoxicity**<br>**Monitor**: CBC, Platelets, LFT<br>(Level 350-830 umol/l – trough)<br>-see comments column & antiepileptics chart p 85 | **DVA**: Common: nausea, tremor, weight gain, alopecia, ↑ LFTs, diarrhea (transient & can be minimized by **starting low & titrating up**); polycystic ovary.<br>**Rare**: ↓ **platelets** (↓ dose helps) **& WBC, hepatotoxic**, skin rx's, **pancreatitis.** Neural tube defects→spina bifida 1-2%.<br>------------<br>[Topiramate drop-out rate: ~30%] | ↑ ASA & warfarin effect<br>**↑ Valproic acid level by**: ASA, cimetidine, erythromycin, fluoxetine, isoniazid & salicylates<br>**↓ Valproic acid level by**: carbamazepine, cholestryramine, lamotrigine, phenobarbital, phenytoin, primidone, rifampin & topiramate<br>**Valproic acid ↑'s levels of**: amitriptyline, carbamazepine epoxide (ie.↑ SE), clonazepam, diazepam, **lamotrigine** lorazepam, phenobarbital **& warfarin** | **Anticonvulsants**: effective NNT=3.8,SE's common SE⇨DC:NNH=2.4-33 [19]<br>•**Divalproex less GI effects** than valproic acid<br>•Monitor LFTs initially: if ↑ enzymes, then ↓ dose; if 2-3x normal→stop drug; Mech: Modulation of GABA receptors?<br>**Gabapentin** effective at 2,400mg/day [20]<br>(Gabapentin & Topiramate are Peds options – see antiepileptic chart for dosing)<br>**Topiramate** (↓dose for renal dysfx) effective [11,12,13,14]; **100mg/day** equal to propranolol 160mg/day [15]; no studies compared to valproate; expensive but new generic avail; SE's common (e.g. paresthesias, cognitive, taste, anorexia, fatigue, wt loss) | *500-1500mg /d*<br>125mg po bid cc<br>250mg po bid-tid cc<br>500mg bid cc with meals<br>{Initiate:300mg tid}<br>600-800mg po tid<br>{Initiate:25mg po hs , ↑ by 25mg/wk}<br>**50-100mg po bid**<br>{may give 100mg at HS to ↓SE} | <br>**15**<br>**22-28**<br>**35**<br>**56**<br>**115-126**<br>**29**generic<br>**73-90** |
| 5HT-2 | **Pizotyline/pizotifen**<br>SANDOMIGRAN C<br>(0.5mg, DS =1ς mg tab) | **2nd line** (seldom used)<br>**CI**•?diabetes, heart disease, glaucoma, urinary retention, prostatic hypertrophy, renal/hepatic dysfunction | Weight gain, fatigue, weak anticholinergic effects | Additive effects with:<br>**CNS depressants, anticholinergics** | •Serotonin-2 receptor antagonist<br>•Somnolence so begin low & dose at bedtime (ie 0.5mg hs). | **Start** 0.5mg po hs<br>**titrate to** 0.5mg tid<br>(or 1.5mg po hs)<br>**MAX 6 mg/day** | **20**<br>**47**<br>**1mg tid** 70 |
| ERGOTS | **Methysergide** X<br>SANSERT<br>(2mg tab ☎▼) **-D/C** by Co | **3rd line** - for prevention of severe recurrent migraine unresponsive to other agents (seldom used)<br>**CI** •hypertension, cardiac, liver,kidney, lung & collagen dx; þ -porphyria concern. •thrombophlebitis & pregnancy | **Retroperitoneal, cardiac & pulmonary fibrosis**<br>**⇨ do not use for >6 months duration without weaning & a 1-2 month drug holiday!**<br>Nausea, muscle cramps, ↑weight, ↓hair, claudication, hallucinations | •Do NOT use within 24hr of **triptans** (risk of ↑ vasoconstriction/spasm)<br>↑ toxicity of ergots with: clarithromycin,erythromycin, propranolol & protease inhibitors | •Serotonin-2 receptor antagonist with carotid vasoconstrictor effect<br>•Active metabolite<br>•If no effect after 3 week trial,not likely to help<br>•Taper dose over 2-3 weeks before stopping! | *2-8mg/d*<br>2mg po bid cc<br>2mg po tid cc | <br>**76**<br>**110** |

**OTHER**: **candesartan** ATACAND 16mg daily Norway trial; **venlafaxine** EFFEXOR XR 75mg – 150mg daily (similar use as TCAs, less evidence, less anticholinergic SEs); **Coenzyme Q10** 75mg BID -100mg TID. •Acupuncture?[18]; Spinal manipulation? **riboflavin** (Vit B2) 400mg/d $10, **magnesium** ~500mg/d$10, **feverfew** TANACET 6.25-18.75mg TID; ≤125mg/d ?, **butterbur** (petasites) **extract** PETADOLEX 100mg/d [16] •**BOTOX** injection 25-100 IU ~q3mons[17] ? (but appears not effective for most chronic daily HA & chronic tension type HA per CADTH - HTIS )[86]

**PROPHYLACTIC THERAPY should be considered if**: • migraines **severe enough to impair quality of life** or patient has **≥ 3 severe attacks per month which fail to respond to abortive therapy.**

**TIPS**: •use one prophylactic agent at a time •**start low & titrate up**; once effective dose reached, continue for **minimum 3 month trial** to evaluate effectiveness (benefits usually seen after 1-2 months) • efficacy depends on **withdrawal of analgesics** causing rebound or chronic daily headache •if single agent ineffective, may try a **combination** (eg beta blocker + TCA); consider neuro consult if no response •continue effective tx for **9-12mon** or indefinitely if severe/recurrence; **discontinue gradually** to prevent rebound •before NSAID/triptan consider metoclopramide or domperidone •in some ♀ **long cycle continuous birth control pills** can help ↓ migraines but may avoid OCs if aura (↑risk) •**Success of prophylaxis** considered to be ↓ **in severity or frequency of headache by 50%** •reassess in teens (eg nearly 40% of teens esp if no migraine family history, no longer had headaches 10 years later Monastero 2006)

**CI** =contraindication **CNS**=central nervous system **DI**=drug interaction **LFT**=liver function test **SE**=side effect **SR**=sustained release. χNon-formulary in SK ☎EDS status SK ▼covered NIHB ⊗not NIHB ✓prior NIHB ς =scored tab (kidney symbol) =↓dose for renal dysfx

**Migraine headache:** prevalence peaks in midlife, ~12% of population affected, with females 3-4 times more often than males, 5-10% of children & adolescents, & 1/3 experience an aura (flashing lights, numb/tingle in face/extremities, disturbed smell or difficulty speaking).

| Generic/TRADE (Strength & forms) | Class/Mechanism of Action/ Pregnancy category [7] | Side effects / Contraindications CI | √ = Therapeutic Use / Comments / Drug Interactions DI | INITIAL & MAX DOSE | USUAL DOSE RANGE | $ /30d |
|---|---|---|---|---|---|---|
| **Levodopa/benserazide**<br>PROLOPA =P<br>50/12.5, 100/25, 200/50mg cap<br>**Levodopa/carbidopa** [8]<br>SINEMET/generic =S<br>100/10ˢ,100/25ˢ,250/25ˢmg IR tab;<br>100/25ˢ·ᵍ,200/50mgˢ·ᵍ CR tab:<br>70% bioavailable vs immediate release<br>**Oral liquid form** [9,10]<br>manufactured by some pharmacies<br>**carbidopa/levodopa/ entacapone** STALEVO [11]<br>50= 12.5/50/200<br>100= 25/100/200<br>150= 37.5/150/200mg tab<br>{75=18.75/75/200;125=31.25/125/200} ®<br>(don't cut these doses in half)<br>(PARCOPA: rapid dissolving form of levo/carbidopa avail in USA only [12],<br>DUODOPA: x® levo/carbidopa 20mg/5mg/ml gel Intraduodenal infusion new in Canada [13]) | **Dopamine precursor**:<br>Levodopa (LD): **most** potent med available for PD<br>{regular tab/cap: peak level at ~30minutes & ~4hr duration}<br><br>Benserazide & carbidopa are peripheral dopamine **decarboxylation inhibitors** which ↓ nausea from levodopa.<br>(≥75mg **carbidopa** [14] blocks enzyme; may need up to 200mg)<br><br>**C** – all | Common: GI: **nausea**, vomiting, anorexia; CNS: headache, confusion, dizziness, **hallucinations**, mood changes, **nightmares**, insomnia, depression; rash, alopecia, discolored urine, dark saliva/sweat & ↑**libido.**<br>**Dose unresponsiveness** & freezing, **fluctuations** (**wearing off**, on-off), **dyskinesia** (chorea, **peak dose**, diphasic & dystonia off period; hand/foot in AM).<br>Serious: dyskinesia, ↓**BP**, psychosis, arrhythmias, sudden sleep, blood dyscrasia, neuroleptic malignant syndrome (esp. after abrupt D/C med), malignant melanoma, anemia & possible ↑ gambling behavior.<br>CI: MAOI use, caution if psychosis history, glaucoma,sympathomimetic amines & may activate melanoma.<br>Correct ↓BP SE by: ↑water & salt intake, midodrine 2.5 - 5 - 10mg bid-tid, domperidone,fludrocortisone 0.05-0.4mg/d & adjust antihypertensive & TCA doses. | √ idiopathic, postencephalitic & symptomatic PD esp. if pt rigid, bradykinesia or **elderly**. Not useful for freezing. For restless leg sx (eg. 100/25@hs).<br>-initiate PD tx with either levodopa **or** a DA; levodopa provides **superior motor benefit** but is assoc. with an ↑**risk of dyskinesia**. [1 American 2002]<br>-**wearing off**, on-off phenomena, sudden offs & freezing & dyskinesia incl. painful dystonia affect ≤ 70% of pts **within 5yr of starting** levodopa. [15]<br>-**No** evidence that CR levodopa [16 (Koller)] better than regular release, but may help to **give CR @HS if early morning OFF** episodes occurring<br>-**on-off** phenomenon (reduced by giving smaller, more frequent levodopa doses **or** adding DA)<br>-can be given up to 4hrs before surgery<br>-may slow progression or ↓ severity of sx (NEJM'04) [17]<br>-avoid abrupt withdrawal→worsen PD/cause NMS<br>DI: ↓ effect of l-dopa: antipsychotics, iron ↓absorption, isoniazid, metoclopramide & pyridoxine only if levodopa alone; no effect if bens./carbidopa used·<br>↑ toxicity: MAOI's, antihypertensive agents,?caffeine ↑L-dopa absorption | **P** 50/12.5mg bid<br>↑q3-7d Max 2g/d<br><br>**S** 50/12.5mg bid<br>↑q3-7d Max 2g/d<br><br>Dosing frequency is 3-6x/day for regular release.<br>An adequate trial is often ~3months of 200/50mg qid, but most pts. respond to lower dosages.<br><br>↑ **dose** by **20-30% if switching** to **CR** if want equivalent dose. CR useful sometimes since duration of action is 25% longer [2] | 100/25mg tid-qid cc<br>200/50mg tid cc<br>(contains phenylalanine)<br><br>100/25mg tid-qid cc<br>250/25mg tid cc<br>100/25mg CR tid cc<br>200/50mg CR bid-tid cc<br>Chew tabs & carbonated drink will ↑absorption even useful for IR tab esp. **good for severe early morning** Sx.<br><br>↑ **protein** foods [18] may ↓ absorption.<br><br>Take **cc** if nausea; **ac** for ↑ absorption of regular formulation<br><br>**Domperidone** 5-10-20mg tid ac to ↓ nausea / hypotension | 54-70<br>87<br><br><br>42-54<br>46<br>58<br>69-99<br><br><br><br><br><br><br><br>~20 |
| **Bromocriptine** [19,20,21,22,23]<br>PARLODEL/generic<br>2.5ˢ mg tab; 5mg cap<br>ergot derivative to D1,2<br>**Cabergoline** [24,25,26]<br>DOSTINEX/generic<br>0.5ˢ mg tab {hyperprolactinemia}<br>ergot derivative to D2<br>**Pergolide** [27,28,29,30]<br>PERMAX/generic D/C by Co<br>0.05ˢ,0.25ˢ,1ˢ mg tabs<br>ergot derivative to D1,2<br>**Pramipexole** [31,32,33,34,35,36]<br>MIRAPEX/generic<br>0.125x®,0.25ˢ,0.5ˢ,1ˢ,1.5ˢ mg tab<br>non-ergot derivative to D2,3,4<br>{starter packs may be available for dose titration}<br>**Ropinirole** [37,38,39,40]<br>REQUIP,g(Requip-24x®)<br>0.25,1,2,5mg tab<br>non-ergot derivative D2,3,4<br>New in USA: Rotigotine Neupro x® a non-ergot DA1,2,3 as 2,4,6mg daily patch aluminum (but recalled→crystals) May ↓ early Sx & ↓ off time in advanced dx. SE: N/V,↑HR/BP/weight,skin rx, dizzy,insomnia | **Dopamine agonist** [41,42] **(DA)**<br>-no disease modifying effects PDRG-UK 14YR<br>(active at various receptors eg. $D_{1,2,3}$ or $_4$ subtype)<br>**B** for bromocriptine, cabergoline & pergolide; but pramipexole & ropinirole are a **C**<br>{lack evidence for any one being better than another} | Common: GI: **nausea**, vomiting, constipation<br>{**may use domperidone to ↓nausea**}, anorexia; CNS: headache, **confusion**, dizziness, depression, **dyskinesia**, **hallucinations**; ↓**BP**,alopecia & ankle **edema.**<br>Serious: seizures, stroke, MI, sudden **onset of sleep** episodes [43,44,45],punding, **gambling** [46,47], ↑ **libido & spending** &<br>{(**ergot derivatives**: pulmonary & retroperitoneal fibrosis, digital spasms, limb/skin pain & Raynaud's like phenomena may occur); & Cardiac valve dx 0.005% with pergolide [48,49,50] & cabergoline [51] ? an $5HT_{2B}$ effect, greater at 3mg/d & at >6month tx. Consider echo at baseline.}<br>CI: protease inhibitors & sibutramine with ergot agents; caution if psychosis & if uncontrolled hypertension | √idiopathic PD, (galactorrhea +/- amenorrhea, hypogonadism, prolactin-secreting adenoma, acromegaly, prevent postpartum lactation, NMS bromocriptine), restless leg Sx<br>-initiate at low dose & ↑ gradually **over 4-6weeks**<br>-for initial PD, levodopa **or** a DA can be used; but DA may have **less motor complications** with tx, but ↑ hallucinations, nausea, dizziness, somnolence & edema than levodopa tx. [1,42 American'02] Not useful for freezing.<br>-at low doses DA have less benefit but still ↑SE<br>-↓ levodopa dose often possible after adding DA<br>-possible preference in **young** (**<50yrs**) PD pts [2,52]<br>-can be given up to 4hrs before surgery<br>-taper dose if D/C med, to prevent withdrawal Sx's<br>DI: ↓ effect therapy: antipsychotics, metoclopramide, nitroglycerin ↓benefit of NTG & omeprazole for ropinirole<br>↑ toxicity: (amantadine, **cimetidine**, diltiazem, quinidine, quinine, ranitidine, triamterene & verapamil with pramipexole only), ciprofloxacin with ropinirole, (clarithromycin, erythromycin, fluvoxamine also with ropinirole, itraconazole, propranolol & protease inhibitors esp with bromocriptine, cabergoline & pergolide), serotonin meds like SSRIs/MAOI ↑risk of serotonin syndrome & sibutramine. | 1.25-2.5mg bid<br>↑q1-2wk<br>Usual 2.5-20mg bid<br><br>0.25mg od ↑q2wk<br>Max 5mg od<br>Pergolide removed USA Mar'07 & CDN Aug'07<br>0.05mg od ↑q7d<br>Max 1.5mg tid<br>{use lower doses if also on Sinemet}<br>0.125mg tid ↑q7d<br>Max 1.5mg tid<br><br>0.25mg tid ↑q7d<br>Max 8mg tid | 5mg tid cc<br>10mg tid cc<br>-less useful as mono tx [2]<br><br>1mg od<br>3mg od<br><br>0.25mg tid<br>0.5mg tid<br>1mg tid<br><br>0.5-1mg tid cc<br>1.5mg tid cc<br>(0.5,1,1.5mg tabs same $ & now new generic)<br><br>1-2mg po tid cc<br>Brand name (higher price)<br>3mg tid cc<br>5mg tid cc<br>now new generic | 103<br>200<br><br><br>558<br>1621<br><br>75<br>144<br>239<br><br>133<br>133<br><br><br>63-69g<br>130-141<br>115/138<br>163/363 |
| **Benztropine**<br>COGENTIN/generic<br>2ˢ mg tab; 2mg/2ml inj<br>**Ethopropazine**<br>PARSITAN<br>50ˢ mg tab<br>**Procyclidine**<br>KEMADRIN/generic<br>5ˢmg,2.5mgx▼tab;2.5mg/5ml elixir<br>**Trihexyphenidyl**<br>ARTANE/generic<br>2ˢ, 5ˢ mg tabs | **Anticholinergics**<br><br>**C** – all<br>**-blocks cholinergic activity in the brain**<br><br>**Best to taper & discontinue over several days (~7) when stopping!** | **Common: CNS: confusion** [53], **drowsiness**, headache, **slow memory; anticholinergic**: dry mouth, blurred vision, urinary retention, **constipation** etc.; rash, ↑ HR & ↓ sweating (over heating).<br><br>Serious: ↑ HR, delirium & psychosis<br><br>CI: narrow angle glaucoma, ileus, BPH, myasthenia gravis, obstructive uropathy | √PD **tremor** (unknown if better for tremor vs other Sx) [54 Cochrane'03], useful for **foot dystonia**, ↓**drooling** [3] & drug induced EPS.<br>As mono or adjunct tx more effective than placebo in improving motor fx. [1 American 2002]<br>Neuropsychiatric & **cognitive SE esp in elderly.**<br>Withdraw very slowly to prevent PD exacerbations.<br>Switching to another anticholinergic may be of use.<br>DI: Worsen Parkinson's Sx with: antipsychotics, cholinergics (eg. donepezil, galantamine, rivastigmine)<br>↑ toxicity with: anticholinergics (eg. amantadine, TCA's, OTCs)<br>(Blind as a bat, mad as a hatter, red as a beet, hot as a hare & dry as a bone) | 0.5-1mg hs ↑q5d<br>Max 2mg tid<br><br>25mg od<br>Max 500mg/d<br><br>2.5mg bid ↑q5d<br>Max 5mg qid<br>↑**salivation**: reports of sublingually Tx with **atropine** eye drops, Atrovent nasal spray, or glycopyrrolate orally.<br>1-2mg hs ↑5qd<br>Max 5mg tid | 1mg bid<br>2mg bid<br><br>50mg bid<br>100mg bid<br><br>2.5mg tid cc<br>5mg tid cc<br><br>2mg tid cc<br>5mg bid cc | 9<br>11<br><br>21<br>36<br><br>9<br>10<br><br>11<br>14 |

| Generic/TRADE (Strength & forms) | Class/Mechanism of Action/ Pregnancy category [7] | Side effects / Contraindications CI | √ = Therapeutic Use / Comments / Drug Interactions DI | INITIAL & MAX DOSE | USUAL DOSE RANGE | $ /30d |
|---|---|---|---|---|---|---|
| **Amantadine** [55,56]<br>**SYMMETREL**/generic<br>100mg cap; 100mg/10ml syrup | **NMDA receptor antagonist**<br>blocks reuptake/↑ release of dopamine via N-methyl-D-aspartate antagonist (NMDA)<br>C | **Common**: **CNS**: (esp in elderly) **confusion**, drowsiness, nightmares, light headedness, **insomnia**; anticholinergic effects, irritability, (less when ↓ dose for age & renal fx); GI upset, ↓BP, ankle **edema** & rose colored mottling on legs.<br>**Serious**: seizures, psychiatric illness, arrhythmias, visual impairment, neutropenia, hallucinations & **↓BP.** | √ PD-modest effect (early to help with **tremor**, later to **↓ dyskinesia**, may help ON effect, better tolerated in young PD pts), antiviral-influenza A, drug induced EPS<br>-300 mg/d ↓dyskinesias ~45% but lasted ≤8months [57]<br>- unknown whether safe & effective for levodopa induced dyskinesias [58 Cochrane 2003]; may ↓fatigue?<br>-avoid abrupt withdrawal→worsen PD/cause NMS<br>DI: ↓ effect of therapy with : antipsychotics & live influenza vaccine may be less effective<br>↑ amantadine levels with: triamterene | 100mg od ↑7qd<br>Max 200mg bid | 100mg bid (8am & 12 noon; or od)<br>100mg tid<br>Trial for ~2weeks before deciding if tx ineffective. [3] | 33<br>45 |
| **Entacapone** [59,60,61,62,63]<br>**COMTAN**<br>200mg tab<br>**Tolcapone TASMAR** 200mg tab -restricted for only previous pts (b/c of ↑LFT's) Phone: 613-941-2108<br>**carbidopa/levodopa/ entacapone STALEVO**<br>-new in Canada<br>50= 12.5/50/200<br>100= 25/100/200<br>150=37.5/150/200mg tab<br>{75=18.75/75/200;125=31.25/125/200} ⊗<br>(do not cut dose in half) | **Inhibits reversible COMT**<br>(peripheral catechol O-methyl-transferase: decreases the GI metabolism of levodopa to prolong the half life & area under the curve without affecting the peak concentration; therefore ↑ effect in the brain)<br>C | **Common**: **nausea**, vomiting, ↑ **dyskinesias**, **urine discoloration**, abdominal pain, ↑ sweating, mood changes & daytime sleepiness.<br>**Serious**: dyskinesia, **↓BP**, **diarrhea** (may present even weeks to months after starting), **hallucinations** & NMS.<br>?? higher prostate cancer with Stalevo [FDA]<br>CI: dobutamine, dopamine, epinephrine, isoproterenol, MAOIs, history of NMS | √ idiopathic PD with wearing-off Sx at end of dose<br>-for **motor complications** to **↓ off time** ~1.5hrs/day (eg. end of dose wearing off), to ↓ levodopa dose, & modestly improve motor & disability [64 Cochrane 2004]<br>-in pts who are **not** experiencing motor fluctuations while on levodopa, entacapone does **not** improve motor scores but improves some quality-of-life measures [65]<br>-combo with levodopa can ↑ levodopa levels ~25% thus **↓ levodopa dose to minimize dyskinesias** & this combo prolongs the levodopa effect<br>DI: ↑HR with dobutamine, dopamine, ephedrine, epinephrine & isoproterenol; chelates with iron; MAOIs a theoretical concern | 100-200mg<br>Max 1.6 g/d | 200mg po tid<br>200mg po qid<br>(with **each** levodopa dose given)<br>**Stalevo**: (Max 8 tabs/d)<br>50= 12.5/50/200 po tid<br>100= 25/100/200 po tid<br>150=37.5/150/200mg tid | 179<br>236<br>175<br>175<br>175 |
| **Selegiline** [66,67,68,69,70,71,72]<br>**ELDEPRYL**/generic<br>5ς mg tab ☎ ▼<br>(also known as deprenyl) | **Irreversibly inhibits monamine oxidase type B** (MAO-B) to decrease the metabolism of dopamine C | **Common**: **nausea**, dizziness, orthostatic **hypotension**, abdominal pain, hallucinations, dyskinesia, rash, **insomnia** & alopecia.<br>**Serious**: arrhythmia,↑HR,↑BP esp. with doses >10mg/d, anemia<br>CI: meperidine | √ adjunct for PD (may aid wearing off effects)<br>-improves disability scores & delays need for ↑levodopa without ↑mortality [73,74]; may ↓freezing?<br>-has very mild symptomatic benefit with **no evidence** for neuroprotective benefit [1 American 2002]<br>-stop 10days before anesthetic (has amphetamine metabolites)<br>DI: ↑ toxicity with: atomoxetine, **amphetamines**, bupropion, buspirone, **dextromethorphan**, entacapone, ephedrine, **meperidine**, methylphenidate, miconazole, mirtazapine, phenylephrine, pseudoephedrine, **SSRI's**, TCA's, venlafaxine | 2.5-5mg od<br>**Max 5mg bid**<br>(given earlier in the day to ↓ insomnia) | 5mg po od cc<br>5mg am & noon<br>(Often used in earlier rather than later PD)<br>Tyramine intake should not be a concern with typical doses | 49<br>90 |
| Rasagiline AZILECT ⊗ 0.5-1mg od $250; 0.5 & 1mg tabs; ↓'s off time<br>SE: headache, arthralgia, ↓BP, dyspepsia, depression,hallucinations & falls.<br>DI: cipro & ↓liver function ↑ rasa level, possible tyramine hypertensive crisis; (renal)<br>↑CNS SE: TCA,MAOI,SSRI,SNRI,cyclobenzaprine,DM,meperidine,methadone, mirtazapine, propoxyphene, St. John's wort, tramadol & vasoconstrictors.<br>Use alone or with levodopa/carbidopa. (high fat-meal ↓'s rasa levels) | | | | | | |

(renal) =↓ dose for renal dysfx ς=scored tab χ=Non-formulary Sask ☎=Exception Drug Status Sask. ⊗=not covered NIHB ✆=prior NIHB ▼=covered by NIHB **ac**=before meals **BP**=blood pressure **cc**=with meal CI=contraindication **CR**=control release d=day **DA**=dopamine agonist **D1,2,3,4**= dopamine receptors subtypes D/C=discontinue **DI**=drug interaction **Dx**=disease **EPS**=Extrapyramidal symptoms **fx**=function **HS**=bedtime **HR**=heart rate **IR**=immediate release **NMS**=neuroleptic malignant syndrome **n/v**=nausea/vomiting **pc**=after meal **PD**=Parkinson's disease **Pt**=patient **Sx**=symptoms **Sz**=seizure **SE**=side effect **UPDRS**=Unified Parkinson's Disease Rating Scale (0=no disability;199=total disability) **Tx**=treatment **wt**=weight

**Epidemiologic**: 100,000 Canadians affected, 0.4% general population, ~3% in >65yr age group, lack of substantia nigra dopamine containing neurons. Website of interest: **www.parkinson.ca**

**Symptoms**: **Resting** rhythmic asymmetric **tremor** (~70% of pts) hands (pill rolling), feet, lips or jaw (not usually head or neck). **Rigidity** (~90% of pts) -lead pipe, cogwheel often in neck, trunk & limbs. **Bradykinesia** (~70% of pts)-slowness of all movements incl. walking. **Postural instability**-often later presentation, shuffling gait, narrow base, festination, freezing & falls. **Micrographia** frequently present.

**Diagnosis**: **Classic**-one-sided signs, resting tremor & good tx response. **Atypical** ~20%, early falls,↓BP, bladder dysfx & lack resting tremor. **Drug Induced**: [75] may take2-6 months to resolve amphotericin B, calcium channel blockers, chemotherapy, cholinergic, lithium,manganese,meperidine,**metoclopramide**, **neuroleptics**, reserpine, SSRI & valproate. **Assoc. problems**: [76] depression/anxiety/psychosis, ↓BP,neurogenic bladder,sexual dysfx,dementia,dysarthia,dysphagia,dermatitis seborrheic, sleep & bowel Δ's.

**Adjunct Meds**: Psychotic Sx: clozapine ☎▼ (~6.25-75mg/d, agranulocytosis 0.6%) [77] or quetiapine (~25-150mg/d) [78]; botox focal dystonia & sialorrhea [79]; Dementia Sx: donepezil & rivastigmine ☎ ✆ but ↑ N/V/ tremor [80]; modafinil ALERTEC ☎▼ 200mg/d may ↓ daytime sleepiness) [81]; beta blocker lack evidence [82]; apomorphine special access (DA:2-6mg SC 3-5x/d prn with domperidone for off-state episodes) [83]; sildenafil erectile dysfx; polyethylene glycol constipation; methylphenidate fatigue but abuse; & Vit E (NOT benefit: [84] DATATOP)

**Red Flags**: early severe dementia; prominent early instability; early autonomic dysfx; no response to levodopa ~1g/d; presence of extra ocular movements, ataxia or corticospinal tract signs.

**Rule out**: Alzheimer with EPS, Benign essential tremor, Corticobasal degeneration, Diffuse Lewy body dx, Drug-induced EPS, Focal lesions, Infectious-postencephalitic, Multisystem atrophy postural hypotension, cerebellar ataxia, Progressive supranuclear palsy early swallowing difficulties, gaze paresis, ? do olfaction test, vascular-lacunar state & Wilson dx.

**Non Drug**: involve patient & family for education, support, **exercise**, physiotherapy, **speech** therapy, occupational therapists (for mobility, safety & driving skills) & nutrition counselling.

**Progression** of the disease- may be more rapid if: onset >70yr, rigid, bradykinesia, dementia, or previous levodopa use but NOT as rapid progression if: male, or resting tremor dominant.

| |
|---|
| **Wearing off**: [1-5] consider **smaller & more frequent LD** dosing liquid form option, an **addition of Sinemet CR**, **combo DA & levodopa**, **COMT inhibitor**, amantadine, selegiline or apomorphine SC. (↓ protein in diet may help) |
| **Dyskinesia**: [1-5] If bothersome consider ↓levodopa dose CR form hard to adjust dose, add amantadine, add/↑/switch DA, possibly D/C COMT/selegiline or consider surgery. **Tremor**: if predominant consider amantadine/anticholinergics esp. in young. |
| If **drug induced confusion/hallucination**: [1-5] May take 1-4 wk to resolve ↓meds in following order→anticholinergic, selegiline, amantadine, DA & then levodopa. Consider tx with quetiapine or clozapine after other possible offending drugs are D/C. |
| Treat when disability present, to control Sx & ↑function, add meds slowly, good history & listen to timing of Sx; deterioration may be due to stress, ↓ sleep, new med or ?H. pylori. If poor medical control may consider surgery. [85,86] |

| Generic/ g=generic TRADE / form | SIDE EFFECTS | MONITOR Annually/if indicated | USES √ COMMENTS/ DRUG LEVEL | DRUG INTERACTIONS (DI) | INITIAL & MAX DOSE | USUAL SEIZURE DOSE RANGE | $ /100day |
|---|---|---|---|---|---|---|---|
| **Carbamazepine** TEGRETOL/generic **CBZ** (100g,200gX▼mg chew tab; 200g mg tab) (200g,400g mg CR tab ☎▼) -avoid humid storage conditions (20mg/ml susp; used in loading dose adult protocol at 8mg/kg Purcell'07) | Common: GI N/V, drowsy, dizzy, **unsteady**, pruritic **rash<10%** may cross react with phenytoin & phenobarb; ↓WBC dose related. **CR tab: less SE** GI/CNS. Rare: aplastic anemia, ↑ **liver enzymes** (GGT/ALK some ↑normally),cardiac abnormalities; **↓serum Na** (SIADH) mild often, but <**125** important; SLE, exfoliative dermatitis, alopecia, ocular effects,↓ **WBC** persistent ~2%, ↓ T3/T4 & Vit K, osteomalacia & neural tube defects (<1%). **Asians** with HLA-B* 1502, ↑↑risk of skin rx. **WEIGHT GAIN = minimal** | CBC q3-6months, Platelets, TSH,LFT, Lytes, **Level** ? ECG for pts >45yrs D Pregnancy Malformation 5% | √**2° Generalized tonic-clonic Sz**, **Partial (1-18yr)**. Not myoclonic Sz; may worsen absence Sz. √ BPAD -acute mania, rapid cycle, mixed & prophylaxis √ trigeminal neuralgia Option: for **aggressive** patients & neurologic dx & cognitive impaired CI: hepatic/porphyria dx; safe in renal dx **Level 17-54** umol/l **-trough** | **↑ Carbamazepine level by:** cimetidine, **clarithro/erythromycin, danazol, diltiazem, felodipine, fluoxetine, fluvoxamine,** grapefruit juice, isoniazid, ketoconazole, lamotrigine, metronidazole, nefazodone, phenobarbital, **propoxyphene,** ritonavir,**verapamil** & valproate **↓ Carbamazepine level by:** phenytoin,phenobarb,St.Johns wort,theophylline **Carbamazepine ↓'s levels of:** **BCP's ~40%,** lamotrigine, phenytoin, theophylline,topiramate,valproate & **warfarin**. **INDUCES P450 3A4 System^** | 100mg bid ↑ 200mg/d q5-7day (to ↓SE) ~2800mg/day **(autoinduction** of P450 system complete in 4 weeks) | 200mg po tid<br>400mg po tid<br>600mg po bid (some clinicians give regular release **bid** in select situations)<br>400mg CR bid (600-1800mg/d) Peds:10-20→35mg/kg/d Mainly an enzyme **inducer** | 33<br>59<br>59<br>90 |
| **Clobazam** FRISIUM/generic (10g mg tab) | Benzo Common: **Drowsiness** (tolerance develops), dizziness, ↓ concentration, anterograde amnesia,↑traffic accidents. Rare: skin rash, paradoxical anger, thrombocytopenia & depression. | ? Platelets U | Alt: generalized tonic-clonic, myoclonic & atonic, partial & absence Sz Broad spectum→tolerance develops | **Few** drug interactions **↓ clobazam level by:** carbamazepine **clobazam ↑ level of:** phenytoin | 5-10mg od 80mg/day | 10mg po bid<br>30mg po hs (20-30mg/d) Peds:0.5-1.5mg/kg/d | 54<br>78 |
| **Clonazepam** RIVOTRIL/ generic (0.5g,1,2g mg tab; 0.25X▼ mg tab) Other Benzo's: **status epilepticus** etc…SE:↓BP,↓resp rate & sedation **Diazepam VALIUM** 2g,5g,10g mg tab; 10mg/2ml **amp** IV at 2mg/min; 5,10,15mg **rectal gel DIASTAT**;10mg/2ml emulsion **DIAZEMULS**. **Lorazepam**[60] **ATIVAN** 0.5,1g,2g mg **po/slX** tab;4mg/ml **amp** IV at 2mg/min **Midazolam VERSED** 1 & 5mg/ml vial, buccal/IM/IV nasal;propofol if refractory | | ? Platelets D | √Myoclonic Sz;Alt→tonic & atonic, absence & infantile spasms +; Panic attack Option: sedative, social phobia, akathisia, acute mania, restless leg syndrome & neuralgic pain | **Few drug interactions.** Tolerance in 1/3 pts in 6 months. ? ↑ Generalized tonic clonic Sz. **Level clonazepam 40-230nmo/l** -useful for compliance, not efficacy | 0.5mg po tid ↑ 0.5-1mg/d q3d 20mg/day | 0.5mg po tid<br>1mg po tid<br>2mg po tid (1.5-8mg/d) Peds:0.01-0.3mg/kg/d | **36**<br>68<br>54 |
| **Divalproex (DVA)** EPIVAL/generic (125,250,500mg EC tab); 1000mg/10 ml vial X⊗) **-prodrug** of VPA; see **valproic acid below** | Common:nausea, diarrhea,dizzy,sedation, somnolence,**tremor** essential ≤20%, dose related, ataxia, fatigue, confusion, headache, abd cramps, hair loss often temp.,**hyperammonemia**,enuresis, menstrual disturbances & ?↑ osteoporosis. **Rare: ↓ platelets**(↓ dose helps) **& WBC, hepatotoxic** esp <2yr,**pancreatitis**,↑blood insulin, neural tube defects→spina bifida 1-2%. **Caution: polycystic ovaries** **WEIGHT GAIN**= ++ (up to 59%, more common in ♀;mean ↑ of **8-14kg**) Pregnancy registry: heart defect & spina bifida 10.7vs2.9% in control gp ↑malformations with valproate Artama05 esp>1g/d[61], eg. neural tube,facial cleft,?hypospadias May↓ **IQ** in newborns. Add **folate** 5mg/d if tx. Concern 1st trimester | CBC,Platelets, LFT **Valproic level** Correct levels up for ↓**albumin** D | √**1°Generalized tonic-clonic**,[127] **Partial, Absence,Myoclonic& Atonic,** myoclonic Juvenile,photosensitive & **LGS** √ BPAD **acute mania,rapid cycle, mixed, prophylaxis** & depression √ migraine prophylaxis; Option: for aggression; Acute Mania -Oral LD 20mg/kg CI in hepatic dx **ADV**: safe in renal dx, ↓ **rash** & less cognitive impairment. **Level 350-830** umol/l **-trough** | **↑ Valproic acid level by:** aspirin, cimetidine, erythromycin, felbamate, fluoxetine, isoniazid & salicylates **↓ Valproic acid level by:** carbamazepine, carbapenems meropenem, chitosan, cholestryramine, lamotrigine, phenobarbital, phenytoin, primidone, rifampin, ritonavir & topiramate **Valproic acid ↑'s levels of:** amitriptyline, carbamazepine epoxide (ie.↑ SE), clonazepam, diazepam, ethosuximide, **lamotrigine** lorazepam, **phenobarbital, rufinamide, &warfarin** **Does not ↓ effect of BCP's** | 250-500mg bid ↑ 250mg/d q1 week 3-5g/day | 250mg po tid cc<br>**500mg po bid cc**<br>500mg po tid cc (1-3g/day) cc= with food Peds:10-15→60mg/kg/d but if <2yr can ↑↑LFT's Mainly an enzyme **inhibitor** | 75<br>**97**<br>142 |
| **Ethosuximide** ZARONTIN (250mg cap;50mg/ml syrup) | Common: nausea, diarrhea, anorexia, drowsiness, hiccups & **headache**. Rare:skin rash Stevens-Johnson, blood dyscrasias, lupus & behavioral changes esp. kids; þ. | CBC,Platelets, **Level** C | √Only for uncomplicated **Absence** Sz. **Does not** protect for generalized tonic clonic Sz.; ↑ breast milk levels **Ethosuximide** good vs DVA & lamotrigine.[197] **Level 280-710** umol/l **-trough** | **↓ ethosuximide levels by:** carbamazepine **↑ ethosuximide levels by:** ritonavir & valproic acid | 250mg od/bid ↑ 250mg/d q1week 2000mg/day | 250mg po bid<br>**500mg po bid** (750-1500mg/d) Peds: 10-15→20-40mg/kg/d | 86<br>**165** |
| **Gabapentin** NEURONTIN/generic (100,300,400mg cap) (600g,800g mg tab X▼,↑cost) **Pregabalin LYRICA** 75-300mg bid ≈$360-500 –partial Sz adult, diabetic neuropathy,neuralgia post herpetic,fibromyalgia 25,50,75,150,& 300mg caps SE: dizzy, ataxia, edema, ↑weight; Rare: **euphoria**, angioedema,gynecomastia DI: glitazones | Common: somnolence, dizzy, ataxia, headache, nystagmus, n/v, blurred vision, tremor, slurred speech, edema, rash ~1%, **behavioral changes** in kids emotional lability, hostility & aggression; {↓WBC≤1%}, **euphoria** **WEIGHT GAIN**= + (appears dose related) | Scr C Teratogenic at tx dosages | Alt: **Partial** & 2° generalized Sz. ≥3yr **-not for generalized Sz** such as juvenile **myoclonic** etc. Option: Neuropathic pain & **Anxiolytic in severe Panic dx & social phobia,** & restless leg Sx Well **tolerated in the elderly**[39] **ADV:↓ rash & safe in liver failure** **DIS**: Myoclonus may be ↑ **3-25** umol/l for compliance, not efficacy | Antacids ↓ by 20% absorption (space by 2hr) NO other signif. interactions With doses >600mg less is absorbed since mechanism is saturated **Does not ↓ effect of BCP's** | 100-300mg tid (↑ 300mg q1day) 3.6-4.8g/d (up to 6.4g) | 400mg po tid<br>**600mg po tid**<br>800mg po tid ↓dose in renal dysfx (900-3600mg/d) Peds:10-15→25-40mg/kg/d | 205<br>**321**<br>387 |
| **Lamotrigine** LAMICTAL/generic (25g,100g,150g mg tab; 5g mg chewable tab) (2mg chewable tab X▼) | **Common:** dizzy, nausea, vomiting, ataxia, asthenia, headache, somnolence, fatigue, ↑ alertness, diplopia, abd pain, rash (1st month→gen. red morbilliform) & ↓ hair. Rare:**Stevens-Johnson syndrome**#, 1st 2months & toxic epidermal necrolysis, ? hepatotoxic, tics in kids & leukopenia, ?? cardiomyopathy. **WEIGHT Gain=neutral effect** **Broad spectrum of Sz activity** Not teratogenic in animals[35], but ↑ risk of fetal death. ↑ non-syndromic **oral clefts**.[89] Pregnancy: ↓ levels considered one of the most safe; ↑ levels in breast milk. | CBC,LFT, **Scr** to ↓ dose if necessary C | √Mono→**Partial** age≥2yr [128] & **LGS.** ADJ: 1°**Generalized tonic-clonic**≥2yr, Alt: **Absence, Myoclonic & Atonic** Option: **BPAD I** acute depression & **Bipolar II** rapid cycling FDA Jun03 Option in new onset geriatric Sz[39] **Rash** 5-10%→life threatening 0.3%#[33] **(If drug related→ D/C at first sign of rash)** **ADV:↓hormonal** dysfx&more **alert** **4-39** umol/l for compliance, not efficacy | **↑ Lamotrigine level by:** sertraline & **valproate** **↓ Lamotrigine level by: BCP's, carbamazepine**,oxcarbazepine,**phenytoin**, phenobarb., primidone, rifampin, ritonavir & topiramate **NO EFFECT ON** P450 enzyme system **With carbamazepine:** ↑ **dizziness.** **Rarely ↓ effect of BCP's**[59]**&folic acid** | 12.5-50mg bid ↑ by 50mg/day **every 1-2weeks** **(to ↓ rash rate)** Peds:0.15-0.6 mg/kg/d start 500-800mg/d | **100mg po bid**<br>150mg po bid (100-500mg/d) Peds: 0.6-15mg/kg/d **If with valproate:** 25mg hs ↑12.5mg/wk→<br>100mg po hs (50-200mg/d) Peds: 0.15-5mg/kg/d | **194**<br>278<br>30<br>99 |

| Drug | Side effects | Monitoring | Indications | Drug interactions | Titration | Dose | Cost |
|---|---|---|---|---|---|---|---|
| **Levetiracetam** KEPPRA g 250, 500, 750mg tab | **Common**: drowsy, dizzy, asthenia, fatigue; depression, psychosis & rarely ↓WBC/Hg. Pregnancy: level may↓, ↑breast milk | **CBC,Scr** C | Adj: Partial Sz→age≥4yr, JME ≥12yr[FDA] Adj: 1° GTC [≥6yr]; option if LGS & absence **ADV**: ↓ rash. **Dose** ↓ if renal dysfx. | **Few drug interactions** **Does not ↓ effect of BCP's** | 500mg bid ↑ 1g/d q2wk 3g/day | 500mg po bid 1000mg po bid (1-3g/d) Ped: 10-60 mg/kg/d | **450** 300 g 873 573 g |
| **Methsuximide** CELONTIN (300mg cap) | **Common**: nausea, diarrhea, drowsiness, hiccups & **headache**. **Rare**: skin rash, blood dyscrasias, lupus & behavioral changes esp. kids; Þ -porphyria concern. | CBC, Platelets, **Level** C | √Only for **Absence Sz**. **Does not** protect for generalized tonic clonic Sz. **Level 53-212** umol/l **-trough** | **methsuximide ↑'s levels of**: phenobarbital, phenytoin & primidone **methsuximide ↓'s levels of**: CBZ, lamotrigine **↓ methsuximide levels by**: carbamazepine, phenobarbital & phenytoin | 300mg od ↑ 300mg/d q1week 1200mg/day | **300mg po tid** 300mg po qid (300-1200mg/d) Peds: 10-30mg/kg/d | **369** 483 |
| **Oxcarbazepine** ⊗ TRILEPTAL/generic 150ς,300ς,600ς mg tab; 60mg/ml susp | **Common**: GI upset, sedation, diplopia, ↓**sodium** >3% & **rash**. A relative of CBZ. **Rare**: skin [SJS&TEN]; Þ concern, angio[edema]. Pregnancy: level may↓. Convert CBZ→ this drug by 1.5xCBZ | As per CBZ C | √Mono→**Partial** Sz in adults & ≥6yr √2° Generalized, not myoclonic/absence **ADV**: ? ↓ CNS SE & rash vs CBZ | Similiar DI's as per CBZ but less. (**BCP's** levels ↓; phenytoin levels↑) Cross sensitivity with CBZ of **25%** | 150mg bid ↑ 300-600mg/d q1week | 600mg po bid 900mg po bid (600-2400mg/d) Peds: 8→10-50 mg/kg/d | **745** 523 g **1100** 771 g |
| **Nitrazepam** MOGADON/generic (5,10mg tab) — Benzo | **Common**: **Drowsiness** (tolerance develops), dizziness, amnesia [anterograde], ↑traffic accidents, dependence, drooling & paradoxical anger. **Rare**: skin rash & thrombocytopenia. | ? Platelets U | √myoclonic & infantile spasms + & sedative/**hypnotic** | Few drug interactions. Tolerance in 1/3 pts in 6 months. ? ↑ Generalized tonic clonic Sz. | 5mg po hs 60mg | 2.5mg po tid 5mg po tid Peds: 0.25-1.2mg/kg/d | 22 **35** |
| **Phenobarbital** generic (15,30ς,60,100mg tab; 5mg/ml soln; 30⊗, 120mg/ml⊗ amp) Special access: 60mg/ml inj | **Common**: **sedation**, **rash** [5-10%], ataxia, dizzy, ↓concentration & cognition, sleep problems, nystagmus, **hyperactive**, ↓Vit D&K, & **behavioral** changes esp. in **kids**. [not ↑ vs CBZ 93] **Rare**: blood dyscrasias, SJS & liver [toxic], Þ | CBC,LFT **Level** D Pregnancy registry: malformations 6.5 vs 2.9% [in control gp]. May↓ IQ. | √Partial seizures (1-12months) Neonatal Sz [Drug of choice], ↑breast milk levels 2° Generalized tonic-clonic (1mo-6yr) LD 20mg/kg **IV**@ 50-100mg/min **Level 65-150** umol/l **-trough** | **↑ phenobarbital level by**: cimetidine, felbamate & **valproate** **phenobarbital ↓'s levels of**: acetaminophen, **BCP's**, carbam&oxcarb-azepine, cyclosporin, dasatinib, estrogen, lamotrigine, rufinamide, theophylline, verapamil & **warfarin** | 60-90mg hs ↑ 30mg/d q1month 240mg/day | 60mg po hs **90mg po hs** (90-180mg/d) Peds: 2-8mg/kg/d | 19 **25** |
| **Phenytoin** DILANTIN (30,100mg cap; 50ς mg chew tab; 6 & 25mg/ml susp; 100mg/2ml vial ✗⊗) (92% phenytoin→ cap & inj; 100% phenytoin→tab & susp) | **Common**: nausea, diarrhea, dizzy, ataxia, ↓ coordination & concentration, sedation, somnolence, tremor, **rash** 5-10% [rarely serious], ↑ LFT [GGT etc], blood dyscrasias, **gingival hyperplasia** [~50%], nystagmus, ↑**body hair**, acne; ↓folic/T4/Vit D&K levels; lupus like rx & **osteomalacia**. Fetal Hydantoin Sx: ↓IQ, nails, face. Fosphenytoin [CEREBYX ✗] IV friendly [at 150mg/min] **150mg Fosphenytoin=100mg Phenytoin** Asians with HLA-B* 1502, ? ↑↑risk of skin rx; Þ concern. | CBC, LFT, **Level** **Folate level** D -May↓ IQ | √**2° Generalized tonic-clonic & Partial** (Not for absence Sz) **LD** 15-20mg/kg **IV** @ 50mg/min (LD option 400mg po stat, then 300mg po q2h x2 doses) **Saturable** kinetics ↑dose→ ↑↑level IV→Purple glove syndrome occurs Correct level up for low **albumin** (**Alb=20g/l→100%;30g/l→40%;>36g/l**→none) **Level 40-80** umol/l **-trough** [steady state >7days] | **↑ phenytoin level by**: amiodarone, cimetidine, cipro, clobazam, **disulfiram**, felbamate, fluconazole, **isoniazid**, methsuximide, oxcarbazepine, propoxyphene, rufinamide SSRIs & **topiramate** **↓ phenytoin level by**: antacid, CBZ, folic acid, **nasogastric feeds** (caps daily in slurry an option, space 2hr), ritonavir, valproate & vigabatrin **phenytoin ↓'s levels of**: amiodarone, **BCP**, CBZ, clonazepam, dasatinib, dexamethasone, folate, irinotecan, **itra-vori-conazole**, lamotrigine, **methadone**, mexiletine, nevirapine, quinidine, rufinamide, theophylline, tiagabine, topiramate, Vit D & warfarin | 300mg hs ↑ 50-100mg/d q1month 400-600mg/d | **300mg po hs** 200mg po bid (300-400mg/d) Peds: 4→8 mg/kg/d IM→ crystallization Caps→like SR product Susp→shake very well | **33** 41 |
| **Primidone** MYSOLINE/generic (125ς,250ς mg tab; 125mg chew tab ✗⊗) | **Common**: **sedation**, rash~5%, depression, nausea, dizzy, ↓Vit D&K level & ↓ libido. {potential 1st dose reaction ∴ start low dose} **-metabolized to phenobarbital & PEMA** - Þ porphyria concern | CBC,LFT **Level** D | √ Partial & 2° Generalized tonic clonic (less effective vs partial Sz than phenobarbital) √ Essential tremor CI: porphyria Þ, ↑breast milk levels **Level 28-55** umol/l **-trough** | **↑ primidone level by**: isoniazid & valproate **↓ primidone level by**: acetazolamide, carbamazepine, phenobarbital (but ↑ phenob. conversion) & phenytoin **primidone ↓ levels of**: **BCP's**, chlorpromaz., furosemide, **lamotrigine**, quinidine, steroids & TCA | 62.5mg hs ↑ by 62.5 - 125mg/d q3d 2000mg/day | 125mg po tid **250mg po tid** (500-1250mg/d) Peds: 50mg start, 10-25mg/kg/d | 25 **36** |
| **Topiramate** TOPAMAX/generic (25,50⊗,100,200mg tab; 15, 25mg sprinkle cap) Caution: metabolic acidosis & ↓ **sweating** [esp. in kids] | **Common**: nausea, dizzy, tremor, ataxia, somnolence, **cognitive dysfunction**, headache, **paresthesias** [-fingers & toes], fatigue, behavioral change, diarrhea, ↓word finding, ↑LFT's rare, **nephrolithiasis&glaucoma**. **WEIGHT GAIN= loss possible** (seems dose & duration dependent & > in ♀) **Renal stones** 1.5% thus ↑ **fluid intake.** | CNS SE ↑ with agents such as DVA. Adjust dose for **Scr** C ♂infant: Hypospadias -Teratogenic at tx dosage; ?concern [144] | √ Mono→Partial & 1° GTC ≥6yrs Alt: **1° Generalized tonic-clonic & Partial** ≥2yr, Atonic & Lennox-Gastaut (LGS) →Age 2-16 ? √ myoclonic & absence Sz √Migraine prophylaxis; √ ↓EtOH [126] **Weight loss ~4kg** ? dose related **Broad spectrum of Sz activity** | **↓ topiramate level by**: carbamazepine & phenytoin (~40%), valproate (~15%) **↑ renal stones with topiramate &**: Aceta, dor & metho-zolamide; & ketogenic diet [?+Kcitrate] **topiramate ↓'s level of**: **BCP's~30%** [esp.>200mg/d], lamotrigine & dva. + dva→ ↓platelet & ↑ encephalopathy | 25mg bid ↑ 25-50mg/d q1week 400-1000mg/d | **100mg po bid** 200mg po bid (200-600mg/d) Peds: 0.5 mg/kg/d start → 5-9 mg/kg/d | **278/542** 424/796 generic/Trade |
| **Valproic acid -VPA** DEPAKENE/generic (250mg cap; 500mg EC cap; 250mg/5ml syrup) | As per **divalproex above** **Depakene generally has more GI side effects than Epival.** | CBC, Platelets, LFT **Level** D Pregnancy registry: heart defect & spina bifida 10.7vs2.9% [in control gp]. May↓IQ [in newborn]. Concern 1st trimester. ↑ malformations with valproate [Artama 05], esp >1g/d [61] | divalproex & valproic acid are therapeutically, but not technically interchangeable meds since they are distinct generic products | As per **divalproex above** | | **500mg po bid** 500mg po tid (1-3g/d) | **121** 179 |
| **Vigabatrin** SABRIL (500ς mg tab, 500mg sachet) | **Common**: drowsy, dizzy, weight gain, fatigue, tremor, psychosis & depression ≤2%, ↑ **behavioral changes** in kids, tremor & **peripheral vision Δ's**. [some are permanent] | Adjust dose for **Scr** U Visual field | Alt: Complex partial & infantile spasm [≥100mg/kg/d may be needed] +. May worsen absence & myoclonus. **ADV**: No skin, blood or liver SE. | **vigabatrin ↓'s levels of**: phenytoin ~30% **Does not ↓ effect of BCP's** | 500mg bid ↑ 1g/d q1week 4000mg/d | 1000mg po bid 1500mg po bid (2-3g/d) Peds: 30-150 mg/kg/d | 422 620 |
| Tiagabine GABITRIL 2,4,12,16mg tab — NOT IN Canada | **Common**: ↓ coordination, drowsy, dizzy, headache, fatigue, asthenia, tremor, stupor nausea & depression. Rare new onset Sz's. | C | Adj: Partial Sz (≥ 12yr) May ↑generalized & absence Sx **ADV**: low incidence of rash | **↓ tiagabine levels by**: carbamazepine, phenobarbital & phenytoin **Does not ↓ effect of BCP's** | 2mg bid ↑ 4-8mg/d q1week | 16mg po bid cc 16mg po tid cc (32-56mg/d) Peds: 0.1→0.4-0.7 mg/kg/d | |
| Zonisamide ZONEGRAN 100mg cap (Special Access) — NOT IN Canada | **Common**: drowsy, ataxia, anorexia, fatigue, rash [<2%] →**sulfa med**, hyperthermia, **psychosis**, **renal stones** [~<4%], ↓weight, ↓WBC, SJS & ↑LFT. | CBC, LFT, **Scr** -harm animal fetus C | Adj: Partial Sz (≥ 16yr) ?√ Generalized, infantile spasms, atypical absence & myoclonic Sz. | **↓ zonisamide levels by**: carbamazepine, phenobarbital & phenytoin **↑ renal stones with topiramate** | 100mg od/bid ↑ 100mg/d q2week | 200mg po bid cc (100-600mg/d) 300mg po bid cc (od/bid) Peds: 1-2→6-8mg/kg/d | |

^ **Carbamazepine ↓level of**: alprazolam, bendamustine, bupropion, clonazepam, cyclosporine, dexamethasone, diazepam, diltiazem, doxycycline, ethosuximide, fentanyl, haloperidol, irinotecan, l-thyroxine, nevirapine, phenobarb, phenothiazines, pregnancy [test], rufinamide, steroid, theophylline, triazolam, tricyclics, verapamil, voriconazole & **warfarin**.

**PREGNANCY**: C=possible risk [evident in animals] D=fetal human risk U=unknown. Registry [N.A. Pregnancy Registry 1-888-233-2334]. Risk ↑if on multiple agents & ↑dose; try for mono tx, split doses & ↓serum level [check level each trimester]. Try to **avoid in 1st trimester. Vit K** [≥10mg/day] in last month.

**GENERAL**: Mono Tx if possible. If ↑Sz or ↑SE: switch. Combos last resort. If stop Sz meds taper ≥2-3months, to ↓Sz relapse risk. Consider stop Sz meds if: Kids Sz free for 1-2yr OR Adults Sz free for 3-5yr. New onset Sz [38]: delaying tx not ↑risk of chronic Sz. Consider **surgery** if refractory Sz.

# **Rash:** ↑dose, ↑too quick, if with valproic or in kids→ ↑rash. **Absence Sz**: **ethosuximide, valproate**, clonazepam, lamotrigine, levetira., clobazam. **Myoclonus**: **valproate**, lamotrigine, levetira., clonazepam, clobazam & topiramate. **1° Generalized tonic-clonic**: **valproate, carbamazepine**, lamotrigine, levetira., oxcarb., phenytoin & topiramate. **Partial & 2° Sz**: **CBZ, lamotrigine, oxcarb., levetiracetam**, valproate, gabapentin, topiramate, pregabalin, phenytoin, clobazam, phenobarb., primidone & vigabatrin. **Young female**: use ↑BCP [50ug dose]/alternate contraception; give **folic acid** ≤5mg/d.

**Drug induced Sz**: amoxapine, amphetamines, antipsychotics, benzo [withdrawal], bupropion, cocaine, dalfampridine, ginkgo, imipenem [& other carbapenems], lithium, maprotiline, meperidine, quinolones & theophylline. **Febrile Sz**: fever provokes Sz [≤5% of kids], often benign & no Tx [acetaminophen or ibuprofen→comfort], phenobarb & DVA but ↑SE.

Þ -porphyria concern √Useful for/in **ADJ**=adjunctive **ADV**=advantage **Alt**=alternate **BCP**=birth control pill **CI**=contraindication **CNS**=central nervous sx **CR**=control release **DIS**=disadvantage **Dx**=disease **EC**=enteric coated **fx**=function **GTC**=generalized tonic clonic **LD**=loading dose **LGS**=Lennox-Gastaut **LFT**=liver function test **N/A**=not applicable **Peds**=pediatric dose **SE**=side effect

FDA Warning [Jan'08]: trials with 11 antiepileptics had baseline ↑ from 0.2% to 0.4% risk for **suicidal behavior** [or ideation]. (Also new is ↑**drowning** risk) =exception drug SK =prior NIHB χ=Non formulary SK. ⊗=not NIHB ▼=covered NIHB =↓dose for renal dysfx ς=scored tab **SR**=sustained release **Sz**=seizure + Consider ACTH [or ketogenic diet]

New [USA]: **Lacosamide Vimpat** ≥17yr add-on partial onset sz, works on slow sodium channel inactivation; 50,100,150,200mg tabs, 50-200mg po bid; ,200mg inj. **SE**: dizzy, fatigue, ataxia, vision [abnormal], headache, nausea, tremor, ↑PR [interval (caution: beta-blocker & calcium channel blocker)], euphoria, ?↓cognition; 2C19 metabolism to inactivate metabolite.

## Table 1: Benefits & Risks [1,2,11]

**Benefits:**

- Simple & highly effective (99.7% if *perfect* use; >92% if *typical* use) {inhibit ovulation, endometrial effects, cervical mucus effects, tubal peristalsis}
- Reduces need for sterilization & abortion
- **Significantly improves menstrual symptoms & regularity**
  - Reduces dysmenorrhea and mittelschmerz, & dysfunctional uterine bleeding
  - ↓ menstrual blood loss (up to 50%), risk of anemia & PMS
  - Alleviates menorrhagia/hot flashes in perimenopausal
  - Convenience of cycle control
- **Decreases incidence of disease**
  - bacterial pelvic inflammatory disease (60%)
  - ectopic pregnancy
  - endometriosis; salpingitis
  - **endometrial** cancer ( >50%) * {*Benefit within 1year of use & persist after DC}
  - **ovarian** cancer (>40%) *
  - ovarian cysts (possible; >60%)
  - acne and hirsutism
  - fibrocystic, benign breast disease (possible; 50-75%)
  - **osteoporosis** (↑ bone density)
  - colorectal cancer (possible) ◆overall cancer

*benefit greatest with long term use (>5yr) & persists up to 15 yrs after discontinuing

**Risks:**

- **venous thromboembolism (VTE)** = ↑ 3-4x with low dose {Absolute risk 1-1.5 per 10,000/year; highest in 1st year}; this risk is lower than risk of VTE in pregnancy (6 per 10,000/yr); ↑ to 10 per 10,000 /yr in women >39yrs of age Kaunitz NEJM Mar/08 (estrogens ↓ activation of Protein C so ↑ risk of thrombus)[3,4,5] May ↓risk: ↓estrogen dose & levonorgestrel/norethindrone/norgestimate. Vlieg '09
- **arterial thrombosis (myocardial infarction and stroke)** - related to estrogen dose ≥50 ug , age >35, smoking, hypertension, and other risk factors for CVD (↑~2-3x); otherwise no ↑ risk over baseline in young non-smoking ♀[6]
- **breast cancer** = controversial; ↑ 1.3x ?; persists for <10yrs after d/c (also may relate to nulliparity/delay in childbearing);
- **cervical cancer** = ↑ 1.5x with long term use (>5yr)[7]; {but may relate to early sexual activity & multiple partners ⇨HPV human papillomaviris} (10yrs' use starting at age 20 may ↑cumulative cancer incidence at age 50 from 3.8 to 4.5/ 1000 ♀)
- **gall bladder disease** = theoretical, but no significant ↑
- does **not** protect against sexually transmitted infections
- may ↑&/or precipitate: hypertension, heart failure, diabetes, gallbladder/liver disease, severe SLE, migraine headaches, depression, GERD, vaginal yeast infections, ↑ triglycerides
- failure esp. if missed doses with ≤20ug estrogen formulations

Tables adapted from RxFiles newsletter – *Hormonal Contraception* – Jan 00

**Drug causes of OC failure**: alcohol -excessive chronic, aprepitant
**Antibiotics: griseofulvin, rifampin** (Others ???: ampicillin, cotrimoxazole, , metronidazole, nitrofurantoin, neomycin, penicillin, rifabutin, tetracycline & tigecycline), **anticonvulsants** (**carbamazepine**, ethosuximide, oxcarbazepine, phenobarbital, **phenytoin**, primidone & topiramate ↑ dose eg. >200mg/day), **antivirals** (nelfinavir & ritonavir), aprepitant, bosentan, modafinil, red clover & St. John's wort.

## Table 2: Contraindications and Precautions [1]

**Contraindications:**

- active thromboembolic disease; current or past VTE
- heart disease: ischemic or complicated valvular
- hypertension (systolic ≥160 mmHg; diastolic ≥100 mmHg)
- history of cerebrovascular accident
- diabetes with retinopathy/nephropathy/neuropathy
- undiagnosed vaginal bleeding
- severe cirrhosis, liver tumour (adenoma, hepatoma)
- known or suspected breast cancer or pregnancy
- < 4-6 weeks postpartum if breastfeeding
- smoker over age 35 and ≥15 cigarettes/day

**Precautions :**

- **Hypertension**-may use OCs EE ≤35ug if hypertension controlled
- **Diabetes** - low dose OCs unlikely to affect glucose control but estrogen may complicate vascular disease
- **Epilepsy** - some anticonvulsants ↓OCs efficacy ↑ OC metabolism; may use backup birth-control method (or OC with ≥ 30ug EE?)
- **Hepatitis, cirrhosis** - avoid OCs if active disease; may use if liver enzymes returned to normal / mild cirrhosis
- **Symptomatic Gallbladder disease** - may be exacerbated
- **Migraine** - avoid OCs if classic aura, complex, age≥35 (↑stroke)
- **Inflammatory bowel disease** - diarrhea may ↓ absorption of OCs requiring backup method; also ↑VTE risk if mod-severe IBD
- **Systemic lupus erythematosus** – inactive/stable SLE ok, but unknown for severe active or if antiphospholipid antibodies/hypercoagulable states
- **Smokers over age 35** - if light smoker (<15cigs/day) or on nicotine patch, can use 20 ug EE product **but still ↑ risk**
- **Older age** eg. 35-55yr & if **obese** BMI>30 due to ↑DVT risk Kaunitz NEJM'08
- **Bariatric Surgery** – may ↓ absorption of OC

## Table 3: Starting Hormonal Contraceptives

**Starting Combined OCs:**

- **most effective if started Day 1 of menstrual period**
- can be started any day up to Day 6
- to avoid weekend period, start on 1st Sunday after period begins
- if started after Day 5 use backup method for first 7 -10 days

**Starting Progestin-only Pill (POP):** irregular bleeding common

- start on Day 1 of menstrual period and daily thereafter
- use backup method for first month
- take pills at the same time each day to ↓ BTB & pregnancy[11]

**Starting Depo-Provera:**

- inject during 1st 5days of menses or anytime if pregnancy ruled out
- repeat inj q12wks ?10 weeks if on meds which ↓MPA level -effective up to 14wk
- return of fertility delayed 4-31(median 10) months after last inj[11]

**Starting Nuvaring:** (if no preceding hormonal contraceptive use in the past month)

- inserted on or prior to Day 5 of the cycle (even if the patient has not finished bleeding). Backup barrier method recommended until after the first 7 days during the 1st cycle.

**Starting Evra Patch:**

- apply on Day 1 of menstrual period; or to avoid weekend period, start on 1st Sunday after period begins & use backup method for 1st wk of 1st cycle only. "Patch Change Day" will be on same day every week.

## Table 4: ACHES - OCs Early Danger Signs [8]

| SIGN | PROBLEM |
|---|---|
| **A**bdominal pain (severe) | Gallbladder disease, pancreatitis, hepatic adenoma, thrombosis |
| **C**hest pain (severe), SOB | Pulmonary embolus or acute MI |
| **H**eadaches (severe) | Stroke, hypertension, migraine |
| **E**ye problems - blurred vision, flashing lights, blindness | Stroke, hypertension, vascular insufficiency |
| **S**evere leg pain (calf or thigh) | Deep vein thrombosis (DVT) |

## Table 5: Side Effects & Their Management [1,9]

- **Breakthru bleeding** (BTB) -most common in 1st 3 months; if persists beyond 3-6 months check for other causes (eg. chlamydia). Change to OC with ↑ estrogen/progestin depending on when BTB occurs in the cycle; may also be related to poor compliance, smoking, DIs
- **Breast tenderness** - if persists beyond 1st 3months rule out pathologic causes; change to OC with less estrogen
- **Weight gain** - may ↑ appetite in 1st month but overall little or no weight gain with low dose OCs & within normal limits for age-related gain; may be cyclical due to Na+ & $H_20$ retention
- **Nausea** - often subsides within 3 months; take at hs with food or change to lower estrogen content
- **Headache** - tension headaches unaffected but hormone related or vascular migraines may ↑ or ↓ esp. with continuous long-cycle; if precipitated or exacerbated by OCs should avoid their use
- **Acne** - sometimes worsens initially but usually improves in the long term; change to ↓ androgenic OC or use topical therapy
- **Mood Changes** – reported; no different than placebo in trials
- **Chloasma** - irreversible and idiosyncratic; exacerbated by sunlight so use sunscreen & reduce exposure; ↓ estrogen dose


**References:**

1. Society of Obstetricians and Gynaecologists of Canada (**SOGC**). The Canadian Consensus Conference on Contraception. J Obstet Gynaecol Can. **2004** Mar;26(3):219-96.
2. Sherif K. Benefits and risks of oral contraceptives. Am J Obstet Gynecol. 1999; 180: S343-8.
3. Venous thromboembolic disease and combined oral contraceptives: results of international multicentre case-control study. World Health Organization Collaborative Study of Cardiovascular Disease and Steroid Hormone Contraception. Lancet. 1995; 346: 1575-82
4. Effect of different progestagens in low estrogen oral contraceptives on venous thromboembolic disease. World Health Organization Collaborative Study of Cardiovascular Disease and Steroid Hormone Contraception. Lancet. 1995; 346: 1582-8.
5. Kemmeren JM, Algra A, Grobbee DE. Third generation oral contraceptives and risk of venous thrombosis: meta-analysis. BMJ. 2001 Jul 21;323(7305):131-4.
6. Acute myocardial infarction and combined oral contraceptives: results of international multicentre case-control study. World Health Organization Collaborative Study of Cardiovascular Disease and Steroid Hormone Contraception. Lancet. 1997; 349: 1202-9
7. Schlesselman J. Net effect of oral contraceptive use in risk or cancer in women in United States. Obstet Gynecol. 1995; 85: 793-801.
8. Hatcher R et al. Contraceptive Technology, 16th edition. New York, Irvington, 1994.
9. Dickey R. Managing Oral Contraceptive Patients, 9th edition. Essential Medical Information Systems, Durant, OK. 1998.
10. Petitti, Diana B. Combo Estrogen-Progestin Oral Contraceptives. NEJM 2003;349:1443-1450.
11. Treatment Guidelines: Choice of Contraceptives. Medical Letter: Dec **2007**; p. 101-108.

| Generation | BRAND NAME Oral Contraceptives (OC) | COMPONENTS E=estrogen P=Progestin A=Androgen | Hormonal Activity E | P | A | $ Cost (12mon) |
|---|---|---|---|---|---|---|
| 1st Generation | MINESTRIN 1/20 ✗▼ | Ethinyl estradiol **20** ug<br>Norethindrone 1 mg | + | +++ | +++ | 225 |
| | LOESTRIN 1.5/30 ✗▼ | Ethinyl estradiol 30 ug<br>Norethindrone 1.5 mg | + | +++ | ++++ | 225 |
| | DEMULEN 30 | Ethinyl estradiol 30 ug<br>Ethynodiol diacetate 2 mg | + | ++++ | +++ | 216 (229 for 28's) |
| | BREVICON 0.5/35<br>ORTHO 0.5/35 | Ethinyl estradiol 35 ug<br>Norethindrone 0.5 mg | +++ | + | + | 202<br>276 |
| | SYNPHASIC (Biphasic) | Ethinyl estradiol 35 ug<br>Norethindrone 0.5 mg x12; 1mg x 9tab | +++ | ++ | ++ | 189 |
| | BREVICON 1/35,<br>ORTHO 1/35, SELECT 1/35 | Ethinyl estradiol 35 ug<br>Norethindrone 1mg | +++ | +++ | +++ | 202-276<br>SELECT **149** |
| | ORTHO-NOVUM 1/50 | Mestranol 50 ug Norethindrone 1mg | +++ | +++ | +++ | 222 Discontinued |
| | ORTHO 7/7/7 (Triphasic) | Ethinyl estradiol 35 ug<br>Norethindrone 0.5 - 0.75 -1 mg | ++++ | ++ | ++ | 276 |
| | | | {7 tabs of each in sequence} | | | |
| 2nd Generation | ALESSE (Aviane $170) | Ethinyl estradiol **20** ug<br>Levonorgestrel 0.1 mg | + | + | ++ | 250 |
| | TRIQUILAR,<br>TRIPHASIL-D/C (Triphasic) | Ethinyl estradiol 30 - 40 - 30 ug<br>Levonorgestrel 0.05 - 0.075 -0.125 mg | ++ | + | ++ | 245<br>228 |
| | | | {7 tabs of each in sequence} | | | |
| | MIN-OVRAL (Portia $170) | Ethinyl estradiol 30 ug<br>Levonorgestrel 0.15 mg | ++ | ++ | +++ | 250 |
| | OVRAL (contains more 'E' than usually recommended) | Ethinyl estradiol **50 ug**<br>Norgestrel 0.25 mg | +++ | +++ | ++++ | 250 |
| 3rd Generation | MARVELON (Apri $163),<br>ORTHO-CEPT | Ethinyl estradiol 30 ug<br>Desogestrel 0.15 mg | ++ | +++ | + | 245,<br>276 |
| | CYCLEN | Ethinyl estradiol 35 ug<br>Norgestimate 0.25 mg | +++ | + | + | 276 |
| | LINESSA (New 2006) | Ethinyl estradiol **25** ug<br>Desogestrel 0.1 Yellow - 0.125 Orange - 0.15 Red mg | ++ | +++ | + | 234 |
| | | | {7 tabs of each in sequence} | | | |
| | TRI-CYCLEN (Triphasic)<br>{TRI-CYCLEN-LO} | Ethinyl estradiol 35ug {TRI-CYCLEN-**LO** 25ug}<br>Norgestimate 0.18 White - 0.215 Lt Blue - 0.25 Blue mg | +++ | + | + | 276<br>LO 217 |
| | | | {7 tabs of each in sequence} | | | |
| | YASMIN (Contain antiandrogenic drospirenone) | Ethinyl estradiol 30ug<br>Drospirenone 3mg {spironolactone derivative & may ↑K+; check K+ x1 e.g. @ 4wks} | ++ | ++ (?) | - | 208 |
| | YAZ ⊗ (Contain antiandrogenic drospirenone) | Ethinyl estradiol **20** ug<br>Drospirenone 3mg | + | ++ (?) | - | 250 |
| | | | **24/4 pill regimen**: 24 active, 4 placebo | | | |

•**VTE**: slight ↑ risk, ? esp. with desogestrel (16 vs 6 cases/100,000 ♀/year, age 20-24) BMJ 2001;323:131-4; NEJM 2003;349:1443-50. {VTE in pregnancy ~ 60/100,000} BNF05

## New Ways and Means…

**Extended Dosing of OC's:** {↓ in menses & associated symptoms}

- **Bi-cycling or Tri-cycling** refers to taking 2-3 consecutive packages of active pills (ie 42-63 days) followed by a week off for menstruation (menses is no different than with traditional dosing)
- method safe & effective {less or shorter hormone free intervals may ↓risk of ovulation}
- **A monophasic product must be used** (bi- and tri-phasics can cause spotting)
  - **SEASONALE (84 day pack:** 84 x Levo 0.15mg + EE 30ug & 7 placebos $250/yr) ✗⊗; & in the USA **SEASONIQUE (91 day pack**: 84 x Levo 0.15 + EE 30ug & 7x EE 10ug)
  - LYBREL ✗NA in USA:FDA approved continuous cycle COC 365 days/year; Levonorgestrel 90ug + EE 20ug

**New Products:**

- YASMIN OC, advantages=less weight gain diuretic effect? & ↓breakthru bleeding
- YAZ OC, acne & PMDD (see chart)
- **MIRCETTE** ✗NA = 28day pill pack with 21 active tabs followed by 2 placebo tabs ; then 5 tabs of estradiol 10ug (↓ risk of missing first active pills of 21day cycle with ultra low dose products)
- **MIRENA Intrauterine System** is a T-shaped IUD with a levonorgestrel reservoir that releases 20ug daily and last up to 5yrs. Decreases menstrual periods (frequency & duration); 20% of users amenorrheic within 1st year. Fertility returns immediately after removal. ($370/**5**yrs)
- **IMPLANON** ✗NA (similar to NORPLANT DC'd Aug02): implantable single rod system **68ug etonogestrol** (a progestin); releases 60-70mcg/d initially, declining to 25-30mcg/d at 3yrs.. **Effective for ~3yrs**. SE: irregular bleeding; .amenorrhea-20% of users at 1st yr; headache, ↑wt, acne, breast pain, mood swings. DI: Cyp3A inhibitors & inducers.
- **LUNELLE** ✗NA (not in Canada) is a monthly injection of estradiol cypionate (5mg) with medroxy-progesterone (25mg); rapid return to fertility

**NA= not available in Canada** ⊘=prior approval NIHB ▼=covered NIHB **HFI**=hormone free interval

**Missed pills:** SOGC Nov08 {#Consider emergency contraception (EC) in 1st week if unprotected intercourse in last 5 days}

- **If 1 pill delayed <24hrs**: take ASAP (as soon as possible). No backup method or emergency contraception necessary.
- **Week 1**: If ≥1 pill missed, take 1 pill ASAP & continue till end of pack. Back-up method x7days. ?EC#
- **Week 2 or 3**: If **<3 pills** missed, take 1 pill ASAP & daily till end of pack; Start new cycle without HFI.
  If **≥3 pills** missed, take 1 pill ASAP & daily till end of pack; Start new cycle without HFI; Backup method for 7 days; consider emergency contraception if repeated or prolonged omission.

Discard any placebo pills. http://www.sogc.org/jogc/abstracts/200811_SOGCClinicalPracticeGuidelines_1.pdf

## Product Selection guided by Signs & Symptoms of…

**Estrogen Deficiency**
- early bleeding & spotting days 1-9
- continuous bleeding or spotting
- ↓ in flow
- absence of withdrawal bleeding
- nervousness
- pelvic relaxation Sx
- atrophic vaginitis
- vasomotor symptoms

**Progestin Deficiency**
- late bleeding and spotting days 10-21
- delayed withdrawal bleeding

**Estrogen Excess +/or Progestin Deficiency**
- PMS
- bloating, edema
- headache (cyclic)
- dizziness
- irritability
- nausea, vomiting
- visual changes (cyclic)
- weight gain (cyclic)
- leg cramps
- dysmenorrhea
- hypermenorrhea, menorrhagia

**Excess Estrogen**
- hypermenorrhea, clotting, menorrhagia
- dysmenorrhea
- mucorrhea
- ↑breast size or cystic change
- cervical extrophy
- ↑uterine or fibroid growth
- thromboembolism
- UTI
- hypertension
- chloasma
- vascular headaches

**Excess Progestin**
- depression
- fatigue
- breast tenderness
- libido decrease
- weight gain (non-cyclic)
- ↑ appetite
- Sx: hypoglycemia, dizzy
- leg vein dilation
- hypertension
- cervicitis
- yeast infection

**Excess Androgen**
- libido increase
- oily skin / scalp
- acne
- edema
- rash & pruritus
- hirsutism (Tx options: OC, Spironolactone 25-100mg BID, cyproterone, drospirenone, eflornithine ✗⊗ Vaniqa Cream BID.)
- cholestatic jaundice

## ACNE

- **All OCs** can be beneficial in acne - due to estrogen binding to sex hormone binding globulin (SHBG)
- Official Acne Indication Alesse, Tri-cyclen, Yasmin, Yaz⊗ & Diane 35/Cyestra-35 ✗▼ $345 g, $425

(Diane 35: ethinyl estradiol 35ug + cyproterone 2mg; Health Canada April 2003 warning:- **not for contraception only**; stop within 4months of acne resolution) *

**Cost** =total 1yr Sask cost ✗ =non-formulary Sk. ▼=covered NIHB ⊘=prior NIHB Sx=symptom Note: **both 21 & 28 tablet packages avail.** for most products (28 packages incl. 7 inert tablets; usually 28 & 21 tablet packages cost the same)

* **Diane 35**: officially indicated for women with severe acne, unresponsive to oral antibiotic & other available treatments, with associated symptoms of androgenization, including seborrhea and mild hirsuitism.

**Emergency Contraception** (EC) within **3**-5days; may interfere with ovulation, fertilization or implantation; drug will not terminate an existing pregnancy; malformations not reported after unsuccessful use; ↓'S from an expected ~8% to ~1% pregnancy rate Med Let 06; **1)Levonorgestrel Plan B** NorLevo OTC ▼$17: 0.75mg tab stat, repeat in 12hr. or 1.5mg x1 only or **2)Yuzpe**: Ovral 2 tabs stat, repeat in 12hr; {or 4 OC pills with ≥35ug EE for each dose}. Gravol to ↓nausea may need to rpt tx if n/v within 1hr. In 2-3wk expect menses 3)Copper T intrauterine ↓$ Flexi-T, Nova-T.

**Compassionate Contraceptive Assistance Program** SOGC Forms & Enrolment Criteria : http://www.sogc.org/projects/ccap_e.asp

{**Multiphasic** pills may have lower hormone dose per cycle, but lack evidence for less adverse effects or advantage over monophasic}

**References**: 1. Biological activity and therapeutic management. OC Chart. Organon Canada Ltd. 1997. 2. Dickey R. Managing Oral Contraceptive Patients, 9th edition. Essential Medical Information Systems, Durant, OK. 1998. 3. Product monographs. 4. www.RxFiles.ca-Jan00.

# Hormonal Birth Control Options [1,2,3,4]

L. Regier © www.rxfiles.ca Jun 10

| | Advantages | Disadvantages & Contraindications (CI) | Failure Rate (% pregnancy in 1st year) / Comments |
|---|---|---|---|
| **Combined OC's**<br>**- typical sequential use** | see RxFiles – Hormonal Contraception. & Supplementary Tables (reversible; other benefits) | @ http://www.rxfiles.ca/rxfiles/uploads/documents/members/CHT-OCs-Color.pdf<br>◆less effective in overweight women [5]<br>CI: several; refer to OC chart – Pg 87 | ◆Failure rate: ≤0.3% perfect use; 3-8% typical use (may be higher with low-dose preps if doses missed) **~ $230/yr** |
| **Continuous Use OC** [6]<br>◆**long-cycle** regimens: continuous administration of monophasic OC for **3**-6[12] months, followed by 7 day hormone-free interval {"missed pills"- management concern after 7 consecutive days}<br>◆any OC with <50ug EE can be used | ◆↓ adverse **symptoms** during pill-free interval (e.g. pelvic pain, **headache**, bloating, swelling, breast tenderness)<br>◆↓endometriosis & ↓polycystic ovary sx<br>◆fewer mod/heavy withdrawal bleeds Legro 07<br>◆♀ convenience: sports, vacations & events | ◆lack long-term safety data (extra 9 wks/yr hormonal exposure)<br>◆slightly higher cost than typical OC regimen (offset by ↓ in feminine hygiene product use)<br>◆initially more **breakthrough bleeding**, but decreases with time (∴long-term ↑quality of life)<br>◆possible delay in recognition of pregnancy | ◆may increase typical contraceptive efficacy<br>◆more amenorrhea days can be achieved with OCs containing 1mg norethindrone acetate NETA than with OCs containing 100ug levonorgestrel [7]<br>◆SEASONALE (84 day pack 84 x Levo 0.15mg + EE 30ug & 7 placebos); equal to taking 4 Min-Ovral packs in a row, avail. CDN. ✗⊗ **~ $260yr** |
| **Vaginal admin of OC's**<br>(short or long-cycle) | ◆avoid 1st pass metabolism which may ↓side effects and improve tolerance. | ◆limited data ◆hormone absorption can be quite high; unknown safety profile for this route.<br>CI: several; refer to OC chart – Pg 87 | **~ $220/yr** |
| EVRA **Transdermal Patch**<br>(3+1 week cycles: 1 patch weekly x3 weeks; off for one week ; can be used consecutively for 9-12 weeks)<br>(Average daily release rate of estradiol 35ug + norelgestromin 200ug) | ◆effectiveness less dependent on compliance (daily action not required)<br>{Missed dose change: ~ 48hr "window of forgiveness"; e.g. patch effective for up to 9 days. If patch comes off or becomes detached for <24hrs, reapply ASAP; patch change day will remain the same. If ≥24hr: Week 1: If 1 day, reapply ASAP & continue; back-up method x7day. ?EC#<br>Week 2 or 3: If <3 days missed, reapply ASAP & continue; Finish cycle & start new without HFI. If ≥3 days missed, reapply ASAP finish cycle & start new without HFI; Backup method x7d; consider emergency contraception if prolonged | ◆less effective if weighing ≥90kg & at ↑ clot risk<br>◆CI: similar to OC's (unclear if risk of **VTE greater**)<br>◆application site skin reactions in up to 20% of ♀<br>◆cycles 1&2:↑spotting rate 18 vs 11% & breast symptoms<br>◆USA patch total levels ↑60% vs 35ug OC, yet 25% lower peak level exposure; **CDN patch different** only 0.6 vs 0.75mg EE | ◆Failure rate: 0.3-0.7% failure rate with perfect use; up to 8% with typical use ✗⊗ **~ $245/yr**<br>◆adhesive works well (<2% of patches required replacement due to detachment)<br>◆similar lipid effects as OC's<br>◆Initiation: 1st day of menses (or 1st Sunday after) |
| **Vaginal Ring**<br>NUVARING<br>(3+1 week cycles: insert flexible ring vaginally for 3 wks; remove for 1 wk)<br>(estradiol 15ug + etonogestrel 120ug released daily)<br>-Store in pharmacy fridge; but stable 4months at room temp. | ◆does not require daily attention {missed dose change: ~ 1 week "window of forgiveness", although serum levels begin to fall in 4th week}<br>◆↓irregular bleeding compare to OC in the 1st cycle<br>◆excellent cycle control & rapid return to fertility | ◆compliance may affect efficacy<br>◆CI: similar to OC's; also uterovaginal prolapse or vaginal stenosis<br>◆vaginitis: ~5-13% of users ◆DI: rifampin ↓level of OC<br>◆foreign body sensation, discomfort, coital problems, expulsion requiring discontinuation:<4% | ◆Failure rate: 0.3-0.8% failure rate with perfect use; up to 8% with typical use<br>◆Initiation: insert between day 1-5 of cycle; in for 3weeks; remove for 7days<br>◆ring expulsion of >3hr a concern ✓ **~$245/yr**<br>{Week 1: backup method required for 7 days after new ring in place. ?EC#.<br>Week 2 & 3: - if <3 days missed; start new cycle & skip HFI; if ≥3 days missed: start new cycle & skip HFI; backup method x7d. EC if prolonged} |
| **Progestin Injection**<br>– IM **q12weeks** for contraception<br>- {q10weeks if on meds that ↓MPA level; e.g. carbamazepine, griseofulvin, phenobarb, phenytoin, rifampin, St John's wort & some other drugs aprepitant, aminoglutethimide, bexarotene, bosentan, felbamate, nevirapine}<br>-max effectiveness considered to be ≤q14weeks (but 2wk grace period option for q13wk regimen WHO/08)<br>**DEPO-PROVERA, generic**<br>(medroxyprogesterone acetate 150mg IM) {USA: Depo-SubQ Provera 104} | ◆effective without daily compliance issues<br>◆option in ♀ with:<br>CI to estrogen,smoker age ≥35, migraine, breast-feeding but may ↑↑ spotting if <6wk post partum, endometriosis, sickle cell disease, on anticonvulsants (↓ drug interactions)<br>◆amenorrhea (~60% at 12 months)<br>◆↓ risk of **endometrial** cancer<br>◆↓symptoms of endometriosis, PMS, pelvic pain, ? ↓PID, ?sickle cell crisis<br>◆↓ incidence of seizures<br>◆few drug interactions | ◆CI: pregnancy, unexplained vaginal bleeding, current breast cancer; current VTE (DVT, PE)<br>◆Relative CI: severe cirrhosis, active viral hepatitis, benign hepatic adenoma, risk for osteoporosis<br>◆disruption of menstrual patterns; unpredictable bleeding in early months, ↓'ing with time<br>◆headache, acne, ↓libido, nausea, breast tenderness<br>◆**weight** gain {56% of users in one study; mean gain 4.1kg; a gain of 5% at 6 months predicts further excessive gain}; but some may lose weight<br>◆mood effects somewhat uncertain<br>◆delayed return to fertility: 4-11months average 9 mo; rate of conception within 24mo of stopping is 90%<br>◆↓ bone mineral density esp. 1st 2yrs; but lack data on fractures | ◆Failure rate 0.3% / year; typical use 3-6.7%<br>◆counsel regarding exercise & diet<br>◆Initiation: administer during first 5 days of menses or anytime if pregnancy ruled out.<br>◆↓ HDL; unknown significance<br>**Risk Factors for osteoporosis**: low body weight (esp. with eating disorders - anorexia), family history, low **calcium** intake, **smoking** & concurrent corticosteroid use.<br>**~ $152/yr, $125/yr g** |
| **Progestin Only Pill (POP) "mini-pill"**<br>MICRONOR<br>(norethindrone 0.35mg tab; taken daily without a hormone free interval) | ◆option in ♀ with:<br>CI to estrogen; smoker age≥35;? for older **obese** ♀; migraine; breast-feeding, may start immediately post-partum (COCs can be considered after 4wks); endometriosis & if sickle cell anemia<br>◆↓menstrual flow, cramping & PMS | ◆CI & Relative CI: as for Progestin Injection above<br>◆headache,bloating,acne,breast tenderness but <than Depo-Provera<br>◆irregular bleeding {may treat with NSAID x10day, low-dose combined OC, or short course estrogen<br>◆missed pill by more than **3 hours** ⇨ requires alternate/backup contraceptive method | ◆Failure rate 0.5% perfect use; 5-10% with typical use **~ $260/yr**<br>◆amenorrhea (~10% of users)<br>◆Recommended Initiation: start on 1st day of cycle or anytime if R/O pregnancy. Taken every day; no pill free interval |
| **IUD-Levonorgestrel (q5 yrs)**<br>MIRENA {20ug/d initial;↓ to 10ug/d} | ◆very effective <7yrs, without daily compliance<br>◆↓**bleeding** (↓menorrhagia & dysmenorrhea)[8] CI=many<br>◆almost half pts eventually become amenorrheic | ◆↑bleeding first 3-6 months; ↓bleeding long-term; cramping<br>◆ high initial cost low-cost long-term; rare uterine perforation | ◆Failure rate 0.2% perfect use; 0.2% typical use<br>◆expulsion can occur (~6%/5yr)<br>◆up-front cost, but eventually less **~ $75/yr** |

Progestin only formulations best hormonal option if **VTE** risk!

✗ =non form SK ✓=prior NIHB ⊗=not NIHB ♀=female CI=contraindication EC=emergency contraception #may EC in 1st week if unprotected sex in last 5 day HFI=hormone free interval OC=oral contraceptive PID=pelvic inflammatory dx PMS=premenstrual Sx POP=progestin only pill Sx=syndrome

**Compassionate Contraceptive Assistance Program** SOGC Form/Info: http://www.sogc.org/projects/ccap_e.asp; **Barrier Method**: {often preferred in breastfeeding}; ♂ **Condom** 85-98% effective, ♀ **Condom** 79-95% effective, **Diaphragm** 84-94% effective, **Sponge** Nulliparous 84-91% effective; Parous 68-80% effective **Spermicide** 75-82% effective (Nonoxynol-9 foam,film,gel,cream,supp,tab; must be in vagina no more than 1hr pre-intercourse; not protect for STDs; irritation may ↑risk of HIV); **Lactational amenorrhea method** 98% during first 6 month after childbirth; day & night only breastfed; & mom amenorrhoeic; **Fertility awareness-based method** typical 75% effective; **No method** 15% effective.

# HERBAL OPTIONS for POSTMENOPAUSAL WOMEN

Originally prepared by: Anne Nguyen PharmD www.cdup.org for the *RxFiles* - © www.RxFiles.ca May 10

| Common name *botanical name* | PURPORTED USE, SELECTED DOSES #, MECHANISM OF ACTION | TOXICITY + | DRUG INTERACTIONS |
|---|---|---|---|
| **Black cohosh** *Actaea (Cimicifuga) racemosa* **NUFEM**, generics, (REMIFEMIN not available in Can.) rhizome/root | vasomotor Sx: **no better** than placebo worse than HT, Newton AnnIntMed'06, Geller'09<br>• limited studies show comparable efficacy to estrogen; one study, showed better efficacy[1]. Not effective in breast cancer survivors.[2]<br>• Onset of action: 2-4 weeks<br>**Dose**: **20mg po bid** (20mg tablet = 1mg triterpene glycoside. Improved manufacturing processes of some products permits this lower dosing instead of **40-80mg** po bid.)[3,4]<br>Proposed MOA: uncertain; may or may not have estrogenic effects[1] | Has been used safely in trials up to 6 months[1,4] (2 months in women with history of breast cancer[2]; does not cause proliferation of breast tissue in vitro[5])<br>Documented: headache, dizziness, GI upset, weight gain, heaviness in legs, cramping[4], rare **liver toxicity** Health Canada '05 & '10, but some products did **not** contain authentic black cohosh (eg. Swiss Herbal) ; 6 liver toxicity reports in Canada.<br>Potential: contains salicylic acid; short term data (12-24 wk) did not show endometrial thickening[3,6] | Documented: black cohosh with chasteberry & evening primrose oil – nocturnal seizures[7]<br>Potential: tamoxifen, antihypertensive - ↑ drug effects[1]; Iron – may ↓ absorption of iron[8] Cisplatin: ↓ cytotoxic effect Rockwell 2005<br>Note: Some Black Cohosh products have DINs (Drug Identification Numbers) and are subject to regulations by Health Canada. Recent trial positive n=304 12wk Osmers 2005 |
| **Chasteberry** a phytoestrogen (chaste tree berry) *Vitex agnus-castus* fruit[4] | ↓ libido, vaginal dryness, dyspareunia (difficult/painful coitus)<br>• although possibly effective for **PMS**, insufficient evidence to support use in postmenopausal women [4,9]<br>Proposed MOA: various effects on FSH, LH, dopamine[4] | Generally well tolerated[4]; used safely in trials up to 1.5yr[4]<br>Documented: headache, GI upset, itching, urticaria, rash, acne, intermenstrual bleeding[4]<br>Potential: avoid in hormone sensitive conditions*[4] | Documented: black cohosh with chasteberry & evening primrose oil – nocturnal seizures[7]<br>Potential: neuroleptics, metoclopramide, oral contraceptives, hormone replacement therapy – interfere with effect |
| **Dong quai** *Angelica sinensis* root | vasomotor symptoms: not better than placebo[10]<br>Proposed MOA: estrogenic effects[4] | Generally well tolerated[4]<br>Potential: **photosensitization**[11], carcinogenic, mutagenic[4] antiarrhythmic[12]; avoid in hormone sensitive conditions* | Documented: **warfarin** – ↑ drug effects[13,14]<br>Potential: anticoagulant, antiplatelet – ↑ drug effects[4] |
| **Evening primrose oil** *Oenothera biennis* seeds | vasomotor symptoms: not better than placebo[15]<br>Proposed MOA: An essential fatty acid, gamma-linolenic acid (GLA) is thought to be the active ingredient, however no good scientific data exists for benefit in postmenopausal women.[15] ?Dose 4-6g/day. | Generally safe[4]<br>Documented: headache, indigestion, nausea, soft stools[4]<br>Potential: unknown | Documented: **phenothiazine** neuroleptic, anesthesia – seizures[4] ; black cohosh with chasteberry & evening primrose oil – nocturnal **seizures** [7]<br>Potential: anticoagulant, antiplatelet – ↑ drug effects[4] |
| **Red clover** a phytoestrogen (isoflavone source) *Trifolium pratense* Flower top | vasomotor Sx: **no** better than placebo to ↓ hot flashes JAMA Jul03, Geller'09<br>cardiovascular disease: ↑HDL; insufficient evidence to support use[9,16]<br>**bone loss:** may ↑ BMD[4,16] ; **Dose**: 4g flower tops po tid,[4]<br>**PROMENSIL** 40mg od (vasomotor); **RIMOSTIL** 1 tablet od (bone/heart)<br>Proposed MOA: contains isoflavaones, has weak estrogenic effect[4] | Documented: rash[4]<br>Potential: avoid in hormone sensitive conditions*[4] | Potential:<br>anticoagulant, antiplatelet – ↑ risk of bleeding; estrogen, oral contraceptives – interfere with effect; fexofenadine, itraconazole, ketoconazole, lovastatin, triazolam – may see ↑ effects of these medications; [4] tamoxifen & letrozole- may interfere with their effects |
| **Soy** (a phytoestrogen; **25g soy protein =50mg isoflavones**) ipriflavone =synthetic isoflavone derivative<br>**-not benefit** hot flushes or symptoms Krebs 2004 Amer J Obstet Gynecol; Cochrane: Lethaby 2007 | **vasomotor symptoms**: conflicting results whether better than placebo for hot flashes.[17,18] Not effective in breast cancer survivors.[18]<br>**heart disease:** Lipids: **no/?** benefit AHA '06; JAMA July7/04; prev ↓cholesterol, LDL&TG [19]<br>**Dose**: **20-50g po od soy protein**[4] (up to 60g for hot flashes)<br>**bone loss: no** benefit JAMA July 7/04; previous results ↑lumbar BMD [20]; but ipriflavone no effect on fracture [21]<br>Proposed MOA: contains isoflavones, has weak estrogenic effects; may block production of thyroid hormone[4] | Has been used safely in trials up to 2 months[4]<br>Documented: constipation, bloating, mood Casini'06, nausea[4]<br>Potential: conflicting results Trock06, thus best to avoid use in patients with breast cancer[4]<br>(preliminary studies did not show endometrial effects[22,23])<br>• 240ml (1 cup) **soy milk** contains ~ 6-9g soy protein<br>• 100g **tofu** contains ~8-14g soy protein (16-28mg isoflavone) | Documented:<br>theophylline - ↑ theophylline by ipriflavone (semisynthetic isoflavone soy derivative)[11]<br>thyroxine – ↓ thyroxine levels[24]<br>**Food source may be preferred over supplements**<br>Potential:<br>estrogen – ?antagonize estrogen replacement therapy<br>tamoxifen – ↓ effect of tamoxifen<br>warfarin -↓ anticoagulant effect Cambria-Kiely 2002 |
| **Wild yam** *Dioscorea villosa* Rhizome/root | ↓ libido, vaginal dryness: insufficient evidence to support use[4,9]<br>Proposed MOA: progesterone precursor; note that conversion to progesterone does not occur in the human body, ∴ may not be of value. Less useful than compounded progesterone cream.[3,4] | Generally well tolerated<br>Documented: emesis (large doses)[4]<br>Potential: avoid in hormone sensitive conditions*[4] | none reported[4] |
| **VALERIAN** *Valeriana officinalis* root[25] | **insomnia**:[26] {NYTOL NATURAL SOURCE, UNISOM NATURAL SOURCE}<br>**Dose**: 400-800mg po hs<br>Proposed MOA: mediate release of GABA.[24] | Has been used safely in trials up to 28 days.[4]<br>Documented: Withdrawal symptoms (cardiac failure, delirium)[27], ataxia, hallucination, ↑ muscle relaxation, hypothermia[23], restlessness & palpitations (paradoxical)[23] | Documented: none[25]<br>Potential: alcohol, barbiturates, benzodiazepines, opiates – ↑ CNS effects[25] |

BMD=bone mineral density **MOA**=mechanism of action **Sx**=symptoms * **hormone sensitive conditions** = breast, uterine or ovarian cancer, endometriosis & uterine fibroids[28] + Avoid herbal products in pregnancy/lactation.

# **Doses** provided only for products which **may** be more effective than placebo. **Purity** of compounds a concern & may affect dosing. **Herbal products: little evidence to support use.**

**Ginseng:** limited evidence for or against benefit; SE: headache, sleep problems & GI effects, DI: warfarin (may ↓ INR)

**Ginkgo biloba:** not included as not efficacious for memory enhancement in a 6 week trial.[29] The longest study conducted by National Institute of Aging was ineffective. Dekosky GEM n=3,069 6.1yr follow-up. Jama/08

**Kava kava:** not included as it was pulled off the Canadian market in August 2002 due to liver toxicity.

**St. John's Wort:** sometimes for mild-moderate depression (not major depression JAMA APR01 & APR02), but has many drug interactions.

Original Reviewers: **Janet Webb** BSc(Pharm), MSc(Med) (drug information pharmacist,BC); **Brent Jensen** BSP (The RxFiles); **Suzanne Montemuro**, MD, CCFP (FM Vancouver, BC)

**Review**: Complementary & alternative medicine for menopausal symptoms (Ann Intern Med 2002 & Arch Intern Med 2006). 30 **StopFlash**: contains 8 herbs eg. black cohosh, valerian, dong quai etc & 3 essential oils; no good evidence for efficacy.

**Non-Hormonal Hot Flush Options**: stop smoking; some evidence: SSRIs eg. paroxetine in breast cancer pts, SNRIs venlafaxine, gabapentin & soy isoflavones (generally less effective than estrogen); conflicting data for clonidine Nelson JAMA 2006; Huang '08

# POSTMENOPAUSAL PHARMACOTHERAPY Comparison Chart

## ESTROGEN -ORAL (3A4 inhibitors may ↑estrogen level)

- ↓MP Sx -short term,low dose & ↓hip fracture risk (↑biliary tract Dx)
- ↑stroke/clot HR1.4; ↔CHD or breast cancer;WHI estrogen only 48
- start low-dose 0.3mg to ↓SE uterine bleed; tender breast→↑cancer risk • +Ca &Vit D
- tapering when DCing 49; option but similar SE to just stopping

**Combination HT: RISKS > benefit over 5+ yrs** WHI: NNH=88 ; **see note†**. risk less in young 50-59yr ♀. Additional benefit of estrogen: prevent PMO/fractures, ?↓colo-rectal cancer. Many possible benefits have been called into question following large scale RCTs (HERS, WHI, WHIMS, HABITS).

| Source | Generic Name | TRADE Name / Strength | Equivalent / Usual Dose | $/Yr |
|---|---|---|---|---|
| Equine | Conjugated equine est. (CEE) | PREMARIN 0.3, 0.625 WHI estrogen only, 1.25 mg tab ⊗ | 0.625mg po OD | 160 |
| plant | Conjugated estrogen sulfate | C.E.S. 0.3, 0.625, 0.9, (1.25 D/C by Co) mg tab | 0.625mg po OD | 84 |
| plant | Micronized estradiol-17β | ESTRACE 0.5, 1 WELL-HART 50, 2 mg (scored tabs) | 1mg po OD | 146 |
| plant | Estropipate (estrone sulfate) | OGEN 0.625, 1.25, 2.5mg (scored tabs) D/C by Co ✗ | 0.625mg po OD | 109 |
| equine | CEE + MPA (Blister-card) † | PREMPLUS 0.625mg tab + 2.5mg tab (or 5mg tab) | 1 tab of each OD ?soon D/C | 175 |
| synth | Ethinyl estradiol EE /norethindrone NE | FemHRT EE 5μg/d + NE 1mg/d tab ✗▼ | 1 tab po daily | 315 |

Estradiol/norethindrone 0.5/0.1mg & 1/0.5mg tab OD Activelle & LD ✗ ⊗ $440. Estradiol/drospirenone 1/1mg tab OD Angeliq ✗ ⊗ $315

## ESTROGEN -TRANSDERMAL/TOPICAL

- ↓MP Sx; prevent PMO; ↓gallbladder dx & VTE than oral
- alternative to oral; maybe preferred if liver dysfx, smoker or hypertriglyceridemia {↓LDL, ↔/↑HDL, ↓TGs}; but long-term risk/benefit still unknown.
- **patch**: rotate sites (abdomen/thighs/buttocks)
- **gel: do not rotate sites** (arm, abdomen or thigh)
- **TRI-EST Cr.** -controversial: promoted as "bio-identical"; SOGC: *no advantages & expensive*

| Source | Generic Name | TRADE Name / Strength | Equivalent / Usual Dose | $/Yr |
|---|---|---|---|---|
| plant | Estradiol-17β **Patch** | ESTRADERM 25, 50, 100 μg/d Reservoir (cannot be cut) ☎▼ | 50μg twice/wk | 430 |
| plant | ESTALIS-SEQUI = $387 ☎▼ | ESTRADOT 25, 37.5, 50, 75, 100 μg/d Matrix (Inter-changeable) ☎▼ | 50μg twice/wk smallest size | 355 |
| plant | VIVELLE DC 2003 50μg/d x14d, then | SANDOZ-ESTRADIOL DERM 50,75,100 μg/d Matrix ☎▼ | 50μg twice/wk | 287 |
| plant | ESTALIS 140/50 or 250/50μg/d x14d | OESCLIM 25, 50 μg/d Matrix ☎▼ | 50μg twice/wk | 330 |
| plant | {CLIMARA Pro E2 45ug, levonorgestrel 15ug; Apply once a week ✗ ⊗ $510} | CLIMARA 25, 50, 75, 100 μg/d Matrix ☎▼ | 50μg **weekly** | 343 |
| pl/syn | **Combination Patch** | ESTRACOMB D/C by Co 1.2 50... x14d; 1.2: NE 250... x14d ☎▼ | twice wk (cyclic) | 366 |
| pl/syn | Estradiol-17β/norethindrone | ESTALIS E2 50μg/d + NE 140μg or 250μg Matrix ☎▼ | twice/wk **(continuous)** | 387 |
| plant | Estradiol-17β **Topical Gel** | ESTROGEL 0.75mg/1.25g {to each arm daily} ☎▼ | 2.5g(1.5mg) daily (as directed) | 410 |
| plant | Estriol/Estrone/Estradiol Crm. | TRI-EST Cr 2.5mg/g **compounded** - 80/10/10% ✗ ⊗ | Apply ~ 1g daily | ~ 285 |

## ESTROGEN -VAGINAL –with ↑tx transmucosal absorption↓

- for **urogenital** Sxs: Cody'09 atrophy/dryness/stress incont.
- **less systemic** effect (but creams may require progesterone)

| Source | Generic Name | TRADE Name / Strength | Equivalent / Usual Dose | $/Yr |
|---|---|---|---|---|
| equine | Conjugated estrogens | PREMARIN Vag. Cr 0.625mg/g Off-label use: apply to nostrils to ↓ nosebleeds | 0.5-2g pv HS(cyclic 3wk/1wk ✱) | 92-250 |
| plant | Estradiol-17β | VAGIFEM Vag. Tab 25μg {initial: 1tab vag OD x2wks} | 1 tab per vag twice/wk | 359 |
| plant | Estradiol-17β | ESTRING Vag. Ring 2mg (7.5μg/day) | vaginally every 90 days | 343 |

## PROGESTAGENS - ORAL

- for endometrial protection in women on ERT with an intact uterus; dose required depends on ERT
- if continuous regimen, will prevent bleeding • þ concern

| Source | Generic Name | TRADE Name / Strength | Equivalent / Usual Dose | $/Yr |
|---|---|---|---|---|
| synth | Medroxyprogesterone (MPA) • may ↓HDL; † | PROVERA 2.5, 5, 10 mg scored tabs (14days Tx q 3 months ??use limited) ← | 2.5mg po OD promotes amenorrhea; 5-10mg po X10-14 d/mo | 73; 63-84 |
| plant | Micronized progesterone • less breakthrough bleeding | PROMETRIUM 100mg cap • has peanut oil • sedating (give doses ≥200mg at HS); ?less SE's ☎✆ | 100-200mg po HS; 200-300mg po X10-14 d/mo | 520-999; 360-617 |

- **Progesterone cream** 2.5, 5 &10% can be **compounded**; lack data on absorption, serum levels & efficacy (apply to thigh, inside of upper arm, abdomen) ✗ ⊗ — Apply ~ 1g daily — ~ 260

## ANDROGENS (T=testosterone)

- for symptoms of androgen deficiency post bilateral oophorectomy & post-menopause; ↓ abdom. fat & TBW.[51]
- studies re. optimal prep, dose & long-term safety are lacking

Testosterone 1% Gel ANDROGEL ✗ ⊗; ♂ 2.5-5g od $130; data lacking in ♀

| Generic Name | TRADE Name / Strength | Equivalent / Usual Dose | $/Yr |
|---|---|---|---|
| Testosterone & Estradiol Inj. | CLIMACTERON inj D/C Dec'05 testosterone enanth. 150mg † + estradiol dienanthate 7.5mg/1&5ml vial ✗▼ | **0.5ml** IM Q4-6 wks (+/- 0.5ml DELESTROGEN †) | 175 (<200) |
| Testosterone undecanoate | ANDRIOL 40mg cap (data lacking in ♀) | 40mg po alternate days | 244 |
| Testosterone Vag. Ointment | T-propionate 2%; Micronized-T 0.125% (compounded) ✗ ⊗ | M-T 0.125%: 0.2-0.4ml per vag. OD | 500 |

## SERMs (2nd generation) (antiresorptive)

- prevent/treat PMO; no stimulation of breast or endometrium
- SE: flashes hot, cramps leg, edema peripheral • ?use to ↓breast ca postmenopausal

| Generic Name | TRADE Name / Strength | Equivalent / Usual Dose | $/Yr |
|---|---|---|---|
| Raloxifene ✗ | EVISTA 60mg tab (new generic) | 60mg po OD | 870 630 generic |

• does not control ♀ MP symptoms, may worsen them • no breakthru bleeding • ↓vertebral #only • ↓LDL, ↔HDL or TG; ↑VTE NNH=143 8yr CORE like estrogen; ↔CV events in low more/ high (Ruth: but ↑fatal stroke NNH=250 5.6yr) CV risk♀; ↓invasive breast ca MORE/STAR but ↑non-invasive breast ca. ☎ for pts unable to tolerate, or not respond in 1yr to etidronate & calcium DIDROCAL

## Parathyroid hormone

osteosarcoma in rats; leg cramps, ↑Ca++, ↓BP, ↓back pain. Bisphosphonate given pre or concurrently may blunt PTH tx effect. For **GIO** this is a tx option.

| Generic Name | TRADE Name / Strength | Equivalent / Usual Dose | $/Yr |
|---|---|---|---|
| Teriparatide (1-34 of PTH) [52,53] (anabolic agent) | FORTEO 750ug/3 ml pen store in fridge ↓ vertebral & non vertebral # (↑osteosarcoma risk: Paget's pts, unexplained ↑AlkPhos & Hx bone radiotherapy) ✗ ⊗ | 20ug SC OD (Max ≤ 18mo tx) -some inj site reactions | 9,000 |

## BISPHOSPHONATES

- ↓vertebral, non-vertebral & hip # 2° prevention
- most effective agents in preventing/treating PMO (antiresorptive)
- minimal SE (altered taste, GI irritation & bone pain; rare: ocular disorder, jaw necrosis, ?A fib)
- no effect on MP symptoms, CHD, lipids, breast, endometrium
- long term: alendronate x10yr seems safe, approved 1996 (but ? bone suppression, ? cyclic q 5yr) [54]

| Generic Name | TRADE Name / Strength | Equivalent / Usual Dose | $/Yr |
|---|---|---|---|
| Etidronate ↓ vertebral # only & Calcium | DIDROCAL etidronate 400mg **x14d**; then Ca++ 500mg **x76d** | po daily (hs or ~2hr ac) | 230 160 generic |
| Alendronate $360 (C) Fosavance 70mg alen+Vit D5600 (• ↓ risk of esophageal irritation: give 250ml water only & sit up ≥30min) | FOSAMAX 10&70mg tab; 40mg tab Paget's; (5mg tab ✗ & 70mg soln ☎) ⊗ (**PMO prevention**: 5mg/day, ~35mg/wk; **PMO Tx**: ≥70mg/wk) ☎✆ | 10 mg po OD am ~1hr ac; 70mg po weekly ~1hr ac | 520; 710 400 generic |
| Risedronate Actonel Plus Ca 35mg rise+Calcium ✗ ⊗ | ACTONEL 5,35, 75 D/C, 150mg PMO Tx; 75mg odx2 qmon $690 ⊗; 5mg od=$445, 30 Paget's mg tab ☎✆ | 35mg po weekly ~1hr ac | 710 360 generic |
| Pamidronate (D) | AREDIA 30,60,90mg IV {zoledronic Aclasta 5mg IV/yr ☎✆ Paget's $740} √GIO ?q2yr ☎▼ | 30mg IV 2hr D5W q3mon | 450 |

• **HTA Evidence:** 1) Teriparatide & some bisphosphonates alend. & rised. have a demonstrated direct impact on 2° prevention of clinically important #; 2) Neither teriparatide nor bisphosphonates have a demonstrated impact on 1° prevention of clinically important #; 3) Alendronate generic most cost-effective.[55]

## MISC

**Vaginal Moisturizer** REPLENS • useful alternative to vaginal estrogen for urogenital symptoms (**vaginal dryness**)[56] ; ?↓sperm motility • Apply HS ~3X/week; 8pack = $20 ✗ ⊗

**Calcitonin (Salmon) Nasal** MIACALCINg ☎✆ pts unable to tolerate/not responding in 1yr to bisphosphonates • ↓vertebral #only • ↓vertebral # pain acute • Dose: 200IU OD (alternate nostrils) $720/yr (C)

**Oral Contraceptives (low-dose)** • perimenopause option for symptomatic, healthy non-smokers level I evidence; HT also used to control symptoms level III evidence (less effective for cycle control/contraception)

**Calcium** ▼ 1000-**1500mg** daily (Foods Ca++: Milk 1 cup=~300mg, cheese 30g=~200mg, tofu 1/2 cup=~200mg). PMO: Stop smoking! **Vit D** 400-**800 IU/d** esp D3 (often in **multivitamin** & Ca++ products); **800** -1000-2000 **IU/d** in elderly/dietary deficiency[57]

☎ =EDS ✗ =non-formulary Sask ✆ prior approval NIHB ⊗not covered NIHB ▼covered NIHB **Cost**=retail cost Sask **BP**=blood pressure **CHD**=coronary heart dx **CV**=cardiovascular **E2**=estradiol 17β **GIO**=glucocorticoid-induced osteoporosis **GI**=stomach **HT**=hormone tx **MP**=menopausal **PMO**=postmenopausal osteoporosis **SE**=side effect **TBW**=total body weight **VTE**=venous thromboembolism #=fracture † may add 0.5ml estradiol valerate inj. Delestrogen in same syringe to ensure estrogen component; requires progestagen opposition in ♀ with uterus. =↓dose for renal dysfx

✱ after initial, short-term tx ~1-2 wk, often taper/↓ to lowest effective dose (eg. 1-3Xper wk); **DI**: ↑estrogen level by 3A4 inhibitors or ↓level by inducers. **Other**: HT Estrogen regimens generally are **1/6-1/3 the estrogen** found in oral contraceptives.

NEW: **Denosumab Prolia** Not in Canada target RANK ligand inhibit osteoclasts, 60mg SC q6month; may ↑infection, & ??jaw necrosis & cancer. **† Combo HT (CEE 0.625mg+MPA 2.5mg od)**: ↑MI, stroke, clot, biliary tract dx, dementia & ovarian/?lung/breast ca 2x risk; NNH=50 if older & family ca hx & density WHI '02 58

**Drug induced** osteoporosis: ↑alcohol, antacid aluminum, antiepileptic carbamaz., phenobarb, phenytoin & primidone, antineoplastic eg. aromatase inhibitor, LHRH agonist, **corticosteroid**, glitazone rosi & pio, heparin if Tx>30d, levothyroxine ↑dose, medroxyprogesterone >2yr Tx, ?PPI, smoking, tenofovir & ↓testosterone in ♂.

**10yr ♀ Absolute # Risk**: **High** >20%→Age T Score=Age 50 T-3.9, Age 55 T-3.4, Age 60 T-3, Age 65 T-2.6, Age 70 T-2.2, Age 75 T-2.1, Age 80 T-2, Age 85 T-2.2. **Low or moderate**: ↑to next level if on prednisone >2.5mg for >3mon or if fragility # after age 40. Frax: http://www.shef.ac.uk/FRAX/index.htm

**WHO FRAX # Risk**: age, gender, personal # history, BMD femoral neck, ↓body mass index kg/m², steroid use, 2° Osteo eg. rheumatoid arthritis, parental hip #, current smoker, alcohol ≥3drink/day. Consider **Tx**: if **hip or spine #**; or if **HIGH** # risk: ↓BMD ♀PM,♂≥50yr & ↑risk-eg. 10yr Risk→hip ≥3% or major # ≥20%.

There has been renewed interest in herbal products. Two recent randomized trials have shown no effect in adults [2] & kids [3] with **Echinacea** for the common cold. For **ginseng** in the form of Cold-fX a recent cold trial [4] is promising, but has limitations [5]. Plus we await publication of the NIH sponsored osteoarthritis GAIT [6] trial with **glucosamine & chondroitin**. Even despite no direct evidence, Lakota's (which contains glucosamine plus **8** other ingredients) continued marketing efforts has generated much interest in herbal remedies.

**Herbal Products:**

| AGENT | POSSIBLE USE / LIMITED EVIDENCE | SIDE EFFECTS, CI, DI | DOSE | COST |
|---|---|---|---|---|
| **Ginseng** root extract χ ⊗<br><br>**Cold-fX** [4,5,8,9]<br>200mg CVT-E002® cap<br>300mg CVT-E002® Extra strength cap<br>Liquid available<br>(~95%Panax quinquefolium)<br>North American ginseng<br><br>(CVT-EOO2= **Immunity-FX**) | **Treat** at onset of cold/flu symptoms or help **prevent** cold/flu symptoms<br><br>(?? Activates macrophages / ??enhance acquired immune response, only preliminary not conclusive evidence)<br><br>Less people acquired at least 1 cold in the treatment group, although any difference did not reach significance. Differences were statistically significant (in favor of treatment) for those suffering recurring colds. Cold duration was ↓. However, cold or flu confirmation testing was not done.[4] | SE: From other ginseng products reports of→ nervousness, excitation, diarrhea, insomnia, inability to concentrate, headache, hypertension, epistaxis, allergies & skin eruptions.<br>CI: pregnant & lactating women, kids <12 or if allergy to herb<br>DI: **alcohol**→ may ↑ alcohol clearance from the body<br>**corticosteroids** →herb may affect steroid concentrations<br>**estrogens/corticosteroids**→ herb may have additive effects (reported mastalgia & postmenopausal bleeding)<br>**furosemide**→ report of diminishing furosemide effect<br>**heart & blood pressure meds**→ herb has negative chronotropic & inotropic activity, as well as possible ↓BP<br>**hypoglycemics** → herb may add to hypoglycemic effect<br>**MAOI's/neuroleptics**→may inhibit reuptake of neurotransmitters & ↑ tremor/mania thus contraindicated<br>**mood stabilizers**→herb may induce mania<br>**oral contraceptives**→ herb may interfere in effectiveness of sex hormone treatment<br>**sedatives**→ herb may potentiate/antagonize sedative SE<br>**warfarin ↑↓ INR** → herb may cause ↑ bleeding by itself or ↓ INR (Case reports [10]) | **200mg caps as follows:**<br>Treat: Day 1→ 3cap tid<br>Day 2→ 2 cap tid<br>Day 3→ 1 cap tid<br>then 1 or 2 caps/d until feeling better (7d=~25 caps)<br>(Not labeled indication by Health Canada)<br><br>Prevent: 1 cap bid x 8-12wk (USA study [22])<br><br>New cold **Prevention** CDN trial dose used: [4]<br>2cap od x **4 month**<br><br>(on an empty stomach) | $14/ 18 caps<br><br>$25/ 60 caps<br><br>$55/ 150 caps |
| **Glucosamine** χ ⊗<br>500mg tab/cap...<br>Currently better evidence with the **sulfate** Guide 12, Cochrane 18 **salt** than the hydrochloride salt Gait, 18, 19 | Adjunctive symptomatic relief of osteoarthritis. (may have some efficacy in a small group of pts with moderate to severe pain [6,11,12])<br>-Consider stopping IF not some relieve of pain after 3months therapy | SE: may cause GI side effects such as diarrhea.<br>CI: allergy (shellfish), pregnant & lactating women<br>DI:<br>**Hypoglycemics/insulin**→does not ↑HgA1C [13], may cause insulin resistance<br>? ↑ resistance to doxorubicin & etoposide. | 500mg po tid<br><br>Max 1500mg/day<br><br>(Well absorbed) | $12/ 120 caps |
| **Lakota Joint Care Formula** [7] χ ⊗<br><br>Capsule contains:<br>(**Glucosamine Sulfate** 150mg & **Glucosamine HCL** 150mg, Boswellian extract, Collagen type 2, White Willow bark powder, Devil's Claw, Sarsparilla, Yucca root, Feverfew leaf & Bromelain) | For arthritis pain & to ↓ cartilage breakdown<br><br>(?possibly effective; some evidence for **glucosamine,** but at higher doses; but also contains **8** other ingredients lacking outcome evidence).<br>Consider stopping IF not some relieve of pain after 3months therapy | Some GI irritaion (caution if peptic ulcer)<br>CI: pregnant & lactating women, Reye's syndrome, kids <12 or if allergy (to herbs , shellfish or ASA)<br>DI:<br>**Antihypertensives**→ Devil's Claw may further ↓BP & can affect HR & contractility<br>**ASA/Warfarin**→White Willow Bark - contains salicin & therefore may have additive effect to ASA; Feverfew - may inhibit platelet aggregration; Bromelain - may have additive anticoagulant/platelet effects (↑ bleeding risk)<br>**Digoxin**: Sarsparilla may ↑digoxin absorption<br>**Hypoglycemics/insulin**→glucosamine may cause insulin resistance<br>**Iron**→may precipitate because of high tannin content | Initially 4-6 capsules/d with meals, then decrease to 2-4caps/d to maintain benefit<br><br>Max 9 capsules/d | $40/ 120 caps |
| **Lakota Osteo** χ ⊗: contains only Collagen type 2 & L-proline | | | | |

**ac**=before **ASA**=aspirin **BP**=blood pressure **CI**=contraindication **DI**=drug interaction **Dx**=disease **Fx**=function **HR**=heart rate **hx**=history **NS**=non significant **pts**=patients **rx**=reaction **SE**=side effects χ not Sask. formulary ⊗ not NIHB

**Summary of the recent Cold-fX trial for PREVENTING colds** (American Ginseng: Panax quinquefolium) [4,5]

General: Cold-fX was studied in 323 adults (age 18-65) with a history of 2 colds in the previous year; Cold-fX was given 400mg (2 caps)/day vs placebo for ~4months from Sep 2003 to April 2004 in Edmonton Alberta. (Trial funded by CV Technologies Afexa; 4 of 6 authors have connection with company)

Results: 55 vs 64% NS had 1 cold Jackson defined; 10 vs 22.8 % had ≥2 colds during the 4 months; & Duration of cold: 8.7 vs 11.1days (2.4 days less)

Limitations: ? what is the active ingredient & mechanism; Jackson 2 vs 6 day score used thus only more severe illness were evaluated; not intention to treat analysis, symptom self-reporting & many excluded (if vaccinated against influenza in the previous 6 months; if MS, TB, diabetes, cancer, lupus, HIV, heart/lung/renal/liver/neurological diseases; if on immunosuppressives, corticosteroids, wafarin, phenalzine, pentobarbital, haloperidol or cyclosporine; & if pregnant, lactating or heavy smokers).

In adults, Cold-fX **↓'d by 0.25** colds/person in those who **had ≥2 colds** in the previous year. Thus we await further verification of this result.

✓ Handwashing, [14] possibly gargling, [15] & the influenza vaccine [16] are proven to prevent upper respiratory infections. (others lack evidence)[17,20]


References:

1. Natural Medicines Comprehensive Database 2005 & 2. Turner RB, Bauer R, Woelkart K, Hulsey TC, Gangemi JD. An evaluation of **Echinacea** angustifolia in experimental rhinovirus infections. N Engl J Med. 2005 Jul 28;353(4):341-8.
3. Taylor JA, Weber W, Standish L, Quinn H, Goesling J, McGann M, Calabrese C. Efficacy and safety of **echinacea** in treating upper respiratory tract infections in children: a randomized controlled trial (but ↑ rash). JAMA. 2003 Dec 3;290(21):2824-30.
4. Predy GN, Goel V, Lovlin R, Donner A, Stitt L, Basu TK. Efficacy of an extract of North American **ginseng** containing poly-furanosyl-pyranosyl-saccharides for preventing upper respiratory tract infections: a randomized controlled trial. CMAJ. 2005 Oct 25;173(9):1043-8. n=279
5. Turner RB. Studies of "natural" remedies for the common cold: pitfalls and pratfalls. CMAJ. 2005 Oct 25;173(9):1051-2.
6. National Institutes of Health (NIH) **Glucosamine/Chondroitin** Arthritis Intervention Trial (GAIT) (The 1,538-patient GAIT trial compared the effectiveness and safety of these supplements taken alone and in combination in patients with painful knee osteoarthritis (WOMAC Pain 125-400 mm) treated at 16 academic medical centers in the U.S. The response rate for all patients was 60.1% in a placebo group, 64% in a glucosamine **hydrocholoride** arm (500 mg TID); 65.4% in a chondroitin alone arm (400 mg TID); & 66.6% in a glucosamine-plus-chondroitin arm (500 mg/400mg TID) (p=0.09), according to a study results reported at the American College of Rheumatology, San Diego Nov/05) http://nccam.nih.gov/news/19972000/121100/qa.htm
7. **Lakota** web site: http://www.lakotaherbs.com/english/2_rheumatoid.php
8. Cold-fX (Standardized Oligo/polysaccharide Extract of **Panax quinquefolium**) Pharmacist Letter. Jan 2005 & Dec 2005. & 9. ColdfX website http://www.cvtechnologies.com/coldfx/default.aspx
10. Yuan CS, Wei G, Dey L, et al. Brief communication: American **ginseng** reduces **warfarin's** effect in healthy patients: a randomized, controlled Trial. Ann Intern Med. 2004 Jul 6;141(1):23-7.
11. Richy F, Bruyere O, Ethgen O, Cucherat M, Henrotin Y, Reginster JY. Structural and symptomatic efficacy of **glucosamine and chondroitin** in knee osteoarthritis: a comprehensive meta-analysis. Arch Intern Med. 2003 Jul 14;163(13):1514-22.
12. Herrero-Beaumont G et al. Effects of **glucosamine sulfate** on a 6-month control of knee osteoarthritis symptoms vs placebo & acetaminophen: Results from the Glucose Unum in Die Efficacy (**GUIDE**) Trial. ACR Meeting Nov 2005.
13. Scroggie DA, et al. The effect of **glucosamine-chondroitin** supplementation on glycosylated hemoglobin levels in patients with type 2 diabetes mellitus: a placebo-controlled, double-blinded, randomized clinical trial. Arch Intern Med. 2003 Jul 14;163(13):1587-90.
14. Ryan MA, Christian RS, Wohlrabe J. **Handwashing** and respiratory illness among young adults in military training. Am J Prev Med. 2001 Aug;21(2):79-83.
15. Satomura K, et al.; Great Cold Investigators-I. Prevention of upper respiratory tract infections by **gargling** a randomized trial. Am J Prev Med. 2005 Nov;29(4):302-7. (InfoPOEMs: Gargling with water effectively reduces the risk of developing an upper respiratory tract infection (URTI). Nine individuals will need to gargle with water for 1 minute 3 times daily for 60 days to prevent 1 additional person from developing a URTI. Gargling with povidone-iodine was no more effective than usual care. (LOE = 1b-) )
16. **Influenza vaccine** 2005-2006. Med Lett Drugs Ther. 2005 Oct 24;47(1220):85-7 & Jefferson T, Rivetti D, Rivetti A, et al. Efficacy and effectiveness of **influenza vaccines** in elderly people: a systematic review. Lancet. 2005 Oct 1;366(9492):1165-74. Epub 2005 Sep 22.
17. Arroll B. Non-antibiotic treatments for upper-respiratory tract infections (common cold). Respir Med. 2005 Dec;99(12):1477-84. CONCLUSION: Most non-antibiotic treatments for the common cold are **probably not effective**. The most promising are dextromethorphan, bisolvon and guaifenesin for cough, antihistamine-decongestant combinations for a wide range of symptoms, nasal decongestants (at least for the first dose) and possibly zinc lozenges.
18. Towheed TE, et al. Glucosamine therapy for treating osteoarthritis. Cochrane Database Syst Rev. Apr 18, 2005 & 19. Glucosamine & chondroitin: recent osteoarthritis research. Pharmacist's Letter Jan 2006.


**Prepared by**: Brent Jensen BSP, Loren Regier BSP BA

## HERBAL Drug Interaction Chart [1,2,3,4,8,10,11,12]

| Herb (botanical name) | Interaction/Side effects (SE) |
|---|---|
| **Agrimony** | warfarin ↓ INR → herb may be a coagulant **SE**: photo dermatitis |
| **Alfalfa** ♣ po (Medicago sativa) | cholesterol meds→ herb may further ↓ lipid levels<br>cyclosporin/steroids→ ? herb immuno-stimulating<br>**hypoglycemic** meds→herb may cause further hypoglycemia<br>warfarin ↑↓ INR → herb may contain warfarin constituents or ↓ effect because of Vitamin K content in herb<br>**SE**: May ↑K+, rare pancytopenia & worsening of lupus **CI**: Lupus |
| **Aloe** (Aloe vera) ♣ top; ♣ po (non-latex) | digoxin & thiazide↑cardiac SE→ b/c electrolyte imbalance; thyroid dysfunction<br>Not if breastfeeding. **SE**: contact dermatitis, ↓K+ esp with insulin |
| **Angelica** ♣ po,top | warfarin ↑ **INR** → herb may contain warfarin constituents<br>Not recommended with breastfeeding. **SE**: photo dermatitis |
| **Anise** po (Aniseed) | MAOI's→ herb may ↑ risk of hypertensive crisis<br>warfarin ↑ INR → herb may contain warfarin constituents |
| **Aristolochia** (found in Xie Gan Wan) | amiodarone, anabolic steroids, ketoconazole, methotrexate→ additive **hepatotoxicity** effect **SE**: **nephrotoxic, cancer** (Canada warning Mar'05) |
| **Arnica** (Wolf bane) | warfarin ↑ INR → herb may contain warfarin constituents |
| **Asafoetida** ♣ po | warfarin ↑ INR → herb may contain warfarin constituents- in vivo |
| **Ayurvedic syrup** | phenytoin→herb **may ↓ phenytoin levels** as well as ↓ efficacy<br>**SE**: heavy metal poisoning. **20% of products** have lead/mercury/arsenic Saper04 & 08 |
| **Betel nut** (Areca catechu) | antipsychotics→herb may **↑ extrapyramidal SE** (strong cholinergic effects); **asthmatics**→ inadequate control of asthma |
| **Black cohosh** ♣ po (Cimicifuga racemosa) Remifemin 20mg bid | hormones→ herb may have **estrogen**-like effect.Dose: 40-80mg/day.<br>iron→ herb has tannic acids which may ↓ iron absorption; cisplatin?<br>warfarin ↑INR→herb may contain **salicylates.** Rare ↑**LFT** Health CND05<br>**SE**:For menopausal symptoms→ may cause mild GI effects & ↓ **BP** |
| **Bladderwrack** (Fucus,Kelp) | warfarin ↑ INR → herb may have anticoagulant action<br>levothyroxine→herb is a source of iodine→caused **hyperthyroidism** |
| **Bogbean** | warfarin ↑ INR → herb may have hemolytic activity |
| **Borage** | antipsychotics/anticonvulsants/TCA's→herb may ↑ **seizures**<br>amiodarone, steroids anabolic, ketoconazole, methotrexate→ herb may ↑ **hepatotoxicity** effect. Generally **unsafe**. Not help atopic dermatitis Takwale 2003 |
| **Broom** | Antihypertensive meds→ herb may ↑ BP by itself |
| **Calamus** | Sedatives→ herb may potentiate sedation. Generally **unsafe** |
| **Capsicum** ♣ po,top (Chili peppers) | MAOI's→ herb ↑ risk of hypertensive crisis SE:dermatitis,GI upset.<br>**ACE inhibitor**→ may ↑ **cough**; **theophylline**→ may ↑ absorption |
| **Cascara** ♣ po (Rhamnus purshiana) | Various meds→ ↓ absorption since going quicker via GI system<br>Digoxin/thiazides/steroids→ herb may potentiate **hypokalemia** |
| **Cassia** po | warfarin ↑ INR → herb may inhibit platelet aggregation |
| **Celery** ♣ po (seed/extract) | warfarin ↑ INR → herb may contain warfarin constituents<br>sedatives→ herb may potentiate sedation. Herb→ ? diuretic action. |
| **Cereus** | MAOI's/SSRI's/TCA's→herb may ↑ risk of serotonin syndrome |
| **Chamomile** ♣ po,top (Matricaria recutita) (German/Roman) | warfarin ↑INR →herb may contain warfarin constituents,↑**bleed** Segal'06<br>iron→ has tannic acids which may ↓iron absorption; may help anxiety Amsterdam'09<br>**sedatives**→ herb may ↑ sedation; allergic reactions, conjunctivitis |
| **Chaparral** (Larrea tridentata) | amiodarone, anabolic steroids, ketoconazole, methotrexate→ herb may have additive **hepatotoxicity** effect. Generally unsafe Health CND'05 |
| **Chinese herb mixture** | Rare: heavy metal **contamination**. Not help Hepatits C Jakkula 04 |
| **Chondroitin** ♣ **1200mg/day** Reichenbach'07-?no benefit;?Kahan | warfarin ↑**INR**→ herb may ↑bleeds & chondroitin sulfate is part of the antithrombotic-danaparoid.?bovine cartilage & ?Prostate cancer concern.<br>SE:GI.↓**oral** absorption ~10%,IM form in other countries-?minimal effect Michel'05. |
| **Chromium** picolinate ♣ po May↓insulin resistance FDA | nephrotoxic drugs→herb may ↑renal failure & rhabdomyolysis,not ↓$A_1C$ Kleefstra 06<br>hypoglycemic→may cause ↓glucose Nahas'09;not help impaired glucose tol. Gunton'05 |
| **Clove** ♣ top | warfarin ↑ INR → herb contains eugenol –a platelet inhibitor |
| **Coltsfoot** (Tussilago farfar) | amiodarone, anabolic steroids, ketoconazole, methotrexate→ herb may have additive **hepatotoxicity** effect. Not rec. with breastfeeding |
| **Comfrey** (Symphytum species) | herb may have additive or as monotherapy a **hepatotoxic** effect (Health Canada warning Dec 2003). Generally **unsafe (FDA 2001).** |
| **Co-enzyme $Q_{10}$** (Ubiquinone) po<br>-see Bonakdar'05, Young'07 & Med Let Feb06 | betablockers,phenothiazines,TCA's,doxorubicin→ herb may ↓ cardiac side effects from these medications {60-200mg daily} limited studies in heart failure<br>cardiac & antihypertensives → may improve effect of cardiac meds<br>HMG-Co A & hypoglycemics→ may ↓ natural levels of $Q_{10}$ in body<br>warfarin ↓ INR → herb may decrease effect of warfarin. Watch LFTs. |
| **Couchgrass** | diuretics→herb may ↑ potassium loss; lithium→herb may alter level.<br>sedatives→ herb may potentiate sedation |
| **Dandelion** ♣ po | diuretics & lithium→herb may ↑ diuretic effect & ↑ lithium toxicity<br>warfarin ↓ INR→↓ effect due to Vitamin K content in the herb; ↑K+ |
| **Danshen** | warfarin ↑ **INR** → **clinical bleed** due to ? acetylsalvianolic acid |
| **DHEA** Dehydroepian-drosterone ♣ po | warfarin ↑ INR → herb may have fibrinolytic potential. Watch LFTs.<br>triazolam ↑level due to DHEA. Banned by the NFL/Olympics. Med Let05 |
| **Devil's Claw** ♣ po (Harpagophytum procumbens) | heart & BP meds→ herb may interfere (↑↓ ) with BP<br>hypoglycemics → herb may ↑↓**glucose.** ??help low back pain Gagnier 07<br>**warfarin→?purpura** SE:headache, ringing ears,↓ appetite,↓ taste |
| **Dong Quai** ♣ po,top (Angelica sinensis) | heart meds→ herb has **quinidine** like activity<br>warfarin ↑ **INR** →herb ?contain warfarin constituent-**Case reports**<br>Not recommended with breastfeeding. **SE**: photosensitive |

| Herb | Interaction/Side effects (SE) |
|---|---|
| **Echinacea** po Ⓟ **Purple coneflower**<br>**E. purpurea, pallida & angustifolia** North America<br>**No ↓ in infection:** kids -Taylor JAMA 2003; or adult colds -Turner NEJM 05 | amiodarone, anabolic steroids, ketoconazole, methotrexate→ herb may have additive **hepatotoxicity** if used for > 8 weeks<br>**corticosteroids/cyclosporin**→ avoid combination<br>glycemic control → herb may cause hypo/hyperglycemia<br>warfarin ↑ INR→ herb in vitro ?↑ INR →by ↓ warfarin metabolism<br>**SE**: Often used for 2 weeks for an acute infection but can cause rash, **allergic** reaction,tiredness,somnolence,dizziness,headache&GI upset.<br>**CI**: HIV,TB,transplant pts, RA,MS,lupus →herb immunostimulant |
| **Elecampane** | sedatives→ herb may potentiate sedation |
| **Ephedra** Ⓟ (Ma huang) **Herbal Ecstasy** **Ephedrine/ Pseudoephedrine** (Ban in olympics) **?~1% ephedrine.** **Tea~15-30mg ephedrine/cup.** | anticonvulsants→↑ **seizure**; urine→may false positive with amphetamine;<br>**caffeine**,decongestants,stimulants→herb may ↑nervousness, ↑BP & tremor;<br>**heart & blood pressure** meds→ herb may ↑ heart rate & BP;<br>hypoglycemics → herb may cause hypo/**hyper**glycemia;<br>**SE**: Used in many weight loss or energy products but **over 800 reports** of nervousness, insomnia, irritability, psychosis, headache, dizziness, seizures, stroke, premature ventricular contraction, hypertension, **MI & death** esp. with caffeine. **FDA ban Apr/04.**<br>FDA max: 8mg/dose & 24mg/day for ≤1week. May ↓dexamethasone level<br>Not if breastfeeding. **NOT considered SAFE**. May ↑thyroid hormones |
| **Evening Primrose oil** ♣ po (Oenothera biennis) | **anaesthetics/antipsychotics**/anticonvulsants→herb may ↑**seizures**<br>? For menopause/itch, EFA omega-6 source **SE**: nausea, headache, ↓BP & soft stool |
| **Fenugreek** | warfarin ↑INR →herb may contain warfarin constituents; may↓glucose Nahas'09 |
| **Feverfew** po **Tanacet 125mg od** (Tanacetum parthenium)<br>-only 6 of 30 lots had labeled content CPJ Draves 2003/2004 | iron→ herb contains tannic acids which may ↓ iron absorption<br>**NSAIDS/STEROIDS**→ may ↓ the therapeutic **effect** of feverfew<br>warfarin ↑ **INR** → herb in vitro ? inhibit binding of platelets<br>Recommend 0.2% but most products contain <0.1% parthenolide<br>**SE**: Often used for migraines ? benefit Pittler 04 but can cause gastric discomfort, oral **ulcers**, lip & tongue swelling & rebound headache when herb stopped. Not recommended with breastfeeding. |
| **Flaxseed** ♣ (has ALA fatty acid) | warfarin ↑ INR →herb may ↑ bleeding time **(Linum usitatissimum).**<br>May ↓LDL, but not triglycerides. **SE**: gas, bloating, allergy |
| **Garlic** po Ⓟ (Allium sativum)<br>**Active agents: allicin & ajoene**<br>**Need high doses to work. Only short 3hr half life & acid labile → enteric coated better**<br>**No lipid effect** Gardner'07 | antihypertensive meds→ herb may ↓ **BP** thus caution advised<br>aspirin/warfarin ↑**INR** → ajoene from allicin breakdown is ? responsible for **reversible** inhibition of platelet aggregation-**bleeding**→**Case reports**<br>hypoglycemics→herb may ↓glucose;<br>**ritonavir, saquinavir** & isoniazid →↓ level.<br>**SE**: Often in the past used for hypertension & ↑**cholesterol**, but can cause burning sensation, nausea, heartburn, menorrhagia, diaphoresis, lightheadedness, **odor**iferous skin & breath, & contact dermatitis. |
| **Germander** (Teucrium chamaedrys) | amiodarone, anabolic steroids, ketoconazole, methotrexate→ herb may have additive **hepatotoxicity** effect<br>Generally considered **unsafe- 30 cases of acute liver failure.** |
| **Ginger** po (Zingiber officinale)<br>~250mg po tid White AFP'07 | heart & antihypertensives→ herb may ↑ or ↓ effect with these meds<br>hypoglycemics → herb may cause hypoglycemia<br>warfarin ↑ **INR** → herb may inhibit platelet aggregation (in vitro)<br>**SE**: an antiemetic Portnoi'03,Smith'04 but some heart burn & allergic reactions. |
| **Ginkgo biloba** Ⓟ (Maidenhair Tree) po<br>-? dementia Birks 2009, **no benefit** DeKosky '08 Snitz '09<br>**~40mg po tid ac**<br>(**not** helpful for mountain sickness) | acetaminophen & ergotamine/caffeine→ subarachnoid **hemorrhage** & subdural hematoma.Caution with bupropion/theophylline/ anticonvulsant/TCA/trazodone→may ↓seizure threshold→↑ seizures.<br>**aspirin/clopidogrel/dipyridamole/ticlopidine/warfarin ↑ INR** → ginkolide B may inhibit platelet activating factor by displacement from its receptor binding site (**Case reports**) . ?more **strokes** in GEM trial<br>thiazides → with herb may lead ↑BP 1 case. May: omeprazole/insulin ↓ levels<br>**SE**: Often used to help circulation & cognition but may cause **headache**, dizziness, restlessness, nausea, vomiting, diarrhea & dermal sensitivity. |
| **Ginseng, Eleuthero or Siberian** po (Eleutherococcus senticosus) | digoxin→ herb **may ↑ digoxin** serum level (? Maybe assay interference with level or from contaminated P. sepium)<br>heart & blood pressure meds→ herb may change **BP**/↑ heart rate<br>warfarin ↑**INR** →herb ? ↓ platelet aggregation & contain coumarin<br>Not recommended with breastfeeding. May ↑K+ |
| **Ginseng,** Ⓟ **American** ♣ po **(Panax quinquefolius)** Cold-fX promising Predy'05<br>**Korean/Asian** ♣ po **(Panax ginseng)**<br>Only 25% of ginseng products actually contained ginseng in a recent study, plus **85% did not contain ginseng in a 1990 survey.**<br>-not heart benefit Buettner05 | alcohol→ may ↑ alcohol clearance from the body<br>corticosteroids → herb may affect steroid concentrations<br>heart & blood pressure meds→ herb has negative chronotropic & inotropic activity, as well as possible ↓ **blood pressure.**<br>May ↑QTc interval→caution with cardiac meds<br>**estrogens/corticosteroids**→ herb may have possible additive effects (reported mastalgia & postmenopausal bleeding)<br>**furosemide**→ case report of diminishing furosemide effect<br>hypoglycemics → herb may have additive **hypoglycemic** effect<br>**MAOI's**→ may inhibit reuptake of various neurotransmitters & ↑ tremor/**mania** thus contraindicated<br>mood stabilizers→herb may **induce mania**<br>oral contraceptives→ herb may interfere in effectiveness of sex hormone tx<br>**sedatives**→ herb may potentiate/antagonize sedative side effects<br>warfarin ↑ ↓ **INR** → herb may cause ↑ bleeding by itself or ↓ **INR** (**Case reports**,Yuan 2004)<br>**SE**: in general for ALL species: **nervousness**, excitation, diarrhea, insomnia, inability to concentrate, headache, hypertension, epistaxis, allergies & skin eruptions.<br>Not recommended with breastfeeding |
| **Glucosamine** sulf/HCL **~500mg po tid** po<br>Lakota has this & 8 other herbs<br>Some benefit Clegg&Herrero06 | Hypoglycemics/insulin→does not ↑$HgA_1C$ Scroggie 2003, may ↑insulin resistance & ? ↑ resistance to doxorubicin & etoposide.?warfarin ↑ INR.<br>Well absorbed ~90%, IV elsewhere.Some efficacy Richy & Towheed.Shellfish allergy maybe.<br>For osteoarthritis. **SE**: GI side effects eg. diarrhea. **Sulfate salt** better evidence! |

⇨Items listed for each herb reflect case reports, sometimes studies but not overall safety & efficacy; (shaded) Likely Safe, but potential drug interactions & side effects ♣ Possibly safe but DI's & SE's.

| | |
|---|---|
| **Goldenseal** (Hydrastis canadensis) | heart & antihypertensives→herb can alter heart & blood pressure<br>heparin → herb can oppose the action of heparin<br>sedatives→ herb may ↑ sedation. **Expensive & often adulterated.** |
| **Gotu kola** | sedatives→ herb may ↑ sedation    statins → herb may ↑ lipids |
| **Green tea** ♣[po,top]<br>?↓hypertension Yang 04<br>?↑LFT's Bonkovsky 06 | iron→herb has tannic acids which may ↓iron [absorption]; ? ↓glucose [Nahas'09]<br>**warfarin ↓ INR** → herb may contain ↑ vitamin K content (in vitro).<br>Contains 10-80mg **caffeine**/cup. **Lithium** level ↑ if stop caffeine. |
| **Guar gum** ♣[po] (Cyamopsis tetragonolobus) | digoxin & penicillin V→slows absorption in the stomach<br>glyburide,iron & **metformin**→ ↓ absorption with some formulations<br>SE: rare gastric obstruction. May ↓ cholesterol levels. |
| **Hawthorn** [Dahmer AFP'10] (Crataegus monogyna) | **digoxin &↓BP meds**→ herb may interfere. Pittler'08 [but SPICE negative trial for HF]<br>MAOI's: may contain tyramine → ↑ risk of hypertensive crisis. ↑K⁺ |
| **Hops** | **sedatives**→ herbs may ↑ sedation; herb has estrogen like chemicals |
| **Horse chestnut**<br>?↓venous insufficiency [Pittlens] | aspirin & warfarin ↑ INR → herb may contain warfarin constituents<br>SE: irritant to stomach & hypoglycemia **(Aesculus hippocastanum)** |
| **Horseradish** ♣[po] | warfarin ↑ INR →peroxidase stimulates arachidonic acid metabolites |
| **Indian snakeroot** | antihypertensives & digoxin→ herb can ↑ effect<br>antidepressants→ herb can ↓ effect (reserpine found in herb) |
| **Jamaican Dogwood** | sedatives→ herb may potentiate sedative SE |
| **Karela** (Bitter melon) | hypoglycemics → herb may affect blood glucose levels [Nahas'09] |
| **Kava kava** Ⓟ (Piper methysticum)<br>**Stop-sale** order in Canada Aug/02, but still avail. [Mills 03]<br>-a social drink in South Pacific | alcohol/antipsychotics/sedatives→ herb may ↑ **sedation**<br>alprazolam /benzodiazepines→ has led to additive depression<br>(Case report of **↑lethargy/?coma** with alprazolam)<br>antiparkinsonian meds→herb may exacerbate Parkinson's–case report<br>SE: Often used for anxiolytic but causes headache,dizziness,GI discomfort & local numbess after oral ingestion; **dry scaly skin** & discoloration (**yellow**), leukopenia, **thrombocytopenia**, photosensitivity & eye redness with long term use or high dosages.<br>Reports of **hepatotoxicity** [FDA Mar/02].Not recomm. with breastfeeding |
| **Kelp** | levothyroxine→herb source of iodine→caused **hyperthyroidism** |
| **Kombucha** | amiodarone, anabolic steroids, ketoconazole, methotrexate→ herb may have additive **hepatotoxicity** effect.Source of **anthrax** outbreak. |
| **Kyushin** | digoxin→herb may interfere with dynamics/monitoring |
| **Life root** (Senecio aureus) | amiodarone, anabolic steroids, ketoconazole, methotrexate→ herb may have additive **hepatotoxicity** effect. Generally **unsafe** |
| **Licorice** ♣[po (<30g/day)] (Glcyrrhiza glabra)<br>**High dose is >50 grams/day**<br>**Most licorice in the USA contains anise oil rather than licorice.** | antihypertensives/digoxin/loop diuretics/spironolactone/thiazides → herb may cause **hypokalemia**, plus **sodium & fluid retention** which can ↑ **blood pressure** (ie. Pseudoaldosteronism)<br>**corticosteroids**→herb **may ↑ oral & topical steroid** effects<br>**digoxin**→herb may interfere with pharmacodynamically/monitoring<br>hypoglycemics → herb may cause ↓ glucose tolerance thus caution<br>oral contraceptive→ may lead to hypertension,edema & ↓ potassium<br>warfarin ↑ INR → herb may inhibit platelet activity<br>SE: lethargy, headache & electrolyte imbalances. ??help liver [Dhiman'05]<br>Not recommended with breastfeeding. Generally **unsafe** |
| **Meadowsweet** | warfarin ↑ INR → herb may contain salicylate constituents |
| **Melilot** (Sweet clover) ♣[po] | warfarin ↑ INR → herb may contain warfarin constituents |
| **Milk thistle** ♣[po] (Silybum marianum) | **hypoglycemics** → herb may have additive hypoglycemic effect<br>SE: Gastric pain, diarrhea, vomiting & allergic rx.   May ↓indinavir.<br>In Europe avail. IV to "detoxify the liver??[Rambaldi'05]".Oral ~25% [absorbed]. |
| **Mistletow** | warfarin ↓ INR → herb may contain lectins → ↓ agglutination |
| **Nettle** | iron→ herb contains tannic acids which may ↓ iron absorption<br>sedatives→ herb may potentiate sedation<br>warfarin ↓ INR → herb may contain Vitamin K; May ↑K⁺ |
| **Papain/Papaya** ♣[po] | warfarin may ↑INR;**(Carica papaya) Allergy:** Digibind **SE:** gastritis |
| **Parsley** ♣[po] | antihypertensives→ herb has sympathomimetics→watch for ↑ BP<br>**MAOI's**→ herb ↑ risk of hypertensive crisis.Herb may contain Vit K |
| **Passionflower** ♣[po] | MAOI's/SSRI's/TCA's→herb may ↑ risk of **serotonin syndrome**<br>**sedative**→ herb↑ sedation;warfarin ↑ INR→may contain coumarins |
| **Pennyroyal** (Mentha puleguim) | amiodarone, anabolic steroids, ketoconazole, methotrexate→ herb may have additive **hepatotoxicity** effect (? Treat → acetylcysteine) |
| **Plantain** ♣[po (with ↑ fluid)] (Black psyllium) [fibre] | carbamazepine/digoxin/iron/lithium/warfarin→ ↓ absorption by herb<br>digoxin→herb may interfere with absorption/dynamics/monitoring |
| **Pleurisy root** | MAOI's→ herb ↑ risk of hypertensive crisis |
| **Poplar** ♣[top] | warfarin ↑ INR → herb may contain salicylate constituents |
| **Prickly Ash** | warfarin ↑ INR → herb may contain warfarin constituents |
| **Psyllium**(P.ovata) | carbamazepine/digoxin/iron/lithium/warfarin→ herb ↓ absorption |
| **Quassia** | warfarin ↑ INR → herb may contain warfarin constituents |
| **Red Clover** ♣[po] (Promensil) | oral contraceptive/tamoxifen/letrozole→ may ↓effect/interfere.<br>warfarin ↑INR→may contain [warfarin]. **SE**:rash. Made cheetah's sterile. |
| **Royal jelly** | asthma meds→ may cause bronchospasm. Expensive source of "B" vitamins. Severe allergies reported with bee products. |
| **Sage** ♣[po,top] | sedatives→ herb may potentiate sedation |

**Web links**: http://www.fda.gov/food/dietarysupplements/default.htm
http://nccam.nih.gov/  www.ars-grin.gov/duke  www.quackwatch.com
www.ncahf.org  www.herbmed.org  www.consumerlab.com
www.camline.ca  www.naturaldatabase.com  www.mskcc.org/aboutherbs
http://www.hc-sc.gc.ca/dhp-mps/prodnatur/index-eng.php  www.herbs.org

| | |
|---|---|
| **Saiboku-to** Asian herb mixture | corticosteroids→herb may ↑ prednisolone levels<br>Same herbs→**sho-saiko-to**,Poria cocos,Mangolia officinalis&Perillae frutescens |
| **Sassafras** | SE: sedation.   Generally considered **unsafe (S. albidum)** |
| **Sauropus androgynus** | amiodarone, anabolic steroids, ketoconazole & methotrexate→ herb may potentiate **hepatotoxicity** |
| **Saw palmetto** ♣[po] (Serenoa repens)<br>**Sabal fruit**<br>May cause false –'ve PSA test & ?make normal prostate cells more sensitive to radiation | **estrogen/contraceptive/hormone**→ herb may have anti-androgen & estrogenic activity. {160mg bid} (? cause of floppy iris Syndrome)<br>iron→herb has tannic acids→may ↓iron [absorption]; may ↑**bleeding** [ASA, warfarin]<br>SE: Used for benign **prostatic hyperplasia** but causes **headache**, GI (nausea, abd pain, constipation & diarrhea), may ↑ **BP** ; & rare hormonal actions (breast tenderness, loss of libido & venous thrombosis) & pancreatitis. Efficacy? [Bent'06]: ≤ Proscar but likely < than ∝1 blockers |
| **Scullcap** | amiodarone, anabolic steroids, ketoconazole, methotrexate→ herb may have additive **hepatotoxicity** effect (? due to adulterants)<br>**sedatives**→ herb may potentiate sedation |
| **Senna** ♣[po] (Cassia senna) | digoxin/thiazides/steroids→ herb may potentiate hypokalemia various meds→ ↓ absorption→going quicker via GI system |
| **Shankapulshpi** | phenytoin→herb **may ↓ phenytoin levels** as well as ↓ efficacy **(Ayurvedic mixed herb syrup)** |
| **Shepherds Purse** | MAOI's→ may contain tyramine thus ↑ risk of hypertensive crisis<br>sedatives→ herb may potentiate sedation |
| **Sho-saiko-to** | prednisolone→↓ levels for prednisolone   **(Asian herb mixture)** |
| **St. John's** ♣[po] Ⓟ **Wort** (Hypericum perforatum)<br>**~300mg po tid -not for major Depression** JAMA 01/& 02 but ?positive→Szegedi05, Linde08 & Gastpar06 for Mild-Moderate depression.<br>**Active agents: 0.3% hypericin & hyperforin (Used commonly –esp. in Germany)**<br>Only **2/54 products** contained within 10% of the labeled amount. [CJC Pharmacol 2003] | Antihypertensive meds→ this herb may ↑ BP thus caution advised<br>barbiturates→ herb may ↓ barbiturate induced sleeping time<br>**amiodarone / cyclosporin / dabigatran / dasa, erlo, ima, lapa, nilo & suni-tinib / dig / exemestane / fexofenadine / indinavir / irinotecan/ maraviroc / midazolam / nevirapine/ omeprazole /oral contraceptive / rivaroxaban /sirolimus/sorafenib /statin/sumatriptan/ theophylline / verapamil / voriconazole / warfarin**→ herb may **↓ levels** of these drugs via ↑ metabolism (P450 3A4 inducer)<br>iron→ herb contains tannic acids which can ↓ iron absorption<br>**MAOI's/SSRI's/TCA's**→herb may ↑ risk of **serotonin syndrome (6 case reports-tremor, delirium…)** by ↑ serotonin levels plus since MAOI action → restriction tyramine food is wise.<br>**narcotics**→ may ↑sleeping time; loperamide: delirium & agitation report<br>piroxicam/tetracyclines→ can ↑ photosensitize reaction<br>sedatives→ herb may potentiate **sedation; Thyroid** meds: may↑ TSH<br>**SE**: Often for mild to moderate depression but may cause allergic reactions, headache, dizziness, restless, fatigue, dry mouth, mania, nausea, vomiting, constipation,dreams, hair loss & **photosensitivity & possible uterotonic activity.** Possible **cataract link** thus rec to wear wrap around sunglasses. Hold for 2 weeks before any surgery. |
| **Tamarind** | aspirin→ ↑ bioavailability of aspirin **(Tamarindus indica)** |
| **Tonka Bean** | warfarin ↑ INR → herb may contain warfarin constituents |
| **Umbelliferae** | warfarin ↑ INR → herb may contain dicumoral constituents |
| **Uzara root** | **digoxin**→herb may have additive effects or interfere with monitoring |
| **Valerian** ♣[po] Ⓟ (Valeriana officinalis)<br>-see Hadley'05 article eg. Nytol Natural Source | sedatives→ herb may potentiate **sedation**<br>Possible acute **hepatitis** reported (? Due to adulterants).<br>**SE**: Often used for sedative & anxiolytic action but may cause headache, excitability, ataxia & gastric complaints. (Case report of withdrawal syndrome involving **cardiac abnormalities & delirium**) |
| **Verbena** (Vervain) ♣[po] | MAOI's→ herb ↑ risk of hypertensive crisis |
| **Vitamin E** ♣[po,top] | warfarin ↑ INR →herb may ↓ platelet aggregation. In **sunflower seeds**. |
| **Wild Carrot** ♣[po] | sedatives→ herb may potentiate sedation |
| **Wild Lettuce** ♣[po] | sedatives→ herb may potentiate sedation |
| **Willow/Wintergreen** | **warfarin ↑INR**→ herb may contain **salicylate** [constituent]; may affect BP |
| **Woodruff** | warfarin ↑ INR → herb may contain warfarin constituents |
| **Yarrow** | warfarin ↓ INR → herb may be a coagulant in vivo |
| **Yohimbe** (Pausinystalia yohimbe) | clonidine & antihypertensives→herb may ↑ BP since is ∝ 2 blocker<br>**TCA antidepressants**→herb may ↑ **risk of hypertension**<br>SE:nervousness, tremor, headache,dizzy,flushing,↑urinary frequency & nausea |
| **Xaio chai hu tang** | corticosteroids→herb may ↓ **blood level of prednisolone** |

**Unsafe Herb list**: (American Journal Health System Pharmacy, Jan 15/1999) borage, calamus, chaparral, coltsfoot, comfrey, ephedra, germander, licorice, life root, sassafras, star anise

**Potentially safe herb** ♣ **but still interactions**: (American Journal Health System Pharmacy, Jan 1999) feverfew, garlic, ginkgo, ginseng-Asian, saw palmetto, St. John's wort [but DI's important], valerian

**Frequently Allergic reactions with**: (American Journal of Medicine, Feb 1998) Agnus,Castus,Angelica,Aniseed,Apricot,Arnica,Artichoke,Asafoetida,Boneset,Cassia,Celery, Cinnamon,Cowslip,Dandelion,Elecampane,Euphobia,Feverfew,Fucus,Gravel Root,Gauicum, Holy Thistle,Hops, Hydrangea,Juniper,Lady's Slipper,Meadowsweet,Motherwort,Parsley, Pilewort,Plantain,Pulsatilla,Rosemary,Royal Jelly,Tansy,Wild Carrot&Yarrow.

Natural medicine does **NOT** guarantee SAFETY. **1/4 of all modern drugs** have a natural/botanical origin. Medicinal herbs are drugs with potential harm & benefit! (Eg. **Red yeast** may contain **lovastatin**). Concerns regarding **purity, potency & quality** are especially important in the herbal industry. A sample of 2609 sample of traditional Chinese medicines collected from 8 hospitals in Taiwan, 23.7% contained pharmaceutical **adulterants**, most commonly **acetaminophen, caffeine, hydrochlorothiazide, indomethacin & prednisolone.**[5,7] Other **NSAIDS & benzodiazepines** found in Chinese patent medicines sold outside Asia[6]. In 24 of 251 Asian patent medicines there was **lead**; 36 **arsenic** & 35 contained **mercury**.[9] Like all drugs there are some **serious side effects & interactions that occur.**

References: 1. Hansten and Horn's Drug Interactions Analysis and Management 2009. 2. AHFS Drug Information 2009. 3. American Family Physcian Mar 1/1999. 4. CPS - Product Monographs, 2009. 5. J Clin Pharmacol 1997;37:344-350. 6. Arthritis Rheum 1995;38:614-617. 7. BMJ 1994;308:1162. 8. The Lancet 2000;355:134-138. 9. NEJM 1998 339:847. 10. Pharmacy Practice June 1999 & June 2000 11. **Natural Medicines Comprehensive Database 2010.** 12. Review of Natural Products 2005.

**BP**-Blood pressure **CI**-Contraindication **GI**-Gastrointestinal **K**=potassium **INR-international normalization ratio (ie.** bleeding risk)
**LFT**=liver function tests Ⓟ**-a concern if given pre-op (JAMA 2001) SE**-side effect ♣ Possibly safe but DI & SE.

| | COMPLAINT & TREATMENT NOTES | GENERIC NAME | Pregnancy category [7,8,9,10,11] ↓ | TRADE NAME | USUAL DOSE Adult / Pediatric (Daily MAXIMUM) | $ / pkg | COMMENTS |
|---|---|---|---|---|---|---|---|
| COLDS | **CONGESTION**<br>• nasal decongestants: Cochrane Review [73]: single dose in adults moderately effective for cold (13% ↓ symptoms); not for children (especially <6yr) with common cold (reports of CNS & CV SE's)<br>• oral – limited data, especially in children [76]<br>• limit **nasal prep** to **~7 days** to **avoid rebound congestion** (≤ 3 days with phenylephrine) Tx: stop preps & ? use nasal steroids<br>• antihistamines of questionable benefit in common cold [72]; anticholinergic activity provides extra drying (? benefit)<br>• **saline** drops/spray: option; some effect<br>• **sinus saline irrigation** (Neti Pots): option<br>• thin film forms: handy, different ingredients | ORAL • Pseudoephedrine<br>-diverted for meth. labs | C | SUDAFED (12hr formulation and pediatric tabs also available) | 60mg q4-6h or 120mg q12h; MAX 240mg/d<br><6 yr (not indicated): 15mg q4-6h; MAX 60mg/day<br>6-11yrs: 30mg q4-6h; MAX 120mg/d | 6-8 | • **SE**= insomnia, tremor, irritability & headache<br>• oral decongestant: **caution** in pts with ↑ BP, heart Dx, β-blockers [56], uncontrolled hyperthyroidism, diabetes, glaucoma narrow angle & prostatic hypertrophy<br>{Phenylpropanolamine: products withdrawn; ↑'d stroke rare in ♀<50yrs}[64]<br>• **nasal agents**: less systemic absorption & SE |
| | | • Phenylephrine (Note: short acting) | C | DIMETAPP ▼ Cold versions<br>DRISTAN reg tabs<br>SUDAFED PE | 10mg q4h; MAX 60mg/day<br><6 yr (not indicated): 2.5mg q4h; MAX 15mg/day<br>6-11yrs: 5mg q4h; MAX 30mg/day | 5-7 | |
| | | NASAL • Oxymetazoline<br>-topical may ↓rosacea erythema | C | DRISTAN LONG LASTING NASAL MIST | 2-3 drops or sprays q10-12h up to BID<br>MAX 2 applications/24hrs<br>Adults: 0.05% | 5-7 | **COMBINATION PRODUCTS:** generally not recommended - less flexibility in dosing, more adverse effects; however, convenient for multiple symptoms e.g. acute sinusitis & associated headache {ADVIL COLD & SINUS ibuprofen 200mg + pseudoephedrine 30mg}<br>• decongestant + antihistamine 1st Gen most common, some benefit in acute cough due to common cold & cough due to post-nasal drip [13] (effective in older children & adults, but **not in <6yrs** [72,76])<br>• expectorant + cough suppressant may not be rational<br>• Some products have 4 drugs in one formulation: e.g. TYLENOL COLD (acetaminophen, chlorpheniramine, pseudoephedrine, DM)<br>• Pediatric Cautions: lack of efficacy data; toxicity & overdose potential if using multiple cold products [76,77]<br>⇨ Health Canada [177]: **not** to use cough & cold drugs in kids **<6yr old** [2008]; due to safety & efficacy concerns. |
| | | • Xylometazoline | C | OTRIVIN | 2-3 drops or sprays q8-10h up to TID<br>Adults: 0.1% | 5-7 | |
| | | • Saline Nasal Spray | A | SALINEX ▼ ✓ Pediatric option | 1 spray TID-QID PRN | 5 | |
| | | • **Nasal Phenylephrine (eg.** REGULAR DRISTAN NASAL MIST ) not recommended **- short duration, frequent admin, rebound congestion more likely** | | | | 9 | |
| | **COUGH** [174]<br>• **acute** (ie. <3-8wks duration) usually due to self-limiting viral infection<br>• chronic [13,86] (>8wk) usually symptom of underlying resolvable cause:<br>-drugs (ACEI's- persists <4wks after stopping)<br>-GERD, asthma, COPD (smokers), allergy<br>- postnasal drip (UACS) upper airway cough syndrome<br>Treat underlying cause; interim use of antitussives may be warranted.<br>• hydration: oral liquids & humidified air<br>• honey: Age 2-5: ½ teaspoonful; Avoid in infants: botulism<br>• **Rx** prep (TYLENOL #3 but caution acetominophen dose); (hydrocodone combos-Tussionex, Novahistex DH) (hydrocodone: HYCODAN 5mg tab; 1mg/ml susp) | • Dextromethorphan (**DM**)<br>abuse concerns [117]<br>**Evidence for clinical effectiveness of OTC products in acute cough is limited & conflicting.** [12,74,92] | C | BENYLIN DM ▼<br>{12hr formulations: ▼<br>BENYLIN DM 12hr ,<br>DELSYM DM 12hr…<br>2 tsp (60mg) po BID} | 10-20mg q4h; 30mg q6-8h MAX 120mg/d<br>2-5yr (not indicated): 2.5-5mg q4h or 7.5mg q6-8h; MAX 30mg/d; 6-11yrs: 5-10mg q4h or 15mg q6-8h; MAX 60mg/d | 6-10 | |
| | | • Guaifenesin - not a suppressant but reduces viscosity & may aid in expectoration of sputum | C | ROBITUSSIN (plain) | 200-400mg q4-6h; MAX 2.4g/day<br>2-5yr (not indicated): 50-100mg q4-6h; MAX 600 mg/day<br>6-11yrs: 100-200mg q4-6h; MAX 1.2 g/day | 6-10 | • sugar & alcohol in some products, but minimal **concern** in diabetes & kids (some >14 kcal/dose)<br>• Codeine preps: **SE**= drowsiness, nausea, constipation; not recommended in asthmatics; caution if breastfeeding<br>• Rx Salbutamol VENTOLIN may help: cough if also airway obstruction in acute bronchitis [14,15]; or for cough due to chronic bronchitis. [13] |
| | | • Codeine – avail. OTC in 3.3mg/tsp liquid formulas with ≥ 2 other active ingredients (eg. **Benylin Codeine, Robitussin with Codeine**)<br>• **Diphenhydramine** also option | C/D | **Effective dose of codeine** = 10-20mg q4h; MAX 120mg/d<br>2-5 yrs: 1-1.5mg/kg/d (use calibrated syringe for measuring); 6-11yrs: 5-10mg q4-6h; MAX 60mg/d. Contraindicated: <2yrs. Label dosing guidelines of most OTC [codiene containing] cough syrups results in subtherapeutic levels of codeine in adults.<br>**Effective dose of hydrocodone** more potent: ≥12yrs 5mg q4-6h prn; 2-12yrs: 1mg - 2.5mg q4-8h; MAX 15mg/day (use calibrated syringe for measuring) | | 5-9 | • **in general, products designated with:**<br>**DM** contain **Dextromethorphan** (suppressant)<br>**D** contain a **decongestant**<br>**E** contain an **expectorant (ie. Guaifenesin)** |
| ALLERGY | **ALLERGY –SYSTEMIC** [5,16-24,99,142]<br>• **oral antihistamines** relieve all (to some extent) allergic symptoms except nasal congestion (exceptions: desloratadine [25] & cetirizine [26] may aid congestion). If acute congestion, consider short-term oral decongestant (avoid topical decongestants).<br>• ↑ **efficacy if used prophylactically**<br>{Terfenadine SELDANE, astemizole HISMANAL no longer marketed due to rare risk of arrhythmias}<br>• **Rx** SINGULAIR - less effective than INCSs. [27-29] | ***1st Generation oral:***<br>• Chlorpheniramine | B | CHLORTRIPOLON ▼ (12hr Repetabs also – 1 tab (12mg) po BID; syrup; tabs) | 4mg q4-6h; 4-8mg @hs; MAX 24mg/day<br>2-5yrs (not indicated): 1mg q4-6h; MAX 6mg/d<br>6-11yrs: 2mg q4-6h; MAX 12mg/d | 8-12 | • USEFUL for itch, sneeze & **urticaria** symptoms<br>• NOT very USEFUL for sinonasal congestion<br>• **Pregnancy**: 1st gen chlorpheniramine preferred or **B** agents<br>• 1st generation **caution** in narrow angle glaucoma, bladder neck obstruction, heart disease, hyperthyroidism & prostatic hypertrophy<br>• **SE**: **sedation** esp. 1st gen (May not be an issue at low [63] doses –most Benadryl studies used 50mg as a comparator [21]) (paradoxical **stimulation** possible in kids & elderly) & **anticholinergic** (eg. dry mouth & nose, constipation, ↑ heart rate & ? ↓ lactation). Effects more common with 1st gen. antihistamines; negligible with more costly 2nd gen. 1st gen. start dose low & taper up depending on sedation / diagnosis<br>• headache = common ≤10% with 2nd gen agents<br>• rare seizures reported with 1st & 2nd generation [55]<br>• **2nd gen favored** by experts [5,17] due to less cognitive impairment, long acting & less SE. |
| | | • Diphenhydramine | B | BENADRYL ▼ syrup,cap,tab<br>-esp. for anaphylactic reactions | 25-50mg q4-6h; MAX 150mg/day<br>2-5yr (not indicated): 6.25mg q4-6h; MAX 25mg/d<br>6-11yrs: 12.5mg q4-6h; MAX 75mg/d | 6-8 | |
| | | ***2nd Generation oral:***<br>• Cetirizine hydroxyzine metabolite<br>Useful: nasal congestion, sedating @ ↑ doses | B | REACTINE ▼ tab ; syrup | 5-10mg OD; 2-5yrs: 2.5mg OD-BID | 10-15 | |
| | | • Fexofenadine terfenadine metabolite<br>DI: grapefruit & other juices, antacids | C | ALLEGRA tabs | 60mg BID or 120mg OD<br>6-11yrs: 30mg BID; <6yr not recommended | 10-15 | |
| | | • Loratadine<br>-possibly sedating @ ↑ doses | B | CLARITIN ▼ reg. & dissolve tabs; syrup | 10mg OD (kids >30kg: 10mg od)<br>2-9yrs: 5mg OD (tabs: tasteless & chewable) | 12-15 | |
| | **TOPICAL (Nasal/Ophthalmic)**<br>• Sinus saline irrigation Neti Pots: works<br>• **Rx preps** generally more efficacious [30-34] | • Desloratadine loratadine metabolite<br>Useful: nasal congestion [22]<br>-possibly sedating @ ↑ doses | C | AERIUS 5mg tabs, liquid | 5mg OD 2-5yr: 1.25mg OD; 6-11yr: 2.5mg | 18 | |
| | | Also remember environmental factor modification! | | | | | |
| | **Rx Intranasal Steroid (INCS):** (for allergic rhinitis) Beclomethasone ▼, FLONASE ▼, NASOCORT ▼, NASONEX ▼, RHINOCORT ▼, RHINALAR ▼; AVAMYS, OMNARIS. Rx anticholinergic nasal for rhinorrhea: ATROVENT ▼.<br>**Rx Ophthalmics: $H_1$ blockers:** LIVOSTIN ▼ expiry 30day (also Livostin nasal), EMADINE; **$H_1$ & Mast Cell:** ZADITOR, PATANOL; **Mast Cell** slow onset: ALOMIDE ▼, ALOCRIL ▼. | | | | | | |
| | • **Avoid** OTC topical decongestants due to rebound (**Vasocon-A, Naphcon-A, Albalon-A▼…**).<br>• may require short term oral decongestants | • Sodium cromoglycate | B | CROMOLYN ▼<br>OPTICROM ▼ Mast cell stabilizer | Adults & ≥2yr: 1 spray each nostril QID [3,5]<br>1-2 eye drops qid expiry in 1 month after opened | 15-17 | • prophylatic if used before allergen exposure but slow onset |
| | **• Saline/Lubricating Sprays/Drops** | • Saline solution<br>• Methylcellulose… | B | EYE STREAM<br>ISOPTOTEARS ▼ | Use, wash out & flush as necessary<br>- also Eyelube ▼, GenTeal Gel, Lacrilube, Refresh PM ▼ | 7<br>9 | Home-made saline generally not recommended as lack of sterility is a concern for nasal/ophthalmic preparations {level teaspoon of salt mixed in 250ml warm water} |

**Rx** = non-OTC products available by prescription in Canada; see page 97 for description of additional abbreviations

OTC Products

**GASTRO-INTESTINAL**

| COMPLAINT & TREATMENT NOTES | DRUGS OF CHOICE | | USUAL DOSE Adult / Pediatrics (Daily MAXIMUM) | $ | COMMENTS |
|---|---|---|---|---|---|
| **DYSPEPSIA** [35,36,57] **(non-ulcer)**<br>◆antacids & OTC histamine-2 receptor antagonists (H2RAs) effective for mild-moderate **episodic** heartburn & GERD; more severe cases require appropriate assessment + Rx therapy<br>◆important to avoid precipitating and aggravating factors (eg. stop smoking)<br>◆**persistent symptoms** should be self-medicated for **no longer than 2wks before seeking medical evaluation** | ***Antacids/Protectants***<br>◆Magnesium-aluminum hydroxide antacids **B** | **MAALOX**<br>**MYLANTA**<br>In both tablet & liquid form; liquid most efficacious. | 50-100MEq QID (see label instructions for dosing) (1hr after meals & HS)<br>***RULE OUT* organic disease if >50yrs or any patient with alarm symptoms** {VBAD: persistent Vomiting, Bleeding / hematemisis / melena, Abdominal mass, Dysphagia; radiating chest pain, ↓weight, fatigue} | 4-10 | ◆Mg+Al antacids preferred as constipating effect of $Al^{+2}$ counterbalanced by laxative effect of $Mg^{+2}$; AVOID Sodium Bicarbonate products<br>◆**Pregnancy**: antacids & alginates preferred<br>◆antacids interfere with **absorption** of some drugs (bisphosphonates, digoxin, iron, tetracyclines & quinolone antibiotics); space **2hrs apart**<br>◆**OTC H2RAs comparable but NOT superior to antacids for episodic heartburn & GERD**<br>◆ranitidine may ↑ blood alcohol level<br>◆dyspepsia may be **drug induced**: e.g. alendronate, amiodarone, antibiotics eg. erythromycin..., acarbose, herbs, iron, K+ tabs, metformin, orlistat, NSAIDs, steroids & theophylline |
| | **Pepcid Complete** = (famotidine/calcium carb./magnesium hydroxide; 10 tabs ≅ $9) | | | | |
| | ◆Calcium carbonate | **TUMS**▼ 200mg Reg., 300mg Extra, 400mg Ultra | 200-400mg PRN (Max 2g elemental Ca++ in 24hrs) | 4-12 | |
| | ◆Alginates **B** | **GAVISCON** | 2-4tsp QID (after meals & HS) | 8-12 | |
| | ***OTC H2RAs***<br>◆Famotidine **B** | **PEPCID AC** | >12yrs: 10mg OD; can repeat x1<br>MAX 20mg/d; 2wk trial | 6-10 | |
| | ◆Ranitidine | **ZANTAC 75** | >16yrs: 75mg OD; may repeat x1<br>MAX 150mg/d; 2wk trial | 4-6 | |
| | ◆Bismuth Subsalicylate **C/D** | Peptol Bismol▼, Maalox Multi-Action | 30ml or 2 tabs q0.5-1 hr prn; MAX 8doses/day | 5-10 | |
| **CONSTIPATION** [37,65,101,120,123,137]<br>◆ensure adequate FIBRE (~25g/day); slowly ↑ intake of fruits & vegetables; begin with 1-2 TBSP/day wheat bran & ↑ up to 2-4 TBSP/day with FLUID<br>◆FLUID INTAKE & regular EXERCISE is important (but not adequate for all)<br>◆rule out impaction; treat underlying causes where possible<br>◆may be **drug-induced** (anticholinergics, analgesics esp. opiates, antacids with $Al^{+2}$, calcium and iron supplements, high dose diuretics, clonidine, calcium channel blockers esp. verapamil, & tricyclic antidepressants) | ***Bulk forming (fiber)***<br>◆Psyllium, other **B** | **METAMUCIL**▼ psyllium<br>**PRODIEM** polycarbophil cap or methylcelulose powder | 4.5-20g/day ↑ gradually with adequate fluid (bacteria degrade fiber→ gas & bloating possible) | 8-18 | ◆**bulk-forming** agents**, stool softeners, lactulose & polyethylene** glycol: Lax-A-Day, RestoraLAX **OK for chronic use; stimulant,** other **osmotic** preps **for short-term occasional use** (1-2 days duration, one course/wk) EXCEPT stimulants useful with opioid therapy<br>◆**Pregnancy**: bulk, lactulose & docusate preferred<br>◆**SE**: bloating, abdominal discomfort, flatulence common with most; stimulants & osmotics can cause cramping, abdominal pain & diarrhea. Abuse & habit forming potential with stimulants.<br>◆ONSET: bulking & softening agents work over days; lactulose & sorbitol in 24-48hrs; stimulants & MOM within hrs (overnight); Oral Fleet [154], suppositories & **GOLYTELY**▼ within ~1hr. |
| | ◆New fiber products: inulin FiberSure, BeneFiber. ◆Lax-A-Day 17g/day in water/juice/coffee | | | | |
| | ***Stool softeners***<br>◆Docusate **C** | **COLACE**▼ | 1-2 caps OD-BID **(not laxative per se & not effective except for softening)** | 4-8 | |
| | ***Stimulant***: tend to ↑cramps<br>◆Senna: benign melanosis coli **C** | **SENOKOT**▼, **EXLAX**<br>**SENOKOT-S**▼ +docusate | 1-2 tabs OD-BID (if OD, give at HS) | 5-10 | |
| | ◆Bisacodyl **C** | **DULCOLAX**▼ | 5-15mg tab HS/OD; 10mg supp OD | 5-10 | |
| | ***Osmotic***<br>◆Peg-3350 Polyethylene Glycol | **MIRALAX** | 1 packet, stirred into beverage once daily | | |
| | ◆GLYCERIN **C** | **GLYCERIN** supp▼ | for immediate relief | 4 | |
| | ◆MOM | *Milk of Magnesia*▼ | 15-30mls OD-BID Risk of hypermagnesemia | 5-10 | |
| | ◆phosphate | **FLEET**▼(oral & enema) | for immediate relief Risk of hyperphosphatemia | 7 | |
| | ◆Lactulose: Poorly absorbed sugar **B** | **CHRONULAC, gen**▼ | 15-30mls OD-BID | 30 | |
| **DIARRHEA**<br>◆common CAUSES = infections, food, water, drugs (antibiotics, acarbose, chemotherapy, cholinergics, laxatives, Mg++, misoprostol & orlistat, SSRIs), lactose intolerance & IBS<br>◆**rehydration** [114] **critical** esp. in infants & elderly; **PEDIALYTE**▼ suitable for infants {Home made option: 1 tsp salt+8 tsp sugar in 1 liter water.}; **GATORADE** suitable for mild-moderate dehydration in adults<br>◆OTC therapy is for mild-moderate cases only (ie. otherwise healthy adult, no fever, <2days duration, no blood)!<br>◆antibiotic-induced usually self-limiting; live culture yogurt 100 million bacteria/gram or<br>◆if prolonged/severe, assess for C. difficile<br>◆Other: probiotics may help; po Zinc in developing countries WHO | ◆Bismuth Subsalicylate **C** | **PEPTO-BISMOL**▼<br>generics | Tx: 30ml or 2 tabs q30mins x 8doses/d<br>Prophylaxis Travelers Diarrhea: QID<br>**Contraindicated in children esp≤3yrs** | 5-10 | ◆**antidiarrheals are contraindicated in ≤2yrs**; treatment of infantile diarrhea should be rehydration & appropriate dietary measures, treatment of underlying causes<br>◆AVOID sorbitol, xylitol, lactose, any food triggers<br>◆Traveller's Diarrhea prevention: Dukoral Vaccine (for cholera & E. coli). *Boil it, Cook it, Peel it or Forget it!*<br>◆bismuth subsalicylate can turn tongue & stools black; beware salicylate overdose & Reye's Sx<br>◆kaolin not particularly effective but attapulgite (KAOPECTATE Canada **B**) of limited usefulness for symptoms; psyllium (METAMUCIL **B**) also useful for symptom control - absorbs fluids, adds bulk<br>◆**avoid loperamide if dysenteric symptoms or high fever; can lead to retention of pathogens** |
| | ◆**Probiotics**: (*Saccharomyces boulardii* FLORASTOR; *Lactobacillus rhamnosus GG* CULTURELLE; probiotic mixtures): ↓ the development of antibiotic-associated diarrhea. Only *S. boulardii* 1g od effective for *C. difficile* diarrhea. [165] Also caution if immunocompromised & concerns with lack of live bacteria in some products. | | | | |
| | ◆Loperamide **B** | **IMODIUM**▼<br>generics | 4mg stat; 2mg after each loose bowel movement to max of 16mg (8tabs)/day<br>Use cautiously in kids <12yrs;<br>**Contraindicated if ≤2yrs old** | 8-12 | |
| | ◆Rx preps: codeine & **LOMOTIL** available | | | | |
| | **Irritable Bowel Syndrome (IBS)** [58-61,106] is characterized by disordered intestinal motility & alternating bouts of constipation & diarrhea. Organic causes must be ruled out. Therapy is symptomatic (loperamide for diarrhea, fiber for constipation, antispasmodics if indicated). **Lifestyle** changes are as important as drug therapy (avoid food triggers, adequate diet, fibre, fluids & exercise, reducing stress); underlying psychosocial co-morbidity should also be treated. Rx products such as antidepressants (**Elavil**), antispasmodics (**Buscopan, Bentylol**⊗, **Modulon**✗, **Dicetel**✗⊗, **Zelnorm**✗⊗ for constipation, FDA D/C Mar 2007 but now avail. for specific criteria, 82) may help. | | | | |

**PAIN**

| COMPLAINT & TREATMENT NOTES | DRUGS OF CHOICE | | USUAL DOSE Adult / Pediatrics (Daily MAXIMUM) | $ | COMMENTS |
|---|---|---|---|---|---|
| **PAIN RELIEF – GENERAL**<br>◆for conditions self-limiting and of short duration including: lower back, dental, headache<br>◆**Caution**: many strengths, formulations and combination products available | ◆Acetaminophen **B**<br>Acetaminophen available in many combo products. Ensure total MAX <4grams/day. | **TYLENOL**▼ generics | 325-1000mg q4-6h; MAX 3.2 - 4g/day (≤12yrs: 10-**15**mg/kg q4-6h: **MAX 75mg/kg/day; liver concerns** [152]) | 5-9 | ◆for more complete discussion of analgesic agents, see other ***Rx Files*** Comparative Charts: *NSAIDs and other Analgesics*, *Opiates*, *Migraine Treatment & Prophylaxis*, *Back Pain*<br>◆maximum OTC ibuprofen dose provides analgesia but anti-inflammatory effect requires ≥1600mg/day - regular<br>**Caution:** chronic use can lead to rebound headache; NSAIDS: ↑ heart failure & hypertension, ↑GI ulcers.<br>◆non drug treatments (massage, hot/cold therapy, resuming activity, physiotherapy...) are sometimes useful |
| | ◆ASA **C/D** | **ASPIRIN**▼, **ANACIN**, g | 325-1000mg q4-6h; MAX 4g/day<br>**Avoid** in children due to Reyes | 5-9<br>50-100 t | |
| | ◆Ibuprofen **B/D** | ***ADVIL***▼, ***MOTRIN***▼, g | 200-400mg q6-8h; MAX^OTC 1.2g/d<br>6mon-12yrs: 5-10mg/kg q6-8h MAX <40mg/kg/day OTC | 4-12<br>50-100 t | |
| | ◆Naproxen▼ | **ALEVE** | 220mg q8-12h; MAX^OTC 660mg/d (may give 440mg with first dose; Not indicated OTC for <12yrs) | 9-17<br>50-100 t | |

Codeine available OTC only in combination products (eg. **TYLENOL #1, ATASOL 8**) or ASA (eg. **222s**) in a dose of 8mg codeine /tablet.

DERMATOLOGY

| COMPLAINT & TREATMENT NOTES | DRUGS OF CHOICE | | USUAL DOSE Adult / Pediatrics (Daily MAXIMUM) | $ | COMMENTS OTC Products |
|---|---|---|---|---|---|
| **ACNE** (noninflammatory;papulopustular)[38-40,87-89]<br>Mild – moderate cases may be treated with OTC preps & non-drug therapy:<br>•balanced diet✓; (food "triggers" *e.g. ?milk*, likely have minimal direct affect)<br>•wash ≤ BID (mild soap/soapless cleanser)<br>•wash hair frequently & keep off the face & forehead<br>•use oil-free cosmetics<br>•control stress factors<br>•avoid picking & squeezing lesions to prevent scarring<br>•while somewhat useful to cosmetically dry oily skin, **antiseptic** cleansers often ineffective (as surface bacteria not causative agent), costly & irritate skin | •Benzoyl Peroxide (**BP**) 2.5-5% OTC in lotions, creams, gels (>5% products by Rx only)<br><br>•Glycolic Acid (eg. alpha hydroxy acid)<br>•Salicylic Acid (**SA**)- up to 5% | 2.5%, 5% lotion or gel<br>**BENZAGEL**▼,<br>**PanOxyl Aquagel**▼<br>**Spectro AcneCare; Proactive** (wash & soap also available)<br><br>**NeoStrata..., Reversa...**<br><br>Lotion, 1% or 2%<br>**Acnex**▼**; Clearasil; Oxy Control** | General Directions:<br>•begin with water based lotion or cream with BP 2.5% (or maybe SA)<br>•apply at HS after washing, increase to BID if needed; wash off in am<br>•allow a trial of 6-8wks; if no improvement increase to BP 5% lotion or cream at hs (can ↑ to BID) or can use water based BP gel<br>• if no improvement, consider Rx products: topical antibiotics eryc & clindamycin, or oral; oral contraceptives Tri-Cyclen, Alesse; Diane-35 ✗, **Stieva-A**▼ comedogenic, **Differin**▼ fast onset & less skin irritation but expensive, **Tazorac**▼ effective but skin irritation & expensive, or **Accutane**▼ severe, nodulocystic cases; monitor for lipid & liver effects) **X** | 8-15<br><br>25<br><br>8-10 | •**BP most effective OTC** agent; ↓sebum production & has both exfoliant & antibacterial effects *P. acnes*<br>•glycolic acids: ? better than SA with ↓ irritation<br>•SA preps less potent exfoliant but still effective for mild cases, less irritating than BP<br>•**SE**: all preps cause stinging, reddening, peeling of skin esp. BP; BP can bleach hair & clothing<br>•all products: begin @low concentration & ↑ up; potency greatest with: **gels > creams > lotion**<br>•**applying to entire affected area more effective** than "spot treating"<br>•warn patients they may look **worse before better**; **may take 6-12 weeks for improvement** |
| | **Drug induced acne**: **anabolic steroids**, azathioprine, bromides, **carbamazepine**, cetuximab, **corticosteroids**, corticotropin, cyclosporine, disulfiram, erlotinib, gefitinib, isoniazid, **lithium**, phenobarbital, **phenytoin**, quinidine, sirolimus, tetracycline & vitamins $B_{1, 6, \& 12}$ & $D_2$. | | | | BP tolerability improved if applied for only 15 min. initially before removing, then double contact time qhs up to 4hrs, then can leave on overnight. |
| **FUNGAL Infections** [41-44, 100]<br>(acute, superficial)<br>•**Athlete's Foot (Tinea pedis)**<br>•**Jock Itch (Tinea cruris)**<br>•**Ringworm (Tinea corporis)**<br>Nystatin▼ – 2nd ary choice as must be applied 3-4x daily; treats yeast (candida, pityrosporum) but not dermatophyte fungi, thus not useful for most cases of jock itch, athlete's foot or ringworm | •Clotrimazole 1% cream<br>•Miconazole 2% cream<br>Rx: Terbinafine (LAMISIL) 1% cream or 1% spray soln: Apply BID **x1**-2 wks (Max 4wks) $23/30g<br>•Tolnaftate – slightly less effective,higher recurrence | **CANESTEN**▼ **B**<br>**MICATIN**▼ **C**<br><br>**TINACTIN**▼ – crm, aerosol, powder **U** | Apply BID (am + hs) x 2-6weeks<br>Apply to affected as well as surrounding area. Continue application for at least 1 week after symptoms disappear to ensure eradication (10-14 days preferred) | 7-13<br>8-14<br><br>9-14 | •keep area clean and dry (use non-scented talc or medicated powder as prophylaxis)<br>•do not share towels or personal items<br>•improve ventilation of affected area –wear loose clothing, cotton fabrics etc<br>•launder affected linens and clothing in hot water; dry in hot dryer or line dry to expose to UV rays<br>•foul odor may indicate secondary bacterial infection<br>•if recurring tinea pedis & cruris → possibly a sign of toenail infection requiring Rx systemic therapy<br>•Rx systemic products: **Diflucan**☎▼, **Nizoral**☎▼, **Lamisil**▼, **Sporanox**☎▼ & **Terazol**▼ may be needed, esp. for non-responsive/non-albicans infections. |
| •**Candidiasis -Vaginal**<br>-Cochrane Review: no difference in effectiveness of oral Rx vs intra-vaginal OTC routes; oral route often preferred by pts.[71]<br>-fluconazole 150mg po weekly effective in ↓ recurrent vaginal candidiasis but expensive & DIs possible [93] | •Clotrimazole<br>•Miconazole<br><br>•Fluconazole +/- clotrimazole vag crm | **CANESTEN**▼ 1,3,6 day **B**<br>**MONISTAT**▼ 1,3,7 day **C**<br><br>CanesOral 1day | Vaginal: Insert one applicatorful or one vag supp at hs x 1-7 days; apply cream to external perineum & vulvar area BID<br>150mg tab x1; may follow with clotrimazole vag crm | 16-18<br>14-16<br>25-33 | **Vaginal candidiasis**<br>• **1-3 days regimens as effective** as 6-7days with **better compliance**; recurrent resistant cases may need 3-4weeks therapy. If pregnancy, tx 7 days.<br>•dietary yogurt (with live culture) or oral bacilli caps may help restore Lactobacilli colonization, but not prevent post-antibiotic vulvovaginitis [94] |
| | Vaginal products: {CANESTEN 3 Combi Pak▼, CANESTEN 1 Combi Pak▼; CANESTEN 3 Cream 2%▼, CANESTEN 6 Cream 1%▼; MONISTAT 3 Dual Pak▼, MONISTAT 7 Dual Pak▼; MONISTAT 3 Vag Supp▼; MONISTAT 2% Cr.▼} | | | | |
| **Diaper** – see below; usually secondary infection after 2-3days of general diaper dermatitis (shiny red patches with satellite lesions; can affect folds | | | | | |
| **DERMATITIS** - **mild-moderate**<br>**Atopic**[45,46,112,116] **(eczema)**–unknown cause<br>•hydration therapy •itch control<br>•simple emollients underutilized HEO<br>**Contact**– allergens & irritants eg. nickel,detergents [163]<br>•acute – cool compress (+/- astringent eg. Buro-Sol solution)<br>•chronic – hydration as per atopic | •Hydrating creams,lotions<br>•Colloidal oatmeal preps<br>•Petroleum jelly<br>•Hydrocortisone ½ %<br>•Oral Antihistamines (limited efficacy; 1st gen H1 preferred; ATARAX Rx useful for itch; sedation effect); H2's also option | Lubriderm,Nutraderm Moisturel, Sarna-P, Uremol<br>**AVEENO BATH**<br>**VASELINE; {PREVEX**▼**}**<br>**CORTATE**▼ see comments<br>Chlorpheniramine **B**<br>Diphenhydramine **B**<br>Cetirizine [24] :blocks mast cell release **B** | Apply BID-QID<br>Use in the bath as directed (If severe atopic: ½ cup Clorox **bleach** in bath 10min twice/wk may help)<br>See allergy section; **1st gen**: effective for **both** allergic & non allergic rash but sedating give @ hs & thus esp. **useful** for **non-allergic rash** eg. eczema. **2nd gen**: less useful for non allergic rash but ↓sedation; **useful** for **allergic rash** eg. hives & bites. | 8-12 ~400ml<br>8-14<br>3-5<br>5-8<br>8-12<br>18<br>8-10 | **Non drug treatment:**<br>•avoid known triggers, irritants, stress; minimize soap use & hot water contact (bathing, showering)<br>•cool room temp with adequate humidity<br>•loose cotton clothing; avoid wool & synthetics<br>•use laundry soap vs detergent; double rinse cycle (or vinegar in the rinse for diapers); avoid fabric softener<br>**Topical corticosteroids** (eg. hydrocortisone **CORTATE**, clobetasone **SPECTRO ECZEMA CARE**):<br>**Use lowest effective potency for as short duration as possible** (Rx strength may be required for flare-ups and acute contact dermatitis; **apply sparingly BID and change to hydrating lubricants once acute symptoms under control)**<br>**Rx products**: topical corticosteroids (Betaderm, Diprosone, Dermovate); non-steroidal anti-inflammatories (Protopic ☎, Elidel ☎); antibiotics (Fucidin 2%Cr/Oint, Cloxacillin, Bactroban) |
| | •Aluminum acetate (astringent) compresses<br>•anti-staphylococcal | **BURO-SOL COMPRESS**▼ | If oozing vesicles, apply **BURO-SOL** for 10 minutes 3-4x/day; otherwise cool H2O or saline compresses for 20min 4-6x/day. | 10-12 | |
| **Diaper** – prevention key:<br>•change diapers often; keep area clean and dry; •disposable diapers good & often better than cloth<br>•some baby wipes may be irritating; try other brand or use wash cloth and water<br>•increase air exposure time<br>•use protectants as prophylaxis<br>•avoid potent corticosteroids!!! | •Petroleum jelly<br>•Baby or talc powder (avoid use of corn starch)<br>•Zinc Oxide cream, paste [181]<br>•Hydrocortisone ½%<br>•Antifungals (clotrimazole,miconazole) | **VASELINE**<br><br>**ZINCOFAX**▼**,PENATEN**<br>**CORTATE**▼<br>**CANESTEN**▼ **B**<br>**MICATIN**▼ **C** | **Protectants** should be applied liberally to diaper area with each change; for steroids and antifungals (for candidal cases) – may rub in small amount to affected area, cover with protectant (may alternate between steroid and antifungal rather than mixing together which dilutes both) | 3-5<br><br>5-10<br>5-8<br>7-10<br>7-10 | |

| COMPLAINT & TREATMENT | DRUGS OF CHOICE | | USUAL DOSE Adult / Pediatrics | $ | COMMENTS |
|---|---|---|---|---|---|

## DERM.

### PLANTAR WARTS [47-49,70]

-hard, flat with black pinpoint specks in center
- 20-30% resolve within 6 months without tx and 65% within 2yrs
- removal desirable often due to pain and to reduce spread of infection

Rx: Cantharone Plus▼ also an option.

| Drugs of choice | | Usual dose | $ |
|---|---|---|---|
| Salicylic Acid (SA) 12-40% ◆gels, collodions, plasters, discs, pads (weaker preps: less pain but require more reapplication) | COMPOUND W Plus (30% liquid;40% pads)<br>DUOFORTE 27% gel▼<br>DUOFILM 40% patch<br>SCHOLLS Wart Remover 40% disks | ◆Apply daily @hs (patch & disk q48h) until all warty tissue is removed; Presoak area in warm water, then pare away any overlying kera-toma & dead tissue before applying<br>◆may take 8-12 weeks for resolution<br>(more concentrated SA preps used by specialists) | 10-15<br>17<br>20 /14<br>20 |

Laser therapy: expensive & sometimes painful. ??Zinc 10mg/kg od ~60d[84]
??Duct tape: 6days on, 12hrs off; repeat x 5-10 cycles may work [66]

**B**

Comments:
- If diabetes/vascular disorder **do not self treat**
- Rx:Podophyllin&cantharidin CANTHARONE▼ effective single application; delayed[~24hr] pain & blistering
- Cauterization or freezing with liquid nitrogen faster & more efficacious but often more painful
- Avoid walking barefoot (eg. in pool area).
- OTC cryotherapy ~$30 (eg. Lines: Dr. Scholl, Compound W, Wartner)

### HEAD LICE (*P. capitis*) [50-51,124]

- **Notify & examine all contacts** to prevent reinfestation cycle:↑resistance.
- **Reinfestation prevention**: **nit removal**; bedding, clothing, etc.: wash & dry (with heat >15mins), dry clean or seal in plastic bag for ~14 days; vacuum affected rooms; soak combs & brushes in disinfectant solution x 1hr or hot water (65°C for 10min)
- Discourage "no nit" school policies [CDN 124]

| Drugs of choice | | | Usual dose | $ |
|---|---|---|---|---|
| ◆**Permethrin** 1% Cream Rinse | NIX▼, KWELLADA-P▼ | **B** | ◆Apply as directed; ?**REPEAT in 7days.** | 11-14 |
| Cream Rinse: Apply to washed, towel dried hair. Saturate hair & scalp, wait 10 min, rinse. | | | | |
| ◆Pyrethrins & Piperonyl Butoxide | R & C Shampoo▼ | **C** | ◆Apply as directed; **REPEAT in 7 days.** | 9 |
| Apply & saturate dry hair & scalp, wait 10 min, slowly add water to lather, rinse. | | | | |
| ◆Lindane 1% Shampoo | Generic ▼ | **C** | ◆Apply as directed; **REPEAT in 7 days.** | 9 |
| Apply-saturate dry hair & scalp, massage x4 min., add H2O slowly - lather, massage x4 min. then rinse. | | | | |
| ◆ SH-206 - see comments | SH-206 Shampoo | **U** | ◆Apply as directed; **REPEAT in 48 hrs.** | 10 |
| ◆ Isopropyl myristate 50% | RESULTZ ▼ -see comments | | ◆Apply as directed; **REPEAT in 7 days.** | 13 |

Comments:
- Do not sit in bath water as hair is being rinsed.
- R&C Efficacy: 45% on 1st application; 94% on 2nd
- **CI**: Permethrin ↓chance or Pyrethrin: allergy ragweed or chrysanthemum
- **Lindane**: **neurotoxicity/seizure** [133] -ingestion or ↑↑ use; **CI**:young kids, pregnancy, if nursing, elderly, skin dx
- **Long/thick hair pts** may require 2 x ~50ml bottles
- **Tea Tree Oil**: lack of evidence; contact dermatitis
- **SH-206**: a "natural product" **lacking data**; contains acetic acid, citronella, camphor & sodium lauryl ether sulphate
- **Resultz**: dissolves wax louse exoskeleton; for age ≥2yr on SPDP plan; avoid in eyes, may stain fabric, **new & limited trial** data.

## VITAMINS & MINERALS

### VITAMINS/SUPPLEMENTS [129]

**In otherwise healthy subjects, supplementation recommended in**:
- Breast-fed infants -Vitamin D 400IU/d
- Deficient intake or Malabsorption [81]
- Pregnancy - $Ca^{++}$, Vit D, **folate**, iron (possible with diet alone), MV esp in developing countries [52]
- Vegetarians - $Ca^{++}$, Vit B12, D, Iron?
- Alcoholic - Vit B's; multivit. (MV) ?
- Women with heavy menses - Iron
- Non-milk drinkers - $Ca^{++}$, Vit D
- Elderly[126](esp. if poor diet) -B12,D;Ca+MV?
- if on steroids/phenytoin -Vit D, $Ca^{++}$
- HIV -Multivit.(B's,C,E & folic) [91,107]

### IRON ($Fe^{++}$) SUPPLEMENTS

- iron products: use on Dr's advice [113]
- amount of iron in multivitamins OK for chronic daily use; breast-fed infants ≥6mo require $Fe^{++}$ (cereals or supplement)

### CALCIUM & VITAMIN D [109-111]

- adequate intake important throughout life (consider age, bisphosphonates, etc.)
- Vit D essential to ↑active $Ca^{++}$ absorption & use; low in most North Americans esp. above 55th parallel due to ↓ sun.[62] blocked by SPF ≥ 8 (20mins of sun may produce >2,000iu $D_3$/day) Vit D→cod liver oil, herring, salmon, sardines & tuna (25hydroxy Vit D level >75nmol/l may be optimal)
- magnesium supplements not required as deficiency rare (dietary intake sufficient); no proven bone benefit,but laxative effect may counteract constipation from $Ca^{++}$
- ↑Vit A: may ↑bone loss; interfere with Vit D

#### Vitamin Products

Vit $D_3$: D-VI-SOL 400 IU/ml ▼ **Baby Ddrops** 400 IU/drop ; (=10ug cholecalciferol)

**Children's:** Flintstones Extra C▼ chewable CENTRUM JUNIOR ▼

Pregnancy: **MATERNA**▼ $Fe^{++}$ 27mg, Folic 1mg & Vit A 1500iu.
**PregVit folic 5** Rx⊗ Halal,Kosher

Health Canada: recommends a multivitamin with 16-20mg $Fe^{++}$ in pregnancy.[2009]

{**Iron/Folic/Vit C**: **PALAFER CF** $Fe^{++}$ 100mg; Folic 0.5mg; VitC 200mg}

B & C Vitamins: **BEMINAL C FORTIS**

- well formulated multivitamins (**MV**) with both regular and age 50+ formulations:
  - -CENTRUM; ONE-A-DAY; PARAMETTES
  - **-house brands:** most retailers have products comparable to brand name at **lower cost**

Ferrous sulfate ▼ (300mg tab = **60**mg $Fe^{++}$)
Fer-in-Sol drops ▼ ~$20 (75mg/ml = 15mg $Fe^{++}$)
Ferrous sulfate syrup▼ (30mg/ml = 6mg $Fe^{++}$)
**Ferrous gluconate**▼ (300mg tab = **35**mg $Fe^{++}$)
**Ferrous fumarate**▼ (300mg tab = **99**mg $Fe^{++}$)

- **Calcium carbonate** least expensive & highest percentage of avail. elemental $Ca^{++}$ (take with food):
  - calcium **carbonate** ▼ = **40%** elemental $Ca^{++}$ eg. CALTRATE (1500mg = 600mg elemental $Ca^{++}$) TUMS chew (Reg=200mg, Extra=300mg, Ultra=400mg $Ca^{++}$)▼ Combo products with Vit D: eg. Cal-500-D ▼
  - calcium **citrate** = **21%** elemental $Ca^{++}$
  - calcium **lactate** = **13%** elemental $Ca^{++}$
  - calcium **gluconate** = **9%** elemental $Ca^{++}$
- **General multivitamin** good source of **vitamin D** (most have ≥400IU/tablet)
- **Milk:** 1 cup = 300mg $Ca^{++}$ & 100 IU Vit D 30g cheese = 200mg $Ca^{++}$; Tofu 120g = 150mg $Ca^{++}$

#### RDA Recommended Daily Allowance in Adults:

**Fat Soluble Vitamins** — Replace if low fat diet e.g. orlistat patients

| RDA | $ |
|---|---|
| **A** (retinol) 700♀-900♂ ug (~3000 IU) | 15 |
| Beta carotene - 6000 ug (~10000 IU) | 8-12 |
| **D** 400 IU; 600 IU if >70yr; higher often now recommended! CND Cancer Society→ High risk, Adults esp fall & winter: 1000 iu/d. Max 2000iu/d | 15-20 |
| {2010 CND Vit D Osteoporosis Guide [111]: 400-1000 IU men & ♀<50yr; 800-2000 IU if >50yr}▼ **D3 –cholecalciferol** often preferable to D2 ergocalciferol | Vit B&C |
| **E** 22 IU (15mg) *RRR*-α-tocopherol natural▼ {= 67 IU (30mg) of all-rac-α-tocoferol synthetic }[1] | 8-12 /60 tab |

**Water Soluble Vitamins**

| RDA | $ |
|---|---|
| **B1** (thiamine) ~1.2 mg | Multivite |
| **B2** (riboflavin) ~1.3 mg | 10-12 /3 month |
| **B3** (niacin) ~15 mg | |
| **B6** (pyridoxine)~1.5mg replace ≥25mg▼ if on isoniazid | Fe++ |
| **B12** (cyanocobalamine) 2.4 ug Replace if no terminal ileum {OTC: CENTRUM SELECT 25ug▼; Rx: 100&250▼ & 1200ug tab; $10/mo [104-115]} | 5-10 / 60 tab |
| **C** (ascorbic acid[130]) 75-90 mg (Juice ≤100mg) | 12-15 for 30 tab SR products |
| **Folic Acid**[166] ≥400 ug→ Replace if pregnant esp if on anticonvulsants, on methotrexate,phenytoin, or if malabsorption Sx. (cereal grains fortified in Canada) | |
| **Pantothenic acid** 5 mg | Ca++ |

**Minerals** (elemental amounts)

| RDA | $ |
|---|---|
| $Fe^{++}$ 8 mg (men & ♀ post menopausal) 18 mg (women <50yrs) {Treatment: 2-3mg/kg/day e.g. Ferrous Sulfate 300mg (=60mg $Fe^{++}$) po BID-TID} Peds $Fe^{++}$: Treatment 6mg/kg/d; Proph 0.5-2mg/kg/d | 5-12 /100tab |
| $Ca^{++}$ 1000 mg (adults); 1500 mg for postmenopausal ♀ & ♂ >50yrs [6] | Multivite |
| $Mg^{++}$ 310-420 mg | 10-12 /3 month |
| $Zn^{+}$ 8-11 mg (evidence inconclusive in common cold [75], ?eye [85],?↓pneumonia & diarrhea[127]) | |

#### Comments

**GENERAL SUPPLEMENTATION** [103]
- vitamins **not** a substitute for healthy diet
- NO proven benefit to "mega dose" supplements unless true deficiency; excess water soluble vitamins (Bs & C) are lost in the urine, while fat-soluble (A,D,E,K) can accumulate⇨toxicity. Also - ↑ **Vit A**:↑ lung ca in smokers[78,96] & may ↑ fracture risk[80,95]

**ANTI-OXIDANT:** no proven heart/**cancer** benefit for supplemental Vit E, C, beta-Carotene & Selenium [53,54,90,108,161]; Vit E: Alzheimer's limited evidence [67,68,79] & no benefit in mild cognitive impairment [105] & may impair statin benefit [69]; nicotinamide not prevent diabetes [83]; some evidence that ***dietary*** antioxidants ***sources*** may ↓heart risk. Vit E may ↑mortality[97,98],↑heart failure[102] & not ↓cancer in ♀[1 22]. Antioxidants & zinc: may ↓eye macular degeneration.

**IRON:** best on an **empty** stomach (or HS) but GI SE common so OK to take with food but absorption ↓by ≤50% (Vit. C >200-1000mg ↑absorption). SR & enteric forms may cause less GI effects but expensive & poorly absorbed. Tx ~3 months to replace iron stores. Lower dose in anemic elderly may be ok.[113]

**CALCIUM** (DI: ↓ levels of iron, quinolones, tetracyclines, thyroid meds etc.)
- can only absorb ~500mg $Ca^{++}$ at once so best to **split dose** (ie. 1 tab BID); ◆Ca carbonate better **with food** so take with meal (if necessary one bedtime dose is acceptable). Excessive intake→milk alkali syndrome.
- Citrate form – ↑absorption if achlorhydria, ?less GI SE & ↓kidney stones, but caution if ↓ renal fx
- if natural source $Ca^{++}$, use reputable product as **lead** contamination possible esp. with off-shore health food products
- Microcrystalline hydroxyapatite concentrate –MCHC: $Ca^{++}$ from veal bone
- Foods $Ca^{++}$: Milk 1 cup=~300mg, cheese 30g=~200mg, tofu 1/2 cup=~200mg

= ↓ dose for renal dysfx ♀=female ✗ =non formulary in Sask. ☎=EDS ▼ = covered by NIHB
BP=blood pressure COPD=chronic obstructive pulmonary disease CI=contraindication d=days
DI=drug interaction Dx=disease GERD=gastroesophageal reflux disease h=hours hs=bedtime
Rx=prescription SE=side effect SR=sustained release tsp=teaspoon~5ml tbsp=tablespoon~15ml
tx=treatment wk=weeks yr=year; ς= scored; Cost Range: low-end price - generic or smaller size

**References** © www.RxFiles.ca - **OTC Products : 1**. Patient Self-Care, first edition. CPhA; Ottawa, Canada: 2002 **2**. Compendium of Nonprescription Products. CPhA; Ottawa, Canada: 2002-3. **3**. Therapeutic Choices, Fifth edition. CPhA: Ottawa, Canada: 2007. **4**. Drug Information Handbook, 18th edition. APhA; Hudson, Ohio; 2009. **5**. **Treatment Guidelines**: Drugs for Allergic Disorders. The **Medical Letter**: Feb, **2010**; pp. 9-18. **6**. Reid RL, et al. SOGC (Society of Obstetricians and Gynaecologists of Canada)-Menopause and **Osteoporosis Update 2009**. JOGC. **2009**;222:S34-S45.167(S1): 1-34. http://www.sogc.org/guidelines/documents/Menopause_JOGC-Jan_09.pdf **7**. Drugs in Pregnancy and Lactation, 8th ed. Briggs GE; 2008.
Special thanks to Dr. Jeff Taylor, University of Saskatchewan (UofS), College of Pharmacy & Nutrition, as primary reviewer for the OTC Products Chart. Also thanks to specialist reviewers: HM Juma (Podiatry), P. Spafford (ENT), WJ Fenton (Allergy), MP Persaud (Allergy) D. Lichtenwald (Dermatol), WP Olszynski (Rheumatol) & the RxFiles Advisory Committee. 

| Generic/TRADE g=generic avail (Strength & forms) Pregnancy[9] | Side effects / Contraindications CI | √ = therapeutic use / Comments / Drug Interactions DI / Monitor M | Initial[4] / Typical Dose[8] (Max mg/d) * Titration[4] {Child(up to 40 kg); Adolescent; Adult} | $ / 30 days |
|---|---|---|---|---|
| **PSYCHOSTIMULANTS** Response rate ~75%, effect size ~0.9; SHORT-ACTING: (Ritalin, Dexedrine) are less money & flexible during **initial** Tx, esp. in small kids. But, social stigmatization & drug diversion related to in-school dosing.<br>INTERMEDIATE-ACTING: (Ritalin SR, Dexedrine Spansules) may last up to 8 hours. {CADDRA guidelines generally recommend long-acting agents as 1st line; however expert opinion notes role for individualization of therapy.}<br>LONG-ACTING: (Concerta, Biphentin, Adderall XR) are dosed once-daily & have less fluctuation in serum concentrations (may ↑ compliance). May affect evening appetite & sleep, & are more expensive (varying drug plan coverage). Less abuse potential. | | | | |
| **Amphetamine Mixed Salts**<br>dextroamphetamine and levoamphetamine salts (3:1)<br>**ADDERALL XR** χ ⊗<br>5, 10, 15, 20, 25, 30mg cap<br>50% **immediate release** &<br>50% gradual release [MOA:↑ DA,NE]<br>C | **Common**: appetite suppression, ↓ weight, insomnia, headache, dry mouth, rebound irritability, nausea/vomiting, constipation/diarrhea, GI upset, dizziness, anxiety, tremor, ↑BP & ↑HR, emotional lability; slow growth<br>**Infrequent**: uncovering tics, sexual dysfunction, tactile & visual hallucinations, psychosis, ↓ seizure threshold<br>**Serious**: sudden death (see Cardiac Risk note below)<br>CI: advanced arteriosclerosis, symptomatic CV dx, hyperthyroidism ↑BP, hypersensitivity/idiosyncrasy to sympathomimetic amines, glaucoma, agitated states, drug abuse hx, or MAOI use within 14day<br>**Precautions**: **amphetamine misuse or if cardiac dx** → ↑BP/↑HR, serious CV events or even sudden death; **hx of drug dependence**→ ↑ abuse; **hx seizures/EEG changes**→ may ↓seizure threshold; **pre-existing psychosis, bipolar or hx of tics or Tourette's**‡ → may worsen disorder | √ ADHD age ≥ 6yr (narcolepsy in the USA)<br>May be opened & sprinkled on soft foods<br>**Duration: 8-12hr (long-acting)**<br>DI: ↑amphetamines effect: acetazolamide, antacid; MAOI & linezolid ↑effect & ↑BP; sympathomimetics ↑HR & BP, & TCAs ↑CV effects<br>M: ADHD symptoms, behaviour & academic performance; rating scales e.g. SNAP-IV, Conners', CGI; physical exam, patient & family cardiac hx, ECG (at baseline & consider repeat if pt age <12yr at initial ECG or if change in patient symptoms eg. palpitations/syncope)<br>BP, HR: At Day 0, 1 & 3months then q6-12months<br>Pediatric patients: development , weight & growth | Peds: 10mg qam / **30mg qam** (30 mg/d) Titrate 5-10mg q7d<br>Adolescents:<br>10mg qam / **30mg qam** (50mg/d) Titrate 5mg q7d<br>Adults:<br>10mg qam / **60mg qam** (60mg/d) Titrate 5-10mg q7d | 86 / **123** (123)<br>86 / **123** (208)<br>86 / **240** (240) |
| **Dextroamphetamine**<br>**DEXEDRINE** 5g mg tab<br>**DEXEDRINE Spansule**<br>10, 15mg cap<br>[MOA: blocks re-uptake of DA; increases release of DA and NE]<br>C<br>{SK Formulary: max $15/Rx for age ≤14yrs as of Jul/08} | **Common**: *as in Adderall XR*<br>**Infrequent**: *as in Adderall XR*<br>**Serious**: *as in Adderall XR*<br>CI: as in Adderall XR + patients with motor tics or with a family hx of diagnosis of Tourette's Syndrome‡<br>**Precautions**: *as in Adderall XR* + tartrazine (FD&C Yellow No. 5) sensitivity, esp. with aspirin sensitivity; may cause allergic-type reaction (tablets)<br>**Precautions**:<br>**CV disease** (HF, MI, ↑BP, QT syndrome) → ↑BP/↑HR, sudden death reported;<br>**Hx of drug/alcohol dependence**→ ↑ abuse; **Psychosis**→ may worsen Sx; hyperthyroidism;<br>**Seizures/EEG changes** → may ↓ seizure threshold;<br>**Severe depression or normal fatigue** → cautious/avoid use. | √ ADHD age ≥ 6 yr; adjunctive therapy for narcolepsy<br>**Duration: Tab:~4-6hr (short);**<br>**Spansule** both IR & ER pellets: **6-8hr (intermediate)**<br>**More potent than MPH** (10mg MPH ≈ 5mg Dextroamp.)<br>**Short-acting** often used as **initial** Tx in small kids, but bid-tid dosing; **longer acting** greater convenience, confidentiality but may ↓evening appetite & ↓sleep<br>Spansules may be opened & **sprinkled** on soft foods<br>DI: *as in Adderall XR*<br>M: *as in Adderall XR* | Peds: Tab: 2.5mg qam & qnoon / **10mg bid** (30mg/d) Titrate 5mg q7d by adding 4pm dose<br>Spansule: 10mg qam / **15mg qam** (30mg/d) Titrate 10mg q7d by adding 4pm dose<br>Adolescents:<br>Tab: 2.5mg qam & qnoon / **10mg bid** (30 mg/d) Titrate 5mg q7d by adding 4pm dose<br>Spansule: 10mg qam / **15mg qam** (30 mg/d) Titrate 10mg q7d by adding 4pm dose<br>Adult: Tab: 5mg qam & qnoon / **15mg bid** (50 mg/d) Titrate 5mg q7d by adding 4pm dose<br>Spansule: 10mg qam / **30mg qam** (45 mg/d) Titrate 10mg q7d by adding 4pm dose | 27 / **88** (128)<br>36 / **42** (78)<br>27 / **88** (128)<br>36 / **42** (78)<br>47 / **128** (208)<br>36 / **78** (113) |
| **Lisdexamfetamine VYVANSE** χ ⊗; NEW Canada: 20,30,40,50 & 60mg cap daily $110-140 in morning; √ADHD age 6-12yr; caps taken whole or dissolved in water; a prodrug & slower rate controlled absorption thus hope to have ↓abuse. | | | | |
| **Methylphenidate (MPH)**<br>**RITALIN, g** 5, 10g, 20g mg tab<br>**RITALIN SR, g** 20mg tab<br>-do not chew or crush tablet<br>[MOA: blocks DA reuptake] wax matrix<br>C<br>{SK Formulary: max $15/Rx for age ≤14yrs as of Jul/08} | **Common**: Insomnia 13%, ↓appetite 26%, nausea 12%, vomiting 10%, weight loss 9%, tic 7%, emotional instability 6%, anorexia 5%, nasal congestion 6%, nasopharyngitis 5%, headaches<br>**Serious**: blood dyscrasia (very rare), angioedema, hallucinations, sudden death (see Cardiac Risk note below)<br>CI: Anxiety, tension, agitation, thyrotoxicosis, advanced arteriosclerosis, symptomatic CV disease, ↑BP, glaucoma & pheochromocytoma, patients with motor tics or with a family hx or diagnosis of Tourette's syndrome‡, MAOI use within 14 days.<br>**Precautions**:<br>**CV disease** (HF, MI, ↑BP, QT syndrome) → ↑BP/↑HR, sudden death reported;<br>**Hx of drug/alcohol dependence**→ ↑ abuse;<br>**Psychosis**→ may worsen Sx; hyperthyroidism<br>**Seizures/EEG changes** → may ↓ seizure threshold;<br>**Severe depression or normal fatigue** → cautious/avoid use. | √ ADHD age ≥ 6yr (narcolepsy in the USA)<br>**Duration: Tabs**: ~3-5hr (**short**-acting);<br>**SR**: ~3-8hr (**intermediate**-acting)<br>**Short**-acting often used as **initial** Tx in small kids, but bid-tid dosing; **Intermediate acting** ↑convenience & confidentiality but may ↓evening appetite & ↓sleep<br>DI: clonidine ECG changes & sudden death; linezolid & MAOI ↑BP; phenobarbital & phenytoin ↑level; sympathomimetic ↑HR & BP, TCAs ↑TCA levels, warfarin ↑INR ↓ MPH level: carbamazepine<br>M: *as in Adderall XR*. Also CBC, differential & platelets: periodically long-term Tx<br>**Consider abuse & diversion risk** especially with any short acting stimulant (e.g. children may be targeted for the drug). **Take reasonable precautions** to ↓ risk (e.g. use of treatment agreement; refrain from informing others, etc.; consider long-acting stimulant or non-stimulant). | Peds: IR tab: 5mg qam & qnoon 0.3 mg/kg/day / **10mg tid** (60mg/d) Titrate 5-10mg 0.2 mg/kg/day q7d by adding 4pm dose<br>SR tab: 20mg qam / **40mg qam** (60mg/d) Titrate 20mg q7d by adding 2pm dose<br>Adolescents:<br>IR tab: 5mg qam & qnoon / **20mg tid** (60 mg/d) Titrate 5mg q7d by adding 4pm dose<br>SR tab: 20mg qam / **60mg qam** (80 mg/d) Titrate 20mg q7d by adding 2pm dose<br>Adult:<br>IR tab: 10mg qam & qnoon / **20mg tid** (60 mg/d) Titrate 10mg q7d by adding 4pm dose<br>SR tab: 20mg qam / **60mg qam** (100 mg/d) Titrate 20mg q7d by adding 2pm dose<br>**Lower cost options**<br>(**Combo strategies**: e.g. kick start & avoid noon dosing → Ritalin **SR** qam + small Ritalin **IR** dose qam; "rebound" → Ritalin **SR** qam + small Ritalin **IR** dose late afternoon)<br>(Ritalin **no sub** is typically **$15-30 more** than generics/month; may crumble less when tabs split, but has ↑ street abuse value | 14 / **23** (42)<br>18 / **30** (42)<br>14 / **42** (42)<br>18 / **42** (54)<br>18 / **42** (42)<br>18 / **42** (65)<br>(27-39) |
| **Methylphenidate**<br>**BIPHENTIN** χ ⊗<br>C<br>10, 15, 20, 30, 40, 50, 60, 80mg cap<br>Multilayer-release delivery system: 40% **immediate**, 60% gradual | See Methylphenidate above | √ ADHD age ≥ 6yr (somewhat lower cost for once daily)<br>**Duration: 10-12hr (long-acting)**<br>Capsules should be swallowed whole & must never be crushed or chewed. Contents may be **sprinkled** on these soft foods: apple sauce, ice cream or yogurt. | Peds: 10mg qam / **30mg qam** (60mg/d) Titrate 10mg q7d<br>Adolescents:<br>10mg qam / **40mg qam** (80 mg/d) Titrate 10mg q7d<br>Adults:<br>10mg qam / **60mg qam** (80 mg/d) Titrate 10mg q7d | 31 / **66** (114)<br>31 / **82** (146)<br>31 / **114** (146) |
| **Methylphenidate**<br>**CONCERTA** ⊗<br>C<br>18, 27, 36, 54mg tab<br>{New g: Novo-Methylphenidate ER non-OROS}<br>Osmotic release oral system OROS: 22% immediate, 78% **gradual**<br>{SK Formulary: max $15/Rx for age ≤14yrs as of Jul/08} | See Methylphenidate above; tablet does not change in shape in GI tract → should not be administered to pts with pre-existing GI narrowing Dx (e.g. small bowel inflammatory dx, "short gut" syndrome, hx of peritonitis, cystic fibrosis, intestinal pseudo-obstruction, or Meckel's diverticulum).[7]<br>**Dose conversion:**<br>Methylphenidate 5mg bid/tid or 20mg SR od → 18mg qam<br>Methylphenidate 10mg bid/tid or 40mg SR od→ 36mg qam<br>Methylphenidate 15mg bid/tid or 60mg SR od→ 54mg qam<br>(A 27 mg is avail for Drs to prescribe between 18 mg & 36 mg dosages) | √ ADHD age ≥ 6yr<br>**Duration: 8-12hr (long-acting)**<br>Swallow whole with liquids; tablet shell may be in **stool**. Non-deformable shell makes it very difficult to break, cut or crush, which may dramatically ↓ its **abuse risk**<br>(If inadequate immediate effects and/or effects too prolonged esp. at high doses → consider Biphentin) | Peds: 18mg qam / **36mg qam** (54mg/d) Titrate 18mg q7d<br>Adolescents: 18mg qam / **54mg qam** (54 mg/d) Titrate 18mg q7d<br>Adults: 18mg qam / **54mg qam** (108 mg/d) Titrate 18mg q7d<br>****Full formulary SK July/08 in effort to ↓ stimulant abuse & diversion****<br>To get one responder after 6weeks: Concerta NNT=3 vs Strattera NNT=5 Newcom'08 n=516 | 82/ **105** (128)<br>82 / **128** (128)<br>82 / **128** (250)<br>Generic= 30% less costly, but unproven clinically. |

## NON-STIMULANT / SELECTIVE NOREPINEPHRINE REUPTAKE INHIBITOR: Effect size ~0.6

**Consider if…**

Atomoxetine ↓core ADHD Sx by at least ~25% in ~65% of pts after 6-12 weeks of Tx. **Consider if** non-responsive/CIs to stimulants, co-morbid substance **abuse**, anxiety, tics; or stimulant SE (mood lability, tics)

| Drug | Side effects | Comments | Dose | Cost |
|---|---|---|---|---|
| **Atomoxetine** Approved 2005<br>**STRATTERA** ☎ ⊗ C<br>10, 18, 25, 40, 60mg cap<br>(New CDN 80, 100 mg) χ ⊗ USA initially<br>•cap can not be opened/sprinkled<br>[MOA: NE reuptake inhibitor]<br>{SK: if EDS☎ approved, max $15/Rx for age ≤14yrs as of Jul/08} | **Common:** Headache ~20%, insomnia 16%, xerostomia >10%, abdominal pain 20%, vomiting ~10%, ↓appetite ~10%, nausea 12%, cough 11%; mild ↑**BP** ~5% & **HR** 3%; fatigue 8%, ↓weight 2%, urinary hesitation {↑risk of vomiting & somnolence 7% vs MPH-IR; but ↓appetite concern. Poor 2D6 metabolizers have higher rates of ↓appetite}<br>**Serious:** liver toxicity rare, suicidal thinking 0.4%, blackbox warning, sudden death (see below), dyskinesia, seizures peds 0.2%; adults 0.1%, priapism rare<br>**CI:** MAOI within 14days; narrow angle glaucoma; symptomatic CV Dx; ↑BP; advanced arteriosclerosis; uncontrolled hyperthyroidism | √ ADHD age ≥ 6 yrs **Duration: 24hrs (long-acting)**<br>Swallow capsules whole; do not open (GI irritation)<br>**DI:** hepatic CYP450 2D6 metabolism 5-10% are poor metabolizers<br>↑ atomoxetine effect: fluoxetine, linezolid, MAOIs, paroxetine, quinidine; salbutamol ↑HR & BP<br>**M:** weight, height, BMI; attention, hyperactivity, anxiety, worsening of aggressive behaviour or hostility; BP & HR (baseline & following ↑dose & during Tx), emergence of irritability, agitation, changes in behaviour, & suicidal ideation, esp. during initial months of Tx or if ↑ dosage. | Peds: 10mg 0.5mg/kg/d / **25mg qam** 1.2mg/kg/d (Lower of 1.4 mg/kg/d or 60mg/d)<br>Titrate 0.8mg/kg/d at week 2 & 1.2mg/kg/d at week 4 -slower titration to ↓SE | 100 / **125** (150) |
| | | | Adolescents:<br>18mg 0.5mg/kg/d / **40mg qam** 1.2mg/kg/d (Lower of 1.4mg/kg/d or 100mg/d)<br>Titrate 0.8mg/kg/d at week 2 & 1.2mg/kg/d at week 4 -slower titration to ↓SE | 115/ **140** (290 2 cap) |
| | | | Adults:<br>25mg 0.5mg/kg/d / **60-80mg qam** 1.2mg/kg/d (Lower of 100mg/d or 1.4 mg/kg/d)<br>Titrate 40mg, 60mg, 80mg & max 100mg q14days<br>(slower titration will ↓SE or divide dose bid; give at bedtime may ↓nausea & fatigue) | 125/ **150-290**<br>(170 1 cap/290 2 cap) |

**Precautions:** **suicidal ideation/clinical worsening** → ↑risk in kids during first few months of Tx or after ↑dose; **behavioral changes** eg. aggression & hostility → may be precursor to suicidality; **orthostatic hypotension** → use cautiously; **CV disease** (CAD, MI, BP, cardiomyopathy, arrhythmias, QT syndrome)→ risk ↑BP/↑HR & sudden death; **jaundice or liver injury** → risk of liver failure/transplant; **psychotic or bipolar/manic Sx** → hallucinations, delusional thinking or mania may emerge.

## Agents WITHOUT Official Indication for ADHD:

| Generic / TRADE / form | Role in ADHD Adv: Advantages Dis: Disadvantages | Side effects SE / Drug Interactions DI / Comments | Dose |
|---|---|---|---|
| **Bupropion SR**<br>**WELLBUTRIN** g<br>(100,150mg **SR** tab)☎<br>(150,300mg **XL**tab)☎<br>Antidepressant [MOA:↑DA,NE] | Moderately effective for improving the core Sx of ADHD<br>**Adv:** no abuse or diversion risk, not assoc. with rebound hyperactivity, ↓ cost, useful in ADHD pts with comorbid depression &/or nicotine use.<br>**Dis:** 2-4 weeks before effects seen; safety in combo with other ADHD meds not proven. Swallow tablets whole with fluids, & **not** to chew, divide, or crush | **SE:** insomnia, headache, constipation, N/V, nervousness, dizziness, sweating, ↑BP, ↑HR, tics, **suicidal ideation, seizures** 0.5-1%. ↑Seizure with doses > 300 mg/day<br>**DI:** CYP2D6/3A4 Inducers e.g., carbamazepine, phenytoin, rifampin may ↓bupropion level & ↑ level of hydroxybupropion active metabolite. ↑venlafaxine/TCAs eg imipramine, desipramine, nortriptyline levels by bupropion. MAOI ↑ serotonin Sx | SR tab: Peds: 3-6 mg/kg/day; single dose not > 150 mg<br>100-150mg bid 2-3 mg/kg/day; single dose not > 150 mg ;max 450mg/d<br>XL tab:[10]<br>Initial: 150mg XL once daily<br>Usual: 150-300mg XL once daily |
| **Clonidine CATAPRES** g<br>0.1, 0.2mg tab $\alpha_2$-agonist<br>**DIXARIT**, g 0.025 mg tab | ↓ aggression, impulsivity, ↑arousal & ↑activity, but not benefit: inattention or ↓concentration<br>**As an adjunct:** Used concurrently with stimulants, to target **sleep** disruptions, **conduct** issues, aggression, impulsivity, comorbid oppositional defiant disorder & **tics**.<br>**Guanfacine** → available through Health Canada's Special Access Program | **SE:** ↓BP, sedation & dizziness initially; dry mouth; may ↑ depression.<br>**DI:** Avoid use with TCAs. Additive effects with other CNS depressants.<br>**Caution:** CV disease/depression; 2 deaths on MPH & clonidine reported but recent RCT showed clonidine ± MPH to be safe in childhood ADHD[11] | Peds: Usual dose in children: 5-8μg/kg/day; may divide dose<br>Initial 0.05–0.1 mg/day often at bedtime<br>Usual dose in adults: 0.05 – 0.4 mg /day |
| **Desipramine** [MOA: ↑NE]<br>10,25,50,75,100mg tab<br>**Imipramine**<br>10, 25, 50; 75χ▼mg tab<br>**Nortriptyline** 10, 25mg cap<br>Tricyclic antidepressants | TCAs:[1,12] less effective than stimulants at ↓ core ADHD Sx.<br>Beneficial in some pts who cannot take stimulants, atomoxetine or bupropion, or if a concurrent tic Dx, enuresis, sleep problems, anxiety or depression.<br>**Adv:** no abuse potential, not associated with rebound hyperactivity[6]<br>**Dis:** 3-4 weeks before effects seen, risk of overdose, CV side effects<br>Combos with other ADHD meds can be made but referral to ADHD specialist is advised | **SE:** sedation, dizziness, constipation, heart block (check ECG), ↑ weight, overdose toxicity, ↑ HR; sudden death in kids Tx with TCAs reported<br>**DI** see RxFiles Antidepressants DI chart.<br>**Caution:** avoid in pts with a hx of cardiac conduction disorder, urinary retention, seizure disorders or hyperthyroidism.<br>**Monitor:** HR, BP, cardiac exam, weight:baseline→q3-6month while on TCA | **Desipramine** 6–12 y: 10–20 mg/day; adolescent: 30–50 mg/day; (Peds: 2-5 mg/kg/day; Adult dose: 100-300 mg/day).<br>**Imipramine** 6–12 y: 10–20mg/day; adolescent: 30–50 mg/day; max 150 mg/day) (may divide dose)<br>**Nortriptyline** 6–12 y: 10–20mg/day; Adolescent: 30–50mg/day; max 150mg/day (may divide dose) |
| **Risperidone RISPERDAL** g<br>(0.25,0.5ς,1,2ς,3ς,4ς mg tab;<br>{Depot not generally for ADHD}<br>M-TAB melts 0.5,1,2,3,4 mg tab;<br>1mg/ml soln; Antipsychotic | Systematic review: lack of quality evidence.[13] Little effect on inattention.<br>As an adjunct:[1] to target **aggressive**, ↑impulsive or if hyperactive when stimulants alone are ineffective/not tolerated; to ↓ behaviours in kids with comorbid conduct Dx, oppositional defiant Dx, autistic Dx, impulse control Dx & Tourette's Sx. May ↑ compliance | **SE:** Weight gain, drowsiness, headache, orthostatic hypotension, dyspepsia, dose-related extrapyramidal effects; hyperprolactinemia, may negatively affect cognition in pts with ADHD | Initial: 0.25–0.5mg hs; ↑weekly by 0.5 mg/day<br>Usual maintenance dose 0.75–1.5 mg/day |
| **Modafanil ALERTEC** g[4]<br>100mg tab☎▼; (Provigil in US)<br>CNS stimulant non-controlled substance | For narcolepsy, but some evidence modafinil is superior to placebo in ↓core ADHD Sx kids& adults<br>**Adv:** mild abuse potential; samples avail. & anecdotally a weaker stimulant effect & ↓ SE's<br>**Dis: serious skin rx**; not ADHD approved; **SE** when combined with stimulants e.g.↑BP | **SE:** headache, nausea, rhinitis & anxiety & rare psychiatric Sx<br>**Caution:** Serious skin reaction, including erythema multiforme, Stevens-Johnson syndrome, & toxic epidermal necrolysis reported.[14] | Adult: 100mg BID $70/month; max 400mg/day |

=↓ dose for renal dysfx ς=scored tab χ=Non-formulary Sask ☎=Exception Drug Status Sask ⊗=not covered by NIHB ▼=covered by NIHB **ac**=before meals **BMI**=body mass index **BP**=blood pressure **cc**=with meal **CGI**=Clinical Global Impression scale **CV**=cardiovascular disease **CI**=contraindication **DA**=dopamine **DI**=drug interaction **Dx**=diagnosis **fx**=function **HF**=heart failure **HR**=heart rate **ht**=height **IR**=immediate release **M**: monitor **MAOI**=monoamine oxidase inhibitor **MI**=myocardial infarction **MOA**=mechanism of action **MPH**=methylphenidate **NE**=norepinephrine **Pt**=patient **Rx**=reactions **SNAP-IV**=revised version of Swanson, Nolan & Pelham Questionnaire **SR**=sustained release **Sx**=symptoms **SE**=side effect **Tx**=treatment **wt**=weight * MAX dose listed in 2007-08 Canadian ADHD Guidelines, which may differ from product monograph
‡Psychostimulants are used with precaution in tic spectrum disorders but the Canadian guidelines committee agrees that use can be indicated if ADHD symptoms warrant treatment. Medications for ADHD may be combined with other drugs for tics.[4]

**PREVALENCE:** worldwide prevalence 5%[15]; 3-7% of children[16], 4% of adults[4]; boys > girls (9:1 to 2.5:1)[10] **SYMPTOMS:** Core Sx: inattention, hyperactivity, impulsiveness. Other: impaired behavioural, cognitive, academic, emotion &/or social.

**COMORBID/ RESEMBLING CONDITIONS:** age-appropriate behaviour, mental retardation, understimulating environments, learning disabilities; disorders {conduct, oppositional defiant, stereotypic movement, mood (e.g. bipolar), anxiety, personality (e.g. narcissistic, antisocial, borderline, passive-aggressive personality), substance-related, pervasive developmental, psychotic, depression, of impulse control}; chronic fatigue, fetal alcohol syndrome, hyper- or hypothyroidism, drug/substance-induced (see below), OCD, pathological gambling, pheochromocytoma, PTSD, seizure, situational disturbances, Tourette's[17,18]

**DRUG/SUBSTANCE-INDUCED:** anticonvulsants, antihistamines, bronchodilators, caffeinism, decongestants, isoniazid, lead poisoning, neuroleptics (from akathisia), phenobarbital, phenytoin[19,20]

**DIAGNOSIS:**[21] a) Inattentive subtype (10-20%): ≥ 6 (of 9) inattentive Sx: inattention to details/makes careless mistakes, difficulty sustaining attention, seem not to listen, fail to finish tasks, difficulty organizing, avoid tasks requiring sustained attention, lose things, easily distracted, forgetful;
b) hyperactive-impulsive subtype (5-10%): ≥ 6 (of 9) hyperactive-impulsive Sx: fidgety, unable to stay seated, inappropriate running/climbing, difficulty engaging in leisure activities quietly, "on the go", talks excessively, blurt out answers before question finished, difficulty waiting turn, interrupt/intrude others;
c) combined subtype (70-80%): if criteria met for **both** inattentive & hyperactive-impulsive subtypes. ADHD Sx must: persist for ≥ 6months, present prior to age 7, & present in ≥ 1 setting. Evidence of significant impairment in social, academic or occupational fx. Sx not explained by another mental dx.

**SCREENING Tools:** SNAP-IV, T-CAPS, Weiss Symptom Screen, Weiss Functional Impairment Rating Scale; psychoeducational testing. **Tools: http://www.caddra.ca/ Tx GOALS:** ↓ core Sx; improve behaviour, academic, social & self-esteem; minimize med SE

**NON-DRUG Interventions:** behavioural therapy may be considered: for milder ADHD; when psychosocial Tx preferred; in preschool-age children; & adult ADHD[22,23] In kids with ADHD & comorbid dxs, behavioural therapy alone was less effective than meds alone in ↓ ADHD core Sx.[24] Combined medication & behavioural Tx do not offer substantial improvement over meds alone in ↓ ADHD Sx, but may add benefit for some non-ADHD Sx areas[25,26,27,28]; (eg. parent training, contingency management, daily school report cards) **environmental interventions**, e.g adherence to regular daily schedules, structured home & school settings, sitting at the front of the classroom, using white noise during homework time; role for academic remediation, social skills training, etc.; **diet modifications** has limited anecdotal evidence supporting benefits but ↓food additives, preservatives (eg. sodium benzoate) & food colourings may be useful if true sensitivities; **complementary & alternative medicine lack evidence:**[29] natural health products (St. John's Wort, chamomile, melatonin, valerian for calming/sedating; others: blue-green algae, B vitamins, pycnogenol, omega-3), homeopathy, neurofeedback, hyponosis.

**CARDIAC Risk:** 45 deaths (31 kids, 14 adults), Jan 1992 to Feb 2005, related to stimulants or atomoxetine.[30] But the rate of sudden death in those taking psychostimulants or atomoxetine did **not exceed the background rate**.[31] Pts with known CV diseases should not be prescribed these drugs.[32]
AHA cardiovascular guidelines suggest: prior to initiation of Tx to ↑chance of identifying CV conditions: i) pt & family history, ii) physical examination, & iii) ECG, read by a Dr with expertise in pediatric ECGs. Consult pediatric cardiology if significant finding.[33] Routine ECG **not** necessary AAP'08.CCS & CPS'09.

**PSYCHIATRIC Risk:** Suicidal thinking atomoxetine 0.4%; 55 Canadian cases reported. Although risk is small, it should be discussed with pts & family, & kids should be monitored for this esp. in the first few months of Tx.[5] Aggression/emotional lability: Stimulants & atomexetine trials show not ↑aggression[5,34].
Clinicians should distinguish between aggression/ emotional lability that is present when the stimulant is active & ↑ hyperactivity/impulsivity in the evening when the stimulant is no longer effective.[5] Note: oppositional-defiant Sx usually decrease with therapy.

**GROWTH Suppression Risk:** Stimulant Tx may be assoc. with a ↓ in height, at least in the first 1-3 yrs of Tx.[35] One study had ↓growth rates after 3yrs of stimulant Tx compared to those with no meds (average growth of 2 cm & 2.7 kg less than non-med subgroup).[36,37]
Most kids achieve a satisfactory adult height but some growth may be permanently attenuated. **Monitor:** ht, wt & BMI at baseline & 1-2 times/yr during Tx. If pt has a change in height, weight or BMI that crosses two percentile lines, a **drug holiday** during weekends, summer or consider switching to an alternative med.[5]

**MISUSE/DIVERSION:** Lifetime diversion rates: 16-29% of students with stimulant scripts asked to give, sell, or trade their meds.[38] Strategies to ↓ risk → **see ADHD Newsletter/Treatment Agreement**. Stimulant Tx does not appear to ↑ risk for substance use Dx. It is unclear whether Tx ↓ risk.[39,40,41]
**Other Strategies: 1)** Educate patient/family: *handle medication like you would your wallet!!!*; **2)** Refrain from informing others about being on the drug; **3)** Remove labels when discarding; **4)** Use random pill counts; **5)** Weekly dispensing; **6)** School program & collaboration; **7)** Non-Ritalin options. **8)** …

**SE MANAGEMENT:**[4,6,42] **headaches** → acetaminophen; usually ↓ after meds used for 1-3 weeks; divide dose ↓ **appetite** → give med with meals; give high-calorie meals when stimulant effects are low (breakfast, bedtime); supplemental Boost, Ensure; engage child in meal prep & shopping for favourite foods; manage drug-induced **dry mouth** → ↑fluids intake; **rebound appetite** in the evening → spread out supper into 2 or 3 session to prevent GI distress; ↓ dose &/or titrate dose slowly; **insomnia** → optimal sleep hygiene; give doses earlier in the day; avoid stimulant dose after 2 pm if possible, change to shorter-acting meds; ↓ noon or afternoon stimulant dose; consider clonidine, trazodone, an antihistamine, or melatonin 3-6 mg ½ hr before bedtime; others: benzos, TCAs, atypical antipsychotics; **tics** → switch stimulant or switch to a non-stimulant; add clonidine or an atypical antipsychotic; **irritability** → ↓ dose; adjust longer-acting meds; assess for Sx of comorbid conditions ; **rebound hyperactivity** → Overlap stimulant dosing pattern, switch to longer-acting stimulant, combine IR with SR forms, or add other meds; switch to a non-stimulant.

**In USA:** Dexmethylphenidate: **Focalin** (2.5,5,10mg cap, **XR** 5,10,15,20mg cap); Methylphenidate: **Methylin** 5,10,20mg tab; **Methylin ER** 10,20mg tab; **Metadate ER** 10,20mg tab; **Metadate CD** 10,20,30,40,50,60mg cap can open & sprinkle; **Ritalin LA** 10,20,30,40mg cap; **Daytrana Patch** 10,15,20,30mg; Lisdexamfetamine **Vyvanse** 20,30,50,60,70mg cap; Mixed amphetamine salt: **Adderall** 5,7.5,10,12.5,20,30mg tab; Dextroamphetamine: **Dextrostat** 5,10mg tab; **Medkinet,** Modafinil: **Sparlon** (Skin rx (SJS) → Cephalon not pursue ADHD indication), Guanfacine: **Intuniv** FDA Sep09 Age 6-17yr, **Tenex** 1,2mg tab FDA ADHD pending; Methamphetamine: **Desoxyn** 5mg tab (Biovail: Canadian approval *Attenade* not yet marketed)

| Generic/**TRADE**<br>g=generic avail. | Class | Side effects (SE) | Anxiolytic Uses [1,2,3,4] | Comments<br>(√ = therapeutic use) | INITIAL & MAX DOSE | USUAL DOSE RANGE | $ /30day |
|---|---|---|---|---|---|---|---|
| SSRI'S:<br>**Citalopram =CC** CELEXAg<br>(10x▼, 20, 40mg **scored** tabs)<br>**Fluoxetine = F** PROZACg<br>(10,20,40x▼mg cap & 4mg/ml soln)<br>**Fluvoxamine =X** LUVOXg<br>(50ς,100ς mg tab)<br>**Paroxetine = P** PAXILg<br>(10ς,20ς,30mg tab)<br>**Sertraline = S** ZOLOFTg<br>(25,50,100mg cap) | **SSRI'S:** | **SSRIs SE in General (GI & CNS)**<br>**nausea** {21%(F) - 36% (X)},<br>anxiety, insomnia {~14%},<br>agitation, anorexia, tremor<br>somnolence {11-26%}, sweating,<br>dry mouth, headache, dizziness,<br>diarrhea {12% (F,P)-17% (S),<br>constipation {13-18%}<br>sexual dysfx.[5,6], **D/C Syndrome**<br>**Serotonergic syndrome** with MAOI<br>-↑BP, tremor, agitation, hypomania | PD F,P,S<br>PDA P,S<br>PTSD P,S<br>OCD<br>NNT=6 - 12 F,P,S,X<br>SAD/GAD P,S, Es | CC,Es -**fewest drug interactions**<br>F –most **anorexic** & stimulating<br>F –long half-life (5 week washout)<br>X-most **nausea**, constipating & sedating SSRI, ↑DI's<br>P -most anticholinergic of SSRI's •↑weight & D/C syndrome possible [7]<br>S -most diarrhea & male sexual dysfx of SSRIs<br>S -**few drug interactions**, ?benefit in heart dx pts[8]<br>-**flat dose response curve for depression**; however titration to higher dose & a longer trial [10-12wks] often required for anxiety treatment (**start low, aim high**).<br>- **not too useful for specific phobias** eg. heights, flying, spiders- cognitive behavioral therapy often best | **CC 10-20mg am**<br>60mg/d<br>**F** 10-20mg od<br>80mg/d<br>**X 25-50mg hs**<br>300mg/d<br>**P** 10-20mg am<br>60mg/d<br>**S 25-50mg am**<br>200mg/d,<br>(CAMS 25-200mg/d) | 20mg po od<br>40mg po od<br>20mg po od am<br>40mg po od am<br>100mg po hs<br>150mg po hs<br>20mg po od am<br>40mg po od am<br>100mg po od cc<br>100mg po bid cc | **27**<br>27<br>**30**<br>53<br>**36**<br>51<br>**32**<br>57<br>**34**<br>61 |
| **Escitalopram CIPRALEX ✗** ⊗ S(+)citalopram 10ς-20ςmg od -$60 | | | | | | | |
| **Venlafaxine** EFFEXORg<br>(Reg 37.5ς, 75ςmg tab - D/C Jul04)<br>(XR 37.5,75,150mg caps) g<br>(contents of XR may be sprinkled) | **SNRI**<br>**5HT & NE**<br>(also some DA) | •**As dose↑: ↑BP**, agitation, tremor, sweating, nausea {~37%}, sleep disturbances, headache, "clean TCA"<br>•SE similar to SSRI but ↓sexual dysfx | **GAD/SAD**<br>PD/PDA<br>?PTSD | •**less weight** gain; **few drug** interactions<br>•adjust dose for ↓ renal function<br>•caution: withdrawal syndrome (e.g. agitation, nausea, fatigue, dizziness, headache, etc.) | 18.75-37.5mg<br>375mg/d | 37.5mg **XR** po **daily**<br>75mg **XR** po **daily**<br>150mg **XR** po **daily**<br>225mg **XR** od (if 2-3 cap) | 26<br>46<br>48<br>94-123 |
| **Duloxetine CYMBALTA** (30,60mg cap) ⊗ an SNRI 30-60mg/d $72-138 Max 120mg. SE: insomnia, somnolence, headache, nausea, diarrhea, ↓appetite, fatigue, ↑sweating, ↑BP, ↑**LFTs**, ↑DI & dry mouth. √depression [adult], GAD, diabetic peripheral neuropathic pain, fibromyalgia & ?effective for stress incontinence. | | | | | | | |
| **Alprazolam** XANAXg<br>(0.25ς,0.5ς);(1ς mg tab;TS 2ς mg)x▼ | Triazolo | **Drowsiness** (tolerance develops),<br>**dizziness**, ↓ concentration, falls,<br>anterograde amnesia, ↑ traffic<br>**accidents**, physical **dependence** &<br>rarely paradoxical **anger or hostility**. | PD<br>PDA<br>GAD<br>SAD | √Anxiety but rebound anxiety possible, **Panic attacks**<br>Severe **withdrawal** & some ? antidepressant effect | 0.25mg<br>4-10mg | 0.25mg po tid<br>0.5mg po tid | **16**<br>17 |
| **Clonazepam** RIVOTRILg<br>(0.25x▼,0.5ς,1,2ς mg tab) | Nitro | | | √ Anticonvulsant, Panic attack<br>Other uses long acting an advantage sometimes: **sedative,** social phobia & akathisia, acute mania & neuralgic pain | 0.25mg<br>10-20mg | 0.5mg po tid<br>1mg po bid<br>2mg po tid | **16**<br>20<br>22 |
| **Lorazepam** ATIVANg<br>(0.5,1ς,2ς mg tab;<br>0.5,1,2mg slx▼ tab;4mg/ml **amp**x⊗) | 3- Hydroxy #<br>**Benzodiazepine** | Alprazolam **Level ↑ by:**<br>**fluvoxamine**, grapefruit juice, ketoconazole, **nefazodone**;<br>Alprazolam **Level ↓ by:** theophylline | (**Fast acting**, rebound anxiety) | √ Anxiety, Preanesthetic<br>Other: **sedative**, muscle relaxant, alcohol withdrawal;<br>↓ **DI's**, √Status epilepticus (slower onset, but longer duration vs diazepam) | 0.5mg<br>10mg | 0.5mg po tid<br>1mg po tid<br>2mg po tid<br>(BZs esp. useful for the 1st month, while waiting for antidepressants to work. Less benefit for OCD & PTSD.) | 11<br>**12**<br>14 |
| **Buspirone** BUSPARg<br>(5,10ς mg tab) | **Azapirone**<br>5 $HT_{1a}$ agonist | Nausea, headache, dizziness, restlessness (non-sedating)<br>Onset 1week; Max effect **6 weeks** | GAD<br>(**Delayed** onset) | √ **Anxiety in Bz naive pt.**;Other:alcohol withdrawal<br>**Non-addicting**, DI-fluvoxamine,grapefruit juice;<br>**NO dependency**, No cross tolerance with benzo's | 5mg<br>60-90mg | 5mg po tid<br>10mg po tid-qid | 46<br>55-71 |
| **Hydroxyzine** ATARAXg<br>(10,25,50mg cap,2mg/ml syr);(50mg ampx⊗) | **Antihistamine** | **Drowsiness**, sedation, headache, weakness, anticholinergic,↓ cognition | Anxiety but ↑ SE's; not recommended | √ Sedative/hypnotic, anti-pruritic<br>Tolerance to efficacy | 10mg<br>400mg | 25mg po tid<br>50mg po tid | **23**<br>27 |
| **MAOIs**:non-selective & irreversible;✓ atypical depression/**refractory PD/PDA/PTSD/OCD/SAD**;enzyme effect ~10day; many DI & food cautions(tyramine-hypertensive crisis);phenelzine NARDIL 15mg tab;tranylcypromine PARNATE 10mg tab | | | | | | | |
| **Moclobemide** MANERIXg<br>(100ς,150ς,300ς mg tab) | **RIMA** | Dry mouth, dizzy, headache, nausea, restlessness, tremor, insomnia, **less sexual** dysfunction, insomnia | SAD | • no tyramine dietary precaution if dose ≤600mg/d, enzyme selective & reversible effect lasts ~24hrs,<br>**DI**: dextromethorphan,meperidine,sympathomimetic | 100mg bid<br>600-900mg/d | 150mg po bid pc<br>300mg po bid pc | **26**<br>54 |
| **Propranolol** INDERALg<br>(10ς,20ς,40ς,80ς & 120ς mg tablet;<br>**LA** 60,80,120 & 160mg);<br>(**Vial** 1mg/mlx⊗) | **Beta blocker** | **Hypotension**,bronchospasm,fatigue<br>Contraindicated:asthma,**bradycardia**<br>Caution: diabetes, heart failure<br>Consider: **Atenolol** 25-100mg 60-90 min before task | SAD<br>Anxiety | Other uses: **aggression**(impulsive outbursts), **akathisia,** lithium tremor, **performance anxiety,** panic, stage fright; ✓BP, Angina, Post MI, Arrhythmias<br>✓Atrial Fib, Migraine headache prophylaxis<br>(??PTSD: may help bad memories seem more distant) | 10-40mg bid<br>(10-80mg 30-90min prior to task)<br>320mg/d | 20mg po bid<br>40mg po bid<br>80mg LA po od<br>(somatic Sx relief only) | 10<br>**10**<br>28 |
| **Tricyclic Antidepressants**<br>**Clomipramine =Cl**<br>ANAFRANILg (10, 25, 50mg tab)<br>**Imipramine =I**<br>TOFRANILg<br>(10, 25, 50, 75x▼mg tab)<br>**Desipramine =D**<br>NORPRAMINg<br>(10, 25, 50, 75, 100mg tab) | **TCA's** | **CNS effects** (agitation on initiation of therapy, confusion, drowsiness, headache, tremors, seizures),<br>**anticholinergic effects** ( dry mouth, blurred vision, constipation etc.);<br>nausea, sweating, rash,<br>**cardiovascular effects** ( ↑ heart rate, arrhythmias, orthostatic hypotension); anorgasmia | **PD**<br>PDA<br>PTSD<br>GAD<br>OCD-**esp.Cl**<br>SAD | May ↑ effect of anticholinergic & CNS meds.<br>May take 2-3 months for maximum effect.<br>**clomipramine for OCD** b/c most 5HT agent.<br>Fatal (≥2gm) **overdose** → to heart & CNS<br>•desipramine generally **better tolerated** than clomipramine & imipramine & has most NE activity & the least anticholinergic activity<br>• trough plasma levels can be drawn | 10-25mg<br>300mg<br>(Desipramine cost based on using 50mg tabs which are less) | Cl 150mg po hs<br>Cl 200mg po hs<br>I 150mg po hs<br>I 200mg po hs<br>D 150mg po hs<br>D 200mg po hs | 47<br>**57**<br>45<br>**57**<br>49<br>**64** |

# **Benzodiazepines**: **D/C gradually to avoid rebound anxiety**, avoid in pregnancy & in patients with a history of drug abuse, dose ↑ is rare in patients taking bz's for anxiety, use ↓ dose in elderly. **Pt**=patient x Non-formulary Sask

**Drugs ↑ anxiety Sx:** amphetamines,antipsychotics,anticholinergic-toxicity,caffeine,cocaine,dapsone,digitalis-toxicity,donepezil,dopamine,ephedrine,isoniazid,levodopa,lidocaine,methylphenidate,nicotinic acid,phenylephrine,pseudoephedrine,salbutamol,SSRI's,steroids & theophyline; plus **Withdrawal from** anxiolytics/sedatives,ethanol&narcotics.

**Pregnancy category**[9]: B→ buspirone C→ bupropion ,citalopram, clomipramine, desipramine, **fluoxetine** (has **most** clinical experience), fluvoxamine, hydroxyzine, MAOI's, nefazodone(but ↑LFTs rarely), sertraline & venlafaxine.

**GAD**=generalized anxiety dx [10] **OCD**=obsessive compulsive dx [11,12] **PD**=panic dx **PDA**=panic dx with agoraphobia **PTSD**=post traumatic stress dx [13,14] **SAD**=social anxiety dx; **BP**=blood pressure **DI**=drug interaction **Dx**=disorder

=↓ dose for renal dysfx ς=scored tablet ▼=covered by NIHB ⊗=not covered by NIHB Anxiety Disorders of America www.adaa.org Psychotherapy, **cognitive behavior therapy, medications** [CAMS] & self-help (↓caffeine, relaxation) can be very effective.

Herbal: Kava possible short term use for mild to moderate anxiety, but rare ↑LFTs. Inositol modest effects for panic or OCD disorders. Do not encourage using St. John's wort, valerian, Sympathyl or passionflower. Saeed AFP 2007

## BENZODIAZEPINE (BZ) COMPARISON CHART [1,2,3,4,5,6,7]

| Name: Generic -TRADE<br>(generics avail. for all brands of BZs) | Equivalent Dose/Class | Peak Level/ *ABSORPTION RATE* | Average* Half-life (hr) | Active Metabolites | Comments<br>(√ = therapeutic use) | INITIAL & MAX DOSE | USUAL DOSE RANGE | $ /Month |
|---|---|---|---|---|---|---|---|---|
| **SHORT ACTING:** more **rebound** anxiety effect & **withdrawal reactions, better sedative/hypnotic**; preferred over long acting in **elderly (less accumulation)** & in patients with **liver disorders** (easier metabolism) | | | | | | | | |
| **Alprazolam** -XANAX<br>(0.25ς,0.5ς);(1ς mg tab; TS 2ς mg)ˣ▼ | 0.5mg<br>D (Pregnancy ←category)<br>Triazolo | 1-2 hr<br>*Medium* | 12<br>(9-20) | Minor<br>Oxidation # | √Anxiety but rebound anxiety possible, **Panic attacks**<br>Severe **withdrawal** & some ? antidepressant effect<br>**DIs: Level ↑ by:** diltiazem, fluoxetine, fluvoxamine, ketoconazole, grapefruit juice, nefazodone, ritonavir; **↓ by:** rifampin, theophylline | 0.25mg<br>4-10mg | 0.25mg po tid<br>0.5mg po tid | 15<br>17 |
| **Bromazepam** -LECTOPAM<br>(1.5ς, 3ς, 6ς mg tab) | D 3-6mg<br>2-Keto | 1-4 hr<br>*Medium* | 20<br>(8-30) | Minor<br>Oxidation | √Anxiety<br>? May exacerbate depression | 3mg<br>30-60mg | 3mg po hs<br>6mg po hs | 10<br>12 |
| **Lorazepam** -ATIVAN<br>(0.5,1ς,2ς mg **po** tab);<br>(0.5,1,2mg **sl** tab▼;4mg/ml **amp**⊗)ˣ | D 1mg<br>3-Hydroxy | **PO** 1-4 hr<br>**SL/IM** 1 hr<br>**IV** 5-10 min<br>*Medium* | 15<br>(8-24) | **None**<br>Conjugation # | √ **Anxiety**, Preanesthetic; Other: **sedative**, muscle relaxant,alcohol withdrawal;acute **mania**; **Fewer DI's,** √Status epilepticus -slower onset but longer duration vs diazepam;IM well absorbed | 0.5mg<br>10mg | 0.5mg po tid<br>1mg po tid<br>2mg po tid | 11<br>12<br>15 |
| **Oxazepam** -SERAX<br>(10ς,15ς,30ς mg tab) | D 15mg<br>3-Hydroxy | 1-4 hr<br>*Medium* | 8<br>(3-25) | **None**<br>Conjugation | √ Anxiety, **alcohol withdrawal**<br>Other: **sedative**<br>Less affected by **liver** dysfunction;**Fewer DI's** | 10mg<br>120mg | 15mg po hs<br>30mg po hs<br>30mg po tid | 10<br>11<br>17 |
| **Temazepam** -RESTORIL<br>(15,30mg cap) | X 15mg<br>3-Hydroxy | 2-3 hr<br>*Medium* | 11<br>(3-25) | **None**<br>Conjugation | √ **Sedative/hypnotic;** Other: anxiolytic<br>May delay but not suppress REM sleep<br>**Fewer DI's** | 15mg<br>60mg | 15mg po hs<br>30mg po hs | 11<br>12 |
| **Triazolam** -HALCION<br>(0.125ς,0.25ς mg tab) | X 0.25-0.5mg<br>Triazolo | 1-2 hr<br>*Rapid* | 2<br>(1.5-5) | **None**<br>Oxidation | √ Sedative/**hypnotic**; DI's as per alprazolam.<br>**Behavioral disturbances may occur in elderly. Prone to withdrawal / rebound effects** | 0.125mg<br>0.5mg | 0.125mg po hs<br>0.25mg po hs | 12<br>15 |
| **LONG ACTING: less rebound** symptoms;better choice **when tapering off** of BZs (e.g. clonazepam/diazepam);**withdrawal** may be **delayed** 1-2 wk **for 2-Keto group; bedtime** dose option for hypnotic & **anxiolytic** effect. | | | | | | | | |
| **Chlordiazepoxide** ⚕<br>(5,10,25mg cap) ⊗ -LIBRIUM | D 10-25mg<br>2-Keto | 1-4 hr<br>*Medium* | 100 | Yes<br>Oxidation | √ Anxiety, preanesthetic, **alcohol withdrawal**<br>Other: sedation; Slower onset vs diazepam | 5mg<br>200-400mg | 25mg po tid<br>50mg po tid | 24<br>40 |
| **Clonazepam** -RIVOTRIL<br>(0.25ˣ▼; 0.5ς,1,2ς mg tab) | 0.25-0.5mg<br>D Nitro | 1-4 hr<br>*Rapid* | 34<br>(19-60) | **None**<br>Oxidation & Nitro reduction | √ Anticonvulsant, **Panic** attack<br>Other: **sedative**, social phobia, akathisia, **acute mania,** restless leg syndrome & neuralgic pain ,Used for BZ withdrawal | 0.25mg<br>10-20mg | 0.5mg po tid<br>1mg po bid<br>2mg po tid | 16<br>20<br>22 |
| **Clorazepate** -TRANXENE<br>(3.75,7.5,15mg cap) ⊗ | D 10-15mg<br>2-Keto | 0.5-2 hr<br>*Rapid* | 100<br>Inactive until Metabolized | Yes<br>Oxidation | Hydrolyzed in GI →↓ clorazepate level by **antacids**<br>√ Anxiety, panic, alcohol withdrawal, seizures | 3.75mg<br>60-90mg | 3.75mg po bid<br>7.5mg po bid<br>15mg po bid | 14<br>20<br>32 |
| **Diazepam** -VALIUM<br>(2ς,5ς,10ς mg **tab**; 10mg/2ml **amp**; 5mg/ml **rectal gel** DIASTAT ⊗;<br>{10mg/2ml **emulsion inj** ˣ⊗ DIAZEMULS, Peak effect 15min after IV, & 2hrs after IM} | 5-10mg<br>D 2-Keto<br>X | **PO** 1-2 hr<br>**IM** 1hr<br>**IV** 8 min<br>*Rapid* | 100 | Yes<br>Oxidation | √Anxiety, **muscle relaxant,** seizures, **alcohol withdrawal &** preanesthetic; Other: sedative<br>Quicker onset & **↓duration** of action initially vs lorazepam.DIs<br>**IM** causes pain; **Diazemuls IV** better tolerated ,Used for BZ withdrawal | 2mg<br>40mg | 2mg po tid<br>5mg po tid<br>10mg po tid | 13<br>15<br>16 |
| **Flurazepam** -DALMANE<br>(15,30mg cap) ⊗ | 15-30mg<br>2-Keto | 0.5-1 hr<br>*Rapid* | 100<br>(40-250) | Yes<br>Oxidation | √ Sedative/**hypnotic**; Quick onset but **accumulates →hangover** →confusion, etc. | 15mg<br>60mg | 15mg po hs<br>30mg po hs | 10<br>11 |
| **Nitrazepam** -MOGADON<br>(5ς,10ς mg tab) | U 5-10mg<br>Nitro | 0.5-2 hr<br>*Medium* | 30<br>(15-48) | None<br>Nitro reduction | √ Sedative/**hypnotic**, myoclonic seizures | 5mg<br>10mg | 5mg po hs<br>10mg po hs | 10<br>12 |

**SE**: **drowsy**, dizzy, ataxia, disinhibition, **dependence**, CNS depression, disorientation, **psychomotor impairment**, confusion, aggression, excitement,**↑fall/fracture**[8] & **vehicle accidents** in elderly & anterograde **amnesia**. **Tolerance** to sedative/hypnotic, muscle relaxant & anticonvulsant, but less **tolerance** for the anxiolytic & antipanic effects. No **cross-tolerance** with buspirone & SSRI'S; as well often lacks cross-tolerance with alprazolam.

**Benzo Withdrawal**: Depends on: duration of tx, dose, rate of tapering & BZ t½ life; **Onset:** 1-2d with short t½; 3-8d with long t½ BZ's; **S/Sx:** insomnia, nausea/vomiting, twitching, irritability, ↑anxiety, paresthesias, tinnitus, delirium & seizures.

**When D/C BZ:** If Tx>12wk taper at a rate of 10-25%/wk (esp. **slow** the last 25%) & consider changing to equivalent dose of clonazepam/diazepam (except alprazolam), cognitive behavioral therapy & taper off BZ→ http://www.benzo.org.uk/manual/index.htm A persistent abstinence syndrome can last up to 1yr, which is worse in the first month & may take >6 months before noticeable benefits to the patient/family members. (Gabapentin may be helpful in some situations)

**Length of Therapy**: **Anxiety:** use as an adjunct only & re-evaluate q4-6 weeks; **Hypnotic:** not to exceed 4 week. Caution: BZ & **clozapine** may lead to marked sedation,↑ salivation, & rare respiratory arrest.

**Drug Interactions (DIs)**: **↑CNS depression:** antidepressants, antihistamines, barbiturates, ethanol; Antacids ↓ absorption; **↑'d BZ levels by:** allopurinol, oral contraceptives, cimetidine, estrogen, erythromycin, fluoxetine, fluvoxamine, isoniazid, omeprazole, **Protease inhibitors**, valproic (less DI effect on lorazepam, oxazepam, temazepam, but ↑effect on 2-Keto BZ); **BZ may ↑levels of:** digoxin &phenytoin. **BZ levels ↓'d by:** carbamazepine, phenobarbital, rifampin & smoking.

# **Oxidation** is a high-energy metabolic pathway impaired in liver disease & reduced in elderly; whereas **conjugation** to more water soluble glucuronide derivative allows for excretion (less intensive), thus less affected by DIs.

**Overdose**: safe when taken alone; Tx: flumazenil 0.5mg/5ml $30. **Precaution**: hx of substance abuse, sleep apnea, cognitive/renal/hepatic dx, **elderly**, porphyria, CNS depression, myasthenia & **pregnancy** (floppy infant Sx; possible teratogen oral cleft & can precipitate withdrawal in newborns if used in 3rd trimester). **BZ**=benzodiazepine **DI**=drug interaction **Dx**=disease * t½ average(range) can be ↑↑ in geriatric pts & altered by DIs ˣ Non-formulary in Sask ⚕ =↓ dose for renal dysfx ς=scored ▼covered NIHB ⊗not NIHB

Found in as adulterants in some herbal products: Estazolam found in Eden Herbal Formulations Sleep Ease & Serenity Pills II, Salt Spring Herbals Sleep Well & in Sleepees. Clonazepam found in Optimum Health Care SleePlus TCM & BYL SleePlus.

# BIPOLAR DISORDER: Overview Of Evidence-based Treatment Guidelines & Options[1,2,3,4,5,6]

## MANIA & MIXED STATE ☛

- **Divalproex/valproate: √ mania & mixed** -? use loading dose
- **Lithium: √ mania**
- **Atypical Antipsychotic: √ mania** (esp. for **acute agitation**)
- **Carbamazepine: √ mixed (alternate)** (CBZ can ↓level of DVA, olanzapine & risperidone; thus CBZ not recommended with olanzapine or risperidone) (Oxcarbazepine may be better tolerated than CBZ, but limited clinical evidence)

**Combo of Mood Stabilizers**: consider if poor response to lithium, DVA or CBZ, severe mania or mixed episodes. Balance (Ensure medication trials are adequate: at least **2weeks** before efficacy can be assessed). Consider other causes: antidepressants, caffeine, alcohol, illicit substances & medical.

**Important but select roles:**

**Benzodiazepines** (clonazepam/lorazepam$^{im/po}$): in place or with antipsychotic to **sedate** acutely agitated pt; behavioral control while waiting for mood stabilizer response. Caution resp depression: wait 1-2hrs between IM olanzapine & IM benzo

**Antipsychotics: Typical** (haloperidol$^{im/po}$): for marked psychosis; rarely as sole or primary antimanic except in exceptional circumstances.

**Atypical** (risperidone po/M tab/Consta/olanzapine im/po/Zydis ▼/ ziprasidone / aripiprazole ⊗ /quetiapine): efficacious in acute **mania**, esp. if marked psychotic Sx; FDA: ≥10yr risperidone/quetiapine & ≥13yr olanzapine. or in refractory mania. **Disadv**: tardive dyskinesia possible, extrapyramidal Sx, diabetes, ↑weight/lipids & acute dystonias **Adv:** rapid onset of action

**ECT**: efficacious & broad-spectrum; consider for severe behavioral disturbances/psychosis marked/suicidality, or if poor response to combos.

**Less evidence/less preferable options:**
Gabapentin/lamotrigine/topiramate/verapamil;
Clozapine for the truly refractory patient;
Experimental: calcitonin, levetiracetam, omega 3 fatty acids, phenytoin & **tamoxifen**.

## RAPID CYCLING ☛ (≥4 cycles/year)

- **Divalproex/valproate √ first line**
- **Lithium** or **carbamazepine** √ second line added to DVA if necessary
- **Lamotrigine** (less useful if frequently manic) Risk of life threatening rash ↑'s when combine DVA & lamotrigine.
- ↓ use of antidepressants, nicotine, alcohol & illicit drugs may help

**Combination of Mood Stabilizers:**
Up to 3 combos may be used when necessary

**Important but limited roles:**
**Benzodiazepines** (clonazepam/lorazepam)
**ECT:** consider if fail or poor response to combos

**Less evidence/ less preferable options**:
risperidone/**olanzapine**/quetiapine→ but approved in FDA & Canada
gabapentin/topiramate;
verapamil/nimodipine;
clozapine for the **refractory** patient;
thyroxine –less evidence unless **hypothyroid.**

**Caution: Antidepressants** - particularly TCA's may provoke switch into mania & rapid cycling (**switch** to mania >10% for TCA vs <5% for SSRI) **Bupropion** less switches than sertraline & much less than venlafaxine Leverich'06

## BIPOLAR DEPRESSION ☛ (assess for risk of suicide/self-harm)

- NNT=10 to ↓ depression sx by at least 50% Van Lieshout'10
- Cognitive-behavioral or interpersonal therapy
- **Lithium √ first line** (may protect against suicide)
- **Lamotrigine √ first line** (esp. to prevent depressive; not great if frequently manic)
- **Quetiapine √ first line** FDA indication Oct/06; 2nd line Bipolar II Depression
- **Olanzapine plus SSRI** an option, not Aripiprazole monotherapy
- **ECT**: consider if markedly suicidal, acute psychosis or moderate to severe depression not responding to mood stabilizers/antipsychotics/antidepressants

**If non-psychotic:**
- Mood stabilizer & **antidepressant** -often D/C antidepressant after 3-6months (**bupropion,SSRI** ?not fluoxetine, SNRI, MAOI, RIMA-**avoid TCA's**) **or**
- Two mood stabilizers (LI & DVA, LI & CBZ, DVA & CBZ) **or**
- Mood stabilizer & **lamotrigine**

**If psychotic:** (If mood incongruent, may be poorer prognosis than mood congruent)
- Mood stabilizer & antipsychotic **or**
- Mood stabilizer & antipsychotic & antidepressant **or**
- 2 mood stabilizers & antipsychotic

**Later treatment options:**
- 3 mood stabilizers
- Clozapine for the truly refractory patient
- Other novel treatments: eg. Methylphenidate, **modafanil** & pramipexole

**Therapeutic Drug Levels:**
Take **trough level** PRIOR to the next dose when steady state is achieved ie. after at least **4-5 days** for carbamazepine & valproic acid. Lithium is often a 12hr trough. (Take any time if suspect toxicity/non-compliance.) Anti-manic levels are not established, thus anticonvulsant levels are used as a guide only. Levels for gabapentin & lamotrigine are not readily avail. (ie. sent to provincial lab) & less known about the significance of a particular level. For CBZ, lithium & valproic acid - levels guide in selecting the correct dose, assessment of pt compliance & avoiding excessive SE.

## Continuation/Early Stable Phase:

Acute phase (Duration of **2-10 weeks**) →Medication responder (Euthymia & resolution of Psychosis)
Continuation/Early Stable Phase (Duration of **6-12 weeks**)

**Treatment**: Pharmacotherapy & **psycho-education** & bio-social rhythm normalization +/- psychotherapy (Cognitive behavioural & interpersonal therapy in select patients). Beynon '08

- **Mood stabilizer**: maintain optimal serum level, confirm normal lab investigations, ensure no/minimal tolerable side effects, ensure no toxicity
- **Benzodiazepines**: gradual titration to discontinuation if asymptomatic for 2-3 weeks, or continue at minimum doses for Sx management **Disadv:** tolerance, dependence, withdrawal, falls & accidents.
- **Antipsychotics**: gradual titration to discontinuation if asymptomatic for 2-3 weeks, except in persistent or incongruent psychosis, when longer periods are indicated; or continue at minimum doses for Sx management. **Disadv:** tardive dyskinesia,extrapyramidal Sx, akathisia, diabetes, weight gain & acute dystonias. Gardner CMAJ 2005
- **Antidepressant**: gradual titration to discontinuation if asymptomatic for 6-12 weeks, or continue at minimum doses for Sx management (Taper over a ≥2-4week period)
- **ECT**: possible continuation/maintenance ECT (weekly to monthly ECT) is indicated for patients who respond poorly to continuation medications or prefer ECT.

Abruptly stopping pharmacotherapy provokes relapse; thus **if possible, D/C gradually over 1 month or more**.

## Maintenance/Prophylactic/Late Stable:

Treatment if medication/prophylaxis (eg. lithium, valproate, lamotrigine & olanzapine but use symptoms & past tx hisory to help selection[6]) is acceptable to the pt:

Hx of single episode→Pharmacotherapy, psycho-education & bio-social rhythm normalization, optimally **for 1 year** & preferable not less than 6 months. Gradual discontinuation over a period of 3 months, but not less than 1 month. Annual monitoring & rapid reassessment where indicated.

Hx of recurrent episodes, or single severe episode & a strong family Hx→**indefinite prophylaxis**,psycho-education & bio-social rhythm normalization +/- psychotherapy. **Non adherence** to meds is critical.

## Early symptom Exacerbation:

- Optimize mood stabilizer serum level (repeat ~q6months)
- Adjust for change in bioavailability of active agents (e.g. drug interactions etc…)
- Identify & manage substance abuse & caffeine or nicotine intake
- Modify poor sleep hygiene
- Identify & manage psychosocial precipitants or stressors (e.g. adverse life events, negative expressed emotions or hostility in family, new stressors)

If **non responders** then consider other treatments or combos: Mood stabilizers +/-Benzodiazepine for sleep etc. +/-antipsychotic +/-ECT +/-Antidepressants +/-Lamotrigine

Antipsychotics: haloperidol,olanzapine, risperidone, quetiapine etc… √ therapeutic use **Adv**=advantage **BZ**=benzodiazepine **CBZ**=carbamazepine **Disadv**=disadvantage **DVA**=divalproex/valproate **ECT**=electroconvulsive therapy **LI**=lithium **Sx**=symptoms


**1.** CJPsyc Aug 97 Vol 42 -Supp 2 **2.** Expert Consensus Guideline Series- Bipolar Disorder, Apr 00, Postgraduate Medicine **3.** Practice guideline: Bipolar disorder treatment (revision). Am J Psychiatry. **2002** Apr;159(4 Suppl):1-50. http://www.psych.org/psych_pract/treatg/pg/Practice%20Guidelines8904/BipolarDisorder_2e.pdf **4.** Belmaker RH. Bipolar disorder. N Engl J Med. **2004** Jul 29;351(5):476-86. **5.** NICE UK guidelines 2006 www.nice.org.uk
**6.** Yatham LN, Kennedy SH, Schaffer A, et al. **CANMAT** & International Society for Bipolar Disorders (ISBD) collaborative update of CANMAT guidelines for the management of bipolar disorder: **update 2009**. Bipolar Disord. 2009 May;11(3):225-55.
Yatham LN, Kennedy SH, O'Donovan C, et al., **CANMAT** guidelines for the management of patients with bipolar disorder: **update 2007**. Bipolar Disord. 2006 Dec;8(6):721-39.
Yatham LN, et al.; **Canadian** CANMAT bipolar guideline: consensus & controversies. Bipolar Disord. **2005**;7 Suppl 3:5-69. http://www.canmat.org/MAForum2005/Bipolar_Guidelines.pdf {www.mooddisorderscanada.ca, www.camh.net , www.cmha.ca}
**MDQ** Mood Disorder Questionaire for **Screening** http://www.dbsalliance.org/pdfs/MDQ.pdf

# MOOD STABILIZERS & ADJUNCT AGENTS

 Brent Jensen BSP — May 10

| Generic/Form TRADE g=generic avail. | SIDE EFFECTS | MONITOR Q6-12 Months | COMMENTS/ DRUG LEVEL | DRUG INTERACTIONS | INITIAL & MAX DOSE | USUAL DOSE RANGE | $ /100day |
|---|---|---|---|---|---|---|---|
| **Carbamazepine**<br>**TEGRETOL** g<br>(100ς,200ς χ ▼mg chew tab; 200ς mg tab)<br>(200ς,400ς mg CR tab ☎▼)<br>(20mg/ml susp)<br>Pregnancy category→ Malformation 5% ? cleft palate **D** | **Common**: GI N/V, drowsy, dizzy, **unsteady**, pruritic **rash<10%** may cross react with phenytoin & phenobarb; ↓WBC dose related, **CR tab: less SE** GI/CNS.<br>**Rare**: aplastic anemia, ↑ **liver enzymes**, cardiac abnormalities, ↓ serum sodium, SLE, exfoliative dermatitis, ocular effects, ↓WBC (persistent 2%), ↓ T3/T4, alopecia, Asians with HLA-B* 1502 have ↑↑risk of skin rx.<br>**WEIGHT GAIN = minimal** | CBC,Platelets, TSH,LFT, Lytes, **Level**<br>ECG for pts >45yrs | √ BPAD -acute mania, rapid cycle, **mixed** & prophylaxis<br>√ trigeminal neuralgia, seizures<br>Option for **aggressive** patients & those with **neurologic dx**.<br>CI: **hepatic**/porphyria **dx**; safe in renal dx<br>**17-54 umol/l** | **↑ Carbamazepine level by**: cimetidine, **clarithro/erythromycin, danazol, diltiazem, felodipine,fluoxetine, fluvoxamine**, grapefruit juice, isoniazid, ketoconazole, **lamotrigine**, metronidazole, nefazodone, phenobarbital, **propoxyphene**, ritonavir,**verapamil** & valproate<br>**↓ Carbamazepine level by**: phenytoin,phenobarb,St.Johns wort,theophylline<br>**Carbamazepine ↓ levels of**: Valproate<br>**INDUCES P450 3A4 System**^ | 200mg hs<br>1800mg/day<br>(**autoinduction** of P450 system complete in 4 weeks; may start low-dose & ↑ weekly x4 weeks; also ↓'s SE) | 200mg po bid<br>200mg CR bid<br>200mg po tid<br>400mg po bid<br>400mg CR bid<br>600mg po hs<br>**800mg po hs** | 24<br>49<br>33<br>42<br>90<br>33<br>**42** |
| **Divalproex (DVA)**<br>**EPIVAL** g<br>(125,250,500mg EC tab);<br>1000mg/10 ml vial χ⊗) **D**<br>**-prodrug** of VPA; see **valproic acid below** | **Common**: nausea, diarrhea, dizzy, ataxia, somnolence, sedation, **tremor**, fatigue, confusion, headache, abdominal cramps, hair loss often reversible, menstrual disturbances<br>**Rare**: **↓platelets & WBC, hepatotoxic**, skin rx's,**pancreatitis**,neural tube defects 1-2%<br>**Caution: polycystic ovaries**<br>**WEIGHT GAIN= ++** (up to 59%, more common in ♀; mean ↑ of **8-14kg**)<br>Pregnancy registry: heart defect & spina bifida 10.7 vs 2.9% in control gp. ↑**malformations** with valproate Artama 05. esp >1g/d Perucca 05. Folate 5mg/d if tx. May↓**IQ** in newborn. Concern 1st trimester. eg. neural tube, facial cleft, ?hypospadias | CBC,Platelets, LFT<br>**Level** | √ BPAD **acute mania,rapid cycle, mixed, prophylaxis** & depression<br>√ seizures & migraine prophylaxis;<br>Option for aggression;<br>Safe in renal dx.<br>Acute Mania -Oral load of 20mg/kg has been used<br>CI: **hepatic dx** & **kids≤2yr**<br>**400-700 umol/l** | **↑ Valproic acid level by**: aspirin, cimetidine, erythromycin, felbamate, fluoxetine, isoniazid, salicylates<br>**↓ Valproic acid level by**: carbamazepine, cholestyramine, lamotrigine, meropenem,phenobarbital,phenytoin,rifampin,ritonavir<br>**Valproic acid ↑ levels of**: amitriptyline, carbamazepine epoxide (ie.↑ SE), clonazepam, diazepam,ethosuximide,**lamotrigine**, lorazepam, phenobarbital, **warfarin**<br>**Not ↓ effect of BCP's**<br>Mainly an enzyme **inhibitor** | 250mg od<br>3000mg/day | 250mg po bid<br>250mg po tid<br>**500mg po bid**<br>1gm po hs<br>500mg po tid | 52<br>75<br>**97**<br>97<br>142 |
| **Lamotrigine**<br>**LAMICTAL** g<br>(25ς,100ς,150ς mg tab; 5ς mg chewable tab)<br>(2mg chewable tab χ▼)<br>Not teratogenic in animals, but ↑ risk of fetal death. ↑ non-syndromic **oral clefts**. Pregnancy: ↓ levels & ↑ levels seen in breast milk. **C** | **Common:** dizzy, nausea, vomiting, asthenia, headache, somnolence, ataxia, ↑ alertness, diplopia, abdominal pain, rash<br>**Rare**:**Stevens-Johnson syndrome**#, 1st 2months & toxic epidermal necrolysis, hepatotoxic, leukopenia & tics in kids.<br>**WEIGHT GAIN= neutral effect** | CBC,LFT | √ seizures; Option: Alt./adjunct **for BPAD I for acute depression** & **Bipolar II for rapid cycling** FDA Jun03<br>**Rash** 10% → life threatening 0.3%#<br>(If drug related/severe, D/C at first sign of rash)<br>4-39umol/l (? Sig/not routinely avail.)<br>Breast feeding: caution b/c of rash | **↑ Lamotrigine level by**: sertraline, **valproate**<br>**↓ Lamotrigine level by**: **BCP's**, **carbamazepine**, **phenytoin**, phenobarb, primidone, rifampin, ritonavir<br>NO EFFECT on P450 enzymes<br>**Rarely ↓ effect of BCP's** & **folic acid** | 25mg hs<br>↑ only **25-50mg/week** increments<br>400mg/day | 50mg po bid<br>**100mg po bid**<br>150mg po bid<br>**If using with valproate:**<br>25mg hs start ↑12.5mg/wk<br>100mg po hs<br>Mono Therapy dose 50-400mg/d; 50-200mg/d with **divalproex** | 99<br>**194**<br>278<br><br>30<br>99 |
| **Lithium** carbonate<br>**CARBOLITH** g,<br>**DURALITH** g<br>(150,300,600mg cap;<br>300ς mg SR tab, generic -D/C by Co)<br>**PMS-LITHIUM CITRATE**<br>(300mg/5ml **syrup** χ▼)<br>Ebstein's anomaly0.1% ? Fetal echo if 1st trimester **D** | **Common:** nausea/vomiting/diarrhea, edema, **polyuria**, **polydypsia**, , ↑WBC, alopecia, acne, psoriasis, hypothyroidism, ↑Ca++,↑ K+ & **tremor** propranolol or ↓ Lithium dose helps<br>**Level 1.5-2 mmol/l:** drowsy, ataxia, slurred speech, hypertonicity, tremor dose related,Tx Inderal<br>**Level >2mmol/l:** arrhythmias, ↓ heart rate, myocarditis, seizures, coma & death.<br>**WEIGHT GAIN= +** (25-60% -mean gain **7.5kg**) | CBC,TSH, ECG<br>Urinalysis, Lytes, Ca++<br>**SCr**, **Level Trough** 8-12hr:<br>~0.8-1.1mmol/l<br>(in elderly 0.4-0.7 mmol/l) | √ BPAD FDA ≥12yr: **acute mania & prophylaxis, mild depression**<br>**Suicide reduction** for BPAD pts<br>Option:Cluster headache, OCD, antidepressant augmentation & aggression<br>Safe to use in **liver dx**<br>CI: **↓renal fx**, **breast feeding** caution<br>Acute Mania **0.8-1.2 mmol/l**<br>Maintenance Tx **0.6-1.0 mmol/l** | **↑ Lithium level by**: ACE inhibitors, ARBs,carbamazepine, Ca channel blockers, diuretics, fluoxetine, metronidazole, NSAIDS, sodium depletion, spironolactone<br>**↓ Lithium level by**: caffeine, metamucil, NaCl, theophylline<br>**Lithium↑ toxic** by ↑ **serotonin effect**: l-tryptophan, MAOI's, sibutramine, verapamil<br>With **Antipsychotics**- ↑ neurotoxicity | 300mg hs<br>1800mg/day | 300mg po hs<br>300mg po bid<br>300mg SR bid<br>600mg po hs<br>300mg po tid<br>300mg SR tid<br>**900mg po hs**<br>1200mg po hs | 28<br>34<br>61 generic<br>34<br>39<br>81 generic<br>**39**<br>46 |
| **Valproic acid -VPA**<br>**DEPAKENE** g<br>(250mg cap; 500mg EC cap; 250mg/5ml **syrup**) **D** | As per **divalproex above**<br>**Depakene generally has more GI** side effects than **Epival** | CBC,Platelets, LFT<br>**Level** | Divalproex & valproic acid are **not** interchangeable medications<br>As per **divalproex above** | As per **divalproex above**<br>Pregnancy registry: heart defect & spina bifida 10.7vs2.9% in control gp. ↑ malformations with valproate Artama 05, esp >1g/d Perucca 05. May ↓ IQ in newborns. | 250mg od<br>3000mg/day | 250mg po bid<br>**500mg po bid**<br>1gm po hs<br>500mg po tid | 64<br>**121**<br>121<br>179 |
| **Gabapentin**<br>**NEURONTIN** g<br>(100,300,400 cap)<br>(600ς,800ς mg tab χ▼ ↑cost) **C** | **Common**: somnolence, dizzy, ataxia, nystagmus, n/v, blurred vision, tremor, slurred speech, rash, behavioral changes in kids & ↓WBC **WEIGHT GAIN= +** (appears dose related), **euphoria** | NA<br>**little effect as mood stabilizer** | √seizures; Option:Neuropathic pain &**Anxiolytic in severe Panic dx & social phobia**,↓ dose if ↓ renal fx, 3-25umol/l (? Significance/avail.) | Antacids ↓ by 20% absorption<br>NO other signif. interactions<br>With doses >600mg less is absorbed since mechanism is saturated | 100mg hs<br>(↑ **100-**400mg/day increments)<br>3600mg/day | 100mg po bid<br>300mg po bid<br>**400mg po bid**<br>300mg po tid | 53<br>115<br>**139**<br>169 |
| **Topiramate**<br>**TOPAMAX** g<br>(25,50⊗,100,200mg tab; 15, 25mg sprinkle cap) **C**<br>Hypospadias in male infants | **Common**: nausea, dizzy, tremor, ataxia, somnolence, **cognitive dysfunction**, headache, paresthesias, sedation, fatigue, diarrhea, metabolic acidosis, **nephrolithiasis & glaucoma**.<br>**WEIGHT GAIN=** loss possible<br>(seems dose & duration dependent & > in ♀) | CNS SE synergize with agents such as divalproex | **Weight loss** ~**4kg** ?dose related<br>May minimize weight gain induced by other psychotropics<br>√ seizures; 80% Renal elimination<br>√ migraine prophylaxis<br>+ dva→ ↓ platelet&↑ **encephalopathy**<br>**Renal stones** 1.5% thus try to ↑ **fluid intake** | **↓ Topiramate level by**: **carbamazepine** & phenytoin (40%), valproate (15%)<br>**↑ toxicity of topiramate with**: Ketogenic diet; Aceta-,dor-& metho-zolamide (topiramate has carbonic anhydrase inhib. properties)<br>**Topiramate** >200mg/d **↓ effectiveness** : **oral contraceptive pills** | 25mg hs<br>↑ only by **25-50mg/week** increments<br>**250-400**mg/day | 25mg po bid<br>50mg po bid<br>**100mg po bid**<br>200mg po bid<br>400mg po hs<br>Caution: ↓ **sweating** especially in children | 159/299<br>227/570<br>**278**/542<br>424/796<br>424/796<br>generic/Trade |

(kidney icon)=↓ dose for renal dysfx ς=scored ☎ =Exception Drug Status Sask χ =Non formulary in Sk ▼covered NIHB **CI**=contraindication **CR**=control release **Dx** =disease **EC**=enteric coated **SE**=side effect **SR**=sustained release ^ **Carbamazepine ↓ level of**: alprazolam, clonazepam, cyclosporine, dexamethasone, diazepam, doxycycline, ethosuximide, felodipine, fentanyl, irinotecan, lamotrigine, haloperidol, nefazodone, nevirapine, **OC'S**, phenytoin, phenobarbital, phenothiazines, pregnancy tests, **risperidone**, steroids, theophylline, triazolam, tricyclics, valpro...

**Pregnancy**: Lithium, carbamazepine, valproic acid have teratogenic risk, risk > if on multiple meds; thus try for monotherapy & ↓serum level. Try to **avoid** in **1st trimester**. Consider antipsychotic, benzo...

√ **Useful for/in** # **Rash:** ↑dose, ↑too quickly, if with valproic or in kids → ↑rash rate. **CLONAZEPAM / LORAZEPAM** (0.5-2mg qid) / **antipsychotics** eg. haloperidol, olanzapine☎▼, quetiapine, risperidone, ziprasidone, aripipr...

 Prepared by: Loren Regier, Brent Jensen

## Table 1: Adverse Effects: Management Options [24,25]

- **Dizziness** ☞ check BP for **orthostatic hypotension**; mild symptoms may attenuate over several weeks; ↓ dose or switch agent; encourage adequate fluid intake & avoid excessive salt restriction; Florinef 0.1mg po od & titrate
- **Sedation/foggy** ☞ may attenuate over 1-2weeks; give single dose 1-2 hr prior to bedtime; ↓dose or choose alternative; select pts modafinil or methylphenidate / atomoxetine
- **Peripheral anticholinergic effects** ☞ tolerance may develop over several weeks; switch to alternative agent; treatment options for some Sx:
  - **blurry vision-**pilocarpine eye drops;methylcellulose drops for dry eyes
  - **urinary hesitancy** - bethanechol 25-50mg po tid-qid
  - **abdominal cramps, nausea, diarrhea** - adjust dose
  - **dry mouth** - sugarless gum; saliva substitutes e.g.ORAL balance Gel, Mouth Kote; pilocarpine
  - **constipation** - adequate hydration, activity, bulk forming laxatives
- **Sweating** ☞ ↓dose or change antidepressant; benztropine, cyproheptadine, clonidine
- **Weight gain** ☞ modify & monitor diet & activity; switch to alternate agent
- **Sexual dysfunction** ☞ distinguish etiology (drug vs illness); switch to: (**bupropion**, **mirtazapine**, moclobemide, venlafaxine ↓↓dose); adjust dose; 1day/wk drug holiday, amantadine;
  Other: • ↓ libido → neostigmine 7.5-15mg 30min prior to intercourse
  - impaired erection → bethanechol 10mg po tid
  - anorgasmia → amantadine; cyproheptadine Periactin 4mg po qam, ?**sildenafil** in ♀
  - antidepressant induced erectile dysfunction → sildenafil may help [26]
- **Myoclonus** ☞ ?TCA toxicity; reassess dose/levels; clonazepam 0.25mg tid
- **Insomnia & anxiety (5HT related)** ☞ ↓dose; administer in am; + short course of trazodone 50-100mg hs; switch to alternate agent
- **SIADH (syndrome of inappropriate antidiuretic hormone secretion** esp in elderly**)**: associated with hyponatremia ☞ DC causative agent; fluid restriction (1 liter/d)
- **Serotonin Syndrome**[27]: excitement, anxiety, diaphoresis, rigidity, ↑temp, tremor, clonus, ↑reflexes, ↑HR&BP, delirium; D/C serotonergic meds; Tx: Periactin 4mg po q4h, diazepam
- **Discontinuation syndrome** with abrupt withdrawal eg. paroxetine & venlafaxine a flu-like syndrome x~10day (FINISH: flu, insomnia, nausea, imbalance, sensory disturbances & hyperactivity) may occur. Tx: **TAPER** off original antidepressants slowly over several **days**/? even weeks or give benztropine (for cholinergic rebound→nausea/vomiting, **sweating**), lorazepam (for agitation/insomnia), propranolol (for akathisia) as necessary.

## Table 4: Individualizing Therapy Considerations [28]

| | |
|---|---|
| **Anxiety/Panic** | ✓SSRIs, venlafaxine, mirtazapine |
| **Anxiety, Comorbid** | ✓moclobemide, mirtazapine, duloxetine, ? buspirone |
| **Atypical*** | ✓moclobemide, MAOIs, SSRIs ------→ * |
| **Bipolar** | ✓mood stabilizer e.g. lithium, valproic acid, carbamazepine, quetiapine **+/-** antidepressant |
| **Cardiac Condition** | ✓SSRIs (citalopram,sertraline), MAOIs, bupropion |
| **Chronic Pain/Neuropathy**[29] | ✓TCAs: amitriptyline, nortriptyline; venlafaxine, duloxetine |
| **Drug Induced** [30,31] | stop or reduce offending agent (see bottom) |
| **Elderly** [32,33] | ✓SSRI (CC,P,S); venlafaxine; mirtazapine; RIMA; **2°TCA** e.g. **nortriptyline** |
| **Migraine**[34] | ✓amitriptyline, nortriptyline |
| **Obsessive Compulsive** | ✓SSRI (high dose), clomipramine |
| **Orthostatic Hypotension** | ✓venlafaxine(↑BP); nortriptyline, SSRIs (ambulation, hydration, gradual dose titration) |
| **Phobic** | ✓moclobemide, MAOI, paroxetine? |
| **Psychotic** | ✓+antipsychotic quetiapine, aripiprazole, olanzapine, amoxapine etc., ECT Navarro'08 |
| **Seizure History** | ✓trazodone, SSRIs, moclobemide, venlafaxine |
| **Sleep Disorders**[35] | ✓trazodone, amitriptyline, other TCAs (nortriptyline) |
| **Smoking Cessation**[36] | ✓bupropion ZYBAN 300mg/d, nortriptyline 25-75mg/d |
| **Weight Gain, Less**[37] | ✓bupropion, SSRIs, RIMA, venlafaxine, duloxetine |

## Table 2: Precautions [38,39,40]

**TCAs**: benign prostatic hypertrophy, history of urinary retention, uncorrected angle closure glaucoma, seizure history, post-MI - acute recovery phase, cardiovascular disease, cholinergic rebound upon withdrawal from high doses (dizziness, nausea, diarrhea, insomnia, restlessness, cardiac conduction delays, heart block; arrhythmias)

**SSRIs**: hepatic dysfunction (↑ levels & half-life), irritable bowel syndrome, CNS overstimulation (e.g. ***serotonin syndrome***) [41] especially if used in combination with other serotonergic drugs (buspirone, dextromethorphan, lithium, **MAOI**, meperidine, mirtazapine, MDMA, ondansetron, sibutramine, St. Johns Wort, sumatriptan, tramadol, tryptophan, TCA)[42]; withdrawal syndrome: dizziness, GI upset, headache, sleep disturbance, agitation/restlessness (usually mild & transient; less common with fluoxetine) [43]

**Bleeding & ?↑Fractures**: assoc. by SSRI inhibition; risk of bleeding <0.5% [44]

**MAOIs**: hypertensive crisis can occur secondary to foods containing **tyramine** {e.g. HIGH → Unpasteurized cheese (cheddar, camembert, blue), yeast extract, herring, aged unpasteurized meats, broad bean pods; MODERATE→ avocado, meat extract, certain ales & beer, wine; LOW→ fruit, cream & cottage cheese, distilled spirits, chocolate};
CI: Stroke/heart dx, geriatric or debilitated, pheochromocytoma, or hx of severe headache.

**Bupropion**: avoid if hx of seizures, bulimia or anorexia nervosa

**Pediatrics**: Safety & efficacy **not** well established. [45,46,47,48] CBT, fluoxetine & citalopram 1st line option.[65] (Concern→suicide idea<25yr, aggression & agitation) NNH=143. Imipramine for enuresis kids≥6 yrs. FDA: Fluoxetine depression (49) & OCD; clomipramine, fluvoxamine & sertraline OCD,50.

**Pregnancy**: Consider risk vs benefit! ECT & psychotherapy are non-drug options. TCAs desipramine & SSRIs: most clinical safety data. (Some C agents may be preferable: **fluoxetine** (most experience), paroxetine (no active metabolite, but ?↑harm[51]), sertraline ?↑septal defects & bupropion but less clinical experience). citalopram: ?↑septal defects. Only if low depression risk, consider ↓dose &/or taper off over weeks before delivery.[52] Neonate may have **withdrawal** [53] & pulmonary hypertension with SSRI. [54] Depression serious risk for relapse, hospitalization, suicide: inform ?malformations, monitor u/s, echo.

**Breast feeding**: consider risk vs benefit; psychotherapy; levels often <10% of maternal dose; esp. SSRI's & also nortriptyline used (**sertraline**, paroxetine & fluvoxamine: ↓ levels & no reported adverse effects; fluoxetine, ?citalopram & venlafaxine: ↑breast milk level). [55,56,57,58]

**Elderly**: extra caution required; med dose: start low & go slow

**Relative Seizure Risk**:[59]
HIGH→ maprotiline, amoxapine, clomipramine, bupropion
LOW→ amitripyline, imipramine, trimipramine, nortriptyline, desipramine, doxe
LOWEST→ trazodone, SSRI'S, MAOI'S, moclobemide, venlafaxine

*__*Atypical depression*__ defined as: mood reactivity; irritability; hypersomnia; hyperphagia; psychomotor agitation & hypersensitivity to rejection.

**DRUG INTERACTIONS**: Various cytochrome **P450 inhibition**[60] by SSRI's. Less DI's [61]: **citalopram** escitalopram, **mirtazapine, moclobemide, sertraline & venlafaxine.**

| Drug | CYP450 1A2 | CYP450 2C9 | CYP450 2C19 | CYP450 2D6 | CYP450 3A4 |
|---|---|---|---|---|---|
| **citalopram** | 0 | 0 | 0 | + | 0 |
| fluoxetine | + | ++ | + to ++ | +++ | + to ++ |
| fluvoxamine | +++ | ++ | +++ | + | ++ |
| paroxetine | + | + | + | +++ | + |
| sertraline | + | + | + | + to ++ | + |

Antidepressant Drug Interactions: page **106** Other non P450 reactions possible (eg. Serotonin Sx)

## Table 3: Switching Antidepre[...] periods in DAYS for outpatient[...]

| FROM ↓ / SWITCH TO ☞ New agent | amitriptyline, **clomipramine**, doxepin, Imipramine, desipramine, nortriptyline | mirtazapine, venlafaxine, duloxetine | **fluoxetine**, fluvoxamine, paroxetine, citalopram, sertraline, nefazodone, trazodone | **phenelzine** | **tranylcypromine** | **moclobemide** | **bupropion** |
|---|---|---|---|---|---|---|---|
| amitriptyline | 1* | 1# | 1-7† | 7† | | 1† | 1-7† |
| **clomipramine** | 1* | 1# | **7-14†** | 7† | | 1† | 7-14† |
| doxepin, imipramine | 1* | 1# | 1-7† | 7† | | 1† | 1-7† |
| desipramine | 1* | 1# | 1-7† | 7† | | 1† | 1-7† |
| nortriptyline | 1* | 1# | 1-7† | 7† | | 1† | 1-7† |
| mirtazapine | 1# | 1† | 3† | 7† | | 3† | 3† |
| **duloxetine** | 7# | 5† | 5† | 5† | | 5† | 5† |
| **venlafaxine††** | 7# | 7† | 7† | 7† | | 7† | 7† |
| **fluoxetine** | 35! | 35! | 7! | 35! | | 35! | 7! |
| fluvoxamine | 1-7† | 7† | 1# | 7† | | 1† | 1+ |
| **paroxetine††** | 7† | 7† | 7# | 10† | | 7† | 7+ |
| citalopram/sertraline | 1-7† | 7† | 1# | 10† | | 1† | 1+ |
| nefazodone | 1-3† | 3† | 1# | 7† | | 1† | 1+ |
| trazodone | 1-7† | 7† | 1# | 7† | | 2† | 1+ |
| **phenelzine** | **10-14** | **14** | **10-14** | | **14** | 2## | **14** |
| **tranylcypromine** | **10-14** | **14** | **10-14** | **14** | | 2## | **14** |
| **bupropion** | **1-3†** | **1†** | **1†** | 7† | | **3†** | |
| **moclobemide** | **2** | **2** | **2** | **2** | | | **2** |

The more critical recommendations are in **bold**; risks of toxicity are greater with higher dosage regimens and inadequate washout period. **Some urgent cases may necessitate shorter delays in switching.**
* no washout required; use equivalent dose;
† taper first drug; start 2nd new drug at a low dose;
\# taper first drug over 3-7day prior to initiating 2nd new drug;
\## taper if high dose; maintain dietary restriction for 10d;
! use lower doses of 2nd new drug initially; longer tapering (up to **8** week) may be required for high dose fluoxetine
†† paroxetine & venlafaxine tapered slowly ↓discontinuation rxs.

**Drug induced depression**: ACEI, acetazolamide, amphetamine/ cocaine withdrawal, anticonvulsants, amantadine, barbiturates, BCPs, benzos, bromocriptine, caffeine, chemotherapy some, cimetidine, clonidine, dapsone, digoxin, disulfiram, efavirenz, ethambutol, ethanol, finasteride, griseofulvin, Haldol, hydralazine, interferon, isoniazid, isotretinoin, levodopa, mefloquine, methyldopa, methylphenidate, methysergide, metoclopramide, metronidazole, nitrofurantoin, NSAIDs, opiates, physostigmine, procainamide, progestins, propranolol, reserpine, streptomycin, steroids, sulfas, tetracycline & thiazides.

**General**: Remission ~30%, Response ~50%, Eventually ~80% respond to drug (2-4 wk some & **6-8wk** for major improvement). **Psychotherapy**, **cognitive behavioral therapy (CBT)** +/- drug tx also effective! **ECT** may be effective 6-12 txs over 2-4wk. New: Vagus nerve & transcranial magnetic stimulation

**ACP Guide 2008:** Since drugs are ~equally effective; consider SE, cost, & pt preference. Assess after 1-2 wks & regularly (SE e.g. suicidal, effect). Modify tx if no response within 6-8wks. **Tx Duration**: 1st episodes⇨continue for ~ 6 months 4-9months after response; pts with a hx of 2+ episodes⇨tx longer (years -lifelong)! **CANMAT 2009 Canadian** Guide: Adult Major Depressive Disorder. Pharmacotherapy. Lam RW, et al. J Affect Disord. 2009 Aug 10. {11% of Canadians at some time, 4% during any given year, acute/maintenance tx, psychotherapy –CBT or IPT, ECT, & Complementary-St John's wort, light tx SAD & exercise. } [65]

**Assessment** Questions: **PHQ-9** or 1) In last month, have you often been bothered by "feeling down", depressed or hopeless? 2) In last month, have you been bothered by having little interest or pleasure in doing things? Clinical benefit relates to severity Depression Mild-Mod NNT=16, Severe NNT=11, Very Severe NNT=4 over ~8 wks Fournier'10

# ANTIDEPRESSANT COMPARISON CHART [1,2,3,4,5,6,7]

© www.RxFiles.ca Prepared by Brent Jensen, Loren Regier

May 10

| NAME: Generic / TRADE<br>g=generic availabilty $T_{1/2}$= half-life | RECEPTOR AFFINITY | SIDE EFFECTS: ACH. | SIDE EFFECTS: SED. | SIDE EFFECTS: OTHER | COMMENTS & ADDITIONAL USES (Bold indicates official indication in Canada) | | INITIAL & MAX. DOSE | USUAL ADULT DOSE RANGE | $ /Month |
|---|---|---|---|---|---|---|---|---|---|
| **Citalopram CELEXA**$_g$ $T_{1/2}$=35hr<br>20,40mg **scored** tab (10&30mg)✗▼ abr=**CC**<br>**escitalopram CIPRALEX**✗⊗ S(+)citalopram 10ς-20ςmg od $60 | **5HT SELECTIVE**<br>**SSRI's**<br>(blocks dopamine at high doses:**P,S**)<br>{Women may respond better than ♂} | + | + | **SSRIs SE in General**<br>**nausea** {21%(F) - 36% (X)}, anxiety, insomnia {~14%}, agitation, anorexia, **tremor** somnolence {11-26%}, sweating (all), dry mouth, **headache**, dizziness, enuresis, diarrhea {12% (F,P)-17% (S)}, constipation {13-18%}, EPS sexual dysfx. >30%[8,9], SIADH<br>**Toxicity can→**depression<br>{**D/C Syndrome**[10] →flu-like Sx's '**FINISH**' flu, insomnia, nausea, imbalance, sensory Δ's, hyper} | •**fewest drug** interactions<br>•?benefit heart dx pts[11] | **Therapeutic Uses**:[12,13]<br>√ OCD (esp. **F**, **P**,**S**,**X**)<br>√Panic(esp. **P**,**S**;F,CC,X)<br>√ GAD (**P**,**ES**);?others<br>√ Bulimia nervosa (**F**)<br>√Diabetic neurop.(CC) & deter use of EtOH<br>√PTSD(**P**,S),√PMDD(F,P,S)<br>√Social Phobia (**P**,S)<br>√ Pediatric (ES,F,S,X)<br>+ve effect on headache?<br>•**flat dose response** (majority of depressed pts respond at the **lowest effective dose**) | **10-20mg am**<br>60mg/d | 20mg po od<br>40mg po od Star*D~40-60mg/d | **27**<br>27 |
| **Fluoxetine PROZAC**$_g$<br>(10,20,40✗▼mg **cap** & 4mg/ml **soln**) abr=**F**<br>$T_{1/2}$=4-6days, plus norfluoxetine 4-16days (Approved 1989) | | 0 | 0 | | •**most anorexic** & stimulating<br>•long half-life (5 wk washout)<br>•90mg **weekly** in USA •DI tamoxifen | | 10-20mg od<br>80mg/d | (10mg po od) ✝<br>20mg po od am (Solution $90)<br>40mg po od am | 41<br>**30**<br>53 |
| **Fluvoxamine LUVOX**$_g$<br>(50,100mg scored tabs) abr=**X**<br>$T_{1/2}$=15-26hr | | 0/+ | ++ | | •**most nauseating**, constipating & sedating SSRI; ↑ DI's | | **25-50mg hs**<br>300mg/d | 100mg po hs<br>150mg po hs<br>50mg am & 150mg hs | **36**<br>51<br>66 |
| **Paroxetine PAXIL**$_g$ $T_{1/2}$=21-31hr<br>(10ς,20ς, 30mg tab)(40mg tab✗▼) abr=**P**<br>{**Paxil CR** 12.5,25,37.5mg tab✗⊗ } | | + | + | | •most anticholinergic SSRI<br>•most **anxiety** indications •DI tamoxifen<br>•↑**weight**, D/C reaction possible[14] &<br>•↑sexual dysfx, sedation & constipation | | 10-20mg am<br>60mg/d | 10-**20**mg po od am<br>30mg po od am<br>40mg po od am<br>12.5-25mg **CR** od am ✗⊗ | 44-**32**<br>33<br>57<br>62-67 |
| **Sertraline ZOLOFT**$_g$<br>(25,50,100mg cap) abr=**S**<br>$T_{1/2}$=26hr, plus desmethyl 66hr | | 0 | + | | •most diarrhea & male sexual dysfx of SSRIs •?benefit heart pts[15], **few drug** interactions[16];?↑TG | | **25-50mg am**<br>200mg/d | 100mg po od cc<br>50mg am & 100mg pm StarD<br>100mg po bid cc | **34**<br>59<br>61 |
| Nefazodone SERZONE $T_{1/2}$=2-4hr<br>DISCONTINUED<br>abr-**Z** | **SARI 5HT Selective**<br>SSRI+$5HT_2$ rec. antagonism | + | +++ | As for SSRIs +: ↓ BP<br>Rare: **hepatotoxicity**[17] | •least stimulating serotonergic<br>•**less wt** gain;**less sex** dysfx,**DI**'s | •↓anxiety/insomnia {Still avail. in USA} | 50-100mg bid<br>600mg/d | 100mg po bid<br>150mg po bid<br>**DISCONTINUED Canada NOV03** | |
| **Trazodone DESYREL**$_g$ $T_{1/2}$=6-11hr<br>(50;75✗▼;100mg scored tabs)<br>(150mg Dividose tab:50/75/100/150mg ✗▼) | | **0** | ++++ | ↓↓ **BP**, dizzy, headache, nausea; ($\alpha_1$ blockade); **priapism** 1/6000, (Tx epi) | √dementia 50mg hs (**insomnia, sundowning**, aggression); less cardiac effects than TCAs | √ Panic, chronic pain<br>√ **Sleep disorders:** 50-100mg hs | 50mg bid<br>600mg/d | 50mg po hs<br>100mg po bid pc<br>200mg po bid pc | 14<br>27<br>**48** |
| **Amitriptyline ELAVIL**$_g$ $T_{1/2}$=9-44hr & nortriptyline<br>(10, 25,50mg; 75mg✗▼tab) | **5HT & NE EFFECTS**<br>tertiary (**3°**) amine **TCA's**<br>{Men may respond better than ♀} | +++++ | +++++ | **General TCA SE**:<br>↑HR, ↓BP (Tx: fluid+/- Florinef), **weight gain**, sexual dysfx, sweating, rash, tremors, ECG abnormalities, **seizures**<br>•fatal in overdose [18] (≥2gm) due to **cardiac** & neurologic toxicity.<br>•? rare: anticonvulsant hypersensitivity cross reactions<br>•**2°** amines generally **better tolerated** then 3° amines (less dry mouth, dizziness & weight gain) | •often 10-30⁺mg hs for sleep, **IBS** & chronic pain •Cp | **Therapeutic Uses** [19]<br>√ **IBS, Pain** Syndromes[20] & sleep disorders[21] (amitriptyline; but **nortriptyline** 2°TCA useful & less SE)<br>√ **Neuropathy**<br>√ Agitation & insomnia<br>√ Panic→ imipramine<br>√ **Migraine** prophylaxis[22] (esp. amitrip./nortriptyline)<br>√ Smoke D/C→nortrip.<br>√ ADHD(ie. desipramine) | 10-25mg hs<br>300mg/d | 50 mg po hs<br>200mg po hs | 15<br>**38** |
| **Clomipramine ANAFRANIL**$_g$<br>(10, 25, 50mg tab) $T_{1/2}$=20-32hr & desmethyl 69hr | | +++++ | ++++ | | •esp. effective for **OCD**≥10yrs<br>•Most serotonergic TCA; •Cp<br>•higher risk of seizures | | 10-25mg hs<br>300mg/d | 50 mg po hs<br>150mg po hs<br>200mg po hs | 21<br>47<br>**61** |
| **Doxepin SINEQUAN**$_g$<br>(10,25,50,75,100,150mg cap) $T_{1/2}$=8-52hr with desmethyl | | +++ | ++++ | | •Most histamine block •Cp •Breastfeed concern<br>•√ psychoneurotic/anxious dep. | | 10-25mg hs<br>300mg/d | 50 mg po hs<br>200mg po hs | 22<br>57 |
| **Imipramine TOFRANIL**$_g$<br>(10, 25, 50; 75✗▼mg tab) $T_{1/2}$=6-34hr with desipramine & hydroxy | | +++ | +++ | | •Cp<br>√ Childhood enuresis (age 6+) | | 10-25mg hs<br>300mg/d | 50 mg po hs<br>150-200mg po hs | 18<br>45-**57** |
| **Desipramine NORPRAMIN**$_g$<br>(10,25,50,75,100mg tab)-imipramine derivative<br>(50mg tab **better price** in SK) $T_{1/2}$=12-46hr with hydroxy | **NE > 5HT**<br>secondary (**2°**) amine **TCA's** | ++ | ++ | | •Most NE activity •caution CV hx<br>•**Least ACH** side effects<br>•Cp (used in IBS irritable bowel syndrome) | | 10-25mg hs<br>300mg/d | 50 mg po hs<br>150mg po hs (3x50mg)<br>200mg po hs (4x50mg) | 22<br>48<br>64 |
| **Nortriptyline AVENTYL**$_g$<br>(10, 25mg cap) -amitriptyline derivative<br>$T_{1/2}$=16-88hr & hydroxy | | +++ | ++ | | •**Least hypotensive** TCA. √IBS<br>•Cp (response may be higher at low end ≈50mg of dose range[23]) | | 10mg hs<br>**150mg/d**<br>Star*D <200mg/d | 25mg po hs<br>50mg po hs<br>100mg po hs<br>**75-100mg/d** for neuropathic pain | 17<br>**25**<br>41 |
| Des**venlafaxine ER Pristiq**✗⊗ **50**-100mg po od new-avail; DI: Cyp 3A4 (?clarithromycin) $95 | | | | | | | | | |
| **Venlafaxine EFFEXOR** g<br>(**Reg** 37.5,75mg scored tabs-Co **D/C** Jul04)<br>(**XR** 37.5mg, 75mg, 150mg cap) g<br>-XR cap content may be **sprinkled** $T_{1/2}$=5hr & desmethyl 11hr | **SNRI**<br>**5HT & NE**<br>(also some DA) | ++ | + | •**As dose↑: ↑BP**&HR, agitation, tremor, sweating, nausea~37%, headache, sleep disturbances<br>•caution:**withdrawal effects** | •initial nausea; "clean TCA"<br>•side effects similar to SSRIs;<br>•**low wt** gain; **few drug** interactions<br>•↓renal fx adjust dose;overdose concern>1g | √GAD, Panic & social anxiety disorder<br>√for BPAD depressed; relapse prevents & ↓recurrence | 18.75-**37.5**mg<br>375mg/d | 37.5mg **XR** po od<br>75mg **XR** po od<br>150mg **XR** od Star*D ~200mg/d<br>225mg **XR** od (150mg+75mg cap) | 26<br>46<br>48<br>94 |
| **Duloxetine CYMBALTA** SNRI 30,60mg cap **SE**: nausea, insomnia, somnolence, headache, diarrhea, ↓appetite, fatigue, ↑sweat, ↑BP, ↑**LFTs**, ↑DI 1A2,2D6, dry mouth; urinary retention FDA?. √depression adult & maintenance, GAD, diabetic neuropathic pain, fibromyalgia & ?stress incontinence ☎⊗ 30-**60**mg/d $72-138 Max 120mg. | | | | | | | | | |
| **Bupropion SR WELLBUTRIN**$_g$<br>(100,150mg tab)☎(150,300mg **XL**tab)☎ $T_{1/2}$=21hr | **NDRI**<br>**DA & NE** | 0 | 0 | agitation, insomnia, tremor, sweating, ↓**appetite**, GI upset, psychos. | •↑'d risk of **seizure** ~0.4% 400mg/d<br>•**less sex dysfx**, **low wt. gain** | =**ZYBAN**✗▼→D/C smoking;<br>√ BPAD & Seasonal AD | 100mg od am<br>450mg/d | 100-150mg bid Star*D~300mg/d<br>150-300mg XL po od | 32-40<br>26-44 |
| **MAOIs**: non-selective & irreversible; ✓ atypical/refractory depression; enzyme effect ~10days; many DIs & food cautions (tyramine-hypertensive **crisis**);phenelzine *NARDIL* 15mg tab bid-tid; tranylcypromine *PARNATE* 10mg tab bid-tid | | | | | | | | | |
| **Mirtazapine REMERON**$_g$ $T_{1/2}$=20-40hr<br>15ς,30ς,45mg tabs (**RD**$_g$ 15,30,45mg tab) | **NaSSA** 5HT & NE | +++ | ++++ | Dry mouth, **sedation**, edema, arthralgias, dizzy. DI-clonidine | ↑appetite&weight ;↓sexual dysfx; rare neutropenia; RD if difficulty swallowing | √Anxiety, Somatization | ≤7.5-45mg/day<br>Star*D <60mg/d | 15-30mg po hs (RD & reg)<br>Generic RD Novo-mirtaz OD is ↓$ | 20-33 |
| **Moclobemide MANERIX**$_g$ $T_{1/2}$=1-2hr<br>(100,150,300mg scored tabs)<br>(2x150mg tabs **cheaper** than 300mg tab) | **RIMA**<br>Selective & Reversible | + | 0 | Dry mouth, dizzy, headache, nausea, tremor, restless, **less sex dysfx** | •no tyramine dietary precaution if <600mg/d<br>•enzyme effect lasts ~24hrs<br>**DI**:meperidine, sympathomimetics, DM… | √Atypical,<br>√**Anxious-phobic**,<br>√Co-morbid anxiety | 100mg bid<br>600-900mg/d | 150mg po bid pc<br>300mg am&150pm pc<br>300mg po bid pc | **26**<br>36<br>54 |

=↓ dose for renal dysfx ς=scored tab ☎ **EDS** ✗ non-formulary in SK =prior approval NIHB ▼=covered by NIHB ⊗=not NIHB **COST**=total cost **5HT**=serotonin **ACH**=anticholinergic effects (dry mouth, constipation, urinary hesitancy, blurred vision) **ADD**=attention deficit disorder **BP**=blood pressure **Cp**=plasma level avail **DA**=dopamine **D/C**=discontinuation **DI**=drug interactions **epi** =epinephrine **GI**=stomach **HR**=heart rate **MAOI**=monoamine oxidase inhibitors **NE**=norepinephrine **OCD**=obsessive compulsive dx **RIMA** reversible inhibitor of MAO-A **SE**=side effect **SED**=sedation **SSRI**=selective 5HT reuptake inhibitor **Sx**=symptoms **TCA**=tricyclic antidepressant **Tx**=treatment **wk**=week **wt**=weight **INITIAL DOSE** -Lower initial dose for elderly/sensitive pts. ✝ =initial dose lower than usual effective dose. **Pregnancy**: C agents: fluoxetine (**most** clinical experience), sertraline & bupropion but less clinical experience. **Treatment Duration**: at full dose for at least ≥6-12months after remission (if recurrence tx longer)

**Add-on** Augment/Combo→if **partial** respond: some evidence ECT,(esp. with TCA + lithium ~600-900mg/d or l-thyroxine ≤100ug/d; buspirone Star*D, pindolol, quetiapine XR/olanzapine/risperidone/aripiprazole & tryptophan with SSRI). **B**upropion Star*D or mirtazapine (with SSRI or venlafaxine).

| Column 1 AD | Column 2- AVOID Combination with: | Column 3- CAUTION: MINIMIZE RISK (dose adjustment; monitor effects) with: |
|---|---|---|
| **citalopram** CELEXA | linezolid③ moclobemide②③ pimozide⑥② | buspirone ③; carbamazepine ⑥⑨; cimetidine ⑧; metoprolol ⑥ |
| **fluoxetine** 2D6,2C19<br>PROZAC | cisapride ⑥②cv<br>dexfenfluramine & fenfluramine ③<br>L-tryptophan ③<br>linezolid ③<br>MAOI's ③<br>rasagiline②<br>selegiline ③<br>sibutramine ③<br>sumatriptan ③<br>thioridazine⑥② | alprazolam ⑥<br>amitriptyline⑥ / aripiprazole ⑥<br>atomoxetine②<br>beta blocker⑥ (Atenolol unaffected)<br>buspirone ③<br>carbamazepine ⑥<br>carvedilol ⑥ / clopidogrel ④<br>codeine ⑥ (↓ pain control)<br>cyclobenzaprine ⑥②<br>cyproheptadine (↓ effect of Prozac)<br>desipramine ⑥②<br>dextromethorphan ③<br>diazepam ⑥<br>digoxin ⑥②<br>doxepin ⑥②<br>flecainide ⑥②<br>furosemide ②↓Na+/SIADH<br>haloperidol ②EPS<br>imipramine ⑥②③<br>labetolol ⑥<br>lithium ③⑥ or ⑦<br>lovastatin & simvastatin⑥(rhabdo)<br>L-tryptophan ③<br>methadone ⑥②<br>metoprolol ⑥<br>mexiletine ⑥②<br>midazolam⑥<br>nifedipine ⑥②<br>nortriptyline⑥②<br>perphenazine⑥<br>phenytoin ⑥②<br>pindolol ⑥<br>propafenone⑥②<br>propranolol ⑥<br>risperidone ⑥<br>ritonavir ⑥②<br>tamoxifen④<br>TCA's ⑥<br>timolol ⑥<br>tramadol ③④<br>trazodone ⑥③<br>verapamil ⑥②<br>warfarin ⑥ |
| **fluvoxamine** 1A2,2C19,3A4<br>LUVOX | alosetron ⑥②<br>cisapride ⑥②cv<br>clozapine ⑥②<br>dex-&fenfluramine③<br>linezolid ③<br>MAOI's③ pimozide ⑥②<br>rasagiline② ramelteon⑥②<br>selegiline ③<br>sibutramine/sumatriptan ③<br>tacrine ⑥②<br>theophylline ⑥<br>thioridazine/tizanidine⑥② | alprazolam ⑥<br>amitriptyline⑥, asenapine ⑥<br>bendamustine ⑥②<br>caffeine ⑥<br>calcium channel bl. ⑥<br>carbamazepine ⑥<br>clomipramine ③<br>clopidogrel ④<br>desipramine ⑥<br>diazepam ⑥<br>duloxetine⑥②<br>grapefruit juice ⑧<br>haloperidol ⑥<br>imipramine ⑥<br>lithium ③⑥ or ⑦<br>L-tryptophan ③<br>methadone ⑥②<br>mexiletine ⑥②<br>midazolam ⑥<br>nifedipine ⑥②<br>olanzapine ⑥②<br>propranolol ⑥<br>quinidine ⑥②<br>rifampin ⑨<br>smoking ⑨<br>theophylline ⑥②<br>tizanidine ⑥②<br>triazolam ⑥<br>verapamil ⑥②<br>warfarin ⑥ |
| **paroxetine** 2D6, p glycoprotein<br>PAXIL | dexfenfluramine & fenfluramine ③<br>linezolid ③<br>MAOI's ③<br>pimozide ⑥QT prolongation<br>rasagiline②<br>selegiline ③<br>sibutramine ③<br>sumatriptan ③<br>thioridazine ⑥② | amitriptyline ⑥①<br>anticholinergics ①<br>aripiprazole⑥, asenapine⑧<br>atomoxetine②/B-blocker⑥<br>bupropion ⑧<br>buspirone ③<br>carvedilol ⑥ /cimetidine ⑧<br>codeine ⑥ (↓ pain control)<br>desipramine ⑥<br>dextromethorphan ③<br>doxepin ⑥ , duloxetine⑥②<br>flecainide ⑥②<br>furosemide ②↓Na+/SIADH<br>haloperidol ②EPS<br>imipramine ⑥<br>labetalol ⑥<br>lithium ③<br>L-tryptophan ③<br>metoprolol ⑥<br>mexiletine ⑥②<br>nefazodone ③<br>nortriptyline ⑥<br>paliperidone⑥②<br>perphenazine ⑥<br>phenytoin ⑨⑥<br>pindolol ⑥; procyclidine ⑥<br>propafenone ⑥②<br>propranolol ⑥<br>risperidone ⑥<br>ritonavir ⑧, tamoxifen④<br>timolol ⑥<br>tramadol ③④<br>trazodone ⑥<br>TCA's ⑥<br>warfarin ⑥ |
| **sertraline** 2D6, p glycoprotein<br>ZOLOFT | dexfenfluramine & fenfluramine ③<br>linezolid ③<br>MAOI's ③<br>pimozide ⑥②<br>selegiline ③<br>sibutramine ③<br>sumatriptan ③ | carbamazepine ⑨⑥<br>erythromycin ⑧③<br>furosemide ②↓Na+/SIADH<br>grapefruit juice ⑧<br>lithium ③<br>L-tryptophan ③<br>phenytoin ⑨⑥<br>ritonavir ⑧<br>St. John's Wort ③<br>tamoxifen?④<br>tramadol ③④<br>warfarin ⑥ |
| **trazodone**<br>DESYREL | moclobemide ②③<br>MAOI's ②③<br>sibutramine ③<br>sumatriptan ③ | amiodarone②; buspirone③<br>carbamazepine ⑨<br>chlorpromazine①(hypotension)<br>cimetidine ⑧<br>clonidine ④<br>digoxin ⑥<br>fluoxetine ③<br>hypotensives ①BP<br>ampren-,indin-,riton-saqu-avir⑧3A4<br>ketoconazole ⑧ 3A4<br>lithium ③<br>L-tryptophan ③<br>phenytoin ⑥<br>sedatives ①<br>venlafaxine ③ |
| **TCA's - 1°**<br>amitriptyline, clomipramine, doxepin, imipramine<br>**TCA's - 2°**<br>desipramine, nortriptyline | clonidine ④<br>epinephine ②<br>guanethidine ④<br>MAOI's ②③<br>moclobemide ②③<br>rasagiline② | **anticholinergics**/1° ②<br>carbamazepine ⑨⑥<br>chlorpromazine ①⑧<br>chlorpropamide ⑤<br>cholestyramine ⑨<br>cimetidine ⑧<br>diltiazem ⑤(hypotension)<br>duloxetine⑧②, ethanol ②<br>fluconazole ⑧<br>fluoxetine ⑧<br>fluphenazine ①⑧<br>fluvoxamine ⑧ (clomip)<br>grapefruit juice ⑧ (clomip)<br>indinavir ⑧ (desip)<br>isoproterenol ②cv<br>lithium ③ (neuro)<br>L-tryptophan ③ (clomip)<br>perphenazine ①⑧<br>phenobarb/primidone ②⑨<br>phenylephrine & sympathomimetics ②cv<br>phenytoin ⑨<br>propantheline ②ACH<br>propoxyphene⑧(doxepin)<br>propafenone ⑥② (desip)<br>propranolol ⑤<br>quinidine ⑧ (desip/imip)<br>rifampin ⑨<br>ritonavir ⑧ (desip)<br>**sedatives** ①<br>SSRI③(1°TCA),terbinafine ①⑧<br>trifluoperazine①⑧<br>valproic acid ⑧<br>venlafaxine ⑧<br>verapamil ②cv |
| **mirtazapine**<br>REMERON | MAOI's ②<br>clonidine ④ (HTN crisis)<br>desipramine fatal in OD ②<br>sibutramine ③ | cimetidine ⑧<br>ethanol ② |
| **duloxetine** 2D6,1A2<br>CYMBALTA | MAOI's ②<br>cyclobenzaprine ③<br>fluvoxamine ⑧<br>paroxetine ⑧<br>thioridazine ⑥ | cimetidine ⑧<br>ciprofloxacin ⑧<br>propafenone ⑥②<br>linezoid ③<br>lithium ③<br>phenothiazines ⑥<br>propafenone ⑥②<br>Quinidine ⑧<br>St. John's Wort ③<br>TCAs ⑥<br>tramadol ③<br>tryptophan ③ |
| **venlafaxine**<br>EFFEXOR | MAOI's ②<br>rasagiline②<br>sibutramine ③ | cimetidine ⑧<br>desipramine ⑥<br>imipramine ⑥<br>ketoconazole ⑧<br>moclobemide ③<br>selegiline ③<br>SSRI's ①③<br>TCA's ②③ |
| **bupropion** 2D6<br>WELLBUTRIN/ ZYBAN | MAOI's ②<br>thioridazine ⑥② | other drugs affecting **seizure** threshold ②<br>amantadine ② CNS<br>cimetidine ⑧<br>carbamazepine ⑨<br>cyclophosphamide ⑥②<br>desipramine ⑥<br>ifosphamide ⑥②<br>levodopa ①<br>orphenadrine ⑥<br>phenobarbital ⑨<br>phenytoin ⑨<br>rifampin ⑨ , ritonavir ⑧<br>SSRIs ⑧<br>TCAs ⑧ |
| **moclobemide**<br>MANERIX<br>(MAOI precautions) | amitriptyline ②③<br>atomoxetine ②<br>clomipramine ②③<br>citalopram ②③<br>dextromethorphan ③<br>ephedrine②BP<br>imipramine②③<br>meperidine ②<br>phenylpropanolamine②BP<br>rasagiline②<br>pseudoephedrine ②BP<br>rizatriptan ⑥③ (naratriptan less affected)<br>thioridazine⑥②<br>trazodone ③ | **antihypertensives** ②<br>antipsychotics②<br>cimetidine ⑧<br>clopidogrel ④<br>levodopa ③<br>opioids ③ (morphine slightly safer)<br>selegiline ③<br>SSRI's ③<br>tyramine ② (↑ BP @ ↑↑ dose) |
| **MAOI's**<br>phenelzine<br>NARDIL<br>tranylcypromine<br>PARNATE | atomoxetine ②<br>bupropion & buspirone②<br>clomipramine ②③<br>cyclobenzaprine ②③<br>dexfenfluramine & fenfluramine ③<br>dextromethorphan ③<br>duloxetine ③<br>ethanol ②<br>lithium ③ linezolid ③<br>maxindol ②<br>meperidine ②<br>methotrimeprazine ②<br>methylphenidate ②<br>mirtazapine②<br>phenylephrine ②BP<br>phenylpropanolamine②BP<br>pseudoephedrine ②BP<br>reserpine ② (hypertension)<br>rizatriptan ⑥③<br>sumatriptan ⑥③<br>SSRI's ③<br>TCA's ②③<br>tramadol ②③<br>trazodone ③<br>venlafaxine ②③<br>zolmitriptan ⑥③ | chlorpropamide ⑤<br>entacapone ②<br>insulin ⑤<br>levodopa ②<br>moclobemide ②<br>morphine ②<br>tolbutamide⑤<br>tyramine ② (↑ BP @ small dose)<br>**MAOI's include**: isocarboxazid, linezolid, moclobemide, phenelzine, rasagiline, selegiline & tranylcypromine.<br>**Many other MAOI interactions possible!** |

① increased side effects ② increased risk of toxicity ③ risk of serotonin syndrome ④ reduced effect column 2 or 3 drug ⑤ increased effect of column 2 or 3 drug
⑥ metabolic: ↑ level of column 2 or 3 drug ⑦ metabolic: ↓ level of column 2 or 3 drug ⑧ metabolic: ↑ level of column 1 AD ⑨ metabolic: ↓ level of column 1 AD

Hypersexuality or paraphilic behavior are extremely difficult to manage. Before initiating pharmacotherapy to control unwanted sexual behaviors, the current drug regimen should be evaluated for drugs that may **cause/exacerbate** the behavior (eg. amphetamines/anticholinergic/antiparkinson meds). **Cognitive behavioral modification, psychotherapy & environmental changes** should be implemented **first for treatment. Some modification strategies include**: correct any misidentification by the patient of other residents as their spouse or lover, increase attention & appropriate activities, make certain behaviors such as disrobing more difficult, move patient to different room if location is problematic . Attempts to distract & redirect their behavior with conversation, food or other activities can be successful. **Case reports** suggest that antiandrogens, estrogens, LHRH agonists & serotonergic medications may be **useful when other methods have failed.** **Baseline labwork** may include: free androgen index & total testosterone, FSH, LH, estradiol, prolactin & progesterone. Of note - following surgical castration & hyperprolactinemia, sexual behavior declines. The aim of pharmacological treatment is to suppress sexual fantasies, to suppress sexual urges & behavior, & to reduce the risk of recidivism & further victimization. We wish to thank those who have assisted with this Q&A: Dr. L Thorpe, Dr. R Menzies & RxFiles advisors.)

| Drug/Forms/Reason for use g=generic avail. | Side effects(SE) / Comments | Young patients[3,4,7] Dose Cost/month | Older patients[1,2,5,6] Dose Cost/month |
|---|---|---|---|
| **SSRI's**- considered possible **first line**<br>**citalopram** (Celexa)g 10✗▼,20,40mg scored tabs<br>**paroxetine** (Paxil)g 10ς,20ς, 30mg tab (renal)<br>**sertraline**# (Zoloft)g 25,50,100mg cap<br>-better impulse control, or for possible anti-compulsion effect & to ↓ sexual desire | **SE**: Especially early in therapy: insomnia, fatigue, headache, tremor, nausea, vomiting, diarrhea, falls, decreased concentration, confusion, SIADH & rarely extrapyramidal reactions.<br>Titrate dose up as tolerated & **wait 4-6 weeks** for effect.<br>Fluoxetine (Prozac) frequently studied in younger patients but due to weight loss & long half life often not recommended in elderly. Also tried has been clomipramine ~150mg/day & fluvoxamine (Luvox). | 20mg po od $27 Celexa<br>40mg po od $27 Max:60mg/day<br>20mg po od $32 Paxil<br>40mg po od $57 Max:60mg/day<br>50mg po od $32 Zoloft<br>100mg po od $34 Max:200mg/day | 10mg po od $18<br>20mg po od $27 Max:30mg/d<br>10mg po od $41 ($20 if 1/2x20mg tab)<br>20mg po od $32 Max:30mg/d<br>50mg po od $32<br>100mg po od $34 Max:100mg/d |
| **buspirone** (Buspar)g 5,10ς mg tab<br>-for ? anticompulsion & ↓ deviant fantasies | **SE**: Nausea, headache, dizziness, restlessness. **Non-sedating & non-addicting.** Onset 1week; Max effect **6** weeks.<br>Drug interactions:fluvoxamine, grapefruit juice. NO dependency & no cross tolerance with benzodiazepines. | | 5mg po tid $46 Max:60-90mg/d<br>10mg po tid $55 |
| **Add to SSRI's if limited response:**<br>**cyproterone**## (Androcur)g (☎→hirsuitism) ▼<br>50ς mg tab (300mg/3ml amp ⊗)<br>-antiandrogen;possible ↓ sexual fantasies, behavior, masturbation, intercourse & impact on erections | **SE:** hepatic dysfunction, fatigue, **weight gain**, transient depression ~5-10%, ↓ in body hair, gynecomastia ~15% & feminization, as well as cardiovascular toxicity including fluid retention, thromboembolism, myocardial ischemia. Alterations in glucose and cerebrovascular accidents have occurred.<br>Dose to maintain testosterone concentration in a range that prevents feminization. Onset ~<1 month | **PO** Initial 50mg po od $ 53<br>100mg po bid $193<br>Range 50-500mg/day<br>**IM** Usual 200mg **q2wk** $184<br>300-400mg qwk $350<br>Range 100-600mg qwk | **PO** Initial 50mg po od $ 53<br>100mg po od $100<br>**IM** Usual 200mg q2wk $184<br>300-400mg qwk $350 |
| **Monitor**:serum testosterone, LH,BP,weight,LFT,BG q3-6months or as needed.Consider obtaining informed **consent** before start tx. | | | |
| **Add to SSRI's if limited response:**<br>**medroxyprogesterone** (Provera )g;<br>(Depo-Provera) g<br>2.5ς,5ς,10ς (100mg tab✗▼); 150mg/1ml & 250mg/5ml vial<br>-antiandrogenic; ? ↓ libido, sexual arousal, fantasies, urges & behavior | **Caution**: with depression, diabetes, or conditions which may be worsened by fluid retention **SE**: **weight gain**, lethargy, headache, ↓ sperm production, hot & cold flashes, hepatic dysfunction, nightmares, dyspnea, loss of body hair, hyperglycemia, leg cramps, GI disturbances, fluid retention, menstrual disorders, thromboembolism, feminization, depression, osteoporosis >2yr tx & dermatologic effects. In clinical trials the concern of an ↑ risk for breast, uterine, or ovarian cancer has not been shown. Onset ~<1 month<br>**CI**: hypersensitivity, DVT hx, liver/heart dx, breast cancer, vaginal bleeding | **PO** Initial 50mg po od $59<br>100mg po tid $312<br>Range 50-600mg/day<br>**IM** Usual 300mg **qwk** $260/203 g<br>then ?↓100mg/wk maint. after wks<br>Range: 75-700mg/wk | **PO** Initial 5mg po od $13<br>100mg po od $112<br>**IM** Usual 100mg q2wk $71/55 g<br>150mg q2wk $71/55 g<br>200mg q2wk $136/104 g |
| **MISC**:<br>**cimetidine** (Tagamet)g (renal)<br>200✗▼,300,400,600,800✗▼mg tab; 300mg/5ml liquid | Common **SE**: headache, arthralgia & nausea. Serious adverse effects of cimetidine are blood dyscrasias, hypotension, arrhythmias, CNS effects (delirium, confusion, depression), gynecomastia, renal dysfunction and hepatotoxicity. ?antiandrogen effects possible for efficacy. | 300-800mg po bid $13-23<br>Neurology 2000 → 14 of 20 demented ~73 yr old pts responded. The other six pts responded to adding ketoconazole 100-200mg/day or sprionolactone 75mg/day; or both to cimetidine. Response time in ~1-8 weeks[1] | 300-600mg po bid $13-17 |
| **Antipsychotics - limited usefulness**<br>**risperidone**(Risperdal) g (renal) (**Consta** 12.5,25,37.5,50mg vial ☎); 0.25,0.5ς,1,2ς,3ς,4ςmg tab;M-TAB 0.5,1,2,3,4mg;1mg/ml soln) | **SE**: hypotension, sedation, anticholinergic, delirium, confusion, headache, dry mouth, constipation, asthenia, nausea, akathisia, neuroleptic malignant syndrome, phototoxicity, parkinsonian side effects & tardive dyskinesia. | 1mg po bid $47<br>2mg po bid $87 | 0.25mg po bid $25<br>1mg po bid $47 |
| LHRH agonist (☎:endometriosis,fibroids & menorrhagia)<br>**Leuprolide** acetate (Lupron & Depot) ☎ ▼<br>5mg/ml vial ⊗; Depot: 3.75,7.5,11.25,22.5 &30mg<br>**Goserelin** acetate (Zoladex & LA) ☎ ▼<br>Depot: 3.6mg & 10.8mg vial<br>antiandrogen;?↓ exhibitionist, fantasies & urges | **SE**: hot flashes, erectile dysfx, ↓ libido, ↓ sperm count, ↓ body hair, injection site irritation & rare anaphylaxis (consider first a 1mg SC Lupron test dose), **renal dysfx**, flare reaction-a transient ↑ testosterone level when initiating treatment & possible worsening of patient's condition. May ↑ blood glucose.<br>-Goserelin pellet SC into anterior abdominal wall<br>Long term risk of **osteoporosis** with these agents & others if testosterone levels are dramatically reduced for an extended period of time.<br>**CI**: hypersensitivity, vaginal bleeding undiagnosed, pregnancy, breast feeding. | 3.75/7.5mg IM q month $390-450<br>11.25/22.5mg IM q3month ~$350-360 ($1000-1140 per 3 months)<br>3.6mg SC q month $441<br>10.8mg SC q3month ~$360 ($1114 per 3 months)<br>**Monitor**: serum testosterone,LH,CBC,BUN,Scr q 6 months | |

1. Neurology 2000 May 23;54(10):2024 Hypersexuality in patients with dementia: possible response to cimetidine. Wiseman SV, McAuley JW, Freidenberg GR, Freidenberg DL. 2. J Am Geriatr Soc 1999 Feb;47(2):231-4 Pharmacologic treatment of hypersexuality and paraphilias in nursing home residents. Levitsky AM, Owens NJ. 3. Can J Psychiatry 2001 Feb;46(1):26-34 The neurobiology, neuropharmacology, & pharmacological treatment of the paraphilias & compulsive sexual behaviour. Bradford JM. 4. Can J Psyc 2000 Aug;45:559-563. Protocols for the use of cyproterone,medroxyprogeserone & leuprolide in the treatment of paraphilia. 5. J Gerontol Nurs1998 Apr;24(4):44-50Addressing hypersexuality in Alzheimer's dx. Kuhn DR, et al. 6. From very limited case reports 7. Clinical Handbook of Psychotropic Drugs,Bezchlibnyk-Butler 17th Ed. 8. Dyer O. Drug treatment is proposed to manage child sex offenders. BMJ. 2007 Jun 30;334(7608):1343.

⊗ not covered NIHB ▼ covered by NIHB

**#** most studied SSRI for **hypersexuality** **##** **most studied antiandrogen** in terms of its effects as a treatment for **sexual deviation (often in pedophiles)**

(renal symbol) = ↓ dose for renal dysfx ς =scored ☎ =Exception Drug Status in Sask ✗ = Non-formulary in Sk **BG**=blood glucose **BUN**=blood urea nitrogen **CBC**=complete blood count **DVT**=deep vein thrombosis **Dx**=disease **Hx**=history **LFT**=liver function tests **LH**=luteinizing hormone **LHRH**= Luteinizing-hormone-releasing hormone **Scr**=serum creatinine **SE**=side effects

# ANTIPSYCHOTICS: Frequently asked Questions.

## 1. What is the difference in WEIGHT GAIN among the different antipsychotics?[1]

**Estimated weight Δ at 10 weeks:** [1,2] using a Fixed effects Model

| | kg | |
|---|---|---|
| **loxapine** | minimal | |
| **haloperidol** | 0.48 | |
| **aripiprazole** | | 4.4 |
| **risperidone** | 2.0 | 5.3 |
| chlorpromazine | 2.1 | |
| quetiapine | ~2.5 | 6.1 |
| thioridazine | 3.49 | |
| olanzapine | 3.51 | 8.5 |
| clozapine | 3.9 | |

*Allison, David Am J Psyc Nov 99,JCP 2001;*

*Correll JAMA Oct 2009* in kids over 10.8 weeks

The following statements from the CPS or specific studies state:

**Risperidone** RISPERDAL -can ↑ weight by 2 kg at 10 weeks, then 2.3kg after long term treatment
-**18%** of pts vs 9% of placebo pts ↑ by >7% from baseline (Catie[18months]: 14% ↑ by >7%; Mean change **0.8** lbs)

**quetiapine** SEROQUEL -can ↑ weight by 2 kg at 4-8 weeks, 3.5kg at 18-26 week & 5.6kg at 1year
-**25%** of pts vs 4% of placebo pts ↑ by >7% from baseline (Catie[18months]: 16% ↑ by >7%; Mean change **1.1** lbs)

**olanzapine** ZYPREXA -can ↑ weight by ~3.5kg at 10 weeks, then 5.4kg at 6-8months
-**29%** of pts vs 3% of placebo pts ↑ by >7% from baseline (Catie[18months]: 30% ↑ by >7%; Mean change **9.4** lbs)

**clozapine** CLOZARIL -can ↑ weight by 4 kg at 10 weeks, dose related.

## 2. What are the different EXTRAPYRAMIDAL SIDE EFFECTS (EPS) and COSTS?

| Atypical agent | EPS effect | Prolactin levels | Younger patients (Dose & Cost/month) | Geriatric patients (Dose & Cost/month) |
|---|---|---|---|---|
| haloperidol | High | ↑↑ | 5mg po bid $18 | 1mg po hs $10 |
| risperidone RISPERDAL | Low[+] | ↑ | 1mg po bid $47<br>2mg po bid $87 | 0.5mg po hs $22<br>1mg po hs $27 New generics cheaper. M-tab more expensive. |
| olanzapine ZYPREXA | Lower[+] | ↑ ↔ | 10mg po od $125<br>15mg po od $185 | 2.5mg po od $37 (generics:↓↓$ now)<br>5mg po od $66 |
| quetiapine SEROQUEL | Even lower | ↔ | 100mg po tid $ 98<br>200mg po bid $129 | 25mg po hs $19 (generics:↓↓$ now)<br>50mg po hs $30 |
| clozapine | Lowest* | ↔ | 100mg po tid $265 | 100mg po hs $94 |

[+] dose dependent *even some anti- tremor effect

## 3. Are there any SPECIAL SITUATIONS where one agent differs from the other agents?

| Atypical agent | Liver Enzymes (↑ALT 2-3x) | Seizure Risk | Neutro -penia | Special differences |
|---|---|---|---|---|
| risperidone RISPERDAL | Rare | ≤ 0.3% | Rare<br>Health Canada as of Nov'08 received 69 total reports of agranulocytosis / neutropenia for olanzapine, quetiapine & risperidone. | Approved→behavioral disturbances in severe dementia (BPSD) & for acute treatment of mania; Liquid formulation, M tab & **depot** forms available; Parkinson's motor function worse esp. if >2mg/d |
| olanzapine ZYPREXA | ↑ ≤ 6% | ≤ 0.9% | Rare | Approved for acute treatment of mania, ↑ diabetes, ↑ weight, anticholinergic & ↑lipid. Zydis wafer avail. |
| quetiapine SEROQUEL<br>Useful agent if Parkinson's psychosis or Lewy Body dementia. | ↑ ≤ 9% | ≤ 0.8% | Rare | Approved for acute mania. ↑ cholesterol (11%), ↑ triglycerides (17%), TSH changes (ie hypothroidism ~0.4%) Eye lens changes→ cataracts in beagle dogs |
| clozapine CLOZARIL<br>Most effective agent but ↑SE, withdrawal/delirium possible if stop med abruptly. But may have lower mortality Tiihonen '09 | ↑ ≤ 37% | ≤ 5% dose dependent | YES 1% (esp. ↑ in kids & elderly) Death <0.02%pt/yr | Anti-tremor effects, Useful for Parkinson's induced psychosis but ADR's & weekly q 2-4week if stable blood tests discourage its use. Approved to ↓suicide risk in schizophrenics CSAN: 1-800-267-2726 Gen: 1-866-501-3338 Apo: 1-877-276-2569 |
| haloperidol | ↑ ≤ 16% | <1% | NO | Available in **IV/IM & depot** formulations, Useful option for acute treatment of delirium |


1. Allison DB et al. Antipsychotic Induced Weight Gain: A comprehensive Research Synthesis. Am J Psychiatry 1999;156(11):1686-96.
2. Allison DB, Casey DE. Antipsychotic-induced weight gain: a review of the literature. J Clin Psychiatry. 2001;62 Suppl 7:22-31.
3. Expert Consensus Guideline Series- Treatment of Schizophrenia 1999. J Clin Psychiatry 1999;60 (Suppl 11)
4. Switching Antipsychotics- Canadian Expert Consensus Panel July 2000
5 Canadian Clinical Practice Guidelines for the Treatment of Schizophrenia, Nov 1998, Vol 43, Supp 2; Can J Psyc Vol 50 Suppl 1 Nov **2005** http://www.cpa -apc.org/Publications/Clinical_Guidelines/schizophrenia/november2005/cjp-cpg-suppl1-05_full_spread.pdf
6. Lehman AF, et al. APA:Practice guideline for the treatment of patients with schizophrenia, 2nd Ed. Am J Psychiatry. 2004 Feb;161(2 Supp):1-56. http://www.psych.org/psych_pract/treatg/pg/Practice%20Guidelines8904/Schizophrenia_2e.pdf


## 4. What DEPOT MEDICATIONS are available?

| MEDICATION | | DEPOT SOLUTION |
|---|---|---|
| flupenthixol - FLUANXOL<br>haloperidol - HALDOL LA (preserv. benzyl alcohol) | fluphenazine-MODECATE (preserv. benzyl alc.)<br>pipotiazine -PIPORTIL | **sesame oil** |
| zuclopenthixol - CLOPIXOL Depot | | **coconut oil** but highly refined |
| risperidone - RISPERDAL CONSTA Depot | {Paliperidone palmitate IM monthly in USA} | **microspheres** in diluent |

## 5. Selecting Medications for SPECIFIC COMPLICATING PROBLEMS [3,4,5,6]

| | Recommended antipsychotic medication choices | Recommended adjunctive medication |
|---|---|---|
| **Aggression/violence Agitation/excitement** | haloperidol 2-5mg IM/1-2mg IV q1h prn Max 20mg/d (**with** promethazine 25-50mg IM prn useful)<br>lorazepam 1-4mg IV/IM/ q1h prn Max 8mg/d<br>zuclopenthixol accuphase 50-150mg IM q2d prn Max total cumulative dose ≤ 400mg & ≤ 4 inj<br>Olanzapine 10mg IM prn (but ↑$) inj ziprasidone & aripiprazole in USA<br>High potency CAP or AAP (ie. risperidone) | valproic acid<br>Possibly lithium, carbamazepine, propranolol, BZ(if no hx of substance abuse) |
| **Insomnia** | AAP (quetiapine,olanzapine ) or low potency CAP preferred | Bz -short term use of Tema-/ lora-/ oxa-zepam |
| | ♦ **if** history of abuse consider **trazodone**, diphenhydramine, hydroxyzine & methotrimeprazine | |
| **Dysphoria** | AAP strongly preferred over CAP | SSRI |
| **Suicidal behavior** | AAP strongly preferred over CAP | SSRI-if in the context of postpsychotic depression |
| **Comorbid substance abuse** | AAP preferred over CAP<br>Depot meds may be helpful for non-compliance | |
| **Cognitive problems** | AAP strongly preferred over CAP | |
| **Compulsive water drinking (psychogenic polydipsia)** | AAP preferred over CAP<br>clozapine (but not for initial treatment) | |

## 6. Selecting Medications to Avoid SIDE EFFECTS [3,4,5,6]

| | LEAST likely to cause | MOST likely to cause |
|---|---|---|
| **Sedation** | Risperidone, high potency CAP (aripiprazole & ziprasidone seem less) | Low potency CAP<br>clozapine, quetiapine, olanzapine |
| **Weight Gain /hyperglycemia-** esp in 1st time antipsyc users & diabetes | haloperidol,perphenazine,risperidone (aripiprazole & ziprasidone seem less) | clozapine most, then olanzapine, then quetiapine (not always dose related except clozapine) |
| **Extrapyramidal effects (EPS side effects)** | clozapine Less EPS<br>quetiapine ↓<br>olanzapine<br>risperidone More EPS | Mid & high potency CAP |
| **Anticholinergic side effects & Cognitive side effects** | risperidone<br>quetiapine, high potency CAP | Low potency CAP<br>clozapine |
| **Sexual side effects** | quetiapine,olanzapine,clozapine | CAP |
| **Cardiovascular SE (eg. QT effect), concern if cardiac risk /DIs/elderly, consider ECG testing in select pts** | risperidone<br>olanzapine, high potency CAP,<br>quetiapine | Low potency CAP (eg. thioridazine),<br>clozapine, pimozide & ziprasidone |
| | | **Sudden cardiac death:** ?dose-related class effect; ~0.3% of pts tx for 1yr. (3 deaths per 1000 person-years of tx) |
| **Tardive dyskinesia (TD)**<br>-Vitamin B6 1200mg/d may help<br>-Levetiracetam may help Woods '08<br>-**Atypicals** may be similar to CAP Woods '10 | clozapine Likely Less TD<br>quetiapine ↓<br>olanzapine<br>risperidone Likely More TD | CAP |
| **Recurrence of neuroleptic malignant syndrome** | olanzapine Less recurrence<br>clozapine ? ↓<br>quetiapine,risperidone More | CAP |
| **Prolactin Elevation** | cloz- olanz- & queti -apine;<br>aripiprazole | Risperidone, CAP |

**AAP** -atypical antipsychotics (clozapine, olanzapine, quetiapine & risperidone); **BZ** -benzodiazepines;
**CAP** -conventional antipsychotics ( chlorpromazine,haloperidol,zuclopenthixol etc…);
**Low potency CAP** - chlorpromazine, methotrimeprazine, & thioridazine etc.;
**Mid potency CAP** - perphenazine; **High potency CAP** - flupenthixol, fluphenazine, haloperidol, loxapine, trifluoperazine etc.

**Drug induced psychosis:** ACEI, acetazolamide, acyclovir, amantadine , amphetamine & cocaine withdrawal, anticholinergics, anticonvulsants, antidepressants, baclofen, barbiturates, benzodiazepines, beta-blockers, bromocriptine, bupropion, caffeine, calcium channel blockers, cephalosporins, chemo some, chloroquine, cimetidine, clonidine, cyclobenzaprine, dapsone, DEET, digoxin, diphenhydramine, disopyramide, disulfiram, DM, dopamine agonists, dronabinol, efavirenz, EPO, ethanol, fluoroquinolones, ganciclovir, ifosfamide, interleukin-2, interferon, isoniazid, isotretinoin, ketamine, levodopa, lidocaine, mefloquine, methyldopa, methylphenidate, methysergide, metronidazole, nevirapine, nitrofurantoin, NSAIDs, opiates, procainamide, propafenone, pseudoephedrine, quinidine, selegiline, sildenafil, steroids, sulfas, tizanidine & zaleplon.

May 10

| Name: Generic/TRADE (& receptor activity) g=generic | GROUP | Clinical Equivalency (mg) | SIDE EFFECTS -SE (%) Anticholinergic | Sedation | Hypotension | EPS | ANTI-EMETIC | DOSE: INITIAL; MAX; {elderly} | USUAL DOSE RANGE | $ /Month |
|---|---|---|---|---|---|---|---|---|---|---|
| **Chlorpromazine** LARGACTIL g (25ς,50ς,100ς mg tab)(liquid made by some pharmacies) 50mg/2ml amp); (100mg supp X▼) | Aliphatic Phenothiazine | **100** | >30<br>Cholestatic jaundice <1%, **Weight gain** ~3-5kg, Seizures <1%, Photosensitivity <3%. Hiccups [Intractable: may help] | >30 | >30 | >10 | ++++ (Pregnancy category→ C) | 25mg<br>1200mg | 50mg po bid<br>100mg po bid | 20<br>29 |
| **Methotrimeprazine** NOZINAN g (2,5,25,50mg tab) (25mg/ml amp X⊗) | | 70 | >30 | **>30** | >30 | >10 | + C | 5mg<br>1000mg | 25mg po bid<br>50mg po bid | 25<br>32 |
| **Pericyazine** NEULEPTIL (5,10,20mg cap; 10mg/ml liquid) | Piperidine | 15 | >30 | >30 | >10 | >2 | ++++ U | 5mg; (max 60mg) | 10mg po bid | 35 |
| **Pipotiazine** PIPORTIL (DEPOT 25mg/ml,50mg/ml,100mg/2ml X Amp) | | 20mg IM q4week | >10<br>Less akathisia & dystonic reactions than other DEPOT medications | >10 | >2 | 10-30 | + U | 25-250mg **IM** q4w | 25mg IM q10d<br>50-75mg IM q2-4w | 63<br>67 |
| Thioridazine MELLARIL g (10,25,50,100mg tab; 30mg/ml liquid) **Discontinued -Canada Sept/05** | Phenothiazine | 100 | >30<br>**ECG: ↑ QT interval (sertindole >thioridazine >ziprasidone)**, T wave ⌂'s,priapism, retrograde ejaculation; FDA: kids >2 approved | >30 | >30 | >2 | + C | 25mg<br>800mg→Retinal pigmentosa | 50mg po bid<br>100mg po bid | Available in USA |
| **Fluphenazine** MODECATE,MODITEN g (DEPOT with preservative 125mg/5ml Vial & 100mg/1ml Amp; 1, 2 , 5mg tab) | Piperazine | 5<br>15mg IM q4week | >2 | >2 | >2 | >30 | + C | 1-40mg PO<br>12.5-75mg**IM/SC**q2w | 2-5mg po bid<br>25-50mg IMq**2-4w** | 23-19<br>32 /5ml vial |
| **Perphenazine** TRILAFON g (2,4,8,16mg tab); (5mg/ml amp X⊗) | | 8 | >2 | >10 | >2 | >30 | ++++ C | 2mg<br>64mg | 4mg po bid<br>8mg po bid ~20mg/d CATIE | 13<br>13 |
| **Trifluoperazine** STELAZINE g (1,2,5,10, 20X▼ mg tab; 10mg/ml soln) | | 6 | >2 | >2 | >10 | >30 | ++++ C | 2mg<br>40mg | 2mg po bid<br>5mg po bid | 19<br>23 |
| **Flupenthixol** FLUANXOL (DEPOT 20mg/1ml amp, 100mg/1ml amp g; 0.5,3mg tab) | Thioxanthene | 10<br>24mg IM q4week | >10 | >2 | >2 | >30 | ++ C | 2-12mg po<br>10-80mg **IM** q2-3w | 3mg po bid<br>20-40mg Im**q2-3w** | 45<br>24-40 |
| **Zuclopenthixol** CLOPIXOL ☎ ✆ (10,25mg tabs), **Accuphase** (50mg/1 ml amp) DEPOT 200mg/1 ml amp) | | 50<br>120mg IM q4week | >10 | >30 | >2 | >30 (LESS with DEPOT) | ++ C | 20-100mg po<br>50-400mg **IM** q2w | 10mg po bid<br>25mg po bid<br>100-200mgIMq2-3w | 34<br>76<br>31 |
| **Clozapine** ☎▼ CLOZARIL,g (25ς, 50ς, 100ς, 200ς mg tab) D1-5,5HT1&2,α1,α2,H1,M1-5 | Dibenzodiazepine | 50 | >30<br>SE:Dizzy,constipation,N/V,fever,↑sweat,↑HR,↓BP,↑**salivation** [Tx: Atropine eye drop/Atrovent nasal spray], enuresis [nocturnal], **seizure**(≤5%-dose related),agranulocytosis [1%]→**CBC qweek**(q2→4week if stable), **weight** ↑↑↑,ECG ⌂'s, cardiomyopathy; ↑ALT≤ 37%, **diabetes**, ↑ lipids, akathisia [>10%]. DIs: ↓ clozapine [level]: **carbamazepine**(&↑ neutropenia) & smoking; **Cipro, fluvoxamine & eryc** ↑clozapine [level]; **benzodiazepines** -rare resp. arrest. ↔ **prolactin** effect | >30 | >30 | **>2** | + | 6.25-25mg (↑25-50mg/d)<br>900mg U<br>No breast feeding | 100mg po tid<br>200mg po bid<br>FDA: ↓ suicide risk in schizophrenics | $265_g$,396<br>$344_g$,519 |
| **Haloperidol** HALDOL g (0.5ς,1ς,2ς,5ς,10ς mg tab; 2mg/ml soln; DEPOT with preservative 250mg/5ml, 500mg/5ml Vial, 100mg/1ml Amp X⊗; 5mg/ml amp) D2>D1 | Butyrophenone | **2 - 6**<br>40mg IM q4week | >2<br>↑QT interval esp. with IV dosing, ↑ ALT ≤ 16%, **Weight gain** ≤ 1 kg; FDA: kids >3 approved | **>2** | >2 | >30 (LESS with DEPOT) | +++ C | 1-100mg PO<br>25-300mg **IM** q4w<br>*{0.25-2mg/d}* | 2mg po bid<br>5mg po bid<br>50-100mgIMq2-4w | 15<br>18<br>15-22 |
| **Loxapine** LOXAPAC g (5ς,10ς,25ς,50ς mg tab); (2.5ςmg tab X▼) (25mg/ml soln X▼; 50mg/ml amp X⊗) | Dibenzoxapine | 15 | >10<br>**Weight gain minimal** | >30 | >10 | 10-30 | + C | 5mg<br>250mg | 5mg po bid<br>25mg po bid | 17<br>34 |
| **Olanzapine** ZYPREXA g [Reg + Zydis g] ☎▼ (2.5,5,7.5,10,15mg tab)(ZYDIS 5,10,15mg tab ↑$) 10mg IM X⊗:D1-4, 5HT2,α1,H1,M1-3&5(approved 1996) | Thienobenzodiazepine | 2.5 - **5** | >10<br>SE:somnolence, dry mouth, dizzy, headache, asthenia, constipation, blurred vision, urinary incontinence, dyspepsia, ↑ ALT ≤ 6%, **diabetes**, **weight** ↑↑, ↑BP, **akathisia** >10%, postural hypotension, seizures 0.9%, ?↑stroke/death, ↑↑**triglycerides**, ↑↑**cholesterol**. DIs: ↓ olanzapine by: [smoking], ↑ by fluvoxamine ↔ ↑ **prolactin** | >30 | >2 | **>2** | + C | 2.5-5mg *{1.25-7.5mg/d}*<br>20-30mg<br>√ BPAD 1: acute Tx of manic & mixed episodes≥13yr [FDA]; Schizophrenia Age ≥13yr [FDA] SE: esp ↑weight,TG,diabetes | 10mg od (generic:↓↓$)<br>15-20mg CATIE po od | $125_g$,255<br>$185\text{-}240_g$, [360-480] |
| **Pimozide** ORAP g (2,4mg tab) | Diphenylbutyl piperidine | 2 | >2<br>↑QTc with >8mg/d or azole antifungals, diltiazem, fluvoxamine, macrolides, sertraline, paroxetine, PI's [HIV] & verapamil. FDA: kids >12 approved | >10 | >2 | >10 | + C | 2mg<br>8-20mg | 2mg po bid<br>4mg po bid | 23<br>34 |
| **Quetiapine** SEROQUEL g (25,100,200,300mg tab);(**XR**:50,150,200,300,400mg)⊗ D1-2, 5HT1&2,α1,H1 (approved 1998) | Dibenzothiazepine | 60 - **75** | >2-10<br>SE: **somnolence**, dizzy, drowsy, constipation, dry mouth, **lens changes** [beagles]-annual slit lamp exam, ↓ BP, **weight** ↑, seizures ≤0.8%, dyspepsia, headache,urinary, **abuse**, incontinence,diabetes,↑ALT≤ 9%,akathisia **>2%**,?↑stroke/death,↑triglyceride [17%],↑cholesterol [11%],hypothyroidism [0.4%],?pancreatitis/↓platelet, **low EPS** effect, ↔**prolactin** effect | **>10-30** | >10 | >2 | + C | 12.5mg *{12.5-150mg/d}*<br>800mg<br>√ BPAD: acute Tx of manic, depressive & mixed ≥10yr [FDA]<br>√ Schizo: ≥13yr [FDA]; 600mg XR od $275, 800mg XR od $370 | 200mg po tid ac<br>600mg hs ~540mg/d CATIE<br>300mg po bid ac<br>300mg po tid ac | $190_g$,285<br>$185_g$,277<br>$185_g$,277<br>$270_g$,400 |
| **Risperidone** RISPERDAL g (0.25,0.5ς,1,2ς,3ς,4ς mg tab; DEPOT 12.5,25,37.5,50mg vial) M-TAB melts 0.5,1,2,3,4 mg tab; 1mg/ml soln) D1-4, 5HT1&2,α1,α2,H1 -little M1(approved 1993) | Benzisoxazole | **2** | >2<br>SE: sedation, headache, dry mouth, constipation, blurred vision, urinary incontinence, insomnia, agitation, asthenia, **↓BP**, akathisia >10%, ↓appetite, TTP, seizures ≤0.3%, photosensitive, ?↑ stroke/death, **weight** ↑. Oral liquid **not** mix with cola/ tea. **DI:** ?furosemide. ↑ **EPS doses >2-4mg/day & ↑prolactin** & TG. | >2-10 | >10-30 | >10 | + C | 0.25-1mg *{0.25-2mg/d}*<br>6-10mg<br>Max:50mg **IM** q2w $750<br>√ BPSD; √ BPAD: acute manic & mixed tx ≥10yr [FDA]; Autism:irritability Age 5-16yr [FDA]; Schizophrenia Age ≥13yr [FDA] | 1mg po bid M-tab=$81<br>2mg bid CATIE M-tab=$153<br>25-50mg IM q2w CONSTA | 47<br>87<br>370-700 |

**General:** Onset 7day; good trial is 4-6wk. 25% of pts. respond poorly to Tx, yet 30% of these respond to clozapine. ♀ may need ↓dose than ♂ Positive S/Sx: hallucinations, delusions, thought disorders; Negative S/Sx: social withdrawal, isolation & apathy. =↓ dose for renal dysfx ς=scored

**Neuroleptic Malignant Syndrome**-upto 1%, often within 30day;esp. younger males,high potency depot; mortality of 10%,S/SX: >39°C,muscle rigidity,delirium,autonomic instability(ie.↑↓ BP),↑CPK,↑HR,arrhythmias,tremors,seizures & coma.TX: D/C neuroleptic,cooling blanket,hydrate,dantrolene,bromocriptine &benzodiazepines.

**Tardive dyskinesia**-after months to yrs of neuroleptics,↑ in elderly.S/Sx: fly catching/protruding motions of tongue, tics of the face, chewing motions or excessive blinking.TX: D/C/change/↓ neuroleptic,↓anticholinergics, tetrabenazine, donepezil, Vit E 400-1600iu/d.

**Depot Medications**-after 3-6 months many accumulate;thereby, requiring ↓ dose,onset of action for most are 2-3 days (Peak 4-7day),except **Clopixol Accuphase** with onset: 2-4hr,duration: 2-3days and max. sedation at 8hr.

**Pregnancy**- Consider the risk versus benefit! -use lowest possible dose, high potency agent preferred (ie. haloperidol FDA Category C), if possible try to D/C before delivery. Avoid if possible especially during first trimester.

**Level ↓ by:** antacid,cholestyramine,**carbamazepine**,phenobarbital,phenytoin,rifampin&**smoking**. **Level ↑ by:** amitripyline,amiodarone,cimetidine,ciprofloxacin,diltiazem,erythromycin,fluoxetine,fluvoxamine,grapefruit juice,isoniazid,ketoconazole,nefazodone, paroxetine,propranolol,quinidine&ritonavir.

**EPS** Acute dystonia-spasm of face,neck&back-like seizure(Onset 1-5day esp. young male,Tx:**benztropine**) Akathisia-motor restless-not verbal,pacing,fidgety(Onset 5-60day,esp. old female;Tx:↓dose/△ low potency,lorazepam,**propranolol,**diphenhydramine)

Parkinsonism-rigid,bradykinesia,shuffling gait,tremor (Onset 5-30day esp. old female;Tx:**benztropine**, amantadine) Rabbit Syndrome-rapid chewing movements (Onset after months esp. old females; Tx: **benztropine**). ☎ =**EDS** X = Non-formulary Sask

New: **Aripiprazole ABILIFY**: D2, 5HT1A & 2A (2,5,10,15,20,30mg tab) X⊗ 10-15mg od in morning $135-155. Max 30mg/d $215; FDA 2002: adult & kid ≥13yr, autistic irritability 6-17yr; minimal ↑weight, ↑anxiety/tremor, stimulating, akathisia, EPS, ↓BP; DI 3A4 & 2D6: carbamazepine, fluoxetine, erythromycin & paroxetine.

**Paliperidone INVEGA**: (3,6,9mg XR tabs) X⊗ 3-6-9mg od $120-170-230. Max 12mg ; active **metabolite of risperidone**; ↑ absorption ~50% with high fat meal; ↑ QT; limited short trials to date; DI: carbamazepine, paroxetine, & ↑QT interval meds.

**Ziprasidone ZELDOX**, GEODON: 20,40,60,80mg cap on SPDP, ✆ 40-80mg bid $140 with **meal** & earlier in the day CATIE 110mg/d; ↑**QT** interval 5%,DI's↑, EPS ~5%,minimal ↑weight, stimulating.

New in USA **Asenapine Saphris**: 5,10mg **SL** tab BID. May↑**QT** interval,**EPS**, akathisia, somnolence, minimal ↑wt; DI:↑ level by fluvoxamine, ↑paroxetine level by asenapine. **Iloperidone Fanapt**: 1,2,4,6,8,10,12mg tab; 6-12mg po bid; May↑**QT** interval ,EPS, ↓**BP**, may ↑wt, fatigue. DI:↑ level by paroxetine & clarithromycin.

# SEDATIVES: A CONCISE OVERVIEW

## GOALS OF THERAPY FOR INSOMNIA:

- To improve sleep (ie. decrease time it takes to fall asleep, decrease the frequency of nighttime awakenings & increase the duration of sleep) without dependence on drug therapy
- To improve daytime functioning
- To avoid daytime drowsiness & psychomotor impairment (caution when driving if affected)

## GENERAL APPROACH TO INSOMNIA:

**Non-pharmacologic**

- Resolve any **underlying medical, psychiatric or environmental** causes {e.g. HF, anxiety, depression, sleep apnea, nocturia, pain, thyroid fx, RLS, anemia & chronic pain (for nighttime pain consider long-acting HS analgesic e.g.acetaminophen ER)} {A 24hr Sleep History: useful in evaluating patterns}
- Consider **drug causes** (See Table 1); note common social drug causes (caffeine, alcohol & nicotine)
- **Changing sleep habits, relaxation techniques and cognitive therapy are preferred** for chronic insomnia & often more effective than drugs
- Consider restricting/avoiding daytime naps
- Provide counseling, encouragement & reinforcement

**Pharmacologic**

- Sedatives should only be used in combination with non-drug measures to promote sleep (see Table 2 - Sleep Hygiene)
- Ideally, sedatives should be taken only for short periods depending on the medication (2-4 weeks)
- Rx sedatives are all equally effective; all to varying degrees, cause daytime drowsiness & confusion {In elderly: benzo-like; **NNT=13**; **NNH=6**; ↑sleep time ½hr; ↓ wakings/night 0.6}Glass
- Low doses of short-acting sedatives have a lower risk for side effects when taken on a short-term basis
- Sedatives can be **"habit forming". Expect 2-3 nights** of **poor sleep** when stopped. One suggestion is to decrease total sleep time by 20mins 2 nights before stopping the medication. Consider stopping at a low stress time such as on a weekend. Cognitive behavioral techniques can be helpful in 1° insomnia.
- Use the lowest dose possible & only when required; intermittent use (e.g. up to 4 nights/week) sometimes recommended to minimize tolerance & dependence
- Generally, begin with mild agents, and gradually move to more potent medications as necessary
- **Restless Leg Syndrome (RLS)** – see Q&A/Chart – page 78. {dopaminergics (levodopa, pramipexole, ropinirole); clonazepam?. If painful, may consider gabapentin or opiates.}

**Table 1: Drug Causes of Insomnia**

| | | |
|---|---|---|
| alcohol -disrupts sleep | $H_2$ blockers eg. cimetidine | pseudoephedrine |
| amantadine | interferon | quinidine |
| amphetamines | ipratropium | salbutamol |
| aripiprazole* | lamotrigine | salmeterol |
| atenolol | leuprolide | selegiline |
| bupropion | levodopa | senna stimulant laxatives |
| caffeine effect may last 8-14hr in elderly e.g. coffee, tea, colas | medroxyprogesterone | sibutramine |
| clonidine | methyldopa | SSRI's* (eg. fluoxetine, paroxetine, sertraline) |
| corticosteroids | methylphenidate | terbutaline |
| daunorubicin | modafinil | theophylline |
| decongestants | nicotine | thyroid hormones |
| dextroamphetamine | oral contraceptives | tranylcypromine |
| diuretics* if late in the day | phenylephrine | venlafaxine |
| donepezil* | phenytoin | ziprasidone |
| fluoxetine | pindolol | |
| flutamide | progesterone | |
| | propranolol | |

* consider dosing in AM

**Table 2: Good Sleep Hygiene Measures**

- Maintain a regular schedule for bedtime and awakening
- Go to bed only when sleepy
- Avoid daytime naps or going to bed too early in evening.
- Reserve the bedroom for sleep & sexual activity (no TV)
- Avoid **caffeine** & nicotine especially within 4-6hrs of bedtime
- Do not drink alcohol (especially within 4hrs of bedtime), since it causes fragmented sleep
- Avoid heavy meals before going to bed, but a light carbohydrate snack before bedtime is acceptable
- Do not eat chocolate or large amounts of sugar before bedtime
- Avoid drinking excessive amounts of fluid in the evening
- Take "water pills" in the morning or early afternoon
- Exercise regularly during the day, but avoid vigorous exercise within 3 hrs of retiring (eg. a **walk** after supper is a great idea)
- Minimize noise, light & extreme temperature in the bedroom
- Develop relaxing bedtime rituals (eg. reading, listening to music)
- Get the clock out of visible range to avoid watching!
- Get out of bed & go to another room if unable to sleep within 20 minutes. Return when sleepy.

**Table 3: Sedatives – General Classification & Comments**

| Classification | Examples | | Comments (see also detailed comparison chart ) |
|---|---|---|---|
| **Non-BZ but BZ-Like MOA** (mechanism of action) | Zopiclone (z) | Imovane | • SysRev's & RCTs: AE$^z$ rates =BZ rates, ↓rebound insomnia & withdrawal<br>• NICE Appraisal: lack of clinically useful differences with short acting BZs<br>• **Less problem with tolerance** than BZ; still have problem with **dependence** |
| **Benzodiazepines (BZ)** | Temazepam<br>Oxazepam<br>Lorazepam | Restoril<br>Serax<br>Ativan | • Significant adverse effects on sleep structure (e.g. ↓ REM & Delta sleep)<br>• Option for transient, short-term insomnia; clonazepam if long-term/anxiety<br>• Problems: **tolerance**, **dependence**, **withdrawal**, ↓ cognition/coordination, disinhibition, ↑risk of accidents & falls; "hangover effect" =residual sedation |
| **Antidepressants - Non-TCA** | Trazodone | Desyrel | • Trazodone preserves **sleep structure**; REM neutral; may ↑Δwave/deep sleep<br>• Useful **low-dose** (≤50-100mg) for long-term sedation in agitated dementia (e.g. sundowning) & antidepressant induced insomnia; non-habit forming |
| **Antidepressants - TCAs**<br>Avoid amitriptyline in elderly! | Amitriptyline(3°)<br>trimipramine (3°)<br>nortriptyline (2°) | Elavil<br>Surmontil<br>Aventyl | • Some effect on sleep structure; may ↑Δwave/deep sleep; may be helpful<br>• Low-doses of 3° TCAs (e.g. amitriptyline/trimipramine 10-50mg) useful for sleep disorders especially in patients with **chronic pain,** depression, etc.<br>• 2° TCAs such as **nortriptyline** are an alternative for patients who are elderly, intolerant of amitriptyline or have concomitant pain |
| **Antipsychotics** Highly sedating SE profile | methotrimeprazine | Nozinan | • Potent/useful in **severe cases of insomnia**; non-dependent; rare ↑liver tests<br>• Atypical antispychotics an option; eg. **low-dose quetiapine** 12.5-100mg hs Seroquel |
| **Miscellaneous** | see chart | | • Most other sedatives have limited evidence / usefulness; see chart |

AE= adverse event; NNT=number needed to treat to benefit; NNH=number needed to treat to harm; RCT=randomized controlled trial; SysRev=systematic review

Prepared by Loren Regier & Brent Jensen in consultation with RxFiles advisors & reviewers.
We would especially like to thank Dr. V. Bennett, Dr. L. Thorpe, Dr. M. Baetz & Dr. F. Remillard for their assistance.

 SEDATIVE COMPARISON CHART  Brent Jensen BSP, Loren Regier BSP May 10

| Generic -TRADE g=generic avail. | Equivalent Dose /Class | Peak Levels/ Onset of action | Average t½* /Active Metabolite | COMMENTS | Pregnancy category | INITIAL & (MAX DOSE) | USUAL SEDATIVE DOSE | $ /MONTH |
|---|---|---|---|---|---|---|---|---|
| Zaleplon -STARNOC (5,10mg cap) ✗ DISCONTINUED ❊? | 5mg pyrazolopyrimidine Gaba A1 α1 | 0.9-1.5hr Rapid(15-30min) | 1 hr None | Duration of action of ~4 hrs; little tolerance SE: headache, somnolence, dizziness, dependence Least hangover effect; DI:cimetidine & rifampin | C | 5mg (20mg) | 5mg po hs 10mg po hs may give on waking during night | 24 32 Company D/C '06 |
| In USA: Ramelteon ROZEREM✗⊗ 8mg po hs DI:cipro,Luvox,rifampin; ↑prolactin; works→ melatonin | | | | | | | | |
| Zopiclone -IMOVANE / RHOVANE g (5, 7.5ς mg tab) ✗⊗ ❊? | 5mg cyclopyrrolone Gaba A1 | 1-1.5hr Rapid (30min) | 5 hr / Yes | √Sedative-Good Choice:↓tolerance & withdrawal? SE:dry mouth, bitter taste, residual sedation DI's: erythromycin, ketoconazole, rifampin. Dependence | U | 3.75mg (15mg) | 5mg po hs 7.5mg po hs (Rhovane & g less money) | 15 22 |
| In USA: Eszopiclone LUNESTA✗⊗ 1-3mg po hs (S-isomer) | | | | | | | | |
| Clonazepam -RIVOTRIL g (0.25✗▼; 0.5ς,1,2ς mg tab) | 0.25mg Nitro | 1-4hr Intermed.(20-60min) | 34 (19-60) hr None | CAUTION: ↑falls/fractures, accidents esp. elderly, dependence; ↓cognition long-term use; dizzy, incoordination | D | 0.25mg (10mg) | 0.5mg po hs 1mg po hs | 10 15 |
| Flurazepam -DALMANE g (15,30mg cap) ⊗ | 15mg 2-Keto | 0.5-1hr Intermed.(30-60min) | 100 (40-250) hr Yes-Desalkyl | √Sedatives/hypnotic-Good BZ choices: temazepam; possibly oxazepam, lorazepam | X | 15mg (60mg) | 15mg po hs 30mg po hs | 10 11 |
| Lorazepam -ATIVAN g (0.5,1ς,2ς mg tab); (0.5,1,2mg sl▼ tab;4mg/ml amp⊗) ✗ | 1mg 3- Hydroxy | PO 1-4hr, SL/IM 1hr, IV 5 min Intermed.(30-60min) | 15 (8-24) hr None | Clonazepam good sedative if daytime anxiety; √Anticonvulsant, Panic; (Also used: social phobia, BPAD manic phase, restless leg syndrome & akathisia) | D | 0.5mg (10mg) | 0.5mg po hs 1mg po hs | 8 9 |
| Oxazepam -SERAX g (10ς,15ς,30ς mg tab) | 15 3-Hydroxy | 1-4hr Intermediate→slow | 8 (3-25) hr None | Flurazepam not recommended, Accumulation/hangover→confusion; impairment | D | 10mg (120mg) | 15mg po hs 30mg po hs | 10 11 |
| Temazepam -RESTORIL g (15,30mg cap) | 10mg 3- Hydroxy | 2-3hr Intermediate→slow | 11 (3-25) hr None | Triazolam (not recommended, Behavioral changes/anterograde amnesia, DI's & withdrawal; marked rebound insomnia) | X | 15mg (60mg) | 15mg po hs 30mg po hs | 12 13 |
| Triazolam -HALCION g (0.125ς,0.25ς mg tab) | 0.25mg Triazolo | 1-2hr Rapid (15-30min) | 2 (1.5-5) hr None | Less DI'S: temazepam, oxazepam & lorazepam | X | 0.125mg (0.5mg) | 0.125mg po hs 0.25mg po hs | 12 15 |
| Chloral hydrate - NOCTEC g (500mg/5ml syrup) ⊗ | 500mg | 30-60min Rapid (30min) | 4 - 8 hr Yes | √Sedative {not recommended:Fatal ≥4gm; DI's; SE: gastric irritation, arrhythmias, rash} | C | 500mg (2gm) | 500mg po hs 1gm po hs | 15 23 |
| Diphenhydramine OTC✗▼ -Benadryl, Nytol, Simply Sleep, Sleep aid, Sleepeze D, Sominex, Unisom g (12.5mg chew⊗; 25,50mg cap/tab, 1.25mg/ml liquid, 2.5mg/ml elix, 50mg/ml inj) | 50mg Antihistamine | 1-4 hrs Slow(60-180min) | 4 - 8hr None | √ Allergic reactions, sleep aid SE: anticholinergic (dry mouth, urinary retention), cognitive impairment; residual daytime sedation & tolerance | B | 25mg (200-300mg) | 25mg po hs 50mg po hs | <10 <10 |
| Doxylamine OTC -UNISOM-2 g(25 mg tab) ✗⊗ | 25mg Antihistamine | 2-4hr Slow(60-120min) | 10 hr Yes-? Active | √ Sedative/hypnotic -but residual daytime sedation SE: anticholinergic, cognitive impairment | A | 25mg (75-150mg) | 25mg po hs 50mg po hs | 10 20 |
| Methotrimeprazine NOZINAN g (2,5,25,50 mg tab, 5mg/ml& 40mg/ml soln); (25mg/ml amp✗) | Phenothiazine Neuroleptic | 1-3hr Slow | 15-30 hr None | √Antipsychotic,sedative(non addictive),analgesia SE: hypotension, extrapyramidal reactions, anticholinergic,cognitive impairment | C | 5mg (1000mg) | 5-10mg po hs 25-50mg po hs | 12 12 |
| Or - Quetiapine Seroquel 12.5-50mg po hs ≤$30 | | | | | | | | |
| Trazodone -DESYREL g (50ς,100ς mg tab); (75mg, Dividose 150mg)✗▼ ❊ | 50mg Antidepressant | 0.5-2 hr Intermediate | 4 - 7.5hr Yes | √ Antidepressant, Agitated dementia, √Sedative-antidepressant induced insomnia SE: orthostatic ↓BP; headache, rare priapism in ♂ | C | 25mg (600mg) | 50mg po hs 100mg po hs | 14 18 |
| Or - Mirtazapine Remeron 7.5-15mg po hs ≤$20 | | | | | | | | |
| Amitriptyline ELAVIL g (10,25,50); (75mg✗▼) | Antidepressant | <4 hr Slow | 15hr Yes- nortriptyline -26hr | √ Antidepressant, Sedative-but performance impairment SE: hypotension, anticholinergic,cognitive impairment | C | 10mg (300mg ~2hr pre hs | 10-25mg po hs 50mg po hs | 9-11 15 |
| Or less SE's - Nortriptyline 10-25mg po hs ≤$15 | | | | | | | | |
| L-Tryptophan-TRYPTAN g (250,500,750mg,1gm tab, 500mg cap)✗⊗ ❊ | Watch for serotonin syndrome esp. if used with SSRI or MAOI's. Eosinophilia-myalgia syndrome before due to impurities. | | | √Adjunct in BPAD Bipolar/may potentiate lithium √ Sedative- no tolerance reported SE: GI upset, dry mouth, dizzy, headache | U | 500mg (5gm) | 500mg po hs 1g po hs | 20 35 |
| Melatonin OTC ❊? (1, 3mg cap, 2mg CR cap; 3mg SL)✗⊗ | manufactured synthetic metabolite of 5HT | 0.5-2hr Slow(60-120min) | 1 hr None | Limited studies-conflicting data; ?dose; ?jet lag SE: headache,↑ heart rate, pruritis, nightmares | U | 1mg give 2hr before hs (5-10mg) | 0.5-3mg po hs 2mg CR po hs | 3 5 |
| Valerian Root OTC-VALERIAN, NYTOL & UNISOM NATURAL SOURCE (400 mg tab)✗⊗ ❊? | ? valepotriates ? valerenic acid ? pyridine alkaloids | Not known (mild effect) | Not known | Limited studies-? dose/sleep aid; Purity concerns SE: nausea, headache, morning hangover, hepatotoxic report | U | 400mg (800mg) | 400mg po hs 800mg po hs | 6 10 |

Benzodiazepine: Clonazepam, Flurazepam, Lorazepam, Oxazepam, Temazepam, Triazolam.

**Guidelines:** Use lowest dose, use agents with short/intermediate half lives to avoid daytime sedation, use intermittent dosing (2-4 x/wk), use for no more than 3-4 weeks, D/C gradually, & be aware of rebound insomnia.
**Consider/Rule Out:** Depression insomnia may be first Sx, Mania/hypomania, primary sleep disorder (eg **sleep apnea**) altered sleep cycle & other drug use (Decrease total daily dose/change timing of other meds/agents as in Table 1).
**Misc products:** *Herbal Sleep Aid*: valerian, hops flower, passion flower; *Naturarest*: valerian, St. Johns wort, catnip herb; *Nighty Night Herbal tea*: passion flower chamomile, catnip, hops. ❊ little effect on sleep structure
√official indication (TPB/FDA) or use **BZ**=benzodiazepines **DI**=drug interaction **SE**=side effect * **t ½ average(range)** half-life:↑ in geriatric pts & altered by drug interactions ✗ =non-formulary Sask. =↓ dose for renal dysfx ς =scored ⊗=not covered NIHB ▼=covered NIHB
Found in as adulterants in some herbal products: Estazolam found in Eden Herbal Formulations Sleep Ease & Serenity Pills II, Salt Spring Herbals Sleep Well & in Sleepees. Other: avoid Kava hepatotoxicity risk without benefit. St John's wort useful only if depressed.

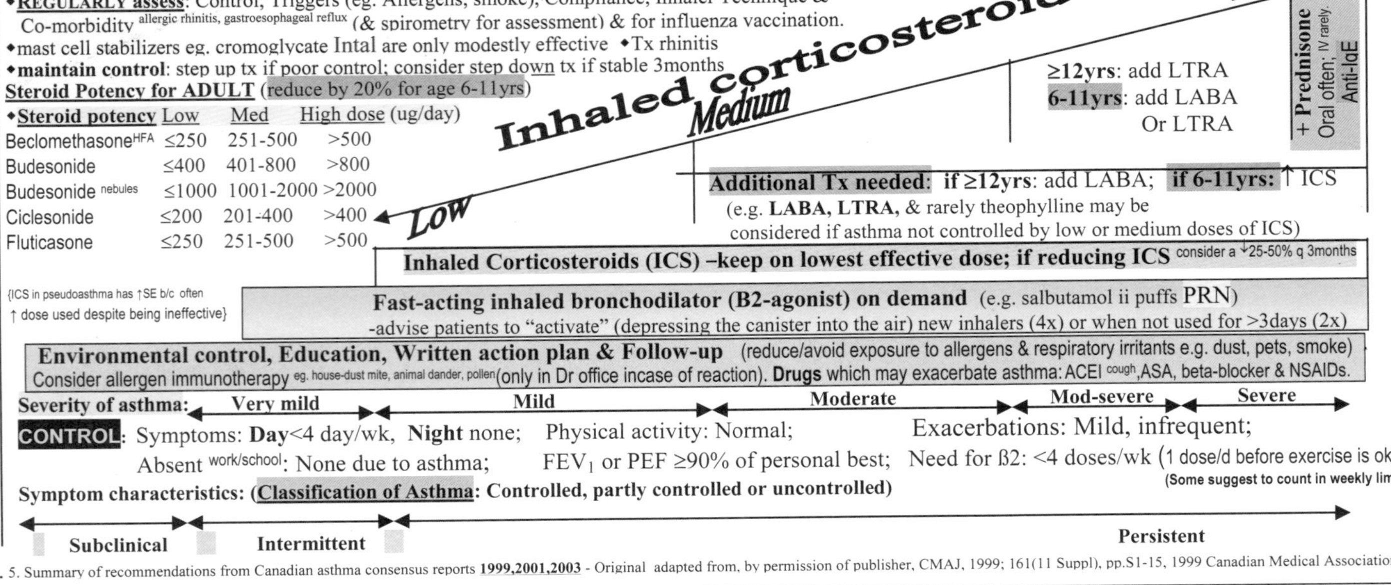

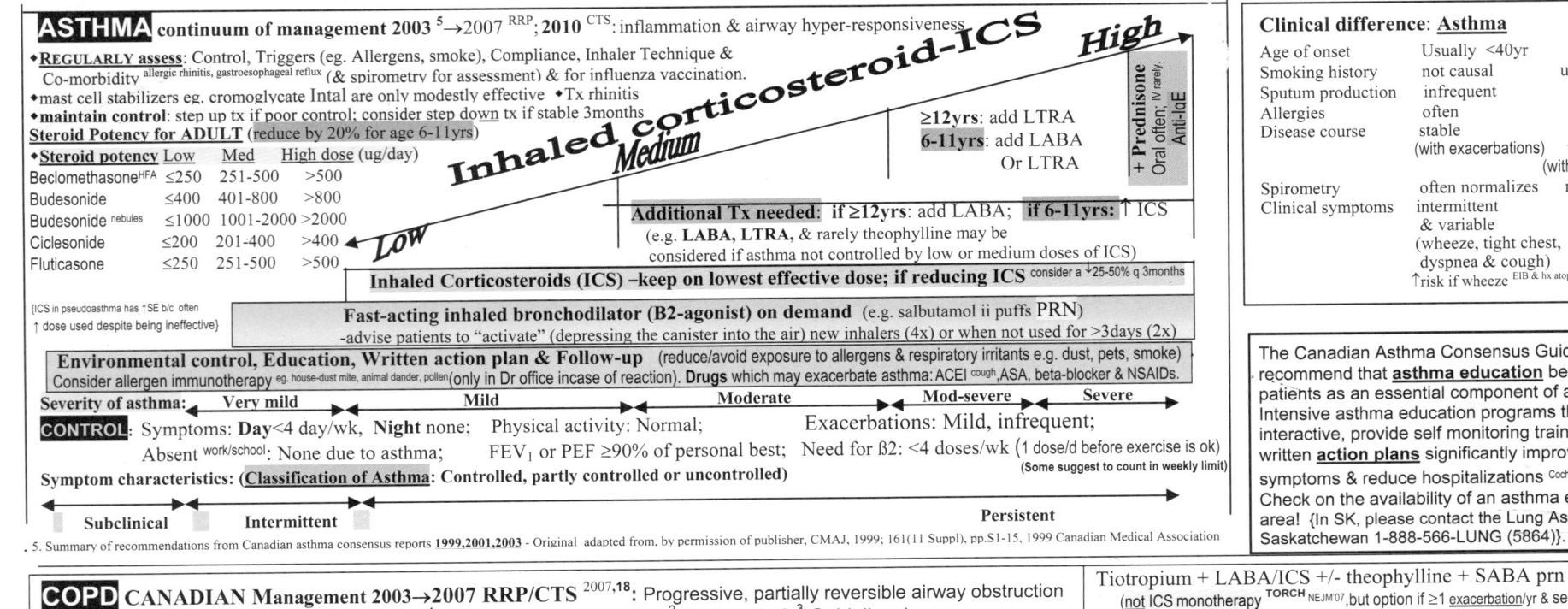

**ASTHMA** continuum of management 2003 [5]→2007 [RRP]; **2010** [CTS]: inflammation & airway hyper-responsiveness

- **REGULARLY assess**: Control, Triggers (eg. Allergens, smoke), Compliance, Inhaler Technique & Co-morbidity allergic rhinitis, gastroesophageal reflux (& spirometry for assessment) & for influenza vaccination.
- mast cell stabilizers eg. cromoglycate Intal are only modestly effective • Tx rhinitis
- **maintain control**: step up tx if poor control; consider step down tx if stable 3months

**Steroid Potency for ADULT** (reduce by 20% for age 6-11yrs)

| • Steroid potency | Low | Med | High dose (ug/day) |
|---|---|---|---|
| Beclomethasone HFA | ≤250 | 251-500 | >500 |
| Budesonide | ≤400 | 401-800 | >800 |
| Budesonide nebules | ≤1000 | 1001-2000 | >2000 |
| Ciclesonide | ≤200 | 201-400 | >400 |
| Fluticasone | ≤250 | 251-500 | >500 |



**Additional Tx needed**: if ≥12yrs: add LABA; if 6-11yrs: ↑ ICS (e.g. **LABA, LTRA,** & rarely theophylline may be considered if asthma not controlled by low or medium doses of ICS)

**Inhaled Corticosteroids (ICS) –keep on lowest effective dose; if reducing ICS** consider a ↓25-50% q 3months

{ICS in pseudoasthma has ↑SE b/c often ↑ dose used despite being ineffective}

**Fast-acting inhaled bronchodilator (B2-agonist) on demand** (e.g. salbutamol ii puffs PRN)
-advise patients to "activate" (depressing the canister into the air) new inhalers (4x) or when not used for >3days (2x)

**Environmental control, Education, Written action plan & Follow-up** (reduce/avoid exposure to allergens & respiratory irritants e.g. dust, pets, smoke)
Consider allergen immunotherapy eg. house-dust mite, animal dander, pollen (only in Dr office incase of reaction). **Drugs** which may exacerbate asthma: ACEI cough, ASA, beta-blocker & NSAIDs.

**Severity of asthma:** Very mild ↔ Mild ↔ Moderate ↔ Mod-severe ↔ Severe

**CONTROL**: Symptoms: **Day**<4 day/wk, **Night** none; Physical activity: Normal; Exacerbations: Mild, infrequent;
Absent work/school: None due to asthma; $FEV_1$ or PEF ≥90% of personal best; Need for ß2: <4 doses/wk (1 dose/d before exercise is ok) (Some suggest to count in weekly limit)

**Symptom characteristics: (Classification of Asthma: Controlled, partly controlled or uncontrolled)**

Subclinical — Intermittent — Persistent

. 5. Summary of recommendations from Canadian asthma consensus reports **1999,2001,2003** - Original adapted from, by permission of publisher, CMAJ, 1999; 161(11 Suppl), pp.S1-15, 1999 Canadian Medical Association

| **Clinical difference**: | **Asthma** | **COPD** |
|---|---|---|
| Age of onset | Usually <40yr | usually >40yr |
| Smoking history | not causal | usually>10pk yrs |
| Sputum production | infrequent | often |
| Allergies | often | infrequent |
| Disease course | stable (with exacerbations) | progressive worsening (with exacerbations) |
| Spirometry | often normalizes | never normalizes |
| Clinical symptoms | intermittent & variable (wheeze, tight chest, dyspnea & cough) ↑risk if wheeze EIB & hx atopic dx | persistent (dyspnea & activity limitation) |

The Canadian Asthma Consensus Guidelines recommend that **asthma education** be offered to all patients as an essential component of asthma therapy. Intensive asthma education programs that are interactive, provide self monitoring training, & that use written **action plans** significantly improve asthma symptoms & reduce hospitalizations Cochrane Review - 2003. Check on the availability of an asthma educator in your area! {In SK, please contact the Lung Association of Saskatchewan 1-888-566-LUNG (5864)}.

**COPD** CANADIAN **Management 2003→2007 RRP/CTS** [2007,18]: Progressive, partially reversible airway obstruction
(Other recent guidelines: Global Gold 2009 [1], American Thoracic 2004 [2] & Nice 2010 [3] Guidelines)
Management: 1) Evaluate & monitor dx Bode (BMI, FEV1,dyspnea,exercise-6min walk) & Ado index 2) ↓ preventable & treatable risks 3) Managing stable COPD 4) Manage exacerbations

Screen: for $\alpha_1$-antitrypsin deficiency Silverman '09 in select pts (eg. if atypical features, disease onset <45yr).
↑ COPD probability with multiple indicators: **dyspnea** eg. progressive, usually worse with exercise, persistent, gasping; **chronic cough; chronic sputum production; & history of exposure** eg. smoke, dust, chemicals.

Goals: ↓dyspnea, ↑exercise tolerance & ↑quality of life & ↓complications such as exacerbations & cor pulmonale.

Chronic Disease Management Program / Education benefits patients on components such as action plans, smoking cessation after 1yr ↓FEV1 normalizes to that of a nonsmoker, disease info, inhaler technique & self management. (eg. Saskatoon Health Region call 655-LIVE) Helping reduce the current **4th leading cause of death** in Canada! Prevalence about 5% in Canada.

**Increasing Dyspnea & Disability**

Tiotropium + LABA/ICS +/- theophylline + SABA prn
(not ICS monotherapy TORCH NEJM'07, but option if ≥1 exacerbation/yr & severe COPD, but associated with ↑ risk of non-fatal pneumonia by about 4% with high steroid dosages)
Consider long term OXYGEN if Pao2 ≤55 at rest (survival benefit if used ≥15hr/d & FEV1 <30%) or
SURGICAL tx if chronic resp. failure. (transplant or lung volume reduction)
End of life: Control DYSPNEA Sx (eg. morphine, lorazepam, diazepam, midazolam, chlorpromazine), COUGH (eg.codeine, morphine, bupivacaine) & SECRETIONS (eg. scopolamine patch, atropine, N-acetylcysteine).

Tiotropium # + LABA + SABA prn {Ipratropium ATROVENT an alternative to tiotropium #}
↓ {NOTE: Guideline recommendation for tiotropium + LABA not based on high quality evidence} Dalhousie ADS
Tiotropium + LABA [+ long acting theophylline (watch blood levels,DIs &SEs)] + SABA prn
Consider **pulmonary rehabilitation** (exercise eg walking, biking, treadmill for stable pts, nutrition & education)

Salbutamol +/or ipratropium prn → SABA prn &/or regular ipratropium 2-4 puffs qid or (Combivent neb prn→ regular)
↓ {Recommended to use **regularly scheduled** tiotropium with or without LABA if **$FEV_1$ <60%**)
(Tiotropium &/or LABA) + SABA prn

| **Pharmacotherapy** | None but avoid risk factors (**smoking**, occupational dusts & chemicals, indoor air pollution from biomass cooking & heating in poorly ventilated dwellings); Consider annual **influenza VACCINCATION**; **pneumococcal** vaccine at least once in their lifetime; possible revaccination after 5yrs (more than 1 revaccination may be counterproductive). **Stop smoking** & COPD education. Treat acute exacerbations -AECOPD (**antibiotics** for purulent/severe exacerbations; **prednisone** 30-40mg **po** od x 10-14days watch for hyperglycemia). | | | | |
|---|---|---|---|---|---|
| **Spirometry** (to diagnose, not screen) | Normal spirometry (post bronchodilator $FEV_1/FVC$≥ 0.7 +/- $FEV_1$≥ 80% predicted) | $FEV_1$ ≥80% predicted $FEV_1/FVC$< 0.7 | ≤50% $FEV_1$ <80% predicted $FEV_1/FVC$< 0.7 | ≤30% $FEV_1$ <50% predicted $FEV_1/FVC$< 0.7 | $FEV_1$ <30% predicted $FEV_1/FVC$< 0.7 |
| Symptoms | Asymptomatic smoker, ex-smoker or chronic cough/sputum | Shortness of breath from COPD when hurrying on the level or walking up a slight hill (**MRC** 2) | Shortness of breath from COPD causing the pt to stop walking after ~100m (or after a few mins) on the level (**MRC** 3-4) | Shortness of breath from COPD resulting in the patient too breathless to leave house, breathlessness after undressing (**MRC** 5) or the presence of chronic respiratory failure or clinical signs of right heart failure | |
| **COPD Stage** | **O: At risk- may not progress to mild** | **1: Mild** | **II: Moderate** | **III: Severe** | **IV: Very severe** |

**#**: **tiotropium** reduced the number of exacerbations vs ipratropium at the dose used; however **no significant** differences in the number of **hospitalizations**. Vincken W, et al. Tiotropium Study Group (1 yr trial). Eur Respir J. 2002 Feb;19(2):209-16. Weigh benefit/risk/cost.

**$FEV_1$**=forced expiratory volume in 1 second **FVC**=forced vital capacity **LABA/ICS** =LABA combination with an inhaled corticosteroid (eg. Advair, Symbicort) **LABA**=long acting beta 2 agonist (ie. formoterol or salmeterol) **LAMA**=long acting muscarinic antagonist **MRC**= Medical Research Council dyspnea scale **SABA**= short acting beta2 agonist (eg. salbutamol) **SABD**= short acting bronchodilator (eg. beta2 agonist like salbutamol or anticholinergics like ipratropium) **SAMA**=short acting muscarinic antagonist eg. ipratropium

18. Can Respir J. 2003 May-Jun; Suppl A. Canadian Thoracic Society COPD Guidelines: **2003**. (**Updated 2007** http://www.copdguidelines.ca/pdf/07CODP%20guidelines.pdf , **2008** Highlights http://www.copdguidelines.ca/pdf/COPD-Highlights.pdf )

# ASTHMA & COPD PHARMACOTHERAPY: Comparison Chart [4,5,6,7,8,9,10,11]

Prepared by: Loren Regier, Sharon Downey  May 10

| Generic /Pregnancy code | Dosage Form & Strength | TRADE | Dose Range / day | Usual Adult Asthma Dose | $/30d | Comments |
|---|---|---|---|---|---|---|
| **Corticosteroid-Inhaled** •1st line:prevent asthma (not for acute); regular use at lowest effective dose to prevent Sx •caution: growth kids ↓1cm short term, & if ↑dose long-term for adrenal fx, ↑glucose eg. 4mmol/l & osteoporosis [12] •Intermittent ICS 2wk courses → no effect on progression from episodic to persistent wheezing in first 3yrs of life. Bisgaard06 Preschool high risk asthma kids → 2yrs of ICS did not alter development of asthma Sx or lung fx during a 3rd tx-free yr. Guilbert06 but FEV1 benefit seen in START trial n=7165 3yr O'Byrne06 | | | | | | |
| **Beclomethasone** diprop. (BDP) **C** | MDI 50ug, 100ug Age≥5yr | *QVAR* -shaking not required (HFA CFC free) | 100-800 ug | ii 50-100ug puffs BID | $ 29-50 | •**SE**: <5%: oral thrush, & dysphonia; to ↓SE's use **spacer & rinse** mouth •QVAR=↑potency due to ↑lung deposition; •if ↑dose required, ? add **LABA** or LTRA •**DI**: itraconazole & ataza/rito-navir ↑Cushing's risk 13 •Pulmicort 400ug turbo ↓$ than 2 x 200ug •Dose flexibility if using 1-2 puffs bid with Flovent 125 MDI or Pulmicort 200 strengths •Aphthous ulcers alt use: ≤2day may work |
| | BDP products from GlaxoSmithKline (e.g. *Beclofort, Beclodisk, Beclovent Rotacaps*) have been **discontinued**. | | | | | |
| **Budesonide** **B** NAEPP'04 -preferred steroid | Turbuhaler 100,200,400ug Age≥6yr *Nebs 0.25, 0.5, 1 mg/2ml | *PULMICORT* *PULMICORT NEBUAMP* | 400-2400 ug 0.5 - 4mg | 100-**200**-400ug puffs BID 1mg per neb BID | $18-29-46 $125 | |
| **Fluticasone** propionate **C** | MDI 50,125,250ug Age≥1yr Diskus 50, 100, 250, 500ug Age≥4yr | *FLOVENT HFA -CFC free* *FLOVENT Diskus* -contains lactose | 100-2000 ug | ii 50-**125**-250ug puffs BID 250-500ug inhaled BID | $36-56-105 $ 56-106 | |
| Ciclesonide Alvesco HFA ≥6yr 100-200-400ug od ($20-31-49); Max 400ug bid ($91), new ▼ 100,200ug aerosol soln; a prodrug; metabolite deactivated by cyp 3A4 | | | | | | |
| **SABA** -Inhaled Short-Acting B2 Agonist •effective for **acute** asthma; control if use <4X/week;poor control if frequent use → add inhaled steroid; ✓ prevent exercise-induced bronchospasm; flat dose response | | | | | | |
| **Salbutamol** (R + S isomers) **C** NAEPP'04 -preferred SABA (also avail. as 2ς,4ς mg tab; 0.4mg/ml oral liquid; IV/IM D/C 2007 amps & Ventolin **Diskus** 200ug) | MDI 100ug CFC free Age≥4yr | *VENTOLIN, APO-,RATIO-* *Airomir/Ratio Salbutamol HFA* CFC free | prn - 1200ug | **i-ii puffs PRN** i-ii puffs PRN (Cost calculated based on QID use) | $ 16 $ 19 | •EIB: ii puffs 15min pre-exercise •**SE**: tremor, ↑nervous, ↑HR esp neb, ↑QT, headache, ↓K+, ↑ insulin secretion, hyperglycemia esp. in diabetics •oral agents available but have slower onset and cause more SE's •PF = "preservative free" nebs |
| | Diskhaler 200,400ug Age≥4yr | *VENTODISK* -contains lactose (D/C 2006); Diskus 200ug | prn - 1600ug | 200ug inhaled PRN | $ 56 | |
| | Inhal'n sol'n 5mg/ml | *VENTOLIN INHAL'N SOLN* | prn - 15mg | 2.5mg per neb PRN | $ 46 | |
| | *Nebs 1.25, 2.5, 5mg/2.5ml | *VENTOLIN NEBULES P.F.* | prn - 15mg | 2.5mg per neb PRN | $ 90 | |
| **Terbutaline** **B** | Turbuhaler 500ug Age≥6yr | *BRICANYL* | prn - 4000ug | 500ug inhaled PRN | $ 18 | |
| **Fenoterol** | MDI 100ug; 0.1% inhalation soln | *BEROTEC* (D/C by company 2007) | prn - 1600ug | i-ii puffs PRN | D/C by co | |
| **LABA** -Inhaled Long-Acting B2 Agonist •add-on agent not monotherapy in pts on higher-dose steroid steroid sparing effect; ✓ nocturnal asthma & EIB but duration not >5hr with regular use; not for acute asthma but formoterol approved for PRN use | | | | | | |
| **Formoterol** **C** (nebs avail. USA: arformoterol is R isomer) | Inhal'n Capsules 12ug Age≥6yr Turbuhaler 6ug, 12ug Age≥6yr | *FORADIL CAPS for inhal'n* *OXEZE* -contains lactose | 24-48ug (max 72ug/24hr) | 12ug **inhaled** BID 6-12ug puff BID | $ 63 EDS ✆ $46-59 EDS ✆ | •full B2 agonist (∴ caution **SE**: tremor / ↑ HR in elderly); fast ONSET ~5min |
| **Formoterol+Budesonide** **C** | Turbuhaler 6ug/100ug, 6ug/200ug Age≥12yr | *SYMBICORT 100,200* -contains lactose & possibly milk protein | Range 1-4 puffs BID | 100ug/6ug 2 puff BID 200ug/6ug 2 puff BID | $ 79 EDS ✆ $100 EDS ✆ | •**combo** convenient but only some flexible dose;may be ↓$, COPD mod-severe dx 14,15 |
| **Salmeterol Xinafoate** **C** | MDI 25ug Age≥4yr Diskus 50ug Torch Age≥4yr | *SEREVENT*-**D/C** June'06 b/c of CFC *SEREVENT Diskus* -contains lactose | 100ug | ii puffs BID → 50ug inhaled BID | D/C by co $ 72 EDS ✆ | •partial B2 agonist; slower onset ~15min; DI 3A4 inhibitor → ↑SE •↑asthma deaths esp. African American (SMART trial 16), & kids. |
| **Salmeterol//Fluticasone** **C** | Diskus 50ug // 100/250/500ug Torch Age≥4yr **MDI** 25ug/125ug, 25ug/250ug Age≥12yr | *ADVAIR Diskus* 100,250,500 -contains lactose *ADVAIR HFA* CFC free 125,250 dose counter | 1 diskus BID 1-**2** inh BID | ADVAIR 100-250 DISKUS 1 inh BID ADVAIR 125-250 MDI 2 inh BID | 103-122 EDS ✆ 122-170 EDS ✆ | •**combo** convenient but less flexible dosing; maybe ↓$, COPD mod-severe dx14 |
| **Mast cell stabilizers** •efficacy highly variable from pt to pt; not for acute attacks; may taper to BID over several weeks after effect achieved; role in pediatric, cold air induced asthma & EIB | | | | | | |
| **Sodium Cromoglycate** (*Cromolyn* nebs 20mg/2ml) **B** | MDI 1mg/puff 20mg Spincap for inhal'n | *INTAL Inhaler* → **D/C** product *INTAL Spincaps* → **D/C** product | 2-8mg 40-160mg | ii puff QID (Up to 16puffs/day) 1 cap for inhal'n QID | $ 64 ✗ ▼ $ 73 | •~4week trial needed to evaluate effect; safe in children |
| **Nedocromil** | MDI 2mg/puff | *TILADE* → **D/C** product | 4-16mg | ii puffs QID | $ 73 | •taste may limit compliance |
| **Anticholinergics** •role in COPD & B-blocker bronchospasm •possible "add on" to SABA in asthma esp. in Emerg. (delayed onset; longer duration); •**SE**: dry mouth, taste changes; (Avoid eye contact: mydriasis/glaucoma) | | | | | | |
| **Ipratropium bromide** **B** -SAMA short acting muscarinic antagonist | MDI 20 ug ⊗ -not nut allergy for HFA; *Nebs 250ug/2ml;500ug/2ml Inhalation soln (must be diluted) | *ATROVENT, ATROVENT HFA* | 80-320ug 375-2000ug | ii puffs TID-QID (Max **3-4 qid**) 250ug per nebule TID 250ug inhalation soln TID | $ 26-32 $ 82 $ 62 | • > effect in elderly than SABA's •caution: glaucoma, urine retention •useful COPD [17] up to 4puffs; ↓cough post-infectious |
| **Ipratropium bromide + Salbutamol** -Combo **C** | MDI 20ug/100ug ⊗; *Nebs **500ug**+2.5mg / 2ml | *MDI* - **D/C'd** June'07 b/c of CFC *COMBIVENT Neb* | 6-12 puffs | ii puffs TID(shake well before use) 1 neb TID | $ 32 $ 100 | •use only if combo indicated •PRN use in asthma |
| **Tiotropium** -LAMA long acting MA **C** | 18ug cap for inhalation | *SPIRIVA HandiHaler* -contains lactose | 1 inhaled cap | 1 cap **inhaled** -not swallow **OD** UPLIFT | $ 82 EDS ✆ | •dose od,slower onset,↑$, for COPD [18,19] |
| **LTRA** -Leukotriene Receptor Antagonists •not 1st line [20,21]; not for acute asthma; steroid sparing effect?; **oral tx option**; ✓ EIB & ASA sensitive pts, or if pt refuses steroids, or for allergic rhinitis. Trial 4-6wks. | | | | | | |
| **Montelukast** (4mg ✆ oral granule) **B** | 4 & 5mg chew-tab [22]; 10mg tab | *SINGULAIR* (age 1-5⇨4mg; 6-14⇨ 5mg) | 10mg | 10mg po HS (or AM if for EIB) | $ 90 EDS ✆ | •rare eosinophilic vasculitis rx?,Psyc SE |
| **Zafirlukast** [23] | 20mg tab | *ACCOLATE* (only for age ≥**12**yrs) | 40mg | 20mg po BID on empty stomach | $ 59 EDS ✆ | •Zafirlukast: DI warf/theoph, & ↑ LFT's |
| **Theophylline** Preparations (Oral) •3rd line therapy due to systemic toxicity and mild bronchodilator activity; useful as 'add on' agent in some pts requiring high dose corticosteroids | | | | | | |
| **Aminophylline** =80%theoph. **C** | 225ς, 350ς mg SR tab | *PHYLLOCONTIN* (**IV** form avail.) | 450-1250mg | 350mg po BID (Individualize **dose** for age, CHF, smoking, liver failure etc.) | $ 26 | •**SE**: N&V, abdom. cramps, HA, nervousness, tremor, insomnia,↑HR Serious: arrhythmias & seizures •DI 1A2,3A4: ↓ theo level: carbamazepine, phenytoin, rifampin ↑ theo level: cimetidine, ciprofloxacin, erythromycin, fluvoxamine, norfloxacin & verapamil |
| **Oxtriphylline** =64%theoph. | 300mg tab | *CHOLEDYL* (also 100mg/5ml elixir) | 600-1600mg | 300mg po TID | $ 19 | |
| **Theophylline** [24,25] **C** (many products avail. such as SR bid agents) | 5.33mg/ml elixir; SR tab (q12h) 400ς, 600ς mg SR tab (q24h) | *Apo-Theo-LA, Novo-Theophyl SR* *UNIPHYL (SR products can be halved)* | 300-1000mg (Toxic Cp >110 umol/l) Level ≤55 effective & ↓SE | 300mg SR po BID 200-400mg po **HS** | $ 17 $ 16 -25 | |

**Cost**: markup & dispensing fee ✆ prior approval NIHB ✗ Non Forumulary Sask EDS=**EDS** **B2**=beta-2 **DI**=drug interaction **EIB**=exercise-induced bronchospasm **fx**=function **HA**=headache **HR**=heart rate **MDI**=metered dose inhaler **SE**=side effect Sx=symptoms

**Spacer** eg *AEROCHAMBER* ▼esp. in kids & elderly will optimize MDIs delivery, ↑efficiency, ↓pharyngeal & systemic SE; *"MDI+Spacer" or "dry powder systems" generally preferable to nebs. ⊗ Avoid → soybean & peanut allergy ς=scored tab

Systemic glucocorticoids-indicated in & following acute asthma exacerbations e.g. **Prednisone**: Adult 30-60mg/d x7-10d; Children 1-2mg/kg OD x3-5d (max 50mg/d); Prednisolone *PEDIAPRED* 1mg/ml oral liquid avail. Not taper usually.

Environment concerns → CFC propellants replaced by hydrofluoroalkanes (**HFA**): ↓particle size, deliver ↑drug to lower airway, ethanol as an excipient in some & spray often softer & warmer than CFC inhaler; prime x4 initially or if not used for several days.

NEW: Omalizumab *XOLAIR* blocks **IgE**; 150mg vial=**$640** ✗ ⊗; a controller several wks to work for mod-severe persistent allergic asthma ≥12yr: 150-375mg SC q2-4wk; SE: anaphylaxis <0.2%,up to 2hr-4day; inj site rx ↓d if clear soln injected, rash, h/a, ?↑infections.

# INHALATIONAL DEVICES and MONITORING TOOLS

Prepared by Donna Turner (RRT), L. Regier BSP, B. Jensen BSP © www.RxFiles.ca May 2010

| References available online | | | | | | |
|---|---|---|---|---|---|---|
| **DEVICE** | **SPIROMETER** | **PEAK FLOW METER** | **TURBUHALER** | **PUFFER** | **DISKUS** | **SPACER** |
| **USES** | •Measures the amount of air one can blow out (FVC) & how fast it comes out of the small airways(FEV1).The ratio FEV1/FVC useful lung function indicator | •Measures maximum force one can blow out of the larger airways (PEF:Peak Expiratory Flow). A tool to help determine lung function | •Dry powder inhaler device used to deliver bronchodilators & corticosteroids (not anticholinergics)<br>**Devices**: there is no evidence to suggest one delivery device works better than another →choose by **characteristics below & patient preference** | •CFC-free pressurized device to deliver bronchodilators & corticosteroids | •Dry powder inhaler device used to deliver bronchodilators & corticosteroids | •Holding chamber used with puffers to improve drug deposition<br>•Comes in various sizes<br>-Adult<br>-Child (~1-5yr) 3-6inhalations / actuation recommended<br>-Infant (0-18months) |
| **ADVANTAGES** | •Gives accurate lung function results<br>•Allows for screening of early lung disease<br>•Allows for diagnosis of some lung diseases<br>•Some units are easy to maintain & portable<br>**Spirometry:** for diagnosis & for possibly yearly monitoring in asthma<br>**Peak flow meters**(PFM): no evidence to show PFM-monitoring is any better than using symptoms as a guide; considered useful in select patients | •Portable, inexpensive handheld device<br>•Simple to use<br>•Different flow ranges for all age groups | •Breath-actuated, so reduces need for hand-breath coordination<br>• "Turbuhaler trainer" to assess flow - **60L/min** optimal; {Note: one whistle device whistles at ≥30L/min; a lower flow rate will result in lower lung deposition}<br>• a colored wheel indicates when 20 doses are left in device | •The aerosol of medication produced has a high percentage of particles the proper size to be drawn into the lower airways<br>•Low inspiratory flow **~20L/min** required<br>•Suitable for **all ages**, incl. children, when used with spacer (e.g. Aerochamber®) | •**Breath-actuated**, so reduces need for hand-breath coordination<br>•"In-check DIAL" trainer assesses adequate inspiratory flow- **30L/min** required)<br>•Exact number of doses left are indicated on a dose counter | •Equal or superior drug delivery to puffer alone or nebules<br>•Reduces need for hand-breath coordination<br>•Size variety allows use with all age groups<br>•Reduces local effects of meds eg. hoarseness, thrush<br>•more efficient lung delivery may allow for ↓ in # of puffs & cost |
| **DISADVANTAGES** | •Most units need to be calibrated daily<br>•Tester training is required<br>•Generally useful if >5yr (some even at age 7yr have difficulty) | •Coughing into unit elicits a false high reading<br>•Some patients are poor peak flow responders<br>•Patients can have a normal PEF giving them a false sense of control- when lung function poor | •<u>Not</u> suitable for children <5yr & in some elderly with poor inspiratory effort<br>•Humidity can clump drug & ↓ delivery<br>•Tipping of device before inhalation can expel dose<br>•Lactose Oxeze & Symbicort | •Cumbersome when used with spacer<br>•Susceptible to freezing<br>•Difficult to assess doses left (track doses used or use the DOSER attachment)<br>•Some have ↓↓ethanol (eg. Airomir 5 ul/puff) as an excipient in HFA formulations | •<u>Not</u> suitable for children <5yr & in some elderly with poor inspiratory effort<br>•Tipping of device before inhalation can expel dose<br>•contains lactose as a non-medicinal filler | •Cumbersome to carry {If unable to carry during the day, may preferably use with ICS/LABA/SABAs at home}<br>•Needs to be cleaned (e.g. every ~week; soak in soapy a few drops water & air dry)<br>•Suggest replacing q2yr |
| **COMMENTS** | •Validation of accurate results needs to be incorporated in program<br>•Physicians can bill (only 9% of Sask. asthmatics had spirometry done in the HQC'05 report) | •Symptom monitoring should be used along with PFM to better monitor asthma control<br>•Used in some action plans to direct therapy | •Turbuhaler trainer is helpful to ensure the proper inspiratory flow is being achieved<br>•Turbuhaler avail. for all inhaled meds-SABA, LABA, Steroids & LABA/Steroid combo | •Puffers, esp. steroids should be used with a spacer at any age to ↑ drug delivery<br>•Advair MDI has dose counter mechanism<br>•CFC free prime x4 times initially or if not used for several days | •In-check DIAL trainer helpful to ensure the proper inspiratory flow is being achieved<br>•Diskus avail. for all inhaled meds-SABA, LABA, Steroids & LABA/Steroid combo | •Should **preferably** be used with any puffer<br>•Pt should demonstrate use of device at visit<br>•Different sizes have different one-way valve weights to ensure proper drug deposit |
| **COST** | $500-2000 / unit | $20-60 / unit | $20-100 / month | $20-150 / month | $50-100 / month | $25-50 / **unit** covered by NIHB |

**DPI**=dry powder inhaler **ICS**=inhaled corticosteroids **LABA**=long acting beta2 agonist **SABA**=short acting beta2 agonist **yr**=year; **Spiriva HandiHaler** (tiotropium): useful ≥20L/min, contains lactose

•Have all inhalers as <u>same device</u> to avoid confusion. **Nebulizer/compressor solution** avail.; expensive without added benefit except possibly in <u>very</u> young & old; significant drug enters room air may ↑ infection transmission, time consuming & can affect eyes.

If on more than one inhaler use the bronchodilator first & the anti-inflammatory last. Best to wait ~1min between puffs & ~5mins between different medications.

# TOBACCO / SMOKING CESSATION PHARMACOTHERAPY-never too late to quit [1,2]

Prepared by L. Regier, B. Jensen, W. Chan; Reviewer: Dr. J. Taylor © www.RxFiles.ca May 10

| Generic/TRADE (Strength & forms) g=generic avail. | Class / Pregnancy category [1,3] | Side Effects (SE) - common Contraindications CI [3] Monitor M | √ = Advantages / ☒=Disadvantages; Comments {NNT: number needed to treat for one patient to be successful at 1 year based on systematic review} | Dosing Schedule | $ ~12 weeks |
|---|---|---|---|---|---|
| **NICOTINE REPLACEMENT (NRT): Patch, Gum or Inhaler**<br>**OTC**<br>{USA: nasal inhaler also available}<br>**(General NRT comments; more information below)** | NRT- assist in reducing craving. Lack of trials; but nicotine levels generally lower than with smoking; ↑'d malformations musculoskeletal with nicotine substitutes[4] | **General NRT SE**: arthralgias/back pain ≥5%, GI – flatulence 4%, diarrhea, nausea, taste change, etc.; acne 3%; dysmenorrhea 3%;<br>⇨Individualize dose: ↑ if withdrawal, ↓ if SE<br>CI caution in post MI or angina/CAD [5] (however some would suggest safer than smoking); hypersensitivity to components, eczema<br>M if no response in 4wks, stop, reassess, reinitiate?<br>**Peak**: N/H 6-12 hrs, I 15 min; **T½**: N/H 4hrs, I 1-2 hrs | **NRT:** ↑in abstinence rates by 30-80% compared to Pl; **NNT~10** [6]<br>**[Abstinence rate vs Pl @12 months: N** ≤11% vs 5.5% NNT=18; **I** 17% vs 9%, NNT=13; **G** ≤27% vs 16.5 %, NNT=9] [7]<br>No statistical difference between formulations. Choose specific formulation based on SE's, CI's & patient preferences.<br>{Some real-life studies have found long-term results no better than placebo. [8] Effectiveness may depend on co-interventions &/or highly motivated patients!}<br>**Combos: NRT+ Bupropion** may be better than either alone[9,10]; NRT+CBT, no added benefit to adding bupropion[11] | | |
| **Nicotine Patch**(clear or flesh color)<br>**NICODERM** Reservoir =N<br>7,14,21mg/d patch χ{▼Max 70 patch/yr} g<br>**HABITROL** Matrix =H<br>7,14,21mg patch χ{▼Max 84 patch/yr}<br>Both contain aluminum → remove prior to a MRI procedure | N = D<br>**PATCH** | **SE**: skin irritations 32%{May Tx with ICS}, headache ~20%; insomnia & nightmares (if worn at night)<br>NOT contraindicated in pts with CV disease [12]<br>◆If insomnia/disturbing dreams, remove patch @HS; if morning craving, keep patch on 24hrs or **consider adding** gum or inhaler.<br>{Unlabeled use: Ulcerative Colitis ~21 mg/day} | √ Convenient once daily dosing, slow constant release rate, more tolerable SE; fewer CV events, option after MI officially **if >2 wks** [5].<br>☒ no spikes in concentrations to correspond with cravings<br>◆Individualize dose; **combo** with gum or lozenge may be more effective<br>◆ two patches may be required in heavy smokers.<br>◆Smoking with patch: may ↑nicotine risks, but not CI | **N&H Smoking Hx <10cig/d, <45kg &/or CHD:** 14mg od x 6wk; 7mg od x 2wk<br>**N** Smoking Hx **>10cig/d**:21mg od x 6wk; 14mg od x 2wk; 7mg od x 2wk<br>**H** Smoking Hx **>20cig/d**:21mg od x3-4wk; 14mg od x3-4wk; 7mg od x3-4wk<br>Manufacturer recommendations; no difference between N & H. Individualize tx. New **Nicorette** patch 15mg x 6wk, 10mg x 2wk, 5mg x 2wk | **$300-$360**<br>g = ~$300<br>(~$30/7 patches)<br>Apply new patch to clean, dry, non-hairy area every day.<br>Tapering not always necessary<br>Start 1-4wk before quit date may↑ |
| **Nicotine Gum** {▼Max 945 pieces/yr}<br>**NICORETTE Gum** =G<br>2mg gum; **PLUS**=4mg χ▼<br>(g; sugar free; Flavors: menthol, original, freshmint, orange, cherry) g<br>**THRIVE** 2,4mg gum sucrose free;mint | G = C<br>**GUM**<br>Pregnancy?: Some prefer acute source (gum or inhaler) over a constant source (patch). | **SE**: cough, throat irritation - usually mild (absorb ~1/2 the nicotine in the gum)[3];<br>CI dental problems, TMJ temporomandibular joint syndrome<br>DI: coffee & acidic beverages e.g. juice, pop impair absorption; space by ≥15minutes | √ Quick delivery via buccal mucosa; ***Park & Chew** Strategy* – chew gum few times, then hold in side of mouth x1min; repeat<br>☒ Patient compliance: unpleasant taste; but high abstinence rate<br>☒ Not advised for ↑risk cardiac pts ☒ Risk of dependence[13]<br>**30 minute chew**: peak level 5→10ng/ml (for the 2mg→4mg gum)<br>◆Reduce to quit ↓ smoking 50% between 6-16wk or Stop to quit after 3mon→↓≥1 gum q4-7days | ~1piece/hr PRN; max 20 pieces/d; ave 10-16/d. individual taper.<br>{Use 4mg if ≥15cigs/d}<br>May use **prn** while **on patch** | **~$140-$250**<br>g=~$160-240<br>($35/2mg 105pcs; $45/4mg 105pcs)<br>**Use 4 mg if hx of smoking within 30min of waking!** |
| **Nicotine Oral Inhaler**<br>**NICORETTE Inhaler** =I<br>4mg {10mg cartridge gives 4mg nicotine} ✗ ⊗ | I = D<br>**INHALER** | **SE**: throat irritation 66%, cough 32%, rhinitis 23%, dyspepsia 18%<br>**10 puffs =1 puff from cigarette:** cartridge has **20min** continuous puffing; once punctured, cartridge viable for **24 hrs**; buccal absorption | √ Quick delivery of high dose convenient for severe cravings habitual hand-to-mouth motion (max absorption with ~20min short continuous frequent puffing) √ Flexible dosing schedule<br>☒ Not recommended for high risk cardiac patients | 6-16 cartridges/d x12 wk; indiv. taper; max 16cart/d. Use 12 wks then taper over 6-12 wks | **~$550-$900**<br>(start kit $40; $30/30 cart's) |
| **Nicotine Lozenges** ✗ ⊗<br>Nicorette SF, cherry, mint g 2,4mg; Thrive mint 1,2mg | **LOZENGE** | **SE**: soreness in gums, teeth, throat, hiccups & heartburn/indigestion. {More potent than gum} | √ Convenient, inconspicuous √ Flexible dosing schedule ◆ Strength depends on time to first craving upon awakening (<30min⇨use **4**mg; >30min⇨use **2**mg)<br>Park & Suck: suck until strong taste, then park, & repeat; lozenge lasts ~30min, don't chew/drink | 1 loz. q1-2hr x6 wk, q2-4hr x3wk, q4-8hr x3wk<br>Max:15 x 2mg lozenges | **~$100-$350**<br>($29 g -45/2mg 96pcs; $31 g -50/4mg 96pcs) |
| **Bupropion SR** =B<br>**ZYBAN** ✗▼150mg tab {Indication: smoking cessation}; 1-800-489-8424<br>WELLBUTRIN {Not officially indicated for smoking cessation}<br>100,150mg SR tab g ☎ ;<br>150,300mg tab **XL** ☎ | **TABLET**<br>**Antidepressant**<br>↓ dopamine reuptake mesolimbic system<br>www.zybannet.com<br>C | **SE**: **insomnia, agitation**, tremor, ↓appetite & GI upset, dry mouth, seizure 1/1000 at 300mg/d, aggression/suicide? n=14<br>CI personal/family hx of **seizures**, ↑risk for seizures (eg. eating disorders); head trauma, pts on MAO inhibitors within 14 days<br>{✗ Zyban not covered for smoking cessation in SK}<br>DI: induce CBZ, phenytoin, phenobarb., rifampin; inhibit cimetidine, cyclophosphamide | **Abstinence Rate at 12 months: 18.5% vs 6.6%** Pl, **NNT=8** [14]<br>{Observational study found 21% abstinent @12mo; 29% stopped due to SE's}[15]<br>May combine bupropion & NRT in patients with ↑↑cravings/withdrawal symptoms<br>◆no significant difference between 150mg/d & 300mg/d at 12 mo?[14]<br>☒ slower onset (1-2 weeks) √ option in concomitant **depression**<br>√ may **delay weight gain & cravings** post-smoking cessation<br>√ not CI in pts with hx of cardiovascular disease[16] or on SSRIs[17] | 150mg SR od x3 days, 150mg SR bid **x7**-12wks<br>Begin 1 week before cessation of smoking.<br>◆For SR: allow at least 8hrs between doses; take 2nd dose early pm to minimize insomnia | **$200 Zyban**<br>{**$135** 300mg od Wellbutrin XL} |
| **Varenicline** ✗ {▼Max 165 tab/yr} =V<br>**CHAMPIX** CHANTIX USA [18]<br>{2wk Starter Pack; 2wk Continuous Pack}<br>C | activate **nicotinic receptors** $\alpha 4\beta 2$ | **SE**: nausea 30%, sleep/dream 18%, taste disturbance; aggression?<br>{↑Weight @12wk: Pl 3kg >V 2.6kg >B 2kg}. Less SE requiring DC than B NNT >15, SJS?<br>DI: NRT-↑nausea. CI: end stage renal?; epilepsy?; suicidal? n=98 FDA | Abstinence Rate continuous @12 months: V: 22% vs B: 15% vs Pl: 9% [19,20]; 1 of 2 trials NS with 12 wk tx **{NNT=14 vs B; NNT=8 vs Pl}**; additional 12wks may ↑ success in 1/15 pts. [21] Start 1wk before quit; total 12wks tx ± 12wks if successful. | 0.5mg tab od x3days, 0.5mg bid x4-7day; then may↑ 1mg tab bid {2 wk Starter Pack avail.} | **$355**<br>{with food & H20}<br>(FAA pilot ban May/08) |
| **Nortriptyline**<br>**AVENTYL** g (10, 25mg cap)<br>(Full formulary in SK) | D<br>**CAPSULE**<br>**Antidepressant** | **SE**: dry mouth, dizziness, drowsiness, ↑weight; ↓SE's than amitriptyline Note: an option when breastfeeding [22,23]<br>CI ECG abnormalities rare, suicidal/seizure risk | **Abstinence Rate 12 months: 17% vs 7%** Pl, **NNT=10** [24]<br>CBT + (Bupropion 300mg/d vs Nortriptyline 75mg/d vs Pl): **NS** 42%vs31%vs22%; 6mo; n=156. [25]<br>◆Consider if also: **Pain, Migraine**, depression, neuropathy, insomnia. | 25–50-**75mg** po hs<br>(25mg-75mg/d for ~2wks before quit-date; continue ≥12wks after) | $48-76-**105** /14 wks |
| **SMOKING / Tobacco – all forms** | | **Quit smoking advice from a clinician, even brief, can increase cessation rates by 30%.**[26] Some attempt 10 x before successfully quitting!<br>(Cigarette Trivia: 1-3mg nicotine/cigarette; ~4000 chemicals/cigarette; 1pack/day = 20-40mg nicotine; 1pack= ~25 cigarettes)[3] Withdrawal Sx better after 1-3 wks. | | 1 pack/day cost–savings⇒ | ($925+) 12wk |

=↓dose for renal dysfx χ=Non-form Sk ☎=Exception Drug Status Sk ⊗=not covered NIHB ▼=covered NIHB ☒=Disadvantage **CBT**=cognitive behavioral therapy CI=contraindication **CV**=cardiovascular **DI**=drug interaction g=generics avail. **HA**=headache **Hx**=history **MI**=myocardial infarction **NS**=not statistically significant **Pl** = placebo **Pt**=patient **Sx**=symptom **SE**=side effect **T½**=half life **wk**=weeks NICE: http://www.nice.org.uk/page.aspx?o=PHI001 Health Canada: www.gosmokefree.ca **Smokers' Helpline** 1-877-513-5333 fax referral option

**Other:** **Psych Considerations:** smoking can ↓ some antipsychotic drug levels by up to 50%-dose adjustment required if smoking stopped/restarted[27] Behavioral therapy best in pts with a hx of depression. **Rimonabant** ACOMPLIA (production suspended)
**Anti-nicotine vaccines (investigational):** Celtic, Nabi, Cytos: reducing nicotine distribution to brain, ↓reinforcing effect of nicotine. **Herbal**: RESOLVE lozenge: CESTEMENOL-350 150 mg Passiflora incarnate, Abies balsamea L: lacks efficacy data & may↑ toxicity.

**Non-Drug Measures:** [5,28,29,30] Consider exercise, counseling & support groups; avoid situations that trigger smoking urge. **DI:** if stop smoking drug level ↑ for caffeine, clozapine, fluvoxamine, haloperidol, olanzapine & theophylline. Other Links: www.can-adaptt.net

**HARMS/Reasons to Stop:** [31,32,33] **Leading cause of preventable death** (45,000 CND/yr); ~50% of long-term smokers die prematurely from cancer, heart, stroke & lung disease yet **~18% CND's smoke**. Smokers die ~10-17yrs younger than non-smokers. Quitting gives a 36% relative reduction in total mortality & ↓ cardiac events in CHD pts by ~50%.[34] **Cost**: 1 pk/d cost **~$3600/yr**. **Other**: impotence, osteoporosis & SIDS sudden infant death syndrome

**Weight Gain:** Average <5 kg/1st yr; ↑ exercise to lessen; health benefits persist despite weight gain (RRR 15-61% in mortality after MI). Consider strategies to avoid weight gain as part of the "Quit Plan".

**5 A's to Smoking Cessation:** **ASK** – about tobacco use at every visit; **ADVISE** - to quit; **ASSESS** - willingness to quit; **ASSIST** -implement plan; **ARRANGE** - follow-up visits, phone; & cessation counseling.

# CANNABINOIDS - An Overview

Cannabis contains hundreds of compounds including ~70 cannabinoids. The most psychoactive cannabinoid is Delta-9-tetrahydrocannabinol (also known as dronabinol or THC). The other 2 less psychoactive cannabinoids are Delta-8-THC & cannabinol. Another active agent is cannabidiol (CBD) which may have analgesic & anti-inflammatory activity. Cannabinoid receptors ($CB_1$ & $CB_2$) are where these agents work.
General dosing considerations: start low & go slow.

## Cannabinoid Comparisons:

| Agent | Possible use | Side effects, CI, DI | Dose | Cost 30d |
|---|---|---|---|---|
| **Dronabinol MARINOL** χ⊗<br>-synthetic THC<br>2.5, 5 mg cap (sesame oil)<br>-store in fridge | Treat severe **N&V** from cancer chemo<br>Treat AIDS related **anorexia**<br>{Oral form – some abuse potential} | N&V, ataxia, confusion, coordination problems, dizziness, somnolence, vertigo, red eyes, ↑ or↓ BP, palpitations, ↑HR, flushing, panic rx, delusion of persecution, depersonalization, depression, disturbance in thinking & euphoria & still an abuse potential<br>CI:pregnant,breast feeding, ?Sz,psyc hx<br>DI: ↑ SE: disulfiram, ethanol, fluoxetine, sleep meds. Theophylline↓theo level | 2.5-5mg po TID-QID chemo N&V (~5mg/m²)<br>2.5mg bid ac lunch & supper to ↑ appetite [AIDS 3]<br>**Start** 2.5mg po HS Max 20mg/d | $202-500<br>$137<br>$72 |
| **Marijuana**[4] χ⊗<br>(Banji, Cannabis sativa, Grass, Pot, Weed etc..:<br>Cost ~$10-20/g)<br>Contains:<br>Delta-9-THC esp♀flowers & leaves ~10-20%THC,<br>Delta-8-THC, cannabinol & CBD<br>{USA 2010: 14 states permit medical use} | An euphoriant. (recreational use)<br>Possibly effective: ↑ appetite [AIDS], ↓ pressure for glaucoma, MS neuropathic pain & tics [20]<br>-see **Category 1** MMAR list below<br>Unknown: dandruff, hemorrhoids, obesity, asthma, urinary infections, leprosy, preventing rejection after kidney transplants …<br>------------------------<br>Sometimes used in baking for medicinal effect without risks of smoking. | Dry mouth, N&V, red eyes; heart, lung [29] & BP dx, ↓mental fx, panic rx, ↑ weight & appetite, hallucinations, flashbacks, sedation; ?depression & sexual problems; ?cancer;<br>?↑ steatosis with hepatitis C, ? psychosis<br>CI: pregnant, breast feeding, ?seizures, ?psych hx (↑ periodontal disease)<br>DI: ↑ SE: disulfiram, ethanol, fluoxetine, sleep meds. Theophylline↓theo level, warfarin?<br>•potency/purity concern if unregulated<br>•1 joint= ≤5 cigarettes from lung fx view [29] | 1-3 grains (65-195mg) for smoking;<br>Hashish plant resin 1 grain (16-65mg)<br>Rare: Lead adulteration to THC | Health Canada (~12.5%THC) $5/gram<br>1-866-337-7705<br>Authorized producers & possession<br>>2400 people approved Feb'08<br>-Dose as a proposed daily amount<br>eg. ≤ 5g/day [10]<br>{Ave 2.5g/day in pain} |
| **Nabilone** ☎▼ **CESAMET**<br>0.5,1mg cap (0.25mg) χ▼<br>(compound for low-dose e.g. simple syrup 5mg/50ml) | Treat severe **N&V** from cancer chemo<br>☎ EDS Sask.=nausea/anorexia in AIDS<br>{Sleep benefit in small fibromyalgia trial} [47 n=31]<br>{Oral form – some abuse potential} | Drowsiness, vertigo, psych high/euphoria, dry mouth, depression, ataxia, ↑HR, ↓BP, blurred vision, hallucinations, sedation, headache & still an abuse potential<br>CI: pregnant, breast feeding, ?Sz,psyc hx<br>DI: ↑ SE: disulfiram, ethanol, fluoxetine, sleep meds. Theophylline↓theo level | 1-2mg OD-BID for chemo N&V<br>**Start** 0.25-0.5mg po HS ↑ by 0.5mg q2days Max 6mg/d | $230-830<br>$60-120 |
| **Tetranabinex/ nabidiolex** [11] **SATIVEX** χ⊗<br>Buccal spray soln 5.5ml= ~51 sprays<br>Natural extract contains:<br>Delta-9-THC 2.7mg & CBD 2.5mg/spray peppermint flavor | **Adjunctive** relief of **advanced cancer pain**; & **neuropathic pain** in **MS** pts >18yrs<br>•Trial n=**66** 5wk aided approval for this indication[18]; but product studied in 5 short trials with a total of 368 pts.<br>•Trial n=38 10wk in diabetic peripheral neuropathy; no better than placebo in pts with pain despite prior TCA tx.[54]<br>Approved as a narcotic April05 with CONDITIONS<br>(promising evidence must be further confirmed)<br>Canada **first** country in the world to approve its use. | mouth irritation~20%, dizziness, ↑HR, euphoric mood, changes in mood & concentration, drowsiness, bad taste, vertigo, reaction time<br>CI: allergy cannabinoids, propylene glycol, ethanol or pepermint oil, pts with severe heart, liver or kidney impairment, pregnant; ? psyc hx<br>DI: ↑ SE: disulfiram, ethanol, fluoxetine, sleep meds. Theophylline↓theo level; may ↑ levels of amitriptyline & fentanyl | Buccal 1 spray q4h<br>directed below the tongue/or side cheek<br>(often use 4 - **5** sprays/day for MS)<br>(often use ≥8 sprays/day for cancer)<br>Initial: 1 spray/day; ↑ q2d<br>Max ~12 sprays/day<br>Prime: 2-3 times initially<br>Unopened: Refrigerate<br>Room temp: stable for 28days<br>Low dose: may spray into milk | $575<br>per 4 bottles (~200doses or ~40 days) |

ac=before **BP**=blood pressure **CBD**=cannabidiol **CI**=contraindication **DI**=drug interaction **BP**=blood pressure **Dx**=disease **Fx**=function **HR**=heart rate **hx**=history **MS**=multiple sclerosis **N&V**=nausea & vomiting **Sz**=seizures **rx**=reaction **THC**=delta-9-tetrahydrocannabinol χ not Sask. formulary ⊗ not NIHB ▼=covered by NIHB ☎=Exception Drug Status Sk ♀=female

## Canadian Society of Addiction Medicine Statement: Oct, 1999

- "Cannabis is chemically classified in the **hallucinogen** category of psychoactive substances. The regular use of cannabis products is known to cause harmful health effects, including **addiction**, with its associated consequences to individuals, communities & society, among those that are susceptible. Currently, available scientific information and clinical practice experience indicate that overall, there is more risk than benefit, in the use of cannabis products for medicinal purposes. Ongoing well-designed clinical research into the possible medicinal uses of cannabis products is essential, using the same rigorous standards that are applied to any therapeutic agent prior to its introduction into general clinical practice."

**Other issues to consider**: (consider using CMPA release form http://www.cmpa-acpm.ca/portal/cmpa_docs/english/content/issues/common/pdf/com_release_form_for_medical_practitioners-e.pdf )

- bill to **decriminalize** appears to be shelved until the next election (likely fines rather than criminal charges for possession but heavier penalties for grow-ops)
- Marijuana Medical Access Regulations (**MMAR** July/2001,Revised June/05)[10] defines specific circumstances for medical use of marijuana:
  - **Category 1**: compassionate end-of-life care; pain/spasms from MS, spinal cord injury or disease; pain/cachexia/anorexia/weight loss/nausea from cancer or AIDS; pain from severe arthritis; or seizures from epilepsy {use **Form B1**}. Application by a medical practitioner (a GP **or** a specialist in the area of the condition)
  - **Category 2**: other serious conditions {use **Form B2**}. A family doctor or specialist can sign the medical declaration. However an **assessment** of the case by a specialist is needed if the medical practitioner is not already a specialist for the patient's medical condition.

## Broader Considerations:

- Pain→ based on very limited evidence: no more effective than codeine, ↑ side effects & **need larger trials** [5]
  → cannabis is moderately efficacious for chronic pain, but benefit may be partially (or completely) offset by potentially serious harms. [51,55 limited evidence]
- MS → modest therapeutic effect & risk of side effects thus **be cautious** about using cannabinoids [7,8,9]
  {Small spasticity benefit & possible less disability & no major safety concerns in a 12 month CAMS MS trial n=502 follow up; pts felt these drugs helped their disease.} [12]

## Limits of the Evidence: [2-4, 9, 12, 47, 51]

- limited RCT's, small short trials, differing routes, forms & types of cannabinoids makes assessing efficacy almost impossible

**Possible approach**: A close review of 1) the indications, 2) what meds were previously used & 3) the context of the "therapeutic trial" of marijuana. These people should have 4) a random urine screen & 5) an addictions assessment/addiction services, complete with 6) collateral information from family & others. Then 7) a focused case management discussion should be held, with all the assessors & care providers, before any decision is made. 8) Consider using "treatment agreement", structured approach for non-oral formulations. 9) Start low dose at HS to minimize side effects.
{Consideration: **Fourth line** analgesic for the management of chronic neuropathic pain.} [50 Canadian Pain Society 2007]

## National Departments / Organizations

### Health Canada: www.hc-sc.gc.ca

The Federal department responsible for helping Canadians maintain & improve their health, while respecting individual choices & circumstances.

**The Health Products and Food Branch** (HPFB)'s mandate is to take an integrated approach to managing the health-related risks & benefits of health products & food by:

- minimizing health risk factors to Canadians while maximizing the safety provided by the regulatory system for health products & food; and,
- promoting conditions that enable Canadians to make healthy choices and providing information so that they can make informed decisions about their health.
- **List of Directorates**: (http://www.hc-sc.gc.ca/ahc-asc/branch-dirgen/hpfb-dgpsa/index_e.html)
  Biologics and Genetic Therapies Directorate ; Food Directorate
  Health Products and Food Branch Inspectorate ; Health Products and Food Litigation Secretariat ; Marketed Health Products Directorate ;
  **Natural Health Products Directorate** : As part of the Health Products & Food Branch of Health Canada, the Natural Health Products Directorate (NHPD) is the regulating authority for natural health products for sale in Canada. Our role is to ensure that Canadians have ready access to natural health products that are safe, effective & of high quality while respecting freedom of choice & philosophical & cultural diversity.
  Office of Biotechnology and Science ; Office of Consumer and Public Involvement ; Office of Management Services ; Office of Nutrition Policy and Promotion ; Office of Regulatory and International Affairs ; Office of the Assistant Deputy Minister ; Policy and Strategic Planning Directorate ; Regional Operations ; Veterinary Drugs Directorate
  **Therapeutic Products Directorate** : Health Canada's Therapeutic Products Directorate (TPD) is the Canadian federal authority that regulates pharmaceutical drugs & medical devices for human use. Prior to being given market authorization, a manufacturer must present substantive scientific evidence of a product's safety, efficacy & quality as required by the Food & Drugs Act & Regulations .

### CADTH (Canadian Agency for Drugs & Technologies in Health): www.cadth.ca

⇨an independent, not-for-profit agency funded by Canadian federal, provincial, & territorial governments to provide credible, impartial advice & evidence-based information about the effectiveness of drugs & other health technologies to Canadian health care decision makers. Programs:

- Health Technology Assessment (HTA): assessing drugs & health technologies
- Common Drug Review (CDR): reviewing clinical evidence on new drugs
- Canadian Optimal Medication Prescribing and Utilization Service (COMPUS) identifying & promoting best practices in drug prescribing & use

### NAPRA: http://www.napra.org/

The National Association of Pharmacy Regulatory Authorities (NAPRA) enhances the activities of the pharmacy regulatory authorities by:

- Representing common interests of member organizations
- Serving as a national resource centre
- Promoting the national implementation of progressive regulatory programs & standards

### Various:

- **AFMC**: Assoc. of Faculties of Medicine of Canada www.afmc.ca
- **AFPC**: Assoc. of Faculties of Pharmacy of Canada www.afpc.info
- **CFPC**: College of Family Physicians of Canada www.cfpc.ca
- **CPhA**: Canadian Pharmacists Association http://www.pharmacists.ca/
- **CSHP**: Canadian Society of Hospital Pharmacists www.cshp.ca
- **CMA**: Canadian Medical Association www.cma.ca
- **HCC**: Health Council of Canada www.healthcouncilcanada.ca
- **PEBC**: Pharmacy Examining Board of Canada www.pebc.ca
- **RCPSC**: Royal College of Physicians and Surgeons of Canada www.rcpsc.medical.org

## Regulations & AR Reporting

**Overview**: The legal framework for drugs in Canada is a mix between Federal and Provincial legislation. Provincial regulations supplement and must be in concordance with the Federal Acts.

### Controlled Drugs and Substances Act http://laws.justice.gc.ca/en/c-38.8/

- Canada: federal drug control act providing regulations/listings related to narcotic, psychotropic and other drugs of abuse (e.g. opioids, cocaine, cannabis, amphetamines, anabolic steroids, benzodiazepines). Various sub-classifications e.g. Narcotic; Controlled I,II,III; Benzodiazepine & other.

### Food and Drug Act

- Canada's federal legislation regarding the production, import, export, transport and sale of food, drugs, contraceptive devices and cosmetics. {Note: it states that cures for Schedule A diseases e.g. cancer cannot be advertised to the general public.}

### NAPRA Drug Schedules http://www.napra.org/

- **Schedule I Drugs**: require a prescription for sale; are provided by pharmacist; require diagnosis & professional intervention of a practitioner. Sale controlled; regulations defined by provincial pharmacy legislation
- **Schedule II Drugs**: while less strictly regulated, do require professional intervention from the pharmacist at the point of sale and possibly referral to a practitioner. While a prescription is not required, the drugs are available only from the pharmacist and must be retained within an area of the pharmacy where there is no public access and no opportunity for patient self-selection
- **Schedule III Drugs**: may present risks to certain populations in self-selection. Although available without a prescription, these drugs are to be sold from the self-selection area of the pharmacy which is operated under the direct supervision of the pharmacist, subject to any local professional discretionary requirements which may ↑ the degree of control. Such an environment is accessible to the patient and clearly identified as the "professional services area" of the pharmacy. The pharmacist is available, accessible & approachable to assist the patient in making an appropriate self-medication selection.
- **Unscheduled drugs**: can be sold without professional supervision. Adequate information is available for the patient to make a safe and effective choice & labeling is deemed sufficient to ensure the appropriate use of the drug. These are not included in Schedules I, II or III & may be sold from any retail outlet.

### Adverse Reaction (AR) Reporting

- **What kind of adverse reactions should be reported?**
  - Any temporal or possible association (no proof required) especially:
    -reactions to Recently Marketed Drugs <5yrs
    -Serious (resulting in hospitalization, disability, life-threatening, death)
    -Unexpected Reactions incl. to immunizations (regardless of severity)
- **Reports can be submitted by** mail, fax, phone or online.
- **Canadian Vigilance** MedEffect Website: info reporting; sign-up for mailed warnings & advisories! http://www.hc-sc.gc.ca/dhp-mps/medeff/index_e.html
  -FAX - Toll-free Canada **1-866-678-6789**
  -Telephone - Toll-free Canada **1-866-234-2345**
- **AR forms:** Compendium of Pharmaceuticals & Specialties (CPS); Other (e.g. Saskatchewan Prescription Drug Plan Formulary Appendix)

## Canada Health Act & Agencies

### Canada Health Act Overview:

- The *Canada Health Act* is Canada's federal health insurance legislation. The provinces of Canada are constitutionally responsible for the administration and delivery of health care services. They decide where their hospitals will be located, how many physicians they will need, and how much money they will spend on their health care systems. The *Act* establishes the criteria and conditions related to insured health care services-the national standards-that the provinces and territories must meet in order to receive the full federal cash transfer contribution under the transfer mechanism, that is, the Canada Health & Social Transfer (CHST).
- The aim of Canada's health care system is to ensure that all residents of Canada have reasonable access to medically necessary insured services without direct charges.

### Five Principles of the Canada Health Act - Overview:

1) **Public Administration:**. The health care insurance plans of the provinces and territories are to be administered and operated on a non-profit basis by a public authority, responsible to the provincial/territorial governments & subject to audits of their accounts & financial transactions.
2) **Comprehensiveness:** The health insurance plans of the provinces & territories must ensure all insured health services* (hospital, physician, surgical-dental) &, where permitted, services rendered by other health care practitioners. *See definition under Health Care Services Covered by the Act.
3) **Universality:** One hundred percent of the insured residents of a province or territory must be entitled to the insured health services provided by the plans on uniform terms and conditions. Provinces and territories generally require that residents register with the plans to establish entitlement.
4) **Portability:** Residents moving from one province or territory to another must continue to be covered for insured health care services by the "home" province during any minimum waiting period, not to exceed three months, imposed by the new province of residence. After the waiting period, the new province or territory of residence assumes health care coverage.
5) **Accessibility:** Health insurance plans of provinces & territories must provide:
   -reasonable access to insured health care services ...
   -reasonable access in terms of physical availability of medically necessary services ..."where and as available".
   -reasonable compensation to physicians and dentists ...
   -payment to hospitals to cover the cost of insured services.

### Health Canada - Agencies (online links):

Public Health Agency of Canada: http://www.phac-aspc.gc.ca/new_e.html
Canadian Health Network: http://www.canadianhealthnetwork.ca/
Canada Health Portal: http://chp-pcs.gc.ca/CHP/index_e.jsp
Canadian Institutes of Health Research (CIHR): http://www.cihr.ca/
Patented Medicine Prices Review Board (PMPRB)

- **Drug Information Services** (may be available in local area):
  -e.g. **DIRC: Drug Information and Research Centre (Ontario)** Ph: 1-800-268-8058; Toronto Area (416)-385-3472 ; www.dirc-canada.org
- **Travel Clinics** - CDN listing: http://www.phac-aspc.gc.ca/tmp-pmv/travel/clinic_e.html
- **CIHI:** an independent, not-for-profit organization that provides essential data & analysis on Canada's health system & the health of Canadians. www.cihi.ca

**Saskatchewan**: **Poison Control Center**: Ph. 1-866-454-1212 **Saskatchewan Drug Information Service (SDIS)**: www.usask.ca/druginfo, Ph 1-800-667-3425 or 966-6340 (Saskatoon)
**Canadian Drug Coverage Links**: (including Provincial, NIHB, Veterans): www.drugcoverage.ca **SK Drug Schedule Summary Link**: http://napra.ca/pdfs/provinces/sk/37.pdf

**Classification of Anemias** [1,2] {Normal hemoglobin (Hgb) Male: **130-180g**/L; Female:**120-160** g/L; ↑ Hgb if live at high altitude, ↓ Hgb if live near the coast}.

| Red Cell Indices | Laboratory Investigations | Findings | Differential Diagnosis |
|---|---|---|---|
| MCV <80 fL<br>**Microcytic** anemia | Serum **ferritin** preferred, Serum iron, TIBC, RDW<br>(Ferritin: is an acute phase reactant that may be ↑ if concurrent liver congestion/dx, collagen dx, malignancy, infection or inflammation | Ferritin <20mcg/L ⇒<br>Ferritin >20mcg/L ⇒ | Iron deficiency anemia (IDA) high RDW, low-normal reticulocyte, low serum iron with high TIBC, ↑ transferrin, ↓ transferrin saturation & ferritin.<br>Anemia chronic dx normal-↑ RDW, low serum iron, low-normal TIBC, only ~25% microcytic, Thalassemia major high RDW & minor normal RDW,<br>Hemoglobinopathy, Lead Overload |
| MCV 80-100 fL<br>**Normocytic** anemia | Consider loss of blood, **Reticulocyte** count | Blood loss, Hemolysis⇒<br>No blood loss ⇒ | Treat cause GI or menstrual bleed (Use of ASA/NSAIDs, warfarin etc.), high reticulocyte<br>Anemia of chronic dx normal-↑ RDW, low serum iron, low-normal TIBC, ↓or normal transferrin, normal-↑ ferritin; **Tx disease**, ?transfusion,?Epo & not iron if ↑ or normal ferritin.<br>Aplastic anemia, Mixed deficiency anemia, Endocrine hypothyroidism, Hemoglobinopathy |
| MCV >100 fL<br>**Macrocytic** anemia | Consider loss of blood, Reticulocyte count, Vitamin $B_{12}$ & folate level,<br>**Blood film,** TSH, LFTs | Blood loss ⇒<br>No Blood loss ⇒ | Treat cause GI or menstrual bleed (Use of ASA/NSAIDs, warfarin etc.), high reticulocyte<br>Liver dx normal RDW, Myelodysplasia high RDW, Folate or Vit $B_{12}$ deficiency high RDW, low-normal reticulocyte, Hemolytic anemia |

**Drug induced Aplastic anemia:** allopurinol, antithyroid meds, **chemo**, chloramphenicol, chlorpromazine, clopidogrel, corticosteroids, furosemide, gold, indomethacin, interferon α2a&2b, isoniazid, methyldopa, NSAIDs, penicillamine, phenothiazines, procainamide, sulfonamides & ticlopidine.
**Drug induced Hemolysis in G6PD Deficiency:** ascorbic acid, benzocaine, chloroquine, dapsone, hydroxychloroqine, nitrofurantoin, phenazopyridine, primaquine, sulfacetamide, sulfamethoxazole, sulfanilamide & sulfapyridine.
**Drug induced Hemolytic anemia:** ACEI, acetaminophen, ASA/NSAIDs, cephalosporins, chlorpromazine, chlorpropamide, diclofenac, hydrochlorothiazide, interferon α2a&2b, isoniazid, levodopa, levofloxacin, mefenamic acid, methadone, methyldopa, penicillins, probenecid, procainamide, quinine, quinidine, ribavirin, rifampin, sulfonamides, & tetracycline. (Direct antiglobulin test-DAT or Coomb's test is used to detect cause of hemolytic anemia)
**Drug induced Megaloblastic anemia:** Direct inhibitors of DNA synthesis– azathioprine, **chemo meds**, hydroxyurea & zidovudine. Folate antagonists- carbamazepine, methotrexate, pentamidine, phenobarbital, phenytoin fosphenytoin, primidone, trimethoprim & valproic acid. Reduced Folate or Vitamin $B_{12}$ absorption- alcohol, aminosalicylic acid, colchicine, cotrimoxazole, $H_2$ blockers, metformin, neomycin, nitrofurantoin, oral contraceptives, proton pump inhibitors, sulfasalazine & triamterene.

## Anemia of CKD - Hemoglobin Control: Key Outcome Trials – Summary

Zack Dumont, Peter Ricci, Linda Gross, Bruce Lang – **www.RxFiles.ca** **May 10**

| | Trials<br>Mean follow-up, n | Intervention | Population<br>CKD stage, age, etc. | Key Baseline Indices<br>(e.g. Iron Studies) | Results | Comments |
|---|---|---|---|---|---|---|
| Iron Trials | **Charytan et al.** [3]<br>43 days; n=96; RCT, OL | **Oral vs IV iron** for ND-CKD<br>FeSO4 325mg po TID x 29 days vs Iron sucrose 200mg IV weekly x 5 doses; assessments made up to 14 days after last dose | ND-CKD; Age mean ~61; mostly ♀, (71% oral, 60% IV); multi-racial<br>Included: CrCl(C-G)≤40ml/min, Hgb<105g/L, TSAT<25%, ferritin<300ug/L \| Excluded: iron tx or blood transfusion w/in last month, apparent GI bleed, alb<30g/L | Hgb (g/L): 97 oral vs 98 IV<br>Ferritin (ng/mL): 103 oral vs 125 IV<br>TSAT (%): 15.6 oral vs 16.6 IV | •△Hgb (g/L): +7 oral vs +10 IV; NS<br>•△Ferritin (ng/mL): -5.1 oral vs 288 IV; p<0.0001<br>•Change in TSAT (%): day 36=2.1 oral vs 5.1 IV \| day 43=0.5 oral vs 4.5 IV; sig increase for IV, but not oral<br>•# of pts achieved Hgb >110g/L: 31.3% vs 54.2% IV (p=0.028)<br>•SE: similar btwn groups, most common is GI in oral group, & taste-disturbances more common in IV group | **Iron therapy**<br>•Should be guided by iron status tests, Hgb levels, ESA dose, & pt status CSN 2008 Guidelines<br>**Iron Therapy in *Non*-hemodialysis CKD pts (ND-CKD)** |
| | **Van Wyck et al.** [4]<br>~56 days; n=161; RCT, OL, ITT | **Oral vs IV iron** for ND-CKD pts<br>FeSO4 325mg po TID for 56 days vs Iron sucrose 1g IV x2 doses over 14 days | Stage 3-5 ND-CKD; Age mean ~63; mean eGFR ml/min/1.73m2: 28.5 oral vs 30.4 IV; 98 pts *NOT* on ESAs<br>Included: Hgb≤110g/L, TSAT≤25%, ferritin≤300ug/L; if on Epo, no △ for 8wks prior or during study | Hgb (g/L): 101 oral vs 102 IV<br>Ferritin (ug/L): 104 oral vs 93 IV<br>TSAT (%): 17 oral vs 16 IV | •% of pts w/Hgb ↑ of ≥10g/L: 28% oral vs 44.3% IV; p=0.0344<br>•% of IV pts with outcome: 53.1 ESA-use oral vs 38.3 no ESA; NS<br>•% of oral pts with outcome: 32.2 ESA-use oral vs 25.5 no ESA; NS<br>{Primary outcome was a Hgb increase > or =1 g/dL}<br>•△eGFR (ml/min/1.73m2): -4.4 oral vs -1.45 IV; p=0.01<br>•△QOL: no statistically significant differences | •Route of admin has been shown to have no difference in reaching Hgb targets Charytan, & IV is superior to oral Van Wyck; but in light of lack of conclusive superiority evidence & due to ↑access risk problems & ↑ cost, recommend **oral iron first** CSN 2008 Guideline<br>•QOL has not been shown to differ between pts |
| | **DeVita et al.** [5]<br>~5mos; n=36; RCT | **IV iron to high>400 vs low>200 ferritin** for HD-CKD pts on ESAs<br>Each subject below target received an IV iron dextran load, HCT was maintained between 32.5-36% by adjusting Epo dose | HD-CKD; Age mean ~66.5;<br>Included: HCT≤33, Ferritin 70-400 | HCT (%): 30.5 High vs 29.5 Low<br>**Ferritin (ug/L): 203.7 High vs 166.4 Low** | •HCT (%): 34.0 High vs 36.1 Low {no sig. dif.}<br>•**Mean Ferritin (ug/L): 387 high-ferritin vs 261 low-ferritin**<br>•**End Ferritin (ug/L): 298.6 high-ferritin vs 469.4 low-ferritin**<br>•△Epo dose (u/kg/wk): -154 high-ferritin vs -31 low-ferritin; p<0.001 | treated with oral or IV iron Van Wyck<br>•Studies show that ↑ Hgb may occur following iron tx with **ferritin ~100ug/L** Charytan & Van Wyck<br>•IV iron produces greater results regardless of ESA use Van Wyck |
| | **Besarab et al.** [6]<br>~6mos; n=42; RCT, OL, ITT, single-centre | **IV iron to high30-50 vs low20-30 TSAT** for HD-CKD pts on ESAs<br>{16-20wk run-in period with IV iron dextran & erythropoietin to get to study levels of TSAT=20-30% & Hgb=95-120}<br>25-150mg IV iron dextran control VS load of 100mg x6 doses for 2wk then 25-150mg/wk study | HD-CKD; Age mean ~60.8;<br>25 males, 17 females | Hgb (g/L): 105 control vs 106 study<br>Ferritin (ug/L): 287 control vs 285 study<br>**TSAT (%): 23.9 control vs 24.6 study**<br>Epo dose (units 3X/wk): 3782 control vs 3625 study | •Hgb (g/L): 103 control vs 104 study<br>•Ferritin (ug/L): 298 control vs 731 study<br>•**TSAT (%): 27.6 control vs 32.6 study**<br>•Epo dose @6mos: 40% lower dose for study group vs control group (significant) | **Iron Therapy in Hemodialysis CKD pts (HD-CKD)**<br>•Pts with higher ferritin (~400 vs 200 ug/L) require lower doses of ESAs DeVita, thus it is |
| | **Macdougall et al.** [7]<br>~4mos; n=25; RCT | **Oral vs IV iron vs No iron** for HD-CKD pts on ESAs<br>Oral ferrous sulfate 200mg TID vs iron dextran 250mg q2wks vs no iron | HD-CKD; Age mean ~58<br>oral, 47 IV, & 54 no iron | Hgb(g/L): 72 oral vs 73 IV vs 73 no iron<br>Ferritin (ug/L): 309 oral vs 345 IV vs 458 no iron | •Hgb (g/L): 102 oral vs 119 IV vs 99 no iron; p<0.05<br>•ESA dose (unit/dose): 1294 oral vs 1202 IV vs 1475 no iron; NS | recommended to target **ferritin >200 ug/L** with iron therapy CSN 2008 Guidelines<br>•Weigh benefits vs risks of initiating iron tx in pts with ferritin >800ug/L & TSAT <25% DRIVE |
| | **Fishbane et al.** [8]<br>~4mos; n=52 | **Oral vs IV iron** for HD-CKD pts on ESAs<br>Oral iron vs Iron dextran 100mg IV x2 weekly | HD-CKD; Age mean ~49.5<br>Included: TSAT>15%, ferritin<100ng/ml | Hgb (g/L): 106 oral vs 108 IV<br>ESA dose (units/treatment): 6750 oral vs 7100 IV | •Hgb (g/L): 106 oral vs 115 IV; p<0.05<br>•HCT (%): 31.8 oral vs 34.4 IV; p<0.05<br>•ESA dose (units/treatment): 7563 oral vs 4050 IV; p<0.05<br>•Serum ferritin (ng/mL): 157.3 oral vs 753.9 IV; p<0.05 | •Pts with higher TSAT% (30-50 vs 20-30) maintain Hgb with lower doses of ESAs Besarab, therefore recommend to target **TSAT >20%** with iron therapy CSN 2008 Guidelines |
| | **DRIVE I** [9]<br>~6wks; n=129 **modified ITT**; RCT, OL, multi-centre | **IV iron vs No iron** in HD-CKD pts with high ferritin, low TSAT<br>Ferrous gluconate 125mg IV with 8 consecutive HD sessions vs no iron; epo doses ↑ 25% in both groups at trial onset (no other △ permitted) | HD-CKD; Age mean ~59-60; ~1:1 male:female; multi-racial<br>Included: Hgb≤110g/L, TSAT≤25%, ferritin=500-1200ug/L (stratified before rand'n to < or > 800ug/L) | Hgb (g/L): 104 IV vs 102 no iron<br>Ferritin (ug/L): 759 IV vs 765 no iron<br>TSAT (%): 18 IV vs 19 no iron | •△Hgb (g/dL): 1.6 IV vs 1.1 no iron; p=0.028<br>•% of responders ≥20g/L ↑ (%): 49.6 IV vs 29.2 no iron; p=0.041<br>•△ferritin (ug/L): 173 IV vs -174 no iron; p<0.001<br>•baseline ferritin was not predictive of iron response<br>•safety was no different if < or > 800 baseline ferritin (not powered to show safety)<br>•△TSAT (%): 7.5 IV vs 1.8 no iron; p<0.001 | •Studies looking at oral iron vs placebo have shown that oral iron is no better than placebo (in Hgb improvements Mcdougall or ESA dose minimization) |
| | **DRIVE II** [10]<br>~6wks; n=129 | Observational study of duration of effect from IV iron under usual clinical mgt | Extension (i.e. used same DRIVE pts) | Epo dose in DRIVE (units/wk): 45,000 IV vs 43,700 no iron | •△Epo dose (units/wk) from dose given in DRIVE: -7527 IV (p=0.003) vs 649 no iron (p=0.809)<br>•% of pts with Hgb>110(g/L): 83.9 IV vs 67.9 no iron; p<0.05 | •**IV iron** has been shown to be superior to oral iron with respect to ↑Hgb Fishbane & Besarab & ↓ESA dose Fishbane |
| ESA | **Revicki et al.** [11]<br>~48wks; n=83; RCT, OL, ITT | **Erythropoietin vs placebo** in ND-CKD pts on health-related QOL HRQL<br>Intially erythropoietin 50u/kg/dose SubQ 3xweekly or untreated; all treated pts could have dosage ↑ (max 450u/kg/wk) until HCT reached 36, then titrated to target 35 | ND-CKD; Age mean ~57, ~67.5% female, mean GFR~10.1ml/min | HCT (%): 26.8 ESA & untreated gp<br>Physical function score (/100): 44.3 ESA vs 49.1 untreated | •**HRQL** Physical function: +7.8 ESA vs -4.8 untreated; p=0.006 / all other tests NS<br>•△HCT (%): +4.7 ESA vs -1 untreated (P < 0.0001)<br>•Withdrawals: 53.5 % (23/43) ESA vs 62.5% (25/40) untreated | **ESA Therapy**<br>•Goal of treating iron-replete pts with ESAs is to improve QOL, while minimizing any SE of the drug & decreasing the need for transfusions<br>•ESAs: ↑ blood pressure; caution |

| Study | Intervention | Population | Baseline | Results |
|---|---|---|---|---|
| **Roth *et al.*** [12]<br>(as with Revicki *et al.*) | **Erythropoietin vs placebo** in ND-CKD pts, effect on rate of CKD decline | Used same pt population as Revicki | GFR (ml/min): 10.2 ESA vs 10 untreated | • △GFR (ml/min): -2.1 ESA vs -2.8 untreated; NS $_{p=0.376}$ |
| **Levin *et al.*** [13]<br>~24mos; n=152;<br>RCT, OL, ITT 🍁 | **Early$_{\&High}$ vs Delayed$_{\&Low}$ ESA** in ND-CKD pts<br>Erythropoietin 2000IU/wk initial dose given to:<br>1) study group to maintain Hgb 120-140g/L,<br>2) control group with a Hgb of 90g/L or less before treatment with a target of 90-105g/L | ND-CKD; Age $_{mean}$ ~57,<br>~30% female, 38% DM,<br>GFR$_{mean}$~29$_{ml/min}$; all pts "iron replete" (TSAT>20%, ferritin>60$_{ug/L}$) | Hgb (g/L): 117.3 delayed vs 117.6 early<br>**LVMI (g/m²): 98.3 delayed vs 100.6 early** | • △Hgb (g/L): -3 delayed vs 9.8 early<br>• **△LVMI@24mos(g/m²):+5.2 delayed vs +0.4 early;NS $_{p=0.28}$** |
| **CREATE** [14]<br>~3yrs; n=603;<br>RCT, OL | **Early/High-Hgb vs Late/Low-Hgb Erythropoietin** in CKD pts<br>Erythropoietin given to target:<br>1) start when Hgb 110-125g/L, target 130-150g/L<br>2) start when Hgb 100g/L, target 105-115g/L | Stage 3-4 ND-CKD; Age $_{mean}$ ~59,<br>~46% female, 26% DM<br>Included: CrCl=15-35$_{ml/min}$, Hgb<110$_{g/L}$<br>Excluded: uncontrolled HTN<br>**Of Note:** Wt (kg): 74.7 early/high-hgb vs 71.8 late/low-hgb; p=0.05 | Hgb (g/L): 116 early/high vs 116 late/low<br>Ferritin (ug/L): 174 early/high vs 189 late/low<br>TSAT (%):25.6 early/high vs 38.1 late/low<br>LVMI (g/m²): 120 early/high vs 118 late/low<br>GFR (ml/min): 24.9 early/high vs 24.2 late/low | • CV Composite (sudden death, MI, acute HF, stroke, TIA, hosp'n for angina, complication of PVD, or hosp'n for arrhythmia): 18% $^{58\ events}$ early/high vs 14% $^{47\ events}$ late/low; HR=0.78, NS $_{p=0.20}$<br>• △LVMI @2yrs(g/m2): -4.6 early/high vs -3.3 late/low; NS<br>• △QOL@2yr(SF-36): better general health with early/high $_{p=0.008}$ & **vitality $_{p=0.01}$**<br>• △eGFR (ml/min/yr): -3.6 early/high vs -3.1 late/low; NS<br>• **Dialysis: 127 early/high vs 111 late/low; p=0.03**<br>• **HTN (sys>160): 89 early/high vs 59 late/low; p=0.005** |
| **CHOIR** [15]<br>Median 16mos;<br>n=1432; RCT, OL<br>**EARLY TERMINATION** | **Erythropoietin to High-** $_{130\ (130\text{-}135)}$ **vs Low-Hgb** $_{113\ (105\text{-}110)}$ in CKD pts | Stage 3-4 ND-CKD; Age $_{mean}$ ~66,<br>~55% female, GFR~27$_{ml/min}$<br>Included: CrCl=15-50$_{ml/min}$, Hgb<110$_{g/L}$<br>Excluded: uncontrolled HTN<br>**Of Note:**<br>HTN (%): 95.8 high-hgb vs 93.2 low-hgb; p=0.03<br>CABG (%): 17.4 vs 13.5; p=0.05 | Hgb (g/L): 101 high vs 101 low<br>Ferritin (ug/L): 168 high vs 179 low<br>TSAT (%): 25.2 high vs 24.6 low | • Composite (death, MI, hosp'n for CHF, stroke): 125 events (18%) high vs 97 events (14%) low; HR=1.34, **p=0.03**, NNH=25 over 16months (driven by death & hosp's)<br>• Death: 52 high vs 36 low; NS, HR=1.48, **p=0.07**<br>• △QOL: significant differences in only 1 of 12 categories (emotional role)<br>• Any serious AE: 376 (54.8%) high vs 334 (48.5%) low; p=0.02<br>• Any serious AE assoc'd w/ESA: 10 (1.5%) high vs 3 (0.4%) low; p=0.05<br>• CHF: 77 (11.2%) high vs 51 (7.4%) low; p=0.02 |
| **Canadian EPO Study group** [16]<br>~6mos; n=118;<br>RCT, DB 🍁 | **Erythropoietin to high-Hgb** $_{115\text{-}130}$ **vs Erythropoietin to low-Hgb** $_{95\text{-}110}$ **vs Placebo** in HD-CKD pts<br>Intially erythropoietin 100u/kg/dose 3xweekly; all pts with ferritin<250ug/L received oral or IV iron 1 month prior, & prn during the study | HD-CKD;<br>Age $_{mean}$ ~43-44 epo vs 48 placebo;<br>Hgb<90g/L | Hgb (g/L): 71 high vs 69 low vs 71 placebo | • △Sickness $^{impact\ profile}$: 7.8 high vs 5.3 low vs 2.9 placebo<br>• △ Stress test $^{m\ walked}$: 51 high vs 33 low vs 19 placebo<br>• Mean dose (units/kg/wk): 248 high vs 204 low<br>• Hgb (g/L): 117 high vs 102 low vs 74 placebo<br>• Dialysis access site clots: 7/38 high vs 4/40 low vs 1/40 placebo<br>• △BP (sys/dia): 0/+7 high vs 0/+2 low vs -4/-1 placebo |
| **Parfrey *et al.*** [17]<br>~96wks; n=596;<br>RCT, DB 🍁 | **Erythropoietin to High$_{135\text{-}145}$- vs Low $_{95\text{-}115}$ Hgb** in dialysis pts without symptomatic heart dx or LV dilation<br>Arms divided into "concentric LVH" & "LV dilation" | HD-CKD; Age $_{mean}$ ~50.8,<br>~60% male<br>**Of Note:**<br>Age: 52.2 high-hgb vs 49.4 low-hgb; p=0.02<br>SBP $_{mmHg}$: 144 high-hgb vs 140 low-hgb; p=0.02 | LVVI (ml/m²) gp: 296 high vs 300 $^{low}$<br>LVMI (g/m²) gp: 122 high vs 123 low<br>Hgb (g/L): 110 high vs 110 low<br>TSAT (%): 35.7 high vs 36.8 low | • %△LVVI (%): 7.6 high-hgb vs 8.3 low-hgb; NS<br>• %△LVMI (%): 16.8 high vs 14.2 low; NS<br>• Mean Hgb (g/L) @24wks: 133 high vs 109 low<br>• **△QOL @ (SF-36): 1.21 high vs -2.31 low; p=0.036**<br>• TSAT (%): 34.6 high vs 34.2 low |
| **Foley *et al.*** [18]<br>~48wks; n=146;<br>RCT 🍁 | **Erythropoietin to High**$_{135\ (130\text{-}140)}$ **vs Low**$_{100\ (95\text{-}105)}$ **Hgb** effect on cardiomyopathy in dialysis pts | HD-CKD; Age $_{mean}$ ~62,<br>~45% male in LVH group,<br>~78% male in dilation group | LVMI (g/m²): 147 high vs 139 low<br>LVCVI (g/m²): 122 high vs 123 low | • △LVMI @48wks (g/m²): NS; p=0.35$_{Mann\text{-}Whitney\ U\text{-}test}$<br>• △LVCVI @48wks (g/m²): NS; p=0.13$_{Mann\text{-}Whitney\ U\text{-}test}$<br>• △Hgb (g/L): 122.5 high vs 104 low<br>• Improvement in high group: fatigue $_{p=0.009}$, depression $_{p=0.02}$, & relationship $_{p=0.004}$ |
| **Besarab** [19]<br>Median 14mos; n=1233;<br>**EARLY TERMINATION** | **Erythropoietin to "Normal"-** $_{42\%}$ **vs Low-HCT** $_{30\%}$ in CKD pts w/ clinical evidence of HF or ischemic heart dx<br>"Normal Hematocrit Study" | HD-CKD; Age $_{mean}$ ~65,<br>~50% female,<br>Dialysis duration ~3.2yrs, ~44% DM,<br>~51% Class II $_{NYHA\ HF}$ (no class IV) | HCT (%): 30.5 high vs 30.5 low | • Time to death or 1st non-fatal MI: didn't reach SS, term'd early<br>• Death/1st non-fatal MI: 202 high vs 164 $^{low}$; RR=1.3 $_{95\%\ CI\ 0.9\text{-}1.9}$;<br>Deaths: 183 high vs 150 low; Non-fatal MI: 19 high vs 14 low<br>• improved physical functioning |
| **Tonelli *et al.*** [20] 🍁 | **Erythropoietin to High- vs Low-Hgb** in CKD pts: Cost-effectiveness<br>Target Hgb $_{g/L}$: 110-120, 120-125, 140 vs 95-105 | HD-CKD;<br>"typical US dialysis centre" population | IV Dose $^{(units\ 3X/wk)}$ to achieve Hgb targets: 95-105=3523, 110-120=5078, 120-125=6097, 140=9341 | • Cost/QALY: 110-120 vs 95-105 =$ 55,295;<br>120-125 vs 110-120 =$ 613,015;<br>140 vs 120-125 = $ 828,215 |
| **TREAT** [21] 🍁<br>Median 29mos;<br>n~4038;<br>RCT, DB, ITT, multi-centred | **Darbepoetin to High- vs Low-Hgb in CKD pts with type 2 diabetes**<br>Target Hgb $_{g/L}$: **130** in study group vs "placebo" control (**≥90** placebo or if <90, then darbepoetin to >90) | ND-CKD & diabetes<br>Age $_{mean}$ ~68yrs, ~56% female, eGFR ~33ml/min, BMI=30, CV hx ~65%, DM: 15yr history, A1C ~7%, on iron tx ~44%<br>Included: eGFR$_{MDRD}$ 20-60$_{ml/min/1.73m^2}$, Hgb<110$_{g/L}$, TSAT>15%<br>Excluded: uncontrolled HTN, kidney transplant, CA, HIV, bleeding, preg | Hgb (g/L): 105 High vs 104 Low<br>Ferritin (ug/L): 131 darbe vs 137 Low<br>TSAT (%): 23 High vs 23 Low<br>Heart Failure (%): 31.5 High vs 35.2 low; p=0.01<br>FACT-Fatigue score (0$^{least\ tired}$-52$^{most\ tired}$): 30.2 High vs 30.4 Low; | • 1⁰ outcome (death or CV event nonfatal MI, CHF, stroke, hosp'n for angina): 632 $^{31.4\%}$ High $_{130\ Target}$ vs 302 $^{29.7\%}$Low $_{90\ Target}$; NS<br>• 1⁰ outcome (death or ESRD): 652 $^{32.4\%}$ High vs 618 $^{30.5\%}$ Low; NS<br>• **↑stroke 101 $^{5\%}$ High vs 53 $^{2.6\%}$ Low, HR=1.92 $_{95\%CI\ 1.38\text{-}2.68}$; p<0.001, NNH=42 / 2.4yr**<br>• Hgb (g/L) achieved: **125** High vs **106** Low<br>• **Venous Thromboembolisms: 41 $^{2.0\%}$ High vs. 23 $^{1.1\%}$Low; p=0.02**<br>• **Arterial Thromboembolisms: 178 $^{8.9\%}$ High vs. 144 $^{7.1\%}$Low; p=0.04**<br>• **ESRD: 338 $^{16.8\%}$ High vs. 330 $^{16.3\%}$ Low; NS**<br>• **Transfusions: 15% High vs. 25% Low; p<0.001**<br>• **Fatigue: +4.2 High vs. +2.8 Low; p<0.001**<br>**Note: 46% "placebo" had darbepoetin rescue, but ↓QALY** |

• ESAs: ↓ need for blood **transfusions**, which come with their own set of complications
• No clinical benefit has been shown with tx with ESAs early Levin & CREATE, therefore
**Tx should be withheld until Hgb is sustained below 100g/L & iron stores are repleted & other causes of anemia considered** CSN 2008 Guidelines
• LV mass: Pts treated to low or high Hgb targets do not show difference in progression of LV mass in HD-CKD Parfrey & Foley or ND-CKD Levin & CREATE
• QOL in HD-CKD: high Hgb showed improvement in quality of life, but the effect **waned** over time Parfrey & Foley
• QOL in ND-CKD: Varying results show few areas are improved by treating with ESAs early & to higher targets CREATE, CHOIR, & TREAT, & what effects are seen do **diminish** over time CREATE
• Worsening kidney function in ND-CKD: No studies have shown significant difference in tx to high vs low Hgb targets & the contribution to worsening eGFR Roth & TREAT (may ↑ dialysis if tx to higher targets CREATE, or may have no association TREAT)
• Hard endpoints in HD-CKD: Studies showing hard endpoints, such as time to death or 1st MI Besarab, show treating to high Hgb targets >130 may produce more **harm** than good FDA warnings
• Hard(er) endpoints in ND-CKD: Studies comparing composite CV endpoints show tx to high Hgb targets >130 may lead to **↑CV events** CREATE & CHOIR and stroke TREAT, though there are some limitations to studies {CREATE: ?under-powered, CHOIR: see "Of note"; no iron protocol used, TREAT: 46% of "placebo" group received study drug for rescue}
• Meta-analysis of 9 RCTs (all n>100, follow-up >12wks) with CKD pts who were randomly assigned to receive ESAs showed that targeting higher Hgb levels lead to ↑ all-cause mortality (RR=1.17, p=0.031) & AV access thrombosis (RR=1.34, p=0.0001)
• Results of **TREAT** reinforce that treating to higher i.e. physiologic Hgb levels Target: 130 g/L, achieved 125 may come with **significant risks** & only modest improvements in quality of life

**CKD**=chronic kidney dx **ESRD**=end-stage renal dx **C-G**=Cockroft-Gault **dx**=disease **ESA**=Erythropoiesis stimulating agent **FeSO4**=ferrous sulfate **Hct**=hematocrit **HD-CKD**=dialysis-CKD **HF**=heart failure **Hgb**=hemoglobin **HRQL**=health-related QOL **ITT**=intention to treat **LFT**=liver function tests **LVMI**=left ventricular mass index **LVVI**=left ventricular volume index **LVCVI**=left ventricular cavity volume index **MCV**=Mean corpuscular volume **MI**=myocardial infarction **ND-CKD**=non-dialysis CKD **OL**=open label **pt**=patient **QALY**=quality-adjusted life year **QOL**=quality of life **RCT**=randomized control trial **RDW**=Red cell distribution width **TIBC**=total iron binding capacity **TSAT**=transferrin saturation **TSH**=thyroid stimulating hormone ♀=female △=changes

| **Anemia Management Recommendations** | **CSN 2008 Guideline** [22] | **K/DOQI 2007 Guideline** Update [23] | **EBPG 2004 Guideline** [24] | **UK-RA 2006 Guideline** [25] | **CARI 2008 Hgb & 2006 Iron Guideline** [26] | **CADTH 2008** Systematic Review & Economic Evaluation [27] | **K/DIGO Summary** [28] |
|---|---|---|---|---|---|---|---|
| ☆ Hgb (g/L) target | 110 | 110-120 | >110 | 105-125 | 110-120 (120-140 if no CV dx) | 110 | • Hgb>130 can be associated with harm<br>• Hgb=95-115g/L associated with better outcomes than >130<br>• For Hgb=115-130 there is no evidence to suggest harm or benefit compared with ↑ or ↓ levels<br>• Recommended iron levels are directed at optimizing ESA use & target hgb levels<br>• Lack of info comparing efficacy/safety of various iron preps, regimens & administration routes |
| range | 100-120 | <130 | <120 if severe CV dx<br><140 pre-dialysis | Adjust dose when <110 or >120 | <130g/L | | |
| TSAT (%) | >20 | >20 | | | >20 consider 30-40 in HD | | |
| Ferritin (ug/L) in ND-CKD | >100 | >100 | | | >100 | | |
| Ferritin (ug/L) in HD-CKD | >200 | >200 | | | 200-500 | | |

**CADTH**=Canadian Agency for Drugs & Technologies in Health **CARI**=Caring for Australians with Renal Insufficiency **CSN**=Canadian Society of Nephrologists **EBPG**=European Best Practice guidelines **K/DIGO**=Kidney Disease Improving Global Outcomes **K/DOQI**=Kidney Disease Outcomes Quality Initiative **UK-RA**=United Kingdom Renal Assoc.

## When should ESAs be initiated?

- **Start ESAs when Hgb sustained below 100g/L & all other causes of anemia have been corrected** including IDA Opinion/CSN2008
- **Adequate response requires**:
  1) Maintain sufficient **iron stores**: Attempt with oral iron, but **IV** necessary if SE & in most HD-CKD pts; Supplemental iron replacement useful if serum **transferrin saturation (TSAT) is <20%**, or **serum ferritin** <100 ug/L in ND-CKD or <200 ug/L in HD-CKD; or {assess serum Vit B12 & folate}.
  2) Other causes of anemia should be corrected before ESA treatment started.

## How should ESAs be dosed?

- **USUAL Dose**: Individualized to achieve & maintain Hgb 100-120g/L { HD-CKD:draw Hgb level mid-week pre-dialysis}. For many pts, the **maintenance dose will be lower than starting dose** (esp. for ND-CKD). The optimal Hgb in ESRD is **unknown**; however, in pts with a Hgb <100g/L, there is some evidence of deterioration in left ventricular hypertrophy, cerebral function, & quality of life 1999 CSN.

## How can ESA therapy be monitored? What are the goals?

- Hgb q1-2 wk during tx **initiation** or after major ESA/iron dose **adjustment** (if unexpected rapid ↑ occurs).
- Hgb q1mon, Ferritin & TSAT (=serum iron/TIBC) q1-3mos

**Once stable** Hgb achieved with ESA/iron in ND-CKD or HD-CKD, monitor **Hgb MONTHLY** prudent given possible fluctuations as pts get ill, GI bleeds or ESA adverse effects (ND-CKD: less likely to have rapidly changing Hgb if clinically stable, therefore, if stable Hgb & stable ESA dose over several months, consider Hgb less than monthly CSN Guidelines 2008).

**Goals: If on ESA Hgb target = 100 – 120g/L** Grade A/CSN Guidelines 2008 **, and,**
**ND-CKD: maintain TSAT >20% & ferritin >100 ug/L; HD-CKD: maintain TSAT >20% & ferritin >200 ug/L.**
**Transfusions: reduce number & risk of complications.**
**Improve quality of life.**

## How should doses be adjusted?

- **Dose adjustment** should not be made **more than once/month**, unless clinically indicated. Dose adjust ESA in **outpatient setting ~q2months**, since most Hgb changes not seen for 2-6 weeks. KDOQI 2007, 1
- **Hgb Deviations** away from target=110g/L or Hgb rise >10g/l: (**Small** dose **adjustments** 10-20% prevent large fluctuations)
  - If no significant Hgb change >10 g/L over previous month, **adjust ESA only when Hgb outside of 100-120g/L** 2008 CSN. (↓ **ESA** dose if Hgb >115g/L & trending higher, or Hgb >10g/L over previous month; ↑ **ESA** if Hgb <105g/L & trending lower.)
  - If **Hgb 120-140** g/L – ↓ dose. If **Hgb >140** g/L consider holding, until Hgb approaches upper end of range ~120, then restart ESA at a lower dose (Consider monitoring Hgb every 2 weeks in these pts).
- **Timeline- from initiation to reach target**: Optimal to reach Hgb target **within 2-4 months**. If **Hgb** rise **inadequate** (<5g/L in 1month), then ↑dose by **25-50%**. (Smaller dose adjustments ⇒ less fluctuation) If **Hgb** rise is **excessive** (>10 g/L in 1 month), ↓ dose by **20-30%** 2008 CSN.
- If holding, use caution, since impact of holding is most evident ~2 months later. If ESA is held, Hgb may roller coaster or cycle to > or < than target KDOQI. ie. Lower ESA dose, not hold, when a ↓ Hgb is needed.

## What about ESA resistance? (May be due to a chronic inflammatory state due to dialysis)

**Suggested when**: **Eprex** ≥300 units/kg/wk or ≥20,000 units/wk or **Aranesp** ≥1.5 mcg/kg/wk or ≥100 mcg/wk[5].

**Etiologies**: 1) Patient non-compliance Iron or epoetin. 2) **Iron deficiency** Most pts will require iron tx. 3) Underlying **infection**, inflammation, or malignancy Inhibits iron transfer from storage to bone marrow; suppresses erythropoiesis through activated macrophages. 4) Occult blood loss counteracts epoetin-stimulated erythropoiesis. 5) Dialysis adequacy. 6) Underlying hematologic dx E.g. thalassemia, refractory anemia, or other myelodysplastic dx. 7) Vitamin deficient – **folic acid** or B12 Limits Hgb synthesis. 8) Hemolysis Counteracts epoetin-stimulated erythropoiesis. 9) Drug therapy – marrow suppressants, ACE-I, calcium-iron DIs. 10) Aluminum intoxication Inhibits iron incorporation into heme protein. 11) Pure Red Cell Aplasia PRCA. 12) Bone marrow replacement; hyperparathyroidism Osteitis fibrosa cystica; metastatic, neoplastic limits bone marrow volume. 13) TSH level – hypothyroidism anemia can mimic erythropoietin deficiency. 14) Albumin level nutrition status.

<table>
<tr><th>Generic / TRADE<br>Strength/Forms, Pregnancy</th><th>Indications, Administration, Storage</th><th>Side effects SE, Contraindications CI,<br>Drug Interactions DI</th><th>Dose, Monitoring</th><th>Cost $</th></tr>
<tr><td colspan="5">ESAs- Erythropoiesis Stimulating Agent; ↓transfusion & ↑quality of life; Erthropoiesis Regulating Hormone = Glycoprotein: stimulates RBC production. Produced in kidney & elsewhere, stimulates division & differentiation of erythroid progenitors in bone marrow.</td></tr>
<tr><td>Epoetin alfa EPREX Approved FDA 1989<br><br>Single-use pre-filled syringes with PROTECS needle guard: (HSA-free) C<br>1,000 IU/0.5 mL, 2,000 IU/0.5 mL, 3,000 IU/0.3 mL, 4,000 IU/0.4 mL, 5,000 IU/0.5 mL, 6,000 IU/0.6 mL, 8,000 IU/0.8 mL, 10,000 IU/mL, 20,000 IU/0.5 mL, 30,000 IU/0.75 mL, 40,000 IU/mL<br><br>Unavailable: Eprex® Multi-use Vial 20,000 IU/mL which had benzyl alcohol.</td><td>✓ ↑/maintain RBC level (via HCT/Hgb & ↓transfusions)<br>✓ Tx Anemia of Chronic Renal Failure (dialysis & non)<br>✓ Zidovudine-treated HIV pts, Chemotherapy in pts with non-myeloid malignancies but >$70,000/QALY, ↓allogeneic blood exposure & facilitate autologous blood collection<br>Administration: DO NOT SHAKE<br>IV: over 1-5min depending on dose/previous SE. Admin is independent of dialysis procedure, may give into venous line during dialysis to obviate need for additional venous access.<br>SubQ Inj: Max inj volume is 1 mL. If >1ml, use more than 1 site.<br>Storage (Pre-filled syringe): No preservative. Discard if unused. May remove from fridge & store @room temp not >25° C max 7day.</td><td rowspan="2">SE: Well-tolerated but at ↑Hgb i.e. >120g/L higher death, stroke, cancer & clot.<br>Hypertension 5-24%, dose dependent BP ↑ or aggravate existing HTN, ↑ monitoring {Do not stop tx if uncontrolled HTN develops}; ↑death if HD-CKD with symptomatic cardiac dx & ND-CKD pts when Hgb >120g/L CHOIR; ↑stroke if ND-CKD when Hgb>120 g/L TREAT; hemodialysis access thrombosis 7-8%; lower hemodialysis adequacy if ↑Hgb targets;<br>Pure Red Cell Aplasia (PRCA), seizures very rare;<br>Influenza-like illness h/a's, joint pain, myalgia & pyrexia – esp @ start of treatment, If giving IV, a slower injection may be preferred (e.g. 5mins) for 1st 2 doses to avoid flu-like reaction,<br>Hypersensitivity reactions rash, urticaria, angioneurotic edema & anaphylactic reaction<br>Suspect PRCA: in any pt on ESA for > 4wks who develops a sudden, rapid ↓Hgb level (>5 g/L/wk) or transfusion at >1 UNIT red cell/wk while showing a normal white cell & platelet, & a low absolute reticulocyte count <10 x 109/L. Incidence ~0.5 cases/10,000 pt yrs. Cases only reported after SubQ exposure. Epoetin alfa: >200 cases worldwide. Anemia after 3-67 months of tx.[1]<br>CI: uncontrolled HTN >180/110, previous PRCA following ESA tx, hypersensitivity to drug/excipient mammalian cell-derived meds; EPREX in pts scheduled for elective surgery & not with an autologous blood donation program if severe coronary, peripheral arterial, carotid, or cerebral vascular dx.<br>Caution: Cancer, cardiac disease, seizure history, underlying hematologic disease (e.g. hemolytic anemia, sickle cell anemia, thalassemia, porphyria).<br>DI: ACE-Inhibitors–reversible resistance case reports. Caution with myelosuppressive agents – azathioprine, chemotherapy & cyclophosphamide.<br>Benefit: less transfusions & less fatigue</td><td>SubQ in ND-CKD & PD-CKD;<br>IV or SubQ in HD-CKD 2,3<br>Initial: 50-100 units/kg IV or SubQ 2-3x/wk [1]<br>Option: HD-CKD: 75 units/kg 2x/week IV or ND-CKD: 50-100 units/kg SubQ once weekly<br><br>Epoetin often 1-3 x/week, but in ND-CKD may give once per week or q2-4 weeks limited evidence.<br><br>IV: requires ↑ dose vs SubQ (a ~30% ↑ in dose)</td><td>$16 / 1,000 IU syringe<br>$5000-10,000/yr<br>☎ & Φ: 1st choice; -Anemia in chronic renal dx pts prior to dialysis initiation, or AIDs, or transplant pts.<br>NIHB-on CRF formulary.<br>100% covered by SPDP for SAIL pts.</td></tr>
<tr><td>Darbepoetin alfa ARANESP<br>Approved FDA 2001 C<br><br>SingleJect Prefilled Syringes:<br>10, 20, 30, 40, 50, 60, 80, 100, 130, 150, 200, 300, 500 mcg/syringe</td><td>✓ Tx Anemia of Chronic Renal Failure (dialysis & non)<br>✓Tx of anemia in nonmyeloid malignancies<br><br>Storage: at 2-8°C. Do not freeze or shake. Protect from light. (Does not contain preservatives; do not use if left at room temperature up to 25°C for >24 hours)</td><td>SubQ in ND-CKD & PD-CKD; IV or SubQ in HD-CKD.<br>CKD Anemia: 0.45 mcg/kg IV or SubQ once weekly. SQ every 2-4 weeks in some<br><br>If on Eprex 2-3x/week, change to qweekly Aranesp at a dose equivalent to the total weekly Eprex dose.<br>If on Eprex 1x/week, change to q2wks Aranesp at a dose equivalent to 2x the weekly Eprex dose.<br><br><table><tr><th colspan="2">Conversion between Exprex & Aranesp</th></tr><tr><th>Eprex (units/wk)</th><th>Aranesp (mcg/wk)</th></tr><tr><td><2,500</td><td>~10</td></tr><tr><td>2,500-4,999</td><td>10-20</td></tr><tr><td>5,000-10,999</td><td>20-30</td></tr><tr><td>11,000-17,999</td><td>40</td></tr><tr><td>18,000-33,999</td><td>60</td></tr><tr><td>34,000-89,999</td><td>100</td></tr><tr><td>>90,000</td><td>200</td></tr></table></td><td>$29 - 570 per syringe<br>$5000-10,000/yr<br>☎ & Φ: if Eprex intolerant/ineffective; Anemia in chronic renal dx pts prior to dialysis.<br>NIHB-on CRF formulary.<br>100% if covered by SPDP for SAIL pts.<br>Aranesp AIDE Info: 1-800-665-4273</td></tr>
<tr><td>Methoxy polyethylene glycol-epoetin beta[4] MIRCERA Approved FDA 2007 C</td><td>✓ Tx of anemia with CKD</td><td colspan="3">✗ ⊗ Not on formulary. Not yet available in Canada {NOC received Mar 2008, but ongoing patent-infringement lawsuit with Amgen makers of Aranesp has halted advancement}.</td></tr>
</table>

=↓dose renal dysfx Φ =SAIL Sk Program ☎ =Exception Drug Status in SK ✗ =Non-formulary SK ✓ =prior approval for NIHB ⊗=not covered NIHB ▼ covered NIHB; **BP**=blood pressure **CKD**=chronic kidney dx **CRF**=chronic renal failure **DX**=disease **ESAs**=Erythropoiesis stimulating agent **ESRD**=end stage renal dx **h/a**=headache **HCT**=hemocrit **HD**=hemo-dialysis **Hgb**=hemoglobin **HTN**=hypertension **HSA**=human serum albumin **IDA**=iron deficiency anemia **inj**=injection **ND-CKD**=Non-Dialysis-CKD **PD**=Peritoneal Dialysis **Pt**=patient **QALY**=quality adjusted life year **RBC**=red blood cell **Rx**=reaction **SE**=side effects **SubQ**=subcutaneous **Tx**=treat.

**Health Canada Warning** 2007 **Hgb** levels during ESA tx should **not be >120**g/L (May not be applicable to all surgery pts). Patients treated with EPREX before elective surgery should receive antithrombotic therapy to ↓ blood clots. A ↑risk of **death** & CV events (stroke, heart attack & clots) seen in cancer & CKD pts. A ↑ risk of **death** seen in pts with **cancer** & anemia who were not on radiation or chemotherapy. (ESAs are not authorized for use in these pts). Tumor growth progression in pts with head & neck cancer with radiation treatment only. Also ↑ death in pts with metastatic breast cancer receiving chemo. 5,6,7

**Initiate** ESA treatment when iron stores are corrected, other reversible causes of anemia treated, & Hgb is sustained <100 g/L.

**Target Hgb 110 g/L Range: 100-120 g/L** 8 CSN 2008 (Target Hgb: 110-120g/L; not >130g/L 9 KDOQI 2007; Hgb Level >130g/L→ assoc. with harm; Hgb 95-115g/L→ assoc. with better outcomes vs >130g/L; Hgb 115-130g/L→ no evidence for harm/benefit vs other level 10 KDIGO 2008)

Amy Wiebe, Peter Ricci, Bonnie Geall, Linda Gross, Zack Dumont May 10

## What is CKD-IDA? What are the categories?

- Causes incl.: ↑blood loss from dialyzer/phlebotomies, ↓iron absorption, ↑intestinal blood loss, & demand of ESA tx. **Ferritin** is the first marker to fall in IDA; low levels correlate with Fe deficiency; **high levels do not correlate well with Fe overload** {(Ferritin is an acute phase reactant: may ↑in renal / liver disease, cancer, infection, RA, SLE, recent surgery, etc). Upper ferritin limit=500ug/L opinion only, KDOQI 2007. If elevated, look for signs of inflammation before assuming overload.}

1) **Absolute** = low Fe stores (TSAT<20%, ferritin<100ug/L).
2) **Functional** =Fe stores normal, but not meet ESA's need TSAT<20%, ferritin normal or ↑.
3) **Reticuloendothelial**(blockade) = ↓iron delivery due to ↑acute phase reactants CRP, TNF, interleukins; TSAT ↓, & ferritin abruptly ↑.

## When should I treat with supplemental iron? Oral or IV?

- Assess iron status in all anemic pts with CKD; If poor/no response **noted after 3 weeks** of oral iron therapy, consider possibility of pt noncompliance, simultaneous blood loss, additional complicating factors, or incorrect diagnosis.
- In ND-CKD, start with oral iron; if poor response or SE, switch to IV.
- In HD-CKD, oral can be used Expert opinion, but IV may be necessary CSN Guideline.

## Which oral iron? How should patients take it?

- Absorption depends on iron form heme vs. non-heme, IR vs. SR, dose, degree of erythropoiesis, diet, stomach acidity, GI diseases, ferritin level & iron stores
- If difficulty tolerating, ↓dose & ↑frequency; start with **lower dose & ↑slowly** to the target dose; try a **different form** or preparation; take with or after meals or **at bedtime**. Usually given **2hr before** or **1hr after meals**, but may be given **with food** to prevent GI irritation; however, **avoid** with cereals, dietary fiber, tea, coffee, eggs, or milk (formation of insoluble complexes with non-heme iron)
- Oral iron best absorbs on an empty stomach. [bioavailability 1% to 50%}.

## What options for loading IV iron? (Not essential for most pts)

- The following regimens may be used to give **~1gram of iron** (=usual load):

ND-CKD or PD-CKD: VENOFER: 300mg IV over 1hr weekly or daily x 3doses;
**Iron Dextran**: Dose(mL) = 0.0442 (Desired Hgb-Observed Hgb) x LBW + (0.26xLBW) {Total Dose Infusion Load: ~1-1.5g/500ml NS over ≥3hr (CKD: reload periodically)};
FERRLECIT: 125mg IV 2x / week x 6 doses.
HD-CKD: VENOFER: 100mg IV qdialysis x 10dose; OR 200mg IV qdialysis x 5 dose;
FERRLECIT: 125mg IV qdialysis x 8 doses;
**Iron Dextran** DEXIRON, INFUFER: 100-400mg IV q2-4wks.

## What are the options for maintaining with IV iron?

1) **Periodic iron repletion:** series of IV iron doses given episodically to replenish stores.
2) **Continuous maintenance tx:** smaller doses given at regular intervals to maintain stores. (ie. once monthly or every 2 weeks)

- For more information see RxFiles "Anemia-Hgb Key Outcome trials Summary"

## How can iron therapy be monitored? What are the goals?

- Monitoring frequency depends on pt clinical status, response to iron (ΔHgb), ESA dose; ↑monitoring if recent ESA tx initiation or ESA hyporesponse.
- **If on ESA**: **Hgb q1mon**, Ferritin & TSAT (=serum iron/TIBC) q1-3month
- **Goals**:
  - ND-CKD: maintain ferritin >100 ug/L & **TSAT >20%.**
  - HD-CKD: maintain ferritin >200 ug/L & **TSAT >20%.**
- **Minimum time to wait after IV admin before re-assessing:**
  a) TSAT: iron sucrose/gluconate wait 48hr, iron dextran wait 1-2 weeks.
  b) Ferritin: wait ≥1 week

**Approach** ND-CKD & PD: **a)** start oral iron if **Hgb<100g/l & have IDA**, or for pt on **ESAs** **b)** use cheapest oral iron eg. **ferrous sulfate**, then expensive oral irons if not tolerated. **c)** if pts remain iron deficient on oral iron, or if not tolerate oral, consider iv but hard on veins
HD: attempt oral, but may need iv iron. Use less expensive iron **dextran**, or sucrose if react

| Generic/TRADE (Strength & forms) g=generic — pregnancy | Side effects SE, Contraindications CI | √ = Therapeutic use / Comments / Drug Interactions DI | Elemental Iron Content/ Half-life | Usual DOSE | $ / dose (Fe content) |
|---|---|---|---|---|---|
| **Ferrous sulfate** OTC χ▼ Φg<br>FER-IN-SOL 300mg tab; 15 & 75mg/ml drop;<br>SLOW FE 6 & 30mg/ml syrup; 150mg tab | **Common**: dark stools will not subside with tx; Generally dose related & ↓with time: constipation, nausea, epigastric pain>10%, diarrhea1-10% {Safer than IV iron forms}<br>CI: hemochromatosis primary, active peptic ulcer, regional enteritis, colitis ulcerative<br>**Precaution**: ↓iron absorption: if partial gastrectomy steatorrhea, or with ER/EC forms which may transport iron past the duodenum & proximal jejunum; **liquid preps** may **stain** teeth with ongoing use (mix with juice/water & drink thru a straw may ↓staining; baking soda may help remove stains).<br>Testing: False positive blood in stool. | √ Prevent & Tx iron deficiency, ND-CKD anemia<br>Anemia of chronic dx-Tx disease, ?transfusion, ?ESA & not iron if ↑ or normal ferritin. (**Disease causes**: infection, cancer, arthritis, lupus, IBD, post transplantation etc.)<br>√ Correct erythropoietic abnormality caused by ↓iron<br>Admin: **hs preferred** to ↑absorption, ↓SE & ↓DI's<br>**Heme iron:** derived from animal proteins, **expensive**, largely unaffected by dietary factors. Better/**more consistent absorption** (~23% more) than non-heme iron.[9]<br>**Non-heme iron:** present in grains & vegetables. Requires acidic GI pH for absorption (**Poor bioavailability**)<br>**Polysaccharide:** Bioavailability questionable, **expensive**<br>DI: ↓ iron absorption: Aluminum containing phosphate binders, antacids, calcium supplements, cholestyramine, **food** ↓absorption by ~50% {Space med by >2-12hr}; $H_2RA$'s & PPI's.<br>↓ drug absorption: bisphosphonates, fluoroquinolones, levothyroxine, methyldopa, penicillamine & tetracyclines.<br>Consider holding iron until antibiotic tx completed. | **Ferrous sulfate** 20% Fe<br>(300mg tab = **60**mg Fe)<br>**Fer-in-Sol drops** ~$20<br>{breast-fed infants ≥6months}<br>(75mg/ml = 15mg Fe)<br>Syrup(30mg/ml = 6mg Fe)<br>**Slow Fe** (160mg tab = 50mg Fe) ~$13/30tabs, 31% Fe -questionable absorption | **Target=180-200mg *elemental* Fe/day or** 2-3mg/kg/day (HD pts may require high dose)<br>{Elderly: lower dose of 15-50mg/day may be effective}<br>Peds: Treat 3-6mg/kg/day; Proph 0.5-2mg/kg/day<br>Titrate dose q3-7d as tolerated (start low go slow)<br>Tx ~3months *after* anemia corrected<br>Tx to target & as tolerated treat pt, not labs<br>{take on empty stomach to ↑absorption, but **with meals to ↓GI SE**}<br>Vit C >100mg marginal ↑absorption (Apple juice with iron may help)<br>Suggested dosing:<br>**Ferrous Sulfate:** 300-600-**900mg po hs**<br>**Ferrous Fumarate:** 300-600**mg po hs**<br>**Oral can be used in HD pts** Expert opinion, **but IV may be necessary.** CSN Guideline | 3 tab sulfate (180mg) =$ 0.18 |
| **Ferrous gluconate** OTC χ▼ Φg<br>FERGON 300 & 324mg tab | | | **Ferrous gluconate** 11% Fe<br>(300mg tab = 35mg Fe) | | 5 tab gluconate (175mg) =$ 0.35 |
| **Ferrous fumarate** OTC χ▼<br>PALAFER Φg<br>300mg cap; 60mg/ml susp; 200 & 300mg tab | | | **Ferrous fumarate** 33% Fe<br>(300mg tab/cap = 100mg Fe) | | 2 tab fumarate (200mg) =$ 0.18 |
| **Polysaccharide iron complex**<br>OTC χ⊗ TRIFEREXX, Polyride Fe<br>150mg cap, 50mg coated tab, 100mg/5ml sol'n | | | **Triferexx** 100% Fe<br>(150mg tab = 150mg Fe) | | 1 cap Complex (150mg) =$ 0.80<br>2 tabs =$ 0.73 |
| **Heme iron polypeptide** OTC χ⊗<br>PROFERRIN 398mg tab<br>-bovine hemoglobin | | | **Proferrin** 100% Fe<br>(398mg tab=11mg heme Fe) | | 3 tabs Heme (33mg heme) =$ 2.25 |
| **IV Products**<br>**Iron sucrose** ☎⊗Φ<br>VENOFER<br>100mg/5 ml vial<br>B | SE: Generally well tolerated. ↓BP, cramps & leg cramps, nausea, headache, fever, vomiting, diarrhea, arthralgia, flushing, back pain, **may impair host defense** (consider holding IV iron during severe infections)<br>**Serious**: rare sensitivity reactions: **Dextran** 0.1-0.6% > >Sucrose or gluconate. (anaphylactoid = **bronchospasm**, **pruritis**, ↓BP, anaphylactic shock, LOC, dyspnea, collapse) allergies or inflammatory conditions may ↑ risk, chest pain, tremor, sweating, seizures.<br>CI: anemia not associated with iron deficiency, acute phase of infectious dx, hemochromatosis, severe hepatic dysfx<br>**Precaution**: iron overload (po & IV iron not tx concomitantly), & with history of allergies/asthma/arthritis (possible fever & exacerbation or reactivation of joint swelling) | √ Recommended route in HD pts oral iron loss > iron absorption<br>√ Prevent functional & absolute iron deficiency & promote erythropoiesis in HD pts on ESA tx KDOQI '06<br>√ Indications: if oral not tolerated, inadequate response to oral Fe, inadequate response to ESA, severe anemia, or if very low Fe stores.<br>√ Efficacious for ↑Hgb & ↓ESA use in HD pts Fishbane<br>Administration: Slow inj to ↓the risk of ↓BP<br>Reassess iron therapy if: TSAT ≥50% or serum ferritin ≥500 ug/L KDOQI 2006<br>"If below target Hgb, or requiring high ESA doses, **consider iron tx** to ↑Hgb if serum ferritin is >800 ug/L & TSAT is <25%. In this circumstance, physicians should carefully assess the risks & benefits of ongoing iron administration" CSN guidelines, DRIVE<br>DI: none known; do not mix with other IVs/TPN solution (Iron dextran has been added to some TPN solutions) | (100mg inj = 100mg Fe)<br>T ½ = ~6h | ND-CKD: **LD=**300mg IV in 250mL **NS over 1hr** qwk x 3wk;<br>**MD=**200mg IV undiluted over ≥15min q1-3mon (Dose Individualized based on TSAT)<br>HD-CKD: **LD=**100mg IV undiluted over 2-5 min OR diluted in 100ml **NS** over 15min qdialysis x 10dose; *OR*, 200mg IV undiluted over 2-5 min qdialysis x5dose;<br>**MD=**100-**200**mg IV undiluted over 2-5 min q2-4wk Max 300mg | $41/ 100mg dose |
| **Iron dextran** ☎▼Φ<br>DEXIRON, INFUFER<br>50mg/ml injection (2 & 5ml vials)<br>C | | | (100mg inj = 100mg Fe)<br>T ½ = ~40-60h<br>{**IM**- if route chosen give deep via Z track; needle ~20g, 5cm; but not usually recommended} | **Test dose required: 25mg IV/IM→wait 1hr** see bottom note +<br>ND-CKD: **LD=**Dose (mL) = ~1-1.5g/500ml NS over ≥3hr ⇒ 0.0442 (Desired Hgb – Observed Hgb) x LBW + (0.26xLBW)<br>**MD=**100-400mg IV in 100mL **NS** over 1hr q2-3mon<br>HD-CKD: Calculate pt dose based on wt, age, sex, degree of anemia by table/formula, *OR*, 100-400mg IV in 100ml **NS** over 1hr q2-**4**wks<br>**Max=1-1.5g/dose; some require a lower dose** | $28/ 100mg dose |
| **Iron sodium ferric gluconate** ☎⊗Φ+ benzyl alcohol<br>FERRLECIT<br>12.5mg/ml inj (5ml amp)<br>B | | | (100mg inj = 100mg Fe)<br>T ½ = ~1h | ND-CKD: **LD=**125mg IV undiluted over ≥10 min 2x/wk x 6dose;<br>**MD=**125mg IV undiluted over ≥10 min qmonth<br>HD-CKD: **LD=**125mg IV undiluted over ≥10 min OR diluted in 100ml **NS** over 1hr qdialysis x 8 dose;<br>**MD=**125mg IV undiluted over ≥10 min q2weeks<br>**Max=125mg/dose; severe SE with ↑ doses** | $51/ 125mg dose |

χ=Non-formulary Sk ☎=Exception Drug Status Sk ⊗=not covered NIHB ▼=covered NIHB **BP**=blood pressure **CKD**=chronic kidney dx **CRI**=chronic renal insufficiency **HD-CKD**=dialysis CKD **Dx**=diagnosis/disease **EC**=enteric coated **Epo**=erythropoietin **ESA**=erythropoietin-stimulating agent **ER**=extended release **Fe**=iron **Fx**=function **Hgb**=hemoglobin **IBD**=inflammatory bowel dx **IDA**=iron deficiency anemia **LOC**=loss of consciousness **LD**=loading dose **MD**=maintenance dose **ND-CKD**=non-dialysis CKD **NS**=normal saline **PD-CKD**=peritoneal-dialysis CKD **Pt**=patient **SE**=side effect **TIBC**=total iron binding capacity **TSAT**=transferrin saturation **T ½**=half-life **Tx**=treat **wk**=week **wt**=weight

**Coverage**: Dialysis pts coverage is provided under Sask. Aids to Independent Living (SAIL) Program Φ (EDS coverage not required for SAIL). **In USA**: ferumoxytol 510mg fe/17ml vial, IV at ≤ 1ml/sec Feraheme. **PD-CKD** is dosed like **ND-CKD**.

**+ Dextran Sensitivity Test**: Give initial **test dose**: Administer slow IV >5 min of 0.5 mL 25 mg iron, observe ≥1hr for sensitivity reactions before giving remainder. Subsequent test not needed if no immediate reaction with initial dose. Resuscitative meds & personnel trained in anaphylaxis need to be available. Observe for signs of anaphylactoid reactions for first 15 mins after initiation of all IV iron doses & q15-30 mins thereafter until end of infusion.

## Adverse Events

### What is an Adverse Reaction (AR)?

Health Canada defines an AR as "a noxious and unintended response to a drug which occurs with use or testing for the diagnosis, treatment, or prophylaxis of a disease or modification of an organic function. This includes **any** undesirable patient effect suspected to be associated with drug use."

### Overview of the Problem

**Canadian Adverse Events (AEs) Study** [1]

- *By the numbers…*
  - **7.5%** is the overall incidence of AEs for patients admitted into Canadian hospitals
  - **185,000** of 2.5 million annual hospital admissions in Canada were due to AEs
  - **70,000 (37%) AE related admissions were** potentially preventable
  - **23.6%** were drug or fluid related
  - **1 in 9** ER visits are drug related events 68% preventable ; ZED CMAJ'08
- AEs are reported in 6% of patients taking **1-3 medications** and in **52%** of patients taking **8 or more medications.**[2]
- Incidence of AE in ambulatory patients is from **3-68%.**[3,4]
- Antibiotic AE visits to US Emergency rooms 140,000/yr Shehab'08

### Addressing the Problem: ISMP www.ismp-canada.org

- The Institute for Safe medication Practices (ISMP) is an organization seeking to address drug safety issues. See website!

### Problem Medications

**Drugs most likely to land a patient in the Emergency Room [5]:**

- **anti-platelet agents** (ASA, clopidogrel PLAVIX & **pain-killers** (acetaminophen, NSAIDS, opioids)
- 1/3 of events are due to **allergies (antibiotics)**
- 1/3 of events are due to **unintentional overdose**
  - **acetaminophen, anticonvulsants, diabetes meds, digoxin, lithium, theophylline & warfarin**

Signals for ARs: eg. leucopenia, hypoglycemia, hyperkalemia, falls, & use of naloxone, dextrose or Vitamin K. Handler'08

### Problem Meds in Elderly (comorbidity important)

**Almost 1/3 of adverse drug events in the elderly are caused by just 3 drugs: digoxin, insulin & warfarin.**

Watch to make sure doses are appropriate, esp. for these drugs, and especially in **seniors**. Up to 1/2 of adverse drug events may be due to **too much drug** for the patient's **age, weight, renal function, or diseases.** Be aware of ***Beers** list.* Fick '03

### DRUG INTERACTIONS can be a major factor!

- clinically important CYP450 DI table[6] http://medicine.iupui.edu/flockhart/
- Be on the alert for polypharmacy increasing potential for interactions.

## Minimizing Risk

### High-Alert Medications

High-alert Medications are drugs which bear a heightened risk of causing significant patient harm if used in error.

#### High Alert Medications (adapted from ISMP lists) 7

- Amiodarone, Colchicine, Epoprostenol, Oxytocin IV
- Chemotherapeutic agents
- Heparin (bleeding, thrombocytopenia) protamine sulfate will reverse effect
- Hypoglycemics, oral (e.g. glyburide)
- Insulin SC & IV (severe hypoglycemia)
- Injectables: Lidocaine, Magnesium sulfate inj, Nitroprusside, Potassium, Hypertonic Saline (> 0.9%)
- Methotrexate, oral (non-oncologic)
- Narrow Therapeutic Window Drugs e.g.:
  - Anticonvulsants: Carbamazepine, Phenytoin, Phenobarbital & Valproic Acid
  - Digoxin, Lithium, Theophylline & Warfarin
- Opioids/Narcotics {special caution: **methadone**} DI:alcohol,sedatives
  - (eg. fentanyl, hydromorphone, morphine & oxycodone)

### What can you do? (Minimize interruptions/distractions)

- Make sure patients are **not doubling up** by continuing a **similar drug that should be discontinued or changed.**
- Emphasize close monitoring for patients on warfarin or insulin. Ask them what their last blood work showed.
- Avoid abbreviations (i.e. write "units" instead of "U").
- Use a leading zero before a decimal place (i.e. 0.5mg) and stop using trailing zeros on a dosage (i.e. 5.0mg).
- Write out prescription **legibly** including **indication** for use (especially with look alike, sound alike drugs)
- Always repeat the prescription back a 2nd time when giving/receiving a verbal order.
- When giving a verbal order for dosages such as 15, state one five to prevent interpretations as 50.
- Dose kids by weight & use calibrated measuring devices. Use oral syringes for oral meds, so can't be injected.
- Perform an independent **DOUBLE CHECK** prior to the administration of all high-alert medications. Before giving >3 tabs, caps, amps, syringes TRIPLE check !!!
- Watch out for Dual brand names (eg. Viagra + Revatio)
- Check for **allergies** before writing or filling script

### Medication Reconciliation

- During transfer of care (eg. from home to hospital & back; to new unit or facility; perioperative) communication between health professionals is critical to minimize errors.

### On the Alert for Polypharmacy

- Insure you have complete drug list when writing new Rx!
- Insure patients are not still taking previously stopped meds!

## New Medications to the Market

### Use Caution until Proven Otherwise

- When a new drug comes on the market, little is known about potentially rare and serious adverse events. Most of this information comes with post-marketing surveillance.
- New drugs are heavily marketed during product launch & there may be a tendency to believe newer is better.
- A heightened degree of caution is often warranted over the first 2 - 5 years of a drug coming on the market.
- When looking for drug safety, look for effectiveness evidence on important **clinical outcomes** such as heart disease, stroke and death (if available). Remember the adverse event profile of new drugs may be quite incomplete.
- FYI: **Black Box** warnings: http://www.formularyproductions.com/blackbox/

#### Drugs Recently Removed From The Market

| Drug | Brand | Reason |
|---|---|---|
| Trovafloxacin | *Trovan* | (Hepatic) |
| Cisapride | *Prepulsid* | (Cardiac-QT) |
| Fenfluramine/Dexfenfluramine | *Phen-Fen* | (Cardiac-Valves) |
| Astemizole | *Hismanal* | (Cardiac-QT DI) |
| Grepafloxacin | *Raxar* | (Cardiac-QT) |
| Troglitazone | *Resulin* | (Hepatic) |
| Rofecoxib | *Vioxx* | (Cardiac-MI) |
| Valdecoxib | *Bextra* | (Skin & Cardiac) |

**DI**=drug interaction **QT**=prolong QT interval & Torsades

***New & approved* does not always mean *new and improved.***

### Other:

- **"The Future of Drug Safety: Promoting and Protecting the Health of the Public"** report from the Institute of Medicine (IOM) Committee on the Assessment of the US Drug Safety System September 22, 2006. Link: http://www.iom.edu/CMS/3793/26341/37329.aspx
- **FDA: Potential watch list:** http://www.fda.gov/cder/aers/potential_signals/
- **FDA: Drug Safety:** http://www.fda.gov/Cder/drugSafety.htm
- **FDA Bad Drug Ads:** http://www.fda.gov/Drugs/GuidanceComplianceRegulatoryInformation/Surveillance/DrugMarketingAdvertisingandCommunications/ucm209384.htm

### Reporting an Adverse Reaction

- **What kind of adverse reactions should be reported?**
  - Any temporal/possible/suspected association – drug or natural product, (no proof required) especially:
    - -Reactions to Recently Marketed drugs <5yrs
    - -Serious (resulting in hospitalization, disability, life-threatening, death)
    - -Unexpected Reactions (regardless of severity)
    - -Immunization reactions http://www.phac-aspc.gc.ca/im/aefi-form_e.html
- **Reports** can be submitted by mail, fax, phone or online.
- **MedEffect Website:** reporting; sign-up for mailed warnings & advisories! FAX **1-866-678-6789** Phone **1-866-234-2345**
  - http://www.hc-sc.gc.ca/dhp-mps/medeff/index_e.html
- **AR forms – available from:**
  Compendium of Pharmaceuticals & Specialties (CPS); Other (e.g. Saskatchewan Prescription Drug Plan Formulary Appendix)
  Pdf: http://www.hc-sc.gc.ca/dhp-mps/alt_formats/hpfb-dgpsa/pdf/medeff/ar-ei_form_e.pdf

**Saskatchewan**: **Poison Control Center**: Ph. 1-866-454-1212 **Saskatchewan Drug Information Service (SDIS)**: www.usask.ca/druginfo, Ph 1-800-667-3425 or 966-6340 (Saskatoon)
**Canadian Drug Coverage Links**: (including Provincial, NIHB, Veterans): www.drugcoverage.ca **SK Drug Schedule Summary Link**: http://napra.ca/pdfs/provinces/sk/37.pdf
**Safer Health Care Now!** http://www.saferhealthcarenow.ca/ **Canadian Patient Safety Institute:** http://www.patientsafetyinstitute.ca/index.html

## *A Short History: Academic Detailing in Saskatchewan*

### How did RxFiles begin?

- The roots of RxFiles go back to 1996 when a guest from North Vancouver spoke on the academic detailing service established out of Lion's Gate Hospital for physicians on the North Shore. Within a year a pilot project was convened between Saskatoon's Family Medicine group and the Department of Pharmaceutical Services for Saskatoon Health Region.
- The academic detailing program officially began in May 1997. First up was training in N. Vancouver, followed by launch of the first newsletter & academic detailing sessions in July 1997. Loren Regier and Sharon Downey shared the 1 FTE allocated.
- The program materials and visits were well received, and participation grew over 3 years of program development in Saskatoon.
- By 2000, some were asking "how come Saskatoon has this service and we don't?" This led to a gradual expansion to cover Regina, Prince Albert, Battlefords and several other rural Saskatchewan areas.
- As of March, 2010 – RxFiles employs or contracts with 10 SK pharmacists for 4 FTE academic detailing positions. In addition, several family physicians, specialists, nurse practitioners and others contribute to the content, review & training in each topic area. RxFiles does not receive any industry funding.

### Was academic detailing an easy sell?

- Thanks for asking! The first years were a lot of work as the service built goodwill and established credibility. Fortunately, academic detailing, although short on pizza and samples has a lot of other things going for it:
  1) a high value on independently assessing evidence, clinical opinion and providing a balanced, non-commercial perspective.
  2) the physician office visits enhance the value of the printed material, ensuring that the information gets a good hearing.
  3) academic detailing preserves physician autonomy and flexibility in prescribing – so at the end of the discussion, the physician decides how to best apply the information for each individual patient.

## *RxFiles Drug Comparison Charts*

### There sure is a lot of information on each page!

- Agreed. At first glance, there is an overwhelming amount of information, but after diving in, the detail is what provides the extra value. After sifting through the evidence, pulling together a vast spectrum of information and running it by various specialists, the only way to simplify it would be to oversimplify it. Although they take a bit of getting used to, those who do, find many drug questions answered!

### Who's idea were the drug charts?

- Brent Jensen drafted several psychiatry drug charts in the mid-1990's after City Hospital pharmacists were asked to regularly attend psychiatry rounds. Having a wealth of "answers" and comparisons at a glance was invaluable in contributing to patient therapy decisions. The charts idea was applied to the academic detailing material and soon they could be found posted on walls and bulletin boards in several physicians offices. In addition, physicians started asking for back issues once they realized how useful and unique the information was. PS – Brent still masterminds keeping the charts excellent, up-to-date & small-print! Thanks Brent!
- In 2000, a collection of psychiatry charts – 12 pages – was published along with the topic of "Psychotropics in the Elderly". The booklet was a hit! It was decided that since the charts seemed to be getting so much front line use, that we should pull all our updated charts together and publish. 10 years later, the RxFiles Drug Comparison Charts book is in its 8th Edition, covering many drug therapy areas and being used throughout Canada and even beyond. The book and website are self sustaining – "not for profit; not for loss" as revenue from sales is used to keep the extensive amount of information up-to-date.
- *As for the small print…* the strength and weakness of the charts is that a lot of information is compared side-by-side on one page. Reviewers usually want to add and not subtract information, so that's just the way these charts have evolved. As for the academic detailing – it won't feel so cramped – in fact – there's lots of room to roam to the most practical point of discussion.

Enjoy!

## *A Few Perspectives…& Anecdotes*

### On evidence and information…

- *Seek simplicity, and mistrust it!* Alfred North Whitehead Mathematician (1861–1947) (passed on to RxFiles by the Dalhousie Academic Detailing Service)
- *Education is a progressive discovery of our own ignorance.* Will Durant, 19th Century Historian
- *Figures don't lie, but liars figure.* Mark Twain (1835-1910) (& a favourite quote of one of our Pharmacology professors)
- *Looking at the pharmacology texts of 20 years ago, I am reminded that while a lot has changed, some information stands the test of time. Theories come and go, but evidence based on clinical outcomes is more likely to stand in the long run.*
- *When Vioxx (rofecoxib) was pulled off the market in 2004 for concerns about increased thrombotic events, a prominent physician called to ask us when we first warned physicians about this potential adverse event. A quick look found that we included cautionary notes in 2001, and included "??cardiac/serious events" in our 2002 book. In 2004, we only had to remove the question marks with the breaking news.*

### On Samples

- *On the plus side, samples are a way to initiate a new drug, and it's nice to offer our patients something for free. So – do samples serve our patients needs well? It all depends… If the drug given is the best drug one would have chosen anyway, then that's a positive. But let's say you are going on "life-saving medication" that you will likely need to take for the rest of your life. Would you want the one that is a free sample for 30 days, or would you want the one that has good outcome evidence, an established safety record, and possibly a few thousand dollars less over then next 5 years? Sometimes we serve the sampler, rather than allowing the sample to serve us. And sometimes the best drug isn't in the sample cupboard!*
- *Other factors to consider include the impact of packaging & disposal of unused samples on the environment and patient safety concerns given one less check at the pharmacy level.*[i]

### On Life and Medicine

- *Even when I'm sure I'm right, I remember I could be wrong.*
- *A merry heart is a good medicine; a broken spirit drys the bones.* Proverbs 17:22

### On the RxFiles Charts

- *Thanks. These are getting me through med school!*
- *No margin for error, when there are no margins!*
- *Important enough to keep in my purse!*

### On the RxFiles Office

- *I was expecting mahogany, & …a little more space…*

FTE= full time equivalent SK=Saskatchewan www.RxFiles.ca

*When a drug is doing more "to you" than "for you", it's time to reconsider the course of therapy.*[ii]

## 1) Definitions [1]

**Use:** sporadic consumption without apparent adverse consequences

**Abuse:** frequency of consumption may vary, some adverse consequences / clinical impairment are experienced by user (*dominos begin to fall*)

**Addiction's 4C's**: LOSS of **control** over substance use WITH **craving** &/or **compulsive** use which is **continued despite harm**. (*major domino effect*)

**Pseudoaddiction**: drug seeking behavior mimicking addiction resulting from under-treatment of pain. {But r/o pain + addiction, e.g. dual diagnosis.}

**Dependence, physical**: a state of adaptation resulting in drug class-specific withdrawal symptoms upon abrupt dose reduction, decreasing drug levels or antagonist administration. (Not to be confused with addiction!)

**Detoxification-managing acute withdrawal**: treatment intended to remove the physiological effects of the addictive substances (protocols)

- **Social Detox**: managed & engaged in recovery; 3-10day stay.
- **Brief Detox:** ~ 24hr observation; not medically managed.

**Harm Reduction:** measures taken to address problems (e.g. social) that are open to outcomes other than abstinence or cessation of drug use

**Tolerance**: decreasing effect of a drug over time.

⇨**Tolerance & physical dependence should not be confused with addiction.** Addiction is characterized by compulsive use of a substance or preoccupation with obtaining it despite evidence that continued use causes harm (physical, emotional, social or economic) [2]

## 2) Statistics From the Literature (CADUMS 2008) [3]

- The prevalence of past 12 month cocaine (1.6%), ecstasy (1.4%), speed (1.1%) and methamphetamine (0.2%) use in 2008; comparable to rates reported in 2004.
- The rate of drug use by youth 15-24 years of age remains much higher than that reported by adults 25 years and older: 4x higher for cannabis use (32.7% versus 7.3%), & 9x higher for past-year use of any other illicit drug (15.4% versus 1.7%).
- 72% of non-medical opioids used by students was obtained from home [4]
- The prevalence of harm experienced during the past year due to one's drug use was ~10x higher among youth age 15-24yrs, than among adults age ≥ 25 (10.8% vs 1.1%) {*Harm* related to social life, health, work, studies, or employment, financial, legal, housing or learning.}
- age adjusted mortality ↑ 5x in urban drug addicts Boston [5]
- ~10% report drugs/alcohol as reason for 1st ever sexual intercourse [6]

## 3) Alcohol (EtOH) Abuse

◆**A standard drink** = 13.7 grams (0.6 ounces) of pure alcohol or:

- 12-ounces 341mL of regular beer (5% EtOH)
- 5-ounces 142mL of wine (12% EtOH)
- 1.5-ounces or a "shot" of 80-proof (40% EtOH) distilled spirits or liquor (e.g. gin, rum, vodka, or whiskey).

[Also significant caloric intake!!! Evening planner see: http://www.educalcool.qc.ca/en/evening-planner/]

◆**Moderate drinking** = describes a lower risk pattern of drinking.

- No more than 2 drinks in any one day & no more than 9 drinks per week for women & 14 drinks per week for men.
- This definition is referring to the amount consumed on any single day & is not intended as an average over several days. See: http://www.educalcool.qc.ca/en/

◆**Those who should not drink:**

- Children and adolescents.
- Individuals of any age who cannot limit their drinking to low levels.
- Women **who may become pregnant** or who are pregnant.
- Individuals **who plan to drive**, operate machinery, or take part in other activities that require attention, skill, or coordination.
- Those at high risk of DI's: Rx or OTC drugs e.g. disulfiram, metronidazole, CNS depressants? Precaution also in those with chronic/high-dose **acetaminophen** use.
- Individuals with certain medical conditions e.g. pancreatitis, cirrhosis, hepatitis?
- Persons recovering from alcoholism.

◆**Binge drinking:** a pattern of consumption that brings the blood EtOH level to ≥0.08%. Usually corresponds to >4 drinks on one occasion for men; or >3 drinks/single occasion for women, generally within about 2 hours.

**Related issues:** ◆ maltreatment of others (e.g. child abuse by caregiver) [7]

- Psychosocial issues: "escape", depression, self esteem, suicidal ideation
- High risk behaviours: sexual (abuse, unplanned/unwanted/unprotected), financial, criminal; driving with intoxicated driver; cutting & suicide attempts
- Adolescents: especially vulnerable (neurodevelopment & behaviour)[8]
- Problems: health, ↓ inhibition (violence, aggression), impaired driving…
- **Recovery** must be functional not just stopping or decreasing use {e.g. identify life skills lacking & move client toward achieving/functioning.}

## 4) Addiction Screening: CAGE, AUDIT, Other e.g. SASSI [9]

**C** – have you ever felt the need to <u>C</u>ut down or <u>C</u>hange your drinking/drug use?
**A** – do you get <u>A</u>nnoyed when others criticize your drinking/drug use?
**G** – have you ever felt <u>G</u>uilty about your drinking/drug use for any reason?
**E** – <u>E</u>ye-opener: Have you ever felt the need for a drink early in the morning to decrease hangover or withdrawal?

When assessing a patient's answers to the above questions: one YES suggests caution; ≥ 2 YES' suggests strong caution/need for vigilance.

| **AUDIT: 10 questions to assess alcohol use patterns.** [10] | 0 | 1 | 2 | 3 | 4 |
|---|---|---|---|---|---|
| 1) How often do you have 1 drink containing alcohol? | Never | ≥monthly | 2-4x/mo | 2-3x/wk | 4+x/wk |
| 2) How many drinks do you have on a typical day? | 1-2 | 3-4 | 5-6 | 7-9 | 10+ |
| 3) How often do you have 4+ drinks on one occasion? | Never | < 1/mo | 1/mo | 1/wk | ~daily |
| 4) How often last year were you not able to stop drinking? | Never | < 1/mo | 1/mo | 1/wk | ~daily |
| 5) How often last year did you fail to do what was expected…? | Never | < 1/mo | 1/mo | 1/wk | ~daily |
| 6) How often last year have you needed a 1st drink in the AM…? | Never | < 1/mo | 1/mo | 1/wk | ~daily |
| 7) How often last year have you had a feeling of guilt after drinking? | Never | < 1/mo | 1/mo | 1/wk | ~daily |
| 8) How often last year have you not remembered the night before…? | Never | < 1/mo | 1/mo | 1/wk | ~daily |
| 9) Have you/someone else been injured as a result of drinking? | No | | Yes, not this yr. | | Yes, this yr |
| 10) Has a relative, friend or doctor been concerned about your drinking? | No | | | | |
| Total score: 0-7=low risk; 8-15=at risk; >16 likely problems | | | | | |

**Single Question Screen:** How many times in the past year have you had x or more drinks in a day? (where x = **4** drinks for ♀, & **5** drinks for ♂)
(How many times in the past year have you used an illegal drug or used a prescription med for nonmedical reasons?)

**<u>History</u>** (Useful questions asked in a non-judgemental fashion):

Ask 1st about socially acceptable drugs: nicotine, caffeine.
Ask next about alcohol, specifically beer & wine; quantity used.
Then ask about illicit drugs, beginning with marijuana.
⇨Are illicit drugs available at school/work? Any close friends who use drugs?
Obtain collateral information from family & friends as necessary; confirm patient history & assess for recent/sudden behaviour changes.
Ask regarding weight loss, sleep disturbance, impotence, gambling, porn.

**<u>Physical findings</u>** (intoxication or withdrawal):

- Evidence of associated infections, hepatitis, HIV, oral thrush
- Needle marks (including "hidden" sites), STDs; pupil size, ↑HR, sweating, watery eyes, runny nose, slurred speech, yawning, unsteady gait.
- Lab: LFTs, Hep B & C screen; drug screens (e.g. UDT as at bottom of page).

## 5) Universal Precautions in Pain Medicine [11,12,13]

- assumes that one can not always determine who will become a problem user; thus, suggests a minimum level to assess & manage risk.

1. **Make a Diagnosis** with Appropriate Differential
2. Psychological Assessment Including **Risk of Addictive Disorders**; include discussion of urine drug testing (**UDT**)
3. Informed Consent &/or Use of a **Treatment Agreement** (sample[14])
4. Pre/Post-Intervention Assessment of **Pain & Function**
5. Appropriate Trial of Opioid Therapy +/- Adjuncts +/- Non-drug Tx
6. Have an "**Exit Strategy**" for discontinuing an opioid if lack benefit.[11]
7. Reassessment of Pain Score and Level of Function
8. Regularly Assess the **"five A's"**: <u>A</u>nalgesia, <u>A</u>ctivity, <u>A</u>dverse effects, <u>A</u>berrant behavior & <u>A</u>ccurate medical records.
9. Periodically Review Pain Diagnosis & Comorbid Conditions, Including Addictive Disorders. Use a *Termination of Controlled Substances Agreement* as needed.
10. **Document** Assessment, Discussions and Progress

## 6) Red Flags – Aberrant Rx Drug Use [15,16]

### Consider Discontinuation / Specialist Referral

1. Prescriptions from multiple physicians (check profile when available)
2. Frequent visits to emergency room requesting drugs of abuse
3. Requests from patients from outside of local area
4. Stolen, modification or tampering of prescriptions
5. Polypharmacy with CNS depressants, habituating substances
6. Forgery, selling, stealing, or using other persons medications
7. Injecting oral or chewing long acting formulations

### Reassess Regimen and/or Treatment Agreement

1. Rapid escalation of opioid doses in chronic non-cancer pain
2. Frequent excuses for running out of medication or losing Rx's
3. Frequent changes of the opioid prescribed
4. Aversion to concurrent recommended treatments or UDT
5. Request for brand-name vs generic & short vs long-acting products
6. Lack of request for adjunct analgesic refills.
7. Missed follow-up visits. 8) Unsanctioned non-compliance with regimen

## 7) Principles of Addiction Treatment [17]

1) No single treatment is appropriate for all; concomitant medications are useful for many; treatment needs to be readily available
2) Attend to multiple needs, not just drug use
3) Assess for medical, family, vocational, social & legal services
4) Ensure adequate time in treatment (≥3 months)
5) Arrange for counselling & behavioural therapies individual or group
6) Integrate treatment for those with mental disorders
7) Acute detoxification is only the 1st stage in long-term tx
8) Treatment does <u>not</u> need to be voluntary to be effective
9) Drug & alcohol use monitoring should be ongoing
10) Assess for HIV/AIDS, hepatitis B & C, etc. & provide counselling regarding risk behaviours (sexual contacts, drug use, etc.)
11) Expect a long-term process with possible relapses. *Addiction is chronic relapsing*
12) Individualize "self-help" & spiritual adjunct support programs

**Presentations: Possible Causes:** ◆<u>**Unresponsive**</u>: hypoglycemics, opioids, EtOH, cyanide, CO, tranquilizers, hydrocarbons, barbs. ◆<u>**Seizures**</u>: hypoglycemics, amphetamines, cocaine, hallucinogens, anticonvulsants, TCAs, PCP, mescaline. ◆<u>**Hyperthermia**</u>: salicylates, Ecstasy, atropine, phenytoin. ◆<u>**Hypothermia**</u>: EtOH, opioids, sedative/hypnotics, TCAs, barbs, CO.

**Links**: WHO: http://www.who.int/topics/substance_abuse/en/; Medline Plus: http://www.nlm.nih.gov/medlineplus/substanceabuseproblems.html; AAFP: http://familydoctor.org/online/famdocen/home/common/addictions/basics/586.html; National Institute on Drug Abuse: http://www.nida.nih.gov/ ; Community Learning Network (CLN): http://www.cln.org/themes/substance_abuse.html; Opioid & Stimulant Identification pics: [19]

**Links-CDN**: Canadian Centre on Substance Abuse (CCSA): http://www.ccsa.ca/eng/Pages/Home.aspx ; CAMH: http://www.camh.net/, http://knowledgex.camh.net/primary_care/Pages/default.aspx ; SK link[20] Pregnancy/Lactation: http://www.camh.net/Publications/Resources_for_Professionals/Pregnancy_Lactation/index.html; National Anti-drug Strategy: http://www.nationalantidrugstrategy.gc.ca/index.html; Éduc'alcool: http://www.educalcool.qc.ca/en/

**Tips for Legitimate Rx's** of drugs causing physical/psychological dependence: 1) <u>**Interval dispensing**</u> to limit the "pill-load"; 2) Determine if <u>**specialist support**</u> needed.

**Responding to aberrant behaviour**: **Do not debate the motive**; rather get agreement that such behaviour is problematic. Then delve into the root cause of the problem!

**Urine Drug Testing (UDT)**: useful to monitor medication compliance & manage potential drug abuse risk. [18]

- <u>Immunoassay</u>: rapid, inexpensive & preferred for initial screening. <u>Chromatography</u>: ↑$, delay but ↑ accuracy. Amphetamines: detectable 2-3 days; Benzos: 3 days for short acting; Cocaine: 2-8days; Opiates: 1-3days; THC: 3days if single use, ~15days if daily use, 60+ days if long-term/heavy use. ◆False negatives possible.
- Assess drug causes for false positives. ◆ Ensure proper collection technique & integrity of specimen.
- Goal is to improve patient care & communication, not to police!!! Discuss unexpected results with patient.
- If abuse risk is high, advise of consequences, tighten boundaries, refer to addiction specialist or taper/DC if necessary.

Is drug prescribed there? Are any non-prescribed drugs there?

# Substance Abuse & Treatment Options Chart [21,22,23,24]

Loren Regier - www.RxFiles.ca - July 2010

| Drugs/Substances of Abuse & slang terms | Signs/Symptoms, Overuse; Health Concerns | Management & Treatment Options; Comments [25,26] Acute intoxication; Long-term Withdrawal |
|---|---|---|
| **Cannabinoids** [27] {THC = delta-9-tetrahydrocannabinol}<br>**Hashish** dried hemp flower resin - boom, hash, hemp<br>**Marijuana** dried hemp - dope, grass, joints, pot, weed<br>{typically↑↑ potency than previous ∴↑ risk} - cannabis<br>{may be "spiked" with cocaine, meth, methylphenidate} | ⇨euphoria, impair learning & reaction time; confusion, panic, ↓ balance, coordination; ↑ HR, ↓BP orthostatic, ↑appetite<br>➔pulmonary disease & cancer (unfiltered smoke); psychosis<br>➔associated problems: physical, psychological, financial, legal & social (e.g. failure to achieve/fulfill responsibilities), ↓testosterone | Acute intoxication: 1-3hr; similar to alcohol; changes in mood, perception & functioning can persist<br>Withdrawal syndrome: controversial. ⇨Cognitive Behavioural Therapy (CBT) & supportive treatment.<br>Legal "medicinal" cannabinoid alternatives:⇨consider if indicated: see RxFiles Cannabinoids Chart [28]<br>{Illegal use of marijuana may be sign of ↑ risk for other substance abuse; urine drug testing (UDT) available but may remain positive for ~10 days in casual user, 2-4 wks in heavy user, & months in chronic heavy user} |
| **Hallucinogens** {perceptual, cognitive & ECG △'s}<br>**LSD** lysergic acid diethylamide - acid, cubes, microdot, ...<br>**Mescaline** - buttons, cactus, mesc, peyote | ⇨altered state of perception & feeling; persisting flashbacks<br>⇨↑body temp, HR, BP; ↓ appetite, sleeplessness, weakness, tremors (LSD & mescaline); mental disorders long-term (LSD) | LSD: most potent; psychedelic effects: onset <1hr; duration <8hrs; psychotic effects persist 2+ days<br>Tx: ⇨provide calm, supportive environment [still used in college; squares on eyes to absorb]<br>{**Psilocybin** - magic mushroom, purple passion; chewed ⇨nervousness & paranoia} |
| **Opioid/Opiate**<br>**Codeine** - doors & fours, loads, ...<br>**Fentanyl** Duragesic - China girl, TNT, Tango & Cash<br>**Heroin** - brown sugar, H, junk, smack<br>**Hydromorphone** - Dilaudid, dillies, dilly-2 or -4, beads<br>**Hydrocodone** comboS - vike, Watson-387<br>**Meperidine** - Demerol, demmies<br>**Morphine** MS Contin - M, the down, Miss Emma,...<br>{red's=200mg; grey's=100mg; peach's=60mg; purples=30mg}<br>**Opium** - big O, black stuff, gum, hop<br>**Oxycodone** Oxy-Contin (part rapid release) - Oxy, O.C., killer.<br>{Contaminants may also be an issue; e.g. heroin-anthrax.[29] When prescribing, counsel to store properly & avoid sharing!!! } | ⇨analgesia, euphoria, drowsiness/sedation, nausea, constipation, confusion. On overdose: respiratory depression, coma, death. (with heroin: ⇨staggering gait.)<br>⇨seizures (especially propoxyphene Darvon-N, meperidine Demerol, tramadol, combo pentazocine Talwin + tripelennamine T's & blues)<br>➔long-term tolerance, hyperalgesia; ↑death esp with benzos [30]<br>◆Important to distinguish short-term SEs from appropriate use with short & long-term SEs from abuse/addiction<br>◆Always check med profile for hx of opioid, benzo, etc. use!<br>◆Minimize withdrawal by tapering LA opioids over 7-14+ days<br>◆Overdose risk if restart same dose after abstinence period! | Acute toxicity: ⇨ reversed by naloxone NARCAN, a narcotic antagonist 0.4 - 2mg IV, may repeat after 2-3minutes, Max 10mg. May precipitate withdrawal (severe agitation, anxiety, N&V, diarrhea, yawn, sneeze, rhinorrhea, cramps). (Deaths often associated with co-use/abuse/Rx of benzodiazepines; Contaminants: MPTP parkinsonism, quinine, strychnine).<br>Withdrawal: lacrimation, rhinorrhea, yawn, dilated pupils, N&V, diaphoresis, chills, ↑HR & BP, myalgia, cramps, diarrhea; anxiety, dysphoria, craving, restless, insomnia, fatigue. Not life-threatening! ◆onset < 8hrs from last use; peaking between 36-72hr; physical withdrawal resolves in 5-10days; longer with methadone onset in 24-48hrs; persists 2-3 wks.<br>◆ Symptom Tx: *N&V* – dimenhydrinate or prochloroperazine; *diarrhea* – loperamide; *myalgias* – acetaminophen, naproxen; *anxiety, dysphoria, lacrimation, rhinorrhea* – hydroxyzine; *insomnia* – trazodone. Clonidine: see protocols[31]<br>Methadone: very LA opioid; daily admin; prevent withdrawal without intoxication/sedation. TID if for pain. Many DIs: e.g.↑QT<br>Buprenorphine: partial μ agonist; rapid withdrawal symptom alleviation; but withdrawal if highly dependent<br>Clonidine: α-2 adrenergic agonist; non-opioid tx option; not effective for aches, craving & insomnia. (May be abused.)<br>Naltrexone: opioid μ antagonist preventing analgesia & euphoria; useful after detox; hepatotoxicity FDA. |
| **Sedatives** CNS Depressants<br>**Alcohol** [32,33,34] - EtOH, booze, liquor ...<br>⇨major fetal effects (e.g. FAS)<br>**GHB** Gammahydroxybutyrate - G, grievous bodily harm, liquid ecstasy - "date rape" drug; clear liquid<br>**Flunitrazepam** ROHYPNOL - R2, Roche, roofies/roofied, rope - "date rape" drug<br>**Barbiturates** - barbs, reds, phennies, yellows<br>**Benzodiazepines** - candy, downers, sleeping pills<br>Ativan, Halcion, Librium, Valium, Xanax Alprazolam [benzo's]<br>**Methaqualone** - ludes, mandrex, quad, quay | Alcohol: ⇨withdrawal esp if >40drinks/wk: tremor; Lab clues: ↑MCV, ↑GGT<br>GHB: ⇨HA, loss of reflexes, memory; seizures, coma, death Resp depr<br>Flunitrazepam: ⇨visual & GI disturbance; urinary retention; memory loss<br>Barbiturates: ⇨depression, irritable, dizzy<br>Benzodiazepines: ⇨sedation, dizzy; ➔tolerance/dependence<br>Methaqualone: ⇨euphoria, depression; coma<br>General: ⇨↓ inhibitions (may result in ↑ anger/violence, unplanned sex, inappropriate speech)<br>⇨↓HR, BP & RR<br>⇨drowsy, ↓concentration; fatigue, confusion<br>⇨impaired coordination, memory & judgement<br>⇨slurred speech<br>[Seizures on withdrawal, esp if previous hx; alprazolam particularly of concern.] | Respiratory Depression & Coma: ⇨tx intubation & ventilation; Hypoglycemia (e.g. with excessive EtOH in kids): ⇨tx IV glucose<br>Alcohol: Social Norms Interventions (limit to "moderate drinking" & avoid binge drinking.) Consider cultural factors.<br>Long-term: Skills Interventions (e.g. drinking myths, drink refusal & assertiveness skills): ↓ over drinking risk<br>Stimulus Control (avoid/limit friends & places visited); Coping Skills; 12 Step Facilitation Therapy<br>Drug Tx: Acute: benzos for tremor (diazepam; lorazepam if hepatic dysfx or elderly; gabapentin[35]; pregabalin[36]); thiamine 50mg/d x3.<br>Long-term: Disulfiram compounded from powder ANTABUSE: blocks ALDH enzyme inducing dizziness, flushing, N&V, ↓BP (aversion tx)<br>Naltrexone ReVia, Depade: ↓ reinforcing effects via ↓response to endogenous opioid. Topiramate: ✓ but SEs.[37] Acamprosate Campral: conflicting data.<br>GBH: rapid onset ~10min; duration ≤2-4hrs. Flunitrazepam: rapid onset ~15min; duration ≤6hrs;<br>Oral benzodiazepine: Acute intox. rarely lethal, except with alcohol or CNS depressants; ⇨flumazenil ANEXATE inj (benzo antagonist): useful but may cause acute withdrawal/seizures; avoid routine use. Long-term withdrawal: diazepam or clonazepam tapering protocol |
| **Stimulants**<br>**Amphetamine** DEXEDRINE - bennies, speed, uppers,...<br>**Methylphenidate** RITALIN (Concerta has ↓ abuse risk!)<br>**MDMA** 3,4-methylenedioxymethamphetamine, **Ecstasy** - E, X<br>adulterants common; addictive! - X-TC, Adam, lover's speed<br>**Methamphetamine** - crystal meth, speed, ice, jib,<br>{made from pseudoephedrine} gak, glass, white, lady, girls<br>{Amphetamine analogues designer drugs: [MDA love drug, MDEA Eve]; [PMA Death (similar to MDMA)]}<br>**Cocaine** Erythrolum coca leaf - blow, C, candy, coke, snow, rock<br>adulterants common (e.g. levamisole, benzocaine, sugar, talc)[43,44] crack solid 92% pure | Amphetamine/Methylphenidate: ⇨tremor, ↓coordination, irritable, restless, aggressive; IV trackmarks<br>MDMA: ⇨hallucinogen mild; impaired cognition; ↑temp; toxicity (cardiac, renal & hepatic)<br>Methamphetamine: ⇨aggression, violence, psychotic behaviour; CV & neurological damage<br>General: (↑5-HT) ⇨↑HR, BP, energy, wt loss; ↑alertness; ↓appetite, nervousness, insomnia, ➔HF; hyperthermia<br>Cocaine: ⇨↑temp, chest/GI pain, resp failure; HA, seizure, panic; MI, vasoconstriction; talc⇨pulm fibrosis, HTN; long-term➔excited delirium, rhabdomyolysis | Cocaine: onset 5min; peak & duration: snort <30-60min, oral <90min, IV <5min; {t ½=1 hr; longer in *body packers*} most toxicity too brief to treat; anxiety/seizures/↑temp ⇨benzodiazepine; ↑BP⇨nitroprusside; CV toxicity⇨benzo ↓ sympathetic stimulation, ASA ↓thrombus, NTG or CCB (verapamil or diltiazem) ↓vasoconstriction, $O_2$<br>Amphetamines other: similar toxicity (& tx) as cocaine but ↑ duration. Strokes: hemorrhagic & ischemic. Life-threatening hyperthermia! Severe psych sx's may persist. Meth: duration 6-8hr. Ritonavir: DI & ↑risk fatal overdose.[38]<br>Ecstasy: onset: 20min; peak: 2-3hrs; duration: ~4hrs. Amphetamine like CV effects, rhabdomyolysis, stroke, death [39] Seizures common cause of ER visits ⇨ usual tx; persisting cognitive impairment. Contaminants (amphetamines common) ⇨ lethal overdose (hyperthermia: tx with rapid cooling +/- dantrolene). Ritonavir: DI & ↑risk fatal overdose.[40] Young-healthy: high risk!<br>➔Long-term: memory & motor impairment; psychosis (grey matter deficit); MI chest pain, stroke. (↑↑DA & ↑NE release.)<br>⇨Tx: behavioural therapies; the antidepressant bupropion may be useful. [Explosive/fire risk when making!] [41,42] |
| **Various**<br>**Dissociative Anesthetics** (floating, out of body)<br>◆ **Ketamine** Ketalar SV - K, Kat, cat Valiums, Special K<br>◆ **PCP** Phencyclidine - angel dust, love boat, peace pill | ⇨↑HR, ↑BP; impaired motor fx, memory loss, numbness<br>⇨ketamine: delirium, depression, respiratory depression, ↓bladder capacity<br>⇨PCP: ↓BP, ↓HR; panic, aggression, violence; ↓appetite | Ketamine: duration <1hr, dose dependant.<br>PCP overdose: may last several days causing psychosis & violence; ⇨ restraints & benzodiazepines ⇨ supportive tx: benzos for seizures, external cooling for hyperthermia (block NMDA receptors) |
| **Steroids, Anabolic** - Andriol, testosterone, etc.<br>{may be common in unapproved products} | ⇨acne, hostility, aggression; long term ↑BP, ↓clotting, ↑stroke, hepatic cysts/ca, renal ca; premature growth stagnation. | Abused: by athletes/body-builders<br>♂: prostate ca, ↓sperm, ↓testicular size, gynecomastia; ♀: menstrual irregularities, hirsutism, etc. |
| **Volatile Inhalants** - solvents, gases, nitrites whippits N2O<br>{toluene: paint, lacquer, glue}, poppers liquid gold, rush; puffers | ⇨stimulation, ↓inhibition, HA, N&V, slurred speech, ataxia, ↓coordination, cramps, ↓wt, depression; resp depr, coma | ➔damage to CV & brain/nervous system; ↑ sudden death CV. {Toluene: ↓K+, ↓ phosphate, renal tubular acidosis, abdominal pain, ataxia (may be permanent), resp failure ⇨ supportive tx; avoid arrhythmogenics e.g. epinephrine.} |

**Other Substances**: Bupropion WELLBUTRIN; Caffeine: see wt loss chart [45], withdrawal esp if >100mg/day (HA 50%, fatigue, drowsy, irritable), over ≤ 9 days. Dextromethorphan (DM): euphoria at 5-10x usual dose – *Robotripping* (sweat, ↑HR, ↑BP, dyskinesias, speech disorders, N&V, mydriasis, photophobia, resp depression), ↑5HT; blocks NMDA. Dimenhydrinate; Gabapentin NEURONTIN: snort or inject high doses for cocaine like euphoria (400mg caps of choice); potentiate or ease withdrawal from alcohol, cocaine, etc.[46]; Pregabalin LYRICA: ~ euphoria ~4%. Quetiapine SEROQUEL [47]: (quell, baby heroin, Susie-Q; Q-ball = Q + cocaine); oral, intranasal, & IV cooked, then injected; use to ↓ benzo withdrawal or as sedative/anxiolytic; dose reported ~ 200mg-2400mg/d; consider alternatives antipsychotics, SSRIs, buspirone, VPA, lithium; ➔↑ lethal arrhythmia, ↓BP, ↑wt, ↑DM.

BP=blood pressure ca=cancer CV=cardiovascular DM=diabetes FAS=fetal alcohol syndrome fx=function HA=headache HCV=hepatitis C Hep=hepatitis HR=heart rate LA=long-acting LFTs=liver fx tests N&V=nausea & vomiting SE=side effects Sx= symptoms Tx=treatment wt=weight

**Other Addictions**: Gambling, gaming, porn & sexual addictions/behaviours may also be present & require tx. **Club Drugs (raves)**: include Ecstasy, Rohypnol, ketamine, crystal meth, GHB, poppers. **Nicotine** [See chart [48]] - cigarettes, cigars, snuff, chew; ⇨↑CV/ca

**Contaminants**: impurities & adulterants common! Consider risk of: bacterial (endocarditis, osteomyelitis, sepsis), fungal, viral (HIV/AIDS) infection in IV drug abusers (needle sharing) & crack cocaine smoking[49]. Talc from tablets crushed for injection causes pulmonary granulomas. Lead.

**Pregnancy**:[50] **Club drugs** (MDMA, Rohypnol, GHB, ketamine), **Cocaine**, & **Alcohol**: avoid (malformations/abortion). **Amphetamines**: weigh benefit/risk;not teratogenic. **Cannabis**: avoid or ↓ (↓ long-term development). **Opioids**: may use; consider methadone, or ?buprenorphine [51].

## Table 1: Immunosuppressants (IS): In General [4]

- **The complexities of SOT requires patients to be treated by physicians/clinics with expertise in SOT.**
- IS goals: prevent acute & chronic rejection, while minimizing toxicity. High IS required initially=rationale for induction therapy, risk of rejection ↓'s (but is not eliminated) with time; maintenance IS tx may gradually be tapered by transplant specialist
- Multidrug approach using various agents, permits lower doses of IS agents; may combine 2-3 drugs from various classes (ie: CNI or SRL +/- MMF or AZA +/- steroid)
- IS blood level goals are patient & organ specific
- Cyclosporine (CSA) – trough or C2 levels (C2 – 2hr post dose, absorptive test) establish dose timing prior to interpreting level
- Tacrolimus (TAC), Sirolimus (SRL) - trough levels only
- IS predispose pts to **infection, malignancy**; & may require more aggressive therapy
- **Drug interactions** (DI): critical; review with new or change in meds

## Table 2: Transplantation – General Information for the Health Care Professional Providing Care to SOT Recipients

- Complex patients often with multiple medical issues.
- Many potential drug interactions! Always check for interactions prior to prescribing meds (consider expected as well as reported eg. TAC)
- Avoid **NSAIDs** (use acetaminophen, opiate option if indicated except avoid meperidine), aminoglycosides- additive nephrotoxicity with IS!
- Avoid **herbal** products (may interact or stimulate immune system)
- Do not ignore strange symptoms, which may indicate rejection (see table 5)
- **Immunocompromised status**: fever & other symptoms of infection should be investigated promptly
- Malignancy-↑'d risk (3-4x general public [4])! Encourage routine screening & lifestyle factors: routine dermatologic exams, important to use sunscreen, & regular screening tests as indicated eg. PAP smear, colonoscopy
- Frequency of IS drug level monitoring in stable patients is based on Transplant Center Protocols (eg **monthly**). Increased frequency is required in new patients or when medications/medical condition changes.
- **Drug levels are assay specific** – use caution comparing levels from different labs
- **Initial Treatment –3 drug regimen** (eg CNI+MMF+prednisone) common, patient specific **modifications made by Transplant Specialist**.
- Rejection Episodes – should be managed by Transplant Specialist & may include treatment with high dose steroids, mono/polyclonal antibodies, immunoglobulins, & IS regimen modification.

## Table 3: Drug Treatment Comparison Chart [1,2,3]

| Generic/TRADE (Strength & forms) g=generic avail. | Dosing (Adult) considerations | $/mo | Side effects SE / Monitoring M | P (Pregnancy Category) [1,2] | Drug Interactions DI {key/select: not exhaustive!} General Comments & Considerations |
|---|---|---|---|---|---|
| **⇨ CALCINEURIN INHIBITORS= CNI** | | | | | |
| **Cyclosporine** NEORAL **CSA**<br>(10, 25, 50, 100mg cap; 100mg/ml liquid generic)<br>50mg/ml IV (1 & 5 ml vials) - Sandimmune IV<br>(IV to oral conversion is 1:3 eg. 300mg per day= 100mg IV per day) | *Dosed BID; Peds: q8-12h*<br>Titrate to maintain trough or C2 level as determined by transplant center.<br>Routine monitoring essential to maintain level within narrow window.<br>Intra & inter pt variability with bioavailability! | 100mg q12h $400<br>150mg q12h $580 | **SE**: Nephrotoxicity acute & chronic, HTN common-esp heart pts, Neurologic sx's often dose related: tremor 3-55%, headache 2-25%, paresthesia, dizziness, fatigue, encephalopathy; GI-N,V,D; Gingival hyperplasia: tx azithromycin, d/c nifedipine if possible. Metabolic: ↑ (lipid, uric acid, K+), ↓ Mg; Hypertrichosis, hepatotoxicity<br>**M**: drug **level**, SCr, lipids, K, Mg, uric acid, BP, liver function (possibly monthly) | C | • Take consistently with regard to time of day & meals.<br>• Similar SE profile for both CNIs but:<br>CSA⇒ ↑lipid & BP, gingival hyperplasia, hypertrichosis, nephrotoxic & hyperuricemia<br>TAC⇒ headache, GI SE (esp diarrhea), hyperglycemia/diabetes & alopecia<br>**DI**: CNIs are metabolized by CYP450 **3A4** & have **many potential DI's** !!<br>↑ CNI level by: allopurinol, amiodarone, clarithromycin, danazol, diltiazem, erythromycin; flu-, keto-, posa-, vori -conazole; grapefruit juice, verapamil.<br>↓ CNI level by: aluminum, bosentan, carbamazepine, orlistat, phenobarbital, phenytoin, rifampin, St. Johns Wort, sulfasalazine.<br>↑ nephrotoxicity: aminoglycoside, amphotericin, melphalan, MTX, NSAIDs<br>CSA & TAC are also metabolized by p-glycoprotein, drugs that affect P-gp will interact (clarithromycin, colchicine, digoxin, verapamil)<br>CSA: ↑level of aliskiren, colchicine, dabigatran, dronedarone & statins (see Table 4) |
| **Tacrolimus** (FK506) PROGRAF **TAC**<br>(0.5,1,5mg cap; 5mg/ml amp) **FK**<br>(IV to oral conversion is 1:4 eg. 4mg per day= 1mg IV per day)<br>ADVAGRAF extended release<br>(0.5,1,5mg cap) {Not Interchangeable, if decision to switch product is made by Transplant Specialist, initial dose 1:1 ratio}<br>Suspension made by some pharmacies. | *PROGRAF = BID*<br>*ADVAGRAF = Daily*<br>Titrate to maintain trough levels as determined by transplant center. | 2.5mg q12h $480<br>5mg q12h $810<br>5mg daily $430<br>10mg daily $830 | **SE**: Nephrotoxicity acute & chronic, Neurologic: **headache** 37-64%, **tremor**, insomnia, paresthesia, dizziness, seizures rarely. GI: **diarrhea** 37-72%, N&V or constipation. Metabolic: ↑**BG**–may lead to DM, ↑K+, ↓ Mg, hypophosphatemia<br>CV: HTN, ↑lipid, cardiomegaly, ↑QT ,alopecia<br>Anemias, leukocytosis, thrombocytopenia, abnormal liver enzymes?<br>**M**: drug **level**, SCr, K+, Mg, blood glucose, CBC, liver function (possibly monthly) | C | |
| **⇨ m-TOR INHIBITORS** | | | | | |
| **Sirolimus** rapamycin RAPAMUNE **SRL**<br>(1mg tab, 1mg/ml po suspension)<br>Covered 100%: kidney tpt SAIL program; other organs must pay EDS copay | *Dosed Daily*<br>Titrate to maintain trough levels as determined by transplant center.<br>Loading dose often given initially.<br>-long t1/2 (57-63hr), when dose adjustments are made, new dose should be maintained for 7-14day prior to additional adjustment | 3mg od $740<br>5mg od $1210 | **SE**: ↑lipid TG ~50%, ↑cholesterol ~45%; dose related & may need tx), ↑BP, proteinuria, hypersensitivity angioedema caution with ACEI, exfoliative dermatitis, vasculitis, impaired wound healing >risk if BMI>30kg/m2, ↑fluid/edema, mucosal ulcers in mouth & under tongue; dose related, acne, rash, **anemia**/leuco-,thrombo-cytopenia, pneumonitis interstitial rare & serious<br>Black box warning: Lung tpt- bronchial anastomotic dehiscense;<br>Liver tpt- ↑mortality, graft loss & artery thrombosis hepatic (in combo with CSA or TAC)<br>**M**: drug **level**, Scr, lipid profile, urine albumin/creatinine ratio, CBC (possibly monthly) | C | • Take consistently with regard to food (with or without food)<br>• Solution: dilute in H20/orange juice, take immediately; protect from light, refrigerate<br>• Mouth ulcers: mucositis mouthwash or Oracort Kenalog Dental paste useful<br>• May have immunosuppression conversion role for malignant pts eg. SCC/BCC,RCC,HCC<br>**DI**: SRL is a CYP450 3A4 & p-glycoprotein substrate: similar DI's as with CNI's<br>SRL should be administered 4 hours after CSA, due to ↑absorption of SRL<br>SRL + CNI combination has additional nephrotoxicity risk |
| **Everolimus** CERTICAN (RAD-001) | -approved in Europe in 2003 & USA 2010 Zortress, not yet approved in Canada; available in Canada as Afinitor for use in refractory metastatic renal carcinoma. | | | | |
| **⇨ ANTIPROLIFERATIVES** | | | | | |
| **Mycophenolate Mofetil** CELLCEPT<br>(250, 500mg tab; 200mg/ml po sol; **MMF**<br>500mg vial for inj)<br>(IV to oral conversion is 1:1 )<br>**Mycophenolate Sodium** MYFORTIC<br>(180, 360mg EC tabs) | *Dosed BID*<br>Usual Cellcept dose is 500mg-1.5g bid depending on organ, time post transplant & other factors<br>Cellcept 500mg = Myfortic 360mg | 500mg q12h $300<br>1gm q12h $560<br>360mg q12h $290<br>720mg q12h $540 | **SE**: NVD, abdominal pain, gastritis ↑↑ incidence; divide dose, take with food; ?change to myfortic, ↓ dose as advised by transplant physician 10;<br>**neutropenia** {↑ with antivirals or may be due to viral infection; dose reduction, interruption or filgrastim options (dose manipulation only done under advice from transplant center)}; pure red cell aplasia,<br>GI perforation/ulcer rare, more likely in active serious GI dx,<br>**M**: **pregnancy test** prior to tx; CBC, ANC qwkx4, q2wkx4, →qmonthly | D | • MMF is rapidly hydrolyzed to mycophenolic acid (MPA), which is subsequently metabolized to mycophenolic acid glucaronide (MPAG)<br>• May measure MPA level, but not routinely done poor correlation of MPA level to efficacy or toxicity<br>• Manufacturer suggests empty stomach since food ↓'s Cmax, but many GI SE, thus often recommend taking **with meals** for pt convenience & compliance<br>**DI**: cholestyramine-avoid ↓ AUC: interruption enterohepatic recycling; antacids, iron & sevalamer separate doses; & other drugs that inhibit tubular secretion or enterohepatic recycling. PPI's may ↓ MMF slightly. |
| **Azathioprine IMURAN** g **AZA**<br>50 g mg tab dumbbell shape (Can make susp)<br>50mg/17ml vial; 6-MP prodrug | *Dosed Daily:*<br>Dose required to prevent rejection & minimize SE varies with each pt<br>Typical maintenance dose=1-3mg/kg | 50mg od $25<br>100mg od $43 | **SE**: flu-like fever 2-3 wks into tx, infections, hepatotoxic onset usually within 6 months, bone marrow suppression 2-5%, dose related, unpredictable esp. leukopenia, allergy <5%, pancreatitis as hypersensitivity rxn 2% -occurs within 1st month, GI SE dose-related & improve with time 26<br>**M**: CBC every other week while doses adjusted, then qmonth; LFTs | D | • MMF use often preferred over AZA lower rejection rates with MMF • With meals may ↓GI SE<br>**DI**: **allopurinol** (↑↑ levels/toxicity), ↑infections with steroids;<br>ACEI (↑ leukopenia/anemia);<br>{5-ASA, sulfasalazine & olsalazine may inhibit thiopurine methyltransferase}. |
| **⇨ CORTICOSTEROIDS** | | | | | |
| **Prednisone** g<br>1, 5 g & 50 g mg tabs<br>**Prednisolone** g<br>1mg/ml Oral Solution PEDIAPRED | Taper as per transplant center's protocol; dose varies on organ, time post tpt, pt factors & other meds used. | 5-10mg po daily $9 | **SE**: cushingoid features, ↑ BG, infections, skin thinning, psychiatric SE, insomnia, impaired wound healing, GI bleeds, cataracts, osteoporosis/osteopenia, fluid & electrolyte imbalances, fat redistribution<br>**M**: annual eye exam, HPA axis suppression, BG, CBC, electrolytes; BMD | C | • ↑ BG, weight gain, mood changes, insomnia more apparent early post transplant, when doses are higher<br>• With meals may ↓GI SE<br>• IV Solumedrol: may be used if unable to give oral or if rejection suspected<br>**DI**: aspirin GI SE, carbamazepine, fluoroquinolone ↑ tendon rupture, phenytoin ↓ steroid effect. |
| **⇨ OTHER** | | | | | |
| **Belatacept** LEA-29Y | -an **investigational** biologic compound under development for use in SOT; fusion protein; CD28 antagonist; potential use as a replacement for CNI's (in combo with MMF + steroids) | | | | |

## Table 4 : Other Disease Considerations

**Anemia** may contribute to CV disease[7] ♦may require treatment with epoetin/darbepoetin ♦may be drug related ( MMF, SRL)

**Cardiovascular disease** [5,6,7,8]
- major cause of morbidity/mortality in SOT recipients ♦ absolute death rate from CVD in SOT is 2x general population [8]
- Framingham may underestimate risk [7] ♦ all heart recipients should receive **statin** regardless of LDL [5, lacks outcome data]
- kidney recipients tx as high CV risk [6,7] ♦↓risk factors (control BP, diabetes, stop smoking, weight loss, achieve lipid targets) [7]
- ASA for known ischemic heart disease or if high CV risk [7] ♦ clopidogrel: reports of rhabdomyolysis with CSA & statin [29]

**Cholesterol** [6,28]
- **Statins**-first line but ↑ risk of myopathy/rhabdomyolysis; ♦ DI's: CSA ↑serum levels of all statins, start with ½ dose & titrate pending effect/tolerance; ♦<u>avoid</u> rosuvastatin- 10x Cmax elevation [25]; ♦ statin + TAC: adverse events reported
- muscle pain/weakness frequent, but serious reports of unexpected hepatic SE in liver recipients are very rare
- Fibrates (fenofibrate [Diabetes: Accord NS], gemfibrozil [minimal CYP 3A4 effect]) are only tx options for ↑↑ triglycerides [eg. >10mmol/L to ↓ pancreatitis]
- Cholestyramine/colestipol adversely affect absorption of CSA, MMF
- Ezetimibe [lacks outcome data] in combo with CSA can increase levels of both drugs – caution with CNIs! [1]

**Fertility considerations** [9] ♦ consult transplant center if pregnant or considering pregnancy
- improved health post SOT may lead to return to fertility ♦pregnancy may pose risk to mother & organ ♦ options **IUD** (good), progestin injection/implant device (good, but ↓BMD concern), combined hormonal methods (good but consider estrogen risks CVD, clot, cancer) ♦ **DI**: minor with IS meds, contraceptives remain effective despite slightly altered circulating hormone levels
- Other issues: Men also require contraception during & for 90days after valganciclovir therapy; MMF: reports of birth defects

**GI Complications** [10,21]
- GI complications frequent & can include oral lesions, esophagitis, peptic ulcer, diarrhea, colon disorders, malignancy
- may be related to meds, infection or pre-existing GI pathology ♦ Rule out all infectious causes (see Table 6)
- many programs routinely prophylaxis with **PPI or H2RA** to ↓drug side effects (PPIs may ↓ MMF, but clinically still utilized).
- MMF-↑↑ GI SE, TAC>CSA, SRL-mouth ulcer, steroid-ulcerogenic; other: Mg/PO4 supplements, antibiotic, antidiabetic, colchicine…

**Gout** [11, 27]
- hyperuricemia CSA>TAC ♦avoid treating hyperuricemia if asymptomatic ♦treatment –see RxFiles gout chart, avoid NSAIDs (additive nephrotoxicity); <u>**Acute Tx**</u>: steroid [IA/oral], colchicine (DI: CSA ↑both levels; manufacturer suggest: 0.6mg po x1, no repeat x3day); <u>**Prophylaxis**</u>: allopurinol (but **↓AZA dose** by 75%); adjust doses in renal dysfunction.

**Hypertension** [23]
- occurs in 50-90% kidney & liver, & almost all heart pts. May be difficult to treat ↑BP SE of CNI ♦optimal target unknown, extrapolate from general public; some authors suggest tx to high risk targets (BP <130/80) ♦follow JNC-7 guidelines & consider side effects:
  - <u>ACE/ARB</u>: may affect renal function, ↑K, anemia {<u>Aliskiren</u>: avoid in transplant patients [5x increase in AUC of aliskiren in combo with CSA.]}
  - <u>CCB</u>: ↑CNI levels (verapamil & diltiazem) [some specialists use DI to ↓CNI dose, to achieve the same drug level], peripheral edema, gingival hyperplasia
  - <u>Diuretics</u>: ↓renal function if hypovolemic, ↓K , ↑uric acid <u>Other agents</u>: check for DI's & SE drug profile before initiating.

**Immunizations** [12,13]
- attempt to fully immunize **prior** to transplant ♦<u>**avoid**</u> **live vaccine** post SOT eg. BCG, MMR, typhoid [oral], yellow fever, Varicella, Zoster
- vaccine response post SOT may be **blunted** ♦**influenza** vaccine should be administered yearly ♦ <u>seek advice prior to travel</u>

**Infection**
- risk is related to overall level of IS & is generally greater the first 3 months postop & following tx for acute rejection
- Pathogens may be viral (CMV, EBV, herpes), bacterial, or parasitic [10]; SOT pts are also uniquely susceptible to emerging pathogens (e.g. West Nile virus, H1N1 influenza)
- if using macrolide in SOT patient, <u>**avoid**</u> **clarithromycin/erythromycin** due to ↑ Cyp 3A4 DI's! Consider **azithromycin** instead
- All rifamycins have major DI's with CNIs
- Quinolones: theoretical concern over ↑risk of QT prolongation in combo with TAC, but often used in practice

**Osteoporosis** / osteopenia is a metabolic complication of transplantation[14] ♦highest rate of bone loss/fracture in first year post SOT [14]
- periodically assess pts for low BMD & risk factors (↑ age & steroid exposure; ↓ body weight, low BMI, smoking/alcohol)
- Bisphosphonates or Vit D analogues **targeted tx for high risk pts**. Optimize **calcium** 1-1.5 g Ca/day & **Vit D** 400-1000 IU/day for all.

**PTLD** [15,16] (Post-transplant lymphoproliferative disorders): diverse spectrum of disease with varied clinical presentation, may be nodal/extranodal, may localize in allograft, or disseminated, may be indistinguishable from Non-Hodgkin's Lymphoma
- <u>Diagnosis</u>: pathology, EBV viral load (high load often precedes presentation, low load has good negative predictive value, high load has poor positive predictive value)
- <u>Incidence</u>: highest in pediatrics, varies with organ transplanted (small intestine > pancreas, heart, lung, liver > kidney)

**Renal Insufficiency** [22]
- complication of all SOT, CKD affects 30-50% of non-renal SOT, associated with ↑hospitalizations, infections & allograft dysfunction
- modify medications/procedures to minimize renal adverse effects, refer to nephrology if kidney function declines

## Table 5 : Organ Specific Concerns

**KIDNEY**

<u>Rejection</u>: <u>Acute</u>: abrupt ↑in Scr ≥ 30% baseline[4], fever, ↓urine output, weight gain, hypertension, edema, pain over the kidney.
<u>Chronic</u>: hypertension, proteinuria, progressive decline in renal function
- Original cause of renal failure can be an issue (eg. hypertension, diabetes, Focal Segmental Glomerulosclerosis)
- BK virus- a type of polyomavirus; common cause of kidney allograft dysfunction & graft loss; Management: ↓overall IS load, leflunomide possibly

**LUNG** [24]

<u>Rejection</u>: <u>Acute</u>: fever, flu-like sx's, ↑chest pain, cough, short of breath, ↓pulmonary function test, ↑↓body weight or >2kg/24hr
<u>Chronic</u>: Bronchiolitis obliterans syndrome (BOS)-leading cause of morbidity/mortality [long term], occurs up to 64% by 5yr ♦Azithromycin 250mg every other day – potential use in BOS
- Infection: lung transplants have additional susceptibility vs other allografts Factors: exposure via direct inhalation, high IS load, & denervation which inhibits cough reflex.

**HEART**

<u>Rejection</u>: majority of episodes are asymptomatic!
Symptoms could include fever, malaise, ↓exercise tolerance, hypotension, congestive/heart failure sx's [5]
<u>Chronic</u>: coronary graft vasculopathy (specific pathology unique to transplanted vessels) is the leading cause of death after 1yr
- Scheduled endomyocardial biopsies often done by transplant center early post transplant, due to ↑↑rejection & lack of clinical sx's
- Transplanted heart is denervated; ↑'d resting heart rate (90-110 bpm), decreasing ability to rise quickly with exercise
- MI may be asymptomatic; altered response to drugs that work via the autonomic nervous system
- All patients should receive a **statin**, (regardless of LDL) to prevent CVD [5], plus **ASA** & **ACE** inhibitors for cardioprotection

**LIVER** (5yr survival 80%)

<u>Rejection</u>: ↑bili, ↑LFTs, leukocytosis <u>Chronic</u>: 'Vanishing bile duct syndrome', ↑LFTs, ↑bili leading to jaundice, itching
- least immunogenic organ[4]: less (eg. 1-2 IS meds) & simplified IS required to prevent rejection
- Recurrence of disease can be an issue: Hepatitis C, primary biliary cirrhosis

## Table 6: New Recipient Considerations

- **Anticoagulation** - (Aspirin etc) used routinely in some centers/organs to prevent clots
- **Diarrhea** - frequent in SOT recipients, often med related but important to rule out infectious etiologies (e.g. CMV, C.difficile, Norwalk, etc.); avoid dehydration (important in pts receiving nehprotoxic meds), loperamide may be used when all possible causes are excluded/managed –use only in consultation with Transplant Specialist.
- **Electrolyte abnormalities** - extremely common, esp early post transplant (↑ or ↓K, ↓Mg, ↓P04): multifactorial; follow labs & treat as necessary
- **Induction therapy** involves the use of a high level of immunosuppression at the time of transplant & may involve the use of a monoclonal or polyclonal antibody: {Daclizimab [Zenepax] - discontinued 2009}
  Basiliximab [Simulect] - monoclonal antibody; IL-2 receptor [antagonist]; 20mg IV pre-transplant & day 4
  Anti-thymocyte Globulin: targets T cell antigen, polyclonal antibody: Rabbit Thymoglobulin 1.5mg/kg/d IV x ≥ 7day;
  Equine-Atgam - 15mg/kg/d IV x14d, then every other day x 14day.
- **Diabetes Mellitus: New Onset After Transplantation (NODAT)** [19,20] - rates 2-53%, most cases in the 1st yr post transplant, pts with NODAT are at high CVD risk, NODAT associated with reduced graft function & survival; corticosteroids associated with highest risk; CNIs are diabetogenic with TAC>CSA;
  <u>Management</u>: should employ a multidisciplinary approach: patient education is important!
- **Prophylaxis** is <u>routinely</u> administered to SOT recipients to protect against common opportunistic pathogens. Protocols may vary & are center & organ specific.
  - <u>**CMV prophylaxis**</u> [17,18]- CMV most common opportunistic infection post transplant, & ↑'s other complications (bacteremia, fungemia, EBV related PTLD, acute/chronic allograft injury, rejection), risk dependent on donor/recipient serology.
    Prophylaxis: Valganciclovir 900mg od [adjust for renal dysfx] x 100-200 days; or screening & preemptive treatment (CMV PCR).
    Treatment: IV ganciclovir, po valganciclovir, ? CMV immunoglobulin as adjunct; IS adjustments may be needed (eg. MMF).
  - <u>**PCP/PJP prophylaxis**</u> - for at least 1 year post transplant, **cotrimoxazole**, or dapsone if cotrimoxazole allergic; if intolerant of both oral options then inhaled pentamidine administered monthly x 6
    (Cotrimoxazole may also be used indefinitely for prevention of toxoplasmosis in heart pts in some centers)
- **Vision** may change post transplant, suggest no change to prescription lenses for 6 months

ς =scored tablet χ=Non-formulary Sask ☎=Exception Drug Status SK ✆ =prior approval for NIHB ⊗=not covered by NIHB ▼covered by NIHB **ANC**=absolute neutrophil count **AZA**=azathioprine **BG**=blood glucose **BMD**=bone mineral density **BOS**=bronchiolitis obliterans syndrome **BP**=blood pressure **Ca**=Calcium **CMV**=Cytomegalovirus **CSA**=cyclosporine **CNI**=calcineurin inhibitors **CV**=cardiovascular **DI**=drug interaction **DM**=diabetes mellitus **DX**=disease **EBV**=Epstein-Barr Virus **GERD/GI**=stomach **GI**=stomach **H2RA**=H2 receptor antagonist eg. ranitidine **HTN**=hypertension **IA**=intra-articular **IS**=immunosuppressants **K+**=potassium **LFT**=liver function tests **Mg**=magnesium **MMF**=mycophenolate mofetil **NODM**=new onset diabetes mellitus **NVD**=nausea, vomiting, diarrhea **P**=pregnancy category **PCP/PJP**=Pneumocystis jiroveci / carinii pneumonia **PCR**=polymerase chain reaction **PPI**=proton pump inhibitor **PTLD**=Post-transplant lymphoproliferative disorders **SAP**=special access program **Scr**=serum creatinine **SE**=side effect **SRL**=sirolimus **SOT**=solid organ transplant **SX**=symptoms **TAC**=tacrolimus **TG**=Triglycerides **tpt**=transplant **Tx**=Treatment <u>Website</u>: <u>www.transplant.ca</u>, <u>http://www.a-s-t.org/</u>

**RxFiles** Saskatoon City Hospital 701 Queen Street, Saskatoon, SK Canada S7K 0M7
TEL: (306) 655-8505 FAX: (306) 655-7980 Email: info@RxFiles.ca Internet: www.RxFiles.ca ©

## Newsletters

Apr/10 **Onychomycosis Treatment Newsletter and Antifungal Drug Chart**
Oct/09 **Gout Newsletter and Chart**
May/09 **Chronic Heart Failure- Improving Outcomes and Preventing Admissions & Chart**
Oct/08 **Type 2 Diabetes (T2DM) Update & Focus on Insulin Management Issues**
Aug/08 **ADHD Drug Therapy Newsletter & Chart**
Mar/08 **Overactive Bladder & Urinary Incontinence Comparison Chart**
Mar/08 **Nausea & Vomiting Treatment Options Chart**
Feb/08 **IBS: Irritable Bowel Syndrome Newsletter & Drug Comparison Chart**
Sept/07 **Navigating Acid Suppression Options –Optimal PPI Therapy**
Mar/07 **Acne Therapy Newsletter & Comparison Chart**
Oct 06 **Weight Loss Drugs & Smoking Cessation Pharmacotherapy**
Mar 06 **Asthma Treatment "Questions, Tips, Pearls & Comparisons"**
Oct 05 **Opioids in Chronic Non-Malignant Pain -Troubleshooting Drug Therapy Issues**
June 05 **Parkinson's Disease "Tips & Pearls" & Comparison Chart**
Feb 05 **Fluoroquinolones – "Too Valuable to Overuse"**
Oct 04 **POST-MI Troubleshooting Practical Issues**
May 04 **Drug Resources for Hand-held PDA**
Jan 04 **Intranasal Corticosteroids (a Supplement to the OTC Products Chart)**
Jan 04 **OTC (Over-The-Counter) Products**
May/03 **Drug Therapy Issues** •**Androgens in the Aging Male / Topical Corticosteroids on the Face / Adverse Reaction Reporting**
Feb 03 **HYPERTENSION UPDATE: Is anyone leaving samples of thiazide diuretics?**
•See also: Landmark Trials Summary (Jan 03); Antihypertension Selection Guide & 1 Page Summary of Agents
•See Q&A: How does the Australian (ANBP2) trial compare to ALLHAT? (Mar 03)
•See also: Comparison Charts (Diuretics, Beta-blockers, ACE-Inhibitors & Calcium Channel Blockers)

May 02 **HRT Alternatives in Light of the WHI**
• See Q&A: HRT in Light of the WHI –Data in Perspective (Sept 02)
• See Q&A: HRT: Age & the WHI (including a Patient Handout) (Nov 02)
•See also: Postmenopausal & Herbal Options Comparison Charts

May 02 **COXIB'S In Clinical Practice: Towards a Saskatchewan Consensus**
•See also: NSAID Comparison Chart

Feb 02 **Lipid Lowering Agents & Comparison Chart**
•See also: Q&A-An Overview of ASCOT-LLA - Atorvastatin in Primary Prevention (Apr 03)
•See also: Q&A-Monitoring of Creatine Kinase (CK) in Patients on Statin Therapy (Mar 02)

Oct 01 **Agents for Type 2 Diabetes & Hypoglycemic Comparison Chart**
•See also: Q&A-Hypoglycemic Drug Interactions (Oct/01); Insulin Comparison Chart;
Q&A: Renal Function Monitoring in Diabetes (Oct 01)

Jul 01 **Glaucoma: Topical Treatment Tips & Comparison Chart**
May 01 **Psychotropic Drugs in the Elderly**
•See also: Chart Updates - Antidepressants, Antipsychotics, Anxiety, Mood Stabilizer,
Sedation; Q&A-Pharmacological Treatment of Hypersexuality

Feb 01 **Acute Otitis Media** •See also: Anti-infectives, Oral Comparison Chart Update
Jan 01 **Community Acquired Pneumonia**
•See also: CAP Comparison Chart Update; CAP-Pocket Card (Prediction Tool/Treatment)

Sep 00 **Drugs for Influenza** •See also: Antivirals Comparison Chart
May 00 **Asthma Pharmacotherapy**
•See also: Asthma Q&A's (Feb 00); Q&A: COPD - Pharmacotherapy Overview (Feb 00);
Q&A: COPD & Corticosteroids (Feb 00); Comparison Chart Update

Mar 00 **Antihypertensive Pharmacotherapy Update**
•See also: Comparison Charts (Diuretics, Beta-blockers, ACE-Inhibitors & Calcium Channel Blockers
Q&A: Alternatives to Nifedipine in the Oral Treatment of Hypertensive Urgencies (Nov 98)

Jan 00 **COX-2 Specific Inhibitors & NSAID Comparison Chart**
•See also: Q&A: Update on Meloxicam (Mobicox) & COX-2 Selectivity (Feb 01);
Q&A: Brexidol - Uncloaked!" {piroxicam-beta-cyclodextrin};Q&A: Back Pain Treatment Chart

Jan 00 **Hormonal Contraception & Comparison Chart**
•See also: Q&A: Diane 35 {ethinyl estradiol 35 ug; cyproterone 2mg} (Mar 00)

Sep 99 **Postmenopausal Pharmacotherapy & Comparison Chart**
• See also: Q&A: Chronic Unopposed Vaginal Estrogen Therapy (Oct 99); Q&A: Natural' Hormone Replacement Therapy (NHRT) (Sep 99); Comparison Chart Update

May 99 **Acid Suppression & Comparison Chart**
Mar 99 **H. pylori Eradication Regimens & Comparison Chart**
Oct 98 **Antidepressants:** Interactions Chart; Antidepressant Chart Update
•See also: Q&A: Is Fluoxetine Effective in the Treatment of PMS? (Dec 98); Q&A: St. John's Wort in the Treatment of Depression (Nov 98); Q&A: Can Zyban (bupropion/Wellbutrin) be given with SSRIs? (Sept 06)

May 98 **Topical Corticosteroids & Comparison Chart**
Apr 98 **Beta Blockers** Dec 97 **Calcium Channel Blockers**
Oct 97 ACE Inhibitors & Angiotensin II Antagonists Jul 97 NSAIDs, Dare to Compare

## Q&A Summaries

Dec/09 **Thyroid Management: Hypo & Hyperthyroid Treatment Chart**
Oct/09 **Antifungal Treatment Chart**
Oct/09 **Influenza – Overview Chart 2009 - With Consideration for Pandemic H1N1 (pH1N1)**
Oct/09 **Zostavax (Shingles prevention vaccine)**
Sept/09 **Active A (ASA vs ASA+clopidogrel) & W (ASA+clopidogrel vs warfarin) trials in atrial fibrillation**
July/09 **Saskatchewan Drug/Health Information Links**
July/09 **H1N1 (Swine Flu) Links; Record Trial Summary- Rosiglitazone for cardiovascular outcomes in T2DM**
May/09 **HIV Drug Management Comparison Chart**
April/09 **Vaccines- Ault Comparison Chart**
Jan/09 **PPIs May Reduce Effectiveness Of Clopidogrel (PLAVIX)**
Jan/09 **What's the scoop on ACEI & ARB combinations causing harm?**
Dec/08 **Accomplish** (Benazepril + amlodipine **vs** benazepril + hydrochlorothiazide in high cardiac risk hypertensive patients)
Nov/08 **Jupiter Trial Overview** (Rosuvastatin Vs Placebo For Primary Prevention In Low-Moderate Risk Older Adults With Normal LDL, ↑CRP)
Oct/08 **Diabetes in Pregnancy and Gestational Diabetes Mellitus (GDM) & Insulin Pen Delivery Devices**
Oct/08 **Diabetes: Metformin Precautions (Renal, Hepatic & Heart failure); Sitagliptin (Januvia)**
June/08 **The Enhance Trial Summary (Ezetimibe)**
June/08 **The Gout Treatment Chart**
June/08 **Pediatric Pain Comparison Chart**
June/08 **Diabetes Landmark Trials Summary: Advance & Accord**
Feb/08 **Darifenacin (Enablex) vs Oxybutynin on Memory Impairment**
Aug/07 **Lumiracoxib (Prexige) and Hepatotoxicity**
May 07 **Rosiglitazone (Avandia) Cardiovascular Risk**
May 07 **Dream Trial Overview**
May 07 **Diabetes Prevention Summary**
Sept 06 **Malaria Prophylaxis**
Jan 06 **IDEAL- an Overview.** **Herbal: Recent Developments (Cold-fX, glucosamine & Lakota)**
Sept 05 **Ascot-BPLA trial summary.** **Cannabinoids: an overview.**
**Chronic Non-Malignant Pain General Pharmacological Considerations Tables.**
June 05 **Restless Leg Syndrome & Essential Tremor**
Feb 05 **QT Prolongation and Torsades de Pointes: Drugs and Sudden Death**
Nov 04 **Lipid Therapy Update**
Aug 04 **An Overview of CARDS - Atorvastatin in Type 2 Diabetes**
May 04 **An Overview of PROVE IT-TIMI 22 - Atorvastatin high-dose in ACS**
Dec 03 **ARBs in Heart Failure (HF) - Observations on CHARM Data**
Apr 03 **An Overview of ASCOT-LLA - Atorvastatin in Primary Prevention**
Mar 03 **How does the Australian (ANBP2) trial compare to ALLHAT?**
Nov 02 **Age & the WHI (including a Patient Handout)**
Sept 02 **HRT in Light of the WHI –Data in Perspective**
Mar 02 **Monitoring of Creatine Kinase (CK) in Patients on Statin Therapy**
Dec 01 **Handling Back Pain Up-Front; Treatment Options**
Oct 01 **Hypoglycemic Drug Interactions**
July 01 **Treatment of Hypersexuality Patients**
Feb 01 **Update on Meloxicam (Mobicox) & COX-2 Selectivity**
Nov 00 **Selecting Cold Products Post-PPA**
May 00 **Asthma Q&A's; COPD - Pharmacotherapy Overview**
Feb 00 **COPD & Corticosteroids; Brexidol - Uncloaked! {piroxicam-beta-cyclodextrin}**
Mar 00 **Diane 35 {Ethinyl estradiol 35 ug; Cyproterone 2mg}**
Sept-Oct 99 **Chronic Unopposed Vaginal Estrogen Therapy;** **'Natural' Hormone Replacement Therapy (NHRT)**
Mar- Dec 98 **Is Fluoxetine Effective in the Treatment of PMS?** **Can Zyban (bupropion) be given with SSRIs?**
**St. John's Wort in the Treatment of Depression** **Antidepressant Drug Interactions**
**Alternatives to Nifedipine for Hypertensive Urgencies** **Diuretics for Hypertension**

**RxFiles 8th Edition** Comparison Charts – All Updated to May/10 (138 pages, 88 charts, with 14 new charts)

The Standard 8th Edition book is ~9 x 11 inches, full color print, tabbed and indexed.
The Pocket 8th Edition is 5.5 x 7.5 inches (color, tabbed, indexed) –but it has much smaller print.
The Combo Pak is one of the Standard & one of the Pocket books together.
An Oversize Edition is extra LARGE 15 x 12 inches (color, tabbed, indexed) .

The RxFiles

*Also available at - www.RxFiles.ca*
•**Program Information** •**References** • **Links**
•**RxFiles Email Notification** - whenever something new is posted to the web
•**Online Subscription**- access to all the most recent charts & newsletters
•**Search Feature** – for quick information access to RxFiles website information

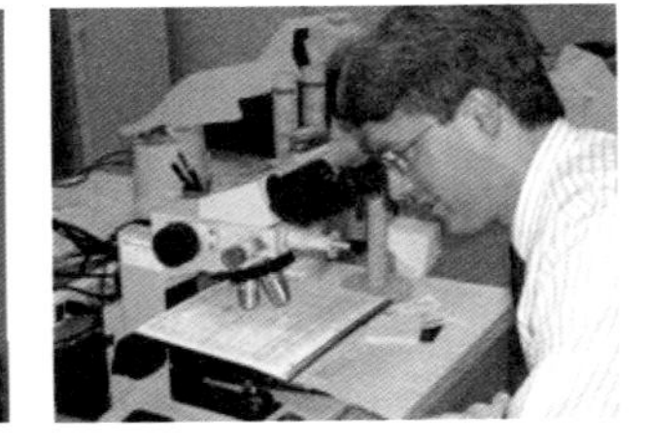

# Drugs in Pregnancy Risk Classification [1,2,3,4]

The following are the codes that appear on some of our charts. This table explains the rating system used.

| RISK FACTOR | CLASSIFICATION | COMMENTS * Weight risk vs benefit esp. in some diseases eg. diabetes, asthma, hypertension, psychiatry. Benefit of treatment in these conditions, may outweight the risks of not treating. |
|---|---|---|
| A | SAFE | **No risk.** Considered safe in all trimesters. No evidence of fetal risk in controlled studies in humans. |
| B | LIKELY SAFE | **Minimal risk.** Either no evidence of risk in animals or risk found in animal studies not reproduced in humans. |
| B/D | | **With higher dose, longer duration of drug exposure or near term the risk becomes D** |
| C | CAUTION | **Potential risk.** Risk evident from studies in animals and/ or no human studies available. Use only if benefit outweighs risk. May be more or less safe depending on trimester. |
| C/D | | **With higher dose, longer duration of drug exposure or near term the risk becomes D** |
| D | EXTREME CAUTION | **Positive evidence of risk.** Use only if benefit outweighs risk. |
| X | CONTRAINDICATED | **++ Positive evidence of risk.** Avoid in women who are or may become pregnant as risk of use outweighs any benefit. |
| U | UNKNOWN | **Risk unknown or untested.** Information unavailable / inadequate at this time. |

**Colors**: used within the charts
**Green** Shading usually **HERBAL/Lifestyle** related
**Blue** Shading usually indicates **PEDIATRIC** related
**Purple** script usually indicates TRADE NAMES
**Yellow is highlighted clinical differences, practice gaps & common questions.**
**Navy** script usually indicates **MAJOR TRIALS**

* Rating system has limitations eg. antidepressant frequently used like fluoxetine has a C rating; yet maprotiline (B rating) has less clinical experience

General Info: **Pregnancy Exposure Registries** http://www.fda.gov/womens/registries/default.htm **LactMed** [Lactation] http://toxnet.nlm.nih.gov/cgi-bin/sis/htmlgen?LACT


1. Drugs in Pregnancy and Lactation, 8th ed. Briggs GE, Freeman RK, Yaffe SJ, editors. Williams and Wilkins; Baltimore, MD: 2008.
2. Drug Information Handbook, 17th ed. Lacy CF, Armstrong LL, Goldman MP and Lance LL, editors. Lexi-Comp Inc; Hudson, Ohio: 2008-2009.
3. Individual Drug Product Monographs. 4. Micromedex 2010 {NOTE: for additional Canadian information on drugs in **pregnancy & lactation** see **http://www.motherisk.org/index.jsp** }


**WHO Essential Medicines List** http://www.who.int/medicines/publications/essentialmedicines/en/index.html

**Common RxFiles ABBREVIATIONS & SYMBOLS –most of our charts have footnotes to explain unique abbreviations.**

☎ =Exception Drug Status (**EDS**) in Saskatchewan (1-800-667-2549)
✗ =non-formulary in Saskatchewan
$ Retail *Cost to Consumer* based on acquisition cost, markup & dispensing fee in Saskatchewan. Lowest generic price used where available

**BID**=twice daily **BP** =blood pressure **Bz** =benzodiazepine **CI** =contraindication
**HF** =heart failure **HR** =Heart rate **HSR** =Hypersensitivity reaction
**SE** =side effect **SJS** =Stevens Johnson Sx **Sx** =syndrome/symptom **Sz** =seizure
ς =indicates strength of tablet is scored ☺ = tastes good

=prior approval required by **NIHB** (Non-Insured Health Benefits) coverage for eligible **First Nations & Inuit** 1-800-580-0950
⊗ =not covered by NIHB http://www.hc-sc.gc.ca/fnih-spni/pubs/nihb-ssna_e.html#drug-med_bull-lebull
▼ =covered by NIHB for the **OTC charts** p70-73 & identified **ONLY** for those drugs which have **Sask**. Formulary restrictions such as **EDS or non formulary status**

**CV** =cardiovascular **DI** =drug interaction **Dx** =diagnosis/disease **g** =generic avail. **GI** =Gastrointestinal **HA** =headache
**LFT** =Liver Function tests **M** =Monitoring **OD**=daily **P** =concern if given **Pre-Op** þ=Porphyria **QID**=four times daily
**TID**=three times daily **Tx** =treatment **Units**= uses SI but can convert (cholesterol x 38.6=mg/dL; glucose x 18=mg/dL)
= CDN (We are **Canadian**) ⊗ =Avoid → soybean & peanut allergy ♂ =male ♀ =women

=↓ dose required for **Renal** dysfunction [1] if 1) ≥ 75% renal excretion 2) toxic if accumulates 3) an active metabolite requiring dose adjustment. [CrCl <60ml/min shows impaired renal function] =↓ dose required for **Liver** dysfunction

**CrCl** ml/min **Male**={(140-age) x **ABW** weight in Kg } / {serum creatinine in umol/l x 0.814}
**Female**= 0.85 x CrCl male
Adjusted body weight in kg (**ABW**) = {Ideal body weight (**IBW**) + 0.4 (Actual body weight-**IBW**)}
**IBW** (Males)= 50kg + 0.906 (Height in cm - 152.4cm); **IBW** (Females)= 45kg + 0.906 (Height in cm - 152.4cm)
**MDRD** (eGFR)= accurate, but need PDA with MedCalc to do the calculation. **CKD-EPI** eGFR= new accurate for CKD



**Newsletters, Charts & References** are available **online** at **www.RxFiles.ca**


***RxFiles Academic Detailing Program***

***Objective comparisons for optimal drug therapy. For more information check our website - www.RxFiles.ca or, contact Loren Regier BSP, BA RxFiles, c/o , Saskatoon City Hospital***
**701 Queen Street Saskatoon, SK S7K 0M7 Canada; Ph (306) 655-8505, Fax (306) 655-7980**

RxFiles Program Pharmacists: **North Battleford** (P. Karlson), **Prince Albert** (J. Bareham), **Regina/Moose Jaw** (Z. Dumont, B. Schuster), **Estevan/Weyburn** (V. Johnson), **Swift Current** (L. Butt), **Yorkton** (T. Nystrom). **Saskatoon & Other Saskatchewan Areas** (B. Jensen, L. Regier, S. Stone). Thanks to the many physician/program advisors & specialist reviewers for their ongoing assistance.

# DRUG COMPARISON CHARTS 8TH EDITION

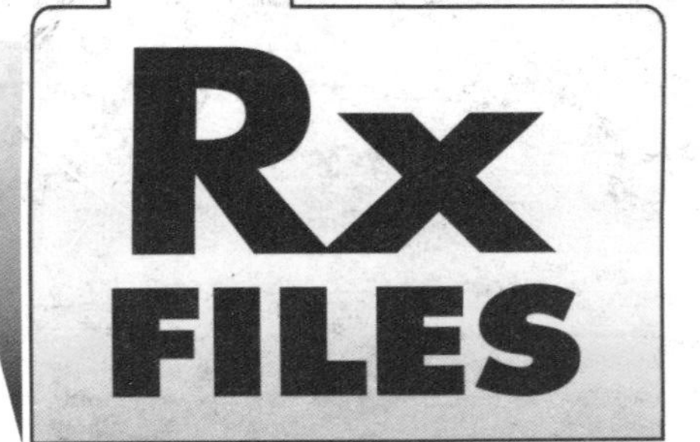

## OBJECTIVE COMPARISONS FOR OPTIMAL DRUG THERAPY

The *RxFiles Academic Detailing Program* exists to help physicians and other healthcare professionals make the best possible drug therapy choices for their patients. To do this, we take a balanced look at effectiveness, safety, cost and patient considerations, weeding through the evidence as well as the marketing hype.

**More information is available on our website,** which is updated regularly as new evidence and clinical information emerges.

**The highlight of the program is the interactive discussions "academic detailing" we have with family physicians, specialists and others in our home province of Saskatchewan, Canada; this is what makes our program unique.**

**Information Exchange**

RxFiles Drug Comparison Charts available as:

- **Standard** Size Chart Book (readable; ~ 9"x11")
- **Pocket** Size (same content; smaller size; 5.5" x 7.5")
- **Oversize** (extra large; ~ 15"x12")
- **Website**: subscriber access area for pdf charts, as well as newsletters, Q&As, trial summaries, etc. **Ongoing updates**: get on the RxFiles Email Update List for notification of new postings.

*...no free lunch or samples, just objective, comparative drug information!*

*Vaughn, Julia, Tanya, Brenda, Leah, Shannon, Zack, Pam, Brent, Loren*
*"It's all in the detail"*

**RxFiles**

**ACADEMIC DETAILING PROGRAM**

c/o Saskatoon City Hospital
701 Queen Street
Saskatoon, SK S7K 0M7
CANADA

Phone: 306-655-8505
Fax: 306-655-7980
E-mail: info@RxFiles.ca

**www.RxFiles.ca**

Academic detailing — Family Med Forum—Best Ed Booth — Lucky students @PDW — Brent's paper trail — AD Workshop 2009 — Teacher(s) of the Year